MAN IN CONTEMPORARY SOCIETY

A SOURCE BOOK

Man in Contemporary Society

A SOURCE BOOK PREPARED BY THE CONTEMPORARY CIVILIZATION STAFF OF COLUMBIA COLLEGE, COLUMBIA UNIVERSITY

Volume II

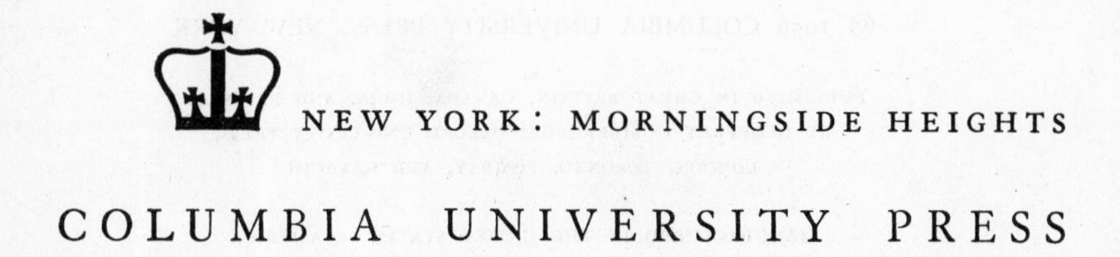

NEW YORK: MORNINGSIDE HEIGHTS

COLUMBIA UNIVERSITY PRESS

LIBRARY OF CONGRESS CATALOG CARD NUMBER: 55-9067

PUBLISHED IN GREAT BRITAIN, CANADA, INDIA, AND PAKISTAN
BY GEOFFREY CUMBERLEGE: OXFORD UNIVERSITY PRESS,
LONDON, TORONTO, BOMBAY, AND KARACHI

MANUFACTURED IN THE UNITED STATES OF AMERICA

CONTENTS

THE ANATOMY OF SOCIETY: ECONOMY

THE ANATOMY OF SOCIETY: ECONOMY

1. TECHNOLOGY AND INDUSTRIAL SOCIETY

MELVILLE J. HERSKOVITS

THE SCIENCES of economics and anthropology have rarely been directly and formally joined. On the one hand, economics, in its systematic aspects, has tended to universalize conceptions founded upon data and assumptions characteristic of the economic life of post-eighteenth-century Western civilization. Although the "classical" economists clearly understood the limited distribution of specifically European economic attitudes and institutions, when they turned to primitive cultures they sought to discover in these alien societies the economic behavior familiar to them in their own cultural setting. On the other hand, anthropologists have always had an intense interest in the technological equipment of primitive cultures, but, until recently, did not attempt to conceptualize the total economic systems in which the technologies functioned only as parts. In recent years, however, interest in comparative economics has spread, with the result that many of the assumptions of Western economic thought have been critically reexamined, while many areas of the study of primitive cultures have been illuminated.

In this interdisciplinary work Melville J. Herskovits (b. 1895), professor of anthropology at Northwestern University and specialist in the Negro cultures of West Africa, South America, and the Caribbean, has made significant contributions. The following selection has been taken from Herskovits's *Economic Anthropology: A Study in Comparative Economics* (1952), which is a second, revised edition of his *The Economic Life of Primitive Peoples* (1940). Among the other works of Herskovits, *Trinidad Village* (1947), written in collaboration with his wife, Frances S. Herskovits, and *Man and His Works: The Science of Cultural Anthropology* (1949) have been most important.

ECONOMIC ANTHROPOLOGY: A STUDY IN COMPARATIVE ECONOMICS

CHAPTER I: ECONOMIZING AND RATIONAL BEHAVIOR

The elements of scarcity and choice, which are the outstanding factors in human experience that give economic science its reason for being, rest psychologically on firm ground. It is a truism that wants are capable of a degree of expansion the end of which has not been reached by any known society. Wants, that is, apparently manifest a certain dynamic quality, which seems to derive from the inventiveness and receptivity of man, and are ultimately to be referred to the cumulative nature of human culture itself. Each generation takes for granted the cultural setting of the society into which it is born. And each, because of the creative restlessness of man, adds its contribution to the total culture of the group it comprises. . . .

Our primary concern . . . is to understand the cross-cultural implications of the process of economizing. We may begin our analysis by considering the concept of a free good. It is a commonplace in economic theory, for example, that no economic value can be assigned to a sunset or the view of a mountain, since these are to be had for the taking. It is only when a given good is not available in quantities to supply every desire for it that the economizing process comes into play. Even in the case of the utilization of what would seem to be a free good, however, some economic factors may enter. There may be more than enough animals available, and no restrictions on the member of the tribe as to where and what he will hunt; but choices will nonetheless have to be made. These considerations cannot be overlooked if the free good is not to lie, inert, as a theoretical concept and not as a functioning element in the daily life of the people. . . .

Beyond whatever free goods may be available, even to members of societies with the smallest numbers, the simplest technologies and the most direct economic systems, the far greater number of goods are not free. Even the provision of basic needs, food and shelter and clothing and implements, must inevitably involve choice; moreover, these choices are dictated not only by the alternatives between available items, but by the patterns of the culture of the individual who, in the final analysis, must do the choosing. Choice between alternatives is limited not only by the goods and services available to satisfy wants. The nature of the available goods and of the wants they satisfy is likewise restricted. Economizing, that is, is carried on in a cultural matrix. The matter has been phrased cogently in considering the economy of southern Bougainville, Solomon Islands: "At the present, in answer to the problem of discrepancy between needs and resources, it is sufficient to recall that these needs are *cultural* rather than *nutritional,* and to state the conviction that there will always be discrepancies between cultural needs and available resources." Social conventions, religious beliefs, aesthetic conceptions, and ethical prescriptions all function in shaping the wants of peoples and the times and places and circumstances in which they can be satisfied.

. . . [For] example, certain West African peoples conventionally and traditionally expend food so liberally on feasts that must be given during the dry season that at the beginning of the rainy season, when hard labor of breaking the ground for the new planting has to be performed, there is an actual inadequacy of caloric intake that could easily be supplied if food resources had been conserved. It must be emphasized that there is no question of lack of foresight, for it is well established that these peoples are aware of the alternate possibility. It is rather a question of economic choice dictated by the drive to maximize satisfactions in terms of the traditional values of the culture. . . .

One of the principles of early economic theory was to regard the individual as the point from which all development of theoretical principles must begin. We have come to realize that the individual never exists alone; that a society, as it has been put, is more than an aggregate of Robinson Crusoes; and that social interaction in terms of cultural tradition dictates reconsideration of the earlier starting-point. The process of economizing, we recognize, is essentially based on the broader organization of society. Yet the individual cannot be left out of the picture, for all forms of social behavior, in the final analysis, must be referred to the behavior of individual members of a given society in specific situations. . . .

In short, we must not reject Economic Man only to substitute Society as an exclusive formula for understanding economic behavior and as a base-point for analysis. Economizing is never carried on *unilaterally*. The choices of the individual must always be limited by the resources of society and the values of his culture. But the factors of variation to be found even within the smallest, most homogeneous, and most conservative society must not be lost sight of. The economic unit, we must conclude, is the individual operating as a member of his society, in terms of the culture of his group.

This implies that any analysis of the schedule of wants of a given society which projects these wants against the supply of goods and services available to satisfy them must be supplemented by introducing a third term into the equation; the cultural definition of wants and the conventions that dictate how and when they are to be regarded as adequately satisfied. . . .

. . . [The] scarcity of goods in the face of the wants of a given people at a given time is a universal fact of human experience; . . . no economy has been discovered wherein enough goods are produced in enough variety to satisfy all the wants of all the members of any society. This is true whether the group is small or large, the mechanisms of its economic system simple or complex.

More important, it is true whether the society is undisturbed and the differences in its way of life from one generation to another slight, or whether it is in a state of dynamic change. The dissimilarities between any society and any other in these respects is one of degree and not of kind. The general principle, therefore, stands, despite the many changes that are rung on the basic theme manifested in the particular forms it assumes in functioning economies.

It can also be taken as cross-culturally acceptable that, on the whole, the individual tends to maximize his satisfactions in terms of the choices he makes. Where the gap between utility and disutility is appreciable, and the producer or consumer of a good or service is free to make his choice, then, other things being equal, he will make his choice in terms of utility rather than disutility. One need not accept the hedonism of classical economics to recognize the validity, on broad lines, of the proposition, at least in the terms in which we have phrased it here.

Yet it should be apparent that the two basic postulates of economic science —the allocation of scarce resources among alternative ends and the conscious determination of the choices made in maximizing satisfactions—are not of the same order. The first is a statement of fact that can be objectively verified. In pecuniary, machine economies this can be done by means of price analysis which shows how the market responds to scarcities or overproduction of given commodities. In non-pecuniary, non-machine, and nonliterate societies we can have recourse to ethnographic descriptions of the range of goods produced by a people and record the choices that are actually reached. The empirical nature of analyses that press the point further, inquiring into the kind of resources a people can draw on, and how they are utilized in producing ultimate consumption goods, is likewise apparent. The forms taken by competitive striving for a good in short supply, if competitive patterns are present, and the degree to which this striving stimulates to further production, can also be objectively described. We can determine whether bidding will be in terms of prestige or price. We can ascertain whether a failure to increase supply is due to lack of ultimate resources, or to non-economic causes of a social or religious order. Or, where the response to increased demand is increase in supply, we can find out how this increase has occurred and, given time and resources for adequate investigation of the problem, the extent to which the supply has increased.

The second proposition, however, lies in the realm of values, not only in the technical sense of economic science, but in the broader philosophical connotation of those ultimate sanctions to behavior that give meaning to life.

It is possible to bring objective proof, that is, as to *what* men do in the way of economizing; the question *why* they do it rests on subjective and cultural factors. It is significant that so much of that aspect of economic theory that bears on this latter point derives from assumptions of a psychological nature. It is more than a figure of speech when economists speak of "rationalizing" production or distribution. The usage derives logically and semantically from the prominence traditionally given the view that man, in his economic behavior, acts rationally.

The earlier concept of Economic Man, the most extreme expression of this position, has long since been given over by economists, together with any conclusions that may have been drawn concerning the relevance of this concept as indicative of Human Nature in the large. The influence of the earlier economic historians was important in bringing about this changed point of view. They indicated the need to take time and place into full account if the economies of earlier periods of western European society were to be understood. The process of refining the conception of the role of rational choice has continued, with stress being laid on non-economic choices to be made in "the business of living," or by successively eliminating more and more variables in drawing assumptions so that the choices to be made rationally are restricted not only as to time and place but to the economic as against other aspects of living as well.

We may take as an example the case of the Kwakiutl of the Northwest Coast of North America, whose economy has been the subject of much study, earlier in terms of its dramatic prestige give-away rituals termed potlatches, and in later years concerning the productive and social system that made this institution possible. As a result of these investigations, an inner dynamic of considerable significance for the point under discussion has been revealed. Codere has phrased the matter in these terms: "In what might be called their 'economic life' the Kwakiutl are virtuoso technicians and extravagant producers and storers. It is in their 'social life' that they 'economize.'" In this society, that is, a basic aim was the attainment and maintenance of position, to be achieved only through the expenditure of valuable goods. . . . This was carried on by certain financial mechanisms—investment, credit, and the payment of interest, which, as it is phrased, "maximized the potlatch." The underlying drive in this complex system, therefore, "is to be found in the relation of the arbitrarily determined scarcity of potlatch positions to the superabundance of some economic goods."

The factor of rational choice, even when its applicability is narrowed, still remains as an element in the basic postulates of economic science. . . .

. . . [But] it is essential at this point to consider the problem of rationality in the light of our knowledge of the psychology of culture. The concept of culture . . . includes all phases of the learned, traditionally sanctioned behavior of human beings. These phases are conceived as aspects of culture, which are universals in the ways of life of all human groups—technology, economics, social organization, political structures, religious beliefs and institutions, language, art, music, and literary modes of expression being the broadest categories. These universal aspects, in their institutionalized forms, are different in all of the many different societies found over the earth. Yet each of these *forms* represents the working out, in terms of its own particular historical stream, of universal *processes* of cultural dynamics which have brought about the results to be observed in the life of any given people at any given point in time. . . .

. . . This brings us to *cultural relativism,* which stresses the validity of the most diverse kinds of value-systems for the peoples who live in accord with them. It derives from the following proposition in cultural psychology: "Judgments are based on experience, and experience is interpreted by each individual in terms of his own enculturation." Its documentation is vast, and derives principally from much research that has established the devotion of every people to their own way of life, and the extent to which the malfunctioning of culture can be ascribed to a break-down in the value-systems of a people.

. . . This relativistic approach to the comparative study of economic behavior and institutions provides the epistemological foundation essential if the differences between different ways of life are not to be analyzed and assessed in terms of principles that derive from a single culture—in this case, our own. The point of view this latter engenders is called ethnocentrism, the roots of which, in Euroamerican cultures, will be considered . . . [directly]. Here it need merely be pointed out that this is a habit of thought that must be guarded against if understanding of any modes of behavior and value-systems other than those of one's own group is to be attained.

The principle of maximizing satisfactions by the conscious exercise of choice between scarce means is valid because we find that this does occur in all societies. The cross-cultural perspective, however, gives us pause when defining "rationality." We are tempted to consider as rational the behavior that represents only the typical reactions to be expected of those who order their lives in terms of economic systems of Europe and America, where it is rational to defer the gratification of wants, to accumulate resources, to produce more goods and multiply services. Yet . . . there are many cultures, if not a majority of them, where the deferment of wants is held to be disadvantageous, where best judgment dictates that resources be expended, where there is no tradition of expanding production and increasing services. . . .

CHAPTER II: BEFORE THE MACHINE

Though man has inhabited the earth for more than half a million years, the invention of the steam engine, which introduced the machine age, occurred less than two hundred years ago. In this mere instant, as the life of the human race is counted, the machine has come to hold a place of such importance in present-day America and Europe that it is not easy for us to imagine a machineless existence.

Yet for much of mankind the machine holds little significance. Even in America and in Europe, where the influence of a mechanized technology invades all phases of life, quiet backwaters still exist where farming folk or village communities live lives relatively little touched by the machine. More important are the untold millions who today follow patterns of life almost entirely different from those by which we order our lives and who, in the Americas, the South Seas, Australia, Asia, and Africa, meet their needs without the use of any of those complex mechanical aids we hold essential.

The term "primitive" has been applied to most of these folk. Because with but few exceptions, they have developed no written language, the word thus became synonymous with "non-historic" or "nonliterate." These terms, however, are actually to be preferred because they do not carry the connotations of inferiority, simplicity, and lack of sophistication that have come to cluster about the word "primitive," and thus to obscure its meaning. Such large differences are, indeed, to be found among nonliterate societies that to characterize them in any general manner is exceedingly difficult. Every institution shows a tremendously wide range of variation in its "primitive" manifestations. It has therefore become a truism that there is no generic difference between "primitive" societies and literate ones, but that, the world over, all cultures represent specialized local developments which have come into being as a result of the unique historical developments that . . . mark the past of each of them.

This being the case, we may find it worth while to sketch the characteristics of the nonliterate societies that justify us in marking them off for special study. We will, in particular, consider those traits that will occupy us in contrasting and comparing their economics with those of the literate, machine cultures.

At the outset, we are struck by the differences in population size between "primitive" and literate groups. This is true not only where density is concerned, but in the numbers of those who make up the self-conscious social entities which we variously designate as "band" or "tribe" or "kingdom." Another difference between nonliterate and literate folk lies in the respective degree of contact they have with the outside world. In supplying their wants, what the nonliterate tribesman could obtain "was usually near at hand," as it has been put. On the other hand, "the whole world . . . contributes to our needs. A complicated business organization makes this possible, one that stands out in marked contrast to the simple system" of these folk. Even in pre-machine days in Europe, or in the non-machine but literate cultures of Asia, the range of communication and the consequent breadth of horizon of these peoples were and are in general greater than those of an African or a North American Indian tribe, or even, for all their voyaging, of the inhabitants of the Polynesian islands. Literate societies . . . also manifest a greater degree of specialization of labor, a greater emphasis on the market and on a standard medium of exchange—money—as an expression of value to facilitate market operations, and a resultant greater economic complexity than do nonliterate communities.

The machine, however, most highly developed in the cultures of North America and Europe, has been the outstanding factor in accentuating all those characteristics of an economic order that have been mentioned as distinguishing the lives of literate from nonliterate peoples. The implications of the machine for human society are therefore greatest in these cultures, and it is between these machine cultures and all others, especially the nonliterate ones, that the differences are widest. That is why, at the outset, the role of the machine must be emphasized as a factor in differentiating their life from ours.

In considering the influence of the machine in our lives, we must constantly bear in mind the effect the technological perfections that have gone with its development, the greater degree of productivity these have permitted, and the changes they have wrought in the economic sphere have had on some of the more important currents of thought of our day. Especially important is the fact that the achievements of the machine are objectively demonstrable, from which it follows that technological and economic gains can most readily be used when evaluating different cultures. The mechanistic philosophy of our day, when raised in the field of method to a tradition of objective observation, is readily contrasted with the mystical elements in the technology and economic order of nonliterate societies.

This is one of the principal reasons why the identification of the word "primitive" with the concept "lower" as regards social development—or its converse, the use of "civilized" in the sense of something "higher"—has been so convincing and, as expressed in the term "progress," has come to lodge so deeply in our everyday manner of thought. Here is the apparent documentation of the ethnocentrism that makes the appreciation of the values of other cultures than our own so difficult. Descriptions of our technological achievement can seemingly be employed to demonstrate the more complex nature of our culture as compared with the cultures of all other peoples, especially of nonliterate folk. That such a demonstration has had so great an appeal and has been so difficult to dislodge from the popular mind is not strange. It was such an assumption that gave the attempts to establish an evolutionary sequence for human civilizations their greatest psychological force. . . .

In the same way, the concept of progress, so deeply rooted in our habits of thought, has derived its most important sanctions from demonstrations in the field of technology and economics. That a man, working with a machine, can produce more in given units of time with a given expenditure of energy than when working by hand, is not difficult to prove. It is not so easy, however, to show that one set of religious beliefs is more adequate than another, or one type of family organization more effective than the next. Here the validation of judgment must derive from assumptions that lie quite outside objective proof. Even in the economic and technological spheres the argument couched in terms of relative powers of productivity is by no means self-evident when the ultimate ends toward which such activities are directed—as against the values that guide day-to-day living—come to be analyzed. In all societies, that is, the technological and economic order must at least be efficient enough to permit survival. Granting this, we know enough about the psychology of culture to understand that the satisfaction of human wants is by no means dependent upon an abundance of goods. Increased efficiency in production is likewise not necessarily accompanied by a corresponding efficiency in achieving an effective distribution of what the technological system is capable of producing. . . .

Another instance of how pervasive the indirect influence of the machine has been may be introduced here. . . . This concerns the theory of economic determinism. The increased productivity of our technology and the accompanying complexity of economic organization has resulted in a corresponding increase in the interdependence of individuals and communities. But it was just when the industrial revolution was at its height, and the economic problems presented by it had attained an order of difficulty perhaps never before experienced, that this theory in its present form, was developed. It seems, therefore, that there might well be a discernible relationship between a point of view that holds economic phenomena to be basic in shaping other aspects of life and the historical setting of the period during which this concept was developed.

There can be little doubt that economic factors do play an important rôle in influencing non-economic aspects of culture; but this merely recognizes the fact that all phases of life are closely interrelated and, because of this, tend to modify each other. In these terms, ours is by no means the only culture where economic factors are preponderant in influencing the other facets of culture. Yet it does remain an historic fact that it was only among a people—ourselves—whose economy had become more complex than any before experienced by man, and at a time when the problems presented by the economic order were becoming most serious, that this theory made its appearance. . . .

The relationship between the machine technology and the pecuniary organization of our economy has by no means been made clear. Yet it is apparent that this relationship has given rise to certain special kinds of economic phenomena such as the business cycle, and the periodic unemployment that has followed on technological advances. These phenomena are the direct result of the increased productivity of the machine, coupled with a system whereby the sale of goods for profit as a technique for amassing wealth has become an end rather than a means of life. This entire complex operates so as to deprive many persons of an opportunity to obtain the basic necessities of living, no matter how willing they may be to work or how able.

Such conditions are unknown to nonliterate man. These smaller groups may live on a level but little removed from subsistence needs, where the margin between starvation and survival is slight. Yet even in such societies, the individual who, as an individual, is reduced to such straits that he must either depend on some agency set up for the purpose of preventing his giving way before the harsh dicta of the economic system, or starve, is rarely, if ever, encountered. In societies existing on the subsistence margin, rather, it is generally the rule that when there is not enough, all hunger alike; when there is plenty, all participate.

This does not mean that in cultures where the margin of available goods is greater than in those existing on such a low economic plane, an equal distribution of available resources exists. Practically all societies where life is lived on more than a subsistence level know the concepts of rich and poor, of leader and follower. But even in societies with relatively complex economies, such as those of West Africa and Melanesia, where buying to sell at a profit is of some importance and the hiring of labor is not unknown, the phenomena of the business cycle, of technological unemployment, and of malnutrition resulting from an inability to obtain the necessities of life are not found. . . .

Among nonliterate folk we encounter conditions in many respects analogous to the economic system of the Middle Ages and before. As in pre-machine-age Europe, the laborer is almost invariably the owner of the means of production and to that extent is the master of his own economic destiny. That is, capitalism, as we have come to know it since the advent of power machinery, is foreign to non-machine economies. Capital goods may be concentrated in the hands of individual members of certain communities of this type, but this merely signifies that the difference between these systems and our machine economy is one of degree rather than of kind. In nonliterate societies, we do find men who control the labor of others, whether completely, as under the institution of slavery, or for limited periods of time, under forms of employment for wages. We can even encounter, in Samoa, something akin to an organized body of workers who do not hesitate to interrupt their labor where this is necessary to enforce their demands, or even to indulge in sabotage. But the demands to be enforced are demands of prestige and not of livelihood, for among these workers there is no one to whom the return for his labor is essential to his existence.

Another outstanding difference between machine and non-machine cultures is found in their degree of specialization. In the latter, as has been noted, almost every person controls all the techniques essential for his own support and for the support of those dependent upon him. Even the man who excels in building a canoe, or hunting game, or weaving, or iron-working will, with the aid of members of his family, also carry on agriculture or tend the herds, and he can, when necessary, build a house and fashion household utensils, or make the clothing that habitat and tradition dictate as necessities. Similarly, though some women may be better potters than others, or may excel in basketry or in some other occupation, yet all women will know how to do the household tasks and other kinds of work that are allotted to women under the prevalent patterns of labor. Conversely, it is rare, even where individuals surpass in certain skills, that these skills are restricted to them alone. . . .

We must recognize that all men and women in non-machine societies can control the techniques essential for obtaining a living, and, where there are specialized crafts, that the craftsmen are never dependent for their livelihood solely upon what they produce. These are sufficiently striking differences between nonliterate economies and our own. Even more striking, however, are the implications of the fact that among nonliterate peoples the extreme forms of specialization known to us, where the worker must restrict his activities to minor operations in the entire production process, is but rarely encountered. Specialization within one industry does occur in non-machine societies, as where an individual will be expert at making one special part of a canoe. But, again, almost without exception, such a worker is found to be a full-fledged member of a larger co-operative work group, and psychologically has no difficulty in identifying himself with the finished product. . . .

Certainly the resources an individual in a non-machine society brings to his task must be greater and more varied, in terms of productive activity, than when he carries on the intense specialization demanded of him in a machine technology. What in the field of art has been termed the drive toward virtuosity can be given full play where every step in a process is in the hands of the producer, from the gathering of the raw materials to the finished product that may be admired by the worker's fellows.

Yet another distinction between machine and non-machine societies lies in the development of the tradition of business enterprise, as we know it. . . . Practically no present-day human group is entirely self-supporting, and there is good reason to believe that trade existed in quite early prehistoric times. Where tribal specialization has followed on the localization of natural resources, the needs of a people for those goods they cannot produce because of a lack of essential raw materials cause them to trade for what they desire, and much of their own productive activity is devoted to the making of their own speciality for the same market. A comparable phenomenon is found within certain tribal economies, as where the makers of iron objects, to the degree that they devote their time to this work, must exchange their products for such food, utensils, or non-utilitarian objects as they need or desire if they are to have them. In a number of nonliterate societies where trading is a recognized occupation, and where, as in West Africa, trade is carried on by the use of money rather than by barter, buying in order to sell at a profit, or manufacture of goods primarily for disposal in the market, is well known. . . . But the role which these aspects of trade play in the economic life of such peoples does not have an importance comparable in any way to that held by business in our own economy.

Though in non-industrial societies sparring between traders for advantage does, of course, mark their operations, sometimes even this seems to be absent where values in terms of goods exchanged by direct barter are fixed by traditional usage. Nonetheless, among nonliterate groups the conduct of business transactions has nothing of the impersonal quality that has come to be an outstanding characteristic of our economic system. It is well known that where a non-European has to deal with a European in a matter involving trade, both parties to the transaction are often subject to no little irritation because of differing traditions of trading. Among many who live in non-machine societies, sparring for advantage in the exchange of goods is something of a pleasurable contest of wits.

Nonliterate societies also differ from our own in the relative stress they lay on pecuniary standards of evaluation. Among ourselves, these standards assume such importance that values in terms of money not only dictate our economic judgments, but tend to invade evaluations of all other phases of our culture as well. This has brought it about that money, by and of itself, has come to have a place quite aside from its function as the least common denominator of the market-place. As a matter of fact, it is not easy for us to think of ends that are not expressed as monetary values, even though they concern art or religion or family relations. That we use phrases such as "to have a heart of gold," or to "give a gilt-edged promise," means only that our linguistic usage, like that of all peoples, reflects our standard of values—not as this standard may operate in an economic sense, but as the phrase is applied to moral and personal judgments of the broadest sort.

Now this kind of evaluation is a rarity in nonliterate societies. It is found, notably in Melanesia and in northwestern North America, where outward emblems of wealth are psychologically as important as among ourselves. Yet, in general, there are many more of these groupings where goods, to say nothing of people, are not to be bought at a price, than where the opposite is true. Many instances have been recorded where objects desired by a purchaser have been refused him in the face of fabulous offers—fabulous, that is, in terms of the values set by the people among whom the owner of that desired object lived. It is more revealing of our own psychology than that of those against whom the charge of economic irresponsibility has been laid that the basis of this charge, so often repeated in the accounts of contacts between natives and Europeans, is that these peoples are prone to accept trifles, such as beads, in recompense for objects which we hold to have the highest value, such as golden ornaments or precious stones. In reality, this merely means that in such cases the standards of value brought into play differ from our own.

One of the most widely spread traits of human beings, manifest under the most diverse types of social order, is the desire for prestige. . . . [There] is an intimate relationship between prestige and the control of economic resources in most societies living above a subsistence level. The degree to which those who live under the regime of the machine are dependent upon others for almost every necessity of life, whether material or psychological, and the extent to which it has become necessary to translate experience into terms of those monetary units on which we are so dependent for the goods and services we find essential or desirable, demonstrate the economic consequence of extreme specialization. Here we see money assuming an importance out of all proportion to its manifestation in other cultures or at other times.

It is a commonplace that Europe of the Middle Ages stressed other-worldliness in evaluating its satisfactions and directives. This, however, is merely one way of recalling to ourselves that prestige and the resultant power associated with it can and, in most societies, is to be gained through excellence in other fields than the accumulation of wealth, that the rewards for outstanding accomplishment can be conceived in terms other than those of money. . . .

A final distinction between machine and non-machine societies has to do with the utilization of economic resources for the support of non-subsistence activities. Because of greater powers of production, the goods available under a machine technology to release man-power from direct concern with the tasks of producing the necessities of life are more numerous among ourselves than in any other society. The conversion of these resources into what is to be termed social leisure is of the highest importance for the understanding of many aspects of the organization of human societies, wherever they are found and whatever their complexity. . . . Here we will consider only that phase of the development of a mechanistic approach to life that accompanied the advent and growth of a machine technology, which finds its most characteristic expression in the scientific tradition.

From the beginning of the industrial revolution, the amount of economic resources devoted to the support of the scientific investigation of the world in which we live has become ever larger. This in turn has so helped to increase the efficiency of the processes of production that much more consumption and capital goods have been available than ever before. But the relationship is a reciprocal one, which has released an ever increasing measure of social leisure; and this, in turn, has permitted the investigation of a constantly wider range of problems.

Science, of course, did not begin with the machine age, as is apparent when we consider the history of physics and mathematics. Medicine, one of the scientific disciplines that has most flowered in our culture, also has a history that long antedates the coming of the machine. Those whose task it is to care for human life and assuage human suffering, whether as practitioners of scientific medicine or as magic healers, are in all societies held to be worthy of support out of the subsistence goods produced by those who are always potentially, at least, in need of them. As regards science in general, however, since there was more to consume, more social leisure has been available since the advent of the machine age to release scientists for the pursuit of their investigations. The increased efficiency of the productive processes that have resulted from the application of discoveries in the fields of the exact and mechanical sciences to industry is striking. In such matters as housing and all its related conveniences, or quantity and variety of foods, or aids to health and the prolongation of the life-span, or the wider recreational facilities and opportunities for a broader outlook in the world, the resources of machine societies are not to be compared with those where the technology does not permit an equivalent production of material goods.

There is no intention to suggest in what has just been set forth that the machine technology, by and of itself, causes the societies in which it develops to live under optimum conditions, any more than there is of indicating that the societies in which man lived or lives in what is sometimes termed a state of nature—in non-machine cultures, that is—represent a golden age.

What is meant is that the more admirable developments of science and the multiplication of resources, like those less desirable aspects of life under this same order of society, are concomitants of the machine as against other technologies. In non-machine cultures, life, though lived at a slower pace, must be lived with far more constant regard for the demands of the natural environment, and often in actual fear of not surviving. That is perhaps why the most convincing exposition of the values of our culture to native peoples is on the technological and scientific level; and this is also why we are so prone to insist that our way of life is the best. . . .

LEWIS MUMFORD

LEWIS MUMFORD, born in 1895 in Flushing, Long Island, is one of the few American students of society who has not maintained a continuous connection with an academic institution. However, he has lectured at various colleges and universities and was professor of humanities at Stanford in 1942–44. In 1951 he accepted the professorship of regional planning at the University of Pennsylvania. Mumford consistently has refused to be identified with a single scholarly "department," for his interests require a synthesis of various academic disciplines. The range of his works has been considerable. At an early age he produced *The Story of Utopias* (1922). In *Sticks and Stones* (1924) he began concentrating upon the theme with which his name is most identified: the relation of technology to the common values of civilization and to the social destiny of man. The theme was developed further in *Technics and Civilization* (1934). In *The Culture of Cities* (1938), Mumford emerged as a major critic of contemporary urban life and a strong advocate of metropolitan replanning and reconstruction. In recent years—as evidenced by his works *The Condition of Man* (1944) and *The Conduct of Life* (1951)—he has been devoted to the formulation of an ethical evaluation of man's progress.

In *Technics and Civilization*, from which the following selection has been drawn, Mumford is concerned not merely to recount the history of technological development, but to analyze the relation between "technics"—the "translation into appropriate, practical forms of the theoretic truths . . . of science"—and the humane values connoted by the concept of civilization. Mumford has been strongly influenced by the notion that the form of a machine should follow its function—function as defined not only technologically but also socially and culturally. For Mumford the great era of technological innovation began about 1000 A.D. and is certain to continue into the future. He discerns three phases in the history of modern machine civilization. The first, which he calls the "eotechnic," occurred approximately between 1000 and 1700 and was a time when "the dispersed technical advances and suggestions of other civilizations were brought together and the process of invention and experimental adaptation went on at a slowly accelerating pace. . . . This complex reached its climax . . . in the seventeenth century." In the following selection, Mumford deals with the second, or "paleotechnic," phase, and with the beginnings of the third, or "neotechnic," phase.

TECHNICS AND CIVILIZATION

The Paleotechnic Phase

2. THE NEW BARBARISM

. . . Paleotechnic industry . . . arose out of the breakdown of European society and carried the process of disruption to a finish. There was a sharp shift in interest from life values to pecuniary values: the system of interests which only had been latent and which had been restricted in great measure to the merchant and leisure classes now pervaded every walk of life. It was no longer sufficient for industry to provide a livelihood: it must create an independent fortune: work was no longer a necessary part of living: it became an all important end. Industry shifted to new regional centers in England: it tended to slip away from the established cities and to escape to decayed boroughs or to rural districts which were outside the field of regulation. Bleak valleys in Yorkshire that supplied water-power, dirtier bleaker valleys in other parts of the land which disclosed seams of coal, became the environment of the new industrialism. A landless, traditionless proletariat, which had been steadily gathering since the sixteenth century, was drawn into these new areas and put to work in these new industries: if peasants were not handy, paupers were supplied by willing municipal authorities: if male adults could be dispensed with, women and children were used. These new mill villages and milltowns, barren of even the dead memorials of an older humaner culture, knew no other round and suggested no other outlet, than steady unremitting toil. The operations themselves were repetitive and monotonous: the environment was sordid; the life that was lived in these new centers was empty and barbarous to the last degree. Here the break with the past was complete. People lived and died within sight of the coal pit or the cotton mill in which they spent from fourteen to sixteen hours of their daily life, lived and died without either memory or hope, happy for the crusts that kept them alive or the sleep that brought them the brief uneasy solace of dreams.

Wages, never far above the level of subsistence, were driven down in the new industries by the competition of the machine. So low were they in the early part of the nineteenth century that in the textile trades they even for a while retarded the introduction of the power loom. As if the surplus of workers, ensured by the disfranchisement and pauperization of the agricul-

---

This selection has been reprinted from Lewis Mumford, *Technics and Civilization* (pp. 153–155, 168–172, 178–181, 210–211, 212–215, 221–223, 263–264, 265–267, 373–380, Harcourt, Brace and Co., New York, 1934) by permission of the publisher.

tural workers, were not enough to re-enforce the Iron Law of Wages, there was an extraordinary rise in the birth-rate. The causes of this initial rise are still obscure; no present theory fully accounts for it. But one of the tangible motives was the fact that unemployed parents were forced to live upon the wages of the young they had begotten. From the chains of poverty and perpetual destitution there was no escape for the new mine worker or factory worker: the servility of the mine, deeply engrained in that occupation, spread to all the accessory employments. It needed both luck and cunning to escape those shackles.

Here was something almost without parallel in the history of civilization: not a lapse into barbarism through the enfeeblement of a higher civilization, but an upthrust into barbarism, aided by the very forces and interests which originally had been directed toward the conquest of the environment and the perfection of human culture. Where and under what conditions did this change take place? And how, when it represented in fact the lowest point in social development Europe had known since the Dark Ages did it come to be looked upon as a humane and beneficial advance? We must answer those questions.

The phase one here defines as paleotechnic reached its highest point, in terms of its own concepts and ends, in England in the middle of the nineteenth century: its cock-crow of triumph was the great industrial exhibition in the new Crystal Palace at Hyde Park in 1851: the first World Exposition, an apparent victory for free trade, free enterprise, free invention, and free access to all the world's markets by the country that boasted already that it was the workshop of the world. From around 1870 onwards the typical interests and preoccupations of the paleotechnic phase have been challenged by later developments in technics itself, and modified by various counterpoises in society. But like the eotechnic phase, it is still with us: indeed, in certain parts of the world, like Japan and China, it even passes for the new, the progressive, the modern, while in Russia an unfortunate residue of paleotechnic concepts and methods has helped misdirect, even partly cripple, the otherwise advanced economy projected by the disciples of Lenin. In the United States the paleotechnic régime did not get under way until the eighteen fifties, almost a century after England; and it reached its highest point at the beginning of the present century, whereas in Germany it dominated the years between 1870 and 1914, and, being carried to perhaps fuller and completer expression, has collapsed with greater rapidity there than in any other part of the world. France, except for its special coal and iron centers, escaped some of the worst defects of the period; while Holland, like Denmark and in part Switzerland, skipped almost directly from an eotechnic into a neotechnic economy, and except in ports like Rotterdam and in the mining districts, vigorously resisted the paleotechnic blight.

In short, one is dealing with a technical complex that cannot be strictly placed within a time belt; but if one takes 1700 as a beginning, 1870 as the high point of the upward curve, and 1900 as the start of an accelerating downward movement, one will have a sufficiently close approximation to fact. Without accepting any of the implications of Henry Adams's attempt to apply the phase rule of physics to the facts of history, one may grant an increasing rate of change to the processes of invention and technical improvement, at least up to the present; and if eight hundred years almost defines the eotechnic phase, one should expect a much shorter term for the paleotechnic one.

6. THE DESTRUCTION OF ENVIRONMENT

. . . In this paleotechnic world the realities were money, prices, capital, shares: the environment itself, like most of human existence, was treated as an abstraction. Air and sunlight, because of their deplorable lack of value in exchange, had no reality at all. Andrew Ure, the great British apologist for Victorian capitalism, was aghast at the excellent physician who testified before Sadler's Factory Investigating Commission on the basis of experiments made by Dr. Edwards in Paris with tadpoles, that sunlight was essential to the growth of children: a belief which he backed up—a century before the effect of sunlight in preventing rickets was established—by pointing to the absence of deformities of growth, such as were common in milltowns, among the Mexicans and Peruvians, regularly exposed to sunlight. In response to this Ure proudly exhibited the illustration of a factory room without windows as an example of the excellent gas-lighting which served as a substitute for the sun!

The values of the paleotechnic economy were topsy-turvy. Its abstractions were reverenced as "hard facts" and ultimate realities; whereas the realities of existence were treated by the Gradgrinds and Bounderbys as abstractions, as sentimental fancies, even as aberrations. So this period was marked throughout the Western World by the widespread perversion and destruction of environment: the tactics of mining and the debris of the mine spread everywhere. The current annual wastage through smoke in the United States is huge—one estimate is as high as approximately $200,000,000. In all too literal sense, the paleotechnic economy had money to burn.

In the new chemical industries that sprang up during this period no serious effort was made to control either air pollution or stream pollution, nor was any effort made to separate such industries from the dwelling-quarters of the town. From the soda works, the ammonia works, the cement-making works, the gas plant, there emerged dust, fumes, effluvia, sometimes noxious for human organisms. In 1930 the upper Meuse district in Belgium was in a state of panic because a heavy fog resulted in widespread choking and in the death of 65 people: on careful examination it turned out that there had been only a particularly heavy concentration of the *usual* poison gases, chiefly sulphurous anhydride. Even where the chemical factories were not conspicuously present, the railroad distributed smut and dirt: the reek of coal was the very incense of the new industrialism. A clear sky in an industrial district was the sign of a strike or a lockout or an industrial depression.

If atmospheric sewage was the first mark of paleotechnic industry, stream pollution was the second. The dumping of the industrial and chemical waste-products into the streams was a characteristic mark of the new order. Whereever the factories went, the streams became foul and poisonous: the fish died or were forced, like the Hudson shad, to migrate, and the water became unfit for either drinking or bathing. In many cases the refuse so wantonly disposed of was in fact capable of being used: but the whole method of industry was so short-sighted and so unscientific that the full utilization of by-products did not concern anyone for the first century or so. What the streams could not transport away remained in piles and hillocks on the outskirts of the industrial plant, unless it could be used to fill in the water-courses or the swamps on the new sites of the industrial city. These forms of industrial pollution of course go back very far in the history of paleotechnic industry: Agricola makes mention of them, and they remain to this day one of the most durable attributes of the mining economy.

But with the new concentration of industry in the industrial city there was still a third source of stream pollution. This was from human excrement, recklessly dumped into the rivers and tidal waters without any preliminary treatment, to say nothing of attempts to conserve the valuable nitrogenous elements for fertilizer. The smaller rivers, like the Thames and later the Chicago River became little less than open sewers. Lacking the first elements of cleanliness, lacking even a water supply, lacking sanitary regulations of any kind, lacking the open spaces and gardens of the early medieval city, which made cruder forms of sewage disposal possible, the new industrial towns became breeding places for disease: typhoid bacteria filtered through the soil from privy and open sewer into the wells from which the poorer classes got their water, or they were pumped out of the river which served equally as a reservoir for drinking water and a sewage outlet: sometimes, before the chlorine treatment was introduced, the municipal waterworks were the chief source of infection. Diseases of dirt and diseases of darkness flourished: smallpox, typhus, typhoid, rickets, tuberculosis. In the very hospitals, the prevalent dirt counteracted the mechanical advances of surgery: a great part of those who survived the surgeon's scalpel succumbed to "hospital fever." Sir Frederick Treves remembered how the surgeons of Guy's Hospital boasted of the incrustations of blood and dirt on their operating coats, as a mark of long practice! If that was surgical cleanliness, what could one expect of the impoverished workers in the new slums?

But there were other types of environmental degradation besides these forms of pollution. Foremost among these was that resulting from the regional specialization of industry. Natural regional specializations exist by reason of strong differences in climate and geological formation and topography: under natural conditions, no one attempts to grow coffee in Iceland. But the new specialization was based, not upon conforming to regional opportunities, but upon concentrating upon a single aspect of industry and pushing this to the exclusion of every other form of art and work. Thus England, the home of the new specialization, turned all its resources and energy and man-power into mechanical industry and permitted agriculture to languish: similarly, within the new industrial complex, one locality specialized in steel and another in cotton, with no attempt at diversification of manufacture. The result was a poor and constricted social life and a precarious industry. By reason of specialization a variety of regional opportunities were neglected, and the amount of wasteful cross-haulage in commodities that could be produced with equal efficiency in any locality was increased; while the shutting down of the single industry meant the collapse of the entire local community. Above all, the psychological and social stimulus derived from cultivating numerous different occupations and different modes of thought and living disappeared. Result: an insecure industry, a lop-sided social life, an impoverishment of intellectual resources, and often a physically depleted environment. This intensive regional specialization at first brought huge pecuniary profits to the masters of industry; but the price it exacted was too high. Even in terms of mechanical efficiency the process was a doubtful one, because it was a barrier against that borrowing from foreign processes which is one of the principal means of effecting new inventions and creating industries. While when one considers the environment as an element in human ecology, the sacrifice of its varied potentialities to mechanical industries alone was highly inimical to human welfare: the usurpation of park sites and bathing sites by the new steel works and coke-ovens, the reckless placement of railroad yards with no respect to any fact except cheapness and convenience for the railroad itself, the destruction of forests, and the building up of solid masses of brick and paving stone without regard for the special qualities of site and soil—all these were forms of environmental destruction and waste. The cost of this indifference to the environment as a human resource—who can measure it? But who can doubt that it offsets a large part of the otherwise real gains in producing cheap textiles and transporting surplus foods?

8. THE STARVATION OF LIFE

. . . [A] wide-spread starvation of life . . . took place during the paleotechnic régime, and . . . still continues in those many areas and occupations where paleotechnic habits predominate.

In the depauperate homes of the workers in Birmingham and Leeds and Glasgow, in New York and Philadelphia and Pittsburgh, in Hamburg and Elberfeld-Barmen and Lille and Lyons, and in similar centers from Bombay to Moscow, rickety and undernourished children grew up: dirt and squalor were the constant facts of their environment. Shut off from the country by miles of paved streets, the most common sights of field and farm might be strange to them: the sight of violets, buttercups, day-lilies, the smell of mint, honeysuckle, the locust trees, the raw earth opened by the plow, the warm hay piled up in the sun, or the fishy tang of beach and salt-marsh. Overcast by the smoke-pall, the sky itself might be shut out and the sunlight diminished; even the stars at night became dim.

The essential pattern set by paleotechnic industry in England, with its great technical lead and its sedate, well-disciplined operatives, was repeated in every new region, as the machine girdled the globe.

Under the stress of competition, adulterants in food became a commonplace of Victorian industry: flour was supplemented with plaster, pepper with wood, rancid bacon was treated with boric acid, milk was kept from souring with embalming fluid, and thousands of medical nostrums flourished under the protection of patents, bilge-water or poison whose sole efficacy resided in the autohypnotism produced by the glowing lies on their labels. Stale and rancid food degraded the sense of taste and upset the digestion: gin, rum, whisky, strong tobacco made the palate less sensitive and befuddled the senses: but drink still remained the "quickest way of getting out of Manchester." Religion ceased in large groups to be the opiate of the poor: indeed the mines and the textile mills often lacked even the barest elements of the older Christian culture: and it would be more nearly true to say that opiates became the religion of the poor.

Add to the lack of light a lack of color: except for the advertisements on the boardings, the prevailing tones were dingy ones: in a murky atmosphere even the shadows lose their rich ultramarine or violet colors. The rhythm of movement disappeared: within the factory the quick staccato of the machine displaced the organic rhythms, measured to song, that characterized the old workshop, as Bücher has pointed out: while the dejected and the outcast shuffled along the streets in *Cities of Dreadful Night,* and the sharp athletic movements of the sword dances and the morris dances disappeared in the surviving dances of the working classes, who began to imitate clumsily the graceful boredom of the idle and the leisured.

Sex, above all, was starved and degraded in this environment. In the mines and factories an indiscriminate sexual intercourse of the most brutish kind was the only relief from the tedium and drudgery of the day: in some of the English mines the women pulling the carts even worked completely naked—dirty, wild, and degraded as only the worst slaves of antiquity had been. Among the agricultural population in England sexual experience before marriage was a period of experimental grace before settling down: among the new industrial workers, it was often preliminary to abortion, as contemporary evidence proves. The organization of the early factories, which threw girls and boys into the same sleeping quarters, also gave power to the overseers of the children which they frequently abused: sadisms and perversions of every kind were common. Home life was crowded out of existence; the very ability to cook disappeared among the women workers.

Even among the more prosperous middle classes, sex lost both its intensity and its priapic sting. A cold rape followed the prudent continences and avoidances of the pre-marital state of women. The secrets of sexual stimulation and sexual pleasure were confined to the specialists in the brothels, and garbled knowledge about the possibilities of intercourse were conveyed by well-meaning amateurs or by quacks whose books on sexology acted as an additional bait, frequently, for their patent medicines. The sight of the naked body, so necessary for its proud exercise and dilation, was discreetly prohibited even in the form of undraped statues: moralists looked upon it as a lewd distraction that would take the mind off work and undermine the systematic inhibitions of machine industry. Sex had no industrial value. The ideal paleotechnic figure did not even have legs, to say nothing of breasts and sexual organs: even the bustle disguised and deformed the rich curve of the buttocks in the act of making them monstrous.

This starvation of the senses, this restriction and depletion of the physical body, created a race of invalids: people who knew only partial health, partial physical strength, partial sexual potency: it was the rural types, far from the paleotechnic environment, the country squire and the parson and the agricultural laborer, who had in the life insurance tables the possibility of a long life and a healthy one. Ironically enough, the dominant figures in the new struggle for existence lacked biological survival value: biologically the balance of power was in the countryside, and it was only by faking the statistics—that is, by failing to correct them for age-groups—that the weaknesses of the new industrial towns could be concealed.

With the starvation of the senses went a general starvation of the mind: mere literacy, the ability to read signs, shop notices, newspapers, took the place of that general sensory and motor training that went with the handicraft and the agricultural industries. In vain did the educators of the period, like Schreber in Germany with his projects for Schrebergärten as necessary elements in an integral education, and like Spencer in England with his praise of leisure, idleness, and pleasant sport, attempt to combat this desiccation of the mind and this drying up of life at the roots. The manual training that was introduced was as abstract as drill; the art fostered by South Kensington was more dead and dull than the untutored products of the machine.

The eye, the ear, the touch, starved and battered by the external environment, took refuge in the filtered medium of print; and the sad constraint of the blind applied to all the avenues of experience. The museum took the place of concrete reality; the guidebook took the place of the museum; the criticism took the place of the picture; the written description took the place of the building, the scene in nature, the adventure, the living act. This exaggerates and caricatures the paleotechnic state of mind; but it does not essentially falsify it. Could it have been otherwise? The new environment did not lend itself to first hand exploration and reception. To take it at second hand, to put at least a psychological distance between the observer and the horrors and deformities observed, was really to make the best of it. The starvation and diminution of life was universal: a certain dullness and irresponsiveness, in short, a state of partial anesthesia, became a condition of survival. At the very height of England's industrial squalor, when the houses for the working classes were frequently built beside open sewers and when rows of them were being built back to back—at that very moment complacent scholars writing in middle-class libraries could dwell upon the "filth" and "dirt" and "ignorance" of the Middle Ages, as compared with the enlightenment and cleanliness of their own. . . .

16. THE PALEOTECHNIC PASSAGE

The paleotechnic phase . . . [however] did two things. It explored the blind alleys, the ultimate abysses, of a quantitative conception of life, stimulated by the will-to-power and regulated only by the conflict of one power-unit—an individual, a class, a state—with another power-unit. And in the mass-production of goods it showed that mechanical improvements alone were not sufficient to produce socially valuable results—or even the highest degree of industrial efficiency. . . .

. . . [Thus] the truly significant part of the paleotechnic phase lay not in what it produced but in what it led to: it was a period of transition, a busy, congested, rubbish-strewn avenue between the eotechnic and the neotechnic economies. Institutions do not affect human life only directly: they also affect it by reason of the contrary reactions they produce. While humanly speaking the paleotechnic phase was a disastrous interlude, it helped by its very disorder to intensify the search for order, and by its special forms of brutality to clarify the goals of humane living. Action and reaction were equal—and in opposite directions.

The Neotechnic Phase

1. THE BEGINNINGS OF NEOTECHNICS

The neotechnic phase represents a third definite development in the machine during the last thousand years. It is a true mutation: it differs from the paleotechnic phase almost as white differs from black. But on the other hand, it bears the same relation to the eotechnic phase as the adult form does to the baby.

During the neotechnic phase, the conceptions, the anticipations, the imperious visions of Roger Bacon, Leonardo, Lord Verulam, Porta, Glanvill, and the other philosophers and technicians of that day at last found a local habitation. The first hasty sketches of the fifteenth century were not turned into working drawings: the first guesses were now re-enforced with a technique of verification: the first crude machines were at last carried to perfection in the exquisite mechanical technology of the new age, which gave to motors and turbines properties that had but a century earlier belonged almost exclusively to the clock. The superb animal audacity of Cellini, about to cast his difficult Perseus, or the scarcely less daring work of Michelangelo, constructing the dome of St. Peter's, was replaced by a patient co-operative experimentalism:

a whole society was now prepared to do what had heretofore been the burden of solitary individuals.

Now, while the neotechnic phase is a definite physical and social complex, one cannot define it as a period, partly because it has not yet developed its own form and organization, partly because we are still in the midst of it and cannot see its details in their ultimate relationships, and partly because it has not displaced the older régime with anything like the speed and decisiveness that characterized the transformation of the eotechnic order in the late eighteenth century. Emerging from the paleotechnic order, the neotechnic institutions have nevertheless in many cases compromised with it, given way before it, lost their identity by reason of the weight of vested interests that continued to support the obsolete instruments and the anti-social aims of the middle industrial era. *Paleotechnic ideals still largely dominate the industry and the politics of the Western World:* the class struggles and the national struggles are still pushed with relentless vigor. While eotechnic practices linger on as civilizing influences, in gardens and parks and painting and music and the theater, the paleotechnic remains a barbarizing influence. To deny this would be to cling to a fool's paradise. In the seventies Melville framed a question in fumbling verse whose significance has deepened with the intervening years:

> . . . Arts are tools;
> But tools, they say, are to the strong:
> Is Satan weak? Weak is the wrong?
> No blessed augury overrules:
> Your arts advanced in faith's decay:
> You are but drilling the new Hun
> Whose growl even now can some dismay.

To the extent that neotechnic industry has failed to transform the coal-and-iron complex, to the extent that it has failed to secure an adequate foundation for its humaner technology in the community as a whole, to the extent that it has lent its heightened powers to the miner, the financier, the militarist, the possibilities of disruption and chaos have increased.

But the beginnings of the neotechnic phase can nevertheless be approximately fixed. The first definite change, which increased the efficiency of prime movers enormously, multiplying it from three to nine times, was the perfection of the water-turbine by Fourneyron in 1832. This came at the end of a long series of studies, begun empirically in the development of the spoon-wheel in the sixteenth century and carried on scientifically by a series of investigators, notably Euler in the middle of the eighteenth century. Burdin,

Fourneyron's master, had made a series of improvements in the turbine type of water-wheel—a development for which one may perhaps thank France's relative backwardness in paleotechnic industry—and Fourneyron built a single turbine of 50 H.P. as early as 1832. With this, one must associate a series of important scientific discoveries made by Faraday during the same decade. One of these was his isolation of benzine: a liquid that made possible the commercial utilization of rubber. The other was his work on electro-magnetic currents, beginning with his discovery in 1831 that a conductor cutting the lines of force of a magnet created a difference in potential: shortly after he made this purely scientific discovery, he received an anonymous letter suggesting that the principle might be applied to the creation of great machines. Coming on top of the important work done by Volta, Galvani, Oersted, Ohm, and Ampère, Faraday's work on electricity, coupled with Joseph Henry's exactly contemporary research on the electro-magnet, erected a new basis for the conversion and distribution of energy and for most of the decisive neotechnic inventions.

By 1850 a good part of the fundamental scientific discoveries and inventions of the new phase had been made: the electric cell, the storage cell, the dynamo, the motor, the electric lamp, the spectroscope, the doctrine of the conservation of energy. Between 1875 and 1900 the detailed application of these inventions, the phonograph, the moving picture, the gasoline engine, the steam turbine, the airplane, were all sketched in, if not perfected, by 1900: these in turn effected a radical transformation of the power plant and the factory, and they had further effects in suggesting new principles for the design of cities and for the utilization of the environment as a whole. By 1910 a definite countermarch against paleotechnic methods began in industry itself.

The outlines of the process were blurred by the explosion of the World War and by the sordid disorders and reversions and compensations that followed it. Though the instruments of a neotechnic civilization are now at hand, and though many definite signs of an integration are not lacking, one cannot say confidently that a single region, much less our Western Civilization as a whole, has entirely embraced the neotechnic complex: for the necessary social institutions and the explicit social purposes requisite even for complete technological fulfillment are lacking. The gains in technics are never registered automatically in society: they require equally adroit inventions and adaptations in politics; and the careless habit of attributing to mechanical improvements a direct rôle as instruments of culture and civilization puts a demand upon the machine to which it cannot respond. Lacking a cooperative social intelligence and good-will, our most refined technics promises no more for society's improvement than an electric bulb would promise to a monkey in the midst of a jungle.

True: the industrial world produced during the nineteenth century is either technologically obsolete or socially dead. But unfortunately, its maggoty corpse has produced organisms which in turn may debilitate or possibly kill the new order that should take its place: perhaps leave it a hopeless cripple. One of the first steps, however, toward combating such disastrous results is to realize that even technically the Machine Age does not form a continuous and harmonious unit, that there is a deep gap between the paleotechnic and neotechnic phases, and that the habits of mind and the tactics we have carried over from the old order are obstacles in the way of our developing the new. . . .

3. NEW SOURCES OF ENERGY

The neotechnic phase was marked, to begin with, by the conquest of a new form of energy: electricity. The lodestone and the properties of amber when rubbed were both known to the Greeks; but the first modern treatise on electricity dates back to Dr. John Gilbert's *De Magnete,* published in 1600. Dr. Gilbert related frictional electricity to magnetism, and after him the redoubtable burgomaster of Magdeburg, Otto von Guericke, he of the Magdeburg hemispheres, recognized the phenomenon of repulsion, as well as attraction, while Leibniz apparently was the first to observe the electric spark. In the eighteenth century, with the invention of the Leyden jar, and with Franklin's discovery that lightning and electricity were one, the experimental work in this field began to take shape. By 1840 the preliminary scientific exploration was done, thanks to Oersted, Ohm, and above all, to Faraday; and in 1838 Joseph Henry had even observed the inductive effects at a distance from a Leyden jar: the first hint of radio communication.

Technics did not lag behind science. By 1838 Professor Jacobi, at St. Petersburg, had succeeded in propelling a boat on the Neva at four miles an hour by means of an "electro-magnetic engine," Davidson on the Edinburgh and Glasgow Railway achieved the same speed; while in 1849 Professor Page attained a speed of 19 miles per hour on a car on the Baltimore and Washington Railroad. The electric arc light was patented in 1846 and applied to the lighthouse at Dungeness, England, in 1862. Meanwhile, a dozen forms of the electric telegraph had been invented: by 1839 Morse and Steinheil had made possible instantaneous communication over long distances, using grounded wires at either end. The practical development of the dynamo by Werner Siemens (1866) and the alternator by Nikola Tesla (1887) were the two necessary steps in the substitution of electricity for steam: the central power station and distribution system, invented by Edison (1882), presently developed.

In the application of power, electricity effected revolutionary changes: these touched the location and the concentration of industries and the detailed organization of the factory—as well as a multitude of inter-related services and institutions. The metallurgical industries were transformed and certain industries like rubber production were stimulated. Let us look more closely at some of these changes.

During the paleotechnic phase, industry depended completely upon the coal mine as a source of power. Heavy industries were compelled to settle close to the mine itself, or to cheap means of transportation by means of the canal and the railroad. Electricity, on the other hand, can be developed by energy from a large number of sources: not merely coal, but the rapidly running river, the falls, the swift tidal estuary are available for energy; so are the direct rays of the sunlight (7000 H.P. per sun-acre) for the sun-batteries that have been built in Egypt; so too is the windmill, when accumulators are provided. Inaccessible mountain areas, like those in the Alps, the Tyrol, Norway, the Rockies, interior Africa, became for the first time potential sources of power and potential sites for modern industry: the harnessing of water-power, thanks to the supreme efficiency of the water-turbine, which rates around 90 per cent, opened up new sources of energy and new areas for colonization—areas more irregular in topography and often more salubrious in climate than the valley-bottoms and lowlands of the earlier eras. Because of the enormous vested interest in coal measures, the cheaper sources of energy have not received sufficient systematic attention upon the part of inventors: but the present utilization of solar energy in agriculture—about 0.13 per cent of the total amount of solar energy received—presents a challenge to the scientific engineer; while the possibility of using differences of temperature between the upper and lower levels of sea water in the tropics offers still another prospect for escaping servitude to coal.

The availability of water-power for producing energy, finally, changes the potential distribution of modern industry throughout the planet and reduces the peculiar industrial dominance that Europe and the United States held under the coal-and-iron régime. For Asia and South America are almost as well endowed with water-power—over fifty million horsepower each—as the older industrial regions, and Africa has three times as much as either Europe or North America. Even within Europe and the United States a shifting of the industrial center of gravity is taking place: thus the leadership in hydroelectric power development has gone to Italy, France, Norway, Switzerland and Sweden in the order named, and a similar shift is taking place toward the two great spinal mountain-systems of the United States. The coal measures are no longer the exclusive measures of industrial power.

Unlike coal in long distance transportation, or like steam in local distribution, electricity is much easier to transmit without heavy losses of energy and higher costs. Wires carrying high tension alternating currents can cut across mountains which no road vehicle can pass over; and once an electric power utility is established the rate of deterioration is slow. Moreover, electricity is readily convertible into various forms: the motor, to do mechanical work, the electric lamp, to light, the electric radiator, to heat, the x-ray tube and the ultra-violet light, to penetrate and explore, and the selenium cell, to effect automatic control. . . .

16. THE PRESENT PSEUDOMORPH

So far, in treating the neotechnic phase, I have concerned myself more with description and actuality rather than with prophecy and potentiality. But he who says A in neotechnics has already said B, and it is with the social implications and consequences of the neotechnic economy, rather than with its typical technical instruments, that I purpose to . . . [concern myself now].

There is, however . . . [a fundamental] difficulty in dealing with . . . [the neotechnic] phase: namely, we are still in the midst of the transition. The scientific knowledge, the machines and the utilities, the technological methods, the habits of life and the human ends that belong to this economy are far from being dominant in our present civilization. The fact is that in the great industrial areas of Western Europe and America and in the exploitable territories that are under the control of these centers, the paleotechnic phase is still intact and all its essential characteristics are uppermost, even though many of the machines it uses are neotechnic ones or have been made over—as in the electrification of railroad systems—by neotechnic methods. In this persistence of paleotechnic practices the original anti-vital bias of the machine is evident: bellicose, money-centred, life-curbing, we continue to worship the twin deities, Mammon and Moloch, to say nothing of more abysmally savage tribal gods. . . .

. . . [This fact] is best explained, I think, by a concept put forward by Oswald Spengler in the second volume of the *Decline of the West:* the concept of the cultural pseudomorph. Spengler points to the common fact in geology that a rock may retain its structure after certain elements have been leached out of it and been replaced by an entirely different kind of material.

Since the apparent structure of the old rock remains, the new product is termed a pseudomorph. A similar metamorphosis is possible in culture: new forces, activities, institutions, instead of crystallizing independently into their own appropriate forms, may creep into the structure of an existing civilization. This perhaps is the essential fact of our present situation. As a civilization, we have not yet entered the neotechnic phase; and should a future historian use the present terminology, he would undoubtedly have to characterize the current transition as a mesotechnic period: we are still living, in Matthew Arnold's words, between two worlds, one dead, the other powerless to be born.

. . . The examples of pseudomorphic forms can be drawn from every department. In city growth, for instance, we have utilized electric and gasoline transportation to increase the congestion which was the original result of the capitalistic concentrations of coal and steam power: the new means have been used to extend the area and population of these obsolete and inefficient and humanly defective metropolitan centers. Similarly the steel frame construction in architecture, which permits the fullest use of glass and the most complete utilization of sunlight, has been used in America to increase the overcrowding of buildings and the obliteration of sunlight. The psychological study of human behavior is used to condition people to accept the goods offered by the canny advertisers, despite the fact that science, as applied in the National Bureau of Standards at Washington, gives measurable and rateable levels of performance for commodities whose worth is now putatively established by purely subjective methods. The planning and coordination of productive enterprise, in the hands of private bankers rather than public servants, becomes a method of preserving monopoly control for privileged financial groups or privileged countries. Labor saving devices, instead of spreading the total amount of leisure, become means of keeping at a depauperate level an increasing part of the population. The airplane, instead of merely increasing the amount of travel and intercourse between countries, has increased their fear of each other: as an instrument of war, in combination with the latest chemical achievements in poison gas, it promises a ruthlessness of extermination that man has heretofore not been able to apply to either bugs or rats. The neotechnic refinement of the machine, without a coordinate development of higher social purposes, has only magnified the possibilities of depravity and barbarism.

Not alone have the older forms of technics served to constrain the development of the neotechnic economy: but the new inventions and devices have been frequently used to maintain, renew, and stabilize the structure of the old order. There is a political and financial vested interest in obsolete technical equipment: that underlying conflict between business interests and industrial interests, which Veblen analyzed with great acuteness in *The Theory of Business Enterprise,* is accentuated by the fact that vast amounts of capital are sunk in antiquated machines and burdensome utilities. Financial acquisitiveness which had originally speeded invention now furthers technical inertia. Hence the tardiness in introducing the automatic telephone: hence the continued design of automobiles in terms of superficial fashions, rather than with any readiness to take advantage of aero-dynamic principles in building for comfort and speed and economy: hence the continued purchase of patent rights for improvements which are then quietly extirpated by the monopoly holding them.

And this reluctance, this resistance, this inertia have good reason: the old has every cause to fear the superiority of the new. The planned and integrated industry of neotechnic design promises so much greater efficiency than the old that not a single institution appropriate to an economy of parsimony will remain unaltered in an economy of surplus: particularly the institutions limiting ownership and dividends to a small fragment of the population, who thus absorb the purchasing power by excessive re-investment in industrial enterprise and add to its over-expansion. These institutions, indeed, are incompatible with a planned production and distribution of the necessaries of life, for financial values and real goods cannot be equated to the advantage of the whole community on terms that will benefit chiefly the private capitalists by and for whom the original structure of capitalism was created.

One need not wonder that those who affect to control the destinies of industrial society, the bankers, the business men, and the politicians, have steadily put the brakes upon the transition and have sought to limit the neotechnic developments and avoid the drastic changes that must be effected throughout the entire social milieu. The present pseudomorph is, socially and technically, third-rate. It has only a fraction of the efficiency that the neotechnic civilization as a whole may possess, provided it finally produces its own institutional forms and controls and directions and patterns. At present, instead of finding these forms, we have applied our skill and invention in such a manner as to give a fresh lease of life to many of the obsolete capitalist and militarist institutions of the older period. Paleotechnic purposes with neotechnic means: that is the most obvious characteristic of the present order. And that is why a good part of the machines and institutions that boast of being "new" or "advanced" or "progressive" are often so only in the way that a modern battleship is new and advanced: they may in fact be reactionary, and they may stand in the way of the fresh integration of work and art and life that we must seek and create.

3. THE ELEMENTS OF SOCIAL ENERGETICS

Let us examine the implications of neotechnic developments, within the machine itself, upon our economic objectives, upon the organization of work, upon the direction of industry and the goals of consumption, upon the emerging social purposes of the neotechnic phase of civilization. . . .

In the course of capitalistic enterprise, which accompanied the widespread introduction of machines and machine-methods in the fifteenth and sixteenth centuries, the focus of industry shifted from the craft guild to the merchant guild or the livery company or the company of merchant adventurers, or to the special organization for exploiting patent monopolies. The means of exchange usurped the function and meaning of the things that were exchanged: money itself became a commodity and money-getting became a specialized form of activity. Under capitalism profit reigned as the main economic objective; and profit became the decisive factor in all industrial enterprise. Inventions that promised profits, industries that produced profits, were fostered. The reward of capital, if not the first claim upon productive enterprise, was at all events the dominating one: the service of the consumer and the support of the worker were entirely secondary. Even in a period of crisis and breakdown . . . dividends continue to be paid to rentiers out of past accumulation while the industry itself often operates at a loss, or the mass of workers are turned out to starve. Sometimes profits were obtained by lowering the costs and spreading the product: but if they could be had only by offering inferior or adulterated goods—as in the sale of medical nostrums or the slum housing of the underpaid worker—health and well-being were sacrificed to gain. The community, instead of receiving a full return for its goods and services, permitted a portion of the product to be diverted for the private gratification of the holders of land and capital. These holders of land and capital, backed up by the law and all the instruments of government, determined privately and solely in accordance with the canon of profit what should be produced and how much and where and how and by whom and on what terms.

In the economic analysis of the society that grew up on this basis, the three main terms in industrial activity were production, distribution, and consumption. Profits were to be increased by cheaper production, by wider and multifold distribution, and by a steadily rising standard of consumptive expenditure, with—sometimes in lieu of that, sometimes accompanying it—an enlarging market of consumers. Saving labor, or cheapening labor by a superiority of bargaining power—obtained by withholding land from the laborer and monopolizing the new instruments of production—were the two chief means, from the capitalist's standpoint, of increasing the margin of profits. Saving labor by rationalization was a real improvement which bettered everything but the position of the laborer. The stimulation of the demand for goods was the chief means of increasing the turnover: hence the problem of capitalism was essentially not to satisfy needs but to create demands. And the attempt to represent this process of private aggrandizement and class-advantage as a natural and socially beneficent one was perhaps the main labor of political economists during the nineteenth century.

When one examines economic activities from the standpoint of the employment of energy and the service of human life, this whole financial structure of production and consumption turns out to have mainly a superstitious basis. At the bottom of the structure are farmer and peasant, who during the entire course of the industrial revolution, which their increase of the food supply has made possible, have scarcely ever received an adequate return for their products—at least on the basis of pecuniary accountancy by which the rest of this society was run. Furthermore: what are called gains in capitalist economics often turn out, from the standpoint of social energetics, to be losses; while the real gains, the gains upon which all the activities of life, civilization, and culture ultimately depend were either counted as losses, or were ignored, because they remained outside the commercial scheme of accountancy.

What are, then, the essentials of the economic processes in relation to energy and to life? The essential processes are conversion, production, consumption, and creation. In the first two steps energy is seized and prepared for the sustenance of life. In the third stage, life is supported and renewed in order that it may wind itself up, so to speak, on the higher levels of thought and culture, instead of being short-circuited at once back into the preparatory functions. Normal human societies exhibit all four stages of the economic processes: but their absolute quantities and their proportions vary with the social milieu.

Conversion has to do with the utilization of the environment as a source of energy. The prime fact of all economic activity, from that of the lower organisms up to the most advanced human cultures, is the conversion of the sun's energies: this transformation depends upon the heat-conserving properties of the atmosphere, upon the geological processes of uplift and erosion and soil-building, upon the conditions of climate and local topography, and —most important of all—upon the green leaf reaction in growing plants. This seizure of energy is the original source of all our gains: on a purely energetic interpretation of the process, all that happens after this is a dissipation of energy—a dissipation that may be retarded, that may be dammed up, that may be temporarily diverted by human ingenuity, but in the long run cannot be averted. All the permanent monuments of human culture are attempts, by using more attenuated physical means of preserving and transmitting this energy, to avert the hour of ultimate extinction. The most important conquest of energy was man's original discovery and utilization of fire; after that, the most significant transformation of the environment came through the cultivation of the grain-bearing grasses, the vegetables, and the domestic animals. Indeed, the enormous increase in population which took place at the beginning of the nineteenth century, *before* the machine had made any appreciable change in agriculture, was due to the opening of immense areas of free land for grain cultivation and cattle raising and the better provision of winter fodder crops, combined with the addition of three new energy crops —sugar cane, sugar beet, and potato—to the diet of the industrial population.

The mechanical conversion of energy is second in importance to the organic conversion. But in the development of technics the invention of the water-wheel, the water-turbine, the steam engine, and the gas engine multiplied the energies that were available to man through the use of foods grown for himself and his domestic animals. Without the magnification of human energy made possible through this series of prime movers, our apparatus of production and transport could not have reached the gigantic scale it attained in the nineteenth century. All the further steps in the economic process depend upon the original act of conversion: the level of achievement can never rise higher than the level of the energy originally converted, and just as only an insignificant part of the sun's energy available is utilized in conversion, so only a small part of this, in turn, finally is utilized in consumption and creation.

Conversion lifts the energy available to a peak: from that point on energy runs down hill, in gathering and shaping the raw materials, in transporting supplies and products, and in the processes of consumption itself. Not until the economic process reaches the stage of creation—not until it supplies the human animal with more energy than he needs to maintain his physical existence, and not until still other energies are transformed into the more durable media of art and science and philosophy, of books, buildings and symbols —is there anything that can be called, even within a limited span of time, a gain. At one end of the process is the conversion of the free energy of nature and its transformation into forms usable by agriculture and technology: at the other end of the process is the conversion of the intermediate, preparatory products into human subsistence, and into those cultural forms that are usable by succeeding generations of men. . . .

The permanent gain that emerges from the whole economic process is in the relatively non-material elements in culture—in the social heritage itself, in the arts and sciences, in the traditions and processes of technology, or directly in life itself, in those real enrichments that come from the free exploitation of organic energy in thought and action and emotional experience, in play and adventure and drama and personal development—gains that last through memory and communication beyond the immediate moment in which they are enjoyed. In short, as John Ruskin put it, *There is no Wealth but Life;* and what we call wealth is in fact wealth only when it is a sign of potential or actual vitality.

An economic process that did not produce this margin for leisure, enjoyment, absorption, creative activity, communication and transmission would completely lack human meaning and reference. In the histories of human groups there are of course periods, periods of starvation, periods of flood and earthquake and war, when man fights a losing fight with his environment, and does not even secure bare physical survival; and there are moments when the complete social process is brutally cut short. But even in the most perverse and degraded forms of life, there is an aspect that corresponds, vitally and psychically speaking, to "creation," and even in the most inadequate forms of production, such as that which prevailed during the paleotechnic phase, there remains a surplus not arrogated by industry. Whether this surplus goes to increase the preparatory processes, or whether it is to be spent on creation, is a choice that cannot be automatically decided; and the tendency in capitalist society to put it back quickly into the preparatory processes, and to make possible increased production by applying pressure to consumption, is merely a further indication of its absence of social criteria.

The real significance of the machine, socially speaking, does not consist either in the multiplication of goods or the multiplication of wants, real or illusory. Its significance lies in the gains of energy through increased conversion, through efficient production, through balanced consumption, and through socialized creation. The test of economic success does not, therefore, lie in the industrial process alone, and it cannot be measured by the amount of horsepower converted or by the amount commanded by an individual user: for the important factors here are not quantities but ratios: ratios of mechanical effort to social and cultural results. A society in which production and consumption completely cancelled out the gains of conversion—in which people worked to live and lived to work—would remain socially inefficient, even if the entire population were constantly employed, and adequately fed, clothed, and sheltered.

The ultimate test of an efficient industry is the ratio between productive means and the achieved ends. Hence a society with a low scale of conversion but with a high amount of creation is humanly speaking superior to a society with an enormous panoply of converters and a small and inadequate army of creators. By the ruthless pillage of the food-producing territories of Asia and Africa, the Roman Empire appropriated far more energy than Greece, with its sparse abstemious dietary and its low standard of living. But Rome produced no poem, no statue, no original architecture, no work of science, no philosophy comparable to the Odyssey, the Parthenon, the works of the sixth and fifth century sculptors, and the science of Pythagoras, Euclid, Archimedes, Hero: and so the quantitative grandeur and luxury and power of the Romans, despite their extraordinary capacity as engineers, remained relatively meaningless: even for the continued development of technics the work of the Greek mathematicians and physicists was more important.

This is why no working ideal for machine production can be based solely on the gospel of work: still less can it be based upon an uncritical belief in constantly raising the quantitative standard of consumption. If we are to achieve a purposive and cultivated use of the enormous energies now happily at our disposal, we must examine in detail the processes that lead up to the final state of leisure, free activity, creation. It is because of the lapse and mismanagement of these processes that we have not reached the desirable end; and it is because of our failure to frame a comprehensive scheme of ends that we have not succeeded in achieving even the beginnings of social efficiency in the preparatory work.

How is this margin to be achieved and how is it to be applied? Already we are faced with political and moral problems as well as technological ones. There is nothing in the nature of the machine as such, nothing in the training of the technician as such, that will provide us with a sufficient answer. We shall of course need his help: but in turn *he* will need help from other quarters of the compass, far beyond the province of technology.

THORSTEIN VEBLEN

THORSTEIN VEBLEN was born in 1857 on a frontier farm in Wisconsin, the fourth son of Norwegian immigrant parents. His youth was spent in a pioneer farming community in Minnesota. It was clear from the outset that Veblen was not interested either in farming or the ministry, the only occupations open to him if he continued to live in this settlement. It was also evident that he was endowed with an exceptionally gifted intellect. He attended, and in 1880 was graduated from, Carleton College in Minnesota. His teacher, John Bates Clark (1847–1938), with whose economic theory he later came to disagree completely, encouraged him to take up a career in teaching and scholarship. For graduate study he went to Johns Hopkins and later to Yale, where he received his doctorate in 1884. He taught in several universities, Cornell from 1890 to 1892, the University of Chicago from 1892 to 1906, Stanford from 1906 to 1910, and Missouri from 1911 to 1918. From 1918 to his retirement in 1927 he served as a lecturer at the New School for Social Research in New York City. Ironically, he died in 1929, the year of the Wall Street "crash," when general confidence in so many of the institutions and conventions of the business civilization he criticized was profoundly shaken.

Although Veblen never wished to be considered primarily as a critic, it was in this role that he made his lasting impression as the most original of American economists. He saw society as a complex of habitual customs or conventions (he defined a custom or convention as an "institution," that is, a "widely spread, or social, habit of thought") which exercises prescriptive authority over the behavior of individuals and groups. In his view, the main task of economic science is to explain the origin and development of the "institutions" of Western culture and to use such explanations for interpreting current economic activity. The "institutional" framework of a culture is then the fact of paramount importance. Behavior patterns of individuals and groups are impossible to understand apart from an analysis of the socio-economic context in which they exist and function.

Among the many "institutions" which Veblen discerned in modern capitalist society, none were so important as (1) the "business enterprise" or the "pecuniary habit of thought" which directs social activity to the pursuit of money profits in an economy of private means of production, and (2) the "machine process" or "the widely spread habit of thought" which increasingly entrusts the production of goods and services to the machine methods of modern technological industrialism. The dichotomy which Veblen conceived to exist between these two "institutions" of business and industry is found in all his writings and is fundamental to his criticism of contemporary society. For he deeply felt that the ends of business (pecuniary gains) would always be in sharp conflict with the ends of industry (maximum efficiency in production). Envisioning industrial society as a "comprehensive, balanced mechanical process," Veblen saw the community's welfare as increasingly dependent upon the smooth articulation and coordination of its technological parts. "It therefore rests with the business men to make or mar the running adjustments of industry." Although Veblen's estimation of the possibility that business might develop ways to allow industry to function at maximum efficiency varied during his scholarly career, in the last analysis the influence of early twentieth-century "muckraking" never left him. He was skeptical that "business enterprise" could ever fully liberate "the machine process," for he felt that in the fundamental conflict between the profit-making necessities of business and the "instinct of workmanship" upon which technology depended (a conflict often fought within the personality of individual "captains of industry"), creative values were most likely to be subordinated and frustrated by pecuniary motives.

A prolific writer in various media, Veblen is best known today for a series of remarkable books which started with the publication of *The Theory of the Leisure Class* (1899) and continued with *The Theory of Business Enterprise* (1904), from which the following selection has been taken. Other works were *The Instinct of Workmanship and the State of the Industrial Arts* (1914), *Imperial Germany and the Industrial Revolution* (1915), *An Inquiry into the Nature of Peace* (1917), *The Higher Learning in America* (1919), *The Place of Science in Modern Civilization* (1919), *The Vested Interests and the State of the Industrial Arts* (1919), *The Engineers and the Price System* (1921), and *Absentee Ownership and Business Enterprise in Recent Times* (1923).

THE THEORY OF BUSINESS ENTERPRISE

CHAPTER I: INTRODUCTORY

. . . The scope and method of modern industry are given by the machine. This may not seem to hold true for all industries, perhaps not for the greater part of industry as rated by the bulk of the output or by the aggregate volume of labor expended. But it holds true to such an extent and in such a pervasive manner that a modern industrial community cannot go on except by the help of the accepted mechanical appliances and processes. The machine industries—those portions of the industrial system in which the machine process is paramount—are in a dominant position; they set the pace for the rest of the industrial system. In this sense the present is the age of the machine process. This dominance of the machine process in industry marks off the present industrial situation from all else of its kind. . . .

This selection has been reprinted from *The Theory of Business Enterprise* by Thorstein Veblen, Copyright 1904 by Charles Scribner's Sons, Copyright 1932 by Ann Bevans and Becky Veblen; used by permission of the publishers, Charles Scribner's Sons, New York (1921 edition, pp. 1–2, 5–18).

CHAPTER II: THE MACHINE PROCESS

In its bearing on modern life and modern business, the "machine process" means something more comprehensive and less external than a mere aggregate of mechanical appliances for the mediation of human labor. It means that, but it means something more than that. The civil engineer, the mechanical engineer, the navigator, the mining expert, the industrial chemist and mineralogist, the electrician,—the work of all these falls within the lines of the modern machine process, as well as the work of the inventor who devises the appliances of that process and that of the mechanician who puts the inventions into effect and oversees their working. The scope of the process is larger than the machine. In those branches of industry in which machine methods have been introduced, many agencies which are not to be classed as mechanical appliances, simply, have been drawn into the process, and have become integral factors in it. Chemical properties of minerals, *e.g.,* are counted on in the carrying out of metallurgical processes with much the same certainty and calculable effect as are the motions of those mechanical appliances by whose use the minerals are handled. The sequence of the process involves both the one and the other, both the apparatus and the materials, in such intimate interaction that the process cannot be spoken of simply as an action of the apparatus upon the materials. It is not simply that the apparatus reshapes the materials; the materials reshape themselves by the help of the apparatus. Similarly in such other processes as the refining of petroleum, oil, or sugar; in the work of the industrial chemical laboratories; in the use of wind, water, or electricity, etc.

Wherever manual dexterity, the rule of thumb, and the fortuitous conjunctures of the seasons have been supplanted by a reasoned procedure on the basis of a systematic knowledge of the forces employed, there the mechanical industry is to be found, even in the absence of intricate mechanical contrivances. It is a question of the character of the process rather than a question of the complexity of the contrivances employed. Chemical, agricultural, and animal industries, as carried on by the characteristically modern methods and in due touch with the market, are to be included in the modern complex of mechanical industry.

No one of the mechanical processes carried on by the use of a given outfit of appliances is independent of other processes going on elsewhere. Each draws upon and presupposes the proper working of many other processes of a similarly mechanical character. None of the processes in the mechanical industries is self-sufficing. Each follows some and precedes other processes in an endless sequence, into which each fits and to the requirements of which each must adapt its own working. The whole concert of industrial operations is to be taken as a machine process, made up of interlocking detail processes, rather than as a multiplicity of mechanical appliances each doing its particular work in severalty. This comprehensive industrial process draws into its scope and turns to account all branches of knowledge that have to do with the material sciences, and the whole makes a more or less delicately balanced complex of sub-processes.

Looked at in this way the industrial process shows two well-marked general characteristics: (a) the running maintenance of interstitial adjustments between the several sub-processes or branches of industry, wherever in their working they touch one another in the sequence of industrial elaboration; and (b) an unremitting requirement of quantitative precision, accuracy in point of time and sequence, in the proper inclusion and exclusion of forces affecting the outcome, in the magnitude of the various physical characteristics (weight, size, density, hardness, tensile strength, elasticity, temperature, chemical reaction, actinic sensitiveness, etc.) of the materials handled as well as of the appliances employed. This requirement of mechanical accuracy and nice adaptation to specific uses has led to a gradual pervading enforcement of uniformity, to a reduction to staple grades and staple character in the materials handled, and to a thorough standardizing of tools and units of measurement. Standard physical measurements are of the essence of the machine's régime.

The modern industrial communities show an unprecedented uniformity and precise equivalence in legally adopted weights and measures. Something of this kind would be brought about by the needs of commerce, even without the urgency given to the movement for uniformity by the requirements of the machine industry. But within the industrial field the movement for standardization has outrun the urging of commercial needs, and has penetrated every corner of the mechanical industries. The specifically commercial need of uniformity in weights and measures of merchantable goods and in monetary units has not carried standardization in these items to the extent to which the mechanical need of the industrial process has carried out a sweeping standardization in the means by which the machine process works, as well as in the products which it turns out.

As a matter of course, tools and the various structural materials used are made of standard sizes, shapes, and gauges. When the dimensions, in fractions of an inch or in millimetres, and the weight, in fractions of a pound or in grammes, are given, the expert foreman or workman, confidently and without reflection, infers the rest of what need be known of the uses to which any given item that passes under his hand may be turned. The adjustment and adaptation of part to part and of process to process has passed out of the category of craftsmanlike skill into the category of mechanical standardization. Hence, perhaps, the greatest, most wide-reaching gain in productive celerity and efficiency through modern methods, and hence the largest saving of labor in modern industry.

Tools, mechanical appliances and movements, and structural materials are scheduled by certain conventional scales and gauges; and modern industry has little use for, and can make little use of, what does not conform to the standard. What is not competently standardized calls for too much of craftsmanlike skill, reflection, and individual elaboration, and is therefore not available for economical use in the processes. Irregularity, departure from standard measurements in any of the measurable facts, is of itself a fault in any item that is to find a use in the industrial process, for it brings delay, it detracts from its ready usability in the nicely adjusted process into which it is to go; and a delay at any point means a more or less far-reaching and intolerable retardation of the comprehensive industrial process at large. Irregularity in products intended for industrial use carries a penalty to the nonconforming producer which urges him to fall into line and submit to the required standardization.

The materials and moving forces of industry are undergoing a like reduction to staple kinds, styles, grades, and gauge. Even such forces as would seem at first sight not to lend themselves to standardization, either in their production or their use, are subjected to uniform scales of measurement; as, *e.g.,* water-power, steam, electricity, and human labor. The latter is perhaps the least amenable to standardization, but, for all that, it is bargained for, delivered, and turned to account on schedules of time, speed, and intensity which are continually sought to be reduced to a more precise measurement and a more sweeping uniformity.

The like is true of the finished products. Modern consumers in great part supply their wants with commodities that conform to certain staple specifications of size, weight, and grade. The consumer (that is to say the vulgar consumer) furnishes his house, his table, and his person with supplies of standard weight and measure, and he can to an appreciable degree specify his needs and his consumption in the notation of the standard gauge. As regards the mass of civilized mankind, the idiosyncrasies of the individual consumers are required to conform to the uniform gradations imposed upon consumable goods by the comprehensive mechanical processes of industry.

"Local color," it is said, is falling into abeyance in modern life, and where it is still found it tends to assert itself in units of the standard gauge.

From this mechanical standardization of consumable goods it follows, on the one hand, that the demand for goods settles upon certain defined lines of production which handle certain materials of definite grade, in certain, somewhat invariable forms and proportions; which leads to well-defined methods and measurements in the processes of production, shortening the average period of "ripening" that intervenes between the first raw stage of the product and its finished shape, and reducing the aggregate stock of goods necessary to be carried for the supply of current wants, whether in the raw or in the finished form. Standardization means economy at nearly all points of the process of supplying goods, and at the same time it means certainty and expedition at nearly all points in the business operations involved in meeting current wants. Besides this, the standardization of goods means that the interdependence of industrial processes is reduced to more definite terms than before the mechanical standardization came to its present degree of elaborateness and rigor. The margin of admissible variation, in time, place, form, and amount, is narrowed. Materials, to answer the needs of standardized industry, must be drawn from certain standard sources at a definite rate of supply. Hence any given detail industry depends closely on receiving its supplies from certain, relatively few, industrial establishments whose work belongs earlier in the process of elaboration. And it may similarly depend on certain other, closely defined, industrial establishments for a vent of its own specialized and standardized product. It may likewise depend in a strict manner on special means of transportation.

Machine production leads to a standardization of services as well as of goods. So, for instance, the modern means of communication and the system into which these means are organized are also of the nature of a mechanical process, and in this mechanical process of service and intercourse the life of all civilized men is more or less intimately involved. To make effective use of the modern system of communication in any or all of its ramifications (streets, railways, steamship lines, telephone, telegraph, postal service, etc.), men are required to adapt their needs and their motions to the exigencies of the process whereby this civilized method of intercourse is carried into effect. The service is standardized, and therefore the use of it is standardized also. Schedules of time, place, and circumstance rule throughout. The scheme of everyday life must be arranged with a strict regard to the exigencies of the process whereby this range of human needs is served, if full advantage is to be taken of this system of intercourse, which means that, in so far, one's plans and projects must be conceived and worked out in terms of those standard units which the system imposes.

For the population of the towns and cities, at least, much the same rule holds true of the distribution of consumable goods. So, also, amusements and diversions, much of the current amenities of life, are organized into a more or less sweeping process to which those who would benefit by the advantages offered must adapt their schedule of wants and the disposition of their time and effort. The frequency, duration, intensity, grade, and sequence are not, in the main, matters for the free discretion of the individuals who participate. Throughout the scheme of life of that portion of mankind that clusters about the centers of modern culture the industrial process makes itself felt and enforces a degree of conformity to the canon of accurate quantitative measurement. There comes to prevail a degree of standardization and precise mechanical adjustment of the details of everyday life, which presumes a facile and unbroken working of all those processes that minister to these standardized human wants.

As a result of this superinduced mechanical regularity of life, the livelihood of individuals is, over large areas, affected in an approximately uniform manner by any incident which at all seriously affects the industrial process at any point.

As was noted above, each industrial unit, represented by a given industrial "plant," stands in close relations of interdependence with other industrial processes going forward elsewhere, near or far away, from which it receives supplies—materials, apparatus, and the like—and to which it turns over its output of products and waste, or on which it depends for auxiliary work, such as transportation. The resulting concatenation of industries has been noticed by most modern writers. It is commonly discussed under the head of the division of labor. Evidently the prevalent standardization of industrial means, methods, and products greatly increases the reach of this concatenation of industries, at the same time that it enforces a close conformity in point of time, volume, and character of the product, whether the product is goods or services.

By virtue of this concatenation of processes the modern industrial system at large bears the character of a comprehensive, balanced mechanical process. In order to an efficient working of this industrial process at large, the various constituent sub-processes must work in due coördination throughout the whole. Any degree of maladjustment in the interstitial coördinations of this industrial process at large in some degree hinders its working. Similarly, any given detail process or any industrial plant will do its work to full advantage only when due adjustment is had between its work and the work done by the rest. The higher the degree of development reached by a given industrial community, the more comprehensive and urgent becomes this requirement of interstitial adjustment. And the more fully a given industry has taken on the character of a mechanical process, and the more extensively and closely it is correlated in its work with other industries that precede or follow it in the sequence of elaboration, the more urgent, other things equal, is the need of maintaining the proper working relations with these other industries, the greater is the industrial detriment suffered from any derangement of the accustomed working relations, and the greater is the industrial gain to be derived from a closer adaptation and a more facile method of readjustment in the event of a disturbance,—the greater is also the chance for an effectual disturbance of industry at the particular point. This mechanical concatenation of industrial processes makes for solidarity in the administration of any group of related industries, and more remotely it makes for solidarity in the management of the entire industrial traffic of the community.

A disturbance at any point, whereby any given branch of industry fails to do its share in the work of the system at large, immediately affects the neighboring or related branches which come before or after it in the sequence, and is transmitted through their derangement to the remoter portions of the system. The disturbance is rarely confined to the single plant or the single line of production first affected, but spreads in some measure to the rest. A disturbance at any point brings more or less derangement to the industrial process at large. So that any maladjustment of the system involves a larger waste than simply the disabling of one or two members in the complex industrial structure. So much is clear, that the keeping of the balance in the comprehensive machine process of industry is a matter of the gravest urgency if the productive mechanism is to proceed with its work in an efficient manner, so as to avoid idleness, waste, and hardship. The management of the various industrial plants and processes in due correlation with all the rest, and the supervision of the interstitial adjustments of the system, are commonly conceived to be a work of greater consequence to the community's well-being than any of the detail work involved in carrying on a given process of production. This work of interstitial adjustment, and in great part also the more immediate supervision of the various industrial processes, have become urgent only since the advent of the machine industry and in proportion as the machine industry has advanced in compass and consistency. . . .

HARRISON BROWN

FROM the point of view of the ordinary observer in Europe or America at the end of the nineteenth century, the world still seemed a place of unlimited resources. As fast as population multiplied, new industries seemed always to develop to give employment and provide the goods required to sustain men in increasingly higher standards of material life. As fast as certain specialists could forecast the imminent exhaustion of mineral, forest, and energy resources, new veins of ore were discovered and new types of fuels perfected. Agronomy always seemed able to enrich the yield, at decreasing cost, of the arable acres at man's disposal. The tragic view of the human race, described and analyzed by Thomas Malthus (1766–1834), as pressed inexorably into moral dilemma by the weight of population bearing upon a limited food supply, seemed farfetched. There was the feeling that resources were incalculably great, that productive land was unbounded, that science and industry would indeed be able always to provide sufficiently for the growing needs of man.

In the mid-twentieth century students of science and society have tended to view man's relation to his natural and industrial environment less sanguinely. Medical and hygienic science had succeeded, in the Western world, in drastically decreasing death rates and increasing life expectancies, and the demand of poorer areas—often regions only newly entering political life as independent nation-states—to receive like benefits was rising on every hand. Industry, dependent upon increasingly complex, and increasingly fragile, networks of markets and methods of transportation, consumed enormous quantities of raw materials even as it entered a new phase of productivity which seemed only to forecast things to come. As standards of life rose in the European-American sectors of the globe, "underdeveloped" areas, clamoring either for the material well-being, or for the military power which industrialization seemed to guarantee, were precipitated into a race to "catch up" with technological civilization. At the same time, it became apparent that the growth of population, which in Europe had stabilized after the upward surge of the nineteenth century, was becoming a world-wide phenomenon. Industrial societies, thoroughly grounded in "scientific" techniques and attitudes, alone seemed to offer the possibility of providing sustenance for these masses of men; yet it was clear that industrialization, if not a cause, was a powerful factor in the population growth to begin with. It was equally clear that any slowing down of the pace of production increase was dangerous; yet the industrial system was becoming so complicated and interdependent as to be vulnerable, in an unprecedented degree, to disruption, war, and economic depression.

In these circumstances, thoughtful men have reexamined the basic ideas of Malthus. Most of these are not prophets of despair; on the contrary they plead only for intelligence and caution, for objective study and for human discipline and solidarity, in the task of making available the benefits of industry and science to wider groups of men. Harrison Brown, author of *The Challenge of Man's Future* (1954), from which the following selection has been taken, does not sound false alarms, but points to the pitfalls as well as the promises of world-wide industrialization, and underscores the fact that the industrialization of present-day agrarian societies entails patterns of socio-economic change that are in many ways not comparable with those familiar to Western man.

Harrison Brown was born in Wyoming in 1917, studied at the University of California, and received a Ph.D. in chemistry at Johns Hopkins. A leading geochemist, he has been associated with the Oak Ridge Plutonium Project and taught at the University of Chicago. Since 1951 he has been professor of geochemistry at the California Institute of Technology. His first book was *Must Destruction Be Our Destiny?* (1946).

THE CHALLENGE OF MAN'S FUTURE

CHAPTER VII: PATTERNS OF THE FUTURE

. . . [The] resources available to man are being rapidly consumed, but . . . at the same time, new resources are being made available by our increased knowledge and improved technology. Given adequate supplies of energy, man can, in principle, extract everything that he needs for his existence at a high standard of living from substances which exist abundantly on the earth's surface—air, sea water, and ordinary rock. . . . Within the rock itself there is sufficient energy to carry out the processing and also to provide power for the operation of industrial machinery. At the same time, man can extract energy from sunlight and use it to operate his factories. When we look at the situation solely from the point of view of technological and energetic feasibility, we must conclude that the resources available to man permit him, in principle, to provide adequately for a very large population for a very long period of time.

There are, of course, physical limitations of some sort which will determine the maximum number of human beings who can live on the earth's surface. But at the present time we are far from the ultimate limit of the number of persons who could be provided for. If we were willing to be crowded together closely enough, to eat foods which would bear little resemblance to the foods we eat today, and to be deprived of simple but satisfying luxuries such as fireplaces, gardens, and lawns, a world population of 50 billion persons would

This selection has been reprinted from *The Challenge of Man's Future* by Harrison Brown, Copyright 1954 by Harrison Brown and used by permission of The Viking Press, Inc., New York (pp. 220–228, 243–246, 248–249, 254–258).

not be out of the question. And if we really put our minds to the problem we could construct floating islands where people might live and where algae farms could function, and perhaps 100 billion persons could be provided for. If we set strict limits to physical activities so that caloric requirements could be kept at very low levels, perhaps we could provide for 200 billion persons.

At this point the reader is probably saying to himself that he would have little desire to live in such a world, and he can rest assured that the author is thinking exactly the same thing. But a substantial fraction of humanity today is behaving as if it would like to create such a world. It is behaving as if it were engaged in a contest to test nature's willingness to support humanity and, if it had its way, it would not rest content until the earth is covered completely and to a considerable depth with a writhing mass of human beings, much as a dead cow is covered with a pulsating mass of maggots.

For population densities to reach levels much higher than those which exist in present-day agrarian cultures, a great deal of technology is required. India, for example, could not possibly support her existing high population density without the benefit of the knowledge and materials she obtains from the industrialized society of the West. Without the existence of an industrialized society somewhere in the world, disease could not be effectively controlled and transportation would not be in existence which would permit shipment of food from areas of surplus to areas of deficiency. In the absence of the availability of the products of industrialization, the population of the Indian sub-continent would probably not exceed about 100 million persons. Similarly, if industrialization should for some reason cease to exist in the world, and human life were to be supported entirely by intensive agriculture, the population of human beings would probably never exceed about 5 billion persons. This represents about the maximum number that could be supported on a bare subsistence basis in the absence of the means to construct elaborate transportation and irrigation systems, and provide artificial fertilizers and chemicals and other weapons for combating animals and insects which compete with man for food.

. . . [Within] a period of time which is very short compared with the total span of human history, supplies of fossil fuels will almost certainly be exhausted. This loss will make man completely dependent upon waterpower, atomic energy, and solar energy—including that made available by burning vegetation—for driving his machines. There are no fundamental physical laws which prevent such a transition, and it is quite possible that society will be able to make the change smoothly. But it is a transition that will happen only once during the lifetime of the human species. We are quickly approaching the point where, if machine civilization should, because of some catastrophe, stop functioning, it will probably never again come into existence.

It is not difficult to see why this should be so if we compare the resources and procedures of the past with those of the present.

Our ancestors had available large resources of high-grade ores and fuels that could be processed by the most primitive technology—crystals of copper and pieces of coal that lay on the surface of the earth, easily mined iron, and petroleum in generous pools reached by shallow drilling. Now we must dig huge caverns and follow seams ever further underground, drill oil wells thousands of feet deep, many of them under the bed of the ocean, and find ways of extracting elements from the leanest of ores—procedures that are possible only because of our highly complex modern techniques, and practical only to an intricately mechanized culture which could not have been developed without the high-grade resources that are so rapidly vanishing.

As our dependence shifts to such resources as low-grade ores, rock, sea water, and the sun, the conversion of energy into useful work will require ever more intricate technical activity, which would be impossible in the absence of a variety of complex machines and their products—all of which are the result of our intricate industrial civilization, and which would be impossible without it. Thus, if a machine civilization were to stop functioning as the result of some catastrophe, it is difficult to see how man would again be able to start along the path of industrialization with the resources that would then be available to him.

The situation is a little like that of a child who has been given a set of simple blocks—all the blocks of one type which exist—with which to learn to build, and to make the foundation for a structure, the upper reaches of which must consist of more intricate, more difficult-to-handle forms, themselves quite unsuited for the base. If, when the foundation was built, he conserved it, he could go on building. But if he had wasted and destroyed the foundation blocks, he would have "had it," as the British Royal Air Force would say. His one chance would have been wasted, his structure of the future would be a vanished dream, because there would be nothing left with which to rebuild the foundation.

Our present industrialization, itself the result of a combination of no longer existent circumstances, is the only foundation on which it seems possible that a future civilization capable of utilizing the vast resources of energy now hidden in rocks and sea water, and unutilized in the sun, can be built. If this foundation is destroyed, in all probability the human race has "had it."

Perhaps there is possible a sort of halfway station, in which retrogression stops short of a complete extinction of civilization, but even this is not pleasant to contemplate.

Once a machine civilization has been in operation for some time, the lives of the people within the society become dependent upon the machines. The vast interlocking industrial network provides them with food, vaccines, antibiotics, and hospitals. If such a population should suddenly be deprived of a substantial fraction of its machines and forced to revert to an agrarian society, the resultant havoc would be enormous. Indeed, it is quite possible that a society within which there has been little natural selection based upon disease resistance for several generations, a society in which the people have come to depend increasingly upon surgery for repairs during early life and where there is little natural selection operating among women, relative to the ability to bear children—such a society could easily become extinct in a relatively short time following the disruption of the machine network.

Should a great catastrophe strike mankind, the agrarian cultures which exist at the time will clearly stand the greatest chance of survival and will probably inherit the earth. Indeed, the less a given society has been influenced by machine civilization, the greater will be the probability of its survival. Although agrarian societies offer little security to the individual, they are nevertheless far more stable than industrial ones from a long-range point of view.

Is it possible to visualize a catastrophe of sufficient magnitude to obliterate industrial civilization? Here the answer must clearly be in the affirmative, for, in 1954, it takes no extraordinary imagination to foresee such a situation. Practically all major industrial countries are now aligned on one side or the other of a major dispute. Weapons of such power that whole cities can be destroyed in a few minutes are in the hands of the disputants, and, should a major war break out, those weapons, which become more powerful every year, will almost certainly be used. It is clearly within the realm of possibility that another war would so disrupt existing industrial societies that recovery would be impossible and the societies would either revert to agrarian cultures or become extinct. Indications of the possibilities that confront us are offered by the catastrophe which paralyzed Western Europe in World War II, and the slow process of its postwar recovery—a process which would have been very much slower had the highly industrialized United States not been in existence, relatively unscarred and prepared to give aid. And the damage and disruption of industrial activity we witnessed then are insignificant when compared with the disruption that might be suffered by all participants in an "atomic" war.

It is quite possible that a war fought at the present time, even with existing powerful weapons of mass destruction, would not bring industrial civilization to an end. With America and Europe prostrate, the people of Asia would have room into which they could expand and thus accelerate the evolution of their own industrial society. It is also quite possible that the West would recover from a major war, although admittedly recovery would be a far slower process than it was after World War II. But with each passing year, as populations become larger, as the industrial network becomes more complex, and as high-grade resources dwindle, recovery from a major war will become increasingly difficult.

It must be emphasized, however, that industrial civilization can come to an end even in the absence of a major catastrophe. Continuance of vigorous machine culture beyond another century or so is clearly dependent upon the development and utilization of atomic or solar power. If these sources of newly applied energy are to be available in time, the basic research and development must be pursued actively during the coming decades. And even if the knowledge is available soon enough, it is quite possible that the political and economic situation in the world at the time the new transition becomes necessary will be of such a nature that the transition will be effectively hindered. Time and again during the course of human history we have seen advance halted by unfavorable political and economic conditions. We have seen societies in which technical knowledge and resources were both present, but where adequate capital and organization were not in existence and could not be accumulated sufficiently rapidly.

At the present time a part of the world is agrarian and another part is either already industrialized or in the process of industrialization. It appears most unlikely that these two greatly different ways of life can co-exist for long. A world containing two major patterns of existence is fundamentally unstable—either the agrarian regions of the world will industrialize or, in the long run, the industrial regions will revert to agrarian existence.

That the agrarian regions of the world will attempt to industrialize is unquestionable. We see about us today signs of revolution, of reorganization, and of reorientation of goals leading toward the creation of local counterparts of Western machine culture. The reasons underlying the trend are obvious. It is in the nature of man not to want to die early and to look enviously at his neighbor who possesses greater wealth than his. A longer life, greater personal security, and more material comforts are looked upon as harbingers of greater happiness, and although this premise is by no means necessarily true, the fact that the individual believes it to be true is the important consideration that confronts us.

The search for greater personal security, longer life, and more material possessions will force the agrarian regions of the world to attempt to industrialize. But, as is indicated here, the probability of their succeeding in the absence of a major world catastrophe in the near future is small. There are clearly paths that could be taken which would lead to a successful transition in the world as a whole. But the nature of man makes remote the possibility that the steps necessary for complete transition will be taken. The picture would change considerably if Western machine civilization were to collapse, thus giving the present agrarian cultures room into which they could expand. But the collapse of Western culture would have to come well in advance of the time when high-grade ore and fuel deposits disappear. We have seen that a collapse of machine civilization after the disappearance of high-grade ore deposits would probably be irreversible, and the world as a whole would be covered with people living an agrarian existence.

It is clear that machine civilization as it is organized at the present time may revert to agrarian culture. In view of this possibility, the most probable pattern for the future of mankind is that sooner or later the entire world will become an agrarian one. This could come about in one of several ways. The status quo could be maintained with abortive attempts on the part of agrarian regions to industrialize, leading eventually to depletion of ore deposits, followed by the decline and eventual decay of machine culture. The regions of advanced machine culture might fight one another and so disrupt the elaborate machine network that recovery would be impossible. The greater part of the world might actually succeed in industrializing, but a catastrophe could bring about reversion to agrarian existence.

Collapse of machine civilization would be accompanied by starvation, disease, and death on a scale difficult to comprehend. In the absence of adequate sanitation facilities, the ability to inoculate against disease, facilities for food transportation and storage, factories for producing items which are essential for the maintenance of life, the death rate would reduce the population to a level far below that which could be supported by a stable agrarian society which practices intensive agricultural techniques. There would be such violent competition for food that savagery would be the heritage of the survivors. Human life would be confined once again to those areas which can be most easily cultivated, watered, and fertilized, and the principles enunciated by Malthus would once again become the major force operating upon human populations. Only very slowly would the number of persons climb to the level which could be supported by a world-wide agrarian culture—about 5 billion.

The characteristics of the agrarian society of the future would probably be very much like those of most parts of China today or like those of societies which existed in Europe as late as the early eighteenth century. The ratio of available food to total population would be low. There would be no large-scale industries, for metals would be practically non-existent and the only sources of energy would be wood and waterpower. Lack of adequate supplies of metals would prevent the widespread use of electricity. Although parts of society would benefit from accumulated knowledge concerning public health and human biology, death rates would be high. Antibiotics and vaccines would be non-existent. Birth rates would almost certainly lie close to the biological maximum.

In the agrarian world of the future, as in the world prior to 1750, there would be very little difference in the manner of life of all civilized people. This fact is vividly illustrated by a story told recently by a well-known demographer:

> I remember walking down a street in Nanking, China, one afternoon nearly twenty years ago with the eminent English economic historian R. H. Tawney, and remarking to him that Chinese cities often reminded me of his description of early eighteenth-century English economic life. He replied in effect: "I was just thinking that the English workmen of that age would have been very much at home in the economy as well as in the living conditions we have just been observing, but so also would the Frenchman from Paris or the Italian from Florence. The farmers would have wondered at some of the crops raised here, but they would have understood the Chinese methods of cultivation and the care given the soil."

Although the world as a whole would be predominantly agrarian, it is possible that small pockets of semi-industrialized society would survive. These would be centered largely around areas where waterpower is available and limited quantities of metals such as magnesium from sea water could be produced. But in the absence of a broader industrial base, per capita production of such materials would be extremely small. These semi-industrial areas, centered around regions of waterpower, might well become the wealthiest regions of the world, and it is in such regions that we might expect the traditions of the arts and the sciences to be perpetuated. But in such a world the sciences almost certainly would not flourish to the extent to which they do today or even to that which distinguished the ancient empires. Material wealth would be too rare and the struggle for food too intense to permit many persons to engage in such activities.

Much of the knowledge existing at the time when industrial civilization reached its peak would probably be preserved, taught in schools, and passed on from generation to generation. But much of it would be valueless and, as time went on, would be lost. We know from observations of past societies that knowledge and techniques can be lost rather quickly. In order to appreciate this, we have only to contrast the superb engineering techniques of the Romans with those of the residents of the Italian peninsula early in the Renaissance.

It is of course possible that, starting from a base of knowledge accumulated by previous society, and the abilities to utilize waterpower and to extract magnesium from sea water, man might once again learn to process rock, harness solar power, and extract energy from uranium. In such an eventuality a world-wide industrial civilization would arise once again and cover the earth, perhaps later to crumble under pressures similar to those which now confront humanity. But the probabilities of a second emergence would be remote. The advantages gained by the existence of previously accumulated knowledge would probably be offset by the scarcity of the number of raw materials necessary for the smooth functioning of an industrial society. . . .

Industrialization of the underdeveloped areas of the world is perhaps the most formidable task confronting mankind today. We must now ask: Can we visualize ways and means by which existing primitive agrarian societies can be transformed reasonably rapidly and smoothly into modern industrial societies? . . . [And] we must recognize that even if family-limitation techniques should receive widespread acceptance, the path of industrialization would still be extremely difficult, and it would still be fraught with innumerable dangers.

An industrialization program must possess many interlocking features, no one of which can be divorced from the others. The ultimate goal of such a program would be to manufacture goods in sufficient quantity so that every person would have adequate housing, clothing, education, medical and public-health facilities, and at the same time receive adequate nutrition. In order to accomplish this, factory buildings and production machines must be built, building materials must be produced, machines must be fabricated which in turn can be used to fabricate machines, metals must be produced, ores must be mined, fuels must be obtained, and transportation systems must be extended. Men must be trained to build and to operate the factories and transportation systems. These men must come from the farms, but they cannot leave the farms until food production per man-hour has been increased without decreasing crop yields—otherwise there would be a lowering of food production and more widespread starvation. In turn, a significantly increased food production per man-hour requires mechanization of farms. Mechanization of farms in turn requires machines, which in turn require a certain degree of industrialization if they are to be manufactured and properly maintained. Thus, in a sense, the inhabitants of underdeveloped areas find themselves in a vicious circle which cannot easily be broken.

Industrialization requires enormous investments of materials and labor before goods can actually be produced, transported, and used. Obviously, if all persons in a given society must spend all of their working hours producing food for their own consumption, accumulation of a surplus becomes impossible. . . . If a surplus of food can be produced, some members of the society can engage in occupations other than farming and can manufacture goods. But unless a mechanism is available whereby a part of the effort can be channeled into the production of capital goods such as machines and factory buildings, which are not consumer items but which will later enable greater production of such items, industrialization cannot expand. In other words, mechanisms must be available which enable persons to deprive themselves of consumer goods and instead to use a part of the surplus food and goods which they have produced for the purchase of capital items which are not immediately useful but which will eventually result in increased consumer production. Translated into terms of money, persons must refrain from spending all the money they derive from the sale of goods and other services, and the "savings" must be invested in capital goods that will result in increased production.

We can obtain some idea of the amount of capital investment that is required in a highly industrialized society by examining the capital resources of the United States. Prior to World War II, the real capital resources, exclusive of land, amounted to about 250 billion dollars, corresponding to an average of 2000 dollars for every person in the country. At the same time the average per capita income in the United States amounted to about 550 dollars per year. Simultaneously, the average per capita income in the underdeveloped areas of the world amounted to little more than 40 dollars per year.

The greater part of the incomes of the inhabitants of the underdeveloped areas must be spent on food, and there is practically no surplus that can be saved for capital investment. In India, for example, voluntary savings amounted to only 2 to 3 per cent of the national income, compared with savings rates of between 10 and 15 per cent in the United States, the United Kingdom, and Canada. When we couple the respective savings rates with the respective per capita income we see that available capital per person can increase in the United States at a rate about 70 times more rapid than the rate in India.

In many underdeveloped areas only a small fraction of the voluntary savings available are channeled into productive uses at home. Many savings are hoarded in the form of precious stones, gold, and silver. Other funds are often sent abroad for investment in industrialized countries. For example, during the period 1936–1947, there was a net inflow to United States banking funds of over 2 billion dollars from Latin America and from the Far East. An additional handicap in the underdeveloped countries is the lack of adequate facilities for collecting and investing voluntary savings. Commercial bank facilities do not exist in most such areas, and there are few investment banks and other forms of private credit institutions.

If all underdeveloped areas at their existing population levels were to possess the per capita capital investment enjoyed by the United States immediately prior to World War II, the total investment in those countries would amount to about 3600 billion dollars. It has been estimated that a sum corresponding to about one-seventh that amount—about 500 billion dollars—would suffice over a 50-year period to switch about one-fourth of the labor force and their families from agricultural to industrial and commercial occupations. This would give them an economic situation similar to that which existed in prewar Japan.

In view of the low incomes of underdeveloped areas, it is clear that industrialization requires either outside financing during the initial stages, or forced savings well above the voluntary rate, similar to the compulsory savings in the Soviet Union. However, even with strict totalitarian regimes of the Russian type, industrialization would necessarily proceed slowly in the absence of help from the outside, largely as the result of the unfavorable population-land-resource situations in most underdeveloped areas.

The most difficult part of an industrialization program is that of getting started. Once industrialization is well under way and goods begin to flow in increasing quantity, both per capita incomes and savings can increase rapidly. Substantial help from the outside can contribute greatly toward overcoming the initial hurdles and can accelerate the whole industrialization process.

It seems likely that, given concerted efforts of both underdeveloped areas and the industrialized regions of the world, the standards of living of the underprivileged two-thirds of humanity could be raised significantly in about 50 years, and standards of living characteristic of the industrialized West of today might be attained in an additional 50 years without resorting to totalitarian methods. But it is equally likely that in the absence of concerted efforts and vigorous application of imagination and ingenuity to the problem, the programs would be doomed to failure. The chance of success of a vigorous program is much greater than that of a half-hearted one. . . .

It is clear that the nations of the West possess sufficient resources and productive capacity to catalyze a successful world development program at the present time. Our physical ability to bring about successful transition is not one of the unknowns. We have the ability to do it; whether we have the vision and the will is another matter. Have the people of the industrialized areas the foresight to launch a major effort to elevate standards of living in the underdeveloped regions? Will they be able to subordinate immediate selfish interests to the goal of achieving an abundant life for humanity as a whole? Will the people of the underdeveloped areas in turn have the vision to guide their own destinies wisely? Will they be able to discourage detrimental action of self-seeking minority groups? Will they be able to plan intelligently their own programs of development of basic industries, transportation, agriculture, public health, education, and culture?

. . . Areas which attempt to industrialize within the framework of the existing world situation will experience many difficulties that have not been experienced heretofore by nations undergoing the industrialization process. These difficulties stem from the unfavorable ratios of men to easily cultivable land and to resources. The difficulties will be offset to a certain extent by our increased knowledge and technological development. But even so, problems will quickly arise which will be far outside the realm of our previous experience. As we know, for example, India cannot maintain a large per capita production level for a prolonged period of time with her existing energy resources. This means that if India's transition is to be successful she must utilize atomic or solar energy long before the United States is forced to take equivalent steps. Similarly, in order to produce sufficient food, the people of India will have to utilize new types of agricultural technology such as algae culture and food-yeast production long before the United States is in a similar position of necessity. Similar problems will be encountered in practically all areas of resource development.

Problems such as these will create many serious economic and political situations. On the economic side, is it possible for a region, in the interests of self-sufficiency, to devise ways and means of manufacturing and utilizing fuels and foods if they are more expensive than those which are used elsewhere in the world but which would otherwise have to be imported? Is it possible for a nation such as India to organize her economic and political structure in such a way that she can utilize on a large scale power which might cost her perhaps two to three times as much as power derived from imported coal? Such steps will clearly be necessary if the industrial transitions in most such areas are to be successful, for in general there is little that can be exported which will not be needed, in the long run, at home.

From the point of view of long-range world stability, regional self-sufficiency would appear to be a goal toward which all major areas of the world should move as rapidly as possible. If the world as a whole were to have a common government and a political and economic structure that would permit India to produce food and Iraq to produce oil for the great world industrial centers, much as Iowa produces food and Texas produces oil for the industrial centers of the United States, stability might be achieved. But in the absence of such structures and in view of the fact that surpluses of any description are becoming rarities on the world scene, regional self-sufficiency appears to be a highly desirable goal even at the expense of utilizing resources temporarily more expensive than those used in other parts of the world at the time. . . .

If industrial civilization eventually succumbs to the forces that are relentlessly operating to make its position more precarious, the world as a whole will probably revert to an agrarian existence. In such an event history will continue for as long a time as man exists. Empires, republics, and military states will rise and fall. There will be wars, migrations, and revolutions. Art, music, and literature will flourish, wane, then flourish again. As in the histories of the past and of the present, there will be unceasing change. Yet, looked upon over a period of thousands of years, history will have a sameness like the repeated performances of a series of elaborate epic plays in which, over the centuries, the actors change, the languages change, the scenery changes, but the basic plots remain invariant.

But if industrial civilization survives—if wars are eliminated, if the population of the world as a whole is stabilized within a framework of low death rates and low birth rates—will there continue to be a human history? The terms "stability" and "security" imply predictability, sameness, lack of change. And these terms further imply a high degree of organization—universal organization to avoid war, local organization to produce goods efficiently, and organization to control the distribution of goods. Organization in turn implies subjugation of the individual to the state, confinement and regimentation of the activities of the individual for the benefit of society as a whole.

Today we see about us on all sides a steady drift toward increased human organization. Governments are becoming more centralized and universal. In practically all areas of endeavor within industrial society—in our systems of production, in the fields of labor, capital, commerce, agriculture, science, education, and art—we see the emergence of new levels of organization designed to coordinate, integrate, bind, and regulate men's actions. The justifications for this increasing degree of organization to which man must accommodate himself are expressed in terms such as "stability," "security," and "efficiency." The end result of this rapid transition might well be the emergence of a universal, stable, efficient, industrial society within which, although all persons have complete personal security, their actions are completely controlled. Should that time arrive, society will have become static, devoid of movement, fixed and permanent. History will have stopped.

Here we indeed find ourselves on the horns of the dilemma. To what purpose is industrialization if we end up by replacing rigid confinement of man's actions by nature with rigid confinement of man's actions by man? To what purpose is industrialization if the price we pay for longer life, material possessions, and personal security is regimentation, controlled thoughts, and controlled actions? Would the lives of well-fed, wealthy, but regimented human robots be better than the lives of their malnourished, poverty-stricken ancestors? At least the latter could look forward to the unexpected happening—to events and situations which previously had been outside the realm of their experiences.

In a modern industrial society the road toward totalitarianism is unidirectional. In days gone by men could revolt against despotism. People could arise against their governments in the absence of legal recourse, and with muskets, sticks, knives, and stones as their weapons they could often defeat the military forces of the central authorities. But today our science and our technology have placed in the hands of rulers of nations weapons and tools of control, persuasion, and coercion of unprecedented power. We have reached the point where, once totalitarian power is seized in a highly industrialized society, successful revolt becomes practically impossible. Totalitarian power, once it is gained, can be perpetuated almost indefinitely in the absence of outside forces, and can lead to progressively more rapid robotization of the individual.

Thus we see that, just as industrial society is fundamentally unstable and subject to reversion to agrarian existence, so within it the conditions which offer individual freedom are unstable in their ability to avoid the conditions which impose rigid organization and totalitarian control. Indeed, when we examine all of the foreseeable difficulties which threaten the survival of industrial civilization, it is difficult to see how the achievement of stability and the maintenance of individual liberty can be made compatible.

The view is widely held in our society that the powers of the machine will eventually free man from the burden of eking out an existence and will provide him with leisure time for the development of his creativity and enjoyment of the fruits of his creative efforts. Pleasant though this prospect may be, it is clear that such a state cannot come into existence automatically; the pressures forcing man into devising more highly organized institutions are too great to permit it. If he is to attain such an idyllic existence for more than a transitory period he must plan for that existence carefully, and in particular he must do everything within his power to reduce the pressures that are forcing him to become more highly organized.

One of the major pressures that give rise to the need for increasing numbers of laws, more elaborate organization, and more centralized government is increase of population. Increase of numbers of people and of population density results in greater complexities in day-to-day living and in decreased opportunities for personal expression concerning the activities of government. But even more important, as populations increase and as they press more heavily upon the available resources there arises the need for increased efficiency, and more elaborate organizations are required to produce sufficient food, to extract the necessary raw materials, and to fabricate and distribute the finished products. In the future we can expect that the greater the population density of an industrial society becomes, the more elaborate will be its organizational structure and the more regimented will be its people.

A second pressure, not unrelated to the first, results from the centralization of industrial and agricultural activity and from regional specialization in various aspects of those activities. One region produces textiles, another produces coal, another automobiles, another corn, and another wheat. Mammoth factories require mammoth local organizations. Centralized industries must be connected, and this requires elaborate transportation systems. Regional localization of industries gives rise to gigantic cities, which in turn give rise to elaborate organization for the purpose of providing the inhabitants with the necessary food, water, and services. All of these factors combine to produce vulnerability to disruption from the outside, increased local organization and regimentation, more highly centralized government, and increasing vulnerability to the evolution of totalitarianism.

A third pressure results from increasing individual specialization and the resultant need for "integration," "coordination," and "direction" of activities in practically all spheres of vocational and leisure activity. It results in the placing of unwarranted trust in "integrators," "coordinators," and "directors." Early specialization results in lack of broad interests, lessened ability to engage in creative activity during leisure hours, decreased interest in the creative activities of other individuals, and lessened abilities to interpret events and make sound judgments. All of these factors combine to pave the way for collectivization, the emergence of strong organization, and, with it, the great leader.

Strong arguments can be presented to the effect that collectivization of humanity is inevitable, that the drift toward an ultimate state of automatism cannot be halted, that existing human values such as freedom, love, and conscience must eventually disappear. Certainly if we used the present trends in industrial society as our major premises, the conclusion would appear to be inescapable. Yet is it not possible that human beings, recognizing this threat to the canons of humanism, can devise ways and means of escaping the danger and at the same time manage to preserve those features of industrial civilization which can contribute to a rich, full life? Is it really axiomatic that the present trends must continue and that in the long run industrial civilization and human values are incompatible? Here, in truth, we are confronted with the gravest and most difficult of all human problems, for it is one that cannot be solved by mathematics or by machines, nor can it even be precisely defined. Solutions, if they exist, can arise only in the hearts and minds of individual men.

The machine has divorced man from the world of nature to which he belongs, and in the process he has lost in large measure the powers of contemplation with which he was endowed. A prerequisite for the preservation of the canons of humanism is a reestablishment of organic roots with our natural environment and, related to it, the evolution of ways of life which encourage contemplation and the search for truth and knowledge. The flower and vegetable garden, green grass, the fireplace, the primeval forest with its wondrous assemblage of living things, the uninhabited hilltop where one can silently look at the stars and wonder—all of these things and many others are necessary for the fulfillment of man's psychological and spiritual needs. To be sure, they are of no "practical value" and are seemingly unrelated to man's pressing need for food and living space. But they are as necessary to the preservation of humanism as food is necessary to the preservation of human life.

I can imagine a world within which machines function solely for man's benefit, turning out those goods which are necessary for his well-being, relieving him of the necessity for heavy physical labor and dull, routine, meaningless activity. The world I imagine is one in which people are well fed, well clothed, and well housed. Man, in this world, lives in balance with his environment, nourished by nature in harmony with the myriads of other life forms that are beneficial to him. He treats his land wisely, halts erosion and overcropping, and returns all organic waste matter to the soil from which it sprung. He lives efficiently, yet minimizes artificiality. It is not an overcrowded world; people can, if they wish, isolate themselves in the silence of a mountaintop, or they can walk through primeval forests or across wooded plains. In the world of my imagination there is an organization, but it is as decentralized as possible, compatible with the requirements for survival. There is a world government, but it exists solely for the purpose of preventing war and stabilizing population, and its powers are irrevocably restricted. The government exists for man rather than man for the government.

In the world of my imagination the various regions are self-sufficient, and the people are free to govern themselves as they choose and to establish their own cultural patterns. All people have a voice in the government, and individuals can move about when and where they please. It is a world where man's creativity is blended with the creativity of nature, and where a moderate degree of organization is blended with a moderate degree of anarchy.

Is such a world impossible of realization? Perhaps it is, but who among us can really say? At least if we try to create such a world there is a chance that we will succeed. But if we let the present trend continue it is all too clear that we will lose forever those qualities of mind and spirit which distinguish the human being from the automaton.

THE ANATOMY OF SOCIETY: ECONOMY

2. WORK AND WEALTH: MOTIVATIONS IN SOCIAL ECONOMY

MAX WEBER

THE PROTESTANT ETHIC AND THE SPIRIT OF CAPITALISM by Max Weber (1864–1924) contains a dramatic historical hypothesis concerning the origins of modern capitalism. It also exhibits a preoccupation with certain concepts which, like bureaucracy and charisma, routine and authority, rational and nonrational behavior, social theory and social action, and especially the relationship between religious values and economic conduct, animated Weber's inquiries throughout his intellectual life. The work is really more than a historical treatise and an account of "what really happened": It is a concrete application of a complex social theory, and it implies a moral judgment on modern society as well. Thus, though it is but one of a number of persuasively argued and well-documented, but differing, explanations of capitalism's origin, rise, and character, the importance of Weber's work is not altogether a matter of its historical veracity. For Weber is presenting here a general theory of social causation which has philosophical overtones and methodological significance, and a critical evaluation of social institutions which is based upon a profound moral insight into the possibilities of human nature and the cast of human destiny. Like Marx, Weber appears to have both admired and deplored the accomplishments of capitalism. Like Marx again, Weber displayed an almost prophetic intuition of the dynamics of economic history. But unlike Marx, Weber could not support the jubilantly fatalistic view that capitalism is but a transient episode of world history, foreordained to an apocalyptic doom; nor did he accept class struggle as the sole agency of social change. It is partly as a critique of historical materialism—as evidenced perhaps by the deliberate use of the term "spirit" in its title—that Weber's essay may be read. For Marx's theoretic system is an explicit disavowal of the causal efficacy of the human spirit, all of whose manifestations—politics, art, law, literature, and religion —are "mere ideologies," functions and reflections of subjacent economic foundations. With the change of these foundations, the entire superstructure is "more or less rapidly transformed," while the economic foundations themselves are subject to irrepressible and irreversible forces, "working with iron necessity toward inevitable results." Weber's analysis of society was a subtler one than Marx's, revealing distinctions which cut across strict economic lines; and though his sense of reality was at least as keen as Marx's, Weber discerned possibilities of social action which Marx's categories precluded. What if it could be shown that a set of ideas, an "ideology," once modified the course of historical development, and reenforced the trends of economic development in such a way that the latter would be historically unintelligible without reference to the ideas themselves? What if it could be shown that the antecedent economic circumstances, however necessary, were not sufficient conditions for the emergence of a certain type of human experience and a certain set of moral attitudes? Might it not then be possible that another set of ideas, if powerfully enough felt, could once again have an impact on the material basis of economic existence? Weber's theoretical and historical analyses were in part a justification of his belief in social action: He himself had always displayed a taste for the active political life as well as for the more remote endeavors of the scholar. To be sure, he who would alter the context of social action would necessarily run counter to a pattern of behavior which had become established in the minds of men as the natural way, and which had crystallized into habit and routine with the sanction of tradition. And to be sure, the pattern might persist indefinitely, there being no inevitable force which must, as Marx believed, destroy and replace it. It might go on, bringing more and more of human activity into its rigidly specified forms. But if the charismatic spirit has wrought change once before, might it not do so again, breaking through routine and providing modern society with a set of rejuvenating values and a new meaning for life? These are but some of the searching queries that Weber raises here.

The following selections were part of those originally published by Weber as "Die protestantische Ethik und der Geist des Kapitalismus" in two articles in the *Archiv für Sozialwissenschaft und Sozialpolitik* in 1904 and 1905. He later revised the manuscript and incorporated it as "Die protestantische Ethik" in the first volume of his *Gesammelte Aufsätze zur Religionssoziologie* (1920). The complete essay was translated into English as *The Protestant Ethic and the Spirit of Capitalism* (1930) by Talcott Parsons. The present selection has been newly translated especially for this volume by Peter J. Gay.

THE PROTESTANT ETHIC AND THE SPIRIT OF CAPITALISM

Part One

RELIGIOUS AFFILIATION AND SOCIAL STRATIFICATION

A look at the occupational statistics of a country with mixed religious affiliation presents one fact with striking frequency: capitalists, entrepreneurs, and the most highly skilled workers—especially the highly trained technical or commercial personnel of modern enterprises—are overwhelmingly Protestant. This phenomenon has been ardently discussed in the Catholic press and literature and at German Catholic Congresses. Its finds expression in the statistics on religion of countries where differences in religious affiliation coincide with differences in nationality and hence cultural development (such as in Eastern Germany between Germans and Poles). It is equally true in almost every area where capitalist development in its opening

This selection has been translated from Max Weber "Die protestantische Ethik," *Gesammelte Aufsätze zur Religionssoziologie* (Tubingen, 1920), Vol. I, pp. 17–26, 163–204.

phase had been free to transform the social structure and occupational composition of a population in accordance with its needs. The freer the hand of capitalism during the period of its growth, the more obvious is this fact.

Now it is true that the greater relative participation of Protestants in capital ownership, in management, and in the upper ranks of labor in the great modern industrial and commercial enterprises can be traced back, in part, to historic circumstances which lie deep in the past and which cannot be said to be caused by religious affiliation, for this affiliation appears, to a certain degree, to be the result of economic forces. Participation in the economic functions listed above presupposes ownership of property, an expensive education, or both, and is today frequently bound up with inherited wealth. It is of course patent that most of the areas of Germany which turned to Protestantism in the sixteenth century were in economically favored positions, as, for example, the majority of the wealthy cities. The consequences of this circumstance still favor the Protestants in the present-day economic struggle for existence. The following historical question then arises: Why did these economically most highly developed areas show an especially strong predisposition in favor of the Reformation?

The answer is by no means as simple as it appears at first glance. It would seem that liberation from economic traditionalism is a factor conducive to religious skepticism and rebellion against all traditional authority. But one must take into account what is often overlooked, that the Reformation did not mean the elimination of the domination of the Church over everyday life, but the substitution of one form of control for another. The new authority which replaced an easy, and largely formal, regime entered into all spheres of life whether public or private and came to control the whole range of human conduct with far-reaching, earnest, and terribly burdensome regulations. The rule of the Catholic Church—"punishment for the heretic but indulgence to the sinner" (as it was then even more than now)—is being tolerated at present by nations of thoroughly modern economic character. It was borne equally easily by the richest and economically most highly-developed countries in the world at the close of the fifteenth century. The rule of Calvinism, which was in full sway in the sixteenth century in Geneva and Scotland, at the turn of the sixteenth and seventeenth centuries in the Netherlands, in the seventeenth century in New England, and, for a time, in England itself, would be for us today the most unbearable kind of ecclesiastical control over the individual. Many of the old patrician families in those countries shared this modern view of Calvinism. For what the Reformers criticized when they arose in the highly developed countries was not an excess but a deficiency of religious control over life. Now, how does it happen that these very countries, and within them the economically rising bourgeois middle class, not only tolerated the hitherto unknown puritanical tyranny but developed such heroism in its defence as the bourgeoisie had rarely shown earlier and was never to show later? What spurred on what Carlyle has called, not without reason, "the last of our heroisms?"

But even more important: If, as has been said, the greater number of Protestants in positions of leadership and capital ownership in modern industry can be explained in part simply as the consequence of inherited wealth, there are other phenomena which cannot be explained in this fashion. For example, take the demonstrable difference observable in Baden, Bavaria, and Hungary between the kind of higher education which Catholic and Protestant parents give their children. That the percentage of Catholic high school students and graduates is far smaller than the percentage of Catholics in the total population may in large part be due to the superior wealth of the Protestants. But this does not explain the fact that the percentage of Catholic graduates who prepare themselves for technical studies and industrial or commercial careers is even smaller. Catholics seem to prefer humanistic studies. This cannot be explained alone by the lesser role they play in capitalistic enterprises. It is the other way around. This lesser role is partly a result of their training.

Even more striking is an observation which helps us to understand why we find only a limited number of Catholics among skilled workers in modern industry. It is noteworthy that factories draw their skilled labor from the ranks of young artisans, but more Protestants than Catholics leave their handicrafts for industry. In other words, Catholic artisans have a far stronger propensity to remain in their crafts, and thus they more frequently become master craftsmen. The Protestants, on the other hand, are more likely to stream into the factories where they eventually fill the upper ranks of skilled labor and the industrial bureaucracy. Why this is so may be discovered if we study the kind of personality created by the educational atmosphere, especially the religious tone of community and home. The direction which the education of the child takes determines his choice of profession and his subsequent career.

This scanty participation of Catholics in the modern economic life of Germany is especially striking because it contradicts an observation which has frequently been made that national or religious minorities are driven compulsively into commercial careers, because the ambitions of their most talented members cannot find an outlet in service to the state. In their position as the oppressed, they seek satisfaction in economic activity. This has unquestionably been true of the economically progressive Poles in Russia and East Prussia (in contrast to Galicia which they themselves dominate); it has equally been true of the Huguenots in France under Louis XIV, of the nonconformists and Quakers in England, and—last but not least—of the Jews for two thousand years. But in the case of German Catholics this effect cannot be observed, and even in the past, when Catholics were persecuted or barely tolerated (as at times in Holland and England), they did not play a vital economic role.

On the other hand, the Protestants—whether dominating or dominated, majority or minority—have always shown a specific inclination to economic rationality not observable among Catholics regardless of their status. The explanation of this divergent behavior must then be sought in the abiding inner character of their religions, and not in their temporary external historical or political position, although the latter has, of course, had important consequences, too.

We are thus led to investigate these religions and ask what the elements in them are that have had—or still have—the economic effects we have been discussing. There is great temptation to give way to superficial observations and certain contemporary impressions and to formulate the contrast by saying that Catholicism shows a greater otherworldliness, and that the ascetic nature of its highest ideals leads its adherents to a real indifference to worldly goods. This reasoning corresponds to the currently popular appraisal of Catholicism as against Protestantism. Protestants use this argument in criticizing the (real or imaginary) ascetic ideals of the Catholic way of life. Catholics reply in kind by blaming Protestants for "materialism," which is supposed to be the result of their secularization of life. Thus a modern writer believes he can characterize the contrasting attitudes of the two groups towards economic life in this fashion. "The Catholic . . ." he writes, "is calmer. He is equipped with less economic drive, and is more concerned with a secure existence—even if accompanied by a smaller income—than with a dangerous, exciting life which might bring fame and fortune. The proverb says jokingly: 'Either eat well or sleep well.' In this case, the Protestant likes to eat well, whereas the Catholic likes to sleep well." Indeed, the desire "to eat well" may pretty well characterize the religiously indifferent Protestant of Germany of the present time. But in the past, very different; English, Dutch, and American Puritans were typically anything but joyful in life. As a matter of fact, this character trait is of the highest importance for our study. French Protestants have in some measure maintained this character, acquired by all Calvinist Churches at the time of the religious struggles of the Reformation, up to the present day. And yet, in spite of this characteristic —or, perhaps because of it—Protestantism was one of the most important factors in the industrial and capitalist development of France. If we give the name "otherworldliness" to this seriousness and predominance of religious interests in the conduct of life, then French Calvinists were, and are, at least as "otherworldly" as, say, the North German Catholics whose Catholicism is as close to their hearts as to no other people in the world. Both groups can be distinguished from the dominating religious elements in their countries in the same way. French Catholics are, in the lower strata, filled with *joie de vivre;* the upper groups are openly antireligious. German Protestants, for their part, are immersed in worldly economic life, and the upper strata are largely indifferent to religion.

These parallels demonstrate clearly that vague concepts such as the alleged otherworldliness of Catholicism and the alleged materialist joy of life of Protestantism are of no use in our investigation. These generalizations are at best only partly correct for the present day; they certainly do not hold for the past. If we wish to employ them we should speculate as to whether this whole contrast between otherworldliness, asceticism, and clerical piety on the one hand and participation in capitalist life on the other might not be converted into an intimate relationship.

THE SPIRIT OF CAPITALISM

The title of this study contains a somewhat pretentious phrase, "the *spirit* of capitalism." What can we understand by it? The attempt to define it shows certain difficulties which are inherent in the very nature of our investigation.

If we can find any object to which that description can be meaningfully applied, it can only be a historical individual, that is, a complex of relations in historical reality which we combine into a conceptual whole from the point of view of their cultural significance.

Such a historical concept cannot be defined according to the formula of first finding the general classification and then differentiating by detail since it refers to a phenomenon significant for its individual characteristics. It must be gradually composed from elements which are derived from historical reality. Therefore, the definitive concept cannot come at the beginning but at the conclusion of the investigation. In other words, we shall learn only during the course of our investigations just what we understand by the spirit of capitalism and how we can formulate it most adequately for our purposes.

The point of view here employed is, of course, not the only possible one from which the historical phenomena we are studying can be analyzed. Other viewpoints would bring out other features as essential. It follows that what we shall here understand by the spirit of capitalism is by no means an interpretation that excludes other analyses. The essence of the act of forming historical concepts for methodological purposes is not to attempt pigeonholing reality in abstract categories but to bring out the concrete pattern of its origins, the source of its individual flavor.

Thus, if we wish to determine the object, the analysis and historical explanation of which we are concerned with, we cannot use a conceptual definition, but must begin with a provisional description of what we mean by the spirit of capitalism. Such a description is indeed indispensable for an understanding of the object of our investigation. Let us turn to a document which perfectly embodies this spirit. It has the double advantage of expressing it in nearly classical purity, and of being free from all religious connotations and hence for our purposes, of being free from preconceptions.

Remember, that *time* is money. He that can earn ten shillings a day by his labour, and goes abroad, or sits idle, one half of that day, though he spends but sixpence during his diversion or idleness, ought not to reckon *that* the only expense; he has really spent, or rather thrown away, five shillings besides.

Remember, that *credit* is money. If a man lets his money lie in my hands after it is due, he gives me the interest, or so much as I can make of it during that time. This amounts to a considerable sum where a man has good and large credit, and makes good use of it.

Remember, that money is of the prolific, generating nature. Money can beget money, and its offspring can beget more, and so on. Five shillings turned is six, turned again it is seven and threepence, and so on, till it becomes a hundred pounds. The more there is of it, the more it produces at every turning, so that the profits rise quicker and quicker. He that kills a breeding-sow, destroys all her offspring to the thousandth generation. He that murders a crown, destroys all that it might have produced, even scores of pounds.

Remember this saying, *The good paymaster is lord of another man's purse*. He that is known to pay punctually and exactly to the time he promises, may at any time, and on any occasion, raise all the money his friends can spare. This is sometimes of great use. After industry and frugality, nothing contributes more to the raising of a young man in the world than punctuality and justice in all his dealings; therefore never keep borrowed money an hour beyond the time you promised, lest a disappointment shut up your friend's purse for ever.

The most trifling actions that affect a man's credit are to be regarded. The sound of your hammer at five in the morning, or eight at night, heard by a creditor, makes him easy six months longer; but if he sees you at a billiard-table, or hears your voice at a tavern, when you should be at work, he sends for his money the next day; demands it, before he can receive it, in a lump.

It shows, besides, that you are mindful of what you owe; it makes you appear a careful as well as an honest man, and that still increases your credit.

Beware of thinking all your own that you possess, and of living accordingly. It is a mistake that many people who have credit fall into. To prevent this, keep an exact account for some time both of your expenses and your income. If you take the pains at first to mention particulars, it will have this good effect: you will discover how wonderfully small, trifling expenses mount up to large sums, and will discern what might have been, and may for the future be saved, without occasioning any great inconvenience.

For six pounds a year you may have the use of one hundred pounds, provided you are a man of known prudence and honesty.

He that spends a groat a day idly, spends idly above six pounds a year, which is the price for the use of one hundred pounds.

He that wastes idly a groat's worth of his time per day, one day with another, wastes the privilege of using one hundred pounds each day.

He that idly loses five shillings' worth of time, loses five shillings, and might as prudently throw five shillings into the sea.

He that loses five shillings, not only loses that sum, but all the advantage that might be made by turning it in dealing, which by the time that a young man becomes old, will amount to a considerable sum of money.

It is Benjamin Franklin who preaches to us in these words. No one can doubt that the spirit of capitalism speaks through them in characteristic fashion, although we cannot claim that they express the whole of that spirit. Let us dwell for a moment on this passage; one writer sums up its philosophy in a single phrase: "They make tallow out of cattle, and money out of men." What strikes us in this philosophy of avarice is the ideal of the solvent gentleman and above all the idea of the obligation of the individual to increase his capital, which is regarded as an end in itself. Indeed, not a mere technique of the art of living is being preached here but a peculiar form of ethics. Its violation is looked upon not only as foolishness but as a kind of neglect of duty. This is of fundamental importance. Not only commercial wisdom is being taught in this passage—that we find frequently enough—but a whole ethos comes to light here, and this is the very quality in which we are interested.

A colleague who had retired once urged Jakob Fugger to do the same since he had made enough money and should give others a chance to profit. Fugger rejected this advice as the counsel of despair, and told his friend that he felt quite differently about the matter: he wanted to make money as long as he could. The spirit of Fugger's reply can be distinguished from Franklin's words, for while the former is the expression of commercial daring and a personal inclination indifferent to morality the latter takes the character of ethically tinged maxims for the conduct of life.[1] It is in this sense that the term spirit of capitalism will be used. We are, of course, concerned with *modern* capitalism in Western Europe and the United States. "Capitalism" has existed in China, India, Babylonia, in the ancient and medieval world. But, as we shall see, it lacked the particular ethics we are now discussing.

It is true that all of Franklin's moral maxims maintain a utilitarian tone, for example, honesty is *useful* because it assures credit. This fact applies equally to punctuality, industry, and moderation, and that is why they are virtues. It follows that where the *appearance* of honesty fulfills the same purpose it suffices, and an unnecessary surplus of this virtue would obviously be condemned by Franklin as unproductive waste. This deduction is substantiated by reference to his *Autobiography*. There he recounts his "conversion" to the above-mentioned virtues:

I grew convinced that truth, sincerity, and integrity in dealings between man and man were of the utmost importance to the felicity of life; and I formed written resolutions, which still remain in my journal book, to practise them ever while I lived. Revelation had indeed no weight with me as such; but I entertained an opinion that, though certain actions might not be bad because they were forbidden by it, or good because it commanded them, yet probably these actions might be forbidden because they were bad for us, or commanded because they were beneficial to us in their own nature, all the circumstances of things considered.

Another example can be found in his discussion of the utility of consistently maintaining the *appearance* of modesty, and belittling one's own merits in order to achieve ultimate general recognition.

I therefore put myself as much as I could out of sight and started it (that is, the project of a library which he had initiated) as a scheme of a *number of friends,* who had requested me to go about and propose it to such as they thought lovers of reading. In this way my affair went on smoothly and I ever after practised it on such occasions; and from my frequent successes, can heartily recommend it. The present little sacrifice of your vanity will afterwards be amply repaid. If it remains awhile uncertain to whom the merit belongs, some one more vain than yourself will be encouraged to claim it, and then even envy will be disposed to do you justice by plucking those assumed feathers and restoring them to their right owner.

We are then forced to the conclusion that, according to Franklin, virtues are virtues only insofar as they are concretely useful to the individual, and that mere appearance is sufficient wherever it serves the same purpose as the

[1] This, of course, does not mean that Fugger was indifferent to morality or religion. Nor does it mean that Franklin's ethics are fully expressed in the passage here quoted. But the problem is just this: How can such a philanthropist write such sentences in the manner of a moralist?

real thing. This, be it noted, is an inevitable consequence of strict utilitarianism. What Germans like to regard as the hypocrisy of the virtues of Americanism thus seems confirmed.

But the matter is by no means so simple. Benjamin Franklin's own character, which emerges from the rare honesty of his *Autobiography,* and the fact that he derives his insight into the utility of virtue from a divine revelation, show that there is more here than disguised egocentrism. Above all, the *summum bonum* of this ethic—the acquisition of money and ever more money with the strictest avoidance of innocent enjoyment—is devoid of eudaemonistic or even hedonistic ideas. It is so strongly regarded as an end in itself that from the point of view of individual happiness or usefulness it appears to be downright irrational.

Acquisition has become the ultimate purpose of man; it is no longer a means to the satisfaction of his material wants. This irrational reversal of what we might call the "natural" state of affairs is clearly one of the chief motivating forces of capitalism, alien to those not touched by capitalistic influence. But at the same time it contains emotions which are closely related to religious beliefs. If we ask why money should be made out of men, Benjamin Franklin, although he was a colorless Deist, replies with a Biblical citation which, he says, his devoutly Calvinist father had impressed upon him in his youth: "Seest thou a man diligent in his *business?* He shall stand before kings." (Prov. xxii, 29). The earning of money within the modern economic order is—as long as it is acquired legally—the result and the expression of proficiency in a calling. This skill, as can easily be recognized now, since it reveals itself to us in all his writing without exception, is the real Alpha and Omega of Franklin's ethic.

That peculiar idea, of a duty to a calling, today so current yet really not self-evident at all, is characteristic of the social ethic of capitalistic culture. Indeed, this obligation, which the individual is supposed to feel, and does feel, towards the content of his professional activity, no matter of what it consists, no matter whether it appears as the utilization of his labor power or only his material possessions (his "capital"), is, in a sense, of the essence of capitalism. Nor has this feeling grown *only* upon capitalistic soil; it can be traced back to the distant past. And even less can we claim, of course, that it is essential for the continued existence of present-day capitalism that today's workers or employees subjectively accept these ethical maxims. The modern capitalistic economic order is a huge universe into which the individual is born and in which he must live and which is for him, as an individual, given and unalterable. Capitalism forces the standards of economic behavior upon the individual to the extent of his involvement in market relations. The manufacturer who constantly contravenes these norms will be as infallibly eliminated from the economic scene as the worker who cannot fit himself to them and has to walk the streets without a job.

Thus, present-day capitalism, which dominates economic life, educates and creates those economic subjects which it needs—employers and workers—by a kind of economic survival of the fittest. But this is the point at which one can grasp the limitations of the concept of Selection of the Fittest as an explanation of historical processes. In order that the selection of a kind of conduct of life and concept of calling best adapted to the character of capitalism be possible at all, it must first have *arisen,* and not among isolated individuals, but as a point of view held by the whole groups. How this view of life originates is, of course, what needs explaining. The concept of naïve historical materialism, that such "ideas" become active only as "mirrors" or "superstructures" of economic relations, will be discussed later in detail. Suffice it here to say that there can be no doubt that the capitalist spirit existed in the state of Benjamin Franklin's birth, Massachusetts, *before* capitalistic development. In contrast to other areas of North America, we find complaints against calculating profit-hunger in New England as early as 1632. In neighboring colonies which were to become the Southern States of the United States, the capitalist spirit lagged. This was true in spite of the fact that the South was developed by great capitalists for business reasons, while the New England colonies had been founded by ministers and seminary graduates with the aid of the petty bourgeoisie, craftsmen, and yeomen, for *religious* purposes. In *this* case, at least, the causal connection is the direct opposite of the one that the materialist viewpoint would affirm. Generally, the early history and development of such ideas are much more complex than the theoreticians of the "superstructure" (that is, the Marxists) assume.

The capitalistic spirit, in the meaning which we have so far established for it, had to fight its way to success in bitter battle against a world of hostile powers. Convictions such as the ones expressed in the quotations from Franklin, which were applauded by a whole people, would have been condemned in the ancient world as well as the Middle Ages as an expression of filthy avarice and the most undignified of attitudes. This hostile view is still maintained by those social groups who have only the slightest involvement with the modern economic order, or who have adapted themselves to it least. This was not so because the profit motive had been unknown or undeveloped in the precapitalist era, as has so often been said. Nor was the lust for gold less strong outside of the capitalistic sphere than inside. To believe that is a common illusion of modern Romantics. It is not at this point that the difference between the capitalist and precapitalist spirit can be found, for the greed of the Chinese Mandarin, the aristocrat of Ancient Rome, or the modern farmer can stand up to any comparison. Besides, the lust for gold of a Neapolitan cabdriver or craftsman of southern Europe or Asia expresses itself, as everyone may observe for himself, much more intensely and unscrupulously than, say, that of an Englishman in similar situations.

The universal domination of *absolute* unscrupulousness in bringing selfish interests to bear in money-making was a specific characteristic of the very countries whose bourgeois-capitalistic development had remained backward, as measured by Occidental standards. Every manufacturer knows that the absence of *conscienziosità* of the workers of such countries was, and in some degrees still is, one of the chief obstacles to their capitalist growth; just compare Italy and Germany. Capitalism has no more use for the worker who wants unbridled freedom to do as he chooses than it has for the businessman who is openly unscrupulous, as Franklin has already taught us.

Thus, the difference between the capitalistic and noncapitalistic spirit is not to be found in any difference between a more or less highly developed drive for money. The lust for gold is as old as the history of men. However, we shall see that those who gave way to this drive most completely (like the Dutch captain who was willing to sail through Hell itself for profit, even though he might singe his sails) were in no way the representatives of that state of mind for which the specifically modern spirit of capitalism emerged as a mass phenomenon. Ruthless acquisition, bound to no inner ethical norms, has existed at all times in history, wherever it was made possible. Much in the manner of war and piracy, free trade had no holds barred if conducted with foreigners or outsiders. Morality for strangers permitted acts forbidden in the dealings of kinsmen with each other. Capitalistic gain has been looked upon as an adventure in all societies which have known money as an object of wealth and where the chance presented itself to make profit through various devices—*commenda,* tax farming, loans to states, and the financing of wars, noble courts, and bureaucrats. Equally widespread has been the inner attitude of the adventurer which laughed at ethical limitations. Absolute and conscious ruthlessness in economic acquisition has often been intimately bound up with the strictest traditionalism. With the breakdown of tradition and the growing pervasiveness of free acquisition the new circumstances have not been ethically justified or encouraged. They have been merely viewed as ethically neutral and unpleasant, though inevitable. This has been not only the general position of all ethical teachings but also, what is more important, the practical attitude of the average person in the precapitalistic epoch ("pre-capitalistic" in the sense that rational utilization of capital on an industrial basis and rational capitalist organization of labor were not yet the dominant forces in the orientation of economic activity). But precisely this attitude was one of the strongest inhibitions against adjustment to the conditions of orderly bourgeois-capitalist economy.

Part Two

ASCETICISM AND THE ETHOS OF WORK

If we want to discover the connections between the basic religious concepts of ascetic Protestantism and its maxims of economic conduct, we must necessarily draw upon writings which have emerged from ministerial practice. For modern man has simply no idea how great the influence of the clergy was at a time when the next world was everything, and when the social position of the Christian depended upon his being admitted to communion. This power of religion, which made itself felt in practice through the ministerial office, church discipline, and sermons, was the decisive molder of national character.

For our present purposes let us consider ascetic Protestantism as a single whole. Since English Puritanism, as an outgrowth of Calvinism, demonstrates the most consistent working out of the idea of the "calling," we shall use one of its representatives as the pivotal figure in this discussion. Richard Baxter stands out among many literary proponents of the Puritan ethic for his eminently practical and peaceable point of view and the universal recognition given to his widely reprinted and translated works. He was a Presbyterian and an apologist for the Westminster Synod, but, like so many of the leading spirits of his time, he gradually outgrew dogmatic Calvinism. He was secretly an opponent of Cromwell's usurpation, since he was opposed to all revolutions, and had no use for sectarianism and the fanaticism of the "saints." He displayed generosity toward eccentricity, showed objectivity toward opponents, and sought to orient his work toward a practical promotion of a churchly, moral life. One of the most effective ministers of all time, he made his services available to Parliament, to Cromwell, and to the Restoration, resigning under the last. His *Christian Directory* is the most comprehensive compendium of Puritan moral theology and is guided by the practical experiences of his own ministerial work. For purposes of comparison, we shall use Spener's *Theologische Bedenken* [2] as representative of German Pietism and Barclay's *Apology* for Quakerdom, as well as other proponents of ascetic ethics.

[2] [*Theological Reflections.*]

If we examine Baxter's *Saints' Everlasting Rest* and his *Christian Directory*, or related works of other writers, we are struck from the outset by their stress on the Ebionitic elements of the New Testament in their discussion of economic acquisition and of wealth. Wealth as such is a grave danger; its temptations are constant. Striving toward it is not only senseless as against the overwhelming significance of the Kingdom of God, but also morally questionable. This attitude against any drive toward the acquisition of temporal goods is far more marked in this asceticism than in Calvin. Calvin saw no hindrance to the effectiveness of clergymen who were wealthy, but, on the contrary, a thoroughly desirable enhancement of their reputation, and he permitted them to invest their fortunes profitably as long as they avoided scandal. Puritan writings, however, are filled with examples of condemnations of the pursuit of money and worldly goods. They may be contrasted with the literature of the late Middle Ages which was far more openminded on this subject.

These scruples were meant seriously, but we must look closely to discover their real ethical meaning and context. What is to be morally condemned is relaxation after acquisition, the enjoyment of wealth, with its attendant consequences of idleness and lust, and above all, the diversion of man from his search for a holy life. Property is dangerous only because it brings with it this danger of relaxation. For the "saints' everlasting rest" lies in the next world; on earth man must "do the work of him who sent him, as long as it is yet day," if he wishes to be certain of his state of grace. Not idleness and enjoyment, but only activity can serve to enhance the glory of God, as His will has revealed beyond question. As Baxter says: "It is for action that God maintaineth us and our activities; work is the moral as well as the natural end of power. . . . It is action that God is most served and honoured by. . . . The public welfare or the good of the many is to be valued above our own."

Thus wasting time is the first and essentially the gravest of all sins. The span of life is unthinkably brief and precious, so we must make sure of our salvation. Loss of time through sociability, idle talk, luxury, even longer sleep than necessary for health (six to at most eight hours) deserves absolute moral condemnation. We do not yet have here Franklin's formulation, "Time is money," but the sentence is, so to speak, valid in a spiritual sense, that is, time is of infinite value since every wasted hour is an hour lost to the service of the glory of God. To quote Baxter again: "Keep up a high esteem of time and be every day more careful that you lose none of your time, than you are that you lose none of your gold and silver. And if vain recreation, dressings, feastings, idle talk, unprofitable company, or sleep be any of them temptations to rob you of any of your time, accordingly heighten your watchfulness."

Idle contemplation is of no value and must be condemned, at least if it interferes with professional activity. In Baxter's discussion of calling, there occurs this passage:

Question: But may I not cast off the world that I may only think of my salvation? Answer: You may cast off all such excess of worldly cares or business as unnecessarily hinder you in spiritual things. But you may not cast off all bodily employment and mental labour in which you may serve the common good. Everyone as a member of Church or Commonwealth must employ their parts to the utmost for the good of the Church and the Commonwealth. To neglect this and say: I will pray and meditate, is as if your servant should refuse his greatest work and tie himself to some lesser, easier part. And God hath commanded you some way or other to labour for your daily bread and not to live as drones of the sweat of others only.

Thus contemplation is less pleasing to God than man's active carrying out of His will in a calling. Sundays are provided for that and, according to Baxter, "It's they that are lazy in their callings that can find no time for holy duties."

Consequently, Baxter's chief work is filled with repeated, even passionate preachings in favor of hard and steady work, physical and mental. Two motives can be discerned here. In the first place, work is highly regarded throughout the Western Church (in sharp contrast not only to the Orient, but to the rules of monasteries all over the world) as a well-tested, ascetic device. Work is regarded as a specific preventive measure against all those major temptations which Puritanism puts into the category, "the unclean life." Puritan sexual asceticism differs from the asceticism of the monastery only in degree, not in fundamental principle. Since it also covers married life, it is more extensive than the latter. Sexual relations, even within marriage, are acceptable only as the means designed by God to enhance His glory according to the commandment, "Be fruitful and multiply." As Baxter says, conjugal sexual relations have as their purpose, "a sober procreation of children."

Spener, be it noted here, follows similar reasoning, but makes concessions to Luther's crude view which makes the avoidance of irrepressible immorality a secondary aim. Carnal lust is sinful even within marriage where it may occur as an accompaniment to conception. It is, according to Spener, only the consequence of the Fall which converted such a natural and divinely prescribed act into a sin, inevitably bound to sinful emotions. According to the opinion of a few Pietists, the highest form of Christian marriage is the one in which the bride retains her virginity, the next highest, the one in which sexual intercourse serves exclusively for procreation, and so on down to those marriages which were concluded for purely erotic or external reasons which must ethically be regarded as living in sin. In these lower grades of marriage, one entered into for materialistic reasons is to be preferred to one entered into for erotic reasons, since it has at least sprung from rational considerations.

To return to Baxter, he continually prescribes labor, along with a sober diet, vegetarianism, and cold baths, against all sexual temptation, as well as against religious doubts and self-torments: "Work hard in your calling."

But beyond all that, work was regarded as the divinely prescribed purpose of life itself. St. Paul's sentence, "He who will not work, neither shall he eat," applies to everybody without qualification. Unwillingness to work is a symptom of the absence of the state of grace. Sloth and idleness are such great sins because they are cumulative. Baxter looks upon them as "destroyers of grace."

The divergence from medieval concepts is clear. Thomas Aquinas, too, has interpreted St. Paul's statement. But, according to him, work is necessary only by natural reason for the maintenance of the life of the individual and of the community. Where that purpose is absent, the precept becomes invalid. It applies only to society as a whole, not to every individual. It does not cover the man who can afford to live on his wealth without working. It is also true that contemplation, as a spiritual form of activity in the kingdom of God, has primacy over a literal interpretation of this commandment. For the popular theology of the Middle Ages, the highest form of monastic "productivity" lay in the increase of the *Thesaurus ecclesiae* [3] through prayer and choir service.

It is obvious that these exemptions from the ethical duty to work are not admitted by Baxter. He insists with the greatest emphasis that even wealth does not absolve man from that unqualified commandment. As he puts it: "Question: But will not wealth excuse us?— Answer: It may excuse you from some sordid sort of work, by making you more serviceable to another, but you are no more excused from service of work . . . than the poorest man." Even the wealthy man shall not eat without working, because though he may not need labor to supply his needs, he must obey God's commandment as surely as the poor man. Divine Providence has assigned a calling to everyone without distinction, and man must recognize it and labor within it. This calling is not, as in Lutheranism, a fate to which one must submit and with which one must be satisfied. It is an order of God to the individual to labor for His glory. This apparently trifling nuance had far-reaching psychological consequences and is connected with the development of the providential interpretation of the economic universe which had already been begun by the Scholastics.

The phenomenon of the division of labor and stratification of professions

[3] [That is, the Church's treasury of grace and merit.]

within society had already been noted by Thomas Aquinas, among others, as a direct result of the divine plan for the world. But man's station in this cosmos follows from natural causes and is accidental ("contingent," as the Scholastics would have said). But Luther, as we have seen, explained existing class stratification as the direct result of God's will. It thus became a religious duty for man to remain in the station in which he had actually been placed by objective historical circumstances as though it had been divinely prescribed. This was especially the case since the relation of Lutheran piety to worldly things was an uncertain one from the beginning and remained so. Luther's thought, which never quite sloughed off St. Paul's indifference to this world, did not lend itself to the formation of ethical principles which could be employed to shape the temporal world. One had to take the world as it was; *this* was a religious duty.

The providential character of the interplay of private economic interests takes a slightly different form in the Puritan world view. The vocational stratification designed by Providence can be discovered, true to the Puritan form of pragmatism, in its *results.* Baxter discusses this matter in terms which frequently remind the reader of Adam Smith's famous apotheosis of the division of labor. Specialization of labor leads to a quantitative and qualitative improvement in production because it makes skilled labor possible. In this way it serves the common welfare, which is identical with the welfare of the greatest possible number. While the motivation is purely utilitarian and closely related to a viewpoint that is popular in the secular literature of the time, the characteristically Puritan influence emerges when Baxter sets the following motto at the head of his discussion: "Outside of a well-marked calling the accomplishments of a man are only casual and irregular, and he spends more time in idleness than at work," and when he concluded it as follows: "and he (the specialized worker) will carry out his work in order while another remains in constant confusion, and his business knows neither time nor place . . . therefore is a certain calling the best for everyone."

Irregular work, into which the ordinary laborer is forced, is a frequently inevitable, but always undesirable, condition. The life of the man without a calling lacks that systematic, methodical character which, as we have seen, worldly asceticism requires. Quaker ethics, too, demand that the occupational life of man be viewed as a constant exercise in ascetic virtue. This conscientiousness, which shows its results in the care and methodical way with which he pursues his calling, should be a confirmation of his state of grace. God does not demand work in itself, but rational work in one's calling. It is this methodical nature of earthly asceticism which is constantly emphasized in the Puritan idea of the calling, not, as in Luther, the acceptance of the lot ordained for man by God. Thus, Puritanism affirms without question that man may combine several callings as long as he adds to the general or his personal welfare, and as long as he does not harm anyone else or is led to become unfaithful to one of his several pursuits. Similarly, change of calling is by no means to be condemned if it is not undertaken lightly, and if it results in the pursuit of an occupation more pleasing to God, that is, following the general principle, one that is more useful.

The usefulness of a calling and whether it is thus pleasing to God is measured in the first place by ethical considerations, and secondly by the importance to the community of the goods produced. The third consideration has the greatest practical importance, namely, private profitableness. For when that deity whose actions the Puritans see in all the dispensations of life shows one of His elect a chance for profit, He must have His reasons. And the pious Christian must follow this call by taking the opportunity:

If God show you a way in which you may lawfully get more than in another way (without wrong to your soul or to any other), if you refuse this, and choose the less gainful way, you cross one of the ends of your calling, and you refuse to be God's steward, and to accept His gifts and use them for Him when He requireth it: you may labour to be rich for God, though not for the flesh and sin.

Wealth is thus ethically doubtful only inasmuch as it presents a temptation to idle relaxation and a sinful enjoyment of life. Striving for wealth is objectionable only when it has the aim of a carefree and merry existence. But as exercise of duty in a calling it is not only morally permitted but actually *commanded*. This point is crucial for our purposes.

The parable of the servant who was rejected because he did not increase the talent entrusted to him seems to bear this out directly. To desire to be poor, so the argument ran frequently, was the same thing as desiring to be ill; it must be condemned as a glorification of works deprecatory to the glory of God. Finally, begging by a man capable of labor is sinful not only as idleness, but because it violates the Apostles' word on brotherly love. (Under the Stuarts, especially Laud's regime under Charles I, the principle of public aid to the poor and finding of work for the unemployed was developed systematically. The Puritan campaign slogan against such aid was, "Giving alms is no charity.")

The stressing of the ascetic significance of a steady calling provided an ethical glorification of modern specialized man (*Fachmenschentum*). The providential interpretation of profit-making does the same for the businessman. The refined idleness of the *seigneur* and the parvenu-like ostentation of the newly-rich snob are equally distasteful to the ascetic. But the bright light of ethical approval falls upon the sober bourgeois self-made man. "God blesseth his trade" is a phrase regularly employed to describe those elect who successfully followed these divine decrees. The whole force of the God of the Old Testament who rewards His followers' piety in *this life* must have affected the Puritans in the same way. After all, did not the Puritan, following Baxter's advice, measure his state of grace by comparison with that of Biblical heroes, and did he not interpret the pronouncement of the Bible like sections of a legal code?

Of course, the attitude of the Old Testament was by no means clear-cut. We saw that Luther interpreted the word "calling" in a worldly sense for the first time in a translation of a passage from Jesus Sirach.[4] In spite of Hellenistic influence, this book belongs, in its whole tenor, to those parts of the enlarged Old Testament that have a traditionalist bent. It is characteristic that the book, Jesus Sirach, seems to have enjoyed considerable popularity with Lutheran German peasants up to the present time as it has with large segments of German Pietism.

The Puritans rejected the Apocrypha as not divinely inspired, following their harsh differentiation between divine and fleshly things. Among the canonical books, the Book of Job had the strongest effect with its combination of two important elements. On the one hand, it contains a gratuitous glorification of God as absolutely sovereign and majestic beyond human comprehension (so congenial to Calvinism); on the other hand, it stresses the certainty (as unimportant to Calvin as it was important to the Puritans) that God blesses His followers in this life, too—*only* in this life, in the Book of Job—and also in material matters. Oriental quietism, which emerges in some of the most eloquent verses of the Psalms and the Song of Songs, was interpreted away. Similarly, Baxter placed less emphasis on the traditionalist meaning of that section of the First Epistle to the Corinthians which was decisive for the concept of calling. Instead, those parts of the Old Testament were emphasized which praised formal legalism as a mark of conduct pleasing to God. The theory that only those parts of the Mosaic Law had lost their validity which contained ceremonial or historically conditioned precepts for the Jewish people, but that the rest had continuing validity as an expression of natural law, made possible the elimination of those rules that could not be fitted into modern life. At the same time, it permitted a powerful strengthening of that spirit of self-righteous and sober legalism which was an intimate part of the worldly asceticism of this kind of Protestantism,

[4] [The Wisdom of Jesus ben Sirach (Ecclesiasticus) is an apocryphal Wisdom Book which most Christian denominations do not consider canonical.]

and which possessed numerous traits closely related to the morality of the Old Testament.

The description of the fundamental ethical attitude of Puritanism, especially the English variety, as "English Hebraism," frequently employed by contemporaries as well as by more recent writers, is quite fitting if correctly understood. One must use extreme caution with these parallels, and should think of Jewry as it had developed after hundreds of years of formalistic, legalistic, and Talmudic education, not of the Judaism of Palestine at the time of the writing of the Old Testament. The unsophisticated valuing of life, per se, which ancient Jewry displayed, is far removed from the distinctive views of Puritanism. It is equally remote, be it noted, from the economic ethic of medieval and modern Jewry which was decisive for its development within the capitalist ethos. The Jews were to be found on the side of the politically or speculatively oriented form of venture-capitalism. In a word, their ethos was that of pariah-capitalism. Puritanism, on the other hand, carried the ethos of the rational bourgeois enterprise and the rational organization of labor. It borrowed from the Jewish ethic only what would fit into this framework.

It would be impossible to demonstrate within the limits of this sketch the consequences for human character of the penetration of life of Old Testament norms. But it would be a fascinating task which has not even really been accomplished for the Jewish people. In addition to the connections which have already been hinted at, we may remark that it was important for the Puritan world view that the belief in a chosen people saw a tremendous revival among them. Even the mild-mannered Baxter thanked God that He had allowed him to be born in England, and a member of the True Church, rather than elsewhere. This gratitude for personal blamelessness, granted by the grace of God, runs through the whole mood of the Puritan bourgeoisie. It conditioned that formal, correct, and harsh character that was so prevalent among representatives of this heroic epoch of capitalism.

Let us now clarify those points in which the Puritan concept of calling and the demands of an ascetic life directly influenced the development of the capitalist way of life. Asceticism, as we have seen, turned with full force against one thing above all—the innocent enjoyment of earthly existence and of the joys it has to offer. Most characteristic of this trait was the struggle over the *Book of Sports,* which James I and Charles I raised to the status of a law for the express purpose of fighting Puritanism, and which Charles had ordered to be read from all pulpits. When the Puritans fought like demons against the royal edict that certain popular amusements be legally permitted on Sundays outside of church time, they objected so strongly, not only because this represented a disturbance of the Sabbath, but also because it was an open diversion from the well-ordered conduct of life of the saint. And when the king threatened harsh penalties against those who attacked the legality of Sunday sports, it was precisely because he wished to destroy this antiauthoritarian, ascetic trait which represented such a danger to the state. The monastical, feudal society protected pleasure seekers against the rising bourgeois morality and the ascetic conventicle which was hostile to authority, just as present-day capitalist society protects those "willing to work" (that is, scabs) against the class morality of the workers and the trade union which is hostile to established authority.

Over against this, the Puritans championed their most salient characteristic, which was the principle of the ascetic conduct of life. As a matter of fact, their dislike of sports was, even with the Quakers, by no means a fundamental one. Their only requirement was that the sport serve a rational purpose—recreation necessary for physical efficiency. The Puritans were suspicious of it, however, when it served as a means of the innocent self-expression of untamed drives. As soon as sports became an instrument of pleasure, or wakened competitive ambitions, raw instincts, or the irrational desire to gamble, they were of course to be condemned outright. Impulsive enjoyment of life, which withdrew man's attention from his calling as well as his piety, was the enemy of rational asceticism, no matter whether it took the form of "aristocratic" sport, or the pleasures of dancing or pub-crawling of the common man.

Accordingly, Puritans viewed with suspicion or hostility all those cultural goods that did not have a directly religious reference. Not that the life ideal of Puritanism was a gloomy and narrow-minded philistinism; the very opposite is true, at least for science, with the exception of contempt for Scholasticism. The outstanding exemplars of the Puritan movement were deeply affected by the Renaissance. The sermons of the Presbyterian preachers are studded with classical allusions, and even the Radicals did not hesitate to use such learning in their theological polemics, although they considered it objectionable. Perhaps never has a country been so richly endowed with graduates as New England in the first generation of its existence. The satire of their opponents, such as Butler's *Hudibras,* centered on the ivory tower erudition and learned dialectic of the Puritans. This can partly be explained by the Puritans' esteem for knowledge in religious terms, a consequence of their attitude toward the Catholic "fides implicita." [5]

[5] [*Unquestioning faith.*]

But the situation changes when we enter the fields of nonscientific literature and art. According to Baxter, novels and similar works should not be read, since they were a "waste of time." Here asceticism weighs like a deadly chill upon the life of "Merry Old England." Not only worldly feasts were touched by it. The Puritans' angry hatred of all "superstition," as well as all vestiges of magic and salvation through the sacraments, was leveled at the celebrations of Christmas as well as the Maypole and innocent church art. That Puritans allowed the development of a great, frequently bluntly realistic art in Holland merely proves that ascetic Calvinism had lost its power of attraction in that country. After the brief rule of a Calvinist theocracy, which soon dissolved into a sober state church, the authoritarian regimentation over morals could do little against the love of life of the Court and the estate of the Regents (significantly a group of *rentiers*) as well as the wealthy petty bourgeoisie.

Puritans condemned the theatre, and we are reminded that the Puritan city government of Stratford-on-Avon closed its theatres during Shakespeare's last years, and that Shakespeare's hatred and contempt of Puritanism is apparent everywhere. The radicals did not content themselves with the rigid elimination of the erotic and of nudity from the realm of permissible subjects in the fields of literature and art. Terms such as "idle talk," "superfluities," and "vain ostentation"—all descriptions of irrational and aimless conduct which was not ascetic and not directed to the glory of God, but toward man—were generously employed to oppose the use of artistic motifs and favor sober functionalism.

This was especially true where direct adornment of the person was involved, as in dress. That powerful tendency toward uniformity of life, which buttresses the present-day capitalist interest in the "standardization" of production, has its intellectual foundation in the Puritan rejection of the deification of things of the flesh (*Kreaturvergötterung*).

This point emerges again and again in our study. It explains such sayings as Baxter's: "Every penny which is paid upon yourselves and children and friends must be done as by God's own appointment and to serve and please Him. Watch narrowly, or else that thievish carnal self will leave God nothing." It is fundamental that what is used for personal purposes is withdrawn from the service of the glory of God.

Of course, we must not forget that Puritanism contains within itself a world of contradictions. Certainly it is true that its leaders had a more highly developed instinct for timeless greatness in art than the Cavaliers. A unique genius, such as Rembrandt, as little as his conduct might have found favor with the Puritan God, was still significantly influenced in his creative work by his Puritan environment. But this does not alter the general picture that the powerful spiritualization of human personality which the Puritan atmosphere helped to create was to be of benefit to literature only in later generations.

Without pursuing the considerations of the influence of Puritanism on these fields any further, we can say that cultural goods acquired for aesthetic or sporting purposes are always confronted by the one characteristic limitation that they must not cost anything. Man is looked upon as the administrator of goods which have been put to his use by the grace of God; he must, as the servant in the Biblical parable, give an account of every penny. It is, to say the least, doubtful morally to spend anything for purposes of personal pleasure, rather than for the glory of God. Who has not observed exponents of this attitude even today? The individual's consciousness of the *obligation* to the wealth which he has only in trust, and to which he subordinates himself as a mere "machine for acquisition," weighs heavily on his shoulders. If the ascetic attitude of life can stand the test, it follows that the greater the property, the heavier the feeling of responsibility to maintain it inviolate and to increase it through restless labor for the glory of God. The genesis of this mode of life goes back, like so many other components of the spirit of capitalism, to the Middle Ages, but its ethical basis can be found only in the ethic of ascetic Protestantism. Its significance for the development of capitalism is obvious.

To recapitulate: Worldly Protestant asceticism acted effectively against the spontaneous *enjoyment* of wealth; it limited consumption, especially that of luxuries. On the other hand, it eliminated traditional inhibitions against the acquisition of property; it burst the bonds of the profit motive by not only legalizing it, but even viewing it as directly willed by God. The struggle against carnal lust and the fondness for worldly goods was, as the Puritans and the great Quaker apologist Barclay expressly testified, *not* a struggle against rational acquisition but against the irrational use of wealth. The latter was above all to be found in the obvious forms of luxury, which were condemned as the glorification of fleshly things, which was so congenial to the feudal age. God did not look with favor upon luxury; He desired rational and utilitarian use of wealth for the purposes of the individual and the community. This did not mean mortification of the wealthy man, but the employment of his property for necessary and practically useful things. The concept of comfort characteristically limits the range of ethically acceptable usages of wealth. It is, of course, no accident that the development of the mode of life most closely approximating the idea of comfort can be found first and most clearly among the most consistent representatives of Puritanism—the Quakers. Their ideal was the clean and solid comfort of the bourgeois home, rather than the tinsel and pretense of feudal splendor which rested on an unsound economic basis and preferred shabby elegance to sober simplicity.

In the realm of the production of private riches, asceticism fought against dishonesty as well as instinctive greed. "Covetousness" and "Mammonism" were condemned as the pursuit of wealth for its own sake. For wealth, as such, was a temptation. But here asceticism acted as the force which "ever seeks the good and ever creates evil," because its very attitude created wealth and its temptations. The striving for possessions as an end in itself was highly reprehensible to asceticism, a view in accord with the Old Testament and the ethical valuation of "good works." But acquisition as the fruit of labor in one's calling represented God's blessing. Even more important was the fact that the religious value placed upon restless, steady, systematic secular labor in a calling as the highest means of asceticism and, at the same time, as the surest and most visible confirmation of man's rebirth and proof of his faith must have acted as the mightiest support imaginable for the strengthening of that attitude toward life which we have here designated as the spirit of capitalism.[6]

When the limitation of consumption is combined with the release of the drive toward acquisition, the result is obvious—the formation of capital through forced savings. This is what Eduard Bernstein meant when he wrote, "Asceticism is a bourgeois virtue." While his writings are the first to hint at these important relations, they are much more comprehensive than he imagined. Not the mere accumulation of capital, but the ascetic rationalization of economic life as a whole is the important point. The inhibitions standing in the way of the consumption of acquired wealth must perforce benefit production by its use as investment capital.

Of course, the impact of this influence cannot be determined accurately. In New England the relationship is so apparent that it did not escape the eye of such an observant historian as John Andrew Doyle (in his *The English in America*). But the simplicity of life introduced into the serious religious circles in Holland by a strict Calvinism which ruled for only seven years

[6] For the benefit of those whose consciences would be uneasy without an "economic" (or, if you insist, "materialist") interpretation, let me say that I regard the influence of economic development upon the fate of religious thought as very considerable . . . but the contents of religious thought cannot simply be deduced "economically." They are—and this cannot be helped—of themselves the most powerful molders of "national character," and carry their own laws of development.

led to enormous wealth with an excessive drive for capital accumulation. It is obvious, furthermore, that the tendency toward the absorption of bourgeois fortunes in the nobility (always strong, and even conspicuous in Germany today) was definitely checked by the antipathy of Puritanism toward the feudal way of life. English mercantilist writers of the seventeenth century traced the superiority of Dutch capital as against that of England to the fact that in the latter country, unlike Holland, new fortunes regularly were invested in land. Thus the English sought to acquire a feudal, noble existence and withdrew money from capitalist investment.

The Puritans, Baxter observes, did not fail to appreciate agriculture as a pursuit of special importance, well suited to piety. While the landlord did not feel this way, the yeoman and farmer did, and in the eighteenth century, not the Junker, but the rational agriculturist subscribed to this viewpoint. Since the seventeenth century there has been a deep rift in English society between the "squirearchy," the pillar of "Merry Old England," and Puritan circles whose social power has gone through great fluctuations. Two traits, a constant naïve joy of life, and a strictly regulated, reserved self-control, and conventional ethic, go hand in hand in the picture of the British "national character." A similar sharp contrast can be observed in the early history of the North American colonies between the "adventurers," who desired a seignorial plantation life based upon the labor of indentured servants, and the thoroughly bourgeois Puritans.

As far as the power of the Puritan view of life extended, it sanctioned under all circumstances the tendency toward a bourgeois, rationally economic conduct of life (far more important than the mere encouragement of capital formation). Indeed, it could be called its most significant and, above all, most consistent influence. It presided at the birth of modern economic man.

Of course, these Puritan ideals failed when the temptations of wealth, well recognized by the Puritans, grew too powerful. We frequently find the most genuine supporters of the Puritan spirit among the members of the rising strata of the petty bourgeoisie and farmers. On the other hand, the "blessed rich," even among the Quakers, were often ready to forswear the old ideals. This had happened again and again to the predecessors of worldly asceticism, medieval monastic asceticism. When the rational conduct of economic existence had had its full impact through a strictly regulated life and limited consumption, the wealth acquired succumbed to the nobility (as before the Reformation) or threatened to break down monastic discipline. Then one of the numerous "Reformations" had to check this development. In a certain sense, the whole history of monastic orders can be looked at as a steadily renewed battle with the secularizing effect of wealth.

The same is true of the worldly asceticism of Puritanism. The mighty "revival" staged by Methodism, which antedates the flowering of British industry at the end of the eighteenth century, may well be compared with the earlier reforms of monastic orders. A quotation from John Wesley is in order here. It could serve as a gloss on what has been said so far, for it shows that the leaders of asceticism were fully aware of the apparently paradoxical relationships which have been discussed here. These leaders understood them in the way in which they have been developed in this paper. Wesley writes:

I fear, wherever riches have increased, the essence of religion has decreased in the same proportion. Therefore I do not see how it is possible, in the nature of things, for any revival of true religion to continue long. For religion must necessarily produce both industry and frugality, and these cannot but produce riches. But as riches increase, so will pride, anger, and love of the world in all its branches. How then is it possible that Methodism, that is, a religion of the heart, though it flourishes now as a green bay tree, should continue in this state? For the Methodists in every place grow diligent and frugal; consequently they increase in goods. Hence they proportionately increase in pride, in anger, in the desire of the flesh, the desire of the eyes, and the pride of life. So, although the form of religion remains, the spirit is swiftly vanishing away. Is there no way to prevent this—this continual decay of pure religion? We ought not to prevent people from being diligent and frugal; *we must exhort all Christians to gain all they can, and to save all they can; that is, in effect, to grow rich.*

Then there follows the warning that those who gain all they can and save as much as they can should also give as much as they can, that they may grow in grace and lay up treasure in heaven. This shows, to the last detail, the relations I have tried to explain.

Just as Wesley said, these mighty religious movements, whose significance for economic development lay chiefly in their education for asceticism, achieved their full effect on the economic scene only after the peak of pure religious enthusiasm had been left behind. Then, the feverishly intense search for the Kingdom of God gradually dissolved into sober virtue in one's calling, the religious roots slowly died off, and made way for utilitarian worldliness. We may say, with Dowden, that Robinson Crusoe, the isolated economic man who did missionary work as a sideline, replaced in the popular imagination Bunyan's pilgrim, who had striven in his loneliness for the Kingdom of God, hurrying through Vanity Fair. And again, as Dowden has remarked, as the maxim, "to make the best of *both* worlds" became predominant, man's clear conscience had to be ranked as one of the means to bourgeois comfort. The German proverb, "A good conscience is a soft pillow," expresses this very well. The legacy that a religiously active seventeenth century handed down to its utilitarian successor was above all a completely clear, even a pharisaically good conscience in money-making, as long as it did not transcend the bounds of legality. All traces of apologies for money-making had disappeared; a specifically bourgeois ethic of the calling had been created.

The bourgeois entrepreneur could, and felt that he ought to, follow his economic self-interest in the certainty of being in God's good grace, and of being visibly blessed by Him. This remained true as long as he observed the formal rules of the game, kept his morals spotless, and did not make objectionable use of his wealth. In addition, the power of religious asceticism made available to him sober, conscientious, eminently capable workers who regarded their labor as their divinely ordained purpose in life. Even more, it gave him the comforting assurance that the unequal distribution of the goods of this world was the direct consequence of God's Providence which followed out His unknown aims by these distinctions as well as by this selective show of grace. Calvin had already made the frequently cited remark that only if the "people" (that is, the masses of workers and artisans) were kept poor, would they remain faithful to God. The Dutch (Pieter de la Court and others) secularized this statement to run: the masses worked only if driven to it by necessity. This formulation of a key motif of capitalist economy contributed to the theory of the productivity of low wages. This utilitarian manner of phrasing the matter imperceptibly coincided with the withering away of its roots in religious thought, which corresponded to the pattern of development that we have repeatedly observed elsewhere. Medieval ethics did not merely tolerate begging, it actually glorified the mendicant orders. Even secular beggars were valued, and occasionally described as an "estate," because they gave the wealthy an opportunity for performing good works. The Anglican social ethic of the Stuarts was quite close to this attitude. It remained for Puritan asceticism to collaborate in the writing of those harsh English Poor Laws which fundamentally changed matters. This was easy for the Puritans, since the Protestant sects and strict congregations actually had no beggars among them.

On the other hand, if we look at the situation from the standpoint of the worker, we find, for example, the Zinzendorf version of Pietism regarding the worker who is faithful to his profession and does not strive for gain as a man who follows the example of the Apostles and is thus endowed with the charismatic power [7] of the disciples. At the beginning, the Baptists held similar views in even more radical form.

Of course, all of the ascetic literature of almost every denomination is saturated with the notion that faithful labor is always pleasing to God, even if the worker receives low wages and has had no opportunities in life. Protestant asceticism did not add anything here, but it deepened the attitude most effectively. It created for this attitude a most powerful basis in supplying its psychological drive by viewing this labor as a *calling*, as the best, often sole, means of assuring the state of grace. And it legitimized, on the other hand, the exploitation of this specific willingness to work by interpreting the entrepreneurs' acquisition of riches as a calling, too. Moreover, it is possible to doubt that the "joy of the medieval laborer in his creation," which is so frequently cited, was a very powerful psychological agent, although there was certainly something to it. But in any case, asceticism robs work of this worldly charm and directs labor to the next world. Modern capitalism has destroyed its attraction forever. Work in a calling is willed by God. The impersonality of modern work and what can only be called its joyless meaninglessness when viewed from the eye of the individual then still has a religious aura. Capitalism in its infancy needed workers who were available for economic exploitation for conscience's sake. Today, capitalism is in the saddle and may enforce willingness to work without otherworldly inducements.

It is obvious that this exclusive striving after the Kingdom of God through fulfillment of the duty to work at a calling and the strict asceticism which church discipline naturally imposed, particularly upon the propertyless classes, powerfully furthered the productivity of labor in the capitalist sense of that term.

The treatment of work as a calling was to become as characteristic for the modern worker as the corresponding concept of acquisition for the entrepreneur. It was an accurate judgment of what was then a novel state of affairs when so keen an Anglican observer as Sir William Petty attributed Dutch economic power of the seventeenth century to the large number of

[7] ["Charisma," meaning "gift of grace," is a sociological concept used with great insight by Weber. It is a power of domination inherent in leaders which is the direct opposite of routine or legality. Its origin may be supernatural; its impact is always an irrational one. In his *Wirtschaft und Gesellschaft* Weber defines charisma as "an extraordinary personal quality whose owner is regarded as being endowed with supernatural or superhuman or at least specifically extraordinary forces or qualities not available to all, and for whose sake he is esteemed as divinely inspired, or as an example to all, and therefore regarded as a leader. It is, of course, completely unimportant what ethical, aesthetic, or any other value this quality has from an objective point of view. The only thing that matters is how those who are dominated by the charisma, the 'followers,' feel about it."]

Dissenters in that country (Calvinists and Baptists). These people, he said, saw their duty toward God in work and industry.

The Puritans were passionately opposed to the organic concept of society in that fiscal-monopolistic version which Anglicanism accepted under the Stuarts, especially under Laud. Against that alliance of church and state with the monopolists, based on a social-Christian substructure, with state privileges for commercial, financial, and colonial capitalism, the Puritans offered their views of an individualist drive of rational, legal acquisition through personal ability and initiative. This latter attitude made a basic contribution to the rise of industries which developed without state aid, and sometimes in the face of official opposition. The privileged monopoly industries, meanwhile, soon disappeared from the English scene.

The Puritans, such as Prynne and Parker, refused to have truck with the schemes of large-scale capitalistic courtiers. These capitalists were ethically under suspicion, while the Puritans were proud of their own superior bourgeois morality in business, and this superiority was the real reason for their persecution by these people.

Defoe even suggested that the struggle against dissent could be won by a boycott of bank credit and through the withdrawal of deposits. The contrast between these two kinds of capitalist behavior went hand in hand largely with differing religious affiliations. In the eighteenth century, the opponents of the nonconformists again and again scoffed at them as the carriers of the "spirit of shopkeepers," and accused them of being the ruination of the Old English ideals. Herein, too, lay the contrast between the Puritan and the Jewish economic ethics, and such contemporaries as Prynne realized that the former, not the latter, could be described as the bourgeois economic ethic.

One of the basic elements of the spirit of modern capitalism and of modern culture generally, the rational conduct of life based on the idea of the calling, sprang from the spirit of Christian asceticism. It is this point which this paper has sought to prove. If we take another glance at the quotations from Benjamin Franklin, quoted at the beginning of this essay, we see that the essential elements of what was there described as the spirit of capitalism were the very thing that we have discovered to be the content of the Puritan ethic of the calling. The difference is that the religious foundation has disappeared; it had already died off by Franklin's time.

The idea that modern economic labor is stamped with asceticism is, of course, not new. Goethe attempted to teach us, at the height of his worldly wisdom, in *Wilhelm Meisters Wanderjahre,* and in the ending which he gave his *Faust,* that the delimiting of man to a specialized pursuit, with the renunciation of the Faustian universality of man which it necessitates, is the absolute prerequisite of valuable activity in the modern world. Activity and renunciation, both are essential to each other. This is the fundamental, ascetic motif of the bourgeois way of life. For Goethe, this insight meant a sad farewell to an epoch of rich and beautiful humanity which can no more repeat itself in the course of our cultural development than can the period that saw the flowering of ancient Athens.

The Puritan *desired* to be a man with a calling; we are forced into it. For as asceticism emerged from the monastery to enter into secular economic life, it began to dominate inner morality and played its part in the building of that mighty universe of the modern economic order which was bound to the technical and economic prerequisites of mechanical, machine production. This order determines with overwhelming force the way of life of the individual; not only those who are directly connected with the economy, but everyone who is born into this machine, feels its power. In truth, it may determine man's fate until the last ton of coal has burned out.

According to Baxter, the worry over worldly goods should lie over the shoulders of his saints like a light cloak, which may be thrown off at any time. But fate has decreed that this cloak become a strait jacket. Through the attempt of asceticism to rebuild the world and to be active in that world, material goods have gained ever-growing power over man until they have acquired an inescapable might, as never before in history.

Today, the spirit of asceticism has escaped from its strait jacket, whether permanently, no man can say. In any case, victorious capitalism, since it now rests upon a mechanical basis, no longer needs this prop. Even the rosy mood of its smiling heiress, the Enlightenment, seems to have paled permanently, and the concept of the duty of one's calling, once so filled with religious meaning, haunts our life like a ghost. Where the fulfillment of one's calling cannot be directly related to the highest spiritual and cultural values, or where it is not simply felt as economic coercion, the individual has abandoned all attempts at its justification.

In the country of its most untrammeled activity, the United States, the acquisitive drive, freed from its religious and ethical connotations, has had the tendency of associating itself with purely worldly passions, which frequently gives it the character of a sport. To cite but one example, the German immigrant son-in-law of the leading dry-goods man in an Ohio town had this to say about his father-in-law: "Couldn't the old man retire with his $75,000 a year? No! The store front must now be enlarged to 400 feet. Why? That beats everything, he says. In the evening, when his wife and daughter read, he yearns for bed. On Sunday, he looks at his watch every five minutes to see when the day will be over. What a futile life!" It is obvious that the "old man," for his part, would be unable to comprehend such a judgment and would regard it merely as a symptom of German lassitude.

No one knows today who will inhabit the strait jacket hereafter or whether new prophets will arise at the end of this colossal development or whether old ideas and ideals will have a mighty revival. If neither of these should come to pass, we may experience a mechanization and petrification, adorned with a kind of feverish self-conceit. Then, indeed, this saying shall be true of the last period of this cultural epoch: "Specialists without spirit, sensualists without heart; a nothingness caught in the delusion that it has reached a degree of development never before achieved by mankind."

WERNER SOMBART

THOUGH known officially as an economist, Werner Sombart (1863–1941) always tended to treat formal economics as a vestibule for the discussion of other things, such as the nature of scientific thought, the secularization of culture, and the place and nature of values in society. All of his works have a marked historical and sociological turn. His great work, *Der moderne Kapitalismus* (Vols. I and II, 1902; Vol. III, 1928), a study of the "stages" of capitalism, is footnoted, as it were, with separate works on the connection between war, luxury, and capitalism, and on the role which he felt the Jews played in the historical emergence of the capitalist structure. Of these, his *Der Bourgeois: Zur Geistesgeschichte des modernen Wirtschaftsmenschen* (1913) dealt with the social psychology of the bourgeoisie. The following selection has been taken from the English edition, entitled *The Quintessence of Capitalism* (1915), which was translated and edited by M. Epstein.

Like many German scholars of his time, Sombart was convinced that the subject matter of the cultural sciences—history, sociology, economics, and anthropology—is incapable of quantitative expression and precise prediction; that the cultural sciences aim primarily to "understand," through intuition, sympathy, and insight, the spiritual content of human minds; and that these sciences are not only autonomous with respect to the natural sciences, but are intimately related to one another. It was these methodological assumptions which Sombart brought to the study of economic history and in terms of which he sought to define, in a succession of different works, his own precise relationship to Karl Marx. He was inclined to be skeptical of Marx's prophecy of the inevitable advent of socialism, feeling that, though the twentieth century must witness the ascendancy of the proletariat, Marxian socialism need by no means be the destined form of consciousness for this movement. Marx's great discovery, according to Sombart, was his recognition that capitalism is an existing social system with a history, with its own laws of development, with a characteristic consciousness of itself; and that it, like all economic systems, is relative to a historical time and place. It is neither eternal nor ideal, but is one of a number of economic systems which have existed, or could exist. Such a system must have (1) a characteristic spirit or outlook; (2) a certain "form," by which Sombart meant an elaborated system of market relationships; and (3) a specific "technique" or mode of production. Generalizing the concept of "economic system" in this manner, Sombart departed from Marx by insisting that economic study is primarily concerned with the *spirit* of any economic system, so that economic history is in a sense applied social psychology. The economic historian thus would seek to understand the psychological states and transformations of such a system, rather than externally examine the expansion of market relationships or the development of modes of production. Any economic theory, classical economics included, is to be construed, not as a set of statements which is true or false in any absolute sense, but rather as reflecting the spirit of the system from which it springs. And so the universal history of society and economy would have, as its central theme, not the progressive satisfaction of material wants, but rather the struggle between contrasting human types—the warrior, the pirate, the trader, the entrepreneur—and the successive dominions of their separate and distinctive spirits.

Save for a brief period as counselor to the Bremen Chamber of Commerce, Sombart was a teacher all his life, first at the University of Breslau, then at the College of Commerce in Berlin, and finally at the University of Berlin, where, in 1917, he succeeded his former teacher, Adolf Wagner (1835–1917). His academic commitments and scholarly pursuits notwithstanding, Sombart was never the completely dispassionate student, and his life and works reflect a fear of parochialism. A popular lecturer and writer, he was never far from the public eye as a foe of orthodoxy, known as the "red professor" until World War I, and after it as an eloquent antagonist of communism and a proponent of "German Socialism" and "autarchy." His capacity for forceful statement, his sophisticated eclecticism, created for him a number of different audiences and a number of different reputations. Friedrich Engels claimed that, with Sombart, for "the first time a German university professor has achieved the feat of seeing in Marx's writings . . . what Marx actually said." In America, he is sometimes known as the "German Veblen." Between the wars, social conservatives in the Balkans looked to him as the advocate of re-agrarianization. And his book *Deutscher Sozialismus* (1934) carried some overtones of Nazism.

THE QUINTESSENCE OF CAPITALISM: A STUDY OF THE HISTORY AND PSYCHOLOGY OF THE MODERN BUSINESS MAN.

Book I. The Spirit of Enterprise

IV. THE SPIRIT OF CAPITALISTIC ENTERPRISE

Undertaking [1] in its broadest conception means the realization of a well-considered plan, for the carrying out of which it is needful to have the continued co-operation of many individuals under the guidance of a single will.

The plan must be well defined. Hence sudden instinctive actions are ex-

---

This selection has been reprinted from Werner Sombart, *The Quintessence of Capitalism,* T. Fisher Unwin, London, 1915 (pp. 51–65, 153–189) by permission of The Free Press, Chicago, Ill., holder of American rights.

[1] [In the German, *die Unternehmung* connotes an undertaking, or enterprise, of a definite economic character. The translator has often rendered *der Unternehmer* literally as undertaker, rather than the more common entrepreneur or enterpriser.]

cluded. You don't talk of an "undertaking" when a few tramps quickly resolve there and then to set upon and rob a passing traveller. On the other hand, it is distinctly an "undertaking" when a gang of desperadoes calmly decide on a burglary on a certain day, and resolve to meet to do the job.

Item, the plan must needs be realized. It is not enough merely to conceive the idea, or even to decide upon its realization. The action must be consummated.

Item, it must be a plan, "for the carrying out of which it is needful to have the continued co-operation of many individuals." Your plan may be ever so well considered, but if only a single person carries it out, it is not an "undertaking." Accordingly, every artistic effort and every handicraft production is thus excluded from the conception.

And the plan must be carried out under the guidance of a single will, which may be embodied in more than one person. If a number of friends plan to take a walk, that is not an "undertaking." But an African expedition, or a Cook's tour, undoubtedly is.

Note that the possibilities of undertaking are co-extensive with all human activities, and are not by any means limited to those only that have reference to wealth. Undertaking in the economic sense is merely a sub-division of undertaking as a whole; and capitalist undertaking is a branch of undertaking in the economic sense.

And how shall we describe the spirit of enterprise? It is the resultant of the combination of all the qualities of the soul necessary for the successful consummation of an undertaking. These qualities may be divided, on the one hand, according to the different functions an undertaker has to carry out; and on the other, according to their importance, which varies with the varying work of the undertaker. But in every case, the successful undertaker must be a trinity composed of (1) conqueror, (2) organizer, (3) trader.

1. The Conqueror. What are the psychological qualities necessary for carrying out an enterprise? I should say they are three in number. (1) To make plans is one. Which is to say, that you must have ideas. The undertaker must thus possess a certain measure of intellectual freedom. (2) The will to carry out the plan—the will to do. The inventor does not possess this characteristic. For him the discovery or invention suffices. But the undertaker must needs reproduce the invention, must duplicate and multiply it. His one thought is the realization of his plan. What he needs above all is intellectual energy. (3) But he must also have the capacity to carry his scheme through. In other words, he must possess diligent application, turning from his goal neither to the right nor the left. Your true undertaker, who is a conqueror, will have sufficient determination and strength to break down any obstacle that stands in his way. But he must be a conqueror also in his ability to take high risks, and to stake his all in order to achieve greatly. In this he is akin to the gambler.

Sum it all up, and what is his mental outfit? Intellectual elasticity, mental energy, and intensity and constancy of will.

2. *The Organizer*. Seeing that the work on which an undertaker is engaged always requires other people to work with him and be subservient to his will, it follows that the undertaker must above all be a successful organizer. And organizing means so to dovetail the work of many persons as to produce the most efficient results; so to dispose of human beings and commodities as to effect the desired creation of utilities. Now, obviously, this requires a complex of qualities for its achievement. For one thing, your successful organizer must have the knack of taking exact stock of people, that is, he must be able to pick out of a crowd just those individuals that are going to serve his purpose. For another, he must have the capacity of letting others do his work, putting each one in the place best suited for him, in order to obtain the maximum possible result, and also of getting the most from each. Thirdly, and lastly, it is the organizer's business to see to it that the co-operating individual units form a productive whole, that the complex relationships are properly corelated. As Clausewitz says of the ideal military commander, what he needs is to gather his forces in the right place, and to have them ready at the right time.

3. *The Trader*. But organizing ability does not complete the undertaker's outfit. His contact with human beings calls for much besides. In the first place, he must obtain the services of his employees. Next, he must by peaceful means influence masses of people whom he does not know, so to shape their conduct that he will derive benefits from it. That is precisely what is done by the leader of an expedition, who obtains leave to pass through a strange territory, or get provisions for his party; or by a capitalist undertaker who disposes of his goods; or by a statesman who arranges a commercial treaty. In all these cases negotiation is necessary, and negotiation means to confer with another, and, by making the best of your own case and demonstrating the weakness of his, get him to adopt what you propose. Negotiation is but an intellectual sparring match.

Thus, the undertaker must be a skilful negotiator and dealer; and a dealer in the broadest economic sense is a trader. Trading, then, means negotiating concerning the buying and selling of commodities, shares, capital, or businesses. The rag-and-bone man at the backdoor, higgling with cook for a rabbit-skin; the old-clo' dealer who spends his eloquence for hours together in order to get the country yokel to buy a pair of his trousers; a Rothschild conferring with an agent of some South American Republic in order to arrange for the floating of a large loan; the representative of the Standard Oil Trust obtaining special freight rates from all the railways in the States; Carnegie and his associates discussing with J. Pierpont Morgan a plan for the taking over by the latter of the Carnegie Works, at a price that ran into thousands of millions, and of which the historian of the United States Steel Corporation remarks, "it was the most masterly piece of diplomacy in the history of American industry";—all these are instances of trading. The difference between them is merely quantitative; the thing is the same in each case. For the essence of all modern trading is negotiating, though not necessarily face to face. It may even be achieved impersonally, as when a shopkeeper resorts to all manner of tricks in order to try and induce the public to buy his wares. What else is advertising?

In every case, the end in view is to convince buyer or seller of the advantage of the contract. And when the populace is convinced, and hastens in crowds to some particular shop, the shopkeeper's ideal has been realized. To arouse interest, to win confidence, to stir up the desire to purchase—such is the goal of the successful trader. How he reaches it is immaterial, so long as he does reach it by any method except the appeal to force. He must make the other party eager to complete the bargain. The trader must work by suggestion; and one of the most effective suggestions is to convey to the mind the vital importance of closing with the deal at once. "'It looks like snow, boys,' said the Finns, for they had Aander (a kind of snow-shoe) to sell." So we read in the Magnus Barford Saga (1006 A.D.), and the story summarizes all trading, and is an instance of one of the earliest advertisements—that weapon of every modern trader, who no longer dwells in a strongly fortified house, as did his predecessors in Genoa in the days of Benjamin of Tudela; nor does he use cannon to force the natives of some newly discovered territory to trade with him, as did the East India merchants in the seventeenth century. . . .

That every enterprise may be affected by unforeseen circumstances goes without saying. Hence the undertaker must be capable of accommodating himself to changing conditions, must keep his nerve, must be able to do the right thing at the right time. *Coup d'oeil* Frederick the Great called the quality, which he regarded as an essential in his generals (and a general, remember, is also an undertaker in the broad sense); and its realization is assured by determination. . . .

XI. THE BOURGEOIS—OLD STYLE

. . . Is the capitalist spirit constant? Does the bourgeois remain immutably the same? In other words, is there anything common to all the types . . . and to all the national expressions of capitalism, so that it may be possible to sketch the picture of the bourgeois from them?

With one qualification the answer is in the affirmative. And the qualification is that we should be allowed to divide one age of capitalist growth from another according to its characteristic spirit, for it was this that marked off one type of bourgeois or undertaker from another. This means that there was not one persistent type of undertaker at all times, but different sorts at different times.

Now, so far as I can judge, capitalist undertakers from the first dawn of capitalism to about the middle of the eighteenth century—the period which I have christened that of early capitalism—had, with all their variation in details, a good many characteristics in common. These were so definite that they form a clear dividing line between the undertaker of the early capitalist period and his prototype in modern times. What manner of man, then, was he, this bourgeois of old?

To begin with, he also was a capitalist undertaker. Profit was his end, undertakings his means; he speculated and calculated; and ultimately he cultivated the middle-class virtues, though not all in the same degree. What, then, was his distinguishing mark, you ask? How did he differ from his modern brother? You may sum it up in a sentence: in all his thoughts and actions, in all that he did or left undone, he was actuated by the weal or woe of the living, breathing human being. The central doctrine of the pre-capitalist period had not lost its efficacy. *Omnium rerum mensura homo;* man still continued to be the measure of all things. Life was still natural. Even the bourgeois as yet walked bolt-upright on his two feet; he did not yet run about on all fours.

Of course, only fragments remained of the pre-capitalist man who was still met with in the first faint beginnings of capitalism, when the Genoese noble merchants built them towers, or when Sir Walter Raleigh sallied forth in search of El Dorado. These fragments you may come across in Defoe or Benjamin Franklin. But the remainder of that early natural man with his healthy appetites has disappeared; he has been forced to accustom himself to the strait-waistcoat of middle-class respectability and the tyranny of the calculating habit. His claws have been trimmed, his carnivorous teeth blunted, and his horns encased in leather.

But all those who bowed the knee to capitalism—the rich landowner and the great oversea trader, the banker and the speculator, the manufacturer and the draper—all these never ceased to accommodate their economic activities to the healthy demands of life; for all of them business was but a means of livelihood. Their own interests and those of their fellow-men, for whom and with whom they laboured, determined the extent and direction of what they did. In support of this, you need only examine the views of these old-fashioned bourgeois.

1. First and foremost, consider their conception of riches and their attitude towards profit. Wealth was undoubtedly prized, and to obtain it was the passionate desire of every heart. But wealth was not an end in itself. Its only virtue lay in the creation or preservation of life-values. This is the tune on which all our informants harp, from Alberti to Defoe and Franklin.

The true value of money, says Alberti, can be appreciated only by him who has at any time been obliged to say to another "that bitter word, which all free spirits hate—'I pray thee.'" Riches should bring you independence and liberty, should get you friends, should make you honoured and renowned. On the other hand, "What you cannot make use of is but a heavy burden."

It will suffice to add to these expressions of opinion, dating from the childhood of capitalism, others that were current in the latest period of this early capitalist era. The similarity in sentiment will be apparent.

Our first witness shall be Benjamin Franklin. A man, he says, who has been granted wealth and a soul to use it aright has received a special and splendid gift of grace. Once in possession of riches it is a paramount duty to use them well. "A wise man will desire no more than what he may get justly, use soberly, distribute cheerfully, and live upon contentedly." Riches must be constantly increasing through industry and skilful application. They should never be allowed to lie fallow, but always be adding to their owner's wealth and spreading happiness all around. It is sensible to accumulate goods and money; but to use them well is wise. It is not riches that give happiness, but rather their proper utilization. Riches bring fame, guarantee security, and provide means for many an honourable and useful undertaking. Moreover, wealth must be acquired in just and right ways, for only those riches bring joy that are gotten honestly, or *onestamente,* as Alberti says. If you are selling anything for profit, hearken to the still, small voice of conscience, and be content with fair gain; and take no advantage of the buyer's ignorance.

Now, it may quite rightly be objected that this wise counsel is easily given.

In all probability it is the leisure-thought of the writers; possibly the voice of conscience heard in the quiet of the study but neglected in the stress and heat of the day. Consequently, it is evidence that must be ruled out of court.

2. To see that such an objection would be invalid, observe (and this is the second point) the attitude of all our authorities to business itself, their conduct as business men, the way they carried on their affairs; in a word, their "style" (as it may be called), and you shall find the same spirit in it as that in their attitude towards wealth.

Their business pace was as yet slow; their whole activity was calm and unruffled. There was no stormy whirlwind in their work. Recall Franklin's decision to spend his time as profitably as possible and his view that industry was the prime virtue. His working-day was mapped out thus: six full hours were devoted to his business; seven to sleep; and the rest he gave up to prayer, reading, and social diversions. And this was the type of the diligent undertaker, though Franklin was then only in a small way of business.

Leisure was thus appreciated. And just the same as you left yourself an abundance of it during the day and during the year, so, too, you sought to obtain the maximum amount of leisure for life as a whole. It was a common practice for people who had amassed a fortune in business or in industry (even though it were not of great proportions) to retire in middle age, and if possible purchase a country seat where they might end their days in contemplative ease. Jacob Fugger with his "Let me earn so long as I am able"—a dictum typically characteristic for a full-blown capitalist economic outlook—was undoubtedly far in advance of his age. It was for holding such a view that Anthony Fugger described him as a queer fish. He was regarded as abnormal. And so he was, judged from the standpoint of those who in their demands on life placed the ideal of the retired private gentleman first and foremost.

This yearning for a peaceful existence in a country house may be found in all the Italian books on trade; in the German Renaissance there was the same tendency to feudalize the traders; and in the eighteenth century the English commercial world still continued to look longingly at this end-all of business. The ideal of the retired private gentleman may thus be regarded as an article of faith in the early capitalist economic creed everywhere. That it had yet another significance we shall see presently.

The domination of this ideal in England in the first half of the eighteenth century is attested by Defoe's remarks on the common English practice to retire from business comparatively early. When a man has amassed £20,000, "why should he trade any farther? and what need he desire any more that has such a bank? 'Tis time to leave off and have done; 'tis time to leave labouring for the world, when he has the world, as they call it, on a string." Such a one "changes his situation in the world, that is to say, he lays down the tradesman and takes up the gentleman with a £1,000 a year estate." Defoe gives him two "seasonable hints." Let him live within the compass of his income. Of his £1,000 a year he should spend half and lay up the remainder, thus ensuring "a rising family under him." Secondly, he should keep far from speculation, for has he not retired from business to enjoy what he has got? Why then adventure it? All he has to do is to be "quiet when he is arrived at this station of life." After all, "if a tradesman is leaving off, it is with the usual saying of the rich men that withdraw from the world— That he may enjoy himself; that he may live in quiet and peace at the latter end of his days, without noise and without hurry."

That was all very well when they had made their fortune. But while making it, what of their work? Let it be said at once that it was slow. Business methods were such that in any given time you accomplished the least possible transactions. The extensive development of commerce was small; its intensive development was only in accord with it. The spirit in which business was carried on appears to me to be exemplified in the ancient saw to demand as high prices as possible so as to obtain a great rate of profit on a small capital. Small turnover, large profits, seems to have been the ruling principle of the undertakers of those days. And not merely of the lesser men, some of whom had not yet thrown off entirely the shackles of the gild system; the very big trading companies had it too. Thus it was the policy of the Dutch East India Company to carry on "small transactions that brought in a great deal." That was why it always destroyed spice plants, burned rich harvests and the like; though another motive was to deprive the poor of the opportunity of enjoying colonial products.

Quite generally it was the aim of all business to satisfy the demands of the wealthy, which is always easier than to deal with the demand on a large scale. This was quite justifiable according to the economic theory of the seventeenth and eighteenth centuries, which made out a good case for high prices.

The dignified aspect of the old-fashioned bourgeois, his stiff and pedantic bearing, were only the outward garb of his inward calm. Can you imagine a man in the long fur cloak of the Renaissance, or in the knee-breeches and powdered wig of the subsequent centuries, as ever being in a hurry? Reliable authorities, indeed, describe the old-fashioned tradesman as one who walks with careful step and slow, who is never in haste just because he is occupied.

Messer Alberti, himself a very busy man, tells us that he had never observed a busy person walking otherwise than at a slow pace, and this applied to fifteenth-century Florence. Of eighteenth-century Lyons a contemporary tells the same tale. "Here," he says, "our walk is slow because every one is busy; in Paris people are in one continuous haste—because there is nothing to do there." So in Glasgow about the same time. We read of its merchants "how in scarlet coats, cocked hats, and powdered wigs, they strutted up and down the Planistanes, the only bit of pavement then in Glasgow, covering three or four hundred yards of road in front of the Town Hall and the adjoining offices, talking grandly to one another and nodding haughtily to the humbler folk who came to do them homage."

3. The attitude of the old-fashioned traders towards competition and to their customers sprang naturally from their business style. Above all else they wanted quiet. This "static principle," which had dominated the whole of pre-capitalist economic activities, had not yet lost all its influence in the early capitalist period. And the circle of your customers was like a fenced-off preserve; it was wholly yours—to be compared to the territory assigned to the trading company in lands beyond the sea for its exclusive exploitation.

. . . Let me refer to one or two business principles, all of them naturally resulting from a static economic order, all of them included in the economic outlook of the old-fashioned bourgeois.

All "custom hunting" was looked at askance; to take away your neighbour's customers was contemptible, unchristian, and immoral. A rule for "Merchants who traded in commodities" was: "Turn no man's customers away from him, either by word of mouth or by letter, and do not to another what you would not have another do to you." It was, however, more than a rule; it became an ordinance, and is met with over and over again. In Mayence its wording was as follows: "No one shall prevent another from buying, or by offering a higher price make a commodity dearer, on pain of losing his purchase; no one shall interfere in another's business undertaking or carry on his own on so large a scale as to ruin other traders." In Saxony it was much the same. In the Ordinances of 1672, 1682, and 1692, paragraph 18 reads: "No shopkeeper shall call away the customers from another's shop, nor shall he by signs or motions keep them from buying."

It followed from this that all tricks to increase your custom, of whatever sort they were, were rather despised. Right into the nineteenth century there was still a certain prejudice in many a high-class firm against even the simplest form of advertisement. Some houses in New York had not got rid of the prejudice by the middle of the century. "No respectable house would overdo the thing. There was a sort of self-respect about the articles advertised."

But even in an advertising age it was for long considered nefarious to praise your goods or to point out wherein your business was superior to others. The last word in commercial impropriety was to announce that your prices were lower than those of the man opposite. "To undersell" was most ungentlemanly: "No blessing will come from harming your neighbour by underselling and cutting prices."

Bad as underselling itself was, it was beneath contempt to advertise it. "Since the days of our author," remark the editors of the fifth edition (1745) of Defoe's *Complete English Tradesman* (Defoe died in 1731), "this underselling practice is grown to such a shameful height that particular persons publicly advertise that they undersell the rest of the trade."

For France there is extant a particularly valuable document, dating from the second half of the eighteenth century, which proves even more strikingly how heinous this offence was thought to be, even in Paris. It is an ordinance of the year 1761, and it proclaims to all and sundry in the French capital that to advertise that you are selling your goods at a price below the customary one must be regarded as the last resource of a merchant in difficulties, and that such action deserved severe condemnation. The ordinance proceeded to forbid the wholesale and retail traders of Paris and its suburbs "to run after one another" trying to find customers, and above all to distribute handbills calling attention to their wares.

Other methods of drawing advantages for yourself at the expense of your neighbours or of poaching on others' preserves were equally disreputable. The author of the *Complete English Tradesman* has some reflections on this manner of competition which help us exceedingly in gaining a true estimate of the business ethics of those days. They prove that economic activities were still in a static state and that tradition and custom ruled them. Remember that Defoe was not unskilled as a trader, and that generally he is filled with the capitalist spirit.

This is his story. Before Wiltshire broadcloth reaches Northampton, where it is retailed, four people find employment.

> The clothier, when it is finished, sends it up by the carrier to London to Mr. A, the Blackwell Hall factor, to be sold. Mr. A, the factor, sells it to Mr. B, the woollen-draper; Mr. B, the woollen-draper, sells it to Mr. C, the shopkeeper at Northampton, and he cuts it out in his shop and sells it to the country gentlemen about him . . . also 'tis sent down by the carrier from London to Northampton.

Now in Northampton is another shopkeeper, "perhaps an Alderman, a rich overgrown Tradesman," who has more money than his neighbours and therefore wants no credit. "Prying about into all the secrets of the trade," he discovers where the cloth comes from, communicates with the clothier in Wiltshire, and buys his goods direct, then has them brought by horse-packs to Northampton. Possibly by tempting the clothier with ready money he obtains the cloth a penny per yard cheaper than the factor in London sold it to the woollen-draper. What is the result? The overgrown tradesman will save in cost of transport, so much so that his cloth will cost him half-a-crown per yard less than his neighbour. Hence he will be able to undersell, and thus obtain his neighbour's custom. Not only that, but he will have taken away the occupation of several people: the carrier who brought the goods to London from Wiltshire, the carrier who took them from London to Northampton, and finally Mr. A, the Blackwell Hall factor, who "also loses his employment and may sit and blow his fingers for want of trade." Mr. B likewise is ruined by the loss of his wholesale trade. "And what is all the benefit which is made by this spoil upon trade? Only this, that Squire D. E. of Northamptonshire buys his suits half-a-crown a yard cheaper," and a covetous man has been made richer. And the moral? "This is cutting off the circulation of trade; this is managing trade with a few hands; and if this practice, which is indeed evidently begun, was to come to be universal, a million of people in England that now live handsomely by trade would be destitute of employment and their families in time might want bread."

This passage speaks volumes. How utterly inconceivable must the line of thought appear to a modern business man!

Like the producers, the consumers also received attention. In a certain sense the consumer received even more, for the conception that all production was in the interests of consumption had not yet disappeared. It was the old "natural" view; production for use was still the rule of all economic activities. Hence the stress laid throughout the whole of the early capitalist period on *good* wares, and on the principle that commodities should really be what they pretended. Innumerable were the ordinances that were everywhere promulgated to this intent, more especially in the seventeenth and eighteenth centuries; and the state deemed it part of its work itself to regulate the quality of wares. It is idle to assert that this very state control is evidence of the decline of the "natural" view; in other words, that the custom of producing for use was on the decline. Such was not the case. The interference of the state was intended to check the conduct of some few unscrupulous manufacturers. For the rest, the old tradition prevailed that you should make good and genuine commodities; it was the tradition of the gild system, and industry in the early capitalist period continued to be tinged with it.

It was long before the purely capitalist notion gained acceptance that the exchange value of any commodity was what influenced the undertaker most. We may observe how slow its progress was from the conflicting opinions on the subject in the eighteenth century. Sir Josiah Child appears to have been in the minority on this, as on most other questions, when he formulated the demand that every manufacturer should be allowed to judge for himself as to the kind of commodity, and the quality, that he brought into the market. It is curious enough now-a-days to read Child's plea for the right of the manufacturer to make shoddy goods. "If we intend to have the trade of the world," he cries, "we must imitate the Dutch, who make the worst as well as the best of all manufactures, that we may be in a capacity of serving all markets and all humours."

4. Finally, the attitude of the old-fashioned bourgeois to technical inventions is significant for the spirit within him. The old view of life appears once more: technical improvements are to be welcomed if only they do not overthrow man's happiness. True, they may cheapen commodities; but the odd pence thus gained are too high a price for the tears and the sufferings of the families of the workmen who are thrown out of employment. Once more, then, human welfare is the pivot of the whole economic organism, even though this time it be but the welfare of the wage-earning class. The interests of this class were by no means absent from men's thoughts in those days, although the reason for this may have been a selfish one.

There is abundant testimony to the dislike of labour-saving machinery in the early capitalist period. Let us glance at one or two instances.

In the second year of Elizabeth's reign a Venetian inventor . . . offered a labour-saving machine to the Court of the London Clothworkers' Company (whose industry by that time was already capitalistic in its organization). The Court carefully considered the offer and decided to refuse it, for the new invention would probably have deprived many a workman of his living. "It wolde be a grete decay unto the companye, whereupon the Master and Wardens gave the stranger grete thanks and also xxs. in money towards his charge, and so parted."

In 1684 the knitting-frame for stockings was forbidden to be used (again in a capitalistically organized industry), and once more the reason was that it might reduce the wages of the craftsmen. Even a professional "projector" and inventor like John Joachim Becher shared this view. "I should certainly advise no one to invent instruments that might do away with human labour or reduce wages; but there can be no objection to such as are of advantage and utility, especially in those places where there is more work than workers can accomplish." Colbert's language is stronger still; the inventor of time-saving devices is a "foe of work." And these are the sentiments of Frederick the Great: "It is not by any means my intention that the spinning machine should be generally used. . . . If it were, a large number of people who depended for their livelihood on spinning would be thrown out of employment into starvation—which cannot possibly be tolerated." After all this we shall not be surprised to find that a man of such noble sentiments and good taste as Montesquieu should be conservative in this respect. He believed that machines, even including water-mills, were not an unmixed blessing. Finally, so thorough a business man as Postlethwayt is very reserved in his judgment on new inventions. A people without commerce may safely refuse to admit machines, but commercial states should only allow them after careful scrutiny and should anyhow exclude such as manufacture goods for home consumption. "What we gain in expedition, we lose in strength."

What comes to the fore throughout? The old conception of producing in order to satisfy wants, no more and no less, the traditional way of life, or moral scruples. But be the reason what it may, it is always a stumbling-block to the unfettered development of acquisitiveness, of the undertaking spirit, and of economic rationalism.

With the dawn of the nineteenth century all this changed, at first slowly, then with a rush. . . .

XII. THE MODERN BUSINESS MAN

How has the economic outlook changed in the last century? What characterizes the capitalist spirit of our own day—the zenith of capitalism; and how does that spirit differ from the one which filled the old-fashioned bourgeois?

Before attempting to answer these questions, let us realize that there is no one single type of undertaker to-day, any more than in earlier epochs; that, as in the early capitalist period, a different spirit moves different capitalist undertakers. Let us, then, place the various types in groups. Surprising as it may seem, they are the types we already know as having existed in the past. To-day, too, we find the freebooter, the ground landlord, the bureaucrat, the speculator, the trader and the manufacturer.

Recall the career of a Cecil Rhodes. Does it not remind you of the Genoese merchants on their towers, or possibly even more of Sir Walter Raleigh and Sir Francis Drake? Cecil Rhodes was of the stuff that robber-knights were made of. He was a discoverer and a conqueror whom no stumbling-blocks could retard; beside the sword and the rifle he wielded another mighty weapon—modern stock-exchange gambling. He was partly politician, partly capitalist undertaker; rather more of a diplomat than a trader; he recognized no other power than brute force. It is strange to find in him even one iota of the Puritan spirit. And if we are to compare him with earlier generations, he must be placed alongside the men of the Renaissance.

How different from Cecil Rhodes's world is that of (say) Stumm, or some Silesian mine-owner! Here we are in the atmosphere of the old feudal landed nobility; the ancient relationship between master and man is still met with; the staff of the establishments are arranged in a kind of hierarchy, and business is deliberate and cumbersome. Such are a few of the characteristics of these concerns, the directors of which have much in common with the capitalist landed proprietor of days gone by.

Then there is a third kind of undertaker nowadays who reminds us of the bureaucrat of old—exact in his work, methodical to a degree, nicely balanced in his judgments, highly gifted as an organizer, very careful before committing himself, an excellent executive official, who to-day may be town clerk of a large town and to-morrow manager of a bank, who frequently enough gives up the control of a Government department for that of a trust. You will find him at the head of state and municipal enterprises.

Different from all these is the speculator of our time, who appears to be twin-brother to the eighteenth-century projector. Recently the daily papers reported the exploits of a French speculator, and the story is worth recalling. Rochette was the man's name; his age scarcely thirty. Yet he had allowed millions to slip between his fingers. He started life as an under-waiter in a railway station restaurant; before long he was a full-fledged waiter in a café in Melun. Coming to Paris, he made himself acquainted with book-keeping, and entered the service of Berger, the financial swindler. On his master's bankruptcy Rochette took over the business with the 5,000 francs dowry brought him by a typist whom he married. He then began to float companies, and in the space of four years no less than 13 came into existence. There was the Crédit Minier, with a capital of 500,000 francs; the Laviana Coal Mines, with 2 millions; the Liat Coal Mines, with the same amount; the Banque Franco-Espagnole, with 20 millions; the Minier Trust, with 10 millions; the Union Franco-Belge, with 2½ millions; the financial paper *Le Financier,* with 2 millions; a number of copper and tin companies; a Moroccan Fishery Company; an incandescent lamp company, with 4½ millions; and many more. He issued altogether some 60 million francs' worth of shares, which by skilful manipulation rose to 200 millions, though a tenth of that figure was more nearly their true value. He had opened no less than 57 branch establishments in France; and the total number of people who participated in his scheme was close upon 40,000. Most of them were ruined, their total losses amounting to more than 150 millions. Why, it may be asked, was Rochette able to take in so many people? The explanation will be found in his marvellous power of surrounding himself with "solid," respectable folk. Just to show how cunning he was in blinding his victims, it may be mentioned that he founded a large factory for utilizing a filament lamp patent. Everybody rushed to get shares in the company; the huge factory was the talk of the town; its tall chimneys belched forth smoke day and night, to the great satisfaction of the shareholders. In reality, however, there was only one solitary individual working in the building, and he was the stoker!

Does not this story read like a report of doings in England in the 1720's?

How different is the persevering tradesman who makes a fortune because of his sure eye for the right conjuncture, or by clever calculations and advantageous agreements with his wholesale house, his customers, and his employees. What has such a man, say a Berlin draper, in common with Cecil Rhodes? What the director of a multiple shop with a gold-mine speculator? And what all these with the manufacturer who runs his factory as was done 100 or 200 years ago, in Bradford or Sedan?

These old friends are still among us, and seemingly their form is unchanged. Nor are they the only types of the modern undertaker. Others have joined the group, which thus becomes quite picturesque. A very common one, usually found in America, may be termed the master-undertaker (since super-undertaker is an ugly word). His great characteristic is that he unites within himself several independent types. He may be freebooter, unscrupulous calculator, landlord, and speculator all in one. Any trust-magnate will serve as an illustration.

Finally, a phenomenon of our age is the collective undertaker, who is not an individual at all, but a group of capitalist undertakers at the head of a giant enterprise. They form a kind of syndicated undertaker, each of them exercising special functions, and in their corporate capacity they represent undertaking in all its comprehensiveness. We need only think of such industrial organizations as our electrical concerns, our iron foundries, our cannon factories.

In short, modern undertaking in all its types presents a variegated picture. But in our own days, as in those of long ago, all the types have certain features in common, all are filled with the same spirit. It is only a difference of degree that distinguishes the one from the other. In olden times, as we saw, the undertakers were children of the early capitalist spirit; in modern times, they are the children of the perfected capitalist spirit.

What manner of thing is this perfected capitalist spirit? And what have all the types of the modern capitalist undertaker in common?

1. The ideal of both must be our first consideration. What is it? What are the life-values that govern the latter-day business man? What strikes us here is that there has been a peculiar change of perspective in the evaluation of man, a change of perspective which seems to have affected the whole of the rest of life. Man, the flesh-and-blood man, with his joys and sorrows, with his needs and demands, has been forced from his place as the centre round which all economic activities rotate; his throne is now occupied by a few abstractions, such as Acquisitiveness and Business. Man has ceased to be what he was until the end of the early capitalist period—the measure of all things. The economic subjective agent now aims at as high a profit as he can, and strives to make his business flourish exceedingly. The two aims are closely intertwined, as we shall presently observe. Their relationship may be expressed thus: The undertakers wish to see business thriving; as for acquisitiveness, it is forced upon them, even though they may never have set out with that as their goal.

The real interest of undertaking does not always lie in mere gain, certainly not for the dominating personalities who determine the type. Walter Rathenau was, as I think, perfectly right when he once said: "I have never yet met with a business man whose chief aim was to acquire wealth. I will even go so far as to assert that he who is out to make money cannot possibly be a great business man." Something very different occupies the thoughts of the undertaker. His heart is set on seeing his business thrive. Once more Walter Rathenau has expressed it well.

> The object of the business man's work, of his worries, his pride and his aspirations is just his undertaking, be it a commercial company, factory, bank, shipping concern, theatre or railway. The undertaking seems to take form and substance, and to be ever with him, having, as it were, by virtue of his book-keeping, his organization, and his branches, an independent economic existence. The business man is wholly devoted to making his business a flourishing, healthy, living organism.

This view is shared by all the capitalist undertakers of the day in so far as they have expressed themselves on the inner meaning of their activity.

Now, what is really meant by making a business, that is, a capitalist undertaking, flourish? Observe that a business begins with a sum of money and ends with the same, and that therefore its existence is bound up with the realization of a surplus. Success in business can only mean success in realizing this surplus. No profits, no business success. A factory may make very dear or very cheap goods, and their quality may establish their maker's name as a household word throughout the globe, but if the business continues to show a deficit from year to year, it is a failure from the capitalist point of view. To flourish, a concern must be profitable; to prosper, it must pay.

You see now what I meant when I made the statement that the undertakers wish to see business thriving, and as for acquisitiveness, it is forced upon them.

Such being the goal of the capitalist undertaker, the end of his activities is necessarily projected into infinity. In earlier times, when the needs of the community determined economic activities, these had natural boundaries or limits. There can be no such limits when economic activities are determined by acquisitiveness and by flourishing businesses. There is never a point in the future when the total profits are sufficiently great for the undertaker to say: It is enough. Should the development of a business be such that its prosperity ceases to increase, the many-sidedness of modern enterprise will see to it that before long a second, and possibly a third, business is added to the original one. Thus it is that in modern days two equally strong tendencies show themselves—expansion of one and the same business, and the branching out into subsidiary or additional businesses. This very often leads to a kind of inner pressure in the mind of the undertaker. It frequently happens that he really does not want to expand further, but he must. Many a captain of industry has confessed as much. We were always hoping, says Andrew Carnegie in his *Autobiography,* that there would come a time when extension of business would no longer be necessary; but we invariably found that to put off expanding would mean retrogression. Rockefeller tells the same tale. The first reason for starting his trusts was the desire to unite his capital and his capacities

> to carry on a business of some magnitude and importance in place of the small business that each separately had heretofore carried. After some time, when the possibilities of the new conditions became apparent, we found that more capital was necessary. This we provided, as also the people, and founded the Standard Oil Company with a capital of a million dollars. Later we discovered that even more money could be profitably invested, and we raised our capital to 3½ millions. The more the business grew the more capital we put into it, the object being always the same: to extend our business by furnishing the best and cheapest products.

A kind of monomania this; capital is piled on capital *because* the business grows. Extension of business is the end; furnishing cheap and good products the means. A famous German undertaker—Strousberg—says exactly the same thing. "The first wedge calls as a rule for a second, and so the great railway I was building made further demands upon me. To satisfy these I extended my activities, departed more and more from my original intention, and, finding so much promise in the new prospect, I devoted myself wholly to my business."

Most capitalist undertakers think of nothing else but this constant desire for extension and expansion, which to the outside observer appears so meaningless. If you ask them what purpose the expansion is intended to serve, they will regard you with a kind of mild surprise and reply a little testily that the purpose is self-evident; it is to make economic life more vigorous, and, moreover, is demanded by economic progress.

But what is meant by "economic progress" in this quite general and fairly stereotyped answer? What is the association of ideas in the minds of the people who give it? Examine carefully and you shall find that it means an expansion in what may be called the "economic apparatus"—the production of largely increased quantities at the cheapest possible price; enormous output; enormous extent of communications; the quickest transportation of goods, people, and news.

But the answer, like the phenomena that prompted the question, sounds meaningless too. It is therefore unsatisfactory. There must be method in all this madness; it must surely be explicable. The people concerned in the activities do not seem to be alive to any life-values at their base. But life-values in them there must be, or you would not find whole generations of men intellectually sound and strong engaged in the activities mentioned. An analysis of the soul of the modern capitalist undertaker therefore repays the trouble, and at the very outset you stumble across—the child. In very truth, the psychology of the modern undertaker appears to me to resemble greatly that of the child. Understand the one and you will understand the other. For all the processes in the mind of the undertaker (and indeed of modern man generally), if reduced to their simplest elements, show a kind of relapse into the days of childhood.

Let us consider the matter more in detail.

The child possesses four elementary "values"; four ideals dominate its existence. They are—

(a) Physical bigness, as seen in grown-ups and imagined in giants;

(b) Quick movement—in running, bowling a hoop, riding on a roundabout;

(c) Novelty—it changes its toys very quickly; it begins something and never completes it because another occupation attracts it; and

(d) Sense of power—that is why it pulls out the legs of a fly, makes Towzer stand on his hind legs and beg nicely, and flies its kite as high as it can.

Curious as it may sound, these ideals, and these only, will be found in all modern "values." Let us take them in turn.

(a) We attach importance to quantities, to mere size. It is what interests us, what we admire most. That, I fancy, will be generally admitted. There is a universal tendency (to use the words of Lord Bryce) "to mistake bigness for greatness." It matters not wherein the bigness consists: it may be the population of a town or a country, the height of a monument, the breadth of a river, the frequency of suicide, the passengers carried by a railway, the size of a ship, the number of players in an orchestra, or what not. Of course our greatest admiration is reserved for a huge sum of money. Besides, money makes it possible to measure the size of otherwise unmeasurable things and to compare them. It is a natural and easy step from this to the belief that that is valuable which costs much. We say this picture or this jewellery is twice as valuable as that. In America, where this modern tendency may be studied better than anywhere else because there it has reached its greatest perfection, people come to the point at once, and prefix to every commodity its monetary value. "Have you seen the 50,000-dollar Rembrandt at Mr. A's house?" is a not unusual question. "To-day Mr. Carnegie's 500,000-dollar yacht entered the harbour of" (say) Boston—so you may read in the daily paper.

Get into the habit of looking at the mere quantity of things and you will naturally tend to compare any two phenomena that may come under your notice; you will weigh the one against the other and pronounce the larger to be the more valuable. Again, if of two things the one becomes larger than the other in a given space of time, it is said to have been successful. So that the inclination towards what is measurably big brings with it necessarily another tendency—worship of success. The modern business man is appraised only in accordance with his success. Now success means to overtake others; to do more, to achieve more, to possess more than others; in a word, to be great. The pursuit of success holds out the same unlimited possibilities as the chase of profits; the one complements the other.

To illustrate the influence on the inner workings of the mind of this quantitative valuation of things, so characteristic of our day, let us refer to the attitude of people to sport. What is invariably the main question of interest? Is it not, who will win? Who will score most? A match is but a quantitative balance between two results. Imagine such a standpoint in an ancient Greek wrestling school! Imagine it at a Spanish bull-fight! The thing is impossible.

In both these cases qualitative values were looked for, e.g., the highest personal artistic skill.

(b) Speed is of almost the same consequence to the modern man as massivity. To rush on in a 100-h.p. motor-car is one of the supremest ideals of our age; and he who cannot speed madly along contents himself with reading of record-breaking velocity. Perhaps the express between Hamburg and Berlin was ten minutes in advance of its scheduled time; perhaps the latest ocean-liner reached New York three hours earlier than it was expected; perhaps the postman now comes at 7:30 instead of at the customary 8 o'clock; perhaps one newspaper published a declaration of war (probably a fictitious one) an hour before its competitor—all these things are of tremendous interest to the queerly constituted folk of our day; they seem to be of vital importance to them.

Moreover, a curious concept has sprung into existence, that of "beating the record." In terms of record-breaking you impress on your memory the speediest achievements as the most valuable ones. In its fullest meaning the new concept refers to great size and great speed combined. All the megalomania, all the mad hurry of our time, is expressed in record-beating. I think it most likely that the future historian of our time will speak of it as "The Age of Record-breaking."

(c) Whatever is new nowadays attracts merely because it is a novelty. It attracts most when the assurance is possible, "There never has been anything like it." Sensational we call its effect on the mind. That the love of sensation is a marked feature of the age requires no expatiation. Modern journalism is perhaps the best proof. But recall also how fashions in dances, no less than in clothes, change from season to season. Is it not because nothing is so attractive as what is new?

(d) The sense of power is the fourth characteristic of the modern spirit; it is felt in the consciousness of superiority over others. But in reality it is only an expression of weakness; hence its importance in the child's world. For, after all, any one gifted with true greatness, which is usually inward, will be hardly likely to estimate the outward semblance of power at all highly. Power has no temptation for Siegfried; only a Mime thirsts for it. Bismarck in all probability did not bother much about the power he exercised; but in Lassalle the desire for power must have been tremendous. A king possesses power; it is therefore of small moment in his sight. But the financier of humble origin, who keeps a kingly borrower waiting in his ante-chamber for some little time, suns himself in this power because his soul has none of it. An undertaker who employs 10,000 men and experiences a sense of power in consequence is like a little boy who makes his doggie bring back the stick he keeps on throwing from him. Moreover, when neither by money nor any other outward force power over mankind is given us, we talk of the conquest of nature. That is why our age is so childishly delighted with epoch-making discoveries—say, the mastery of the air, and such-like achievements. The truly great man, however, will be comparatively unmoved at the sight of a biplane in the air. A truly great generation concerned with the deepest problems of life will not be enraptured because it made some discoveries in technical science. Power of this sort it will assuredly regard as "superficial." Our own age lacks true greatness; accordingly, like a child it admires the power which new inventions bestow, and it overrates those who possess it. Hence the high esteem in which the populace holds inventors and millionaires.

It is just possible that these visions float before the gaze of the undertaker more or less clearly. But certain it is that they take form and substance in his goal—the expansion and growth of his business. Acquisitiveness and interest in his enterprise thus direct his activities as a capitalist undertaker.

2. His ideal we have reviewed. It remains now to review these activities as influenced by the ideal. In essence the activities of the modern capitalist undertaker remain the same as before. He must conquer, organize, deal, speculate, and calculate. But the extent of each of these factors varies, and consequently the resultant whole is not quite like that of an earlier age.

In modern times the trading function has become of more and more significance. I use the word "trading" in the sense . . . of dealing or negotiating. It is on this that commercial success now increasingly depends; on the skill and strength of suggestion in making contracts of all kinds. In olden days knots were cut; to-day they must be unravelled.

Next in importance to dealing comes skilful speculation—by which I mean stock-exchange manipulations. Modern undertakings are drawn more and more into the vortex of stock-exchange activities. Trust development such as we find in the United States is in reality only the transformation of manufacturing and commercial enterprises into purely stock-exchange speculative concerns. Consequently the directors and managers of such businesses have new problems to solve, and this opens up new activities for them.

As for calculation, it becomes more and more delicate as well as increasingly difficult, both because of the need for absolute exactitude and also because it has become so extensive.

Finally, the activities of the capitalist undertaker have become much more many-sided; that is to say, in so far as specialization has not set in. Economic activities have branched out in all directions; what wonder then that those who direct them should be called upon to be many-sided?

So much for the nature of the activity itself. What is new is its boundlessness. So long as the needs of the living human being governed economic activities, so long did these have a limit. But with the disappearance of the governing factor, the natural limit fell away. Accordingly the activities of the capitalist undertaker have no bounds. . . . Which means that the expenditure of human energy in modern economic activities, extensively and intensively, is strained to the uttermost. Every minute of the day, of the year, nay, of life itself, is devoted to work; and during this working period every power is occupied at highest pressure. Everybody is acquainted with the hard-worked man of to-day. Whether employer or employed, he is constantly on the verge of a breakdown owing to overwork. That he tends to be excited, that he is always on the move, is generally known too. Speed and yet more speed—such is the cry of the age. It rushes onward in one mad race.

The influence of such a life on body and soul is not difficult to gauge. It corrodes the former and dries up the latter. Everything is sacrificed to the Moloch of work; all the higher instincts of heart and mind are crushed out by devotion to business. How much the inner life of modern man has been shattered is best seen if we cast a glance at the kernel of all natural life—the relationship to women. These men have no time for the enjoyment of delicate passions, nor even for gallant flirtations. They seem to be quite incapable of deep erotic emotions. Either they are wholly apathetic so far as love is concerned, or they are content with a brief sensual intoxication. They either do not bother about women at all, or they buy what they require in this respect.

3. Business principles likewise have undergone a change. That was only to be expected when the goal of enterprise has become different. To-day, it may be said, five main rules regulate economic activities.

(a) Absolute rationalism is the first. Economic activities are ruled by cold reason, by thought. . . . [That] has always been the case; it showed itself in the making of plans, in considering whether any policy was likely to be successful or no, and in calculation generally. The modern capitalist spirit differs from its predecessors only in the degree in which this rule is obeyed. To-day the rule is strictly, one might almost say sternly, enforced. The last trace of traditionalism has vanished. The man of to-day (and the American undertaker may stand as the most perfect type) is filled with the will to apply cold reason to economic activities; moreover, he possesses the determination to make the will effective. Accordingly, he is ever ready to adopt a newer method if it is more rational, whether in the sphere of organization, of production, or of calculation. This naturally implies that, no matter what the cost may be, he is able to leave the old methods the moment the newer ones are available.

(b) Production for exchange (as opposed to production for use) is the motto of economic activities. As much profit as possible is their ideal; consequently what matters is not the goodness or the kind of commodities produced but their saleability. How they are sold is secondary, so long as they are sold. Consequently the undertaker is wholly indifferent to the quality of his wares; he will make shoddy goods or cheap substitutes, if only it pays. If cheap and nasty boots yield more profit than good ones, it would be a deadly sin against the holy spirit of capitalism to manufacture good ones. It is no argument against the truth of this to point to a movement in certain industries (the chemical industry is one), the object of which is to improve quality. As well say that the bonuses which the general store offers to its employees on the sale of more expensive articles proves the same thing. What both instances do prove is that they are cases where there is more profit from high-class goods than from inferior articles. The greatest gain is the only criterion in these matters, and an undertaker will make now cheap goods, now dearer, according as the one or the other yields more profit. From the capitalist's standpoint that is only natural.

What follows from this is plain. Since it is inherent in acquisitiveness to enlarge incomings to the uttermost; and since, again, the greater the sale the larger the profits, it is only to be expected that the undertaker will try all he can to increase his sales. Apart from the greater gain, more extended sales will give him certain advantages over competitors. Hence it is by no means remarkable that the desire for greater sales, for new markets, for more customers, is one of the mightiest motive powers in modern capitalism. It is directly responsible for a number of business principles, all of which have one end in view—to make the public buy. The more important of these principles deserve to be mentioned.

(c) The first (and the third in the general scheme) may be enunciated as follows: Search out the customer and attack him. That is to-day as self-evident a maxim in all branches of business as it was strange and wrong in the age of early capitalism. In practice it means that you set out to attract the customer's attention and to stir up within him the desire to purchase. You attract his attention by shouting in his ears, or catching his eye, by loud, coloured indicators; you strive to make him purchase by suggestion; you seek to convince him that the articles for sale are extraordinarily good or valuable.

Advertisement serves both ends—as every one knows; and advertisements, as every one knows also, shatter all sense of propriety, of taste, of good manners, and of dignity. Is it not true to say that modern advertising in its extreme forms is both unaesthetic and immoral?

(d) Secondly, sell as cheaply as you can; reduce price to the lowest possible figure so as to attract the public. In the early capitalist age low prices were an abomination. The motto then was . . . little business but great profits. To-day we are at the opposite extreme: as much business as possible but small profits. Small profits, quick returns—is not this nowadays the universal motto?

(e) Elbow-room is demanded in order to arrive at the wished-for goal. Which means, first, that you require freedom of action, liberty to enter upon or to abstain from any course, as seems best to you. It means emancipation from the trammels of law or morality; it means that you should be allowed to poach on your neighbour's preserves just as he may be allowed to poach on yours; it means that you should be allowed to oust him if you can; it means that you object to interference either from the state or from working men's organizations in making your contracts. You want none of the restraints of an earlier age. The free exercise of your powers shall alone determine economic success or failure.

And in the second place it means—what follows quite naturally—unrestricted competition. If acquisition is the first consideration, unrestricted competition is a matter of course. You need no longer be bound by considerations of any kind, whether moral, aesthetic or social. Unscrupulous is the adjective for your actions.

Look at the extensive American trusts and you will see what unrestricted competition means. The . . . doings of the American Tobacco Company are a case in point; they outdistanced the accepted practices of Europe and illustrate to what lengths an unscrupulous undertaker will go. No considerations give him pause; he leaves no road untried that promises success. The trust threw its goods away at ridiculous prices in order to conquer new markets; middlemen received enormous commissions; well-known brands were imitated and poor quality wares were sold in wrappers that misled the public. If it became involved in litigation, the trust by its superior financial strength was able to draw out the cases until its opponents were utterly exhausted. Even retail trading received careful attention, for the trust opened shops at effective points, and by underselling forced the old-established tobacconists to close their doors. Finally, the trust monopolized the raw material, and so came into conflict with the tobacco-growers of Kentucky. In 1911 the trust was proceeded against under the Sherman Law, and the presiding judge in delivering sentence characterized the activities of the undertaking against their competitors as having been carried on with extraordinary cunning, precaution, and devilry. Every human creature that by energy or skill threatened to stand in the way of the trust was mercilessly crushed.

Perhaps the most perfect type of unscrupulous, smart business man was Edward H. Harriman . . . the secret of . . . [whose] victorious career was his utter lack of moral scruples. Had he not cast these overboard he would have stumbled almost at the very first step he took. He began by breaking the man who had opened for him the gates of the railway paradise; following this up by his brutal campaign against Morgan, who, however, knew how to utilize for his own ends the capacities of his opponent. Harriman's fight with Hill was as unscrupulous as the policy that brought him into the Standard Oil Trust. But Harriman's delinquencies were not merely personal; they form part and parcel of American speculation.

Of the great victors on the racecourse of modern capitalism it may be asserted, what was recently said of Rockefeller, that they know how to glide over every moral restraint with almost childlike disregard. The mirror of this naïve view of life will be found in the memoirs of John Rockefeller, who once summed up the faith within him by saying that he was willing to pay a substitute a salary of a million dollars, if beside other positive qualities he had no scruples whatsoever, and was ready to kill off thousands of victims without a murmur.

Another undertaker, this time a German, who considered himself rather backward in this respect because he was "too good-natured and considerate" —I refer to Werner Siemens—urged his brother Charles to become a smart business man in these terms: "Always be determined and unscrupulous. That in so large a concern is called for. Once begin to be considerate of private interests and you will fall into a morass of demands and intrigues" (letter of March 31, 1856).

4. The middle-class virtues—industry, frugality, and honesty—are they of any consequence for the modern capitalist undertaker? It is as difficult to reply to the question in the affirmative as in the negative. The place of these virtues in modern economic life is so very different from what they occupied in the early capitalist system. As a matter of fact, they have ceased to be necessary to the undertaker. Nevertheless, they still play their part in undertaking. Before these virtues were still in the sphere wherein personal will-power was exercised; now they have become part of the mechanism of business. Before, they were characteristic of living beings; now, they have turned into objective principles of business methods.

This may sound difficult. I will explain my meaning by considering each of the virtues in turn.

In the olden days when industry was preached as a prime virtue in the tradesman, it was necessary to implant a solid foundation of duties in the inner consciousness of men. Everybody had to be urged to exercise his will-power in a certain direction, and when the habit was once formed the industrious tradesman went through his day's work in conscious self-mastery. To-day all this is changed. The business man works at high pressure because the stress of economic activities carries him along in spite of himself. He is no longer exercising a virtue; necessity drives him to this particular course. The general business pace determines what his own business pace shall be. He can no more be idle than a man at a machine; whereas a craftsman with his tools can be idle or industrious as he chooses.

The objectiveness of frugality is even more marked, for the private and the business "housekeeping" of the undertaker are now separate. In the latter frugality is needful more than ever. "Extravagance even in the smallest things should be avoided. It is not petty to have a care of this, for extravagance is a consuming disease difficult to localize. There are great undertakings whose existence depends on whether all the sand is removed from the carts or whether one shovelfull is left behind." Recall the careful, almost miserly, economy of Rockefeller in his management of the Standard Oil Company; recall how not a drop of oil was wasted; the wooden boxes in which tin was brought from Europe were sold to florists or were used as firewood. But in the private housekeeping of the undertaker you will find none of this fanatical thrift. Neither Rathenau's nor Rockefeller's castle is a center of that frugality so much beloved of Benjamin Franklin; and the festive boards of our rich undertakers know nothing of sufficiency and moderation. And if the head of the family is content to go on in the old-fashioned bourgeois style of his youth, his wife, his sons, and his daughters will all see to it that luxury and superfluity and pomp become part and parcel of the new bourgeois spirit. Bourgeois the style of life still is, even in the case of the wealthiest. The old doctrines of Alberti still hold sway. Never let your expenditure exceed your income, he urged his disciples. And calculate. To-day this advice is faithfully obeyed by the modern bourgeois. Herein his mode of living differs from the seignorial. The seigneur scorns money.

Commercial honesty comes last. Can any one doubt that honesty is to-day—to-day perhaps more than ever—a factor in business life? In business life only, however. For the conduct of the undertaker as a man may differ widely from his conduct as a tradesman. Commercial honesty is a complexity of principles that are intended to apply to business but not to the personal conduct of the business subject. An honest tradesman to-day may certainly be unmoral in his private life. When you say he is "good," you mean that he is reliable in his business; that he will pay; that his firm has a good name. You pass no judgment on his personal conduct, which is governed by other principles. Indeed, the firm may not have an individual head at all. It may be an impersonal limited company, the directors of which change from time to time. Their personal morality stands in no relationship to the business. The "name" of the business is all that matters. Thus, here, too, what before was a personal quality has now become a matter of business routine. You can see it best by considering modern credit. A bank in olden days was relied upon because it could point to an ancient and honoured name; it was "good" for personal reasons. To-day a bank inspires confidence by the size of its invested capital and its reserves. To-day you assume that business is carried on honestly—anyhow until some swindle comes to light to prove the contrary. In this virtue then, as in the others, what before was organic has now become mechanical.

All this applies to the large undertakings. In the small and middle-sized enterprises, however, you may still find the principles prevalent in the early days of capitalism. The middle-class virtues are still cultivated, and the undertaker's personal characteristics determine his economic progress. It is in the large undertakings and their directors and managers that we find the spirit of capitalism fully developed in all its shining purity. . . .

THORSTEIN VEBLEN

THE ascetic doctrine of work which Max Weber saw as the mainspring of the capitalist spirit was particularly suited to a productive economy vitally dependent upon savings as the chief source of capital accumulation. But other modes of behavior are equally necessary in a market economy dependent upon high standards of consumption to maintain an increasing rate of machine production. The injunction constantly to convert profits into capital improvements is paralleled in Western civilization by a similarly powerful injunction to spend freely upon personal comfort, even to indulge a taste for luxury and display.

In *The Theory of the Leisure Class* (1899), from which the following selection has been taken, Thorstein Veblen, not without malice toward the "gilded age" society of *nouveaux riches* so conspicuous in America at the turn of the twentieth century, attempted to formulate an explanation of the folkways of irrational consumer behavior. For Veblen social stratification inevitably gives rise to "invidious comparisons" among the several levels of the graduated social system. Low-status groups tend to emulate the manners and standards of consumption of the high status groups. In a pecuniary culture honor resides in money; in order to assert their claims to honor, the wealthy must advertise their riches. This results in an elaborate ceremony of "conspicuous consumption and conspicuous waste," the most evident trait of which is the "ostentatious display" of leisure. The "pecuniary canons of taste" thus established by the highest leisure class permeate the entire community of consumers. They reach down to the lowest income scales, create needs and desires, stimulate social envy, force expenditures, and drive the "underprivileged" into competitive habits of industry to gain money so as, in the end, to purchase the symbols of honor in society. Emulation, which Veblen considered to be an economic motive second only to self-preservation, thus becomes the motor force of the "business enterprise."

THE THEORY OF THE LEISURE CLASS

CHAPTER II: PECUNIARY EMULATION

In the sequence of cultural evolution the emergence of a leisure class coincides with the beginning of ownership. This is necessarily the case, for these

This selection is from *The Theory of the Leisure Class* by Thorstein Veblen, Copyright 1899 by The Macmillan Company, and has been reprinted by permission of The Viking Press, Inc., New York (1931 Modern Library ed., pp. 23–34, 68–101).

two institutions result from the same set of economic forces. In the inchoate phase of their development they are but different aspects of the same general facts of social structure.

It is as elements of social structure—conventional facts—that leisure and ownership are matters of interest for the purpose in hand. An habitual neglect of work does not constitute a leisure class; neither does the mechanical fact of use and consumption constitute ownership. The present inquiry, therefore, is not concerned with the beginning of indolence, nor with the beginning of the appropriation of useful articles to individual consumption. The point in question is the origin and nature of a conventional leisure class on the one hand and the beginnings of individual ownership as a conventional right or equitable claim on the other hand.

The early differentiation out of which the distinction between a leisure and a working class arises is a division maintained between men's and women's work in the lower stages of barbarism. Likewise the earliest form of ownership is an ownership of the women by the able-bodied men of the community. The facts may be expressed in more general terms, and truer to the import of the barbarian theory of life, by saying that it is an ownership of the woman by the man.

There was undoubtedly some appropriation of useful articles before the custom of appropriating women arose. The usages of existing archaic communities in which there is no ownership of women is warrant for such a view. In all communities the members, both male and female, habitually appropriate to their individual use a variety of useful things; but these useful things are not thought of as owned by the person who appropriates and consumes them. The habitual appropriation and consumption of certain slight personal effects goes on without raising the question of ownership; that is to say, the question of a conventional, equitable claim to extraneous things.

The ownership of women begins in the lower barbarian stages of culture, apparently with the seizure of female captives. The original reason for the seizure and appropriation of women seems to have been their usefulness as trophies. The practice of seizing women from the enemy as trophies, gave rise to a form of ownership-marriage, resulting in a household with a male head. This was followed by an extension of slavery to other captives and inferiors, besides women, and by an extension of ownership-marriage to other women than those seized from the enemy. The outcome of emulation under the circumstances of a predatory life, therefore, has been on the one hand a form of marriage resting on coercion and on the other hand the custom of ownership. The two institutions are not distinguishable in the initial phase of their development; both arise from the desire of the successful men to put their prowess in evidence by exhibiting some durable result of their exploits. Both also minister to that propensity for mastery which pervades all predatory communities. From the ownership of women the concept of ownership extends itself to include the products of their industry, and so there arises the ownership of things as well as persons.

In this way a consistent system of property in goods is gradually installed. And although in the latest stages of the development, the serviceability of goods for consumption has come to be the most obtrusive element of their value, still, wealth has by no means yet lost its utility as a honorific evidence of the owner's prepotence.

Wherever the institution of private property is found, even in a slightly developed form, the economic process bears the character of a struggle between men for the possession of goods. It has been customary in economic theory, and especially among those economists who adhere with least faltering to the body of modernised classical doctrines, to construe this struggle for wealth as being substantially a struggle for subsistence. Such is, no doubt, its character in large part during the earlier and less efficient phases of industry. Such is also its character in all cases where the "niggardliness of nature" is so strict as to afford but a scanty livelihood to the community in return for strenuous and unremitting application to the business of getting the means of subsistence. But in all progressing communities an advance is presently made beyond this early stage of technological development. Industrial efficiency is presently carried to such a pitch as to afford something appreciably more than a bare livelihood to those engaged in the industrial process. It has not been unusual for economic theory to speak of the further struggle for wealth on this new industrial basis as a competition for an increase of the comforts of life,—primarily for an increase of the physical comforts which the consumption of goods affords.

The end of acquisition and accumulation is conventionally held to be the consumption of the goods accumulated—whether it is consumption directly by the owner of the goods or by the household attached to him and for this purpose identified with him in theory. This is at least felt to be the economically legitimate end of acquisition, which alone it is incumbent on the theory to take account of. Such consumption may of course be conceived to serve the consumer's physical wants—his physical comfort—or his so-called higher wants—spiritual, aesthetic, intellectual, or what not; the latter class of wants being served indirectly by an expenditure of goods, after the fashion familiar to all economic readers.

But it is only when taken in a sense far removed from its naïve meaning that consumption of goods can be said to afford the incentive from which accumulation invariably proceeds. The motive that lies at the root of ownership is emulation; and the same motive of emulation continues active in the further development of the institution to which it has given rise and in the development of all those features of the social structure which this institution of ownership touches. The possession of wealth confers honour; it is an invidious distinction. Nothing equally cogent can be said for the consumption of goods, nor for any other conceivable incentive to acquisition, and especially not for any incentive to the accumulation of wealth.

It is of course not to be overlooked that in a community where nearly all goods are private property the necessity of earning a livelihood is a powerful and ever-present incentive for the poorer members of the community. The need of subsistence and of an increase of physical comfort may for a time be the dominant motive of acquisition for those classes who are habitually employed at manual labour, whose subsistence is on a precarious footing, who possess little and ordinarily accumulate little; but . . . even in the case of these impecunious classes the predominance of the motive of physical want is not so decided as has sometimes been assumed. On the other hand, so far as regards those members and classes of the community who are chiefly concerned in the accumulation of wealth, the incentive of subsistence or of physical comfort never plays a considerable part. Ownership began and grew into a human institution on grounds unrelated to the subsistence minimum. The dominant incentive was from the outset the invidious distinction attaching to wealth, and, save temporarily and by exception, no other motive has usurped the primacy at any later stage of the development.

Property set out with being booty held as trophies of the successful raid. So long as the group had departed but little from the primitive communal organisation, and so long as it still stood in close contact with other hostile groups, the utility of things or persons owned lay chiefly in an invidious comparison between their possessor and the enemy from whom they were taken. The habit of distinguishing between the interests of the individual and those of the group to which he belongs is apparently a later growth. Invidious comparison between the possessor of the honorific booty and his less successful neighbours within the group was no doubt present early as an element of the utility of the things possessed, though this was not at the outset the chief element of their value. The man's prowess was still primarily the group's prowess, and the possessor of the booty felt himself to be primarily the keeper of the honour of his group. This appreciation of exploit from the communal point of view is met with also at later stages of social growth, especially as regards the laurels of war.

But so soon as the custom of individual ownership begins to gain consistency, the point of view taken in making the invidious comparison on which private property rests will begin to change. Indeed, the one change is but the reflex of the other. The initial phase of ownership, the phase of acquisition by naïve seizure and conversion, begins to pass into the subsequent state of an incipient organisation of industry on the basis of private property (in slaves); the horde develops into a more or less self-sufficing industrial community; possessions then come to be valued not so much as evidence of successful foray, but rather as evidence of the prepotence of the possessor of these goods over other individuals within the community. The invidious comparison now becomes primarily a comparison of the owner with the other members of the group. Property is still of the nature of trophy, but, with the cultural advance, it becomes more and more a trophy of successes scored in the game of ownership carried on between the members of the group under the quasi-peaceable methods of nomadic life.

Gradually, as industrial activity further displaces predatory activity in the community's everyday life and in men's habits of thought, accumulated property more and more replaces trophies of predatory exploit as the conventional exponent of prepotence and success. With the growth of settled industry, therefore, the possession of wealth gains in relative importance and effectiveness as a customary basis of repute and esteem. Not that esteem ceases to be awarded on the basis of other, more direct evidence of prowess; not that successful predatory aggression or warlike exploit ceases to call out the approval and admiration of the crowd, or to stir the envy of the less successful competitors; but the opportunities for gaining distinction by means of this direct manifestation of superior force grow less available both in scope and frequency. At the same time opportunities for industrial aggression, and for the accumulation of property by the quasi-peaceable methods of nomadic industry, increase in scope and availability. And it is even more to the point that property now becomes the most easily recognised evidence of a reputable degree of success as distinguished from heroic or signal achievement. It therefore becomes the conventional basis of esteem. Its possession in some amount becomes necessary in order to any reputable standing in the community. It becomes indispensable to accumulate, to acquire property, in order to retain one's good name. When accumulated goods have in this way once become the accepted badge of efficiency, the possession of wealth presently assumes the character of an independent and definitive basis of esteem. The possession of goods, whether acquired aggressively by one's own exertion or passively by transmission through inheritance from others, becomes a conventional basis of reputability. The possession of wealth, which was at the outset valued simply as an evidence of efficiency, becomes, in popular apprehension, itself a meritorious act. Wealth is now itself intrinsically honourable and confers honour on its possessor. By a further refinement, wealth acquired passively by transmission from ancestors or other antecedents presently becomes even more honorific than wealth acquired by the possessor's own effort. . . .

Prowess and exploit may still remain the basis of award of the highest popular esteem, although the possession of wealth has become the basis of commonplace reputability and of a blameless social standing. The predatory instinct and the consequent approbation of predatory efficiency are deeply ingrained in the habits of thought of those peoples who have passed under the discipline of a protracted predatory culture. According to popular award, the highest honours within human reach may, even yet, be those gained by an unfolding of extraordinary predatory efficiency in war, or by a quasi-predatory efficiency in statecraft; but for the purposes of a commonplace decent standing in the community these means of repute have been replaced by the acquisition and accumulation of goods. In order to stand well in the eyes of the community, it is necessary to come up to a certain, somewhat indefinite, conventional standard of wealth; just as in the earlier predatory stage it is necessary for the barbarian man to come up to the tribe's standard of physical endurance, cunning, and skill at arms. A certain standard of wealth in the one case, and of prowess in the other, is a necessary condition of reputability, and anything in excess of this normal amount is meritorious.

Those members of the community who fall short of this, somewhat indefinite, normal degree of prowess or of property suffer in the esteem of their fellow-men; and consequently they suffer also in their own esteem, since the usual basis of self-respect is the respect accorded by one's neighbours. Only individuals with an aberrant temperament can in the long run retain their self-esteem in the face of the disesteem of their fellows. Apparent exceptions to the rule are met with, especially among people with strong religious convictions. But these apparent exceptions are scarcely real exceptions, since such persons commonly fall back on the putative approbation of some supernatural witness of their deeds.

So soon as the possession of property becomes the basis of popular esteem, therefore, it becomes also a requisite to that complacency which we call self-respect. In any community where goods are held in severalty it is necessary, in order to his own peace of mind, that an individual should possess as large a portion of goods as others with whom he is accustomed to class himself; and it is extremely gratifying to possess something more than others. But as fast as a person makes new acquisitions, and becomes accustomed to the resulting new standard of wealth, the new standard forthwith ceases to afford appreciably greater satisfaction than the earlier standard did. The tendency in any case is constantly to make the present pecuniary standard the point of departure for a fresh increase of wealth; and this in turn gives rise to a new standard of sufficiency and a new pecuniary classification of one's self as compared with one's neighbours. So far as concerns the present question, the end sought by accumulation is to rank high in comparison with the rest of the community in point of pecuniary strength. So long as the comparison is distinctly unfavourable to himself, the normal, average individual will live in chronic dissatisfaction with his present lot; and when he has reached what may be called the normal pecuniary standard of the community, or of his class in the community, this chronic dissatisfaction will give place to a restless straining to place a wider and ever-widening pecuniary interval between himself and this average standard. The invidious comparison can never become so favourable to the individual making it that he would not gladly rate himself still higher relatively to his competitors in the struggle for pecuniary reputability.

In the nature of the case, the desire for wealth can scarcely be satiated in any individual instance, and evidently a satiation of the average or general desire for wealth is out of the question. However widely, or equally, or "fairly," it may be distributed, no general increase of the community's wealth can make any approach to satiating this need, the ground of which is the desire of every one to excel every one else in the accumulation of goods. If, as is sometimes assumed, the incentive to accumulation were the want of subsistence or of physical comfort, then the aggregate economic wants of a community might conceivably be satisfied at some point in the advance of industrial efficiency; but since the struggle is substantially a race for reputability on the basis of an invidious comparison, no approach to a definitive attainment is possible.

What has just been said must not be taken to mean that there are no other incentives to acquisition and accumulation than this desire to excel in pecuniary standing and so gain the esteem and envy of one's fellow-men. The desire for added comfort and security from want is present as a motive at every stage of the process of accumulation in a modern industrial community; although the standard of sufficiency in these respects is in turn greatly affected by the habit of pecuniary emulation. To a great extent this emulation shapes the methods and selects the objects of expenditure for personal comfort and decent livelihood.

Besides this, the power conferred by wealth also affords a motive to accumulation. That propensity for purposeful activity and that repugnance to all futility of effort which belong to man by virtue of his character as an agent do not desert him when he emerges from the naïve communal culture where the dominant note of life is the unanalysed and undifferentiated solidarity of the individual with the group with which his life is bound up. When he enters upon the predatory stage, where self-seeking in the narrower sense becomes the dominant note, this propensity goes with him still, as the pervasive trait that shapes his scheme of life. The propensity for achievement and the repugnance to futility remain the underlying economic motive. The propensity changes only in the form of its expression and in the proximate objects to which it directs the man's activity. Under the regime of individual ownership the most available means of visibly achieving a purpose is that afforded by the acquisition and accumulation of goods; and as the self-regarding antithesis between man and man reaches fuller consciousness, the propensity for achievement—the instinct of workmanship—tends more and more to shape itself into a straining to excel others in pecuniary achievement. Relative success, tested by an invidious pecuniary comparison with other men, becomes the conventional end of action. The currently accepted legitimate end of effort becomes the achievement of a favourable comparison with other men; and therefore the repugnance to futility to a good extent coalesces with the incentive of emulation. It acts to accentuate the struggle for pecuniary reputability by visiting with a sharper disapproval all shortcoming and all evidence of shortcoming in point of pecuniary success. Purposeful effort comes to mean, primarily, effort directed to or resulting in a more creditable showing of accumulated wealth. Among the motives which lead men to accumulate wealth, the primacy, both in scope and intensity, therefore, continues to belong to this motive of pecuniary emulation.

In making use of the term "invidious," it may perhaps be unnecessary to remark, there is no intention to extol or depreciate, or to commend or deplore any of the phenomena which the word is used to characterise. The term is used in a technical sense as describing a comparison of persons with a view to rating and grading them in respect of relative worth or value—in an aesthetic or moral sense—and so awarding and defining the relative degrees of complacency with which they may legitimately be contemplated by themselves and by others. An invidious comparison is a process of valuation of persons in respect of worth.

CHAPTER IV: CONSPICUOUS CONSUMPTION

In . . . [discussing] the evolution of the vicarious leisure class and its differentiation from the general body of the working classes, reference . . . [may be] made to a further division of labour,—that between different servant classes. One portion of the servant class, chiefly those persons whose occupation is vicarious leisure, come to undertake a new, subsidiary range of duties—the vicarious consumption of goods. The most obvious form in which this consumption occurs is seen in the wearing of liveries and the occupation of spacious servants' quarters. Another, scarcely less obtrusive or less effective form of vicarious consumption, and a much more widely prevalent one, is the consumption of food, clothing, dwelling, and furniture by the lady and the rest of the domestic establishment.

But already at a point in economic evolution far antedating the emergence of the lady, specialised consumption of goods as an evidence of pecuniary strength had begun to work out in a more or less elaborate system. The beginning of a differentiation in consumption even antedates the appearance of anything that can fairly be called pecuniary strength. It is traceable back to the initial phase of predatory culture, and there is even a suggestion that an incipient differentiation in this respect lies back of the beginnings of the predatory life. This most primitive differentiation in the consumption of goods is like the later differentiation with which we are all so intimately familiar, in that it is largely of a ceremonial character, but unlike the latter it does not rest on a difference in accumulated wealth. The utility of consumption as an evidence of wealth is to be classed as a derivative growth. It is an adaptation to a new end, by a selective process, of a distinction previously existing and well established in men's habits of thought.

In the earlier phases of the predatory culture the only economic differentiation is a broad distinction between an honourable superior class made up of the able-bodied men on the one side, and a base inferior class of labouring women on the other. According to the ideal scheme of life in force at that time it is the office of the men to consume what the women produce. Such consumption as falls to the women is merely incidental to their work; it is a means to their continued labour, and not a consumption directed to their own comfort and fulness of life. Unproductive consumption of goods is honourable, primarily as a mark of prowess and a perquisite of human dignity;

secondarily it becomes substantially honourable in itself, especially the consumption of the more desirable things. The consumption of choice articles of food, and frequently also of rare articles of adornment, becomes tabu to the women and children; and if there is a base (servile) class of men, the tabu holds also for them. With a further advance in culture this tabu may change into simple custom of a more or less rigorous character; but whatever be the theoretical basis of the distinction which is maintained, whether it be a tabu or a larger conventionality, the features of the conventional scheme of consumption do not change easily. When the quasi-peaceable stage of industry is reached, with its fundamental institution of chattel slavery, the general principle, more or less rigorously applied is that the base, industrious class should consume only what may be necessary to their subsistence. In the nature of things, luxuries and the comforts of life belong to the leisure class. Under the tabu, certain victuals, and more particularly certain beverages, are strictly reserved for the use of the superior class.

The ceremonial differentiation of the dietary is best seen in the use of intoxicating beverages and narcotics. If these articles of consumption are costly, they are felt to be noble and honorific. Therefore the base classes, primarily the women, practise an enforced continence with respect to these stimulants, except in countries where they are obtainable at a very low cost. From archaic times down through all the length of the patriarchal régime it has been the office of the women to prepare and administer these luxuries, and it has been the perquisite of the men of gentle birth and breeding to consume them. Drunkenness and the other pathological consequences of the free use of stimulants therefore tend in their turn to become honorific, as being a mark, at the second remove, of the superior status of those who are able to afford the indulgence. Infirmities induced by over-indulgence are among some peoples freely recognised as manly attributes. It has even happened that the name for certain diseased conditions of the body arising from such an origin has passed into everyday speech as a synonym for "noble" or "gentle." It is only at a relatively early stage of culture that the symptoms of expensive vice are conventionally accepted as marks of a superior status, and so tend to become virtues and command the deference of the community; but the reputability that attaches to certain expensive vices long retains so much of its force as to appreciably lessen the disapprobation visited upon the men of the wealth or noble class for any excessive indulgence. The same invidious distinction adds force to the current disapproval of any indulgence of this kind on the part of women, minors, and inferiors. This invidious traditional distinction has not lost its force even among the more advanced peoples of today. Where the example set by the leisure class retains its imperative force in the regulation of the conventionalities, it is observable that the women still in great measure practise the same traditional continence with regard to stimulants.

This characterisation of the greater continence in the use of stimulants practised by the women of the reputable classes may seem an excessive refinement of logic at the expense of common sense. But facts within easy reach of any one who cares to know them go to say that the greater abstinence of women is in some part due to an imperative conventionality; and this conventionality is, in a general way, strongest where the patriarchal tradition—the tradition that the woman is a chattel—has retained its hold in greatest vigour. In a sense which has been greatly qualified in scope and rigour, but which has by no means lost its meaning even yet, this tradition says that the woman, being a chattel, should consume only what is necessary to her sustenance,—except so far as her further consumption contributes to the comfort or the good repute of her master. The consumption of luxuries, in the true sense, is a consumption directed to the comfort of the consumer himself, and is, therefore, a mark of the master. Any such consumption by others can take place only on a basis of sufferance. In communities where the popular habits of thought have been profoundly shaped by the patriarchal tradition we may accordingly look for survivals of the tabu on luxuries at least to the extent of a conventional deprecation of their use by the unfree and dependent class. This is more particularly true as regards certain luxuries, the use of which by the dependent class would detract sensibly from the comfort or pleasure of their masters, or which are held to be of doubtful legitimacy on other grounds. In the apprehension of the great conservative middle class of Western civilisation the use of these various stimulants is obnoxious to at least one, if not both, of these objections; and it is a fact too significant to be passed over that it is precisely among these middle classes of the Germanic culture, with their strong surviving sense of the patriarchal proprieties, that the women are to the greatest extent subject to a qualified tabu on narcotics and alcoholic beverages. With many qualifications—with more qualifications as the patriarchal tradition has gradually weakened—the general rule is felt to be right and binding that women should consume only for the benefit of their masters. The objection of course presents itself that expenditure on women's dress and household paraphernalia is an obvious exception to this rule; but it will appear in the sequel that this exception is much more obvious than substantial.

During the earlier stages of economic development, consumption of goods without stint, especially consumption of the better grades of goods,—ideally all consumption in excess of the subsistence minimum,—pertains normally to the leisure class. This restriction tends to disappear, at least formally, after the later peaceable stage has been reached, with private ownership of goods and an industrial system based on wage labour or on the petty household economy. But during the earlier quasi-peaceable stage, when so many of the traditions through which the institution of a leisure class has affected the economic life of later times were taking form and consistency, this principle has had the force of a conventional law. It has served as the norm to which consumption has tended to conform, and any appreciable departure from it is to be regarded as an aberrant form, sure to be eliminated sooner or later in the further course of development.

The quasi-peaceable gentleman of leisure, then, not only consumes of the staff of life beyond the minimum required for subsistence and physical efficiency, but his consumption also undergoes a specialisation as regards the quality of the goods consumed. He consumes freely and of the best, in food, drink, narcotics, shelter, services, ornaments, apparel, weapons and accoutrements, amusements, amulets, and idols or divinities. In the process of gradual amelioration which takes place in the articles of his consumption, the motive principle and the proximate aim of innovation is no doubt the higher efficiency of the improved and more elaborate products for personal comfort and well-being. But that does not remain the sole purpose of their consumption. The canon of reputability is at hand and seizes upon such innovations as are, according to its standard, fit to survive. Since the consumption of these more excellent goods is an evidence of wealth, it becomes honorific; and conversely, the failure to consume in due quantity and quality becomes a mark of inferiority and demerit.

This growth of punctilious discrimination as to qualitative excellence in eating, drinking, etc., presently affects not only the manner of life, but also the training and intellectual activity of the gentleman of leisure. He is no longer simply the successful, aggressive male,—the man of strength, resource, and intrepidity. In order to avoid stultification he must also cultivate his tastes, for it now becomes incumbent on him to discriminate with some nicety between the noble and the ignoble in consumable goods. He becomes a connoisseur in creditable viands of various degrees of merit, in manly beverages and trinkets, in seemly apparel and architecture, in weapons, games, dancers, and the narcotics. This cultivation of the aesthetic faculty requires time and application, and the demands made upon the gentleman in this direction therefore tend to change his life of leisure into a more or less arduous application to the business of learning how to live a life of ostensible leisure in a becoming way. Closely related to the requirement that the gentleman must consume freely and of the right kind of goods, there is the requirement that he must know how to consume them in a seemly manner. His life of leisure must be conducted in due form. Hence arise good manners. . . . High-bred manners and ways of living are items of conformity to the norm of conspicuous leisure and conspicuous consumption.

Conspicuous consumption of valuable goods is a means of reputability to the gentleman of leisure. As wealth accumulates on his hands, his own unaided effort will not avail to sufficiently put his opulence in evidence by this method. The aid of friends and competitors is therefore brought in by resorting to the giving of valuable presents and expensive feasts and entertainments. Presents and feasts had probably another origin than that of naïve ostentation, but they acquired their utility for this purpose very early, and they have retained that character to the present; so that their utility in this respect has now long been the substantial ground on which these usages rest. Costly entertainments, such as the potlatch or the ball, are peculiarly adapted to serve this end. The competitor with whom the entertainer wishes to institute a comparison is, by this method, made to serve as a means to the end. He consumes vicariously for his host at the same time that he is a witness to the consumption of that excess of good things which his host is unable to dispose of single-handed, and he is also made to witness his host's facility in etiquette.

In the giving of costly entertainments other motives, of a more genial kind, are of course also present. The custom of festive gatherings probably originated in motives of conviviality and religion; these motives are also present in the later development, but they do not continue to be the sole motives. The latter-day leisure-class festivities and entertainments may continue in some slight degree to serve the religious need and in a higher degree the needs of recreation and conviviality, but they also serve an invidious purpose; and they serve it none the less effectually for having a colourable non-invidious ground in these more avowable motives. But the economic effect of these social amenities is not therefore lessened, either in the vicarious consumption of goods or in the exhibition of difficult and costly achievements in etiquette.

As wealth accumulates, the leisure class develops further in function and structure, and there arises a differentiation within the class. There is a more or less elaborate system of rank and grades. This differentiation is furthered by the inheritance of wealth and the consequent inheritance of gentility. With the inheritance of gentility goes the inheritance of obligatory leisure; and gentility of a sufficient potency to entail a life of leisure may be inherited without the complement of wealth required to maintain a dignified leisure. Gentle blood may be transmitted without goods enough to afford a reputably free consumption at one's ease. Hence results a class of impecunious gentlemen of leisure. . . . These half-caste gentlemen of leisure fall into a system of hierarchical gradations. Those who stand near the higher and the highest grades of the wealthy leisure class, in point of birth, or in point of wealth, or both, outrank the remoter-born and the pecuniarily weaker. These lower grades, especially the impecunious, or marginal, gentlemen of leisure, affiliate themselves by a system of dependence or fealty to the great ones; by so doing they gain an increment of repute, or of the means with which to lead a life of leisure, from their patron. They become his courtiers or retainers, servants; and being fed and countenanced by their patron they are indices of his rank and vicarious consumers of his superfluous wealth. Many of these affiliated gentlemen of leisure are at the same time lesser men of substance in their own right; so that some of them are scarcely at all, others only partially, to be rated as vicarious consumers. So many of them, however, as make up the retainers and hangers-on of the patron may be classed as vicarious consumers without qualification. Many of these again, and also many of the other aristocracy of less degree, have in turn attached to their persons a more or less comprehensive group of vicarious consumers in the persons of wives and children, their servants, retainers, etc.

Throughout this graduated scheme of vicarious leisure and vicarious consumption the rule holds that these offices must be performed in some such manner, or under some such circumstance or insignia, as shall point plainly to the master to whom this leisure or consumption pertains, and to whom therefore the resulting increment of good repute of right inures. The consumption and leisure executed by these persons for their master or patron represents an investment on his part with a view to an increase of good fame. As regards feasts and largesses this is obvious enough, and the imputation of repute to the host or patron here takes place immediately, on the ground of common notoriety. Where leisure and consumption is performed vicariously by henchmen and retainers, imputation of the resulting repute to the patron is effected by their residing near his person so that it may be plain to all men from what source they draw. As the group whose good esteem is to be secured in this way grows larger, more patent means are required to indicate the imputation of merit for the leisure performed, and to this end uniforms, badges, and liveries come into vogue. The wearing of uniforms or liveries implies a considerable degree of dependence, and may even be said to be a mark of servitude, real or ostensible. The wearers of uniforms and liveries may be roughly divided into two classes—the free and the servile, or the noble and the ignoble. The services performed by them are likewise divisible into noble and ignoble. Of course, the distinction is not observed with strict consistency in practice; the less debasing of the base services and the less honorific of the noble functions are not infrequently merged in the same person. But the general distinction is not on that account to be overlooked. What may add some perplexity is the fact that this fundamental distinction between noble and ignoble, which rests on the nature of the ostensible service performed, is traversed by a secondary distinction into honorific and humiliating, resting on the rank of the person for whom the service is performed or whose livery is worn. So, those offices which are by right the proper employment of the leisure class are noble; such are government, fighting, hunting, the care of arms and accoutrements, and the like,—in short, those which may be classed as ostensibly predatory employments. On the other hand, those employments which properly fall to the industrious class are ignoble; such as handicraft or other productive labour, menial services, and the like. But a base service performed for a person of a very high degree may become a very honorific office; as for instance the office of a Maid of Honour or of a Lady in Waiting to the Queen, or the King's Master of the Horse or his Keeper of the Hounds. The two offices last named suggest a principle of some general bearing. Whenever, as in these cases, the menial service in question has to do directly with the primary leisure employments of fighting and hunting, it easily acquired a reflected honorific character. In this way great honour may come to attach to an employment which in its own nature belongs to the baser sort.

In the later development of peaceable industry, the usage of employing an idle corps of uniformed men-at-arms gradually lapses. Vicarious consumption by dependents bearing the insignia of their patron or master narrows down to a corps of liveried menials. In a heightened degree, therefore, the livery comes to be a badge of servitude, or rather of servility. Something of a honorific character always attached to the livery of the armed retainer, but this honorific character disappears when the livery becomes the exclusive badge of the menial. The livery becomes obnoxious to nearly all who are required to wear it. We are yet so little removed from a state of effective slavery as still to be fully sensitive to the sting of any imputation of servility. This antipathy asserts itself even in the case of the liveries or uniforms which some corporations prescribe as the distinctive dress of their employees. In this country the aversion even goes the length of discrediting—in a mild and uncertain way—those government employments, military and civil, which require the wearing of a livery or uniform.

With the disappearance of servitude, the number of vicarious consumers attached to any one gentleman tends, on the whole, to decrease. The like is of course true, and perhaps in a still higher degree, of the number of dependents who perform vicarious leisure for him. In a general way, though not wholly nor consistently, these two groups coincide. The dependent who was first delegated for these duties was the wife, or the chief wife; and, as would be expected, in the later development of the institution, when the number of persons by whom these duties are customarily performed gradually narrows, the wife remains the last. In the higher grades of society a large volume of both these kinds of service is required; and here the wife is of course still assisted in the work by a more or less numerous corps of menials. But as we descend the social scale, the point is presently reached where the duties of vicarious leisure and consumption devolve upon the wife alone. In the communities of the Western culture, this point is at present found among the lower middle class.

And here occurs a curious inversion. It is a fact of common observation that in this lower middle class there is no pretence of leisure on the part of the head of the household. Through force of circumstances it has fallen into disuse. But the middle-class wife still carries on the business of vicarious leisure, for the good name of the household and its master. In descending the social scale in any modern industrial community, the primary fact—the conspicuous leisure of the master of the household—disappears at a relatively high point. The head of the middle-class household has been reduced by economic circumstances to turn his hand to gaining a livelihood by occupations which often partake largely of the character of industry, as in the case of the ordinary business man of to-day. But the derivative fact—the vicarious leisure and consumption rendered by the wife, and the auxiliary vicarious performance of leisure by menials—remains in vogue as a conventionality which the demands of reputability will not suffer to be slighted. It is by no means an uncommon spectacle to find a man applying himself to work with the utmost assiduity, in order that his wife may in due form render for him that degree of vicarious leisure which the common sense of the time demands.

The leisure rendered by the wife in such cases is, of course, not a simple manifestation of idleness or indolence. It almost invariably occurs disguised under some form of work or household duties or social amenities, which prove on analysis to serve little or no ulterior end beyond showing that she does not and need not occupy herself with anything that is gainful or that is of substantial use. . . . [The] greater part of the customary round of domestic cares to which the middle-class housewife gives her time and effort is of this character. Not that the result of her attention to household matters, of a decorative and mundificatory character, are not pleasing to the sense of men trained in middle-class proprieties; but the taste to which these effects of household adornment and tidiness appeal is a taste which has been formed under the selective guidance of a canon of propriety that demands just these evidences of wasted effort. The effects are pleasing to us chiefly because we have been taught to find them pleasing. There goes into these domestic duties much solicitude for the proper combination of form and colour, and for other ends that are to be classed as aesthetic in the proper sense of the term; and it is not denied that effects having some substantial aesthetic value are sometimes attained. Pretty much all that is here insisted on is that, as regards these amenities of life, the housewife's efforts are under the guidance of traditions that have been shaped by the law of conspicuously wasteful expenditure of time and substance. If beauty or comfort is achieved,—and it is a more or less fortuitous circumstance if they are,—they must be achieved by means and methods that commend themselves to the great economic law of wasted effort. The more reputable, "presentable" portion of middle-class household paraphernalia are, on the one hand, items of conspicuous consumption, and on the other hand, apparatus for putting in evidence the vicarious leisure rendered by the housewife.

The requirement of vicarious consumption at the hands of the wife continues in force even at a lower point in the pecuniary scale than the requirement of vicarious leisure. At a point below which little if any pretence of wasted effort, in ceremonial cleanness and the like, is observable, and where there is assuredly no conscious attempt at ostensible leisure, decency still requires the wife to consume some goods conspicuously for the reputability of the household and its head. So that, as the latter-day outcome of this evolution of an archaic institution, the wife, who was at the outset the drudge and chattel of the man, both in fact and in theory,—the producer of goods for him to consume,—has become the ceremonial consumer of goods which he produces. But she still quite unmistakably remains his chattel in theory; for the habitual rendering of vicarious leisure and consumption is the abiding mark of the unfree servant.

This vicarious consumption practised by the household of the middle and lower classes can not be counted as a direct expression of the leisure-class scheme of life, since the household of this pecuniary grade does not belong within the leisure class. It is rather that the leisure-class scheme of life here comes to an expression at the second remove. The leisure class stands at the head of the social structure in point of reputability; and its manner of life and its standards of worth therefore afford the norm of reputability for the community. The observance of these standards, in some degree of approximation, becomes incumbent upon all classes lower in the scale. In modern civilized communities the lines of demarcation between social classes have grown vague and transient, and wherever this happens the norm of reputability imposed by the upper class extends its coercive influence with but slight hindrance down through the social structure to the lowest strata. The result is that the members of each stratum accept as their ideal of decency the scheme of life in vogue in the next higher stratum, and bend their energies to live up to that ideal. On pain of forfeiting their good name and their self-respect in case of failure, they must conform to the accepted code, at least in appearance.

The basis on which good repute in any highly organised industrial community ultimately rests is pecuniary strength; and the means of showing pecuniary strength, and so of gaining or retaining a good name, are leisure and a conspicuous consumption of goods. Accordingly, both of these methods are in vogue as far down the scale as it remains possible; and in the lower strata in which the two methods are employed, both offices are in great part delegated to the wife and children of the household. Lower still, where any degree of leisure, even ostensible, has become impracticable for the wife, the conspicuous consumption of goods remains and is carried on by the wife and children. The man of the household also can do something in this direction, and, indeed, he commonly does; but with a still lower descent into the levels of indigence—along the margin of the slums—the man, and presently also the children, virtually cease to consume valuable goods for appearances, and the woman remains virtually the sole exponent of the household's pecuniary decency. No class of society, not even the most abjectly poor, foregoes all customary conspicuous consumption. The last items of this category of consumption are not given up except under stress of the direst necessity. Very much of squalor and discomfort will be endured before the last trinket or the last pretence of pecuniary decency is put away. There is no class and no country that has yielded so abjectly before the pressure of physical want as to deny themselves all gratification of this higher or spiritual need.

From the foregoing survey of the growth of conspicuous leisure and consumption, it appears that the utility of both alike for the purpose of reputability lies in the element of waste that is common to both. In the one case it is a waste of time and effort, in the other it is a waste of goods. Both are methods of demonstrating the possession of wealth, and the two are conventionally accepted as equivalents. The choice between them is a question of advertising expediency simply, except so far as it may be affected by other standards of propriety, springing from a different source. On grounds of expediency the preference may be given to the one or the other at different stages of the economic development. The question is, which of the two methods will most effectively reach the persons whose convictions it is desired to affect. Usage has answered this question in different ways under different circumstances.

So long as the community or social group is small enough and compact enough to be effectually reached by common notoriety alone,—that is to say, so long as the human environment to which the individual is required to adapt himself in respect of reputability is comprised within his sphere of personal acquaintance and neighbourhood gossip,—so long the one method is about as effective as the other. Each will therefore serve about equally well during the earlier stages of social growth. But when the differentiation has gone farther and it becomes necessary to reach a wider human environment, consumption begins to hold over leisure as an ordinary means of decency. This is especially true during the later, peaceable economic stage. The means of communication and the mobility of the population now expose the individual to the observation of many persons who have no other means of judging of his reputability than the display of goods (and perhaps of breeding) which he is able to make while he is under their direct observation.

The modern organisation of industry works in the same direction also by another line. The exigencies of the modern industrial system frequently place individuals and households in juxtaposition between whom there is little contact in any other sense than that of juxtaposition. One's neighbours, mechanically speaking, often are socially not one's neighbours, or even acquaintances; and still their transient good opinion has a high degree of utility. The only practicable means of impressing one's pecuniary ability on these unsympathetic observers of one's everyday life is an unremitting demonstration of ability to pay. In the modern community there is also a more frequent attendance at large gatherings of people to whom one's everyday life is unknown; in such places as churches, theatres, ballrooms, hotels, parks, shops, and the like. In order to impress these transient observers, and to retain one's self-complacency under their observation, the signature of one's pecuniary strength should be written in characters which he who runs may read. It is evident, therefore, that the present trend of the development is in the direction of heightening the utility of conspicuous consumption as compared with leisure.

It is also noticeable that the serviceability of consumption as a means of repute, as well as the insistence on it as an element of decency, is at its best in those portions of the community where the human contact of the individual is widest and the mobility of the population is greatest. Conspicuous consumption claims a relatively larger portion of the income of the urban than of the rural population, and the claim is also more imperative. The result is that in order to keep up a decent appearance, the former habitually live hand-to-mouth to a greater extent than the latter. So it comes, for instance, that the American farmer and his wife and daughters are notoriously less modish in their dress, as well as less urbane in their manners, than the city artisan's family with an equal income. It is not that the city population is by nature much more eager for the peculiar complacency that comes of a conspicuous consumption, nor has the rural population less regard for pecuniary decency. But the provocation to this line of evidence, as well as its transient effectiveness, are more decided in the city. This method is therefore more readily resorted to, and in the struggle to outdo one another the city population push their normal standard of conspicuous consumption to a higher point, with the result that a relatively greater expenditure in this direction is required to indicate a given degree of pecuniary decency in the city. The requirement of conformity to this higher conventional standard becomes mandatory. The standard of decency is higher, class for class, and this requirement of decent appearance must be lived up to on pain of losing caste.

Consumption becomes a larger element in the standard of living in the city than in the country. Among the country population its place is to some extent taken by savings and home comforts known through the medium of neighbourhood gossip sufficiently to serve the like general purpose of pecuniary repute. These home comforts and the leisure indulged in—where the indulgence is found—are of course also in great part to be classed as items of conspicuous consumption; and much the same is to be said of the savings. The smaller amount of the savings laid by by the artisan class is no doubt due, in some measure, to the fact that in the case of the artisan the savings are a less effective means of advertisement, relative to the environment in which he is placed, than are the savings of the people living on farms and in the small villages. Among the latter, everybody's affairs, especially everybody's pecuniary status, are known to everybody else. Considered by itself simply—taken in the first degree—this added provocation to which the artisan and the urban labouring classes are exposed may not very seriously decrease the amount of savings; but in its cumulative action, through raising the standard of decent expenditure, its deterrent effect on the tendency to save cannot but be very great.

A felicitous illustration of the manner in which this canon of reputability works out its results is seen in the practice of dram-drinking, "treating," and smoking in public places, which is customary among the labourers and handicraftsmen of the towns, and among the lower middle class of the urban population generally. Journeymen printers may be named as a class among whom this form of conspicuous consumption has a great vogue, and among whom it carries with it certain well-marked consequences that are often deprecated. The peculiar habits of the class in this respect are commonly set down to some kind of an ill-defined moral deficiency with which this class is credited, or to a morally deleterious influence which their occupation is supposed to exert, in some unascertainable way, upon the men employed in it. The state of the case for the men who work in the composition and press rooms of the common run of printing-houses may be summed up as follows. Skill acquired in any printing-house or any city is easily turned to account in almost any other house or city; that is to say, the inertia due to special training is slight. Also, this occupation requires more than the average of intelligence and general information, and the men employed in it are therefore ordinarily more ready than many others to take advantage of any slight variation in the demand for their labour from one place to another. The inertia due to the home feeling is consequently also slight. At the same time the wages in the trade are high enough to make movement from place to place relatively easy. The result is a great mobility of the labour employed in printing; perhaps greater than in any other equally well-defined and considerable body of workmen. These men are constantly thrown in contact with new groups of acquaintances, with whom the relations established are transient or ephemeral, but whose good opinion is valued none the less for the time being. The human proclivity to ostentation, reenforced by sentiments of goodfellowship, leads them to spend freely in those directions which will best serve these needs. Here as elsewhere prescription seizes upon the custom as soon as it gains a vogue, and incorporates it in the accredited standard of decency. The next step is to make this standard of decency the point of departure for a new move in advance in the same direction,—for there is no merit in simple spiritless conformity to a standard of dissipation that is lived up to as a matter of course by every one in the trade.

The greater prevalence of dissipation among printers than among the average of workmen is accordingly attributable, at least in some measure, to the greater ease of movement and the more transient character of acquaintance and human contact in this trade. But the substantial ground of this high requirement in dissipation is in the last analysis no other than that same propensity for a manifestation of dominance and pecuniary decency which makes the French peasant-proprietor parsimonious and frugal, and induces the American millionaire to found colleges, hospitals and museums. If the canon of conspicuous consumption were not offset to a considerable extent by other features of human nature, alien to it, any saving should logically be impossible for a population situated as the artisan and labouring classes of the cities are at present, however high their wages or their income might be.

But there are other standards of repute and other, more or less imperative canons of conduct, besides wealth and its manifestation, and some of these come in to accentuate or to qualify the broad, fundamental canon of conspicuous waste. Under the simple test of effectiveness for advertising, we should expect to find leisure and the conspicuous consumption of goods dividing the field of pecuniary emulation pretty evenly between them at the outset. Leisure might then be expected gradually to yield ground and tend to obsolescence as the economic development goes forward, and the community increases in size; while the conspicuous consumption of goods should gradually gain in importance, both absolutely and relatively, until it had absorbed all the available product, leaving nothing over beyond a bare livelihood. But the actual course of development has been somewhat different from this ideal scheme. Leisure held the first place at the start, and came to hold a rank very much above wasteful consumption of goods, both as a direct exponent of wealth and as an element in the standard of decency, during the quasi-peaceable culture. From that point onward, consumption has gained ground, until, at present, it unquestionably holds the primacy, though it is still far from absorbing the entire margin of production above the subsistence minimum.

The early ascendency of leisure as a means of reputability is traceable to the archaic distinction between noble and ignoble employments. Leisure is honourable and becomes imperative partly because it shows exemption from ignoble labour. The archaic differentiation into noble and ignoble classes is based on an invidious distinction between employments as honorific or debasing, and this traditional distinction grows into an imperative canon of decency during the early quasi-peaceable stage. Its ascendency is furthered by the fact that leisure is still fully as effective an evidence of wealth as consumption. Indeed, so effective is it in the relatively small and stable human environment to which the individual is exposed at that cultural stage, that, with the aid of the archaic tradition which deprecates all productive labour, it gives rise to a large impecunious leisure class, and it even tends to limit the production of the community's industry to the subsistence minimum.

This extreme inhibition of industry is avoided because slave labour, working under a compulsion more rigorous than that of reputability, is forced to turn out a product in excess of the subsistence minimum of the working class. The subsequent relative decline in the use of conspicuous leisure as a basis of repute is due partly to an increasing relative effectiveness of consumption as an evidence of wealth; but in part it is traceable to another force, alien, and in some degree antagonistic, to the usage of conspicuous waste.

This alien factor is the instinct of workmanship. Other circumstances permitting, that instinct disposes men to look with favour upon productive efficiency and on whatever is of human use. It disposes them to deprecate waste of substance or effort. The instinct of workmanship is present in all men, and asserts itself even under very adverse circumstances. So that however wasteful a given expenditure may be in reality, it must at least have some colourable excuse in the way of an ostensible purpose. . . . The instinct [often] eventuates in a taste for exploit and an invidious discrimination between noble and ignoble classes. . . . In so far as it comes into conflict with the law of conspicuous waste, the instinct of workmanship expresses itself not so much in insistence on substantial usefulness as in an abiding sense of the odiousness and aesthetic impossibility of what is obviously futile. Being of the nature of an instinctive affection, its guidance touches chiefly and immediately the obvious and apparent violations of its requirements. It is only less promptly and with less constraining force that it reaches such substantial violations of its requirements as are appreciated only upon reflection.

So long as all labour continues to be performed exclusively or usually by slaves, the baseness of all productive effort is too constantly and deterrently present in the mind of men to allow the instinct of workmanship seriously to take effect in the direction of industrial usefulness; but when the quasi-peaceable stage (with slavery and status) passes into the peaceable stage of industry (with wage labour and cash payment) the instinct comes more effectively into play. It then begins aggressively to shape men's views of what is meritorious, and asserts itself at least as an auxiliary canon of self-complacency. All extraneous considerations apart, those persons (adults) are but a vanishing minority today who harbour no inclination to the accomplishment of some end, or who are not impelled of their own motion to shape some object or fact or relation for human use. The propensity may in large measure be overborne by the more immediately constraining incentive to a reputable leisure and an avoidance of indecorous usefulness, and it may therefore work itself out in make-believe only; as for instance in "social duties," and in quasi-artistic or quasi-scholarly accomplishments, in the care and decoration of the house, in sewing-circle activity or dress reform, in proficiency at dress, cards, yachting, golf, and various sports. But the fact that it may under stress of circumstances eventuate in inanities no more disproves the presence of the instinct than the reality of the brooding instinct is disproved by inducing a hen to sit on a nestful of china eggs.

This latter-day uneasy reaching-out for some form of purposeful activity that shall at the same time not be indecorously productive of either individual or collective gain marks a difference of attitude between the modern leisure class and that of the quasi-peaceable stage. At the earlier stage, as was said above, the all-dominating institution of slavery and status acted resistlessly to discountenance exertion directed to other than naïvely predatory ends. It was still possible to find some habitual employment for the inclination to action in the way of forcible aggression or repression directed against hostile groups or against the subject classes within the group; and this served to relieve the pressure and draw off the energy of the leisure class without a resort to actually useful, or even ostensibly useful employments. The practice of hunting also served the same purpose in some degree. When the community developed into a peaceful industrial organisation, and when fuller occupation of the land had reduced the opportunities for the hunt to an inconsiderable residue, the pressure of energy seeking purposeful employment was left to find an outlet in some other direction. The ignominy which attaches to useful effort also entered upon a less acute phase with the disappearance of compulsory labour; and the instinct of workmanship then came to assert itself with more persistence and consistency.

The line of least resistance has changed in some measure, and the energy which formerly found a vent in predatory activity, now in part takes the direction of some ostensibly useful end. Ostensibly purposeless leisure has come to be deprecated, especially among that large portion of the leisure class whose plebeian origin acts to set them at variance with the tradition of the *otium cum dignitate*.[1] But that canon of reputability which discountenances all employment that is of the nature of productive effort is still at hand, and will permit nothing beyond the most transient vogue to any employment that is substantially useful or productive. The consequence is that a change has been wrought in the conspicuous leisure practised by the leisure class; not so much in substance as in form. A reconciliation between the two conflicting requirements is effected by a resort to make-believe. Many and intricate polite observances and social duties of a ceremonial nature are

[1] [*Dignified idleness.*]

developed; many organisations are founded, with some specious object of amelioration embodied in their official style and title; there is much coming and going, and a deal of talk; to the end that the talkers may not have occasion to reflect on what is the effectual economic value of their traffic. And along with the make-believe of purposeful employment, and woven inextricably into its texture, there is commonly, if not invariably, a more or less appreciable element of purposeful effort directed to some serious end.

In the narrower sphere of vicarious leisure a similar change has gone forward. Instead of simply passing her time in visible idleness, as in the best days of the patriarchal régime, the housewife of the advanced peaceable stage applies herself assiduously to household cares. The salient features of this development of domestic service have already been indicated.

Throughout the entire evolution of conspicuous expenditure, whether of goods or of services or human life, runs the obvious implication that in order to effectually mend the consumer's good fame, it must be an expenditure of superfluities. In order to be reputable it must be wasteful. No merit would accrue from the consumption of the bare necessaries of life, except by comparison with the abjectly poor who fall short even of the subsistence minimum; and no standard of expenditure could result from such a comparison, except the most prosaic and unattractive level of decency. A standard of life would still be possible which should admit of invidious comparison in other respects than that of opulence; as, for instance, a comparison in various directions in the manifestation of moral, physical, intellectual, or aesthetic force. Comparison in all these directions is in vogue to-day; and the comparison made in these respects is commonly so inextricably bound up with the pecuniary comparison as to be scarcely distinguishable from the latter. This is especially true as regards the current rating of expressions of intellectual and aesthetic force or proficiency; so that we frequently interpret as aesthetic or intellectual a difference which in substance is pecuniary only.

The use of the term "waste" is in one respect an unfortunate one. As used in the speech of everyday life the word carries an undertone of deprecation. It is here used for want of a better term that will adequately describe the same range of motives and of phenomena, and it is not to be taken in an odious sense, as implying an illegitimate expenditure of human products or of human life. In the view of economic theory the expenditure in question is no more and no less legitimate than any other expenditure. It is here called "waste" because this expenditure does not serve human life or human well-being on the whole, not because it is waste or misdirection of effort or expenditure as viewed from the standpoint of the individual consumer who chooses it. If he chooses it, that disposes of the question of its relative utility to him, as compared with other forms of consumption that would not be deprecated on account of their wastefulness. Whatever form of expenditure the consumer chooses, or whatever end he seeks in making his choice, has utility to him by virtue of his preference. As seen from the point of view of the individual consumer, the question of wastefulness does not arise within the scope of economic theory proper. The use of the word "waste" as a technical term, therefore, implies no deprecation of the motives or of the ends sought by the consumer under this canon of conspicuous waste.

But it is, on other grounds, worth noting that the term "waste" in the language of everyday life implies deprecation of what is characterised as wasteful. This common-sense implication is itself an outcropping of the instinct of workmanship. The popular reprobation of waste goes to say that in order to be at peace with himself the common man must be able to see in any and all human effort and human enjoyment an enhancement of life and well-being on the whole. In order to meet with unqualified approval, any economic fact must approve itself under the test of impersonal usefulness—usefulness as seen from the point of view of the generically human. Relative or competitive advantage of one individual in comparison with another does not satisfy the economic conscience, and therefore competitive expenditure has not the approval of this conscience.

In strict accuracy nothing should be included under the head of conspicuous waste but such expenditure as is incurred on the ground of an invidious pecuniary comparison. But in order to bring any given item or element in under this head it is not necessary that it should be recognised as waste in this sense by the person incurring the expenditure. It frequently happens that an element of the standard of living which set out with being primarily wasteful, ends with becoming, in the apprehension of the consumer, a necessary of life; and it may in this way become as indispensable as any other item of the consumer's habitual expenditure. As items which sometimes fall under this head, and are therefore available as illustrations of the manner in which this principle applies, may be cited carpets and tapestries, silver table service, waiter's services, silk hats, starched linen, many articles of jewellery and of dress. The indispensability of these things after the habit and the convention have been formed, however, has little to say in the classification of expenditures as waste or not waste in the technical meaning of the word. The test to which all expenditure must be brought in an attempt to decide that point is the question whether it serves directly to enhance human life on the whole—whether it furthers the life process taken impersonally. For this is the basis of award of the instinct of workmanship, and that instinct is the court of final appeal in any question of economic truth or adequacy. It is a question as to the award rendered by a dispassionate common sense. The question is, therefore, not whether, under the existing circumstances of individual habit and social custom, a given expenditure conduces to the particular consumer's gratification or peace of mind; but whether, aside from acquired tastes and from the canons of usage and conventional decency, its result is a net gain in comfort or in the fulness of life. Customary expenditure must be classed under the head of waste in so far as the custom on which it rests is traceable to the habit of making an invidious pecuniary comparison—in so far as it is conceived that it could not have become customary and prescriptive without the backing of this principle of pecuniary reputability or relative economic success.

It is obviously not necessary that a given object of expenditure should be exclusively wasteful in order to come in under the category of conspicuous waste. An article may be useful and wasteful both, and its utility to the consumer may be made up of use and waste in the most varying proportions. Consumable goods, and even productive goods, generally show the two elements in combination, as constituents of their utility; although, in a general way, the element of waste tends to predominate in articles of consumption, while the contrary is true of articles designed for productive use. Even in articles which appear at first glance to serve for pure ostentation only, it is always possible to detect the presence of some, at least ostensible, useful purpose; and on the other hand, even in special machinery and tools contrived for some particular industrial process, as well as in the rudest appliances of human industry, the traces of conspicuous waste, or at least of the habit of ostentation, usually become evident on a close scrutiny. It would be hazardous to assert that a useful purpose is ever absent from the utility of any article or of any service, however obviously its prime purpose and chief element is conspicuous waste; and it would be only less hazardous to assert of any primarily useful product that the element of waste is in no way concerned in its value, immediately or remotely.

THE ANATOMY OF SOCIETY: ECONOMY

3. THE CATEGORIES OF ECONOMIC UNDERSTANDING

JOHN K. GALBRAITH

AMERICAN CAPITALISM: The Concept of Countervailing Power (1954) by John Kenneth Galbraith (b. 1908), professor of economics at Harvard and specialist in agricultural economics and government economic controls, has been one of the most provocative of recent attempts to offer a new rationale of capitalism's role in contributing to economic progress and social welfare. The Galbraith study focuses on the issue of monopoly versus competition and deals only subordinately with such problems as instability and unequal distribution of income. Yet its central constructive thesis, which is highly sympathetic to capitalism, carries implications that tend to affirm the ability of American capitalism to sustain high levels of employment under equitable conditions of income distribution.

The major argument of the book contains two basic propositions. The first is that a pervasive sense of insecurity characterizes the attitudes of Americans toward their economic system and the expectations they hold with respect to their future under it, and that this sense of insecurity stems from a misconception of its workings. The second proposition is that a new conception of the working of the economic system can be offered that not only is more accurate but also justifies optimism about future performance. Another way to put this is that the first part of Galbraith's book is devoted to a diagnosis of American attitudes toward the national economy, while the second part offers an original diagnosis of the economy itself.

The following selection, taken from *American Capitalism,* contains the core of Galbraith's development of the first proposition. It is characterized by a high degree of selectivity and simplification and should consequently be understood as a ground-clearing operation designed to facilitate the later study of an admittedly skeletal, analytical hypothesis about American capitalism.

Before reading Galbraith's version of the grip that "the competitive model" has held over men's minds and emotions, it is well to recall the general nineteenth-century background of industrial development and positive state action for social purposes. The historical fact is that nineteenth-century Britain, original homeland of the "laissez-faire" economy, actually saw a remarkable amount of state intervention. Professor J. Bartlet Brebner has noted that, "as the state took its fingers off commerce during the first half of the nineteenth century, it simultaneously put them on industry and its accompaniments." Moreover the nineteenth- and early twentieth-century American economy was marked by a considerable amount of state intervention: tariff protection, government sponsorship of canals, turnpikes, and railroads, state regulation of railroads and other public utilities, and regulation of banking practices. Indeed, although the ideal of a competitive economy was certainly reflected in the passage of the Sherman Antitrust Act of 1890, the passage only three years earlier of the Interstate Commerce Act suggested the conviction that, in some economic areas at least, competition could not be expected at all, and that governmental regulation was necessary to advance the general welfare.

Although the foregoing considerations suggest that the influence of "the competitive model" may have been less pervasive than Galbraith believes it to have been, they are not the only questions one might profitably bring to bear in the study of Galbraith's first proposition. His development of that proposition exposes a puzzle too important to neglect. Why, if Galbraith's diagnosis is correct, do many businessmen and others respect the competitive model today despite persuasive arguments that its premises do not fit the facts of contemporary economic life? Or despite the fact that a predominantly private-market economy has not assured continuous full employment? Or despite the fact that preceding generations of Americans did not subscribe to the competitive ideal in anything like the degree represented by Galbraith?

A clue to the answer to these queries may be found in the fact that the competitive model, as Galbraith propounds it, is a strictly twentieth-century model. It was not until the 1930's that economists worked out the abstract model of which he writes. They worked it out, moreover, in order to clarify the terms of a description of economic activity that would take account not only of the market consequences of competition (these had been traced out, although not with the thoroughness later shown to be possible, decades earlier), but also of the consequences of markets featured by large-sized economic units, concentrations of economic power, and tendencies toward extreme economic fluctuation. Before the 1930's no very heavy interpretative burden was put upon "the competitive model." During and after the thirties the competitive model has been used by economists as a standard of comparison fully as much as it has been employed as a policy goal. And if "the competitive model" has been considered by businessmen to be a descriptive phrase and the expression of an ideal, it has also provided the material for a slogan that might rally opposition to many forms of governmental economic intervention, even if not, as Galbraith notes, to the antitrust laws.

Yet even if one attributes more importance than does Galbraith to the utility of the competitive model as an analytical tool and as a symbol of opposition to state interventionism—indeed, even if one believed that freer competition in international trade and investment is still a desirable policy objective—he must return to Galbraith's argument more than once if his own understanding of current attitudes toward capitalism is to advance as far as it may.

AMERICAN CAPITALISM: THE CONCEPT OF COUNTERVAILING POWER [I]

CHAPTER II: THE FOUNDATIONS OF FAITH

II

[In America, liberals and conservatives alike share a common heritage of economic ideas.] . . . These derive from a theory of capitalism which has deeply shaped the attitudes of both. This is the system of classical economics which was constructed in the latter part of the eighteenth and during the nineteenth century, primarily in England. Those who would make its acceptance a test of sound Americanism should know that, to a singular degree, it is an alien doctrine. Its principal early architects were Englishmen and Scots. American economists, although they added some important amendments and reproduced it in countless textbooks, contributed comparatively little to the structure itself. Until fairly recent times Americans have not shown high originality in economic theory, and the habit of looking abroad for authority is still strong. It was the classical system, as imported from nineteenth-century England, that became the explicit and remains the implicit interpretation of American capitalism. . . .

. . . Given this system, or more accurately, an economy constructed to its specifications where there is stout observance of its rules of behavior, all . . . [worries about the insecurity and instability of capitalism dissolve]. It described an economic system of high social efficiency—that is to say one in which all incentives encouraged the employment of men, capital and natural resources in producing most efficiently what people most wanted. There could be no misuse of private power because no one had power to misuse. An innocuous role was assigned to government because there was little that was useful that a government could do. There was no place in the theory for depression or inflation. The system worked. This was the promise, but it was a promise made only to a society with the proper economic institutions and the proper respect for the rules of behavior which the classical system required. In the contemporary United States few of the preconditions for the system can seriously be supposed to exist. Nor do we pretend to live by its rules. Accordingly, it can only be assumed that we stand constantly in danger of reaping the terrible reward of our neglect and our disobedience.

This selection has been reprinted from J. K. Galbraith, *American Capitalism: The Concept of Countervailing Power* (pp. 12–25, 35–52, Copyright 1952 by John Kenneth Galbraith) by permission of the Houghton Mifflin Company, Boston, publisher.

The dangers and even the disasters we risk are no less fearsome because we do not know their precise shape or why they do not come.

III

The first requirement of the classical system, as everyone is aware, is competition. In the design of the system this was fundamental and, if it was present in a sufficiently rigorous form, it was also sufficient. In practice, another condition, more properly an assertion, was added in the form of Say's Law of Markets. This held that the act of producing goods provided the purchasing power, neither too much nor too little, for buying them. Thus there was invariable equivalence between the value of what was produced and the purchasing power available to buy that production. It will be evident, even from the most casual reflection, that this comforting doctrine went far to preclude either a serious depression or a violent inflation.

The kind of competition that was necessary for this system was rigorous or, rather, there was a tendency to specify an increasingly rigorous form of competition with the passage of time. The classical economists—Adam Smith, Ricardo and Mill—were not especially self-conscious in their use of the term. Competition was the rivalry of the merchants of the town or of the cotton manufacturers or pit proprietors of nineteenth-century England. Adam Smith contented himself with distinguishing competition from monopoly by its consequences: "The price of monopoly is upon every occasion the highest which can be got. . . . The price of free competition, on the contrary, is the lowest which can be taken, not upon every occasion indeed, but for any considerable time together." But toward the end of the nineteenth century, writers began to make explicit what had previously been implied; namely, that competition required that there be a considerable number of sellers in any trade or industry in informed communication with each other. In more recent times this has been crystallized into the notion of many sellers doing business with many buyers. Each is well informed as to the prices at which others are selling and buying—there is a going price of which everyone is aware. Most important of all, no buyer or seller is large enough to control or exercise an appreciable influence on the common price. In the language of the most distinguished modern exponent of the classical system as an economic and political goal, "The price system will fulfill (its) function only if competition prevails, that is, if the individual producer has to adapt himself to price changes and cannot control them." The rigor of this definition of competition must be stressed especially to the business reader, for it has been the source of an endless amount of misunderstanding between businessmen and economists. After spending the day contemplating the sales force, advertising agency, engineers and research men of his rivals the businessman is likely to go home feeling considerably harassed by competition. Yet if it happens that he has measurable control over his prices he obviously falls short of being competitive in the foregoing sense. No one should be surprised if he feels some annoyance toward scholars who appropriate words in common English usage and, for their own purposes, give them what seems to be an inordinately restricted meaning.

Yet the notion of a market for an industry in which no producer or buyer has *any* influence on price is not as improbable as appears at first glance. There is no wheat or cotton grower in the United States whose contribution to the wheat or cotton market is appreciable in relation to the total supply. In January 1949, a Missouri cotton planter made what was believed to be the largest sale of cotton in the history of the Memphis spot market. But the 9400 bales he sold for $1,400,000 was an almost infinitesimal six tenths of one per cent of the 1949 supply. This planter could have gone to heaven with his cotton instead of to Memphis and there would have been no noticeable tremor on any earthly market.

So it is with most other agricultural products. In the nineteenth century, when the classical system was taking form, agriculture contributed a considerably larger share of the national product than at present. Moreover the burgeoning cotton industry, coal-mining and metal and metal-working industries of England of the time were all shared by numerous producers. The production of each was small in relation to that of all. None could much influence the common price. Finally, in England of the day sellers were exposed to prices that were made in the markets of the world at large. The kind of competition that was implicit in the pioneering designs of the classical economists of the nineteenth century was not unrealistic. It described a world that existed; those who formulated the theory were practical men.

This did not remain the case. Economists, as noted, in seeking to give precision to their language, added rigor to the notion of competition. They also began to require of competition a meaning which would cause it, in turn, to produce the economic and social consequences which earlier economists had associated with it. The definition of competition was gradually accommodated to the requirements of a model economic society; it became not the definition that described reality but the one that produced ideal results. The preoccupation ceased to be with interpreting reality and came to be with building a model economic society. The definition of competition was, in effect, accommodated to the requirements of that model. Its nexus with the competition of the real world, which itself was in process of change, was no longer maintained.

By the early decades of the present century the task of constructing this model of a capitalist society regulated by competition was virtually complete. It was an intellectual achievement of a high order. As a device, in theory, for ordering the economic relations between mankind, it was very nearly perfect. Socialist theorists—Enrico Barone the great Italian scholar and Oskar Lange the equally notable Polish economist—used the theoretical performance of the competitive model as the goal of a socialist state. Few of the original architects of the competitive model would have defended it as a description of the world as it is—or was. For some the competitive model was a first approximation to reality—it departed from real life only to the extent that there was monopoly in industry or over natural resources, including land, or that government or custom interposed barriers to competition. For others it was the goal toward which capitalism might be expected to move or toward which it might be guided or a standard by which it might be appraised. For yet others the construction and refinement of the competitive model was a challenging intellectual exercise.

The birth, development and subsequent career of an idea is something like that of a human. The parents have measurable control over the first two stages but not the third. Once constructed, the competitive model passed into the textbooks and the classrooms. In the absence of any alternative interpretation of economic life, it became the exclusive system of all who undertook to teach economics. It was and remains the economics of those who essay to popularize the subject—to instruct in one lesson. The qualifications, and especially the warnings that there had been an abstraction from reality, were lost or neglected. To this day the abstraction, largely undiluted and unqualified, is the principal residuum of the considerable expense that has gone into the effort to teach economics to Americans.

Man cannot live without an economic theology—without some rationalization of the abstract and seemingly inchoate arrangements which provide him with his livelihood. For this purpose the competitive or classical model had many advantages. It was comprehensive and internally consistent. By asserting that it was a description of reality the conservative could use it as the justification of the existing order. For the reformer it could be a goal, a beacon to mark the path of needed change. Both could be united in the central faith at least so long as nothing happened to strain unduly their capacity for belief.

It is now necessary to examine the performance of the model in more detail.

IV

The notion of efficiency as applied to an economic system is many-sided. There is the matter of getting the most for the least—the commonplace engineering view of efficiency. There is also the problem of getting the particular things that are wanted by the community in the particular amounts that they are wanted. In addition some reasonably full use must be made of the available, or at least of the willing, labor supply. There must be some satisfactory allocation of resources, between present and future production—between what is produced for consumption and what is invested in new plant and processes to enlarge future consumption. There must also be appropriate incentive to change—the adoption of new and more efficient methods of production must be encouraged.

Finally—a somewhat different requirement and one that went long unrecognized—there must be adequate provisions for the research and technological development which brings new methods and (though one is permitted to deplore them on occasion) new products into existence. All this makes a large bill of requirements.

The peculiar fascination of the competitive model was that, given its particular form of competition—that of many sellers, none of whom was large enough to influence the price—all the requirements for efficiency, with the exception of the very last, were met. No producer—no more than the Kansas wheat grower of fact—could gain additional revenue for himself by raising or otherwise manipulating his price. This opportunity was denied to him by the kind of competition assumed, the competition of producers no one of whom was large enough in relation to all to influence the common price. He could gain an advantage only by reducing cost. Were there even a few ambitious men in the business he would have to do so to survive, for if he neglected his opportunities others would seize them. If there are already many in a business it can be assumed that there is no serious bar to others entering it. Given an opportunity for improving efficiency of production, those who seized it, and the imitators they would attract from within and without, would expand production and lower prices. The rest, to survive at these lower prices, would have to conform to the best and most efficient practices. In such manner a Darwinian struggle for business survival concentrated all energies on the reduction of costs and prices.

In this model, producer effort and consumer wants were also effectively related by the price that no producer and no consumer controlled or influenced. The price that would just compensate some producer for added labor, or justify some other cost, was also the one which it was just worth the while of some consumer to pay for the product in question. Any diminution in consumer desire for the item would be impersonally communicated through lower price to producers. By no longer paying for marginal labor or other productive resources the consumer would free these resources for other and more wanted employment. Thus energies were also efficiently concentrated on producing what was most wanted.

In the competitive model these changes did not raise the threat of unemployment. When the tastes of the consumer waned for one product they waxed for another; the higher price for the second product communicated to the producers in that industry the information that they could profitably expand their production and employment. They took in the slack that had been created in the first industry. Even had the consumer decided to save, the saving was for investment—for another kind of expenditure. In any case it was always open to the worker in this system to insure his own employment. Any particular employer was restrained from expanding employment only because the outlay for the added employment was not covered by the resulting increase in income at the going price. The worker seeking employment had it within his own power to alter this delicate balance by offering to work for a lower wage. By doing so he could always make it worth the while of an employer to give him a job. A union, by restraining this wage-cutting, could obviously do damage in this delicately adjusted Elysium. But unions were not a part of the system.

V

There was never full agreement among the architects of the model on the manner in which labor and the other productive resources of the community were allotted as between consumption and investment—between current use and the production of plant, equipment, utilities and public works which would yield their return only over a period of time in the future. However, despite sectarian disputes on details, there was something close to a consensus on the nature of the underlying process. Here as elsewhere competition rendered efficient service. The competition of those who sought the prospective return from plant, machinery, utility or other investment established a price, in the form of the rate of interest, for those who were willing to save from current consumption and thereby make these investments possible. A high return from additional investment would bid up the price for savings. This would lead to more savings and less current consumption. Resources would thus be freed for investment. By the same process the community's desire for goods for current consumption would be balanced against the prospect of having more and different goods as the result of investment.

If it is assumed that immediate consumption is man's normal preference, and that he will only save if he is paid to do so, it is wholly unnatural to suppose that anyone would first deprive himself of consumers' goods and then, by not turning over his savings for investment, deprive himself also of the reward for his thrift. Accordingly, whether a man consumed or saved, his income was in either case spent. But even the stubborn hoarder—and no one was quite so scorned by the nineteenth-century builders of the competitive model—did no irreparable damage. By getting income and neither spending it nor allowing others to do so he withheld some demand from the market. The only effect of this was that the impersonally determined prices for goods fell as supply exceeded demand. Others then found their current income buying more than before. Their spending offset the additions to the miser's hoard.

Here was the basis of the notion that there could never be an excess of savings—that the aggregate of demand for all goods must always equal their supply. This was Say's Law—the claim upon immortality of Jean Baptiste Say, the French interpreter of Adam Smith. Few ideas have ever gripped the minds of economists so firmly as Say's Law; for well over a hundred years it enjoyed the standing of an article of faith. Whether a man accepted or rejected Say's Law was, until well into the nineteen-thirties, the test of whether he was qualified for the companionship of reputable scholars or should be dismissed as a monetary crank.

Say's Law reinforced the conclusion that, in the competitive model, there would always be full use of willing labor. As a result, to the extent that the model was taken to be an approximation to reality, no serious consideration could be given to the possibility or fact of a bad depression. A depression must involve some interruption in the flow of spending—some general reduction in demand for goods below the capacity of the economy to supply them. What is being spent at any given time for consumers' goods is obviously being spent. Interruptions between the receipt of income and its ultimate disposal must be sought for in that part of income that is saved. But Say's Law arrested any search for trouble in this area by declaring that savings or their equivalent must also be spent. A decrease in expenditures by consumers would only mean an increase in saving and investment expenditure. Under such circumstances it was impossible to suppose that a general and progressive reduction in spending—without which there could be no depression—could get under way.

There was room in this system for rhythmic cycles of good business and bad. So long as the principal effect of such movements was on profits and the rate of economic growth, rather than on employment, no serious collision with Say's Law occurred. And, in fact, the business cycle became the object of a good deal of statistical study, especially in the United States. Much data could be gathered, and many charts could be drawn without trespassing on Say. But until the mid-thirties, in both England and the United States, the notion of the grave depression was not only foreign to the accepted system of economics but its admission was largely barred to analysis. Unemployment, which was sufficiently a fact so that it could not be ignored, was generally associated with the activities of unions. Unions prevented the worker from getting himself employed by preventing him from reducing the wage at which he offered to work and so making it worth the while of an employer to hire him. This was not the dogma of mossbacks; it was the only important avenue to an explanation left by Say and the competitive model. As late as 1930, Sir William Beveridge, a modern symbol of unorthodoxy, firmly asserted that the effect, at least potentially, "of high wages policy in causing unemployment is not denied by any competent authority."

Say's Law and the resulting sterility of the interpretations of business fluctuations helps explain the rather passive role played by economists in the very early years of the Great Depression. Many men of reputation either said nothing or vigorously but unhelpfully condemned unbalanced budgets or relief to farmers, businessmen, banks and the unemployed. Politics, in all cases, dictated another course—and the judgments of politicians not of economists, as viewed in retrospect, reflected the course of wisdom. Fortunately the economists were soon to be rehabilitated by the intellectual repeal of Say's Law.

To return to the competitive model. Clearly it either solved the operating problems of the economy, including the great questions of social efficiency, or, as in the case of the severe depression, it excluded the problem from consideration. Efficiency in its various forms was assured by the pressure on the individual firm to produce cheaply, to keep abreast of others in progress, and by the role of an impersonally determined price in passing gains along to consumers and in passing their demands back to producers. The same price structure, abetted by flexible wages and a theory which identified the act of saving with the fact of investment, went far to preclude unemployment. Say's Law canonized the doubtful points. It is already easy to understand the depths of the nostalgia for such a mechanism, however rigorous its requirements. It is also possible to understand how the conviction that its rules were being violated, or the admission that the model could never be achieved in practice, could leave a community, which had long used this system as a reference point in interpreting its economy, with a sense of profound disquiet.

CHAPTER IV: THE ABANDONMENT OF THE MODEL

I

The system of ideas just outlined—the theory of capitalism . . . —was vulnerable at two points. In the realm of ideas there was its pivotal dependence on competition, on a definition of competition that had tended to become increasingly precise and hence increasingly brittle. Even the staunchest defenders of the doctrine required a rigorous form of competition—with Professor Hayek they held that it had to be the competition in which "the individual producer has to adapt himself to price changes and cannot control them." There was also, in the world of reality, the need for performance. The system had to work. Were the assumption of competition to be undermined, it would be a devastating blow. So, equally, would be a failure in performance. Both blows fell simultaneously in the decade of the thirties.

The first blow had been in the making for many years—that it would come sooner or later was implicit in the pattern of industrial growth that has occurred both in the United States and throughout the western world. With many notable exceptions—agriculture, the textile and garment industries, soft-coal mining, wholesale and retail trade, shoe manufacturing—the number of firms participating in a business is likely to be at its maximum within a few years or even a few months after the business is born. Thereafter there is, typically, a steady decline until a point of stability is reached with a handful of massive survivors and, usually, a fringe of smaller hangers-on. Thenceforward the changes in the industry are in the relative positions of the established firms. This is not a universal pattern of development but it is a typical one. The automobile, steel, rubber, farm implement, tobacco, liquor, chemical and radio industries all took such a course. Of the several-score firms now making television sets, there is a good chance that all but a handful will disappear within the next decade.

The process by which the typical industry passes from the hands of the many to the few has not been well understood. Not infrequently in the

United States it has been identified with a design by someone to acquire monopoly control of enterprise. There have been spectacular searches for the devils. The Muckrakers and the Pujo investigation of 1912 looked for the *deus ex machina* of the consolidation movement of the preceding decades —and thought they found it in the bankers. (These were the years which produced International Harvester, International Nickel, International Paper, International Silver and International Salt, as well as the more modestly titled United States Steel, all attesting by their names the generous horizons of the men who put them together.) In the thirties the Pecora investigations and the Temporary National Economic Committee looked, somewhat less specifically, for the architects of the utilities combines, the big motion-picture companies, the theater chains and the burgeoning chain store systems.

To regard the tendency toward concentration of ownership in an industry as the result of some individual's imperial design is to miss the point. In fact, the causes are deeply organic. Except in industries where the maximum advantages of size are realized at a relatively small volume of production—agriculture, some types of trade, and some few fields of mining and manufacture—entry into an industry is easy only when it is very new. Then the recruitment of capital by all is based on hope and promise and it is impossible to distinguish the promise of an embryo Ford from that of an embryo Preston Tucker. No aspirant has the advantage of organization and experience; none has achieved the status of a comparatively sure thing. Since all are beginners all are small, and the capital requirements for any one are modest.

With the growth of the industry the firms already in operation also grow. In doing so they realize whatever technical economies there may be in larger-scale production and the successful ones also acquire, either directly from earnings or from their reputation for making them, the wherewithal in new capital for further growth.

These firms also acquire—a point somewhat neglected by economists—the economies of experience. The development of an industrial enterprise is a fairly intricate task in organization and administration. It can only be accomplished easily when it is accomplished slowly—when there is opportunity to search for talent, to try new men out a few at a time, and when there is leisure to reassign, promote to innocuousness, or detach with regrets, the inevitable mistakes. Only a little of this can be afforded at any given time.

The result is a passive but highly effective handicap on the latecomer. In this race the horse with the poorest record, or no record, must carry the greatest weight. Capital must be found in spite of the fact that there are other firms that are a better prospect for the investor. In recent times the Reconstruction Finance Corporation has eased the problem of entry of new firms and it is indeed significant that the new arrivals in such industries as automobile, steel and aluminum production in the last ten years have all had capital from this source. But even if the aspirant has the necessary merit and friendships to obtain government funds he must still contend with new foremen and untried supervisors and engineers and he must risk the *gaucheries*[1] of untried executives. An old firm may have a few neophytes; the new firm has few others. It must accomplish, often in a few months, the tasks of organization which those already in the field have worked out, step by step, over many years. As a result, in an established industry, where the scale of production is considerable, there is no such thing as freedom of entry. On the contrary, time and circumstances combine to bar the effective entry of new firms.

At the same time that entry becomes difficult or impossible, the forces which tend to reduce the number already in the industry continue. Weaklings may still fail, and disappear especially in bad times. Good times make it easy to finance consolidations and tempting for the strong company to expand and the weak to sell out. Thus, both depression and prosperity work, alike, to reduce the number of firms in an industry. The combination of a low or zero birthrate and a continuing death rate must always be a declining population.

The growth pattern here described is not peculiar to the United States. Industrial development appears to have followed a roughly similar path in other advanced countries. There may, however, be something distinctive about the final equilibrium in the United States. In Western Europe the end result, abetted by cartel agreements, has frequently been a single massive survivor or combination. With us it is far more typically a few large firms together with a fringe of small ones. This equilibrium is apparently associated with a certain equality of strength among the major survivors coupled with a measure of equality of size that makes it difficult for any one large firm to buy another out. At this stage, too, consolidation is consolidation of giants. It has become a sufficiently massive and spectacular affair so that public opinion and the possibility of adverse attention from the Department of Justice both act as deterrents. At the same time the price competition of the large firms is likely to be sufficiently circumscribed by caution so that the smaller fringe can live, albeit often precariously, under the umbrella the large firms provide.

[1] [*Clumsy blunders.*]

Having reached this stage, little further change occurs in the membership of the typical industry. There is no more cherished view of the American economy than that which regards it as a biological process in which the old and the senile are continually being replaced by the young and vigorous. It is a pleasant but almost certainly a far-fetched fiction. In fact the present generation of Americans, if it survives, will buy its steel, copper, brass, automobiles, tires, soap, shortening, breakfast food, bacon, cigarettes, whiskey, cash registers and caskets from one or another of the handful of firms that now supply these staples. As a moment's reflection will establish, there hasn't been much change in the firms supplying these products for several decades.

II

An economy where the typical industry is shared by a few firms is awkwardly inconsistent with a theory of capitalism which requires that power to affect prices or wages or output or investment be impersonally governed by the reactions of the many. During the thirties, as the result of a singularly important series of studies, the notion that there was extensive concentration in American industry gained wide acceptance. The first of these studies was the epochal investigation by Adolf A. Berle and Gardiner C. Means into the proportion of national wealth, industrial wealth and corporate assets owned by the two hundred largest non-financial corporations. This was followed by further investigations under government auspices by Means, more yet by the Temporary National Economic Committee and, since World War II, still further studies by the Federal Trade Commission and the Department of Commerce.

Three questions were at issue in these studies, namely: how important are a minority of very, *very* big corporations in the American economy? To what extent are markets divided between a relatively small number of large firms—large, that is, in relation to the markets they share? Does concentration become greater year by year?

There is still something less than complete agreement on the answers and not all of the discussion which these studies have provoked has been of Olympian objectivity. The government, so often inclined in economic matters to assert that all is for the best in the best of all worlds, has, in this case, shown no disposition to minimize the extent of the concentration or the need for vigorous counteraction through the antitrust laws. The critics of the figures have, with a few exceptions, been men who are deeply devoted to the economic and political system identified with the competitive model as an economic and political goal. They have been in the always equivocal position of the man who must testify to the virtue of a well-loved mistress.

Yet the principal conclusions, if stated with reasonable moderation, are not subject to serious challenge and have gained wide acceptance. The importance of the large corporation, and the large proportion of manufacturing, transportation, utilities service and mining which a comparatively small number perform, is clear. Means calculated that for 1933 the 200 largest non-financial (i.e., producing or controlling as distinct from financing) corporations and their subsidiaries had approximately fifty-seven per cent of the total assets of such corporations. A recent investigation by the Federal Trade Commission shows, for the year 1947, that the 113 largest manufacturing corporations owned forty-six per cent of the property, plant and equipment employed in manufacturing.

Whatever the margin of error in these figures, it cannot be great enough to alter the essential conclusion which is that a small number of large corporations are responsible for a very substantial proportion of all industrial activity. And, in fact, this conclusion has not been seriously challenged.

That the typical industry is shared by a relatively small number of corporations—that there is concentration in individual markets as well as in the aggregate—has provided more opportunity for debate. So, also, have the attempts to show that concentration is increasing year by year. With reference to the latter the evidence is, in fact, decidedly dubious. It may well be that the appearance of new industries—television, air freight carriage, specialized gambling services are notable post-World War II examples—is sufficient to offset the consolidation that goes on within older industries.

The measurement of the concentration within industries has run afoul of the imprecision of the word industry. As this term is used in everyday discourse and as it is used for statistical purposes, it groups together the production of some highly unrelated products and it runs boundaries between products that are closely interchangeable. Crosleys and Cadillacs are both products of the automobile industry, but a cut in price or a doubling of output of Crosleys is not a datum of perceptible importance to the Cadillac Division of General Motors. Copper, brass and aluminum, which are closely interchangeable for many uses, are products of different industries. Withal, the notion of an industry as a group of firms supplying roughly the same market has practical usefulness and it would be impossible to get along without it.

In spite of these problems, which have provided an almost unparalleled opportunity for quibbles, these studies affirm, at least, that over an important sector of the American economy individual markets are shared by a small number of producers. In the production of motor vehicles, agricultural machinery, rubber tires, cigarettes, aluminum, liquor, meat products, copper, tin containers and office machinery the largest three firms in 1947 did two thirds or more of all business. In steel, glass, industrial chemicals, and dairy products the largest six accounted for two thirds. There is a similar degree of concentration in a host of less important or derivative industries. And in a number more—gasoline, cement, mixed fertilizer and milk distribution—markets that are necessarily regional or local are typically divided between a similarly small number of sellers.

There are numerous industries where the number of firms serving the same market remains large and where no one or no small number have any considerable proportion of the total business. But for a large and important sector of the economy—indeed for the industries which are commonly supposed to typify American capitalism—this is clearly not the case. On the contrary, as one of the leading contemporary students of market organization has concluded, "The principal general indications of studies of American market structure are (among others) that concentration of output among relatively few sellers is the dominant pattern." The acceptance of such a conclusion could not but be damaging to a theory of capitalism based on the notion that markets were shared by many producers no one of them large enough to influence the common prices paid or received.

III

Meanwhile economic theory, as distinct from economic statistics, had also dealt the competitive model a serious blow. Economists had anciently recognized one major exception to the competition of the many. That was the limiting case of monopoly—the case where one firm was in complete control of all the product of an industry. So long as economists held to this bipolar classification of industries—competition *or* monopoly—the position of competition as a valid assumption concerning the economy was relatively secure. That was because monopoly—the absolute monopoly of the single firm—was so rare as to have the standing only of a curiosity. Apart from the public utilities there was, before World War II, only one example that could easily be brought to mind, namely the Aluminum Company of America. So long as monopoly was so exceptional, competition must be the rule. The economy as a whole must be competitive.

In 1932–33, under the combined attack of an American and a British economist (Professor E. H. Chamberlin of Harvard University and Mrs. Joan Robinson of Cambridge University) the old bipolar classification of markets, competition *or* monopoly, was abandoned. New categories of markets, neither purely competitive nor fully monopolized, were recognized between the two. In this intermediate zone were industries whose markets had the characteristics of both competition and monopoly. They were monopolistically or imperfectly competitive.

The establishment of a multiple, rather than a double classification of markets was the most far-reaching contribution of the new theory. It meant, although it wasn't wholly foreseen at the time, the end of the faith in competition in the old sense. Now there were alternatives to the implausible assumption of competition without going to the implausible case of monopoly. The competition of many sellers, like the control of a market by one, soon came to be regarded as an extreme or limiting case. From the statistical investigations as well as from everyday observation it was evident, moreover, that one of the intermediate types of markets—that of few sellers or oligopoly as it came to be called—was of commanding importance. No sooner had oligopoly been recognized as something different from either competition or monopoly than it was on its way to replace competition as the principal assumption by which the industrial economy was interpreted.

However, a vast distance separates oligopoly from the competition of the competitive model. Price-making in markets where there are a few sellers is not only measurably influenced by the action of any individual firm but the individual must take into consideration the response of others to his initiative. If he correctly appraises what is advantageous for the industry as a whole, the others presumably will follow his lead. Otherwise they will not. When each seller considers the advantage of any action from the viewpoint of the profits of the industry as a whole he is obviously thinking much as would a monopolist. To assume that oligopoly was general in the economy was to assume that power akin to that of a monopolist was exercised in many, perhaps even a majority of markets.

In actual practice things are both simpler and more complicated. They are simpler because in most industries where there are few sellers there soon develops a tacit understanding which allows one firm to assume some measure of leadership. This firm makes an appraisal of the price policy that is appropriate for itself with greater or less consideration of what will be acceptable to the other members of the industry. The others follow its lead. Things are more complicated because, except under conditions of very strong demand, any firm in an industry can initiate price reductions. This normally forces others to follow suit. There is no similar compulsion to follow a price increase. Any one of the large cigarette companies can bring down cigarette prices by lowering its own price. It cannot as certainly bring the others up by raising its prices. As compared with monopoly, one of the mitigating facts about oligopoly is the commanding position of the firm which sees the greatest advantage in low prices.

Price-making under oligopoly is further complicated by the fact that there is never complete substitutability between the products of different sellers. A Ford differs from a Chevrolet and the differences are energetically magnified by the advertising of the companies. This gives to Ford and General Motors a measure of independence in their prices. The same is true, though in small degree, even of chemically identical products like steel or sulphur. Habit, corporate personality, terms and promptness of delivery will hold customers even in face of minor price differentials. However, these are details. The important thing is that the doctrines of a monopolistic or imperfect competition paved the way for a destruction of the old assumption of competition on which the competitive model was erected. It is now time to see what took its place.

IV

It is a measure of the magnitude of the disaster to the old system that when oligopoly or crypto-monopoly is assumed it no longer follows that any of the old goals of social efficiency are realized. The producer now has measurable control over his prices. Hence prices are no longer an impersonal force selecting the efficient man, forcing him to adopt the most efficient mode and scale of operations and driving out the inefficient and incompetent. One can as well suppose that prices will be an umbrella which efficient and inefficient producers alike will tacitly agree to hold at a safe level over their heads and under which all will live comfortably, profitably and inefficiently. There is no longer, by the old line of argument, any certainty of technical advance. When there are many producers in an industry, some one of them will certainly seize upon any known innovation. In so doing, the pioneer forces others to follow. To resist progress is to perish. If there is only a handful of producers, there is a chance that none will assume the initiative. There is at least the possibility that all will prefer and concur in choosing profitable stagnation.

When sellers have gained authority over prices, prices no longer reflect the ebb and flow of consumer demand. It was such price movements in the competitive model which equated consumer desires—as evidenced by their willingness to pay—with what producers found it worth while to supply. When prices are tacitly administered by a few large firms they no longer move freely and production no longer responds automatically to price changes. An increase in demand may bring increased production at the old prices; it may just as well lead to a decision to increase prices and profits with production remaining as before.

In any case it must be assumed that prices will be set and production will be managed, however imperfectly, with an eye to the profits of the industry. One of the oldest conclusions of economics is that a price so set—a monopoly price—must be higher and the resulting output smaller than under conditions of competition. Thus not only does oligopoly lead away from the world of competition, with its promise of efficiency, but it leads toward the world of monopoly. This, anciently, had been viewed as the very antithesis of social efficiency.

There were other bitter consequences of the new assumptions. A close examination of oligopoly showed that price competition, the very motor of the competitive model, was not only sharply circumscribed but had to be. When there are only a few firms in an industry and their products are closely substitutable, a price cut by one company must, as just noted, be matched by the others. Otherwise the firm with the lower price will draw a disproportionate share of the business in the short run and, through operation of habit and customer good will, may well retain it in the long run. This the other firms must prevent. An aggressive and persistent price-cutter can, accordingly, affect the level of prices and return of the entire industry. Should he persist and provoke retributive action, the ensuing price warfare can be ruinous to all. There is no point set by cost or any other consideration below which prices cannot go. Cuts must be matched and, if the game is fully played through, all can be ruined.

Businessmen who live in the shadow of this disaster, as do all who share markets with a few firms, protect themselves by a convention. This convention simply outlaws the use of prices as a weapon of competitive warfare. The convention against price competition, when there are only a few sellers in a market, is a matter of great importance. It is also so much a part of customary business practice that where it is well observed its very existence is often unnoticed even by those who adhere to it. Prices continue to change and they may be changed, at the instance of an aggressive and efficient leader, when that firm knows that the result will be uncomfortable for other firms. But this is very different from using prices as a sanguinary weapon for invading another's markets or separating him from his customers. This the convention prohibits and there is nothing more frightening, in industries where the convention is not rigidly observed, than the news that a price war has broken out. Quite typically the individual who resorts to price competition does so surreptitiously and the opprobrious character of his action is suggested by the terms in which he is normally described: he is irresponsible, a chiseler, an unfair competitor, a man who is guilty of unsound or even un-American business practices. The primitive defender of the convention against price competition does not hesitate to use racial epithets to assail the unorthodox competitor.

Nevertheless, the convention against price competition is inevitable under oligopoly. The alternative is self-destruction, which cannot be expected of men with a normal desire to remain solvent and which in any case would serve no useful purpose. Although the structure of the market of small numbers precludes aggressive price competition—the uninhibited price movements which the competitive model requires—economists have been reluctant to concede the fact. They have regularly rebuked the businessman who foreswears price competition as a traitor to the price system. The businessman has been understandably mystified by these attacks. Evidently the test of his faith in competition is his willingness to court disaster in its name.

The final embarrassment from the unraveling of the new ideas was that as price competition in its pristine form disappeared, other forms of competition become suspect. The convention against retributive price competition in the market shared by a few large firms does not extend to other forms of commercial rivalry. Individual firms retain their desire to keep and even to enlarge their share of the market. The first is important for survival, the second for both profits and prestige. With price competition ruled out, competitive energies are normally concentrated on persuasion and, especially in consumers' goods, on salesmanship and advertising. The cigarette manufacturer recruits customers, not by the self-defeating and dangerous device of cutting cigarette prices but, with the unreluctant aid of his advertising agency, by recourse to the radio, billboards and television screens and through magazines and the press. This is competition but no longer the kind of competition that is eligible for a blanket defense. On the contrary, the very instrument which once rewarded the community with lower prices and greater efficiency now turns up assailing its ears with rhymed commercials and soap opera and rendering the countryside hideous with commercial art. What hath Adam Smith wrought?

In any case no one could any longer argue very seriously that the cost and volume of even the comparatively inoffensive forms of competitive selling and advertising were in response to popular demand. Not only had the old pressure for efficiency in production been lost, but there appeared to be a positive premium on expenditures on distribution. This was all readily assimilated to the new theory. Indeed, given the market of the few it was normal and natural.

One consequence of the new ideas was to place economic theory sharply in opposition to the burgeoning advertising industry. Not unnaturally, those advertising men who take their profession seriously, and have the normal human wish to be wanted, have not found it pleasant to be considered extraneous. Since they were hardly in a position to devise a new system of theory which would re-establish their place in the scheme of things, they have been reduced to stating, often with some vigor, that it is advertising that made this country what it is today. Perhaps it was a mark of their good nature that they weren't more put out with economists than they were. The adman was one of the many displaced persons who was caught up in the retreat from the competitive model.

V

Such was the general state of ideas on economic efficiency in the main tradition of economics—in the impeccable line of descent from Adam Smith, Ricardo and Alfred Marshall—at the beginning of World War II. Such, with relatively few modifications, is where the main ideas concerning what economists call value or market theory remain today. By evolution, from a system where nearly everything worked out for the best, economists found themselves with a system where nearly everything seemed to work out for the worst.

It would be a mistake to exaggerate the alarm with which the generality of economists viewed this result. One author did go so far as to plead with his colleagues "to recognize that the concept of a system of monopoly is self-contradictory and the very negation of everything economics stands for." They were adjured to see no evil. In a great personal tragedy, Heinrich von Stackelberg, a brilliant German contributor to the new theory, apparently lost all hope of any order in the economy except as might be provided by the state. Almost alone among the German economists of any distinction he became an active National Socialist.

A certain number of economists have also undertaken to revive the faith of their colleagues in the existence, actual or potential, of the competitive model. But even this task has been assumed, in the main, by popular writers whose faith in pure competition has not been weakened by contact with the new ideas.

This philosophical detachment of the economists is to be explained by their much greater interest in the last fifteen years in the problem of depression and by their preoccupation with factors bearing more directly on the total performance of the economy. Nonetheless the new market theory had a profound effect. A generation ago American economists, an inconvenient bias toward free trade apart, were counted among the staunchest allies of the businessman and among the nation's most notable defenders of the *status quo*. Partly as the result of the new ideas, they have since acquired an almost unexcelled reputation for waspishness. The very term economics has come to be identified in the minds of many conservatives, if not with radicalism, at least with an inordinate capacity to find fault. This by itself is of little consequence, and in any case, men who afflict the comfortable serve equally with those who comfort the afflicted. One cannot suppose that American capitalism would long prosper without the critics its leaders find such a profound source of annoyance. Nonetheless, the new ideas had the far-reaching consequence of bringing into question a basic supposition of capitalism—the supposition of efficiency. . .

THOMAS WOLFE

ECONOMIC depression, rendered doubly ominous by the rise of European dictatorship and ended only in the early years of World War II, was the common experience of the 1930's. It was in that decade that many Americans, not for the first time, but for the first time without the feeling that an inexhaustible future lay ahead of present difficulties, came to reexamine the easy confidence which for long had distinguished them among the peoples of the world.

"Brother, can you spare a dime?" The bewildered nation listened to and sang those bitter words during 1932. Four years before, President Herbert Hoover (b. 1874) had told the country that "we shall soon with the help of God be within sight of the day when poverty will be banished from the nation." In fact, as late as October 31, 1932, Hoover had repeated the same words with the significant omission of "soon." What had happened to the golden promise of the twenties? Or as many were asking, "Were the twenties golden?" For depressions do not come as sudden catastrophes. They give ample warning that the economy is sick, although most frequently the attending physicians—professional social scientists, economists, and statesmen—do not agree in time on the meaning of the symptoms.

Black Thursday, October 29, 1929, had marked the beginning of the credit-ridden economy's collapse. On that day alone, 16,410,000 shares had been sold on the stock market. In two days $15 billion worth of paper value had been wiped out; by year's end an additional $25 billion had gone down the drain. What millions of families had known for a decade now became common knowledge to the entire nation. America was an ironic contradiction; want existed amidst extraordinary plenty. The Brookings Institute observed that in 1921 the 24,000 families with an income of over $100,000 apiece received a total income three times that of the 6 million poorest families. During the same year, twenty per cent of the population received 51.3 per cent of the total national income. For the fortunate few the twenties had been truly golden; for the many it had been a long and losing struggle to make ends meet.

The bulk of the population had managed to meet their needs by assuming an ever-increasing burden of indebtedness. They had mortgaged their future earnings to meet their immediate needs. The depression spelled disaster to these debtors. Not only did they find themselves with rapidly dwindling incomes—between 1929 and 1932 salaries declined 40 per cent, dividends 56.6 per cent, and wages 60 per cent—but also with debts that were rapidly increasing in value as the national income declined from $81 billion in 1929 to $41 billion in 1932. In effect, as the money supply deflated, its value increased. Consequently, a dollar borrowed in 1929 but repaid in 1932 brought considerably more upon repayment than on borrowing.

Concurrently with the decline in income came the decline in consumption and subsequently in production. By the spring of 1930 more than 3 million were unemployed; once started the army of "expendables" grew with terrifying speed until it reached 15 million in late autumn of 1932. Throughout it all, the bulk of the population behaved with surprising restraint. Bred to think in terms of self-reliance and individual responsibility, the average American came only reluctantly to understand that he was not individually responsible for his plight. As meager resources were consumed, the specter of want ceased to be an impending possibility and became a grim fact. Pork might sell for eight cents a pound or milk for six cents a quart, but increasing numbers of Americans were forced to consider what one does when money is no longer obtainable. To accept private charity had always carried with it the stigma of individual failure, and only with difficulty did most Americans overcome their distaste for such an admission. But private charity itself proved unable to meet the need.

Three and four decades previously social legislation guaranteeing against want in old age and unemployment had become common in western Europe. America, smug in its conviction of an innate moral superiority, had declined to assume similar responsibilities. Slowly the hollowness of the old myths revealed themselves to the national consciousness. Hoover defended "rugged individualism," but for the hungry the term seemed a callous indifference to their misery. They listened for the "voice from the wilderness" that would tell them that the old truths were mere shibboleths designed to safeguard vested interests. No longer could they live in hope of a golden tomorrow that God would bring in good time; they needed help and *soon*. The mood to try something, anything, had arrived.

The overwhelming rejection of Hoover in November, 1932, brought to the forefront Franklin Delano Roosevelt (1882–1945). Prepared to abandon past methods, to experiment with the novel, he sought to preserve political liberty while sacrificing economic license. To the depressed third of the nation he brought immediate economic relief in the form of an emergency relief program. The sacred cow of private enterprise found itself circumscribed by law and forced to compete with governmentally subsidized projects such as TVA. The farmer, blinded by the "black blizzards" of parched soil being blown from the southwestern reaches of the Great Plains, received government subsidies guaranteeing him a reasonable price for his produce. The millions of unorganized industrial workers received government backing for their unions. Long-needed social legislation guaranteeing each person a measure of security against unemployment and during old age was finally passed. The walls of the past had been breached.

But it would be mistaken to assume that the New Deal did more than dent the problems of the depression. It had mitigated want rather than ended it. Only war brought the dormant economy back into full operation. For all their efforts, the men of the New Deal had been unable to answer the fundamental question. What happens to capitalism when it has solved its problems of production and is confronted with the problems of distribution?

The experience of the 1930's generated many forms of self-examination among the American people. Artists and writers turned to the life around them, and of which they were a part, for themes. Much of literature became "realist" in tone; some of it expressed direct concern with "social consciousness." In travail, the sights, sounds, and smells of America seemed magnified and charged with special significance. Among the novelists, Thomas Wolfe (1900–1938), born in Asheville,

North Carolina, author of *Look Homeward, Angel* (1929), *Of Time and the River* (1935), and *The Web and the Rock* (1940), was especially sensitive to the surface textures of life in the 1930's. It is from his last novel, *You Can't Go Home Again* (1940), published posthumously, that the following selection has been taken. Wolfe wrote with passion of an America which seemed to have lost its sense of community. He attempts to convey what it meant to "come of age" in the decade of depression.

YOU CAN'T GO HOME AGAIN

. . . George was reading the *New York Times* one morning when his eye was caught by a small news item on an inside page. It occupied only a scant two inches or so at the bottom of a column, but the Libya Hill date line leaped out at him:

BANK FAILS IN SOUTH. Libya Hill, O.C., Mar. 12.—The Citizens Trust Company of this city failed to open its doors for business this morning, and throughout the day, as news of its closing spread, conditions of near-panic mounted steadily here and in all the surrounding region. The bank was one of the largest in western Old Catawba and for years had been generally regarded as a model of conservative management and financial strength. The cause of its failure is not yet known. It is feared that the losses to the people of this community may be extensive.

The alarm occasioned by the closing of the bank was heightened later in the day by the discovery of the sudden and rather mysterious death of Mayor Baxter Kennedy. His body was found with a bullet through his head, and all the available evidence seems to point to suicide. Mayor Kennedy was a man of exceptionally genial and cheerful disposition, and is said to have had no enemies.

Whether there is any connection between the two events which have so profoundly disturbed the accustomed calm of this mountain district is not known, although their close coincidence has given rise to much excited conjecture.

"So," thought George, laying down the paper with a stunned and thoughtful air, "it has come at last! . . . What was it that Judge Rumford Bland had said to them?"

The whole scene in the Pullman washroom came back to him. He saw again the stark and speechless terror in the faces of Libya Hill's leaders and rulers as the frail but terrible old blind man suddenly confronted them and held them with his sightless eyes and openly accused them of ruining the

---

town. As George remembered this and sat there thinking about the news he had just read, he felt quite sure there must be some direct relation between the failure of the bank and the Mayor's suicide.

There was, indeed. Things had been building up to this double climax for a long time.

Jarvis Riggs, the banker, had come from a poor but thoroughly respectable family in the town. When he was fifteen his father died and he had to quit school and go to work to support his mother. He held a succession of small jobs until, at eighteen, he was offered a modest but steady position in the Merchants National Bank.

He was a bright young fellow and a "hustler," and step by step he worked his way up until he became a teller. Mark Joyner kept a deposit at the Merchants National and used to come home and talk about Jarvis Riggs. In those days he had none of the brittle manner and pompous assurance that were to characterize him later, after he had risen to greatness. His hair, which was afterwards to turn a dead and lifeless sandy color, had glints of gold in it then, his cheeks were full and rosy, he had a bright and smiling face, and it was always briskly and cheerfully—"Good morning, Mr. Joyner!" or "Good morning, Mr. Shepperton!"—when a customer came in. He was friendly, helpful, courteous, eager to please, and withal businesslike and knowing. He also dressed neatly and was known to be supporting his mother. All these things made people like him and respect him. They wanted to see him succeed. For Jarvis Riggs was a living vindication of an American legend—that of the poor boy who profits from the hardships of his early life and "makes good." People would nod knowingly to one another and say of him:

"That young man has his feet on the ground."

"Yes," they would say, "he's *going* somewhere."

So when, along about 1912, the word began to go around that a small group of conservative business men were talking of starting a new bank, and that Jarvis Riggs was going to be its cashier, the feeling was most favorable. The backers explained that they were not going to compete with the established banks. It was simply their feeling that a growing town like Libya Hill, with its steady increase in population and in its business interests, could use another bank. And the new bank, one gathered, was to be conducted according to the most eminently approved principles of sound finance. But it was to be a progressive bank, too, a forward-looking bank, mindful of the future, the great, golden, magnificent future that Libya Hill was sure to have—that it was even heresy to doubt. In this way it was also to be a young man's bank. And this was where Jarvis Riggs came in.

It is not too much to say that the greatest asset the new enterprise had from the beginning was Jarvis Riggs. He had played his cards well. He had offended no one, he had made no enemies, he had always remained modest, friendly, and yet impersonal, as if not wishing to intrude himself too much on the attention of men who stood for substance and authority in the town's life. The general opinion was that he knew what he was doing. He had learned about life in the highly-thought-of "university of hard knocks," he had learned business and banking in "the hard school of experience," so everybody felt that if Jarvis Riggs was going to be cashier of the new bank, then the new bank was pretty sure to be all right.

Jarvis himself went around town and sold stock in the bank. He had no difficulty at all. He made it quite plain that he did not think anyone was going to make a fortune. He simply sold the stock as a safe and sound investment, and that was how everybody felt about it. The bank was modestly capitalized at $25,000, and there were 250 shares at $100 each. The sponsors, including Jarvis, took 100 shares between them, and the remaining 150 shares were divided among "a selected group of leading business men." As Jarvis said, the bank was really "a community project whose first and only purpose is to serve the community," so no one was allowed to acquire too large an interest.

This was the way the Citizens Trust Company got started. And in no time at all, it seemed, Jarvis Riggs was advanced from cashier to vice-president, and then to president. The poor boy had come into his own.

In its early years the bank prospered modestly and conservatively. Its growth was steady but not spectacular. After the United States entered the war, it got its share of the nation's prosperity. But after the war, in 1921, there was a temporary lull, a period of "adjustment." Then the 1920's began in earnest.

The only way to explain what happened then is to say that there was "a feeling in the air." Everybody seemed to sense a prospect of quick and easy money. There was thrilling and rapid expansion in all directions, and it seemed that there were possibilities of wealth, luxury, and economic power hitherto undreamed of just lying around waiting for anyone who was bold enough to seize them.

Jarvis Riggs was no more insensible to these beckoning opportunities than the next man. The time had come, he decided, to step out and show the world what he could do. The Citizens Trust began to advertize itself as "the fastest-growing bank in the state." But it did not advertize what it was growing on.

That was the time when the political and business clique which dominated the destinies of the town, and which had put amiable Baxter Kennedy in the Mayor's office as its "front," began to focus its activities around the bank. The town was burgeoning rapidly and pushing out into the wilderness, people were confident of a golden future, no one gave a second thought to the reckless increase in public borrowing. Bond issues involving staggering sums were being constantly "floated" until the credit structure of the town was built up into a teetering inverted pyramid and the citizens of Libya Hill no longer owned the streets they walked on. The proceeds of these enormous borrowings were deposited with the bank. The bank, for its part, then returned these deposits to the politicians, or to their business friends, supporters, allies, and adherents—in the form of tremendous loans, made upon the most flimsy and tenuous security, for purposes of private and personal speculation. In this way "The Ring," as it was called, which had begun as an inner circle of a few ambitious men, became in time a vast and complex web that wove through the entire social structure of the town and involved the lives of thousands of people. And all of it now centered in the bank.

But the weaving of this complicated web of frenzied finance and speculation and special favors to "The Ring" could not go on forever, though there were many who thought it could. There had to come a time when the internal strains and stresses became too great to sustain the load, a time when there would be ominous preliminary tremors to give warning of the crash that was to come. Just when this time arrived is pretty hard to say. One can observe a soldier moving forward in a battle and see him spin and tumble, and know the moment he is hit. But one cannot observe so exactly the moment when a man has been shot down by life.

So it was with the bank and with Jarvis Riggs. All that one can be sure of is that their moment came. And it came long before the mighty roar of tumbling stocks in Wall Street echoed throughout the nation. That event, which had its repercussions in Libya Hill as elsewhere, was not the *prime cause* of anything. What happened in Wall Street was only the initial explosion which in the course of the next few years was to set off a train of lesser explosions all over the land—explosions which at last revealed beyond all further doubting and denial the hidden pockets of lethal gases which a false, vicious, and putrescent scheme of things had released beneath the surface of American life.

Long before the explosion came that was to blow *him* sky-high, and the whole town with him, Jarvis Riggs had felt the tremors in the thing he had created, and he knew he was a doomed and ruined man. Before long others knew it, too, and knew that they were ruined with him. But they would not let themselves believe it. They did not dare. Instead, they sought to exorcise the thing they feared by pretending it wasn't there. Their speculations only grew madder, fiercer.

And then, somehow, the cheerful, easy-going Mayor found out what some of those around him must have known for months. That was in the spring of 1928, two years before the failure of the bank. At that time he went to Jarvis Riggs and told him what he knew, and then demanded to withdraw the city's funds. The banker looked the frightened Mayor in the eye and laughed at him.

"What are you afraid of, Baxter?" he said. "Are you showing the white feather now that the pinch is on? You say you are going to withdraw the deposits of the city? All right—withdraw them. But I warn you, if you do the bank is ruined. It will have to close its doors tomorrow. And if it closes its doors, where is your town? Your precious town is also ruined."

The Mayor looked at the banker with a white face and stricken eyes. Jarvis Riggs leaned forward and his tones became more persuasive:

"Pull out your money if you like, and wreck your town. But why not play along with us, Baxter? We're going to see this thing through." He was smiling now, and wearing his most winning manner. "We're in a temporary depression—yes. But six months from now we'll be out of the woods. I know we will. We're coming back stronger than ever. You can't sell Libya Hill short," he said, using a phrase that was in great vogue just then. "We've not begun to see the progress we're going to make. But the salvation and future of this town rests in your hands. So make up your mind about it. What are you going to do?"

The Mayor made up his mind. Unhappy man.

Things drifted along. Time passed. The sands were running low.

By the fall of 1929 there began to be a vague rumor going about that all was not well at the Citizens Trust. George Webber had heard it himself when he went home in September. But it was a nebulous thing, and as often as not the person who whispered it fearfully would catch himself and say:

"Oh, pshaw! There's nothing in it. There couldn't be! You know how people talk."

But the rumor persisted through the winter, and by early March it had became a disturbing and sinister contagion. No one could say where it came from. It seemed to be distilled like a poison out of the mind and heart and spirit of the whole town.

On the surface there was nothing to account for it. The Citizens Trust maintained its usual appearance of solid substance, businesslike efficiency, and Greek-templed sanctity. Its broad plate-glass windows opening out upon the Square let in a flood of light, and the whole atmosphere was one of utter clarity. The very breadth of those windows seemed to proclaim to the world the complete openness and integrity of the bank's purpose. They seemed to say:

"Here is the bank, and here are all the people in the bank, and all the people in the bank are openly at work. Look, citizens, and see for yourselves. You see there is nothing hidden here. The bank is Libya, and Libya is the bank."

It was all so open that one did not have to go inside to know what was going on. One could stand on the sidewalk outside and look in and see everything. To the right were the tellers' cages, and to the left there was a railed-off space in which the officers sat at their sumptuous mahogany flat-topped desks. At the largest of these desks, just inside the low enclosure, sat Jarvis Riggs himself. There he sat, talking importantly and pompously, as though laying down the law, to one of his customers. There he sat, briskly reading through the pile of papers on his desk. There he sat, pausing in his work now and then to look up at the ceiling in deep thought, or to lean back in his swivel chair and gently rock in meditation.

It was all just as it had always been.

Then it happened.

March 12, 1930 was a day that will be long remembered in the annals of Libya Hill. The double tragedy set the stage as nothing else could have done for the macabre weeks to follow.

If all the fire bells in town had suddenly begun to ring out their alarm at nine o'clock that morning, the news could not have spread more rapidly that the Citizens Trust Company was closed. Word of it leapt from mouth to mouth. And almost instantly, from every direction, white-faced men and women came running toward the Square. There were housewives with their aprons on, their hands still dripping dishwater; workmen and mechanics with their warm tools in their hands; hatless business men and clerks; young mothers carrying babies in their arms. Everyone in town, it seemed, had dropped whatever he was doing and rushed out in the streets the moment the news had reached him.

The Square itself was soon a seething mass of frenzied people. Frantically, over and over, they asked each other the same questions: Was it really true? How had it happened? How bad was it?

In front of the bank itself the crowd was quieter, more stunned. To this spot, sooner or later, they all came, drawn by a common desperate hope that they would yet be able to see with their own eyes that it was not so. Like a sluggish current within that seething mass the queue moved slowly past, and as the people saw those locked and darkened doors they knew that all hope was gone. Some just stared with stricken faces, some of the women moaned and wailed, from the eyes of strong men silent tears coursed down, and from the mouths of others came the rumble of angry mutterings.

For their ruin had caught up with them. Many of the people in that throng had lost their life savings. But it was not only the bank's depositors who were ruined. Everyone now knew that their boom was over. They knew that the closing of the bank had frozen all their speculations just as they were, beyond the possibility of extricating themselves. Yesterday they could count their paper riches by ten thousands and by millions; today they owned nothing, their wealth had vanished, and they were left saddled with debts that they could never pay.

And they did not yet know that their city government was bankrupt, too—that six million dollars of public money had been lost behind those closed and silent doors.

It was a little before noon on that ill-omened day that Mayor Kennedy was found dead. And, just to put the final touch of gruesome irony upon the whole event, a blind man found him.

Judge Rumford Bland testified at the inquest that he left his front office, upstairs in the ramshackle building that he owned there on the Square, and went out in the hall, heading in the direction of the toilet, where he proposed to perform an essential function of nature. It was dark out there, he said with his ghostly smile, and the floors creaked, but this didn't matter to him—he knew the way. He said he couldn't have lost his way even if he had wanted to. At the end of the hall he could hear a punctual drip of water, dropping with its slow, incessant monotone; and besides, there was the pervasive smell of the tin urinal—all he had to do was to follow his nose.

He arrived in darkness and pushed open the door, and suddenly his foot touched something. He leaned over, his white, thin fingers groped down, and all at once they were plunged—wet, warm, sticky, reeking—into the foundering mass of what just five minutes before had been the face and brains of a living man.

—No, he hadn't heard the shot—there was all that infernal commotion out in the Square.

—No, he had no idea how *he* had got there—walked it, he supposed—the City Hall was only twenty yards away.

—No, he couldn't say why His Honor should have picked that spot to blow his brains out—there was no accounting for tastes—but if a man wanted to do it, that was probably as good a place as any.

So it was that weak, easy-going, procrastinating, good-natured Baxter Kennedy, Mayor of Libya Hill, was found—all that was left of him—in darkness, by an evil old blind man.

In the days and weeks that followed the closing of the bank, Libya Hill presented a tragic spectacle the like of which had probably never before been seen in America. But it was a spectacle that was to be repeated over and over again, with local variations, in many another town and city within the next few years.

The ruin of Libya Hill was much more than the ruin of the bank and the breakdown of the economic and financial order. True, when the bank failed, all that vast and complicated scheme of things which had been built upon it, the ramifications of which extended into every element of the community's life, toppled and crashed. But the closing of the bank was only like the action of a rip cord which, once jerked, brought the whole thing down, and in doing so laid bare the deeper and more corrosive ruin within. And this deeper ruin —the essence of the catastrophe—was the ruin of the human conscience.

Here was a town of fifty thousand people who had so abdicated every principle of personal and communal rectitude, to say nothing of common sense and decency, that when the blow fell they had no inner resources with which to meet it. The town almost literally blew its brains out. Forty people shot themselves within ten days, and others did so later. And, as so often happens, many of those who destroyed themselves were among the least guilty of the lot. The rest—and this was the most shocking part of it—suddenly realizing their devastating guilt to such a degree that they could not face the results of it, now turned like a pack of howling dogs to rend each other. Cries of vengeance rose up from all their throats, and they howled for the blood of Jarvis Riggs. But these cries proceeded not so much from a conviction of wounded justice and deceived innocence as from their opposites. It was the sublime, ironic, and irrevocable justice of what had happened to them and their knowledge that they alone had been responsible for it, that maddened them. From this arose their sense of outrage and their cries of vengeance.

What happened in Libya Hill and elsewhere has been described in the learned tomes of the overnight economists as a breakdown of "the system, the capitalist system." Yes, it was that. But it was also much more than that. In Libya Hill it was the total disintegration of what, in so many different ways, the lives of all these people had come to be. It went much deeper than the mere obliteration of bank accounts, the extinction of paper profits, and the loss of property. It was the ruin of men who found out, as soon as these symbols of their outward success had been destroyed, that they had nothing left—no inner equivalent from which they might now draw new strength. It was the ruin of men who, discovering not only that their values were false but that they had never had any substance whatsoever, now saw at last the emptiness and hollowness of their lives. Therefore they killed themselves; and those who did not die by their own hands died by the knowledge that they were already dead. . . .

Below the starred immensity of mountain night old Rumford Bland, he that is called "The Judge," strokes his sunken jaws reflectively as he stands at the darkened window of his front office and looks out with sightless eyes upon the ruined town. It is cool and sweet tonight, the myriad promises of life are lyric in the air. Gem-strewn in viewless linkage on the hills the lights make a bracelet for the town. The blind man knows that they are there, although he cannot see them. He strokes his sunken jaws reflectively and smiles his ghostly smile.

It is so cool and sweet tonight, and spring has come. There never was a year like this, they say, for dogwood in the hills. There are so many thrilling, secret things upon the air tonight—a burst of laughter, and young voices, faint, half-broken, and the music of a dance—how could one know that when the blind man smiles and strokes his sunken jaws reflectively, he is looking out upon a ruined town?

The new Court House and City Hall are very splendid in the dark tonight. But he has never seen them—they were built since he went blind. Their fronts are bathed, so people say, in steady, secret light just like the nation's dome at Washington. The blind man strokes his sunken jaws reflectively. Well, they *should* be splendid—they cost enough.

Beneath the starred immensity of mountain night there is something stirring in the air, a rustling of young leaves. And around the grass roots there is something stirring in the earth tonight. And below the grass roots and the sod, below the dew-wet pollen of young flowers, there is something alive and stirring. The blind man strokes his sunken jaws reflectively. Aye, there below, where the eternal worm keeps vigil, there is something stirring in the earth. Down, down below, where the worm incessant through the ruined house makes stir.

What lies there stir-less in the earth tonight, down where the worm keeps vigil?

The blind man smiles his ghostly smile. In his eternal vigil the worm stirs, but many men are rotting in their graves tonight, and sixty-four have bullet fractures in their skulls. Ten thousand more are lying in their beds tonight, living as shells live. They, too, are dead, though yet unburied. They have been dead so long they can't remember how it was to live. And many weary nights must pass before they can join the buried dead, down where the worm keeps vigil.

Meanwhile, the everlasting worm keeps vigil, and the blind man strokes his sunken jaws, and slowly now he shifts his sightless gaze and turns his back upon the ruined town.

Ten days after the failure of the bank in Libya Hill, Randy Shepperton arrived in New York. He had made up his mind suddenly, without letting George know, and the motives that brought him were mixed. For one thing, he wanted to talk to George and see if he couldn't help to get him straightened out. His letters had been so desperate that Randy was beginning to be worried about him. Then, too, Randy felt he just had to get away from Libya Hill for a few days and out of that atmosphere of doom and ruin and death. And he was free now, there was nothing to keep him from coming, so he came. . . .

George was full of his own problems and talked about them constantly. Randy was an understanding listener. But suddenly one day, toward the end of Randy's visit, the thought struck George as strange that his friend should be taking so much time off from his job. He asked Randy about it. How had he managed it?

"I haven't got a job," Randy answered quietly with his little embarrassed laugh. "They threw me out."

"You mean to say that that bastard Merrit—" George began, hot with instant anger.

"Oh, don't blame him," Randy broke in. "He couldn't help it. The higher-ups were on his tail and he had to do it. He said I wasn't getting the business, and it's true—I wasn't. But what the Company doesn't know is that nobody can get the business any more. It isn't there, and hasn't been for the last year or so. You saw how it was when you were home. Every penny anybody could get hold of went into real estate speculation. That was the only business they had left down there. And now, of course, that's gone, too, since the bank failed."

"And do you mean to say," George commented, speaking the words slowly and with emphasis—"do you mean to say that Merrit seized that moment to throw you out on your ear? Why, the dirty—"

"Yes," said Randy. "I got the sack just a week after the bank closed. I don't know whether Merrit figured that was the best time to get rid of me or whether it just happened so. But what's the difference? It's been coming for a long time. I've seen it coming for a year or more. It was just a question of when. And believe me," he said with quiet emphasis, "I've been through hell. I lived from day to day in fear and dread of it, knowing it was coming and knowing there wasn't anything I could do to head it off. But the funny thing is, now it's happened I feel relieved." He smiled his old clear smile. "It's the truth," he said. "I never would have had the guts to quit—I was making pretty good money, you know—but now that I'm out, I'm glad. I'd forgotten how it felt to be a free man. Now I can hold my head up and look anybody in the eye and tell the Great Man, Paul S. Appleton himself, to go to the devil. It's a good feeling. I like it."

"But what are you going to do, Randy?" asked George with evident concern.

"I don't know," said Randy cheerfully. "I haven't any plans. All the years I was with the Company I lived pretty well, but I also managed to save a little something. And, luckily, I didn't put it in the Citizens Trust, or in real estate either, so I've still got it. And I own the old family house. Margaret and I can get along all right for a while. Of course jobs that pay as well as the one I had don't turn up around every corner, but this is a big country and there's always a place for a good man. Did you ever hear of a good man who couldn't find work?" he said.

"Well, you can't be too sure of that," said George, shaking his head dubiously. "Maybe I'm wrong," he went on, pausing and frowning thoughtfully, "but I don't think the Stock Market crash and the bank failure in Libya Hill were isolated events. I'm coming to feel," he said, "that we may be up against something new—something that's going to cut deeper than anything America has experienced before. The papers are beginning to take it seriously. They're calling it a depression. Everybody seems to be scared."

"Oh, pshaw!" Randy said with a laugh. "You *are* feeling low. That's because you live in New York. Here the Stock Market is everything. When it's high, times are good; when it's low, they're bad. But New York is not America."

"I know," said George. "But I'm not thinking about the Stock Market. I'm thinking about America. . . . Sometimes it seems to me," he continued slowly, like a man who gropes his way in darkness over an unfamiliar road, "that America went off the track somewhere—back around the time of the Civil War, or pretty soon afterwards. Instead of going ahead and developing along the line in which the country started out, it got shunted off in another direction—and now we look around and see we've gone places we didn't mean to go. Suddenly we realize that America has turned into something ugly—and vicious—and corroded at the heart of its power with easy wealth and graft and special privilege. . . . And the worst of it is the intellectual dishonesty which all this corruption has bred. People are *afraid* to think straight —*afraid* to face themselves—*afraid* to look at things and see them as they are. We've become like a nation of advertising men, all hiding behind catch phrases like 'prosperity' and 'rugged individualism' and 'the American way.' And the real things like freedom, and equal opportunity, and the integrity and worth of the individual—things that have belonged to the American dream since the beginning—they have become just words, too. The substance has gone out of them—they're not real any more. . . . Take your own case. You say you feel free at last because you've lost your job. I don't doubt it—but it's a funny kind of freedom. And just how free *are* you?"

"Well, free enough to suit me," said Randy heartily. "And, funny or not, I'm freer than I've ever been before. Free enough to take my time and look around a bit before I make a new connection. I don't want to get in with another outfit like the old one. I'll land on my feet," he said serenely.

"But how are you going to do it?" asked George. "There can't be anything for you in Libya Hill, with the bottom dropped out of everything down there."

"Hell, I'm not wedded to the place!" said Randy. "I'll go anywhere. Remember, I've been a salesman all my life— I'm used to traveling around. And I have friends in the game—in other lines—who'll help me. That's one good thing about being a salesman: if you can sell one thing, you can sell anything, and it's easy to switch products. I know my way around," he concluded with strong confidence. "Don't you worry about me."

They said very little more about it. And when Randy left, his parting words at the station were:

"Well, so long, fellow! *You're* going to be all right. But don't forget to kill that wounded faun! As for me, I don't know just what the next move is, but I'm on my way!"

With that he got aboard his train, and was gone.

But George wasn't too sure about Randy. And the more he thought about him, the less sure he became. Randy had certainly not been licked by what had happened to him, and that was good; but there was something about his attitude—his cheerful optimism in the face of disaster—that seemed spurious. He had the clearest head of anybody George knew, but it was almost as if he had shut off one compartment of his brain and wasn't using it. It was all very puzzling.

"There are tides in the affairs of men," George thought musingly—"definite periods of ebb and flow. . . . And when they come, they come, and can't be held back by wishing."

That was it, perhaps. It seemed to George that Randy was caught in the ebb and didn't know it. And that was what made it so queer and puzzling—that *he,* of all people, shouldn't know it.

Also, he had spoken about not wanting to get mixed up with another outfit like the old one. Did he think the fearful pressures he had been subject to were peculiar to the company he had been working for, and that their counterparts existed nowhere else? Did he suppose he could escape those conditions just by changing jobs? Did he believe it was possible by such a shift to enjoy all the glorious advantages he had ever dreamed of as a bright, ambitious youth—high income and good living far beyond what most men are accustomed to—and to do it without paying the cost in other ways?

"What will you have? quoth God; pay for it, and take it," said Emerson, in that wonderful essay on "Compensation" that every American ought to be required by law to read . . . Well, that was true. One always paid for it . . .

Good Lord! Didn't Randy know you can't go home again?

The next few years were terrible ones for all America, and especially terrible for Randy Shepperton.

He didn't get another job. He tried everything, but nothing worked. There just weren't any jobs. Men were being let off by the thousands everywhere, and nowhere were new ones being taken on.

After eighteen months his savings were gone, and he was desperate. He had to sell the old family house, and what he got for it was a mere pittance. He and Margaret rented a small apartment, and for another year or so, by careful management, they lived on what the house had brought them. Then that, too, was gone. Randy was on his uppers now. He fell ill, and it was an illness of the spirit more than of the flesh. At last, when there was nothing else to do, he and Margaret moved away from Libya Hill and went to live with the older sister who was married, and stayed there with her husband's family—dependents on the bounty of these kindly strangers.

And at the end of all of this, Randy—he of the clear eyes and the quick intelligence—he who was nobody's fool—he who thought he loved the truth and had always been able to see straight to the heart of most things—Randy went on relief.

And by that time George thought he understood it. Behind Randy's tragedy

George thought he could see a personal devil in the form of a very bright and plausible young man, oozing confidence and crying, "Faith!" when there was no faith, and dressed like a traveling salesman. Yes, salesmanship had done its job too well. Salesmanship—that commercial brand of special pleading—that devoted servant of self-interest—that sworn enemy of truth. George remembered how Randy had been able to look at *his* alien problem and see it in the abstract, whole and clear, because there was no self-interest to cast its shadow on his vision. He could save others—himself he could not save, because he could no longer see the truth about himself.

And it seemed to George that Randy's tragedy was the essential tragedy of America. America—the magnificent, unrivaled, unequaled, unbeatable, unshrinkable, supercolossal, 99-and-44-one-hundredths-per-cent-pure, schoolgirl-complexion, covers-the-earth, I'd-walk-a-mile-for-it, four-out-of-five-have-it, his-master's-voice, ask-the-man-who-owns-one, blueplate-special home of advertising, salesmanship, and special pleading in all its many catchy and beguiling forms.

Had not the real rulers of America—the business men—been wrong about the depression from the start? Had they not pooh-poohed it and tried to wipe it out with words, refusing to see it for what it was? Had they not kept saying that prosperity was just around the corner—long after "prosperity," so called, had vanished, and the very corner it was supposed to be around had flattened out and bent into a precipitate downward curve of hunger, want, and desperation? . . .

It was a process of discovery in its most naked, literal, and primitive terms. He was just beginning really to see thousands of things for the first time, to see the relations between them, to see here and there whole series and systems of relations. He was like a scientist in some new field of chemistry who for the first time realizes that he has stumbled upon a vast new world, and who will then pick out identities, establish affiliations, define here and there the outlines of sub-systems in crystalline union, without yet being aware what the structure of the whole is like, or what the final end will be.

The same processes now began to inform his direct observation of the life around him. Thus, on his nocturnal ramblings about New York, he would observe the homeless men who prowled in the vicinity of restaurants, lifting the lids of garbage cans and searching around inside for morsels of rotten food. He saw them everywhere, and noticed how their numbers increased during the hard and desperate days of 1932. He knew what kind of men they were, for he talked to many of them; he knew what they had been, where they had come from, and even what kind of scraps they could expect to dig out of the garbage cans. He found out the various places all over the city where such men slept at night. A favorite rendezvous was a corridor of the subway station at Thirty-third Street and Park Avenue in Manhattan. There one night he counted thirty-four huddled together on the cold concrete, wrapped up in sheathings of old newspaper.

It was his custom almost every night, at one o'clock or later, to walk across the Brooklyn Bridge, and night after night, with a horrible fascination, he used to go to the public latrine or "comfort station" which was directly in front of the New York City Hall. One descended to this place down a steep flight of stairs from the street, and on bitter nights he would find the place crowded with homeless men who had sought refuge there. Some were those shambling hulks that one sees everywhere, in Paris as well as New York, in good times as well as bad—old men, all rags and bags and long white hair and bushy beards stained dirty yellow, wearing tattered overcoats in the cavernous pockets of which they carefully stored away all the little rubbish they lived on and spent their days collecting in the streets—crusts of bread, old bones with rancid shreds of meat still clinging to them, and dozens of cigarette butts. Some were the "stumble bums" from the Bowery, criminal, fumed with drink or drugs, or half insane with "smoke." But most of them were just flotsam of the general ruin of the time—honest, decent, middle-aged men with faces seamed by toil and want, and young men, many of them mere boys in their teens, with thick, unkempt hair. These were the wanderers from town to town, the riders of freight trains, the thumbers of rides on highways, the uprooted, unwanted male population of America. They drifted across the land and gathered in the big cities when winter came, hungry, defeated, empty, hopeless, restless, driven by they knew not what, always on the move, looking everywhere for work, for the bare crumbs to support their miserable lives, and finding neither work nor crumbs. Here in New York, to this obscene meeting place, these derelicts came, drawn into a common stew of rest and warmth and a little surcease from their desperation.

George had never before witnessed anything to equal the indignity and sheer animal horror of the scene. There was even a kind of devil's comedy in the sight of all these filthy men squatting upon those open, doorless stools. Arguments and savage disputes and fights would sometimes break out among them over the possession of these stools, which all of them wanted more for rest than for necessity. The sight was revolting, disgusting, enough to render a man forever speechless with very pity.

He would talk to the men and find out all he could about them, and when he could stand it no more he would come out of this hole of filth and suffering, and there, twenty feet above it, he would see the giant hackles of Manhattan shining coldly in the cruel brightness of the winter night. The Woolworth Building was not fifty yards away, and a little farther down were the silvery spires and needles of Wall Street, great fortresses of stone and steel that housed enormous banks. The blind injustice of this contrast seemed the most brutal part of the whole experience, for there, all around him in the cold moonlight, only a few blocks away from this abyss of human wretchedness and misery, blazed the pinnacles of power where a large portion of the entire world's wealth was locked in mighty vaults. . . .

K. WILLIAM KAPP

TO an economist a cost always entails an alternative. For example, if it is decided to produce a pair of shoes, then resources must be employed which might have produced other articles. Those other articles given up to produce the shoes are said to constitute the cost of the shoes. But when "harm to third persons or the community as a result of the productive process" is defined as *social* costs, then a different judgment is involved. All may agree that air pollution, city traffic, or industrial accidents are harmful consequences of some new private undertaking, but these become costs in the economic sense just indicated only if we say what the alternative to this use of resources might have been. To list the incidence of accidents, air pollution, or even technological unemployment as *social* costs is not to prove that a venture should be banned to avoid such undesired concomitants, just as a reminder that work is required to produce shoes does not itself mean that the effort is not worth making.

Many of the phenomena studied by Professor Kapp in *The Social Costs of Private Enterprise* (1950), from which the following selection has been taken, *are* costs in the sense that they represent alternative opportunities foregone. Damage from smoke of industrial plants is such a cost. For the public might be willing to pay (give up resources in taxes or higher prices) what it would cost for the nuisance to be eliminated by some expenditure for technological improvement. But interesting questions arise in an effort to relate the existence of such costs to a judgment about private enterprise. Would a social-planning board necessarily choose to avoid such costs? Would a state commission be as likely to act to abate a nuisance created by its own enterprise as to restrict entrepreneurs in a separate and private sector of the community? And, if attention to such real costs is persistently frustrated by the market mechanism, might not traditional devices be utilized to reconcile the conflict between public and private interest? The most sanguine exponents of the free enterprise system have accepted the need for an appropriate institutional setting within which the private market must operate—state provision for defense, education, and public health, for sanctity of contracts and a reliable exchange medium, for punishment of fraud and dissolution of monopoly, even for monetary and fiscal programs to insure price and employment stability.

Clearly, however, some items on Professor Kapp's list *are not* costs in the narrowly economic sense. Obsolescence of a skill or of capital equipment, the wasteful utilization of a resource because of ignorance or shortsightedness, or the hurt of an accident caused by personal carelessness are experiences all might agree are regrettable, while accepting them as the price of any enterprise, public or private. If Kapp's extensive survey of such "costs" of private enterprise urges us to judgment of its market institutions, it is in part because of the importance he attaches to social evaluation and social preferences as distinguished from individual evaluations and preferences. He acknowledges that assessment of an unplanned system requires a parallel inquiry into the social *returns* of private enterprise. It may be added that a final choice between planned and unplanned economic systems would also call for consideration of the "private costs—and private returns—of public enterprise."

Karl William Kapp was born in Germany in 1910. He received a degree of *docteur à science* from the University of Geneva in 1936 on the basis of his dissertation *Planwirtschaft und Aussenhandel* (1936). Coming to the United States, he taught in Columbia College as an instructor and then at Wesleyan University as an assistant professor of economics. He is currently professor of economics at Brooklyn College. He has also written *The League of Nations and Raw Materials* (1941) and, with his wife, Lore L. Kapp, *A Graphic Approach to Economics* (1951).

THE SOCIAL COSTS OF PRIVATE ENTERPRISE

Introduction: Ever since the human mind conceived the idea that production and distribution are fundamentally self-regulating processes capable of achieving the optimum solution of the economic problem without positive direction by public authority, individual economists as well as entire schools of doctrine have questioned the general validity of such an optimistic interpretation. In dissenting from the tenets of the classical school the critics made extensive references to what can be considered as social costs in the broad sense in which the term will be used here. Indeed, confronted with the mass of factual evidence unearthed by the critics, one wonders why the older optimistic preconceptions of a natural regularity and orderliness of the competitive process were not abandoned long ago and replaced by premises postulating instead basic tendencies toward disorder and waste which could have served as a basis either for a far-reaching critique of the existing order or for a new system of theoretical conclusions in favor of economic planning.

There seem to be three reasons why the critics did not carry their discussion to this conclusion. First, most critics shared the basic pre-suppositions of their time, which made them unable to reject the rationalistic and optimistic notion of a "natural" order in social and economic affairs. Second, old preconceptions die slowly, especially if they reflect deep-seated political creeds

---

This selection has been reprinted by permission of the publishers from Karl William Kapp, *The Social Costs of Private Enterprise,* Cambridge, Mass.: Harvard University Press, Copyright 1950, by The President and Fellows of Harvard College (pp. 26–27, 4–6, 8–9, 10–12, 13–15, 16–17, 20–22, 24, 47–50, 65–69, 127–130, 131–139, 163–168, 228–231). Rearrangement of material is with permission of the author.

and ideologies. And third, it is much easier to build a system of theoretical generalizations upon the notion of natural law and rational economic conduct than it is to build a system of liberal economic thought upon the conception of a tendency toward disorder and waste in economic affairs. It is thus not surprising that the factual evidence unearthed by the critics in contradiction to the basic presuppositions of classical and neo-classical economic thought has as yet not led to the elaboration of a new and equally systematic body of doctrine. . . .

Social Costs and Economic Science: It is not difficult to show that the classical approach to the study of economic life has had far-reaching consequences for the subsequent development of economic science. In the first place, economics has been preoccupied, from the very beginning, with a search for an assumed orderliness in economic life or, as J. M. Clark puts it, with "a search for levels of equilibrium." Second, it was inevitable that economists, in their search for natural orderliness in economic life, began to see both reality as a whole and specific phenomena in a light which tended to confirm their philosophical preconceptions. Indeed, "the details of economic life [were] construed for purposes of general theory, in terms of their subservience to the aims imputed to the collective life process." Basic concepts such as wealth, production, utility, costs, returns, etc., were formulated in such a manner as to make them integral parts of the general scheme of thinking. In addition, economists concentrated their attention on those phenomena which could be shown to serve the purpose which they imputed to the economic process. In fact, "those features of detail which will bear construction as links in the process whereby the collective welfare is furthered, are magnified and brought into the foreground." In contrast, other phenomena which could not be shown to be integral parts of the system of natural liberty because they upset rather than furthered its assumed orderliness were presented as untypical exceptions or minor disturbances. In other words, the philosophical presuppositions of classical economics determined the selection of the phenomena to be studied by economic science, the scope of which was thus more and more adapted to its original (normative) aim of demonstrating both the existence and the superiority of the system of natural liberty over alternative forms of economic organization.

Furthermore, under the influence of the rationalistic presuppositions of the eighteenth century, theoretical economic analysis, especially value theory, confined itself more and more to the study of market phenomena. In fact, political economy became "economics," which was said to be concerned only with those ends (and means) whose importance could be measured in terms of exchange values. That is to say, those ends and means which could not be expressed in terms of market prices came to be regarded as "noneconomic" and as such outside the proper scope of economic analysis. Thus, only rational behavior was said to be relevant for purposes of economic analysis. In other words, nonrational behavior was assumed to be either nonexistent or at least of no importance in connection with the analysis of the conditions of equilibrium in an essentially stationary economy which required study only at a given point of time (instead of a dynamic, irregularly expanding economy which would call for analysis of the processes of adjustment extending over different points of time). Merely another aspect of this procedure which tended to eliminate the dynamic and less congenial factors of reality from economic analysis is the theoretical economist's preoccupation with money costs and returns and his tacit assumption that entrepreneurial outlays and private returns constitute a theoretically adequate measure of the costs and benefits of productive activities.

The dominant neoclassical system of thought is no exception in this respect. On the contrary, it has continued and completed the demonstration that the natural law operates for the good of mankind in the economic life of nations and the world; its subjectivism permitted the most systematic application of rationalistic conceptions of human behavior to economic analysis and prepared the way for a new classicism designed to demonstrate, on the basis of the mechanics of private interests, that social justice is possible without socialism. More specifically, the new classicism, which views the market situation as the outcome of forces set into motion by the action of rational individuals, was dominated from the very outset by the desire to demonstrate that "free competition procures the maximum of utility," and that under static conditions labor receives what it produces. . . .

In any event, as far as the basic philosophy of neoclassical theory is concerned there is as yet little evidence that social costs (and social returns) have found the full recognition which they deserve. The implicit identification of entrepreneurial costs and returns with total costs and total benefits has continued to govern the methodological approaches of one generation of economists after another. Perhaps this is inevitable. After all, most economic theory reflects the historically given social conditions and patterns of behavior at any given time; it endeavors to give more or less systematic expression to a particular way of solving the economic problems of the time. In this sense economic theory merely "describes" what is happening in the economy. Neither social costs nor social returns enter into the cost-price calculations of the private firm unless special provisions to this effect are made by law and by the systematic application of the principles of social insurance, as in the case of workmen's compensation acts. Fundamentally, therefore, the treatment of social costs as a minor and exceptional disturbance rather than as a characteristic phenomenon of the market economy reflects merely the very imperfect way in which these costs are taken into consideration in the present system of economic calculation of costs and returns. . . .

In the light of this brief survey of the evolution of classical economic analysis, the phenomenon of social costs assumes a much broader significance than that of a specific technical question related to private cost accounting. Indeed, a detailed analysis of social costs opens the way for the demonstration that the social performance of the free market economy would still fall short of the economic optimum even if it should be possible to achieve an approximation to perfect competition and to counteract the cumulative and self-sustaining tendencies toward general disequilibrium in modern capitalism which have preoccupied economists in recent years. For the fact that private entrepreneurs are able to shift part of the total costs of production to other persons, or to the community as a whole, points to one of the most important limitations of the present scope of neoclassical value theory, which, because it is confined to exchange value, has so far been incapable of assimilating to its reasoning and to its conceptual system many of the costs (and returns) which cannot easily be expressed in dollars and cents.

However, the demonstration that private enterprise tends to shift part of the costs of production to third persons and to the community as a whole constitutes only one of the reasons why the original presumption against governmental regulation and the bias against planning which still pervades much of neoclassical value theory must be abandoned. There are two further reasons why, in our estimation, the unplanned market economy fails to achieve the maximization of the want-satisfying power of scarce resources: (1) obstacles to rational behavior of consumers and entrepreneurs as well as outright nonrational behavior patterns in modern industrial society; (2) the existence of social returns which diffuse themselves throughout society and, since they cannot be sold in markets and cannot be appraised in terms of dollars and cents, are largely neglected by private enterprise. The first of these factors has been analyzed by the author in some detail. The much more important analysis of social returns and the related subjects of public investments which likewise seem to break out of the framework of traditional neoclassical economic analysis has to be reserved to a separate study. The present work must thus be understood as part of a larger inquiry, the purpose of which is twofold: to measure the performance of the economy by yardsticks which transcend those of the market, and to prepare the ground for a broadening of the scope of economic analysis so as to include those omitted aspects of reality which many economists have been inclined to dismiss or neglect as "noneconomic." Such a new science of economics will have to be based upon the recognition that we are able to obtain a valid picture of a situation and a real understanding of reality only if we view them as a whole, i.e., in their totality. Only by overcoming the present departmentalization of our knowledge in the social sciences or, more specifically, by accepting the fact that the "economic" and the "noneconomic" are intrinsically interrelated and must be studied together, will we be able to lay the foundation for a new science of economics which will be "political economy" in an even more comprehensive sense than the term was ever understood by the classical economists and their predecessors. . . .

The Nature and Significance of Social Costs: The term social costs refers to a wide variety of cost elements. In fact, for the purposes of our investigation the term covers all direct and indirect losses suffered by third persons or the general public as a result of private economic activities. These social losses may be reflected in damages to human health; they may find their expression in the destruction or deterioration of property values and the premature depletion of natural wealth; they may also be evidenced in an impairment of less tangible values. As an instrument of analysis the concept carries no quantitative connotation; it will serve its purpose if it helps to trace and to reveal a substantial proportion of the social losses of production for which neither law nor custom has as yet established an adequate responsibility of the individual producer.

Social losses may arise in different ways. Some clearly have their origin in individual industries and can be traced to particular productive processes and business practices. Other social costs arise in the operation of the competitive system within a given framework of generally accepted institutions and government policies. This institutional origin of some social costs raises a number of interesting and important issues. . . .

In some cases, the social costs of production are felt immediately; in other instances the ill effects of private production remain hidden for considerable periods of time, so that the injured persons do not become immediately aware of their losses. Furthermore, certain social losses affect only a limited group, whereas others may be felt by all members of society. Indeed, the actual damages caused by private productive activities may be distributed over so many persons that any one of them may individually sustain only a relatively small loss. Although aware of his losses, the individual may not consider it worthwhile to take defensive action against the particular industrial concern responsible for his losses. In short, the term social costs refers to all those harmful consequences and damages which third persons or the community sustain as a result of the productive process, and for which private entrepreneurs are not easily held accountable.

This concept of social costs is comprehensive enough to include even certain "social opportunity costs," that is, those social cost elements which take the form of wastes or inefficiencies of various kinds. As will be seen later, the elimination of these wastes and inefficiencies represents an opportunity for genuine economies; it is doubtful whether a private-enterprise economy can avail itself of these economies without a radical change in its basic structure.

It would be easy to show that an increasing proportion of public policy in a liberal democratic state is devoted to the prevention and repair of various social losses caused by private producers. In the absence of these preventive measures private business would continue to shift part of the costs of production to society. Fundamentally, the adoption of such preventive measures and the need for remedial action may be considered as the most convincing evidence for the occurrence of social costs in the competitive market economy. However, as far as economic theory is concerned, this recognition of the phenomenon of social costs has been confined mostly to A. C. Pigou's welfare economics and several critics of formal equilibrium theory. As pointed out before, the main body of neoclassical value theory has continued to regard such losses as accidental and exceptional cases or as minor disturbances. At best, social losses are considered as "external" costs falling outside the scope of economics proper.

To dismiss the entire problem of social costs in this manner is, however, to beg the question. For whether or not these costs are "external" in character and fall outside the scope of economics can be decided only after their general nature, their significance, and their probable magnitude have been thoroughly explored. Similarly, to dismiss the problem of social costs on the grounds that measures are constantly being taken not only by governments but also by private organizations with a view to minimizing or remedying their negative effects, is to miss the most important issue, namely, the question of the extent to which such interference with the economic process is justified and economically worthwhile. This question, too, can be answered only after an attempt has been made to apprehend the nature and possible magnitude of the social costs of production. In any event, the existence of preventive regulations and private restrictions in some spheres of economic life has as yet not led to the elimination of social costs. Indeed, in many instances closer analysis of existing legislation reveals that present measures and private restraints do not prevent the occurrence of social losses and that there are still many cases of social costs which have found either no or only inadequate recognition. . . .

The above thesis may be extended to include the proposition that the growing recognition given in recent years to the phenomenon of social costs reflects merely a shift in the balance of power from those groups in society responsible for initiating economic change to those who bore the brunt of the social losses in the past and who now are using their growing political and economic power in an effort to protect themselves against the undesirable consequences of progress. This broader thesis raises a number of issues which are of the greatest significance. The political history of the last 150 years can be fully understood only as a revolt of large masses of people (including business) against the shifting of part of the social costs of production to third persons or to society. And it is also obvious that the steady increase of protective social legislation, the enforcement of minimum standards of health and efficiency, the prohibition of destructive practices in many fields of production, or even the efforts of farmers, business men, and labor to peg the prices of their products by means of oligopolistic restraints of trade, reflect at least in part a gradual shift of the balance of power away from those producers and innovators who were formerly able to transfer part of the costs of production to the community. Viewed in this fashion, however, the struggle for a more equal distribution of social costs or their prevention and the shift in the balance of power are nothing but an integral part of the general expansion of democracy which has marked the history of the last 150 years.

Of course, this is not to say that the means used as protective measures against the shifting of some of the costs of rapid economic change have always halted at the point of social optimum (whatever definition we care to give to this important concept). Pressure groups and vested interests have doubtless been able to distort and abuse the legitimate struggle for a more equal distribution of social costs to the detriment of society. Most certainly not every oligopolistic restraint of trade can be interpreted merely as a measure designed to remedy the wastes of unregulated competition. In many instances these restraints are techniques of plundering the consumer and as such must themselves be regarded as the sources of important social costs. And yet, after everything has been said about the misuse of power by vested interests, the fact remains that, on the whole, the increased emphasis on the elimination of and protection against social losses and the shift in the balance of power referred to above are direct results of an expansion of democracy in the sense of popular control over economic institutions and policy. . . .

There are, however, some philosophical considerations which make the study of social costs a matter of concern for the social scientist. It is these considerations which, more than any other single factor, have motivated the present investigation. An economic system which shifts part of the costs of production to third persons, and a body of doctrine which disregards these social costs, are in opposition to one of the most fundamental tenets of our professed humanistic ideals: respect for the human personality. Instead of being treated in his own right the individual becomes a mere instrument in the interest of long-run progress or whatever other "cause" if we fail to consider the human costs of production. This neglect of the individual needs to be remedied not only at the level of social legislation but also at that of economic theory, and it is within this broader context that the analysis and elimination of social costs offers a challenge to the economist.

Turning now to the practical problem of elimination or repairing social losses caused by private production, or to the reduction of social costs to a minimum by making private producers as fully accountable for them as possible, it will not suffice to indicate merely the general nature of the harmful consequences and possible damages which third persons or the public in general might suffer as a result of productive activities; what is required for these purposes of policy making is some kind of quantitative measurement of the social costs of production. As a first step toward such a quantitative determination of the possible magnitude of the social costs of production, the general discussion of specific cases of social losses in the subsequent . . . [sections] is followed, as far as possible, by brief summaries of factual evidence of social losses and short résumés of available estimates of their relative magnitude expressed in monetary terms. These estimates are based largely on data published by various private and public agencies during the last 30 years. If some of the estimates appear to be out of date, for example in comparison with current series of prices and production, it is well to remember that data on social costs are found only occasionally in publications dealing with particular phases of industrial production; they are neither gathered nor kept up to date as systematically as are other statistical series. . . .

The ultimate authority and responsibility for these quantitative estimates rests, moreover, with the original authors and sources from which they are quoted. If the available figures seem to indicate that the social costs of production are substantial, it is important to emphasize again that they represent, at best, only an incomplete picture of such costs inasmuch as so far no systematic study of social costs has been made with a view to ascertaining their full magnitude for any particular industry. Moreover, even if the available monetary estimates of social losses were complete, they would still have to be considered as fragmentary, because some of the social losses are intangible in character and have to be evaluated in other than monetary terms.

In the light of these considerations it becomes evident that the final determination of the magnitude of social costs of production is ultimately a matter of social evaluation; i.e. the magnitude of the social costs depends upon the importance which organized society attributes to both the tangible and the intangible values involved. Such social evaluations do not, however, pose an entirely *new* problem. For the formulation of public policy nearly always requires a general evaluation of "means" and "ends" whose relative importance can only be estimated, since a substantial proportion of all "costs" and "returns" of economic policies are "political" and intangible in character. Of course, this is not to say that the problem of policy formulation on the basis of general estimates of possible costs and returns has been fully explored and offers no further theoretical difficulties. Quite on the contrary, the issues raised by the concept of "social value" and "social evaluation" belong to the most important unsolved problems of economic science. . . .

We wish to make it clear that in tracing the social costs of private enterprise we are not implying that regulation and economic planning would necessarily eliminate these costs. Nor are we comparing unregulated private enterprise with a system of economic planning. Whether or not a system of economic planning would avoid the social costs of production depends upon whether the planners wish to avoid or neglect them. In the last analysis this is probably a matter of the political structure of the planned economy; that is to say, whether or not the social costs of production will be avoided under alternative forms of organization depends upon whether or not the content of the economic plan as an essentially political act of decision making is subject to review at the polls. . . .

The Social Costs Resulting from the Impairment of the Human Factor of Production: Perhaps the most generally recognized case of social costs of competition is the impairment of the physical and mental health of laborers in the course of the productive process. These so-called human costs of production have found widespread recognition in various kinds of protective labor legislation and social insurance, so that their inclusion in a study on social costs calls for special explanation. It might be argued, for example, that existing protective labor legislation tends either to prevent the occurrence of social losses or to translate these losses if they do occur into entrepreneurial outlays. Such reasoning neglects, however, a number of things. In the first place, it is a mistake to assume that the enactment of preventive social legislation is a guarantee of its effectiveness in the prevention of social losses. As a matter of fact, the present system of social and labor legislation represents, at best, only a first step toward the elimination of the phenomenon of social costs. There are numerous instances in which the impairment of the human factor continues to be borne by the injured worker and remains either partly or entirely unaccounted for in entrepreneurial outlays.

Moreover, the present study is concerned with the general thesis that the entrepreneurial outlays do not measure the actual total costs of production; . . . this thesis is not invalidated but rather confirmed by the existence of and need for protective legislation designed to prevent or minimize specific social losses caused by private production. Finally, even if the present system of protective labor legislation were successful in translating all human costs of production into entrepreneurial outlays, the impairment of the human factor would still offer the best starting point for our discussion because it represents a particularly simple and typical case of social costs. . . .

In its economic implications, the impairment of the health and efficiency of human beings in the course of the productive process does not differ from the gradual deterioration of durable agents of production. In both cases a progressive reduction or even complete destruction of the economic usefulness of valuable factors of production is taking place. And yet, in the absence of a comprehensive system of social insurance, the market economy, operating as it does within a given framework of contractual obligations, tends to deal with these two cases of deterioration of valuable factors of production in an entirely different manner. Indeed, no owner of durable factors of production would be willing to make use of such agents, if some provision were not made to compensate him for the deterioration of his asset. Such provision is usually achieved by depreciation charges designed to furnish the funds required for the replacement of any given fixed agent of production or, in the terminology of accounting, "to maintain intact the value of the original capital investment." In any event, by furnishing a convenient and more or less satisfactory method of accounting for that part of the costs of production which results from the use of durable agents of production, depreciation charges enable the individual producer to see to it that his total monetary outlays do not exceed the returns obtainable from the goods and services produced.

In sharp contrast with this treatment of durable agents of production is the manner in which the competitive process deals with the impairment of the human factor. This difference is largely due to the fact that laborers, as human beings, are not subject to private ownership rights. They are free persons whose services may be hired but who have to provide for their own livelihood. If these free laborers are affected adversely by the productive process, there is nobody—except perhaps the laborer himself—who has any interest in seeing to it that an adequate "depreciation charge" is made for the impairment of his physical and mental health. In fact, the entrepreneur, in his desire to reduce costs of production as far as possible, will generally be reluctant to consider the impairment of the physical and mental capacities of his laborers as part of the costs of his enterprise. His unwillingness to do so will be the greater the easier he finds it to replace "worn-out" workers by new laborers. On the other hand, the laborer, because of his relatively weaker bargaining position, will find it difficult to have his claim to special financial compensation in case of hazardous occupations recognized by the entrepreneur, particularly in times of widespread unemployment. Under such conditions, therefore, it is unlikely that wages will include an adequate or even any compensation for the possible impairment of the worker's health in the productive process.

It might be argued that entrepreneurs, in their own interest, will tend to provide for healthy and safe working conditions because damages to the workers' health reduce efficiency and, by the same token, increase the costs of production. However, this argument neglects two things. First, the private producer is under no obligation to keep inefficient laborers, but may simply hire new workers whose efficiency has not yet been affected by unhealthy working conditions. Second, the introduction of safety and health-protective devices, though ultimately contributing to a higher labor efficiency and lower costs, will necessarily add to the producer's present costs and thus affect adversely his competitive position. Or, it might simply be more profitable to operate the plant without safety devices—considering even adverse effects on labor efficiency—than to introduce such devices (still assuming their introduction to be worth while in terms of outlays and expected "returns" in the form of greater efficiency and good will). In this case, as well as in the probably much greater number of cases where the provision of healthier working conditions is directly unprofitable in terms of entrepreneurial outlays and returns, the deterioration and even destruction of the human factor are likely to become chronic features in competitive economies if not corrected by comprehensive social legislation.

The losses caused by such impairment of the human factor will be borne either by the injured worker or by the taxpayer in the form of greater public expenditures for medical care, hospitals and relief. The fact that these losses, in the absence of adequate social legislation, are not charged against the operating costs of private enterprise but are borne largely by the laborer or the community makes them typical social costs in the sense in which the term is used in this study. . . .

The most significant aspect of the "human costs" of production is the fact that they are avoidable. Competent authorities have estimated that from 70 to 90 per cent of all work injuries could be prevented by proper safety devices. If instead of being prevented they are permitted to occur and to cause social costs of considerable magnitude, that is due to a combination of ignorance of the actual costs of work injuries and unwillingness and inability of the individual firm to bear, under conditions of competitive enterprise, the costs of adequate safety and accident-prevention programs. As it is, therefore, it may be said that to the extent of the social losses caused by the impairment of the human factor private enterprise has been subsidized by the men and women who make up the labor force employed in modern industry. While there is at least a presumption that the value of the original capital equipment is being kept intact through the use of depreciation charges, the "capital value" of the human factor of production has certainly not been maintained in the relatively short history of industrial society. If instead of 20,000 workers, 20,000 head of cattle were exposed to certain death due to an epidemic and recurrent disease, there would be an easily calculable incentive to adopt required preventive measures. It is the fact, then, that the human factor of production has no capital value, which places it in a market economy in a less favorable position than nonhuman means of production.

Summarizing the preceding discussion, it may be said that modern industrial production tends to give rise to a serious impairment of the physical and mental health of the individual worker. Among the more important of these human costs of production are the ill effects of industrial accidents, occupational diseases and the employment of women and children. In its economic implications, such impairment of the physical and mental health of human beings does not differ from the deterioration of nonhuman durable agents of production. And yet, whereas the depreciation of the latter tends to be translated into entrepreneurial outlays by means of depreciation charges, damages to persons would remain unaccounted for in private costs if the competitive process were left to itself. As a matter of fact, in the absence of protective labor legislation and compulsory social insurance, these human costs of production not only would be shifted to and borne by the individual but would also be considerably greater than they are at present. Workmen's compensation acts, by placing upon the employer the financial responsibility for work injuries regardless of fault, have had the effect of translating some of these human costs of production into entrepreneurial expenditures. Despite the fact that a considerable extension of protective labor legislation has taken place in recent decades, all available evidence points to the conclusion that the present scope and operation of existing laws still permit the shifting of the major part of the human costs of production to the injured worker and his dependents, or the community.

The Social Costs of Air Pollution: In contrast to the widespread recognition of the losses caused by the impairment of the human factor, the social costs of air and water pollution have attracted much less attention. This is probably due to the fact that the causal relation between productive activities and air and water pollution is more complex and less easily seen than the relatively clear connection that exists between private production and, say, industrial accidents. Moreover, whereas the impairment of human health by industrial accidents and occupational diseases tends to affect a relatively well-organized group of persons all of whom have a strong interest in the prevention of the risks and dangers to which they are exposed in their daily work, the harmful consequences of the pollution of the atmosphere and the contamination of water by various kinds of industrial waste products are usually felt by a highly heterogeneous, unorganized group of persons. Their reaction is, therefore, less articulate than that of injured workers in the case of industrial accidents and occupational diseases. Nevertheless, there can be no doubt that the social costs of air and water pollution are considerable. In the United States these costs may well reach several billion dollars annually. . . .

While the domestic use of coal continues to be a contributing cause of atmospheric pollution, it is primarily the emanations of smoke and gas from industrial establishments, railroads and large heating plants which, at present, cause most of the prevailing air pollution. Indeed, the large-scale replacement of man and horse power by such energy resources as bituminous coal and oil has made air pollution a common and characteristic phenomenon around many industrial centers. Nor can it be assumed that the replacement of coal and oil by atomic energy may one day eliminate the pollution of the atmosphere. On the contrary, recent experiments with radioactive disposal systems seem to indicate that radioactive waste materials—solids, liquids and gases—may get into the air and represent not only short-lived but long-lived risks for neighboring cities and countries. In fact, if not properly controlled, the problem of air pollution in the atomic age may well become world-wide.

The manner in which present industrial production tends to give rise to air pollution need not occupy us to any great extent. Suffice it to point out that the formation of smoke and other gaseous emanations is almost invariably a sign of improper and incomplete combustion of fuels; in other words, the existence of smoke is always indicative of technical inefficiencies in the use of energy resources. Such inefficiencies fail to be eliminated whenever the private returns (or savings) obtainable from their elimination are not high enough to cover the private costs involved. The fact that the resulting pollution of the atmosphere may cause substantial losses to other people will not and cannot normally be considered in the cost-return calculations of private enterprise. . . .

Soil Erosion, Soil Depletion, and Deforestation: As was pointed out by Fourier, and more systematically by Liebig, agricultural production and the competitive exploitation of forest land offer dramatic illustrations of the fact that private productive activities may give rise to substantial social losses that are not reflected in entrepreneurial outlays. Both agriculture and private forestry draw upon natural resources which are subject to depletion and destruction. Just as the fertility of the soil may be depleted if proper care is not taken to maintain it, so may timber resources be destroyed if lumbering operations are permitted to interfere with the normal renewal of trees and other plants. The fact that both soil fertility and forest growth (unlike petroleum and coal) would remain dependable "flow resources" as long as certain ecological relationships are not disturbed tends to emphasize the wasteful character of productive activities leading to their destruction. However, whereas the social losses arising from the destruction of wildlife and the premature depletion of energy resources are largely confined to, and measured by, the value of the capital asset which they represent, soil-depleting methods of cultivation and forest depletion may have consequences which exceed in importance those bound up with the loss of soil fertility and forest resources. In particular, they may give rise to social damage such as floods, the silting of streams and reservoirs, the diminution of ground-water stores, the pollution of rivers, the destruction of irrigation schemes, the harmful effects of dust storms and the disappearance of wildlife. . . .

Nothing in the following discussion should be interpreted to imply that soil erosion and soil depletion are social costs which occur only in competitively organized market economies. It is well known that precapitalist societies have suffered from similar social losses, and the decline of whole civilizations can in fact be traced to an over-utilization of land. However, whereas these earlier cases of social costs arising from the destruction of land resources were unavoidable, inasmuch as they resulted from overpopulation or destruction by enemy forces, and were rarely fully understood in all their implications, they are now not only understood but susceptible to control by appropriate conservation practices.

In order to explain the manner in which the competitive process in agriculture and private forestry tends to cause social losses, it is necessary to stress the close interdependence and relationship which exists between the land and its natural vegetative cover at any given place. For anything that upsets this interrelationship may lead to costly disturbances of several kinds. In fact, a combination of natural factors such as the topography of the land, its surface configuration, the quality of the soil and the amount and distribution of rainfall all determine the vegetation in any given area. For instance, "long droughts or rainfall so light as to leave the subsoil dry may exclude forest growth." Under these conditions, grassland will be dominant, the natural forest being found chiefly along the streams. On the other hand, "trees can grow on slopes far too steep for farming, and most species do not make great demands on soil fertility, but nearly all are rather exacting in their moisture requirements." The vegetative cover of any given area of land performs important soil-protecting functions. For vegetation determines the capacity of the soil to absorb rainfall, regulates infiltration of water, keeps ground-water stores at the proper level and equalizes runoff and stream flow. Normal geological erosion of the land is thus kept at a minimum, or at least reduced to a pace at which it does not seriously interfere with natural vegetative growth and the slow process of soil formation.

Anything that destroys this natural balance is likely to interfere with the protective influence which the vegetative cover exercises upon the land. Such interference may come even before the land is being used for farming and forestry. Indeed, the very process of bringing virgin land into cultivation by plowing under the natural sod, by removing the forest cover or by draining ponds and other wet lands may have harmful effects which are usually ignored by those interested only in increasing the area of tillable land. If carried out on a large scale in response to a rapidly growing demand for farm products, the process of bringing virgin soil into use may endanger the very prosperity which it seeks to promote. Thus, the removal of the virgin sod and forest cover tends to accelerate the flow of water to the seas, with . . . harmful consequences. . . . Drainage for both agricultural and transportation purposes (e.g., for highway and railroad construction) also has contributed to accelerated runoff of rainfall and a substantial diminution of ground-water stores, "which once gradually fed their waters to the streams by seepage and springs through the dry season. . . ." This, in turn, has caused streams, ponds, and lakes to become low during the dry season and in some instances to disappear entirely, thus creating "serious problems of pure water supply for agricultural and municipal uses, and . . . excessive pollution of streams no longer sufficient in flow to carry the burden which public works placed upon them at a time when their capacity appeared adequate." Another consequence of ill-considered drainage has been the fact that with the decreasing and irregular level or complete disappearance of streams, fish and wildlife have partly died out because of increasing difficulties in finding breeding, feeding and resting places. Although most of these losses cannot be measured in dollars and cents, the fact remains that the worthwhileness of bringing new land into use is inadequately appraised if the social losses resulting from the removal of virgin vegetation and drainage are completely disregarded. . . .

Even more detrimental and far-reaching in its effects than the losses resulting from soil depletion may be the damages caused by man-induced soil erosion. As long as the land is protected by its natural vegetative cover, no serious erosion is likely to take place. As already pointed out, such vegetation permits proper absorption and infiltration of precipitation. Moreover, the roots of the plants possess the required soil-binding capacity and prevent any excessive runoff of rainfall. However, if this protective cover is removed, the absorptive capacity of land and infiltration of water are reduced and the soil is exposed to, and may be carried away by, water and wind. For example, "when an excessive number of cattle and sheep are permitted to graze on pasture land, or on native grassland, or in forest openings, the vegetative cover is destroyed to the very roots, runoff is accelerated and [water] erosion begins its destructive work." The same thing is likely to happen if sloping land is plowed so that furrows run up and down the hill, especially when the land is cultivated with clean-tilled crops such as corn and cotton. In all these cases accelerated runoff may start "dissolving [the soil], carrying soil particles in suspension, or merely . . . rolling them along the surface of the ground. . . ."

These natural factors are, however, given and not subject to human control. In other words, in order to avoid soil erosion, methods of cultivation have to be adapted to the conditions of the natural environment. If the farmer fails to do so and if rapid erosion sets in as a result of a combination of natural factors and farm practices, it is obviously the latter which must be considered as the cause of the devastation of the land and not the high rainfall or the steepness of the slope.

Fundamentally, there are two kinds of erosion: water and wind erosion. Water erosion implies a more or less complete destruction of the top soil. Severe gully erosion, which develops primarily in hilly regions, may render the land permanently unsuited for any kind of utilization, be it for farming, pasture or forests. Even more far-reaching are the indirect effects of water erosion. The lowered permeability of eroded soils increases the frequency and height of floods and reduces the natural replenishment of ground-water stores, thereby affecting the water supply for domestic and irrigation purposes. Finally, the deposition of erosion debris may lead to the sedimentation of bottom lands, reservoirs and stream channels. . . .

The destructive effects of wind erosion not only will be felt by farmers responsible for it but may be carried into regions located at considerable distances from the original erosion area. One of the outstanding examples of erosion is the development of the so-called dust bowl in the arid regions of the American plains and the subsequent migration of hundreds of thousands of impoverished farmers from the central states to the Pacific coast. These conditions were brought about by certain farm and grazing practices of the early settlers, the lowering of the ground-water level by drainage of swamps several hundreds of miles away, and the removal of the natural grass cover during the first World War in response to the increasing demand for bread grains and the use of the land for the growing of wheat. While the individual farmer may have been able to recover his private outlays in these cases, his production caused substantial social losses which the price mechanism failed to record entirely. . . .

The depletion of American timber resources within a relatively short period of time strongly suggests that private forestry may also give rise to social losses of considerable magnitude. Here too, however, it is necessary to keep in mind the special conditions which characterized the American scene until recently. Forests were at first obstacles to the development and proper utilization of the land. In fact, the early settlers viewed forests with a certain hostility which, it is said, became "ingrained in the American spirit," and hastened the removal of forests even long after the forests had ceased to be barriers to the settlement of the country. Moreover, the depletion of forest resources was also encouraged by two misconceptions: first, the common assumption that all forest land was fundamentally suited for agriculture, and second,

> the firm conviction that our timber resources were inexhaustible. The early settlers came from countries where woodland was scarce, to a land of untold forest riches. It was only natural that they should have firmly believed that the forests of America could never be brought visibly close to exhaustion. The nineteenth century was nearly over before this misconception was seriously challenged.

As a result of these ideas, the removal of the forest cover proceeded rapidly and by 1880 "about 24 per cent of the original eastern forest had been cleared for farms . . . most of the timber being burned or left to decay in heaps on the ground or in the valley bottoms." And yet, it must be realized that the clearing of the land in response to the growing need for farm land alone could never have produced the present depletion of the great forest resources on the American continent. It was only when lumbering operations began to be carried out on a large-scale commercial basis that serious deforestation of vast areas began to develop. The desire of private owners of forest lands to realize as quickly as possible a maximum income upon their initial investment resulted in a rapid expansion of lumbering and tended to intensify the competitive struggle for producing timber. Indeed, competition between different timber-producing regions soon became ruinous and led to depressed prices which, in turn, caused the use of destructive methods of production. Instead of applying methods of selective logging and systematic tree renewal, without which forest resources deteriorate and sooner or later tend to be exhausted, lumber companies found it more profitable, at last in the short run, to cut trees indiscriminately. Thus, in some cases only the best trees were taken, whereas in other instances it was found more profitable to cut even smaller and younger trees, especially if the latter were found in more accessible regions. Moreover, low and depressed prices of lumber made it impossible to apply conservational practices such as proper disposal of slash (a substantial fire hazard), the elimination of insect pests and plant diseases, and the prevention of forest fires. That many of the destructive practices in private forestry stem directly from the small-scale and competitive character of the industry is revealed by the fact that three-fourths of the forest land is owned by more than four million small owners and that it is primarily the small owner who finds it difficult to adopt yield-sustaining cutting practices. Whether this is due to the lack of capital, the pressure for current earnings, the uneconomic size of the holdings or the lack of skill with which these holdings are handled, the result is the same: timber-cutting practices on about 71 per cent of the small holdings have continued to be poor and destructive and no solution seems to be in sight for this central dilemma of America's private forestry. . . .

The resulting progressive deforestation had the direct effect of raising the costs of timber, especially that of high quality, and made it necessary to use inferior woods. Furthermore, lumbering operations had to be shifted to areas far removed from the principal markets—a procedure which not only involve higher freight charges but also caused the migration of entire wood industries. As a result of the transient nature of the lumber industries, whole forest communities have suffered and not infrequently were left stranded. At present, it is not so much the large private holder, such as the big pulp and lumber manufacturers, but farmers and other small owners whose cutting practices leave the land either without or with limited means for natural reproduction. Here, as in the case of other social costs, it is the more highly competitive sector of the industry, consisting mostly of small-scale operators, which is the greatest offender.

The full extent of the social losses which arise from the competitive exploitation of private forest resources is realized only if we consider once more that forests, in addition to being a source of timber, also perform important protective and economic functions. More than any other vegetative cover "forests retard runoff during heavy rains and periods of rapid melting snows, and increase the amount of water that percolates into the ground." This quality of forest vegetation, together with the soil-binding capacity of the plant roots, not only prevents erosion and minimizes the sediment load of rivers and lakes, but, at the same time, equalizes the flow of streams and thereby reduces the frequency and height of floods. In addition, forests provide habitat, feeding ground and refuge for wildlife with its important economic and recreational values. To these values must be added the utility derived from the use of the forest ranges for grazing livestock and the income which thousands of persons obtain from the commercial exploitation of various minor forest by-products, such as turpentine, nuts, fruits, sugar, syrup, tan bark, cascara bark, dyestuffs, pharmaceuticals, etc. It has even been suggested that forests are conducive to favorable weather conditions by exerting a beneficial influence on wind velocity, humidity and temperature. However, these beneficial influences of forests on climate are in no way definitively established, and, indeed, it is more likely that climatic conditions determine the existence and location of forests. Nevertheless, the importance of forests as windbreaks has been emphasized by experiences in Soviet Russia and the systematic establishment of tree belts at the Western border of the American plain.

Most of the aforementioned utilities and protective functions of the forest remain inappropriable by the private owner of the forest land. He is not able to exact a remuneration for the soil-binding and flood-preventing capacity of his trees. Nor does he usually receive any returns from those who gather the various minor forest by-products mentioned above. It is, therefore, not surprising to find that private management of forests tends to neglect these inappropriable utilities in its economic decisions and may sacrifice them completely in the course of intensive lumbering operations.

Such neglect and disregard of the protective functions of forests may have all the far-reaching harmful consequences which we have just discussed in connection with the problem of erosion. Thus, after the progressive clearing of the land of its forest cover, infiltration of precipitation is reduced, water runoff is increased and valuable soil elements begin to be washed away. Such "sediment is carried into streams where it silts up reservoirs used for irrigation, for water-power development and for water supply; impairs the navigability of streams; injures their habitat value for fish; and spoils the recreational qualities of the water. During flood periods, moreover, the sediment may be spread over fertile lowland farms ruining or seriously injuring them." Furthermore, forest depletion and the subsequent excessive runoff in periods of torrential downpours and melting snow tend to increase the extent and magnitude of floods. In addition, if lumbering operations clear the land faster than it can be taken into cultivation vast areas of cutover land or "slashing" are created. These slashings are especially susceptible to fire which destroys not only the remaining scrub but causes damage to litter and humus under timber. The destructive effects of such fires again open the way for an acceleration of runoff which, in turn, may cause serious damage to the soil by exposing it to erosion. Finally, deforestation of coastal dunes in the past menaces present-day harbor installations, transportation systems, agricultural lands, summer homes and other improvements. If to these social damages caused by deforestation are added the losses resulting from the destruction of forest grazing ranges and the disappearance of valuable forest by-products, one finally obtains an approximate idea of the possible social losses resulting from the competitive exploitation of forest resources. . . .

The Social Costs of Unemployment and Idle Resources: The most prominent of these forces seem to be the following: the fact that the combined action of producers acting independently of each other may have the effect of distorting and rendering false their own cost and price expectations; the cumulative and self-sustaining nature of price rises and declines; the increasing relative importance of durable goods in modern economic life and the "acceleration" of the demand for and production of producers' goods; the propensity to speculate and the tendency of prices to rise or fall in accordance with speculative expectation and behavior and the disproportions created by innovations giving rise to a depreciation of capital and labor. . . .

Just as the human factor of production is subject to deterioration and impairment in the course of the productive process, so do its "production" and "upkeep" entail certain fixed costs. Not only are monetary outlays involved in raising the new generation of workers, but, in addition, young persons have to be provided with some kind of training, which may vary from the elementary education of the unskilled worker to the highly specialized training of the professional man and intellectual worker. In addition to this fixed investment of time and money in raising the family of the worker, there are the costs of maintaining the worker himself in proper "working conditions." These costs of bringing up the laborer and maintaining his working capacity intact are relatively constant; indeed, a certain minimum of them must be borne under all circumstances "whether the laborer works or not: that is, if it is not borne, if the maintenance is not forthcoming, the community suffers a loss through the deterioration of its working power. . . ." In this sense the costs of labor, or at least a substantial part of them, constitute a kind of overhead cost not only for the individual worker but also and especially for society as a whole. As a matter of fact, the costs of labor are overhead costs in an even more definite sense than are the fixed charges on capital account. Neither the laborer nor the community could escape the burden of these costs even if they wanted to do so.

Under capitalism, these overhead costs of labor are translated into variable costs "in much the same way in which the constant costs of a telephone exchange are translated into a variable charge when the user pays so much per call." In the case of the individual worker, this translation of overhead costs into variable costs is the result of the fact that the laborer under conditions of the present exchange economy is a free person who sells his services by means of a free wage contract. Under this system the burden of all overhead costs of labor is bound to fall upon the individual worker; "he is, under our social system, a free being, responsible for his own continuous support and that of his family; hence his maintenance is his own burden and not an obligation of industry, except so far as he can exact wages that will cover it." This is in marked contrast with the costs of machines and the fixed charges of the borrowed capital which have to be met by industry regardless of business conditions.

It is at this point that the social costs of unemployment become apparent. For, once the fixed overhead costs of labor have been converted into variable costs, the entrepreneur is able to disregard the fixed costs of labor completely. A decline of business will be met first by a reduction of the "variable" costs of labor and thus tends to give rise to a wave of unemployment. This procedure is not only the most convenient for the entrepreneur, but in view of the fixity of most capital outlays it is the only method of reducing costs of production. Periods of depression will thus give rise to a general shift of the fixed burden of labor to the individual worker, his family or the community.

The same disregard of the fixed overhead costs of labor marks all entrepreneurial decisions concerned with the introduction of technological improvements. In this case, too, entrepreneurial outlays are bound to fall short of the actual total costs, part of which have to be borne by the worker or the community in the form of greater expenditures for relief and unemployment. Needless to add, this is not the result of any miscalculation by the entrepreneur but is inherent in the capitalist wage system.

A similar shift and disregard of overhead costs is involved in the nonutilization of nonhuman productive resources. This becomes evident as soon as it is realized that the conversion of fixed into variable costs is not limited to the field of labor but takes place "whenever anybody who has any 'overhead costs' sells his products or his services." For he then "puts the 'overhead costs' into the price he charges and thus they nearly always become a 'variable cost' to the purchaser. Thus, most of the 'constant costs' of business disappear as constant costs and are converted into 'direct' or 'variable' costs. . . ."

In times of depression these direct costs tend to be shifted backward all along the line along which goods move toward the consumer. As soon as business conditions begin to deteriorate, each individual firm reduces its variable expenditures by curtailing as far as possible its purchases of raw materials, semifinished articles, tools and other producers' goods. However, the overhead costs involved in the production of these intermediate goods remain substantially the same. Since their fixed costs have to be borne by a smaller volume of output and sales, unit costs are inevitably increased. It is this increase of costs resulting from any contraction of the demand for intermediate goods by producers closer to the consumer, which is not considered entirely in private business decisions and cost calculations. And inversely, in deciding the question whether or not it is worth while to resume production at full capacity, instead of keeping part of his plant idle, the individual entrepreneur can only disregard the entire series of savings which would accrue in all intermediate stages of production as a result of the fact that with increased production the fixed overhead costs in these industries could again be distributed over a larger total output. This is merely another way of saying that for the economy as a whole the difference in costs involved in partial utilization of available plant equipment as against those involved in full utilization is relatively small—so small, indeed, that as long as the additional products have any want-satisfying power there is a presumption that their production is worth while in terms of total costs and total returns. In other words, the cost calculations of the individual firm fail to record both the social costs resulting from enforced idleness and the economies obtainable from full utilization of productive resources.

It is this "atomistic" method of accounting which tends to distort the economic calculations of the market economy and accounts for the obviously absurd fact that no production and complete idleness are preferred to at least some output and partial utilization of available resources. Another reason for this absurdity, according to which—while millions of persons are unable to satisfy their most elementary needs—nothing seems to be preferable to at least something, is that during the initial stages of the depression many cost prices reflect what the productive resources were worth in the past and not what they are worth under existing conditions. In other words,

> a wage rate of three dollars per day for making shoes ought to mean that there are other opportunities for using this labor to produce something worth three dollars per day. If the worker stands idle because he is not worth three dollars per day at making shoes, that means that the three-dollar alternative does not exist or at least is not available within the limits of existing knowledge. Under these conditions, to act on the assumption that shoes are not worth producing unless they will cover the three-dollar wage is false social accounting, flying in the face of the elementary fact that anything produced is that much more than nothing. It stands

in the way of our making the best available use of our productive resources, whatever that use may be, by insisting that they shall not be used at all unless their use will cover "costs" which changed conditions may have rendered, for this purpose, arbitrary and misleading.

The same applies to interest and rent. They too represent what capital and land were worth in the past in times of prosperity and not what they are worth under the new conditions after business has declined. It is, therefore, "inevitable that productive resources should go to waste, with the further result that they create no purchasing power to buy the products of other productive resources." . . .

Summary and Implications: Each of the preceding [sections] has endeavored to show that private productive activities tend to give rise to a wide variety of social losses not reflected in entrepreneurial outlays. The detailed analysis of these social losses has revealed their heterogeneous origin and character. Thus, whereas some of the social costs of private production could be traced to particular production practices (or neglect of preventive measures) in specific industries, other social losses were seen to arise rather as a result of the workings of the competitive process within the prevailing framework of existing legal and economic institutions.

It was also shown that a considerable proportion of the aforementioned social losses of private production are measurable and can even be expressed in monetary terms. In fact . . . a substantial proportion of social losses are reflected in direct monetary expenditures either by private individuals or by public authorities. The fact that these social costs are ultimately reflected in monetary losses and public expenditures emphasizes their "economic" character even in the narrow sense in which the term is used in neoclassical value theory. Other social costs, however, such as the impairment of aesthetic and recreational values and partly also the impairment of human health, are of a less tangible character and can only be estimated in terms other than market values.

Among . . . social costs of production . . . are the individual and social losses caused by industrial accidents, occupational diseases, woman and child labor; social costs are also reflected in the manifold destructive effects of air and water pollution resulting from inadequate methods of combustion and from the disposal of untreated waste products into streams, rivers and lakes by private firms; moreover, important social costs of production tend to be bound up with the competitive exploitation of both self-renewable and exhaustible natural wealth such as wildlife, petroleum and coal reserves, soil fertility, and forest resources. Social losses also arise in connection with technical changes and the manner and rate of introduction of innovations by private enterprise. . . . [The] social costs of economic depressions as well as the social losses resulting from monopoly . . . in turn set the stage for the social losses arising in the field of distribution. These losses . . . [are] bound up primarily with the wastes and inefficiencies of excessive duplication of retail services and the high costs of sales promotion. . . .

What these losses have in common and what makes them truly *social* costs is the fact that they do not enter into the cost calculations of private firms. They are shifted to and are paid for in one form or another by individuals other than the entrepreneur or by the community as a whole or by both. It is true that social legislation and various kinds of governmental regulations, by making individual firms more fully responsible for the social losses caused by their productive activities, doubtless have had the effect of reducing the magnitude of the social costs of production. The need for, and the increasing scope of, such legislation lends additional support to the general thesis that entrepreneurial outlays are not an adequate measure of the true total costs of production.

Our analysis of the manner in which the productive process tends to give rise to social costs provides also an answer to the optimistic view that the interaction and legal adjustment of conflicting interests in modern society offer a sufficient guarantee against the occurrence or at least for the minimization of social losses. Thus, it may be argued that any attempt on the part of individual producers to shift part of the costs of production to the shoulders of other persons is bound to meet with the decided opposition of the latter. Their resistance, or rather the interaction of the conflicting interests, it may be said, tends to produce a more or less equitable adjustment which has the further effect of keeping the magnitude of the social costs at a minimum. Such reasoning, however, fails to consider a number of important facts. In the first place, it overlooks the fact that some of the social costs (e.g., damage to human health) may remain hidden for considerable periods of time during which the persons affected are unaware of the losses they sustain. In other cases, such as the greater frequency and height of floods resulting from soil erosion, the social losses are catastrophic in character and appear to be the result of *force majeure,* although in reality they are caused or at least aggravated by the productive activities of private entrepreneurs. Moreover, some damages, although substantial if viewed in their totality, are distributed over such a great number of persons that each individual sustains only a relatively small loss, which does not seem to warrant defensive action. In still other cases the injured person may simply be unable, financially or otherwise, to take appropriate defensive steps, or he may find it difficult to prove damages. As noted before, this is of considerable importance inasmuch as "judicial precedent requires the demonstration of specific damage rather than general damage and further requires quantitative estimates of the amount of damage experienced by specified individuals." And even if such evidence is available and damage can be proved, effective prevention of damage by means of an injunction can be secured only if it can be shown that practicable means of prevention exist. Another reason why social damages are often caused with impunity by private producers is the fact that individuals to whose shoulders such costs are shifted have not the same economic power, financial resources and general foresight as the highly organized business units responsible for such losses. Furthermore, industries in which the prevention of social losses would be particularly costly might find it more profitable to fight any existing or suggested regulatory legislation than to take remedial action.

Finally, there are those social losses which are intrinsically connected with the operation of the competitive system as a whole—for example, the competitive depletion of energy resources under the "rule of capture" and the tendency to shift the overhead costs of labor to the individual worker in times of depression or after the introduction of technical improvements. Obviously, there is no defense against these social losses except through the abandonment of the customary wage system. In other words, there is no basis for the belief that the interaction and legal adjustment of conflicting interests offer any guarantee that the social costs of production will be kept at a minimum and adequately assessed against entrepreneurial outlays. In the absence of organized group action, social costs tend to become a common phenomenon in the private enterprise economy. Indeed, generally speaking, capitalism must be regarded as an economy of unpaid costs, "unpaid" in so far as a substantial proportion of the actual costs of production remain unaccounted for in entrepreneurial outlays; instead they are shifted to, and ultimately borne by, third persons or by the community as a whole.

A. A. BERLE, JR., AND G. C. MEANS

As a legal concept the corporation antedates both capitalism and industrial society. The idea of *persona ficta,* the fictitious person who in law is endowed with the human capacity to will, to own, and to act, which is the jurisprudential essence of the corporation, was developed in the Middle Ages. As a means of mustering the financial resources of many scattered individuals for a common economic enterprise, the corporation's ancestry lies principally in the joint-stock companies of the late sixteenth and seventeenth centuries. It was not until the eighteenth and early nineteenth centuries that the corporation was finally and sharply distinguished from the partnership through the device of limited liability. It was not until the end of the nineteenth century that the corporation emerged as a principal means of economic organization within the capitalist system.

In 1932 appeared *The Modern Corporation and Private Property,* a joint study by A. A. Berle, Jr., and G. C. Means, from which the following selection has been taken. It was immediately recognized as one of the fundamental books of the times. This work was concerned with many things, not least among them problems of measuring the degree of concentration of economic resources in relatively few corporate hands and problems of determining the extent to which monopoly existed in the American market. But the central thesis of the work—that the modern corporation was becoming the major social and political, as it had already become the dominant economic, institution of the modern world—transcended these themes. As Berle and Means saw it, the rise of the corporation entailed a radical transition in the concepts of property, ownership, and control, even as it also entailed a reorganization of traditional modes of business and work.

Since 1932 many studies, directed at particular aspects of the corporate problem, have challenged the authors' data and some of their specific conclusions with regard to concentration and monopoly. Yet since 1932 nothing has occurred to change the Berle and Means analysis of the corporation's emergence as the prime locus of economic and social power in contemporary America. Despite the difficulty in interpreting complex statistics, the fact is clear, as A. A. Berle, Jr., notes in his most recent book, *The Twentieth Century Capitalist Revolution* (1954), that in the mid-1950's "considerably more than half of all American industry—and that the most important half—is operated by 'concentrates.' Slightly more than half is owned outright by not more than 200 corporations." The impact of these great aggregates of capital, these hierarchies of bureaucratized management and labor, upon society is greater than their mere economic strength would indicate, for they are social and quasi-political institutions as well as economic organizations. That the constituents of the "corporate system" wield critical power in the life of modern America is obvious. However, the question whether that system can adapt itself sufficiently to assume a responsibility commensurate with its power yet remains to be answered in any clear, unmistakable manner.

Adolf Augustus Berle, Jr., was born in 1895 in Boston. After completing legal training at Harvard, he practiced corporation law with various law firms. Since 1927 he has been professor of corporation law at Columbia University, a career punctuated by leaves of absence to enable him to serve as Assistant Secretary of State from 1938 to 1944 and Ambassador to Brazil from 1945 to 1946. Berle frequently contributes articles to magazines and is the author, in addition to the works already cited, of *Studies in the Law of Corporate Finance* (1928), *Cases and Materials in the Law of Corporation Finance* (1930; with G. C. Means), *New Directions in the New World* (1940; with William C. Warren), and *Natural Selection of Political Forces* (1950).

Gardiner Cort Means was born in Windham, Conn., in 1896, and was educated as an economist and lawyer at Harvard University. He has held numerous positions of responsibility in the Federal government and is the author, besides the work already cited, of *The Holding Company--Its Public Significance and Its Regulation* (1932; with J. C. Bonbright), *Modern Economy in Action* (1936; with his wife, Caroline F. Ware), and *The Structure of the American Economy* (1939).

THE MODERN CORPORATION AND PRIVATE PROPERTY

Book I

Property in Flux: Separation of the Attributes of Ownership Under the Corporate System

CHAPTER I: PROPERTY IN TRANSITION

Corporations have ceased to be merely legal devices through which the private business transactions of individuals may be carried on. Though still much used for this purpose, the corporate form has acquired a larger significance. The corporation has, in fact, become both a method of property tenure and a means of organizing economic life. Grown to tremendous proportions, there may be said to have evolved a "corporate system"—as there was once a feudal system—which has attracted to itself a combination of attributes and powers, and has attained a degree of prominence entitling it to be dealt with as a major social institution.

This selection has been reprinted from A. A. Berle, Jr., and G. C. Means, *The Modern Corporation and Private Property* (pp. 1–9, 333–357, Copyright 1932 by The Macmillan Company, New York) by permission of the publisher.

We are examining this institution probably before it has attained its zenith. Spectacular as its rise has been, every indication seems to be that the system will move forward to proportions which would stagger imagination today; just as the corporate system of today was beyond the imagination of most statesmen and business men at the opening of the present century. Only by remembering that men still living can recall a time when the present situation was hardly dreamed of, can we enforce the conclusion that the new order may easily become completely dominant during the lifetime of our children. For that reason, if for no other, it is desirable to examine this system, bearing in mind that its impact on the life of the country and of every individual is certain to be great; it may even determine a large part of the behaviour of most men living under it.

Organization of property has played a constant part in the balance of powers which go to make up the life of any era. We need not resolve the controversy as to whether property interests are invariably controlling. The cynical view of many historians insists that property interests have at all times, visible or invisible, been dominant. Following this grim analysis, one commentator on the rise of corporations observed that they had become the "master instruments of civilization." Another expressed his depression at the fact that the system had at length reached a point definitely committing civilization to the rule of a plutocracy. Still others have seen in the system a transition phase towards ultimate socialism or communism. Acceptance of any of these beliefs may be delayed; but the underlying thought expressed in them all is that the corporate system has become the principal factor in economic organization through its mobilization of property interests.

In its new aspect the corporation is a means whereby the wealth of innumerable individuals has been concentrated into huge aggregates and whereby control over this wealth has been surrendered to a unified direction. The power attendant upon such concentration has brought forth princes of industry, whose position in the community is yet to be defined. The surrender of control over their wealth by investors has effectively broken the old property relationships and has raised the problem of defining these relationships anew. The direction of industry by persons other than those who have ventured their wealth has raised the question of the motive force back of such direction and the effective distribution of the returns from business enterprise.

These corporations have arisen in field after field as the myriad independent and competing units of private business have given way to the few large groupings of the modern quasi-public corporation. The typical business unit of the 19th century was owned by individuals or small groups; was managed by them or their appointees; and was, in the main, limited in size by the personal wealth of the individuals in control. These units have been supplanted in ever greater measure by great aggregations in which tens and even hundreds of thousands of workers and property worth hundreds of millions of dollars, belonging to tens or even hundreds of thousands of individuals, are combined through the corporate mechanism into a single producing organization under unified control and management. Such a unit is the American Telephone and Telegraph Company, perhaps the most advanced development of the corporate system. With assets of almost five billions of dollars, with 454,000 employees, and stockholders to the number of 567,694, this company may indeed be called an economic empire—an empire bounded by no geographical limits, but held together by centralized control. One hundred companies of this size would control the whole of American wealth; would employ all of the gainfully employed; and if there were no duplication of stockholders, would be owned by practically every family in the country.

Such an organization of economic activity rests upon two developments, each of which has made possible an extension of the area under unified control. The factory system, the basis of the industrial revolution, brought an increasingly large number of workers directly under a single management. Then, the modern corporation, equally revolutionary in its effect, placed the wealth of innumerable individuals under the same central control. By each of these changes the power of those in control was immensely enlarged and the status of those involved, worker or property owner, was radically changed. The independent worker who entered the factory became a wage laborer surrendering the direction of his labor to his industrial master. The property owner who invests in a modern corporation so far surrenders his wealth to those in control of the corporation that he has exchanged the position of independent owner for one in which he may become merely recipient of the wages of capital.

In and of itself, the corporate device does not necessarily bring about this change. It has long been possible for an individual to incorporate his business even though it still represents his own investment, his own activities, and his own business transactions; he has in fact merely created a legal *alter ego* by setting up a corporation as the nominal vehicle. If the corporate form had done nothing more than this, we should have only an interesting custom according to which business would be carried on by individuals adopting for that purpose certain legal clothing. It would involve no radical shift in property tenure or in the organization of economic activity; it would inaugurate no "system" comparable to the institutions of feudalism.

The corporate system appears only when this type of private or "close" corporation has given way to an essentially different form, the quasi-public corporation: a corporation in which a large measure of separation of ownership and control has taken place through the multiplication of owners.

Such separation may exist in varying degrees. Where the men ultimately responsible for running a corporation own a majority of the voting stock while the remainder is widely diffused, control and part ownership are in their hands. Only for the remaining owners is there separation from control. Frequently, however, ownership is so widely scattered that working control can be maintained with but a minority interest. The Rockefeller family, for example, is reported to have retained direct or indirect minority interests in many of the Standard Oil Companies; and in the case of the Standard Oil Company of Indiana, this interest, amounting to only 14.5 per cent, combined with the strategic position of its holders, has proved sufficient for the control of the corporation. In such a case the greater bulk of ownership is virtually without control. Separation of ownership and control becomes almost complete when not even a substantial minority interest exists, as in the American Telephone and Telegraph Company, whose largest holder is reported to own less than one per cent of the company's stock. Under such conditions control may be held by the directors or titular managers who can employ the proxy machinery to become a self-perpetuating body, even though as a group they own but a small fraction of the stock outstanding. In each of these types, majority control, minority control, and management control, the separation of ownership from control has become effective—a large body of security holders has been created who exercise virtually no control over the wealth which they or their predecessors in interest have contributed to the enterprise. In the case of management control, the ownership interest held by the controlling group amounts to but a very small fraction of the total ownership. Corporations where this separation has become an important factor may be classed as quasi-public in character in contradistinction to the private, or closely held corporation in which no important separation of ownership and control has taken place.

Growing out of this separation are two characteristics, almost as typical of the quasi-public corporation as the separation itself—mere size and the public market for its securities. It is precisely this separation of control from ownership which makes possible tremendous aggregations of property. The

Fords and the Mellons, whose personal wealth is sufficient to finance great enterprises, are so few, that they only emphasize the dependence of the large enterprise on the wealth of more than the individual or group of individuals who may be in control. The quasi-public corporation commands its supply of capital from a group of investors frequently described as the "investing public." It draws these savings to itself either directly, as individuals purchase stocks or bonds, or indirectly, as insurance companies, banks, and investment trusts receive these savings and invest them in corporate securities. To secure these funds it must commonly avail itself of an open market in its securities—usually by listing shares on a stock exchange, or, less importantly, by maintaining a private or "unlisted" market. So essential, in fact, is the open market to the quasi-public corporation that it may be considered almost as characteristic of that type of corporation as the separation of ownership from control and the great aggregation of wealth.

These characteristics are not invariable. The private corporation may be, and in a few instances is, exceedingly large: witness the Ford Motor Company, still owned and directed by Mr. Ford and his immediate associates. Private or "close" corporations may and occasionally do avail themselves of a public market for their shares; the Aluminum Company of America, though most of its stock is closely held, has its shares listed on the New York Curb Exchange, and a small fraction of its stock is traded in there. But these instances are so exceptional as to prove the rule. In the overwhelming bulk of cases, corporations fall into the quasi-public class when they represent large aggregations of wealth and their securities are available in the open market; for in such corporations part or most of the owners have almost invariably surrendered control.

Though the American law makes no distinction between the private corporation and the quasi-public, the economics of the two are essentially different. The separation of ownership from control produces a condition where the interests of owner and of ultimate manager may, and often do, diverge, and where many of the checks which formerly operated to limit the use of power disappear. Size alone tends to give these giant corporations a social significance not attached to the smaller units of private enterprise. By the use of the open market for securities, each of these corporations assumes obligations towards the investing public which transform it from a legal method clothing the rule of a few individuals into an institution at least nominally serving investors who have embarked their funds in its enterprise. New responsibilities towards the owners, the workers, the consumers, and the State thus rest upon the shoulders of those in control. In creating these new relationships, the quasi-public corporation may fairly be said to work a revolution. It has destroyed the unity that we commonly call property—has divided ownership into nominal ownership and the power formerly joined to it. Thereby the corporation has changed the nature of profit-seeking enterprise. This revolution forms the subject of the present study.

Examination of the changes produced can properly commence with the new relationships between the owners on the one hand and control on the other. . . . This involves the area roughly termed "corporation finance"—the relations between the corporation as managed by the group in control, and those who hold participations in it—its stockholders, bondholders, and, to some extent, its other creditors. The change in internal organization—the relation of the corporation to its workers, its plant organization and its technical problem of production—we cannot consider at this time. Nor can we here deal with its external relationships, on the one hand with its customers—the terms on which it furnishes to them its products or its services—and on the other hand, with the political state—the government by which it may be in some degree controlled, or over which it may have a measure of dominance. Here we are concerned only with a fundamental change in the form of property, and in the economic relationships which rest upon it.

Outwardly the change is simple enough. Men are less likely to own the physical instruments of production. They are more likely to own pieces of paper, loosely known as stocks, bonds, and other securities, which have become mobile through the machinery of the public markets. Beneath this, however, lies a more fundamental shift. Physical control over the instruments of production has been surrendered in ever growing degree to centralized groups who manage property in bulk, supposedly, but by no means necessarily, for the benefit of the security holders. Power over industrial property has been cut off from the beneficial ownership of this property—or, in less technical language, from the legal right to enjoy its fruits. Control of physical assets has passed from the individual owner to those who direct the quasi-public institutions, while the owner retains an interest in their product and increase. We see, in fact, the surrender and regrouping of the incidence of ownership, which formerly bracketed full power of manual disposition with complete right to enjoy the use, the fruits, and the proceeds of physical assets. There has resulted the dissolution of the old atom of ownership into its component parts, control and beneficial ownership.

This dissolution of the atom of property destroys the very foundation on which the economic order of the past three centuries has rested. Private enterprise, which has molded economic life since the close of the middle ages, has been rooted in the institution of private property. Under the feudal system, its predecessor, economic organization grew out of mutual obligations and privileges derived by various individuals from their relation to property which no one of them owned. Private enterprise, on the other hand, has assumed an ownership of the instruments of production with complete property rights over those instruments. Whereas the organization of feudal economic life rested upon an elaborate system of binding customs, the organization under the system of private enterprise has rested upon the self-interest of the property owner—a self-interest held in check only by competition and the conditions of supply and demand. Such self-interest has long been regarded as the best guarantee of economic efficiency. It has been assumed that, if the individual is protected in the right both to use his own property as he sees fit and to receive the full fruits of its use, his desire for personal gain, for profits, can be relied upon as an effective incentive to his efficient use of any industrial property he may possess.

In the quasi-public corporation, such an assumption no longer holds. As we have seen, it is no longer the individual himself who uses his wealth. Those in control of that wealth, and therefore in a position to secure industrial efficiency and produce profits, are no longer, as owners, entitled to the bulk of such profits. Those who control the destinies of the typical modern corporation own so insignificant a fraction of the company's stock that the returns from running the corporation profitably accrue to them in only a very minor degree. The stockholders, on the other hand, to whom the profits of the corporation go, cannot be motivated by those profits to a more efficient use of the property, since they have surrendered all disposition of it to those in control of the enterprise. The explosion of the atom of property destroys the basis of the old assumption that the quest for profits will spur the owner of industrial property to its effective use. It consequently challenges the fundamental economic principle of individual initiative in industrial enterprise. It raises for reexamination the question of the motive force back of industry, and the ends for which the modern corporation can be or will be run.

The corporate system further commands attention because its development is progressive, as its features become more marked and as new areas come one by one under its sway. Economic power, in terms of control over physical assets, is apparently responding to a centripetal force, tending more and more to concentrate in the hands of a few corporate managements. At the same time, beneficial ownership is centrifugal, tending to divide and subdivide, to split into ever smaller units and to pass freely from hand to hand. In other words, ownership continually becomes more dispersed; the power formerly joined to it becomes increasingly concentrated; and the corporate system is thereby more securely established.

This system bids fair to be as all-embracing as was the feudal system in its time. It demands that we examine both its conditions and its trends, for an understanding of the structure upon which will rest the economic order of the future.

Book IV

Reorientation of Enterprise: Effects of the Corporate System on Fundamental Economic Concepts

CHAPTER I: THE TRADITIONAL LOGIC OF PROPERTY

The shifting relationships of property and enterprise in American industry here described, raise in sharp relief certain legal, economic, and social questions which must now be squarely faced. Of these the greatest is the question in whose interests should the great quasi-public corporations (now representing such a large proportion of industrial wealth) be operated. This problem really asks in a different form the question, who should receive the profits of industry?

It is traditional that a corporation should be run for the benefit of its owners, the stockholders, and that to them should go any profits which are distributed. We now know, however, that a controlling group may hold the power to divert profits into their own pockets. There is no longer any certainty that a corporation will in fact be run primarily in the interests of the stockholders. The extensive separation of ownership and control, and the strengthening of the powers of control, raise a new situation calling for a decision whether social and legal pressure should be applied in an effort to insure corporate operation primarily in the interests of the "owners" or whether such pressure shall be applied in the interests of some other or wider group.

The lawyer answers this question in no uncertain terms by applying to the quasi-public corporation the traditional logic of property. The common law, extended to meet the new situation, logically demands the award of the entire profit to the security holders, and in particular to the stockholders. According to this logic a corporation should be operated primarily in their interests.

The legal argument is largely historical; but it has been built up through a series of phases which make this conclusion inevitable. From earliest times the owner of property has been entitled to the full use or disposal of his property, and in these rights the owner has been protected by law. Since the use of industrial property consists primarily of an effort to increase its value—to make a profit—the owner of such property, in being entitled to its full use, has been entitled to all accretions to its value—to all the profits which it could be made to earn. In so far as he had to pay for the services of other men or other property in order to accomplish this increase in value, these payments operated as deductions; the profit remaining to him was the difference between the added value and the cost of securing these services. To this difference, however, the owner has traditionally been entitled. The state and the law have sought to protect him in this right.

From earliest times, also, the stockholder in the corporation has posed both as the owner of the corporation and the owner of its assets. He was removed slightly from legal ownership in the assets in that he did not have legal "title" to them—that was vested in the corporation; but collectively the stockholders, through their participations, were entitled to the whole of corporate assets and to the whole of any corporate profits which could be made. The corporation was theirs, to be operated for their benefit.

In the development of the corporation, constantly widening powers over the management of the enterprise have been delegated to groups within the corporation. At first these powers concerned mainly the technical (profit-making) activity of the enterprise. Later, powers were delegated which had to do with the distribution of profits and interests among the security holders. With the separation of ownership and control, these powers developed to a stage permitting those in control of a corporation to use them against the interests of ownership. Since powers of control and management were created by law, in some measure this appeared to legalize the diversion of profit into the hands of the controlling group.

Following the traditional logic of property, however, it is clear that these powers are not absolute. They are, rather, powers in trust. The controlling group is, in form at least, managing and controlling a corporation for the benefit of the owners. While insertions might be made in corporation statutes and in corporate charters apparently giving power which could be used against the interests of the owners, these were, in the light of the common law, only grants of power to the controlling group, the better to operate the corporation in the interests of its owners. The very multiplication of absolute powers, including power to shift interests in the corporate assets and profits from security holders to those in control, threw into bold relief the tacit (but by no means fictitious) understanding that all these powers were designed for the benefit of the corporation as a whole, and not for the individual enrichment of the management or control. While the law fumbled in application of this principle, and developed through a series of rules, sometimes inconsistent and often not clear in application, not a single case on record denies the ultimate trusteeship of the controlling group, nor even faintly implies that such a group may use its power for its individual advantage. Fact-situations can be "rigged" whereby the individual profit of this group is made to appear an advantage to the corporation as a whole; advantage may be taken of emergencies in which the management and control present the security-holding group with the alternative of permitting profit to the "control" on the one hand or inviting disaster on the other. Sometimes the courts, shielding themselves behind a consideration of the advantage to the "corporation as a whole," have overlooked the fact that apparent advantage to the mythical corporate entity may mean staggering loss to its separate owners; and that it is often necessary to trace *what group within the corporation* receives the ultimate advantage. Despite these situations, in many of which the controlling group is able, first, to seize a portion of the corporate profits and, second, to hold them against legal attack, the theory of the law seems clear. All the powers granted to management and control are powers in trust.

Tracing this doctrine back into the womb of equity, whence it sprang, the foundation becomes plain. Wherever one man or a group of men entrusted another man or group with the management of property, the second group became fiduciaries. As such they were obliged to act conscionably, which meant in fidelity to the interests of the persons whose wealth they had undertaken to handle. In this respect, the corporation stands on precisely the same footing as the common-law trust. Since the business problems connected with trusts were relatively restricted, a series of fairly accurate regulations could be worked out by the equity courts constraining the trustee to certain standards of conduct. The corporation, which carried on any and every kind of business, raised a set of problems of conduct infinitely more varied, and calling for expert business judgment which courts were not equipped to render. Fixed standards of conduct, therefore, became impossible of development in the corporate situation; such rigid standards as were worked out (for instance, the standard that no stock must be issued unless first offered preemptively to existing shareholders) became arbitrary or inapplicable in the complex corporate structure of today. But though definite rules could not be laid down, the courts have maintained a supervisory jurisdiction; the fundamental principle of equitable control remains unimpaired; and the only question is how it should be applied in each case. Inability to answer these questions has given ample latitude to the control to absorb a portion of the corporate profits. This does not mean, however, that the law concedes them a right to such absorption. It merely means that legal machinery may not be sufficiently developed to accomplish a remedy.

Underlying all this is the ancient preoccupation of the common law with the rights of property. Primarily, the common law did not undertake to set up ideal schemes of government. It aimed to protect men in their own. Only where the property interests conflicted with some very obvious public policy did the law interfere. Its primary design was protecting individual attributes of individual men,—their right to property, to free motion and locomotion, to protection of individual relationships entered into between them. In this aspect the corporation was merely one more bit of machinery by which the property of individuals was managed by other individuals; and the corporate management took its place in the picture alongside of agents, trustees, ship captains, partners, joint adventurers, and other fiduciaries. As the power of the corporate management has increased, and as the control of the individual has sunk into the background, the tendency of the law has been to stiffen its assertion of the rights of the security holder. The thing that it has not been able to stiffen has been its regulation of the conduct of the business by the corporate management. And this omission has resulted, not from lack of logical justification, but from lack of ability to handle the problems involved. The management of an enterprise is, by nature, a task which courts can not assume; and the various devices by which management and control have absorbed a portion of the profit-stream have been so intimately related to the business conduct of an enterprise, that the courts seem to have felt not only reluctant to interfere, but positively afraid to do so.

The result accordingly is that the profits of the enterprise, so far as the law is concerned, belong to the security holders *in toto*. Division of these profits among the various groups of security holders is a matter of private agreement, but they, between them, have the complete right to all of the profits which the corporation has made. Not only that: they are entitled to those profits which the management in reasonable exercise of its powers ought to make. They have further a right that no one shall become a security holder except upon a suitable contribution to the corporate assets—that is, that the security holding group shall be a group of persons who have committed actual property to the administration of the management and control of the corporation.

Such is the view which the law has developed by extending to the new situation the traditional logic of property. The control group is not in a position openly to combat this logic. Constant appeals are made both to this ideology and to its legal basis when corporations go into the market seeking capital. The expectation of the entire profit is the precise lure used to induce investment in corporate enterprises. The possibilities of the situation are continuously stressed by investment bankers who, in turn, act for the corporate management and control when the latter are bidding for the public investor's savings. Whatever their private views or actual practice, the control groups within corporations have estopped themselves from maintaining any other view. The legal hypothesis has been too much the basis of the financial structure of today.

Yet, while this conclusion may result inevitably when the traditional logic of property is applied to the new situation, are we justified in applying this logic? In the past, the ownership of business enterprise, the only form of property with which we are here concerned, has always, at least in theory, involved two attributes, first, the risking of previously collected wealth in profit-seeking enterprise; and, second, the ultimate management of and responsibility for that enterprise. But in the modern corporation, these two attributes of ownership no longer attach to the same individual or group. The stockholder has surrendered control over his wealth. He has become a supplier of capital, a risk-taker pure and simple, while ultimate responsibility and authority are exercised by directors and "control." One traditional attribute of ownership is attached to stock ownership; the other attribute is attached to corporate control. Must we not, therefore, recognize that we are no longer dealing with property in the old sense? Does the traditional logic of property still apply? Because an owner who also exercises control over his wealth is protected in the full receipt of the advantages derived from it, must it *necessarily* follow that an owner who has surrendered control of his wealth should likewise be protected to the full? May not this surrender have so essentially changed his relation to his wealth as to have changed the logic applicable to his interest in that wealth? An answer to this question cannot be found in the law itself. It must be sought in the economic and social background of law.

CHAPTER II: THE TRADITIONAL LOGIC OF PROFITS

The economist, approaching the problems growing out of the shifting relationship of property and enterprise which we have examined, must start from a different background and with a set of interests differing essentially from those of the law. His interest is not primarily in the protection of man in his own, but in the production and distribution of what man desires. He is preoccupied, not with the rights of property, but with the production of wealth and distribution of income. To him property rights are attributes which may be attached to wealth by society and he regards them and their protection, not as the inalienable right of the individual or as an end in themselves, but as a means to a socially desirable end, namely, "a plentiful revenue and subsistence" for the people.

The socially beneficent results to be derived from the protection of property are supposed to arise, not from the wealth itself, but from the efforts to acquire wealth. A long line of economists have developed what might be called the traditional logic of profits. They have held that, in striving to acquire wealth, that is, in seeking profits, the individual would, perhaps unconsciously, satisfy the wants of others. By carrying on enterprise he would employ his energy and wealth in such a way as to obtain more wealth. In this effort, he would tend to make for profit those things which were in most demand. Competition among countless producers could be relied upon in general to maintain profits within reasonable limits while temporarily excessive profits in any one line of production would induce an increase of activity in that line with a consequent drop of profits to more reasonable levels. At the same time it was supposed that the business man's effort to increase his profits would, in general, result in more economical use of the factors of production, each enterprise having to compete with others for the available economic resources. Therefore, it has been argued that by protecting each man in the possession of his wealth and in the possession of any profits he could make from its use, society would encourage enterprise and thereby facilitate the production and distribution of goods desired by the community at reasonable prices with economic use of labor, capital, and business enterprise. By protecting property rights in the instruments of production, the acquisitive interests of man could thus be more effectively harnessed to the benefit of the community.

It must be seen that under the condition just described, profits act as a return for the performance of two separate functions. First, they act as an inducement to the individual to risk his wealth in enterprise, and, second, they act as a spur, driving him to exercise his utmost skill in making his enterprise profitable. In the case of a private enterprise the distinction between these two functions does not assume importance. The owner of a private business receives any profits made and performs the functions not only of risk-taking but of ultimate management as well. It may be that in the past when industry was in the main carried on by a multitude of small private enterprises the community, through protecting property, has induced a large volume of risk-taking and a vigorous conduct of industry in exchange for the profits derived therefrom.

In the modern corporation, with its separation of ownership and control, these two functions of risk and control are, in the main, performed by two different groups of people. Where such a separation is complete one group of individuals, the security holders and in particular the stockholders, performs the function of risk-takers and suppliers of capital, while a separate group exercises control and ultimate management. In such a case, if profits are to be received only by the security holders, as the traditional logic of property would require, how can they perform both of their traditional economic roles? Are no profits to go to those who exercise control and in whose hands the efficient operation of enterprise ultimately rests?

It is clear that the function of capital-supplying and risk-taking must be performed and that the security holder must be compensated if an enterprise is to raise new capital and expand its activity, just as the workers must be paid enough to insure the continued supplying of labor and the taking of the risks involved in that labor and in the life based on it. But what if profits can be made more than sufficient to keep the security holders satisfied, more than sufficient to induce new capital to come into the enterprise? Where is the social advantage in setting aside for the security holder, profits in an amount greater than is sufficient to insure the continued supplying of capital and taking of risk? The prospect of additional profits cannot act as a spur on the security holder to make him *operate* the enterprise with more vigor in a way to serve the wants of the community, since he is no longer in control. Such extra profits if given to the security holders would seem to perform no useful economic function.

Furthermore, if all profits are earmarked for the security holder, where is the inducement for those in control to manage the enterprise efficiently? When none of the profits are to be received by them, why should they exert themselves beyond the amount necessary to maintain a reasonably satisfied group of stockholders? *If* the profit motive is the powerful incentive to action which it is supposed to be, and *if* the community is best served when each enterprise is operated with the aim of making the maximum profit, would there not be great social advantage in encouraging the control to seize for themselves any profits over and above the amount necessary as a satisfactory return to capital? Would not the prospect of this surplus profit act as an incentive to more efficient management by those in control? Certainly, one cannot escape the conclusion that if profits have any influence as a motivating force, any surplus which can be made over a satisfactory return to the investor would be better employed when held out as an incentive to action by control than when handed over to the "owners" who have surrendered control.

This conclusion is somewhat modified by the fact that the separation of ownership and control has not yet become complete. While a large body of stockholders are not in a position to exercise any degree of control over the affairs of their corporation, those actually in control are usually stockholders though in many cases owning but a very small proportion of the total stock. It may be that the prospect of receiving one or two per cent of the total added profit which could be produced by their own more vigorous activity would be sufficient inducement to produce the most efficient operation of which the controlling group are capable. It remains true, however, that profits over enough to keep the remaining stockholders satisfied and to make possible the raising of new capital would still involve an economically wasteful disposal. Only the one or two per cent of profits going to the controlling group would perform both roles traditionally performed by profits.

The traditional logic of profits, when thus applied to the modern corporation, would indicate that *if profits must be distributed either to the owners or to the control,* only a fair return to capital should be distributed to the "owners"; while the remainder should go to the control as an inducement to the most efficient ultimate management. The corporation would thus be operated financially in the interests of control, the stockholders becoming merely the recipients of the wages of capital.

This conclusion runs directly counter to the conclusion reached by applying the traditional logic of property to precisely the same situation—and is equally suspect.

CHAPTER III: THE INADEQUACY OF TRADITIONAL THEORY

When such divergent results are obtained by the application of the logic of two major social disciplines to a new fact situation, we must push our inquiry still further back into the assumptions and concepts of those disciplines.

Underlying the thinking of economists, lawyers and business men during the last century and a half has been the picture of economic life so skillfully painted by Adam Smith. Within his treatise on the "Wealth of Nations" are contained the fundamental concepts which run through most modern thought. Though adjustments in his picture have been made by later writers to account for new conditions, the whole has been painted in the colors which he supplied. Private property, private enterprise, individual initiative, the profit motive, wealth, competition,—these are the concepts which he employed in describing the economy of his time and by means of which he sought to show that the pecuniary self-interest of each individual, if given free play, would lead to the optimum satisfaction of human wants. Most writers of the Nineteenth Century built on these logical foundations, and current economic literature is, in large measure, cast in such terms.

Yet these terms have ceased to be accurate, and therefore tend to mislead in describing modern enterprise as carried on by the great corporations. Though both the terms and the concepts remain, they are inapplicable to a dominant area in American economic organization. New terms, connoting changed relationships, become necessary.

When Adam Smith talked of "enterprise" he had in mind as the typical unit the small individual business in which the owner, perhaps with the aid of a few apprentices or workers, labored to produce goods for market or to carry on commerce. Very emphatically he repudiated the stock corporation as a business mechanism, holding that dispersed ownership made efficient operation impossible. "The directors of such companies . . . ," he pointed out,

> being the managers rather of other people's money than of their own, it cannot well be expected that they should watch over it with the same anxious vigilance with which the partners in a private copartnery frequently watch over their own. Like the stewards of a rich man, they are apt to consider attention to small matters as not for their master's honour, and very easily give themselves a dispensation from having it. Negligence and profusion, therefore, must always prevail, more or less, in the management of the affairs of such a company. It is upon this account that joint stock companies for foreign trade [at the time he was writing the only important manifestation of the corporation outside of banks, insurance companies, and water or canal companies] have seldom been able to maintain the competition against private adventurers. They have, accordingly, very seldom succeeded without an exclusive privilege, and frequently have not succeeded with one. Without an exclusive privilege they have commonly mismanaged the trade. With an exclusive privilege they have both mismanaged and confined it.

Yet when we speak of business enterprise today, we must have in mind primarily these very units which seemed to Adam Smith not to fit into the principles which he was laying down for the conduct of economic activity. How then can we apply the concepts of Adam Smith in discussing our modern economy?

Let us consider each of these concepts in turn.

Private Property. To Adam Smith and to his followers, private property was a unity involving possession. He assumed that ownership and control were combined. Today, in the modern corporation, this unity has been broken. *Passive property,*—specifically shares of stock or bonds,—gives its possessors an interest in an enterprise but gives them practically no control over it, and involves no responsibility. *Active property,*—plant, good will, organization, and so forth which make up the actual enterprise,—is controlled by individuals who, almost invariably, have only minor ownership interests in it. In terms of relationships, the present situation can be described as including:—(1) "passive property," consisting of a set of relationships between an individual and an enterprise, involving rights of the individual toward the enterprise but almost no effective powers over it; and (2) "active property," consisting of a set of relationships under which an individual or set of individuals hold powers over an enterprise but have almost no duties in respect to it which can be effectively enforced. When active and passive property relationships attach to the same individual or group, we have private property as conceived by the older economists. When they attach to different individuals, private property in the instruments of production disappears. Private property in the share of stock still continues, since the owner possesses the share and has power to dispose of it, but his share of stock is only a token representing a bundle of ill-protected rights and expectations. It is the possession of this token which can be transferred, a transfer which has little if any influence on the instruments of production. Whether possession of active property,—power of control over an enterprise, apart from ownership,—will ever be looked upon as private property which can belong to and be disposed of by its possessor is a problem of the future, and no prediction can be made with respect to it. Whatever the answer, it is clear that in dealing with the modern corporation we are not dealing with the old type of private property. Our description of modern economy, in so far as it deals with the quasi-public corporation, must be in terms of the two forms of property, active and passive, which for the most part lie in different hands.

Wealth. In a similar way, the concept "wealth" has been changed and divided. To Adam Smith, wealth was composed of tangible things,—wheat and land and buildings, ships and merchandise,—and for most people wealth is still thought of in physical terms. Yet in connection with the modern corporation, two essentially different types of wealth exist. To the holder of passive property, the stockholder, wealth consists, not of tangible goods,—factories, railroad stations, machinery,—but of a bundle of expectations which have a market value and which, if held, may bring him income and, if sold in the market, may give him power to obtain some other form of wealth. To the possessor of active property,—the "control"—wealth means a great enterprise which he dominates, an enterprise whose value is for the most part composed of the organized relationship of tangible properties, the existence of a functioning organization of workers and the existence of a functioning body of consumers. Instead of having control over a body of tangible wealth with an easily ascertainable market value, the group in control of a large modern corporation is astride an organism which has little value except as it continues to function, and for which there is no ready market. Thus, side by side, these two forms of wealth exist:—on the one hand passive wealth,—liquid, impersonal and involving no responsibility, passing from hand to hand and constantly appraised in the market place; and on the other hand, active wealth,—great, functioning organisms dependent for their lives on their security holders, their workers and consumers, but most of all on their mainspring,—"control." The two forms of wealth are not different aspects of the same thing, but are essentially and functionally distinct.

Private Enterprise. Again, to Adam Smith, private enterprise meant an individual or few partners actively engaged and relying in large part on their own labor or their immediate direction. Today we have tens and hundreds of thousands of owners, of workers and of consumers combined in single enterprises. These great associations are so different from the small, privately owned enterprises of the past as to make the concept of private enterprise an ineffective instrument of analysis. It must be replaced with the concept of corporate enterprise, enterprise which is the organized activity of vast bodies of individuals, workers, consumers and suppliers of capital, under the leadership of the dictators of industry, "control."

Individual Initiative. As private enterprise disappears with increasing size, so also does individual initiative. The idea that an army operates on the basis of "rugged individualism" would be ludicrous. Equally so is the same idea with respect to the modern corporation. Group activity, the coordinating of the different steps in production, the extreme division of labor in large scale enterprise necessarily imply not individualism but cooperation and the acceptance of authority almost to the point of autocracy. Only to the extent that any worker seeks advancement within an organization is there room for individual initiative,—an initiative which can be exercised only within the narrow range of function he is called on to perform. At the very pinnacle of the hierarchy of organization in a great corporation, there alone, can individual initiative have a measure of free play. Yet even there a limit is set by the willingness and ability of subordinates to carry out the will of their superiors. In modern industry, individual liberty is necessarily curbed.

The Profit Motive. Even the motivation of individual activity has changed its aspect. For Adam Smith and his followers, it was possible to abstract one motive, the desire for personal profit, from all the motives driving men to action and to make this the key to man's economic activity. They could conclude that, where true private enterprise existed, personal profit was an effective and socially beneficent motivating force. Yet we have already seen how the profit motive has become distorted in the modern corporation. To the extent that profits induce the risking of capital by investors, they play their customary role. But if the courts, following the traditional logic of property, seek to insure that all profits reach or be held for the security owners, they prevent profits from reaching the very group of men whose action is most important to the efficient conduct of enterprise. Only as profits are diverted into the pockets of control do they, in a measure, perform their second function.

Nor is it clear that even if surplus profits were held out as an incentive to control they would be as effective an instrument as the logic of profits assumes. Presumably the motivating influence of any such huge surplus profits as a modern corporation might be made to produce would be subject to diminishing returns. Certainly it is doubtful if the prospect of a second million dollars of income (and the surplus profits might often amount to much larger sums) would induce activity equal to that induced by the prospect of the first million or even the first hundred thousand. Profits in such terms bear little relation to those envisaged by earlier writers.

Just what motives are effective today, in so far as control is concerned, must be a matter of conjecture. But it is probable that more could be learned regarding them by studying the motives of an Alexander the Great, seeking new worlds to conquer, than by considering the motives of a petty tradesman of the days of Adam Smith.

Competition. Finally, when Adam Smith championed competition as the great regulator of industry, he had in mind units so small that fixed capital and overhead costs played a role so insignificant that costs were in large measure determinate and so numerous that no single unit held an important position in the market. Today competition in markets dominated by a few great enterprises has come to be more often either cut-throat and destructive or so inactive as to make monopoly or duopoly conditions prevail. Competition between a small number of units each involving an organization so complex that costs have become indeterminate does not satisfy the condition assumed by earlier economists, nor does it appear likely to be as effective a regulator of industry and of profits as they had assumed.

In each of the situations to which these fundamental concepts refer, the Modern Corporation has wrought such a change as to make the concepts inapplicable. New concepts must be forged and a new picture of economic relationships created. It is with this in mind that . . . the modern corporation was posed as a major social institution; and its development was envisaged in terms of revolution.

CHAPTER IV: THE NEW CONCEPT OF THE CORPORATION

Most fundamental to the new picture of economic life must be a new concept of business enterprise as concentrated in the corporate organization. In some measure a concept is already emerging. Over a decade ago, Walter Rathenau wrote concerning the German counterpart of our great corporation:

> No one is a permanent owner. The composition of the thousandfold complex which functions as lord of the undertaking is in a state of flux. . . . This condition of things signifies that ownership has been depersonalized. . . . The depersonalization of ownership simultaneously implies the objectification of the thing owned. The claims to ownership are subdivided in such a fashion, and are so mobile, that the enterprise assumes an independent life, as if it belonged to no one; it takes an objective existence, such as in earlier days was embodied only in state and church, in a municipal corporation, in the life of a guild or a religious order. . . . The depersonalization of ownership, the objectification of enterprise, the detachment of property from the possessor, leads to a point where the enterprise becomes transformed into an institution which resembles the state in character.

The institution here envisaged calls for analysis, not in terms of business enterprise but in terms of social organization. On the one hand, it involves a concentration of power in the economic field comparable to the concentration of religious power in the mediaeval church or of political power in the national state. On the other hand, it involves the interrelation of a wide diversity of economic interests,—those of the "owners" who supply capital, those of the workers who "create," those of the consumers who give value to the products of enterprise, and above all those of the control who wield power.

Such a great concentration of power and such a diversity of interests raise the long-fought issue of power and its regulation—of interest and its protection. A constant warfare has existed between the individuals wielding power, in whatever form, and the subjects of that power. Just as there is a continuous desire for power, so also there is a continuous desire to make that power the servant of the bulk of the individuals it affects. The long struggles for the reform of the Catholic Church and for the development of constitutional law in the states are phases of this phenomenon. Absolute power is useful in building the organization. More slow, but equally sure is the development of social pressure demanding that the power shall be used for the benefit of all concerned. This pressure, constant in ecclesiastical and political history, is already making its appearance in many guises in the economic field.

Observable throughout the world, and in varying degrees of intensity, is this insistence that power in economic organization shall be subjected to the same tests of public benefit which have been applied in their turn to power otherwise located. In its most extreme aspect this is exhibited in the communist movement, which in its purest form is an insistence that *all* of the powers and privileges of property shall be used only in the common interest. In less extreme forms of socialist dogma, transfer of economic powers to the state for public service is demanded. In the strictly capitalist countries, and particularly in time of depression, demands are constantly put forward that the men controlling the great economic organisms be made to accept responsibility for the well-being of those who are subject to the organization, whether workers, investors, or consumers. In a sense the difference in all of these demands lies only in degree. In proportion as an economic organism grows in strength and its power is concentrated in a few hands, the possessor of power is more easily located, and the demand for responsible power becomes increasingly direct.

How will this demand be made effective? To answer this question would be to foresee the history of the next century. We can here only consider and appraise certain of the more important lines of possible development.

By tradition, a corporation "belongs" to its shareholders, or, in a wider sense, to its security holders, and theirs is the only interest to be recognized as the object of corporate activity. Following this tradition, and without regard for the changed character of ownership, it would be possible to apply in the interests of the *passive* property owner the doctrine of strict property rights. . . . By the application of this doctrine, the group in control of a corporation would be placed in a position of trusteeship in which it would be called on to operate or arrange for the operation of the corporation for the *sole* benefit of the security owners despite the fact that the latter have ceased to have power over or to accept responsibility for the *active* property in which they have an interest. Were this course followed, the bulk of American industry might soon be operated by trustees for the sole benefit of inactive and irresponsible security owners.

In direct opposition to the above doctrine of strict property rights is the view, apparently held by the great corporation lawyers and by certain students of the field, that corporate development has created a new set of relationships, giving to the groups in control powers which are absolute and not limited by any implied obligation with respect to their use. This logic leads to drastic conclusions. For instance, if, by reason of these new relationships, the men in control of a corporation can operate it in their own interests, and can divert a portion of the asset fund of income stream to their own uses, such is their privilege. Under this view, since the new powers have been acquired on a quasi-contractual basis, the security holders have agreed in advance to any losses which they may suffer by reason of such use. The result is, briefly, that the existence of the legal and economic relationships giving rise to these powers must be frankly recognized as a modification of the principle of private property.

If these were the only alternatives, the former would appear to be the lesser of two evils. Changed corporate relationships have unquestionably involved an essential alteration in the character of property. But such modifications have hitherto been brought about largely on the principle that might makes right. Choice between strengthening the rights of passive property owners, or leaving a set of uncurbed powers in the hands of control, therefore resolves itself into a purely realistic evaluation of different results. We might elect the relative certainty and safety of a trust relationship in favor of a particular group within the corporation, accompanied by a possible diminution of enterprise. Or we may grant the controlling group free rein, with the corresponding danger of a corporate oligarchy coupled with the probability of an era of corporate plundering.

A third possibility exists, however. On the one hand, the owners of passive property, by surrendering control and responsibility over the active property, have surrendered the right that the corporation should be operated in their sole interest,—they have released the community from the obligation to protect them to the full extent implied in the doctrine of strict property rights. At the same time, the controlling groups, by means of the extension of corporate powers, have in their own interest broken the bars of tradition which require that the corporation be operated solely for the benefit of the owners of passive property. Eliminating the sole interest of the passive owner, however, does not necessarily lay a basis for the alternative claim that the new powers should be used in the interest of the controlling groups. The latter have not presented, in acts or words, any acceptable defense of the proposition that these powers should be so used. No tradition supports that proposition. The control groups have, rather, cleared the way for the claims of a group far wider than either the owners or the control. They have placed the community in a position to demand that the modern corporation serve not alone the owners or the control but all society.

This third alternative offers a wholly new concept of corporate activity. Neither the claims of ownership nor those of control can stand against the paramount interests of the community. The present claims of both contending parties now in the field have been weakened by the developments [already] described. . . . It remains only for the claims of the community to be put forward with clarity and force. Rigid enforcement of property rights as a temporary protection against plundering by control would not stand in the way of the modification of these rights in the interest of other groups. When a convincing system of community obligations is worked out and is generally accepted, in that moment the passive property right of today must yield before the larger interests of society. Should the corporate leaders, for example, set forth a program comprising fair wages, security to employees, reasonable service to their public, and stabilization of business, all of which would divert a portion of the profits from the owners of passive property, and should the community generally accept such a scheme as a logical and human solution of industrial difficulties, the interests of passive property owners would have to give way. Courts would almost of necessity be forced to recognize the result, justifying it by whatever of the many legal theories they might choose. It is conceivable,—indeed it seems almost essential if the corporate system is to survive,—that the "control" of the great corporations should develop into a purely neutral technocracy, balancing a variety of claims by various groups in the community and assigning to each a portion of the income stream on the basis of public policy rather than private cupidity.

In still larger view, the modern corporation may be regarded not simply as one form of social organization but potentially (if not yet actually) as the dominant institution of the modern world. In every age, the major concentration of power has been based upon the dominant interest of that age. The strong man has, in his time, striven to be cardinal or pope, prince or cabinet minister, bank president or partner in the House of Morgan. During the Middle Ages, the Church, exercising spiritual power, dominated Europe and gave to it a unity at a time when both political and economic power were diffused. With the rise of the modern state, political power, concentrated into a few large units, challenged the spiritual interest as the strongest bond of human society. Out of the long struggle between church and state which followed, the state emerged victorious; nationalist politics superseded religion as the basis of the major unifying organization of the western world. Economic power still remained diffused.

The rise of the modern corporation has brought a concentration of economic power which can compete on equal terms with the modern state—economic power versus political power, each strong in its own field. The state seeks in some aspects to regulate the corporation, while the corporation, steadily becoming more powerful, makes every effort to avoid such regulation. Where its own interests are concerned, it even attempts to dominate the state. The future may see the economic organism, now typified by the corporation, not only on an equal plane with the state, but possibly even superseding it as the dominant form of social organization. The law of corporations, accordingly, might well be considered as a potential constitutional law for the new economic state, while business practice is increasingly assuming the aspect of economic statesmanship.

KARL POLANYI

KARL POLANYI was born in Vienna, Austria, in 1886. He was trained as a lawyer in the University of Budapest. Always immersed in scholarship, Polanyi nevertheless was active politically in his native Hungary, both as a party leader (Radical Citizens' Party) and as a publicist. Driven out of Central Europe by the advent of Nazism, Polanyi went first to England as a lecturer at Oxford, and then to the United States. Between 1940 and 1943 he was resident scholar at Bennington College, Vermont, and in 1947 was appointed visiting professor of economics at Columbia University. The author of many books, essays, and articles, Polanyi is best known to the English-speaking world for his *Christianity and the Social Revolution* (1935) and *The Great Transformation* (1944). The following selection first appeared in the magazine *Commentary* in 1947 and represents a distillation of the principle argument of *The Great Transformation*.

In his analysis of nineteenth- and twentieth-century society, Polanyi protests the subordination of "social good-will, social status, and social assets" to the economic aspects of life. He decries the practice—common to many non-Marxist and Marxist thinkers alike—of seeing social relationships as exclusively embedded within particular economic systems. The weakness of modern society, to Polanyi, is not industrialization, but the emphasis on the market system; the expression of social, religious, and other noneconomic values in terms of current market price. Indeed, in the modern market economy, nature and man have become transmuted into land and labor, and are regarded as mere factors of production rather than as basic qualities of the social universe.

OUR OBSOLETE MARKET MENTALITY

THE FIRST CENTURY of the Machine Age is drawing to a close amid fear and trepidation. Its fabulous material success was due to the willing, indeed the enthusiastic, subordination of man to the needs of the machine.

Liberal capitalism was in effect man's initial response to the challenge of the Industrial Revolution. In order to allow scope to the use of elaborate, powerful machinery, we transformed human economy into a self-adjusting system of markets, and cast our thoughts and values in the mold of this unique innovation.

This selection has been reprinted from Karl Polanyi, "Our Obsolete Market Mentality," *Commentary,* Vol. 3, No. 2 (February, 1947), 109–116, by permission of the publisher.

Today, we begin to doubt the truth of some of these thoughts and the validity of some of these values. Outside the United States, liberal capitalism can hardly be said to exist any more. How to organize human life in a machine society is a question that confronts us anew. Behind the fading fabric of competitive capitalism there looms the portent of an industrial civilization, with its paralyzing division of labor, standardization of life, supremacy of mechanism over organism, and organization over spontaneity. Science itself is haunted by insanity. This is the abiding concern.

No mere reversion to the ideals of a past century can show us the way. We must brave the future, though this may involve us in an attempt to shift the place of industry in society so that the extraneous fact of the machine can be absorbed. The search for industrial democracy is not merely the search for a solution to the problems of capitalism, as most people imagine. It is a search for an answer to industry itself. Here lies the concrete problem of our civilization.

Such a new dispensation requires an inner freedom for which we are but ill equipped. We find ourselves stultified by the legacy of a market-economy which bequeathed us oversimplified views of the function and role of the economic system in society. If the crisis is to be overcome, we must recapture a more realistic vision of the human world and shape our common purpose in the light of that recognition.

Industrialism is a precariously grafted scion upon man's age-long existence. The outcome of the experiment is still hanging in the balance. But man is not a simple being and can die in more than one way. The question of individual freedom, so passionately raised in our generation, is only one aspect of this anxious problem. In truth, it forms part of a much wider and deeper need—the need for a new response to the total challenge of the machine.

THE FUNDAMENTAL HERESY

Our condition can be described in these terms:

Industrial civilization may yet undo man. But since the venture of a progressively artificial environment cannot, will not, and indeed, should not, be voluntarily discarded, the task of adapting life *in such a surrounding* to the requirements of human existence must be resolved if man is to continue on earth. No one can foretell whether such an adjustment is possible, or whether man must perish in the attempt. Hence the dark undertone of concern.

Meanwhile, the first phase of the Machine Age has run its course. It involved an organization of society that derived its name from its central institution, the market. This system is on the downgrade. Yet our practical philosophy was overwhelmingly shaped by this spectacular episode. Novel notions about man and society become current and gained the status of axioms. Here they are:

As regards *man,* we were made to accept the heresy that his motives can be described as "material" and "ideal," and that the incentives on which everyday life is organized spring from the "material" motives. Both utilitarian liberalism and popular Marxism favored such views.

As regards *society,* the kindred doctrine was propounded that its institutions were "determined" by the economic system. This opinion was even more popular with Marxists than with liberals.

Under a market-economy both assertions were, of course, true. *But only under such an economy*. In regard to the past, such a view was no more than an anachronism. In regard to the future, it was a mere prejudice. Yet under the influence of current schools of thought, reinforced by the authority of science and religion, politics and business, these strictly time-bound phenomena came to be regarded as timeless, as transcending the age of the market.

To overcome such doctrines, which constrict our minds and souls and greatly enhance the difficulty of the life-saving adjustment, may require no less than a reform of our consciousness.

THE MARKET TRAUMA

The birth of laissez faire administered a shock to civilized man's views of himself, from the effects of which he never quite recovered. Only very gradually are we realizing what happened to us as recently as a century ago.

Liberal economy, this primary reaction of man to the machine, was a violent break with the conditions that preceded it. A chain-reaction was started —what before was merely isolated markets was transmuted into a self-regulating *system* of markets. And with the new economy, a new society sprang into being.

The crucial step was this: labor and land were made into commodities, that is, they were treated *as if* produced for sale. Of course, they were not actually commodities, since they were either not produced at all (as land) or, if so, not for sale (as labor).

Yet no more thoroughly effective fiction was ever devised. By buying and selling labor and land freely, the mechanism of the market was made to apply to them. There was now supply of labor, and demand for it; there was supply of land, and demand for it. Accordingly, there was a market price for the use of labor power, called wages, and a market price for the use of land, called rent. Labor and land were provided with markets of their own, similar to the commodities proper that were produced with their help.

The true scope of such a step can be gauged if we remember that labor is only another name for man, and land for nature. The commodity fiction handed over the fate of man and nature to the play of an automaton running in its own grooves and governed by its own laws.

Nothing similar had ever been witnessed before. Under the mercantile regime, though it deliberately pressed for the creation of markets, the converse principle still operated. Labor and land were not entrusted to the market; they formed part of the organic structure of society. Where land was marketable, only the determination of price was, as a rule, left to the parties; where labor was subject to contract, wages themselves were usually assessed by public authority. Land stood under the custom of manor, monastery, and township, under common-law limitations concerning rights of real property; labor was regulated by laws against beggary and vagrancy, statutes of laborers and artificers, poor laws, guild and municipal ordinances. In effect, all societies known to anthropologists and historians restricted markets to commodities in the proper sense of the term.

Market-economy thus created a new type of society. The economic or productive system was here entrusted to a self-acting device. An institutional mechanism controlled human beings in their everyday activities as well as the resources of nature.

This instrument of material welfare was under the sole control of the incentives of hunger and gain—or, more precisely, fear of going without the necessities of life, and expectation of profit. So long as no propertyless person could satisfy his craving for food without first selling his labor in the market, and so long as no propertied person was prevented from buying in the cheapest market and selling in the dearest, the blind mill would turn out ever-increasing amounts of commodities for the benefit of the human race. Fear of starvation with the worker, lure of profit with the employer, would keep the vast establishment running.

In this way an "economic sphere" came into existence that was sharply delimited from other institutions in society. Since no human aggregation can survive without a functioning productive apparatus, its embodiment in a distinct and separate sphere had the effect of making the "rest" of society dependent upon the sphere. This autonomous zone, again, was regulated by a mechanism that controlled its functioning. As a result, the market mechanism became determinative for the life of the body social. No wonder that the emergent human aggregation was an "economic" society to a degree previously never even approximated. "Economic motives" reigned supreme in a world of their own, and the individual was made to act on them under pain of being trodden under foot by the juggernaut market.

Such a forced conversion to a utilitarian outlook fatefully warped Western man's understanding of himself.

HUNGER AND GAIN ENTHRONED

This new world of "economic motives" was based on a fallacy. Intrinsically, hunger and gain are no more "economic" than love or hate, pride or prejudice. No human motive is *per se* economic. There is no such thing as a *sui generis* economic experience in the sense in which man may have a religious, aesthetic, or sexual experience. These latter give rise to motives that broadly aim at evoking similar experiences. In regard to material production these terms lack self-evident meaning.

The economic factor, which underlies all social life, no more gives rise to definite incentives than the equally universal law of gravitation. Assuredly, if we do not eat, we must perish, as much as if we were crushed under the weight of a falling rock. But the pangs of hunger are not automatically translated into an incentive to produce. Production is not an individual, but a collective affair. If an individual is hungry, there is nothing definite for him to do. Made desperate, he might rob or steal, but such an action can hardly be called productive. With man, the political animal, everything is given not by natural, but by social circumstance. What made the 19th century think of hunger and gain as "economic" was simply the organization of production under a market economy.

Hunger and gain are here linked with production through the need of "earning an income." For under such a system, man, if he is to keep alive, is compelled to buy goods on the market with the help of an income derived from selling other goods on the market. The name of these incomes—wages, rent, interest—varies accordingly to what is offered for sale: use of labor power, of land, or of money; the income called profit—the remuneration of the entrepreneur—derives from the sale of goods that fetch a higher price than the goods that go into the producing of them. Thus all incomes derive from sales, and all sales—directly or indirectly—contribute to production. The latter is, in effect, *incidental to the earning of an income*. So long as an individual is "earning an income," he is, automatically, contributing to production.

Obviously, the system works only so long as individuals have a reason to indulge in the activity of "earning an income." The motives of hunger and gain—separately and conjointly—provide them with such a reason. These two motives are thus geared to production and, accordingly, are termed "economic." The semblance is compelling that hunger and gain are *the* incentives on which any economic system must rest.

This assumption is baseless. Ranging over human societies, we find hunger and gain not appealed to as incentives to production, and where so appealed to, they are fused with other powerful motives.

Aristotle was right: man is not an economic, but a social being. He does not aim at safeguarding his individual interest in the acquisition of material possessions, but rather at insuring social good-will, social status, social assets. He values possessions primarily as a means to that end. His incentives are of that "mixed" character which we associate with the endeavor to gain social approval—productive efforts are no more than incidental to this. *Man's economy is, as a rule, submerged in his social relations.* The change from this to a society which was, on the contrary, submerged in the economic system was an entirely novel development.

FACTS

The evidence of facts, I feel, should at this point be adduced.

First, there are the discoveries of primitive economics. Two names are outstanding: Bronislaw Malinowski and Richard Thurnwald. They and some other research workers revolutionized our conceptions in this field and, by so doing, founded a new discipline. The myth of the individualistic savage had been exploded long ago. Neither the crude egotism, nor the apocryphal propensity to barter, truck, and exchange, nor even the tendency to cater to one's self was in evidence. But equally discredited was the legend of the communistic psychology of the savage, his supposed lack of appreciation for his own personal interests. (Roughly, it appeared that man was very much the same all through the ages. Taking his institutions not in isolation, but in their interrelation, he was mostly found to be behaving in a manner broadly comprehensible to us.) What appeared as "communism" was the fact that the productive or economic system was usually arranged in such a fashion as not to threaten any individual with starvation. His place at the camp fire, his share in the common resources, was secure to him, whatever part he happened to have played in hunt, pasture, tillage, or gardening.

Here are a few instances: Under the *kraalland* system of the Kaffirs, "destitution is impossible: whosoever needs assistance receives it unquestioningly" (L. P. Mair, *An African People in the Twentieth Century,* 1934). No Kwakiutl "ever ran the least risk of going hungry" (E. M. Loeb, *The Dis-*

tribution and Function of Money in Early Society, 1936). "There is no starvation in societies living on the subsistence margin" (M. J. Herskovits, *The Economic Life of Primitive Peoples,* 1940). In effect, the individual is not in danger of starving unless the community as a whole is in a like predicament. It is this absence of the menace of individual destitution that makes primitive society, in a sense, more humane than 19th-century society, and at the same time less *"economic."*

The same applies to the stimulus of individual gain. Again, a few quotations: "The characteristic feature of primitive economics is the absence of any desire to make profits from production and exchange" (R. Thurnwald, *Economics in Primitive Communities,* 1932). "Gain, which is often the stimulus for work in more civilized communities, never acts as an impulse to work under the original native conditions" (B. Malinowski, *Argonauts of the Western Pacific,* 1930). If so-called economic motives were natural to man, we would have to judge all early and primitive societies as thoroughly unnatural.

Secondly, there is no difference between primitive and civilized society in this regard. Whether we turn to ancient city-state, despotic empire, feudalism, 13th-century urban life, 16th-century mercantile regime, or 18th-century regulationism—invariably the economic system is found to be merged in the social. Incentives spring from a large variety of sources, such as custom and tradition, public duty and private commitment, religious observance and political allegiance, judicial obligation and administrative regulation as established by prince, municipality, or guild. Rank and status, compulsion of law and threat of punishment, public praise and private reputation, insure that the individual contributes his share to production.

Fear of privation or love of profit need not be altogether absent. Markets occur in all kinds of societies, and the figure of the merchant is familiar to many types of civilization. But isolated markets do not link up into an economy. The motive of gain was specific to merchants, as was valor to the knight, piety to the priest, and pride to the craftsman. The notion of making the motive of gain universal never entered the heads of our ancestors. At no time prior to the second quarter of the 19th century were markets more than a subordinate feature in society.

Thirdly, there was the startling abruptness of the change. Predominance of markets emerged not as a matter of degree, but of kind. Markets through which otherwise self-sufficient householders get rid of their surplus neither direct production nor provide the producer with his income. This is only the case in a market-economy where *all* incomes derive from sales, and commodities are obtainable exclusively by purchase. A free market for labor was born in England only about a century ago. The ill-famed Poor Law Reform (1834) abolished the rough-and-ready provisions made for the paupers by patriarchal governments. The poorhouse was transformed from a refuge of the destitute into an abode of shame and mental torture to which even hunger and misery were preferable. Starvation or work was the alternative left to the poor. Thus was a competitive national market for labor created. Within a decade, the Bank Act (1844) established the principle of the gold standard; the making of money was removed from the hands of the government regardless of the effect upon the level of employment. Simultaneously, reform of land laws mobilized the land, and repeal of the Corn Laws (1846) created a world pool of grain, thereby making the unprotected Continental peasant-farmer subject to the whims of the market.

Thus were established the three tenets of economic liberalism, the principle on which market economy was organized: that labor should find its price on the market; that money should be supplied by a self-adjusting mechanism; that commodities should be free to flow from country to country irrespective of the consequences—in brief, a labor market, the gold standard, and free trade. A self-inflammatory process was induced, as a result of which the formerly harmless market pattern expanded into a sociological enormity.

BIRTH OF A DELUSION

These facts roughly outline the genealogy of an "economic" society. Under such conditions the human world must appear as determined by "economic" motives. It is easy to see why.

Single out whatever motive you please, and organize production in such a manner as to make that motive the individual's incentive to produce, and you will have induced a picture of man as altogether absorbed by that particular motive. Let that motive be religious, political, or aesthetic; let it be pride, prejudice, love, or envy; and man will appear as essentially religious, political, aesthetic, proud, prejudiced, engrossed in love or envy. Other motives, in contrast will appear distant and shadowy since they cannot be relied upon to operate in the vital business of production. The particular motive selected will represent "real" man.

As a matter of fact, human beings will labor for a large variety of reasons as long as things are arranged accordingly. Monks traded for religious reasons, and monasteries became the largest trading establishments in Europe. The Kula trade of the Trobriand Islanders, one of the most intricate barter arrangements known to man, is mainly an aesthetic pursuit. Feudal economy was run on customary lines. With the Kwakiutl, the chief aim of industry seems to be to satisfy a point of honor. Under mercantile despotism, industry was often planned so as to serve power and glory. Accordingly, we tend to think of monks or villeins, western Melanesians, the Kwakiutl, or 17th-century statesmen, as ruled by religion, aesthetics, custom, honor, or politics, respectively.

Under capitalism, every individual has to earn an income. If he is a worker, he has to sell his labor at current prices; if he is an owner, he has to make as high a profit as he can, for his standing with his fellows will depend upon the level of his income. Hunger and gain—even if vicariously—make them plough and sow, spin and weave, mine coal, and pilot planes. Consequently, members of such a society will think of themselves as governed by these twin motives.

In actual fact, man was never as selfish as the theory demanded. Though the market mechanism brought his dependence upon material goods to the fore, "economic" motives never formed with him the sole incentive to work. In vain was he exhorted by economists and utilitarian moralists alike to discount in business all other motives than "material" ones. On closer investigation, he was still found to be acting on remarkably "mixed" motives, not excluding those of duty towards himself and others—and maybe, secretly, even enjoying work for its own sake.

However, we are not here concerned with actual, but with assumed motives, not with the psychology, but with the ideology of business. *Not on the former, but on the latter, are views of man's nature based*. For once society expects a definite behavior on the part of its members, and prevailing institutions become roughly capable of enforcing that behavior, opinions on human nature will tend to mirror the ideal whether it resembles actuality or not.

Accordingly, hunger and gain were defined as "economic" motives, and man was supposed to be acting on them in everyday life, while his other motives appeared more ethereal and removed from humdrum existence. Honor and pride, civic obligation and moral duty, even self-respect and common decency were now deemed irrelevant to production, and were significantly summed up in the word "ideal." Hence man was believed to consist of two components, one more akin to hunger and gain, the other to honor and power. The one was "material," the other "ideal"; the one "economic," the other "non-economic"; the one "rational," the other "non-rational." The Utilitarians went so far as to identify the two sets of terms, thus endowing the "economic" side of man's character with the aura of rationality.

He who would have refused to imagine that he was acting for gain alone was thus considered not only immoral, but also mad.

ECONOMIC DETERMINISM

The market mechanism moreover created the delusion of economic determinism as a general law for all human society.

Under a market-economy, of course, this law holds good. Indeed, the working of the economic system here not only "influences" the rest of society, but determines it—as in a triangle the sides not merely influence, but determine, the angles.

Take the stratification of classes. Supply and demand in the labor market were *identical* with the classes of workers and employers, respectively. The social classes of capitalists, landowners, tenants, brokers, merchants, professionals, and so on, were delimited by the respective markets for land, money and capital and their uses, or for various services. The income of these social classes was fixed by the market, their rank and position by their income.

This was a complete reversal of the secular practice. In Maine's famous phrase, "contractus" replaced "status"; or, as Tönnies preferred to put it, "society" superseded "community"; or, in terms of the present article, *instead of the economic system being embedded in social relationships, these relationships were now embedded in the economic system.*

While social classes were directly, other institutions were indirectly determined by the market mechanism. State and government, marriage and the rearing of children, the organization of science and education, of religion and the arts, the choice of profession, the forms of habitation, the shape of settlements, the very aesthetics of private life—everything had to comply with the utilitarian pattern, or at least not interfere with the working of the market mechanism. But since very few human activities can be carried on in the void, even a saint needing his pillar, the indirect effect of the market system came very near to determining the whole of society. It was almost impossible to avoid the erroneous conclusion that as "economic" man was "real" man, so the economic system was "really" society.

SEX AND HUNGER

Yet it would be truer to say that the basic human institutions abhor unmixed motives. Just as the provisioning of the individual and his family does not commonly rely on the motive of hunger, so the institution of the family is not based on the sexual motive.

Sex, like hunger, is one of the most powerful of incentives when released from the control of other incentives. That is probably why the family in all its variety of forms is never allowed to center on the sexual instinct, with its intermittences and vagaries, but on the combination of a number of effective motives that prevent sex from destroying an institution on which so much of man's happiness depends. Sex in itself will never produce anything better than a brothel, and even then it might have to draw on some incentives of the market mechanism. An economic system actually relying for its mainspring on hunger would be almost as perverse as a family system based on the bare urge of sex.

To attempt to apply economic determinism to all human societies is little short of fantastic. Nothing is more obvious to the student of social anthropology than the variety of institutions found to be compatible with practically identical instruments of production. Only since the market was permitted to grind the human fabric into the featureless uniformity of selenic erosion has man's institutional creativeness been in abeyance. No wonder that his social imagination shows signs of fatigue. It may come to a point where he will no longer be able to recover the elasticity, the imaginative wealth and power, of his savage endowment.

No protest of mine, I realize, will save me from being taken for an "idealist." For he who decries the importance of "material" motives must, it seems, be relying on the strength of "ideal" ones. Yet no worse misunderstanding is possible. Hunger and gain have nothing specifically "material" about them. Pride, honor, and power, on the other hand, are not necessarily "higher" motives than hunger and gain.

The dichotomy itself, we assert, is arbitrary. Let us once more adduce the analogy of sex. Assuredly, a significant distinction between "higher" and "lower" motives can here be drawn. Yet, whether hunger or sex, it is pernicious to *institutionalize* the separation of the "material" and "ideal" components of man's being. As regards sex, this truth, so vital to man's essential wholeness, has been recognized all along; it is at the basis of the institution of marriage. But in the equally strategic field of economy, it has been neglected. This latter field has been "separated out" of society as the realm of hunger and gain. Our animal dependence upon food has been bared and the naked fear of starvation permitted to run loose. Our humiliating enslavement to the "material," which all human culture is designed to mitigate, was deliberately made more rigorous. This is at the root of the "sickness of an acquisitive society" that Tawney warned of. And Robert Owen's genius was at its best when, a century before, he described the profit motive as "a principle entirely unfavorable to individual and public happiness."

THE REALITY OF SOCIETY

I plead for the restoration of that unity of motives which should inform man in his everyday activity as a producer, for the reabsorption of the economic system in society, for the creative adaptation of our ways of life to an industrial environment.

On all these counts, laissez-faire philosophy, with its corollary of a marketing society, falls to the ground. It is responsible for the splitting up of man's vital unity into "real" man, bent on material values, and his "ideal" better self. It is paralyzing our social imagination by more or less unconsciously fostering the prejudice of "economic determinism."

It has done its service in that phase of industrial civilization which is behind us. At the price of impoverishing the individual, it enriched society. Today, we are faced with the vital task of restoring the fullness of life to the person, even though this may mean a technologically less efficient society. In different countries in different ways, classical liberalism is being discarded. On Right and Left and Middle, new avenues are being explored. British Social-Democrats, American New Dealers, and also European fascists and American anti-New Dealers of the various "managerialist" brands, reject the liberal utopia. Nor should the present political mood of rejection of everything Russian blind us to the achievement of the Russians in creative adjustment to some of the fundamental aspects of an industrial environment.

On general grounds, the Communist's expectation of the "withering away of the State" seems to me to combine elements of liberal utopianism with practical indifference to institutional freedoms. As regards the withering State, it is impossible to deny that industrial society is complex society, and no complex society can exist without organized power at the center. Yet, again, this fact is no excuse for the Communist's slurring over the question of concrete institutional freedoms.

It is on this level of realism that the problem of individual freedom should be met. No human society is possible in which power and compulsion are absent, nor is a world in which force has no function. Liberal philosophy gave a false direction to our ideals in seeming to promise the fulfillment of such intrinsically utopian expectations.

But under the market system, society as a whole remained invisible. Anybody could imagine himself free from responsibility for those acts of compulsion on the part of the state which he, personally, repudiated, or for unemployment and destitution from which he, personally, did not benefit. Personally, he remained unentangled in the evils of power and economic value. In good conscience, he could deny their reality in the name of his imaginary freedom.

Power and economic value are, indeed, a paradigm of social reality. Neither power nor economic value spring from human volition; non-cooperation is impossible in regard to them. The function of power is to insure that measure of conformity which is needed for the survival of the group: as David Hume showed, its ultimate source is opinion—and who could help holding opinions of some sort or other? Economic value, in any society, insures the usefulness of the goods produced; it is a seal set on the division of labor. Its source is human wants—and how could we be expected not to prefer one thing to another? Any opinion or desire, no matter what society we live in, will make us participants in the creation of power and the constituting of value. No freedom to do otherwise is conceivable. An ideal that would ban power and compulsion from society is intrinsically invalid. By ignoring this limitation on man's meaningful wishes, the marketing view of society reveals its essential immaturity.

THE PROBLEM OF FREEDOM

The breakdown of market-economy imperils two kinds of freedom: some good, some bad.

That the freedom to exploit one's fellows, or the freedom to make inordinate gains without commensurable service to the community, the freedom to keep technological inventions from being used for the public benefit, or the freedom to profit from public calamities secretly engineered for private advantage, may disappear, together with the free market, is all to the good.

But the market-economy under which these freedoms thrived also produced freedoms that we prize highly. Freedom of conscience, freedom of speech, freedom of meeting, freedom of association, freedom to choose one's job—we cherish them for their own sake. Yet to a large extent they were by-products of the same economy that was also responsible for the evil freedoms.

The existence of a separate economic sphere in society created, as it were, a gap between politics and economics, between government and industry, that was in the nature of a no man's land. As division of sovereignty between pope and emperor left medieval princes in a condition of freedom sometimes bordering on anarchy, so division of sovereignty between government and industry in the 19th century allowed even the poor man to enjoy freedoms that partly compensated for his wretched status.

Current scepticism in regard to the future of freedom largely rests on this.

There are those who argue, like Hayek, that since free institutions were a product of market-economy, they must give place to serfdom once that economy disappears. There are others, like Burnham, who assert the inevitability of some new form of serfdom called "managerialism."

Arguments like these merely prove to what extent economistic prejudice is still rampant. For such determinism, as we have seen, is only another name for the market-mechanism. It is hardly logical to argue the effects of its absence on the strength of an economic necessity which derives from its presence. And it is certainly contrary to Anglo-Saxon experience. Neither the freezing of labor nor selective service abrogated the essential freedoms of the American people, as anybody can witness who spent the crucial years 1940–1943 in these States. Great Britain during the war introduced an all-round planned economy and did away with that separation of government and industry from which 19th-century freedom sprang, yet never were public liberties more securely entrenched than at the height of the emergency. In truth, we will have just as much freedom as we will desire to create and to safeguard. There is no *one* determinant in human society. Institutional guarantees of personal freedom are compatible with any economic system. In market society alone did the economic mechanism lay down the law.

MAN VS. INDUSTRY

What appears to our generation as the problem of capitalism is, in reality, the far greater problem of an industrial civilization. The economic liberal is blind to this fact. In defending capitalism as an economic system, he ignores the challenge of the Machine Age. Yet the dangers that make the bravest quake today transcend economy. The idyllic concerns of trust-busting and Taylorization have been superseded by Hiroshima. Scientific barbarism is dogging our footsteps. The Germans were planning a contrivance to make the sun emanate death rays. We, in fact, produced a burst of death rays that blotted out the sun. Yet the Germans had an evil philosophy and we had a humane philosophy. In this we should learn to see the symbol of our peril.

Among those in America who are aware of the dimensions of the problem, two tendencies are discernible: some believe in elites and aristocracies, in managerialism and the corporation. They feel that the whole of society should be more intimately adjusted to the economic system, which they would wish to maintain unchanged. This is the ideal of the Brave New World, where the individual is conditioned to support an order that has been designed for him by such as are wiser than he. Others, on the contrary, believe that in a truly democratic society, the problem of industry would resolve itself through the planned intervention of the producers and consumers themselves. Such conscious and responsible action is, indeed, one of the embodiments of freedom in a complex society. But, as the contents of this article suggest, such an endeavor cannot be successful unless it is disciplined by a total view of man and society very different from that which we inherited from market-economy.

THE ANATOMY OF SOCIETY: ECONOMY

4. POLITICAL ECONOMY: PROPORTIONING WELFARE, FREEDOM, AND CONTROL

FRIEDRICH ENGELS

FRIEDRICH ENGELS (1820–1895) has often been considered a mere shadow of Karl Marx, but his own writings show considerable independence of mind and suggest rather that he subordinated his career to what he considered Marx's historical mission—the tribute that talent pays to genius. Born in Barmen, Germany, the son of a textile manufacturer, he turned to radicalism early and arrived at a materialist, anti-Utopian socialism similar to Marx's before the two men met in 1844. Their close association began soon after the publication of Engels's first book, *The Condition of the Working-Class in England in 1844* (first brought out in German in 1845), a minutely documented indictment of capitalism.

After the revolutions of 1848, Engels settled in England and in the early 1850's he moved to Manchester as his father's representative. Working with Marx proved an almost full-time occupation. They wrote books and pamphlets together; Engels sent Marx money for many years; he wrote articles to which Marx signed his name; and the two men carried on their voluminous correspondence in which they hammered out the outlines of their doctrine. When Marx died in 1883, Engels became his friend's literary executor and the grand old man of international socialism, with particular influence over the German Social Democrats.

The origins of the present reading furnish a striking commentary on Engels's career and relation to Marx. In the 1870's, the rather confused views of Eugen Dühring (1833–1921), a blind man and an anti-Semitic socialist academician, had found an enthusiastic following among many German Social Democrats. The leaders of that movement, Bebel and Liebknecht, considered themselves inadequately versed in the theory of socialism and begged Marx and Engels to write a statement that would at once refute Dühring and clarify Marxism, since Volume I of Marx's *Capital,* which had come out in 1867, was far too technical to be widely understood or even read. Marx was busy on Volume II of that work, while Engels was unwilling to enter into a polemic with a blind man and anxious to pursue his own researches into natural philosophy. But as so often before, it was Engels who sacrificed his work to the uncongenial task, although Marx wrote sections of the resulting book. The refutation, popularly known as the *Anti-Dühring* (published first as a series of articles and then as a book in 1878), was promptly banned in Germany. In 1882 a Swiss publisher brought out a "thoroughly revised and popularized" version of parts of that book, a pamphlet which became known in its English translation as *Socialism: Utopian and Scientific.* It is possibly the most effective nontechnical summary of Marxism ever written. It was soon translated from the original German into all major languages, and, along with the *Communist Manifesto,* became the classic popular statement of the Marxist theory of dialectical materialism. The following selection has been taken from the 1935 American edition.

1878

SOCIALISM: UTOPIAN AND SCIENTIFIC

I

MODERN socialism is, in its essence, the direct product of the recognition, on the one hand, of the class antagonisms existing in the society of today between proprietors and non-proprietors, between capitalists and wage workers; on the other hand, of the anarchy existing in production. But, in its theoretical form, modern socialism originally appears ostensibly as a more logical extension of the principles laid down by the great French philosophers of the eighteenth century. Like every new theory, modern socialism had, at first, to connect itself with the intellectual stock in trade ready to its hand, however deeply its roots lay in material economic facts.

The great men, who in France prepared men's minds for the coming revolution, were themselves extreme revolutionists. They recognised no external authority of any kind whatever. Religion, natural science, society, political institutions, everything, was subjected to the most unsparing criticism; everything must justify its existence before the judgment seat of reason, or give up existence. Reason became the sole measure of everything. It was the time when, as Hegel says, the world stood upon its head; [1] first, in the sense that the human head, and the principles arrived at by its thought, claimed to be the basis of all human action and association; but by and by, also, in the wider sense that the reality which was in contradiction to these principles had, in fact, to be turned upside down. Every form of society and government then existing, every old traditional notion was flung into the lumber room as irrational; the world had hitherto allowed itself to be led solely by prejudices; everything in the past deserved only pity and contempt. Now, for the first time, appeared the light of day, the kingdom of reason; henceforth

---

[1] This is the passage on the French Revolution: "Thought, the concept of law, all at once made itself felt, and against this the old scaffolding of wrong could make no stand. In this conception of law, therefore, a constitution has now been established, and henceforth everything must be based upon this. Since the sun had been in the firmament, and the planets circled round him, the sight had never been seen of man standing upon his head—i.e., on the idea—and building reality after this image. Anaxagoras first said that the *Nous,* reason, rules the world; but now, for the first time, had man come to recognise that the Idea must rule the mental reality. And this was a magnificent sunrise. All thinking beings have participated in celebrating this holy day. A sublime emotion swayed men at that time, an enthusiasm of reason pervaded the world, as if now had come the reconciliation of the Divine Principle with the world." Hegel: Philosophy of History, 1840, p. 535. Is it not high time to set the Anti-Socialist Law in action against such teachings, subversive and to the common danger, by the late Professor Hegel?

superstition, injustice, privilege, oppression, were to be superseded by eternal truth, eternal right, equality based on nature and the inalienable rights of man.

We know today that this kingdom of reason was nothing more than the idealized kingdom of the bourgeoisie; that this eternal right found its realization in bourgeois justice; that this equality reduced itself to bourgeois equality before the law; that bourgeois property was proclaimed as one of the essential rights of man; and that the government of reason, the *Contrat Social* of Rousseau, came into being, and only could come into being, as a democratic bourgeois republic. The great thinkers of the eighteenth century could, no more than their predecessors, go beyond the limits imposed upon them by their epoch.

But, side by side with the antagonism of the feudal nobility and the burghers, who claimed to represent all the rest of society, was the general antagonism of exploiters and exploited, of rich idlers and poor workers. It was this very circumstance that made it possible for the representatives of the bourgeoisie to put themselves forward as representing not one special class, but the whole of suffering humanity. Still further. From its origin, the bourgeoisie was saddled with its antithesis: capitalists cannot exist without wage workers, and, in the same proportion as the mediaeval burgher of the guild developed into the modern bourgeois, the guild journeyman and the day laborer, outside the guilds, developed into the proletarian. And although, upon the whole, the bourgeoisie, in its struggle with the nobility, could claim to represent at the same time the interests of the different working classes of that period, yet in every great bourgeois movement there were independent outbursts of that class which was the forerunner, more or less developed, of the modern proletariat. For example, at the time of the German reformation and the peasants' war, the Anabaptists and Thomas Münzer; in the great English Revolution, the Levellers; in the great French Revolution, Babeuf.

There were theoretical enunciations corresponding with these revolutionary uprisings of a class not yet developed; in the sixteenth and seventeenth centuries, utopian pictures of ideal social conditions; in the eighteenth, actual communistic theories (Morelly and Mably). The demand for equality was no longer limited to political rights; it was extended also to the social conditions of individuals. It was not simply class privileges that were to be abolished, but class distinctions themselves. A communism, ascetic, denouncing all the pleasures of life, Spartan, was the first form of the new teaching. Then came the three great Utopians: Saint Simon, to whom the middle class movement, side by side with the proletarian, still had a certain significance; Fourier; and Owen, who in the country where capitalist production was most developed, and under the influence of the antagonisms begotten of this, worked out his proposals for the removal of class distinction systematically and in direct relation to French materialism.

One thing is common to all three. Not one of them appears as a representative of the interests of that proletariat which historical development had in the meantime produced. Like the French philosophers, they do not claim to emancipate a particular class to begin with, but all humanity at once. Like them, they wish to bring in the kingdom of reason and eternal justice, but this kingdom, as they see it, is as far as heaven from earth from that of the French philosophers.

For, to our three social reformers, the bourgeois world, based upon the principles of these philosophers, is quite as irrational and unjust, and, therefore, finds its way to the dust hole quite as readily as feudalism and all the earlier stages of society. If pure reason and justice have not, hitherto, ruled the world, this has been the case only because men have not rightly understood them. What was wanted was the individual man of genius, who has now arisen and who understands the truth. That he has now arisen, that the truth has now been clearly understood, is not an inevitable event, following of necessity in the chain of historical development, but a mere happy accident. He might just as well have been born five hundred years earlier, and might then have spared humanity five hundred years of error, strife and suffering.

We saw how the French philosophers of the eighteenth century, the forerunners of the revolution, appealed to reason as the sole judge of all that is. A rational government, rational society, were to be founded; everything that ran counter to eternal reason was to be remorselessly done away with. We saw also that this eternal reason was in reality nothing but the idealized understanding of the eighteenth century citizen, just then evolving into the bourgeois. The French Revolution had realized this rational society and government.

But the new order of things, rational enough as compared with earlier conditions, turned out to be by no means absolutely rational. The state based upon reason completely collapsed. Rousseau's *Contrat Social* had found its realization in the Reign of Terror, from which the bourgeoisie, which had lost confidence in its own political capacity, had taken refuge first in the corruption of the Directorate, and, finally, under the wing of the Napoleonic despotism. The promised eternal peace was turned into an endless war of conquest. The society based upon reason had fared no better. The antagonism between rich and poor, instead of dissolving into general prosperity, had become intensified by the removal of the guild and other privileges, which had to some extent bridged it over, and by the removal of the charitable institutions of the Church. The "freedom of property" from feudal fetters, now veritably accomplished, turned out to be, for the small capitalists and small proprietors, the freedom to sell their small property, crushed under the overmastering competition of the large capitalists and landlords, to these great lords, and thus, as far as the small capitalists and peasant proprietors were concerned, became "freedom *from* property." The development of industry upon a capitalistic basis made poverty and misery of the working masses conditions of existence of society. Cash payment became more and more, in Carlyle's phrase, the sole nexus between man and man. The number of crimes increased from year to year. Formerly, the feudal vices had openly stalked about in broad daylight; though not eradicated, they were now at any rate thrust into the background. In their stead, the bourgeois vices, hitherto practiced in secret, began to blossom all the more luxuriantly. Trade became to a greater and greater extent cheating. The "fraternity" of the revolutionary motto was realized in the chicanery and rivalries of the battle of competition. Oppression by force was replaced by corruption; the sword, as the first social lever, by gold. The right of the first night was transferred from the feudal lords to the bourgeois manufacturers. Prostitution increased to an extent never heard of. Marriage itself remained, as before, the legally recognised form, the official cloak of prostitution, and, moreover, was supplemented by rich crops of adultery.

In a word, compared with the splendid promises of the philosophers, the social and political institutions born of the "triumph of reason" were bitterly disappointing caricatures. All that was wanting was the men to formulate this disappointment, and they came with the turn of the century. In 1802 Saint Simon's *Geneva Letters* appeared; in 1808 appeared Fourier's first work, although the groundwork of his theory dated from 1799; on January 1, 1800, Robert Owen undertook the direction of New Lanark.

At this time, however, the capitalist mode of production, and with it the antagonism between the bourgeoisie and the proletariat, was still very incompletely developed. Modern industry which had just arisen in England was still unknown in France. But modern industry develops, on the one hand, the conflicts which make absolutely necessary a revolution in the mode of production and the doing away with its capitalistic character—conflicts not only between the classes begotten of it, but also between the very productive forces and the forms of exchange created by it. And, on the other hand, it develops, in these very gigantic productive forces, the means of ending these conflicts. If, therefore, about the year 1800, the conflicts arising from the new social order were only just beginning to take shape, this holds still more fully as to the means of ending them. The "have-nothing" masses of Paris during the Reign of Terror were able for a moment to gain the mastery, and thus to lead the bourgeois revolution to victory in spite of the bourgeoisie itself. But, in doing so, they only proved how impossible it was for their domination to last under the conditions then obtaining. The proletariat, which then for the first time evolved itself from these "have-nothing" masses as the nucleus of a new class, as yet quite incapable of independent political action, appeared as an oppressed, suffering order, to whom, in its incapacity to help itself, help could, at best, be brought in from without or down from above.

This historical situation also dominated the founders of socialism. To the crude conditions of capitalistic production and the crude class conditions corresponded crude theories. The solution of the social problems, which as yet lay hidden in undeveloped economic conditions, the utopians attempted to evolve out of the human brain. Society presented nothing but wrongs; to remove these was the task of reason. It was necessary, then, to discover a new and more perfect system of social order and to impose this upon society from without by propaganda, and, wherever it was possible, by the example of model experiments. These new social systems were foredoomed as utopian; the more completely they were worked out in detail, the more they could not avoid drifting off into pure phantasies. . . .

The utopians' mode of thought has for a long time governed the socialist ideas of the nineteenth century, and still governs some of them. Until very recently all French and English socialists did homage to it. The earlier German communism, including that of Weitling, was of the same school. To all these, socialism is the expression of absolute truth, reason, and justice, and has only to be discovered to conquer all the world by virtue of its own power. And as absolute truth is independent of time, space, and of the historical development of man, it is a mere accident when and where it is discovered. With all this, absolute truth, reason, and justice are different with the founder of each different school. And as each one's special kind of absolute truth, reason, and justice is again conditioned by his subjective understanding, his conditions of existence, the measure of his knowledge and his intellectual training, there is no other ending possible in this conflict of absolute truths than that they shall be mutually exclusive one of the other. Hence, from this nothing could come but a kind of eclectic, average socialism, which, as a matter of fact, has up to the present time dominated the minds of most of the socialist workers in France and England. Hence, a mishmash allowing of the most manifold shades of opinion; a mishmash of such critical statements, economic theories, pictures of future society by the founders of different sects, as excite a minimum of opposition; a mishmash which is the more easily brewed the more the definite sharp edges of the individual constituents are rubbed down in the stream of debate, like rounded pebbles in a brook.

To make a science of socialism, it had first to be placed upon a real basis.

II

In the meantime, along with and after the French philosophy of the eighteenth century had arisen the new German philosophy, culminating in Hegel. Its greatest merit was the taking up again of dialectics as the highest form of reasoning. . . .

. . . In [the Hegelian] system—and herein is its great merit—for the first time the whole world, natural, historical, intellectual, is represented as a process, i.e., as in constant motion, change, transformation, development; and the attempt is made to trace out the internal connection that makes a continuous whole of all this movement and development. From this point of view the history of mankind no longer appeared as a wild whirl of senseless deeds of violence, all equally condemnable at the judgment seat of mature philosophic reason, and which are best forgotten as quickly as possible, but as the process of evolution of man himself. It was now the task of the intellect to follow the gradual march of this process through all its devious ways, and to trace out the inner law running through all its apparently accidental phenomena.

That the Hegelian system did not solve the problem it propounded is here immaterial. Its epoch-making merit was that it propounded the problem. This problem is one that no single individual will ever be able to solve. Although Hegel was—with Saint Simon—the most encyclopaedic mind of his time, yet he was limited, first, by the necessarily limited extent of his own knowledge, and, second, by the limited extent and depth of the knowledge and conceptions of his age. To these limits a third must be added. Hegel was an idealist. To him the thoughts within his brain were not the more or less abstract pictures of actual things and processes, but, conversely, things and their evolution were only the realized pictures of the "Idea," existing somewhere from eternity before the world existed. This way of thinking turned everything upside down, and completely reversed the actual connection of things in the world. Correctly and ingeniously as many individual groups of facts were grasped by Hegel, yet, for the reasons just given, there is much that is botched, artificial, labored, in a word, wrong in point of detail. The Hegelian system, in itself, was a colossal miscarriage—but it was also the last of its kind. It was suffering, in fact, from an internal and incurable contradiction. Upon the one hand, its essential proposition was the conception that human history is a process of evolution, which, by its very nature, cannot find its intellectual final term in the discovery of any so-called absolute truth. But, on the other hand, it laid claim to being the very essence of this absolute truth. A system of natural and historical knowledge embracing everything, and final for all time, is a contradiction to the fundamental law of dialectic reasoning. This law, indeed, by no means excludes, but, on the contrary, includes the idea that the systematic knowledge of the external universe can make giant strides from age to age.

The perception of the fundamental contradiction in German idealism led necessarily back to materialism, but *nota bene,* not to the simply metaphysical, exclusively mechanical materialism of the eighteenth century. Old materialism looked upon all previous history as a crude heap of irrationality and violence; modern materialism sees in it the process of evolution of humanity, and aims at discovering the laws thereof. With the French of the eighteenth century, and even with Hegel, the conception obtained of nature as a whole, moving in narrow circles, and forever immutable, with its eternal celestial bodies, as Newton, and unalterable organic species, as Linnaeus, taught. Modern materialism embraces the more recent discoveries of natural science according to which nature also has its history in time, the celestial bodies, like the organic species that, under favorable conditions, people them, being born and perishing. And even if nature, as a whole, must still be said to move in recurrent cycles, these cycles assume infinitely larger dimensions. In both aspects, modern materialism is essentially dialectic, and no longer requires the assistance of that sort of philosophy which, queen-like, pretended to rule the remaining mob of sciences. As soon as each special science is bound to make clear its position in the great totality of things and of our knowledge of things, a special science dealing with this totality is superfluous or unnecessary. That which still survives of all earlier philosophy is the science of thought and its laws—formal logic and dialectics. Everything else is subsumed in the positive science of nature and history.

While, however, the revolution in the conception of nature could only be made in proportion to the corresponding positive materials furnished by research, already much earlier certain historical facts had occurred which led to a decisive change in the conception of history. In 1831, the first working class rising took place in Lyons; between 1838 and 1842, the first national working class movement, that of the English Chartists, reached its height. The class struggle between proletariat and bourgeoisie came to the front in the history of the most advanced countries in Europe, in proportion to the development, upon the one hand, of modern industry, upon the other, of the newly acquired political supremacy of the bourgeoisie. Facts more and more strenuously gave the lie to the teachings of bourgeois economy as to the identity of the interests of capital and labor, as to the universal harmony and universal prosperity that would be the consequence of unbridled competition. All these things could no longer be ignored, any more than the French and English socialism, which was their theoretical, though very imperfect, expression. But the old idealist conception of history, which was not yet dislodged, knew nothing of class struggles based upon economic interests, knew nothing of economic interests; production and all economic relations appeared in it only as incidental, subordinate elements in the "history of civilization."

The new facts made imperative a new examination of all past history. Then it was seen that *all* past history, with the exception of its primitive stages, was the history of class struggles; that these warring classes of society are always the products of the modes of production and of exchange—in a word, of the *economic* conditions of their time; that the economic structure of society always furnishes the real basis, starting from which we can alone work out the ultimate explanation of the whole superstructure of juridical and political institutions as well as of the religious, philosophical, and other ideas of a given historical period. Hegel had freed history from metaphysics—he had made it dialectic; but his conception of history was essentially idealistic. But now idealism was driven from its last refuge, the philosophy of history; now a materialistic treatment of history was propounded, and a method found of explaining man's "knowing" by his "being," instead of, as heretofore, his "being" by his "knowing."

From that time forward socialism was no longer an accidental discovery of this or that ingenious brain, but the necessary outcome of the struggle between two historically developed classes—the proletariat and the bourgeoisie. Its task was no longer to manufacture a system of society as perfect as possible, but to examine the historico-economic succession of events from which these classes and their antagonisms had of necessity sprung, and to discover in the economic conditions thus created the means of ending the conflict. But the socialism of earlier days was as incompatible with this materialistic conception as the conception of nature of the French materialists was with dialectics and modern natural science. The socialism of earlier days certainly criticized the existing capitalistic mode of production and its consequences. But it could not explain them, and, therefore, could not get the mastery of them. It could only simply reject them as bad. The more strongly this earlier socialism denounced the exploitation of the working class, inevitable under capitalism, the less able was it clearly to show in what this exploitation consisted and how it arose. But for this it was necessary—(1) to present the capitalistic method of production in its historical connection and its inevitableness during a particular historical period, and therefore, also to present its inevitable downfall; and (2) to lay bare its essential character, which was still a secret. This was done by the discovery of *surplus value*. It was shown that the appropriation of unpaid labor is the basis of the capitalist mode of production and of the exploitation of the worker that occurs under it; that even if the capitalist buys the labor power of his laborer at its full value as a commodity on the market, he yet extracts more value from it than he paid for; and that in the ultimate analysis this surplus value forms those sums of value from which are heaped up the constantly increasing masses of capital in the hands of the possessing classes. The genesis of capitalist production and the production of capital were both explained.

These two great discoveries, the materialistic conception of history and the revelation of the secret of capitalistic production through surplus value, we owe to Marx. With these discoveries socialism became a science. The next thing was to work out all its details and relations.

III

The materialist conception of history starts from the proposition that the production of the means to support human life and, next to production, the exchange of things produced, is the basis of all social structure; that in every society that has appeared in history, the manner in which wealth is distributed and society divided into classes or orders is dependent upon what is produced, how it is produced, and how the products are exchanged. From this point of view the final causes of all social changes and political revolutions are to be sought, not in men's brains, not in man's better insight into eternal truth and justice, but in changes in the modes of production and exchange. They are to be sought, not in the *philosophy*, but in the *economics* of each particular epoch. The growing perception that existing social institutions are unreasonable and unjust, that reason has become unreason, and right wrong, is only proof that in the modes of production and exchange changes have silently taken place, with which the social order, adapted to earlier economic conditions, is no longer in keeping. From this it also follows that the means of getting rid of the incongruities that have been brought to light must also be present, in a more or less developed condition, within the changed modes of production themselves. These means are not to be invented by deduction from fundamental principles, but are to be discovered in the stubborn facts of the existing system of production.

What is, then, the position of modern socialism in this connection?

The present structure of society—this is now pretty generally conceded—is the creation of the ruling class of today, of the bourgeoisie. The mode of production peculiar to the bourgeoisie, known, since Marx, as the capitalist mode of production, was incompatible with the feudal system, with the privileges it conferred upon individuals, entire social ranks and local corporations, as well as with the hereditary ties of subordination which constituted the framework of its social organization. The bourgeoisie broke up the feudal system and built upon its ruins the capitalist order of society, the kingdom of free competition, of personal liberty, of the equality, before the law, of all commodity owners, of all the rest of the capitalist blessings. Thenceforward the capitalist mode of production could develop in freedom. Since steam, machinery, and the making of machines by machinery transformed the older manufacture into modern industry, the productive forces evolved under the guidance of the bourgeoisie developed with a rapidity and in a degree unheard of before. But just as the older manufacture, in its time, and handicraft, becoming more developed under its influence, had come into collision with the feudal trammels of the guilds, so now modern industry, in its more complete development, comes into collision with the bounds within which the capitalistic mode of production holds it confined. The new productive forces have already outgrown the capitalistic mode of using them. And this conflict between productive forces and modes of production is not a conflict engendered in the mind of man, like that between original sin and divine justice. It exists, in fact, objectively, outside us, independently of the will and actions even of the men that have brought it on. Modern socialism is nothing but the reflex, in thought, of this conflict in fact; its ideal reflection in the minds, first, of the class directly suffering under it, the working class.

Now, in what does this conflict consist?

Before capitalistic production, i.e., in the Middle Ages, the system of petty industry obtained generally, based upon the private property of the laborers in their means of production; in the country, the agriculture of the small peasant, freeman or serf; in the towns, the handicrafts organized in guilds.

The instruments of labor—land, agricultural implements, the workshop, the tool—were the instruments of labor of single individuals, adapted for the use of one worker, and, therefore, of necessity, small, dwarfish, circumscribed. But for this very reason they belonged, as a rule, to the producer himself. To concentrate these scattered, limited means of production, to enlarge them, to turn them into the powerful levers of production of the present day—this was precisely the historic role of capitalist production and of its upholder, the bourgeoisie. In the fourth section of *Capital* Marx has explained in detail, how since the fifteenth century this has been historically worked out through the three phases of simple co-operation, manufacture, and modern industry. But the bourgeoisie, as is also shown there, could not transform these puny means of production into mighty productive forces, without transforming them, at the same time, from means of production of the individual into *social* means of production only workable by a collectivity of men. The spinning wheel, the hand loom, the blacksmith's hammer were replaced by the spinning machine, the power loom, the steam hammer; the individual workshop, by the factory, implying the co-operation of hundreds and thousands of workmen. In like manner, production itself changed from a series of individual into a series of social acts, and the products from individual to social products. The yarn, the cloth, the metal articles that now came out of the factory were the joint product of many workers, through whose hands they had successively to pass before they were ready. No one person could say of them: "I made that; this is *my* product."

But where, in a given society, the fundamental form of production is that spontaneous division of labor which creeps in gradually and not upon any preconceived plan, there the products take on the form of *commodities,* whose mutual exchange, buying and selling, enable the individual producers to satisfy their manifold wants. And this was the case in the Middle Ages. The peasant, e.g., sold to the artisan agricultural products and bought from him the products of handicraft. Into this society of individual producers, of commodity producers, the new mode of production thrust itself. In the midst of the old division of labor, grown up spontaneously and upon *no definite plan,* which had governed the whole of society, now arose divisions of labor upon *a definite plan,* as organized in the factory; side by side with *individual* production appeared *social* production. The products of both were sold in the same market, and, therefore, at prices approximately equal. But organization upon a definite plan was stronger than spontaneous division of labor. The factories working with the combined social forces of a collectivity of individuals produced their commodities far more cheaply than the individual small producers. Individual production succumbed in one department after another. Socialized production revolutionized all the old methods of production. But its revolutionary character was, at the same time, so little recognised, that it was, on the contrary, introduced as a means of increasing and developing the production of commodities. When it arose, it found ready-made, and made liberal use of, certain machinery for the production and exchange of commodities; merchants' capital, handicraft, wage labor. Socialized production thus introducing itself as a new form of the production of commodities, it was a matter of course that under it the old forms of appropriation remained in full swing, and were applied to its products as well.

In the mediaeval stage of evolution of the production of commodities, the question as to the owner of the product of labor could not arise. The individual producer, as a rule, had, from raw material belonging to himself, and generally his own handiwork, produced it with his own tools, by the labor of his own hands or of his family. There was no need for him to appropriate the new product. It belonged wholly to him, as a matter of course. His property in the product was, therefore, based *upon his own labor*. Even where external help was used, this was, as a rule, of little importance, and very generally was compensated by something other than wages. The apprentices and journeymen of the guilds worked less for board and wages than for education, in order that they might become master craftsmen themselves.

Then came the concentration of the means of production and of the producers in large workshops and manufactories, their transformation into actual socialized means of production and socialized producers. But the socialized producers and means of production and their products were still treated, after this change, just as they had been before, i.e., as the means of production and the products of individuals. Hitherto, the owner of the instruments of labor had himself appropriated the product, because as a rule it was his own product and the assistance of others was the exception. Now the owner of the instruments of labor always appropriated to himself the product, although it was no longer *his* product but exclusively the product of the *labor of others*. Thus, the products now produced socially were not appropriated by those who had actually set in motion the means of production and actually produced the commodities, but by the *capitalists*. The means of production, and production itself, had become in essence socialized. But they were subjected to a form of appropriation which presupposes the private production of individuals, under which, therefore, every one owns his own product and brings it to market. The mode of production is subjected to this form of appropriation, although it abolishes the conditions upon which the latter rests.[2]

This contradiction, which gives to the new mode of production its capitalistic character, *contains the germ of the whole of the social antagonisms of today*. The greater the mastery obtained by the new mode of production over all important fields of production and in all manufacturing countries, the more it reduced individual production to an insignificant residuum, *the more clearly was brought out the incompatibility of socialized production with capitalistic appropriation*.

The first capitalists found, as we have said, alongside of other forms of labor, wage labor ready-made for them on the market. But it was exceptional, complementary, necessary, transitory wage labor. The agricultural laborer, though, upon occasion, he hired himself out by the day, had a few acres of his own land on which he could at all events live at a pinch. The guilds were so organized that the journeyman of today became the master of tomorrow. But all this changed as soon as the means of production became socialized and concentrated in the hands of capitalists. The means of production, as well as the product of the individual producer became more and more worthless; there was nothing left for him but to turn wage worker under the capitalist. Wage labor, aforetime the exception and accessory, now became the rule and basis of all production; aforetime complementary, it now became the sole remaining function of the worker. The wage worker for a time became a wage worker for life. The number of these permanent wage workers was further enormously increased by the breaking up of the feudal system that occurred at the same time, by the disbanding of the retainers of the feudal lords, the eviction of the peasants from their homesteads, etc. The separation was made complete between the means of production concentrated in the hands of the capitalists on the one side, and the producers, possessing nothing but their labor power, on the other. *The contradiction between socialized production and capitalistic appropriation manifested itself as the antagonism of proletariat and bourgeoisie.*

We have seen that the capitalistic mode of production thrust its way into

[2] It is hardly necessary in this connection to point out, that, even if the form of appropriation remains the same, the *character* of the appropriation is just as much revolutionized as production is by the changes described above. It is, of course, a very different matter whether I appropriate to myself my own product or that of another. Note in passing that wage labor, which contains the whole capitalistic mode of production in embryo, is very ancient; in a sporadic, scattered form it existed for centuries alongside of slave labor. But the embryo could duly develop into the capitalistic mode of production only when the necessary historical preconditions had been furnished.

a society of commodity producers, of individual producers, whose social bond was the exchange of their products. But every society, based upon the production of commodities, has this peculiarity: that the producers have lost control over their own social inter-relations. Each man produces for himself with such means of production as he may happen to have, and for such exchange as he may require to satisfy his remaining wants. No one knows how much of his particular article is coming on the market, nor how much of it will be wanted. No one knows whether his individual product will meet an actual demand, whether he will be able to make good his cost of production or even to sell his commodity at all. Anarchy reigns in socialized production.

But the production of commodities, like every other form of production, has its peculiar inherent laws inseparable from it; and these laws work, despite anarchy, in and through anarchy. They reveal themselves in the only persistent form of social inter-relations, i.e., in exchange, and here they affect the individual producers as compulsory laws of competition. They are, at first, unknown to these producers themselves, and have to be discovered by them gradually and as the result of experience. They work themselves out, therefore, independently of the producers, and in antagonism to them, as inexorable natural laws of their particular form of production. The product governs the producers.

In mediaeval society, especially in the earlier centuries, production was essentially directed towards satisfying the wants of the individual. It satisfied, in the main, only the wants of the producer and his family. Where relations of personal dependence existed, as in the country, it also helped to satisfy the wants of the feudal lord. In all this there was, therefore, no exchange; the products, consequently, did not assume the character of commodities. The family of the peasant produced almost everything they wanted: clothes and furniture, as well as means of subsistence. Only when it began to produce more than was sufficient to supply its own wants and the payments in kind to the feudal lord, only then did it also produce commodities. This surplus, thrown into socialized exchange and offered for sale, became commodities.

The artisans of the towns, it is true, had from the first to produce for exchange. But they, also, themselves supplied the greatest part of their own individual wants. They had gardens and plots of land. They turned their cattle out into the communal forest, which, also, yielded them timber and firing. The women spun flax, wool, and so forth. Production for the purpose of exchange, production of commodities was only in its infancy. Hence, exchange was restricted, the market narrow, the methods of production stable; there was local exclusiveness without, local unity within; the market in the country, in the town, the guild.

But with the extension of the production of commodities, and especially with the introduction of the capitalist mode of production, the laws of commodity production, hitherto latent, came into action more openly and with greater force. The old bonds were loosened, the old exclusive limits broken through, the producers were more and more turned into independent, isolated producers of commodities. It became apparent that the production of society at large was ruled by absence of plan, by accident, by anarchy; and this anarchy grew to greater and greater height. But the chief means by aid of which the capitalist mode of production intensified this anarchy of socialized production was the exact opposite of anarchy. It was the increasing organization of production, upon a social basis, in every individual productive establishment. By this, the old, peaceful, stable condition of things was ended. Wherever this organization of production was introduced into a branch of industry, it brooked no other method of production by its side. The field of labor became a battle ground. The great geographical discoveries, and the colonization following upon them, multiplied markets and quickened the transformation of handicraft into manufacture. The war did not simply break out between the individual producers of particular localities. The local struggles begat in their turn national conflicts, the commercial wars of the seventeenth and the eighteenth centuries.

Finally, modern industry and the opening of the world market made the struggle universal, and at the same time gave it an unheard-of virulence. Advantages in natural or artificial conditions of production now decide the existence or non-existence of individual capitalists, as well as of whole industries and countries. He that falls is remorsely cast aside. It is the Darwinian struggle of the individual for existence transferred from nature to society with intensified violence. The conditions of existence natural to the animal appear as the final term of human development. The contradiction between socialized production and capitalistic appropriation now presents itself as *an antagonism between the organization of production in the individual workshop and the anarchy of production in society generally*.

The capitalistic mode of production moves in these two forms of the antagonism immanent to it from its very origin. It is never able to get out of that "vicious circle," which Fourier had already discovered. What Fourier could not, indeed, see in his time is: that this circle is gradually narrowing; that the movement becomes more and more a spiral, and must come to an end, like the movement of the planets, by collision with the center. It is the compelling force of anarchy in the production of society at large that more and more completely turns the great majority of men into proletarians; and it is the masses of the proletariat again who will finally put an end to anarchy in production. It is the compelling force of anarchy in social production that turns the limitless perfectibility of machinery under modern industry into a compulsory law by which every individual industrial capitalist must perfect his machinery more and more, under penalty of ruin.

But the perfecting of machinery is making human labor superfluous. If the introduction and increase of machinery mean the displacement of millions of manual, by a few machine workers, improvement in machinery means the displacement of more and more of the machine workers themselves. It means, in the last instance, the production of a number of available wage workers in excess of the average needs of capital, the formation of a complete industrial reserve army, as I called it in 1845, available at the times when industry is working at high pressure, to be cast out upon the street when the inevitable crash comes, a constant dead weight upon the limbs of the working class in its struggle for existence with capital, a regulator for the keeping of wages down to the low level that suits the interests of capital. Thus it comes about, to quote Marx, that machinery becomes the most powerful weapon in the war of capital against the working class; that the instruments of labor constantly tear the means of subsistence out of the hands of the laborer; that the very product of the worker is turned into an instrument for his subjugation. Thus it comes about that the economizing of the instruments of labor becomes at the same time, from the outset, the most reckless waste of labor power, and robbery based upon the normal conditions under which labor functions; that machinery, "the most powerful instrument for shortening labor time, becomes the most unfailing means for placing every moment of the laborer's time and that of his family at the disposal of the capitalist for the purpose of expanding the value of his capital." Thus it comes about that overwork of some becomes the preliminary condition for the idleness of others, and that modern industry, which hunts after new consumers over the whole world, forces the consumption of the masses at home down to a starvation minimum, and in doing this destroys its own home market.

The law . . . that always equilibrates the relative surplus population, or industrial reserve army, to the extent and energy of accumulation, this law rivets the laborer to capital more firmly than the wedges of Vulcan did Prometheus to the rock. It establishes an accumulation of misery, corresponding with accumulation of capital. Accumulation of wealth at one pole is, therefore, at the same time, accumulation of misery, agony of toil, slavery, ignorance, brutality, mental degradation, at the opposite pole, i.e., on the side of the class that produces *its own product in the form of capital.* [Marx, *Capital.*]

And to expect any other division of the products from the capitalistic mode of production is the same as expecting the electrodes of a battery not to decompose acidulated water, not to liberate oxygen at the positive, hydrogen at the negative pole, so long as they are connected with the battery.

We have seen that the ever-increasing perfectibility of modern machinery is, by the anarchy of social production, turned into a compulsory law that forces the individual industrial capitalist always to improve his machinery, always to increase its productive force. The bare possibility of extending the field of production is transformed for him into a similar compulsory law. The enormous expansive force of modern industry, compared with which that of gases is mere child's play, appears to us now as a *necessity* for expansion, both qualitative and quantitative, that laughs at all resistance. Such resistance is offered by consumption, by sales, by the markets for the products of modern industry. But the capacity for extension, extensive and intensive, of the markets is primarily governed by quite different laws, that work much less energetically. The extension of the markets cannot keep pace with the extension of production. The collision becomes inevitable, and as this cannot produce any real solution so long as it does not break in pieces the capitalist mode of production, the collisions become periodic. Capitalist production has begotten another "vicious circle."

As a matter of fact, since 1825, when the first general crisis broke out, the whole industrial and commercial world, production and exchange among all civilized peoples and their more or less barbaric hangers-on, are thrown out of joint about once every ten years. Commerce is at a standstill, the markets are glutted, products accumulate, as multitudinous as they are unsaleable, hard cash disappears, credit vanishes, factories are closed, the mass of the workers are in want of the means of subsistence, because they have produced too much of the means of subsistence; bankruptcy follows upon bankruptcy, execution upon execution. The stagnation lasts for years; productive forces and products are wasted and destroyed wholesale, until the accumulated mass of commodities finally filter off, more or less depreciated in value, until production and exchange gradually begin to move again. Little by little the pace quickens. It becomes a trot. The industrial trot breaks into a canter, the canter in turn grows into the headlong gallop of a perfect steeplechase of industry, commercial credit, and speculation, which finally, after breakneck leaps, ends where it began—in the ditch of a crisis. And so over and over again. We have now, since the year 1825, gone through this five times, and at the present moment (1877) we are going through it for the sixth time. And the character of these crises is so clearly defined that Fourier hit all of them off when he described the first as *"crise pléthorique,"* a crisis from plethora.

In these crises, the contradiction between socialized production and capitalist appropriation ends in a violent explosion. The circulation of commodities is, for the time being, stopped. Money, the means of circulation, becomes a hindrance to circulation. All the laws of production and circulation of commodities are turned upside down. The economic collision has reached its apogee. *The mode of production is in rebellion against the mode of exchange.*

The fact that the socialized organization of production within the factory has developed so far that it has become incompatible with the anarchy of production in society, which exists side by side with and dominates it, is brought home to the capitalists themselves by the violent concentration of capital that occurs during crisis, through the ruin of many large, and a still greater number of small, capitalists. The whole mechanism of the capitalist mode of production breaks down under the pressure of the productive forces, its own creations. It is no longer able to turn all this mass of means of production into capital. They lie fallow, and for that very reason the industrial reserve army must also lie fallow. Means of production, means of subsistence, available laborers, all the elements of production and of general wealth are present in abundance. But "abundance becomes the source of distress and want" (Fourier), because it is the very thing that prevents the transformation of the means of production and subsistence into capital. For in capitalistic society the means of production can only function when they have undergone a preliminary transformation into capital, into the means of exploiting human labor power. The necessity of this transformation into capital of the means of production and subsistence stands like a ghost between these and the workers. It alone prevents the coming together of the material and personal levers of production; it alone forbids the means of production to function, the workers to work and live. On the one hand, therefore, the capitalistic mode of production stands convicted of its own incapacity to direct further these productive forces. On the other, these productive forces themselves, with increasing energy, press forward to the removal of the existing contradiction, to the abolition of their quality as capital, to the *practical recognition of their character as social productive forces.*

This rebellion of the productive forces, as they grow more and more powerful, against their quality as capital, this stronger and stronger command that their social character shall be recognized, forces the capitalist class itself to treat them more and more as social productive forces, so far as this is possible under capitalist conditions. The period of industrial high pressure, with its unbounded inflation of credit, not less than the crash itself, by the collapse of great capitalist establishments, tends to bring about that form of the socialization of great masses of means of production, which we meet with in the different kinds of joint-stock companies. Many of these means of production and of distribution are, from the outset, so colossal, that, like the railroads, they exclude all other forms of capitalistic exploitation. At a further stage of evolution this form also becomes insufficient. The producers on a large scale in a particular branch of industry in a particular country unite in a "trust," a union for the purpose of regulating production. They determine the total amount to be produced, parcel it out among themselves, and thus enforce the selling price fixed beforehand. But trusts of this kind, as soon as business becomes bad, are generally liable to break up, and, on this very account, compel a yet greater concentration of association. The whole of the particular industry is turned into one gigantic joint-stock company; internal competition gives place to the internal monopoly of this one company. This has happened in 1890 with the English *alkali* production, which is now, after the fusion of 48 large works, in the hands of one company, conducted upon a single plan, and with a capital of £6,000,000.

In the trusts, freedom of competition changes into its very opposite—into monopoly; and the production without any definite plan of capitalistic society capitulates to the production upon a definite plan of the invading socialistic society. Certainly this is so far still to the benefit and advantage of the capitalists. But in this case the exploitation is so palpable that it must break down. No nation will put up with production conducted by trusts, with so barefaced an exploitation of the community by a small band of dividend mongers.

In any case, with trusts or without, the official representative of capitalist society—the state—will ultimately have to undertake the direction of production.[3] This necessity of conversion into state property is felt first in the

[3] I say "have to." For only when the means of production and distribution have *actually* outgrown the form of management by joint-stock companies, and when, therefore, the taking them over by the state has become *economically* inevitable, only then—even if it is the state of today that effects this—is there an economic advance, the attainment of another step preliminary to the taking over of all productive forces by society itself. But of late, since Bismarck went in for state ownership of industrial establishments, a kind of spurious socialism has arisen, degenerating, now and again, into something of flunkeyism, that without more ado declares *all*

great institutions for intercourse and communication—the post-office, the telegraphs, the railways.

If the crises demonstrate the incapacity of the bourgeoisie for managing any longer modern productive forces, the transformation of the great establishments for production and distribution into joint-stock companies, trusts, and state property show how unnecessary the bourgeoisie is for that purpose. All the social functions of the capitalist are now performed by salaried employees. The capitalist has no further social function than that of pocketing dividends, tearing off coupons, and gambling on the Stock Exchange, where the different capitalists despoil one another of their capital. At first the capitalistic mode of production forces out the workers. Now it forces out the capitalists, and reduces them, just as it reduced the workers, to the ranks of the surplus population, although not immediately into those of the industrial reserve army.

But the transformation, either into joint-stock companies and trusts, or into state ownership, does not do away with the capitalistic nature of the productive forces. In the joint-stock companies and trusts this is obvious. And the modern state, again, is only the organization that bourgeois society takes on in order to support the external conditions of the capitalist mode of production against the encroachments, as well of the workers as of individual capitalists. The modern state, no matter what its form, is essentially a capitalist machine, the state of the capitalists, the ideal personification of the total national capital. The more it proceeds to the taking over of productive forces, the more does it actually become the national capitalist, the more citizens does it exploit. The workers remain wage workers—proletarians. The capitalist relation is not done away with. It is rather brought to a head. But, brought to a head, it topples over. State ownership of the productive forces is not the solution of the conflict, but concealed within it are the technical conditions that form the elements of that solution.

This solution can only consist in the practical recognition of the social nature of the modern forces of production, and therefore in the harmonizing

state ownership, even of the Bismarckian sort, to be socialistic. Certainly, if the taking over by the state of the tobacco industry is socialistic, then Napoleon and Metternich must be numbered among the founders of socialism. If the Belgian state, for quite ordinary political and financial reasons, itself constructed its chief railway lines; if Bismarck, not under any economic compulsion, took over for the state the chief Prussian lines, simply to be the better able to have them in hand in case of war, to bring up the railway employees as voting cattle for the government, and especially to create for himself a new source of income independent of parliamentary votes—this was, in no sense, a socialistic measure, directly or indirectly, consciously or unconsciously. Otherwise, the Royal Maritime Company, the Royal porcelain manufacture, and even the regimental tailor of the army would also be socialistic institutions, or even, as was seriously proposed by a sly dog in Frederick William III's reign, the taking over by the state of the brothels.

of the modes of production, appropriation, and exchange with the socialized character of the means of production. And this can only come about by society openly and directly taking possession of the productive forces which have outgrown all control except that of society as a whole. The social character of the means of production and of the products today reacts against the producers, periodically disrupts all production and exchange, acts only like a law of nature working blindly, forcibly, destructively. But with the taking over by society of the productive forces, the social character of the means of production and of the products will be utilized by the producers with a perfect understanding of its nature, and instead of being a source of disturbance and periodical collapse, will become the most powerful lever of production itself.

Active social forces work exactly like natural forces, blindly, forcibly, destructively, so long as we do not understand and reckon with them. But when once we understand them, when once we grasp their action, their direction, their effects, it depends only upon ourselves to subject them more and more to our own will, and by means of them to reach our own ends. And this holds quite especially of the mighty productive forces of today. As long as we obstinately refuse to understand the nature and the character of these social means of action—and this understanding goes against the grain of the capitalist mode of production and its defenders—so long these forces are at work in spite of us, in opposition to us, so long they master us, as we have shown above in detail.

But when once their nature is understood, they can, in the hands of the producers working together, be transformed from master demons into willing servants. The difference is as that between the destructive force of electricity in the lightning of the storm, and electricity under command in the telegraph and the voltaic arc; the difference between a conflagration and fire working in the service of man. With this recognition at last of the real nature of the productive forces of today, the social anarchy of production gives place to a social regulation of production upon a definite plan, according to the needs of the community and of each individual. Then the capitalist mode of appropriation, in which the product enslaves first the producer and then the appropriator, is replaced by the mode of appropriation of the products that is based upon the nature of the modern means of production; upon the one hand, direct social appropriation, as means to the maintenance and extension of production—on the other, direct individual appropriation, as means of subsistence and of enjoyment.

While the capitalist mode of production more and more completely transforms the great majority of the population into proletarians, it creates the power which, under penalty of its own destruction, is forced to accomplish this revolution. While it forces on more and more the transformation of the vast means of production, already socialized, into state property, it shows itself the way of accomplishing this revolution. *The proletariat seizes political power and turns the means of production into state property.*

But, in doing this, it abolishes itself as proletariat, abolishes all class distinctions and class antagonisms, abolishes also the state as state. Society thus far, based upon class antagonisms, had need of the state. That is, of an organization of the particular class which was *pro tempore* the exploiting class, an organization for the purpose of preventing any interference from without with the existing conditions of production, and therefore, especially, for the purpose of forcibly keeping the exploited classes in the condition of oppression corresponding with the given mode of production (slavery, serfdom, wage labor). The state was the official representative of society as a whole; the gathering of it together into a visible embodiment. But it was this only in so far as it was the state of that class which itself represented, for the time being, society as a whole; in ancient times, the state of slave-owning citizens; in the Middle Ages, the feudal lords; in our own time, the bourgeoisie. When at last it becomes the real representative of the whole of society, it renders itself unnecessary. As soon as there is no longer any social class to be held in subjection; as soon as class rule and the individual struggle for existence based upon our present anarchy in production, with the collisions and excesses arising from these, are removed, nothing more remains to be repressed, and a special repressive force, a state, is no longer necessary. The first act by virtue of which the state really constitutes itself the representative of the whole of society—the taking possession of the means of production in the name of society—this is, at the same time, its last independent act as a state. State interference in social relations becomes, in one domain after another, superfluous, and then dies out of itself; the government of persons is replaced by the administration of things, and by the conduct of processes of production. The state is not "abolished." *It dies out.* This gives the measure of the value of the phrase "a free state," both as to its justifiable use at times by agitators, and as to its ultimate scientific insufficiency; and also of the demands of the so-called anarchists for the abolition of the state out of hand.

Since the historical appearance of the capitalist mode of production, the appropriation by society of all the means of production has often been dreamed of, more or less vaguely, by individuals, as well as by sects, as the ideal of the future. But it could become possible, could become a historical necessity, only when the actual conditions for its realization were there. Like every other social advance, it becomes practicable, not by men understanding that the existence of classes is in contradiction to justice, equality, etc., not by the mere willingness to abolish these classes, but by virtue of certain new economic conditions. The separation of society into an exploiting and an exploited class, a ruling and an oppressed class, was the necessary consequence of the deficient and restricted development of production in former times. So long as the total social labor only yields a produce which but slightly exceeds that barely necessary for the existence of all; so long, therefore, as labor engages all or almost all the time of the great majority of the members of society—so long, of necessity, this society is divided into classes. Side by side with the great majority, exclusively bond slaves to labor, arises a class freed from directly productive labor, which looks after the general affairs of society, the direction of labor, state business, law, science, art, etc. It is, therefore, the law of division of labor that lies at the basis of the division into classes. But this does not prevent this division into classes from being carried out by means of violence and robbery, trickery and fraud. It does not prevent the ruling class, once having the upper hand, from consolidating its power at the expense of the working class, from turning its social leadership into an intensified exploitation of the masses.

But if, upon this showing, division into classes has a certain historical justification, it has this only for a given period, only under given social conditions. It was based upon the insufficiency of production. It will be swept away by the complete development of modern productive forces. And, in fact, the abolition of classes in society presupposes a degree of historical evolution, at which the existence, not simply of this or that particular ruling class, but of any ruling class at all, and, therefore, the existence of class distinction itself has become an obsolete anachronism. It presupposes, therefore, the development of production carried out to a degree at which appropriation of the means of production and of the products, and, with this, of political domination, of the monopoly of culture, and of intellectual leadership by a particular class of society, has become not only superfluous, but economically, politically, intellectually a hindrance to development.

This point is now reached. Its political and intellectual bankruptcy is scarcely any longer a secret to the bourgeoisie itself. Its economic bankruptcy recurs regularly every ten years. In every crisis, society is suffocated beneath the weight of its own productive forces and products, which it cannot use, and stands helpless, face to face with the absurd contradiction that producers have nothing to consume, because consumers are wanting. The expansive force of the means of production bursts the bonds that the capitalist mode of production had imposed upon them. Their deliverance from these bonds is the one precondition for an unbroken, constantly accelerated development of the productive forces, and therewith for a practically unlimited increase of production itself. Nor is this all. The socialized appropriation of the means of production does away not only with the present artificial restrictions upon production, but also with the positive waste and devastation of productive forces and products that are at the present time the inevitable concomitants of production, and that reach their height in the crises. Further, it sets free for the community at large a mass of means of production and of products, by doing away with the senseless extravagance of the ruling classes of today, and their political representatives. The possibility of securing for every member of society, by means of socialized production, an existence not only fully sufficient materially, and becoming day by day more full, but an existence guaranteeing to all the free development and exercise of their physical and mental faculties —this possibility is now for the first time here, but *it is here*.

With the seizing of the means of production by society, production of commodities is done away with, and, simultaneously, the mastery of the product over the producer. Anarchy in social production is replaced by systematic definite organization. The struggle for individual existence disappears. Then for the first time, man, in a certain sense, is finally marked off from the rest of the animal kingdom, and emerges from mere animal conditions of existence into really human ones. The whole sphere of the conditions of life which environ man, and which have hitherto ruled man, now comes under the dominion and control of man, who for the first time becomes the real, conscious lord of nature, because he has now become master of his own social organization. The laws of his own social action, hitherto standing face to face with man as laws of nature foreign to and dominating him, will then be used with full understanding, and so mastered by him. Man's own social organization, hitherto confronting him as a necessity imposed by nature and history, now becomes the result of his own free action. The extraneous objective forces that have hitherto governed history pass under the control of man himself. Only from that time will man himself, more and more consciously, make his own history—only from that time will the social causes set in movement by him have, in the main and in a constantly growing measure, the results intended by him. It is the ascent of man from the kingdom of necessity to the kingdom of freedom.

Let us briefly sum up our sketch of historical evolution.

I. *Mediaeval Society*.—Individual production on a small scale. Means of production adapted for individual use; hence primitive, ungainly, petty, dwarfed in action. Production for immediate consumption, either of the producer himself or of his feudal lords. Only where an excess of production over this consumption occurs is such excess offered for sale, enters into exchange. Production of commodities, therefore, is only in its infancy. But already it contains within itself, in embryo, *anarchy in the production of society at large.*

II. *Capitalist Revolution.*—Transformation of industry, at first by means of simple co-operation and manufacture. Concentration of the means of production, hitherto scattered, into great workshops. As a consequence, their transformation from individual to social means of production—a transformation which does not, on the whole, affect the form of exchange. The old forms of appropriation remain in force. The capitalist appears. In his capacity as owner of the means of production, he also appropriates the products and turns them into commodities. Production has become a *social* act. Exchange and appropriation continue to be *individual* acts, the acts of individuals. *The social product is appropriated by the individual capitalist.* Fundamental contradiction, whence arise all the contradictions in which our present day society moves, and which modern industry brings to light.

1. Severance of the producer from the means of production. Condemnation of the worker to wage labor for life. *Antagonism between the proletariat and the bourgeoisie.*

2. Growing predominance and increasing effectiveness of the laws governing the production of commodities. Unbridled competition. *Contradiction between socialized organization in the individual factory and social anarchy in production as a whole.*

3. On the one hand, perfecting of machinery, made by competition compulsory for each individual manufacturer, and complemented by a constantly growing displacement of laborers. *Industrial reserve army.* On the other hand, unlimited extension of production, also compulsory under competition, for every manufacturer. On both sides, unheard of development of productive forces, excess of supply over demand, overproduction, glutting of the markets, crises every ten years, the vicious circle: excess here, of means of production and products; excess there, of laborers, without employment and without means of existence. But the two levers of production and of social well being are unable to work together because the capitalist form of production prevents the productive forces from working and the products from circulating, unless they are first turned into capital—which their very superabundance prevents. The contradiction has grown into an absurdity. *The mode of pro-*

duction rises in rebellion against the form of exchange. The bourgeoisie is convicted of incapacity further to manage its own social productive forces.

4. Partial recognition of the social character of the productive forces forced upon the capitalists themselves. Taking over of the great institutions for production and communication, first by joint-stock companies, later on by trusts, then by the state. The bourgeoisie demonstrated to be a superfluous class. All its social functions are now performed by salaried employees.

III. *Proletarian Revolution.*—Solution of the contradictions. The proletariat seizes the public power, and by means of this transforms the socialized means of production, slipping from the hands of the bourgeoisie, into public property. By this act, the proletariat frees the means of production from the character of capital they have thus far borne, and gives their socialized character complete freedom to work itself out. Socialized production upon a predetermined plan becomes henceforth possible. The development of production makes the existence of different classes of society thenceforth an anachronism. In proportion as anarchy in social production vanishes, the political authority of the state dies out. Man, at last the master of his own form of social organization, becomes at the same time the lord over nature, his own master—free.

To accomplish this act of universal emancipation is the historical mission of the modern proletariat. To comprehend thoroughly the historical conditions and thus the very nature of this act, to impart to the now oppressed proletarian class a full knowledge of the conditions and of the meaning of the momentous act it is called upon to accomplish, this is the task of the theoretical expression of the proletarian movement, scientific socialism.

PAUL SERING

PAUL SERING (pseudonym for Richard Loewenthal) was born in 1908. He early became an active member of the German Socialist Party but viewed critically the course pursued by its leadership following World War I. He was attracted to the inner-party oppositional group *Neu Beginnen* (New Beginning), which revolted against the mechanical and rhetorical use of Marxist concepts to which the Party had become accustomed while, in fact, pursuing a moderate and opportunistic course. After the German labor movement was suppressed by the Hitler regime, Sering went into exile, first to Prague—where the Party's émigré leadership had set up headquarters—and subsequently to London. Since the end of World War II, Sering has been active as a journalist for both German and English publications.

Sering's book *Beyond Capitalism* (*Jenseits des Kapitalismus,* published in German in 1948), from which the following selection has been translated by Kurt Shell, is an attempt to redefine the Marxist position under the shattering impact of the defeats and disappointments suffered by the European socialist movements. The developments which shook the socialist, particularly Marxist, position most severely were the rise of totalitarian fascism in Germany, the possibility of non-socialist planning, and the stabilization of the Soviet Union as a terroristic dictatorship. In spite of the sophistication which Marx and some of his disciples had brought to the elaboration of their theory, its basic features were essentially simple. The historical process was conceived as moving inevitably—or almost inevitably—toward the collapse of capitalism and the triumph of a working class united in its antagonism to capitalism and in its rational attachment to the socialist solution. The world-wide economic crisis, however, brought not unity and triumph but near-annihilation to Europe's socialist labor movements.

Before collectivization of the means of production had become an accomplished fact in the Soviet Union, socialists had widely assumed that abolition of private property by a proletarian regime would forever eliminate the problem of power, exploitation, and alienation. The fact that in the Soviet Union seizure of power by a proletarian regime, annihilation of the capitalist class, and abolition of private ownership of the means of production were accompanied by increasing repression not only of the enemies of the proletariat but of the workers and peasants themselves, raised the most profound questions in socialist minds, questions which went to the heart of the socialist assumption that the key to the transformation of man and society lay in the control of property. Not only Marxists like Sering but all socialists who shared the belief that socialization was a means to the achievement of a freer, more rational, and more humane society have been forced to subject their convictions and assumptions to an extensive reexamination.

BEYOND CAPITALISM

I. MARX AND HISTORICAL "NECESSITY"

The basic features of Marx's prophecy have been realized to a surprising degree. Marx claimed to have based socialism on the scientific analysis of the laws of social development. History has proved this claim to be no mere illusion.

But we must warn right here against a fundamental misunderstanding which is found equally among opponents and followers of the socialist cause: the view that Marx attempted to substitute for the will to struggle in the socialist cause, a faith in the "scientifically proved" inevitability of socialism. The motives of the socialist struggle were the same before Marx as they are now: the desire to free men from their dependence on personal repression and impersonal laws of the market; the demand for social justice; the faith in the possibility of an order established not on the coexistence of the ant heap but on the fraternal cooperation of creative men. By means of scientific analysis we can reveal the conditions under which the realization of these goals becomes possible and the forces on which this realization depends. These forces, however, realize themselves through the actions of purposeful men and not without their contribution. The necessity known to history is never the inevitability of a specific outcome to the struggle. It is the necessity implicit in the conditions required for the survival and development of a certain society. . . . Human history is full of dead-end streets, of fossils and ruins of cultures which, at critical points in their development, fell victim to stagnation and thus finally decayed. Historical analysis can show, in each such case, in which direction further development would have been possible, what forces opposed it, and why the forces of progress ultimately succumbed. The outcome of such a struggle can never be predicted in advance—only the struggle's content. For our time Marx formulated it as "socialism or barbarism."

Just as there is no certainty of a specific solution at critical points in the historical process, there is rarely only *one way,* though there is only *one direction* in which the solution lies. Marx explains the historical transition from one form of production to another—envisioned for the future as transition from capitalism to socialism—by the historical example of the development from feudalism to capitalism. The basic lines of this development can be shown to

---

This selection has been reprinted from Paul Sering, *Jenseits des Kapitalismus,* Wiener Volksbuchhandlung, Vienna (1948), by permission of the publisher, pp. 21–26, 58–66, 67–71, 73–74, 75–77, 78, 79–81, 109–113, 146–149, 152–155, 161–162, 165–166, 175, 176, 178, 179–183, 211–212.

have been valid for all of Europe, as are the predicted features of the development of capitalism to socialism. But the details of the process, the political forms of the transition, the groupings of the struggling classes, the duration of the struggle, have differed tremendously from country to country and have contributed decisively toward the different ways in which the histories of Europe's peoples have been shaped. . . . The direction of the development from feudalism to capitalism is the same everywhere; the ways are very diverse and so are the life rhythms of the resulting societies.

It would be unscientific dogmatism to assume that similar divergencies are excluded from the next stage of development. The prediction of the great line of development can be scientific. Formulation of a universal political prescription for the socialists of all countries on the basis of this prediction would be a foolish game. . . .

We cannot hide the fact that large parts of the socialist labor movement have in the past fallen victim to a dogmatic misunderstanding which confused prediction of historical development with a universal political recipe. Certain elements of the socialist movement are still victims of this same confusion. They can be recognized by their Marxist "orthodoxy," by the fundamental tendency to answer concrete questions of everyday politics with the help of quotations from Marx's writings. Such orthodoxy is the very opposite of scientific socialism, just as it is contrary to rational, purposeful action. By linking faith to the letter it empties faith of content and obscures scientific insight by isolating it from ever-changing concrete experience.

These remarks are necessary if the comparison between Marxist prediction and the real development of the past hundred years is to be fruitful. Such a comparison can neither purport to prove that all truth about the present was already written down a hundred years ago, nor can it "revise" Marx. By recalling the basic outline of Marx's prediction we realize that this prediction has been confirmed to an extraordinary extent—up to a certain point. Technical and organizational progress, the increased power of the socialist labor movement, the extension of the new method of production, with its problems, to the entire globe, and finally, the almost unbearably catastrophic character of this development; these are obvious examples. None of these processes has moved in a straight and even line. There were periods of faster and slower external expansion, of shallower and deeper crises, of calmer and stormier progress. Above all, there were periods of success, of revolutionary victories, and of profound setbacks for the socialist labor movement. All in all, however, the actual existence of these tendencies revealed by Marx is today undeniable.

The new problem begins at the point at which socialism actually becomes capable of realization. . . . It is a symptomatic fact that at present everyone speaks of socialism and that everywhere the replacement of the capitalist market economy proves itself as absolutely essential . . . [And, indeed, everywhere controlled, planned economies have made their appearance]. But the goals and methods of this planning in many instances differ fundamentally from the goals and methods which we recognize as the most significant aspects of the socialist idea. Thus there do seem to exist nonsocialist, even antisocialist ways out of the capitalist crisis. What is the nature of these ways? Are they passing, transitory stages, or the beginning of a new social organization unforeseen by socialist theory? Who are its class exponents? What factors are responsible for the frequently heard conclusion that in this age of planning we are as far removed from the classless society as ever? And what role does political power, the state, play as transformer of the economy and society?

II. IMPERIALISM AND THE STRUGGLE FOR POWER IN THE STATE

The general struggle for power over the state's economic policy which ultimately leads to the final paralysis of capitalistic automatism . . . and forces transition to coordinated public planning begins with the state's intervention for specific monopoly-capitalist interest groups. Its first expression is modern imperialism. . . .

With the development of modern industry in the major states—an uneven development moving in spurts—colonial policy and the penetration of backward countries gain a new function: the opening up of export markets, at first for consumer goods. At this level slavery and similar forms of the labor contract become uneconomic from the standpoint of the industrial countries, and it becomes necessary to develop a money economy in the colonial area. In this phase, characteristically, the attempt is made to have colonial countries cultivate raw materials which the industrialized countries can convert into finished textiles for resale to the colonial countries. All this occurs before capitalism in the industrialized countries has reached the monopolistic stage. Attainment of this stage coincides with two other developments: the replacement of England as the unique industrial workshop of the world by . . . a number of highly developed industrial countries (roughly since the 1870s) and the growing importance of the backward countries as spheres for investment of capital accumulated in the industrial countries. Capital export into half-colonial and fully colonial areas, existing previously as a corollary of their technological penetration, gradually becomes the economically most significant function of imperialist economic policy, of the relations between countries with advanced capitalism and the economically backward areas.

Capital export involves a considerable export of the means of production, construction of railroads, power stations, factories in these backward areas, and hence a real transformation of their economic structure. Its motor force is the urge for highly profitable investment opportunities . . . and requires the limitation of risks by means of direct or indirect political control. Capitalists of industry and finance interested in a particular investment project in a country to be opened up will undertake this project only when assured of the powerful support of their own government. This intertwining of economic and political activity is possible only for a monopolistic group, indeed only for modern monopoly with its influence over the state. The connection between the development of monopoly capitalism in industrialized countries, the transition to the preponderance of capital export to backward areas, and modern imperialism aiming at rendering investment spheres secure by political means is thus typical and not fortuitous.

In the historical situation of competitive struggle between several highly developed industrial countries this form of imperialism acts as a powerful stimulus toward the sharpening of international divisions. At first the tendency toward international integration of monopolistic groups counteracts this stimulus: the formation of international cartels . . . again and again creates common capital interests which cut across traditional conflicts frequently in utter disregard of national interests. . . . [But] the tendency toward integration of monopoly with the national state proved far stronger than that toward international integration. Lenin already pointed to an essential cause for this: the unevenness of development in various countries whose respective power position is altered by each new invention and discovery. Every change in the power position of states or industries shatters all existing cartel agreements.

A further cause of the instability of this international integration was its purely financial nature; it had no basis in production and thus was largely destroyed by the currency and credit crisis of 1931. A third element was the need of monopoly-capitalist groups to fight for control of their own states the more the growth of democratic mass organizations and the democratic representation of hostile interests challenged their control. Wherever monopoly capital can secure its influence over the state only by enforcing its own national economic plan, it also becomes tied to this national economic plan.

Normally that industrial monopoly which uses the state's power to secure its imperialist expansion is in the very nature of things the representative of a rising industry. But in old industrial countries the industries which have passed their peak and are increasingly deprived of their markets by international competition are no less numerous and frequently no less strongly organized. They are in need of the state's aid far more urgently—not for purposes of expansion or to secure new profitable investment opportunities, but for the sake of maintaining mere existence. And they command the supreme argument of all those demanding subsidies—that the free play of the laws of the market would not only ruin capitalist owners but would also bring unemployment to large masses of workers.

The older an industrial country, the more limited its capacity for expansion, the more successful is this argument. For, in the first place, in such a country it is not so certain, as it had been in the expansive phase of early capitalism, that those ruined in one sector of industry soon could be usefully employed in another. Secondly, with the growth of democracy and welfare policies the minimum demand for social security has increased, and the sudden ruin of entire branches of industry becomes a political danger for the system. This is particularly true where the oldest branch of industry—agriculture—is concerned. Agriculture has become backward in large parts of Europe in comparison to overseas production, but no modern capitalist state would dare permit a large part of its peasantry to go down in the way England did during the early phase of industrial development. Owners of estates and peasants, though not monopolistically organized, still can organize themselves as political-economic interest groups and hence be in a position to influence effectively public economic policy.

Every measure of economic policy which serves the expansion of a rising, or the protection of a declining, industry is simultaneously an interference in the domestic and international market mechanism and in the domestic distribution of income. . . . Every step away from the liberal idea of free trade not only sharpens internal conflicts but also impedes in one way or another the market's inner automatism. State intervention, irrationally but inevitably responding to every pressure and pull of contradictory interests . . . adds its effects to those of the monopolies' "private planning," their pricing policy and limitations on production. The reality of the economic process is increasingly remote from the theoretical picture of a free market economy. And simultaneously it becomes increasingly evident that the distribution of incomes is not determined by immutable economic laws but can be altered by political struggle and influence over the government's economic policy.

The general spread of the struggle for "political distribution" is thus the necessary consequence of monopoly capitalism, imperialism, and a policy of subsidies. Where great capitalist power groups openly use the state as a milch cow, workers and peasants cannot hang back in the exercise of their democratic rights. It is no accident that the creation of independent labor parties in countries where previously the labor movement had been satisfied by trade-union forms of struggle coincides in time with the first blossoming of modern imperialism and the surrender of free-trade ideology. Nor is it an accident that the growth of labor's parliamentary representation is followed by the formation of interest parties among other strata. Under the impact of universal suffrage and the struggle for political distribution—the political wage, the political wheat price, the political tariff on steel—parliament is transformed into an arena for the struggle of interests. The more highly organized the interests facing each other are, the less predictable the oscillations of public economic policy become under the influence of their alternating combinations, and the more thoroughly the automatic operation of the market disintegrates until it reaches final paralysis.

At no point is this interest struggle sharper and its effect more paralyzing than at the low point of the cyclical economic crisis. The more such artificially supported interest groups are present in an economic system, the more impossible it becomes to drive those groups to bankruptcy by a sudden return to liberalism. The more artificial props are maintained in the crisis, the more impossible it becomes for the market mechanism to do its normal work of overcoming the crisis and providing a stable and calculable basis for new investments. This is why "free" monopoly capitalism at this stage tends to prolong the agony of crisis up to the limits of endurance and, simultaneously, by heaping incompatible demands on top of each other, to render the democratic state incapable of action. Crisis, however, only makes acutely apparent the contradiction here described: the contradiction between the new hierarchical form of production, developed under the cover of monopoly-capitalist property relations, and the anarchy of uncoordinated blocs of factional organizations which in the course of this process have somehow "just growed." The contradiction can be overcome only if the state's organization and the relations of interest groups are adjusted by replacement of the paralyzed "free" market by state planning.

III. THE NEED FOR PLANNING

This transition to a planned economy directed by the state always represents a sharp turn in historical development. It can never be achieved without unequivocal clarification of political power relations. It must become clear *who* plans and *for what;* otherwise there is no plan. And this clarification, which always represents a decision against many partial interests, itself the result of a struggle against the stubborn enemies of planning and frequently of a struggle for leadership among the advocates of planning, does not occur without the pressure of an acute emergency. We can clearly point to the emergency which led to the final collapse of the old capitalist market mechanism and demonstrated the need for planning in some important countries—the global economic crisis of 1929–1932. It gave birth not only to the Hitler regime but also to the American "New Deal," the Empire-Preference System of Ottawa, and to the smaller but highly successful planning experiments in Scandinavia and New Zealand. It brought to an end the attempt, undertaken after World War I, to restore past economic prosperity by return to global currency automatism. The collapse of the world-wide currency system gave the final signal for the first great planning measures in capitalist countries on the basis of the national state. . . .

The crisis in the industrial countries brought home the need for planning in a twofold form. The seemingly never-ending growth of unemployment presented the governments with the unprecedented task not of saving this or that industry or class but of priming an entire economy apparently incapable of recovering by its own strength. The breakdown of international trade for all and of international solvency for some made it necessary to protect their economies against further setbacks of the world market and to insure a minimum of essential imports through direction of foreign trade and currency control. . . .

What in reality was the historical transition to a planned economy thus first appeared in the form of currency maneuvers. Introduction of currency control in Germany in 1931 was the necessary prerequisite for all the planning measures of the Hitler system; the devaluation of the dollar the first step of the New Deal; the depreciation of the pound sterling the starting point of England's turning away from free trade. . . .

We must realize with full clarity the fundamental novelty of this situation from the viewpoint of socialists. Neither Roosevelt nor Hitler, neither New Dealers nor Nazis, were socialists in the [traditional] sense. Neither the one nor the other thought of abolishing monopoly-capitalist property or of establishing the rule of the working class over the exploiters. In the United States a socialist labor movement in our sense did not exist as a political factor. In Germany the transition to planning took place on the basis of a smashing defeat suffered by that movement and of the destruction of its organization by a totalitarian dictatorship. The failure of the capitalist system, the insoluble crisis of the market economy, predicted by socialists became dramatic reality. The transition to a conscious direction of social production, toward a uniform goal with the help of the state, which they had demanded, became inevitable. But it was realized there [in the United States] without the participation and here [in Germany] against the will of socialists, by methods alien to them and for goals which were not theirs.

This is the real problem which the events of 1933 pose for the socialist movement even today, this the fundamental fact which requires a new orientation of socialist thought. For this fact is not extinguished by Hitler's defeat and the collapse of his regime. We repeat once more: the replacement of the capitalist market economy by a system of state planning, predicted by Marx, has become fact in our time—but under conditions differing in decisive points from those foreseen by him. These conditions made it possible to replace the capitalist market economy with nonsocialist planning systems maintaining monopoly-capitalist property. It is these conditions we must now examine.

IV. THE NEW HIERARCHY

Karl Marx's prediction of a development toward a classless society was based on quite specific assumptions about the tendency of technical development in the age of the machine. He expected that mechanization of production and bureaucratic rationalization would simplify the leading functions on all levels of production; while, at the same time, increased productivity and extended leisure would provide workers with the opportunity of reaching a higher educational level, helping them to gain the capacity for taking on complex executive tasks. According to Marx, at the terminal point of this development functional division between labor and supervision would disappear. The classless society would be established when there would be no more street cleaners on the one hand and managing directors on the other, when each member of the work community would be obliged to work as a street cleaner for a time yet would be capable of functioning as a managing director at other times. Naturally Marx did not expect this goal to be realized in the near future. Particularly he believed that the requisite rise of general culture would become possible only after the proletariat had taken power, after the overthrow of capitalism. The taking of power thus represented merely the initial step in the development toward communism.

The technical aspect of this development, however, would already be indicated under capitalism by the increasing simplification of supervisory functions.

Today there can be no argument that technical development has not taken this direction. The increasing role which science plays in production has resulted in increased specialization, increased need for persons with many years of specialized education. The organizational tasks of modern mass production and of public administration concerned with it have not become simpler as organizational scope has expanded, but more complicated. Even where leading functions in the new hierarchy of production management do not primarily demand scientific expertness, they require special capacities which are not only unevenly divided by nature but which, above all, must be developed through continuous experience. The director of a large industrial enterprise, or of a nationalized industry, need not necessarily be a specialist in the technical problems of the particular industry. He may be more easily transferable from one industry into another than many of the experts who are his subordinates. But to a high degree he must possess the power to make decisions and have experience in exercising leadership—he cannot be a dilettante in the *mode* of his activity. It is impossible to "democratize" such leadership function. . . . The director of the plant, of a large enterprise, of an industry, of a regional planning unit, can be bound in his over-all policy directives to the decisions of a democratic body and made responsible to it and be open to public criticism. But the task of day-to-day decisions, the day-to-day exercise of command power over a complex organism, no democratic body can take from him. . . . In highly industrialized countries [however], the masses of the working population have left elementary poverty and ignorance behind them. They are capable of demanding from leading functionaries an accounting about the exercise of functions and of arriving at an informed judgment on the appropriateness of actions—in other words, they are able to exercise effective democratic control. The institutions of political democracy, therefore, do not float in empty space but can become the real instruments for the subjection of the managerial hierarchy to the will of the working community.

From this it follows that the degree of the bureaucracy's authority depends in every country and in every phase of development on the question whether the material and cultural prerequisites for democratic control and the ascent of the gifted from all strata to leading positions exist, and whether liberal social institutions have been developed to make such control over leading personnel and such replenishment possible. Dictatorial planning under conditions of mass poverty and of educational opportunities controlled from above means development toward class rule by the bureaucracy. Democratic planning under conditions of a rising living standard and equal and free educational opportunities means development away from all class rule. . . .

The process [of transition] corresponds neither to the traditional revolutionary concept of the disappearance of the old owners and their replacement by the direct rule of the workers, nor to the contrary concept of the replacement of the old owners by a new bureaucracy. What occurs in reality is that the political advocates of planning attempt to further the process of differentiation within the hierarchy of capitalist production and thus attempt to gain as many "managers" as possible for their purposes. Fundamentally, the great mass of leading executive personnel can be won for any kind of planning which recognizes their own indispensability. An exception is represented by those who at the same time have capitalist property interests. . . . If the direction of planning is socialistic and attacks the nature of capitalist property, the great majority of [these] production executives allied with capital ownership will, with a few exceptions, oppose the plan; and the need for differentiation and "purposes" will be highly acute. If the planning tendency is compatible with the continued existence of monopoly-capitalist property, opposition will come only from those whose special minority interests are harmed by the direction of planning. But in this case, too, the transformation of the top stratum from a capitalist into a bureaucratic one receives new impetus through the mere fact of planning. Production is invaded by many new persons coming from politics and the state machinery free of capitalist tradition and without capital. Here and there capitalists opposed to planning withdraw from active economic life. Newly risen executives feel secure in the new political climate and are ready to take the side of those who plan efficiently. Individual capitalists are ready to profit from the conflict between the state and their competitors opposed to planning by aligning themselves with the plan. All this is true regardless of whether the planners are fascists, democratic socialists, or New Dealers.

V. THE WORKING CLASSES

Our examination of differentiation among the leading strata of production can be summarized by stating that in the decisive crisis of free capitalism the working classes do not face a unified exploiting class. But just as little are the working classes socially unified in the moment of crisis in the sense expected by Marx. It is neither true that the working classes, in the course of capitalist development, have become industrial proletarians nor that the proletariat itself has become a socially unified mass.

The decisive crisis of free capitalism comes everywhere in the world at a time when along with propertyless proletarians there still exist millions of working owners of small property—most of them peasants. While the independent middle strata of craftsmen and traders have indeed suffered decisive losses in numbers and especially in economic weight through the progressive concentration of capital, the overwhelming part of the world's agricultural economy is at present still characterized by peasant ownership. . . . This peasantry is in industrial countries no longer subject to feudal exploitation—it is independent, but its economic existence is not secured. On the contrary, it is most acutely affected by economic crises and its need for economic security is an important element in the transition to planning. The demands of the marginal strata of artisans and petty tradesmen point in the same direction.

Within modern large enterprises in industry, trade, and transportation another unforeseen development has taken place: the relative increase of the importance of office work . . . and with this the growth of white-collar employees as a special social stratum within the proletariat. In part the increase of office work is the automatic consequence of the more complex and scientific organization. Detailed planning of the production process in an enterprise possessing a high degree of division of labor; accounting for the costs and shares of the total income for each department; centralized bookkeeping of the kind developed in banking—these processes necessarily require an increase of office work which is in part the precondition of a modern planned society. The same is largely true of the growth of the machinery of public administration to the extent that it is rooted in the state's increasing economic functions. . . .

The over-all result of these factors is that the percentage of industrial labor in the total population of the advanced countries has declined slightly. The mass of the propertyless who—in Marx's sense—live on the sale of their labor power has continued to grow. But it is *divided* in larger measure among workers, white-collar employees, officials, and unemployed, who live and work under diverse conditions, who in part have diverse backgrounds, who develop diverse class ideologies, and who are often separated from each other by caste barriers.

It is by no means inevitable that all these groups will consider themselves as proletarians. On the contrary, many of them pride themselves on being something "special." But while workers, white-collar employees, unemployed, artisans, small tradesmen, and peasants are neither equally propertyless nor equally exploited nor equal in social position and manner of life, the crisis of capitalism nevertheless unifies them to the utmost degree in one respect: in the insecurity of their existence. A hundred years of industrial development since the Communist Manifesto, a hundred years of rising productivity and living standards, have given to millions of toiling men the means to satisfy demands which they do not wish to renounce again. They now have the feeling that they have indeed more to lose than their chains. But the crisis of capitalism has also made them aware that in this social order they may lose all at any time. Freedom from exploitation and equality of opportunity have remained the essential demands of the labor movement. But the great, unifying slogan for all laboring people . . . is the cry for security. It is a fact of most portentous import that the most effective slogan in the moment of political decision is not one of the traditional slogans of the labor movement. The demand for economic and social security being raised everywhere is addressed to the state and this has two decisive consequences. First, since we are dealing with the national state, the transition to planning thus takes place within a national framework and tends to strengthen the ties of all strata of the population to the distinct interests of the national state. Second, it means that the state is not viewed as the instrument of suppression which must be shattered by the masses, but as the savior-in-need to which the masses are willing to grant increasing power the more desperate they feel their situation to be. . . .

VI. IS CAPITALIST PLANNING POSSIBLE?

[There are four basic methods by which the state can stimulate economic activity within the framework of capitalism.] First, the state can raise mass consumption by increasing consumer power among the poorer strata of the population and can thus stimulate production. Second, it can encourage the production of investment goods in order to increase the general productivity of the economy and thus similarly start an increased flow of consumer goods. Third, it can direct investments toward purposes which are unproductive from the viewpoint of individual consumption and thus of social utility, for instance, armaments or ostentatious public buildings. Fourth, as long as it is not a world power, it can concentrate investment on pushing exports, thus making them equally independent of domestic consumption.

The first two types of stimulation clearly can be continued only on the basis of increasing welfare of the mass of the population within the planning state. The third type depends essentially on a continuation of arms production which is capable of devouring far greater investments than any other form of unproductive expenditure known to modern society. The fourth, based on export, can in the long run be planned only if the importing countries are made economically and finally politically dependent on the planning state. It demands economic and political expansion. The choice thus is only between two main directions of planning: welfare planning on one hand, imperialist planning on the other.

In England's wartime planning such a choice never arose. Planning came about under pressure of external necessity. There was a state of war and the subordination of all other needs to those of war production was required and recognized by all classes. But in 1933 Roosevelt and Hitler had the opportunity to decide freely the direction of their planning. And they chose different ways.

Roosevelt's New Deal administration consciously took the way of adding to the purchasing power of the working masses and of increasing general productive capacity; easing of credit for home building; reducing debts and interest charges for farmers; wage increases for labor directly through arbitration and indirectly through legal recognition of trade unions; attempts at lowering monopoly prices; productive emergency work paid at normal rates; and the gigantic project aiming at the improvement of the Tennessee Valley, a territory comprising several states, by means of dam construction, electrification, irrigation, and distribution of fertilizer at reduced cost.

Hitler's Third Reich equally consciously went the way of rearmament and planned imperialist expansion: super highways, increase of steel-producing capacity, arms production proper, *Ersatz* production, and simultaneous systematic integration of neighboring countries into the German planning system by means of trade treaties of a new type bringing the entire economy of these countries into dependence on German foreign trade planning long before their military occupation.

And here we come to a discovery decisive for the character of planned capitalism: Hitler's planning inevitably led to war and could be maintained only by means of totalitarian dictatorship—but under these conditions it functioned as expected. Roosevelt's planning led to increased welfare and to the President's reelection in four electoral campaigns in spite of the pressure exerted by the great majority of the capitalist press, but it failed to function beyond a certain point. This point can be exactly determined. Roosevelt succeeded in stimulating production from the side of purchasing power, but private investments never reached the scope desired and expected by the administration. Unemployment was reduced by millions, but full employment was never achieved.

The reason for this difference in development is easily seen: Hitler's planning was supported from the beginning by the decisive groups of big German capitalists. In minor questions they had to subordinate themselves, but generally they did not have to be forced to cooperate—the plan was their own plan. Roosevelt's plan, with its stress on mass consumer power, its support for trade unions, and its increase of wages at the expense of profits, from the beginning met the resistance of a large number of capitalists. Though many entrepreneurs had only to gain from economic stimulation, regardless by what method it was achieved, they nevertheless all feared to lose in the long run by Roosevelt's social policy. They felt that his plan did not eliminate their risks but rather increased them from the political side.

Indeed it is impossible for state planning to eliminate the risk for entrepreneurs in production for mass consumption to the same extent as in production of socially useless items for the account of the state. Consumer goods are produced in every modern society—in systems of free capitalism, planned capitalism, and socialism—for a market, which means that the consumers have a choice, within broad limits, on what consumer goods they wish to spend their income. In the case of arms and munitions, fortresses and super-highways, even in the case of production of exports to dependent countries, the state can guarantee in advance the absorption of the product. . . . In the production of consumer goods for the domestic market, particularly the domestic market of a free country, such state guarantees for the absorption of specific goods are impossible.

Even if the state were to buy the entire output of a particular item at profitable prices and then distribute it free or at reduced prices to the consumers—and something of this sort one could imagine in the case of housing, cheap motor cars, etc.—this would hurt rather than help capitalist production in its totality. The market for other goods serving the same needs, old apartment houses, for example, or bicycles, would be seriously shaken; the risk eliminated from one branch of production would be transferred—as is the case with successful monopolies—to other branches, and the total scope of capitalist production would be eliminated. For the extension of such methods to ever larger segments of consumer goods production can only end in the transformation of these branches of production into socialized public services.

But actually more is here at stake than the risk of the individual branch of production. Welfare planning is possible only through direct increase in the worker's share of the national income, which means an automatic lowering of the share derived from capital ownership whose source is capitalist profit. Here we meet the fundamental dilemma of all capitalist production: the dependence of every increase in production on growing consumption on the one hand and growing profit on the other. Elimination of this dilemma by planning can succeed only where an essential part of investment is consciously directed into channels independent of consumption by the working masses. Production of bombs has the advantage over the production of more useful items in that their sale is independent of the level of the wages paid out.

Roosevelt's planning, for the very reason that it aimed at a progressive raising of mass consumption, was incapable of assuring America's capitalists the same freedom from risks which Hitler assured Germany's capitalists. For this reason American capitalists hesitated to undertake new investments—and in a capitalist framework willingness to invest on the part of capitalists is essential for the functioning of the system. Roosevelt could have rendered it unessential only if he had been ready and sufficiently strong to take measures which, instead of merely aiming at encouragement of private investments, had led to their extensive replacement by public investments—socialist measures. Replacement of private profit by social need as the motive power for investment is more than planning within the framework of capitalist property—it requires the shattering of this framework.

While it is thus true that planning within the capitalist framework can be *attempted* by various forces and for diverse purposes, it can be *successfully* carried out in this framework in only one direction, that of imperialist planning. In the opposite direction, that of welfare planning, it must either break through the frame of the profit system or it must fail.

VII. GOALS AND METHODS OF RUSSIAN PLANNING

[For Russia], a huge country, backward compared to industrial Western Europe and the United States, to adopt a policy of independent industrialization, three basic obstacles had to be overcome. In the first place, industrialization had to take place at a forced pace in the interest of independence from the capitalist world and for the sake of creating the groundwork for a socialist development. This meant that, in contrast to the natural growth of industry in the older capitalist countries, stress was put from the beginning on the manufacture of means of production with special efforts devoted to arms production. In other words, millions of new workers were to be drawn from the countryside into the new industries without producing consumer goods in appropriate amounts. For years the country's appetite for goods could not be satisfied; the efforts of the new workers could not be rewarded by any continuing visible rise in their standards of living. Forced industrialization through one's own efforts meant industrialization through the heaviest national sacrifices, sacrifices which had to be made by workers as well as peasants.

The second obstacle lay in the available human resources—in the low average skills of labor, the lack of technical specialists and of trained management personnel. Even the greatest efforts at education could not bridge this gap, for ever new masses of semiliterate peasants were drawn into industry and suddenly had to learn to handle complicated machinery; ever new branches of industry and public activity required management personnel. As a consequence average labor productivity was low, labor discipline was low, efficiency in carrying through the plan in a general administrative sense was low. To overcome these obstacles a continuous effort was required to raise productivity by all sorts of pressures and incentives; it required extreme exertions to improve discipline in factory and administration and to control the execution of orders. Simultaneously the elementary education of the masses had to be undertaken and their interest in production and in the state had to be aroused.

The third obstacle was the tendency of peasant agriculture to produce a new capitalist class. Independent peasants competing in their production for the market do not remain equally well-off nor always independent. Even where the starting point is the same . . . differentiation between well-off, medium, and poor peasants quickly develops. Out of this emerge forms of dependence, forms of tenancy and hired labor, which are difficult to prevent in spite of legal prohibitions. The well-off peasants soon begin to engage in trade on their own and to accumulate capital. At the level at which Russian agriculture found itself after the agrarian revolution of 1917 this was a normal process, a corollary of the growing prosperity of the agrarian economy. But it was a process of capitalist class formation running strictly counter to the aims of planning. The result was a continuous zig-zagging between periods in which peasant initiative was freed for the sake of increasing production and periods of struggle against the newly formed upper strata in the peasantry. This conflict reached its climax in the "de-Kulakization," the systematic liquidation of the top strata in the villages by means of expropriation, exile, and other public measures as well as in the collectivization of the largest part of peasant agriculture under state pressure. Even subsequent to collectivization, however, the tendency toward the emergence of income differences within the collectives and between collectives remained and gave rise to periodic interventions by the state.

To overcome the first obstacle—the country's lack of developed resources—through the construction of heavy industry and armament production required severe sacrifices from the masses of workers and peasants. It also required that the workers' class organizations—the trade unions—and the workers' and peasants' organs of self-rule—the councils—be subordinated to the ruling party which guaranteed the execution of this policy. In the view of the party leaders, long-term material sacrifices were incompatible with free democratic representation.

Overcoming the second obstacle—low labor productivity and the low level of skill in the administrative and managerial apparatus—required the efforts of party and trade unions in repeated educational and propaganda campaigns on behalf of increased productivity; it required diverse appeals to material and ideal motives in order to arouse the workers' technical initiative; it required an attempt at controlling a bureaucracy—uncontrollable by its very nature—by strict, oversimplified directives from above and public criticism from below.

Overcoming the third obstacle—the peasantry's capitalist tendencies—required the periodic mobilization of party and state machinery in the organization of a new phase of the agrarian revolution; the ruthless attack against all strata that had come into existence since the revolution, not on the basis of individual violations of the law but on that of membership in a stratum considered harmful from the standpoint of the state; and, finally, the creation of an agrarian system in which state machine-tractor stations combined in party and state hands effective economic and political control over the collectives.

These are the features which have given the Bolshevist state its totalitarian character. The one-party system is not merely a weapon to defend the new society against a feudal or bourgeois counterrevolution whose prerequisites have long vanished. It is the tool of the state power for the ever-renewed transformation of society toward a goal, once established and stubbornly adhered to. It is the tool used to suppress all partial interests which at one time or another collide with the leadership's concept of this goal; to subordinate all social organizations—councils, trade unions, collectives—to their party line; to mobilize all social energies for the intermediate goal established at any time. It is the tool of a permanent revolution from above demanding active participation of the masses yet excluding their free choice between approval and rejection of the measures proposed. It is the tool of a forced effort extending over decades in which the rights of the individual or the interests of the group count for nothing and the goal set from above counts for everything. . . .

We must ask ourselves what the social characteristics of the system produced by this planning are.

First of all, in this system there exists not the slightest tendency toward a return to a capitalist mode of production, not the slightest tendency toward toleration of a capitalist class. Tremendous differences in incomes, privileges, interest-bearing and inheritable savings do exist, but there is no possible connection between such savings and influence over the direction of production. Planning is the task of party and state and no one else. Leading functionaries may earn a large income, but the recipient of a large income (who may also be an artist, scientist, or author) has no claim to becoming a leading functionary. The manager of a plant or of a larger industrial unit has no more autonomy than is required for the functioning of the plant, frequently less. The state's monopoly in determining the use to which means of production are to be put is untouchable. Basically it exists also for agriculture. The collectives which face the state industry in the market as private producers and which in part accumulate special wealth are not owners of their land but merely have the usufruct of state lands. And the state's supreme authority is safeguarded also in agriculture through the key technical positions previously mentioned.

In the Soviet Union trade and markets exist as technical means of distributing goods and of economic accounting. But there is no autonomy in market relationships. Thus a problem of disposal does not exist. In single instances it is, of course, possible that this or that consumer item may be overproduced (or, more frequently, underproduced). Generally, however, only that will be produced which the state desires and for which therefore some use exists. Such planning in contrast to capitalist planning is fundamentally free. An *economic* reason which would force it to give priority to arms production or to seek territorial expansion does not exist; and no *economic* obstacle exists to the concentration of planning on the task of raising the working masses' living standard. If the government decides to raise the living standard, it has only to order increased production of consumer goods and a simultaneous raising of the wage level and lowering of taxes on the collectives—a problem of disposal cannot arise.

But while Soviet society is free of capitalist tendencies it is by no means classless. On the contrary, the tendency toward the emergence of a new upper social stratum based not on private ownership but on the exercise of essential managerial functions has become increasingly obvious during the past thirty years. Differentiation of incomes has steadily increased since about 1934 and extends to the army as well as public administration and industry. In many instances it is more pronounced today than for corresponding cases in capitalist countries where peak incomes are still derived from ownership but where the highest managerial salaries are not as far above the wages of the ordinary worker as they are in Russia. This income differentiation has assumed increasing weight through the fact that more and more privileges are either obtainable for money or are provided as additions to peak salaries.

Today in Russia fees are again charged for higher education, university scholarships have been reduced, housing privileges are extended to leading functionaries, a free market exists on which scarce goods can be bought at uncontrolled prices, etc. Among these privileges those are the most important which permit inheritance of savings and better education for payment, for they give to the children of leading functionaries if not a monopoly of the chances to advance into high positions at least a considerably better chance than the sons of workers or peasants.

The next fact to which we must pay attention is that the authority of leading functionaries over their subordinates has constantly grown, equally in the army, public administration, and industry. We need not think here of the experiments of the first years of the Revolution when the illusion was widespread that the authority of an officer or manager could be replaced by that of a democratic soldiers' or workers' council. The shattering of this illusion was in any case unavoidable. But it was at first followed by an attempt to safeguard the workers' rights in the plant through effective powers of control for work councils and trade unions, by stress on the social equality between officers and soldiers outside the service, etc. The most important fact is that these attempts were increasingly given up, that in the plant the so-called "unitary power of command" was established for the plant director, that in the army distinctions of social rank were introduced as distinct from mere command functions. The power of the Russian superior over his subordinates is today far greater in all areas than in democratic capitalist countries. . . .

We are aware that our statements are in contrast to all we have so far said about the *intentions* of the Bolshevik dictatorship. The Bolsheviks took power as a socialist party. They stabilized their dictatorship with the aim of creating, through industrialization and modernization of agriculture, the prerequisites of a socialist society; with the aim also of raising the standard of life and culture of the masses, even at the price of heavy temporary sacrifices, far higher than capitalism was capable of doing under equal circumstances. They created an economic order which knows no *economic* obstacles to the improvement of the general standard of welfare. It makes gigantic cultural efforts—to increase labor productivity, to eliminate illiteracy, to educate a new intelligentsia. And yet we affirm that the party monopoly of these Bolsheviks in fact impedes the rise of the Russian masses' standard of life and culture.

The reason is not to be found in the intentions of Stalin and his collaborators, but in the mechanism which every party dictatorship must use to maintain its power position. Control of all forms of social organization by a centralized party, the conscious direction of social development into a path which it would not follow out of its own inner nature, requires a tremendous concentration of power. Every individual claim may be considered an obstruction, every social group a group of wreckers. Dictatorship means the elimination of every legal limitation on the state power. It demands the freedom to move at any time against all individuals not only when they have violated a law but when they threaten to become "objective" obstacles to realization of the state's purposes. The dictatorial state is always right and no one has recourse against it.

This development does not correspond to the intentions of the Russian revolutionaries. But it corresponds to the inner contradictions of the tasks they set for themselves. The history of the Soviet Union is the history of a purposeful minority attempting to create in a backward country by unprecedented efforts the material and cultural conditions for socialism. This effort required the establishment of a totalitarian dictatorship and its development to the ultimate consequence—dictatorship of the party elite. The continuation of this totalitarian dictatorship through the decades made possible, in spite of tremendous difficulties, realization of many of its immediate economic and political goals. It transformed a colossus threatened by collapse into a large industrial power capable of resisting Hitler's attack, one which became a world power by its victory. But this same dictatorship, by the nature of the means it had to use to reach these immediate goals, rendered achievement of its original goal—the development toward socialism—impossible.

This is the real tragedy of the Russian revolution. It teaches us that a necessary connection exists between the economic goal of socialism and the political form. It shows up as an illusion the widespread belief that socialists are free to choose on the basis of practicability between a dictatorial and free form of socialism. Just because modern technology and productive organization tend to create a new hierarchy of managers, the decision whether this hierarchy is to turn into a new upper class or shall be subordinated in its functions to the needs of the working masses depends on the existence of effective democratic controls. In an age of hierarchic organization of production a society can be socialist only if and as far as it is democratic. . . .

The ruthless denial of individual rights and of freedom of opinion, the reduction of human personality to a mere pawn in the process of social transformation may have been possible in Russia without destroying the basis of communal life; in Europe it would unavoidably become a cause of complete demoralization, of complete cultural disintegration. Bolshevism, unlike National Socialism, is not an eruption of barbarism, but the Bolshevization of Europe could only lead to barbarism.

VIII. SOCIALIST PLANNING

The question arises whether under present technical and economic conditions, under conditions of hierarchic and bureaucratic production methods which create the need for planning, a third way actually exists: whether socialism, though not a scientific necessity in the sense of being inevitable, represents nevertheless a scientifically recognizable and politically realizable possibility in our time. . . .

Socialization of the means of production is not identical with their nationalization by law. What is important is the effective control of society over the utilization of the means of production, not their juridical ownership by the state. In a planned economy control over factories which legally still are the property of small owners can be effectively transferred into the hands of the state planning authority.

As long as monopoly ownership is not attacked, all state planning, whether democratic or dictatorial, remains dependent on the cooperation of the monopoly capitalists and therefore more or less subject to the pressure of their interests in contrast to the interests of society. Expropriation of other owners of capital, other owners of the means of production, is not equally a *prerequisite* for the socialist development. . . . The process of substituting salaried managers for private owners in the real direction of production begins under "free" capitalism and is hastened by every form of planned economy. The more effective the planning, the more private ownership of individual enterprises loses its concrete power and functional meaning, the readier is the owner himself to surrender his legal title along with the risk and to transform himself into a state functionary or the functionary of a public enterprise. Such a development is the natural social consequence, not the prerequisite, of socialist planning. Socialists are not interested in forcing . . . the "little man" to surrender rights to which he is still attached. The necessity for expropriation is strictly a question of economic power. Where large property ownership reveals itself as a concentration of power, where it becomes a center of resistance to the socialist planning goals, there this resistance can be broken only through expropriation. Where private ownership of individual enterprises lacks this characteristic of power, there the socialist state power is not interested in creating for itself artificial difficulties by expropriating persons whose productive activities it is incapable of replacing.

Equally, it is not decisive for the nature of planning whether expropriation of monopoly capitalists takes place with or without compensation.

Ownership of a decisive share of a large bank's or a large industry's stock represents a power position. Ownership of government bonds or of bank deposits in the same amount which cannot be transformed into such stock represents no power position but merely a title to income. Practically, the necessity for compensation frequently arises from the impossibility to draw a legally effective distinction between large and small shareholders and from the desire to avoid harm to the small savers.

From the standpoint of the community's effective control over the means of production such compensation is indeed quite harmless. Its danger for the socialist development lies in its effect on income distribution. Large cash capital . . . represents a claim to unearned income. The socialist answer to this danger is the progressive capital levy which taxes away all property above the limit of middle-class well-being. Such a capital levy is an extraordinarily important weapon in the struggle for socialist justice and for equality of opportunity for individual development. It is not however a *precondition* of socialist planning; on the contrary, it is one of the measures which become possible only within the framework of socialist planning and bear witness to the socialist character of this planning.

The second demand, that the state must be democratic, flows from the concept of socialization, from the effective social control over the means of production, and from the bureaucratic tendency inherent in modern organization of production. Only when the bureaucratic hierarchy is subjected to effective democratic control can it be prevented from gradually closing itself off as a caste and from making public planning the instrument for the consolidation of a new class rule. Only when planning is truly and not merely fictionally carried on *by* the people can it in the long run remain planning *for* the people. But the people, society, the working classes, these are millions of people with diverse interests, knowledge, and capacities. Planning is technically a highly complicated process in which comparatively few specialized experts located at decisive points must continually make responsible decisions. The question arises in what sense planning *can* be democratic; in what sense planning by the people can be real.

First of all, the basic decisions of every economic plan are not of a technical but of a political nature. Experts can gauge a country's productive capacity at a particular time and from this calculate what living standard and thus what income level of the working masses is compatible with a given investment program and vice versa. But the decision as to which of the technically possible alternatives is *desirable,* how much should be currently consumed and how much provided for the improvement of the productive apparatus, for the creation of new industries or roads, does not depend on experts. If the alternatives are clearly presented, every citizen is capable of making a decision on these according to his understanding and interest. The people can plan in the sense that they can freely decide in what direction and at what speed they wish to develop their productive apparatus, for what long-term purposes they are willing to make short-term sacrifices or vice versa, when and for the sake of which groups the immediate improvement of the living standard must be given priority vis-à-vis long-term tasks.

The decision is in exactly the same degree a decision between different economic interests as any political decision in a capitalist democracy. It is a decision not only between present and future interests, but also between the interests of peasants and workers, of unskilled helpers and specialized bureaucrats, of welfare recipients in need of support and gainfully employed recipients of wages. It is a dangerous fallacy to assume that with the elimination of monopolistic exploitation all interest conflicts will be submerged in the fraternal unity of all the toilers. Planning, on the contrary, consists in the discovery of a concrete compromise between the continuously conflicting partial interests of various groups of working people. And if planning is to be democratic, it must allow as much play for the representation of these special interests as is in any way compatible with effective planning.

From this it follows that planning cannot be democratic unless freedom exists for organized representation and propagation of diverse viewpoints—thus freedom to form parties. The mere existence of economic group organizations, like trade unions, peasant leagues, etc., is not enough. The same persons often have diverse interests, as producers and consumers, as savers and wage earners, etc., and only the freedom for every individual to decide for himself which interest he gives priority to at any given moment can assure democratic decision-making. Where only economic organizations face each other, as in the "corporate state" conceived by many conservative opponents of democracy, there is no room for influencing public opinion and for the changing balance which the free voter establishes between partial interests. . . . It remains decisive for the democratic character of planning that interests be freely represented, not merely behind closed doors but in the struggle for public opinion, and that the compromise achieved in this struggle be not simply legislated by the leadership of the state.

The Ultimate Goal—Socialism. What do we mean by socialism? To this question the answer is the same today as a hundred years ago: abolition of classes and elimination of wage work. But today, when we live through the first phase of socialist planning, it becomes necessary to explain in somewhat more concrete terms the meaning of these words.

Abolition of classes cannot mean the end of functional division of labor. It must mean that the functional division of labor, and particularly the differences between performance and supervision, must not be profound; that children of diverse occupational backgrounds must have equal opportunities for development, must have an equal chance according to their ability to contribute to the common purposes of society. Beyond this, abolition of social classes must mean that income differences existing at the beginning of socialist planning will steadily diminish. The precondition is, first of all, increase in the productivity of labor, increase in disposable goods and disposable leisure. The classless society can be achieved only to the extent that—in Marx's words—"the springs of wealth flow faster." For the more goods that can be placed at the disposal of each member of society, the less importance attaches to additional income as an incentive to effort; the more must ideal and collective stimulants, the will to contribute to the whole, replace the material stimulus of income and the more easily can they do so.

This replacement, however, is the prerequisite for the real elimination of wage work. After the misery and hopelessness of the recent capitalist crisis the overwhelming majority of people are today satisfied if they are merely assured of a wage sufficient to meet their modest needs. They hardly feel the fundamental indignity implicit in the concept of a wage—namely, that man is worthy to receive the necessities of life from society only in the exact measure in which his contribution to production in the market is deemed worthy of compensation. All work for wages is "dehumanization" in that it transforms man from an end into a means of production—and this is at first just as true for wage work in a planned economy as for wage work under "free" capitalism. The special feature of socialist planning is that it strives to transcend this situation and indeed does lead beyond it.

It can do so in one way, and one way only. The larger a society's resources become, the larger is the share of life's necessities which can be assured to the working member of society independent of the "value" of his labor effort, not as compensation but as a right: "to each according to his needs." That which at present we call public services—the right to free education, to free medical care—is the beginning of this development, like many forms of social insurance. Tomorrow an advanced society can make housing a public service and establish the right to a home along with the other basic rights of a working man. And once this road has been taken, no limit exists to the severance of real income from compensation for labor performed except society's productivity.

E. F. M. DURBIN

E. F. M. DURBIN, who was born in 1906 and died at the early age of forty-two, was one of the outstanding intellectual representatives of English socialism. Like many leading British socialists he was a trained economist who had studied at Oxford and the London School of Economics and later taught economics at those institutions. During World War II he obtained a close-up view of administrative problems by his work in the civil service. The Labor Party's electoral victory of 1945 propelled him into Parliament, where he rapidly advanced to junior governmental position by becoming Parliamentary Secretary in the Ministry of Works. He was one of the Labor Party's "bright young men" who prepared and helped realize Britain's transformation into a welfare state committed to maintenance of full employment and equal opportunity for all her citizens.

Durbin's approach to socialism—and in this he is a typical spokesman for his Party—is characterized by a mixture of moral fervor and practical sense. His humanitarianism was outraged by the misery which he felt industrial capitalism had needlessly inflicted on his countrymen. His aesthetic sensibility was revolted by the damage done to "England's green and pleasant land" by the ravages of a thoughtless and unheeding search for profits. His moral conscience rebelled against the snobbishness and servility of the traditional English class system. He was a Fabian, however, in his conviction that any industrial system working "efficiently" (in the traditional sense) would not be able to do without monetary incentives, and thus differential incomes. Stung by the criticism which the upholders of a free-market economy had directed against earlier socialist schemes for economic planning, Durbin attempted to prove that an efficient market—and price system, with its corollary of consumer freedom—could be maintained under socialism as well as under capitalism.

With Marxist socialism Durbin shared only one basic conviction: that the collective ownership of the means of production was a prerequisite for a society in which social injustice and economic chaos were to be eliminated. In every other respect Marxist categories were alien to his thought, as they were and are to the majority of his fellow socialists in Britain. He lacked belief in a historical process culminating in the inevitable collapse of the capitalist system, rejected the dichotomy of a society divided into two hostile classes whose struggle would lead to the annihilation of one of them, and thus never contemplated the possibility of using force to bring about the transition to socialism. The traditional values of the English society within which Durbin grew up—individual liberty, parliamentary democracy, the rule of law—remained an unquestioned part of his political outlook. If he had conceived of a conflict between them and his socialist ideals, it would undoubtedly have been the socialist ideals which would have had to give way.

Problems of Economic Planning (1949), from which the following selection has been taken, is a collection of articles and essays written by Durbin in the late

1930's and the 1940's which his friends brought together and published after his death in 1948.

PROBLEMS OF ECONOMIC PLANNING

PAPER I: THE CASE FOR SOCIALISM

. . . The most fruitful central idea for our future is, I feel sure, to be found in the main doctrine of the British Labour Party.

I am a member of that Party and I believe that my Party has made, and will continue to make, an invaluable contribution to the political discussion that proceeds continuously within the nation and determines the development of our institutions. In particular, I feel convinced that the faith of the Party in a moderate and democratic form of Socialism is a natural outcome of our slowly growing faith in human liberty, equality and brotherhood and represents the next step in our social emancipation. Let me explain, briefly, what I mean.

The main evil from which we suffer and the main barrier to social progress is the disgraceful inequality in the distribution of income and property that we still tolerate.

We can only remove this evil by abolishing property as a main source of income for anyone. To do this, it will be necessary . . . to modify the right of inheritance so that it is only possible to pass comparatively small sums of money or nothing at all from generation to generation. But this obvious truism leads to a further step in the argument. Property is the present method by which we direct our economic life. The owner of capital wealth controls—at least in legal theory—the administration of industry; and if he is to do so no longer, then he must be replaced by some representative of the State. It is my personal conviction that this growth of social responsibility in the economic sphere—the coming into existence of a planned economy—will greatly improve the efficiency of our industry and finance in the long run. I believe that the substitution of conscious foresight for the instinctive adjustments of the competitive system, and the establishment of social authority in place of the search for private monopolistic control, will bring into existence a better balanced and a more securely progressive economy.

This selection has been reprinted from E. F. M. Durbin, *Problems of Economic Planning* (pp. 3–13, 20–28, 41–57, Copyright 1949 by Routledge and Kegan Paul, Ltd., London) by permission of the publisher.

That is what I mean when I say that I am a Socialist. It is, however, necessary to add two further comments. In the *first* place it is important to emphasise that it is only necessary, and in the modern world it is only possible, to abolish property *as a main source of income*. The time has long gone past when it would be practicable or desirable to get rid of property altogether. Considerably more than half of the electorate now possess a little stock of money—substantial and valuable to them—in a Post Office or Trustee Savings Bank, in a Friendly or Provident Society, in the "Co-op." Property in this sense—i.e. *a small reserve* against a "rainy day"—has come to stay and is now so widely distributed among the population that it has become a means to personal liberty without creating social injustice. If everyone has a little property then no one gains an unfair advantage by the possession of it; while all enjoy a greater freedom. We should, therefore, as Socialists, seek to equalise the distribution of property rather than to liquidate it as an institution. It is too late, in any case, to do anything else.

In the *second* place it is necessary to make plain that the social control (and ownership) of the larger basic industries does not imply, at least in my view, the desirability of setting up vast and cumbersome Government Departments to run each industry. In certain cases—the railways, electrical supply and the public utilities—a single unified plant and corresponding single administration is dictated by technical considerations. But the greater number of our industries (coalmining, textiles, shipbuilding, engineering, vehicles and the distributive trades) require a more divided and flexible arrangement. These commodities should be produced in a number of separate plants with a considerable degree of autonomy preserved for each of them—a de-centralisation of industrial management.

A socialised industry should be owned by the State and its technical management remain responsible to the nation. But it should retain all the advantages of small enterprise: plants that are small enough to be managed efficiently, enough of them to make a comparison between the competence of different managements enlightening, and a pricing and costing system useful. An efficiently planned economy must combine the advantages of unified direction and individual initiative. Like a modern Army or Navy, it should possess unity of command and the power to enforce the execution of a general strategy; but there must be independence, vitality and adaptability in the lower ranks of the administrative hierarchy and in the tactics of enterprise.

This improvement in the efficiency of our economy and in the justice of our distributive arrangements is the beginning of a new social order. It will enable us to abolish unemployment and to extend the social services so that no member of our community need fall below a reasonable minimum of subsistence or live in daily fear of the desperate impoverishment that can still accompany unemployment or illness, old age or the sudden burden of family responsibilities. Moreover, substantial equality in the distribution of property will undermine the degrading differences of hierarchy and opportunity. We shall no longer be divided from one another by accents and education, by differences of economic interest and social class. We can then throw open the gates of knowledge and insist that every child shall receive the training of hand or eye or brain to which his inherited abilities suit him and see to it that the subsequent entry of young men and women into the occupations of lawyer and doctor, university teacher and industrial manager, becomes as easy as it now is difficult. By the same token the calling of the miner and the factory hand, the shopgirl and the railway porter will take on their full dignity: the equal in social honour of any useful service to the economy of a free society.

Economic equality will not only bring justice and social freedom but it will also release immense resources of ability now running to waste. No one can teach, as I have now done for ten years, both inside the walls of the universities and in the various types of extra-mural classes open to adult men and women (who have not taken a university degree), without knowing that we are failing to train a great number of first-class minds; while at the same moment we are allowing persons of third- and fourth-rate intelligence to crowd out our classes and waste our time merely because their parents possess enough money to pay the fees. This is social inefficiency of the worst type. And what is true of the particular natural talent that it is my professional business to train—academic or intellectual intelligence—must be true of all the other human gifts. We are neglecting immense, almost unimaginable, stores of vitality, imagination, executive ability, aesthetic and manual skill. All the ingenuity that we possess—all of which we should mobilise in our battle for happiness—could be brought to a rich harvest if we throw open the door of opportunity to our children.

The citadels of vandalism and the closed mind could then be forced. With knowledge would come power. Better educated men and women, freed from the bonds of social subservience, would see more clearly the society in which they wished to live and guide more firmly the conduct of democratic policy by which alone their hopes can slowly be established in the practice of the nation. Economic planning and social equality are the ideas upon whose slow growth the purification of our social order chiefly depends.

This is, then, what I mean by a new or a better society. I believe we could create in one generation an economic system that provided continuous employment for every able-bodied worker; that maintained a steady and substantial rise in real wages; that would enable us to set a minimum standard of living, well above the present "poverty line," below which no single man, woman or child would be allowed to fall; in which all forms of education were open and free to the talented; in which property was equally distributed, thus becoming a growing source of personal freedom for us all. And upon the same foundation of this stable and progressive economy it would be possible to build a better society from which all educational inferiority had been removed; in which all men and women could live a richer life of friendship, free from the barriers of class distinction; that was able to protect the treasures of its ancient culture in town and country and could free the strong and merciful hand of science to cure physical and mental ill-health—holding back the dark waters of death to give us more life and lifting the burden of guilt and fear from the hearts of children in order that there may be more joy in the longer tale of our years.

This hope is *not* Utopian. It is a moderate and practicable programme of improvement. There is nothing in this list of changes that is not easily within our physical and intellectual powers to bring about. We need only become united in a wish to possess this better order and in understanding that we can have it for the asking.

Let me repeat: there is nothing impossible in this vision. We have done far more difficult things and overcome greater barriers in the past. Lack of faith in the practicability of social progress—at least in this country—is only possible to those who obstinately concentrate their attention upon the great evils of this present time. A wider historical perspective—a single glance into the past—will reveal a wholly different story. Consider for a moment the last century of our social and economic development.

One hundred and one years ago—in 1841—Britain stood at the beginning of the "hungry forties." Let us suppose that a representative member of the toiling and starving industrial proletariat had been told, "In three generations your great-grandchildren will work for eight hours a day (instead of twelve) for an average real wage of three pounds a week (instead of twenty-five shillings); there will be universal adult suffrage (instead of a tiny electorate composed entirely of the rich), and universal and free elementary education (in place of your illiteracy); most of the unemployed will be supported by a state insurance and assistance scheme (instead of being humiliated, as you are, by the Poor Law); there will be regular provision for the sick and the aged (instead of the private charity and starvation from which you suffer); the sons of poor men will go to Oxford and Cambridge at the expense of the state and working men will enter the House of Commons in large numbers and occupy the highest offices in the state; the recognition of Trade Unions will be the rule, and not the exception; and most members of your class will possess a little property."

What would the poor man of 1841 have had to say to all that? He would, I suggest, have laughed bitterly. The prospect would have seemed preposterous to him—unrealisable in its optimism, a foolish dream. Sunk in poverty and ignorance, exhausted by endless hours of monotonous labour, burdened by an immense family, persecuted by the civil law against trade unions, patronised by the charity of the rich, tortured by the Poor Law, weakened throughout life by the horrible sanitary chaos of the early industrial slums and dying at an early age of curable diseases—the working man of 1841 would have been blind to the future—naturally but obstinately and obstructively blind.

So it is with us. Absorbed in the evils of our own time we do not see the great tide of social progress that sweeps slowly but inevitably through the affairs of free peoples. . . .

. . . We must preserve our democratic form of government if our community is to secure a richer life for all its members. The revolutionary improvements that have taken place in the standard of life and the social freedom of our people during the last hundred years have been deeply influenced, and partly caused, by the pressure of common opinion. The mode of its operation has been obscure, devious, and peculiarly British. Public opinion in this country has never, until recent years, been particularly well informed on public policy; and it has never been consciously creative or revolutionary. Yet it has, in fact, been both. By the expression of discontent, by the rejection of unwanted change and the uncovering of secret abuses, by working the unimpressive machinery of meetings, leagues and parties, by inoffensive demonstrations and petitions and by the ballot box, it has slowly, imperceptibly, pressed into existence the society that it desired.

Without this incoherent activity the franchise would never have been extended, Trade Unions would not have been freed from the restrictions of an unfriendly law, primary education, old age pensions, unemployment and health insurance, and the emancipation of economic activity from the dead restrictions of the past, would never have been secured. The case for these reforms was normally crystallised and stated by enlightened minorities (often middle-class and intellectual), but Cobden and Shaftesbury and Gladstone, Peel, Lloyd George and Fisher would never have overcome the immense weight of political inertia and vested interest unless their call had been supported by the deeper sound of the public voice. . . .

PAPER III: THE IMPORTANCE OF PLANNING

"We are all Socialists now," said Sir William Harcourt in 1894. We are certainly not all Socialists in post-war Europe. The last few years have seen a wholesale destruction of Socialist Parties on the continent and the election of an overwhelming anti-Socialist majority to the English House of Commons.

But it would be almost true to say that "we are all *Planners* now." The collapse of the popular faith in *laissez-faire* has proceeded with spectacular rapidity in this country and all over the world since the war. There now exists a completely planned economy in Russia, a bold and far-reaching attempt at general planning in America, an extension of the economic power of authoritarian governments in Italy and Germany, and the rudiments of financial and agricultural planning in England. Indeed, in this country planning has become one of the many subjects that scarcely enters into party controversy. The Labour Party proposes to socialise, and thereafter to plan a large sector of industry by the creation of ten or twelve public corporations. It is unquestionably a planning Party. But it was the Conservative Party which passed the Electrical Supply Act of 1928, placed the London Passenger Transport Bill on the Statute Book, set up the Exchange Equalisation Fund, has cartelised sections of the agricultural industry, is making some attempt to re-organise and unify the iron and steel industry, is subsidising shipping and proposes to begin the first stages of geographical planning. All these measures involve in greater or less degree the social control of industry. There is therefore an important agreement between the largest parties in the State on the supersession of private enterprise in the guidance of economic affairs.

There is, however, no such general agreement about the ends which the growing power of the Central Government shall be made to serve. The Conservative Party is not hypocritical in its opposition to the Labour Party, since it is radically opposed to the reform of society which the Labour Party intends. It is *Socialism,* and not economic planning that is in dispute. These two things are often confused, but they are in fact quite different, and it is of the greatest importance to understand their true relations. In particular it is necessary in this article to consider the importance of planning both to Socialists and to anti-Socialists.

Before this can be done we must define the meaning of economic planning with some precision. The term is used in current speech to describe widely different types of economic reform. It is applied indiscriminately to large-scale and fundamental changes in economic institutions, such as those carried through in the Russian economy, and to the comparatively small alterations which the cartelisation of the English milk industry involves. It is necessary to distinguish between:

(a) Planning, meaning simply the *intervention of the Government in a particular industry* at a time when the greater part of the economy still remains in private hands, and

(b) Planning which results in the *general supersession of individual enterprise* as the source of economic decisions.

This distinction is of importance, because the basis of authority and the probable results of the two types of planning are quite different. It is, for example, quite untrue, as certain opponents of Planning always argue, that *general* planning will be no more than the sum of a large number of interferences with a private enterprise economy. It would be just as sensible to argue that civilisation is nothing more than the destruction of primitive culture. The substitution of one set of institutions for another, whether better or worse, is quite different from the arbitrary frustration of existing arrangements. Thus, while it is easy for certain economists to prove that planning of the first type will result in nothing more than the interference with adjustments to the real situation which would be made by private enterprise and will lead to the use of the new powers created by unification to restrict output and hold up prices, it does not follow that the same thing will be true when central control is generalised and private interest is replaced over a large field of industrial activity. To begin with, in the case of general planning, the source of authority is no longer an industrial corporation, but an *inter-industrial* body. This makes the pull of conflicting interests more apparent and the implication of alternative courses more plain. There is, for example, no evidence that the Russian economy, whatever its other economic shortcomings, has been characterised by any attempt to restrict production. Social interests are necessarily more strongly represented in the machinery of generalised planning than in particular interferences, and it is confusing to call these two types of economic change by the same name.

It is also necessary to be clear about two different uses to which the machinery of centralised control may be put. Planning does not in the least imply the existence of *a* Plan—in the sense of an arbitrary industrial budget which lays down in advance the volume of output for different industries. Planning does not, and should not, imply any dogmatism about the future. It is not possible to tell in detail what will happen to human tastes, to technical invention, to general standards of security and well-being. It would therefore be foolish in the extreme to attempt to lay down plans which could not be amended quickly in the light of changing social requirements. There is no power yet known to man whereby he can foretell the movements of human society with the precision and degree of certainty that is exhibited by the physical sciences. There is as yet no economic astronomer, and until this gentleman has made his appearance there can be no reasonable rigidity or permanence in the absolute and relative outputs of the various industrial products.

What, then, is the true characteristic of Planning? If it does not involve the construction of a single plan, and is nevertheless something more than the cartelisation of particular industries, what is the correct definition of its essential nature? The element common to all the forms of new control we regard as "Planning" is the extension of the size of the unit of management and the consequent enlargement of the field surveyed when any economic decision is taken. The diagnostic property of an unplanned economy is the requirement that all decisions should be taken by individual supervisors in only a small—indeed, an infinitesimal—area of the industrial world. Under conditions of perfect competition—the pure type of the unplanned economy—the individual producer controls so small a part of the total output of a single commodity that he can exert no influence upon the price of anything that he either buys or sells. His field of vision is restricted to the technical organisation of his own factory or workshop, and no individual or corporation possesses any power to control the prices or output of the industry. All forms of planning machinery extend the area of economic life surveyed by the deciding authority and increase the number and importance of the economic quantities that can be controlled by some one.

The extension of control can take place in two stages. There is first the grouping of production units making the same or closely related products into one corporation. This is the case of the cartelisation, incorporation or socialisation of a single industry. Electrical production and London passenger transport are English examples of this type. The second and more important extension is that which brings a group of industries and economic activities, and in the limit the whole economic field, under the survey and control of a single authority—termed the Supreme Economic Authority. . . . It is this extension of the area of survey and control which is the definitive thing about all forms of Planning.

What is the importance of Planning so defined in the first place to Socialists and in the second place to those who are interested in economic efficiency? Socialists may be described as those who believe it to be of ethical and practical importance to remove inequality between persons and classes in so far as it is based upon the inheritance of property and the institutions created for the service of the rich. To people who hold such views the setting up and subsequently the successful operation of a certain form of Planning is of the first importance.

Now, there is nothing in my definition of Planning to say who is to plan and to what end. It is, however, perfectly clear that social equality cannot be achieved in an unplanned economy. The capitalist system depends for its power of adjustment upon the search for the reward distributed to private property in the means of production and for its power to grow upon the savings derived from large private incomes. It is therefore apparent that any sustained attempt to impair the operations of the profit motive and to destroy inequality in the distribution of wealth, without providing an alternative method of accumulating capital, will lead to a breakdown. The time will come when either the scheme of transferring income must be stopped or the capitalist system will cease to function. Such a disastrous alternative must at all costs be prevented, and it can only be done by removing the power to make economic decisions from the hands of property-owners. They must be vested in the State or the representatives of the State.

To a Socialist the mere change in the seat of power is not sufficient. It is a means to an end. The end consists in the creation of a society in which men are both free and equal. But, while the institution of some form of Planning is not the object, it is the indispensable preliminary means for the attainment of the new society. It is indispensable for the reasons just stated. It is preliminary because men must live and work during the period of social change—a period which may be long and difficult. To a Socialist, therefore, the setting up of a comprehensive machinery for the control of the means of production is of the most urgent importance.

But, as we have seen, it is not only Socialists who are interested in Planning—not only Socialists who believe in it. An increasing number of thinking men and women are coming to the conclusion that centralised control is a better method of organising production, apart altogether from the kind of social superstructure subsequently created within it. They believe that Planning is an essentially more *efficient* method of organising economic life.

The matter is, of course, also of the greatest importance for Socialists. If Socialism is to be obtained by democratic methods, it is necessary that, as a system, it should work efficiently from the earliest possible moment—and "work efficiently" in a sense that the ordinary elector can appreciate. Without in the least taking the cynical view that the ordinary elector is indifferent to questions of status and social freedom, it would be flying in the face of plain reality to deny that "the man in the street" judges the economic efficiency of any system by the degree of security in employment and the level of real wages it brings to him. To him Planning will "work" if it brings about a sustained rise in employment and a noticeable increase in the general standard of living. The first stages of Socialism—by which I mean the first period of five years in which a Labour Government seeks to transfer a large sector of industry to social ownership—will be judged by the extent to which "prosperity" is restored during the lifetime of that Government. Any Socialist, therefore, who wishes to secure for the next Labour Government the second period of office necessary for a further advance to social change, and who does not propose to obtain that extended period by unconstitutional and revolutionary methods, will be deeply concerned with the power of Planning to increase the means of livelihood and consumption.

We must therefore examine the efficiency of Planning as a method of directing economic life.

There are three charges which have been brought against Planning—both by professional economists and by business men. It has been argued that a Planned Economy will be a muddled economy because it will lack the automatic guide to productive activity provided by a pricing system; that it will lack the necessary incentives to secure efficient management; and that it will be unable to make adequate provision for the future. These are serious charges and must be considered.

The first of them—that Planning will lead to chaos because it lacks the automatic guidance of prices—can be advanced in two forms. It may either be said that Planned Economy *cannot* have a pricing system because the institutions of central control render accurate prices impossible, or that although prices can exist their guidance *will not,* in fact, be followed by a Planning Authority. These two versions of the argument are radically different. The first assumes that there is some logical contradiction between prices and the central control, while the second argument must be based upon social and psychological assumptions. It could only be justified by a demonstration that people will necessarily be foolish and pigheaded in a society which has chosen to control its economic life. It is of the greatest interest to notice that the arguments of *laissez-faire* economists have recently shifted their emphasis sharply from the one trend of argument to the other. This is so for three reasons:

(a) In the first place, Russia, a centrally Planned economy, is plainly operating a price system of a sort. The Communist Party attempted in the first instance to abandon economic calculus altogether, and the result was unspeakably disastrous. The present Russian system including the Five-Year Plan is therefore one which is based fundamentally upon prices. The Plan or industrial budget is a schedule of total prices; industries are rationed in the monetary funds placed at their disposal; costs are calculated; and prices are charged for finished products at every stage. No one is saying that their price system is accurate or that relative prices are made the sole criterion of productive policy. But that a price system can exist side by side with the central control of production is demonstrated beyond the possibility of refutation by Russian economic history.

(b) And, in the second place, it cannot be denied that any price system, however crude, must result in *some* kind of rational guidance as long as consumers are left free to spend their money as they please and a rough uniformity of costing practice is enforced upon all industries at once. Economists are perfectly right to insist that only the most delicate assessment of the value of economic resources in alternative uses will secure a *perfect* adaptation of production to the needs of society. But the degree of adaptation can vary very greatly, and any Planning Authority which insists upon a uniform assessment of values and costs will be able to make correspondingly wide adjustments to changing tastes and changing conditions. Even in the Russian price system where no payment is made for land or for the differences of individual efficiency within large groups of workers, it is obvious that the Central Authority could detect large divergences between the value produced and the cost incurred in any particular line of production by the tendency for stocks to change or prices to move at any given level of output. And this reasoning applies to every type of product. Crude price systems mean crude adjustment. Delicate price systems mean delicate adjustment. But it is only the absence of any price system which means no adjustment.

(c) From these two lines of investigation it must follow that there is no formal or logical contradiction between planning and pricing. It is perfectly possible for a centralised authority to order a price system to appear and to follow the guidance it necessarily gives. *There is no necessary connection between the form of the authority by which decisions are taken and the principles according to which the decisions are made.* It would be just as sensible to argue that the organisation of the medical profession under a National Council which laid down rules of professional conduct made it impossible to practise sound medicine as to affirm that the creation of a governing body for industry made it *impossible* to take wise economic decisions. It all depends upon what the Central Authority chooses to do.

Consequently the emphasis of the attack upon Planning has, in recent years, shifted back to the second charge, that, despite the logical possibility of pricing and wise planning, such wisdom will not in fact be exhibited by central authorities. I know of no reasoned defence of the view that central control will strengthen social unreason, but the two specific charges that proper incentive will be lacking and that socialist planning will be incapable of capital accumulation have been made and must be met.

The first of these charges can scarcely be sustained after the experience of authoritarian industrial management witnessed in Europe during and after the War. The sanctions against mismanagement provided by capitalism are bankruptcy and unemployment. The incentive for rapid and socially desirable activity is the hope of larger real incomes. There is no conceivable reason why a Central Authority should not impose just as strong, and even stronger, negative checks and provide the same type of positive inducement. Indeed, the experience of Planned Economies suggests that the danger with respect to negative checks is that they will be made too severe rather than too mild. The firing squad and the swamps of Siberia have featured too prominently as a reward for incompetent management in Russia, for example. And in the same way there is no reason in the nature of planning, and no great probability in practice, that differences in earnings will cease to be attached to grades of labour and skill which it is in the interests of society to develop and extend.

The only charge against Planning in which there remains the least shadow of substance is that a democratic and Socialist form of planning will find it difficult to secure funds for capital accumulation. It is obvious that the *authoritarian* economy in Russia has been guilty of *over*-saving rather than *under*-saving, but in this case it was possible to enforce the relative restriction of consumption by the bayonet and machine-gun. Would it be possible to do the same under a democratic régime in which Trade Union influence was strong?

It would be silly to deny that in a Socialist economy the pressure to raise wages in all industries at once would be sustained and grave. Nevertheless, if the natural desire on the part of each group of workers to increase the volume of their consumption is acceded to indefinitely, the rise in wages will eat into and finally altogether destroy the funds out of which the services of the Central Government and the building of new capital can alone be financed. The surplus arising in socialised industries must be owned by society and not by the group of workers in each industry. It must be administered by the Supreme Economic Authority for the good of the whole economy, and not absorbed by the increase in the standard of living of small groups. Otherwise economic progress will cease. . . .

An investigation of the case against Planning leaves us, then, with the conclusion that, while there is no ground for supposing that it is impossible for a centrally controlled system to be as wisely guided as an unplanned system, there is one obvious danger from which a democratically controlled Socialist economy may suffer and must be saved. But we must go on to ask if there are any reasons for supposing that a Planned Economy will be *more* efficient than an unplanned? There are, in my view, at least four reasons for supposing that this will be the case:

(a) To begin with, a centrally controlled economy will be an economy with *open eyes*. It is the essence of an unplanned and competitive arrangement of industry that the persons who take decisions about output and investment should be blind. They control such a small fraction of the output of a single commodity, and, therefore, take into account such a small part of the industrial field, that they are not and cannot be aware of the consequences of their own actions. They are not aware of the economic results. They do not even consider social repercussions. Competitive producers, for example, will tend to instal machinery with a view to increasing output without realising that all their fellow producers will be doing the same thing and that prices will be forced down in consequence. They will, in fact, be forced below the price which would justify the increased output. Moreover, they will throw labour out of employment without any regard to the results of such a step. Since as producers they are not forced to maintain their erstwhile employees until they—the employees—have found new work, no final assessment of the cost of labour displacement is made by the private employer. Nevertheless, *society* has to bear the cost of maintaining the unemployed. Moreover, the sufferings of the displaced individuals as persons are part of the true cost to humanity of the technical change. In this and a thousand other ways the decisions taken in an unplanned economy must be shortsighted, irrational, self-frustrating and socially disastrous. There is no space to describe in detail the prejudice in favour of change, the wastage of human skill, and the continuous maladjustment which competitive industry exhibits under slowly changing conditions.

All these limitations of vision and calculation could be swept away by central control. The consequences of every decision can be estimated however remote from the point of disturbance they may arise. Some allowance for it can then be made. When it is decided to instal an electrical drill in a coal mine it will be possible to take into account not only the immediate effect upon the cost of extracting coal, but also the influence upon market price of an all-round rise in the output of the mines, the opportunities for the re-employment of displaced coal hewers elsewhere, the cost of maintaining them during the transitional period, and even some allowance can be made for the loss of skill and happiness—a loss that can be brought to no direct pecuniary assessment. A central authority, because it is central—because that is to say it can survey the whole industrial field—can see things no individual producer can ever see and give weight to considerations that cannot play any part in the calculations of men engaged in competing with one another. The general officers on the hill must be able to see more than the ensign in the line of battle.

(b) Just as there is an extension of the field of cognition over the breadth of industry, so also is there an increase in the length of foresight in time. A Central Authority can take account of processes which are occurring so slowly, or will begin to occur so far in the future, that no single producer could be aware of their existence.

A Central Authority could have foreseen the long agony of the hand-loom weavers at the beginning of the last century in this country, the slow and cruel pressure upon world agriculture of more recent times, the need for a large-scale redistribution of labour in England in the twenties of this century; and could have made adjustments on a sufficient scale and over a long enough period to prevent much of the suffering and disharmony that have scarred our economic and social life.

A Central Authority can foresee the exhaustion of raw materials, the wastage of natural resources of beauty and health, and the destruction of human life which the blind scrambling of short-period plans continuously ignores. Such an Authority would, if it were in existence, foresee in our own country the tragic waste of the countryside indiscriminate building is everywhere occasioning, discern the disastrous social and economic consequences of the continual movement of industry into the south, and tackle in its greater wisdom the task of assessing the real social requirements in respect of the geographical distribution of industry and employment.

(c) One of the most important matters with which a Planning Authority will have to deal is the relation between finance and production. In no other field has the unplanned economy been less successful. The constant recurrence of depression and the instability of prosperity is one of the most marked features of capitalist society, and there is a virtual unanimity among economists that the wide movements of industrial activity are traceable to the mismanagement of the relation between credit policy and production. Moreover, the whole trend of recent thought on this subject has gone to show that, if it were possible to control one critical relation, the problem would be solved. The crucial relation is that beween the savings of the public—the amount of money income which is not spent on consumption—and the money which is invested in setting up new capital. In an unplanned economy there are two sources of disequilibrium: (i) in the first place, the people who save and the people who invest are in no direct connection with each other, and it is no one's business to see that acts of saving are followed immediately by equal acts of investment; (ii) in the second place, private banking institutions are in a position to vary the volume of investment without any reference to the course of saving. These are two sources of serious instability and are responsible between them for a very considerable proportion of the unemployment which has afflicted Capitalism throughout its history. No doubt there are purely scientific problems of great intricacy which must be resolved before we can hope to create and maintain stable prosperity. In my view, a large proportion of this necessary preliminary scientific work has been brought to a successful conclusion in recent years. But, whether that is the case or not, it is quite certain that whatever the correct monetary policy may be, it can only be enforced upon private corporations by the creation of an Authority in the financial sphere with adequate powers to over-ride all private considerations in the interest of general harmony. It is therefore safe to say that cyclical oscillation—the major cause of unemployment—will never be cured without the creation of the institutions of centralised *monetary* control. The financial field provides one of the most important opportunities for a Planned Economy to prove more efficient than an unplanned.

(d) Finally, there is one way in which a Socialist Economy may expect an increase in the volume and efficiency of the factors of production which is not available for any other sort of economy whatever—and that is in the attitude of the Trade Union worker to production. In an industrial world dominated by the struggle between organised property and organised labour for status and wealth, it is inevitable that all sorts of obstructive regulations should arise and "ca' canny" practices be enforced. These are, no doubt, partly due to the continuously recurring contractions in the demand for labour. But this is not wholly the case. A residuum of such resistance is wholly attributable to the dislike of the employer and the rights of property as such. There is, therefore, every reason to believe that there will be an increased willingness to relax such restrictions and to co-operate more willingly with the management side of industry when a Socialist Authority has raised the status of workers' representation and can provide full employment for the working population. No doubt too much has been made of this "change of spirit" in the Socialist apologetics of the past. The probability of conflicts between the interests of workers organised in industrial groups and the general service of society is very real. But to assert that the socialisation of the means of production and distribution would release *no* new stores of vital productive energy in the labour force, would be to ignore the width and intensity of the Socialist sentiment which consciously or unconsciously animates the whole proletariat of a modern society. . . .

It has been the purpose of this article to emphasize that the importance of Planning to a democratic Socialist is twofold. In the first place, a transference of industry to social control is the pre-requisite political condition for any stable advance to a more just society. In the second place, Planning is vitally important in order to establish a more efficient economic system. This will render the approach to equality popular and, in any case, it is desirable for its own sake. In the establishment of a more efficient economy the most important single change lies undoubtedly in the cure of periodical depressions. But beyond that task, stretching out into the future when full employment is secured, there remains the double task of maintaining economic advance through the accumulation of capital and retaining the flexibility in the arrangement of the factors of production. Now, neither of these tasks can possibly be performed unless there is a willingness on the part of organised labour to adjust itself to the new conditions of national control. As we have already seen, the only way in which the accumulation of capital can be financed is by the withdrawal of part of the funds earned by socialised industries from the workers employed in them to finance the capital items in the industrial budget. Surpluses arising in socialised industries must not belong to the workers in such industries. They must belong to the State. And in the same way, if correct adjustments are to be made within the industrial structure, the vested interests of the workers in any particular industry must never be allowed to prevent contraction of employment if it is making losses or expansion if it is making profits. No one with a knowledge of Trade Union opinions and practices will doubt that this is one of the real problems of Socialist Planning.

The third, and perhaps the most important, requirement of efficient Planning is therefore the supersession in the Trade Union and Labour Movement in practice as well as in theory of the last elements of Syndicalism. All partial groups of workers by hand and brain—lawyers as well as bricklayers, postmen as well as doctors—must be prepared in the last resort to allow their own interests to be subordinated to the interests of the workers as a whole. It is scarcely necessary to point out that this does not mean that no regard is to be paid to the general human desire for stability and security. Nor does it mean that the vast majority of workers will not benefit by the processes of mutual concession that are demanded from us all. On the contrary, a rapid rate of capital accumulation and a reasonable degree of flexibility are of vital importance for the welfare of every single worker in his nature as a consumer. Only within these conditions can any individual enjoy a rapidly rising standard of living. The interests of all persons as consumers may be in conflict with the interests of particular groups of persons as producers. What is requisite for efficiency is that the interests of all should be served by a continuous process of concession on the part of particular groups. We must all mitigate our claims in order that others may mitigate their claims against us and that by compromise we may all live.

The efficiency of Planning depends in the last resort upon the breadth and consistency of the Socialist faith which animates us. The organised workers who claim with justice that the interest of the community should not be over-ridden for the profits of the few should go on to add that those same interests must not be over-ridden for the wages of a few. The interests of the whole are sovereign over the interests of the part. In society we are born; by society we must live. To the centralised control of a democratic community our livelihood and our security must be submitted. It is the business of society to secure the welfare of all. To do so it must be able to set limits to the welfare of each one of us.

FRIEDRICH A. HAYEK

A NOTABLE feature of the past century, and especially of the past fifty years, has been the increase in the scope and extent of intervention by the state in economic affairs. Admittedly such intervention has promoted the growth of bureaucracy and diminished the extent to which, as a society, we rely upon individual initiative and responsibility to get the world's work done. The world's work is not always done so well or so promptly when the slow-moving machinery of the state first must be nudged or appeased. Admirers of Adam Smith and the other economic liberals have not forgotten the arguments in favor of *laissez-faire*. But they reconcile themselves, perhaps too easily, to the scope and extent of modern intervention with the thought that our world is not Adam Smith's world. Modern economic life is so complicated, business firms have become so large, so many diverse interests need to be adjusted, that matters cannot safely be left to work themselves out in the market place. The "common interest" must be protected, the "wastefulness of competition" must be mitigated, the weak must be protected against the strong. Who else can do this but the state?

It is Friedrich A. Hayek's purpose in his book *The Road to Serfdom* (1944), from which the following selection has been taken, to oppose this view, and to argue that most of what Adam Smith said about the dangers of "big government" is as valid today as it was when *The Wealth of Nations* was being written. Hayek is an economist by profession. Born in Vienna in 1899, he was reared in the Austrian tradition of Karl Menger (1840–1921) and Ludwig von Mises (b. 1881). He taught for some years at the University of Vienna and also worked for the Austrian government. In 1931 he was appointed Tooke Professor of Economic Science and Statistics at the University of London where he stayed until 1950, when he became professor of social and moral science at the University of Chicago. Beside works in economic theory, he has written *Individualism and Economic Order* (1948) and *The Counter-Revolution of Science* (1952).

THE ROAD TO SERFDOM

CHAPTER V: PLANNING AND DEMOCRACY

The common features of all collectivist systems may be described, in a phrase ever dear to socialists of all schools, as the deliberate organization of the labors of society for a definite social goal. That our present society

This selection has been reprinted from Friedrich A. Hayek, *The Road to Serfdom* (pp. 56–67, 69–83, 86–90, 92–100, 119–127, Copyright 1944 by The University of Chicago, Chicago, Ill.) by permission of the University of Chicago Press, publisher.

lacks such "conscious" direction toward a single aim, that its activities are guided by the whims and fancies of irresponsible individuals, has always been one of the main complaints of its socialist critics.

In many ways this puts the basic issue very clearly. And it directs us at once to the point where the conflict arises between individual freedom and collectivism. The various kinds of collectivism, communism, fascism, etc., differ among themselves in the nature of the goal toward which they want to direct the efforts of society. But they all differ from liberalism and individualism in wanting to organize the whole of society and all its resources for this unitary end and in refusing to recognize autonomous spheres in which the ends of the individuals are supreme. In short, they are totalitarian in the true sense of this new word which we have adopted to describe the unexpected but nevertheless inseparable manifestations of what in theory we call collectivism.

The "social goal," or "common purpose," for which society is to be organized is usually vaguely described as the "common good," the "general welfare," or the "general interest." . . . To direct all our activities according to a single plan presupposes that every one of our needs is given its rank in an order of values which must be complete enough to make it possible to decide among all the different courses which the planner has to choose. It presupposes, in short, the existence of a complete ethical code in which all the different human values are allotted their due place. . . .

Not only do we not possess such an all-inclusive scale of values: it would be impossible for any mind to comprehend the infinite variety of different needs of different people which compete for the available resources and to attach a definite weight to each. For our problem it is of minor importance whether the ends for which any person cares comprehend only his own individual needs, or whether they include the needs of his closer or even those of his more distant fellows—that is, whether he is egoistic or altruistic in the ordinary senses of these words. The point which is so important is the basic fact that it is impossible for any man to survey more than a limited field, to be aware of the urgency of more than a limited number of needs. . . .

This is the fundamental fact on which the whole philosophy of individualism is based. It does not assume, as is often asserted, that man is egoistic or selfish or ought to be. It merely starts from the indisputable fact that the limits of our powers of imagination make it impossible to include in our scale of values more than a sector of the needs of the whole society, and that, since, strictly speaking, scales of value can exist only in individual minds, nothing but partial scales of values exist—scales which are inevitably different and often inconsistent with each other. From this the individualist concludes that the individuals should be allowed, within defined limits, to follow their own values and preferences rather than somebody else's; that within these spheres the individual's system of ends should be supreme and not subject to any dictation by others. It is this recognition of the individual as the ultimate judge of his ends, the belief that as far as possible his own views ought to govern his actions, that forms the essence of the individualist position.

This view does not, of course, exclude the recognition of social ends, or rather of a coincidence of individual ends which makes it advisable for men to combine for their pursuit. But it limits such common action to the instances where individual views coincide; what are called "social ends" are for it merely identical ends of many individuals—or ends to the achievement of which individuals are willing to contribute in return for the assistance they receive in the satisfaction of their own desires. Common action is thus limited to the fields where people agree on common ends. Very frequently these common ends will not be ultimate ends to the individuals but means which different persons can use for different purposes. In fact, people are most likely to agree on common action where the common end is not an ultimate end to them but a means capable of serving a great variety of purposes.

When individuals combine in a joint effort to realize ends they have in common, the organizations, like the state, that they form for this purpose, are given their own system of ends and their own means. But any organization thus formed remains one "person" among others, in the case of the state much more powerful than any of the others, it is true, yet still with its separate and limited sphere in which alone its ends are supreme. . . .

We can rely on voluntary agreement to guide the action of the state only so long as it is confined to spheres where agreement exists. But not only when the state undertakes direct control in fields where there is no such agreement is it bound to suppress individual freedom. We can unfortunately not indefinitely extend the sphere of common action and still leave the individual free in his own sphere. . . . Where, as was, for example, true in Germany as early as 1928, the central and local authorities directly control the use of more than half the national income (according to an official German estimate then, 53 per cent), they control indirectly almost the whole economic life of the nation. There is, then, scarcely an individual end which is not dependent for its achievement on the action of the state, and the "social scale of values" which guides the state's action must embrace practically all individual ends.

It is not difficult to see what must be the consequences when democracy embarks upon a course of planning which in its execution requires more agreement than in fact exists. The people may have agreed on adopting a system of directed economy because they have been convinced that it will produce great prosperity. In the discussions leading to the decision, the goal of planning will have been described by some such term as "common welfare," which only conceals the absence of real agreement on the ends of planning. . . . The effect of the people's agreeing that there must be central planning, without agreeing on the ends, will be rather as if a group of people were to commit themselves to take a journey together without agreeing where they want to go: with the result that they may all have to make a journey which most of them do not want at all. That planning creates a situation in which it is necessary for us to agree on a much larger number of topics than we have been used to, and that in a planned system we cannot confine collective action to the tasks on which we can agree but are forced to produce agreement on everything in order that any action can be taken at all, is one of the features which contributes more than most to determining the character of a planned system.

It may be the unanimously expressed will of the people that its parliament should prepare a comprehensive economic plan, yet neither the people nor its representatives need therefore be able to agree on any particular plan. . . . Parliaments come to be regarded as ineffective "talking shops," unable or incompetent to carry out the tasks for which they have been chosen. The conviction grows that if efficient planning is to be done, the direction must be "taken out of politics" and placed in the hands of experts—permanent officials or independent autonomous bodies. . . .

It is important clearly to see the causes of this admitted ineffectiveness of parliaments when it comes to a detailed administration of the economic affairs of a nation. The fault is neither with the individual representatives nor with parliamentary institutions as such but with the contradictions inherent in the task with which they are charged. They are not asked to act where they can agree, but to produce agreement on everything—the whole direction of the resources of the nation. For such a task the system of majority decision is, however, not suited. Majorities will be found where it is a choice between limited alternatives; but it is a superstition to believe that there must be a majority view on everything. There is no reason why there should be a majority in favor of any one of the different possible courses of positive action if their number is legion. Every member of the legislative assembly might prefer some particular plan for the direction of economic activity to no plan, yet no one plan may appear preferable to a majority to no plan at all.

Nor can a coherent plan be achieved by breaking it up into parts and voting on particular issues. A democratic assembly voting and amending a comprehensive economic plan clause by clause, as it deliberates on an ordinary bill, makes nonsense. An economic plan, to deserve the name, must have a unitary conception. . . . A complex whole in which all the parts must be most carefully adjusted to each other cannot be achieved through a compromise between conflicting views. To draw up an economic plan in this fashion is even less possible than, for example, successfully to plan a military campaign by democratic procedure. As in strategy it would become inevitable to delegate the task to the experts.

Yet the difference is that, while the general who is put in charge of a campaign is given a single end to which, for the duration of the campaign, all the means under his control have to be exclusively devoted, there can be no such single goal given to the economic planner, and no similar limitation of the means imposed upon him. The general has not got to balance different independent aims against each other; there is for him only one supreme goal. But the ends of an economic plan, or of any part of it, cannot be defined apart from the particular plan. It is the essence of the economic problem that the making of an economic plan involves the choice between conflicting or competing ends—different needs of different people. But which ends do so conflict, which will have to be sacrificed if we want to achieve certain others, in short, which are the alternatives between which we must choose, can only be known to those who know all the facts; and only they, the experts, are in a position to decide which of the different ends are to be given preference. It is inevitable that they should impose their scale of preferences on the community for which they plan.

This is not always clearly recognized, and delegation is usually justified by the technical character of the task. But this does not mean that only the technical detail is delegated, or even that the inability of parliaments to understand the technical detail is the root of the difficulty. Alterations in the structure of civil law are no less technical and no more difficult to appreciate in all their implications; yet nobody has yet seriously suggested that legislation there should be delegated to a body of experts. The fact is that in these fields legislation does not go beyond general rules on which true majority agreement can be achieved, while in the direction of economic activity the interests to be reconciled are so divergent that no true agreement is likely to be reached in a democratic assembly.

It should be recognized, however, that it is not the delegation of law-making power as such which is so objectionable. . . . The objectionable feature is that delegation is so often resorted to because the matter in hand cannot be regulated by general rules but only by the exercise of discretion in the decision of particular cases. In these instances delegation means that some authority is given power to make with the force of law what to all intents and purposes are arbitrary decisions (usually described as "judging the case on its merits").

The delegation of particular technical tasks to separate bodies, while a regular feature, is yet only the first step in the process whereby a democracy which embarks on planning progressively relinquishes its powers. . . . The delegation of particular powers to separate agencies creates a new obstacle to the achievement of a single co-ordinated plan. Even if, by this expedient, a democracy should succeed in planning every sector of economic activity, it would still have to face the problem of integrating these separate plans into a unitary whole. . . . But the democratic legislature will long hesitate to relinquish the decisions on really vital issues, and so long as it does so it makes it impossible for anyone else to provide the comprehensive plan. Yet agreement that planning is necessary, together with the inability of democratic assemblies to produce a plan, will evoke stronger and stronger demands that the government or some single individual should be given powers to act on their own responsibility. The belief is becoming more and more widespread that, if things are to get done, the responsible authorities must be freed from the fetters of democratic procedure. . . .

It is the price of democracy that the possibilities of conscious control are restricted to the fields where true agreement exists and that in some fields things must be left to chance. But in a society which for its functioning depends on central planning this control cannot be made dependent on a majority's being able to agree; it will often be necessary that the will of a small minority be imposed upon the people, because this minority will be the largest group able to agree among themselves on the question at issue. Democratic government has worked successfully where, and so long as, the functions of government were, by a widely accepted creed, restricted to fields where agreement among a majority could be achieved by free discussion; and it is the great merit of the liberal creed that it reduced the range of subjects on which agreement was necessary to one on which it was likely to exist in a society of free men. It is now often said that democracy will not tolerate "capitalism." If "capitalism" means here a competitive system based on free disposal over private property, it is far more important to realize that only within this system is democracy possible. When it becomes dominated by a collectivist creed, democracy will inevitably destroy itself.

We have no intention, however, of making a fetish of democracy. . . . Democracy is essentially a means, a utilitarian device for safeguarding internal peace and individual freedom. As such it is by no means infallible or certain. Nor must we forget that there has often been much more cultural and spiritual freedom under an autocratic rule than under some democracies—and it is at least conceivable that under the government of a very homogeneous and doctrinaire majority democratic government might be as oppressive as the worst dictatorship. Our point, however, is not that dictatorship must inevitably extirpate freedom but rather that planning leads to dictatorship because dictatorship is the most effective instrument of coercion and the enforcement of ideals and, as such, essential if central planning on a large scale is to be possible. The clash between planning and democracy arises simply from the fact that the latter is an obstacle to the suppression of freedom which the direction of economic activity requires. But in so far as democracy ceases to be a guaranty of individual freedom, it may well persist in some form under a totalitarian regime. A true "dictatorship of the proletariat," even if democratic in form, if it undertook centrally to direct the economic system, would probably destroy personal freedom as completely as any autocracy has ever done. . . .

CHAPTER VI: PLANNING AND THE RULE OF LAW

Nothing distinguishes more clearly conditions in a free country from those in a country under arbitrary government than the observance in the former of the great principles known as the Rule of Law. Stripped of all its technicalities, this means that government in all its actions is bound by rules fixed and announced beforehand—rules which make it possible to foresee with fair certainty how the authority will use its coercive powers in given circumstances and to plan one's individual affairs on the basis of this knowledge. Though this ideal can never be perfectly achieved, since legislators as well as those to whom the administration of the law is intrusted are fallible men, the essential point, that the discretion left to the executive organs wielding coercive power should be reduced as much as possible, is clear enough. . . .

Dicey

The distinction . . . between the creation of a permanent framework of laws within which the productive activity is guided by individual decisions and the direction of economic activity by a central authority is thus really a particular case of the more general distinction between the Rule of Law and arbitrary government. Under the first the government confines itself to fixing rules determining the conditions under which the available resources may be used, leaving to the individuals the decision for what ends they are to be used. Under the second the government directs the use of the means of production to particular ends. The first type of rules can be made in advance, in the shape of *formal rules* which do not aim at the wants and needs of particular people. They are intended to be merely instrumental in the pursuit of people's various individual ends. And they are, or ought to be, intended for such long periods that it is impossible to know whether they will assist particular people more than others. They could almost be described as a kind of instrument of production, helping people to predict the behavior of those with whom they must collaborate, rather than as efforts toward the satisfaction of particular needs.

Economic planning of the collectivist kind necessarily involves the very opposite of this. The planning authority cannot confine itself to providing opportunities for unknown people to make whatever use of them they like. It cannot tie itself down in advance to general and formal rules which prevent arbitrariness. It must provide for the actual needs of people as they arise and then choose deliberately between them. It must constantly decide questions which cannot be answered by formal principles only, and, in making these decisions, it must set up distinctions of merit between the needs of different people. When the government has to decide how many pigs are to be raised or how many busses are to be run, which coal mines are to operate, or at what prices shoes are to be sold, these decisions cannot be deduced from formal principles or settled for long periods in advance. . . . In the end somebody's views will have to decide whose interests are more important; and these views must become part of the law of the land, a new distinction of rank which the coercive apparatus of government imposes upon the people.

The distinction we have just used between formal law or justice and substantive rules is very important and at the same time most difficult to draw precisely in practice. Yet the general principle involved is simple enough. The difference between the two kinds of rules is the same as that between laying down a Rule of the Road, as in the Highway Code, and ordering people where to go; or, better still, between providing signposts and commanding people which road to take. . . .

In our age, with its passion for conscious control of everything, it may appear paradoxical to claim as a virtue that under one system we shall know less about the particular effect of the measures the state takes than would be true under most other systems and that a method of social control should be deemed superior because of our ignorance of its precise results. Yet this consideration is in fact the rationale of the great liberal principle of the Rule of Law. And the apparent paradox dissolves rapidly when we follow the argument a little further.

This argument is twofold; the first is economic and can here only briefly be stated. The state should confine itself to establishing rules applying to general types of situations and should allow the individuals freedom in everything which depends on the circumstances of time and place, because only the individuals concerned in each instance can fully know these circumstances and adapt their actions to them. If the individuals are to be able to use their knowledge effectively in making plans, they must be able to predict actions of the state which may affect these plans. But if the actions of the state are to be predictable, they must be determined by rules fixed independently of the concrete circumstances which can be neither foreseen nor taken into account beforehand: and the particular effects of such actions will be unpredictable. . . . Hence the familiar fact that the more the state "plans," the more difficult planning becomes for the individual.

The second, moral or political, argument is even more directly relevant to the point under discussion. If the state is precisely to foresee the incidence of its actions, it means that it can leave those affected no choice. Wherever the state can exactly foresee the effects on particular people of alternative courses of action, it is also the state which chooses between the different ends. . . . In a world where everything was precisely foreseen, the state could hardly do anything and remain impartial.

. . . As soon as the particular effects are foreseen at the time a law is made, it ceases to be a mere instrument to be used by the people and becomes instead an instrument used by the lawgiver upon the people and for his ends. The state ceases to be a piece of utilitarian machinery intended to help individuals in the fullest development of their individual personality and becomes a "moral" institution—where "moral" is not used in contrast to immoral but describes an institution which imposes on its members its views on all moral questions, whether these views be moral or highly immoral. In this sense the Nazi or any other collectivist state is "moral," while the liberal state is not.

Perhaps it will be said that all this raises no serious problem because in the kind of questions which the economic planner would have to decide he need not and should not be guided by his individual prejudices but could rely on the general conviction of what is fair and reasonable. This contention usually receives support from those who have experience of planning in a particular industry and who find that there is no insuperable difficulty about arriving at a decision which all those immediately interested will accept as fair. The reason why this experience proves nothing is, of course, the selection of the "interests" concerned when planning is confined to a particular industry. Those most immediately interested in a particular issue are not necessarily the best judges of the interests of society as a whole. To take only the most characteristic case: when capital and labor in an industry agree on some policy of restriction and thus exploit the consumers, there is usually no difficulty about the division of the spoils in proportion to former earnings or on some similar principle. The loss which is divided between thousands or millions is usually either simply disregarded or quite inadequately considered. If we want to test the usefulness of the principle of "fairness" in deciding the kind of issues which arise in economic planning, we must apply it to some question where the gains and the losses are seen equally clearly. . . . When we have to choose between higher wages for nurses or doctors and more extensive services for the sick, more milk for children and better wages for agricultural workers, or between employment for the unemployed or better wages for those already employed, nothing short of a complete system of values in which every want of every person or group has a definite place is necessary to provide an answer.

In fact, as planning becomes more and more extensive, it becomes regularly necessary to qualify legal provisions increasingly by reference to what is "fair" or "reasonable"; this means that it becomes necessary to leave the decision of the concrete case more and more to the discretion of the judge or authority in question. One could write a history of the decline of the Rule of Law, the disappearance of the *Rechtsstaat,*[1] in terms of the progressive introduction of these vague formulas into legislation and jurisdiction, and of the increasing arbitrariness and uncertainty of, and the consequent disrespect for, the law and the judicature, which in these circumstances could not but become an instrument of policy. It is important to point out once more in this connection that this process of the decline of the Rule of Law had been going on steadily in Germany for some time before Hitler came into power and that a policy well advanced toward totalitarian planning had already done a great deal of the work which Hitler completed. . . .

The unpredictability of the particular effects, which is the distinguishing characteristic of the formal laws of a liberal system, is also important because it helps us to clear up another confusion about the nature of this system: the

[1] [That is, a state founded upon law.]

belief that its characteristic attitude is inaction of the state. The question whether the state should or should not "act" or "interfere" poses an altogether false alternative, and the term "laissez faire" is a highly ambiguous and misleading description of the principles on which a liberal policy is based. Of course, every state must act and every action of the state interferes with something or other. But that is not the point. The important question is whether the individual can foresee the action of the state and make use of this knowledge as a datum in forming his own plans, with the result that the state cannot control the use made of its machinery and that the individual knows precisely how far he will be protected against interference from others, or whether the state is in a position to frustrate individual efforts. The state controlling weights and measures (or preventing fraud and deception in any other way) is certainly acting, while the state permitting the use of violence, for example, by strike pickets, is inactive. Yet it is in the first case that the state observes liberal principles and in the second that it does not. Similarly with respect to most of the general and permanent rules which the state may establish with regard to production, such as building regulations or factory laws: these may be wise or unwise in the particular instance, but they do not conflict with liberal principles so long as they are intended to be permanent and are not used to favor or harm particular people. It is true that in these instances there will, apart from the long-run effects which cannot be predicted, also be short-run effects on particular people which may be clearly known. But with this kind of laws the short-run effects are in general not (or at least ought not to be) the guiding consideration. As these immediate and predictable effects become more important compared with the long-run effects, we approach the border line where the distinction, however clear in principle, becomes blurred in practice. . . .

To say that in a planned society the Rule of Law cannot hold is . . . not to say that the actions of the government will not be legal or that such a society will necessarily be lawless. It means only that the use of the government's coercive powers will no longer be limited and determined by pre-established rules. The law can, and to make a central direction of economic activity possible must, legalize what to all intents and purposes remains arbitrary action. If the law says that such a board or authority may do what it pleases, anything that board or authority does is legal—but its actions are certainly not subject to the Rule of Law. By giving the government unlimited powers, the most arbitrary rule can be made legal; and in this way a democracy may set up the most complete despotism imaginable. . . .

How even a formal recognition of individual rights, or of the equal rights of minorities, loses all significance in a state which embarks on a complete control of economic life, has been amply demonstrated by the experience of the various Central European countries. It has been shown there that it is possible to pursue a policy of ruthless discrimination against national minorities by the use of recognized instruments of economic policy without ever infringing the letter of the statutory protection of minority rights. This oppression by means of economic policy was greatly facilitated by the fact that particular industries or activities were largely in the hands of a national minority, so that many a measure aimed ostensibly against an industry or class was in fact aimed at a national minority. But the almost boundless possibilities for a policy of discrimination and oppression provided by such apparently innocuous principles as "government control of the development of industries" have been amply demonstrated to all those desirous of seeing how the political consequences of planning appear in practice.

CHAPTER VII: ECONOMIC CONTROL AND TOTALITARIANISM

Most planners who have seriously considered the practical aspects of their task have little doubt that a directed economy must be run on more or less dictatorial lines. That the complex system of interrelated activities, if it is to be consciously directed at all, must be directed by a single staff of experts, and that ultimate responsibility and power must rest in the hands of a commander-in-chief whose actions must not be fettered by democratic procedure, is too obvious a consequence of underlying ideas of central planning not to command fairly general assent. The consolation our planners offer us is that this authoritarian direction will apply "only" to economic matters. One of the most prominent economic planners, Stuart Chase, assures us, for instance, that in a planned society "political democracy can remain if it confines itself to all but economic matters." Such assurances are usually accompanied by the suggestion that, by giving up freedom in what are, or ought to be, the less important aspects of our lives, we shall obtain greater freedom in the pursuit of higher values. On this ground people who abhor the idea of a political dictatorship often clamor for a dictator in the economic field. . . .

Unfortunately, the assurance people derive from this belief that the power which is exercised over economic life is a power over matters of secondary importance only, and which makes them take lightly the threat to the freedom of our economic pursuits, is altogether unwarranted. It is largely a consequence of the erroneous belief that there are purely economic ends separate from the other ends of life. Yet, apart from the pathological case of the miser, there is no such thing. . . . What in ordinary language is misleadingly called the "economic motive" means merely the desire for general opportunity, the desire for power to achieve unspecified ends. If we strive for money, it is because it offers us the widest choice in enjoying the fruits of our efforts. Because in modern society it is through the limitation of our money incomes that we are made to feel the restrictions which our relative poverty still imposes upon us, many have come to hate money as the symbol of these restrictions. But this is to mistake for the cause the medium through which a force makes itself felt. It would be much truer to say that money is one of the greatest instruments of freedom ever invented by man. It is money which in existing society opens an astounding range of choice to the poor man—a range greater than that which not many generations ago was open only to the wealthy. We shall better understand the significance of this service of money if we consider what it would really mean if, as so many socialists characteristically propose, the "pecuniary motive" were largely displaced by "non-economic incentives." If all rewards, instead of being offered in money, were offered in the form of public distinctions or privileges, positions of power over other men, or better housing or better food, opportunities for travel or education, this would merely mean that the recipient would no longer be allowed to choose and that whoever fixed the reward determined not only its size but also the particular form in which it should be enjoyed. . . .

The so-called economic freedom which the planners promise us means precisely that we are to be relieved of the necessity of solving our own economic problems and that the bitter choices which this often involves are to be made for us. Since under modern conditions we are for almost everything dependent on means which our fellow-men provide, economic planning would involve direction of almost the whole of our life. There is hardly an aspect of it, from our primary needs to our relations with our family and friends, from the nature of our work to the use of our leisure, over which the planner would not exercise his "conscious control." [2]

The power of the planner over our private lives would be no less complete

[2] The extent of the control over all life that economic control confers is nowhere better illustrated than in the field of foreign exchanges. Nothing would at first seem to affect private life less than a state control of the dealings in foreign exchange, and most people will regard its introduction with complete indifference. Yet the experience of most Continental countries has taught thoughtful people to regard this step as the decisive advance on the path to totalitarianism and the suppression of individual liberty. It is, in fact, the complete delivery of the individual to the tyranny of the state, the final suppression of all means of escape—not merely for the rich but for everybody. Once the individual is no longer free to travel, no longer free to buy foreign books or journals, once all the means of foreign contact can be restricted to those of whom official opinion approves or for whom it is regarded as necessary, the effective control of opinion is much greater than that ever exercised by any of the absolutist governments of the seventeenth and eighteenth centuries.

if he chose not to exercise it by direct control of our consumption. Although a planned society would probably to some extent employ rationing and similar devices, the power of the planner over our private lives does not depend on this and would be hardly less effective if the consumer were nominally free to spend his income as he pleased. The source of this power over all consumption which in a planned society the authority would possess would be its control over production.

Our freedom of choice in a competitive society rests on the fact that, if one person refuses to satisfy our wishes, we can turn to another. But if we face a monopolist we are at his mercy. And an authority directing the whole economic system would be the most powerful monopolist conceivable. . . .

Not only in our capacity as consumers, however, and not even mainly in that capacity, would the will of the authority shape and "guide" our daily lives. It would do so even more in our position as producers. These two aspects of our lives cannot be separated; and as for most of us the time we spend at our work is a large part of our whole lives, and as our job usually also determines the place where and the people among whom we live, some freedom in choosing our work is, probably, even more important for our happiness than freedom to spend our income during the hours of leisure.

No doubt it is true that even in the best of worlds this freedom will be very limited. Few people ever have an abundance of choice of occupation. But what matters is that we have some choice, that we are not absolutely tied to a particular job which has been chosen for us, or which we may have chosen in the past, and that if one position becomes quite intolerable, or if we set our heart on another, there is almost always a way for the able, some sacrifice at the price of which he may achieve his goal. Nothing makes conditions more unbearable than the knowledge that no effort of ours can change them; and even if we should never have the strength of mind to make the necessary sacrifice, the knowledge that we could escape if we only strove hard enough makes many otherwise intolerable positions bearable.

This is not to say that in this respect all is for the best in our present world, or has been so in the most liberal past, and that there is not much that could be done to improve the opportunities of choice open to the people. Here as elsewhere the state can do a great deal to help the spreading of knowledge and information and to assist mobility. But the point is that the kind of state action which really would increase opportunity is almost precisely the opposite of the "planning" which is now generally advocated and practiced. Most planners, it is true, promise that in the new planned world free choice of occupation will be scrupulously preserved or even increased. But there they promise more than they can possibly fulfil. If they want to plan, they must control the entry into the different trades and occupations, or the terms of remuneration, or both. In almost all known instances of planning, the establishment of such controls and restrictions was among the first measures taken. . . .

There would be little difference if the planning authority confined itself to fixing the terms of employment and tried to regulate numbers by adjusting these terms. . . . A rather plain girl who badly wants to become a saleswoman, a weakly boy who has set his heart on a job where his weakness handicaps him, as well as in general the apparently less able or less suitable are not necessarily excluded in a competitive society; if they value the position sufficiently they will frequently be able to get a start by a financial sacrifice and will later make good through qualities which at first are not so obvious. But when the authority fixes the remunerations for a whole category and the selection among the candidates is made by an objective test, the strength of their desire for the job will count for very little. . . . To make this immense task manageable, it will have to reduce the diversity of human capacities and inclinations to a few categories of readily interchangeable units and deliberately to disregard minor personal differences.

Although the professed aim of planning would be that man should cease to be a mere means, in fact—since it would be impossible to take account in the plan of individual likes and dislikes—the individual would more than ever become a mere means, to be used by the authority in the service of such abstractions as the "social welfare" or the "good of the community." . . .

It is significant of the confusion prevailing on all these subjects that it should have become a cause for reproach that in a competitive society almost everything can be had at a price. If the people who protest against having the higher values of life brought into the "cash nexus" really mean that we should not be allowed to sacrifice our lesser needs in order to preserve the higher values, and that the choice should be made for us, this demand must be regarded as rather peculiar and scarcely testifies to great respect for the dignity of the individual. That life and health, beauty and virtue, honor and peace of mind, can often be preserved only at considerable material cost, and that somebody must make the choice, is as undeniable as that we all are sometimes not prepared to make the material sacrifices necessary to protect those higher values against all injury.

To take only one example: We could, of course, reduce casualties by automobile accidents to zero if we were willing to bear the cost—if in no other way—by abolishing automobiles. And the same is true of thousands of other instances in which we are constantly risking life and health and all the fine values of the spirit, of ourselves and of our fellow-men, to further what we at the same time contemptuously describe as our material comfort. Nor can it be otherwise, since all our ends compete for the same means; and we could not strive for anything but these absolute values if they were on no account to be endangered. . . .

The claim that a planned economy would produce a substantially larger output than the competitive system is being progressively abandoned by most students of the problem. Even a good many economists with socialist views who have seriously studied the problems of central planning are now content to hope that a planned society will equal the efficiency of a competitive system; they advocate planning no longer because of its superior productivity but because it will enable us to secure a more just and equitable distribution of wealth. This is, indeed, the only argument for planning which can be seriously pressed. . . . But the question remains whether the price we should have to pay for the realization of somebody's ideal of justice is not bound to be more discontent and more oppression than was ever caused by the much-abused free play of economic forces.

We should be seriously deceiving ourselves if for these apprehensions we sought comfort in the consideration that the adoption of central planning would merely mean a return, after a brief spell of a free economy, to the ties and regulations which have governed economic activity through most ages, and that therefore the infringements of personal liberty need not be greater than they were before the age of laissez faire. This is a dangerous illusion. . . .

The situation is now entirely different. During the liberal era the progressive division of labor has created a situation where almost every one of our activities is part of a social process. This is a development which we cannot reverse, since it is only because of it that we can maintain the vastly increased population at anything like present standards. But, in consequence, the substitution of central planning for competition would require central direction of a much greater part of our lives than was ever attempted before. It could not stop at what we regard as our economic activities, because we are now for almost every part of our lives dependent on somebody else's economic activities.[3] . . .

It is often said that political freedom is meaningless without economic

[3] It is no accident that in the totalitarian countries, be it Russia or Germany or Italy, the question of how to organize the people's leisure has become a problem of planning. The Germans have even invented for this problem the horrible and self-contradictory name of *Freizeitgestaltung* (literally: the shaping of the use made of the people's free time), as if it were still "free time" when it has to be spent in the way ordained by authority.

freedom. This is true enough, but in a sense almost opposite from that in which the phrase is used by our planners. The economic freedom which is the prerequisite of any other freedom cannot be the freedom from economic care which the socialists promise us and which can be obtained only by relieving the individual at the same time of the necessity and of the power of choice; it must be the freedom of our economic activity which, with the right of choice, inevitably also carries the risk and the responsibility of that right.

CHAPTER IX: SECURITY AND FREEDOM

Like the spurious "economic freedom," and with more justice, economic security is often represented as an indispensable condition of real liberty. In a sense this is both true and important. Independence of mind or strength of character is rarely found among those who cannot be confident that they will make their way by their own effort. Yet the idea of economic security is no less vague and ambiguous than most other terms in this field; and because of this the general approval given to the demand for security may become a danger to liberty. Indeed, when security is understood in too absolute a sense, the general striving for it, far from increasing the chances of freedom, becomes the gravest threat to it.

It will be well to contrast at the outset the two kinds of security: the limited one, which can be achieved for all, and which is therefore no privilege but a legitimate object of desire; and absolute security, which in a free society cannot be achieved for all and which ought not to be given as a privilege—except in a few special instances such as that of the judges, where complete independence is of paramount importance. These two kinds of security are, first, security against severe physical privation, the certainty of a given minimum of sustenance for all; and, second, the security of a given standard of life, or of the relative position which one person or group enjoys compared with others; or, as we may put it briefly, the security of a minimum income and the security of the particular income a person is thought to deserve. We shall presently see that this distinction largely coincides with the distinction between the security which can be provided for all outside of and supplementary to the market system and the security which can be provided only for some and only by controlling or abolishing the market.

There is no reason why in a society which has reached the general level of wealth which ours has attained the first kind of security should not be guaranteed to all without endangering general freedom. . . .

Nor is there any reason why the state should not assist the individuals in providing for those common hazards of life against which, because of their uncertainty, few individuals can make adequate provision. Where, as in the case of sickness and accident, neither the desire to avoid such calamities nor the efforts to overcome their consequences are as a rule weakened by the provision of assistance—where, in short, we deal with genuinely insurable risks—the case for the state's helping to organize a comprehensive system of social insurance is very strong. . . . To the same category belongs also the increase of security through the state's rendering assistance to the victims of such "acts of God" as earthquakes and floods. Wherever communal action can mitigate disasters against which the individual can neither attempt to guard himself nor make provision for the consequences, such communal action should undoubtedly be taken.

There is, finally, the supremely important problem of combating general fluctuations of economic activity and the recurrent waves of large-scale unemployment which accompany them. This is, of course, one of the gravest and most pressing problems of our time. But, though its solution will require much planning in the good sense, it does not—or at least need not—require that special kind of planning which according to its advocates is to replace the market. Many economists hope, indeed, that the ultimate remedy may be found in the field of monetary policy, which would involve nothing incompatible even with nineteenth-century liberalism. Others, it is true, believe that real success can be expected only from the skilful timing of public works undertaken on a very large scale. This might lead to much more serious restrictions of the competitive sphere, and, in experimenting in this direction, we shall have carefully to watch our step if we are to avoid making all economic activity progressively more dependent on the direction and volume of government expenditure. But this is neither the only nor, in my opinion, the most promising way of meeting the gravest threat to economic security. In any case, the very necessary efforts to secure protection against these fluctuations do not lead to the kind of planning which constitutes such a threat to our freedom.

The planning for security which has such an insidious effect on liberty is that for security of a different kind. It is planning designed to protect individuals or groups against diminutions of their income, which although in no way deserved yet in a competitive society occur daily, against losses imposing severe hardships having no moral justification yet inseparable from the competitive system. This demand for security is thus another form of the demand for a just remuneration—a remuneration commensurate with the subjective merits and not with the objective results of a man's efforts. This kind of security or justice seems irreconcilable with freedom to choose one's employment.

In any system which for the distribution of men between the different trades and occupations relies on their own choice it is necessary that the remuneration in these trades correspond to their usefulness to the other members of society, even if this should stand in no relation to subjective merit. Although the results achieved will often be commensurate with efforts and intentions, this cannot always be true in any form of society. It will particularly not be true in the many instances where the usefulness of some trade or special skill is changed by circumstances which could not be foreseen. We all know the tragic plight of the highly trained man whose hard-learned skill has suddenly lost its value because of some invention which greatly benefits the rest of society. The history of the last hundred years is full of instances of this kind, some of them affecting hundreds of thousands of people at a time. . . .

Certainty of a given income can, however, not be given to all if any freedom in the choice of one's occupation is to be allowed. And, if it is provided for some, it becomes a privilege at the expense of others whose security is thereby necessarily diminished. . . . What is constantly being done is to grant this kind of security piecemeal, to this group and to that, with the result that for those who are left out in the cold the insecurity constantly increases. No wonder that in consequence the value attached to the privilege of security constantly increases, the demand for it becomes more and more urgent, until in the end no price, not even that of liberty, appears too high.

If those whose usefulness is reduced by circumstances which they could neither foresee nor control were to be protected against undeserved loss, and those whose usefulness has been increased in the same way were prevented from making an unmerited gain, remuneration would soon cease to have any relation to actual usefulness. It would depend on the views held by some authority about what a person ought to have done, what he ought to have foreseen, and how good or bad his intentions were. Such decisions could not but be to a large extent arbitrary. The application of this principle would necessarily bring it about that people doing the same work would receive different remuneration. The differences in remuneration would then no longer present an adequate inducement to people to make the changes which are socially desirable, and it would not even be possible for the individuals affected to judge whether a particular change is worth the trouble it causes. . . .

The problem of adequate incentives which arises here is commonly discussed as if it were a problem mainly of the willingness of people to do their best. But this, although important, is not the whole, nor even the most important, aspect of the problem. It is not merely that if we want people to give their best we must make it worth while for them. What is more important is that if we want to leave them the choice, if they are to be able to judge what they ought to do, they must be given some readily intelligible yardstick by which to measure the social importance of the different occupations. Even with the best will in the world it would be impossible for anyone intelligently to choose between various alternatives if the advantages they offered him stood in no relation to their usefulness to society. To know whether as the result of a change a man ought to leave a trade and an environment which he has come to like, and exchange it for another, it is necessary that the changed relative value of these occupations to society should find expression in the remunerations they offer.

The problem is, of course, even more important because in the world as it is men are, in fact, not likely to give their best for long periods unless their own interests are directly involved. At least for great numbers some external pressure is needed if they are to give their best. The problem of incentives in this sense is a very real one, both in the sphere of ordinary labor and in those of the managerial activities. The application of the engineering technique to a whole nation—and this is what planning means—"raises problems of discipline which are hard to solve," as has been well described by an American engineer with great experience in government planning, who has clearly seen the problem. "In order to do an engineering job," he explains,

> there ought to be surrounding the work a comparatively large area of unplanned economic action. There should be a place from which workers can be drawn, and when a worker is fired he should vanish from the job and from the pay-roll. In the absence of such a free reservoir discipline cannot be maintained without corporal punishment, as with slave labor.

In the sphere of executive work the problem of sanctions for negligence arises in a different but no less serious form. It has been well said that, while the last resort of a competitive economy is the bailiff, the ultimate sanction of a planned economy is the hangman. The powers which the manager of any plant will have to be given will still be considerable. But no more than in the case of the worker can the manager's position and income in a planned system be made to depend merely on the success or failure of the work under his direction. As neither the risk nor the gain is his, it cannot be his personal judgment, but whether he does what he ought to have done according to some established rule, which must decide. A mistake he "ought" to have avoided is not his own affair; it is a crime against the community and must be treated as such. While so long as he keeps to the safe path of objectively ascertainable duty he may be surer of his income than the capitalist entrepreneur, the danger which threatens him in case of real failure is worse than bankruptcy. He may be economically secure so long as he satisfies his superiors, but this security is bought at the price of the safety of freedom and life.

The conflict with which we have to deal is, indeed, a quite fundamental one between two irreconcilable types of social organization, which, from the most characteristic forms in which they appear, have often been described as the commercial and the military type of society. The terms were, perhaps, unfortunate, because they direct attention to unessentials and make it difficult to see that we face a real alternative and that there is no third possibility. Either both the choice and the risk rest with the individual or he is relieved of both. The army does, indeed, in many ways represent the closest approach familiar to us to the second type of organization, where work and worker alike are allotted by authority and where, if the available means are scanty, everybody is alike put on short-commons. This is the only system in which the individual can be conceded full economic security and through the extension of which to the whole of society it can be achieved for all its members. This security is, however, inseparable from the restrictions on liberty and the hierarchical order of military life—it is the security of the barracks. . . .

BARBARA WOOTTON

AMONG Western nations in which the government has come to play a large and increasing role in economic life, Great Britain comes first to mind. By and large it may be said that nineteenth-century *laissez faire* came to an end in Britain with World War I. Managed money, unemployment insurance, and the first protective tariffs since 1846 were each in some sense a wartime legacy. A little later the depression of the 1930's brought with it a full-scale tariff, aid to agriculture, and a measure of exchange control. After World War II a Labor government introduced public ownership of coal mines, railroads, and electric power, together with a health plan often described (not very accurately) as "socialized medicine." Britain, one might suppose, could offer as clear an example as might be found anywhere of the loss of liberty pictured by Friedrich Hayek.

Time will show how well or ill the British experiment turns out. Moreover, it may be said that, even if socialism fails to deprive the British of their liberties, this proves nothing. For, it could be argued, the long experience of the British in managing their own affairs and resisting arbitrary power may delay, if not permanently prevent, the loss of liberty feared by Hayek. However this may be, there has been no dearth of critics to attack Hayek's position on theoretical grounds. Most frequently such writers have denied the existence of any *necessary* connection between state intervention or planning on the one hand and loss of freedom on the other. One such critic, Barbara Wootton, a British economist broadly in sympathy with the program of the Labor Party, is the author of *Freedom under Planning* (1945), from which the following selection has been taken. Born in Cambridge in 1897, she studied and later taught at Girton College, Cambridge University. For some years she was research officer for the Trades Union Congress and Labor Party Joint Research Department, and later became principal of the Morley College for Working Men and Women. She was professor of social studies in the University of London from 1948 to 1952, and since 1952 has been Nuffield Research Fellow at Bedford College of the University of London. Her books include *Plan or No Plan* (1934), *Lament for Economics* (1938), *Testament for Social Science* (1950), and *Faith in Freedom* (1954), all of which defend her thesis that there is nothing in planning incompatible with democratic freedoms.

FREEDOM UNDER PLANNING

CHAPTER II: CULTURAL AND CIVIL FREEDOMS

In the background of any discussion of the compatibility of economic planning and cultural freedom, there lurks a fundamental philosophic issue. Is it in fact possible to plan for indeterminate cultural ends? For real cultural freedom demands not merely variety, but actual indeterminacy, of cultural ends. Such freedom is not achieved, unless economic planning sets people free to do and say things of their own choosing—things which are not known beforehand to, much less decided by, the planners. That would imply a fundamental difference between the political state and all other forms of association which involve organized action. The political state, where there is real cultural freedom, is no more than a convenient instrument for promoting the joint and several purposes of its members, and has no specific, determinate purpose of its own beyond this. A trade union exists to create better conditions of employment for its members, a church to promote the worship of God, a dramatic society to produce, if not to appreciate, drama; but the state exists—for what? To make it possible for men and women to live their own lives in their own way. . . .

. . . The two peculiarities which distinguish the state from all other forms of association [are] the fact that membership is compulsory, and the fact that the rules made by the state are backed up by physical force. An association with both these peculiarities cannot, by definition, both respect cultural freedom and pursue specific cultural ends. It cannot do both these things because minorities who reject these ends neither defy the law nor resign their membership of the state by which the law is enforced: they therefore lose their cultural freedom. For instance, if Parliament should decide that the proper cultural purpose of this country is to exalt the Christian religion and to exterminate atheistic practices, it would be necessary to suppress all agnostic societies and publications, and to take steps to see that every child was taught the Christian doctrine and that every adult took his part in Christian worship. This is not cultural freedom for non-Christians. (If in the two preceding sentences the word "Marxist" is substituted for "Christian" we have a scarcely exaggerated description of the policy of the Soviet government in the early years of the revolution.) There is, moreover, no parallel to this power in

---

This selection has been reprinted from Barbara Wootton, *Freedom under Planning* (pp. 23, 25–34, 36–40, 42–43, 73–78, 84–87, 122–127, Copyright 1945 by The University of North Carolina Press, Chapel Hill, N.C.) by permission of the University of North Carolina Press, publisher.

any form of association other than the political state; for no other society which adopted policies or principles of which even a minority of its members disapproved could prevent those members from resigning their membership, or compel their compliance by law. I think it is still true in this country, though not perhaps as securely true as might be wished, that this incompatibility of freedom with the pursuit of specific ends by the political state is appreciated, so far as religious freedom is concerned. The power of the state is not therefore used, as it was for instance used at one time in Russia, to compel compliance with official doctrine. What we have to do is to accept this as a *general* truth, applicable to cultural freedoms *generally*. Voluntary societies can and should commit themselves to specific cultural ends: compulsory societies should not.

The problem of planning for freedom thus resolves itself into the problem of determinate planning for indeterminate cultural ends. Stated thus it sounds insoluble. Once again, however, a problem which is theoretically insoluble in the limiting case, turns out to be quite tractable in the concrete form in which it is likely to crop up in practice. We need not despair of the possibility of combining useful planning and cultural freedom, provided that certain conditions are observed.

The first condition is the obvious one that such planning must know where to stop. There are few, if any, cultural freedoms which can be enjoyed in such a vacuum that their exercise makes no demands whatever on the productive resources of the community. It follows that determination of economic priorities, carried to the ultimate limit, would prohibit cultural freedom. Freedom of speech, for example, is not the same thing as freedom of soliloquy. If speech is to be more than soliloquy, there must be an audience to hear what is said, or read what is written. That means a building in which an audience can be gathered, or a microphone to reach them in their own homes, or paper on which to write what they can read. Similarly, even the most austere forms of religious worship usually require a building in which they may be conducted, while many rituals demand organs, books, censers, candles, altar cloths. It follows that any government with absolute power to plan the use of the community's resources down to the last detail can make *effective* freedom of speech or of worship impossible for any body, person, or society, of whom it disapproves, merely by withholding such essential materials.

"Can," however, in this context is not, and must not be, the same word as "will." Admittedly it is possible for a state authority responsible for planning the output of the building industry to assign halls to the League of the

Godless and to refuse them to the churches; or vice versa. But it is equally possible to make suitable buildings available for all denominations on the same terms. As Dr. Mannheim has remarked, it is possible to "co-ordinate the time tables of the different railway lines without controlling the topics of conversation inside the carriages."

No one can lay down, in general terms, the exact limitation on the scope of economic planning which the preservation of cultural freedom demands. But the examples just given illustrate the kind of distinction which would need to be drawn in practice; and they serve to show the fallacy of the assumption that extensive economic planning is *inherently* synonymous with uncompromising cultural conformity. As a matter of fact, the policy of the Soviet Union in regard to religious freedom has actually undergone important changes since the early days of the revolution. Religious freedom has been increased without relaxation of state determination of economic priorities. This at least proves that alternative courses are possible.

It is therefore not enough for Professor Hayek to assert (quite correctly) that "the power of the planner over our private lives" rests on his power over production. It does. But power can be exercised in different ways and in different degrees. All extensions of power involve certain risks: some offer advantages also. If the advantages did not sometimes outweigh the risks, complete anarchy would be preferable to any government. In any particular instance it is necessary to weigh the risks against the possible advantages and to decide in the light of this balance. The argument is not advanced by prejudging the issue in favor of the risks. To condemn all economic planning on the ground that if carried to extremes it *can* be used to nullify all freedom of expression is of a piece with forbidding innocent activities on the ground that in certain circumstances they would be anti-social. I have heard it argued, for example, that it is, in all circumstances, wrong to play tennis or golf on Sundays, since, in certain conditions, to do so might disturb a neighbor's devotions, or deprive the caddy of his Sabbath rest. It would be safer to say that Sunday games are wrong because they offend against the will of God: for this argument has at least the advantage of being incapable of disproof. In terms of any rational utilitarian ethic, these all-or-nothing arguments are equally indefensible, whether applied to economic planning or to Sabbatarian principles.

Somewhat similar is the argument which contends that cultural freedom and economic planning are incompatible since an economic plan and a cultural pattern are, for practical purposes, identical. If the term "cultural" is defined sufficiently widely, this is certainly true in part; but there is no reason why it should be wholly true, unless we perversely wish to make it so. Moreover, the points at which cultural freedom is unavoidably restricted by an economic plan are also the points at which it would be restricted in the absence of any such plan. If cultural liberty means individual freedom to determine the whole way of life, we are bound to admit that this freedom must be in great measure foregone in any large and complex society. An example should make the point clear. The size of cities has an important influence on the average citizen's ability to spend life as he pleases. In very large cities (arranged as such cities are now) it is, to mention only one thing, necessary for many to spend much time in traveling. But if you happen to be one of those who wish, say, that London were a smaller city, you are individually powerless to bring this about. You *may* be able to go and live in a smaller place, Letchworth for example: but living in Letchworth is not the same thing as living in a smaller London. The degree of urbanization of the community, with all the limitations on one's personal freedom which that implies, has for practical purposes to be accepted by the ordinary individual.

It is important, however, to repeat that this restriction has nothing to do with economic planning. The size and shape of most of our present cities are, at present, only in a very small degree the result of the conscious determination of economic priorities. London and Liverpool have not been made: they have happened. But the individual is not, on that account, the more able to modify them to suit his own taste. All that he can do to that end is himself to live outside their boundaries. In that way, by lowering the demand for urban accommodation he casts his vote, for what it is worth (in what Professor Mises has called the ballot box of the market place), against the growth of cities. But it is at best a vote in a very large and undemocratic constituency. Similarly, in cases where the size of towns is consciously determined as a matter of deliberate policy he can, in a democratic society, exercise some tiny weight of opinion. It is a matter for argument, in the light of the particular circumstances of particular cases, whether planning increases or diminishes the freedom of the individual to shape his own cultural pattern in such matters as this. Whichever way the argument goes, however, two things are clear. First, so long as we live in large and complex communities, this freedom is unavoidably very narrowly restricted, whatever method is used for determining economic priorities. And second, none of this alters the fact that there is a world of difference between a society in which people are allowed to say what they please and one in which they are not, even though the externals of life in both cases may be much the same, people living in the same sort of cities and following even much the same daily routine. Moscow, Berlin, New York, Mexico City, and London begin to look remarkably alike: the quality of life to be lived in each of them remains different.

It is, therefore, nonsense to assert that comprehensive economic planning *cannot* stop short of the point at which it destroys all cultural freedom. The critical issue is this business of knowing where to stop. While, as has been said, there can be no general answer to this question, there are one or two things that are worth remembering in this context. For instance, the temptation to exact unnecessary cultural uniformity is always likely to be strong amongst those men and women who are personally responsible for making the decisions which constitute economic planning. It will be strong because it is, generally speaking, easier to plan for uniformity than for diversity. It will be strong because people who arrive at positions of power are, inevitably, people who enjoy the exercise of power. This is, of course, as true of the powerful whose intentions are good as of those whose designs are evil. Both are likely to find it more satisfying that people should do what those in authority want them to do or think that they should do, rather than what they themselves want to do.

In practice this means that the lengths to which economic planning can safely be carried depend on a number of intangibles such as the quality of the planners . . . and the general social conditions of the community in which it is conducted. The critical fields are those of the press, broadcasting, education and any other powerful determinants of public opinion. In the case of education, for example, British and Scandinavian experience at least has already demonstrated that a considerable degree of cultural diversity is possible within a system in which most of the schools are owned, and the teachers paid, by public bodies. The same experience has also shown that this freedom has its limits; but there is no reason to suppose that these limits are fixed for all time, and they are certainly not the same in all countries. It is in the light of considerations like this that one must decide on merits in each instance whether it is expedient to retain a privately-owned press, privately-owned schools, or to permit a public monopoly in broadcasting. These are not so much questions of principle as of expediency. They are also specialist questions which need much fuller discussion than I can give them here. I would only hazard the opinion that it is doubtful whether the time has come in this country when educational freedom is sufficiently secure for a complete state monopoly (which would involve, among other things, the abolition or transfer to public ownership of all the present "progressive schools") to be enthusiastically advocated; and that the evils of a privately-owned press could be greatly diminished by control of profits and advertising revenue.

The second condition of successful economic planning for indeterminate cultural ends is that the planners should show a nice discrimination in their methods. There has been some muddled thinking here amongst democrats who have wistfully observed the success of totalitarian regimes in putting over totalitarian ideologies; and who long to enlist some of the same techniques in the cause of democracy. The answer is that many of these techniques are simply not applicable to the promotion of indeterminate ends. The hysterical dramatization of politics, in which the Nazis have specialized, is a terrifyingly powerful instrument for the creation of a mass mind bent on uniformity. Similar methods cannot, in the nature of things, be employed in the service of diversity and freedom. . . .

Of all our liberties those that are least likely to be threatened by economic planning are the civil rights concerned with the method of enforcement of the law, and the position of the actual or supposed lawbreaker. Even Professor Hayek does not specifically suggest that these are in danger. Of course any large extension of the functions of government necessarily multiplies the number of possible offenses against laws and regulations. Everybody is well aware of this from war-time experience: indeed there must be few, even of the most conscientious citizens, who have not, advertently or inadvertently, been guilty of breaking some war-time regulation. This multiplication of the possible occasions of offense is, however, a quite different matter from the procedure adopted to ensure that the law is kept, or the methods of dealing with offenders. There is no logical connection between state regulation of the output of mining or agriculture or any or all industries on the one hand, and the abolition of *habeas corpus* or of trial by jury, or the establishment of a gestapo, on the other. Here again, war-time experience in Britain is, on the whole, comforting. It is true that a serious breach in these civil rights has been made by the Home Secretary's power under Defense Regulation 18b to imprison without charge or trial persons who, in his personal opinion, ought to be incarcerated: but it is also true, both that this power has been sparingly exercised, and that in the stresses of war there may be occasions for suspicion which have nothing whatever to do with state control of economic priorities. . . .

State economic planning does not, in short, alter the fact that power will be used by cruel and tyrannous people in one way, and by the humane and the lovers of liberty in another. We are thus brought back to the distinction between "can" and "will." Just as the power of the state *can* be used to destroy all cultural freedom, so also it *can* be directed against every kind of civil freedom. Whether it *will* be used in either or both of these ways depends on how far political power is in practice absolute, and what kind of people exercise that power for what kind of ends. The judicial species of civil freedom in particular—that is, fundamentally, freedom from arbitrary punishment—is only *necessarily* threatened by economic planning if it is true that a government which takes responsibility for economic decisions is for some reason *necessarily* composed of more dictatorial people than one which leaves these matters alone. In a chapter which carries the question-begging title: *Why the Worst Get on Top,* Professor Hayek has attempted to establish that this is probable.

The whole question of the impact of economic planning upon both cultural and civil freedoms has been greatly confused by ill-considered inferences from the experience of the U.S.S.R. That country offers the one and only example of really comprehensive economic planning in time of peace which the world has yet seen. Throughout this experiment the degree of both civil and cultural freedom permitted to Soviet citizens has been intolerably low by the standards which the British uphold for themselves (though not everywhere for their Empire). The Soviet plans, have, however, from the beginning, been avowedly devoted to promotion of specific cultural ends: first, the promulgation of Marxist-Leninist doctrine, then, in later years, the increase in the military strength and prestige of the Soviet people. . . .

As for civil liberties, let us remember the background. The Soviet system was begotten and born in the violence of revolution and civil war. It was the child, on the one side, of the Czarist Empire, and on the other of an expressly anti-democratic Marxist policy. In a country accustomed to secret police, political imprisonment and assassination, the new government openly set out to establish a particular type of dictatorship. In these conditions, civil liberties, as we understand them, could not be destroyed by the revolution, since they were not there to destroy. Between the introduction of the revised constitution of 1936 and the German invasion of Russia there was indeed a good deal of talk about relaxation of some of the rigors of the dictatorship, especially in the direction of greater political freedom. No one, however, who reads the Soviet authorities' own enthusiastic accounts of the work of their political prisoners, or who has personally known men and women whose relatives disappeared overnight in the great purges, or who has read press summaries of the Moscow trials of the nineteen-thirties, with their fervent denunciations of the treachery of defendants whose cases were still *sub judice*—no one who has given a moment's attention to any of this evidence can pretend that the Soviet range of civil liberties is comparable with that to which we are accustomed in this country. Equally, however, in the light of the declared objectives of the Soviet government, no one can conclude in the light of this experience that the attempt to combine civil liberty and economic planning has been tried and has failed.

Inferences from the Soviet experiment are likely to crop up repeatedly, whatever the particular liberties that may be under discussion. Just as the Soviet plans have been carried out against a certain civil and cultural background, so also their execution has made use of certain economic compulsions, or restrictions on economic liberties which are highly prized elsewhere. It may be useful, therefore, to summarize here what would appear in every case to be the limits of safe inference from Russian practice. In the first place, Soviet experience can be illuminating when there have from time to time been changes in the quantity or quality of liberty allowed under that regime. In such cases we learn, at the least, that it is *possible* to do things in more ways than one, and we may, in addition, have material for instructive comparisons. Second, Soviet experience is useful in so far as it gives positive evidence of the compatibility of planning with particular freedoms. Positive evidence proves that a thing can be done: negative evidence not that it cannot, but that it has not. Thus positive evidence from the U.S.S.R. has established that it is possible to plan at least up to the Soviet level of efficiency in time of peace without recourse to universal industrial conscription. Negative evidence, such as the fact that there are no legal opposition parties in the U.S.S.R., proves nothing except that there are no legal opposition parties in the U.S.S.R.

CHAPTER III: THE FREEDOM OF THE CONSUMER

Freedom to Spend. . . . In this and most other economically developed countries before the war, we should commonly have described freedom of consumption as freedom to "spend our *money* as we like." This phrase is capable, however, of bearing two fundamentally different meanings. First, it may simply mean freedom to distribute a given sum of money in any way that the owner likes amongst all the things that are available for him to buy. Even in time of war, and still more, of course, in the unrestricted markets of peace, a pound in your pocket can be converted into an almost infinite variety of different objects in your house, on your person, in your stomach, or for use in other ways. Used in this way, the phrase "freedom of consumption" takes the productive pattern, so to speak, for granted. In its second meaning, however, this phrase implies a claim that the choices which consumers do actually make should continuously determine this pattern of production. It is an assertion of what has been called "consumers' sovereignty." The second is a much more subtle and sophisticated interpretation of freedom of consumption than the first, and it probably goes a good deal further than what more people mean when they express the wish to spend their money as they please. Full consumers' sovereignty in this sense is, however, definitely not compatible with economic planning as we have defined it. It is not possible for the *same* questions to be settled *both* by the conscious and deliberate decisions of planners, *and* as the unconscious, unforeseen, results of the behavior of millions of consumers acting independently of one another. The planners could of course carefully watch the market and take account of the fads and fancies of consumers there revealed: if they had sense in their heads, they would certainly include this evidence in the material upon which their decisions were based. But if they carried this attention to consumer behavior to such lengths that the final result of planning was just to copy as accurately as possible the picture that would result if no plan were made, the planners would in fact have ceased to plan. Planned decisions and unplanned market reactions are in fact *alternative* ways of determining economic priorities. Use can be made of both in different parts of the economic field (*e.g.,* the output of saucepans can be planned and that of penny-whistles left to the market), but in the determination of any particular issue they are mutually exclusive. The case for planning is not that it is identical with, but that, in certain circumstances, it is superior to, the planless method of settling economic priorities. . . .

CHAPTER V: THE FREEDOM OF THE CONSUMER

Freedom to Save. The fact has . . . to be faced that full employment is impossible, if the timing of *all* outlay is determined by the personal whims of individual consumers. This is one of the occasions when we are at war with ourselves. The liberty of the consumer-self threatens the security of the producer-self; for *the same person* wants both to spend and save as he pleases, and always to be sure of a job. Not enough weight is given to this conflict by the advocates of complete freedom of consumers' choice: it is for instance never so much as mentioned in Professor Hayek's *Road to Serfdom.* For full employment is incompatible, not only with the theoretical ideal of consumers' sovereignty . . . : it is incompatible equally with the bastard sovereignty of the consumer which does duty for this idea in practice—

with any system, in fact, in which production is left to follow the dictates of market purchases. Under any such system not only must the quality and character of production faithfully follow the quality and character of consumer-spending; the total volume of production of all kinds must also shrink and swell as the public happens to tighten or relax its purse strings. And, to judge from experience, even when those strings are at their slackest, and spending is most generous, the total reached will rarely, if ever, be great enough to provide work for all who want and need it. Even in the best years there has usually been far too large a margin of employable unemployed.[1] Full employment does not happen of itself.

Happily there is every reason to hope that this conflict between consumer liberty and producer security can be resolved: and resolved without grave interference with the consumer's liberty to spend as he pleases. But it cannot be resolved without a considerable amount of economic planning. The road out of the difficulty lies not through dictating to the consumer when he may or may not spend his money; but through the state's undertaking both to make good the deficiencies, and to compensate for the vagaries, of consumer spending. The task of adjusting, one way or another, the total amount of spending by public authorities and private persons to the total capacity and demands of the labor market must become a public responsibility. This means that the state must do a new kind of sum. It must add up the total amount of spending (which, we must remember, in this context includes what is generally called investing) necessary to find work for all, estimate the total volume of spending by private and business consumers, and be prepared itself at the least to fill the gap by the purchases of government departments and other public authorities. These purchases will, of course, affect the pattern of production and, as far as they go, amount to a conscious determination of economic priorities. Thus, if the spending of public authorities takes the form of a large building program, unemployed workers (together with some who may be drawn from other employments) will be busy with the manufacture of bricks and mortar (or, alternatively, of prefabricated units). The new houses which result will have come into existence not as the result of the unconscious working of the market, but through the deliberate decision of responsible people. And that is planning.

The theory which underlies this policy of the maintenance of employment by planned public spending is now generally accepted. It is for instance implicit in the government's White Paper on Employment Policy, though the

[1] In the years from 1921 to 1939 inclusive, the annual average percentage of workers unemployed in Great Britain never fell below 9.6 per cent.

practical applications suggested there are decidedly timid. For our purpose it is necessary only to emphasize that there are *two* variables in our sum: —the total of private consumer outlay and the total outlay of public authorities must *together* add up to the amount necessary for full employment. The question, which of these components—consumer or state spending—should take priority, is a question of policy which different communities can decide in different ways according to their several scales of social value. Either component can be taken as a datum and the other adjusted to match. In no country is the need to maintain full employment the sole criterion of when, where, and how much public authorities should spend. Expenditure on the education of children, for instance, is not undertaken simply for the purpose of finding employment for teachers. In the Soviet Union before the war, first priority, particularly in the earlier plans, was given to public outlay on new construction; such resources as were left after provision for the construction program were then available to meet the needs of consumers. In all countries in time of war, first priority goes to government purchase of war materials. In this country, in the absence of any fundamental change of social outlook, it seems likely that the attitude of government towards private spending after the war will be somewhat deferential. The White Paper plainly thinks of a state employment program as supplementing, rather than supplanting, the outlay of private persons and private business.

Experiment will show the conditions for the successful pursuit of such a policy and the possible variations which can be played upon the main theme. After two wars, we do at least *know* that full employment is possible, provided only that the state is prepared, directly or indirectly, to become an employer on a sufficiently large scale. We do not yet know how far full employment can be attained by a delicate balance between employment on government and on private work, or where that balance must be struck. From the angle of consumer-liberty, however, one cheerful forecast can reasonably be made. Of all the different forms of spending, it is, as we have already said, spending for investment which is the most irregular and the most unreliable. The total of what people spend on food and clothes and household goods and holidays and drink and smokes—even on weddings and funerals—is in the aggregate much less liable to unpredictable upheavals—except for one simple and familiar reason. What makes this total go up and down is not our inconstant spending of a given income, so much as fluctuation in the amount of income that we have. But the amount of spendable income that we have itself depends primarily—for the great majority—on work and wages; and work and wages are determined in their turn by the general state of the business world, on the one hand—that is, by the willingness of investors to launch out into new business—and, on the other hand, by the scale of employment offered by the demands of public authorities.

It follows that variations in spending for enjoyment are consequential results, more than primary causes, of unemployment. Of course it is a vicious circle: the greatest cause of unemployment is unemployment. But the unemployed are not the cause of unemployment because of their passion for intermittent saving and irregular spending. They create unemployment by their lack of the wherewithal either to spend or to save. It follows that the timing of the ordinary expenditure of ordinary people is not the critical factor in the causation of unemployment: the critical factor is the timing of investment. Security of employment need not, therefore, and should not, demand interference with the private person's right to distribute his personal expenditure on goods and services for his own immediate consumption through time according to his fancy. How far it will necessitate control of the distribution through time of private *investment* expenditure will depend upon how far the state finds it necessary to adopt an independent role in the planning of production. If the public authorities seek to confine themselves in their employment policy to attempt to counterbalance the ups and downs of private investment, they will be following, not making, a pattern, and such control will be kept to a minimum. This appears to be present Government policy.

Sir William Beveridge, in his *Full Employment in a Free Society,* has forcefully argued that more than this will be necessary if we are to achieve full employment, and not merely to stabilize unemployment at a level halfway between the bad and the not very good years of the past. If, however, such a more active policy is pursued, private persons and concerns cannot retain the freedom to make substantial investments exactly as and when they choose. For public authorities and private purchasers cannot (both) buy the same things at the same time; nor can they even try to do so without disastrous consequences. . . .

CHAPTER VI: FREEDOM OF THE PRODUCER

Choice of Employment. . . . Freedom to *refuse* or to *leave* a job is not quite the same as freedom to *select* either one's job or one's vocation. Happily, there is nothing in the conscious determination of economic priorities which is inconsistent with the first of these freedoms—nothing which threatens the right to refuse or to leave a job, or which demands industrial conscription or compulsory direction. Whenever some industries are expanding and others contracting, there must, in all circumstances, be changes in the occupations of the people: but whether this expansion and contraction is accidental or planned need itself have no effect upon the machinery used to bring those changes about. In the sixteen years between 1923 and 1939, three-quarters of a million *additional* workers found their way into distributive occupations, more than 300,000 into building, and 60,000 into electrical engineering. Conversely, the number of workers classified as coal miners fell by nearly 400,000, the number of shipbuilders by nearly 95,000, and the number of cotton operatives by about 190,000. These changes, which were necessitated by unplanned and unforeseen variations in the prosperity of different industries, came about through the response of individuals to the opportunities, or lack of opportunities, open to them. People gravitate towards, and still more do they encourage their children to gravitate towards, the industries where pay and prospects look most promising. If pay and prospects and other conditions of employment are suitably adjusted, they will respond in just the same way to calls for fresh workers here or for reductions in staff there, when these changing demands reflect, not casual ups and downs of prosperity, but deliberate public policy. The workers necessary to carry through a large public program of housing, electrification, food production, or whatever it may be, can be engaged and employed in the ordinary commercial way. If the conditions of employment are sufficiently attractive (and training is provided where there is a shortage of necessary skills) the necessary labor will be forthcoming.

The parallel here with freedom of consumption is strictly accurate. The way to give free choice of consumption is to price the available goods and leave each consumer free to buy, or not to buy, as he pleases. The way to give free choice of employment is to price the jobs available and leave each worker free to apply for what he prefers. As with consumption, so also with employment, this is the method of inducement. Under this method, if the demand for certain very popular goods threatens to outrun supplies, the price must be raised in order to restrict buying. Under this method, if the demand for certain kinds of labor outruns the supply forthcoming, the price, that is, the wage, must be raised to attract further applicants. In both cases, of course, it is possible to use dictatorial methods instead of the method of inducement. A dictatorial government may prefer the former alternative; but that will be because it is dictatorial, not because it is engaged in economic planning.

It is indeed doubtful whether the method of compulsion in the distribution of workers between occupations and jobs can even plausibly be passed off as less trouble than the method of inducement. The producer freedoms stand, perhaps, here on firmer ground than the liberties of the consumer. The reason is that the direction of people to jobs is a much more complicated affair than the direction of—at any rate a large range of—goods to people. It is so much more difficult to find a satisfactory basis from which to start. To distribute, say, margarine on the basis of half a pound a head per week as the normal ration, with variations upwards or downwards for special classes, is a simple enough business. But you cannot run industry by allocating everybody, correspondingly, to a day's work a week in the mines. Industrial direction means getting down to the selection of the particular individuals destined for particular jobs—a colossal task in any large-scale program of production. Perhaps this is why the Soviet authorities, until war was practically at their frontiers, generally allowed free choice of vocation and employment, and made little use of industrial conscription, except in the case of political prisoners. Their wage and salary scales were deliberately framed so as to pay more for skills which were scarce, and less for those of which there was abundance; and the comrades seem to have responded with appropriate acquisitive alacrity.

From the angle of freedom, it is of course the great strength of selection by inducement that the actual individuals who get on to any particular job select themselves. The task of the planners is simply to estimate what rate of pay and other conditions of employment will attract the number of competent people required by the job in hand. This can be done only by a process of trial and error. It is also done by trial and error where there is no plan. . . .

CHAPTER VIII: THE FREEDOM OF THE PRODUCER

Freedom of Enterprise. Free choice of employment and freedom of collective bargaining are the two producer freedoms of most concern to most people. But they do not exhaust the list: there remain the claims of freedom of enterprise—the freedom to go into business on your own account, to make and sell what you like for the public to buy, whether "going into business" means opening a corner newspaper shop, or floating a giant company. This freedom stands on a different level from those that we have so far discussed, for two reasons. First, it is of practical interest only to a small minority. For every hundred people who work in an employed capacity, there were, in the census of 1931, fewer than eight in business on their own account. Second, freedom of enterprise had suffered many encroachments even before the war. No one, for instance, was free to run buses in competition with London

Transport, or indeed to compete with local public monopolies anywhere, or with the Post Office; and no one was free to build factories on sites scheduled as residential areas under town planning schemes. . . .

The range of inducements by which the production programs of business firms can be brought into line with predetermined Government plans is exceedingly varied. We have already seen, quite apart from war experience, particular industries, notably various branches of agriculture, fostered by subsidies, by restrictions on imports, by guaranteed prices, or by special remissions of taxation. It is, however, significant that most of these experiments have been directed rather towards prosperity than towards production, on the implicit theory that in any given industry there are apt to be alternatives —that the smaller the output, the greater the prosperity. In that way they make pretty dismal reading. . . .

In this context, far and away the greatest *inducement* used has been the assurance of a certain market, guaranteed to every firm on Government work. While the state has not, as in Russia, undertaken anything like all the actual work of production itself, it has pretty well taken over the whole business of giving orders. The peculiar conditions of war certainly make it exceptionally easy for this function to be monopolized by the state; for a very large part of war-time output is not required for the use of the general public at all, but for the peculiar and highly specialized purposes of the state's own employees in the Services. The state is, therefore, placing orders for goods which are to be used directly on its own account, not resold to the public at large; and this makes its business relatively simple. If in peace time we are to give high priority to freedom of consumption, this particular war-time pattern cannot be continued when the war is over. Government contract for goods for Government use does not, however, fill by any means the whole of the present picture. We also have extensive Government buying of goods for civilian use—notably in the food trades; and this may be a useful model for combination of peace-time planning with freedom of enterprise. There is a large field here for experiment and exploration which is already engaging the attention of many economists.

Experience also suggests that inducement can be supplemented by limited, or by negative, compulsions which may still make possible the preservation of a qualified freedom of enterprise, even where there is extensive planning of production. The fact already mentioned that a person cannot be compelled to go into business on his own account does not mean that once in business he must be completely a law to himself. It is still possible for compulsion to be applied (though of necessity only somewhat gingerly) to people who are in a position to clear out altogether if they wish. During the war, extensive use has been made of what may be respectively called negative, and secondary, compulsions. By negative compulsions I mean such methods as the control of business by systems of licensing. A power of licensing is an obvious negative method of controlling economic priorities. Thus nobody can ever be *compelled* to take out a catering license; but without such a license nobody can at present open a restaurant. Licenses can be issued freely where expansion is desired, and sparingly in cases of low priority.

More positive is the obligation now imposed on firms to manufacture or sell a certain quota of goods of a Government-specified design. In this way the production of utility goods of all kinds has been carried out through the channels of private manufacturer. There is nothing in this technique which could not be transferred practically unchanged into the post-war world; and it is a direct and positive method of giving effect to deliberate plans of production.

The whole question of the relation between freedom of enterprise and planning needs to be treated as a matter more of expediency than of principle. The traditional controversies between socialists and non-socialists only obscure the practical issue which we have to face. These controversies are barren, first, because they are framed in terms not of quantitative differences, but of absolute systems. We have not seen, and we shall not see, the ideal socialist state: we have not seen, and we shall not see, unadulterated capitalism. Even the highly planned Russian economy, as has already been remarked, carries its fringe of private enterprise; and the Americans have their public utilities. Just as every economy in the world is a mixture of plan and no-plan, so is every economy in the world a mixture of the same ingredients—private enterprise, state and municipal enterprise, semi-public corporations, and producers and consumers co-operatives, compounded in varying proportions. Realistic discussion must concern itself, not with two extreme alternatives, but with the endless possible quantitative variations of the mixture. . . .

REPORT OF THE AMERICAN ECONOMIC ASSOCIATION

THERE IS substantial agreement among all schools of contemporary socio-economic thought that solution of the problem of economic instability—the problem of the "boom-and-bust" cycle of prosperity and depression, of full employment and mass unemployment—is crucial to the survival of liberal capitalist civilization. In the United States, a country seemingly committed to a "private enterprise system" (a system which in reality is a mixed economy in which the "private" elements predominate), suggested solutions tend to center in the use of certain indirect, governmental controls and policies of a monetary and fiscal nature. Such controls (many of which are already present, to some degree, in the economy) are considered to operate as "built-in," automatic stabilizers which do not command economic behavior on the part of individuals, but rather set certain conditions and limits for the operation of an economy still largely dependent upon the market and individual market decisions for direction. The efficacy of such policies, the specific kinds of such indirect controls, the degree to which they may be desirable, have been subject for much theoretical discussion as well as great political debate for the past decade or more.

The following selection, which first appeared in the *American Economic Review* (1950), is a report issued under the auspices of the American Economic Association through its Committee on Public Issues. It was prepared by a group of distinguished American economists (Emile Despres of Williams College, Milton Friedman of the University of Chicago, Albert G. Hart of Columbia University, Paul A. Samuelson of the Massachusetts Institute of Technology, and the late Donald H. Wallace of Princeton University, chairman), who attempted, in its writing, "to make available to the interested public a summary of expert knowledge . . . on the nature of the problem of economic instability and its treatment" within the institutional framework of existing American society. It represents, as nearly as can be with a complex and contentious subject, what may be called a liberal capitalist reply, in terms of projected public policy, to the neo-Marxist criticism of a Paul Sering, or to the program of direct and overt "planners" such as Barbara Wootton. It is pertinent to observe that its basic assumption—that government action of considerable proportion is essential to the solution of economic instability—also goes far beyond the limits acceptable to *laissez-faire* proponents such as Friedrich Hayek.

THE PROBLEM OF ECONOMIC INSTABILITY

THIS REPORT is about the problem of economic instability in peacetime in the United States—how to avoid mass unemployment and major fluctuations in the price level while maintaining steady growth in production. It was written in 1949, before military action in 1950 transformed the immediate goals of the economy of the United States. It does not deal with problems of economic mobilization and economic stabilization for war, partial or total, although some of the basic facts and analysis presented here are fundamental for wartime economic problems, as well as for those of peacetime.

The report is addressed primarily to the interested public, not to economists. Its purpose is to tell them what economists do and do not know about the problem of economic instability. Its preparation and publication reflect the belief that there is a body of technical knowledge in economics that has a great deal to contribute to the formation of intelligent policy on economic stability.

This is a brief report dealing with complex and complicated problems. The details, refinements, and qualifications needed in their work by experts in economic analysis or administration would be out of place here. Economics can best serve the public only if its useful conclusions can be briefly and simply explained.

This report endeavors to explain the nature of the fluctuating economic pressures which stabilization policy must offset, remove, or divert into useful channels, and to present economists' thinking about policy measures helpful in stabilization and about the problem of building a coherent program. While economists are not unanimous about stabilization problems, the committee which drafted this report believes that there is a broad consensus which the report reflects. Important professional disagreements are also noted, however, and the range of opinions within the committee is wide enough to make it likely that a large share of such disagreements have been located.

This report has been prepared under the auspices of the American Economic Association. It is not, however, to be considered an official utterance of the Association which by provision of its Charter does not "commit its members to any position on practical economic questions."

This selection has been reprinted from "The Problem of Economic Instability," *American Economic Review,* Vol. XL, No. 4 (Sept., 1950), pp. 505–538, by permission of the publisher.

I. Objectives

PRICE AND EMPLOYMENT OBJECTIVES

Domestic economic stability has two major objectives—sustained full employment, and stability of price levels. The importance of full employment was underlined by our experiences in the 1930's, and has been formally recognized in the Employment Act of 1946. The importance of price-level stability, already widely understood before the war, has been emphasized by our experiences in the 1940's.

Full employment means that qualified people who seek jobs at prevailing wage rates can find them in productive activities without considerable delay. It means full-time jobs for people who want to work full time. It does not mean that people like housewives and students are under pressure to take jobs when they do not want jobs, or that workers are under pressure to put in undesired overtime. It does not mean that unemployment is ever zero. People are unemployed for a time while changing jobs. Full employment is the absence of mass unemployment. By this standard, employment was full, and probably overfull, most of the time during the years 1943–1948.

Price-level stability means the absence of any marked trend or sharp, short-term movements in the general level of prices. Marked shifts in *relative prices* of individual commodities, reflecting changes in consumer preferences, or in conditions of production, are, however, entirely compatible with a stable average *price level*—in fact, most economists favor both price-level stability and flexibility of relative prices.

The desirability of full employment is obvious: unemployment means waste of potential output and hardship for the unemployed and their dependents. The desirability of price-level stability is, perhaps, less obvious. But, on the one hand, any large price drop is almost sure to be accompanied by serious unemployment. And, on the other hand, inflation, though pleasant for some people, hurts those whose dollar incomes do not increase or increase less than living costs; and also sharpens conflicts of economic interest and impairs the group consensus necessary for solving national problems.

THE RELATION OF STABILITY TO OTHER OBJECTIVES

Economic stability is but one among a number of widely accepted objectives for social policy. To some extent the attainment of economic stability is likely to promote other objectives as well. But some measures to promote stability may to some extent conflict with them; hence, it must be borne in mind that economic stability is not desired at all costs.

Three other objectives—peace, progress, and freedom—call for special mention, by reason of their importance and their close relation to economic stability.

The strengthening of peaceful and democratic institutions in the rest of the world depends, much more than most Americans realize, on the maintenance of prosperity in the United States. If depressions in the United States undermine the markets of other countries, or if for reasons of domestic policy we do not let imports flow in freely, the prosperity of other countries will be endangered. Instability in the United States is thus likely to generate economic and political reactions abroad that will endanger the preservation of peace.

Progress involves change, reorganization of economic resources, replacement of the old by the new. A dynamic, progressive economy is one in which new techniques are constantly being developed and introduced, new products are seeking to attract public favor and replace old products, new firms are challenging the old. Such an economy cannot be completely stable. Adaptation to change takes time and involves friction, with resulting dips or jogs in production and employment. On the other hand, willingness to venture into new lines and to develop new products and processes is greatly hindered if individuals and business firms must devote a considerable part of their energies and resources to adjusting themselves to substantial fluctuations in the general level of economic activity.

The essence of freedom is the exercise of free choice by individuals with respect to a wide range of their activities—in the economic sphere, a large measure of freedom in choice of goods to consume, of occupations to follow, of ways of investing or using property. Freedom in these respects implies freedom to experiment, and to change one's mind. It also implies that individuals can and will make mistakes. It thus implies change, which in turn forces adaptation to change. On the other hand, marked economic instability creates conflicts and hardships, sets group against group and produces dissatisfaction with the existing structure of society. Thus it may undermine the basic consensus on which freedom and democracy rest.

THE INSTITUTIONAL SETTING

Americans live today in a society with a large measure of personal freedom, a great deal of private enterprise, and a great deal of government activity. This report treats the problems of economic stability in this kind of mixed society. It assumes that, while government will continue to undertake much economic activity directly and to control private activity in many ways, the bulk of our people will be employed by private business or be self-employed; and that decisions on what to consume, where to work, how to use property, and what and how much to produce will be governed primarily by incentives affecting the people making them, rather than by directives from government. At present the great majority of Americans—including the writers of this report—desire these kinds of institutions. Hence this report does not treat proposals for effecting economic stability by extensive government directives requiring economic units to do certain things and forbidding them to do other things.

II. The Historical Record

Section II gives some main facts of the historical record of instability. Section III presents some basic ideas which, with the facts of Section II, form the basis of the discussion of policy measures in Sections IV–VII.

Economic instability has been chronic in America, as in other advanced economies. Price records, going back to colonial days, show at least one sizable swing each decade. Production records, going back to the Civil War, show numerous depressions and booms of output, few long stretches of full-volume production. The records of employment and unemployment, fragmentary until recent years, confirm this picture of instability, as far as they go.

This record of instability is frequently analyzed in terms of "business cycles." In depressions we find a phase of "revival," a few months in which many prices and much non-agricultural employment and output turn upward. Then comes a phase of "expansion," sometimes lasting for years, with output high or rising, and with prices high or rising, or both. Eventually comes a phase of "recession," occasionally dramatic, when within a few months many prices and output and employment in many industries turn downward. This is often followed by a phase of "contraction," with further declines of output, employment, and prices.

DEPRESSIONS

In the Great Depression of the 1930's with its mass unemployment, output was for a decade far below what our labor force and plant could produce. The total loss of output that could have been produced and was not has been estimated as running into the hundreds of billions of dollars—comparable to the volume of output that went into the waging of World War II. But this depression was not our first long and deep depression. There were dismal years after 1837, and the depressions of the 1870's and 1890's were protracted and severe.

Besides these major depressions, sharp minor slumps appear in the records for 1884–1885, 1904, 1908, 1914, 1920–1922, and 1937—not to mention such dips of output as 1924 and 1927, which were picked up in the seismographic records of the business-cycle analysts, but did not involve serious and prolonged unemployment.

It is not necessary first to be prosperous in order to have a slump of output. A depression-within-a-depression can happen, and did happen in 1895–1898 and 1937–1938.

INFLATIONS

Full-blown inflation—a price rise which is widespread, rapid and carries prices to a peak 50 per cent or more above the starting point—has happened in American history only during and after wars. Our only inflations of this sort were linked with the Revolution, the War of 1812, the Civil War, World War I, and World War II. (The Mexican War and Spanish-American War did not subject the United States to enough strain to generate inflation.) However, there have been periods of sustained though less severe price rise during peacetime. For example, between 1899, a year of recovery, and 1909 wholesale prices rose by one-third.

SUSTAINED PROSPERITY

The economic records show few periods of sustained prosperity. Between the big depressions of the 1870's and 1890's, the decade of the 1880's was mostly prosperous, though it contained also a two-year slump with a panic in 1884. Prosperity also reigned in most of the years 1899–1913 although there was a panic in 1907, and brief, sharp slumps in output occurred in 1904, 1908, 1911, and 1914.

The interwar years exhibit the longest record of sustained prosperity, as well as the worst recorded depression. The years 1923–1929 were on the whole years of prosperity. The setbacks of 1924 and 1927 never became serious.

SOME IMPORTANT CHARACTERISTICS OF BUSINESS CYCLES

Some of the most important uniformities found by study of business cycles are the following:

1. Prices and production, outside of agriculture, ordinarily rise and fall together, instead of moving in opposite directions.

2. Total expenditure on durable goods fluctuates by a greater percentage than spending on non-durable goods. Total private spending on capital goods (plant, equipment, housing and the like) fluctuates by a greater percentage than consumption expenditure.

3. Total output and employment fluctuate by a much larger percentage in *durable-goods* industries than in *non-durable-goods* industries. For instance, auto production is more unstable than gasoline production, house construction than the renting of rooms.

4. Total output and employment fluctuate by a much greater percentage in construction and capital equipment than in consumer goods.

5. Current expenditure on business inventories fluctuates by a greater percentage than total sales.

6. Large changes in total output and employment or in the price level are normally accompanied by large changes in the same direction in the volume of money, i.e., currency and bank deposits, and a change in the velocity of circulation of money.

7. Some prices are highly flexible, others highly rigid. Price rigidity centers in manufactured goods, price flexibility in farm products and foods.

8. Total profits fluctuate by a much greater percentage than other types of income.

The lack of uniformity found in some key characteristics of business cycles is equally significant:

1. The *length* of cycles, averaging about 3½ years, varies widely. For example, counting from trough to trough we find a 5-year cycle in 1927–1932, from peak to peak an 8-year cycle from 1929–1937. On the other hand, 1919–1922 and 1920–1923 were 3-year cycles, and shorter ones have been observed. So we can never tell where we are in the cycle by counting the months elapsed since some past event.

2. The *amplitude* of cycle swings is very irregular. The down-swing of 1923–1924, for example, reduced manufacturing output about a tenth; that of 1937–1938, by nearly half. So we cannot count on any particular amplitude as "normal." Moreover, the evidence is not clear whether as time goes on cycles are becoming more or less severe.

3. Expansion in some cycles brings output up to a full-employment level and holds it there for some time, as in 1925–1927. In other cycles, expansion leads only to a "submerged peak," with unemployment still heavy, as in 1895 and 1937. There is evidence that in full-recovery cycles building construction

characteristically contributes heavily to the expansion, while in submerged-peak cycles it does not.

4. No two cycles are exactly alike in the relative roles played by different factors such as commodity prices, security prices, inventories, foreign loans, or construction. Inventory building and commodity price speculation characterized the boom of 1919–1920 followed by a price collapse. Stock market speculation and foreign loans were important elements in the boom preceding the 1929 decline.

5. Numerous attempts have been made to use our knowledge about uniformities in business cycles to "forecast" the future course of business activity. Economic forecasting has not developed to the point where it is a reliable guide for national policy. Even identification of phases of the cycle as they happen, or soon afterward, is far from easy.

In making use of our knowledge of the past we must be careful to give adequate weight also to our knowledge of the present. Changes in political or economic circumstances or in our institutions make older experience partly obsolete. The record suggests that in peacetime our economy is usually less susceptible to inflation than to depression. But the tremendous government requirements on production in "cold war" and the backlog of demands on the "social security state" are new elements that may create inflationary pressure for some years to come. Moreover, the increased power of organized labor added to the power in business and in farm organizations may introduce an inflationary bias.

If we do not have much more difficulty with inflation, it will probably be because world political tension eases and backlogs of demand prove less urgent than they now look; in that event, we may have to make adjustments to a serious decline of private investment and government purchase of goods and services within a few years. Indeed, some economists fear that such a decline might usher in a protracted period in which large unemployment would be chronic, unless overcome by extensive government programs. Other economists see a danger of both chronic unemployment and a persistent inflationary tendency combined.

III. Basic Ideas

Study of business fluctuations has yielded, in addition to the historical knowledge just sketched, a large amount of useful analysis. Together, these two kinds of knowledge afford an adequate basis for framing stabilization policies that can avoid both severe unemployment and severe inflation. The job of this section is to outline some of the ideas most useful in analysis of business fluctuations. First, however, we should dispose of some common misconceptions.

There is a widespread impression that economists disagree so much that they can give no sound guidance on policy. This is erroneous. There is, indeed, a good deal of disagreement, but it is much less than it seems to outsiders. Economists do not spend much time talking or writing about the large part of their subject matter on which they agree. As in all branches of learning, professional discussion relates chiefly to advancing the frontier of knowledge, where controversy and criticism are indispensable for progress; and the part of the discussion most likely to catch the attention of journalists is whatever happens to be least good-tempered or most extreme, rather than most fundamental. Moreover, many disagreements are merely about how to formulate findings which all accept, or about the relative quantitative weight of factors whose importance nobody denies. Again, many differences of opinion among economists on public policy reflect differences in philosophy rather than in economic analysis as such. This does not mean that their views are to be disregarded. The essence of democracy is to permit different opinions on public policy and to provide means of selection and compromise that enable adoption of workable policies and programs in the face of differences. Moreover, disagreements among economists help to mark out the areas where future developments and effects of policy are peculiarly uncertain, and thus show points at which policy must be kept flexible to permit adaptation as a situation develops.

A second misconception is contained in the proposition that effective stabilization policies can be designed only if we understand fully all the causes of fluctuations. Partial knowledge can be very useful for deciding how to act. People need not know just what causes cloud bursts, or just when they will occur, in order to use their knowledge of the course of floods to design safeguards against flood damage. In economics people need not know, for example, just what makes the volume of construction contracts change from time to time, in order to design arrangements to safeguard us against a general economic collapse when construction shrinks. More complete knowledge is, of course, worth seeking in order to improve the design of policy, but as we go along we can effectively use what we do know.

A third misconception is that inability to forecast coming economic changes accurately leaves us helpless in the grip of events. Present limitations on forecasting, and lack of complete understanding of causes, do make it impossible to treat economic instability solely by use of "preventive medicine." This is not to say, however, that it is impossible to tell when the economy is really sick and may get worse unless curative measures are taken; or that it is impossible to design effective cures. We can, in fact, diagnose real trouble soon enough to treat it. And, although we may not be able to prevent mild recessions or inflations, we do know enough to design policies that can keep them from developing into prolonged periods of mass unemployment or violent inflations.

CLASSES OF EXPENDITURE AND DECISIONS

Substantial changes in total expenditure in the whole economy mean substantial changes in total employment or in the price level, or in both.

In studying the course of fluctuations or analyzing policy proposals, economists commonly break down the total expenditure into four main headings: (a) consumption expenditure; (b) domestic private investment spending (or "capital formation") on new buildings, equipment, and additions to inventory; (c) government expenditure on goods and services; and (d) net foreign balance, representing the balance of all the goods and services we sell the rest of the world over what they sell us (an item which may, of course, be positive or negative in any given year).

Each of these major expenditure classes can be further subdivided. These divisions and subdivisions group together expenditures which rest on similar types of *decisions*.

Consumption expenditure represents use of income by households for direct enjoyment. Sub-groupings run in terms of the durability of the things bought. Services and perishable commodities involve little forward-looking calculation. At the other extreme, the buying of new houses is regarded as a business-type of decision and classified with investment. Other durable-goods buying is moderately forward-looking, but is classed as consumption rather than investment.

Domestic private investment represents spending by business of undistributed profits, cash assets or proceeds of new security issues or bank loans to buy additional goods for business use. Its main components are purchase of new plant and equipment, additions to inventories, and purchase of new housing.

Government expenditure on goods and services includes payment for services of government employees and purchase from private business of supplies, equipment, buildings, etc. (including, for example, goods bought under the Marshall Plan). In addition, government makes outlays for interest, veterans, Social Security benefits, and the like, where the government does not get currently produced services or commodities in exchange. These are called "transfer payments," and are treated essentially as taxes with a minus sign.

DECISIONS TO PRODUCE AND TO BUY

Except for the limited sector of direct government employment, output and employment are set in the first instance by private decisions. Business decisions to produce rest largely on the selling market created by non-business purchasers—consumers, the government, and foreigners—and on the buying markets in which materials, property, labor, and funds are obtained.

The amount of consumer expenditure depends largely on the incomes received by people from the proceeds of productive operations. In other words, households get income in the form of wages, salaries, dividends, etc., from business in return for providing services; and the business output of consumer goods and services is sold to households in return for expenditures out of this income. The simple circle of production-income-expenditure-production is, however, modified by saving of individuals and business enterprises and by business spending on plant and equipment and inventories. Business investment spending is forward-looking and is therefore influenced by many diverse factors, not only by the current state of business activity. The fiscal operations of government also modify the circle by taxation, which reduces taxpayers' disposable income, and by government payments such as salaries and "transfer payments" that constitute income for households.

The total stream of income, before taxes and including business profits not distributed to owners, can be shown as a matter of accounting to equal the total value of contemporaneous output, including items added to business inventory and plant and including government services valued at cost. But this is simply a bookkeeping identity following from the fact that what one consumer, business enterprise, or government agency treats as an expenditure is treated by some other unit as a receipt. In this bookkeeping sense any level of output, high or low, is potentially self-financing—that is, it sets up a flow of income out of which that amount of output *could* continuously be bought at current prices. It does not follow, however, that any existing level of output and employment *will* perpetuate itself—the record shows that it never has for long. For example, the accounting identity between income and value of output may reflect the unwilling acceptance of large inventory accumulations by businessmen in consequence of an unexpected decline in consumer expenditures. In this case, the identity conceals forces making for a decline in income. Or, the identity may reflect an unintended piling up of unused profits in the hands of businessmen in consequence of an unexpected rise in consumer expenditures. In this case, the identity conceals forces making for a rise in income.

Changes in total expenditure and income reflect changes in expenditure by some units in the economy. Total consumer expenditure can and may vary in relation to the flow of income set up by production for various reasons, such as a general change in the fraction of their income people desire to save, or a change in tax rates, or in government "transfer payments," or in dividend rates. Business enterprises may decide to increase or decrease expenditure on plant and equipment or on inventories because of changes in the business outlook, technological change, interest rate movements, or other factors. This will set in motion forces that tend toward increase or decrease in total expenditure and income in the whole economy. Changes in tax structures or in the level of government expenditures, and changes in our net foreign balance may also affect the level of total expenditure and income. Political changes abroad may lead to expansion or contraction of government outlays for military and foreign-assistance programs.

In general, a decision by any group to increase its expenditures in relation to its receipts is a force making for an expansion in aggregate expenditures and income, and to decrease its expenditures in relation to its receipts is a force making for a decline in aggregate income. Whenever the net effect of the decisions of consumers, business, and governments is to raise total expenditure and income there will be an increase in output and employment, or in the price level, or in all three—unless some decisions are changed. Similarly, when the effect is toward lower expenditure and income, there will be a decline in output and employment or in the price level or in all three—unless some decisions are changed.

The decisions by firms and households that make for expansion or contraction in total income are influenced not only by the flow of income but also by monetary factors: holdings of cash and of liquid resources (government securities and other securities easily cashed) and the cost and availability of bank and other credit. When firms and households regard the amount of cash and other liquid resources they hold as large relative to their total wealth, they will try to convert part into other forms of wealth; that is, spend more than they are currently receiving, thereby tending to increase total money income in the economy. Similarly, when it is relatively easy and cheap to borrow, firms and individuals who seek to make investments will find it easy to finance them and will thereby add to the upward pressure on income. Conversely, when firms and households regard the amount of cash and other liquid resources they hold as relatively small, they will try to spend less than they receive; when it is relatively difficult to borrow, investment will be discouraged; both of these will tend to reduce aggregate money income.

It follows from these considerations that one way to counter forces making for contraction is by monetary action designed to increase the amount of cash or other liquid resources held by individuals and firms and to reduce the cost and increase the availability of loans. Similarly, one way to offset any forces making for expansion is by monetary action designed to reduce the amount of cash or other liquid resources held by individuals and firms and to increase the cost and reduce the availability of loans.

With an upswing of business activity and rising prices, most borrowers look like better risks, and there is an expansion of bank financing of business and consumer buying. In a business recession the opposite occurs. This instability of bank credit is enhanced by the great elasticity inherent in a banking system with fractional reserves against deposit liabilities. The banks as a whole can, through their loan operations, create a quantity of purchasing power in the form of deposits equal to several times the amount of their reserves. With present legal reserve requirements and habits of the public with respect to holdings of pocket-book cash, the banking system can create new deposits equivalent to four or five times the amount of excess reserves. In a recession, banks may seek to increase their reserves as a fraction of their liabilities, thereby forcing a contraction in deposits, and conversely in an upswing. In addition, there are a number of factors that tend to increase reserves in business expansion when it would be desirable for them not to increase, and to decrease reserves in business recessions when it would be desirable for them not to decrease.

Expansion and contraction of bank credit is in part a reflection of business fluctuations. But most students of business cycles believe that for the reasons just cited, our banking system has an effect in amplifying these fluctuations, although there is wide disagreement on the quantitative importance of this factor. The great depression of the 'thirties was sharpened by credit contraction, and the postwar inflation of 1946–48 was heightened by credit expansion. Many economists regard our present banking system as an automatic destabilizer, unless effectively controlled.

Economists use the analytical tools outlined above to look for elements in the situation that can lead to expansion or contraction. They also rely heavily on the principles of national accounting to check the consistency of their reasoning. Explanations which have not been checked in this way of consistency are only too common—witness the theories underlying the Townsend

Plan, "Thirty Dollars Every Thursday," Social Credit, and many other "schemes"—and would, if used, lead to gross errors in policy.

We can see the shadows of a good many future changes in components of the economy. The postwar boom in housing and automobiles will slacken sooner or later. Easing of international tension would allow armaments to diminish. Developments in atomic energy may some day induce a temporary bulge in capital investment expenditure. The object of stabilization policy is not to prevent all fluctuations in components, but to see that they offset rather than reinforce each other. Reduction of armaments or housing brings a shrinkage of income earned in those sectors, which threatens to induce cutbacks also in things we can then afford to produce in greater quantity, emergency needs having been partly met. The basic strategy of economic stabilization is to mitigate and offset the effect on total expenditure of changes, upward or downward, in particular sectors or components of the economy.

ROOM FOR POLICY

As explained at the outset, this report excludes from consideration stabilization methods which, involving large assumption by government of the decision-making of households, of business firms, of labor, farm, and other groups, would negate basic freedoms. Also, it is plain that governmental decision-making of this sort would be clumsy and ineffectual. Even totalitarian governments which have no objection in principle to this type of "planning," find it necessary to decentralize most decisions to organizations with much the functions of our firms and households, and to guide decisions by "incentives."

See Hayek

Another conceivable method is to attempt stabilization by setting up organizations in each line of production and instructing each to stabilize its own sector. This may sound excellent for a moment, but it does not stand examination. Such a sector-stabilization organization, confronted with changes in the demand for its output, could not stabilize *both* its selling-price *and* its sales and output. The record of behavior of producer organizations suggests that they usually sacrifice output stabilization to price stabilization, or even to price boosting. Moreover, shifts in the *components* of output and the price level are often desirable. New products find their place by expanding their output, bidding up the prices of labor and other resources, and forcing down the prices and outputs of competing products. To stabilize the individual components of the economy, if we could do it, would be to throw away our prospects of progress and scrap the adaptive mechanism which facilitates progress.

Manifestly there is some room for groups and leaders, conscious of the stabilization problem, to modify their decisions in ways that will help to stabilize the economy. But since individual leaders are ordinarily in a relation of stewardship to others, their freedom to modify decisions in this way is limited. The primary responsibility for stabilization policy falls on government, particularly the federal government, and on public bodies such as the Board of Governors of the Federal Reserve System.

In a system where the great majority of workers are in private employment government stabilization policy consists primarily in altering the general economic climate so as to mitigate or offset developing fluctuations in private business. There is a wide variety of measures by which government can do this. Some of the more important are the following:

1. Change in the amount of tax revenue taken by government from incomes of individuals or businesses. Some change occurs automatically with changes in incomes. Alteration of tax rates or of the design of the tax structure could give greater change.

2. Change in government contributions to the income stream through "transfer payments," such as unemployment compensation and farm income supports. Again some change occurs automatically but more can be obtained by change in the rates or structure of "transfer payments."

3. Change in amount of government expenditure on public works or on other things bought by government.

4. Change in the incentives to individuals by changes in tax rates or structure, or in the rates or structure of "transfer payments," or in the kinds of expenditure undertaken.

5. Change in the cost and availability of bank credit, effected through controls of the monetary authorities.

6. Change in the structure of the public's financial assets and liabilities brought about by monetary or debt management policy.

7. Influencing the business outlook by government pronouncements and prospects of future government action, thus affecting investment decisions or current scheduling of output and employment, or both.

8. Government influence on the price-making and wage-making machinery.

9. International economic policy.

IV. Some International Factors

For many centuries, the problem of domestic economic stability has been greatly complicated by high dependence upon external trade. A country that exports a large fraction of its own production and relies heavily upon imports to meet its internal needs will necessarily be quite sensitive to external disturbances influencing its foreign trade. This sensitiveness to outside influences will be further enhanced if its reserves of gold and foreign exchange are small and its ability to obtain aid or credit abroad is limited. A decline in external demand for its export products, owing to depressed conditions in the chief markets to which it sells, imposes upon it the necessity of quickly bringing its external payments into line with its reduced receipts. This must usually be achieved in the main through curtailment of imports, and this by itself may interfere with domestic stability. At times something may be accomplished by improving the competitive position of exports. In this situation it is possible to avert serious internal deflation by resorting to currency depreciation, imposing direct restriction on imports, or subsidizing exports; but under some circumstances such measures may have other disadvantages, so that some internal deflation may be accepted as a consequence of the falling off in external demand for its goods. For such countries the task of adjusting the external balance at least complicates, and may conflict with, the achievement of domestic economic stability.

The United States is not in that position. Indeed, among economically advanced countries the United States is in an almost uniquely fortunate position. Our problem of domestic economic stability is not significantly affected by complicating external factors. This is not due solely to our huge gold reserves. Even more important are the facts that (1) our foreign trade is a relatively small part of our total activity, and (2) at the present time, other countries have such small reserves of gold and foreign exchange and are controlling their imports from the United States so closely through direct measures that any change in our purchases from them is likely to be reflected very rapidly and fully in a corresponding change in our exports. This means that in the event of a depression in the United States, we could not get any substantial over-all domestic stimulus by raising our barriers to imports. Hence, tariffs and import restrictions cannot be an effective anti-depression measure for the United States.

Though our foreign trade is a relatively small fraction of our activity, our imports bulk large in the activity of a considerable number of other countries. This means that the foreign countries have a large stake in stable prosperity in the United States and in a broadening of our market for imports. Our record of economic instability, combined with our traditional policy of tariff protection, obviously makes them reluctant to link their economies too closely to ours. In the event of a serious depression here, other countries eager to avoid a repetition of the experience of the 'thirties would probably unite in imposing specific restrictions against imports of American goods. The result would be a partial quarantining and isolation of the United States. The general objectives of our foreign policy make it essential that we encourage other democratic countries to adopt commercial policies which emphasize interdependence with, rather than insulation from, the United States. Our success on this score will depend, first and foremost, on our actual performance in achieving stable prosperity, and second, on our willingness to have low import duties, and to refrain from such other obstacles to imports as quotas and cumbersome customs procedure. Under present world conditions, the international political importance of our success, or failure, in achieving domestic economic stability can scarcely be overestimated.

Although our domestic economy is unlikely to experience serious disturbance from unpredictable and independent fluctuations in the foreign demand for American goods, our economy is subject to other important forces from abroad. The size of our programs of foreign economic and military aid and of government-fostered private investment abroad must be based mainly on our assessment of world conditions and the requirements of foreign policy, without much reference to considerations of domestic stability. It is the task of domestic stabilization policy to compensate for unstabilizing variations in the size of those programs, as well as in our military expenditures. A worsening of the international situation, resulting in very heavy expenditures for these purposes, might confront us with as difficult a problem of controlling inflation as in wartime. Improvement in the international situation might, on the other hand, permit a sharp curtailment of military expenditures at home and military aid to others. In this event, tax reductions could go far to forestall any deflationary effect.

Although the present U.S. position permits us a wide range of freedom in choosing domestic policies, even this freedom is not complete. And in any case, we must realize when we choose between alternative stabilization programs that they have definite international implications.

V. Fiscal Policy

A. STRATEGIC PRINCIPLES FOR FISCAL AND MONETARY POLICIES

Sections IV and V discuss fiscal policy and monetary policy. In these fields economics provides some strategic principles for achievement of economic stability. The most important are:

1. Government tax revenue should be higher relative to government expenditure in periods of high employment than in periods of substantial unemployment.

2. Money and credit should be relatively tight in periods of high employment and relatively easy in periods of substantial unemployment.

These two principles are intended to counteract fluctuations in total money demand, thereby restraining price fluctuations and promoting stable, high employment. Whatever may be considered the "normal" or desirable level of government tax revenue and expenditure, and whatever may be considered the "normal" or desirable relationship between them—as far as these can be determined from considerations other than stabilization—tax revenue should be higher than this relative to expenditure in times of high employment and lower than this relative to expenditure in times of substantial unemployment. Whatever may be the "normal" or desirable monetary policies, including debt management—and these may be determined in part on the basis of considerations other than stabilization—money and credit conditions should be relatively tight in times of high employment and relatively easy in times of substantial unemployment.

These are principles of operational strategy. The Congress and the Executive can put them into operation.

Nearly all economists agree with these strategic principles of stabilization. Disagreements relate chiefly to tactics, i.e., specific measures to put these strategic principles into operation.

B. IMPORTANCE OF FISCAL POLICIES OF GOVERNMENTS

Despite the primary role of private enterprise in our economy, government expenditures and receipts have reached a scale that makes them a crucial influence on the way the private economy works. In 1949 when the national income was a little more than $200 billion, federal, state, and local governments spent about $60 billion. And there seems little prospect of a large decline in government expenditures in the foreseeable future. Plainly, government fiscal policies and their timing constitute one of the major influences on the state of employment, production, and prices, whether or not they are deliberately framed with that end in view.

Government affects business activity through both sides of its budget. Wages paid to government employees, interest paid to holders of government bonds, and payments to veterans, to the aged, and to the needy, all constitute income that can be used to buy consumption goods from business. Government procurement of goods is a direct market for business. On the other side of the budget, taxes capture funds that consumers might have spent, or that business firms might have spent on plant and equipment. Taken by themselves, tax collections tend to contract the market of business, and thus to reduce employment or lower prices; and government expenditures, taken by themselves, tend to expand the market and thus to increase employment or raise prices.

It is not only the *size* of revenue and expenditure that counts; their qualitative *composition* is also important. For example, the effects of "transfer payments" depend on who gets them and on what terms—for example, whether unemployment compensation goes largely to the poorest workers and whether payments are set so high as to discourage acceptance of job offers. Again, a billion dollars of taxes collected in one way may have different economic effects from those attending a billion dollars levied in another way, because incentives are affected differently. For example, when people must pay one-fifth or more of their extra earnings to the government, their decision as to whether to work longer or shorter hours may be influenced. To take another example, a particular treatment of business losses in the tax laws may affect people's willingness to venture their capital in new activities.

On the other side of the budget, spending to build new roads may stimulate private investment in automobiles, garages, and trucks; some other types of public expenditure may have adverse repercussions on private investment. Some government spending and taxing policies may affect, rationally or irrationally, the psychological climate within which families and businesses make their decisions.

Fiscal measures for stabilization may be divided into three types: (1) those that are built into the fiscal system and operate automatically; (2) measures adopted in advance that are to go into effect promptly in certain specified contingencies; and (3) measures adopted only as the occasion arises.

C. AUTOMATIC STABILIZERS IN THE FISCAL SYSTEM

Since the prewar period the automatic stabilizing effect of federal fiscal operations has become substantial as a result of the increase in built-in stabilizers, including the pay-as-you-go principle, and the great expansion in the scale of the budget. Most economists consider the marked increase in automatic stabilizers a highly favorable development with respect to maintenance of economic stability.

When total income rises, the existing structure of federal taxes and expenditures tends automatically to increase government revenues relative to expenditures, and when total income falls, to increase expenditures relative to revenues. These changes tend to mitigate or offset inflations or depressions, in part at least.

On the spending side, unemployment compensation, relief, farm benefits, and the like tend to rise and fall with unemployment, and so to be higher in depression than in prosperity. Most other federal expenditures would not change much automatically with changes in the level of total income.

On the revenue side, tax receipts vary sharply in the same direction as national income. Revenue from the personal income tax, our largest single tax, varies directly with changes in national income, and in greater proportion owing to the "progression" in the tax structure. The next largest tax, that on corporate income, also varies in greater proportion than national income, since corporate income fluctuates more sharply than national income itself. Social security contributions from payrolls move roughly in proportion to national income.

We may summarize the automatic stabilizing influence of the 1949 federal fiscal system roughly as follows: in the absence of any offsetting action by Congress or the Executive, every drop of $10 billion in national income will lower taxes by something like $3 billion, thereby reducing by $3 billion an existing surplus or increasing by that amount an existing deficit. Similarly, every rise of $10 billion in national income will increase tax receipts by something like $3 billion thereby increasing an existing surplus by $3 billion or reducing an existing deficit by that amount. Moreover, these effects on the condition of the budget will be accentuated by automatic changes in expenditure. As explained above, every drop in national income will tend to raise federal government expenditure and every increase in national income will tend to lower it. Many economists think that some further increase in built-in automatic stabilizers is possible and desirable.

D. NEEDED: A PRINCIPLE TO REPLACE THE ANNUALLY BALANCED BUDGET

Automatic built-in fiscal stabilizers can be either supplemented or thwarted by explicit legislation and administrative action taken in response to changing business conditions. When high incomes cause tax collections to exceed expenditures, legislatures may destroy this automatic anti-inflation effect by cutting tax rates or by spending recklessly. Likewise, the automatic anti-unemployment effect of built-in stabilizers may be lost if, as happened in 1932, falling tax receipts in depression lead to reduced government outlay and higher tax rates. We cannot balance the budget annually and at the same time have a stabilizing fiscal policy—on this almost all economists agree. The tradition of an annually balanced budget calls for discretionary action from time to time that perversely cancels out the effects of the automatic stabilizers now built into the system.

Abandonment of the rule of an annually balanced budget necessitates adoption of other standards of budgetary policy to enable Congress and the electorate to determine when increases in expenditure call for increases in taxes and when decreases in expenditure can safely be balanced by decreases in taxes. Otherwise, there would be no check to waste and inefficiency, or to expenditures exceeding what the people really want, and hence no check to chronic inflation.

One important proposal is to aim at budget balance over a longer period. Nobody would advocate a *monthly* balance irrespective of seasonal changes; why should any special magic be attributed to a yearly balance irrespective of business-cycle changes? The so-called Swedish budget proposal is to balance the budget over a business cycle. Extra spending would call for extra taxes, but not necessarily for an equal amount of tax revenue in the same year. Budget surpluses in some years would cover the deficits of other years. Uncertainties about the length of the "cycle" and about the relative duration of depression and prosperity would, of course, create difficulties in application, but this proposal deserves serious consideration.

Another possiblity is to preserve balance each year in a "target" or "normal" budget in which tax revenues, unemployment compensation and relief expenditures, and other items that must or should vary with business conditions, are always entered at the amounts they would be in a period of high employment and national income without inflation. An increase in the general scale of government activities would then call for a tax rate increase, but a bulge of relief expenditures and a drop in tax revenue because of a business slump would not. Nor would an increase in tax revenue accompanying inflation call for a tax cut. Many economists believe this plan would be a marked improvement over the traditional annual budget balance rule. It would, however, present some difficult problems in application, particularly what levels of employment and national income would be the proper basis for the "target" or "normal" figures of tax revenues, relief expenditures, etc.

A third proposal is a modified version of the annual balance rule, applicable in periods when the economy is prosperous and stable and there is no evident swing toward depression or inflation. In this situation, newly planned increases or decreases in government expenditure would call for tax-rate changes to produce corresponding changes in tax revenue. Thus, proposed increases in government expenditure would have to meet the traditional test of whether they are worth their cost in terms of higher taxes. As far as it goes, this proposal would probably have the approval of most economists. But it provides no standards for appraisal of the existing relation of government expenditures and receipts, whether deficit or surplus, or for fiscal policy in periods of depression or inflation.

Some economists would dispense with any hard-and-fast rule or formula. They would vary total government revenue in relation to expenditure so as to exercise a stabilizing influence on the economy. They claim that it is not possible to say in advance whether such an approach would call for tremendous surpluses and public debt reduction in the years ahead or a predominance of deficit spending.

E. DISCRETIONARY STABILIZING ACTION

Some economists would place exclusive reliance on built-in stabilizers. They believe that these automatic stabilizers are very likely to reduce economic fluctuations to tolerable magnitudes; and they fear that discretionary government actions are likely to do more harm than good, owing to the defects of forecasting, the destabilizing influence of uncertainty about government action, and the political pressures to favor special interests. Most economists approve the greatest possible use of automatic stabilizers, but do not consider it prudent to rely solely on them. Hence they favor use of additional stabilizing measures if unemployment or inflation pass certain points.

The principal types of discretionary fiscal action for stabilization are: (1) changes in tax rates and tax structures; (2) changes in "transfer payments"; (3) changes in expenditure on public works; and (4) general expansion or contraction of government activities.

The stabilizing influence of the present federal tax structure could be increased by reducing tax rates during a slump in order to encourage business and family expenditure; and by raising tax rates when an excess of money expenditure is causing inflation. Tax exemptions could also be varied.

The same logic underlies proposals for increasing "transfer payments" in bad times: e.g., increasing grants-in-aid by the federal government to help carry the local relief load. Some economists even go so far as to advocate that the government send checks to people broadside during times of mass unemployment. The possible abuses of such a program, and an aversion to giving people money they have not in some sense earned, explain the considerable skepticism toward this proposal and the wider approval of work relief as a means of providing incomes for those who cannot, for the time, be employed in private industry or on public works.

Shifts in the timing of construction of some public buildings, river improvements, power facilities, public housing, and the like, would do no great harm. The question is therefore raised whether such heavy public works cannot be hurried forward in case of a slump and slowed down in case of a boom, and thus used to temper economic fluctuations. In the past this sector of government expenditure has often behaved perversely, growing in prosperity and shrinking in slump. There would be widespread agreement among economists that the least that should be done is to correct this destabilizing tendency by a closer approach to regularization of government expenditure on heavy public works. State and local governments face real obstacles to such regularization of expenditure, but it may be possible to remove these in considerable degree by appropriate federal assistance programs or by other devices.

Some economists would go further and seek to increase heavy public works in depression and retard them in prosperity, particularly if the swings in economic activity should be fairly long in duration and substantial in amplitude. However, there seems to be a trend away from the earlier enthusiastic belief that this can go a long way, by itself, in stabilizing business activity. It takes so long to get public-works projects under way, even with a "shelf" planned ahead, that more accurate forecasting than we now have would be needed to guide the timing of such a program.

"Light" public works—road maintenance, earth-moving projects in relation to conservation and flood control, etc.—offer advantages in flexibility of expenditure and timing, and are regarded by many economists as an important part of a stabilization program.

Finally, the federal government could contract or expand the scope and scale of its activities. Few economists would favor the use of such changes to temper mild short-run fluctuations in economic activity. A larger number would use changes in the general level of government activities along with the other devices mentioned above to meet sharp or prolonged unemployment or inflation.

Whether discretionary action is to operate on public works and work relief expenditures, "transfer payments," or tax rates, or on the general level of government activities, two related problems must be solved: (1) Who is to have the authority to decide when action is to be taken and what kind of action is appropriate?; and (2) What criteria can and should this authority use in reaching its decisions? The second problem would be solved and the first would not be serious if we could forecast accurately for a considerable period ahead, since in that case it would make little difference where the authority was lodged. Different authorities would reach much the same decisions, and in any event, success or failure could be easily gauged and thus effective legislature control would be possible. The admitted impossibility of accurate forecasting makes both problems serious. Retention of authority by the legislature is almost certain to mean a substantial lag before action is taken. As a practical matter, the process of changing a tax law or expenditure program usually takes the Congress many months of hearings and debate. Moreover, each separate action is likely to become enmeshed in political controversy. On the other hand, delegation of authority means surrendering in some measure what have hitherto been exclusive prerogatives of the legislature and thus strengthens the executive arm of the government. It means, not the elimination of political pressures, but concentration of these pressures on an executive authority rather than on the legislature.

Difficulties of the sort just mentioned might be overcome in part by the device of advance enactment by Congress of statutes providing for changes in taxes, "transfer payments," or public works expenditures, and setting forth rules or standards for putting those programs into effect. For example, the law could provide that the withholding rate in the personal income tax be raised by a stated amount whenever an appropriate price index had risen by a certain amount in a defined period of months; and be lowered by a stated amount whenever standard indices of production and employment dropped below specified levels or trends. Again, the law could provide that the period during which unemployed workers could receive unemployment compensation be temporarily increased according to a standard index of the volume of unemployment. Another example is found in advance authorization for a specific program of public works, to be put into operation in accordance with changes in standard indices of production and employment and to be curtailed in accordance with changes in the same indices. Standards for application of these measures would have to be quite easily and widely understood. Congress could, if it desired, retain a "legislative veto" on the actual putting into effect of such programs. This device of advance enactment of stabilizing measures shades into the area of built-in, automatic stabilizers.

VI. Monetary Policy

Monetary policy includes policies dealing with banking and credit—the availability of loans to firms and households, and interest rates—the public debt and its management, and the monetary standard.

A. BANKING POLICY

Banking policy has for generations been held responsible for easing financial "panics." After the first World War the rather vague mandates of the Federal Reserve Act—"maintenance of sound credit conditions" and "accommodation of commerce, industry and agriculture"—came to be construed into a general concern with economic stability. During the "New Era" of the 1920's, there was a widespread impression that the policies of the Federal Reserve System were in fact achieving prosperity with steady prices. The breakdown of the "New Era" prosperity, the recurrence of a financial "panic" in 1933, and the incomplete business recovery after 1933 despite expansionist Federal Reserve policy, have raised doubts of the effectiveness of monetary policy as an instrument for maintaining economic stability. Few economists today would rely so heavily on monetary policy as was typical twenty years ago, but few would regard it as unimportant. Experience has shown that appropriate monetary policies can be helpful and that inappropriate policies can be harmful. Most economists agree on the following: (1) Tight money is a deterrent to price inflation accompanying a general excess of demand over supply; (2) Tight money can greatly accentuate a downswing of activity and may convert a mild depression into a deep one; and (3) Easy money by itself is an inadequate remedy for deep depressions, but it is helpful. Some economists think that easy money may be an adequate remedy for mild depressions, and that appropriate monetary policy may prevent mild depressions from becoming deep.

Looking ahead, there are two main lines of bank-credit policy on which to rely—qualitative controls regulating particular types of credit, and quantitative controls to produce a general tightening or easing of credit. Quantitative controls must be the main reliance, but the possibilities and limitations of qualitative controls need to be considered.

Qualitative Controls. Qualitative controls are measures designed to stimulate, restrict, or stabilize loans for particular, specific purposes. Examples of stimulating controls are Federal Housing Authority insurance of mortgages and revision of bank examination standards designed to facilitate credit expansion through consumer loans and "term loans" to business. Such stimulative measures can scarcely be turned on and off on short notice, but may have their uses in case of persistent depression. The use of qualitative controls to reduce the fluctuation in bank credit is illustrated by the amendments of bank-examination standards in the late 1930's, aimed to encourage banks to judge loans and bond investments by their long-run prospects, and thus to make credit standards less cycle-sensitive. Restrictive qualitative controls are illustrated by the control of stock-exchange margins and of installment credit during and since the war.

Some opinion seems to favor primary reliance on qualitative controls in circumstances where inflationary pressures need to be checked by tight credit. Most economists are skeptical on this point, for several reasons. There seems to be no possibility of designing workable controls over loans to finance inventories, a type of loan which contributed to inflation in 1946–48, and probably in 1919–20. In general, when one type of bank credit is restricted, the activities it is hoped to restrict can usually be financed under some other label, thus evading the restriction. Further, qualitative controls necessarily affect only selected lines of activity and many economists think it undesirable that measures designed to control the general level of activity should favor or repress particular lines of activity.

Quantitative Controls. Control of the quantity of bank credit is operated through instruments affecting the reserves of the banks, since the ability of banks to make loans and investments depends on the amount of their reserves in relation to legal requirements. The reserves of the banks are their deposits in the Federal Reserve Banks. A bank cannot expand its loans or investments unless it is prepared to face a loss of reserves as borrowers, or sellers of securities, use the newly acquired funds. To expand credit, therefore, a bank must either have reserves in excess of the required minimum percentage of its deposits, or have ways to get additional reserve funds. A bank which runs short of reserves has to choose between borrowing from the Federal Reserve Bank or reversing the process of credit expansion and cutting down its outstanding loans and investments.

Policy actions by the Federal Reserve System or the United States Treasury can put the banks in an easy reserve position encouraging credit expansion, or a tight reserve position pushing them into credit contraction. The Board of Governors of the Federal Reserve System can, within limits fixed by statute, change the minimum ratio of reserves to deposits that each member bank in the System is legally required to hold. The Board can also change the "rediscount rate"—the cost to commercial banks of borrowing from the Federal Reserve Banks—though this instrument has been of little importance in recent years. The reserve position of the banks can also be altered by shifting the location of Treasury funds from commercial banks to Federal Reserve Banks, or vice versa. A shift of these funds into Federal Reserve Banks reduces deposits and reserves of commercial banks by equal amounts, thus lowering the percentage ratio of their reserves to their deposits.

The most powerful tool of monetary policy is "open market operations"—that is, the sale and purchase of government securities by the Federal Reserve or by the Treasury. A sale of securities by Federal Reserve Banks or by the Treasury results in a flow of checks from buyers to Federal Reserve Banks. These are subtracted from the reserve accounts of commercial banks (i.e., their deposits with the Reserve Banks), with the result that their reserves are lowered by the amount paid for the securities. In the other direction, a purchase of securities by a Federal Reserve Bank leads to issue of a check which, when collected by a bank from the Reserve Bank, adds directly to the reserve of that bank. The Federal Reserve buys and sells large amounts of securities every week, on its own account and as fiscal agent of the Treasury. If the net effect of these operations is an excess of sales over purchases, bank reserves are reduced. If the net effect is an excess of purchases over sales, bank reserves are expanded.

In the years 1946–48, the open-market power was used to support the prices of government securities. This limited its use to check credit expansion, since banks wishing to get more reserves could do so at will by selling such securities.

Experience suggests that quantitative monetary control is more effective in checking undesired credit expansion than in bringing about desired credit expansion. There is always a point at which shortage of reserves will curtail the growth of bank loans and investments. In the other direction, while expanding the reserves of commercial banks *permits* credit expansion, it cannot guarantee it—that depends also on the attitude of borrowers. In recession, the most that monetary policy can do may be to avoid adding credit deflation to the list of forces aiding the downswing. But if a prosperity period takes on an inflationary tinge, monetary policy has a clear responsibility to arrest credit expansion.

The destabilizing tendencies of banking could be reduced by setting higher reserve requirements. A 20 per cent reserve system, which is roughly what we have today cannot inflate itself nearly as far on a given volume of excess reserves, or deflate itself as far in paying off a given amount of bank debt to the Federal Reserve, as the 10 per cent reserve system which we had in the 1920's.

Some economists favor going all the way to a 100 per cent reserve banking system to minimize this source of instability. In this extreme form, the proposal would involve the complete separation of the depository and check-clearance functions of existing banks from their lending functions. The existing lending functions would be taken over by new institutions, many of which, it is expected, would be formed from loan departments of existing banks and all of which would obtain their funds from the flotation of securities rather than from deposits subject to recall on demand. Proponents of this scheme maintain that it would cure the destabilizing influences now built into our banking structure, facilitate control over the quantity of money by either automatic means or discretionary authorities, and avoid excessive government regulation of the lending market. Many economists doubt that this measure would make a significant contribution to economic stability, and feel that the transitional difficulties of such a drastic change would be great and that less drastic measures can put the banking system on a satisfactory footing.

B. PUBLIC DEBT POLICY

The national debt held outside government agencies and Federal Reserve Banks now amounts to approximately $200 billion or about 90 percent of a year's national income. (This compares with a national debt calculated on the same basis of about 50 percent of national income in 1939.) Of the $200 billion, commercial banks hold about $65 billion and other credit institutions about $35 billion, leaving about $100 billion in the hands of individuals, corporations, and local governments. About $60 billion of the debt, including Savings Bonds, is redeemable on demand. Another $40 billion is composed of short-term Treasury securities. Interest charges on $200 billion of the debt in the hands of the public are about $4½ billion a year.

During and shortly after the war there was a standing offer by the Federal Reserve to buy government securities at stated prices. This policy made it impossible to check price inflation by tightening the bank reserve position significantly.

The standing offer of the Federal Reserve to buy government securities at stated prices rendered the large bank holdings of these securities the practical equivalent of excess legal reserves. Any bank that wanted to increase loans, or to buy investments, could get reserves by selling part of its government securities to the Federal Reserve. Thus, public debt policy largely transformed the open market operations of the Federal Reserve System from a means of controlling bank credit to a means of supporting the prices of government securities and holding down interest rates.

The Federal Reserve authorities later substituted a somewhat more flexible policy of maintaining "orderly conditions" in the government security market in place of the wartime and early postwar policy of supporting government securities at stated prices. Although this new formula creates the possibility of using monetary controls as a contra-cyclical stabilizer, there is serious danger that excessive emphasis will be given to stabilization of government security prices.

Many economists advocate that the Federal Reserve abandon the price of government securities as a primary criterion of policy, and decide on the volume of government securities to purchase or sell on the basis of the desired tightness or ease in the money market.

Many other economists see serious drawbacks to this policy: (1) The budgetary cost might be large; (2) If such a policy resulted in disorderly conditions in the market for government securities, there might be serious repercussions on the solvency of our financial institutions—banks, insurance companies, etc.; (3) Moreover, a tightening of the structure of interest rates may take many years to reverse, so that unless the authorities can forecast with confidence that inflation will last a long time, these economists think that such a policy might do more harm than good.

Security-Reserve Possibilities. One method proposed for bringing the reserve position under control while protecting the market for government securities held by banks is to require banks to keep a reserve of government securities against deposits, in addition to present cash reserves. To be effective in controlling credit, such a requirement would have to tie down the bulk of the reserve-eligible government securities. Interest rates on other government securities would then be allowed to vary. Proposals of the Federal Reserve authorities for requirements stopping a good deal short of absorbing bank holdings might well leave banks such a wide margin of cashable securities as to be ineffective.

The security-reserve proposal was advocated during the active inflation of 1946–48 by the Board of Governors of the Federal Reserve System and by some private economists, as an emergency measure to check the inflation and as a contribution to permanent economic stabilization. In all essential respects, raising required reserve ratios by adding a security-reserve requirement is identical with a straight increase of cash reserve requirements, combined with an equivalent purchase of government securities by the Reserve Banks. The only significant difference is that the security-reserve proposal provides the member banks with the equivalent of a subsidy (in the form of interest on the bonds) to compensate for the loss of earnings on additional assets tied up as reserves. Like a straight increase in cash reserve requirements, it would reduce the possible ratio of credit expansion to excess reserves.

C. THE MONETARY STANDARD

The problem of monetary standards is ordinarily discussed in terms of gold. This is likely to be misleading. Gold has an importance in relation to international problems, but in relation to our domestic problems it is not very important. Our gold reserves are so enormous that maintaining the gold standard—that is, keeping gold at a price of $35 per ounce—can be no guarantee against inflation. Nor can the gold standard be any guarantee against deflation and unemployment, as may be seen from our experience of the 1930's and earlier depressions. Moreover, attempts to manage the domestic economy by changing the gold price would be ineffective domestically and ruinous to our international relations.

Gold is a connecting link between domestic monetary policy and international problems. Currently the chief meaning of our standing offer to buy gold at $35 per ounce is that it creates a market for something produced in friendly countries we are trying to help, particularly sterling-area countries, and that it gives a value in American goods to the monetary reserves of our friends. However, political considerations aside, it is more straightforward and economical to make funds available to nations we seek to help in the form of open gifts than to buy gold we do not need and which they must use some of their resources to produce.

In a long-run view, most economists think it wasteful to produce gold destined only to be buried in our monetary hoards. Some urge the return to a situation in which gold plays an essential role in the monetary system, others, the complete elimination of the monetary role of gold. Many feel, however, that present international difficulties make this an inappropriate time to make a fundamental change in the role of gold.

One proposal for a reform of the monetary standard to promote economic stability is the commodity-reserve-currency plan ("Graham Plan"). This is a scheme for giving a stable real value to the dollar by having the government issue a standing offer to buy or sell, at a fixed price, a *composite commodity-bundle* of standardized and storable raw materials. The offer would be backed up on the buying side by the government's power to issue paper money, and by available storage facilities, and on the selling side by a reserve of commodities in storage.

The chief merit claimed for the commodity-reserve scheme is that it could be a powerful automatic stabilizer. In a recession, purchases for the commodity reserve would increase the quantity of money and check the decline in the incomes of raw-material producers and thus help also to maintain markets for goods used by these producers. In an inflationary boom, sale of commodities from the reserve would reduce the quantity of money, absorb excess spending power and add to available supplies of raw materials. This plan needs further exploration and appraisal before its practical potentialities will be clear, particularly with respect to the make-up of the "composite commodity" and its relation to farm and food policy, to international commodity agreements, and to monetary policies of other countries.

D. THE RELATION BETWEEN FISCAL AND MONETARY POLICY

To simplify exposition, fiscal and monetary policy have been treated separately, though they are in fact closely related and decisions about one will inevitably affect the other. Perhaps the point of most direct contact between monetary and fiscal policy is the financing of deficits and the use of surpluses.

We have seen that a stabilizing fiscal policy may call for a deficit at a time of large unemployment and for a surplus at a time of strong inflation. We have also seen that stabilizing monetary policy calls for relatively easy money at a time of large unemployment and for relatively tight money at a time of strong inflation. The two principles together require that a deficit designed to offset depressing influences be financed in a way that would contribute to monetary ease—for example, by the sale of securities to the Federal Reserve System or by the printing of currency. Similarly, the two principles require that a surplus designed to offset expansive influences be used in a way that would contribute to tight money—for example, by retiring securities owned by the Federal Reserve Banks or by destroying currency.

These simple principles have by no means always been followed. The most recent example is the policy of supporting government security prices in 1946–48, which meant that some of the restrictive effect of post-World-War II surpluses was dissipated. The combined effect of monetary and fiscal policy was in consequence to favor capital formation at the expense of consumption.

Coordination between fiscal and monetary policy is also required on a broader level: the two policies must work together and not at cross purposes. This raises broad issues, largely outside the scope of this report, about the appropriate administrative and political arrangements for the control of monetary and fiscal policies and about the standards employed to guide these policies.

In the past, fiscal policy has been directly governed by legislative action; whereas monetary policy has been largely at the discretion of the Federal Reserve System and the Treasury, though a considerable number of other agencies—the Federal Deposit Insurance Corporation, Reconstruction Finance Corporation, Federal Housing Authority, and so on—have exercised some monetary influence. Perhaps most economists feel that control over monetary policy is at present dispersed too widely to permit effective coordination. Some economists would favor concentrating control over monetary policy and adding discretionary control of fiscal policy. Others would favor reducing or eliminating the amount of discretion at present lodged in the monetary authorities—thereby placing major emphasis in both fiscal and monetary policy on essentially automatic reactions.

In the past, also, the standards for monetary action have been very vague and broad. Some economists would favor equally broad standards for governing fiscal policy. Others would favor the acceptance of a single set of more specific standards—such as stability of an index of prices or employment to govern whatever discretionary action is authorized in both monetary and fiscal policy.

VII. Market Policy [1]

Wise use of the instruments of fiscal and monetary control is essential to economic stability, but there is no assurance that, under all circumstances,

[1] Milton Friedman makes the following comment on this section:

"I disagree with the general tenor of this section and one of its major specific conclusions.

"(1) Market policy seems to me to stand in an entirely different relation to economic stability than monetary and fiscal policy. Monetary and fiscal measures are general measures adapted to the problem of countering general changes in employment, output, and prices and are the appropriate techniques to use for that purpose. Changes in particular prices and particular wages are appropriate for achieving a proper allocation of resources and products among different uses; they are entirely inappropriate for countering general changes in employment, output, and prices.

economic stability will be achieved through such controls alone. In a free-enterprise economy private policies of business and labor with respect to prices, wages, and profits have a bearing upon stability, and the same is true of government policies affecting prices and incomes in particular industries, such as agriculture, transportation, and public utilities.

This raises two fundamental questions. First, how should prices, wages, and profits behave? Second, what steps should be taken so that prices, wages, and profits will behave as they should? Since economists have not yet made much progress in analysing the effects on business fluctuations of price, wage, and profit behavior, no comprehensive and precise answer can be given to the first question. And as one might guess, there are widely divergent views on both questions.

The power of organized labor today suggests that we may be faced with the danger of chronic inflation resulting from general wage increases which recurrently outrun the growth in productivity of the economy as a whole. Man-hour productivity for the economy as a whole has increased in the past at an average rate of about 2 per cent per year. A gradual upward trend in average hourly wage rates corresponding approximately to this general growth in productivity—i.e., an increase of about 2 per cent a year, if past

"The chief reason of considering market policy at all in a report on economic instability is that inappropriate market policy—a market policy that enables special groups, whether trade unions, industrial producers, or farmers, to exercise direct control over prices or wages—may render monetary and fiscal policy largely ineffective in attaining its twin objectives of full employment and stable prices, a point that this section quite appropriately makes. The solution is to be sought in the elimination of these direct controls, not in their extension or in the substitution of governmental controls. The problem is not what behavior ought to be imposed on particular prices or wage rates but rather, what the appropriate institutional arrangements are for the determination of prices, wage rates, etc.—the problem considered in the three paragraphs that precede the final paragraph of this section.

"(2) One of the chief specific conclusions of this section is that prices of products and wages of labor require different treatment for the promotion of economic stability; that it is desirable for the general level of product prices to fluctuate over the business cycle but undesirable for the general level of wage rates to do so (paragraphs 8, 9 and 11 of this section). This seems to me false. Prices of products and wages of labor are on the same footing. Our basic objective is to minimize the fluctuations in both. Insofar as the conclusion of this section goes beyond this statement, it necessarily implies substituting rigidity for stability. When a decline in total money demand presses prices and wages down, the wage level can be kept stable only by preventing particular wage rates from falling.

"If fiscal and monetary policy prevent total money demand from falling or rising sharply, they will thereby prevent any general decline or rise in wages and prices from developing into a spiral and becoming cumulative. Declines or rises in particular prices and wage rates can then serve the useful and indispensable function of facilitating adjustments among different sections of the economy. 'The growing strength of organized labor' is, from this point of view, as harmful in periods of business contraction as in periods of business expansion (see paragraph 8 of this section). The alternative solution of a rigid wage level proposed in this section is equivalent to saying that the appropriate way to reduce temperature fluctuations in a room is to break the thermometer which controls the thermostat so it always registers the same temperature."

trends continue—need not result in an upward trend in the average level of prices. But general increases in wage rates exceeding the average growth of productivity raise costs and will ordinarily result in higher prices.

Chronic wage-induced price inflation would pose a dilemma for fiscal and monetary policy. Suppose wages rise at a rate of 10 per cent per year and prices by 7 or 8 per cent. Should we then adopt tight money and a budget surplus to meet this situation? If we do, the result will be not so much control of prices as a reduction of output and employment: business costs and prices will still be high but total money demand will be deficient so that men and machines will have to become unemployed. If we do not, we face the danger that the wage and price increases will continue at a rate that becomes intolerable. Thus, inflation induced by rising costs rather than excess demand offers a very grave dilemma for fiscal and monetary policy.

Opinions of economists differ regarding the likelihood that these problems will be serious. And suggestions for a solution tend to be impractical or rather general and vague. Direct governmental control of wages is incompatible with a free-enterprise economy. Even proposals for compulsory arbitration of wage disputes are opposed by both unions and employers, and there are as yet no agreed principles of income distribution policy that might establish a basis for arbitration. Limited statutory restraints upon the right to strike are unlikely to curtail seriously the bargaining strength of labor organizations. Adoption by labor leaders of a more responsible attitude on wage increases, taking account of the full effects on the economy as a whole, may be impossible unless inter-union competition becomes weaker and economic understanding of the rank and file, as well as the leaders, becomes greater. For the present, reconciling full employment with price level stability within a free-enterprise framework must be regarded as a major unsolved problem.

It should be emphasized that the relationship, noted above, between growth of productivity and increase in wage rates, does not hold for a particular firm or industry. Productivity does not grow uniformly or evenly among industries and firms; the differences in rates of productivity increase are often great. If wage rates in each particular industry or firm were adjusted to the productivity change in that firm or industry, untenable disparities would develop in the wages paid by different industries for the same kind of labor. Instead, wage rates for a particular grade of labor should be approximately uniform throughout all sectors of the economy, except for regional differentials reflecting basic differences. Divergent rates of growth in productivity in particular industries should, in general, be reflected in shifts in the relative prices of their products, involving price reductions in those fields experiencing above-average progress and price increases in those fields where growth in productivity is lagging.

An average increase of about 2 per cent per year in the level of money wage rates does not, however, imply just this rate of increase for each worker or each grade of labor. Existing anomalies in the wage structure are continually being corrected. Also, progress in equalizing educational and training opportunities and in removing discriminatory barriers to entry into the more agreeable and highly paid occupations should result in narrowing somewhat the wage differentials between menial, unskilled jobs and skilled jobs through increases in rates at the lower end of the wage structure. Again, the faster-growing firms and industries may need to raise wages a little faster in order to attract labor. These factors will at times justify increases in particular wage rates of more than 2 per cent per year.

A downward spiral of wages and prices is at least as harmful to economic stability as an upward spiral. General wage cuts are likely to be unstabilizing; they may help to convert a moderate business recession into a severe depression. If such cuts are not accompanied by equivalent reductions in consumer prices, they depress business by reducing the buying power of workers. If, on the other hand, prices are promptly adjusted, the decline in wages and prices together, coming in a period of business contraction, is likely to give rise to expectations of further reductions, producing general postponement of buying, efforts to liquidate inventories, losses, pressure on borrowers to repay, and serious financial difficulties and deflation. The growing strength of organized labor, while it has increased the likelihood that an inflationary wage-price spiral will develop in periods of business expansion, has much reduced the danger that future periods of business contraction will be intensified by deflationary wage-price spirals, such as occurred in the early 'thirties.

Stability of the wage level does not imply that the level of prices must remain rigid; profit margins can and should vary through the cycle.

In a dynamic economy stable prosperity calls for a continuous readaptation and redirection of productive effort in response to the development of new products, new techniques of production, and changing wants. In a free-enterprise economy this kind of dynamic adjustment requires willingness to adjust prices, and sometimes capacity, promptly to changed conditions of demand or supply. Marked stickiness or rigidity of particular prices may be an important factor impeding dynamic adjustment and contributing to over-all economic instability. Attempts to achieve monopoly profits by limiting output and keeping prices high tend to reduce the buying power of consumers. Some economists think that monopolistic action may prevent new investment.

General conclusions are that cumulative wage-price spirals destroy economic stability, and that the task of maintaining stable prosperity will be greatly assisted if a way can be found to combine a steady and gradual upward trend in money wage rates, corresponding to the average over-all growth in productivity, with a considerable degree of flexibility in the prices of particular goods. It is all too evident that the actual behavior of wages and prices does not correspond to this ideal. The tendency of union wages to rise excessively during periods of business expansion, and the tendency of many prices to remain fixed, or decline only sluggishly, in periods of business contraction are obstacles to economic stability. They may put an impracticable burden upon fiscal and monetary policies. There is disagreement among economists, however, on both the magnitude of these problems and the measures which should be taken to meet them.

According to one view, the government should adopt a positive, sweeping program to remove barriers to competition, so that no business corporation and no labor union would have the power to exert any significant influence over the prices of whatever it sells or buys. Prices, wages, and profits would then be determined by the automatic operation of competitive markets. In those industries where economies of mass production or other factors limit the firms to such a small number that competition is not effective, government ownership or regulation would replace free, private enterprise. This approach calls for a destruction of private power over wages and prices, but with no extension of government power except where effective competition is unattainable.

According to another view, the government, instead of relying primarily on measures to enforce competition, would establish selective price and wage controls and rationing and allocation procedures in key sectors of the economy, thus securing a substantial measure of influence over the behavior of prices, wages, and profits. This approach calls for a curtailment of private power, and an extension of government power, over both prices and wages.

According to a third view, powerful private groups, such as large corporations and labor unions, must be accepted as an inherent feature of our kind of society. Instead of undertaking extensive government controls over wages and prices, however, an attempt should be made to formulate rules of responsible private behavior for organized groups, and to secure the voluntary acceptance by these groups of such rules. This approach emphasizes not the curtailment of private power, but its responsible exercise in conformity with accepted rules. It raises the fundamental question whether private groups can satisfactorily discharge public functions. This view does not, of course, rule out attempts to make competition as effective as possible everywhere, or substitution of public ownership and operation in highly monopolistic industries.

This diversity of views and programs is significant in indicating that the problem of prices, wages, and profits is as yet largely unsolved. Difficulties in this field should not, however, prevent us from using fiscal and monetary controls to do the best we can in limiting fluctuations in total income, expenditure, production, and unemployment.

JOHN K. GALBRAITH

THE following selection from *American Capitalism: The Concept of Countervailing Power* contains John Kenneth Galbraith's interpretation of economic equilibrium within a capitalist economy. It is here that he develops the provocative thesis that capitalism's ability to solve the problems of economic efficiency and power distribution can be better understood in terms of checks and balances on opposite sides of the market than in terms of competition among sellers on one side of the market. According to Galbraith, it is not competition among sellers that protects the consumer, competition among employers that assures satisfactory wages to the worker, or competition among their customers that protects farmers from low prices and incomes. Nor is it, of course, the beneficence of monopolists, of small groups of large producers, of large employers, or of the food-processing firms that buy from farmers that protects the little man. Atomistic competition almost nowhere prevails. Large-sized firms dominate our industries. But wherever competition on one side of a market has given way to concentration of production or buying power, a countervailing power is said to have arisen on the other side. Thus big sellers are checked by big buyers, and vice versa. A comfortable balance of economic power results.

Nor, according to Galbraith, is countervailing power an isolated force tending to preserve the vitality of the economy or equity in the distribution of its fruits. The older competition among sellers in terms of price has given way to a less sharply focused but nevertheless socially desirable competition in techniques of production and product innovation.

Large size is consequently justified in two ways. On the one hand, it develops the ever more efficient techniques and ever more varied and useful products that together give economic progress its most important content. On the other hand, it induces the appearance of countervailing aggregations of economic power that assure the equitable distribution of the fruits of production. Thus atomistic competition—and the ideal of "the competitive model"—is repudiated.

There are, to be sure, imperfections in the functioning of countervailing power. In time of inflation, Galbraith notes, large employers cannot be expected to resist the demands of large unions for wage increases. Increased labor costs can be passed on to consumers in the form of higher prices. There is no equilibrium here, but instead, a wage-price spiral that can carry the inflation to destructive lengths. Although this is Galbraith's only important qualification, another needs to be considered as it might apply in time of recession or depression. At such times, the countervailing power of large unions might be great enough to prevent the wage reductions that might be necessary to permit particularly hard-hit industries and firms to effect essential cost adjustments and to lower final product prices. With a wage-price spiral on the upswing and cost rigidity on the downswing, countervailing power might have somewhat restricted periods within which to work its beneficent effects. And in those periods of relatively high-level stability, the possibility that opposing economic forces will inevitably reach a nice balance is hardly the only one to be considered. It is, of course, Galbraith's recognition of the possibility that they may not balance automatically that explains his willingness to use the antitrust laws to combat "original" market power and to urge the intervention of the state to facilitate the growth of countervailing power where that has not sprung up autonomously. These acknowledgments, although they make the concept of countervailing power something less than a perfect replacement for the interpretation of capitalism based upon "the competitive model," serve the eminently useful purpose of exposing more clearly than ever the points at which the most important choices of public policy need to be made.

AMERICAN CAPITALISM: THE CONCEPT OF COUNTERVAILING POWER [II]

CHAPTER IX: THE THEORY OF COUNTERVAILING POWER

II

. . . In the competitive model—the economy of many sellers each with a small share of the total market—the restraint on the private exercise of economic power was provided by other firms on the same side of the market. It was the eagerness of competitors to sell, not the complaints of buyers, that saved the latter from spoliation. It was assumed, no doubt accurately, that the nineteenth-century textile manufacturer who overcharged for his product would promptly lose his market to another manufacturer who did not. If all manufacturers found themselves in a position where they could exploit a strong demand, and mark up their prices accordingly, there would soon be an inflow of new competitors. The resulting increase in supply would bring prices and profits back to normal.

As with the seller who was tempted to use his economic power against the customer, so with the buyer who was tempted to use it against his labor or suppliers. The man who paid less than prevailing wage would lose his labor force to those who paid the worker his full (marginal) contribution to earnings. In all cases the incentive to socially desirable behavior was provided by the competitor. It was to the same side of the market and thus to competition that economists came to look for the self-regulatory mechanism of the economy.

This selection has been reprinted from J. K. Galbraith, *American Capitalism: The Concept of Countervailing Power* (pp. 117–138, 141–157, Copyright 1952 by John Kenneth Galbraith) by permission of the Houghton Mifflin Company, Boston, publisher.

They also came to look to competition exclusively and in formal theory still do. The notion that there might be another regulatory mechanism in the economy has been almost completely excluded from economic thought. Thus with the widespread disappearance of competition in its classical form and its replacement by the small group of firms if not in overt, at least in conventional or tacit collusion, it was easy to suppose that since competition had disappeared, all effective restraint on private power had disappeared. Indeed this conclusion was all but inevitable if no search was made for other restraints and so complete was the preoccupation with competition that none was made.

In fact, new restraints on private power did appear to replace competition. They were nurtured by the same process of concentration which impaired or destroyed competition. But they appeared not on the same side of the market but on the opposite side, not with competitors but with customers or suppliers. It will be convenient to have a name for this counterpart of competition and I shall call it *countervailing power*.

To begin with a broad and somewhat too dogmatically stated proposition, private economic power is held in check by the countervailing power of those who are subject to it. The first begets the second. The long trend toward concentration of industrial enterprise in the hands of a relatively few firms has brought into existence not only strong sellers, as economists have supposed, but also strong buyers, as they have failed to see. The two develop together, not in precise step but in such manner that there can be no doubt that the one is in response to the other.

The fact that a seller enjoys a measure of monopoly power, and is reaping a measure of monopoly return as a result, means that there is an inducement to those firms from whom he buys or those to whom he sells to develop the power with which they can defend themselves against exploitation. It means also that there is a reward to them, in the form of a share of the gains of their opponents' market power, if they are able to do so. In this way the existence of market power creates an incentive to the organization of another position of power that neutralizes it.

The contention I am here making is a formidable one. It comes to this: Competition which, at least since the time of Adam Smith, has been viewed as the autonomous regulator of economic activity and as the only available regulatory mechanism apart from the state, has, in fact, been superseded. Not entirely, to be sure. There are still important markets where the power of the firm as (say) a seller is checked or circumscribed by those who provide a similar or a substitute product or service. This, in the broadest sense that can be meaningful, is the meaning of competition. The role of the buyer on the other side of such markets is essentially a passive one. It consists in looking for, perhaps asking for, and responding to the best bargain. The active restraint is provided by the competitor who offers, or threatens to offer, a better bargain. By contrast, in the typical modern market of few sellers, the active restraint is provided not by competitors but from the other side of the market by strong buyers. Given the convention against price competition, it is the role of the competitor that becomes passive.

It was always one of the basic presuppositions of competition that market power exercised in its absence would invite the competitors who would eliminate such exercise of power. In other words competition was regarded as a *self-generating* regulatory force. The doubt whether this was in fact so after a market had been pre-empted by a few large sellers, after entry of new firms had become difficult and after existing firms had accepted a convention against price competition, was what destroyed the faith in competition as a regulatory mechanism. Countervailing power is also a self-generating force and this is a matter of great importance. Something, although not very much, could be claimed for the regulatory role of the strong buyer in relation to the market power of sellers, did it happen that, as an accident of economic development, such strong buyers were frequently juxtaposed to strong sellers. However it is far more important that, as with the ancient presupposition concerning competition, the regulatory role of the strong buyer, in relation to the market power of the strong seller, is also self-generating. As noted, power on one side of a market creates both the need for, and the prospect of reward to, the exercise of countervailing power from the other side. In the market of small numbers, the self-generating power of competition is a chimera. That of countervailing power, by contrast, is readily assimilated to the common sense of the situation and its existence, once we have learned to look for it, is readily subject to empirical verification.

Market power can be exercised by strong buyers against weak sellers as well as by strong sellers against weak buyers. In the competitive model, competition acted as a restraint on both kinds of exercise of power. This is also the case with countervailing power. In turning to its practical manifestations, it will be convenient, in fact, to begin with a case where it is exercised by weak sellers against strong buyers.

III

The operation of countervailing power is to be seen with the greatest clarity in the labor market where it is also most fully developed. Because of his comparative immobility, the worker has long been highly vulnerable to private economic power. The customer of any particular steel mill, at the turn of the century, could always take himself elsewhere if he felt he was being overcharged. Or he could exercise his sovereign privilege of not buying steel at all. The worker had no comparable freedom if he felt he was being underpaid. Normally he could not move and he had to have work. Not often has the power of one man over another been used more callously than in the American labor market after the rise of the large corporation. As late as the early twenties, the steel industry worked a twelve-hour day and seventy-two-hour week with an incredible twenty-four-hour stint every fortnight when the shift changed.

No such power is exercised today and for the reason that its earlier exercise stimulated the counteraction that brought it to an end. In the ultimate sense it was the power of the steel industry, not the organizing abilities of John L. Lewis and Philip Murray, that brought the United Steel Workers into being. The economic power that the worker faced in the sale of his labor—the competition of many sellers dealing with few buyers—made it necessary that he organize for his own protection. There were rewards to the power of the steel companies in which, when he had successfully developed countervailing power, he could share.

As a general though not invariable rule there are strong unions in the United States only where markets are served by strong corporations. And it is not an accident that the large automobile, steel, electrical, rubber, farm-machinery and non-ferrous metal-mining and smelting companies all bargain with powerful CIO unions. Not only has the strength of the corporations in these industries made it necessary for workers to develop the protection of countervailing power, it has provided unions with the opportunity for getting something more as well. If successful they could share in the fruits of the corporation's market power. By contrast there is not a single union of any consequence in American agriculture, the country's closest approach to the competitive model. The reason lies not in the difficulties in organization; these are considerable, but greater difficulties in organization have been overcome. The reason is that the farmer has not possessed any power over his labor force, and at least until recent times has not had any rewards from market power, which it was worth the while of a union to seek. As an interesting verification of the point, in the Great Valley of California, the large farmers of that area have had considerable power vis-à-vis their labor force. Almost uniquely in the United States, that region has been marked by persistent attempts at organization by farm workers.

The other industries which are not marked by any high degree of concentration, and accordingly are not especially powerful in their labor market, do not normally have strong unions. The textile industry, boot and shoe manufacture, lumbering and other forest industries in most parts of the country, and smaller wholesale and retail enterprises, are all cases in point. I do not advance the theory of countervailing power as a monolithic explanation of trade-union organization; in the case of bituminous-coal mining and the clothing industry, for example, the unions have emerged as a supplement to the weak market position of the operators and manufacturers. They have assumed price- and market-regulating functions that are the normal functions of management. Nevertheless, as an explanation of the incidence of trade-union strength in the American economy, the theory of countervailing power clearly fits the broad contours of experience.

IV

The labor market serves admirably to illustrate the incentives to the development of countervailing power and it is of great importance in this market. However, its development, in response to positions of market power, is pervasive in the economy. As a regulatory device one of its most important manifestations is in the relation of the large retailer to the firms from which it buys. The way in which countervailing power operates in these markets is worth examining in some detail.

One of the seemingly harmless simplifications of formal economic theory has been the assumption that producers of consumers' goods sell their products directly to consumers. All business units are held, for this reason, to have broadly parallel interests. Each buys labor and materials, combines them and passes them along to the public at prices that, in some sense, maximize returns. Were this in fact the case, the lot of the consumer would be an unhappy one.

In practice, goods pass to retailers whose interests, normally, are at sharp variance with those of their suppliers. The typical retailer is deeply concerned with his volume of sales. This is uniquely important for minimizing inventory risk, it is a prime factor in the prestige of the concern, and, of course, it is one of the dimensions of profit. The convention that excludes cutthroat price competition—in the case of retailers the cutting of gross margins—is observed by retailers as by other firms. Nonetheless, lower prices—a low level in general as well as low prices in relation to those of other firms—are regarded by one whole class of retailers as the major device for obtaining and maintaining volume. It is in their interest accordingly to resist any exercise of market power by their suppliers that results in higher prices. More important, any power retailers can exercise to reduce their suppliers' prices will redound to their benefit. It will enable them to use price as an inducement without breaking the convention against destructive cutting of their own margins.

Such an opportunity exists only when their suppliers are enjoying something that can be taken away, i.e., when they are enjoying the fruits of market power from which they can be separated. Thus, in precise parallel with the labor market, we find the retailer with both a protective and profit incentive to develop countervailing power whenever his supplier is in possession of market power. The practical manifestation of this, over the last half-century, has been the spectacular rise of the food chains, the variety chains, the mail-order houses (now graduated into chain stores), the department-store chains, and the co-operative buying organizations of the surviving independent department and food stores.

This development has been the countervailing response to previously established positions of power. The gains from invading these positions have been considerable. The rubber tire industry is a fairly commonplace example of oligopoly. Four large firms are dominant in the market. In the thirties, Sears, Roebuck & Co. was able, by exploiting its role as a large and indispensable customer, to procure tires from Goodyear Tire & Rubber Company at a price from twenty-nine to forty per cent lower than the going market. These it resold to thrifty motorists for from a fifth to a quarter less than the same tires carrying the regular Goodyear brand.

One consequence of the failure of the government to recognize the role of countervailing power is that many hundreds of pages of court records have detailed the exercise of this power by the Great Atlantic & Pacific Tea Company. There is little doubt that this firm has used the countervailing power it has developed with considerable artistry. In 1937, a survey by the company indicated that, for an investment of $175,000, it could supply itself with corn flakes. Assuming that it charged itself the price it then was paying to one of the three companies manufacturing this delicacy, it could earn a modest sixty-eight per cent on the outlay. Armed with this information, and the threat to go into the business which its power could readily make effective, it had no difficulty in bringing down the price by approximately ten per cent. Such gains from the exercise of countervailing power, it will be clear, could only occur where there is an exercise of original market power with which to contend. The A & P could have reaped no comparable gains in buying staple products from the farmer. Committed as he is to the competition of the competitive model, the farmer has no gain to surrender. Provided, as he is, with the opportunity of selling all he produces at the impersonally determined market price, he has not the slightest incentive to make a special price to A & P beyond that which might be associated with the simple economies of bulk sale.

The examples of the exercise of countervailing power by Sears, Roebuck and A & P just cited show how this power is deployed in its most dramatic form. The day-to-day exercise of the buyer's power is a good deal less spectacular but also a good deal more significant. At the end of virtually every channel by which consumers' goods reach the public there is, in practice, a layer of powerful buyers. In the food market there are the great food chains; in clothing there are the department stores, the chain department stores and the department store buying organizations; in appliances there are Sears, Roebuck, and Montgomery Ward and the department stores; these latter firms are also important outlets for furniture and other house furnishings; the drug and cosmetic manufacturer has to seek part of his market through the large drug chains and the department stores; a vast miscellany of consumers' goods pass to the public through Woolworth's, Kresge's and the other variety chains. In all of these cases buyers deal directly with the manufacturer and there are few of the latter who, in setting prices, do not have to reckon with the attitude and reaction of their powerful customers. The retail buyers have a variety of weapons at their disposal to use against the market power of their suppliers. Their ultimate sanction is to develop their own source of supply as the food chains, Sears, Roebuck, and Montgomery Ward have extensively done. They can also concentrate their entire patronage on a single supplier and, in return for a lower price, give him security in his volume and relieve him of selling and advertising costs.

The more commonplace but more important exercise of countervailing power consists, merely, in keeping the seller in a state of uncertainty as to the intentions of a buyer who is indispensable to him. The larger of the retail buying organizations place orders around which the production schedules and occasionally the investment of even the largest manufacturers become organized. A shift in this custom imposes prompt and heavy loss. The threat or even the fear of this sanction is enough to cause the supplier to surrender some or all of the rewards of his market power. He must, frequently, make a more conditional surrender to less potent buyers if he is not to be more than ever in the power of his large customers. It will be clear that in this operation there are rare opportunities for playing one supplier off against another.

A measure of the importance which large retailing organizations attach to the deployment of their countervailing power is the prestige they accord to their buyers. These men (and women) are the key employees of the modern large retail organization; they are highly paid and they are among the most intelligent and resourceful people to be found anywhere in business. In the everyday course of business, they are considerably better known, both for their capacities and their power, than the salesmen from whom they buy.

There are producers of consumers' goods who have secured themselves from exercise of countervailing power. Some, like the automobile and the oil industry, have done so either by integrating their distribution through to the consumer or because they have an organization of small and dependent and therefore fairly powerless dealers. It seems probable that in a few industries, tobacco manufacture for example, the members are strong enough and have sufficient solidarity to withstand any pressure applied to them even by the most powerful buyer. However, even the tobacco manufacturers, under conditions that were especially favorable to the exercise of countervailing power in the thirties, were forced to make liberal price concessions, in the form of advertising allowances, to the A & P and possibly also to other large customers. When the comprehensive representation of large retailers in the various fields of consumers' goods distribution is considered, it is reasonable to conclude—the reader is warned that this is an important generalization—that most positions of market power in the production of consumers' goods are covered by positions of countervailing power.

Countervailing power also manifests itself, although less visibly, in producers' goods markets. For many years the power of the automobile companies, as purchasers of steel, has sharply curbed the power of the steel mills as sellers. Detroit is the only city where the recently outlawed basing-point system was not used to price steel. Under the basing-point system, all producers regardless of location quoted the same price at any particular point of delivery. This minimized the opportunity of a strong buyer to play one seller off against the other. The large firms in the automobile industry had developed the countervailing power which enabled them to do precisely this. They were not disposed to tolerate any limitations on their exercise of such power. In explaining the quotation of "arbitrary prices" on Detroit steel, a leading student of the basing-point system has recently recognized, implicitly, the role of countervailing power by observing that "it is difficult to apply high cartel prices to particularly large and strong customers such as the automobile manufacturers in Detroit."

The more normal operation of countervailing power in producers' goods markets turns on the relatively small number of customers which firms in these industries typically have. Where the cigarette or soap manufacturer numbers his retail outlets by the hundreds of thousands and his final consumers by the millions, the machinery or equipment manufacturers counts his customers by the hundreds or thousands and, very often, his important ones by the dozen. The latter are important to the seller as individuals and are able to collect the rewards of that importance. As elsewhere, the market pays a premium to those who develop power as buyers that is equivalent to the market power of those from whom they buy. The reverse is true where weak sellers do business with strong buyers.

V

There is an old saying, or should be, that it is a wise economist who recognizes the scope of his own generalizations. While countervailing power is of decisive importance in regulating the exercise of private economic power, it is not universally effective. Some industries, because they are integrated through to the consumer or because their product passes through a dependent dealer organization, have not been faced with countervailing power. As noted, there are a few cases where a very strong market position has proven impregnable even against the attacks of strong buyers. And there are cases where the dangers from countervailing power have, apparently, been recognized and where it has been successfully resisted.

An example of successful resistance to countervailing power is the residential-building industry. No segment of American capitalism evokes less pride. Yet anyone approaching the industry with the preconceptions of competition in mind is unlikely to see, very accurately, the reasons for its shortcomings. There are many thousands of individual firms in the business of building houses. Nearly all are small—the capital of the typical housebuilder runs from a few hundred to a few thousand dollars. The members of the industry oppose little market power to the would-be house owner. Except in times of extremely high building activity there is aggressive competition for business.

The industry does show many detailed manifestations of guild restraint. Builders are frequently in alliance with each other, the unions, and local politicians to protect prices, wages and to maintain established building techniques. These derelictions have been seized upon avidly by the critics of the industry. Since they represent its major departure from the competitive model, they have been assumed to be the cause of the poor performance of the housing industry.

Unhappily, were the restraints on contract prices, materials and techniques in the industry swept away, it seems improbable that the prices of new houses would be much changed and the satisfaction of customers with what they get for what they pay much enhanced. The reason is that the typical builder would still be a small and powerless figure contending with unions that are far stronger than he and buying his building materials in small quantities at high cost from suppliers with effective market power. It is these factors which, very largely, determine the cost of the house.

The builder is kept without power. With few exceptions, the manufacturers of building supplies decline to sell direct to the builder. This prevents any one of the latter from bringing pressure to bear on his source of supply; at the same time it helps keep all builders relatively small and powerless by uniformly denying them the economies of direct purchase. All must pay jobbers' and retailers' margins. A few builders—a spectacular case is Levitt & Sons of Long Island—have managed to circumvent this ban. As the result of more effective buying, a much stronger position in dealing with labor, and the savings from large-scale production of houses, they have notably increased the satisfaction of customers with what they receive for their money. Few can doubt that the future of the industry, if its future is to improve on its past, lies with such firms.

Thus it is the notion of countervailing power, not of competition, which points the way to progress in the housing industry. What is needed is fewer firms of far greater scale with resulting capacity to bring power to bear upon unions and suppliers. It is the absence of such firms, and of the resulting economies, which helps explain why one sector of this industry—low-cost housing where cost is especially important in relation to ability-to-pay—has passed under government management. In the absence of an effective regulating mechanism within the industry in the form of countervailing power, private entrepreneurship has been superseded.

VI

The development of countervailing power requires a certain minimum opportunity and capacity for organization, corporate or otherwise. If the large retail buying organizations had not developed the countervailing power which they have used, by proxy, on behalf of the individual consumer, consumers would have been faced with the need to organize the equivalent of the retailers' power. This would be a formidable task but it has been accomplished in Scandinavia and, in lesser measure, in England where the consumers' cooperative, instead of the chain store, is the dominant instrument of countervailing power in consumers' goods markets. Quite probably there could have been similar organizations in the United States. The fact that there are no consumer co-operatives of any importance in the United States is to be explained, not by any inherent incapacity of the American for such organization, but because the chain stores pre-empted the gains of countervailing power first. The counterpart of the Swedish Kooperative Forbundet or the British Co-operative Wholesale Societies has not appeared in the United States simply because it could not compete with the A & P and the other large food chains. The meaning of this, which incidentally has been lost on devotees of the theology of co-operation, is that the chain stores are approximately as efficient in the exercise of countervailing power as a co-operative would be. In parts of the American economy where proprietary mass buyers have not made their appearance, notably in the purchase of farm supplies, individuals (who are also individualists) have shown as much capacity to organize as the Scandinavians and the British and have similarly obtained the protection and rewards of countervailing power. The Grange League Federation, the Eastern States Farmers' Exchange and the Illinois Farm Supply Company, co-operatives with annual sales running to multi-million-dollar figures, are among the illustrations of the point.

However, it must not be assumed that it is easy for great numbers of individuals to coalesce and organize countervailing power. In less developed communities, Puerto Rico for example, one finds people fully exposed to the exactions of strategically situated importers, merchants and wholesalers and without the apparent capacity to develop countervailing power in their own behalf. (Anyone, incidentally, who doubts the force of the countervailing power exercised by large retailer-buying organizations would do well to consider the revolution which the entry of the large chain stores would work in an economy like that of Puerto Rico and also how such an intrusion would be resented and perhaps resisted by importers and merchants now able to exercise their market power with impunity against the thousands of small, independent and inefficient retailers who are their present outlets.)

In light of the difficulty in organizing countervailing power, it is not surprising that the assistance of government has repeatedly been sought in this task. Without the phenomenon itself being fully recognized, the provision of state assistance to the development of countervailing power has become a major function of government—perhaps *the* major domestic function of government. Much of the domestic legislation of the last twenty years, that of the New Deal episode in particular, only becomes fully comprehensible when it is viewed in this light. . . .

VII

I come now to the major limitation on the operation of countervailing power—a matter of much importance in our time. Countervailing power is not exercised uniformly under all conditions of demand. It does not function at all as a restraint on market power when there is inflation or inflationary pressure on markets.

Because the competitive model, in association with Say's Law, was assumed to find its equilibrium at or near full employment levels, economists for a long time were little inclined to inquire whether markets in general, or competition in particular, might behave differently at different levels of economic activity, i.e., whether they might behave differently in prosperity and depression. In any case the conventional division of labor in economics has assigned to one group of scholars the tasks of examining markets and competitive behavior, to another a consideration of the causes of fluctuations in the economy. The two fields of exploration are even today separated by watertight bulkheads, or, more accurately, by professorial division of labor and course requirements. Those who have taught and written on market behavior have assumed a condition of general stability in the economy in which sellers were eager for buyers. To the extent, as in recent years, that they have had to do their teaching or thinking in a time of inflation—in a time when, as the result of strong demand, eager buyers were besieging reluctant sellers—they have dismissed the circumstance as abnormal. They have drawn their classroom and textbook illustrations from the last period of deflation, severe or mild.

So long as competition was assumed to be the basic regulatory force in the economy these simplifications, although they led to some error, were not too serious. There is a broad continuity in competitive behavior from conditions of weak to conditions of strong demand. At any given moment there is a going price in competitive markets that reflects the current equilibrium of supply-and-demand relationships. Even though demand is strong and prices are high and rising, the seller who prices above the going or equilibrium level is punished by the loss of his customers. The buyer still has an incentive to look for the lowest price he can find. Thus market behavior is not fundamentally different from what it is when demand is low and prices are falling.

There are, by contrast, differences of considerable importance in market behavior between conditions of insufficient and excessive demand when there is oligopoly, i.e., when the market has only a small number of sellers. The convention against price competition, when small numbers of sellers share a market, is obviously not very difficult to maintain if all can sell all they produce and none is subject to the temptation to cut prices. Such a device for maintaining the convention against price competition as the basing-point system only has significance when demand is insufficient in relation to capacity. The basing-point system by making known, or easily calculable, the approved prices at every possible point of delivery in the country provided protection against accidental or surreptitious price-cutting. Such protection is not necessary when there is no temptation to cut prices. By an interesting paradox when the basing-point system was attacked by the government in the late depression years it was of great consequence to the steel, cement and other industries that employed it. When, after the deliberate processes of the law, the system was finally abolished by the courts in April 1948, the consequences for the industries in question were rather slight. The steel and cement companies were then straining to meet demand that was in excess of their capacity. They were under no temptation to cut prices and thus had no *current* reason to regret the passing of the basing-point system.

These differences in market behavior under conditions of strong and of weak demand are important and there are grounds for criticizing their neglect—or rather the assumption that there is normally a shortage of buyers—in the conventional market analysis. However, the effect of changes in demand on market behavior becomes of really profound importance only when the role of countervailing power is recognized. Countervailing power, as a restraint on market power, *only* operates when there is a relative scarcity of demand. Only then is the buyer important to the seller and this is an obvious prerequisite for his bringing his power to bear on the market power of the seller. If buyers are plentiful, that is, if supply is small in relation to current demand, the seller is under no compulsion to surrender to the bargaining power of any customer. The countervailing power of the buyer, however great, disappears with an excess of demand. With it goes the regulatory or restraining role of countervailing power in general. Indeed, the best hope of the buyer, under conditions of excess demand, may be to form a coalition with the seller to bring about an agreed division of returns.

Following the useful practice of testing theory against experience, it is worth noting that it was the twenties and the thirties which were the periods of great growth of chain and group buying enterprises. In sharp contrast with most other types of business, the early depression years especially were favorable to the great chain stores. These were years when demand, generally, fell short of the capacity of suppliers to meet it. Thus they were favorable to the exercise of countervailing power. The intensity of the trade agitation against the mass retailers, culminating in 1936 in the passage of the Robinson-Patman Act (designed as we shall see presently to limit their exercise of this power), was itself a measure of the chain's advantage in this period. By contrast, during the years of strong demand and short supply during World War II, the chain stores lost ground, relatively, to independents. As this strong demand in relation to supply destroyed their capacity to exercise countervailing power, their advantage disappeared. It is interesting to note that the trade agitation and resentment against the chains almost completely disappeared during the war and postwar years.

However, it is again in the labor market where the change in the pattern of exercise of countervailing power that accompanies changes in demand can be seen with greatest clarity. Here also it has the most portentous consequences. In industries where strong firms bargain with strong unions, the management of the former has what has come to be considered a normal resistance to wage increases when demand is not pressing upon capacity. To yield is to increase unit costs. The firm cannot with impunity pass along these higher costs to its customers. There may be a question as to whether other firms in the industry will follow suit; there will always be a question of the effect of the higher prices on sales. If the demand for the products is in any measure elastic the consequence of the higher prices will be a loss of volume. This, with its effect on employment in the industry, is something of which modern union leadership, as well as management, is usually conscious. Thus the trial of strength between union and management associated with collective bargaining is, essentially, over the division of profits. When demand is limited, we have, in other words, an essentially healthy manifestation of countervailing power. The union opposes its power as a seller of labor to that of management as a buyer: At stake is the division of the returns. An occasional strike is an indication that countervailing power is being employed in a sound context where the costs of any wage increase cannot readily be passed along to someone else. It should be an occasion for mild rejoicing in the conservative press. The *Daily Worker,* eagerly contemplating the downfall of capitalism, should regret this manifestation of the continued health of the system.

Under conditions of strong demand, however, collective bargaining takes on a radically different form. Then management is no longer constrained to resist union demands on the grounds that higher prices will be reflected in shrinking volume. There is now an adequate supply of eager buyers. The firm that first surrenders to the union need not worry lest it be either the first or the only one to increase prices. There are buyers for all. No one has occasion, as the result of price increases, to worry about a general shrinkage in volume. A strong demand means an inelastic demand. On the other hand, there are grave disadvantages for management in resisting the union. Since profits are not at stake, any time lost as the result of a strike is a dead loss. Worker morale and the actual loss of part of the working force to employers who offer better wages must be reckoned with. Thus when demand is sufficiently strong to press upon the capacity of industry generally to supply it, there is no real conflict of interest between union and employer. It is to their mutual advantage to effect a coalition and to pass the costs of their agreement along in higher prices. Other buyers along the line, who under other circumstances might have exercised their countervailing power against the price increases, are similarly inhibited. Thus under inflationary pressure of demand, the whole structure of countervailing power in the economy dissolves. . . .

CHAPTER X: COUNTERVAILING POWER AND THE STATE

I

In their relations with government, the American people have long shown a considerable ability to temper doctrine by pragmatism. The ruggedly conservative businessman who excoriates Statism, the Welfare State and the State Department, does not allow his convictions to interfere with an application to the RFC if he really needs the money. The impeccably conservative business journal which editorially condemns Keynesians and deficit spending as heralds of disaster does not fail to point out on the financial page that the effect of the new budget, which it so deplores, will be favorable to business volume and earnings. The up-country cotton or tobacco planter whose belief in States' rights is unequaled except by his mistrust of civil rights votes, nonetheless [shows enthusiasm] for federally administered marketing quotas, a remarkably comprehensive form of agricultural regimentation.

Since the phenomenon of countervailing power is of great practical importance, even though it has gone unrecognized in economic or political theory, we should expect, in line with our highly pragmatic approach to government, that it would have been the object of a good deal of legislation and the subject of a good deal of government policy. As . . . has [been] made clear, there are strong incentives in the modern economy for developing countervailing power. Moreover, the group that seeks countervailing power is, initially, a numerous and disadvantaged group which seeks organization because it faces, in its market, a much smaller and much more advantaged group. This situation is well calculated to excite public sympathy and, because there are numerous votes involved, to recruit political support.

In fact, the support of countervailing power has become in the last two decades perhaps the major peacetime function of the federal government. Labor has sought and received it in the protection and assistance which the Wagner Act provided to union organization. Farmers sought and received it in the form of federal price supports to their markets—a direct subsidy of market power. Unorganized workers have sought and received it in the form of minimum wage legislation. The bituminous-coal mines sought and received it in the Bituminous Coal Conservation Act of 1935 and the National Bituminous Coal Act of 1937. In a considerably more tenuous sense, investors have received it, via the Securities and Exchange Commission, in support of their position vis-à-vis the management or control of the large corporation. These measures, all designed to give a group a market power it did not have before, were among the most important legislative acts of the New Deal.

There should be no problem as to why this legislation, and the administration that sponsored it, were keenly controversial. The groups that sought the assistance of government in building countervailing power sought that power in order to use it against market authority to which they had previously been subordinate. Those whose power was thereby inhibited could hardly be expected to welcome this development or the intervention of the government to abet it.

Because the nature of countervailing power has not been firmly grasped, the government's role in relation to it has not only been imperfectly understood but also imperfectly played. One is permitted to hope that a better understanding of countervailing power will contribute to better administration in the future.

II

The role of countervailing power in the economy marks out two broad problems in policy for the government. In all but conditions of inflationary demand, countervailing power performs a valuable—indeed an indispensable—regulatory function in the modern economy. Accordingly it is incumbent upon government to give it freedom to develop and to determine how it may best do so. The government also faces the question of where and how it will affirmatively support the development of countervailing power. It will be convenient to look first at the negative role of the government in allowing the development of countervailing power and then to consider its affirmative role in promoting it.

At the outset a somewhat general distinction . . . must be made between countervailing and original power. When, anywhere in the course of producing, processing or distributing a particular product, one or a few firms first succeed in establishing a strong market position they may be considered to be the possessors of original market power. They are able, as the result of their power over the prices they pay or charge, to obtain more than normal margins and profits. These are at the expense of the weaker suppliers or customers. This is the monopoly position anciently feared by liberals and as anciently condemned by economists. Their instincts were sound. Countervailing power invades such positions of strength, whether they be held by suppliers or customers, and obtains a share in the rewards.

The rule to be followed by government is, in principle, a clear one. There can be very good reason for attacking positions of original market power in the economy if these are not effectively offset by countervailing power. There is at least a theoretical justification for opposing all positions of market power. There is no justification for attacking positions of countervailing power which leaves positions of original market power untouched. On the contrary, damage both in equity and to the operation of the economy will be the normal consequence of doing so.

The problems of practical application of such a rule are mostly in the field of the antitrust laws and they are a good deal more difficult than the simple articulation of the rule implies. However a general distinction between original and countervailing power is, in fact, now made in the antitrust laws —it has been forced, against the accepted current of ideas concerning competition, by the practical reality of the phenomenon itself.

In the first development of positions of market power, a long lead was assumed by industrial corporations. Thus, when workers and farmers sought to develop strength in the sale of their labor power and products, they did so in markets where industrial firms had already achieved positions of original power. It would be broadly in harmony with the distinction between original and countervailing power to exclude labor and farm organizations from prosecution under the antitrust laws. This has been done. While the Sherman Act made no mention of labor, Congress did not have in mind the still modest efforts of unions to lift their bargaining power when it enacted the legislation in 1890. Subsequently, unions became subject to the law by judicial interpretation. Indeed, in the first few decades that the legislation was in effect, unions were a primary target. This led to their exclusion by name in the Clayton Act of 1914. After the Supreme Court had somewhat obdurately reincluded them in 1921 (Justices Brandeis, Holmes and Clarke dissenting) they were again and finally excluded by the Norris-LaGuardia Act of 1932 and by the subsequent and more benign decisions of a New Deal Court.

Similarly, efforts by farm co-operatives to enhance the market power of the farmer, so long as they are held within reason, are excluded by the Clayton Act of 1914, by further legislation (the Capper-Volsted Act) in 1922 and in more specific instances by the Agricultural Marketing Agreement Act of 1937. Congress has thus recognized, implicitly, that the efforts of labor and agriculture to develop market power were different from those of industrial firms. The difference—the only plausible difference—was that these efforts were the response of workers and farmers to the power of those to whom they sold their labor or products.

A more precise and conscious use of the distinction between original and countervailing power would take account of the fact that some trade unions and some farm groups are clearly the possessors of original power. Thus workers in the building trades, although they are not highly organized or exceptionally powerful in any absolute sense, are strong in relation to the small-scale employers with whom they do business. They are clearly the possessors of original market power. The special nature of their power, as compared with that of the trade-union movement generally, explains the distress of men and women who have reacted sympathetically to the role of unions in general but who, in this case, have found themselves on the side of organizations that have plenary power to restrict output and enhance their own income. The obvious solution lies in the distinction between original and countervailing power. This, logically, would make restrictive practices of master plumbers or plasterers a proper object of interest by the Department of Justice while the absolutely (though not relatively) far more powerful unions in steel or automobiles who impose no similar restrictions on the supply of their labor would not be.

Similarly, there are undoubted cases of exercise of original power by groups of agricultural producers. The immunity granted by existing law is not complete—the Secretary of Agriculture is authorized to enter a complaint if, as result of the activities of the co-operative, prices are "unduly enhanced," and a co-operative cannot merge its power with non-agricultural corporations. As a result there have been a scattering of prosecutions of farmers' organizations —of the California Fruit Growers' Exchange (Sunkist Oranges) and of a

Chicago milkshed producers' organization in combination with distributors, unions and even a college professor. But such cases have been infrequent.

However, the more serious consequences of the failure to perceive the role of countervailing power have been within the fabric of industry itself. The antitrust laws have been indiscriminately invoked against firms that have succeeded in building countervailing power, while holders of original market power, against whom the countervailing power was developed, have gone unchallenged. Such action has placed the authority of law on the side of positions of monopoly power and against the interests of the public at large. The effects have been damaging to the economy and also to the prestige of the antitrust laws.

. . . One of the most important instruments for exercise of countervailing power is the large retail organization. These are the public's main line of defense against the market power of those who produce or process consumers' goods. They are an American counterpart—and without doubt an effective one—of the consumer co-operatives which, in other countries, are viewed as an instrument for countering the power of the cartels. Yet the position of the large retail organizations has been not only a general, but also in some measure a unique object of government attack. Chain stores and other large buyers have been frequent recent objects of Sherman Act prosecution and are the special target of the Robinson-Patman Act which is especially designed to inhibit their exercise of countervailing power.

Under the provisions of the Robinson-Patman Act a chain store may receive the benefit of the demonstrably lower costs of filling the large orders which it places; it may not receive concessions that are the result of its superior bargaining power. The effect, since these concessions are important only when won from positions of original economic power, is to discriminate in favor of original power and against countervailing power.

The effects of failure to distinguish between original and countervailing power have been especially noteworthy in the several suits against the Great Atlantic and Pacific Tea Company. This company was prosecuted before the war for violation of the Robinson-Patman Act, was convicted of violation of the Sherman Act in a case brought in 1944 and finally decided in 1949 and is defendant in a further action now before the courts. In spite of its many legal misadventures, the company has not been charged with, or even seriously suspected of, exploiting the consumer. On the contrary, its crime has been too vigorous bargaining, which bargaining was, effectively, on the consumer's behalf. In the case brought in 1944 it was charged with seeking to increase its volume by reducing its margins and with bringing its bargaining power too vigorously to bear upon its suppliers in order to get price reductions. These suppliers—which included such powerful sellers as the large canning companies—had long been involved in a trial of strength with A & P over prices. They were left undisturbed. The government was in the highly equivocal position of prosecuting activities which have the effect of keeping down prices to the consumer. The positions of market power, which had given A & P its opportunity, were left untouched.

The litigation against A & P has been strongly defended. Although the firm does rather less than ten per cent of the food-retailing business, has strong rivals, and is in an industry where the entry of new firms is singularly easy, much stress has been laid on the danger that it might achieve an effective monopoly of food-retailing. Nevertheless one can hardly doubt that these cases have been a source of serious embarrassment to friends of the antitrust laws. No explanation, however elaborate, can quite conceal the fact that the effect of antitrust enforcement, in this case, is to the disadvantage of the public. Viewed in light of the present analysis the reason becomes evident. The prosecution by inhibiting the exercise of countervailing power provides protection to the very positions of market power that are anathema to the defender of the antitrust laws.

No one should conclude, from the foregoing, that an exemption of countervailing power should now be written into the antitrust laws. A considerable gap has always separated useful economic concepts from applicable legal ones. However, a number of conclusions, with immediate bearing on the antitrust laws, do follow from this analysis. In the first place the mere possession and exercise of market power is not a useful criterion for antitrust action. The further and very practical question must be asked: Against whom and for what purposes is the power being exercised? Unless this question is asked and the answer makes clear that the public is the victim, the antitrust laws, by attacking countervailing power, can as well enhance as reduce monopoly power.

Secondly, it is clear that serious damage can be done to the economy by such legislation as the Robinson-Patman Act. This legislation is the culmination of a long and confused legal and legislative struggle dating from 1914 over what economists have come to call price discrimination. The ostensible motive of the legislation is to protect competition. The seller is prevented from giving a lower price to one customer than to another where the lower price cannot be justified by the economies associated with the particular sale and where the effect is "to injure, destroy, or prevent" competition either with the seller or between his customers. The practical effect, reinforced by recent court decisions, is to make any important price concessions to any large buyer of questionable legality.

Even those who are unwavering in their belief in competition have been inclined to doubt whether this legislation does much to protect competition. What is not doubtful at all is that the legislation strikes directly at the effective exercise of countervailing power. To achieve price discrimination—to use bargaining power to get a differentially lower price—is the very essence of the exercise of countervailing power. In trying, with questionable effect, to preserve one of the autonomous regulators of the economy the government is seriously impairing another.

Finally, the theory of countervailing power throws important light on the advantage of different numbers of firms in an industry and on the objectives of the antitrust laws in relation thereto. One of the effects of the new ideas on market theory . . . was to raise serious doubts whether an industry of small numbers was, in fact, socially preferable to a monopoly. Once firms had recognized their interdependence, it was believed that they would find a price, output and profit position not greatly different from that which would be achieved by a single firm. This made it doubtful whether it was worth while to prosecute a monopoly in order to create an oligopoly.

The high technical dynamic of the typical industry that is shared by a few firms will already have raised some questions about this conclusion. There is reason to suppose that such an industry will be more progressive than an industry controlled by one. Recognition of the role of countervailing power suggests a further clear advantage on the side of the oligopoly. One can hardly doubt that, in general, it will be much easier for countervailing power to break into a position of market strength maintained by an imperfect coalition of three, four or a dozen firms than into a position held by one firm. When there is more than one firm in a market there are opportunities for playing one off against another. Such opportunities abruptly disappear when the number is reduced to one.

Thus the theory of countervailing power comes to the defense of the antitrust laws at what has been a very vulnerable point. Efforts to prevent or to disperse single-firm control of an industry can be defended for the greater opening they provide for the exercise of countervailing power. Similar and equally good reasons exist for resisting mergers. Those who have always believed there was something uniquely evil about monopoly are at least partly redeemed by the theory of countervailing power.

III

It must surely be agreed that, during the present century, American economic and political life have gained in strength as the result of the improved position of workers and farmers—two previously disadvantaged groups. In contrast with the sullenness and anger of labor relations or the deep-seated sense of frustration and inferiority of Midwestern farmers of a scant fifty years ago, both groups have now a well-developed sense of confidence and equality. These attitudes have a solid foundation in material well-being. It would seem difficult for anyone to argue that the American economy or polity is anything but stronger as a result.

The government has played an important part in this development. Both farmers and workers have sought and received government assistance, either in the form of direct support to their market power or in support to organizations which in turn made market power possible. In short the government has subsidized, with its own power, the countervailing power of workers and farmers. . . . This assistance, clearly, explains some part of the self-confidence and well-being which these groups display today.

Yet few courses of policy have ever been undertaken more grudgingly and with a greater sense of guilt. One can scarcely imagine a government action which, on the record, has produced more beneficent results in practice in which less pride has been taken. Especially in the case of agriculture, all measures have, until recently, been characterized as "emergency" legislation. This is invariably our label for excusing to our consciences action which seems to be at once wise and unwise.

The reason for this sense of guilt is that the notion of a government subsidy of its power to groups seeking to develop countervailing power has never enjoyed a place in the accredited structure of American economic and political science. Accordingly the unfinished tasks of developing such power have never had a place on the reformer's calendar. The reformer, in fact, has almost invariably been overtaken by the action. When the groups in question have developed enough influence to obtain government assistance on their own behalf they have simply gone ahead and got it without blessing or benefit of doctrine.

What has strengthened the American economy so admirably in the past must be presumed to have an unexploited potential for good in the future. There are still some millions of Americans who are without any organized expression of market power and whose standards of living and welfare are categorical evidence of the consequences. These include, for example, the 2.3

million hired farm workers, the truly forgotten men of American life. They have no security in their employment—there are few that cannot be fired on a day's notice. They do not have unemployment insurance; they are normally unprotected by workmen's compensation in what is a fairly hazardous occupation; many do not have a fixed place of abode; their pay, even in times when there is a strong demand for their services, is far from handsome. A share in the gains from the newly developed market power of the farmer has still to be transmitted to his hired man.

There are also the unorganized urban workers, those on the fringes of the labor movement and, perhaps most important of all, occupational categories which, in the past, have foresworn efforts to develop economic power. Schoolteachers, clerical workers, municipal employees and civil servants have generally avoided organization as something not quite genteel or because it was believed that employers and the community at large would recognize their importance and pay accordingly. In addition the natural leaders among white-collar workers have had, as ordinary workers do not, the clear alternative of obtaining promotion. A ten per cent increase in pay is not of great consequence to a high-school mathematics teacher if he is soon to become principal. This self-denying ordinance by white-collar workers where organization is concerned has invariably been viewed with approval, even as a manifestation of patriotism and sound Americanism, by public authorities and private employers.

Quite possibly the white-collar groups did not suffer too severely from their lack of market power in the years before World War II. In times of stable prices the salaried worker seeks an increase in pay only for the sake of increasing his real income. His weakness is not likely—as with the wage earner contending against pay cuts—to cost him ground. A skillful negotiator can do much for himself. However, in times of rising prices such as we now face and perhaps face for the future, market power will have to be exercised affirmatively if past positions are to be held. It seems to me quite probable—and since the end of the war there have already been indications of a trend—that the next group to seek to assert its market power will be the genteel white-collar class. In any case, we cannot assume that efforts by presently unorganized groups to seek market power, and to seek the assistance of government in their effort, is finished business.

In the actual sequence of events, some measure of organization by the groups themselves must precede any very important government subsidy to their developing market power. Not until farmers and workers achieved some organization on their own behalf were they able to get the state to reinforce their efforts. In the thirties the Farm Security Administration, an idealistic and imaginative effort to help subsistence and tenant farmers and farm workers, largely petered out because those aided lacked the organization to defend in Congress and before the public the efforts being made on their behalf. Support to countervailing power is not endowed, *ad hoc,* by government. It must be sought.

IV

At this point it becomes possible to answer, at least tentatively [one very important question]. . . . That is the meaning of the great expansion of state activity in recent decades—the expansion which conservatives have found so alarming and which many liberals have supported without knowing quite why. We can now see that a large part of the state's new activity—the AAA, the Wagner Act, minimum-wage legislation—is associated with the development of countervailing power. As such it is neither adventitious nor abnormal; the government action supports or supplements a normal economic process. Steps to strengthen countervailing power are not, in principle, different from steps to strengthen competition. Given the existence of private market power in the economy, the growth of countervailing power strengthens the capacity of the economy for autonomous self-regulation and thereby lessens the amount of over-all government control or planning that is required or sought.

Two or three further points may be made. Increasingly, in our time, we may expect domestic political differences to turn on the question of supporting or not supporting efforts to develop countervailing power. Liberalism will be identified with the buttressing of weak bargaining positions in the economy; conservatism—and this is its proper function—will be identified with the protection of positions of original power. There will be debate over whether weak positions have been unduly strengthened. The struggle over the Taft-Hartley Act is an example of the kind of political issue which countervailing power can be expected to develop. The essential question at issue in the Taft-Hartley controversy was whether, in the process of buttressing a weak bargaining position, the government had turned it into an unduly strong one. One is inclined to suppose that popular indignation with the current claims of some farm groups reflects the feeling that a bargaining position that was once unduly weak has now been made unduly strong.

On the whole, the appearance of countervailing power as a political issue cannot be considered especially unhealthy although it will almost certainly be so regarded. At first glance there is something odious about the notion that the poor and the excluded improve their lot in a democracy only by winning power. There is something even more odious about the suggestion that the state can usefully have a part in the process. But so far, at least, there has been less reason to regret than to approve the results of such a policy. The life of farmers and workers, the two great groups that have enjoyed the most obvious subsidy of power, has evidently been improved. It is hard to say that the community at large has suffered.

The concern over economic power is always less a matter of the way it is manifested than of how it *might* be employed. This is an area where anything that is novel has an unparalleled aspect of danger. A leading American industrialist warned in 1903 that:

> Organized labor knows but one law and that is the law of physical force—the law of the Huns and the Vandals, the law of the savage. . . . Composed as it is of the men of muscle rather than the men of intelligence, and commanded by leaders who are at heart disciples of revolution, it is not strange that organized labor stands for principles that are in direct conflict with the natural laws of economics.

Not even the professional alarmist would voice such views of the labor movement today. It is only in light of history that our fear of the countervailing power of weaker groups dissolves, that their effort to establish their power in the market emerges as the stuff of which economic progress consists. It is by our experience, not our fears, that we should be guided.

JOSEPH A. SCHUMPETER

JOSEPH A. SCHUMPETER was born in Triesch, Czechoslovakia, in 1883. He was educated in Vienna as a lawyer. Although he practiced that profession for a time, his real career began when he turned to the study of economics, becoming professor of economics in various Austrian universities. Coming to the United States, he received a Ph.D. degree from Columbia University in 1913. From 1919 to 1920, Schumpeter served as Austrian Minister of Finance and then became professor of economics at the University of Bonn, Germany. In 1932 he accepted the position of professor of economics at Harvard University, a post he occupied until his death in 1950. Professor Schumpeter contributed widely to scientific journals and wrote, among other works, *The Theory of Economic Development* (English edition, 1934) and *Business Cycles* (English edition, 1939). *Capitalism, Socialism, and Democracy,* from which the following selection has been taken, was first published in 1942.

Unlike Karl Marx and John Maynard Keynes (1883–1946), Schumpeter left no disciples. For Marxism and Keynesianism refer to programs as well as to theories, and Schumpeter had no visible program, nor have his provocative theories had any appreciable effect upon politics and policies. This is not surprising. For Schumpeter was a scholar of grand proportions who stood as a detached observer of what he regarded as the self-destruction of capitalism—a way of life he openly admired; yet he was calm and unruffled on the threshold of socialism—a system he admitted could also work, indeed in some ways better than the capitalism he preferred.

Much of contemporary economic thought revolves around the problem of proportioning freedom, welfare, and control in a dynamic rather than a static society. The problem of assuring full social justice in an expanding, risk-filled economy has occupied the attention of Marx and socialists of all schools; it commands the attention also of those who plan for welfare and full employment within a predominantly capitalist order. For Schumpeter, too, the central question was whether costly welfare programs—costly in the sense of capital expended publicly for welfare being diverted from private investment in expansion of production—of social security, with their attendant policies of progressive income and inheritance taxes and discretionary monetary and fiscal controls, are compatible, not merely with political freedom, but with the very economic progress of enterprise capitalism.

In Schumpeter's view, the network of social controls and agencies woven into the capitalist economy to satisfy political demands seeks to make possible broad participation in the humane values of civilized life. This he held to be not only commendable and desirable, but inevitable, since the electorates of modern democracies will find the objectives of social welfare irresistible. Such electorates have the right and the power to insist upon policies designed to secure full employment without recourse to war and imperialism, to equalize income distribution among the classes, to assure to increasing numbers the amenities of life once available only to the few. Contrary to the major current of Marx's thought, Schumpeter believed that all this was possible in political democracy, that the capitalist class would indeed submit, for these objectives not only appeal to the instincts of justice, but seem capable of preserving at least the core of capitalist civilization. But, he insisted, the price will in fact be the devitalization of that civilization. Its entrepreneurial spirit, already suffocating in the world of bureaucratically organized corporations, will be extinguished. Risk capital will cease to flow into the innovating processes upon which the expansion of capitalism depends. Technological innovation, already threatened by the high capital costs of new businesses, will pass into the hands of the state. The economy will cease to grow and the sources of economic wealth, upon which the social program itself depends, will dry up. In other words, Marx was wrong in stating that a program of social welfare could not be instituted over class opposition; but once instituted, that program will not preserve capitalism as the social reformers hope. The Marxist vision of decay is valid, but the diagnosis is wrong. Yet, according to Schumpeter, there is nothing obvious that can be done to reverse the tendencies of the times: the case for short-run stability and welfare is too tempting for the electorate to eschew, while the case for long-run economic growth is too complicated for the electorate to grasp. In either case, for Schumpeter, the five-hundred-year-old civilization of capitalism seems caught in a process of transition to a newer civilization the outlines of which he disliked but still scrutinized with equanimity.

CAPITALISM, SOCIALISM, AND DEMOCRACY

Part II: Can Capitalism Survive?

CHAPTER XI: THE CIVILIZATION OF CAPITALISM

Leaving the precincts of purely economic considerations, we . . . turn to the cultural complement of the capitalist economy—to its socio-psychological *superstructure,* if we wish to speak the Marxian language—and to the mentality that is characteristic of capitalist society and in particular of the bourgeois class. In desperate brevity, the salient facts may be conveyed as follows.

Fifty thousand years ago man confronted the dangers and opportunities of his environment in a way which some "prehistorians," sociologists and ethnologists agree was roughly equivalent to the attitude of modern primitives. Two elements of this attitude are particularly important for us: the "collective" and "affective" nature of the primitive mental process and, partly

This selection has been reprinted from Joseph A. Schumpeter, *Capitalism, Socialism, and Democracy* (3rd ed., pp. 121–130, 131–143, 156–163, Copyright 1942, 1947 by Joseph A. Schumpeter, Copyright 1950 by Harper & Brothers, New York) by permission of the publisher.

overlapping, the role of what, not quite correctly, I shall here call magic. By the first I designate the fact that in small and undifferentiated or not much differentiated social groups collective ideas impose themselves much more stringently on the individual mind than they do in big and complex groups; and that conclusions and decisions are arrived at by methods which for our purpose may be characterized by a negative criterion: the disregard of what we call logic and, in particular, of the rule that excludes contradiction. By the second I designate the use of a set of beliefs which are not indeed completely divorced from experience—no magic device can survive an unbroken sequence of failures—but which insert, into the sequence of observed phenomena, entities or influences derived from non-empirical sources. The similarity of this type of mental process with the mental processes of neurotics . . . [is to be noted]. But it does not follow that it is foreign to the mind of normal man of our own time. On the contrary, any discussion of political issues may convince the reader that a large and—for action—most important body of our own processes is of exactly the same nature.

Rational thought or behavior and a rationalistic civilization therefore do not imply absence of the criteria mentioned but only a slow though incessant widening of the sector of social life within which individuals or groups go about dealing with a given situation, first, by trying to make the best of it more or less—never wholly—according to their own lights; second, by doing so according to those rules of consistency which we call logic; and third, by doing so on assumptions which satisfy two conditions: that their number be a minimum and that every one of them be amenable to expression in terms of potential experience.

All this is very inadequate of course, but it suffices for our purpose. There is however one more point about the concept of rationalist civilizations that I will mention here for future reference. When the habit of rational analysis of, and rational behavior in, the daily tasks of life has gone far enough, it turns back upon the mass of collective ideas and criticizes and to some extent "rationalizes" them by way of such questions as why there should be kings and popes or subordination or tithes or property. . . .

Now the rational attitude presumably forced itself on the human mind primarily from economic necessity; it is the everyday economic task to which we as a race owe our elementary training in rational thought and behavior. . . . This is due to the inexorable definiteness and, in most cases, the quantitative character that distinguish the economic from other spheres of human action, perhaps also to the unemotional drabness of the unending rhythm of economic wants and satisfactions. Once hammered in, the rational habit spreads under the pedagogic influence of favorable experiences to the other spheres and there also opens eyes for that amazing thing, the Fact.

This process is independent of any particular garb, hence also of the capitalistic garb, of economic activity. So is the profit motive and self-interest. Pre-capitalist man is in fact no less "grabbing" than capitalist man. Peasant serfs for instance or warrior lords assert their self-interest with a brutal energy all their own. But capitalism develops rationality and adds a new edge to it in two interconnected ways.

First it exalts the monetary unit—not itself a creation of capitalism—into a unit of account. That is to say, capitalist practice turns the unit of money into a tool of rational cost-profit calculations, of which the towering monument is double entry bookkeeping. Without going into this, we will notice that, primarily a product of the evolution of economic rationality, the cost-profit calculus in turn reacts upon the rationality; by crystallizing and defining numerically, it powerfully propels the logic of enterprise. And thus defined and quantified for the economic sector, this type of logic or attitude or method then starts upon its conqueror's career subjugating—rationalizing—man's tools and philosophies, his medical practice, his picture of the cosmos, his outlook on life, everything in fact including his concepts of beauty and justice and his spiritual ambitions. . . .

Second, rising capitalism produced not only the mental attitude of modern science, the attitude that consists in asking certain questions and in going about answering them in a certain way, but also the men and the means. By breaking up the feudal environment and disturbing the intellectual peace of manor and village . . . but especially by creating the social space for a new class that stood upon individual achievement in the economic field, it in turn attracted to that field the strong wills and the strong intellects. Pre-capitalist economic life left no scope for achievement that would carry over class boundaries or, to put it differently, be adequate to create social positions comparable to those of the members of the then ruling classes. Not that it precluded ascent in general. But business activity was, broadly speaking, essentially subordinate, even at the peak of success within the craft guild, and it hardly ever led out of it. The main avenues to advancement and large gain were the church . . . to which we may add the chanceries of the great territorial magnates, and the hierarchy of warrior lords. . . . It was only when capitalist enterprise . . . unfolded its possibilities that supernormal ability and ambition began to turn to business as a third avenue. Success was quick and conspicuous . . . [and] fascinating enough for everyone excepting the highest strata of feudal society to draw most of the best brains and thus to generate further success—to generate additional steam for the rationalist engine. So, in this sense, capitalism—and not merely economic activity in general—has after all been the propelling force of the rationalization of human behavior. . . .

. . . Not only the modern mechanized plant and the volume of the output that pours forth from it, not only modern technology and economic organization, but all the features and achievements of modern civilization are, directly or indirectly, the products of the capitalist process. They must be included in any balance sheet of it and in any verdict about its deeds or misdeeds.

There is the growth of rational science and the long list of its applications. Airplanes, refrigerators, television and that sort of thing are immediately recognizable as results of the profit economy. But although the modern hospital is not as a rule operated for profit, it is nonetheless the product of capitalism not only, to repeat, because the capitalist process supplies the means and the will, but much more fundamentally because capitalist rationality supplied the habits of mind that evolved the methods used in these hospitals. And the victories, not yet completely won but in the offing, over cancer, syphilis and tuberculosis will be as much capitalist achievements as motorcars or pipe lines or Bessemer steel have been. In the case of medicine, there is a capitalist profession behind the methods, capitalist both because to a large extent it works in a business spirit and because it is an emulsion of the industrial and commercial bourgeoisie. But even if that were not so, modern medicine and hygiene would still be by-products of the capitalist process just as is modern education. . . .

There is . . . [also] all that may be grouped around the symbolic centerpiece of Gladstonian liberalism. The term Individualist Democracy would do just as well—better in fact because we want to cover some things that Gladstone would not have approved and a moral and spiritual attitude which, dwelling in the citadel of faith, he actually hated. At that I could leave this point if radical liturgy did not consist largely in picturesque denials of what I mean to convey. Radicals may insist that the masses are crying for salvation from intolerable sufferings and rattling their chains in darkness and despair, but of course there never was so much personal freedom of mind and body *for all,* never so much readiness to bear with and even to finance the mortal enemies of the leading class, never so much active sympathy with real and faked sufferings, never so much readiness to accept burdens, as there is in modern capitalist society; and whatever democracy there was, outside of peasant communities, developed historically in the wake of both modern and ancient capitalism. . . .

Two points in particular must be mentioned. . . . Social legislation or, more generally, institutional change for the benefit of the masses is not simply something which has been forced upon capitalist society by an ineluctable necessity to alleviate the ever-deepening misery of the poor. . . . Besides raising the standard of living of the masses by virtue of its automatic effects, the capitalist process also provided for that legislation the means "and the will." The words in quotes require further explanation that is to be found in the principle of spreading rationality. The capitalist process rationalizes behavior and ideas and by so doing chases from our minds, along with metaphysical belief, mystic and romantic ideas of all sorts. Thus it reshapes not only our methods of attaining our ends but also these ultimate ends themselves. "Free thinking" in the sense of materialistic monism, laicism and pragmatic acceptance of the world this side of the grave follow from this not indeed by logical necessity but nevertheless very naturally. On the one hand, our inherited sense of duty, deprived of its traditional basis, becomes focused in utilitarian ideas about the betterment of mankind which, quite illogically to be sure, seem to withstand rationalist criticism better than, say, the fear of God does. On the other hand, the same rationalization of the soul rubs off all the glamour of super-empirical sanction from every species of classwise rights. This then, together with the typically capitalist enthusiasm for Efficiency and Service—so completely different from the body of ideas which would have been associated with those terms by the typical knight of old—breeds that "will" within the bourgeoisie itself. . . .

Also, capitalist civilization is rationalistic "and anti-heroic." The two go together of course. Success in industry and commerce requires a lot of stamina, yet industrial and commercial activity is essentially unheroic in the knight's sense . . . and the ideology that glorifies the idea of fighting for fighting's sake and of victory for victory's sake understandably withers in the office among all the columns of figures. Therefore, owning assets that are apt to attract the robber or the tax gatherer and not sharing or even disliking warrior ideology that conflicts with its "rational" utilitarianism, the industrial and commercial bourgeoisie is fundamentally pacifist and inclined to insist on the application of the moral precepts of private life to international relations. . . . Modern pacifism and modern international morality are . . . products of capitalism.

In view of the fact that Marxian doctrine—especially Neo-Marxian doctrine and even a considerable body of non-socialist opinion—is . . . strongly opposed to this proposition it is necessary to point out that the latter is not meant to deny that many a bourgeoisie has put up a splendid fight for hearth and home, or that almost purely bourgeois commonwealths were often aggressive when it seemed to pay . . . or that no bourgeoisie ever disliked war profits and advantages to trade accruing from conquest or refused to be trained in warlike nationalism by its feudal masters or leaders or by the propaganda of some specially interested group. All I hold is, first, that such instances of capitalist combativeness are not, as Marxism has it, to be explained—exclusively or primarily—in terms of class interests or class situations that systematically engender capitalist wars of conquest; second, that there is a difference between doing that which you consider your normal business in life, for which you prepare yourself in season and out of season and in terms of which you define your success or failure, and doing what is not in your line, for which your normal work and your mentality do not fit you and success in which will increase the prestige of the most unbourgeois of professions; and third, that this difference steadily tells—in international as well as in domestic affairs—against the use of military force and for peaceful arrangements, even where the balance of pecuniary advantage is clearly on the side of war which, under modern circumstances, is not in general very likely. As a matter of fact, the more completely capitalist the structure and attitude of a nation, the more pacifist—and the more prone to count the costs of war—we observe it to be. . . .

But I am not going to sum up as the reader presumably expects me to. That is to say, I am not going to invite him, before he decides to put his trust in an untried alternative advocated by untried men, to look once more at the impressive economic and the still more impressive cultural achievement of the capitalist order and at the immense promise held out by both. I am not going to argue that that achievement and that promise are in themselves sufficient to support an argument for allowing the capitalist process to work on and, as it might easily be put, to lift poverty from the shoulders of mankind.

There would be no sense in this. Even if mankind were as free to choose as a businessman is free to choose between two competing pieces of machinery, no determined value judgment necessarily follows from the facts and relations between facts that I have tried to convey. As regards the economic performance, it does not follow that men are "happier" or even "better off" in the industrial society of today than they were in a medieval manor or village. As regards the cultural performance, one may accept every word I have written and yet hate it—its utilitarianism and the wholesale destruction of Meanings incident to it—from the bottom of one's heart. Moreover . . . one may care less for the efficiency of the capitalist process in producing economic and cultural values than for the kind of human beings that it turns out and then leaves to their own devices, free to make a mess of their lives. . . .

However, whether favorable or unfavorable, value judgments about capitalist performance are of little interest. For mankind is not free to choose. This is not only because the mass of people are not in a position to compare alternatives rationally and always accept what they are being told. There is a much deeper reason for it. Things economic and social move by their own momentum and the ensuing situations compel individuals and groups to behave in certain ways whatever they may wish to do—not indeed by destroying their freedom of choice but by shaping the choosing mentalities and by narrowing the list of possibilities from which to choose. If this is the quintessence of Marxism then we all of us have got to be Marxists. In consequence, capitalist performance is not even relevant for prognosis. Most civilizations have disappeared before they had time to fill to the full the measure of their promise. Hence I am not going to argue, on the strength of that performance, that the capitalist intermezzo is likely to be prolonged. In fact, I am now going to draw the exactly opposite inference.

CHAPTER XII: CRUMBLING WALLS

1. The Obsolescence of the Entrepreneurial Function. . . . [It is possible] that the economic wants of humanity might some day be so completely satisfied that little motive would be left to push productive effort still further ahead. Such a state of satiety is no doubt very far off even if we keep within the present scheme of wants; and if we take account of the fact that, as higher standards of life are attained, these wants automatically expand and new wants emerge or are created, satiety becomes a flying goal, particularly if we include leisure among consumers' goods. However, let us glance at that possibility, assuming, still more unrealistically, that methods of production have reached a state of perfection which does not admit of further improvement.

A more or less stationary state would ensue. Capitalism, being essentially an evolutionary process, would become atrophic. There would be nothing left for entrepreneurs to do. They would find themselves in much the same situation as generals would in a society perfectly sure of permanent peace. Profits and along with profits the rate of interest would converge toward zero. The bourgeois strata that live on profits and interest would tend to disappear. The management of industry and trade would become a matter of current administration, and the personnel would unavoidably acquire the characteristics of a bureaucracy. Socialism of a very sober type would almost automatically come into being. Human energy would turn away from business. Other than economic pursuits would attract the brains and provide the adventure.

For the calculable future this vision is of no importance. But all the greater importance attaches to the fact that many of the effects on the structure of society and on the organization of the productive process that we might expect from an approximately complete satisfaction of wants or from absolute technological perfection can also be expected from a development that is clearly observable already. Progress itself may be mechanized as well as the management of a stationary economy, and this mechanization of progress may affect entrepreneurship and capitalist society nearly as much as the cessation of economic progress would. In order to see this it is only necessary to [state], first, what the entrepreneurial function consists in and, secondly, what it means for bourgeois society and the survival of the capitalist order.

. . . The function of entrepreneurs is to reform or revolutionize the pattern of production by exploiting an invention or, more generally, an untried technological possibility for producing a new commodity or producing an old one in a new way, by opening up a new source of supply of materials or a new outlet for products, by reorganizing an industry and so on. Railroad construction in its earlier stages, electrical power production before the First World War, steam and steel, the motorcar, colonial ventures afford spectacular instances of a large genus which comprises innumerable humbler ones —down to such things as making a success of a particular kind of sausage or toothbrush. This kind of activity is primarily responsible for the recurrent "prosperities" that revolutionize the economic organism and the recurrent "recessions" that are due to the disequilibrating impact of the new products or methods. To undertake such new things is difficult and constitutes a distinct economic function, first, because they lie outside of the routine tasks which everybody understands and, secondly, because the environment resists in many ways that vary, according to social conditions, from simple refusal either to finance or to buy a new thing, to physical attack on the man who tries to produce it. To act with confidence beyond the range of familiar beacons and to overcome that resistance requires aptitudes that are present in only a small fraction of the population and that define the entrepreneurial type as well as the entrepreneurial function. This function does not essentially consist in either inventing anything or otherwise creating the conditions which the enterprise exploits. It consists in getting things done.

This social function is already losing importance and is bound to lose it at an accelerating rate in the future even if the economic process itself of which entrepreneurship was the prime mover went on unabated. For, on the one hand, it is much easier now than it has been in the past to do things that lie outside familiar routine—innovation itself is being reduced to routine. Technological progress is increasingly becoming the business of teams of trained specialists who turn out what is required and make it work in predictable ways. The romance of earlier commercial adventure is rapidly wearing away, because so many more things can be strictly calculated that had of old to be visualized in a flash of genius.

On the other hand, personality and will power must count for less in environments which have become accustomed to economic change—best instanced by an incessant stream of new consumers' and producers' goods—and which, instead of resisting, accept it as a matter of course. The resistance which comes from interests threatened by an innovation in the productive process is not likely to die out as long as the capitalist order persists. It is, for instance, the great obstacle on the road toward mass production of cheap housing which presupposes radical mechanization and wholesale elimination of inefficient methods of work on the plot. But every other kind of resistance —the resistance, in particular, of consumers and producers to a new kind of thing because it is new—has well-nigh vanished already.

Thus, economic progress tends to become depersonalized and automatized. Bureau and committee work tends to replace individual action. . . . Reference to the military analogy will help to bring out the essential point.

Of old, roughly up to and including the Napoleonic Wars, generalship meant leadership and success meant the personal success of the man in command who earned corresponding "profits" in terms of social prestige. The technique of warfare and the structure of armies being what they were, the individual decision and driving power of the leading man—even his actual presence on a showy horse—were essential elements in the strategical and tactical situations. Napoleon's presence was, and had to be, actually felt on his battlefields. This is no longer so. Rationalized and specialized office work will eventually blot out personality, the calculable result, the "vision." The leading man no longer has the opportunity to fling himself into the fray. He is becoming just another office worker—and one who is not always difficult to replace. . . .

Now a similar social process—in the last analysis the same social process—undermines the role and, along with the role, the social position of the capitalist entrepreneur. His role . . . is or was just another form of individual leadership acting by virtue of personal force and personal responsibility for success. His position, like that of warrior classes, is threatened as soon as this function in the social process loses its importance, and no less if this is due to the cessation of the social needs it served than if those needs are being served by other, more impersonal, methods.

But this affects the position of the entire bourgeois stratum. Although entrepreneurs are not necessarily or even typically elements of that stratum from the outset, they nevertheless enter it in case of success. Thus, though entrepreneurs do not *per se* form a social class, the bourgeois class absorbs them and their families and connections, thereby recruiting and revitalizing itself currently while at the same time the families that sever their active relation to "business" drop out of it after a generation or two. Between, there is the bulk of what we refer to as industrialists, merchants, financiers and bankers; they are in the intermediate stage between entrepreneurial venture and mere current administration of an inherited domain. The returns on which the class lives are produced by, and the social position of the class rests on, the success of this more or less active sector—which of course may, as it does in this country, form over 90 per cent of the bourgeois stratum—and of the individuals who are in the act of rising into that class. Economically and sociologically, directly and indirectly, the bourgeoisie therefore depends on the entrepreneur and, as a class, lives and will die with him, though a more or less prolonged transitional stage—eventually a stage in which it may feel equally unable to die and to live—is quite likely to occur, as in fact it did occur in the case of the feudal civilization.

To sum up this part of our argument: if capitalist evolution—"progress"—either ceases or becomes completely automatic, the economic basis of the industrial bourgeoisie will be reduced eventually to wages such as are paid for current administrative work excepting remnants of quasi-rents and monopoloid gains that may be expected to linger on for some time. Since capitalist enterprise, by its very achievements, tends to automatize progress, we conclude that it tends to make itself superfluous—to break to pieces under the pressure of its own success. The perfectly bureaucratized giant industrial unit not only ousts the small or medium-sized firm and "expropriates" its owners, but in the end it also ousts the entrepreneur and expropriates the bourgeoisie as a class which in the process stands to lose not only its income but also what is infinitely more important, its function. The true pacemakers of socialism were not the intellectuals or agitators who preached it but the Vanderbilts, Carnegies and Rockefellers. This result may not in every respect be to the taste of Marxian socialists, still less to the taste of socialists of a more popular (Marx would have said, vulgar) description. But so far as prognosis goes, it does not differ from theirs.

2. *The Destruction of the Protecting Strata.* So far we have been considering the effects of the capitalist process upon the economic bases of the upper strata of capitalist society and upon their social position and prestige. But effects further extend to the institutional framework that protected them. In showing this we shall take the term in its widest acceptance so as to include not only legal institutions but also attitudes of the public mind and policies.

a. Capitalist evolution first of all destroyed, or went far toward destroying, the institutional arrangements of the feudal world—the manor, the village, the craft guild. The facts and mechanisms of this process are too familiar to detain us. Destruction was wrought in three ways. The world of the artisan was destroyed primarily by the automatic effects of the competition that came from the capitalist entrepreneur; political action in removing atrophic organizations and regulations only registered results. The world of the lord and the peasant was destroyed primarily by political—in some cases revolutionary—action and capitalism merely presided over adaptive transformations say, of the German manorial organizations into large-scale agricultural units of production. But along with these industrial and agrarian revolutions went a no less revolutionary change in the general attitude of legislative authority and public opinion. Together with the old economic organization vanished the economic and political privileges of the classes or groups that used to play the leading role in it, particularly the tax exemptions and the political prerogatives of the landed nobility and gentry and of the clergy.

Economically all this meant for the bourgeoisie the breaking of so many fetters and the removal of so many barriers. Politically it meant the replacement of an order in which the bourgeois was a humble subject by another that was more congenial to his rationalist mind and to his immediate interests. But, surveying that process from the standpoint of today, the observer might well wonder whether in the end such complete emancipation was good for the bourgeois and his world. For those fetters not only hampered, they also sheltered. Before proceeding further we must carefully clarify and appraise this point.

b. The related processes of the rise of the capitalist bourgeoisie and of the rise of national states produced, in the sixteenth, seventeenth and eighteenth centuries, a social structure that may seem to us amphibial though it was no more amphibial or transitional than any other. Consider the outstanding influence that is afforded by the monarchy of Louis XIV. The royal power had subjugated the landed aristocracy and at the same time conciliated it by proffering employment and pensions and by conditionally accepting its claim to a ruling or leading class position. The same royal power had subjugated and allied itself with the clergy. It had finally strengthened its sway over the bourgeoisie, its old ally in the struggle with the territorial magnates, protecting and propelling its enterprise in order to exploit it the more effectively in turn. Peasants and the (small) industrial proletariat were likewise managed, exploited and protected by public authority . . . and, vicariously, by landlords or industrialists. This was not simply a government in the sense of nineteenth-century liberalism, i.e., a social agency existing for the performance of a few limited functions to be financed by a minimum of revenue. On principle, the monarchy managed everything, from consciences to the patterns of the silk fabrics of Lyons, and financially it aimed at a maximum of revenue. Though the king was never really absolute, public authority was all-comprehensive.

Correct diagnosis of this pattern is of the utmost importance for our subject. The king, the court, the army, the church and the bureaucracy lived to an increasing extent on revenue created by the capitalist process, even purely feudal sources of income being swelled in consequence of contemporaneous capitalist developments. To an increasing extent also, domestic and foreign policies and institutional changes were shaped to suit and propel that development. *As far as that goes,* the feudal elements in the structure of the so-called absolute monarchy come in only under the heading of atavisms which in fact is the diagnosis one would naturally adopt at first sight.

Looking more closely, however, we realize that those elements meant more than that. The steel frame of that structure still consisted of the human material of feudal society and this material still behaved according to pre-capitalist patterns. It filled the offices of state, officered the army, devised policies—it functioned as a *classe dirigente* [1] and, though taking account of bourgeois interests, it took care to distance itself from the bourgeoisie. The centerpiece, the king, was king by the grace of God, and the root of his position was feudal, not only in the historical but also in the sociological sense, however much he availed himself of the economic possibilities offered by capitalism. All this was more than atavism. It was an active symbiosis of two social strata, one of which no doubt supported the other economically but was in turn supported by the other politically. Whatever we may think of the achievements or shortcomings of this arrangement, whatever the bourgeois himself may have thought of it at the time or later—and of the aristocratic scapegrace or idler—it was of the essence of that society.

c. Of *that* society only? The subsequent course of things, best exemplified by the English case, suggests the answer. The aristocratic element continued to rule the roost *right to the end of the period of intact and vital capitalism.*

[1] [*Managing class.*]

No doubt that element—though nowhere so effectively as in England—currently absorbed the brains from other strata that drifted into politics; it made itself the representative of bourgeois interests and fought the battles of the bourgeoisie; it had to surrender its last legal privileges; but with these qualifications, and for ends no longer its own, it continued to man the political engine, to manage the state, to govern.

The economically operative part of the bourgeois strata did not offer much opposition to this. On the whole, that kind of division of labor suited them and they liked it. Where they did revolt against it or where they got into the political saddle without having to revolt, they did not make a conspicuous success of ruling and did not prove able to hold their own. The question arises whether it is really safe to assume that these failures were merely due to lack of opportunity to acquire experience and, with experience, the attitudes of a politically ruling class.

It is not. There is a more fundamental reason for those failures such as are instanced by the French or German experiences with bourgeois attempts at ruling—a reason which again will best be visualized by contrasting the figure of the industrialist or merchant with that of the medieval lord. The latter's "profession" not only qualified him admirably for the defense of his own class interest—he was not only able to fight for it physically—but it also cast a halo around him and made of him a ruler of men. The first was important, but more so were the mystic glamour and the lordly attitude—that ability and habit to command and to be obeyed that carried prestige with all classes of society and in every walk of life. That prestige was so great and that attitude so useful that the class position outlived the social and technological conditions which had given rise to it, and proved adaptable, by means of a transformation of the class function, to quite different social and economic conditions. With the utmost ease and grace the lords and knights metamorphosed themselves into courtiers, administrators, diplomats, politicians and into military officers of a type that had nothing whatever to do with that of the medieval knight. And—most astonishing phenomenon when we come to think of it—a remnant of that old prestige survives even to this day, and not only with our ladies.

Of the industrialist and merchant the opposite is true. There is surely no trace of any mystic glamour about him which is what counts in the ruling of men. The stock exchange is a poor substitute for the Holy Grail. We have seen that the industrialist and merchant, as far as they are entrepreneurs, also fill a function of leadership. But economic leadership of this type does not readily expand, like the medieval lord's military leadership, into the leadership of nations. On the contrary, the ledger and the cost calculation absorb and confine.

I have called the bourgeois rationalist and unheroic. He can only use rationalist and unheroic means to defend his position or to bend a nation to his will. He can impress by what people may expect from his economic performance, he can argue his case, he can promise to pay out money or threaten to withhold it, he can hire the treacherous services of a *condottiere* or politician or journalist. But that is all and all of it is greatly overrated as to its political value. Nor are his experiences and habits of life of the kind that develop personal fascination. A genius in the business office may be, and often is, utterly unable outside of it to say boo to a goose—both in the drawing room and on the platform. Knowing this he wants to be left alone and to leave politics alone. . . .

d. The inference is obvious: . . . the bourgeois class is ill equipped to face the problems, both domestic and international, that have normally to be faced by a country of any importance. The bourgeois themselves feel this in spite of all the phraseology that seems to deny it, and so do the masses. Within a protecting framework not made of bourgeois material, the bourgeoisie may be successful, not only in the political defensive but also in the offensive, especially as an opposition. For a time it felt so safe as to be able to afford the luxury of attacking the protective frame itself; such bourgeois opposition as there was in imperial Germany illustrates this to perfection. But without protection by some non-bourgeois group, the bourgeoisie is politically helpless and unable not only to lead its nation but even to take care of its particular class interest. Which amounts to saying that it needs a master.

But the capitalist process, both by its economic mechanics and by its psycho-sociological effects, did away with this protecting master or, as in this country, never gave him, or a substitute for him, a chance to develop. The implications of this are strengthened by another consequence of the same process. Capitalist evolution eliminates not only the king *Dei Gratia* [2] but also the political entrenchments that, had they proved tenable, would have been formed by the village and the craft guild. Of course, neither organization was tenable in the precise shape in which capitalism found it. But capitalist policies wrought destruction much beyond what was unavoidable. They attacked the artisan in reservations in which he could have survived for an indefinite time. They forced upon the peasant all the blessings of early liberal-

[2] [*By the grace of God.*]

ism—the free and unsheltered holding and all the individualist rope he needed in order to hang himself.

In breaking down the pre-capitalist framework of society, capitalism thus broke not only barriers that impeded its progress but also flying buttresses that prevented its collapse. That process, impressive in its relentless necessity, was not merely a matter of removing institutional deadwood, but of removing partners of the capitalist stratum, symbiosis with whom was an essential element of the capitalist schema. Having discovered this fact which so many slogans obscure, we might well wonder whether it is quite correct to look upon capitalism as a social form *sui generis* or, in fact, as anything else but the last stage of the decomposition of what we have called feudalism. On the whole, I am inclined to believe that its peculiarities suffice to make a type and to accept that symbiosis of classes which owe their existence to different epochs and processes as the rule rather than as an exception—at least it has been the rule these 6000 years, i.e., ever since primitive tillers of the soil became the subjects of mounted nomads. But there is no great objection that I can see against the opposite view alluded to.

3. The Destruction of the Institutional Framework of Capitalist Society. We return from our digression with a load of ominous facts. They are almost, though not quite, sufficient to establish our next point, viz., that the capitalist process in much the same way in which it destroyed the institutional framework of feudal society also undermined its own.

It has been pointed out above that the very success of capitalist enterprise paradoxically tends to impair the prestige or social weight of the class primarily associated with it and that the giant unit of control tends to oust the bourgeoisie from the function to which it owed that social weight. The corresponding change in the meaning, and the incidental loss in vitality, of the institutions of the bourgeois world and of its typical attitudes are easy to trace.

On the one hand, the capitalist process unavoidably attacks the economic standing ground of the small producer and trader. What it did to the pre-capitalist strata it also does—and by the same competitive mechanism—to the lower strata of capitalist industry. Here of course Marx scores. It is true that the facts of industrial concentration do not quite live up to the ideas the public is being taught to entertain about it. The process has gone less far and is less free from setbacks and compensatory tendencies than one would gather from many a popular exposition. In particular, large-scale enterprise not only annihilates but also, to some extent, creates space for the small producing, and especially trading, firm. Also, in the case of the peasants and farmers, the capitalist world has at last proved both willing and able to pursue an expensive but on the whole effective policy of conservation. In the long run, however, there can be little doubt about the fact we are envisaging, or about its consequences. Outside of the agrarian field, moreover, the bourgeoisie has shown but little awareness of the problem or its importance for the survival of the capitalist order. The profits to be made by rationalizing the organization of production and especially by cheapening the tortuous way of commodities from the factory to the ultimate consumer are more than the mind of the typical businessman can resist.

Now it is important to realize precisely what these consequences consist in. A very common type of social criticism . . . laments the "decline of competition" and equates it to the decline of capitalism because of the virtues it attributes to competition and the vices it attributes to modern industrial "monopolies." In this schema of interpretation, monopolization plays the role of arteriosclerosis and reacts upon the fortunes of the capitalist order through increasingly unsatisfactory economic performance. . . . [There are] reasons for rejecting this view. Economically neither the case for competition nor the case against concentration of economic control is anything like as strong as this argument implies. And, whether weak or strong, it misses the salient point. Even if the giant concerns were all managed so perfectly as to call forth applause from the angels in heaven, the political consequences of concentration would still be what they are. The political structure of a nation is profoundly affected by the elimination of a host of small and medium-sized firms the owner-managers of which, together with their dependents, henchmen and connections, count quantitatively at the polls and have a hold on what we may term the foreman class that no management of a large unit can ever have; the very foundation of private property and free contracting wears away in a nation in which its most vital, most concrete, most meaningful types disappear from the moral horizon of the people.

On the other hand, the capitalist process also attacks its own institutional framework . . . within the precincts of the big units. . . . The figure of the proprietor and with it the specifically proprietary interest have vanished from the picture. There are the salaried executives and all the salaried managers and sub-managers. There are the big stockholders. And then there are the small stockholders. The first group tends to acquire the employee attitude and rarely if ever identifies itself with the stockholding interest even in the most favorable cases, i.e., in the cases in which it identifies itself with the interest of the concern as such. The second group, even if it considers its connection with the concern as permanent and even if it actually behaves as financial theory would have stockholders behave, is at one remove from both the functions and the attitudes of an owner. As to the third group, small stockholders often do not care much about what for most of them is but a minor source of income and, whether they care or not, they hardly ever bother, unless they or some representatives of theirs are out to exploit their nuisance value: being often very ill used and still more often thinking themselves ill used, they almost regularly drift into an attitude hostile to "their" corporations, to big business in general and particularly when things look bad, to the capitalist order as such. No element of any of those three groups into which I schematized the typical situation unconditionally takes the attitude characteristic of that curious phenomenon, so full of meaning and so rapidly passing, that is covered by the term Property.

Freedom of contracting is in the same boat. In its full vitality it meant individual contracting regulated by individual choice between an indefinite number of possibilities. The stereotyped, unindividual, impersonal and bureaucratized contract of today . . . which presents but restricted freedom of choice . . . has none of the old features the most important of which become impossible with giant concerns dealing with other giant concerns or impersonal masses of workmen or consumers. The void is being filled by a tropical growth of new legal structures—and a little reflection shows that this could hardly be otherwise.

Thus the capitalist process pushes into the background all those institutions, the institutions of property and free contracting in particular, that expressed the needs and ways of the truly "private" economic activity. Where it does not abolish them, as it already has abolished free contracting in the labor market, it attains the same end by shifting the relative importance of existing legal forms—the legal forms pertaining to corporate business for instance as against those pertaining to the partnership or individual firm—or by changing their contents or meanings. The capitalist process, by substituting a mere parcel of shares for the walls of and the machines in a factory, takes the life out of the idea of property. It loosens the grip that once was so strong—the grip in the sense of the legal right and the actual ability to do as one pleases with one's own; the grip also in the sense that the holder of the title loses the will to fight, economically, physically, politically, for "his" factory and his control over it, to die if necessary on its steps. And this evaporation of what we may term the material substance of property—its visible and touchable reality—affects not only the attitude of holders but also that of the workmen and of the public in general. Dematerialized, defunctionalized, absentee ownership does not impress and call forth moral allegiance as the vital form of property did. Eventually there will be nobody left who really cares to stand for it—nobody within and nobody without the precincts of the big concerns. . . .

CHAPTER XIV: DECOMPOSITION

The modern businessman, whether entrepreneur or mere managing administrator, is the executive type. From the logic of his position he acquires something of the psychology of the salaried employee working in a bureaucratic organization. Whether a stockholder or not, his will to fight and to hold on is not and cannot be what it was with the man who knew ownership and its responsibilities in the full-blooded sense of those words. His system of values and his conception of duty undergo a profound change. . . . Thus the modern corporation, although the product of the capitalist process, socializes the bourgeois mind; it relentlessly narrows the scope of capitalist motivation; not only that, it will eventually kill its roots.

. . . Important . . . [also] is . . . the disintegration of the bourgeois family. The facts to which I am referring are too well known to need explicit statement. To men and women in modern capitalist societies, family life and parenthood mean less than they meant before and hence are less powerful molders of behavior; the rebellious son or daughter who professes contempt for "Victorian" standards is, however incorrectly, expressing an undeniable truth. . . . If in our statistical age readers insist on a statistical measure, the proportion of marriages that produce no children or only one child, though still inadequate to quantify the phenomenon I mean, might come as near as we can hope to come to indicating its numerical importance. The phenomenon by now extends, more or less, to all classes. But it first appeared in the bourgeois (and intellectual) stratum and its symptomatic as well as causal value for our purposes lies entirely there. It is wholly attributable to the rationalization of everything in life, which we have seen is one of the effects of capitalist evolution. In fact, it is but one of the results of the spread of that rationalization to the sphere of private life. All the other factors which are usually adduced in explanation can be readily reduced to that one.

As soon as men and women learn the utilitarian lesson and refuse to take for granted the traditional arrangements that their social environment makes for them, as soon as they acquire the habit of weighing the individual advantages and disadvantages of any prospective course of action—or, as we might also put it, as soon as they introduce into their private life a sort of inarticulate system of cost accounting—they cannot fail to become aware of the heavy personal sacrifices that family ties and especially parenthood entail under modern conditions and of the fact that at the same time, excepting the cases of farmers and peasants, children cease to be economic assets. These sacrifices do not consist only of the items that come within the reach of the measuring rod of money but comprise in addition an indefinite amount of loss of comfort, of freedom from care, and opportunity to enjoy alternatives of increasing attractiveness and variety—alternatives to be compared with joys of parenthood that are being subjected to a critical analysis of increasing severity. . . . The point I wish to convey is, I think, clear without further elaboration. It may be summed up in the question that is so clearly in many potential parents' minds: "Why should we stunt our ambitions and impoverish our lives in order to be insulted and looked down upon in our old age?"

While the capitalist process, by virtue of the psychic attitudes it creates, progressively dims the values of family life and removes the conscientious inhibitions that an old moral tradition would have put in the way toward a different scheme of life, it at the same time implements the new tastes. As regards childlessness, capitalist inventiveness produces contraceptive devices of ever-increasing efficiency that overcome the resistance which the strongest impulse of man would otherwise have put up. As regards the style of life, capitalist evolution decreases the desirability of, and provides alternatives to, the bourgeois family home. I have previously adverted to the Evaporation of Industrial Property; I have now to advert to the Evaporation of Consumers' Property.

Until the later decades of the nineteenth century, the town house and the country place were everywhere not only pleasant and convenient shells of private life on the higher levels of income, but they were indispensable. Not only hospitality on any scale and in any style, but even the comfort, dignity, repose and refinement of the family depended upon its having an adequate *foyer* of its own that was adequately staffed. The arrangements summarized by the term Home were accordingly accepted as a matter of course by the average man and woman of bourgeois standing, exactly as they looked upon marriage and children—the "founding of a family"—as a matter of course.

Now, on the one hand, the amenities of the bourgeois home are becoming less obvious than are its burdens. To the critical eye of a critical age it is likely to appear primarily as a source of trouble and expense which frequently fail to justify themselves. This would be so even independently of modern taxation and wages and of the attitude of modern household personnel, all of which are typical results of the capitalist process and of course greatly strengthen the case against what in the near future will be almost universally recognized as an outmoded and uneconomical way of life. In this respect as in others we are living in a transitional stage. The average family of bourgeois standing tends to reduce the difficulties of running the big house and the big country place by substituting for it small and mechanized establishments plus a maximum of outside service and outside life—hospitality in particular being increasingly shifted to the restaurant or club.

On the other hand, the home of the old type is no longer an indispensable requirement of comfortable and refined living in the bourgeois sphere. The apartment house and the apartment hotel represent a rationalized type of abode and another style of life which when fully developed will no doubt meet the new situation and provide all the essentials of comfort and refinement. To be sure, neither that style nor its shell are fully developed anywhere as yet and they proffer cost advantage only if we count in the trouble and annoyance incident to running a modern home. But other advantages they proffer already—the facility of using to the full the variety of modern enjoyments, of travel, of ready mobility, of shifting the load of the current little things of existence to the powerful shoulders of highly specialized organizations. . . .

I have said that the new style of bourgeois life does not as yet offer any decisive cost advantage. But this refers only to the current or prime costs of servicing the wants of private life. As to overhead, even the purely pecuniary advantage is obvious already. And inasmuch as the outlay on the most durable elements of home life . . . used to be financed mainly from previous earnings we may say that the need for accumulation of "consumers' capital" is drastically reduced by that process. This does not mean of course that demand for "consumers' capital" is at present, even relatively, smaller than it was; the increasing demand for durable consumers' goods from small and medium incomes more than counterbalances this effect. But it does mean that, so far as the hedonistic component in the pattern of acquisitive motives is concerned, the desirability of incomes beyond a certain level is reduced. In order to satisfy himself of this, the reader need only visualize the situation in a thoroughly practical spirit: the successful man or couple or the "society" man or couple who can pay for the best available accommodation in hotel, ship and train, and for the best available qualities of the objects of personal consumption and use—which qualities are increasingly being turned out by the conveyor of mass production—will, things being what they are, as a rule have all they want with any intensity *for themselves*. And it is easy to see that a budget framed on those lines will be far below the requirements of a "seignorial" style of life.

In order to realize what all this means for the efficiency of the capitalist engine of production we need only recall that the family and the family home used to be the mainspring of the typically bourgeois kind of profit motive. Economists have not always given due weight to this fact. When we look more closely at their idea of the self-interest of entrepreneurs and capitalists we cannot fail to discover that the results it was supposed to produce are really not at all what one would expect from the rational self-interest of the detached individual or the childless couple who no longer look at the world through the windows of a family home. Consciously or unconsciously they analyzed the behavior of the man whose views and motives are shaped by such a home and who means to work and to save primarily for wife *and children*. As soon as these fade out from the moral vision of the businessman, we have a different kind of *homo oeconomicus* before us who cares for different things and acts in different ways. For him and from the standpoint of his individualistic utilitarianism, the behavior of that old type would in fact be completely irrational. He loses the only sort of romance and heroism that is left in the unromantic and unheroic civilization of capitalism—the heroism of *navigare necesse est, vivere non necesse est.*[3] And he loses the capitalist ethics that enjoins working for the future irrespective of whether or not one is going to harvest the crop oneself.

The last point may be put more tellingly. . . . The capitalist order entrusts the long-run interests of society to the upper strata of the bourgeoisie. They are really entrusted to the family motive operative in those strata. The bourgeoisie worked primarily in order to invest, and it was not so much a standard of consumption as a standard of accumulation that the bourgeoisie struggled for. . . . With the decline of the driving power supplied by the family motive, the businessman's time-horizon shrinks, roughly, to his life expectation. And he might now be less willing than he was to fulfill that function of earning, saving and investing even if he saw no reason to fear that the results would but swell his tax bills. He drifts into an anti-saving frame of mind and accepts with an increasing readiness anti-saving *theories* that are indicative of a short-run *philosophy*.

But anti-saving theories are not all that he accepts. With a different attitude to the concern he works for and with a different scheme of private life he tends to acquire a different view of the values and standards of the capi-

[3] [*Seafaring is necessary, living is not necessary.*]

talist order of things. Perhaps the most striking feature of the picture is the extent to which the bourgeoisie, besides educating its own enemies, allows itself in turn to be educated by them. It absorbs the slogans of current radicalism and seems quite willing to undergo a process of conversion to a creed hostile to its very existence. Haltingly and grudgingly it concedes in part the implications of that creed. This would be most astonishing and indeed very hard to explain were it not for the fact that the typical bourgeois is rapidly losing faith in his own creed. And this again becomes fully understandable as soon as we realize that the social conditions which account for its emergence are passing.

This is verified by the very characteristic manner in which particular capitalist interests and the bourgeoisie as a whole behave when facing direct attack. They talk and plead—or hire people to do it for them; they snatch at every chance of compromise; they are ever ready to give in; they never put up a fight under the flag of their own ideals and interests—in this country there was no real resistance anywhere against the imposition of crushing financial burdens during the last decade or against labor legislation incompatible with the effective management of industry. Now, as the reader will surely know by this time, I am far from overestimating the political power of either big business or the bourgeoisie in general. Moreover, I am prepared to make large allowances for cowardice. But still, means of defense were not entirely lacking as yet and history is full of examples of the success of small groups who, believing in their cause, were resolved to stand by their guns. The only explanation for the meekness we observe is that the bourgeois order no longer makes any sense to the bourgeoisie itself and that, when all is said and nothing is done, it does not really care.

Thus the same economic process that undermines the position of the bourgeoisie by decreasing the importance of the functions of entrepreneurs and capitalists, by breaking up protective strata and institutions, by creating an atmosphere of hostility, also decomposes the motor forces of capitalism from within. Nothing else shows so well that the capitalist order not only rests on props made of extra-capitalist patterns of behavior which at the same time it is bound to destroy.

We have rediscovered what from different standpoints and, so I believe, on inadequate grounds has often been discovered before: there is inherent in the capitalist system a tendency toward self-destruction which, in its earlier stages, may well assert itself in the form of a tendency toward retardation of progress.

I shall not stay to repeat how objective and subjective, economic and extra-economic factors, reinforcing each other in imposing accord, contribute to that result. Nor shall I stay to show what should be obvious . . . viz., that those factors make not only for the destruction of the capitalist but for the emergence of a socialist civilization. They all point in that direction. The capitalist process not only destroys its own institutional framework but it also creates the conditions for another. Destruction may not be the right word after all. Perhaps I should have spoken of transformation. The outcome of the process is not simply a void that could be filled by whatever might happen to turn up; things and souls are transformed in such a way as to become increasingly amenable to the socialist form of life. With every peg from under the capitalist structure vanishes an impossibility of the socialist plan. In both these respects Marx's *vision* was right. We can also agree with him in linking the particular social transformation that goes on under our eyes with an economic process as its prime mover. What our analysis, if correct, disproves is after all of secondary importance, however essential the role may be which it plays in the socialist credo. In the end there is not so much difference as one might think between saying that the decay of capitalism is due to its success and saying that it is due to its failure.

But our answer to the question . . . ["Can capitalism survive?"] posits far more problems than it solves. . . . The reader should bear in mind:

First, that so far we have not learned anything about the kind of socialism that may be looming in the future. For Marx and for most of his followers—and this was and is one of the most serious shortcomings of their doctrine—socialism meant just one definite thing. But the definiteness really goes no further than nationalization of industry would carry us and with this an indefinite variety of economic and cultural possibilities will be seen to be compatible.

Second, that similarly we know nothing as yet about the precise way by which socialism may be expected to come except that there must be a great many possibilities ranging from a gradual bureaucratization to the most picturesque revolution. Strictly speaking we do not even know whether socialism will actually come to stay. For to repeat: perceiving a tendency and visualizing the goal of it is one thing and predicting that this goal will actually be reached and that the resulting state of things will be workable, let alone permanent, is quite another thing. Before humanity chokes (or basks) in the dungeon (or paradise) of socialism it may well burn up in the horrors (or glories) of imperialist wars.

Third, that the various components of the tendency we have been trying to describe, while everywhere discernible, have as yet nowhere fully revealed themselves. Things have gone to different lengths in different countries but in no country far enough to allow us to say with any confidence precisely how far they will go, or to assert that their "underlying trend" has grown too strong to be subject to anything more serious than temporary reverses. Industrial integration is far from being complete. Competition, actual and potential, is still a major factor in any business situation. Enterprise is still active, the leadership of the bourgeois group still the prime mover of the economic process. The middle class is still a political power. Bourgeois standards and bourgeois motivations though being increasingly impaired are still alive. Survival of traditions—and family ownership of controlling parcels of stock—still make many an executive behave as the owner-manager did of old. The bourgeois family has not yet died; in fact, it clings to life so tenaciously that no responsible politician has as yet dared to touch it by any method other than taxation. From the standpoint of immediate practice as well as for the purposes of short-run forecasting—and in these things, a century is a "short run" [4]—all this surface may be more important than the tendency toward another civilization that slowly works deep down below.

[4] This is why the facts and arguments presented . . . do not invalidate my reasoning about the possible economic results of another fifty years of capitalist evolution. The thirties may well turn out to have been the last gasp of capitalism—the likelihood of this is of course greatly increased by the current war. But again they may not. In any case there are no *purely economic* reasons why capitalism should not have another successful run which is all I wished to establish.

CONTEMPORARY CIVILIZATION: ITS PREDICAMENTS

1. CIVILIZATION AND CRISIS

JOHAN HUIZINGA

IN March of 1935 the Dutch historian Johan Huizinga delivered an address in Brussels, Belgium, for which he chose the somber title *In the Shadow of Tomorrow*. The speech was later elaborated into a book, from the English translation (1936 by J. H. Huizinga) of which the following selection has been taken. *In the Shadow of Tomorrow* reflected the political mood of the day. In Asia Japan was promoting the Manchurian incident into a war of conquest, and in Europe Adolf Hitler (1889–1945) was preparing his own *de facto* revision of the Versailles Treaty by an occupation of the Saar, while Benito Mussolini (1883–1945) was setting himself for the Ethiopian expedition, and Spain was on the eve of its Civil War. Western civilization was passing from the post-World War I to the pre-World War II stage. Social symptoms of crisis abounded: worldwide economic depression, mass unemployment, strikes. Huizinga contrasted this "toboggan slide to disaster" with man's increased power over nature and his conscious desire for improving the world and the human condition. This antithesis between the growing power of man to control his environment and realize his ideals of universal peace and happiness and the actual course of events, the growing threats of war and social disintegration, Huizinga takes as the point of departure for his investigation of the fate of contemporary man in civilization.

The major symptom of the crisis Huizinga locates in the ever-widening gap between the material progress of society and the realization of happiness by the individual. This is a reflection of the growing conflict between what Huizinga calls knowing—the knowledge, tools, institutions by which man understands and manipulates nature—and being—the direction and end which are man's true goals. Civilization is askew, pulled out of alignment with its natural course of development, by the modern obsession with ease of life and the right to happiness. To restore it to its proper channels Huizinga prescribes a healthy dose of self-discipline, *katharsis*. In all ages when others have called for social and institutional reforms, the humanist has urged the individual to look to himself and to change the world through self-reform and self-control.

Huizinga's forebodings about the tomorrow of civilization materialized in the personal and world tragedy of World War II. True to his moral convictions he resisted the Nazis, was seized and held hostage, and died in a concentration camp on the eve of the liberation of The Netherlands.

IN THE SHADOW OF TOMORROW

CHAPTER I: APPREHENSIONS OF DOOM

We are living in a demented world. And we know it. It would not come as a surprise to anyone if tomorrow the madness gave way to a frenzy which would leave our poor Europe in a state of distracted stupor, with engines still turning and flags streaming in the breeze, but with the spirit gone.

Everywhere there are doubts as to the solidity of our social structure, vague fears of the imminent future, a feeling that our civilization is on the way to ruin. They are not merely the shapeless anxieties which beset us in the small hours of the night when the flame of life burns low. They are considered expectations founded on observation and judgment of an overwhelming multitude of facts. How to avoid the recognition that almost all things which once seemed sacred and immutable have now become unsettled, truth and humanity, justice and reason? We see forms of government no longer capable of functioning, production systems on the verge of collapse, social systems gone wild with power. The roaring engine of this tremendous time seems to be heading for a breakdown.

But immediately the antithesis forces itself on our minds. Never has there been a time when men were so clearly conscious of their commanding duty to cooperate in the task of preserving and improving the world's well-being and human civilization. At no time has work been so much honoured as it is to-day. Man was never so ready to apply his full courage and all his powers to a common cause. At least hope has not yet been lost.

If, then, this civilization is to be saved, if it is not to be submerged by centuries of barbarism but to secure the treasures of its inheritance on new and more stable foundations, there is indeed need for those now living to realise how far the decay has already progressed. . . .

CHAPTER III: THE PRESENT CRISIS COMPARED WITH THOSE OF THE PAST

Is it possible to find historical examples of the civilization of a nation, an empire or a continent, passing through as violent a convulsion as that which racks our time? Crisis of civilization is an historical concept. Through historical appreciation, through a comparison of past and present, the concept

---

This selection has been reprinted from *In the Shadow of Tomorrow* by Johan Huizinga by permission of W. W. Norton & Company, Inc., Copyright 1936 by W. W. Norton & Company, Inc., New York (pp. 15–16, 28–36, 52–66, 79–83, 89–92, 99–112, 231–239).

can be given a certain degree of objectivity. For of the earlier crises we not only know the origins and development but also the consummation. Our knowledge of them has an additional dimension. Sometimes an entire civilization perished, sometimes it won its way through to new and different forms of existence. We are able to view the historical case as a closed process. And although such historical autopsy of the past does not hold out the promise of a cure for the present and perhaps not even that of a prognosis, no possible method to gain an insight into the nature of the ailment may be left untried.

Unfortunately the material of comparable cases is rather less plentiful than it might seem at first. However telling the remains of the many civilizations which are daily made to emerge from under the desert sand, tropical vegetation, or the wastes of depopulated regions, we know far too little of their internal history to be able to discern other causes of their decline and downfall than catastrophes of some sort. Even ancient Greece and Egypt afford hardly any material for an accurate comparison. The twenty centuries since the reign of Augustus and the life of Christ alone are sufficiently near to us to allow of fruitful comparison.

It may be asked: has not civilization during these twenty centuries always been in a state of crisis? Is not all mankind's history precarious to the utmost degree? To be sure, but this is wisdom for philosophical declamation, useful on the proper occasion. Viewed historically, however, certain complexes of past events do present themselves as more or less clearly marked-out periods of intensive cultural change. They are: the transition from Antiquity to the Middle Ages; from the Middle Ages to Modern times; and that from the eighteenth to the nineteenth century.

Consider first the period around 1500. The time is one of tremendous changes; the earth discovered in all its fullness, the structure of the planetary system revealed, the Church torn asunder, the power and the range of the written word infinitely extended by the printing press, the means of warfare vastly augmented, credit and finance growing abundantly, Greek learning restored, the old architecture scorned, the arts unfolding in all their splendour. Then look at 1789–1815. Again the current of the world's happenings has swollen to a roaring torrent. The first state of Europe succumbed to the delusions of the "philosophers" and the fury of the mob, but presently resurrected by the deeds and fortune of a military genius. Liberty acclaimed and the Church doctrines forsaken. The continent of Europe thrown into a jumble and finally put together again. Steam engines panting and the crashing rhythm of the new weaving looms. One scientific conquest after another, the world of the spirit enriched by German philosophy and life's charm enhanced by German music. America politically and economically grown-up, culturally still a youngster.

At both times history's seismograph seems to register as violent a disturbance as to-day. On the surface the shocks, the landslides, the tidal waves seem to be no less powerful in their effects than those of the present. Probing deeper, however, it soon appears that in both of the earlier critical periods, that of the Renaissance and Reformation and that of Revolution and Napoleon, the foundations of society have been less convulsed than in our time. And more important, in both the earlier periods hope and faith remained far more dominant than to-day. Even though then, too, there were many who in the passing of the old and cherished order saw the coming of the end, the feeling of a threatening collapse of all civilization was then neither so widespread nor so strongly founded on exact observation. To the historical eye both periods, however critical, bear above all the mark of ascent.

To repeat, around 1500 and again around 1800 the foundations of society have been much less shaken than to-day. Fiercely as the Catholic and the Protestant world after the Reformation hated and fought one another, the common base of their faith and their Churches kept them much more closely related and rendered the breach with the past much less definite than in our time with its cleft between the absolute rejection of religious belief on the one hand and the reconstitution of Christian faith on the old foundations on the other. Apart from certain fantastical excesses, neither the sixteenth century nor the revolutionary era has deliberately attacked or disavowed the Christian system of morals. The changes of the political structure in the period 1789–1815, including all the successive phases of the French Revolution, are far less fundamental than those that have occurred since 1914, while in the sixteenth century the political structure remained virtually unaffected. Neither the sixteenth century nor the first decades of the nineteenth century have known the systematic undermining of the social order by a creed of class struggle and class antagonism. The economy of both periods, while bearing the mark of crisis, fails to show signs of thorough dislocation. The great economic shifts of the sixteenth century, the virulence of capitalism, the great bankruptcies and the rise of prices, never brought on the convulsed paralysis of trade or the wild currency disorders of the present. The confusion caused by the assignats towards the end of the eighteenth century is as nothing compared to the endless monetary ills of our time. Even the so-called Industrial Revolution (the fitness of the term is questionable) was not of the nature of a violent disturbance but of excessive one-sided growth.

If still another sensitive test is wanted to expose the febrile character of the cultural life of our time, consider the course of the arts. All the transitions through which they have passed, from the Quattrocento to Rococo, have been gradual and conservative. During all this time schooling and craftsmanship remained the unquestioningly accepted prerequisites of all true art. Not until the advent of Impressionism does the repudiation of principles set in which opened the way for the burlesque parade of the fashionable and publicity-crazed modernities of our century.

The comparison of the present with the time of 1500 and 1800, then, gives rise to the general impression that the world is now in the throes of a more intense and more fundamental upheaval than at either of the earlier periods.

There remains the question in how far the process through which we are passing resembles that of the transition from Roman civilization to the Middle Ages. Here indeed we see what many now think close at hand: a high and rich civilization gradually ceding to another of unmistakably lower quality and equipment. But at once a great difference between the two cases appears. The lower civilization of about A.D. 500 had emerged out of the older one carrying with it the treasure of the high form of religion on which in a way the old civilization itself had foundered. With all its barbarian qualities this age of Gregory the Great and the Merovingians was permeated with an intense metaphysical element. Christianity, in spite of its renunciation of the world, has been the propelling force in the development of mediaeval culture to the high and harmonious form in which the twelfth and thirteenth centuries displayed it.

Is this same force of Christian faith acting as powerfully for the future in our time?

Apart from the triumph of Christianity, the cultural transformations of the Roman Empire appear to us as a process of stagnation and degeneration. We see high faculties of social organisation and intellectual encompassment and expression shrinking, withering, and dissolving. There was a declining efficiency of government, technology at a standstill, diminishing productivity, and slackening of intellectual curiosity and construction which remained largely confined to preservation and imitation. In all these aspects the development of Roman civilization bears little resemblance to the processes of our time. For to-day most of the above-mentioned faculties still seem to be steadily growing in intensity, diversity and refinement. The general conditions are, moreover, altogether different. Then there was a multiplicity of peoples loosely, imperfectly and yet truly held together in one world-state. To-day we live in a very tightly linked structure of separate competing states. In our world technical ability reigns ever more unchallenged, productive capacity continues to expand, and the power of scientific research triumphs in a seemingly unending succession of new discoveries. Again, the pace of the process of change is an entirely different one; years seem to have replaced centuries as the yardstick of measurement. Briefly, comparison with the history of A.D. 200–600 offers too few points of contact to be of immediate value for an understanding of our present crisis.

And yet, despite all differences, one important point stands out. The road of Roman civilization was a road to barbarism. Will it turn out to be the same road we are on to-day? . . .

CHAPTER V: THE PROBLEMATIC NATURE OF PROGRESS

. . . Our judgment of human affairs and relations can never free itself entirely from the mood of the moment. If it is a negative mood there is an objective probability that it will colour our views a shade too dark. If we are in the habit of viewing past epochs, Hellas in the days of Pericles, the age of the cathedrals or the Renaissance, in the light of harmony and equilibrium while our own time appears full of friction and disturbance, this is no doubt partly because of the soothing effect of remoteness. We must at once, before we consider the symptoms, allow for a margin of error, therefore. There can be no perfect balance of our cool vision of the distant past and our troubled view of a present in which we are ourselves concerned. Perhaps a final retrospective judgment of our time will see the phenomena which now cause us such anxiety as of only passing and superficial importance. An insignificant disturbance may rob one of sleep and appetite, spoil one's temper and hinder one's work while the organism is sound and untouched. Signs are not altogether wanting that beneath all the social and cultural afflictions with which we are plagued, the pulse of society nevertheless continues to beat more vigorously and healthily than we realise. But that there is disease and that the organism does not function normally is certain.

Here we find ourselves carrying on the argument in medical metaphors. Without metaphor the handling of general concepts such as culture and civilization becomes impossible, and that of disease and disorder is the obvious one for the case in point. Is not crisis itself a concept we owe to Hippocrates? In the social and cultural domain no metaphor is more apt than the pathological one. No doubt our time is full of fever. Growing pains? Possibly. There is raving, wild phantasms and senseless expression. Or is it more than a passing over-stimulation of the brain? Is there reason to speak of a derangement caused by a serious lesion of the nerve centre? Every one of these metaphors has its weight of meaning when applied to the aspects of the present state of our culture.

Most visible and most tangible are the disturbances of the economic organism. Everyone feels them daily in his own life. Those of the body politic are only slightly less direct, though the average person observes their presence and effects in general only through the medium of the press. Viewing the political and economic dislocation and its gradual progress as a whole, it seems to come down to this. The world's equipment has been perfected to a point where the social forces, uncontrolled and unco-ordinated by a principle which transgresses the particular purpose of each one of these forces (for the State cannot be considered as such), function each separately with an excess of power which is distinctly harmful to the harmony of the organism as a whole. Equipment here refers to the means of production and technical means in general, the means of communication and transport, of publicity and mass-mobilisation, including education and political organisation.

When one considers the development of each one of these means by itself without introducing a valuation, this development fully warrants the application of the term progress. They have all increased enormously in power. Remember, however, that progress in itself merely indicates a direction without implying anything as to where the road leads, whether to salvation or perdition. We are too apt to forget that alone the shallow optimism of our ancestors of the eighteenth and nineteenth centuries has confused the assurance of the bigger and *better* with the purely directional conception of "further." The expectation that every new discovery or refinement of existing means must contain the promise of higher value or greater happiness is an extremely naïve thought, heirloom of the charming age of intellectual, moral and sentimental optimism. It is not in the least paradoxical to say that a culture may founder on real and tangible progress. William James once said: "Progress is a terrible thing." It is more than that: it is also a highly ambiguous notion. For who knows but that a little further on the way a bridge may not have collapsed or a crevice split the earth?

CHAPTER VI: SCIENCE AT THE LIMITS OF THINKING POWER

The domain of science is the natural starting-point for a description of the outward manifestations of the cultural disorder. For there we find combined unmistakable and steady progress, an equally unmistakable appearance of crisis and an unshaken belief that to preserve and to continue is both imperative and beneficial.

Ever since the seventeenth century the development of scientific and philosophical thought bears the clear mark of positive and uninterrupted progress. Practically every branch of knowledge, philosophy not excluded, is still daily being refined and extended. Astounding discoveries . . . follow one another in close succession. This progress is most evident in the natural sciences, especially because of the immediate technical application of the new discoveries. But also the social sciences and the humanities, as well as the two branches of knowledge which stand apart from all others, mathematics and philosophy, are continuously penetrating ever deeper into the mine of knowledge with ever more refined means of observation and expression.

All this is the more striking when one remembers that the generation of about the period 1890 believed that science had well-nigh reached a point where it could go no further. The structure of human knowledge appeared to be almost completed. There was still a little polishing and finishing to be done and the march of time might bring some new material, but fundamental changes in the constitution and formulation of our knowledge were apparently not to be expected. How very differently it would turn out! Were a scientific Epimenides who had moved into his cave in 1879 and slept his eight times seven years there, to wake up to-day, even the language of almost all branches of science would have become incomprehensible to him. The terminology of physics, chemistry, philosophy, psychology, or linguistics, to mention but a few, would be a meaningless jumble to him. Anyone surveying the nomenclature of his intellectual domain realises at once that he is constantly using words and notions which forty years ago did not exist. If some fields of knowledge such as history constitute an exception in this respect, it is because there the terms of everyday life must generally continue to be the only medium of expression.

When one now compares the present state of all knowledge with that of fifty years ago the conclusion can be no other than that its progress has been synonymous with improvement. Our knowledge has become more extensive as well as deeper and finer. In terms of value there has been a definite increase. This leads directly to a surprising conclusion; on the way of real positive progress the mind neither can nor will ever turn back. The idea that a scientific thinker would willingly renounce all that has been gained through new conquests is absurd, while in the arts, on the other hand, where there is no progressive development in a continuous series, it is quite conceivable that one might want to forget the progress of an entire period. It has happened often enough.

The example of science, then, shows us a highly important field of culture where at least up to the present the progression is unmistakable and, to all appearances, unbroken. It is a field where the spirit finds its way clearly and definitely marked. Whither it will lead us and what the promise which motions us onward, it is not for us to know.

One thing is certain. This undeniable and positive progress, by which I mean penetration, refinement, purification, in short, improvement, has brought scientific thinking to a state of crisis the outcome of which still remains shrouded in uncertainty. The new knowledge has not yet settled in culture. It has not yet been integrated in a new cosmic conception of illuminating harmony. The aggregate of all knowledge has not yet become culture in us. Rather it would seem as if, with the progressive scientific penetration and dissection of reality, the foundations of our thinking grow ever more precarious and unstable. Old truths have to be abandoned, general terms of everyday use which we thought to be the keys to understanding will now no longer fit the lock. Evolution, yes, but be very careful with it, for the concept is slightly rusty. Elements . . . their immutability no longer exists. Causation . . . on the whole there is little one can do with the concept; it breaks at the slightest usage. Natural laws . . . certainly, but better not talk too much of absolute validity. Objectivity . . . it is still our duty as well as our ideal, but its perfect realisation is not possible, at least not for the social sciences and the humanities.

Our Epimenides of a moment ago may well heave sighs of despair at all this. How he will rub his eyes in incredulous wonder when told that in some sciences (it is said of mathematics) analysis has become so diversified and refined that even the closest professional colleagues can no longer fully understand one another. How great will be his joyful surprise, on the other hand, at hearing that the homogeneity of all matter is on the point of being proved, so that chemistry will have to return to the lap of physics from which once it sprang.

But then again there is this: the means of apperception themselves are beginning to fail us. In the field of microphysics the phenomena must begin to escape observation, since the processes under investigation are more delicate than the instruments of observation, limited as the latter's capacities are by the speed of light. In the case of the most minute quantities the disturbance of the process caused by the fact of observation itself is such as to render full objectivity unattainable. Causation then comes to the border-line of its validity behind which there lies a field of undetermined occurrence.

The phenomena which physics embodies in exact formulae are so remote from our plane of life, the relationships established in mathematics lie so far beyond the sphere in which our thinking moves, that both sciences have long since felt themselves forced to recognise the insufficiency of our old and seemingly well-tested logical instrument. We have had to familiarise ourselves with the idea that for an understanding of nature one may have to work with non-Euclidian geometry and more than three dimensions. Reason in its old form, wedded as it is to Aristotelian logic, can no longer keep up with science. Research forces us to think far beyond the limits of the imagination. Formulae afford the medium of expressing the new discoveries, but the imagination is incapable of conveying the particular reality to our mind. The confident "it is" is reduced to a hesitating "it appears to be." A process appears to be the action of waves or of particles depending on the angle from which it is viewed. Dispense with formulae to express a scientific generalisation and only analogy remains. Which of us outsiders has not often longed to hear from the physicist whether he is to take those representations with which the physicist tries to explain the world of atoms, as symbols or as the direct description of actual realities?

Science seems to have approached the very limits of our power of thought. It is a well-known fact that more than one physicist suffers this continuous working in a mental atmosphere for which the human organism does not seem to be adapted, as a heavy burden, oppressing him sometimes to the point of despair. Yet, desist he will not and cannot. The layman may indulge in a longing for the comfortably tangible reality of older days and reach for his Buffon to delight in that simple and serene representation of the world in which there is the scent of new mown hay and the song of a lingering bird. But the science of yesterday has now become poetry and history.

I once asked De Sitter whether this longing for visions of yore ever broke through his thoughts of the expansion, the emptiness, or the spherical shape of the universe. The seriousness of his denial at once showed me the foolishness of my question.

Is the vertigo of our thinking at the infiniteness of knowledge perhaps similar to that which the mind had to conquer to dare to jump from the Ptolemaic to the Copernican view of the universe?

The categories with which thinking has contented itself so far seem to be in dissolution. Limits are effaced, contradictions appear compatible. Interdependence becomes the watchword of all modern observation of human and social processes. In sociology, economics, psychology or history, everywhere explanation in terms of direct orthodox cause and effect has had to make way for the recognition of many-sided composite relationships and mutual dependence. The concept of condition is supplanting that of cause.

One can go even further. Historic thinking is becoming increasingly antinomic and ambivalent. Antinomic: that is, the mind finds itself as it were suspended between two opposites which before seemed to exclude one another. Ambivalent: that is, our judgment, conscious of the relative merits of two opposing decisions, hesitates before the choice like the ass of Buridan.

Indeed, there is sufficient reason to speak of a crisis of modern thought and knowledge so violent and so far-reaching as can hardly be found in any known period of the past. . . .

CHAPTER VIII: THE DECLINE OF THE CRITICAL SPIRIT

. . . There is reason to speak also of a weakening of the critical spirit, a decline of the critical capacities, a diminishing regard for truth . . . not [only] as a mass phenomenon of the consumers of knowledge but as an organic failing on the part of those who produce it. Related to this decadence-symptom there is still another which we may call the perversion of the function of science or the misuse of science as a means. Let us attempt to deal with this group of phenomena.

At the same moment that science began to reveal its formerly undreamt-of potentialities for dominating nature, vastly extending human power by virtue of its new depth of insight, its capacity to serve as a touchstone of pure knowledge and a guide rule for life declined. The proportion between its various functions changed.

These functions have long been threefold: acquisition and extension of knowledge, education of society to higher and purer forms of civilization, and creation of means to adapt and control natural forces. During the rise of modern science in the seventeenth and eighteenth centuries the first two functions generally kept pace with one another while the third still lagged far behind. The advance of knowledge and the recession of ignorance and superstition filled people with enthusiasm. There was not a soul to doubt the high educational and guidance value of science at that time. More was built on it than its foundations could ever support. With every new discovery the world and its processes came to be better understood. A certain ethical gain was implied in this growing lucidity of the enquiring mind. Meanwhile, what we have called the third function of science, the creation of technical means, made relatively little progress. Electricity was a curiosity for the educated public. Up till the beginning of the nineteenth century the age-old forms of traction and transmission of power remained virtually unchallenged. For the eighteenth century one might express the relationship between the three functions of science, extension of knowledge, education, and creation of technical means, in the series 8:4:1.

If one desired to give numerical expression to their relationship in our time it might be 2:16:16, for instance. The proportion between the three functions has become an entirely different one. Perhaps this low estimate of the educational value of science relative to its knowledge and application values will arouse a storm of protest. And yet, could anyone maintain that the marvellous discoveries of modern science, inaccessible to the minds of any but the initiated few, as they necessarily must be, still continue to contribute materially to the general level of culture? Even the best teaching at universities and inferior educational institutions cannot alter the fact that, while the acquisition of knowledge and its technical application are still daily progressing at an astounding pace, the educational value of science is now no greater than it was a century ago.

The human being of to-day seldom, if ever, looks to science for his philosophy of life. It is not science itself which is to blame. There is a strong tendency away from science. People no longer believe in its capacity for guidance, and not altogether without reason; there has been a time when science claimed too large a share of the world's mastery. But there is also something else besides natural reaction: deterioration of the intellectual conscience. The impulse to achieve a maximum of objectivity and exactness in thinking on the rationally comprehensible, and to apply the test of criticism to such thinking, is weakening. A vast and murky twilight seems to have spread over numberless minds. All the delimitations between the logical, the aesthetic and the emotive functions are purposely ignored. Sentiment is allowed to play a part in forming judgment regardless of the object of judgment and in direct negation of the claims of the critical intellect. Intuition is called upon to justify a choice which in reality is based on emotional predisposition. Interest and desire are confused with consciousness of truth. And to justify all this, what actually is the abandonment of the logical principle itself is paraded as the necessary revolt against the supreme rule of reason.

We have all long since outgrown the belief in a tyrannically consistent rationalism. We realise that not everything can be measured by reason. The advance of thought itself has brought us this realisation. A richer and deeper understanding than the solely rational has given greater meaning to our knowledge. But where the wise man, through freer and ampler judgment, finds a deeper sense in things and life, the fool finds in this freedom only license for greater nonsense. It is a truly tragic consequence: in the process of realising the limitations of reason the modern mind has become susceptible to absurdities to which it had long been immune. . . .

The brakes [of criticism] are failing. . . . It is undeniable that with the renewed desire for synthesis in the social sciences, in itself a healthy and beneficial reaction against the excessive analysis of a preceding period, the "hunch" has come to play a growing part in scientific production. There is an unending succession of bold syntheses, often constructed with great skill and erudition, in which the "originality" of the author enjoys greater triumphs than would seem compatible with sober-minded science. The social philosopher sometimes assumes the rôle of the *bel esprit* of former ages, but it is often not quite clear whether in so doing he takes himself seriously, though he certainly intends to be taken seriously by his readers. The result is something which stands in between cultural philosophy and cultural fantasy. A strong tendency towards aesthetic forms of expression often adds still more to the confused character of the product.

The natural sciences are not plagued with afflictions of this type. They have in the mathematical formula the immediate test of the veracity, not of the validity, of their products. In their domain there is no place for the *bel esprit* and the charlatan is immediately expelled. It is both the privilege and the danger of the humanities that for expressing their ideas they need notions lying beyond the sphere of pure reason in the domain of aesthetic perception.

Over the entire range of the non-exact sciences judgment has become less definite, in contrast with the natural sciences which are able to demand ever greater accuracy of statement. The thoroughly rational is no longer the unchallenged instrument it used to be. Judgment is less tempered by formula and tradition than before. How popular and indispensable have words like "vision," "conception" or "introspection" become to indicate the process of forming knowledge! All this has brought a large measure of indefiniteness to judgment. This indefiniteness *may* be beneficial. But it carries with it the danger of intellectual vacillation between steady conviction and an easy toying with ideas. In view of the antinomic quality of thinking in general, already commented upon, the decision: "This I really think" has become greatly more difficult for the rigorously self-critical mind. For the shallow or prejudiced mind it has become all the more easy.

The lowering of the standards of critical judgment has, I think, been promoted in no small degree by the trend of thought which may be called the Freudian. Freudian psychiatry discovered significant data whose interpretation led research from the field of psychology on to that of sociology and culture. Then the not unusual phenomenon occurred that the mind trained in exact observation and analysis, when faced with the task of sociological, that is, inexact interpretation, shows itself completely lacking in norms by which to judge and evaluate scientific evidence. And thus in this unfamiliar field it is led to jump from any "hunch" to the most far-reaching conclusions which would crumble into nothingness the moment they were subjected to the test of the philosophical-historical method. If, then, the constructions so arrived at are furthermore accepted in wide circles as recognised truths, and their technical terms passed about as ready-made instruments of thought, large groups of a low critical average are accordingly given a welcome opportunity to play at science to their hearts' content. Think only of the pitiful exhibitions of the authors of popular dissertations who explain everything about man and his world in psycho-analytical terms, building their spacious theories and conclusions on "symbols," "complexes" and "phases of infantile psychic life"! . . .

CHAPTER X: THE DISAVOWAL OF THE INTELLECTUAL PRINCIPLE

Decline of the critical spirit, weakening of judgment, perversion of the function of science, all point to a serious cultural disorder. To think, however, that in locating these symptoms one is attacking the evil at its roots, is to make a grave mistake. For already we hear the swelling chorus of objections from the self-styled bearers of a new culture: "But we do not want a tried and tested knowledge to rule us and to decide over our actions; our aim is not to think and to know but to live and to do."

Here we have the pivotal point of the present crisis of civilization: the conflict between *knowing* and *being,* between intelligence and existence. There is nothing novel about it. The essential insufficiency of our understanding was already realised in the earliest days of philosophy. The reality in and through which we live is in its essence unknowable, inaccessible to the processes of the mind, absolutely disparate from thought. In the first half of the nineteenth century this old truth, already understood by a Nicolaus Cusanus, is taken up again by Kierkegaard, whose philosophy centres upon the antithesis of existing and thinking. It served him to found his faith all the more firmly. It was not until much later that other thinkers forced this thought on to tracks away from God and let it derail in nihilism and despair, or in worship of earthly life. Nietzsche, deeply convinced of man's tragic exile from truth and interpreting the will to life as will to power, repudiated the intellectual principle with all the poetical vigour of his genius. Pragmatism deprived the concept truth of its claim to absolute validity by placing it in the flow of time. To the pragmatists truth is what has essential validity for those professing it. Something is true when and in so far as it is valid for a particular time. A crude mind could easily think: something is valid, therefore it is true. A truth-concept reduced to only relative value was bound to bring a kind of ideological egalitarianism, an abolition of all differences of rank and value of ideas, in its wake. Sociological thinkers like Max Weber, Max Scheler, Karl Mannheim and Oswald Spengler have of late introduced the term of the *Seinsverbundenheit des Denkens,* which may be very imperfectly rendered with "the environment- or life-conditioned nature of thought." The concept itself makes them next-door neighbours to historical materialism, which is professedly anti-intellectual. Thus the tendencies of a whole age which, to avoid the vagueness of "anti-intellectual," we venture to call anti-noetic, merged into a mighty stream which shortly was to threaten what were long thought to be insurmountable barriers of intellectual culture. It was Georges Sorel who, in his *Réflexions sur la Violence,* formulated the practical political consequences of all this, thereby becoming the spiritual father of all modern dictatorships.

But it is not only the dictators and their followers who desire the subjugation of the will to knowledge to the vital impulse. We have here the most fundamental element of the cultural crisis as a whole. This revulsion of the spirit is the essential process dominating the situation in which we find ourselves to-day.

Was it philosophical thought which led the way and society which followed? or do we have to reverse the order and admit that it is a case of thought dancing to the tune of life? The doctrine itself which subjugates knowledge to life seems to impose the latter view.

Have earlier generations ever renounced the intellectual principle in this way? It seems impossible to find historical parallels. Systematic philosophical and practical anti-intellectualism such as we are witnessing, appears to be something truly novel in the history of human culture. To be sure, the past has often known reactions of thought whereby a too exclusive primacy of the understanding was succeeded by a revindication of the will. This is what happened, for instance, when the thought of Duns Scotus took its place beside that of Thomas Aquinas. These spiritual reactions, however, were not concerned with practical life or the worldly order but with the Faith, the striving for the ultimate meaning of life. And this striving itself always remained an "apprehending," however far reason was left behind. The modern mind too often confuses intellectualism with rationalism. Even those forms of approach which, transgressing the purely intellectual, were intended to attain through insight and contemplation what was inaccessible to the understanding, always remained directed towards knowledge of truth. The Greek or the Indian word for it, *gnosis* or *jnâna,* makes it clear enough that even the purest mysticism remains a "knowing." It is always the spirit which moves in the world of the intelligible. To have truth was always the ideal. There are no instances known to me of cultures having forsaken Truth or renounced the understanding in its widest sense.

When earlier currents of thought repudiated allegiance to Reason it was always in favour of the super-rational. What parades as the culture of to-day does not only disavow Reason but also the knowable itself, and this in favour of the sub-rational, the passions and the instincts. It votes for the will, not in the sense of Duns Scotus, however, but for the will to worldly power for "existence," for "blood and soil," instead of "understanding" and "spirit."

CHAPTER XI: THE WORSHIP OF LIFE

Keen insight

The next addition to the collection of intellectually fashionable words will doubtless be "existential." I can see it springing up on all sides. Before long it will have landed with the public at large. When, in order to convince one's audience of profundity, one has said "dynamic" long enough, it will be "existential." The word will serve to forsake the spirit all the more solemnly, a sneer at all that is knowledge and truth.

At meetings of scholars statements are heard which even a short time ago would have been thought too senseless to be comical. According to newspaper reports, a speaker at the Congress of Philologists held in Treves in October, 1934, declared that what one should expect from science was not so much truth as "whetted swords." When another of those present showed himself lacking in respect for certain instances of nationalist interpretation of history, he was reproached by the chairman with "lack of subjectivity." Note, all this at a congress of scholars.

This is what our civilized world has come to. Let it not be thought that the degeneration of the critical spirit confines itself to the countries where extreme nationalism has triumphed. Any observer can find numerous proofs in his own environment of a certain indifference of large numbers of educated people to the degree of truth embodied in the figures of their world of ideas. The categories fiction and history, in their simple and current meaning, are no longer clearly distinguished. It is no longer asked whether the truth-content of intellectual matter is up to standard. The ascendancy of the concept "mythos" is the clearest example. People accept a representation in which the elements of wish and fantasy are purposely included but which nevertheless proclaims to represent "the past" and to serve as a guide-rule for life, thereby hopelessly confusing the spheres of knowledge and will.

"Existence-conditioned" thought striving for expression allows fanciful allegory to creep into logical argument, unchecked by critical reasoning. If life cannot be expressed in terms of logic, as everyone must admit to be the case, then it is for the poet to step in where the logical approach fails. Thus it has been as long as the world has known the art of poetry. In the process of cultural development, however, thinker and poet came to be clearly distinguished, and each was allotted his own domain. Of late the new "life philosophy" has shown a tendency to relapse into a bewildering confusion of logical and poetical means of expression. Among the latter the blood-metaphor occupies an especially prominent place. The poets and the sages of all peoples and ages have always made a ready use of the image of "the blood" to catch an active principle of life in one striking word. Although, abstractly speaking, other humours would have been just as capable of conveying the suggestion of heredity and relationship, in blood one saw, felt, and heard the flow of life; in the shedding of blood one saw life ebbing away; blood stood for courage and battle. The image of blood has of old had a sacred content also; in fact, it became the expression of the most profound divine mystery while at the same time it remained a meaningful term for the most prosaic proverb. While it should be no cause for surprise, therefore, that this old image of the blood should still enjoy widespread popularity one may, nevertheless, well feel wonder to see it now restored to the rank of an official term in the juridical phraseology of a great modern nation.

The order of precedence of blood and spirit has been completely reversed by the apostles of the life philosophy. Of the philosopher R. Müller-Freienfels I find quoted: "The essence of our mind lies not in purely intellectual understanding, but in its biological function as a means for the preservation of life." Let no one dare to attribute this function to "the blood"!

The obsession with life is to be viewed as a manifestation of excessive full-bloodedness, to remain in the terminology of the life-philosophy. Through the technical perfection of all comforts of life, the in every way increased security of life, the greater accessibility of all types of pleasure, and the vast and still lingering growth of material prosperity, society has got into a state which in the old pathology might have been called a "plethora." We have been living in spiritual and material superabundance. We are so preoccupied with life because it is made so easy for us. The ever-growing power of observation and the facility of intellectual communication have made life strong and bold. Till well into the middle of the nineteenth century even the well-to-do section of European society was in much more direct and constant contact with the miseries of existence than we are to-day and think our due. Our own grandfathers were given only very limited possibilities of killing pain, healing wounds or fractures, shutting out cold, expelling darkness, communicating with others directly or indirectly, avoiding filth and stench. On all sides man was continually made to feel the natural limitations of earthly well-being. The efficient ministering of the technical, hygienic and sanitary appliances with which man has surrounded himself is spoiling him. He is losing the good-humoured resignation in the daily imperfections of human well-being which formed the discipline of earlier generations. But at the same time he runs the risk of losing the natural ability to take human happiness as it offers itself, as well. Life is made too easy. Mankind's moral fibre is giving way under the softening influence of luxury.

In earlier civilizations, whether Christian, Moslem, Buddhist or any other, there was always this contrast: in principle the value of earthly happiness is depreciated relatively to celestial bliss or union with the All. As all these religions, however, do recognise a relative worth of earthly pleasures and consider them as God-given, denial of the value of life meant ingratitude. It was the very realisation of the precariousness of every moment of human well-being which caused it to be appreciated at its true value. A steady orientation on the hereafter may lead to a renunciation of the terrestrial, but it does not permit of *Weltschmerz*.[1]

In the present there is a contrast also, but it is a very different one. The increase of security, of comfort, and of the possibilities of want-gratification, in short the greater ease of living, has had two results. On the one hand, it has prepared the soil for all forms of renunciation of life: philosophical denial of its value, purely emotive spleen or aversion from life; on the other, it has instilled the belief in the right to happiness. It has made people expect things from life. Related to this there is another contrast. The ambivalent attitude which wavers between the renunciation and the enjoyment of life is peculiar to the individual alone. The community, however, without hesitation and with more conviction than ever before, accepts earthly life as the object of all striving and action. It is indeed a true worship of life.

Now it is a question for serious consideration whether any advanced culture can survive without a certain measure of orientation on Death. The great civilizations of the past have all had it. There are signs that the philosophical thought of to-day is also coming to it. It seems only logical, moreover, that a philosophy which rates "living" above "knowing" should also include the end of life in its vision.

These are strange times. Reason, which once combated faith and seemed to have conquered it, now has to look to faith to save it from dissolution. For it is only on the unshaken and unyielding foundation of a living metaphysical

[1] [That is, sentimental pessimism.]

belief that the concept of absolute truth, with its consequence of absolute validity of ethical norms, can withstand the growing pressure of the instinctive will to live.

Wondrous illusion! Knowledge and understanding are violently attacked from all sides, but always with the weapons of semi-knowledge and misunderstanding. To prove the inutility of the intellectual instrument one has no alternative but to appeal to other knowledge than that which is scorned. Reality and life itself remain inscrutable and mute. All speaking implies knowing. Even the poetry which most passionately attempts to penetrate to the core of life itself (I am thinking of Whitman and certain poems of Rilke) remains a product of the mind, a knowing. To take the anti-noetic principle seriously and consistently is to deny oneself the power of speech.

A philosophy which from the outset declares its basic truths to be conditioned by the particular organisation of life which it serves, is really superfluous for the upholders of this organisation and worthless for the rest of the world. It serves only to support and to rationalise the existing order. Why, if it is not knowledge and understanding that matter, why, then, enlist the thinkers in the service of the all-powerful State to prove its value? Give them a spade, a marital bed and a yard of gold braid. . . .

CHAPTER XXI: KATHARSIS

It is not from intervention by social organisations that we must expect deliverance. The foundations of culture are not such that the organs of society, whether they be nations, churches, schools or parties, could reaffirm or strengthen them. What is required is an internal regeneration of the individual. The spiritual *habitus* of man himself will have to change.

The world of to-day has gone far on the road towards a universal disavowal of ethical standards. It no longer draws a clear line between good and evil. It is inclined to view the entire crisis of civilization as simply the conflict of opposing forces, a struggle for power between antagonists. And yet the one and only hope lies in the recognition that in this struggle human action must be governed by a principle of absolute good and evil. From such recognition it follows that deliverance *cannot* lie in the triumph of one State, one people, one race, or one class. To subjugate the criteria of approval and condemnation to a purpose which is based on egotism is to pervert all true feelings of human responsibility.

The dilemma facing our time grows more acute every day. Once again look at the world in its present political confusion. Everywhere there are complications whose solution can hardly be evaded any longer, and of which any impartial observer must admit that a solution satisfying all legitimate interests and meeting all legitimate demands can hardly be devised. They concern problems of national minorities, impossible boundaries, prohibitions of natural unions, intolerable economic conditions. All these situations engender an atmosphere of exasperation which makes them into so many powder magazines threatening to blow off the lid at any moment. In every one of them the opposing interests are deadlocked in the conflict of rightful claims. There appear to be only two solutions. One of them is armed force, the other is adjustment on the basis of real international goodwill, of mutual renunciation of legitimate claims, of respect for the rights and interests of others; briefly, of unselfishness and equitableness.

From these virtues the world of to-day seems further removed than it has been, or at least pretended to be, for many a century. Even in principle the requirement of international equity and of international harmony to-day finds widespread disavowal. The theory of the unbridled authoritarian State provides an *a priori* acquittal for any potential invader. The world remains helplessly threatened by the madness of a devastating war bringing new and greater degeneration in its wake.

Public forces operate to ward off the senseless evil, to bring agreement and consultation. The smallest success of the League of Nations, though Ares greet it with a smirk of derision, to-day means more than the greatest display of power on land or at sea. Still, in the long run, the forces of a sensible internationalism are not enough if there is no change of spirit. Neither the prevention of war by international action nor the restoration of order and prosperity is in itself sufficient to bring a purification of culture. A new culture can only grow up in the soil of a purged humanity.

Katharsis: thus the Greeks called the state of mind produced by the spectacle of the tragedy, the stillness of heart in which compassion and fear have been dissolved, the purification of the soul which springs from having grasped a deeper meaning in things; which creates a grave and new preparedness for acts of duty and the acceptance of fate; which breaks the *hybris* [2] as it was seen to be broken in the tragedy; which liberates from the violent passions of life and leads the soul to peace.

For a spiritual clarification which our time needs, a new *askesis* [3] will be necessary. The bearers of a purified culture will have to be like those waking in an early dawn. They will have to shake off evil dreams. The dream of their soul which grew up out of the mud and would sink back into it. The dream of their brain which was but steel wire and their heart of glass. The dream of

[2] [That is, violence arising from passion or recklessness.]

[3] [That is, a self-imposed discipline.]

their hands growing into claws and the tusks between their lips. They will have to remind themselves that man can *will* himself not to be an animal.

The new *askesis* will not be one of renunciation of the world for heavenly bliss; it will be one of self-domination and tempered appraisal of power and pleasure. The exaltation of life will have to be toned down a little. One will have to remember how Plato already described the occupation of the wise man as a preparation for death. A steady orientation of the life-consciousness of death heightens the proper use of life itself.

The new *askesis* will have to be a surrender, a surrender to all that can be conceived as the highest. That can no more be nation or class than the individual existence of self. Happy those for whom that principle can only bear the name of Him who spoke: "I am the way, the truth, and the life."

The political revivalisms of the day have caught something of the spiritual attitude necessary for the restoration of culture, but it is impure, wrapped up in excessive puerilism, overborne by the cries of the caged animal, sullied by falsehood and deception. The younger generation, which will somehow have to carry on this culture in its next phase, is not lacking in readiness to give itself, to serve and to suffer, to do great deeds and to sacrifice itself. But the general weakening of judgment and the subversion of moral standards prevent it from testing the true worth of the principle which it is asked to serve.

It is difficult to see where the indispensable purification of the spirit will have to set in. Do we have to pass through still greater depths to become pliable? Or has the rallying of men of goodwill all over the world, unseen under the noisy confusion of the day, already begun? To repeat: the cultivation of internationalism is not all that is needed. None the less, it is of the greatest importance that this patient labour of preparing mankind for better times is continued, as it is carried on to-day in many places throughout the world, by small groups of like-minded individuals, by official international organisations, from the religious, political or cultural point of view. Wherever even the frailest flower of true internationalism (better were to call it internation*ality*) raises its head, support it, strengthen it by grafting it on to the national consciousness, provided the latter be pure. It will flourish all the better for it. The international spirit—the word international itself already implies the preservation of nationalities, but of nationalities which tolerate each other and which do not make conflicts out of contrasts—may become the mould for the new ethics in which the opposition collectivism-individualism will have been dissolved. Is it an idle dream that one day this world could know such goodness? Even if it were, we would still have to cling to the ideal.

But does not the expression of these desires and expectations of a purging of the spirit, a *katharsis* which would be like a conversion, a rebirth, a regeneration, involve us in a contradiction with something we established in the beginning of this [essay]? There we said that earlier periods, in their longing for a better society, had fixed their hopes on a reversal, an insight, a regaining of sense and virtue, as a conscious and early change for the better. Our time, however, knows that great spiritual and social changes are realised only through a process of gradual development, at the best temporarily accelerated by some extraordinary sudden impetus. And yet we are now demanding and hoping for a revulsion, in a way even for a return?

We are here faced again with the antinomic determination, the inconclusiveness of all our judgment. We are forced to recognise a certain amount of truth in the older vision. There must be a possibility of conversion and reversal in the development of civilization. We are thinking here of the recognition or retrieval of eternal truths, truths that are above the stream of evolution and change. It is these values that are at stake.

A time of heavy mental pressure such as that in which we are living is easier to bear for the old than the young. The old know that they only have to help carry the burden of the times a little further. Resignedly they review how the world was, or seemed to be, when they began to shoulder their share of the burden, and what it appears to be turning into now. Their yesterday and tomorrow almost fade into one. Their fears and cares grow lighter in the proximity of death; their hope and trust, their will and courage to act, they place in the hands of those who have the task of living still before them. It is for the latter to accept the grave duty of judging, choosing, working, acting. Theirs the heavy responsibility, theirs the knowledge of what is to come.

The writer of these pages belongs to those whose privilege it is in their official occupations and personal life continually to remain in close contact with youth. It is his belief that the now young generation, in fitness for the difficult tasks of life, is fully equal to that which preceded it. The loosening of restraints, the confusion of thought, the diversion of attention and dissipation of energy under which this generation grew up have not made it weak, lax or indifferent. It seems open, generous, spontaneous, ready for pleasure but also for hardships; decisive, courageous and of great purpose. It walks with a lighter step than its predecessors.

To this young generation the task of ruling this world again as it would be ruled, to save it from perishing in pride and folly, to permeate it again with the spirit!

OSWALD SPENGLER

IN THE SUMMER of 1918, at the end of the twentieth century's first world war, there appeared in the bookshops of Germany and Austria a massive volume bearing the ominous title *Der Untergang des Abendlandes* (a second volume followed in 1922). Its author, Oswald Spengler, born in 1880, was an obscure teacher and scholar. After a few weeks of uncertain sales, the work caught on, was read widely in Germany, and then gradually came to the notice of foreign readers. Its popularity spread until at length an English translation by Charles Francis Atkinson, entitled *The Decline of the West,* was published in "prosperous," "optimistic" America in 1926 (volume two appeared in 1928). Although *The Decline of the West,* from which the following selection has been drawn, is looked upon by some scholars as historically inaccurate and philosophically pretentious, even murky and absurd, it has continued to command a considerable, if not always a learned, audience. This is because Spengler, for all his academic inadequacies, was extraordinarily sensitive to the currents of twentieth-century cultural disenchantment and admirably equipped to express them in imaginative metaphor. For the belief in "progress" which, in vulgarized versions, had permeated much of the thinking of the late nineteenth century, he substituted a stoic pessimism. Basically a man of conservative social and political disposition, he expressed, powerfully if not lucidly, a widespread apprehension over the character and quality of a civilization which seemed incapable of solving its problems and which seemed to many to have lost its sense of direction and meaning. A gloomy prophet, Spengler predicted the inevitable decay and death of Western civilization, a victim of urbanization, mass democracy, Caesarism, imperialism, and nationalism. As one recent student of Spengler and his influence has expressed it: "*The Decline of the West . . .* formulated more comprehensively than any other book the modern *malaise* that so many feel and so few can express. It has become the classic summary of the now familiar pessimism of the twentieth-century West with regard to its historical future." (H. Stuart Hughes.)

Spengler lived to see the advent of Nazism with a "Caesar" whose coming he seemed to have prophesied. But it would be a mistake to associate the author of *The Decline of the West* with the rise of fascism, except symptomatically. He distrusted the radical nihilism of the Nazis, and rejected their theories of race. For their part, the Nazis distrusted his conservative, romantic, even aristocratic prejudices. During the Nazi dictatorship, reading of Spengler's works virtually ceased in Germany. He died in 1936, more a disciple of the nineteenth-century Friedrich Nietzche (1844–1900) than a preceptor of the twentieth-century Adolf Hitler.

THE DECLINE OF THE WEST

CHAPTER I: INTRODUCTION

I

. . . Is there a logic of history? Is there, beyond all the casual and incalculable elements of the separate events, something that we may call a metaphysical structure of historic humanity, something that is essentially independent of the outward forms—social, spiritual and political—which we see so clearly? Are not these actualities indeed secondary or derived from that something? Does world-history present to the seeing eye certain grand traits, again and again, with sufficient constancy to justify certain conclusions? And if so, what are the limits to which reasoning from such premises may be pushed?

Is it possible to find in life itself—for human history is the sum of mighty life-courses which already have had to be endowed with ego and personality, in customary thought and expression, by predicating entities of a higher order like "the Classical" or "the Chinese Culture," "Modern Civilization"—a series of stages which must be traversed, and traversed moreover in an ordered and obligatory sequence? For everything organic the notions of birth, death, youth, age, lifetime are fundamentals—may not these notions, in this sphere also, possess a rigorous meaning which no one has as yet extracted? In short, is all history founded upon general biographic archetypes?

The decline of the West, which at first sight may appear, like the corresponding decline of the Classical Culture, a phenomenon limited in time and space, we now perceive to be a philosophical problem that, when comprehended in all its gravity, includes within itself every great question of Being. . . .

III

Thus our theme . . . broadens itself into a new philosophy—*the* philosophy of the future, so far as the metaphysically-exhausted soil of the West can bear such, and in any case the only philosophy which is within the *possibilities* of the West-European mind in its next stages. It expands into the conception of a *morphology of world history,* of the world-as-history in contrast to the morphology of the world-as-nature that hitherto has been almost the only theme of philosophy. And it reviews once again the forms and move-

---

This selection has been reprinted from *The Decline of the West* by Oswald Spengler, by permission of Alfred A. Knopf, Inc., Copyright 1926 by Alfred A. Knopf, Inc., New York, Vol. I, pp. 3–6, 14–23, 25–27, 31–43.

ments of the world in their depths and final significance, but this time according to an entirely different ordering which groups them, not in an ensemble picture inclusive of everything known, but in a picture of *life,* and presents them not as things-become, but as things-becoming. . . .

V

Amongst the Western peoples, it was the Germans who discovered the mechanical *clock,* the dread symbol of the flow of time, and the chimes of countless clock towers that echo day and night over West Europe are perhaps the most wonderful expression of which a historical world-feeling is capable.[1] In the timeless countrysides and cities of the Classical world, we find nothing of the sort. Till the epoch of Pericles, the time of day was estimated merely by the length of shadow, and it was only from that of Aristotle that the word ὥρα received the (Babylonian) significance of "hour"; prior to that there was no exact subdivision of the day. In Babylon and Egypt water-clocks and sun-dials were discovered in the very early stages, yet in Athens it was left to Plato to introduce a practically useful form of clepsydra, and this was merely a minor adjunct of everyday utility which could not have influenced the Classical life-feeling in the smallest degree.

It remains still to mention the corresponding difference, which is very deep and has never yet been properly appreciated, between Classical and modern mathematics. The former conceived of things *as they are,* as *magnitudes,* timeless and purely present, and so it proceeded to Euclidean geometry and mathematical statics, rounding off its intellectual system with the theory of conic sections. We conceive things as they *become* and *behave,* as *function,* and this brought us to dynamics, analytical geometry and thence to the Differential Calculus.[2] The modern theory of functions is the imposing marshalling of this whole mass of thought. It is a bizarre, but nevertheless psychologically exact, fact that the physics of the Greeks—being statics and not dynamics—neither knew the use nor felt the absence of the time-element, whereas we on the other hand work in thousandths of a second. The one and only evolution-idea that is timeless, ahistoric, is Aristotle's entelechy.

[1] It was about 1000 A.D. and therefore contemporaneously with the beginning of the Romanesque style and the Crusades—the first symptoms of a new Soul—that Abbot Gerbert (Pope Sylvester II), the friend of the Emperor Otto III, invented the mechanism of the chiming wheel-clock. In Germany too, the first tower-clocks made their appearance, about 1200, and the pocket watch somewhat later. Observe the significant association of time measurement with the edifices of religion.

[2] Newton's choice of the name "fluxions" for his calculus was meant to imply a standpoint towards certain metaphysical notions as to the nature of time. In Greek mathematics time figures not at all.

This, then, is our task. We men of the Western Culture are, with our historical sense, an exception and not a rule. World-history is *our* world picture and not all mankind's. Indian and Classical man formed no image of a world in progress, and perhaps when in due course the civilization of the West is extinguished, there will never again be a Culture and a human type in which "world-history" is so potent a form of the waking consciousness.

VI

What, then, *is* world-history? Certainly, an ordered presentation of the past, an inner postulate, the expression of a capacity for feeling form. But a feeling for form, however definite, is not the same as form itself. No doubt we feel world-history, experience it, and believe that it is to be read just as a map is read. But, even to-day, it is only forms of it that we know and not *the* form of it, which is the mirror-image of *our own* inner life.

Everyone of course, if asked, would say that he saw the inward form of History quite clearly and definitely. The illusion subsists because no one has seriously reflected on it, still less conceived doubts as to his own knowledge, for no one has the slightest notion how wide a field for doubt there is. In fact, the *lay-out* of world-history is an unproved and subjective notion that has been handed down from generation to generation (not only of laymen but of professional historians) and stands badly in need of a little of that scepticism which from Galileo onward has regulated and deepened our inborn ideas of nature.

Thanks to the subdivision of history into "Ancient," "Mediaeval" and "Modern"—an incredibly jejune and *meaningless* scheme, which has, however, entirely dominated our historical thinking—we have failed to perceive the true position in the general history of higher mankind, of the little part-world which has developed on West-European [3] soil from the time of the

[3] Here the historian is gravely influenced by preconceptions derived from geography, which assumes a *Continent* of Europe and feels himself compelled to draw an ideal frontier corresponding to the physical frontier between "Europe" and "Asia." The word "Europe" ought to be struck out of history. There is historically no "European" type, and it is sheer delusion to speak of the Hellenes as "European Antiquity" (were Homer and Heraclitus and Pythagoras, then, Asiatics?) and to enlarge upon their "mission" as such. These phrases express no realities but merely a sketchy interpretation of the map. It is thanks to this word "Europe" alone, and the complex of ideas resulting from it, that our historical consciousness has come to link Russia with the West in an utterly baseless unity—a mere abstraction derived from the reading of books—that has led to immense real consequences. In the shape of Peter the Great, this word has falsified the historical tendencies of a primitive human mass for two centuries, whereas the Russian *instinct* has very truly and fundamentally divided "Europe" from "Mother Russia" with the hostility that we can see embodied in Tolstoi, Aksakov or Dostoyevski. "East" and "West" are notions that contain real history, whereas "Europe" is an empty sound. Everything great that the Classical world created, it created in pure denial of the existence of any continental barrier

German-Roman Empire, to judge of its relative importance and above all to estimate its direction. The Cultures that are to come will find it difficult to believe that the validity of such a scheme with its simple rectilinear progression and its meaningless proportions, becoming more and more preposterous with each century, incapable of bringing into itself the new fields of history as they successively come into the light of our knowledge, was, in spite of all, never whole-heartedly attacked. The criticism that it has long been the fashion of historical researches to level at the scheme mean nothing; they have only obliterated the one existing plan without substituting for it any other. To toy with phrases such as "the Greek Middle Ages" or "Germanic antiquity" does not in the least help us to form a clear and inwardly-convincing picture in which China and Mexico, the empire of Axum and that of the Sassanids have their proper places. And the expedient of shifting the initial point of "modern history" from the Crusades to the Renaissance, or from the Renissance to the beginning of the 19th Century, only goes to show that the scheme *per se* is regarded as unshakably sound.

It is not only that the scheme circumscribes the area of history. What is worse, it rigs the stage. The ground of West Europe is treated as a steady pole, a unique patch chosen on the surface of the sphere for no better reason, it seems, than because we live on it—and great histories of millennial duration and mighty far-away Cultures are made to revolve around this pole in all modesty. It is a quaintly conceived system of sun and planets! We select a single bit of ground as the natural centre of the historical system, and make it the central sun. From it all the events of history receive their real light, from it their importance is judged in *perspective*. But it is in our own West-European conceit alone that this phantom "world-history," which a breath of scepticism would dissipate, is acted out.

We have to thank that conceit for the immense optical illusion (become natural from long habit) whereby distant histories of thousands of years, such as those of China and Egypt, are made to shrink to the dimensions of mere episodes while in the neighbourhood of our own position the decades since Luther, and particularly since Napoleon, loom large as Brocken-spectres. We know quite well that the slowness with which a high cloud or a railway train in the distance seems to move is only apparent, yet we believe that the *tempo* of all early Indian, Babylonian or Egyptian history was really slower than that of our own recent past. And we think of them as less substantial,

between Rome and Cyprus, Byzantium and Alexandria. Everything that we imply by the term European Culture came into existence between the Vistula and the Adriatic and the Guadalquivir and, even if we were to agree that Greece, the Greece of Pericles, lay in Europe, the Greece of to-day certainly does not.

more damped-down, more diluted, because we have not learned to make the allowance for (inward and outward) distances.

It is self-evident that for the Cultures of the West the existence of Athens, Florence or Paris is more important than that of Lo-Yang or Pataliputra. But is it permissible to found a scheme of world-history on estimates of such a sort? If so, then the Chinese historian is quite entitled to frame a world-history in which the Crusades, the Renaissance, Caesar and Frederick the Great are passed over in silence as insignificant. How, *from the morphological point of view,* should our 18th Century be more important than any other sixty centuries that preceded it? Is it not ridiculous to oppose a "modern" history of a few centuries, and that history to all intents localized in West Europe, to an "ancient" history which covers as many millennia—incidentally dumping into that "ancient history" the whole mass of the pre-Hellenic cultures, unprobed and unordered, as mere appendix-matter? This is no exaggeration. Do we not, for the sake of keeping the hoary scheme, dispose of Egypt and Babylon—each as an individual and self-contained history quite equal in the balance to our so-called "world-history" from Charlemagne to the World-War and well beyond it—as a *prelude* to classical history? Do we not relegate the vast complexes of Indian and Chinese culture to footnotes, with a gesture of embarrassment? As for the great American cultures, do we not, on the ground that they do not "fit in" (with what?), entirely ignore them?

The most appropriate designation for this current West-European scheme of history, in which the great Cultures are made to follow orbits round *us* as the presumed centre of all world-happenings, is the *Ptolemaic system* of history. The system that is put forward in this work in place of it I regard as the *Copernican discovery* in the historical sphere, in that it admits no sort of privileged position to the Classical or the Western Culture as against the Cultures of India, Babylon, China, Egypt, the Arabs, Mexico—separate worlds of dynamic being which in point of mass count for just as much in the general picture of history as the Classical, while frequently surpassing it in point of spiritual greatness and soaring power.

VII

The scheme "ancient-mediaeval-modern" in its first form was a creation of the Magian world-sense. It first appeared in the Persian and Jewish religions after Cyrus, received an apocalyptic sense in the teaching of the Book of Daniel on the four world-eras, and was developed into a world-history in the post-Christian religions of the East, notably the Gnostic systems.

This important conception, within the very narrow limits which fixed its intellectual basis, was unimpeachable. Neither Indian nor even Egyptian history was included in the scope of the proposition. For the Magian thinker the expression "world-history" means a unique and supremely dramatic act, having as its theatre the lands between Hellas and Persia, in which the strictly dualistic world-sense of the East expressed itself not by means of polar conceptions like the "soul and spirit," "good and evil" of contemporary metaphysics, but by the figure of a catastrophe, an epochal change of phase between world-creation and world-decay.

No elements beyond those which we find stabilized in the Classical literature, on the one hand, and the Bible (or other sacred book of the particular system), on the other, came into the picture, which presents (as "The Old" and "The New," respectively) the easily-grasped contrasts of Gentile and Jewish, Christian and Heathen, Classical and Oriental, idol and dogma, nature and spirit *with a time connotation*—that is, as a drama in which the one prevails over the other. The historical change of period wears the characteristic dress of the religious "Redemption." This "world-history" in short was a conception narrow and provincial, but within its limits logical and complete. Necessarily, therefore, it was specific to this region and this humanity, and incapable of any *natural* extension.

But to these two there has been added a third epoch, the epoch that we call "modern," on Western soil, and it is this that for the first time gives the picture of history the look of a progression. The oriental picture was *at rest.* It presented a self-contained antithesis, with equilibrium as its outcome and a unique divine act as its turning-point. But, adopted and assumed by a wholly new type of mankind, it was quickly transformed (without anyone's noticing the oddity of the change) into a conception of a *linear progress:* from Homer or Adam—the modern can substitute for these names the Indo-German, Old Stone Man, or the Pithecanthropus—through Jerusalem, Rome, Florence and Paris according to the taste of the individual historian, thinker or artist, who has unlimited freedom in the interpretation of the three-part scheme.

This third term, "modern times," which in form asserts that it is the last and conclusive term of the series, has in fact, ever since the Crusades, been stretched and stretched again to the elastic limit at which it will bear no more. It was at least implied if not stated in so many words, that here, beyond the ancient and the mediaeval, something definitive was beginning, a Third Kingdom in which, somewhere, there was to be fulfilment and culmination, and which had an objective point.

As to what this objective point is, each thinker, from Schoolman to present-day Socialist, backs his own peculiar discovery. Such a view into the course of things may be both easy and flattering to the patentee, but in fact he has simply taken the spirit of the West, as reflected in his own brain, for the meaning of the world. So it is that great thinkers, making a metaphysical virtue of intellectual necessity, have not only accepted without serious investigation the scheme of history agreed "by common consent" but have made of it the basis of their philosophies and dragged in God as author of this or that "world-plan." Evidently the mystic number three applied to the world-ages has something highly seductive for the metaphysician's taste. History was described by Herder as the education of the human race, by Kant as an evolution of the idea of freedom, by Hegel as a self-expansion of the world-spirit, by others in other terms, but as regards its ground-plan everyone was quite satisfied when he had thought out some abstract meaning for the conventional threefold order.

On the very threshold of the Western Culture we meet the great Joachim of Floris (c. 1145–1202), the first thinker of the Hegelian stamp who shattered the dualistic world-form of Augustine, and with his essentially Gothic intellect stated the new Christianity of his time in the form of a third term to the religions of the Old and the New Testaments, expressing them respectively as the Age of the Father, the Age of the Son and the Age of the Holy Ghost. His teaching moved the best of the Franciscans and the Dominicans, Dante, Thomas Aquinas, in their inmost souls and awakened a world-outlook which slowly but surely took entire possession of the historical sense of our Culture. Lessing—who often designated his own period, with reference to the Classical as the "after-world" (Nachwelt)—took his idea of the "education of the human race" with its three stages of child, youth and man, from the teaching of the Fourteenth Century mystics. Ibsen treats it with thoroughness in his *Emperor and Galilean* (1873), in which he directly presents the Gnostic world-conception through the figure of the wizard Maximus, and advances not a step beyond it in his famous Stockholm address of 1887. It would appear, then, that the Western consciousness feels itself urged to predicate a sort of finality inherent in its own appearance.

But the creation of the Abbot of Floris was a *mystical* glance into the secrets of the divine world-order. It was bound to lose all meaning as soon as it was used in the way of reasoning and made a hypothesis of *scientific* thinking, as it has been—ever more and more frequently—since the 17th Century.

It is a quite indefensible method of presenting world-history to begin by giving rein to one's own religious, political or social convictions and endowing the sacrosanct three-phase system with tendencies that will bring it exactly to one's own standpoint. This is, in effect, making of some formula —say, the "Age of Reason," Humanity, the greatest happiness of the greatest number, enlightenment, economic progress, national freedom, the conquest of nature, or world-peace—a criterion whereby to judge whole millennia of history. And so we judge that they were ignorant of the "true path," or that they failed to follow it, when the fact is simply that their will and purposes were not the same as ours. Goethe's saying, "What is important in life is life and not a result of life," is the answer to any and every senseless attempt to solve the riddle of historical form by means of a *programme.*

It is the same picture that we find when we turn to the historians of each special art or science (and those of national economics and philosophy as well). We find "Painting" from the Egyptians (or the cave-men) to the Impressionists, or "Music" from Homer to Bayreuth and beyond, or "Social Organization" from Lake Dwellings to Socialism, as the case may be, presented as a linear graph which steadily rises in conformity with the values of the (selected) arguments. No one has seriously considered the possibility that arts may have an allotted span of life and may be attached as forms of self-expression to particular types of mankind, and that therefore the total history of an art may be merely an additive compilation of separate developments, of special arts, with no bond of union save the name and some details of craft-technique.

We know it to be true of every organism that the rhythm, form and duration of its life, and all the expression-details of that life as well, are determined by the *properties of its species.* No one, looking at the oak, with its millennial life, dare say that it is at this moment, now, about to start on its true and proper course. No one as he sees a caterpillar grow day by day expects that it will go on doing so for two or three years. In these cases we feel, with an unqualified certainty, a *limit,* and this sense of the limit is identical with our sense of the inward form. In the case of higher human history, on the contrary, we take our ideas as to the course of the future from an unbridled optimism that sets at naught all historical, i.e., *organic,* experience, and everyone therefore sets himself to discover in the accidental present terms that he can expand into some striking progression-series, the existence of which rests not on scientific proof but on predilection. He works upon unlimited possibilities—never a natural end—and from the momentary top-course of his bricks plans artlessly the continuation of his structure.

"Mankind," however, has no aim, no idea, no plan, any more than the family of butterflies or orchids. "Mankind" is a zoological expression, or an empty word. But conjure away the phantom, break the magic circle, and at once there emerges an astonishing wealth of *actual* forms—the Living with all its immense fullness, depth and movement—hitherto veiled by a catchword, a dry-as-dust scheme, and a set of personal "ideals." I see, in place of that empty figment of *one* linear history which can only be kept up by shutting one's eyes to the overwhelming multitude of the facts, the drama of *a number* of mighty Cultures, each springing with primitive strength from the soil of a mother-region to which it remains firmly bound throughout its whole life cycle; each stamping its material, its mankind, in *its own* image; each having *its own* idea, *its own* passions, *its own* life, will and feeling, *its own* death. Here indeed are colours, lights, movements, that no intellectual eye has yet discovered. Here the Cultures, peoples, languages, truths, gods, landscapes bloom and age as the oaks and the stone-pines, the blossoms, twigs and leaves—but there is no ageing "Mankind." Each Culture has its own new possibilities of self-expression which arise, ripen, decay, and never return. There is not *one* sculpture, *one* painting, *one* mathematics, *one* physics, but many, each in its deepest essence different from the others, each limited in duration and self-contained, just as each species of plant has its peculiar blossom or fruit, its special type of growth and decline. These cultures, sublimated life-essences, grow with the same superb aimlessness as the flowers of the field. They belong, like the plants and the animals, to the living Nature of Goethe, and not to the dead Nature of Newton. I see world-history as a picture of endless formations and transformations, of the marvellous waxing and waning of organic forms. The professional historian, on the contrary, sees it as a sort of a tapeworm industriously adding on to itself one epoch after another.

But the series "ancient-mediaeval-modern history" has at last exhausted its usefulness. Angular, narrow, shallow though it was as a scientific foundation, still we possessed no other form that was not wholly unphilosophical in which our data could be arranged, and world-history (as hitherto understood) has to thank it for filtering our classifiable solid residues. But the number of centuries that the scheme can by any stretch be made to cover has long since been exceeded, and with the rapid increase in the volume of our historical material—especially of material that cannot possibly be brought under the scheme—the picture is beginning to dissolve into a chaotic blur. . . .

IX

In opposition to all these arbitrary and narrow schemes, derived from tradition or personal choice, into which history is forced, I put forward the natural, the "Copernican," form of the historical process which lies deep in the essence of that process and reveals itself only to an eye perfectly free from prepossessions.

Such an eye was Goethe's. That which Goethe called *Living Nature* is exactly that which we are calling here world-history, *world-as-history*. . . . And just as [Goethe] followed out the development of the plant-form from the leaf, the birth of the vertebrate type, the process of the geological strata—*the Destiny in nature and not the Causality*—so here we shall develop the form-language of human history, its periodic structure, its *organic logic* out of the profusion of all the challenging details.

In other aspects, mankind is habitually, and rightly, reckoned as one of the organisms of the earth's surface. Its physical structure, its natural functions, the whole phenomenal conception of it, all belong to a more comprehensive unity. Only in *this* aspect is it treated otherwise, despite that deeply-felt relationship of plant destiny and human destiny which is an eternal theme of all lyrical poetry, and despite that similarity of human history to that of any other of the higher life-groups which is the refrain of endless beast-legends, sagas and fables.

But only bring analogy to bear on this aspect as on the rest, letting the world of human Cultures intimately and unreservedly work upon the imagination instead of forcing it into a ready-made scheme. Let the words youth, growth, maturity, decay—hitherto, and to-day more than ever, used to express subjective valuations and entirely personal preferences in sociology, ethics and aesthetics—be taken at last as objective descriptions of organic states. Set forth the Classical Culture as a self-contained phenomenon embodying and expressing the Classical soul, put it beside the Egyptian, the Indian, the Babylonian, the Chinese and the Western, and determine for each of these higher individuals what is typical in their surgings and what is necessary in the riot of incident. And then at last will unfold itself the picture of world-history that is natural to us, men of the West, and to us alone.

X

Our narrower task, then, is primarily to determine, from such a world-survey, the state of West Europe and America as at the epoch of 1800–2000—to establish the chronological position of this period in the ensemble of Western culture-history, its significance as a chapter that is in one or other guise necessarily found in the biography of every Culture, and the organic and symbolic meaning of its political, artistic, intellectual and social expression-forms.

Considered in the spirit of analogy, this period appears as chronologically parallel—"contemporary" in our special sense—with the phase of Hellenism, and its present culmination, marked by the World-War, corresponds with the transition from Hellenistic to the Roman age. *Rome,* with its rigorous realism —uninspired, barbaric, disciplined, practical, Protestant, *Prussian*—will always give us, working as we must by analogies, the key to understanding our own future. *The break of destiny that we express by hyphening the words "Greeks-Romans" is occurring for us also, separating that which is already fulfilled from that which is to come.* Long ago we might and should have seen in the "Classical" world a development which is the complete counterpart of our own Western development, differing from it in every detail of the surface but entirely similar as regards the inward power driving the great organism towards its end. We might have found the constant *alter ego* of our own actuality in establishing the correspondence, item by item, from the "Trojan War" and the Crusades, Homer and the Nibelungenlied, through Doric and Gothic, Dionysian movement and Renaissance, Polycletus and John Sebastian Bach, Athens and Paris, Aristotle and Kant, Alexander and Napoleon, to the world-city and the imperialism common to both Cultures. . . .

XII

Looked at in this way, the "Decline of the West" comprises nothing less than the problem of *Civilization.* We have before us one of the fundamental questions of all higher history. What is Civilization, understood as the organic-logical sequel, fulfilment and finale of a culture?

For every Culture has *its own* Civilization. In this work, for the first time the two words, hitherto used to express an indefinite, more or less ethical, distinction, are used in a *periodic* sense, to express a strict and necessary *organic succession.* The Civilization is the inevitable *destiny* of the Culture, and in this principle we obtain the viewpoint from which the deepest and gravest problems of historical morphology become capable of solution. Civilizations are the most external and artificial states of which a species of developed humanity is capable. They are a conclusion, the thing-become succeeding the thing-becoming, death following life, rigidity following expansion, intellectual age and the stone-built, petrifying world-city following mother-earth and the spiritual childhood of Doric and Gothic. They are an end, irrevocable, yet by inward necessity reached again and again.

So, for the first time, we are enabled to understand the Romans as the *successors* of the Greeks, and light is projected into the deepest secrets of the late-Classical period. What, but this, can be the meaning of the fact—which can only be disputed by vain phrases—that the Romans were barbarians who did not *precede* but *closed* a great development? Unspiritual, unphilosophical, devoid of art, clannish to the point of brutality, aiming relentlessly at tangible successes, they stand between the Hellenic Culture and nothingness. An imagination directed purely to practical objects—they had religious laws governing godward relations as they had other laws governing human relations, but there was no specifically Roman saga of gods—was something which is not found at all in Athens. In a word, Greek *soul*—Roman *intellect;* and this antithesis is the differentia between Culture and Civilization. Nor is it only to the Classical that it applies. Again and again there appears this type of strong-minded, completely non-metaphysical man, and in the hands of this type lies the intellectual and material destiny of each and every "late" period. Such are the men who carried through the Babylonian, the Egyptian, the Indian, the Chinese, the Roman Civilizations, and in such periods do Buddhism, Stoicism, Socialism ripen into definitive world-conceptions which enable a moribund humanity to be attacked and re-formed in its intimate structure. *Pure* Civilization, as a historical process, consists in a progressive *taking-down* of forms that have become inorganic or dead.

The transition from Culture to Civilization was accomplished for the Classical world in the 4th, for the Western in the 19th Century. From these periods onward the great intellectual decisions take place, not as in the days of the Orpheus-movement or the Reformation in the "whole world" where not a hamlet is too small to be unimportant, but in three or four world-cities that have absorbed into themselves the whole content of History, while the old wide landscape of the Culture, become merely provincial, serves only to feed the cities with what remains of its higher mankind.

World-city and province—the two basic ideas of every civilization—bring up a wholly new form-problem of History, the very problem that we are living through to-day with hardly the remotest conception of its immensity. In place of a world, there is a *city, a point,* in which the whole life of broad regions is collecting while the rest dries up. In place of a type-true people, born of and grown on the soil, there is a new sort of nomad, cohering unstably in fluid masses, the parasitical city dweller, traditionless, utterly matter-of-fact, religionless, clever, unfruitful, deeply contemptuous of the countryman and especially that highest form of countryman, the country gentleman. This is a very great stride towards the inorganic, towards the end—what does it signify? France and England have already taken the step and Germany is beginning to do so. After Syracuse, Athens, and Alexandria comes Rome.

After Madrid, Paris, London come Berlin and New York. It is the destiny of whole regions that lie outside the radiation-circle of one of these cities—of old Crete and Macedon and to-day the Scandinavian North—to become "provinces."

Of old, the field on which the opposed conception of an epoch came to battle was some world-problem of a metaphysical, religious or dogmatic kind, and the battle was between the soil-genius of the countryman (noble, priest) and the "worldly" patrician genius of the famous old small towns of Doric or Gothic springtime. Of such a character were the conflicts over the Dionysus religion—as in the tyranny of Kleisthenes of Sikyon—and those of the Reformation in the German free cities and the Huguenot wars. But just as these cities overcame the country-side (already it is a purely civic world-outlook that appears in even Parmenides and Descartes), so in turn the world-city overcame them. It is the common intellectual process of later periods such as the Ionic and the Baroque, and to-day—as in the Hellenistic age which at its outset saw the foundation of artificial, land-alien Alexandria—Culture-cities like Florence, Nürnberg, Salamanca, Bruges and Prag, have become provincial towns and fight inwardly a lost battle against the world-cities. The world-city means cosmopolitanism in place of "home," cold matter-of-fact in place of reverence for tradition and age, scientific irreligion as a fossil representative of the older religion of the heart, "society" in place of the state, natural instead of hard-earned rights. It was in the conception of *money* as an inorganic and abstract magnitude, entirely disconnected from the notion of the fruitful earth and the primitive values, that the Romans had the advantage of the Greeks. Thenceforward any high ideal of life becomes largely a question of money. Unlike the Greek stoicism of Chrysippus, the Roman stoicism of Cato and Seneca presupposes a private income; and, unlike that of the 18th Century, the social-ethical sentiment of the 20th, if it is to be realized at a higher level than that of professional (and lucrative) agitation, is a matter for millionaires. To the world-city belongs not a folk but a mass. Its uncomprehending hostility to all the traditions representative of the Culture (nobility, church, privileges, dynasties, convention in art and limits of knowledge in science), the keen and cold intelligence that confounds the wisdom of the peasant, the new-fashioned naturalism that in relation to all matters of sex and society goes back far beyond Rousseau and Socrates to quite primitive instincts and conditions, the reappearance of the *panem et circenses* [4] in the form of wage-disputes and football-grounds—all these things betoken the definite closing-down of the Culture and the

[4] [*Bread and circuses.*]

opening of a quite new phase of human existence—anti-provincial, late, futureless, but quite inevitable.

This is what has to be *viewed,* and viewed not with the eyes of the partisan, the ideologue, the up-to-date novelist, not from this or that "standpoint," but in a high, time-free perspective embracing whole millenniums of historical world-forms, if we are really to comprehend the great crisis of the present.

To me it is a symbol of the first importance that in the Rome of Crassus—triumvir and all-powerful building-site speculator—the Roman people with its proud inscriptions, the people before whom Gauls, Greeks, Parthians, Syrians afar trembled, lived in appalling misery in the many-storied lodging-houses of dark suburbs,[5] accepting with indifference or even with a sort of sporting interest the consequences of the military expansion: that many famous old-noble families, descendants of the men who defeated the Celts and the Samnites, lost their ancestral homes through standing apart from the wild rush of speculation and were reduced to renting wretched apartments; that, while along the Appian Way there arose the splendid and still wonderful tombs of the financial magnates, the corpses of the people were thrown along with animal carcases and town refuse into a monstrous common grave—till in Augustus's time it was banked over for the avoidance of pestilence and so became the site of Maecenas's renowned park; that in depopulated Athens, which lived on visitors and on the bounty of rich foreigners, the mob of parvenu tourists from Rome gaped at the works of the Periclean age with as little understanding as the American globe-trotter in the Sistine Chapel at those of Michelangelo, every removable artpiece having ere this been taken away or bought at fancy prices to be replaced by the Roman buildings which grew up, colossal and arrogant, by the side of the low and modest structures of the old time. In such things—which it is the historian's business not to praise or to blame but to consider morphologically—there lies, plain and immediate enough for one who has learnt to see, an *idea.*

For it will become manifest that, from this moment on, all great conflicts of world-outlook, of politics, of art, of science, of feeling will be under the influence of this one opposition. What is the hall-mark of a politic of Civilization to-day, in contrast to a politic of Culture yesterday? It is, for the Classical rhetoric, and for the Western journalism, both serving that abstract which

[5] In Rome and Byzantium, lodging-houses of six to ten stories (with street-widths of ten feet at most!) were built without any sort of official supervision, and frequently collapsed with all their inmates. A great part of the *cives Romani,* for whom *panem et circenses* constituted all existence, possessed no more than a high-priced sleeping-berth in one of the swarming ant-hills called *insula.*

represents the power of Civilization—*money*. It is the money-spirit which penetrates unremarked the historical forms of the people's existence, often without destroying or even in the least disturbing these forms—the form of the Roman state, for instance, underwent very much less alteration between the elder Scipio and Augustus than is usually imagined. Though forms subsist, the great political parties nevertheless cease to be more than reputed centres of decision. The decisions in fact lie elsewhere. A small number of superior heads, whose names are very likely not the best-known, settle everything, while below them are the great mass of second-rate politicians—rhetors, tribunes, deputies, journalists—selected through a provincially-conceived franchise to keep alive the illusion of popular self-determination. And art? Philosophy? The ideals of a Platonic or those of a Kantian age had for the higher mankind concerned a general validity. But those of a Hellenistic age, or those of our own, are valid exclusively for the brain of the Megalopolitan. For the villager's or, generally, the nature-man's world-feeling our Socialism—like its near relation Darwinism (how utterly un-Goethian are the formulae of "struggle for existence" and "natural selection"!), like its other relative the woman-and-marriage problem of Ibsen, Strindberg, and Shaw, like the impressionistic tendencies of anarchic sensuousness and the whole bundle of modern longings, temptations and pains expressed in Baudelaire's verse and Wagner's music—are simply non-existent. The smaller the town, the more unmeaning it becomes to busy oneself with painting or with music of these kinds. To the Culture belong gymnastics, the tournament, the agon, and to the Civilization belongs Sport. This is the true distinction between the Hellenic palaestra and the Roman circus. Art itself becomes a sport (hence the phrase "art for art's sake") to be played before a highly-intelligent audience of connoisseurs and buyers, whether the feat consist in mastering absurd instrumental tone-masses and taking harmonic fences, or in some *tour de force* of colouring. Then a new fact-philosophy appears, which can only spare a smile for metaphysical speculation, and a new literature that is a necessity of life for the megalopolitan palate and nerves and both unintelligible and ugly to the provincials. Neither Alexandrine poetry nor *plein-air* painting is anything to the "people." And, then as now, the phase of transition is marked by a series of scandals only to be found at such moments. The anger evoked in the Athenian populace by Euripides and by the "Revolutionary" painting of Apollodorus, for example, is repeated in the opposition to Wagner, Manet, Ibsen, and Nietzsche.

It is possible to understand the Greeks without mentioning their economic relations; the Romans, on the other hand, can *only* be understood through these. Chaeronea and Leipzig were the last battles fought about an idea. In the First Punic War and in 1870 economic motives are no longer to be overlooked. Not till the Romans came with their practical energy was slaveholding given that big collective character which many students regard as the die-stamp of Classical economics, legislation and way of life, and which in any event vastly lowered both the value and the inner worthiness of such free labour as continued to exist side by side with gang-labour. And it was not the Latin, but the Germanic peoples of the West and America who developed out of the steam-engine a big industry that transformed the face of the land. The relation of these phenomena to Stoicism and to Socialism is unmistakable. Not till the Roman Caesarism—foreshadowed by C. Flaminius, shaped first by Marius, handled by strong-minded, large-scale men of fact—did the Classical World learn the *pre-eminence of money*. Without this fact neither Caesar, nor "Rome" generally, is understandable. In every Greek is a Don Quixote, in every Roman a Sancho Panza factor, and these factors are dominants.

XIII

Considered in itself, the Roman world-dominion was a negative phenomenon, being the result not of a surplus of energy on the one side—that the Romans had never had since Zama—but of a deficiency of resistance on the other. That the Romans did *not* conquer the world is certain; they merely took possession of a booty that lay open to everyone. The *Imperium Romanum* came into existence not as the result of such an extremity of military and financial effort as had characterized the Punic Wars, but because the old East forwent all external self-determinations. We must not be deluded by the appearance of brilliant military successes. With a few ill-trained, ill-led, and sullen legions, Lucullus and Pompey conquered whole realms—a phenomenon that in the period of the battle of Ipsus would have been unthinkable. The Mithradatic danger, serious enough for a system of material force which had never been put to any real test, would have been nothing to the conquerors of Hannibal. After Zama, the Romans never again either waged or were capable of waging a war against a great military Power. Their classic wars were those against the Samnites, Pyrrhus and Carthage. Their grand hour was Cannae. To maintain the heroic posture for centuries on end is beyond the power of any people. The Prussian-German people have had three great moments (1813, 1870 and 1914), and that is more than others have had.

Here, then, I lay down that *Imperialism,* of which petrifacts such as the

Egyptian empire, the Roman, the Chinese, the Indian may continue to exist for hundreds or thousands of years—dead bodies, amorphous and dispirited masses of men, scrap-material from a great history—is to be taken as the typical symbol of the passing away. Imperialism is Civilization unadulterated. In this phenomenal form the destiny of the West is now irrevocably set. The energy of culture-man is directed inwards, that of civilization-man outwards. And thus I see in Cecil Rhodes the first man of a new age. He stands for the political style of a far-ranging, Western, Teutonic and especially German future, and his phrase "expansion is everything" is the Napoleonic reassertion of the indwelling tendency of *every* Civilization that has fully ripened—Roman, Arab or Chinese. It is not a matter of choice—it is not the conscious will of individuals, or even that of whole classes or peoples that decides. The expansive tendency is a doom, something daemonic and immense, which grips, forces into service, and uses up the late mankind of the world-city state, willy-nilly, aware or unaware. Life is the process of effecting possibilities, and for the brain-man there are *only extensive* possibilities. Hard as the half-developed Socialism of to-day is fighting against expansion, one day it will become arch-expansionist with all the vehemence of destiny. Here the form-language of politics, as the direct intellectual expression of a certain type of humanity, touches on a deep metaphysical problem—on the fact, affirmed in the grant of unconditioned validity to the causality-principle, that *the soul is the complement of its extension*. . . .

Rhodes is to be regarded as the first precursor of a Western type of Caesars, whose day is to come though yet distant. He stands midway between Napoleon and the force-men of the next centuries, just as Flaminius, who from 232 B.C. onward pressed the Romans to undertake the subjugation of Cisalpine Gaul and so initiated the policy of colonial expansion, stands between Alexander and Caesar. Strictly speaking, Flaminius was a private person—for his real power was of a kind not embodied in any constitutional office—who exercised a dominant influence in the state at a time when the state-idea was giving way to the pressure of economic factors. So far as Rome is concerned, he was the arche-type of opposition Caesarism; with him there came to an end the *idea of state-service* and there began the "will to power" which ignored traditions and reckoned only with forces. Alexander and Napoleon were romantics; though they stood on the threshold of Civilization and in its cold clear air, the one fancied himself an Achilles and the other read Werther. Caesar, on the contrary, was a pure man of fact gifted with immense understanding.

But even for Rhodes political success means territorial and financial success, and only that. Of this Roman-ness within himself he was fully aware. But Western Civilization has not yet taken shape in such strength and purity as this. It was only before his maps that he could fall into a sort of poetic trance, this son of the parsonage who, sent out to South Africa without means, made a gigantic fortune and employed it as the engine of political aims. His idea of a trans-African railway from the Cape to Cairo, his project of a South African empire, his intellectual hold on the hard metal souls of the mining magnates whose wealth he forced into the service of his schemes, his capital Bulawayo, royally planned as a future Residence by a statesman who was all-powerful yet stood in no definite relation to the State, his wars, his diplomatic deals, his road-systems, his syndicates, his armies, his conception of the "great duty to civilization" of the man of brain—all this, broad and imposing, is the prelude of a future which is still in store for us and with which the history of West-European mankind will be definitely *closed*.

He who does not understand that this outcome is obligatory and insusceptible of modification, that our choice is between willing *this* and willing nothing at all, between cleaving to *this* destiny or despairing of the future and of life itself; he who cannot feel that there is grandeur also in the realizations of powerful intelligences, in the energy and discipline of metal-hard natures, in battles fought with the coldest and most abstract means; he who is obsessed with the idealism of a provincial and would pursue the ways of life of past ages—must forgo all desire to comprehend history, to live through history or to make history.

Thus regarded, the Imperium Romanum appears no longer as an isolated phenomenon, but as the normal product of a strict and energetic, megalopolitan, predominantly practical spirituality, as typical of a final and irreversible condition which has occurred often enough though it has only been identified as such in this instance.

Let it be realized, then:

That the secret of historical form does not lie on the surface, that it cannot be grasped by means of similarities of costume and setting, and that in the history of men as in that of animals and plants there occur phenomena showing deceptive similarity but inwardly without any connexion—e.g., Charlemagne and Haroun-al-Raschid, Alexander and Caesar, the German wars upon Rome and the Mongol onslaughts upon West Europe—and other phenomena of extreme outward dissimilarity but of identical import—e.g., Trajan and Rameses II, the Bourbons and the Attic Demos, Mohammed and Pythagoras;

That the 19th and 20th centuries, hitherto looked on as the highest point of an ascending straight line of world-history, are in reality a stage of life which may be observed in every Culture that has ripened to its limit—a stage of life characterized not by Socialists, Impressionists, electric railways, torpedoes and differential equations (for these are only body-constituents of the time), but by a civilized spirituality which possesses not only these but also quite other creative possibilities;

That, as our own time represents a transitional phase which occurs with certainty under particular conditions, there are perfectly well-defined states (such as have occurred more than once in the history of the past) *later* than the present-day state of West Europe;

And therefore that the future of the West is not a limitless tending upwards and onwards for all time towards our present ideals, but a single phenomenon of history, strictly limited and defined as to form and duration, which covers a few centuries and can be viewed and, in essentials, calculated from available precedents.

XIV

This high plane of contemplation once attained, the rest is easy. To this *single* idea one can refer, and by it one can solve, without straining or forcing, all those separate problems of religion, art-history, epistemology, ethics, politics, economics with which the modern intellect has so passionately—and so vainly—busied itself for decades.

This idea is one of those truths that have only to be expressed with full clarity to become indisputable. It is one of the inward necessities of the Western Culture and of its world-feeling. It is capable of entirely transforming the world-outlook of one who fully understands it, i.e., makes it intimately his own. It immensely deepens the world-picture natural and necessary to us in that, already trained to regard world-historical evolution as an organic unit seen backwards from our standpoint in the present, we are enabled by its aid to follow the broad lines into the future—a privilege of dream-calculation till now permitted only to the physicist. It is, I repeat, in effect the substitution of a Copernican for a Ptolemaic aspect of history, that is, an immeasurable widening of horizon.

Up to now everyone has been at liberty to hope what he pleased about the future. Where there are no facts, sentiment rules. But henceforward it will be every man's business to inform himself of what *can* happen and therefore of what with the unalterable necessity of destiny and irrespective of personal ideals, hopes or desires, *will* happen. When we use the risky word "freedom" we shall mean freedom to do, not this or that, but the necessary or nothing.

The feeling that this is "just as it should be" is the hall-mark of the man of fact. To lament it and blame it is not to alter it. To birth belongs death, to youth age, to life generally its form and its allotted span. The present is a civilized, emphatically not a cultured time, and *ipso facto* a great number of life-capacities fall out as impossible. This may be deplorable, and may be and will be deplored in pessimist philosophy and poetry, but it is not in our power to make otherwise. It will not be—already it is not—permissible to defy clear historical experience and to expect, merely because we hope, that this will spring or that will flourish.

It will no doubt be objected that such a world-outlook, which in giving this certainty as to the outlines and tendency of the future cuts off all far-reaching hopes, would be unhealthy for all and fatal for many, once it ceased to be a mere theory and was adopted as a practical scheme of life by the group of personalities effectively moulding the future.

Such is not my opinion. We are civilized, not Gothic or Rococo, people; we have to reckon with the hard cold facts of a *late* life, to which the parallel is to be found not in Pericles's Athens but in Caesar's Rome. Of great painting or great music there can no longer be, for Western people, any question. Their architectural possibilities have been exhausted these hundred years. Only *extensive* possibilities are left to them. Yet, for a sound and vigorous generation that is filled with unlimited hopes, I fail to see that it is any disadvantage to discover betimes that some of these hopes must come to nothing. And if the hopes thus doomed should be those most dear, well, a man who is worth anything will not be dismayed. It is true that the issue may be a tragic one for some individuals who in their decisive years are overpowered by the conviction that in the spheres of architecture, drama, painting, there is nothing left for *them* to conquer. What matter if they do go under! It has been the convention hitherto to admit no limits of any sort in these matters, and to believe that each period had its own task to do in each sphere. Tasks therefore were found by hook or by crook, leaving it to be settled posthumously whether or not the artist's faith was justified and his life-work necessary. Now, nobody but a pure romantic would take this way out. Such a pride is not the pride of a Roman. What are we to think of the individual who, standing before an exhausted quarry, would rather be told that a new vein will be struck to-morrow—the bait offered by the radically false and mannerized art of the moment—than be shown a rich and virgin clay-bed near by? The lesson, I think, would be of benefit to the coming generations, as showing them what is possible—and therefore necessary—and what is excluded from the inward potentialities of their time. Hitherto an incredible total of intellect and power has been squandered in false directions. The West-European, however historically he may think and feel, is at a certain stage of life invariably uncertain of his own direction; he gropes and feels his way and, if unlucky in environment, he loses it. But now at last the work of centuries enables him to view the disposition of his own life in relation to the general culture-scheme and to test his own powers and purposes. And I can only hope that men of the new generation may be moved . . . to devote themselves to technics instead of lyrics, the sea instead of the paint-brush, and politics instead of epistemology. Better they could not do.

XV

. . . To me, the depths and refinement of mathematical and physical theories are a joy; by comparison, the aesthete and the physiologist are fumblers. I would sooner have the fine mind-begotten forms of a fast steamer, a steel structure, a precision-lathe, the subtlety and elegance of many chemical and optical processes, than all the pickings and stealings of present-day "arts and crafts," architecture and painting included. I prefer one Roman aqueduct to all Roman temples and statues. I love the Colosseum and the giant vault of the Palatine, for they display for me to-day in the brown massiveness of their brick construction the *real* Rome and the grand practical sense of her engineers, but it is a matter of indifference to me whether the empty and pretentious marblery of the Caesars—their rows of statuary, their friezes, their overloaded architraves—is preserved or not. Glance at some reconstruction of the Imperial Fora—do we not find them the true counterpart of a modern International Exhibition, obtrusive, bulky, empty, a boasting in materials and dimensions wholly alien to Periclean Greece and the Rococo alike, but exactly paralleled in the Egyptian modernism that is displayed in the ruins of Rameses II (1300 B.C.) at Luxor and Karnak? It was not for nothing that the genuine Roman despised the *Graeculus histrio,* the kind of "artist" and the kind of "philosopher" to be found on the soil of Roman Civilization. The time for art and philosophy had passed; they were exhausted, used up, superfluous, and his instinct for the realities of life told him so. *One* Roman law weighed more than all the lyrics and school-metaphysics of the time together. And I maintain that to-day many an inventor, many a diplomat, many a financier is a sounder philosopher than all those who practise the dull craft of experimental psychology. This is a situation which regularly repeats itself at a certain historical level. It would have been absurd in a Roman of intellectual eminence, who might as Consul or Praetor lead armies, organize provinces, build cities and roads, or even be the Princeps in Rome, to want to hatch out some variant of post-Platonic school philosophy at Athens or Rhodes. Consequently no one did so. It was not in harmony with the tendency of the age, and therefore it only attracted third-class men of the kind that always advances as far as the *Zeitgeist* of the day before yesterday. It is a very grave question whether this stage has or has not set in for us already.

A century of purely extensive effectiveness, excluding big artistic and metaphysical production—let us say frankly an irreligious time which coincides exactly with the idea of the world-city—is a time of decline. True. But we have not *chosen* this time. We cannot help it if we are born as men of the early winter of full Civilization, instead of on the golden summit of a ripe Culture, in a Phidias or a Mozart time. Everything depends on our seeing our own position, our *destiny,* clearly, on our realizing that though we may lie to ourselves about it we cannot evade it. He who does not acknowledge this in his heart, ceases to be counted among the men of his generation, and remains either a simpleton, a charlatan, or a pedant. . . .

(1883-1955)

JOSÉ ORTEGA Y GASSET

BORN in Madrid in 1883, José Ortega y Gasset completed his undergraduate studies with the Jesuits of Miraflores del Palo, in southern Spain, and in 1904 received his doctorate in philosophy and letters from the Central University of Madrid. From there he went to Germany to pursue his philosophic interests at Leipzig, the University of Berlin, and finally Marburg, where he studied under the neo-Kantian, Hermann Cohen (1842–1918). As he reached intellectual maturity, however, Ortega shook off the two varieties of "scholasticism," Jesuit and neo-Kantian, to which he had been exposed, and began to forge a more personalized view of the cosmos and human affairs. One might place him in the line of such thinkers as Friedrich Nietzsche and Henri Bergson (1859–1941), for whom ideals and action, aesthetic insight and reasoned analysis, individual impulse and social realities comprise bonded unities. Ortega addresses artistic, literary, scientific, socio-political, and historical themes as well as strictly philosophic ones; and his intellectual position, however much it has resisted detailed and unequivocal synthesis, flashes time and again in his fresh and penetrating perceptions.

Though already renowned as professor of metaphysics at the University of Madrid, Ortega first caught his countrymen's imagination in March, 1914, when one afternoon, from the stage of Madrid's La Comedia, he addressed them on the grievous condition of "official Spain," with its spectral political parties upholding ghosts of ideas, its shadows of newspapers, its cabinets of hallucination. The theme was later elaborated in *Invertebrate Spain* (1922), which attributed the country's lack of moral tone and of a vital national and liberal spirit to the historic inadequacy of its select minority. The Visigoths, claimed Ortega, had been devitalized by their contact with the Roman Empire when they invaded Spain; they had never implanted a vigorous feudalism, and therefore Spain united too swiftly, too passively, as a nation in the fifteenth century. "Our masses did all that was to be done: they populated, cultivated, sang, groaned and loved," but they could not give to their American colonies what the English gave to theirs: "superior discipline, culture and progressive civilization."

In 1929 was published Ortega's most widely known book, *The Revolt of the Masses,* from which a selection follows. Here he diagnoses the ills of twentieth-century society in the same accents which "invertebrate" Spain had evoked. The nineteenth- and twentieth-century leaders of Europe are for him latter-day Visigoths. They form a minority who are no longer *select*—by criteria, that is, of morality and intellect, not those of lineage; who fail to sustain the fierce, unrelenting vision to which the unresting flux of social forces commits a true leader. "Let it not even be said," Ortega writes in his essay *Concord and Liberty* (1940), in a vein reminiscent of Nietzsche, "that society means the triumph of the social over the antisocial forces. Such triumph has never come to pass. What in fact prevails is an unceasing fight between the two forces, and the ups and downs characteristic of all struggle. . . . Nothing social has ever been good in the sense in which a picture, an idea, a character, or an action is good." To believe that a social order can achieve a stable "goodness" is to feed the complacent, or "hermetic," attitude to which Ortega ascribes the crisis of our times.

Through the journal *Revista de Occidente,* which he founded in 1922, Ortega broadened the largely Gallic intellectual horizons of Spain and the countries of Latin America by introducing the currents of modern German philosophy. His own works, aside from those mentioned, include *Meditations on Quixote* (1914), *The Modern Theme* (1921), *Kant* (1924), *Dehumanization of Art* (1925), and *Goethe from Within* (1934). As a result of the Spanish Civil War Ortega lived for some years in Buenos Aires. He died, after returning to Spain, in 1955.

THE REVOLT OF THE MASSES

CHAPTER I: THE COMING OF THE MASSES

There is one fact which, whether for good or ill, is of utmost importance in the public life of Europe at the present moment. This fact is the accession of the masses to complete social power. As the masses, by definition, neither should nor can direct their own personal existence, and still less rule society in general, this fact means that actually Europe is suffering from the greatest crisis that can afflict peoples, nations, and civilisation. Such a crisis has occurred more than once in history. Its characteristics and its consequences are well known. So also is its name. It is called the rebellion of the masses. In order to understand this formidable fact, it is important from the start to avoid giving to the words "rebellion," "masses," and "social power" a meaning exclusively or primarily political. Public life is not solely political, but equally, and even primarily, intellectual, moral, economic, religious; it comprises all our collective habits, including our fashions both of dress and of amusement. . . .

Agglomeration, fullness, was not frequent before. Why then is it now? The components of the multitudes around us have not sprung from nothing. Approximately the same number of people existed fifteen years ago. Indeed, after the war it might seem natural that their number should be less. Nevertheless, it is here we come up against the first important point. The individ-

---

This selection has been reprinted from *The Revolt of the Masses* by José Ortega y Gasset by permission of W. W. Norton & Company, Inc., Copyright 1932 by W. W. Norton & Company, Inc., New York (pp. 11, 13, 15–19, 21–23, 67–74, 77–82, 107–108, 110–112, 119–125, 201–203).

uals who made up these multitudes existed, but not *qua* multitude. Scattered about the world in small groups, or solitary, they lived a life, to all appearances, divergent, dissociate, apart. Each individual or small group occupied a place, its own, in country, village, town, or quarter of the great city. Now, suddenly, they appear as an agglomeration, and looking in any direction our eyes meet with the multitudes. Not only in any direction, but precisely in the best places, the relatively refined creations of human culture, previously reserved to lesser groups, in a word, to minorities. The multitude has suddenly become visible, installing itself in the preferential positions in society. Before, if it existed, it passed unnoticed, occupying the background of the social stage; now it has advanced to the footlights and is the principal character. There are no longer protagonists; there is only the chorus. . . .

Strictly speaking, the mass, as a psychological fact, can be defined without waiting for individuals to appear in mass formation. In the presence of one individual we can decide whether he is "mass" or not. The mass is all that which sets no value on itself—good or ill—based on specific grounds, but which feels itself "just like everybody," and nevertheless is not concerned about it; is, in fact, quite happy to feel itself as one with everybody else. Imagine a humble-minded man who, having tried to estimate his own worth on specific grounds—asking himself if he has any talent for this or that, if he excels in any direction—realises that he possesses no quality of excellence. Such a man will feel that he is mediocre and commonplace, ill-gifted, but will not feel himself "mass."

When one speaks of "select minorities" it is usual for the evil minded to twist the sense of this expression, pretending to be unaware that the select man is not the petulant person who thinks himself superior to the rest, but the man who demands more of himself than the rest, even though he may not fulfil in his person those higher exigencies. For there is no doubt that the most radical division that it is possible to make of humanity is that which splits it into two classes of creatures: those who make great demands on themselves, piling up difficulties and duties; and those who demand nothing special of themselves, but for whom to live is to be every moment what they already are, without imposing on themselves any effort towards perfection; mere buoys that float on the waves. This reminds me that orthodox Buddhism is composed of two distinct religions: one, more rigorous and difficult, the other easier and more trivial: the Mahayana—"great vehicle" or "great path"—and the Hinayana—"lesser vehicle" or "lesser path." The decisive matter is whether we attach our life to one or the other vehicle, to a maximum or a minimum of demands upon ourselves.

The division of society into masses and select minorities is, then, not a division into social classes, but into classes of men, and cannot coincide with the hierarchic separation of "upper" and "lower" classes. It is, of course, plain that in these "upper" classes, when and as long as they really are so, there is much more likelihood of finding men who adopt the "great vehicle," whereas the "lower" classes normally comprise individuals of minus quality. But, strictly speaking, within both these social classes, there are to be found mass and genuine minority. As we shall see, a characteristic of our times is the predominance, even in groups traditionally selective, of the mass and the vulgar. Thus, in the intellectual life, which of its essence requires and presupposes qualification, one can note the progressive triumph of the pseudo-intellectual, unqualified, unqualifiable, and, by their very mental texture, disqualified. Similarly, in the surviving groups of the "nobility," male and female. On the other hand, it is not rare to find to-day amongst working men, who before might be taken as the best example of what we are calling "mass," nobly disciplined minds.

There exist, then, in society, operations, activities, and functions of the most diverse order, which are of their very nature special, and which consequently cannot be properly carried out without special gifts. For example: certain pleasures of an artistic and refined character, or again the functions of government and of political judgment in public affairs. Previously these special activities were exercised by qualified minorities, or at least by those who claimed such qualification. The mass asserted no right to intervene in them; they realised that if they wished to intervene they would necessarily have to acquire those special qualities and cease being mere mass. They recognised their place in a healthy dynamic social system.

If we now revert to the facts . . . [of modern European society], they will appear clearly as the heralds of a changed attitude in the mass. They all indicate that the mass has decided to advance to the foreground of social life, to occupy the places, to use the instruments and to enjoy the pleasures hitherto reserved to the few. It is evident, for example, that the places were never intended for the multitude, for their dimensions are too limited, and the crowd is continuously overflowing; thus manifesting to our eyes and in the clearest manner the new phenomenon: the mass, without ceasing to be mass, is supplanting the minorities.

No one, I believe, will regret that people are to-day enjoying themselves in greater measure and numbers than before, since they have now both the desire and the means of satisfying it. The evil lies in the fact that this decision taken by the masses to assume the activities proper to the minorities is not, and cannot be, manifested solely in the domain of pleasure, but that it is a general feature of our time. Thus—to anticipate what we shall see later—I believe that the political innovations of recent times signify nothing less than the political domination of the masses. The old democracy was tempered by a generous dose of liberalism and of enthusiasm for law. By serving these principles the individual bound himself to maintain a severe discipline over himself. Under the shelter of liberal principles and the rule of law, minorities could live and act. Democracy and law—life in common under the law—were synonymous. To-day we are witnessing the triumphs of a hyperdemocracy in which the mass acts directly, outside the law, imposing its aspirations and its desires by means of material pressure. It is a false interpretation of the new situation to say that the mass has grown tired of politics and handed over the exercise of it to specialised persons. Quite the contrary. That was what happened previously; that was democracy. The mass took it for granted that after all, in spite of their defects and weaknesses, the minorities understood a little more of public problems than it did itself. Now, on the other hand, the mass believes that it has the right to impose and to give force of law to notions born in the café. I doubt whether there have been other periods of history in which the multitude has come to govern more directly than in our own. That is why I speak of hyperdemocracy.

The same thing is happening in other orders, particularly in the intellectual. I may be mistaken, but the present-day writer, when he takes his pen in hand to treat a subject which he has studied deeply, has to bear in mind that the average reader, who has never concerned himself with this subject, if he reads does so with the view, not of learning something from the writer, but rather, of pronouncing judgment on him when he is not in agreement with the commonplaces that the said reader carries in his head. If the individuals who make up the mass believed themselves specially qualified, it would be a case merely of personal error, not a sociological subversion. *The characteristic of the hour is that the commonplace mind, knowing itself to be commonplace, has the assurance to proclaim the rights of the commonplace and to impose them wherever it will.* As they say in the United States: "to be different is to be indecent." The mass crushes beneath it everything that is different, everything that is excellent, individual, qualified and select. Anybody who is not like everybody, who does not think like everybody, runs the risk of being eliminated. And it is clear, of course, that this "everybody" is not "everybody." "Everybody" was normally the complex unity of the mass and the divergent, specialised minorities. Nowadays, "everybody" is the mass alone. Here we have the formidable fact of our times, described without any concealment of the brutality of its features.

CHAPTER II: THE RISE OF THE HISTORIC LEVEL

. . . We are living, then, under the brutal empire of the masses. Just so; I have now twice called this empire "brutal," and have thus paid my tribute to the god of the commonplace. Now, ticket in hand, I can cheerfully enter into my subject, see the show from inside. Or perhaps it was thought that I was going to be satisfied with that description, possibly exact, but quite external; the mere features, the aspect under which this tremendous fact presents itself when looked at from the view-point of the past? If I were to leave the matter here and strangle off my present essay without more ado, the reader would be left thinking, and quite justly, that this fabulous uprising of the masses above the surface of history inspired me merely with a few petulant, disdainful words, a certain amount of hatred and a certain amount of disgust. This all the more in my case, when it is well known that I uphold a radically aristocratic interpretation of history. Radically, because I have never said that human society *ought* to be aristocratic, but a great deal more than that. What I have said, and still believe with ever-increasing conviction, is that human society *is* always, whether it will or no, aristocratic by its very essence, to the extreme that it is a society in the measure that it is aristocratic, and ceases to be such when it ceases to be aristocratic. Of course I am speaking now of society and not of the State. No one can imagine that, in the face of this fabulous seething of the masses, it is the aristocratic attitude to be satisfied with making a supercilious grimace, like a fine gentleman of Versailles. Versailles—the Versailles of the grimaces—does not represent aristocracy; quite the contrary, it is the death and dissolution of a magnificent aristocracy. For this reason, the only element of aristocracy left in such beings was the dignified grace with which their necks received the attentions of the guillotine; they accepted it as the tumour accepts the lancet. No; for anyone who has a sense of the real mission of aristocracies, the spectacle of the mass incites and enflames him, as the sight of virgin marble does the sculptor. Social aristocracy has no resemblance whatever to that tiny group which claims for itself alone the name of society, which calls itself "Society"; people who live by inviting or not inviting one another. Since everything in the world has its virtue and its mission, so within the vast world this small "smart world" has its own, but it is a very subordinate mission, not to be compared with the herculean task of genuine aristocracies. I should have no objection to discussing the meaning that lies in this smart world, to all appearances so meaningless, but our subject is now one of greater proportions. Of course, this self-same "distinguished society" goes with the times. Much food for thought was given me by a certain *jeune fille en fleur,*[1] full of youth and modernity, a star of the first magnitude in the firmament of "smart" Madrid, when she said to me: "I can't stand a dance to which less than eight hundred people have been invited." Behind this phrase I perceived that the style of the masses is triumphant over the whole area of modern life, and imposes itself even in those sheltered corners which seemed reserved for the "happy few."

I reject equally, then, the interpretation of our times which does not lay clear the positive meaning hidden under the actual rule of the masses and that which accepts it blissfully, without a shudder of horror. Every destiny is dramatic, tragic in its deepest meaning. Whoever has not felt the danger of our times palpitating under his hand, has not really penetrated to the vitals of destiny, he has merely pricked its surface. The element of terror in the destiny of our time is furnished by the overwhelming and violent moral upheaval of the masses; imposing, invincible, and treacherous, as is destiny in every case. Whither is it leading us? Is it an absolute evil or a possible good? There it is, colossal, astride our times like a giant, a cosmic note of interrogation, always of uncertain shape, with something in it of the guillotine or the gallows, but also with something that strives to round itself into a triumphal arch. . . .

CHAPTER VII: NOBLE LIFE AND COMMON LIFE, OR EFFORT AND INERTIA

To start with, we are what our world invites us to be, and the basic features of our soul are impressed upon it by the form of its surroundings as in a mould. Naturally, for our life is no other than our relations with the world around. The general aspect which it presents to us will form the general aspect of our own life. It is for this reason that I stress so much the observation that the world into which the masses of to-day have been born displays features radically new to history. Whereas in past times life for the average man meant finding all around him difficulties, dangers, want, limitations of his destiny, dependence, the new world appears as a sphere of practically limitless possibilities, safe, and independent of anyone. Based on this primary and lasting impression, the mind of every contemporary man will be formed, just as previous minds were formed on the opposite impression. For that basic impression becomes an interior voice which ceaselessly utters certain words

[1] [That is, a girl in first flower of maturity.]

in the depths of each individual, and tenaciously suggests to him a definition of life which is, at the same time, a moral imperative. And if the traditional sentiment whispered: "To live is to feel oneself limited, and therefore to have to count with that which limits us," the newest voice shouts: "To live is to meet with no limitation whatever and, consequently, to abandon oneself calmly to one's self. Practically nothing is impossible, nothing is dangerous, and, in principle, nobody is superior to anybody." This basic experience completely modifies the traditional, persistent structure of the mass-man. For the latter always felt himself, by his nature, confronted with material imitations and higher social powers. Such, in his eyes, was life. If he succeeded in improving his situation, if he climbed the social ladder, he attributed this to a piece of fortune which was favourable to him in particular. And if not to this, then to an enormous effort, of which he knew well what it had cost him. In both cases it was a question of an exception to the general character of life and the world; an exception which, as such, was due to some very special cause.

But the modern mass finds complete freedom as its natural, established condition, without any special cause for it. Nothing from outside incites it to recognise limits to itself and, consequently, to refer at all times to other authorities higher than itself. Until lately, the Chinese peasant believed that the welfare of his existence depended on the private virtues which the Emperor was pleased to possess. Therefore, his life was constantly related to this supreme authority on which it depended. *But the man we are now analysing accustoms himself not to appeal from his own to any authority outside him.* He is satisfied with himself exactly as he is. Ingenuously, without any need of being vain, as the most natural thing in the world, he will tend to consider and affirm as good everything he finds within himself: opinions, appetites, preferences, tastes. Why not, if, as we have seen, nothing and nobody force him to realise that he is a second-class man, subject to many limitations, incapable of creating or conserving that very organisation which gives his life the fullness and contentedness on which he bases this assertion of his personality?

The mass-man would never have accepted authority external to himself had not his surroundings violently forced him to do so. As to-day, his surroundings do not so force him, the everlasting mass-man, true to his character, ceases to appeal to other authority and feels himself lord of his own existence. On the contrary the select man, the excellent man is urged, by interior necessity, to appeal from himself to some standard beyond himself, superior to himself, whose service he freely accepts. Let us recall that at the start we distinguished the excellent man from the common man by saying that the former is the one who makes great demands on himself, and the latter the one who makes no demands on himself, but contents himself with what he is, and is delighted with himself. Contrary to what is usually thought, it is the man of excellence, and not the common man who lives in essential servitude. Life has no savour for him unless he makes it consist in service to something transcendental. Hence he does not look upon the necessity of serving as an oppression. When, by chance, such necessity is lacking, he grows restless and invents some new standard, more difficult, more exigent, with which to coerce himself. This is life lived as a discipline—the noble life. Nobility is defined by the demands it makes on us—by obligations, not by rights. *Noblesse oblige.* "To live as one likes is plebeian; the noble man aspires to order and law" (Goethe). The privileges of nobility are not in their origin concessions or favours; on the contrary, they are conquests. And their maintenance supposes, in principle, that the privileged individual is capable of reconquering them, at any moment, if it were necessary, and anyone were to dispute them. Private rights or *privileges* are not, then, passive possession and mere enjoyment, but they represent the standard attained by personal effort. On the other hand, common rights, such as those "of the man and the citizen," are passive property, pure usufruct and benefit, the generous gift of fate which every man finds before him, and which answers to no effort whatever, unless it be that of breathing and avoiding insanity. I would say, then, that an impersonal right is held, a personal one is upheld.

It is annoying to see the degeneration suffered in ordinary speech by a word so inspiring as "nobility." For, by coming to mean for many people hereditary "noble blood," it is changed into something similar to common rights, into a static, passive quality which is received and transmitted like something inert. But the strict sense, the *etymon* of the word nobility is essentially dynamic. Noble means the "well known," that is, known by everyone, famous, he who has made himself known by excelling the anonymous mass. It implies an unusual effort as the cause of his fame. Noble, then is equivalent to effortful, excellent. The nobility or fame of the son is pure benefit. The son is known because the father made himself famous. He is known by reflection, and in fact, hereditary nobility has an indirect character, it is mirrored light, lunar nobility, something derived from the dead. The only thing left to it of living, authentic, dynamic is the impulse it stirs in the descendant to maintain the level of effort reached by the ancestor. Always, even in this altered sense, *noblesse oblige*. The original noble lays an obligation on himself, the noble heir receives the obligation with his inheritance. But in any case there is a certain contradiction in the passing-on of nobility from the first noble to his successors. The Chinese, more logical, invert the order of transmission; it is not the father who ennobles the son, but the son who, by acquiring noble rank, communicates it to his forbears, by his personal efforts bringing fame to his humble stock. Hence, when granting degrees of nobility, they are graduated by the number of previous generations which are honoured; there are those who ennoble only their fathers, and those who stretch back their fame to the fifth or tenth grandparent. The ancestors live by reason of the actual man, whose nobility is effective, active—in a word: *is,* not was.

"Nobility" does not appear as a formal expression until the Roman Empire, and then precisely in opposition to the hereditary nobles, then in decadence.

For me, then, nobility is synonymous with a life of effort, ever set on excelling oneself, in passing beyond what one is to what one sets up as a duty and an obligation. In this way the noble life stands opposed to the common or inert life, which reclines statically upon itself, condemned to perpetual immobility, unless an external force compels it to come out of itself. Hence we apply the term mass to this kind of man—not so much because of his multitude as because of his inertia.

As one advances in life, one realises more and more that the majority of men—and of women—are incapable of any other effort than that strictly imposed on them as a reaction to external compulsion. And for that reason, the few individuals we have come across who are capable of a spontaneous and joyous effort stand out isolated, monumentalised, so to speak, in our experience. These are the select men, the nobles, the only ones who are active and not merely reactive, for whom life is a perpetual striving, an incessant course of training. Training=*askesis.*[1] These are the ascetics. This apparent digression should not cause surprise. In order to define the actual mass-man, who is as much "mass" as ever, but who wishes to supplant the "excellent," it has been necessary to contrast him with the two pure forms which are mingled in him: the normal mass and the genuine noble or man of effort.

Now we can advance more rapidly, because we are now in possession of what, to my thinking, is the key—the psychological equation—of the human type dominant to-day. All that follows is a consequence, a corollary, of that root-structure, which may be summed up thus: the world as organised by the XIXth Century, when automatically producing a new man, has infused into him formidable appetites and powerful means of every kind for satisfying them. These include the economic, the physical (hygiene, average health higher than any preceding age), the civil and the technical (by which I mean the enormous quantity of partial knowledge and practical efficiency pos-

[1] i.e. self-imposed discipline

sessed by the average man to-day and lacking to him in the past). After having supplied him with all these powers the XIXth Century has abandoned him to himself, and the average man, following his natural disposition, has withdrawn into himself. Hence, we are in the presence of a mass stronger than that of any preceding period, but differing from the traditional type in that it remains, hermetically enclosed within itself, incapable of submitting to anything or anybody, believing itself self-sufficient—in a word, indocile. If things go on as they are at present, it will be every day more noticeable in Europe—and by reflection, throughout the whole world—that the masses are incapable of submitting to direction of any kind. In the difficult times that are at hand . . . it is possible that, under a sudden affliction, they may for a moment have the good will to accept, in certain specially urgent matters, the direction of the superior minorities.

But even that good will will result in failure. For the basic texture of their soul is wrought of hermetism and indocility; they are from birth deficient in the faculty of giving attention to what is outside themselves, be it fact or person. They will wish to follow someone, and they will be unable. They will want to listen, and will discover they are deaf.

On the other hand, it is illusory to imagine that the mass-man of to-day, however superior his vital level may be compared with that of other times, will be able to control, by himself, the process of civilisation. I say process, and not progress. The simple process of preserving our present civilisation is supremely complex, and demands incalculably subtle powers. Ill-fitted to direct it is this average man who has learned to use much of the machinery of civilisation, but who is characterised by root-ignorance of the very principles of that civilisation.

I reiterate to the reader who has patiently followed me up to this point, the importance of not giving to the facts enunciated a primarily political significance. On the contrary, political activities, of all those in public life the most efficient and the most visible, are the final product of others more intimate, more impalpable. Hence, political indocility would not be so grave did it not proceed from a deeper, more decisive intellectual indocility. In consequence, until we have analysed this latter, the thesis of this essay will not stand out in its final clarity.

CHAPTER VIII: WHY THE MASSES INTERVENE IN EVERYTHING, AND WHY THEIR INTERVENTION IS SOLELY BY VIOLENCE

. . . The command over public life exercised to-day by the intellectually vulgar is perhaps the factor of the present situation which is most novel, least assimilable to anything in the past. At least in European history up to the present, the vulgar had never believed itself to have "ideas" on things. It had beliefs, traditions, experiences, proverbs, mental habits, but it never imagined itself in possession of theoretical opinions on what things are or ought to be—for example, on politics or literature. What the politician planned or carried out seemed good or bad to it, it granted or withheld its support, but its action was limited to being an echo, positive or negative, of the creative activity of others. It never occurred to it to oppose to the "ideas" of the politician others of its own, nor even to judge the politician's "ideas" from the tribunal of other "ideas" which it believed itself to possess. Similarly in art and in other aspects of public life. An innate consciousness of its limitation, of its not being qualified to theorise,[2] effectively prevented it doing so. The necessary consequence of this was that the vulgar never thought, even remotely, of making a decision on any one of the public activities, which in their greater part are theoretical in character. To-day, on the other hand, the average man has the most mathematical "ideas" on all that happens or ought to happen in the universe. Hence he has lost the use of his hearing. Why should he listen if he has within him all that is necessary? There is no reason now for listening, but rather for judging, pronouncing, deciding. There is no question concerning public life, in which he does not intervene, blind and deaf as he is, imposing his "opinions."

But, is this not an advantage? Is it not a sign of immense progress that the masses should have "ideas," that is to say, should be cultured? By no means. The "ideas" of the average man are not genuine ideas, nor is their possession culture. An idea is a putting truth in checkmate. Whoever wishes to have ideas must first prepare himself to desire truth and to accept the rules of the game imposed by it. It is no use speaking of ideas when there is no acceptance of a higher authority to regulate them, a series of standards to which it is possible to appeal in a discussion. These standards are the principles on which culture rests. I am not concerned with the form they take. What I affirm is that there is no culture where there are no standards to which our fellow-men can have recourse. There is no culture where there are no principles of legality to which to appeal. There is no culture where there is no acceptance of certain final intellectual positions to which a dispute may be referred. There is no culture where economic relations are not subject to a regulating principle to protect interests involved. There is no culture where aesthetic controversy does not recognise the necessity of justifying the work of art.

[2] There is no getting away from it; every opinion means setting up a theory.

When all these things are lacking there is no culture; there is in the strictest sense of the word, barbarism. And let us not deceive ourselves, this is what is beginning to appear in Europe under the progressive rebellion of the masses. The traveller who arrives in a barbarous country knows that in that territory there are no ruling principles to which it is possible to appeal. Properly speaking, there are no barbarian standards. Barbarism is the absence of standards to which appeal can be made.

The varying degrees of culture are measured by the greater or less precision of the standards. Where there is little such precision, these standards rule existence only *grosso modo;* where there is much they penetrate in detail into the exercise of all the activities.

Anyone can observe that in Europe, for some years past, "strange things" have begun to happen. To give a concrete example of these "strange things" I shall name certain political movements, such as Syndicalism and Fascism. We must not think that they seem strange simply because they are new. The enthusiasm for novelty is so innate in the European that it has resulted in his producing the most unsettled history of all known to us. The element of strangeness in these new facts is not to be attributed to the element of novelty, but to the extraordinary form taken by these new things. Under the species of Syndicalism and Fascism there appears for the first time in Europe a type of man who does not want to give reasons or to be right, but simply shows himself resolved to impose his opinions. This is the new thing: the right not to be reasonable, the "reason of unreason." Here I see the most palpable manifestation of the new mentality of the masses, due to their having decided to rule society without the capacity for doing so. In their political conduct the structure of the new mentality is revealed in the rawest, most convincing manner; but the key to it lies in intellectual hermetism. The average man finds himself with "ideas" in his head, but he lacks the faculty of ideation. He has no conception even of the rare atmosphere in which ideas live. He wishes to have opinions, but is unwilling to accept the conditions and presuppositions that underlie all opinion. Hence his ideas are in effect nothing more than appetites in words, something like musical romanzas.

To have an idea means believing one is in possession of the reasons for having it, and consequently means believing that there is such a thing as reason, a world of intelligible truths. To have ideas, to form opinions, is identical with appealing to such an authority, submitting oneself to it, accepting its code and its decisions, and therefore believing that the highest form of intercommunion is the dialogue in which the reasons for our ideas are discussed.

But the mass-man would feel himself lost if he accepted discussion, and instinctively repudiates the obligation of accepting that supreme authority lying outside himself. Hence the "new thing" in Europe is "to have done with discussions," and detestation is expressed for all forms of intercommunion which imply acceptance of objective standards, ranging from conversation to Parliament, and taking in science. This means that there is a renunciation of the common life based on culture, which is subject to standards, and a return to the common life of barbarism. All the normal processes are suppressed in order to arrive directly at the imposition of what is desired. The hermetism of the soul which, as we have seen before, urges the mass to intervene in the whole of public life, also inevitably leads it to one single process of intervention: direct action.

When the reconstruction of the origins of our epoch is undertaken, it will be observed that the first notes of its special harmony were sounded in those groups of French syndicalists and realists of about 1900, inventors of the method and the name of "direct action." Man has always had recourse to violence; sometimes this recourse was a mere crime, and does not interest us here. But at other times violence was the means resorted to by him who had previously exhausted all others in defence of the rights of justice which he thought he possessed. It may be regrettable that human nature tends on occasion to this form of violence, but it is undeniable that it implies the greatest tribute to reason and justice. For this form of violence is none other than reason exasperated. Force was, in fact, the *ultima ratio.* Rather stupidly it has been the custom to take ironically this expression, which clearly indicates the previous submission of force to methods of reason. Civilisation is nothing else than the attempt to reduce force to being the *ultima ratio.* We are now beginning to realise this with startling clearness, because "direct action" consists in inverting the order and proclaiming violence as *prima ratio,* or strictly as *unica ratio.* It is the norm which proposes the annulment of all norms, which suppresses all intermediate process between our purpose and its execution. It is the Magna Charta of barbarism. . . .

CHAPTER XI: THE SELF-SATISFIED AGE

To resume; the new social fact here analysed is this: European history reveals itself, for the first time, as handed over to the decisions of the ordinary man as such. Or to turn it into the active voice: the ordinary man, hitherto guided by others, has resolved to govern the world himself. This decision to advance to the social foreground has been brought about in him automatically, when the new type of man he represents had barely arrived at maturity. If from the view-point of what concerns public life, the psychological structure of this new type of mass-man be studied, what we find is as follows: (1) An inborn, root-impression that life is easy, plentiful, without any grave limitations; consequently, each average man finds within himself a sensation of power and triumph which, (2) invites him to stand up for himself as he is, to look upon his moral and intellectual endowment as excellent, complete. This contentment with himself leads him to shut himself off from any external court of appeal; not to listen, not to submit his opinions to judgment, not to consider others' existence. His intimate feeling of power urges him always to exercise predominance. He will act then as if he and his like were the only beings existing in the world; and, consequently (3) will intervene in all matters, imposing his own vulgar views without respect or regard for others, without limit or reserve, that is to say, in accordance with a system of "direct action."

It was this series of aspects which made us think of certain defective types of humanity, such as the spoiled child, and the primitive in revolt, that is, the barbarian. (The normal primitive, on the other hand, is the most submissive to external authority ever known, be it religion, taboo, social tradition, or customs.) . . .

. . . This type which at present is to be found everywhere, and everywhere imposes his own spiritual barbarism, is, in fact, the spoiled child of human history. The spoiled child is the heir who behaves exclusively as a mere heir. In this case the inheritance is civilisation—with its conveniences, its security; in a word, with all its advantages. As we have seen, it is only in circumstances of easy existence such as our civilisation has produced, that a type can arise, marked by such a collection of features, inspired by such a character. It is one of a number of deformities produced by luxury in human material. There might be a deceptive tendency to believe that a life born into a world of plenty should be better, more really a life than one which consists in a struggle against scarcity. Such is not the case, for reasons of the strictest and most fundamental nature, which this is not the place to enlarge upon. . . .

. . . [We have a] tendency to believe that a superabundance of resources favours existence. Quite the contrary. A world superabundant in possibilities automatically produces deformities, vicious types of human life, which may be brought under the general class, the "heir-man," of which the "aristocrat" is only one particular case, the spoiled child another, and the mass-man of our time, more fully, more radically, a third. (It would, moreover, be possible to make more detailed use of this last allusion to the "aristocrat," by showing how many of his characteristic traits, in all times and among all peoples, germinate in the mass-man. For example: his propensity to make out of games and sports the central occupation of this life; the cult of the body—hygienic regime and attention to dress; lack of romance in his dealings with woman; his amusing himself with the "intellectual," while at bottom despising him and at times ordering his flunkeys or his bravoes to chastise him; his preference for living under an absolute authority rather than under a regime of free-discussion, etc.)

I persist then, at the risk of boring the reader, in making the point that this man full of uncivilised tendencies, this newest of the barbarians, is an automatic product of modern civilisation, especially of the form taken by this civilisation in the XIXth Century . . . [which is one] of superabundance, . . . [in] which he perceives only the lavishness of the means at his disposal, nothing of the pains involved. He finds himself surrounded by marvellous instruments, healing medicines, watchful governments, comfortable privileges. On the other hand, he is ignorant how difficult it is to invent those medicines and those instruments and to assure their production in the future; he does not realise how unstable is the organisation of the State and is scarcely conscious to himself of any obligations. This lack of balance falsifies his nature, vitiates it in its very roots, causing him to lose contact with the very substance of life, which is made up of absolute danger, is radically problematic. The form most contradictory to human life that can appear among the human species is the "self-satisfied man." Consequently, when he becomes the predominant type, it is time to raise the alarm and to announce that humanity is threatened with degeneration, that is, with relative death. On this view, the vital level represented by Europe at the present day is superior to the whole of the human past, but if we look to the future, we are made to fear that it will neither preserve the level reached nor attain to a higher one, but rather will recede and fall back upon lower heights. . . .

CHAPTER XII: THE BARBARISM OF "SPECIALISATION"

My thesis was that XIXth-Century civilisation has automatically produced the mass-man. It will be well not to close the general exposition without analysing, in a particular case, the mechanism of that production. In this way, by taking concrete form, the thesis gains in persuasive force.

This civilisation of the XIXth Century, I said, may be summed up in the two great dimensions: liberal democracy and technicism. Let us take for the moment only the latter. Modern technicism springs from the union between capitalism and experimental science. Not all technicism is scientific. That which made the stone axe in the Chelian period was lacking in science, and yet a technique was created. China reached a high degree of technique without in the least suspecting the existence of physics. It is only modern European technique that has a scientific basis, from which it derives its specific character, its possibility of limitless progress. All other techniques—Mesopotamian, Egyptian, Greek, Roman, Oriental—reach up to a point of development beyond which they cannot proceed, and hardly do they reach it when they commence to display a lamentable retrogression.

This marvellous Western technique has made possible the proliferation of the European species. . . . From the VIth century to 1800, Europe never succeeds in reaching a population greater than 180 millions. From 1800 to 1914 it rises to more than 460 millions. The jump is unparalleled in our history. There can be no doubt that it is technicism—in combination with liberal democracy—which has engendered mass-man in the quantitative sense of the expression. But these pages have attempted to show that it is also responsible for the existence of mass-man in the qualitative and pejorative sense of the term.

By mass—as I pointed out at the start—is not to be specially understood the workers; it does not indicate a social class, but a kind of man to be found to-day in all social classes, who consequently represents our age, in which he is the predominant, ruling power. We are now about to find abundant evidence for this.

Who is it that exercises social power to-day? Who imposes the forms of his own mind on the period? Without a doubt, the man of the middle class. Which group, within that middle class, is considered the superior, the aristocracy of the present? Without a doubt, the technician: engineer, doctor, financier, teacher, and so on. Who, inside the group of technicians, represents it at its best and purest? Again, without a doubt, the man of science. If an astral personage were to visit Europe to-day and, for the purpose of forming judgment on it, inquire as to the type of man by which it would prefer to be judged, there is no doubt that Europe, pleasantly assured of a favourable judgment, would point to her men of science. Of course, our astral personage would not inquire for exceptional individuals, but would seek the generic type of "man of science," the high-point of European humanity.

And now it turns out that the actual scientific man is the prototype of the mass-man. Not by chance, not through the individual failings of each particular man of science, but because science itself—the root of our civilisation—automatically converts him into mass-man, makes of him a primitive, a modern barbarian. The fact is well known; it has made itself clear over and over again; but only when fitted into its place in the organism of this thesis does it take on its full meaning and its evident seriousness.

Experimental science is initiated towards the end of the XVIth Century (Galileo), it is definitely constituted at the close of the XVIIth (Newton), and it begins to develop in the middle of the XVIIIth. The development of anything is not the same as its constitution; it is subject to different considerations. Thus, the constitution of physics, the collective name of the experimental sciences, rendered necessary an effort towards unification. Such was the work of Newton and other men of his time. But the development of physics introduced a task opposite in character to unification. In order to progress, science demanded specialisation, not in herself, but in men of science. Science is not specialist. If it were, it would *ipso facto* cease to be true. Not even empirical science, taken in its integrity, can be true if separated from mathematics, from logic, from philosophy. But scientific work does, necessarily, require to be specialised.

It would be of great interest, and of greater utility than at first sight appears, to draw up the history of physical and biological sciences, indicating the process of increasing specialisation in the work of investigators. It would then be seen how, generation after generation, the scientist has been gradually restricted and confined into narrower fields of mental occupation. But this is not the important point that such a history would show, but rather the reverse side of the matter: how in each generation the scientist, through having to reduce the sphere of his labour, was progressively losing contact with other branches of science, with that integral interpretation of the universe which is the only thing deserving the names of science, culture, European civilisation.

Specialisation commences precisely at a period which gives to civilised man the title "encyclopaedic." The XIXth Century starts on its course under the direction of beings who lived "encyclopaedically," though their production has already some tinge of specialism. In the following generation, the balance is upset and specialism begins to dislodge culture from the individual scientist. When by 1890 a third generation assumes intellectual command in Europe we meet with a type of scientist unparalleled in history. He is one who, out of all that has to be known in order to be a man of judgment, is only acquainted with one science, and even of that one only knows the small corner in which he is an active investigator. He even proclaims it as a virtue that he takes no cognizance of what lies outside the narrow territory specially cultivated by himself, and gives the name of "dilettantism" to any curiosity for the general scheme of knowledge.

What happens is that, enclosed within the narrow limits of his visual field, he does actually succeed in discovering new facts and advancing the progress of the science which he hardly knows, and incidentally the encyclopedia of thought of which he is conscientiously ignorant. How has such a thing been possible, how is it still possible? For it is necessary to insist upon this extraordinary but undeniable fact: experimental science has progressed thanks in great part to the work of men astoundingly mediocre, and even less than mediocre. That is to say, modern science, the root and symbol of our actual civilisation, finds a place for the intellectually commonplace man and allows him to work therein with success. The reason of this lies in what is at the same time the great advantage and the gravest peril of the new science, and of the civilisation directed and represented by it, namely, mechanisation. A fair amount of the things that have to be done in physics or in biology is mechanical work of the mind which can be done by anyone, or almost anyone. For the purpose of innumerable investigations, it is possible to divide science into small sections, to enclose oneself in one of these, and to leave out of consideration all the rest. The solidity and exactitude of the methods allow of this temporary but quite real disarticulation of knowledge. The work is done under one of these methods as with a machine, and in order to obtain quite abundant results it is not even necessary to have rigorous notions of their meaning and foundations. In this way the majority of scientists help the general advance of science while shut up in the narrow cell of their laboratory, like the bee in the cell of its hive, or the turnspit in its wheel.

But this creates an extraordinarily strange type of man. The investigator who has discovered a new fact of Nature must necessarily experience a feeling of power and self-assurance. With a certain apparent justice he will look upon himself as "a man who knows." And in fact there is in him a portion of something which, added to many other portions not existing in him, does really constitute knowledge. This is the true inner nature of the specialist, who in the first years of this century has reached the wildest stage of exaggeration. The specialist "knows" very well his own, tiny corner of the universe; he is radically ignorant of all the rest.

Here we have a precise example of this strange new man, whom I have attempted to define, from both of his two opposite aspects. I have said that he was a human product unparalleled in history. The specialist serves as a striking concrete example of the species, making clear to us the radical nature of the novelty. For, previously, men could be divided simply into the learned and the ignorant, those more or less the one, and those more or less the other. But your specialist cannot be brought in under either of these two categories. He is not learned, for he is formally ignorant of all that does not enter into his specialty; but neither is he ignorant, because he is "a scientist," and "knows" very well his own tiny portion of the universe. We shall have to say that he is a learned ignoramus, which is a very serious matter, as it implies that he is a person who is ignorant, not in the fashion of the ignorant man, but with all the petulance of one who is learned in his own special line.

And such in fact is the behaviour of the specialist. In politics, in art, in social usages, in the other sciences, he will adopt the attitude of primitive, ignorant man; but he will adopt them forcefully and with self-sufficiency, and will not admit of—this is the paradox—specialists in those matters. By specialising him, civilisation has made him hermetic and self-satisfied within his limitations; but this very inner feeling of dominance and worth will induce him to wish to predominate outside his specialty. The result is that even in this case, representing a maximum of qualification in man—specialisation—and therefore the thing most opposed to the mass-man, the result is that he will behave in almost all spheres of life as does the unqualified, the mass-man.

This is no mere wild statement. Anyone who wishes can observe the stupidity of thought, judgment, and action shown to-day in politics, art, religion, and the general problems of life and the world by the "men of science," and of course, behind them, the doctors, engineers, financiers, teachers, and so on. That state of "not listening," of not submitting to higher courts of appeal which I have repeatedly put forward as characteristic of the mass-man, reaches its height precisely in these partially qualified men. They symbolise, and to a great extent constitute, the actual dominion of the masses, and their barbarism is the most immediate cause of European demoralisation. Furthermore, they afford the clearest, most striking example of how the civilisation of the last century, *abandoned to its own devices,* has brought about this rebirth of primitivism and barbarism.

The most immediate result of this unbalanced specialisation has been that to-day, when there are more "scientists" than ever, there are much less "cultured" men than, for example, about 1750. And the worst is that with these turnspits of science not even the real progress of science itself is assured. For science needs from time to time, as a necessary regulator of its own advance, a labour of reconstitution, and, as I have said, this demands an effort towards unification, which grows more and more difficult, involving, as it does, ever-vaster regions of the world of knowledge. Newton was able to found his system of physics without knowing much philosophy, but Einstein needed to saturate himself with Kant and Mach before he could reach his own keen synthesis. Kant and Mach—the names are mere symbols of the enormous mass of philosophic and psychological thought which has influenced Einstein—have served to *liberate* the mind of the latter and leave the way open for his innovation. But Einstein is not sufficient. Physics is entering on the gravest crisis of its history, and can only be saved by a new "Encyclopaedia" more systematic than the first. . . .

CHAPTER XV: WE ARRIVE AT THE REAL QUESTION

This is the question: Europe has been left without a moral code. It is not that the mass-man has thrown over an antiquated one in exchange for a new one, but that at the centre of his scheme of life there is precisely the aspiration to live without conforming to any moral code. Do not believe a word you hear from the young when they talk about the "new morality." I absolutely deny that there exists to-day in any corner of the Continent a group inspired by a new *ethos* which shows signs of being a moral code. When people talk of the "new morality" they are merely committing a new immorality and looking for a way of introducing contraband goods. Hence it would be a piece of ingenuousness to accuse the man of to-day of his lack of moral code. The accusation would leave him cold, or rather, would flatter him. Immoralism has become a commonplace, and anybody and everybody boasts of practising it.

If we leave out of question, as has been done in this essay, all those groups which imply survivals from the past—Christians, Idealists, the old Liberals—there will not be found, amongst all the representatives of the actual period, a single group whose attitude to life is not limited to believing that it has all the rights and none of the obligations. It is indifferent whether it disguises itself as reactionary or revolutionary; actively or passively, after one or two twists, its state of mind will consist, decisively, in ignoring all obligations, and in feeling itself, without the slightest notion why, possessed of unlimited rights. Whatever be the substance which takes possession of such a soul, it will produce the same result, and will change into a pretext for not conforming to any concrete purpose. If it appears as reactionary or anti-liberal it will be in order to affirm that the salvation of the State gives a right to level down all other standards, and to manhandle one's neighbour, above all if one's neighbour is an outstanding personality. But the same happens if it decides to act the revolutionary; the apparent enthusiasm for the manual worker, for the afflicted and for social justice, serves as a mask to facilitate the refusal of all obligations, such as courtesy, truthfulness and, above all, respect or esteem for superior individuals. I know of quite a few who have entered the ranks of some labour organisation or other merely in order to win for themselves the right to despise intelligence and to avoid paying it any tribute. As regards other kinds of Dictatorship, we have seen only too well how they flatter the mass-man, by trampling on everything that appeared to be above the common level.

This fighting-shy of every obligation partly explains the phenomenon, half ridiculous, half disgraceful, of the setting-up in our days of the platform of "youth" as youth. Perhaps there is no more grotesque spectacle offered by our times. In comic fashion people call themselves "young," because they have heard that youth has more rights than obligations, since it can put off the fulfillment of these latter to the Greek Kalends of maturity. The youth, as such, has always been considered exempt from *doing* or *having done* actions of importance. He has always lived on credit. It was a sort of false right, half ironic, half affectionate, which the no-longer young conceded to their juniors. But the astounding thing at present is that these take it as an effective right precisely in order to claim for themselves all those other rights which only belong to the man who has already done something.

Though it may appear incredible, "youth" has become a *chantage;*[3] we are in truth living in a time when this adopts two complementary attitudes, violence and caricature. One way or the other, the purpose is always the same; that the inferior, the man of the crowd, may feel himself exempt from all submission to superiors.

It will not do, then, to dignify the actual crisis by presenting it as the conflict between two moralities, two civilisations, one in decay, the other at its dawn. The mass-man is simply without morality, which is always, in essence, a sentiment of submission to something, a consciousness of service and obligation. But perhaps it is a mistake to say "simply." For it is not merely a question of this type of creature doing without morality. No, we must not make his task too easy. Morality cannot be eliminated without more ado. What, by a word lacking even in grammar, is called *amorality* is a thing that does not exist. If you are unwilling to submit to any norm, you have, *nolens volens,*[4] to submit to the norm of denying all morality, and this is not amoral, but immoral. It is a negative morality which preserves the empty form of the other. How has it been possible to believe in the amorality of life? Doubtless, because all modern culture and civilisation tend to that conviction. Europe is now reaping the painful results of her spiritual conduct. She has adopted blindly a culture which is magnificent, but has no roots. . . .

[3] [That is, a kind of cultural blackmail.]
[4] [That is, willing or not.]

CONTEMPORARY CIVILIZATION: ITS PREDICAMENTS

2. VIOLENCE AND THE SOCIALIZATION OF FEAR

KARL KAUTSKY

BORN in Prague of Czech-German parents in 1854 and educated at the University of Vienna, Karl Kautsky was first attracted to socialism not by the writings of Marx and Engels but by the novels of George Sand (1804–1876). In 1874, while still a student, he joined the Austrian Social Democratic Party. In 1881 he met Marx and Engels in London—a meeting which he later described as "the most important event in my life." After Marx's death (1883), he spent five years (1885–1890) in London in close association with Engels. In 1883 Kautsky had founded the German Social Democratic journal *Die neue Zeit,* and he continued as its editor until 1917. In 1936, at the time when Hitler's Germany was threatening Austrian independence, Kautsky—already past eighty—was forced to flee from Vienna. He found refuge in Holland, where his last years were passed in relative poverty and obscurity. Kautsky died in 1938 at the age of eighty-four.

After Engels's death in 1895, Kautsky rapidly gained the reputation of chief theoretical spokesman for international Marxism. It was he who led the defense of "orthodox" Marxism against the revisionism of Eduard Bernstein (1850–1932) in the late 1890's and against the Kantian revisionists in ethical theory a decade later. His authority among European Social Democrats is still high; but he has been sharply repudiated by Marxists of the Leninist-Stalinist wing.

An indefatigable scholar and writer, Kautsky produced dozens of learned works in history (including history of religion), economics, sociology, and philosophy. Most of these were translated into the major European languages, including Russian, and Kautsky's influence upon Russian Marxism before 1917 was enormous. His encyclopedic *Materialist Conception of History,* published in 1927, runs to nearly two thousand pages.

Kautsky himself felt that his chief contribution to social thought was to amplify Marxism with an ethics derived from the moral speculation of the biologist Charles Darwin (1809–1882). It is significant that Kautsky read the *Descent of Man* (1871), in which "Darwin's discovery of the character of morality" was set forth, before he had encountered any of the writings of Marx or Engels. Darwin's insight—that altruistic feelings, hence morality, are present in the social animals—struck Kautsky as "one of the greatest and most fruitful discoveries of the human mind." Darwin himself had laid down only the bare outlines of a "Darwinian ethics"; such an ethics was first developed by Walter Bagehot (1826–1877) in his *Physics and Politics* (1872), but Kautsky's own position seems to have been developed independently. The essence of his view is that it is not merely the animal strength and cunning of individuals which have survival value in the struggle for existence, but also—since the basic unit of struggle is the social group—social instincts, co-operative behavior patterns, and altruistic feelings. Kautsky amassed impressive factual evidence for the presence and efficacy of social instincts in animals and primitive men, and offered an interpretation of human history in terms of the strengthening and weakening of these instincts in various periods and classes.

Kautsky's ethical theory, and his related view that the proletarian revolution should gain power through democratic processes rather than violent revolution, came under vigorous attack by various Bolshevik writers after 1917—including V. I. Lenin (1870–1924) and, most incisively, Leon Trotsky (1879–1940). During these polemical exchanges, which stretched from 1919 to 1925 (and Kautsky repeated his charges, bringing them up to date, in 1930, in a brochure entitled *Bolshevism at a Deadlock*), the Bolsheviks defended and Kautsky attacked a Machiavellian position which subordinated all questions of individual and social morality to the tactical problem of the acquisition and maintenance of political power. Holding that the good end justifies any means, the Bolsheviks refused to recognize any moral limitations upon the choice of these means, concluding that terrorism, violence, and fraud were all antecedently justified. Kautsky insisted that Bolshevik terrorism represented not only a reversal of the historical trend of humanization of morals, but also a violation of the sanctity of human life, a failure to regard the human individual as an end in himself. "The end," he declared, "does not sanctify every means, but only those which are in harmony with it." In other words, he held that there are certain moral principles or values which set absolute and inviolable limits to the choice of means for realizing given socio-political ends. He thus came very close to Kant; and Trotsky—who derisively repudiated Kautsky's "Kantian-clerical, vegetarian-Quaker chatter about the 'sanctity of human life,' " could justly charge that his opponent had taken up a position inconsistent with Marxian ethical relativism.

It seems clear, at least, that Kautsky's advocacy of a constitutional winning of power by the socialists through free elections, accompanied by propaganda and education in the aims of socialism, and his insistence that only thus can the end be kept uncorrupted, are much closer to the democratic and humanistic traditions of the West than is Trotsky's Machiavellianism. Kautsky's position, in general, is that of contemporary Social Democrats; Trotsky's is that maintained (implicitly if not explicitly) by contemporary Communists.

The following selection has been taken from the English (1920) edition of Kautsky's *Terrorism and Communism,* which was first published in German in 1919. The translation has been thoroughly revised especially for this volume by George L. Kline.

TERRORISM AND COMMUNISM

The Effect of Civilization on Human Morals: Brutality and Humanity

. . . The massacres of the great French Revolution were not repeated in succeeding revolutions; . . . from 1830 to 1871 . . . the revolutionary fighters, even when they were under the influence of the traditions established by the Reign of Terror, nevertheless in practice strove to be as humane as possible—in contrast to their enemies who, both before and after, developed the worst form of brutality both in June, 1848, and in May, 1871.

During the whole of the nineteenth century we can observe a progressive humanizing taking place among the working classes. Now, at the beginning of the twentieth century, the Revolution in Russia and Germany has come, and has given rein to massacres which remind us of the French Revolution of the eighteenth century. How can we explain this reversal?

It is generally assumed that man's humaneness is a product of culture, that man is by nature an evil and unsociable creature, with predatory instincts, ever ready to attack, oppress, torture, and kill his neighbor. It is further assumed that man acquires social feeling, kindness, a readiness to help others, an abhorrence of cruelty and murder, only after long progress in culture and technology, in other words, in civilization.

This idea is expressed in the language people employ, which uses the word "humaneness" or "humanity" to describe those qualities that we have just mentioned, and distinguishes them from those other features which are stigmatized as bestial ("bestia," the beast) and brutal ("brutus," the brute). . . . [Many anthropologists see] in violent crime . . . [an] atavism, a drop back into the sensient life of the animal precursors of man.

. . . [But in fact] even bloodthirsty beasts of prey do not, as a rule, kill their own kind; and nothing justifies us in assuming that man is really by nature a beast of prey, with violent bloodthirsty instincts. We do not know the animal precursors of the human species, but we must assume that, among the animals of the present day, the anthropoid ape approaches them most nearly. Like the latter, man's ancestor probably lived chiefly on vegetable nourishment, which he occasionally supplemented with small animals, caterpillars, worms, reptiles, even unfledged birds. But he never killed a large mammal in order to devour it. No ape does the like.

This selection has been reprinted from Karl Kautsky, *Terrorism and Communism,* London: George Allen & Unwin, Ltd., 1920, pp. 121–157 by permission of the publisher.

Furthermore, the ape never wages murderous war against its own kind, lacking even the organs necessary for such conflict. Individual apes may fight over their booty, or over a mate, receiving minor scratches; but such scrimmages do not end fatally for either side.

All this is changed in the case of man as soon as his technical knowledge provides him with new "organs" to supplement those given him by nature, namely, tools and cutting and piercing weapons of various kinds. Man, having acquired the organs of a beast of prey, develops the predatory functions and instincts to go with them. He can now kill larger animals and cut them up. Vegetable nourishment thus loses its importance for him; hunting and bloodshed become everyday affairs. Under such conditions conflicts between individuals may lead to the death of one or both. But the murder of entire peoples, namely war, cannot be explained by the invention of weapons alone. War presupposes a further cultivated development, namely, the grouping of people into closed communities.

Since this point has hitherto been very little considered, and as I myself have hitherto not treated it sufficiently, a few remarks may here be made, although they lead us somewhat away from our subject. Without doubt man takes his origin from the social animals but he distinguishes himself from them by the fact that he forms closed communities. . . .

What distinguishes human beings from animals, apart from the use of tools, is articulate speech. . . . This means of communication is not given to the whole species from the start, but is differently formed in different places. Through language, social unity becomes stronger and more intimate, since, through it, understanding and community of labor are rendered easier and more varied. But through these differences the several tribes and groups of mankind are, from the very start, kept apart one from the other. Therefore each individual is forced to remain with that particular tribe or group whose language he has learned. He cannot communicate with others. He feels strange and uncomfortable when he is among them. In addition to this another factor arises. Language makes possible the designation of individuals and their relations with one another. It also permits memories of the past to be recorded. In other words, it acts as a conservative element. The mature animal easily forgets its parents and the members of its family, which it is unable to distinguish from other creatures of its kind. But the human being, his whole life long, is aware of these relations. He can even recognize and remember the parents of his own parents and the children of his own children, as well as the children of his brothers and sisters, and so on.

It is generally assumed that the family is something ordained by nature, and that the "voice of the blood" is proof of this fact. In reality, the family was created by the "voice of language." Without designations of relationships the family cannot exist as a permanent institution. The "voice of the blood" ceases to sound in the case of animals as soon as the young are fledged and independent. This makes it all the more ridiculous when some people today attempt to explain not only *family* but also *national* ties as a result of the "voice of the blood." . . .

The closed and intimate nature of the family was further enhanced by the formation of households and the accumulation of private property in the form of tools, weapons, and utensils of all kinds, which survived the original owner. For, after the owner's death, this private property was passed on to those members of the family who had maintained the closest and most constant ties with him; it was thus a motivation for maintaining such ties up to the time of his death. The closed and intimate nature of the tribe as a whole was also preserved through possessions of another kind, that is, through the ownership of land which was the common property of the tribe. Even animals prefer to live in regions where they have been brought up and where they feel at home, where they know every food source, every safe corner, every dangerous spot. Nevertheless, the boundaries of such regions are not very clear, and an individual member of the herd or flock who is unable to find sufficient food, or encounters too great dangers, can easily extend the range of his operations until he comes to a region that is better suited to his needs. But, once there, he immediately attaches himself to another herd or flock.

The situation is very different in the closed societies of human beings. An individual who strays from his native region finds himself among men and women whom he cannot understand. Primitive populations do not adjust to available means of subsistence by individual migrations from overpopulated to less heavily populated areas. Such movements of individuals are to be found only in a higher state of culture, and even there only to a certain degree. Rather, the tribe stays together and attempts to enlarge its feeding area at the cost of its neighbors. Here we have the beginnings of warfare and mass-murder, as soon as weapons-technology has become sufficiently well developed.

Thus we see that what we call "brutality" is not characteristic of the animal precursors of man, but is rather a product of cultural development. As for ethical feelings, the sense of solidarity, sympathy for others, readiness to help others—all of these change their character in the course of man's development. Among the social animals, these instincts extend to all the individuals of the given species. But in the case of man, their range of application is confined to members of the immediate social group. Anyone who is outside this group remains an object of indifference, treated without sympathy, or else of direct hostility. As commerce and communication develop, the limits of the society of which the individual feels himself to be a member are also enlarged. Today we are, as it were, reverting to the beginnings of human development; the range of our social and ethical feelings is again beginning to include all the individuals of the species, in other words, the whole human race. But, generally speaking, this is rather an ideal toward which we are very slowly striving.

At the same time, economic development, through the division of labor and the increasing variety of social relationships, has led to the formation of closed societies called States, and these, in turn, are broken up into smaller, more or less closed, communities. Among these are clans, families, ecclesiastical organizations, guilds, etc., each of them with its own morality, limited to its own members. And these groups frequently come into conflict with one another. They are capable of developing great solidarity and sympathy within their own narrow circle; at the same time they can be completely relentless toward others. Since each individual may belong to several such groups, having different and often opposed interests and ethical principles, the greater the contradictions within the society as a whole, the greater will be the tensions within the individual.

The wives and daughters of slaveowners in the Southern States were charming and lovable, full of generosity and sympathy, among the members of their own group; but they tortured their slaves unmercifully. A man may show the most delicate feeling for the members of his family and yet, in his business relations, be the most callous of creditors and a pitiless taskmaster. Civilization does not result in a rectilinear and progressive humanizing of conduct. However, it would be absurd to assume the contrary, and to regard the primitive state of nature as an idyllic condition of the Golden Age from which we have been gradually falling away. Here we must distinguish two conflicting tendencies in human history, of which now one, now the other, is prevalent, depending upon the specific conditions of the time.

TWO TENDENCIES

One tendency we have already discussed. It consists in the continuous improvement of the weapons for slaughter and in the increasing of antagonisms among men. It makes for the increase of national antagonism, the opposition that arises between overpopulated and underpopulated regions, between rich and poor nations, between those who monopolize the treasures of nature and those who are forced to remain in sterile deserts. It leads, further, to the opposition between the industrially developed and the industrially backward. And finally, within given nations, it leads to the various forms of exploitation and enslavement of man by man, with its resulting hatred and cruelty.

With the beginning of agriculture, a contrary tendency arises. . . . The husbandman often sees a friend in the wild beast, since it attacks animals which threaten his crops; and the preserving of game animals, which is of primary importance to the hunter, is viewed coolly by the husbandman. The artisan and, later, the intellectual worker, even more than the agricultural worker, view the production of weapons as wasteful and unnecessary. They regard the time and material expended in making and learning how to use weapons as an economic extravagance (unlike the hunter and animal breeder), and would prefer to minimize such expenditure. Thus the peasant, the artisan, and the intellectual become more and more peaceable in nature, especially the last group, for the peasant and the artisan do need muscular strength to carry on their work. Such muscular strength stands in high honor with them and is welcomed, not only in actual work but even in play, and especially in sports that involve competition. The intellectual, on the other hand, needs no strength. The time which others devote to the development of their muscles he devotes to the increase of his knowledge, or the exercise of his wits. Whoever would endeavor to carry on a literary feud with him, using weapons other than those of the mind, would at once betray his inferiority. . . .

The priestly castes of the ancient world, as well as the Christian clergy, were, in general, averse to the shedding of blood and to acts of violence, so long as they had not become ruling or exploiting classes. This was also true of the intellectuals of the eighteenth century. When, however, the intellectuals themselves became exploiters, they did not always give evidence of the same peaceable tendencies. Where they are not exploiters, it is the same with them as with the peasants, the artisans, and the proletarians. Man in such a case is regarded not as a means for the ends of others, but as an end in himself, or as a means for the ends of the community at large; not, however, as means for the ends of other individuals. Kant's ethics corresponds exactly to this standpoint. Only for Kant ethics does not form a mere moral code for particular classes or times, but rather a permanent moral law, beyond the world of appearances, to which the Almighty himself is subject, since even He is forbidden to make use of man as mere means. . . .

Whatever theoretical ground one may offer for such a point of view, its result is a maximum respect for the human person, the sanctity of human life, and human happiness. But these peace-loving tendencies began to show their disadvantages even in the early stages of agriculture and urban life; for the most peaceable classes and nations proved to be the most defenseless. They were subjugated and exploited by more militant groups, which set themselves up over them as a military aristocracy and betook themselves to the hunt, to war, and to slaughter even more intently than the hunters and animal breeders had formerly done. They thus erected into a principle the methods and instincts of beasts of prey, and conducted themselves as such in their dealings with those of their fellow men who were hostilely disposed toward them.

Thus brutality and humanity became two aspects of the same civilized society, and one or the other of them prevailed, according to changing conditions. In Ancient Rome the whole population was involved in a policy of conquest. Thanks to their military superiority, the Romans succeeded in making all the countries of the Mediterranean servile to them. The whole population, living on the exploitation of these lands, became enthusiastic for war and supported its most merciless conduct. As military success put crowds of cheap slaves at the disposal of the Romans, it ultimately became one of their pastimes to force slaves to fight and kill one another in the amphitheaters, to the delight of the populace. Gladiatorial contests, and the murdering of men as a mere pastime for an idle mob of both high and low degree, mark the extreme limit of a most vulgar cruelty. Yet such contests were characteristic of the ancient Roman state not in the condition of barbarism but at the summit of its civilization. And these gladiatorial contests did not cease until the Roman state had been brought down from its high level of "culture" through the incursion of barbarians living at its borders.

In the course of economic development there arose, alongside of the war nobility, a capitalist class with two diverging tendencies. As an exploiter, the capitalist regarded the man on whose exploitation he lived not as an end in himself, but as a means to his own ends. Such an attitude already contains the germs of inhumanity and cruelty; just how far these germs will develop depends entirely upon prevailing conditions. Colonial policy was responsible for the bloodiest and most fearful atrocities. However, during the period of commercial capital, opposition arose between commercial and industrial capital. The former revealed itself to be warlike and unscrupulous. It massacred and plundered the people of India. It carried on slave trade with Negroes, and forced its various governments to embark on bloody and exhausting commercial wars. On the other hand, industrial capital has had to pay the greater part of the costs of these wars, and has been thereby handicapped. It stands, therefore, in direct opposition to such methods and indeed indignantly so. Its sympathy is strongly aroused for the black slaves in the West Indies, but all the while, it cruelly tortures white women and children in England with overwork and starvation wages.

But at this stage not even the proletariat shows any consistent and unified tendency. We have seen that its conditions of life forced it to regard human life as something sacred. Since it is not merely a non-exploiting class, but rather an exploited class, it suffers most from disregard for human life. War brings it, apart from such exceptions as Ancient Rome, nothing but burdens and dangers; the triumphs and spoils of war go to the ruling classes alone. All of this inspires the proletariat with a horror of all slaughter and every kind of cruelty. However, the proletariat does not appear on the stage of history in the form of an industrial proletariat. Tendencies towards proletarianism appeared in the masses long before modern industrial manufacture had become developed, as a result of the decline of feudalism, a system which had been imposing ever heavier taxes upon the peasants so that their earning power was adversely affected and their productivity fell.

More and more laborers were thus forced out of agriculture, and this increased the burden of labor for those who were left behind. At such a time superfluous labor finds little opportunity for employment in industry, since industry itself is circumscribed by the guilds.

Countless masses of the unemployed, starving and despairing proletariat, swarm the country; and because they themselves are excluded from productive labor, they have recourse to all kinds of parasitical means of livelihood, from begging and stealing to downright robbery. Living in filth and misery, excluded from and despised by society, these people are naturally filled with a wild hatred against all society; and the hatred increases, because those in power, unable and unwilling to take measures towards social reform, resort to terrorism. The starving people are supposed to be frightened out of begging, stealing, cheating, prostitution, and robbery. The most fearful punishments were thus inflicted on these unfortunate people. . . . The result was the same as that produced by any reign of terror which attempts to eliminate social products without being able to change the ground from which such products grow. The number of criminals did not diminish, however many they sent to the galleys, or tortured. For those who survived there remained no other choice than that of leading the life of swindlers. Hence arose continual conflict with the police. The only noticeable result was the increasing demoralization of the proletariat, whose hatred and rage, and whose thirst for blood and cruelty, were all increased by the horrors and cruelties of the executions that took place. Of course this was true in the first place only of the criminal section of the proletariat. This very section was at that time so numerous and was connected by so many ties of kinship and comradeship with elements of the wage-earning proletariat (as well as the lower strata of petite bourgeoisie and peasantry, who all stood more or less with one foot in the bog of the *Lumpenproletariat*) that *Lumpenproletariat* ways of thinking and feeling colored the outlook of all of them. As a consequence, humane feelings, at the time of the outbreak of the French Revolution, were confined to the intellectuals and to those among the well-to-do petit bourgeois and industrial capitalists who were influenced by them. In the proletariat itself, and in those strata standing in closest relation to it, the coarsening and brutalizing that had resulted from the bloody legislation often came to the surface as soon as the power of the State, under whose pressure it had been able to find only underground expression, finally broke down.

SLAUGHTER AND TERRORISM

In view of the "educational" influence of the ruling classes upon the poorest strata, it is not to be wondered at that the revolutionary elements, as soon as they could operate more freely, often gave to the struggle a wild and cruel character, thus turning the great revolution into a particularly bloody one. Nevertheless it would be a mistake to class all revolutionary massacres under one head. One must distinguish between excesses to which a brutalized people, in the passion aroused by struggle and despair, or out of thoughtless fear, allows itself to give way, and those excesses which are the result of a well-planned system of intimidation, introduced by the rulers of a State in legislative form in order to grind down elements which they consider dangerous.

Bloody excesses which sprang spontaneously from the masses occurred at the very beginning of the Revolution; but the commencement of the Reign of Terror dates from the summer of 1793, when the Girondists were arrested and executed. The people showed their brutality as early as the day of the storming of the Bastille, when the garrison capitulated. Some were killed; others had their heads hacked off, and triumphantly carried on pikes. This parading of heads on pikes happened often enough during the course of the Revolution.

The thirst for blood and cruelty increased when it came to a war of the Revolution with the monarchs of Europe. When the Prussian army was marching on Paris and the Prussian commander-in-chief, the Duke of Brunswick, in his manifesto, threatened Paris with total destruction, rumors as to a conspiracy of the aristocrats throughout the land in support of the external enemy were rampant. Then Parisians rose up in uncontrolled and fearful rage to murder the political prisoners in the prisons. That took place on September 2, 1792. This massacre, which cost 3,000 men their lives, represented the height of the horrors of the great Revolution. A veritable intoxication for blood seized these crowds of executioners. They were not content with killing. They literally bathed in blood with delirious delight.

The Princess de Lamballe, whose whole crime consisted merely in being a friend of the Queen, was not only killed; her body was cut open and her heart torn out. . . . Her head was put on a pike and brought before the window of the imprisoned Queen. At the sight of this horror the Queen swooned away.

Even acts of mercy took on a cruel form. An example may be found in the experience of Mme. de Sombreuil, who at the time of the September massacres was in prison with her father. A certain M. de Saint Mart, who was near her father, had his skull split open. Her father was to suffer the same fate; whereupon she in desperation covered him with her own body, and fought for a long time, until she succeeded, after having received three wounds, in moving these men to pity.

One of them took a glass, poured therein blood that was flowing from the head of the murdered M. de Saint Mart, mixed it with wine and powder, and said that if she would drink that to the health of the nation she could save her father. She did this without a shudder, and was forthwith carried out by these self-same men. . . .

There is no doubt that the cruelty of the enraged and desperate masses during the Revolution was terrible. But one should not blame this on the Revolution alone—even if one is ever justified in placing blame for elemental occurrences of this kind. They were the result of the "education" that had long been imposed upon the people by high authority. Just one example:

In 1757 a man named Damiens made an attempt upon the life of Louis XV, attacking him with a kind of penknife. The wound proved to be quite harmless. But the revenge for this deed was terrible. Damiens' right hand was hacked off, and burned before his eyes. Wounds were made in his arms, legs, and chest, and boiling oil and molten lead were poured into these wounds. Then they bound each of his limbs to horses, and drove the animals each in different directions, so that his whole body was literally torn to pieces. This infamous torture was executed in public, in order to make an impression on the crowd. What the effect was we now know.

Similar barbarities were perpetrated right up to the time of the Revolution.

In fact, it was the Revolution which finally brought them to an end. As late as August 13, 1789, Gaultier de Biauzat made the following report from Versailles:

> Last Tuesday, about midday, the people of Versailles succeeded in preventing the execution of a criminal who had been condemned, for patricide, to be flayed and burned alive on a wheel. . . .

Among those who were most incensed at the September massacres was Robespierre. He cried bitterly, "Blood, ever and always blood. These miserable people will end in drowning the Revolution in blood."

Even Marat himself recoiled horror-stricken before those massacres.

> It is characteristic of Marat, a fact which, to my knowledge, has not yet been mentioned by any historian, that he openly disavowed the September massacres, or at least bitterly regretted them—the self-same Marat who recommended them in his issue of August 19, and the benefit of which massacres he wished, on September 2, to extend to the whole of France.

However, in the case of Marat it was political considerations rather than regard for humanity that turned him away from the September massacres. Robespierre, on the other hand, belonged to the intellectuals who were fundamentally opposed to any shedding of blood. This he proved in the Constituent Assembly, in the discussion of the new penal code on May 17, 1791. When capital punishment was brought up for discussion, Robespierre was among those who most vehemently opposed it, on the ground that it did not prevent crime, but merely made the populace more brutal and more inclined to deeds of violence. His efforts were frustrated. Capital punishment, restricted to decapitation, remained; the more horrible forms were to be prohibited. This decision provided one of the very rare occasions when Marat expressed his approval of the National Assembly, in opposition to Robespierre. Two years later Robespierre found himself forced to Marat's side, and obliged to renounce his opposition to capital punishment. From that time on the death penalty was his chief political weapon, employed even against his own political friends.

We have already pointed out that the well-planned and orderly execution of terrorist methods should not be classed with the excesses of an excited mob. For these excesses had their origin among the coarsest and most uncultivated elements of the populace, whereas the Reign of Terror was maintained by highly cultivated men who were filled with the most humane feelings. This Reign of Terror sprang from existing conditions in a way very different from the spontaneous atrocities. These latter were a reaction to the merciless legislation of the old regime against the poverty-stricken masses; whereas the Reign of Terror was forced on the Jacobins because they, in the most appalling circumstances and in the midst of war, found themselves face to face—as a result of the misery of the masses and their own position of power—with an insoluble task. The task was to preserve bourgeois society and private property, and at the same time to make an end to the people's misery. In this desperate situation they were able to extricate themselves only by using the very means which they themselves disapproved and the uselessness of which they had themselves declared. It was the very misery of the masses that had caused the old regime to proceed to its bloody legislation, and to have recourse to terrorism. And it was this same misery that gave rise to the bloody legislation and terrorism of the new regime. The only difference was that the old regime had endeavored to control the wretched populace by beheading and mistreating the poor, whereas the new regime sought to diminish the misery of the masses by beheading—without mistreating—the rich and their servants. The one failed of its object just as the other had. But even here there was a difference. The existence of the old regime did not depend upon the success of the Reign of Terror in eliminating the proletariat. The failure of terrorism was certainly a disagreeable fact, but it represented no serious danger for the regime. This was because the class in question, namely the *Lumpenproletariat,* was quite incapable of ever gaining political power on its own, and because, from an economic point of view, it was not at all indispensable. The new regime, on the other hand, became bankrupt and went to pieces as soon as its terrorism failed, for the class that it was trying to keep down, namely the bourgeoisie, was the very one which, under the circumstances, was best suited to rule; moreover, at the time it was economically indispensable. Thus the repression of the bourgeois class hindered social development and economic production, and in this way gave rise to still greater misery among the very people who should have derived advantage from the Reign of Terror.

But there is a still greater difference between the old and the new Reign of Terror. The former was in complete accord with the ethics of the circles that directed it; its perpetrators did not have to be untrue to themselves to resort to terrorism. They regarded it as a perfectly obvious and justifiable means. But the new Reign of Terror was absolutely contrary to the ethics of the class that carried it out. From the very beginning the terrorists suffered from a bad conscience, which they endeavored to salve by all kinds of sophistry, but which nevertheless undermined their moral strength, lessened their self-confidence, increased their irritability and insecurity, and even corrupted many of them. Even if there be no absolute morality existing in a world beyond the stars; even if the morality of a particular time, country, or class, is something relative, still ethics remains the strongest social bond and the stoutest support in all problems and conflicts of life. Nothing can be worse than to be unfaithful to oneself, or to act against those ethical precepts which one accepts as categorical imperatives. It was these factors which contributed in no small measure to the complete destruction of the Reign of Terror as soon as it met with energetic opposition. How quickly the surviving terrorists became converted to quite other views! Napoleon found the legitimate Monarchists a far greater danger than the old Republicans. This is an indication of how seriously the morality of the latter had suffered under the Reign of Terror.

THE HUMANIZING OF CONDUCT IN THE NINETEENTH CENTURY

The great French Revolution marks one of the most bloody periods of world history, and many people have concluded from this that the shedding of blood is an indispensable function of any true revolution. In consequence they have either condemned revolution or glorified slaughter. As a matter of fact, the Revolution of 1789 itself removed the most important factors which had given it such a cruel and violent character, and prepared the way for milder forms of future revolutions. It accomplished this, on the one hand, by eliminating feudalism and encouraging industrial capital, which had the effect of turning the masses of workers from *Lumpenproletariat* to wage earners. On the other hand, it unleashed a movement which was to end, sooner or later, in the triumph of democracy everywhere. Finally, out of the study of the Revolution and of capitalism, a theory arose which enabled the proletarian party, at any given moment, to set itself only such goals of practical action as lay within the bounds of possibility. Thus there was no longer any reason for it to fall into a blind alley from which it would be forced to attempt to extricate itself by recourse to a Reign of Terror.

Through the Revolution the peasant was emancipated and became master of his own land. As a result, land economy reached a higher stage of development and greater productivity, to the benefit of the peasant. This caused a decrease in the number of surplus workers from agriculture. On the other hand, the influx of workers into the cities was now more readily absorbed. Guild restrictions had broken down; artisans were free to do their work without hindrance. It is true that, in one branch after another, artisan labor was adversely affected by the spread of industrial capital; but this itself helped to develop, by its rapid increase, large demands for labor. The industrial proletariat now became a special class with a special class-consciousness, set off ever more sharply from that of the *Lumpenproletariat*.

The position of the industrial proletariat under capitalism was certainly less favorable than that of the independent artisans at the time when artisan labor was most prosperous. On the other hand, this position was clearly an improvement over that of the *Lumpenproletariat*. The latter had been quite incapable of class struggle; but the industrial proletariat, through class struggle and organization, has accomplished a truly remarkable intellectual and moral upsurge. In the beginning it was extraordinarily degraded by capital, not only economically, but also morally. Its housing conditions, the poverty and insecurity of its existence, its ignorance, were not very different from those of the *Lumpenproletariat*. Indeed, it stood lower than the latter with respect to the monotony of its life, the continuous oppression of factory discipline, which excluded all freedom of action, and the callous sweating of women and children. As a result, the wage-earning proletariat lacked the boldness which characterized the more powerful elements of the *Lumpenproletariat*. And it was becoming increasingly insensitive and coarse. At this stage, it would have been quite incapable of emancipating itself. It was only very slowly that strata of the proletariat, one after the other, through continuous class struggle, succeeded in extricating themselves from the seemingly hopeless bog that threatened to engulf them. Hand in hand with this process went the growth and development of the tendencies towards humaneness which were grounded in the proletarian class situation. These tendencies were aided by the fact that, as a consequence of the Revolution and the events which followed it, the penal laws erected against the proletariat gradually began to lose the harsh character that they had previously had.

For all of these reasons, the revolutionary elements of the proletariat, in the movements of the nineteenth century, were filled with the greatest humanity, withdrawing more and more from the brutal savagery that had distinguished their forerunners at the time of the great French Revolution, and which even Engels observed in the early 1840's among the English factory proletariat. At the same time, the causes that had produced the Reign of Terror disappeared. Soon after the collapse of the Reign of Terror, the more farseeing friends of the proletariat clearly recognized that it could not be emancipated as a class on the foundations of bourgeois society. They concluded that this objective could be achieved only by doing away with private ownership of the means of production and introducing social production. But they found neither the necessary material conditions among the capitalists, nor the psychological conditions among the proletariat; and they failed to see that economic development and class struggle were working to produce these conditions. Therefore, they looked for a "solution of the social question," a plan or formula which would be realizable under any conditions once the necessary power had been gained. If revolutionary proletarians have accepted this idea and sought for power, not in some philanthropic millionaire, but in political dictatorship on the pattern of the first Paris Commune, every such attempt, when undertaken by a minority in the State, was of necessity bound to lead to a reign of terror similar to the rule of the first Paris Commune. To be sure, this attempt was a more rational one. It did not seek to escape the consequences of bourgeois society and yet preserve this society; it attempted to remove the consequences by destroying their foundation. But even this endeavor must have come to grief when an attempt was made to put it into practice, so long as the social pre-conditions were lacking, which alone could remove the foundations they were attempting to destroy. It would have meant the attempt of a minority to impose upon a majority something that was impossible, or at least inexpedient, and contrary to the interests of the majority. And that would have been possible only by resorting to the most violent methods, methods which would necessarily have culminated in bloody terrorism.

No such attempt was made—quite apart from the fact that the mass of workers at the time was only gradually adopting Socialist ideas—because the proletariat's position, following its dominance (in conjunction with those elements of the petite bourgeoisie which were closest to it) between 1789 and 1794, remained considerably weaker for a number of decades. The second Commune gave it rule over Paris, to be sure—but not over France; and even in Paris the Socialists were not in the majority. In fact, these latter had no firm theoretical foundation and therefore were very cautious and restrained. They found a firm basis after the Commune, as Marxism began to penetrate into the masses. This was the conception that Marx and Engels had founded in the 1840's and had deepened and extended in the 1850's and 1860's—the materialist conception of history. They introduced the idea of lawlike development into history, which, according to their ideas, is conditioned by the development of economic relations. From this standpoint they recognized that the capitalist means of production generated conditions that ultimately made necessary and inevitable a socialist means of production; but they also recognized the fruitlessness of any attempt to replace the first method of production by the second, so long as the conditions were not ripe for such a change.

For them, the task of the Socialists was no longer to find a plan or formula for general socialization which would immediately introduce Socialism under any and all conditions. Rather, it was to study economic relations and, on the basis of this knowledge, to make clear what was necessary for society at the time and to struggle to bring this about. In other words, the Socialists were no longer concerned merely to establish Socialism. Where conditions were not yet ripe for Socialism they were to concern themselves with the conditions of capitalist industry, attempting to further its development in the interests of the proletariat. However, this was by no means immediately grasped by the Socialists themselves. Even in the International, some years later, Socialists looked with contempt upon such matters as free trade and the strike, because they did not affect the wage system. It was Marx and Engels who taught the workers to grasp the importance of the economic problems and conflicts of the capitalist system of the time of the proletarian struggle for emancipation. Socialism for the proletariat schooled in Marxist thought thus ceased to be something that could be immediately realized everywhere and under all conditions. Even when the proletariat did gain political power, it was to introduce only so much of Socialism as was possible under the existing conditions, and in a form corresponding to those particular conditions. According to this conception, Socialism could not be introduced by means of a *coup d'état.* It was to be the result of a long historical process. At the same time, the Socialists were constantly urged to undertake, in any given moment, only what was possible under the given power relationships and material conditions. If, therefore, everything was to be done with due consideration it would have been impossible for the Socialists to fail of anything they undertook, or for them to find themselves in a desperate situation, which would force them to act contrary to the spirit of the proletariat and of Socialism, and to have recourse to bloody mass terror.

In fact, since Marxism has captured the Socialist movement, this movement, right up to the beginning of the [First] World War, has, in nearly every one of its great conscious actions, been preserved from grave defeats, and the idea of gaining power by means of terrorism has completely disappeared from the minds of its members. This process was greatly facilitated by the circumstance that, at the same time that Marxism was becoming the dominant Socialist doctrine, democracy was taking root in Western Europe; what had previously been a goal for struggle now provided a firm foundation for political life. This not only aided in the enlightenment and organization of the proletariat; it also increased the insight of its members into the economic conditions and power relationships of the opposing classes. In this way, fantastic adventures and civil war as a means of class struggle were alike eliminated. In 1902 I wrote in my pamphlet *The Social Revolution:*

Democracy is of the highest value, if for no other reason, because it makes possible higher forms of revolutionary struggle. This struggle will no longer be, like that of 1789 or 1848, a struggle of unorganized masses without political education, without any insight into the power relationships of the contending elements, and without any deeper understanding of the tasks of the struggle and the means for carrying them out. It will no longer be a struggle of masses that let themselves be carried away confused by every rumor, and by every chance circumstance. It will be a struggle of organized, enlightened, stable, and thoughtful masses, who do not follow every impulse, who do not explode over every disadvantage and who do not become downhearted as the result of failure. On the other hand, electoral contests make it possible to take stock of oneself and one's enemies. They help towards a clear insight into the relative strength of classes and parties, their progress and decline. Further, they guard against over-hasty action, and secure against defeat. They also help to make even the opponent recognize the untenable nature of his position and often cause him voluntarily to abandon it, wherever such is not a matter of life and death for him. Thus the struggle becomes less cruel and merciless, less dependent on blind chance.

As a result of the combined working of all these conditions, of the formation of the industrial proletariat, and of the elevation of this latter above the level of the *Lumpenproletariat;* as a result, further, of the development of Socialist theory and the establishment of democracy, it was possible to put more and more in the background the gloomy fears which Engels even in 1845 expressed in his book, *The Position of the Working-Classes in England,* where he said:

If the English middle class does not come to its senses—and it seems to have no intention of doing so—there will follow a revolution which will bear no comparison with any that has hitherto taken place. The proletariat, driven to despair, will seize their torches. The revenge of the people will express itself with a ferocity of which not even 1793 can give us any idea. The war of the poor against the rich will be the bloodiest war that has ever been waged.

It must be said that Engels himself expected these fears to be borne out only if there was an immediate outbreak of revolution—which he thought would be the case. But even in the 1840's his fears were somewhat exaggerated, despite the mass influx into industry of extremely undeveloped people, especially Irish, who were very close to the *Lumpenproletariat* in status. Engels himself anticipated that, if the revolution did not come soon, and the proletariat thus had time to develop and become imbued with Socialist spirit, the revolution would take milder forms:

In proportion as the proletariat assimilates Socialist and Communist elements, the shedding of blood, vengeance, and ferocity as phenomena of the revolution, will decrease.

The revolution which Engels expected came in 1848, but not in England. After its collapse there began in all countries of Europe a period of capitalist development which was accompanied by a powerful economic, intellectual, and moral strengthening of the working classes.

In the most advanced countries of Europe things changed rapidly. As early as 1872, a year after the Commune, Marx gave expression to the hope that, in countries like America, England, and Holland, the proletarian revolution would assume a peaceful form. Ever since that time, the rise of the proletariat has brought with it further progress. Yet everyone with an insight into the matter recognizes that a monarchy based on militarism, such as the German, Austrian, or Russian, can be overturned only by means of force. But, even in this matter, people thought less of slaughter by actual weapons and more of the specific means best suited to the proletarian power-device, namely, refusal to work, or, in other words, the general strike. It was perfectly clear that the men of the old regime in Germany and in Russia would endeavor to drown any attempt to overthrow them in a bath of blood. But that considerable sections of the proletariat, when once it came to power, should again have recourse to slaughter, revenge, and rage, as did indeed happen at the end of the eighteenth century, was expected by no one. This set the whole development upside down.

In opposition to the views of Engels . . . [who] voiced the belief that there would be a continuous diminution of barbarity and cruelty in future proletarian revolutions, another view has lately been advanced . . . by N. Bucharin:

> The more highly developed capitalism is in any country, the more reckless will be its struggle to defend itself, and the bloodier will be the *proletarian revolution,* the harsher the measures by means of which the victorious working class will tread under foot the defeated capitalists.

This is the very opposite of what Marx and Engels had expected. And it is false in that it erects into a general law applicable to the whole of social development those Bolshevik practices that have prevailed for the past eighteen months. It is also false in declaring these practices to be the outcome of the recklessness and brutality of the capitalists' struggle to defend themselves. There was no sign of such brutality in November, 1917, in Petrograd and Moscow, or more recently in Budapest. But Bucharin is perfectly correct in asserting that the proletarian revolution has once again become bloody in the extreme. The reason for this state of affairs I, in my "senile obstinacy" or "senile stupidity" (as Bucharin calls it), attribute to factors other than capitalist barbarity, which was never less evident in the countries defeated in the [First] World War than at the beginning of the most recent revolution.

THE EFFECTS OF THE WAR

The real cause of the reversal of the trend towards humanization and the movement towards brutality is to be sought in the [First] World War; but even earlier there were other factors that were inimical to the general humanizing tendency. The most important of these was brought into existence by the French Revolution itself. It was *universal military service,* which the revolutionary regime found necessary, in order, by means of a superiority of troops and the continual filling up of vacant appointments, to cope with the professional armies of the united monarchs arrayed against them. There was only one of these monarchic States which took over this system and indeed preserved and developed it at a time when France had already discarded it. This was Prussia, the smallest and youngest of the great powers of Europe, with the most unfavorable frontiers, whose very existence demanded an army, which, in relation to the population, was far greater than that of any other country. Apart from this fact, old Prussia was the poorest in natural resources among the great states. If, therefore, it really wished to assert itself, it had to sacrifice all other considerations in favor of the army. As a consequence, ever since the day of its entry into the ranks of the great powers, it has been a militarist State par excellence. . . .

Thanks to universal military service and the prestige of militarism in general, Prussia won its position of power in wars waged between 1866 and 1870. These wars forced universal military service upon the remaining European states. At about the same time the railway system became a decisive factor in the conduct of war. All military states endeavored to develop such a system to the limit of their powers, and this created the possibility, and, in the case of arms races, the necessity, for a continuous increase in armed forces. This, in turn, resulted in a more rigid application of universal military service. We finally arrived at the glorious result that the whole male population, except for the physically unfit, was pressed into military service. But such service involves becoming accustomed to the shedding of human blood, and to competition in such bloodshed. It means the deadening of human feeling and the cultivation of brutality. In the eighteenth century, when there were only small professional armies, the great mass of the people were spared from such influences on their morality; but, as a consequence of universal military service, the people, in the course of the nineteenth century, became more and more brutalized—most notably in Prussia.

The humanizing tendencies of the nineteenth century were not thereby rendered wholly ineffective; but they were drastically obstructed. These tendencies had become most pronounced in the case of the intellectuals. It was they who remained longest exempt from military service, even at the time when, instead of voluntary enlistment, forced recruiting was resorted to. Under the conscription system, it was primarily the peasants, artisans, and wage laborers who were affected; the middle class and the intellectuals were spared. Universal service, however, could ultimately make no exception in their case. On the contrary, officers to command reserves were required. But now, as before, the educated man occupied a special position in regard to military service. It was not a position that excluded him from the army, but one in which he had certain privileges within the army itself, as a one-year volunteer and reserve officer. As a result, the educated classes were exposed to the influences of militarism on their thoughts and feelings, and indeed to a still higher degree than was the case of the other classes. For it put them in a privileged position and created in them a certain taste for army life. This influence was exercised particularly through the professional officers, who had made military service their life work, for whom it was no mere temporary form of activity. In all military affairs they were expected to take the initiative and to surpass their men in energy and smartness; thus they developed the characteristic traits of militarism in a higher degree than the enlisted men, who had to serve for a relatively short period, and then under compulsion.

As a result, the educated classes were even more strongly influenced by militarism than the rest of the population. Furthermore, their professional activity brings with it a tendency to develop every idea and conception in a more logical and radical way—which, after all, is quite compatible with very reactionary modes of thought—than is the case with men, who, through practical experience, know the obstacles that occur in daily life. Those of the educated classes who wished to become reserve officers, and took as their example the professional officers, easily surpassed the latter in the harshness of their military thinking. Thus the militarized strata among the intellectuals became pioneers in brutality and violence, and this, because of universal military service, soon spread to the whole people. Even in this respect Prussia was ahead of the other States, since it first introduced the system of one-year volunteers and reserve officers, and raised the reserve officer, more than any other State had done, to a privileged and much-coveted position. Yet, in spite of universal military service, the humanizing tendencies in the proletariat were stronger, as a result of its class position, than the brutalizing influence of militarism. In the case of the intellectuals, especially in Prussia, a strong check was put on these humanizing tendencies, which contributed not a little to the bitterness of class opposition and class struggle.

What is here said of the intellectuals applies especially to the capitalists, whose humane instincts, from the outset, find stronger opposing forces to overcome, as a result of their class position. When, therefore, the war broke out and drew into its orbit for four years practically the whole of the healthy male population, the coarsening tendencies of militarism were brought to a pitch of brutality, lack of human feeling, and sentiment. Even the proletariat could no longer escape its influence. It was in a very high degree infected by militarism, and when it returned home again, was in every way brutalized. Habituated to war, the man who had come back from the front was only too often in a state of mind and feeling that made him ready, even in peacetime and among his own people, to enforce his claims and interests by deeds of violence and bloodshed. That became, as it were, an element of the civil war; it also contributed further to making the masses mere savages. Nevertheless, many of the more mature, as soon as they were removed from the influences of war, reverted to the ways of thinking and feeling that they had known in peacetime. It was much worse, however, in the case of the younger men, who, without teachers or guides, were powerless to withstand the brutalizing influences that prevailed during the four years of war; and hence they received impressions which they can never eradicate completely, so long as they live.

Besides all this, there is a very profound change at work in the very composition of the proletariat. The war has affected most seriously the petite bourgeoisie and has claimed many of their ranks, forcing them into the proletariat. Moreover, these elements, which hitherto remained aloof from proletarian class struggle, have not been affected by the education, the discipline, and the capacity for organization which the proletariat had acquired whenever the class struggle was under the leadership of a Socialist Party which was concerned to enlighten and organize the masses. Within the proletariat as it had been previously constituted there were profound dislocations. All workers, including skilled laborers, were greatly reduced in number through injury, sickness, and death—at a much higher rate than during peacetime. At the same time, hardly any provision was made for their replacement. There was no time or energy to devote to educating the young; indeed, the very need for such activity was not felt. The varied industries of peacetime were replaced by a much more monotonous war industry, which produced only a few types of goods, in processes which required of workers only a few motions—well within the ability of the most unskilled apprentices. Thus the number of skilled laborers, who had contributed so much to Germany's industrial development, became very greatly reduced during the war, and were replaced by unskilled laborers, in rapidly increasing numbers. The skilled laborers were the best organized and best educated, and were the clearest thinking of all the workers. The unskilled were unorganized, ignorant, and indifferent. However, their indifference quickly disappeared during the war. This gigantic event, with its fearful consequences, roused even the most backward elements of the people to feverish excitement. At the same time, however, the number of skilled workers brought up on Socialist doctrine, diminished, as against the numbers of those who, in every respect, were ignorant and undisciplined, and also as against the increase of the proletarianized petite bourgeoisie. As a result the minority with superior education and skill, who had hitherto led the proletariat, gradually lost its position of leadership; and in its stead there arose the blind passion of ignorance.

This was all the easier because the war brought in its train the most profound economic chaos, mass unemployment, runaway inflation, and lack of the necessities of life. So the desperate masses demanded the most radical changes, not in order to create a newer and higher form of society to which they, as a matter of fact, had not given a thought, but in order to find an immediate escape from their grinding misery. For the proletariat the abolition of its wretchedness is always an urgent practical matter. This, in addition to the fact that considerable economic and historical knowledge is a necessary prerequisite for the understanding of Marxism, is the chief reason why Marxist thinking does not take easy root among the workers. The masses instinctively prefer a doctrine which does not lead them along the path of development, but rather offers a formula or plan, the carrying out of which promises them immediate relief, in all circumstances, from their suffering. It takes a certain amount of self-denial on the part of a proletarian to accept a doctrine which, though it does not demand a state of mere passive waiting, since it spurs him on to an energetic waging of class warfare, nevertheless makes his ultimate emancipation dependent upon conditions which must be created through a laborious process of development. However difficult it was for the workers in the decades just before the war, their position was such that for them the immediate transformation of society was not a question of life and death—at least not for the skilled laborer, who formed the nucleus of the forces of class struggle and the Socialist movement. Today these men are being replaced in all political and economic struggles by unskilled workers whose situation is so desperate that they cannot afford to wait. Why indeed should they wait, when the conclusion of the war has finally put political power into their hands?

The war has not only brought the most backward elements of the working classes to the forefront of the class struggle; it has also, as the result of the collapse of the armies, especially in those parts of Europe which are economically most backward, made the proletariat the ruling class in the various towns, by the side of which illiterate peasants, such as are to be found in Russia, do not represent any independent political power. No class ever voluntarily renounces the power that it has won for itself, whatever be the circumstances that have brought it to the helm. It would be folly to demand such renunciation from the Russian or Hungarian proletariat on account of the backward state of their countries. But a Socialist Party guided by a truly Marxist spirit would adjust the current tasks confronting the victorious proletariat to the material and psychic conditions at hand, and would not endeavor, without further ado, to introduce complete socialization in a land of undeveloped capitalist production like Russia.

Certainly it is questionable whether such a party could ever assert its leadership over the masses. To the practical politicians it seems more important to rule at the moment than to expose oneself to momentary failure with a view to being ultimately in the right. The practical politician does not like the role of one who, by making clear the inevitable collapse of a policy which exceeds the bounds of possibility—while looking beyond this collapse and refusing to compromise the ideal—invites unpopularity at the present moment. The old antagonism between practical politics and theoretical politics, between Lassalle and Marx, rose again after the revolution in Russia in 1917. Marx declared in his letter to Kugelmann, dated February 23, 1865 . . . that the German workers, as a result of the reaction of 1849–1859, had become too much hampered in their development not to "become jubilant when a deliverer, in the form of a mob orator like Lassalle, comes and promises to help them at one leap to enter the promised land."

Such "leaps" and such "deliverers" were not to Marx's taste. But the situation at the time of the Second Russian Revolution, like that in Lassalle's time, if for quite other reasons, proved to be very unfavorable to Marxist thinking. Those among the laboring classes in Russia who had been trained along Marxist lines, were either dead, or carried away, or confused by the backward masses who had suddenly awakened to life. It was pre-Marxist ways of thinking that gained the upper hand—those represented by Blanqui, Weitling, or Bakunin. These were the conditions under which the Revolution, first of all in Russia and then in the neighboring countries, was carried out. No wonder then that it not only aroused primitive ways of thinking, but also gave rein to brutal and murderous forms of political and economic warfare, forms which we thought had been left behind by the intellectual and moral development of the proletariat.

(1879-1940)

LEON TROTSKY

LEV DAVIDOVICH BRONSTEIN (Leon Trotsky) was born in 1879 in the Ukraine, of humble parents; his formal education was limited to secondary schools in Odessa and Nikolayev. While still in his teens he became involved in the Russian radical movement, first as a *Narodnik* (populist), then as a Marxist. Trotsky's editorship of an underground newspaper led to his arrest (1898) and three years in prison and Siberian exile. Following his escape in 1902, he joined Lenin in London on the staff of *Iskra* (*The Spark*). With the outbreak of the abortive Russian Revolution of 1905, Trotsky returned to St. Petersburg where, as chairman of the Soviet Executive, he played a major part in the further course of the insurrection. With its collapse, he was again arrested and sentenced to life exile, but escaped on the way to Siberia (1907). The next ten years of his life were spent in exile in Europe and America. Trotsky's part in the October Revolution of 1917 was second only to Lenin's (though this has been systematically denied by Stalinist historians); as chairman of the Petrograd Soviet, then Commissar for Foreign Affairs, and finally Commissar of War, he was at the very center of political power and decision throughout the period of revolution and civil war. After Lenin's death in 1924, however, Trotsky's power was gradually undermined. In 1927 he was expelled from the Communist Party and in 1928 exiled to Alma-Ata, then deported to Turkish Buyuk (Prinkipo) Island in the Sea of Marmara. After this he lived successively in France, Norway, and Mexico, where he was assassinated in 1940.

A brilliant orator and polemicist in several languages, Trotsky always managed to find time, even in the midst of the most feverish political activity, to make speeches and write books and pamphlets. His historical studies, *History of the Revolution of 1905–06* (1917) and *History of the Russian Revolution* (3 vols., 1932), are classics of their kind, as is his posthumous, unfinished, and highly partisan biography of Stalin. The chief theoretical contribution associated with Trotsky's name, rather misleadingly called "the theory of permanent revolution," was originated not by Trotsky but A. I. Gelfand (pseudonym: Parvus) about 1905. According to this doctrine, Russia's economic, social, and political backwardness and the weakness of its middle classes are not obstacles in the way of immediate proletarian revolution (as Marx, Engels, and Kautsky had held), but special conditions which facilitate the "telescoping" of two revolutions, the bourgeois and the proletarian, into a single "permanent" revolution—under the leadership of the party of the proletariat.

Trotsky's prestige and polemical brilliance made him a clear choice when it was felt necessary in 1919 to answer the criticisms of Bolshevik terrorism put forward by Kautsky (as spokesman for "orthodox" European Marxism) and by certain Russian Mensheviks and Socialist Revolutionaries. Trotsky developed his "answer" in four theses: (1) Ends and means are separable and a good end justifies any means whatever. Furthermore, different classes may use the same means (e.g., terrorism) to achieve very different, even opposed, ends. (2) Socialism cannot be achieved, at least under present conditions of capitalist encirclement and intervention, without revolutionary violence. And whoever desires the end of socialism must accept the means of terrorism. (3) All governments use violence to stay in power, and all historical revolutions have used violence to break this power. (4) The Reign of Terror was started not by the Bolsheviks, but by the counterrevolutionary forces.

Trotsky differed sharply from later Soviet Marxists (of the Stalinist period) in the candor with which he acknowledged that terroristic methods were being employed by the Bolsheviks, as well as the openness of his repudiation of the principles of democratic government, civil liberties, and human dignity. In opposition to Kautsky he explicitly asserted that, where necessary, individuals should be treated merely as means. This extreme position proved a double-edged weapon, however, when Trotsky later took up the cudgels against Stalinism. Accusing Joseph Stalin (1879–1953) of embodying a new counterrevolution, Trotsky insisted that Stalin's policy was not (as critics like Kautsky had charged) a logical development of "Bolshevik amoralism." Yet it would appear that, from the point of view of ethics, Stalin merely practiced what Trotsky had both practiced and preached. Trotsky openly ridiculed the sanctity of democracy, justice, and individual liberty in the revolutionary situation, and ruled frankly with force and terror; Stalin openly praised these political virtues, while ruling with instruments of physical and psychological violence. But beyond pointing out this hypocrisy, there would seem to be little that Trotsky could say to justify his own "righteous indignation" at Stalinist practice.

As is often the case with vigorous polemicists, both Kautsky and Trotsky are stronger in their critical assaults than in their own constructive contributions. Ultimately, both sides draw their polemical power from the alleged absolutism of their opponents. There is more than a grain of truth in Trotsky's charge that Kautsky had taken an essentially Kantian position. And Kautsky's naturalistic ethical theory provides a dubious ground, at best, for his assertion of such absolute values as the "sanctity of human life." On the other hand, Trotsky offers no satisfactory ground or justification—only doctrinaire assertion—for his own passionate and exclusive commitment to the end of communism and the means of violent class struggle. "History," he once wrote, in a revealing phrase, "is a tremendous mechanism serving our ideals." Trotsky's unsparing candor and incisiveness in polemical assault harden at just this critical point into stubborn and authoritarian dogmatism.

The following selection has been drawn from Trotsky's *Dictatorship vs. Democracy* (English translation, 1922) which was designed to be a direct refutation of *Terrorism and Communism* by Karl Kautsky. The original translation from the Russian has been thoroughly revised by George L. Kline especially for this volume.

DICTATORSHIP VS. DEMOCRACY

The balance of political power at any given moment is formed under the influence of fundamental and secondary factors of differing degrees of effectiveness; only at its deepest level is it determined by the stage of the development of production. The social structure of a people lags extraordinarily behind the development of its productive forces. The petite bourgeoisie, and particularly the peasantry, continue to exist long after their economic methods have been made obsolete, and have been condemned, by the technical development of the productive powers of society. The consciousness of the masses, in its turn, lags extraordinarily behind the development of their social relations; the consciousness of the old Socialist parties is a whole epoch behind the state of mind of the masses, and the consciousness of the old parliamentary and trade-union leaders, more reactionary than the consciousness of their party, represents a petrified mass which history has been unable hitherto either to digest or reject. In the peaceful parliamentary epoch, during the period of stability of social relations, the psychological factor remained—without great error—the foundation upon which all current calculations were based. It was considered that parliamentary elections adequately reflected the balance of power. The imperialist war [World War I], which destroyed the equilibrium of bourgeois society, revealed the complete uselessness of the old criteria. The latter wholly ignored those profound historical factors which had been gradually accumulating in the preceding period, and have now, all at once, appeared on the surface, and are determining the course of history.

The worshipers of political routine, incapable of surveying the historical process in its complexity, in its internal clashes and contradictions, imagined to themselves that history was preparing the way for the Socialist order simultaneously and systematically on all sides, so that concentration of production and the development of a Communist morality in the producer and the consumer would mature simultaneously with the electric plough and a parliamentary majority. Hence the purely mechanical attitude towards parliamentarism, which, in the eyes of the majority of the politicians of the Second International, indicated the degree to which society was prepared for Socialism as accurately as the manometer indicates the pressure of steam. Yet there is nothing more senseless than this mechanized representation of the development of social relations.

This selection has been reprinted from Leon Trotsky, *Dictatorship vs. Democracy,* New York: Workers' Party of America, 1922 (pp. 15–19, 31–41, 48–59).

If, beginning with the productive bases of society, we ascend the rungs of the superstructure—classes, the State, laws, parties, and so on—it may be established that the "sluggishness" of each additional part of the superstructure is not simply added to, but in many cases multiplied by, the "sluggishness" of all the preceding levels. As a result, the political consciousness of groups which long imagined themselves to be among the most advanced, reveals itself, at a moment of critical change, as a colossal obstacle in the path of historical development. Today it is quite beyond doubt that the parties of the Second International, standing at the head of the proletariat, which dared not, could not, and would not take power into their hands at the most critical moment of human history, and which led the proletariat along the road of mutual destruction in the interests of imperialism, proved a *decisive factor* of the counterrevolution.

The great forces of production—that shock factor in historical development—were choked in those obsolete institutions of the superstructure (private property and the national State) in which they found themselves locked by all preceding development. Engendered by capitalism, the forces of production were knocking at all the walls of the bourgeois national State, demanding their emancipation by means of the Socialist organization of economic life on a world scale. The stagnation of social groupings, the stagnation of political forces, which proved themselves incapable of destroying the old class groupings, the stagnation, stupidity, and treachery of the leading Socialist parties, which had in fact undertaken the defense of bourgeois society—all these factors led to an elemental revolt of the forces of production, in the form of the imperialist war. Human technical skill, the most revolutionary factor in history, arose with the might accumulated during scores of years against the disgusting conservatism and criminal stupidity of the Scheidemanns, Kautskys, Renaudels, Vanderveldes, and Longuets, and, by means of its howitzers, machine guns, dreadnoughts, and aeroplanes began a furious pogrom of human culture.

Thus the cause of the misfortunes at present experienced by humanity is precisely that the development of man's technical control of nature has *long ago* grown ripe for the socialization of economic life. The proletariat has occupied a place in production which completely guarantees its dictatorship, while the most "enlightened" forces in history—the parties and their leaders—have been discovered to be still wholly under the yoke of the old prejudices, fostering among the masses a lack of faith in their own power. In quite recent years Kautsky used to understand this. "The proletariat at the present time has grown so strong," wrote Kautsky in his pamphlet, *The Path to*

Power, "that it can calmly await the coming war. There can be no more talk of a *premature revolution,* now that the proletariat has drawn from the present structure of the State such strength as could be drawn therefrom, and now that its reconstruction has become a condition of the proletariat's further progress."

Kautsky

From the moment that the development of productive forces, outgrowing the framework of the bourgeois national State, drew mankind into an epoch of crises and convulsions, the consciousness of the masses was shaken by dreadful shocks out of the comparative equilibrium of the preceding epoch. The routine and stagnation of its mode of living, the hypnotic suggestion of peaceful legality, had already ceased to dominate the proletariat. But it had not yet stepped, consciously and courageously, on to the path of open revolutionary struggle. It wavered, passing through the last moment of unstable equilibrium. At such a moment of psychological change, the part played by the summit—the State, on the one hand, and the revolutionary Party on the other—acquires a colossal importance. A determined push from left or right is sufficient to move the proletariat, for a certain period, to one or the other side. We saw this in 1914, when, under the united pressure of imperialist governments and Socialist patriotic parties, the working class was all at once thrown out of its equilibrium and hurled on to the path of imperialism. We have since seen how the experience of the war, the contrasts between its results and its original slogans, is shaking the masses in a revolutionary sense, making them more and more capable of an open revolt against capitalism. In such conditions, the presence of a revolutionary party, which renders to itself a clear account of the motive forces of the present epoch, and understands the exceptional role among them of a revolutionary class; which knows its inexhaustible, but unrevealed, powers; which believes in that class and believes in itself; which knows the power of revolutionary method in an epoch of instability of all social relations; which is ready to employ that method and carry it through to the end—the presence of such a party represents a factor of incalculable historical importance.

And, on the other hand, the Socialist party, enjoying traditional influence, which does *not* render itself an account of what is going on around it, which does *not* understand the revolutionary situation, and, therefore, finds no key to it, which does *not* believe in either the proletariat or itself—such a party in our time is the most mischievous stumbling block in history, and a source of confusion and inevitable chaos.

Such is now the role of Kautsky and his sympathizers. They teach the proletariat not to believe in itself, but to believe its reflection in the crooked mirror of democracy—a mirror which has been shattered into a thousand fragments by the jack boot of militarism. The decisive factor in the revolutionary policy of the working class must be, in their view, not the international situation, not the actual collapse of capitalism, not that social collapse which is generated thereby, not that objective necessity of the rule of the working class which cries out from the smoking ruins of capitalist civilization —not all this is to determine the policy of the revolutionary party of the proletariat—but that counting of votes which is carried out by the capitalist tellers of parliamentarism. Only a few years ago, we repeat, Kautsky seemed to understand the real nature of the problem of revolution. "Yes, the proletariat represents the sole revolutionary class of the nation," wrote Kautsky in his pamphlet, *The Path to Power*. "It follows that every collapse of the capitalist order, whether it be of a moral, financial, or military character, implies the bankruptcy of all the bourgeois parties responsible for it, and signifies that the sole way out of the blind alley is the establishment of the power of the proletariat."

And today the party of prostration and cowardice, the party of Kautsky, says to the working class: "The question is not whether you today are the sole creative force in history; whether you are capable of throwing aside that ruling band of robbers into which the propertied classes have degenerated; the question is not that no one else can accomplish this task on your behalf; the question is not whether history allows you any postponement (for the present condition of bloody chaos threatens to bury you yourself, in the near future, under the last ruins of capitalism). The question is whether the ruling imperialist bandits have succeeded—yesterday or today—in deceiving, violating, and swindling public opinion, and collected 51 per cent of the votes against your 49. Perish the world, but long live the parliamentary majority! . . ."

THE IMPERIALIST TRANSFORMATION OF DEMOCRACY

It is not for nothing that the word "democracy" has a double meaning in the political vocabulary. On the one hand, it means a state system founded on universal suffrage and the other attributes of formal "popular government." On the other hand, by the word "democracy" is understood the mass of the people itself, in so far as it leads a political existence. In the second sense, as in the first, the meaning of democracy rises above class distinctions.

This peculiarity of terminology has its profound political significance. Democracy as a political system is the more perfect and unshakable the greater is the part played in the life of the country by the intermediate and less differentiated mass of the population—the petite bourgeoisie of the town and the country. Democracy achieved its highest expression in the nineteenth century in Switzerland and the United States of North America. On the other side of the ocean the democratic organization of power in a federal republic was based on the agrarian democracy of the farmers. In the small Helvetian Republic, the petite bourgeoisie of the towns and the rich peasantry constituted the basis of the conservative democracy of the united cantons.

Born of the struggle of the Third Estate against the powers of feudalism, the democratic State very soon becomes a weapon of defense against the class antagonisms generated within bourgeois society. Bourgeois society succeeds in this the more, the wider beneath it is the layer of the petite bourgeoisie, the greater is the importance of the latter in the economic life of the country, and the less advanced, consequently, is the development of class antagonism. However, the intermediate classes lag ever more helplessly behind historical development, and, thereby, become ever more incapable of speaking in the name of the nation. True, the petit-bourgeois doctrinaires (Bernstein and Company) used to demonstrate with satisfaction that the disappearance of the petit-bourgeois classes was not taking place with the speed expected by the Marxist school. And, in fact, one might agree that, numerically, the petit-bourgeois elements in both town and country—but particularly the latter—still maintain an extremely prominent position. But the central fact remains that the contribution which this class makes to the national income has fallen incomparably more rapidly than its numerical strength. And there has been a corresponding decrease in its social, political, and cultural importance. Historical development has been relying more and more on the polar classes of society—the capitalist bourgeoisie and the proletariat—rather than on these conservative elements inherited from the past.

In proportion as the petite bourgeoisie has lost social importance, it has also lost the capacity to serve as an authoritative arbitral judge in the historical conflict between capital and labor. Yet the very considerable numerical proportion of the town middle classes, and still more of the peasantry, continues to find direct expression in the electoral statistics of parliamentarism. The formal equality of all citizens as electors thereby only gives more open indication of the incapacity of "democratic parliamentarism" to settle the root questions of historical evolution. An "equal" vote for the proletariat, the peasant, and the manager of a trust formally placed the peasant in the position of a mediator between the two antagonists; but, in reality, the peasantry, socially and culturally backward and politically helpless, has in all countries always provided support for the most reactionary, filibustering, and mercenary parties which, in the long run, always supported capital against labor.

Absolutely contrary to all the prophecies of Bernstein, Sombart, Tugan-Baranovsky, and others, the continued existence of the middle classes has not softened, but has sharpened to the ultimate degree, the revolutionary crisis of bourgeois society. If the proletarization of the petite bourgeoisie and the peasantry had been proceeding in a chemically purified form, the peaceful conquest of power by the proletariat through the democratic parliamentary apparatus would have been much more probable than we can imagine at present. Just the fact that was seized upon by the partisans of the petite bourgeoisie—its longevity—has proved fatal even for the external forms of political democracy, now that capitalism has undermined its essential foundations. Occupying in parliamentary politics the place which it has lost in production, the petite bourgeoisie has finally and completely compromised parliamentarism, transforming it into an institution of confused chatter and legislative obstruction. This fact alone has brought the proletariat face to face with the problem of seizing the apparatus of state power, as such, independently of the petite bourgeoisie, and even in opposition to it—not in opposition to its interests, but in opposition to its stupidity and its stumbling and bungling policy.

"Imperialism," wrote Marx of the Empire of Napoleon III, "is the most prostituted, and, at the same time, perfected form of state which the bourgeoisie, having attained its fullest development, transforms into a weapon for the enslavement of labor by capital." This definition has a wider significance than for the French Empire alone, and includes the latest form of imperialism, born of the world conflict between the national capitalisms of the great powers. In the economic sphere, imperialism presupposed the final collapse of the rule of the petite bourgeoisie; in the political sphere, it signified the complete destruction of democracy by means of an internal molecular transformation, and a universal subordination of all of democracy's resources to its own ends. Seizing upon all countries, independently of their previous political history, imperialism showed that all political prejudices were foreign to it, and that it was equally ready and able to use, after their transformation and subjection, the monarchy of Nicholas Romanoff or Wilhelm Hohenzollern, the presidential autocracy of the United States of North America, and the helplessness of a few hundred chocolate legislators in the French parliament. The last great slaughter—the bloody font in which the bourgeois world attempted to be rebaptized—presented us with a picture, unparalleled in history, of the mobilization of all state forms, systems of government, political tendencies, religions, and schools of philosophy in the service of imperialism. Even many of those pedants who had slept through the preparatory period of imperialist development during the last decades, and had continued to maintain a traditional attitude towards the ideas of democracy and universal suffrage, began to feel during the war that their accustomed ideas had become fraught with some new meaning. Absolutism, parliamentary monarchy, democracy—in the presence of imperialism (and, consequently, in the presence of the revolution rising to take its place), all the state forms of bourgeois supremacy, from Russian Tsarism to North American quasi-democratic federalism, have been given equal rights, bound up in combinations which supplemented one another in an indivisible whole. Imperialism succeeded by means of all the resources it had at its disposal, including parliamentarism, irrespective of the electoral arithmetic of voting, in subordinating for its own purposes, at the critical moment, the petite bourgeoisie of the towns and country and even the upper layers of the proletariat. The national idea, under aegis of which the Third Estate rose to power, found its rebirth in the imperialist war in the watchword of national defense. With unexpected brilliance, national ideology flamed up for the last time at the expense of class ideology. The collapse of imperialist illusions, not only among the vanquished, but—after a certain delay—among the victorious as well, finally laid low what was once national democracy, and, with it, its main weapon, the democratic parliament. The flabbiness, rottenness, and helplessness of the petite bourgeoisie and their parties everywhere became evident with terrifying clearness. In all countries the question of the control of the State assumed first-class importance as a question of an open measuring of forces between the capitalist clique, openly or secretly supreme and disposing of hundreds of thousands of trained and hardened officers, devoid of all scruple, and the insurgent revolutionary proletariat; while the intermediate classes were living in a state of terror, confusion, and prostration. Under such conditions, what pitiful nonsense are speeches about the peaceful conquest of power by the proletariat through the means of democratic parliamentarism!

The outline of the political situation on a world scale is quite clear. The bourgeoisie, which has brought the nations, exhausted and bled white, to the brink of destruction (I refer particularly to the victorious bourgeoisie), has revealed its utter inability to bring them out of their terrible situation, and thus has shown that its existence and power are incompatible with the future development of humanity. All the intermediate political groups, including, in the first instance, the social-patriotic parties, are rotting alive. The proletariat they have deceived is turning against them more and more every day, and is becoming strengthened in its revolutionary mission as the only power that can save the peoples from savagery and destruction. However, history has not at all secured, just at this moment, a formal parliamentary majority on the side of the party of the social revolution. In other words, history has not transformed the nation into a debating society solemnly voting the transition to the social revolution by a majority of votes. On the contrary, the violent revolution has become a necessity precisely because the undeferable demands of history are powerless to find a road through the apparatus of parliamentary democracy. The capitalist bourgeois calculates: "while I have in my hands lands, factories, workshops, banks; while I possess newspapers, universities, schools; while—and this most important of all—I retain control of the army, the apparatus of democracy, however you reconstruct it, will remain obedient to my will. I subordinate the stupid, conservative, characterless petite bourgeoisie to myself, not only materially but also spiritually. I oppress, and will continue to oppress, its imagination with the gigantic scale of my buildings, my transactions, my plans, and my crimes. For those moments when it becomes dissatisfied and begins to murmur I have created scores of safety valves and lightning rods. At the right moment I will bring into being opposition parties, which will disappear tomorrow, but which today accomplish their function by giving the petite bourgeoisie an opportunity to express their indignation without any injury to capitalism. I shall hold the masses of the people, under cover of compulsory general education, on the brink of total ignorance, giving them no opportunity to rise above the level which my experts in spiritual slavery consider safe. I will corrupt, deceive, and terrorize the more privileged or the more backward among the proletariat itself. Through such measures I shall prevent the vanguard of the working class from gaining the ear of the majority of the working class so long as the necessary weapons of oppression and intimidation remain in my hands."

To this the revolutionary proletarian replies: "Consequently, the first condition of salvation is to tear the weapons of domination out of the hands of the bourgeoisie. It is hopeless to think of a peaceful gaining of power while the bourgeoisie retains in its hands all the apparatus of power. Three times more hopeless is the idea of coming to power by the path which the bourgeoisie itself indicates and, at the same time, barricades—the path of parliamentary democracy. There is only one way: to seize power, taking away from the bourgeoisie the material apparatus of government. Irrespective of the superficial balance of forces in parliament, I shall take over for social administration the chief forces and resources of production. I shall free the mind of the petit-bourgeois classes from their capitalist hypnosis. I shall show them in practice what Socialist production means. Then even the most backward, the most ignorant, or most terrorized sections of the nation will support me, willingly and consciously joining in the work of Socialist construction.

The dissolution of the Constituent Assembly by the Soviet Russian Government seemed to the leading Social Democrats of Western Europe, if not the beginning of the end of the world, at least a rude and arbitrary break with the whole antecedent development of Socialism. In reality, it was only the inevitable outcome of the new position resulting from imperialism and the war. If Russian Communism was the first to enter the path of casting up theoretical and practical accounts, this was due to the same historical reasons which forced the Russian proletariat to be the first to enter the path of the struggle for power.

All that has happened since then in Europe bears witness to the fact that we drew the right conclusion. To imagine that democracy can be restored in its pristine purity is to live in a pitiful, reactionary utopia.

THE METAPHYSICS OF DEMOCRACY

Feeling the historical ground shaking under his feet on the question of democracy, Kautsky crosses to the ground of metaphysics. Instead of inquiring into what is, he deliberates about what ought to be.

The principles of democracy—the sovereignty of the people, universal and equal suffrage, personal liberties—appear, as presented to him, in a halo of moral duty. They are abstracted from their historical meaning and presented as unalterable and sacred things-in-themselves. This metaphysical fall from grace is not accidental. It is instructive that the late Plekhanov, a merciless enemy of Kantism during the best period of his activity, attempted at the end of his life, when the wave of patriotism had washed over him, to clutch at the straw of the categorical imperative.

The real democracy with which the German people is now making practical acquaintance Kautsky confronts with a kind of ideal democracy, as he would confront a common phenomenon with the thing-in-itself. Kautsky does not point clearly to a single country in which democracy is really capable of guaranteeing a painless transition to Socialism. But he does know, and firmly, that such democracy ought to exist. The present German National Assembly, that organ of helplessness, reactionary malice, and degraded solicitations, is confronted by Kautsky with a different, real, true

National Assembly, which possesses all virtues—excepting the small virtue of reality.

The doctrine of formal democracy is not scientific Socialism, but the theory of so-called natural law. The essence of the latter consists in the recognition of eternal and unchanging legal norms, which among different peoples and at different periods find a different, more or less limited and distorted expression. The modern theory of natural law—i. e., the theory as it emerged from the Middle Ages—included first of all a protest against class privileges, the abuse of despotic legislation, and the other "artificial" products of positive feudal law. The theoreticians of the, as yet, weak Third Estate expressed its class interests in a few ideal norms, which later developed into the teaching of democracy, acquiring at the same time an individualist character. The individual is absolute; all persons have the right of expressing their thoughts in speech and print; every man should enjoy equal electoral rights. As a battle cry against feudalism, the demand for democracy had a progressive character. As time went on, however, the metaphysics of natural law (the theory of formal democracy) began to show its reactionary side—the establishment of an ideal standard to control the real demands of the laboring masses and the revolutionary parties.

If we look back to the historical sequence of world concepts, the theory of natural law will prove to be a paraphrase of Christian spiritualism freed from its crude mysticism. The Gospels proclaimed to the slave that he had exactly the same soul as the slave-owner, and in this way established the equality of all men before the heavenly tribunal. In reality, the slave remained a slave, and obedience became for him a religious duty. In the teaching of Christianity, the slave found an expression for his own ignorant protest against his degraded condition. Side by side with the protest was also the consolation. Christianity told him: "You have an immortal soul, but your condition is that of a pack-mule." Here sounded a note of indignation. But the same Christianity also said: "Although you resemble a pack-mule, yet your immortal soul has in store for it an eternal reward." Here is the voice of consolation. These two notes were found in historical Christianity in different proportions at different periods and amongst different classes. But on the whole, Christianity, like all other religions, became a method of deadening the consciousness of the oppressed masses.

Natural law, which developed into the theory of democracy, said to the worker: "all men are equal before the law, irrespective of their origin, their property, and their position; every man has an equal right in determining the fate of the people." This ideal criterion revolutionized the consciousness of the masses in so far as it was a condemnation of absolutism, aristocratic privileges, and the property qualification. But the longer it went on, the more it dulled consciousness, legalizing poverty, slavery, and degradation: for how could one revolt against slavery when every man has an equal right in determining the fate of the nation?

Rothschild, who has coined the blood and tears of the world into the gold napoleons of his income, has one vote at the parliamentary elections. The ignorant tiller of the soil who cannot sign his name, sleeps all his life without taking his clothes off, and wanders through society like an underground mole, plays his part as a trustee of the nation's sovereignty, and is equal to Rothschild in the courts and at the elections. In the real conditions of life, in the economic process, in social relations, in their way of life, people became more and more unequal; dazzling luxury was accumulated at one pole, poverty and hopelessness at the other. But in the sphere of the legal edifice of the State, these glaring contradictions disappeared, and there penetrated thither only unsubstantial legal shadows. The landlord, the laborer, the capitalist, the proletarian, the minister, the bootblack—all are equal as "citizens" and as "legislators." The mystic equality of Christianity has taken one step down from the heavens in the shape of the "natural," "legal" equality of democracy. But it has not yet reached earth, where lie the economic foundations of society. For the ignorant day-laborer, who all his life remains a beast of burden in the service of the bourgeoisie, the ideal right to influence the fate of the nations by means of the parliamentary elections remained little more real than the bliss which he was promised in the kingdom of heaven.

In the practical interests of the development of the working class, the Socialist Party took its stand at a certain period on the path of parliamentarism. But this did not mean in the slightest that it accepted in principle the metaphysical theory of democracy, based on extra-historical, super-class rights. Proletarian doctrine viewed democracy as an instrument of bourgeois society, wholly adapted to the problems and requirements of the ruling classes. But, as bourgeois society lived by the labor of the proletariat and could not deny the latter the legalization of a certain part of its class struggle without destroying itself, this gave the Socialist Party an opportunity to make use, for a certain period and within certain limits, of the mechanism of democracy, without, however, taking any oath of allegiance to democracy as an unshakable principle.

The root problem of the party, at all periods of its struggle, was to create the conditions for real, economic, living equality for mankind as members of a united human commonwealth. It was just for this reason that the theoreticians of the proletariat had to expose the metaphysics of democracy as a philosophic mask for political mystification.

The democratic party during the period of its revolutionary enthusiasm, when exposing the enslaving and stupefying lie of church dogma, preached to the masses:—"You are lulled to sleep by promises of eternal bliss at the end of your life, while here you have no rights and you are bound with the chains of tyranny." The Socialist Party, a few decades later, said to the same masses with no less right:—"You are lulled to sleep with the fiction of civic equality and political rights, but you are deprived of the possibility of realising those rights. Conditional and shadowy legal equality has been transformed into the convicts' chain with which each of you is fastened to the chariot of capitalism."

In the name of its fundamental task, the Socialist Party mobilized the masses on the parliamentary ground as well as on others; but nowhere and at no time did the party bind itself to bring the masses to Socialism only through the gates of democracy. In adapting ourselves to the parliamentary regime, we confined ourselves to a theoretical exposure of democracy, because we were still too weak to overcome it in practice. But the path of Socialist ideas which is visible through all deviations, and even betrayals, foreshadows no other outcome but this: to throw democracy aside and replace it by the mechanism of the proletariat, at the moment when the latter is strong enough to carry out such a task.

We shall offer one piece of evidence, albeit a sufficiently striking one. "Parliamentarism," wrote Paul Lafargue in the Russian review, *Sotsial-demokrat,* in 1888,

> is a system of government in which the people acquires the illusion that it is controlling the forces of the country itself, when, in reality, the actual power is concentrated in the hands of the bourgeoisie—and not even of the whole bourgeoisie, but only of certain sections of that class. In the first period of its supremacy the bourgeoisie does not understand, or, more correctly, does not feel, the necessity for making the people believe in the illusion of self-government. Hence it was that all the parliamentary countries of Europe began with a limited franchise. Everywhere the right of influencing the policy of the country by means of the election of deputies belonged at first only to more or less large property holders, and was only gradually extended to less substantial citizens, until finally in some countries it became from a privilege the universal right of all and sundry.
>
> In bourgeois society, the more considerable becomes the amount of social wealth, the smaller becomes the number of individuals by whom it is appropriated. The same takes place with power: in proportion as the mass of citizens who possess political rights increases, and the number of elected rulers increases, the actual

power is concentrated and becomes the monopoly of a smaller and smaller group of individuals.

Such is the secret of the majority. . . .

TERRORISM

The chief theme of Kautsky's book is terrorism. The view that terrorism is of the essence of revolution Kautsky proclaims to be a widespread delusion. It is untrue that he who desires revolution must put up with terrorism. As far as he, Kautsky, is concerned, he is, generally speaking, for revolution, but decidedly against terrorism. Further on, however, difficulties arise.

"The revolution brings us," Kautsky complains,

a bloody terrorism carried out by Socialist governments. The Bolsheviks in Russia first stepped on to this path, and were, consequently, sternly condemned by all Socialists who had not adopted the Bolshevik point of view, including the Socialists of the German Majority. But as soon as the latter found themselves threatened in their supremacy, they had recourse to the methods of the same terrorist regime which they attacked in the East.

It would seem that from this follows the conclusion that terrorism is much more profoundly bound up with the nature of revolution than certain sages think. But Kautsky draws an absolutely opposite conclusion. The gigantic development of White and Red terrorism in all the recent revolutions—the Russian, the German, the Austrian, and the Hungarian—is evidence to him that these revolutions turned aside from their true path and were not the revolutions they ought to have been according to the theoretical visions of Kautsky. Without going into the question whether terrorism "as such" is "immanent" in revolution "as such," let us consider a few of the revolutions which pass before us in the living history of mankind.

Let us look first at the Reformation, which proved the watershed between the Middle Ages and modern history; the deeper the interests of the masses that it involved, the wider was its sweep, the more fiercely did the civil war develop under the religious banner, and the more merciless did the terror become on the other side.

In the seventeenth century England experienced two revolutions. The first, which brought forth great social upheavals and wars, entailed among other things, the execution of King Charles I, while the second ended happily with the accession of a new dynasty. The British bourgeoisie and its historians take quite different attitudes toward these two revolutions: the first is for them a rising of a mob—the "Great Rebellion"; the second has been commemorated under the title of the "Glorious Revolution." The reason for this difference of evaluation was explained by the French historian, Augustin Thierry. In the first English revolution, the "Great Rebellion," the active force was the people; while in the second the people were almost "silent." Hence, it follows that, in conditions of class slavery, it is difficult to teach the oppressed masses good manners. When provoked to fury they use clubs, stones, fire and the rope. The court historians of the exploiters are offended at this. But the great event in modern "bourgeois" history is, none the less, not the "Glorious Revolution," but the "Great Rebellion."

The greatest event in modern history after the Reformation and the "Great Rebellion," and far surpassing its two predecessors in significance, was the great French Revolution of the eighteenth century. This classical revolution was matched by a corresponding classical terrorism. Kautsky is ready to forgive the terrorism of the Jacobins, acknowledging that they had no other way of saving the republic. But by this justification after the event no one is either helped or hindered. The Kautskys of the end of the eighteenth century (the leaders of the French Girondists) saw in the Jacobins the personification of evil. Here is a comparison, sufficiently instructive in its banality, between the Jacobins and the Girondists from the pen of one of the bourgeois French historians: "Both one side and the other desired the republic." But the Girondists "desired a free, legal, and merciful republic. The Montagnards desired a despotic and terrorist republic. Both stood for the supreme power of the people; but the Girondists justly understood the people to mean everyone, while the Montagnards considered only the working class to be the people. That was why only to such persons, in the opinion of the Montagnards, did rule belong." The antithesis between the noble champions of the Constituent Assembly and the bloodthirsty agents of the revolutionary dictatorship is here outlined fairly clearly, although in the political terms of the epoch.

The iron dictatorship of the Jacobins was evoked by the fantastically difficult position of revolutionary France. Here is what the bourgeois historian says of this period: "Foreign troops had entered French territory from four sides. In the north, the British and the Austrians, in Alsace, the Prussians, in Dauphine and up to Lyons, the Piedmontese, in Roussillon the Spaniards. And this at a time when civil war was raging at four different points: in Normandy, in the Vendée, at Lyons, and at Toulon." To this we must add internal enemies in the form of numerous secret supporters of the old regime, ready to assist the enemy by any and all means.

The severity of the proletarian dictatorship in Russia, let us point out here, was conditioned by no less difficult circumstances. There was one continuous front, on the north and south, in the east and west. Besides the

Russian White Guard armies of Kolchak, Deniken, and others, the following have attacked Soviet Russia, simultaneously or in turn: Germans, Austrians, Czecho-Slovaks, Serbs, Poles, Ukrainians, Roumanians, French, British, Americans, Japanese, Finns, Esthonians, Lithuanians. . . . In a country throttled by a blockade and strangled by hunger, there are conspiracies, insurrections, terrorist acts, and destruction of roads and bridges.

The government which had taken upon itself the struggle with countless external and internal enemies had neither money, nor sufficient troops, nor anything except boundless energy, enthusiastic support on the part of the revolutionary elements of the country, and the gigantic courage to take all measures necessary for the safety of the country, however arbitrary and severe they were.

In such words did Plekhanov once describe the government of the—Jacobins. . . .

Let us now turn to a revolution which took place in the second half of the nineteenth century, in the country of "democracy"—in the United States of North America. Although the question was not the abolition of property altogether, but only of the abolition of property in negroes, nevertheless, the institutions of democracy proved absolutely powerless to settle the argument in a peaceful way. The southern states, defeated at the presidential elections in 1860, decided by all possible means to regain the influence they had hitherto exerted in the question of slaveowning; and uttering, as was right, the proper sounding words about freedom and independence, rose in a slaveowners' insurrection. Hence inevitably followed all the further consequences of civil war. At the very beginning of the struggle, the military government in Baltimore imprisoned in Fort MacHenry a few citizens, sympathizers with the slaveholding South, in spite of habeas corpus. The question of the lawfulness or unlawfulness of such action became the object of fierce disputes between so-called "high authorities." The judges of the Supreme Court decided that the President had neither the right to arrest the operation of habeas corpus nor to give plenipotentiary powers to that end to the military authorities. "Such, in all probability, is the correct Constitutional solution of the question," says one of the first historians of the American Civil War. "But the state of affairs was to such a degree critical, and the necessity of taking decisive measures against the population of Baltimore so great, that not only the Government but the people of the United States also supported the most energetic measures."

Some goods that the rebellious South required were secretly supplied by the merchants of the North. Naturally, the Northerners had no other course but to introduce methods of repression. On August 6, 1861, the President confirmed a resolution of Congress as to "the confiscation of property used for insurrectionary purposes." The people, in the shape of the most democratic elements, were in favor of extreme measures. The Republican Party had a decided majority in the North, and persons suspected of secessionism, i.e., of sympathizing with the rebellious Southern states, were subjected to violence. In some northern towns, and even in the states of New England, famous for their order, the people frequently burst into the offices of newspapers which supported the revolting slave-owners and smashed their printing presses. It occasionally happened that reactionary publishers were smeared with tar, decorated with feathers, and carried in such array through the public squares until they swore an oath of loyalty to the Union. The personality of a planter smeared in tar bore little resemblance to an "end-in-itself"; so that the categorical imperative of Kautsky suffered in the civil war of the states a considerable blow. But this is not all. "The government, on its part," the historian tells us, "adopted repressive measures of various kinds against publications holding views opposed to its own: and in a short time the hitherto free American press was reduced to a condition *scarcely superior to that prevailing in the autocratic European States.*" The same fate overtook the freedom of speech. "In this way," Lieut.-Colonel Fletcher continues, "the American people at this time denied itself the greater part of its freedom. It should be observed," he moralizes, "that *the majority of the people* was to such an extent occupied with the war, and to such a degree imbued with the readiness for any kind of sacrifice to attain its end, that it not only did not regret its vanished liberties, but scarcely even noticed their disappearance."

Infinitely more ruthlessly did the bloodthirsty slaveowners of the South employ their uncontrollable hordes. "Wherever there was a majority in favor of slavery," writes the Count of Paris,

> public opinion behaved despotically to the minority. All who expressed sympathy for the national banner . . . were forced to be silent. But soon this itself became insufficient; as in all revolutions, the indifferent were forced to express their loyalty to the new order of things. . . . Those who did not agree to this were given up as a sacrifice to the hatred and violence of the mass of the people. . . . In each centre of growing civilization (South-Western states) vigilance committees were formed, composed of all those who had been distinguished by their extreme views in the electoral struggle. . . . A tavern was the usual place of their sessions, and a noisy orgy was mingled with a contemptible parody of public form of justice. A few madmen sitting around a desk on which gin and whisky flowed judged their present and absent fellow-citizens. The accused, even before having been questioned, could see the rope being prepared. He who did not appear at the court learned his sentence when falling under the bullets of the executioner concealed in the forest.

This picture is extremely reminiscent of the scenes which day by day took place in the camps of Denikin, Kolchak, Yudenich, and the other heroes of Anglo-Franco-American "democracy."

We shall see later how the question of terrorism stood in regard to the Paris Commune of 1871. In any case, the attempts of Kautsky to contrast the Commune with us are false at their very root, and reduce the author to a juggling with words of the most petty character.

The institution of hostages apparently must be recognized as "immanent" in the terrorism of the civil war. Kautsky is against terrorism and against the institution of hostages, but in favor of the Paris Commune. (N.B.—The Commune existed fifty years ago.) Yet the Commune took hostages. A difficulty arises. But what does the art of exegesis exist for?

The decree of the Commune concerning hostages and their execution in reply to the atrocities of the Versaillese arose, according to the profound explanation of Kautsky, "from a striving to preserve human life, not to destroy it." A marvellous discovery! It only requires to be developed. It could, and must, be explained that in the civil war we destroyed White Guards in order that they should not destroy the workers. Consequently, our problem is not the destruction of human life, but its preservation. But as we have to struggle for the preservation of human life with arms in our hands, this leads to the destruction of human life—a puzzle the dialectical secret of which was explained by old Hegel, without reckoning other still more ancient sages.

The Commune could maintain itself and consolidate its position only by a determined struggle with the Versaillese. The latter, on the other hand, had a large number of agents in Paris. Fighting with the agents of Thiers, the Commune could not abstain from destroying the Versaillese at the front and in the rear. If its rule had crossed the bounds of Paris, in the provinces it would have found—during the process of the civil war with the Army of the National Assembly—still more determined foes in the midst of the peaceful population. The Commune when fighting the royalists could not allow freedom of speech to royalist agents in the rear.

Kautsky, in spite of all the happenings in the world today, completely fails to realize what war is in general, and civil war in particular. He does not understand that every, or nearly every, sympathizer with Thiers in Paris was not merely an "opponent" of the Communards in ideas, but an agent and spy of Thiers, a ferocious enemy ready to shoot one in the back. The enemy must be made harmless, and in wartime this means that he must be destroyed.

The problem of revolution, as of war, consists in breaking the will of the foe, forcing him to capitulate and to accept the conditions of the conqueror. The will, of course, is a phenomenon of the psychic world, but in contradistinction to a meeting, a dispute, or a congress, the revolution carries out its object by means of the employment of material resources—though to a less degree than war. The bourgeoisie itself conquered power by means of revolts, and consolidated it by civil war. In peacetime, it retains power by means of a system of repression. As long as class society, founded on the most deep-rooted antagonisms, continues to exist, repression remains a necessary means of breaking the will of the opposing side.

Even if, in one country or another, the dictatorship of the proletariat grew up within the external framework of democracy, this would by no means avert the civil war. The question as to who is to rule the country, i.e., the question of the life or death of the bourgeoisie, will be decided on either side, not by references to the paragraphs of the constitution, but by the employment of all forms of violence. However deeply Kautsky goes into the question of the food of the anthropopithecus . . . and other immediate and remote causes of human cruelty, he will find in history no other way of breaking the class will of the enemy except the systematic and energetic use of violence.

The degree of ferocity of the struggle depends on a series of foreign and domestic circumstances. The more ferocious and dangerous is the resistance of the class enemy who has been overthrown, the more inevitably does the system of repression harden into a system of terror.

But here Kautsky unexpectedly takes up a new position in his struggle with Soviet terrorism. He simply waves aside all reference to the brutality of the counterrevolutionary opposition of the Russian bourgeoisie.

"There was no sign," he says, "of such brutality in November, 1917, in Petrograd and Moscow, or more recently in Budapest." Such a happy formulation of the question makes revolutionary terrorism an exclusive product of the bloodthirstiness of the Bolsheviks, who have, at a single stroke, abandoned both the traditions of the vegetarian anthropopithecus and the moral lessons of Kautsky.

The first conquest of power by the Soviets at the beginning of November, 1917 (new style), was actually accomplished with insignificant sacrifices. The Russian bourgeoisie found itself to such a degree estranged from the masses of the people, so internally helpless, so compromised by the course and the result of the war, so demoralized by the regime of Kerensky, that it scarcely dared show any resistance. In Petrograd the power of Kerensky was overthrown almost without a fight. In Moscow its resistance was dragged out, mainly owing to the indecisive character of our own actions. In the majority of the provincial towns power was transferred to the Soviet on the mere receipt of a telegram from Petrograd or Moscow. If the matter had ended there, there would have been no word of the Red Terror. But in November, 1917, there was already evidence of the beginning of the resistance of the propertied classes. True, the intervention of the imperialist governments of the West was required, to give the Russian counterrevolution faith in itself, and to add ever-increasing power to its resistance. This can be shown from facts, both important and insignificant, day by day during the whole epoch of the Soviet revolution.

Kerensky's "Staff" felt no support forthcoming from the mass of the soldiery, and was inclined to recognize the Soviet Government, which had begun negotiations for an armistice with the Germans. But there followed the protest of the military missions of the Entente, followed by open threats. The Staff was frightened; incited by "Allied" officers, it entered the path of opposition. This led to armed conflict and to the murder of the chief of the field staff, General Dukhonin, by a group of revolutionary sailors.

In Petrograd, the official agents of the Entente, especially the French Military Mission, hand in hand with the S. R.s and the Mensheviks, openly organized the opposition, mobilizing, arming, inciting against us the cadets, and the bourgeois youth generally, from the second day of the Soviet revolution. The rising of the cadets on November 10 resulted in a hundred times more victims than the revolution of November 7. The campaign of the adventurers Kerensky and Krasnov against Petrograd, organized at the same time by the Entente, naturally introduced into the struggle the first elements of savagery. Nevertheless, General Krasnov was set free on his word of honor. The Yaroslav rising (in the summer of 1918) which involved so many victims, was organized by Savinkov on the instructions of the French Embassy, and with its resources. Archangel was captured according to the plans of British naval agents, with the help of British warships and aeroplanes. The beginning of the empire of Kolchak, the nominee of the American Stock Exchange, was brought about by the foreign Czecho-Slovak Corps maintained by the resources of the French Government. Kaledin and Krasnov (liberated by us), the first leaders of the counterrevolution on the Don, could enjoy partial success only thanks to the open military and financial aid of Germany. In the Ukraine the Soviet power was overthrown in the beginning of 1918 by German militarism. The Volunteer Army of Denikin was created with the financial and technical help of Great Britain and

France. Only in the hope of British intervention and British military support was Yudenich's army created. The politicians, the diplomats, and the journalists of the Entente have for two years on end been debating with complete frankness the question of whether the financing of the civil war in Russia is a sufficiently profitable enterprise. In such circumstances, one needs to be truly thickheaded to seek the reason for the sanguinary character of the civil war in Russia in the malevolence of the Bolsheviks, rather than in the international situation.

The Russian proletariat was the first to enter the path of the social revolution, and the Russian bourgeoisie, politically helpless, was emboldened to struggle against its political and economic expropriation only because it saw its elder sister in all countries still in power, and still maintaining economic, political, and, to a certain extent, military supremacy.

If our November revolution had taken place a few months, or even a few weeks, after the establishment of the rule of the proletariat in Germany, France, and England, there can be no doubt that our revolution would have been the most "peaceful," the most "bloodless" of all possible revolutions on this sinful earth. But this historical sequence—the most "natural" at the first glance, and, in any case, the most beneficial for the Russian working class—found itself infringed—not through our fault, but through the will of events. Instead of being the last, the Russian proletariat proved to be the first. It was just this circumstance, after the first period of confusion, that imparted desperation to the character of the resistance of the classes which had ruled in Russia previously, and forced the Russian proletariat, in a moment of the greatest peril, foreign attacks, and internal plots and insurrections, to have recourse to severe measures of State terror. No one will now say that those measures proved futile. But, perhaps, we are expected to consider them "inadmissible"?

The working class, which seized power in battle, had as its task and its duty to establish that power unshakably, to guarantee its own supremacy beyond question, to destroy its enemies' hankering for a new overthrow of the state, and thereby to make sure of carrying out Socialist reforms. Otherwise there would have been no point in seizing power.

The revolution does not "logically" demand terrorism, just as it does not "logically" demand an armed insurrection. What a profound commonplace! But the revolution does require of the revolutionary class that it should attain its end by all methods at its disposal—if necessary, by an armed rising: if required, by terrorism. A revolutionary class which has conquered power with arms in its hands is bound to, and will, suppress, rifle in hand, all attempts to tear the power out of its hands. Where it has against it a hostile army, it will oppose to it its own army. Where it is confronted with armed conspiracy, attempts at murder, or insurrection, it will hurl at the heads of its enemies an unsparing penalty. Perhaps Kautsky has invented other methods? Or does he reduce the whole question to the *degree* of repression, and recommend in all circumstances imprisonment instead of execution?

The question of the form of repression, or of its degree, of course, is not one of "principle." It is a question of expediency. In a revolutionary period, the party which has been thrown from power, which does not reconcile itself with the stability of the ruling class, and which proves this by its desperate struggle against the latter, cannot be terrorized by the threat of imprisonment, as it does not believe in its duration. It is just this simple but decisive fact that explains the widespread recourse to shooting in the civil war.

Or, perhaps, Kautsky wishes to say that execution is not expedient, that "classes cannot be cowed." This is untrue. Terror is helpless—and then only "in the long run"—if it is employed by reaction against a historically rising class. But terror can be very efficient against a reactionary class which is unwilling to leave the scene of operations. *Intimidation* is a powerful weapon of both foreign and domestic policy. War, like revolution, is founded upon intimidation. A victorious war, generally speaking, destroys only an insignificant part of the conquered army, intimidating the remainder and breaking their will. The revolution works in the same way: it kills individuals, and intimidates thousands. In this sense, the Red Terror is not distinguishable from the armed insurrection of which it is a direct continuation. The State terror of a revolutionary class can be "morally" condemned only by a man who rejects (in words) every form of violence, consequently every war and every insurrection, as a matter of principle. To do this, however, one would have to be nothing less than a hypocritical Quaker.

"But, in that case, how do your tactics differ from the tactics of Tsarism?" we are asked by the high priests of Liberalism and Kautskianism.

You do not understand this, holy men? We shall explain it to you. The terror of Tsarism was directed against the proletariat. The gendarmerie of Tsarism throttled the workers who were fighting for the Socialist order. Our Cheka-ists shoot landlords, capitalists, and generals who are striving to restore the capitalist order. Do you grasp this . . . subtle distinction? Yes? For us Communists it is quite sufficient.

IGNAZIO SILONE

THE GOD THAT FAILED (1949), from which the following selection has been made, is a collection of six essays, written by distinguished European and American men of letters all of whom had, in the years between the Russian Revolution of 1917 and the Stalin-Hitler Pact of 1939, joined the Communist Party only to be disillusioned. Conceived and edited by Richard Crossman (b. 1907), Labor Member of Parliament, British socialist, and an editor of the left-wing journal of opinion *New Statesman and Nation* of London, the book was first published in America in 1950. The careers and experiences of the six contributors—Arthur Koestler, Hungarian-born British subject and novelist, Ignazio Silone, Italian novelist and critic, Richard Wright, American Negro novelist, André Gide, French novelist, essayist, and critic, Louis Fischer, American journalist, and Stephen Spender, British poet—display little in common save that all are imaginative writers who took the journey into Communism and returned. It was to gain a clearer understanding of the circumstances of their conversion, and perhaps even more pertinently, of their final abjuration, that these men were asked to write their political-psychological autobiographies for the volume.

Of the six essays that comprise *The God That Failed,* the one by Ignazio Silone has been chosen for the following selection. Silone was born at Pescina dei Marsi, a village in the Abruzzi Apennines in Italy, in 1900. His father was a small peasant landowner and his mother a cottage weaver. During World War I, at the age of seventeen, he was appointed secretary of land workers for the Abruzzi district and had to appear in court to face charges in connection with a violent demonstration against the war, a demonstration which he organized. In 1921 he participated in the formation of the Italian Communist Party, and became editor of the weekly *Avanguardia* of Rome and the *Lavoratore,* a daily published in Trieste. Even after the seizure of power by the Fascists, and the proscription of the Communist Party in Italy, Silone remained in his native country, printing illegal newspapers in the underground. He was arrested, imprisoned, and then exiled. But during his exile he came to distrust and finally to hate the party which he had adopted so early in his life. Finally, in 1930—just at the moment when so many writers were joining the Communists—Silone severed his connections with the organization. But he did not, as so many ex-Communists have done, abjure his faith in socialism. On the contrary, he became a leading figure in the Italian Socialist Party, for which he formulated the political program known as the "Third Front." He returned from exile only in 1944, with the defeat and collapse of the Fascist regime which he passionately despised. In addition to his political activity, Silone is one of Italy's most distinguished novelists. Among his works are *Fontamara* (1934), *Bread and Wine* (1936), *The School for Dictators* (1938), *The Seed beneath the Snow* (1942), and the play *And He Hid Himself* (1946).

THE GOD THAT FAILED

. . . I grew up in a mountainous district of southern Italy. The phenomenon which most impressed me, when I arrived at the age of reason, was the violent contrast, the incomprehensible, absurd, monstrous contrast between family and private life—in the main decent, honest, and well-conducted—and social relations, which were very often crude and full of hatred and deceit. Many terrifying stories are known of the misery and desperation of the southern provinces (I have told some myself), but I do not intend to refer now to events that caused a stir, so much as to the little occurrences of daily life. It was these commonplace minor events that showed up the strange double existence of the people among whom I grew up, the observation of which was one of the agonizing secrets of my adolescence.

I was a child just five years old when, one Sunday, while crossing the little square of my native village with my mother leading me by the hand, I witnessed the cruel, stupid spectacle of one of the local gentry setting his great dog at a poor woman, a seamstress, who was just coming out of church. The wretched woman was flung to the ground, badly mauled, and her dress was torn to ribbons. Indignation in the village was general, but silent. I have never understood how the poor woman ever got the unhappy idea of taking proceedings against the squire; but the only result was to add a mockery of justice to the harm already done. Although, I must repeat, everybody pitied her and many people helped her secretly, the unfortunate woman could not find a single witness prepared to give evidence before the magistrate, nor a lawyer to conduct the prosecution. On the other hand, the squire's supposedly Left-Wing lawyer turned up punctually, and so did a number of bribed witnesses who perjured themselves by giving a grotesque version of what had happened, and accusing the woman of having provoked the dog. The magistrate—a most worthy, honest person in private life—acquitted the squire and condemned the poor woman to pay the costs.

"It went very much against the grain with me," he excused himself a few days later at our house. "On my word of honor, I do assure you, I was very sorry about it. But even if I had been present at the disgusting incident as a private citizen and couldn't have avoided blaming him, still as a judge I had to go by the evidence of the case, and unfortunately it was in favor of the

---

dog." "A real judge," he used to love to say, sententiously, "must be able to conceal his own egoistic feelings, and be impartial." "Really, you know," my mother used to comment, "it's a horrible profession. Better to keep ourselves to ourselves at home. My son," she used to say to me, "when you're grown up, be whatever you like, but not a judge."

I can remember other typical little incidents like that of the squire, the dog, and the seamstress. But I should not like to suggest, by quoting such episodes, that we were ignorant of the sacred concepts of Justice and Truth or that we held them in contempt. On the contrary; at school, in church, and at public celebrations they were often discussed with eloquence and veneration, but in rather abstract terms. To define our curious situation more exactly, I should add that it was based on a deception of which all of us, even the children, were aware; and yet it still persisted, being built on something quite apart from the ignorance and stupidity of individuals. . . .

. . . The so-called democratic system had, however, introduced a new technical detail into the relations between citizen and State. This was the secret vote, which though not in itself enough to change things radically, sometimes produced results which were surprising, and, as far as public order was concerned, scandalous. Though these incidents were isolate and had no immediate sequel, they were none the less disturbing.

I was seven years old when the first election campaign, which I can remember, took place in my district. At that time we still had no political parties, so the announcement of this campaign was received with very little interest. But popular feeling ran high when it was disclosed that one of the candidates was "the Prince." There was no need to add Christian and surname to realize which Prince was meant. He was the owner of the great estate formed by the arbitrary occupation of the vast tracts of land reclaimed in the previous century from the Lake of Fucino. About eight thousand families (that is, the majority of the local population) are still employed today in cultivating the estate's fourteen thousand hectares. The Prince was deigning to solicit "his" families for their vote so that he could become their deputy in parliament. The agents of the estate, who were working for the Prince, talked in impeccably liberal phrases: "Naturally," said they, "naturally, no one will be forced to vote for the Prince, that's understood; in the same way that no one, naturally, can force the Prince to allow people who don't vote for him to work on his land. This is the period of real liberty for everybody; you're free, and so is the Prince." The announcement of these "liberal" principles produced general and understandable consternation among the peasants. For, as may easily be guessed, the Prince was the most hated person in our part of the country. As long as he remained in the invisible Olympus of the great feudal proprietor (none of the eight thousand tenants had seen him, up to then, even from afar) public hatred for him was allowed, and belonged to the same category as curses against hostile deities; such curses, though useless, are satisfying. But now the clouds were being rent, and the Prince was coming down within reach of mortal men. From now on, consequently, they would have to keep their expressions of hatred within the narrow circle of private life and get ready to welcome him with due honors in the village streets.

My father seemed reluctant to accept this kind of logic. He was the youngest of several brothers, all of them peasant proprietors; the youngest, the most restless, and the only one with any inclinations toward insubordination. One evening his older brothers came and urged him, in the common interest, to be prudent and careful. For me (to whom no one paid any attention, for grown-ups think that children don't understand such things) it was a most instructive evening. "The Prince being a candidate is a real farce," the eldest brother admitted. "Political candidatures should be reserved for lawyers and other such windbags. But as the Prince is a candidate, all we can do is support him." "If the Prince's candidature is a farce," replied my father, "I don't understand why we should support him." "Because we're his dependents, as you know perfectly well." "Not in politics," said my father. "In politics we're free." "We don't cultivate politics, we cultivate the land," they answered him. "As cultivators of the land we depend on the Prince." "There's no mention of politics in our contracts for the land, only of potatoes and beetroots. As voters we're free." "The Prince's bailiff will also be free not to renew our contracts," they answered him. "That's why we're forced to be on his side." "I can't vote for someone merely because I'm forced to," said my father. "I'd feel humiliated." "No one will know how you vote," they answered him. "In the secrecy of the polling booth you can vote as you like, freely. But during the electioneering campaign we must be on the Prince's side, all of us together." "I'd be pleased to do it if I wasn't ashamed to," said my father, "but, do believe me, I'd be too much ashamed." To settle it, my uncles and my father reached this compromise: he would not come out either on the Prince's side or against him.

The Prince's election tour was prepared by the civil authorities, the police, the carabineers, and the agents of the estate. One Sunday, the Prince deigned to pass through the principal villages in the constituency, without stopping and without making any speeches. This tour of his was remembered for a long time in our district, mainly because he made it in a motorcar, and it was the first time we had seen one. The word "motorcar" itself had not yet found a place in our everyday language, and the peasants called it a "horseless carriage." Strange legends were current among the people about the invisible motive force which took the place of the horses, about the diabolical speed which the new vehicle could reach, and about the ruinous effect, particularly on the vines, of the stink it left behind it. That Sunday the entire population of the village had gone to meet the Prince on the road by which he was due to arrive. There were numerous visible signs of the collective admiration and affection for the Prince. The crowds were dressed up in their best, and were in a perfectly understandable state of excitement. The "horseless carriage" arrived late, and roared through the crowd and the village, without stopping and without even slowing down, leaving a thick white dust cloud behind it. The Prince's agents then explained, to anyone who cared to listen, that the "horseless carriage" went by "petrol vapor" and could only stop when the petrol had finished. "It isn't like horses," they explained, "where all one need do is to pull on the reins. There aren't any reins at all. Did you notice any reins?"

Two days later a strange little old man arrived from Rome; he wore glasses, and had a black stick and a small suitcase. Nobody knew him. He said he was an oculist and had put himself up as candidate against the Prince. A few people gathered round him out of curiosity, mainly children and women, who had not the right to vote. I was among the children, in my short trousers and with my schoolbooks under my arm. We begged the old man to make a speech. He said to us: "Remind your parents that the vote is secret. Nothing else." Then he said, "I am poor; I live by being an oculist; but if any of you have anything wrong with your eyes I'm willing to treat them for nothing." So we brought him an old woman who sold vegetables. She had bad eyes, and he cleaned them up and gave her a little phial with drops in it and explained how to use it. Then he said to us (we were only a group of children): "Remind your parents that the vote is secret," and he went away. But the Prince's election was so certain, to judge by the festive throngs which had welcomed him during his electioneering tour, that the authorities and the agents of the estate had announced in advance a whole program for the celebration of the inevitable victory. My father, according to the agreement with his brothers, did not side with either candidate, but managed to get himself included among the scrutineers of the ballot-papers. Great was everybody's surprise when it became known that in the secrecy of the polling booths an enormous majority had voted against the Prince and for the unknown oculist. It was a great scandal; the authorities called it sheer treachery. But the treachery was of such proportions that the agents of the estate could not take any reprisals against anyone.

After this, social life went back to normal. Nobody asked himself: Why can the will of the people only express itself sporadically? Why can it not become a permanent and stable basis for the reorganization of public life? And yet, it would be incorrect to conclude, from a false interpretation of the episode I have just recorded, that the major obstacle was fear. Our people have never been cowardly or spineless or weak. On the contrary the rigors of the climate, the heaviness of the work, the harsh conditions of the struggle for existence, have made them into one of the toughest, hardest, and most enduring peoples in the whole of Italy. So much so, that there are fewer references in our local annals to political surprises resulting from the secret vote than there are to revolts, localized and shortlived, but violent, destructive and almost savage. These humiliated and downtrodden people could endure the worst abuses without complaint, but then they would break out on unforeseen occasions. . . .

In 1915 an earthquake of exceptional violence destroyed a large part of our province and killed, in thirty seconds, about fifty thousand people. I was surprised to see how much my fellow-villagers took this appalling catastrophe as a matter of course. The geologists' complicated explanations, reported in the newspapers, aroused their contempt. In a district like ours, where so many injustices go unpunished, people regarded the recurrent earthquakes as a phenomenon requiring no further explanation. In fact, it was astonishing that earthquakes were not more frequent. An earthquake buries rich and poor, learned and illiterate, authorities and subjects alike beneath its ruined houses. Here lies, moreover, the real explanation of the Italians' well-known powers of endurance when faced with the cataclysms of nature. An earthquake achieves what the law promises but does not in practice maintain—the equality of all men. A neighbor of ours, a woman who kept a bakery, lay buried, but not hurt, for several days after the earthquake, when her house was completely destroyed. Not realizing that the disaster was general, and imagining that it was only her own house which had fallen down, either because of some defect in its construction or because someone had put a curse on it, the poor woman was greatly distressed; so much so that when a rescue party wanted to drag her out of the ruins she absolutely refused. She calmed down, however, and quickly regained her strength and her wish to live and to rebuild her house, the moment she was told there had been an earthquake and that an enormous number of other houses had collapsed as well.

What seemed to the poor people of our part of the world a much more serious calamity than any natural cataclysm was what happened *after* the earthquake. The State reconstruction program was carried out to the accompaniment of innumerable intrigues, frauds, thefts, swindles, embezzlements, and dishonesty of every kind. An acquaintance of mine, who had been sacked by one of the government departments concerned, gave me some information of this sort about certain criminal acts which were being committed by the head engineers of the department. Impressed rather than surprised, I hastened to pass on the facts to some persons in authority, whom I knew to be upright and honest, so that they could denounce the criminals. Far from denying the truth of what I told them, my honorable friends were in a position to confirm it. But, even then, they advised me not to get mixed up in it or to get worked up, in my simplicity, about things of that kind. "You're young," they said to me affectionately, "you must finish your studies, you've got your career to think of, you shouldn't compromise yourself with things that don't concern you." "Of course," I said, "it would be better for the denunciation to come from grown-up people like yourselves, people with authority, rather than from a boy of seventeen."

They were horrified. "We are not madmen," they answered. "We shall mind our own business and nobody else's."

I then talked the matter over with some reverend priests, and then with some of my more courageous relations. All of them, while admitting that they were already aware of the shameful things that were happening, begged me not to get mixed up in that hornets' nest, but to think of my studies, of my career, and of my future. "With pleasure," I replied, "but isn't one of you ready to denounce the thieves?" "We are not madmen," they replied, scandalized, "these things have nothing to do with us."

I then began to wonder seriously whether it mightn't be a good thing to organize, together with some other boys, a . . . "revolution" that would end up with a good bonfire of the corrupt engineers' offices; but I was dissuaded by the acquaintance who had given me the proof of their crooked dealings: a bonfire, he pointed out, would destroy the proofs of the crimes. He was older and more experienced than myself; he suggested I should get the denunciation printed in some newspaper. But which newspaper? "There's only one," he explained, "which could have any interest in publishing your denunciation, and that's the Socialist paper." So I set to work and wrote three articles, the first of my life, giving a detailed exposure of the corrupt behavior of State engineers in my part of the country, and sent them off to *Avanti*. The first two were printed at once and aroused much comment among the readers of the paper, but none at all among the authorities. The third article did not appear, because, as I learned later, a leading Socialist intervened with the editorial staff. This showed me that the system of deception and fraud oppressing us was much vaster than at first appeared, and that its invisible ramifications extended even into Socialism. However, the partial denunciation which had appeared unexpectedly in the press contained enough material for a number of lawsuits, or at least for a board of enquiry; but nothing happened. The engineers, whom I had denounced as thieves and bandits and against whom quite specific charges had been leveled, did not even attempt to justify themselves or to issue a general denial. There was a short period of expectancy, and then everyone went back to his own affairs.

The student who had dared to throw down the challenge was considered, by the most charitably-minded, an impulsive and strange boy. One must remember that the economic poverty of the southern provinces offers small scope for a career to the youths leaving school by the thousand every year. Our only important industry is State employment. This does not require exceptional intelligence, merely a docile disposition and a readiness to toe the line in politics. The young men of the South, who have grown up in the atmosphere I have briefly described, tend naturally, if they have a minimum of sensitiveness in human relationships, toward anarchy and rebellion. For those still on the threshold of youth, to become a civil servant means renunciation, capitulation, and the mortification of their souls. That is why people say: anarchists at twenty, conservatives at thirty. Nor is the education imparted in the schools, whether public or private, designed to strengthen character. Most of the later years of my school-life I spent in private Catholic institutions. Latin and Greek were excellently taught there; the education in private or personal habits was simple and clean; but civic instruction and training were deplorable. Our history teachers were openly critical of the official views; the mythology of the Risorgimento and its heroes (Mazzini, Garibaldi, Victor Emmanuel II, Cavour) were the objects of derision and disparagement; the literature prevalent at the time (Carducci, D'Annunzio) was despised.

Insofar as this method of teaching developed the pupils' critical spirit, it had its advantages. But the same priestly schoolmasters, since they had to prepare us for the State school examinations—and the fame and prosperity of their academies depended on the results we achieved—also taught us, and recommended us to uphold in our examinations, the points of view completely opposed to their own convictions. Meanwhile, the State examiners, who knew we came from confessional schools, enjoyed questioning us on the most controversial subjects, and then praising us ironically for the liberal and unprejudiced way in which we had been taught. The falseness, hypocrisy, and double-facedness of all this were so blatant that they could not but perturb anyone with the slightest inborn respect for culture. But it was equally inevitable that the average unfortunate student ended by considering diplomas, and his future job in a government office, as the supreme realities of life.

"People who are born in this district are really out of luck," Dr. F. J., a doctor in a village near mine, used to say. "There's no halfway house here; you've got either to rebel or become an accomplice." He rebelled. He declared himself an anarchist. He made Tolstoyan speeches to the poor. He was the scandal of the entire neighborhood, loathed by the rich, despised by the poor, and secretly pitied by a few. His post as panel-doctor was finally taken away from him, and he literally died of hunger.

I realize that the progress which I have been tracing in these pages is too summary to seem anything but strained. And if I touch on this objection now, it is not to refute it or to swear to the absolute truth of my explanations; I can guarantee their sincerity, not their objectivity. I am myself sometimes astonished to find, when I go back over that remote, almost prehistoric, period of our lives with my contemporaries, how they cannot remember at all, or only very vaguely, incidents which had a decisive influence on me; whereas on the contrary, they can clearly recall other circumstances which to me were pointless and insignificant. Are they, these contemporaries of mine, all "unconscious accomplices"? And by what destiny or virtue does one, at a certain age, make the important choice, and become "accomplice" or "rebel"? From what source do some people derive their spontaneous intolerance of injustice, even though the injustice affects only others? And that sudden feeling of guilt at sitting down to a well-laden table, when others are having to go hungry? And that pride which makes poverty and prison preferable to contempt?

I don't know. Perhaps no one knows. At a certain point, even the fullest and deepest confession becomes a mere statement of fact and not an answer. Anyone who has reflected seriously about himself or others knows how profoundly secret are certain decisions, how mysterious and unaccountable certain vocations.

There was a point in my rebellion where hatred and love coincided; both the facts which justified my indignation and the moral motives which demanded it stemmed directly from the district where I was born. This explains, too, why everything I have happened to write up to now, and probably everything I shall ever write, although I have traveled and lived abroad, is concerned solely with this same district, or more precisely with the part of it which can be seen from the house where I was born—not more than thirty or forty kilometers on one side or the other. It is a district, like the rest of the Abruzzi, poor in secular history, and almost entirely Christian and medieval in its formation. The only buildings worthy of note are churches and monasteries. Its only illustrious sons for many centuries have been saints and stone-carvers. The conditions of human existence have always been particularly difficult there; pain has always been accepted there as first among the laws of nature, and the Cross welcomed and honored because of it. Franciscanism and anarchy have always been the two most accessible forms of rebellion for lively spirits in our part of the world. The ashes of skepticism have never suffocated, in the hearts of those who suffered most, the ancient hope of the Kingdom of God on earth, the old expectation of charity taking the place of law, the old dream of Gioacchino da Fiore, of the "Spirituali," of the Celestimisto.[1] And this is a fact of enormous fundamental importance; in a disappointed, arid, exhausted, weary country such as ours, it constitutes real riches, it is a miraculous reserve. The politicians are unaware of its existence, the clergy are afraid of it; only the saints, perhaps, know where to find it. What for us has always been much more difficult, if not impossible, has been to discern the ways and means to a political revolution, *hic et nunc,*[2] to the creation of a free and ordered society.

I thought I had reached this discovery, when I moved to the town and made my first contact with the workers' movement. It was a kind of flight, a safety exit from unbearable solitude, the sighting of *terra firma,* the discovery of a new continent. But it was not easy to reconcile a spirit in moral mutiny against an unacceptable long-established social reality with the "scientific" demands of a minutely codified political doctrine.

For me to join the Party of Proletarian Revolution was not just a simple

[1] Followers of Pope Celestine V, an Abruzzi hermit who, elected Pope in August, 1294, abdicated three and a half months later. He was canonized in 1313.

[2] [*Here and now.*]

matter of signing up with a political organization; it meant a conversion, a complete dedication. Those were still the days when to declare oneself a Socialist or a Communist was equivalent to throwing oneself to the winds, and meant breaking with one's parents and not finding a job. If the material consequences were harsh and hard, the difficulties of spiritual adaptation were no less painful. My own internal world, the "Middle Ages," which I had inherited and which were rooted in my soul, and from which, in the last analysis, I had derived my initial aspiration to revolt, were shaken to their foundations, as though by an earthquake. Everything was thrown into the melting-pot, everything became a problem. Life, death, love, good, evil, truth, all changed their meaning or lost it altogether. It is easy enough to court danger when one is no longer alone; but who can describe the dismay of once and for all renouncing one's faith in the individual immortality of the soul? It was too serious for me to be able to discuss it with anyone; my Party comrades would have found it a subject for mockery, and I no longer had any other friends. So, unknown to anyone, the whole world took on a different aspect. How men are to be pitied!

The conditions of life imposed on the Communists by the Fascist conquest of the State were very hard. But they also served to confirm some of the Communists' political theses, and provided an opportunity to create a type of organization which was in no way incompatible with the Communist mentality. So I too had to adapt myself, for a number of years, to living like a foreigner in my own country. One had to change one's name, abandon every former link with family and friends, and live a false life to remove any suspicion of conspiratorial activity. The Party became family, school, church, barracks; the world that lay beyond it was to be destroyed and built anew. The psychological mechanism whereby each single militant becomes progressively identified with the collective organization is the same as that used in certain religious orders and military colleges, with almost identical results. Every sacrifice was welcomed as a personal contribution to the "price of collective redemption"; and it should be emphasized that the links which bound us to the Party grew steadily firmer, not in spite of the dangers and sacrifices involved, but because of them. This explains the attraction exercised by Communism on certain categories of young men and of women, on intellectuals, and on the highly sensitive and generous people who suffer most from the wastefulness of bourgeois society. Anyone who thinks he can wean the best and most serious-minded young people away from Communism by enticing them into a well-warmed hall to play billiards, starts from an extremely limited and unintelligent conception of mankind.

It is not surprising that the first internal crises which shook the Communist International left me more or less indifferent. These crises originated from the fact that the main parties which had adhered to the new International, even after the formal acceptance of the twenty-one conditions laid down by Lenin to govern admission, were far from homogeneous. They had in common a hatred of imperialist war and of its results; they united in criticizing the reformist ideas of the Second International; but, as to the rest, for good or ill, each reflected its own country's unequal degree of historical development. That is why there were notable differences of opinion between Russian Bolshevism, formed in an atmosphere in which political liberty and a differentiated social structure were both alien concepts, and the Left-Wing Socialist groups of the Western countries. The history of the Communist International was therefore a history of schisms, a history of intrigues and of arrogance on the part of the directing Russian group toward every independent expression of opinion by the other affiliated parties. One after another, they were forced to break with the Communist International: the currents most attached to democratic and parliamentary forms (Frossard), the groups most attached to legality and most opposed to attempts at *coups d'état* (Paul Levi), the libertarian elements who deluded themselves about Soviet Democracy (Roland-Holst), the revolutionary trade-unionists who opposed the bureaucratic submission of the trade unions to the Communist Party (Pierre Monatte, Andres Nin), the groups most reluctant to break off all collaboration with Social Democracy (Brandier, Bringolf, Tasca), and the extreme Left Wing which was intolerant of any opportunist move (Bordiga, Ruth Fischer, Boris Souvarine).

These internal crises took place in a sphere far removed from my own and so I was not involved. I do not say this boastfully; on the contrary, I am merely trying to explain the situation. The increasing degeneration of the Communist International into a tyranny and a bureaucracy filled me with repulsion and disgust, but there were some compelling reasons which made me hesitate to break with it: solidarity with comrades who were dead or in prison, the nonexistence at that time of any other organized anti-Fascist force in Italy, the rapid political, and in some cases also moral, degeneration of many who had already left Communism, and finally the illusion that the International might be made healthy again by the proletariat of the West, in the event of some crisis occurring within the Soviet regime.

Between 1921 and 1927, I had repeated occasion to go to Moscow and take part, as a member of Italian Communist delegations, in a number of congresses and meetings of the Executive. What struck me most about the Russian Communists, even in such really exceptional personalities as Lenin and Trotsky, was their utter incapacity to be fair in discussing opinions that conflicted with their own. The adversary, simply for daring to contradict, at once became a traitor, an opportunist, a hireling. *An adversary in good faith* is inconceivable to the Russian Communists. What an aberration of conscience this is, for so-called materialists and rationalists absolutely in their polemics to uphold the primacy of morals over intelligence! To find a comparable infatuation one has to go back to the Inquisition.

Just as I was leaving Moscow, in 1922, Alexandra Kollontaj said to me: "If you happen to read in the papers that Lenin has had me arrested for stealing the silver spoons in the Kremlin, that simply means that I'm not entirely in agreement with him about some little problem of agricultural or industrial policy." Kollontaj had acquired her sense of irony in the West and so only used it with people from the West. But even then, in those feverish years of building the new regime, when the new orthodoxy had not yet taken complete possession of cultural life, how difficult it was to reach an understanding with a Russian Communist on the simplest, and for us most obvious, questions; how difficult, I don't say to agree, but at least to understand each other, when talking of what liberty means for a man of the West, even for a worker. I spent hours one day trying to explain to one of the directors of the State publishing house, why she ought at least to be ashamed of the atmosphere of discouragement and intimidation in which Soviet writers lived. She could not understand what I was trying to tell her.

"Liberty"—I had to give examples—"is the possibility of doubting, the possibility of making a mistake, the possibility of searching and experimenting, the possibility of saying 'no' to any authority—literary, artistic, philosophic, religious, social, and even political." "But that," murmured this eminent functionary of Soviet culture in horror, "that is counter-revolution." Then she added, to get a little of her own back, "We're glad we haven't got your liberty, but we've got the sanatoria in exchange." When I observed that the expression "in exchange" had no meaning, "liberty not being merchandise that could be exchanged," and that I had seen sanatoria in other countries, she laughed in my face. "You're in the mood for joking with me today," she said to me. And I was so taken aback by her candor that I no longer dared to contradict her.

The spectacle of the enthusiasm of Russian youth in those first years of the creation of a new world, which we all hoped would be more humane than the old one, was utterly convincing. And what a bitter disillusionment it was, as the years went by and the new regime strengthened itself and its economic system got into shape and the armed attacks from abroad ceased, to see the long-promised ultimate democratization failing to come, and, instead, the dictatorship accentuating its repressive character.

One of my best friends, the head of the Russian Communist Youth, Lazar Schatzky, one evening confided to me how sad he was to have been born too late, and not to have taken part either in the 1905 or the 1917 Revolutions. "But there'll still be revolutions," I said to console him, "there'll always be need of revolutions, even in Russia." We were in the Red Square, not far from the tomb of Lenin. "What kind?" he wanted to know. "And how long have we got to wait?" Then I pointed to the tomb, which was still made of wood at that time, and before which we used every day to see an interminable procession of poor ragged peasants slowly filing.

"I presume you love Lenin," I said to him. "I knew him too and have a very vivid recollection of him. You must admit with me that this superstitious cult of his mummy is an insult to his memory and a disgrace to a revolutionary city like Moscow." I suggested to him, in short, that we should get hold of a tin or two of petrol and make a "little revolution" on our own, by burning the totem-hut. I did not, to be frank, expect him to accept my proposal there and then, but at least I thought he would laugh about it; instead of which my poor friend went very pale and began to tremble violently. Then he begged me not to say dreadful things of that kind, either to him or still less to others. (Ten years later, when he was being searched for as an accomplice of Zinoviev, he committed suicide by throwing himself from the fifth floor of the house he lived in.) I have been present at the march post of immense parades of people and armies in the Red Square, but, in my mind, the recollection of that young friend's emotion and of his frightened and affectionate voice, has remained stronger than any other image. It may be that that memory is "objectively" more important.

It is not easy to trace the history of the Communist International, and it would be undoubtedly premature. How can one separate the fatuous from the essential in the interminable discussions at its congresses and meetings? What speeches should be left to the mice in the archives to criticize, and which should be recommended to intelligent people anxious to understand? I do not know. What my memory prefers to recall may to some people seem only bizarre. They were discussing one day, in a special commission of the Executive, the ultimatum issued by the central committee of the British trade unions, ordering its local branches not to support the Communist-led minority movement on pain of expulsion. After the representative of the English Communist Party had explained the serious disadvantages of both solutions—because one meant the liquidation of the minority movement and the other the exit of the minority from the Trades Unions—the Russian delegate Piatnisky put forward a suggestion which seemed as obvious to him as Columbus' egg. "The branches," he suggested, "should declare that they submit to the discipline demanded, and then, in practice, should do exactly the contrary." The English Communist interrupted, "But that would be a lie." Loud laughter greeted this ingenuous objection, frank, cordial, interminable laughter, the like of which the gloomy offices of the Communist International had perhaps never heard before. The joke quickly spread all over Moscow, for the Englishman's entertaining and incredible reply was telephoned at once to Stalin and to the most important offices of State, provoking new waves of mirth everywhere. The general hilarity gave the English Communist's timid, ingenuous objection its true meaning. And that is why, in my memory, the storm of laughter aroused by that short, almost childishly simple little expression—"But that would be a lie"—outweighs all the long heavy oppressive speeches I heard during sittings of the Communist International, and has become a kind of symbol for me.

My visits to Moscow, as I have already said, were few, and limited to my functions as a member of the Italian Communist delegations. I have never been part of the organization of the Communist International, but I could follow its rapid corruption by observing a few acquaintances of mine who belonged to it. Among them, an outstanding example was the Frenchman Jacques Doriot. I had met him for the first time in Moscow in 1921; he was then a modest, willing and sentimental young working-man, and it was for his obvious docility and easy-going nature that he was chosen for the international organization in preference to other young French Communists, who were more intelligent and better educated than himself, but also less conventional. He lived up fully to expectation. Year by year, he became an increasingly important figure in the hierarchy of International Communism, and, year by year, each time I came across him, I found him changed for the worse, skeptical, cynical, unscrupulous, and rapidly becoming Fascist in his political attitude toward men and the State. If I could triumph over my natural repugnance and write a biography of Jacques Doriot, my theme would be: "Militant Communist into Fascist."

Once I met Doriot in Moscow, just after his return from a political mission in China. He gave a few friends and myself a disturbing account of the mistakes of the Communist International in the Far East. The next day, however, speaking before the Executive in full session, he affirmed the exact opposite. "It was an act of political wisdom," he confided to me after the meeting with a slight and superior smile. His case is worth mentioning because it was not isolated. Internal changes in French Communism later led Jacques Doriot to leave the Communist International, and gave him a chance to show himself openly in what had already been, for a long time, his true colors; but many others, who basically are no different from Doriot, have remained at the head of Communist Parties. Palmiro Togliatti, the Italian, referred to this phenomenon of duplicity and demoralization among the personnel of the Communist International in his speech before its Sixth Congress, and asked permission to repeat the words of the dying Goethe: "Light, more light."

In a certain sense, that speech was Togliatti's swan-song; for another year or two he kept up the effort to follow his inmost promptings and to reconcile being a Communist with speaking his mind frankly, but, in the end, even he had to capitulate and submit.

Besides internal differences resulting from its own heterogeneous composition, the Communist International felt the repercussions of every difficulty of the Soviet State. After Lenin's death, it was clear that the Soviet State could not avoid what seems to be the destiny of every dictatorship: the gradual and inexorable narrowing of its political pyramid. The Russian Communist Party, which had suppressed all rival parties and abolished any possibility of general political discussion in the Soviet assemblies, itself suffered a similar fate, and its members' political views were rapidly ousted by the policy of the Party machine. From that moment, every difference of opinion in the controlling body was destined to end in the physical extinction of the minority. The Revolution, which had extinguished its enemies, began to devour its favorite sons. The thirsty gods gave no more truce.

In May, 1927, as a representative of the Italian Communist Party, I took part with Togliatti in an extraordinary session of the enlarged Executive of the Communist International. Togliatti had come from Paris, where he was running the political secretariat of the Party, and I from Italy, where I was in charge of the underground organization. We met in Berlin and went on to Moscow together. The meeting—ostensibly summoned for an urgent discussion of what direction should be given to the Communist Parties in the struggle "against the imminent imperialist war"—was actually designed to begin the "liquidation" of Trotsky and Zinoviev, who were still members of the International Executive. As usual, to avoid surprises, the full session had been preceded and every detail prepared by the so-called Senior-convent, consisting of the heads of the most important delegations. Togliatti, on that occasion, insisted that I should accompany him to these restricted sittings.

According to the rules, only he had a right to attend on behalf of the Italian delegation; but, rightly foreseeing what complications were about to arise, he preferred to have the support of the representative of the clandestine organization. At the first sitting which we attended, I had the impression that we had arrived too late. We were in a small office in the Communist International Headquarters. The German Thälmann was presiding, and immediately began reading out a proposed resolution against Trotsky, to be presented at the full session. This resolution condemned, in the most violent terms, a document which Trotsky had addressed to the Political Office of the Russian Communist Party. The Russian delegation at that day's session of the Senior-convent was an exceptional one: Stalin, Rikov, Bukharin and Manuilsky. At the end of the reading Thälmann asked if we were in agreement with the proposed resolution. The Finn Ottomar Kuusinen found that it was not strong enough. "It should be said openly," he suggested, "that the document sent by Trotsky to the Political Office of the Russian Communist Party is of an entirely counter-revolutionary character and constitutes clear proof that the man who wrote it no longer has anything in common with the working class." As no one else asked to speak, after consulting Togliatti, I made my apologies for having arrived late and so not having been able to see the document which was to be condemned. "To tell the truth," Thälmann declared candidly, "we haven't seen the document either."

Preferring not to believe my ears, I repeated my objection in other words: "It may very well be true," I said, "that Trotsky's document should be condemned, but obviously I cannot condemn it before I've read it."

"Neither have we," repeated Thälmann, "neither have the majority of the delegates present here, except for the Russians, read the document." Thälmann spoke in German and his words were translated into Russian for Stalin, and into French for two or three of us. The reply given to me was so incredible that I rounded on the translator. "It's impossible," I said, "that Thälmann should have said that. I must ask you to repeat his answer word for word."

At this point Stalin intervened. He was standing over at one side of the room, and seemed the only person present who was calm and unruffled.

"The Political Office of the Party," said Stalin, "has considered that it would not be expedient to translate and distribute Trotsky's document to the delegates of the International Executive, because there are various allusions in it to the policy of the Soviet State." (The mysterious document was later published abroad by Trotsky himself, in a booklet entitled *Problems of the Chinese Revolution,* and as anyone can today still see for himself, it contains no mention of the policy of the Soviet State, but a closely reasoned attack on the policy practiced in China by Stalin and the Communist International. In a speech of April 15, 1927, in the presence of the Moscow Soviets, Stalin had sung the praises of Chiang Kai-shek, and confirmed his personal confidence in the Kuomintang; this was barely a week before the famous anti-Communist *volte face* of the Chinese Nationalist leader and of his party; the Communists were expelled from the Kuomintang overnight, tens of thousands of workers were massacred in Shanghai and, a month later, in Wuhan. It was natural therefore that Stalin should have been anxious to avoid a debate on these matters, seeking to protect himself behind a screen of *raison d'état.*)

Ernst Thälmann asked me if I were satisfied with Stalin's explanation. "I do not contest the right of the Political Office of the Russian Communist Party to keep any document secret," I said. "But I do not understand how others can be asked to condemn an unknown document." At this, indignation against myself and Togliatti, who appeared to agree with what I had said, knew no bounds; it was especially violent on the part of the Finn, whom I have already mentioned, a Bulgarian and one or two Hungarians.

"It's unheard-of," cried Kuusinen, very red in the face, "that we still have such petty bourgeois in the fortress of the World Revolution." He pronounced the words petty bourgeois with an extremely comical expression of contempt and disgust. The only person who remained calm and imperturbable was Stalin. He said, "If a single delegate is against the proposed resolution, it should not be presented." Then he added, "Perhaps our Italian comrades are not fully aware of our internal situation. I propose that the sitting be suspended until tomorrow and that one of those present should be assigned the task of spending the evening with our Italian comrades and explaining our internal situation to them." The Bulgarian Vasil Kolarov was given this ungrateful task.

He carried it out with tact and good humor. He invited us to have a glass of tea that evening in his room at the Hotel Lux. And he faced up to the thorny subject without much preamble. "Let's be frank," he said to us with a smile. "Do you think I've read that document? No, I haven't. To tell you the whole truth, I can add that that document doesn't even interest me. Shall I go further? Even if Trotsky sent me a copy here, secretly, I'd refuse to read it. My dear Italian friends, this isn't a question of documents. I know that Italy is the classic country of academies, but we aren't in an academy here. Here we are in the thick of a struggle for power between two rival groups of the Russian Central Directorate. Which of the two groups do we want to line up with? That's the point. Documents don't come into it. It's not a question of finding the historic truth about an unsuccessful Chinese revolution. It's a question of a struggle for power between two hostile, irreconcilable groups. One's got to choose. I, for my part, have already chosen, I'm for the majority group. Whatever the minority says or does, whatever document it draws up against the majority, I repeat to you that I'm for the majority. Documents don't interest me. We aren't in an academy here." He refilled our glasses with tea and scrutinized us with the air of a schoolmaster obliged to deal with two unruly youngsters. "Do I make myself clear?" he asked, addressing me specifically.

"Certainly," I replied, "very clear indeed." "Have I persuaded you?" he asked again. "No," I said. "And why not?" he wanted to know. "I should have to explain to you," I said, "why I'm against Fascism." Kolarov pretended to be indignant, while Togliatti expressed his opinion in more moderate, but no less succinct, terms. "One can't just declare oneself for the majority or for the minority in advance," he said. "One can't ignore the political basis of the question."

Kolarov listened to us with a benevolent smile of pity. "You're still too young," he explained, as he accompanied us to the door. "You haven't yet understood what politics are all about."

Next morning, in the Senior-convent, the scene of the day before was repeated. An unusual atmosphere of nervousness pervaded the little room into which a dozen of us were packed. "Have you explained the situation to our Italian comrades?" Stalin asked Kolarov. "Fully," the Bulgarian assured him. "If a single delegate," Stalin repeated, "is against the proposed resolution, it cannot be presented in the full session. A resolution against Trotsky can only be taken unanimously. Are our Italian comrades," he added turning to us, "favorable to the proposed resolution?"

After consulting Togliatti, I declared: "Before taking the resolution into consideration, we must see the document concerned." The Frenchman Albert Treint and the Swiss Jules Humbert-Droz made identical declarations. (Both of them, a few years later, also ended outside the Communist International.)

"The proposed resolution is withdrawn," said Stalin. After which, we had the same hysterical scene as the day before, with the indignant, angry protests of Kuusinen, Rakosi, Pepper and the others. Thälmann argued from our "scandalous" attitude that the whole trend of our anti-Fascist activity in Italy was most probably wrong, and that if Fascism was still so firmly entrenched in Italy it must be our fault. He asked because of this that the policy of the Italian Communist Party should be subjected to a thorough sifting.

This was done; and as a reprisal for our "impertinent" conduct those fanatical censors discovered that the fundamental guiding lines of our activity, traced in the course of the previous years by Antonio Gramoci, were seriously contaminated by a petty-bourgeois spirit. Togliatti decided that it would be prudent for us both to address a letter to the Political Office of the Russian Communist Party explaining the reason for our attitude at that meeting of the Executive. No Communist, the letter said in effect, would presume to question the historical pre-eminence of our Russian comrades in the leadership of the International; but this pre-eminence imposed special duties on our Russian comrades; they could not apply the rights it gave them in a mechanical and authoritarian way. The letter was received by Bukharin, who sent for us at once and advised us to withdraw it so as not to worsen our already appalling political situation.

Days of somber discouragement followed for me. I asked myself: Have we sunk to this? Those who are dead, those who are dying in prison, have sacrificed themselves for this? The vagabond, lonely, perilous lives that we ourselves are leading, strangers in our own countries—is it all for this? My depression soon reached that extreme stage when the will is paralyzed and physical resistance suddenly gives way.

Before I left Moscow an Italian working-man came to see me. He had been a refugee in Russia for some years to avoid the long term of imprisonment to which a Fascist tribunal had sentenced him. (He is still, I believe, a Communist today.) He came to complain of the humiliating conditions of the workers in the Moscow factory to which he was attached. He was ready to put up with the material shortages of every kind, since to remedy them was clearly beyond the power of individuals, but he could not understand why the workmen were entirely at the mercy of the factory directorate and had no effective organization to protect their interests; why, in this respect also, they should be much worse off than in capitalist countries. Most of the much-vaunted rights of the working class were purely theoretical.

In Berlin, on my way back, I read in the paper that the Executive of the Communist International had severely rebuked Trotsky for a document he had prepared about recent events in China. I went to the offices of the German Communist Party and asked Thälmann for an explanation. "This is untrue," I said to him sharply.

But he explained that the statutes of the International authorized the Presidium, in case of urgency, to adopt any resolution in the name of the Executive. During the few days I had to stay in Berlin, while waiting for my false documents to be put in order, I read in the papers that the American,

Hungarian and Czechoslovakian Communist Parties had energetically deplored Trotsky's letter. "Has the mysterious document finally been produced, then?" "No," he answered me. "But I hope the example set by the American, Hungarian and Czechoslovakian Communists has shown you what Communist discipline means." These things were said with no hint of irony, but indeed with dismal seriousness that befitted the nightmare reality to which they referred.

For reasons of health I had to go straight into a Swiss sanatorium, and all political decisions were suspended. One day, in a village not far from where I was taking my cure, I had a meeting with Togliatti. He explained to me at great length, clearly and frankly, the reasons for the line of conduct he had chosen. The present state of the International, he said in brief, was certainly neither satisfactory nor agreeable. But all our good intentions were powerless to change it; objective historical conditions were involved and must be taken into account. The forms of the Proletarian Revolution were not arbitrary. If they did not accord with our preferences, so much the worse for us. And besides, what alternative remained? Other Communists who had broken with the Party, how had they ended up? Consider, he said, the appalling condition of Social Democracy.

My objections to these arguments were not very coherent, mainly because Togliatti's arguments were purely political, whereas the agitation which my recent experiences had aroused in me went far beyond politics. These "inexcusable historical forms" to which we must bow down—what were they but a new version of the inhuman reality against which, in declaring ourselves Socialists, we had rebelled? I felt at that time like someone who has had a tremendous blow on the head and keeps on his feet, walking, talking and gesticulating, but without fully realizing what has happened.

Realization came, however, slowly and with difficulty during the course of the succeeding years. And to this day I go on thinking it over, trying to understand better. If I have written books, it has been to try and understand and to make others understand. I am not at all certain that I have reached the end of my efforts. The truth is this: the day I left the Communist Party was a very sad one for me, it was like a day of deep mourning, the mourning for my lost youth. And I come from a district where mourning is worn longer than elsewhere. It is not easy to free oneself from an experience as intense as that of the underground organization of the Communist Party. Something of it remains and leaves a mark on the character which lasts all one's life. One can, in fact, notice how recognizable the ex-Communists are. They constitute a category apart, like ex-priests and ex-regular officers. The number of ex-

Communists is legion today. "The final struggle," I said jokingly to Togliatti recently, "will be between the Communists and the ex-Communists."

However, I carefully avoided, after I had left the Communist Party, ending up in one of the many groups and splinter-groups of ex-Communists; and I have never regretted this in any way, as I know well the kind of fate which rules over these groups and splinter-groups, and makes little sects of them which have all the defects of official Communism—the fanaticism, the centralization, the abstraction—without the qualities and advantages which the latter derives from its vast working-class following. The logic of opposition at all costs has carried many ex-Communists far from their starting-points, in some cases as far as Fascism.

Consideration of the experience I have been through has led me to a deepening of the motives for my separation which go very much further than the circumstantial ones by which it was produced. But my faith in Socialism (to which I think I can say my entire life bears testimony) has remained more alive than ever in me. In its essence, it has gone back to what it was when I first revolted against the old social order; a refusal to admit the existence of destiny, an extension of the ethical impulse from the restricted individual and family sphere to the whole domain of human activity, a need for effective brotherhood, an affirmation of the superiority of the human person over all the economic and social mechanisms which oppress him. As the years have gone by, there has been added to this an intuition of man's dignity and a feeling of reverence for that which in man is always trying to outdistance itself, and lies at the root of his eternal disquiet. But I do not think that this kind of Socialism is in any way peculiar to me. The "mad truths" recorded above are older than Marxism; toward the second half of the last century they took refuge in the workers' movement born of industrial capitalism, and continue to remain one of its most enduring founts of inspiration. I have repeatedly expressed my opinion on the relations between the Socialist Movement and the theories of Socialism; these relations are by no means rigid or immutable. With the development of new studies, the theories may go out of fashion or be discarded, but the movement goes on. It would be inaccurate, however, with regard to the old quarrel between the doctrinaires and the empiricists of the workers' movement, to include me among the latter. I do not conceive Socialist policy as tied to any particular theory, but to a faith. The more Socialist theories claim to be "scientific," the more transitory they are; but Socialist values are permanent. The distinction between theories and values is not sufficiently recognized, but it is fundamental. On a group of theories one can found a school; but on a group of values one can found a culture, a civilization, a new way of living together among men.

CZESLAW MILOSZ

IN THE DECADES between World Wars, there was an element of choice for those who considered affiliation with the Communist movement in Western Europe and America. Such intellectuals as Silone were impelled rather than compelled to join the Party. Moreover, when they decided to leave the Party, although certain psychological hazards were involved in their decision, once it had been made it was capable of execution. The situation is quite different for those who have found themselves, since World War II, in East European countries dominated by the Soviet Union. Yet it would be a mistake to think that the adherents, especially the intellectuals—writers, artists, and scholars—of the various "Communist" parties of the satellite countries have declared their conversion to "dialectical materialism" (Russian style), simply to avoid physical punishment or to gain the preferential treatment which Communist regimes generally make available to the loyal intelligentsia. As the following selection, taken from *The Captive Mind* (English translation by Jane Zielonko, 1953) by Czeslaw Milosz attempts to demonstrate, the reasons for, and consequences of, a declaration of allegiance to "Stalinism" involve many complex social, moral, and psychological factors. Soviet rule is not merely a tyranny of brute force over unwilling victims. It seeks also to bend the will and the mind into attitudes, not of resignation and submission, but of positive acceptance.

Czeslaw Milosz, one of the best known modern Polish poets, was born in Lithuania of Polish parents in 1911. Educated in Polish and French universities, Milosz spent the years immediately prior to World War II in the employ of the Polish State Broadcasting Company. Upon the occupation of Poland by the Nazis in 1939, he became active in the Warsaw underground resistance, fighting, editing clandestine publications, and writing poetry. In 1946 Milosz entered the diplomatic service of the new, and at that time still moderate, post-war Polish government. He served as a cultural attaché of the Polish Embassy, first in Washington and later in Paris. Becoming increasingly discontented with the reduction of Poland to a position of mere satellite to the Soviet Union and with the overt domination of its government by Russian-trained Communists, Milosz finally broke with the Warsaw authorities in 1951. Since then he has lived as a political refugee in Paris.

THE CAPTIVE MIND

The Pill of Murti-Bing

. . . A curious book appeared in Warsaw in 1932. It was a novel, in two volumes, entitled *Insatiability*. Its author was Stanislaw Ignacy Witkiewicz, a painter, writer, and philosopher, who had constructed a philosophical system akin to the monadology of Leibnitz. As in his earlier novel, *Farewell to Autumn,* his language was difficult, full of neologisms. Brutal descriptions of erotic scenes alternated with whole pages of discussions on Husserl, Carnap, and other contemporary philosophers. Besides, one could not always tell whether the author was serious or joking; and the subject matter seemed to be pure fantasy.

The action of the book took place in Europe, more precisely in Poland, at some time in the near future or even in the present, that is, in the thirties, forties, or fifties. The social group it portrayed was that of musicians, painters, philosophers, aristocrats, and higher-ranking military officers. The whole book was nothing but a study of decay: mad, dissonant music, erotic perversion; widespread use of narcotics; dispossessed thinking; false conversions to Catholicism; and complex psychopathic personalities. This decadence reigned at a time when western civilization was said to be threatened by an army from the East, a Sino-Mongolian army that dominated all the territory stretching from the Pacific to the Baltic.

Witkiewicz's heroes are unhappy in that they have no faith and no sense of meaning in their work. This atmosphere of decay and senselessness extends throughout the entire country. And at that moment, a great number of hawkers appear in the cities peddling Murti-Bing pills. Murti-Bing was a Mongolian philosopher who had succeeded in producing an organic means of transporting a philosophy of life. This Murti-Bing "philosophy of life," which constituted the strength of the Sino-Mongolian army, was contained in pills in an extremely condensed form. A man who used these pills changed completely. He became serene and happy. The problems he had struggled with until then suddenly appeared to be superficial and unimportant. He smiled indulgently at those who continued to worry about them. Most affected were all questions pertaining to unsolvable ontological difficulties. A man who swallowed Murti-Bing pills became impervious to any metaphysical

---

This selection has been reprinted from *The Captive Mind* by Czeslaw Milosz, by permission of Alfred A. Knopf, Inc., New York, Copyright 1951, 1953 by Czeslaw Milosz (pp. 3–9, 11–15, 16–18, 20, 22–24, 197–204, 207–215, 218–222).

concerns. The excesses into which art falls when people vainly seek in form the wherewithal to appease their spiritual hunger were but outmoded stupidities for him. He no longer considered the approach of the Sino-Mongolian army as a tragedy for his own civilization. He lived in the midst of his compatriots like a healthy individual surrounded by madmen. More and more people took the Murti-Bing cure, and their resultant calm contrasted sharply with the nervousness of their environment.

The epilogue, in a few words: the outbreak of the war led to a meeting of the armies of the West with those of the East. In the decisive moment, just before the great battle, the leader of the Western army surrendered to the enemy; and in exchange, though with the greatest honors, he was beheaded. The Eastern army occupied the country and the new life, that of Murti-Bingism, began. The heroes of the novel, once tormented by philosophical "insatiety," now entered the service of the new society. Instead of writing the dissonant music of former days, they composed marches and odes. Instead of painting abstractions as before, they turned out socially useful pictures. But since they could not rid themselves completely of their former personalities, they became schizophrenics.

So much for the novel. Its author often expressed his belief that religion, philosophy, and art are living out their last days. Yet he found life without them worthless. On September 17, 1939, learning that the Red Army had crossed the eastern border of Poland, he committed suicide by taking veronal and cutting his wrists.

Today, Witkiewicz's vision is being fulfilled in the minutest detail throughout a large part of the European continent. Perhaps sunlight, the smell of the earth, little everyday pleasures, and the forgetfulness that work brings can ease somewhat the tensions created by this process of fulfillment. But beneath the activity and bustle of daily life is the constant awareness of an irrevocable choice to be made. One must either die (physically or spiritually), or else one must be reborn according to a prescribed method, namely, the taking of Murti-Bing pills. People in the West are often inclined to consider the lot of converted countries in terms of might and coercion. That is wrong. There is an internal longing for harmony and happiness that lies deeper than ordinary fear or the desire to escape misery or physical destruction. The fate of completely consistent, non-dialectical people like Witkiewicz is a warning for many an intellectual. All about him, in the city streets, he sees the frightening shadows of internal exiles, irreconcilable, non-participating, eroded by hatred.

In order to understand the situation of a writer in a people's democracy, one must seek the reasons for his activity and ask how he maintains his equilibrium. Whatever one may say, the New Faith affords great possibilities for an active and positive life. And Murti-Bing is more tempting to an intellectual than to a peasant or laborer. For the intellectual, the New Faith is a candle that he circles like a moth. In the end, he throws himself into the flame for the glory of mankind. We must not treat this desire for self-immolation lightly. Blood flowed freely in Europe during the religious wars, and he who joins the New Faith today is paying off a debt to that European tradition. We are concerned here with questions more significant than mere force. . . .

THE VOID

The society portrayed by Witkiewicz is distinguished by the fact that in it religion has ceased to exist as a force. And it is true that religion long ago lost its hold on men's minds not only in the people's democracies, but elsewhere as well. As long as a society's best minds were occupied by theological questions, it was possible to speak of a given religion as the way of thinking of the whole social organism. All the matters which most actively concerned the people were referred to it and discussed in its terms. But that belongs to a dying era. We have come by easy stages to a lack of a common system of thought that could unite the peasant cutting his hay, the student poring over formal logic, and the mechanic working in an automobile factory. Out of this lack arises the painful sense of detachment or abstraction that oppresses the "creators of culture." . . .

To belong to the masses is the great longing of the "alienated" intellectual. It is such a powerful longing that, in trying to appease it, a great many of them who once looked to Germany or Italy for inspiration have now become converted to the New Faith. Actually, the rightist totalitarian program was exceptionally poor. The only gratification it offered came from collective *warmth:* crowds, red faces, mouths open in a shout, marches, arms brandishing sticks; but little rational satisfaction. Neither racist doctrines, nor hatred of foreigners, nor the glorification of one's own national traditions could efface the feeling that the entire program was improvised to deal with problems of the moment. But Murti-Bing is different. It lays scientific foundations. At the same time, it scraps all vestiges of the past. Post-Kantian philosophy, fallen into disrepute because of its remoteness from the life of men; art designed for those who, having no religion, dare not admit that to seek the "absolute" through a juxtaposition of colors and sounds is cowardly and inconclusive thinking; and the semi-magic, semi-religious mentality of the peasants—these are replaced by a *single* system, a single language of ideas. The truck driver and elevator operator employed by a publishing firm now read the same Marxist classics as its director or staff writers. A day laborer and a historian can reach an understanding on this basis of common reading. Obviously, the difference that may exist between them in mental level is no smaller than that which separated a theologian from a village blacksmith in the middle ages.

But the fundamental principles are universal; the great spiritual schism has been obliterated. Dialectical materialism has united everyone, and philosophy (i.e., dialectics) once more determines the patterns of life. It is beginning to be regarded with a respect one reserves only for a force on which important things depend: bread and milk for one's children, one's own happiness and safety. The intellectual has once more become *useful.* He who may once have done his thinking and writing in his free moments away from a paying job in a bank or post office, has now found his rightful place on earth. He has been restored to society, whereas the businessmen, aristocrats, and tradespeople who once considered him a harmless blunderer have now been dispossessed. They are indeed delighted to find work as cloakroom attendants and to hold the coat of a former employee of whom they said, in pre-war days, "It seems he writes." We must not oversimplify, however, the gratifications of personal ambition; they are merely the outward and visible signs of social usefulness, symbols of a recognition that strengthens the intellectual's feeling of *belonging.* . . .

NECESSITY

. . . We are not concerned with the question of how one finds the courage to oppose the majority. Instead we are concerned with a much more poignant question: can one write well outside that one real stream whose vitality springs from its harmony with historical laws and the dynamics of reality? Rilke's poems may be very good, but if they are, that means there must have been some reason for them in his day. Contemplative poems, such as his, could never appear in a people's democracy, not only because it would be difficult to publish them, but because the writer's impulse to write them would be destroyed at its very root. The objective conditions for such poetry have disappeared, and the intellectual of whom I speak is not one who believes in writing for the bureau drawer. He curses and despairs over the censorship and demands of the publishing trusts. Yet at the same time, he is profoundly suspicious of unlicensed literature. The publishing license he himself receives does not mean that the editor appreciates the artistic merits of his book, nor that he expects it to be popular with the public. That license is simply a sign that its author reflects the transformation of reality with scientific exactness. Dialectical materialism in the Stalinist version both reflects and directs this transformation. It creates social and political conditions in which a man ceases to think and write otherwise than as necessary. He accepts this "must" because nothing worth while can exist outside its limits. Herein lie the claws of dialectics. The writer does not surrender to this "must" merely because he fears for his own skin. He fears for something much more precious—the significance of his work. He believes that the by-ways of "philosophizing" lead to a greater or lesser degree of graphomania. Anyone gripped in the claws of dialectics is forced to admit that the thinking of private philosophers, unsupported by citations from authorities, is sheer nonsense. If this is so, then one's total effort must be directed toward following the line, and there is no point at which one can stop.

The pressure of the state machine is nothing compared with the pressure of a convincing argument. I attended the artists' congresses in Poland in which the theories of socialist realism were first discussed. The attitude of the audience toward the speakers delivering the required reports was decidedly hostile. Everyone considered socialist realism an officially imposed theory that would have, as Russian art demonstrates, deplorable results. Attempts to provoke discussion failed. The listeners remained silent. Usually, however, one daring artist would launch an attack, full of restrained sarcasm, with the silent but obvious support of the entire audience. He would invariably be crushed by superior reasoning plus practicable threats against the future career of an undisciplined individual. Given the conditions of convincing argument plus such threats, the necessary conversion will take place. That is mathematically certain.

The faces of the listeners at these congresses were not completely legible, for the art of masking one's feelings had already been perfected to a considerable degree. Still one was aware of successive waves of emotion: anger, fear, amazement, distrust, and finally thoughtfulness. I had the impression that I was participating in a demonstration of mass hypnosis. These people could laugh and joke afterwards in the corridors. But the harpoon had hit its mark, and henceforth wherever they may go, they will always carry it with them. Do I believe that the dialectic of the speakers was unanswerable? Yes, as long as there was no fundamental discussion of methodology. No one among those present was prepared for such a discussion. It would probably have been a debate on Hegel, whose reading public was not made up of painters and writers. Moreover, even if someone had wanted to start it, he would have been silenced, for such discussions are permitted—and even then, fearfully—only in the upper circles of the Party.

These artists' congresses reveal the inequality between the weapons of the dialectician and those of his adversary. A match between the two is like a duel between a foot soldier and a tank. Not that every dialectician is so very intelligent or so very well educated, but all his statements are enriched by the cumulated thought of the masters and their commentators. If every sentence he speaks is compact and effective, that is not due to his own merits, but to those of the classics he has studied. His listeners are defenseless. They could, it is true, resort to arguments derived from their observations of life, but such arguments are just as badly countenanced as any questioning of fundamental methodology. The dialectician rubs up against his public at innumerable meetings of professional organizations and youthful groups in clubs, factories, office buildings, and village huts throughout the entire converted area of Europe. And there is no doubt that he emerges the victor in these encounters.

It is no wonder that a writer or painter doubts the wisdom of resistance. If he were sure that art opposed to the official line could have a lasting value, he probably would not hesitate. He would earn his living through some more menial job within his profession, write or paint in his spare time, and never worry about publishing or exhibiting his work. He believes, however, that in most cases such work would be artistically poor, and he is not far wrong. As we have already said, the objective conditions he once knew have disappeared. The objective conditions necessary to the realization of a work of art are, as we know, a highly complex phenomenon, involving one's public, the possibility of contact with it, the general atmosphere, and above all freedom from involuntary subjective control. "I can't write as I would like to," a young Polish poet admitted to me. "My own stream of thought has so many tributaries, that I barely succeed in damming off one, when a second, third, or fourth overflows. I get halfway through a phrase, and already I submit it to Marxist criticism. I imagine what X or Y will say about it, and I change the ending."

Paradoxical as it may seem, it is this subjective impotence that convinces the intellectual that the one Method is right. Everything proves it is right. Dialectics: I predict the house will burn; then I pour gasoline over the stove. The house burns; my prediction is fulfilled. Dialectics: I predict that a work of art incompatible with socialist realism will be worthless. Then I place the artist in conditions in which such a work *is* worthless. My prediction is fulfilled. . . .

SUCCESS

A patient has a hard time, however, when the moment comes for him to swallow Murti-Bing in its *entirety*. He becomes such a nervous wreck that he may actually fall ill. He knows it means a definitive parting with his former self, his former ties and habits. If he is a writer, he cannot hold a pencil in his hand. The whole world seems dark and hopeless. Until now, he paid a minimal tribute: in his articles and novels, he described the evils of capitalist society. But after all, it isn't difficult to criticize capitalism, and it can be done honestly. The charlatans of the stock exchange, feudal barons, self-deluding artists, and the instigators of nationalistic wars are figures who lend themselves readily to his pen. But now he must begin to *approve*. (In official terminology this is known as a transition from the stage of critical realism to that of socialist realism. It occurred in the newly-established people's democracies about the year 1950.) The operation he must perform on himself is one that some of his friends have already undergone, more or less painfully. They shake their heads sympathetically, knowing the process and its outcome. "I have passed the crisis," they say serenely. "But how he is suffering. He sits at home all day with his head in his hands."

The hardest thing to conquer is his feeling of *guilt*. No matter what his convictions, every man in the countries of which I speak is a part of an ancient civilization. His parents were attached to religion, or at least regarded it with respect. In school, much attention was devoted to his religious upbringing. Some emotional traces of this early training necessarily remain. In any case, he believes that injury to one's fellow-man, lies, murder, and the encouragement of hatred are evil, even if they serve to accomplish sublime ends. Obviously, too, he studied the history of his country. He read its former poets and philosophers with pleasure and pride. He was proud of its century-long battle to defend its frontiers and of its struggle for independence in the dark periods of foreign occupation. Consciously or unconsciously, he feels a certain loyalty to his forefathers because of the history of toil and sacrifice on their part. Moreover, from earliest childhood, he has been taught that his country belongs to a civilization that has been derived from Rome rather than Byzantium.

Now, knowing that he must enter a gate through which he can never return, he feels he is doing *something wrong*. He explains to himself that he must destroy this irrational and childish feeling. He can become free only by weeding out the roots of what is irretrievably past. Still the battle continues. A cruel battle—a battle between an angel and a demon. True, but which is the angel and which the demon? One has a bright face he has known since his childhood—this must be the angel. No, for this face bears hideous scars. It is the face of the old order, of stupid college fraternities, of the senile imbecility of politicians, or the decrepitude of Western Europe. This is death and decadence. The other face is strong and self-contained, and face of a tomorrow that beckons. Angelic? That is doubtful. . . .

The writer, in his fury and frustration, turns his thought to Western Communists. What fools they are. He can forgive their oratory if it is necessary as propaganda. But they believe most of what they proclaim about the sacred Center, and that is unforgivable. Nothing can compare to the contempt he feels for these sentimental fools.

Nevertheless, despite his resistance and despair, the crisis approaches. It can come in the middle of the night, at his breakfast table, or on the street. It comes with a metallic click as of engaged gears. *But there is no other way.* That much is clear. There is no other salvation on the face of the earth. This revelation lasts a second; but from that second on, the patient begins to recover. For the first time in a long while, he eats with relish, his movements take on vigor, his color returns. He sits down and writes a "positive" article, marveling at the ease with which he writes it. In the last analysis, there was no reason for raising such a fuss. Everything is in order. He is past the "crisis."

He does not emerge unscathed, however. The after-effects manifest themselves in a particular kind of extinguishment that is often perceptible in the twist of his lips. His face expresses the peaceful sadness of one who has tasted the fruit from the Tree of the Knowledge of Good and Evil, of one who knows he lies and who feels compassion for those who have been spared full knowledge. He has already gone through what still awaits so many others. . . .

In the epilogue of Witkiewicz's novel, his heroes, who have gone over to the service of Murti-Bing, become schizophrenics. The events of today bear out his vision, even in this respect. One can survive the "crisis" and function perfectly, writing or painting as one must, but the old moral and aesthetic standards continue to exist on some deep inner plane. Out of this arises a split within the individual that makes for many difficulties in his daily life. It facilitates the task of ferreting out heretical thoughts and inclinations; for thanks to it, the Murti-Bingist can feel himself into his opponent with great acuteness. The new phase and the old phase exist simultaneously in him, and together they render him an experienced psychologist, a keeper of his brother's conscience.

One can expect that the new generation, raised from the start in the new society will be free of this split. But that cannot be brought about quickly. One would have to eradicate the Church completely, which is a difficult matter and one that demands patience and tact. And even if one could eliminate this reverenced mainstay of irrational impulses, national literatures would remain to exert their malignant influence. For example, the works of the greatest Polish poets are marked by a dislike of Russia, and the dose of Catholic philosophy one finds in them is alarming. Yet the state must publish certain of these poets and must teach them in its schools for they are the classics, the creators of the literary language, and are considered the forerunners of the Revolution. To place them on the index would be to think non-dialectically and to fall into the sin of "leftism." It is a difficult dilemma, more difficult in the converted countries than in the Center, where the identification of national culture with the interests of humanity has been achieved to a great degree. Probably, therefore, the schizophrenic as a type will not disappear in the near future.

Someone might contend that Murti-Bing is a medicine that is incompatible with human nature. That is not a very strong argument. The Aztecs' custom of offering human sacrifices to their gods, or the mortification of the flesh practiced by the early Christian hermits scarcely seem praiseworthy. The worship of gold has become a motive power second to none in its brutality. Seen from this perspective, Murti-Bing does not violate the nature of humankind.

Whether a man who has taken the Murti-Bing cure attains internal peace and harmony is another question. He attains a relative degree of harmony, just enough to render him active. It is preferable to the torment of pointless rebellion and groundless hope. The peasants, who are incorrigible in their petty bourgeois attachments, assert that "a change must come, because this can't go *on*." This is an amusing belief in the natural order of things. A tourist, as an anecdote tells us, wanted to go up into the mountains, but it had been raining for a week. He met a mountaineer walking by a stream, and asked him if it would continue to pour. The mountaineer looked at the rising waters and voiced the opinion that it would not. When asked on what basis he had made his prediction, he said, "Because the stream would overflow." Murti-Bing holds such magic judgments to be phantoms of a dying era. The "new" is striving to overcome the "old," but the "old" cannot be eliminated all at once.

The one thing that seems to deny the perfection of Murti-Bing is the apathy that is born in people, and that lives on in spite of their feverish activity. It is hard to define, and at times one might suppose it to be a mere optical illusion. After all, people bestir themselves, work, go to the theater, applaud speakers, take excursions, fall in love, and have children. Yet there is something impalpable and unpleasant in the human climate of such cities as Warsaw or Prague. The collective atmosphere, resulting from an exchange and a re-combination of individual fluids, is bad. It is an aura of strength and unhappiness, of internal paralysis and external mobility. Whatever we may call it, this much is certain: if Hell should guarantee its lodgers magnificent quarters, beautiful clothes, the tastiest food, and all possible amusements, but condemn them to breathe in this aura forever, that would be punishment enough.

No propaganda, either pro or con, can capture so elusive and little-known a phenomenon. It escapes all calculations. It cannot exist on paper. Admitting in whispered conversation, that something of the sort does exist, one must seek a rational explanation for it. Undoubtedly the "old," fearful and oppressed, is taking its vengeance by spilling forth its inky fluid like a wounded octopus. But surely the socialist organism, in its growth toward a future of guaranteed prosperity, is already strong enough to counteract this poison; or perhaps it is too early for that. When the younger generation, free from the malevolent influence of the "old," arises, everything will change. Only, whoever has observed the younger generation in the Center is reluctant to cast such a horoscope. Then we must postpone our hopes to the remote future, to a time when the Center and every dependent state will supply its citizens with refrigerators and automobiles, with white bread and a handsome ration of butter. Maybe then, at last, they will be satisfied.

Why won't the equation work out as it should, when every step is logical? Do we have to use non-Euclidian geometry on material as classic, as adaptable, and as plastic as a human being? Won't the ordinary variety satisfy him? What the devil does a man need? . . .

Man, This Enemy

. . . Everything, thus, takes us back to the question of mastery over the mind. Every possible opportunity for education and advancement is offered to the more energetic and active individuals among the workers. The new, incredibly extensive bureaucracy is recruited from among the young people of working-class origin. The road before them is open, open but guarded: their thinking must be based on the firm principles of dialectical materialism.

Schools, theaters, films, painting, literature, and the press all shape their thinking.

We should also call attention to a new institution, the "club," whose significance is comparable to that of the chapel in the middle ages. It exists in every factory, every school, every office. On its walls hang portraits of Party leaders draped with red bunting. Every few days, meetings following prearranged agendas take place, meetings that are as potent as religious rites. The Catholic Church wisely recognized that faith is more a matter of collective suggestion than of individual conviction. Collective religious ceremonies induce a state of belief. Folding one's hands in prayer, kneeling, singing hymns *precede* faith, for faith is a psycho-physical and not simply a psychological phenomenon. . . . The Party has learned this wise lesson from the Church. People who attend a "club" submit to a collective rhythm, and so come to feel that it is absurd to think differently from the collective. The collective is composed of units that doubt; but as these individuals pronounce the ritual phrases and sing the ritual songs, they create a collective aura to which they in turn surrender. Despite its apparent appeal to reason, the "club's" activity comes under the heading of collective magic. The rationalism of the doctrine is fused with sorcery, and the two strengthen each other. Free discussion is, of course, eliminated. If what the doctrine proclaims is as true as the fact that 2×2 equals 4, to tolerate the opinion that 2×2 equals 5 would be indecent.

From his first day of school, the young citizen receives an education based on this truth. There is a great difference between schools in the people's democracies and schools in the West, for example the schools I attended in pre-war Poland. My friends and I were exposed to a dual system of values. Mathematics, physics and biology taught us scientific laws, and inculcated respect for a materialistic outlook inherited from the nineteenth century. History and Letters seemed to elude scientific laws, while the history of the Catholic Church and Apologetics cast doubt, though often naïvely, on what physics and biology taught. In the people's democracies, the materialistic outlook of the nineteenth century has been extended consistently to every subject; history and every branch of human creativity are presented as governed by unshakeable and *already known* laws.

In the nineteenth century, with the rise of literacy, brochures popularizing scientific theories made their appearance. Regardless of the intrinsic worth of these theories, we must grant that from the moment they take on a popular form they become something other than what they were as hypotheses of scientific research. For example, the simplified and vulgarized version of Darwin's theory of the origin of species and the struggle for existence is not the same concept that it was for Darwin or for his scholarly opponents. It takes on emotional coloration, and changes into an important sociological element. The leaders of the twentieth century, like Hitler for instance, drew their knowledge from popular brochures, which explains the incredible confusion in their minds. Evidently, there is no place in such digests for the humble remarks of true scientists who assure us that the laws discovered are hypothetical and relative to the method chosen and the system of symbols used. Vulgarized knowledge characteristically gives birth to a feeling that *everything* is understandable and explained. It is like a system of bridges built over chasms. One can travel boldly ahead over these bridges, ignoring the chasms. It is forbidden to look down into them; but that, alas, does not alter the fact that they exist.

Once the science of nature taught that a forest was a collective of trees governed by a few elementary laws. It seemed that if one cut out the forest and replanted it, after a definite period of years a new forest, exactly like the old, would appear. Today we know this is not so; a forest is an organism arising out of complicated interactions of mosses, soil, fungi, trees, and grasses. The moment these mosses and fungi are destroyed by the cutting out of the forest, the symbiotic pattern is disturbed and the new forest is a completely different organism from what might be expected by someone who ignored the sociology of plants. Stalinists have no knowledge of the conditions human plants need in order to thrive. Forbidding any research in this direction because such study contradicts orthodoxy, they bar mankind from the possibility of acquiring fuller knowledge of itself.

Dialectical materialism, Russian-style, is nothing more than nineteenth-century science vulgarized to the second power. Its emotional and didactic components are so strong that they change all proportions. Although the Method was scientific at its origins, when it is applied to humanistic disciplines it often transforms them into edifying stories adapted to the needs of the moment. But there is no escape once a man enters upon these convenient bridges. Centuries of human history, with their thousands upon thousands of intricate affairs, are reduced to a few, most generalized terms. Undoubtedly, one comes closer to the truth when one sees history as the expression of the class struggle rather than a series of private quarrels among kings and nobles. But precisely because such an analysis of history comes closer to the truth, it is more dangerous. It gives the illusion of *full knowledge;* it supplies answers to all questions, answers which merely run around in a circle repeating a few formulas. What's more, the humanities get connected with the natural sciences thanks to the materialistic outlook (as, for example, in theories of "eternal matter"), and so we see the circle closing perfectly and logically. Then, Stalin becomes the crowning point of the evolution of life on our planet.

The son of a worker, subjected to such an education, cannot think otherwise than as the school demands. Two times two equals four. The press, literature, painting, films, and theater all illustrate what he learns, just as the lives of saints and martyrs serve as illustrations of theology. It would be wrong to assert that a dual set of values no longer exists. The resistance against the new set of values is, however, emotional. It survives, but it is beaten whenever it has to explain itself in rational terms. A man's subconscious or not-quite-conscious life is richer than his vocabulary. His opposition to this new philosophy of life is much like a toothache. Not only can he not express the pain in words, but he cannot even tell you which tooth is aching.

Thanks to excellent means of vulgarization, unprepared people (i.e., those whose minds work feebly) are taught to reason. Their training convinces them that what is happening in the people's democracies is necessary, even if temporarily bad. The greater the number of people who "participate in culture"—i.e. pass through the schools, read books and magazines, attend theaters and exhibitions—the further the doctrine reaches and the smaller grows the threat to the rule of philosophers.

But some people, even with sufficient education, reason "badly." They are impervious to the influence of Hegelian philosophy. A chicken cannot be taught to swim; just so, those who belong to the social groups condemned to disappear cannot be convinced of the truth of dialectics. According to the Party, if these people were clearly aware of their situation, they would have to confess that there is no hope for them. Therefore they look for mental subterfuges. Those people are enemies. They must be ejected to the margins of society not because of what they do, but because of what they *are*. Despite the fact that their intentions may be subjectively good, their guilt has an *objective* character.

Dialecticians have to know the enemy's mentality. Studying the reactionary as a social type, they establish certain features by which he can be recognized. The reactionary, they argue, even though he be an educated man, is incapable of grasping the concept of the interdependence of phenomena. Therefore his political imagination is limited. A man who has been trained sociologically can deduce a whole line of reasoning as to the causes and consequences of every phenomenon. Like a paleontologist, he can divine a whole formation from a single fossil. Show him the verse of a poet from any country, a picture, even an item of clothing and he immediately fits it into a historical context. His line of reasoning may be false; nonetheless he sees everything within the sphere of a given civilization as a symptom, not an accident. The reactionary, incapable of this type of thinking, see the world as a series of unrelated, parallel occurrences.

Thus, Nazism was for the reactionary merely the result of the activity of Hitler and his clique; revolutionary movements are the effects of Moscow's machinations, etc. All the changes occurring in the people's democracies seem to him to resolve themselves into a question of superior force; if some miraculous accident were to remove this force, everything would return to "normal." He is like a man whose garden has been inundated by a raging river, and who expects to find his old flower beds intact after the waters subside. But a flooding river does not merely *exist;* it tears up and carries away whole banks of soil, fells trees, piles up layers of mud, overturns stones, until the garden of old becomes nothing more than a given number of square meters of unrecognizable land. The reactionary cannot grasp movement. His very language is static; his concepts, unchangeable, never renewed by observation. Laurel and Hardy once made a film in which Laurel, an American soldier in the First World War, is ordered to remain in the trench at his machine-gun post when the company moves to attack. Immediately thereafter the Armistice is signed, and in the resultant confusion he is forgotten. They find him twenty years later, his trench surrounded by a mountain of empty cans. He is still at his post, shooting at every commercial airplane that flies by. The reactionary, like Laurel, knows he must shoot, and he cannot realize that the plane is no longer what it was when he got his orders.

No matter how many books the reactionary reads about the dialectical method, he cannot understand its essence. Some little spring is missing in his mind. As a result he cannot properly evaluate human psychology. Dialecticians work on the premise that a man's mental and emotional life is in constant motion, that it is senseless to treat individuals as if they retained a certain stable, innate character in all circumstances. They know that by changing living conditions they change people's beliefs and reflexes. The reactionary is amazed by the changes people undergo. He awkwardly explains his friends' gradual conversion to the system as "opportunism," "cowardice," "treachery." Without such labels he feels lost. Reasoning on the principle of "either—or," he tries to divide the people about him into "Communists" and "non-Communists"; but such a differentiation loses all meaning in a people's democracy. Where dialectics shape life whoever tries to resort to old-world logic must feel completely out of his depth.

Such misfortune always befalls the reactionary. The content suddenly flees from his concepts, and all he has left are empty words and phrases. His friends, who only a year ago used these words and phrases fondly, have rejected them as too general, too ill-defined, too remote from reality. He despairingly repeats "honor," "fatherland," "nation," "freedom," without comprehending that for people living in a changed (and daily changing) situation these abstractions take on a concrete and totally different meaning than before.

Because they so define a reactionary, dialecticians consider him a mentally inferior, and therefore not very dangerous, creature. He is no match for them. Once the propertied class is liquidated, the old intelligentsia (which was reactionary in these terms) can be brought to heel with no great difficulty. Its more vigorous representatives cross over to new ideological positions, while the rest lag further and further behind the transformations occurring all about them and so sink ever lower both socially and mentally. . . .

In its own fashion, the Party . . . is a church. Its dictatorship over the earth and its transformation of the human species depend on the success with which it can channel irrational human drives and use them to its own ends. No, logical arguments are not enough. "Club" ceremonies, poetry, novels, films are so important because they reach deeper into the stratum on which the emotional conflict rages. No other church can be tolerated; Christianity is Public Enemy No. 1. It fosters all the skepticism of the masses as to the radical transformation of mankind. If, as the Gospel teaches, we must not do harm unto others, then perhaps we must not harm kulaks? If the highest glory does not belong to man, then perhaps worship of Lenin and Stalin is idolatry?

I have known many Christians—Poles, Frenchmen, Spaniards—who were strict Stalinists in the field of politics but who retained certain inner reservations, believing God would make corrections once the bloody sentences of the all-mighties of History were carried out. They pushed their reasoning rather far. They argue that history develops according to immutable laws that exist by the will of God; one of these laws is the class struggle; the twentieth century marks the victory of the proletariat, which is led in its struggle by the Communist Party; Stalin, the leader of the Communist Party, fulfills the law of history, or in other words acts by the will of God; therefore one must obey him. Mankind can be renewed only on the Russian pattern; that is why no Christian can oppose the one—cruel, it is true—idea which will create a new kind of man over the entire planet. Such reasoning is often used by clerics who are Party tools. "Christ is a new man. The new man is the Soviet man. Therefore Christ is a Soviet man!" said Justinian Marina, the Rumanian patriarch.

In reality, such Christians (even omitting men like Marina) perpetuate one of the greatest lies of all centuries. They renounce their faith but are ashamed to admit it. The contradiction between Christianity and Stalinist philosophy cannot be overcome. Christianity is based on a concept of *individual* merit and guilt; the New Faith, on *historical* merit and guilt. The Christian who rejects individual merit and guilt denies the work of Jesus, and the God he calls upon slowly transforms himself into History. If he admits that only individual merit and guilt exist, how can he gaze indifferently at the suffering of people whose only sin was that they blocked the path of "historical processes"? To lull his conscience he resorts to the thesis that a reactionary cannot be a good man.

Who is the reactionary? Everyone who opposes the inevitable historical processes, i.e. the Politburo police. The thesis of the "sin of the reactionary" is argued very cleverly: every perception is "oriented," i.e. at the very moment of perceiving we introduce our ideas into the material of our observations; only he sees reality truly who evaluates it in terms of the interests of the class that is the lever of the future, i.e. the proletariat. The writings of Lenin and Stalin teach us what the interests of the proletariat are. Whoever sees reality otherwise than as the proletariat sees it falsely; in other words, his picture of reality is deformed by the pressure of the interests of classes that are backward and so destined to disappear. Whoever sees the world falsely necessarily acts badly; whoever acts badly is a bad man; therefore the reactionary is a bad man, and one should not feel sorry for him.

This line of reasoning has at least one flaw—it ignores the facts. The pressure of an all-powerful totalitarian state creates an emotional tension in its citizens that determines their acts. When people are divided into "loyalists" and "criminals" a premium is placed on every type of conformist, coward, and hireling; whereas among the "criminals" one finds a singularly high percentage of people who are direct, sincere, and true to themselves. From the social point of view these persons would constitute the best guarantee that the future development of the social organism would be toward good. From the Christian point of view they have no other sin on their conscience save their contempt for Caesar, or their incorrect evaluation of his might.

The assertion that historical guilt is individual guilt *per se* is nothing more than a subterfuge of a guilty and lying conscience. This does not mean that one can put off the problem of historical guilt with easy generalizations. Stupidity, i.e. inability to understand the mechanism of events, can cause tremendous suffering. In this sense, the Polish commanders who gave the order to start the Warsaw uprising in 1944 are guilty of stupidity, and their guilt has an individual character. Another individual guilt, however, weighs upon the command of the Red Army which refused to aid the insurgents—not out of stupidity, but on the contrary out of a full understanding of "historical processes," i.e. a correct evaluation of power.

One more example of guilt through stupidity is the attitude of various societies toward thinkers, writers, or artists whose vision reached into the future and whose works were largely incomprehensible to their contemporaries. The critic who denied the value of these works might have acted in good faith, but by his stupidity he condemned men of incomparably greater worth than himself to poverty, even persecution. The specific trick of the Christian-Stalinists is to lump these two concepts of guilt, individual and historical, together, while it is only in a few instances that these concepts coincide.

Catholics who accept the Party line gradually lose everything except the phraseology of their Christian metaphysics. The true content of their faith becomes the Method by a psychological process well-known to Christians in the people's democracies. The existence of a large number of loyal half-Christians in the subjugated part of Europe could have a tremendous effect on the Imperium's political plans. Toleration and even support of these "Christian-patriots," as they are called, enables the Center to avoid a dangerous conflict. The transition from Christianity to a cult of History takes place imperceptibly. Without doubt, the greatest success of the Imperium would come if it could install a Party-line pope in the Vatican. A mass in the Basilica of St. Peter in Rome performed by such a pope, with the assistance of dignitaries from those subjugated countries which are predominately Catholic, would be one of the most important steps toward the consolidation of the world empire.

Christians who serve the Eastern Imperium ingeniously resolve the problem posed by Jesus' words, "Render therefore unto Caesar the things that are Caesar's; and unto God the things that are God's." Until now the contrast between the ordinary man and Caesar has never been effaced. Christianity guaranteed this division by teaching that every man had his own history, distinct from the history of the social group or the nation to which he belonged. If, as is taught today from the Elbe to Vladivostok, the history of every man is nothing more than the reflection of the history of his class, and if his class is personified in Caesar, then it is clear that the man who rebels against Caesar rebels against himself. Christians who agree to this thesis prove they no longer believe in God's judgment of each man's acts. Fear that History will damn them eternally motivates their submission.

The Party knows that the conflict between true Christianity and the Revolution is fundamental. The Revolution aims at the highest goal the human species has ever set for itself on earth, the end of "man's exploitation of man." To do this, it must replace man's desire for profit with a feeling of collective responsibility as a motive for action. This is a distant and honorable goal. Probably it will not be reached quickly; and probably, too, for a long period it will be necessary to maintain a constant terror in order to instill that feeling of responsibility by force. But Christianity contains a dual set of values; it recognizes man to be a "child of God" and also a member of society. As a member of society, he must submit to the established order so long as that order does not hinder him in his prime task of saving his soul. Only by effacing this dualism, i.e. raising man as a purely social creature, can the Party release the forces of hatred in him that are necessary to the realization of the new world.

The masses in highly industrialized countries like England, the United States, or France are largely de-Christianized. Technology, and the way of life it produces, undermines Christianity far more effectively than do violent measures. The erosion of religious beliefs is also taking place in Central and Eastern Europe. There, the core of the problem is to avoid galvanizing the forces of Christianity by some careless misstep. It would be an act of unforgivable carelessness, for example, to close the churches suddenly and prohibit all religious practice. Instead, one should try to split the Church in two. Part of the clergy must be compromised as reactionaries and "foreign agents" —a rather easy task, given the utterly conservative mentality of many priests. The other part must be bound to the state as closely as the Orthodox Church is in Russia, so that it becomes a tool of the government. A completely submissive Church—one that may on occasion collaborate with the security police—loses authority in the eyes of the pious. Such a Church can be preserved for decades, until the moment when it dies a natural death due to a lack of adherents.

So there are measures that can be taken even against the Church, this last stronghold of opposition. Nevertheless, the masses in the people's democracies behave like a man who wants to cry out in his sleep and cannot find his voice. They not only dare not speak, they do not know *what* to say. Logically, everything is as it should be. From the philosophical premises to the collectivization of the farms, everything makes up a single closed whole, a solid and imposing pyramid. The lone individual inevitably asks himself if his antagonism is not wrong; all he can oppose to the entire propaganda apparatus are simply his irrational desires. Should he not, in fact, be ashamed of them?

The Party is vigilantly on guard lest these longings be transmuted into new and vital intellectual formulas adapted to new conditions and therefore capable of winning over the masses. Neither the reaction nor the Church are as great a menace as is *heresy*. If men familiar with dialectics and able to present dialectical materialism in a new light appear, they must be rendered harmless at once. A professor of philosophy who clings to obsolete "idealistic" concepts is not particularly dangerous. He loses his lectureship, but he is allowed to earn a living by editing texts, etc. Whereas a professor who, using the names of Marx and Engels, permits himself departures from orthodoxy, sows seeds from which alarming crops may grow.

Only the bourgeois persists in thinking that nothing results from these nuances of thought. The Party knows that much can come of them; there was a time when the Revolution was merely a nuance in the thinking of a little group of theoreticians led by Lenin, quarreling around a café table in Switzerland. The most neuralgic points of the doctrine are philosophy, literature, the history of art, and literary criticism; those are the points where man in his unfortunate complexity enters the equation. The difference of a tiny fraction in the premises yields dizzying differences after the calculation is completed. A deviation from the line in the evaluation of some work of art may become the leaven of a political upheaval. The Party rightly and logically condemned the foremost Marxist literary scholar of the twentieth century, the Hungarian professor Lukacs. Deep, hidden reasons lay behind the enthusiasm his works aroused in the Marxists of the people's democracies. They saw in him the harbinger of a new philosophy and a new literature. The dislike of "socialist realism" that he betrayed corresponded to the belief, prevalent in the first years after the Second World War, that in the people's democracies the science of Marx and Engels would blaze new paths, unknown in Russia. Because Lukacs expressed this belief in his books, the Party had no course but to stigmatize him.

When one considers the matter logically, it becomes obvious that intellectual terror is a principle that Leninism-Stalinism can never forsake, even if it should achieve victory on a world scale. The enemy, in a potential form, will *always* be there; the only friend will be the man who accepts the doctrine 100 per cent. If he accepts only 99 per cent, he will necessarily have to be considered a foe, for from that remaining 1 per cent a new church can arise. The explanation Stalinists often advance, that this is only a *stage* resulting from "capitalist encirclement," is self-contradictory. The concept of a *stage* presupposes planning from the top, absolute control now and always. Eastern rulers are aware of this contradiction. If they were not, they would not have to present forced participation in clubs and parades, forced voting for a single list, forced raising of production norms, etc. as spontaneous and voluntary acts. This is a dark, unpleasant point for even the most passionate believers.

This way of posing the problem discloses the madness of the doctrines. Party dialecticians know that similar attempts on the part of other orthodoxies have always failed. In fact, History itself exploded one after another the formulas that have been considered binding. This time, however, the rulers have mastered dialectics so, they assert, they will know how to modify the doctrine as new necessities arise. The judgments of an individual man can always be wrong; the only solution is to submit unreservedly to an authority that claims to be unerring.

But what can the doctrine do about the unformulated longings of men? Why does a good Communist, without any apparent reason, suddenly put a pistol to his head? Why does he escape abroad? Isn't this one of those chasms over which the scientifically constructed bridges pass? People who flee from the people's democracies usually give as their chief motive the fact that life in these countries is psychically unbearable. They stammer out their efforts to explain: "The dreadful sadness of life over there"; "I felt I was turning into a machine." It is impossible to communicate to people who have not experienced it the undefinable menace of total rationalism.

To forestall doubt, the Party fights any tendency to delve into the depths of a human being, especially in literature and art. Whoever reflects on "man" in general, on his inner needs and longings, is accused of bourgeois sentimentality. Nothing must ever go beyond the description of man's behavior as a member of a social group. This is necessary because the Party, treating man exclusively as the by-product of social forces, believes that he becomes the type of being he pictures himself to be. He is a social monkey. *What is not expressed does not exist.* Therefore if one forbids men to explore the depths of human nature, one destroys in them the urge to make such explorations; and the depths in themselves slowly become unreal. . . .

The citizen of the people's democracies is immune to the kind of neurosis that takes such manifold forms in capitalist countries. In the West a man subconsciously regards society as unrelated to him. Society indicates the limits he must not exceed; in exchange for this he receives a guarantee that no one will meddle excessively in his affairs. If he loses it's his own fault; let psychoanalysis help him. In the East there is no boundary between man and society. His game, and whether he loses or wins, is a public matter. He is never alone. If he loses it is not because of indifference on the part of his environment, but because his environment keeps him under such minute scrutiny. Neuroses as they are known in the West result, above all, from man's aloneness; so even if they were allowed to practice, psychoanalysts would not earn a penny in the people's democracies.

The torment of a man in the East is . . . of a new, hitherto unknown variety. Humanity devised effective measures against smallpox, typhus, syphilis; but life in big cities or giant collectives breeds new diseases. Russian revolutionists discovered what they claimed were effectual means of mastering the forces of History. They proclaimed they had found the panacea for the ills of society. But History itself repays them in jeers.

The supreme goal of doing away with the struggle for existence—which was the theoretician's dream—has not been and cannot be achieved while every man fears every other man. The state which, according to Lenin, was supposed to wither away gradually is now all-powerful. It holds a sword over the head of every citizen; it punishes him for every careless word. The promises made from time to time that the state will begin to wither away when the entire earth is conquered lack any foundation. Orthodoxy cannot release its pressure on men's minds; it would no longer be an orthodoxy. There is always some disparity between facts and theories. The world is full of contradictions. Their constant struggle is what Hegel called dialectic. That dialectic of reality turns against the dialectic fashioned by the Center; but then so much the worse for reality. It has been said that the twentieth century is notable for its synthetic products—synthetic rubber, synthetic gasoline, etc. Not to be outdone, the Party has processed an artificial dialectic whose only resemblance to Hegel's philosophy is purely superficial. The Method is effective just so long as it wages war against an enemy. A man exposed to its influence is helpless. How can he fight a system of symbols? In the end he submits; and this is the secret of the Party's power, not some fantastic narcotic.

There is a species of insect which injects its venom into a caterpillar; thus inoculated, the caterpillar lives on though it is paralyzed. The poisonous insect then lays its eggs in it, and the body of the caterpillar serves as living larder for the young brood. Just so (though Marx and Engels never foresaw this use for their doctrine), the anaesthetic of dialectical materialism is injected into the mind of a man in the people's democracies. When his brain is duly paralyzed, the eggs of Stalinism are laid in it. As soon as you are a Marxist, the Party says to the patient, you *must* be a Stalinist, for there is no Marxism outside of Stalinism.

Naïve enemies of the poison may think that they can rid themselves of the danger by locking up the works of Marx and Engels in burglar-proof safes and never allowing anyone to read them. They fail to consider that the very course of history leads people to think about the subject matter of these works. Those who have never personally experienced the magnetic attraction and force of the problems posed in these books can count themselves lucky. Though that does not necessarily mean that they should feel proud of themselves.

Only the blind can fail to see the irony of the situation the human species brought upon itself when it tried to master its own fate and to eliminate accident. It bent its knee to History; and History is a cruel god. Today, the commandments that fall from his lips are uttered by clever chaplains hiding in his empty interior. The eyes of the god are so constructed that they see wherever a man may go; there is no shelter from them. Lovers in bed perform their amorous rites under his mocking glance; a child plays in the sand, not knowing that his future life has been weighed and written into the general account; only the aged, who have but a few days left before they die, can justly feel that they have to a large extent escaped his rule.

The philosophy of History emanating from Moscow is not just an abstract theory, it is a material force that uses guns, tanks, planes, and all the machines of war and oppression. All the crushing might of an armed state is hurled against any man who refuses to accept the New Faith. At the same time, Stalinism attacks him from within, saying his opposition is caused by his "class consciousness," just as psychoanalysts accuse their foes of wanting to preserve their complexes.

Still, it is not hard to imagine the day when millions of obedient followers of the New Faith may suddenly turn against it. That day would come the moment the Center lost its material might, not only because fear of military force would vanish, but because success is an integral part of this philosophy's argument. If it lost, it would prove itself wrong by its own definition; it would stand revealed as a false faith, defeated by its own god, reality. The citizens of the Imperium of the East long for nothing so much as liberation from the terror their own thoughts create.

In the Central Committee buildings, strategists move the little flags on the battle map of the war for men's minds. They can pinpoint ever greater successes; the red color, which in 1944 and 1945 was limited to a handful of believers coming from the East, spreads farther every day. But even sages are men, and even they fall prey to anxiety and dread. They compare themselves to the early Christians; they liken the march of the New Faith over the planet to the march of Christianity throughout the decaying Roman Empire. But they envy the Apostles their gift of reaching deep into the human heart. "*They* knew how to make propaganda! How can we compare ourselves with them?" mourned a certain Party dignitary hearing the Gospel read over the radio. The new (anti-) religion performs miracles. It shows the doubters new buildings and new tanks. But what would happen if these miracles suddenly stopped? Knives and pistols would appear in the hands that applaud today. The pyramid of thought would topple. For a long time, on the ground where once it stood there would be nothing save blood and chaos.

THE SOVIET LINGUISTIC CONTROVERSY

APPEAL to dogma to settle controversy is not new in the history of science. But in the twentieth century science is more often called upon to serve political than religious orthodoxy. The need for conformity in modern "totalitarian" regimes is expressed in the attempt to force scientific investigation and speculation into the mold of an ideology. Since the collapse of Nazism in Germany, this tendency has been most apparent in the Soviet Union, homeland of Marxist-Leninist-Stalinist "dialectical materialism."

The selection which follows presents a study of the process whereby a "line"—an official position on a controversial subject—is established. The subject dealt with, linguistics, is more politically sensitive—in view of the multitude of languages spoken in the complex of cultures embraced by the Soviet Union—than, for example, physics. Yet even in the science of physics, theoretical and philosophical discussion is, in Russia, couched in the terms of Marxist rhetoric. To the secular orthodoxies of the twentieth-century world, no area of intellectual expression can be granted true autonomy, and all questions assume a political dimension. Problems are ultimately resolved not through the interplay of disciplined inquiry, but by political dictate.

The linguistic controversy, which was extremely virulent in the Soviet Union in the spring and summer of 1950, centered around the figure of Nikolai Yakovlevich Marr (1864–1934), a philologist who had adapted the science of linguistics to a proper "Marxist" mold. In the early period of the Soviet regime, Marr's doctrines had been subjected to severe criticism within Russia. But in the late 1920's and early 1930's his teaching was elevated to the dignity of a "line," and so assumed the character of dogma, sanctified by its avowed "Marxist" content and approved by the Party. Marrism became the official style of linguistic investigation and instruction in the Soviet Union. Academic posts concerned with languages and literature were monopolized by Marrists. Scholarly disagreement with Marrism was regarded not merely as erroneous, but as heretical.

However, during a congress of scholars gathered in Moscow in January, 1950, to celebrate Marr's memory, observers sensitive to the signs that often signal a change of "line" noted that certain philologists, presumably with powerful support within the Party-Government hierarchy, were beginning to cast doubt upon the adequacy and orthodoxy of Marrism. By May 9, the drift of official support away from the Marrist position became apparent when *Pravda* called for "free" discussion of the linguistics question. There followed a brief, but bitter and abusive, public controversy, which terminated in the establishment of a new "line" announced by Joseph Stalin.

That the controversy and its outcome were more than a scholars' quarrel was soon evident from the fact that universities, academies, and other pedagogical institutes quickly removed from their faculties scholars tainted with the now discredited Marrism. At the same time representatives of the anti-Marrist faction were called in as replacements. New linguistics and literature curricula were developed in accordance with the new "line." New textbooks were written, printed, and distributed while the old were withdrawn from libraries and bookshops. Finally the Presidium of the U.S.S.R. Academy of Sciences and the Ministry of Higher Education rescinded important decrees of July, 1949, and April, 1950, favorable to Marrism, and substituted promulgations designed to cast the new linguistic dogma in the form of bureaucratic regulation. The controversy was over.

This selection has been taken from *The Soviet Linguistic Controversy* (1951), a collection of relevant documents drawn from translations of articles appearing originally in Russian in *Pravda* and the magazine *Voprosy filosofii,* which were published by *The Current Digest of the Soviet Press.* The translators are John V. Murra, Robert M. Hankin, and Fred Holling; Ernest J. Simmons was the editor.

THE SOVIET LINGUISTIC CONTROVERSY

Scientific Session Devoted to Marr Anniversary [1]

A. G. SPIRKIN

The Soviet public observed extensively the 85th anniversary of the birth and 15th anniversary of the death of N. Ya. Marr, inspired Soviet scientist and founder of the new, materialist teachings on language who brought fame to our fatherland's science through his outstanding scientific works.

Academician Marr's teaching on language, erected on the firm base of dialectical and historical materialism, constitutes a genuine, revolutionary upheaval in linguistics. The new teaching on language formulated by N. Ya. Marr, ardent patriot and true son of the party of Lenin and Stalin, is the product of the great October socialist revolution. Nikolai Yakovlevich Marr himself frequently emphasized that the new teaching on language could have developed only under conditions of the Soviet social system with its new, revolutionary world viewpoint and its solution of the national question on the basis of new principles. Academician Marr worked tirelessly for the socialist system, participating directly in national-cultural construction, carrying out the great ideas of Marx, Engels, Lenin and Stalin on the fraternal cooperation of peoples.

This selection has been reprinted from *The Soviet Linguistic Controversy,* New York, King's Crown Press, 1951 (pp. 1, 8–9, 70–76, 91–92) by permission of the publisher.

[1] From *Voprosy filosofii,* No. 3, 1949 (published in April, 1950), pp. 326–327.

Since Marr's death, the materialist teaching on language which he formulated has been creatively developed by his pupils and followers.

The Soviet people profoundly revere the memory of their glorious son. Scientific sessions devoted to the memory of the inspired scientist and ardent Bolshevist patriot N. Ya. Marr have been organized in all linguistics institutes of the Soviet Union, in all academies of sciences of the union republics and higher educational institutions of our country during [the observance of] the 85th anniversary of N. Ya. Marr's birth and the 15th anniversary of his death. Scientific sessions of nationwide importance and devoted to this noteworthy date were held in Leningrad and Moscow.

The task of the scientific sessions in both Moscow and Leningrad was to sum up the work of Soviet linguistics, to subject the shortcomings which exist in this work to sharp Party criticism, and to indicate paths of future creative development of Marr's heritage in connection with profound tasks in studying the language and writing systems of the peoples of the U.S.S.R., in the field of language development.

In Moscow, the scientific session devoted to N. Ya. Marr's memory lasted from Jan. 24 to Jan. 27.

The following persons gave reports at the special session called by the N. Ya. Marr Institute of Language and Thought in Moscow on a joint resolution of the Presidium of the U.S.S.R. Academy of Sciences and representatives of institutes of the union republics working on problems of linguistics in the national republics: Academician I. I. Meshchaninov, Profs. G. P. Serdyuchenko, N. S. Chemodanov and I. M. Oshanin, Corresponding Member of the Armenian Republic Academy of Sciences Prof. A. S. Garibyan, Corresponding Member of the Azerbaidzhan Academy of Sciences M. A. Shiraliyev, Member of the Kazakh Academy of Sciences S. K. Kenesbayev, Comrade V. M. Alatyrev, D. I. Mikhalchi and others. Staff members of the Institute of Language and Thought, Institute of Philosophy of the U.S.S.R. Academy of Sciences, Moscow State University and the academies of sciences of the union republics took part in the debates. All participants stated that creative development of linguistic problems is possible only on the basis of the materialist teaching on language formulated by N. Ya. Marr which has played such a tremendous role in the development of the national languages of the peoples of the U.S.S.R. All participants unanimously demanded that a most resolute struggle be waged against attempts to resurrect reactionary, bourgeois theories of linguistics, the formal-comparative method in linguistics.

Participants in the sessions stressed in their remarks that N. Ya. Marr's works, based on the firm foundation of dialectical and historical materialism, are a most sharp ideological weapon against bourgeois, idealistic linguistics which propagandizes reactionary, racist theories.

The session was opened by A. V. Topchiyev, Chief Learned Secretary of the U.S.S.R. Academy of Sciences who called for development of Bolshevist criticism and self-criticism as making it possible to remedy existing shortcomings in linguistic work and to raise the Soviet materialist science of language to a new, higher level.

In his report "N. Ya. Marr as a Scholar and Teacher," N. Ya. Marr's closest pupil and follower Academician I. I. Meshchaninov brilliantly characterized the creative path followed by the inspired Soviet linguist. Academician Meshchaninov demonstrated on the basis of extensive specific factual material that even prior to the great October socialist revolution N. Ya. Marr adopted a very hostile attitude toward reactionary, bourgeois science. The conditions under which N. Ya. Marr worked in the prerevolutionary university did not permit him to develop his tremendous creative talent. This talent blossomed with unusual force after the great October [revolution] when N. Ya. Marr became an active participant in cultural construction in our country.

Reforms in university teaching and reorganization of the work of an entire series of scientific institutions after the great October socialist revolution advanced N. Ya. Marr to first place in the university world and made him a most active participant in the development of a new, Soviet science. He raised archeology to the level of a genuinely scientific discipline, becoming head of the archeological commission which he reorganized into the Academy of the History of Material Culture. . . .

Note by the Editors of Voprosy filosofii

The session's work showed that on the basis of Marr's heritage a large number of Soviet linguists are performing fruitful work on studying and developing the languages and writing systems of the peoples of the U.S.S.R.

The overwhelming majority of Soviet linguists relies on the theory of linguistics based on the principles of dialectical and historical materialism.

However, the work of this session revealed the generally unsatisfactory situation in the field of linguistics.

The work of the session likewise revealed that there are major shortcomings in the field of linguistics.

The state of affairs is most unsatisfactory in the important field of the study of the Russian language. Research work and textbooks on the Russian language make entirely insufficient use of Marr's basic postulates on language.

The session also disclosed a serious lag in the theoretical sector of the linguistic front. The Institute of Language and Thought was unable to present a single report throwing light on the basic theoretical questions of Marr's teaching.

A number of theoretical reports delivered at the session did not give a sufficiently profound analysis of the ideological wealth of the teaching of the inspired Soviet scientist N. Ya. Marr.

The session was mainly commemorative in nature. The session did not reflect the creative development of N. Ya. Marr's theoretical heritage by his pupils and followers in the 15 years since the founder of materialist linguistics died. The prospects for further development of the Soviet science of language were not precisely indicated. The session did not subject to principled Bolshevist criticism the attacks on Marr made by several Soviet linguists and did not entirely expose the attempts to revise Marr's teaching and to reconcile it with idealist bourgeois linguistics.

Reports by the heads of the Institute of Language and Thought were not sufficiently self-critical. These reports, as well as the speeches by participants in the session, did not disclose the errors of the speakers themselves.

The session failed to pose the most important theoretical problems of materialist linguistics—the problem of stages in the development of language, form and content in language, language and thought, the question of the unity of the glottogonic process, the problem of relationship of the teachings of N. Ya. Marr and I. P. Pavlov and others. This lamentable fact attests that questions of the theory of linguistics are not receiving proper attention in the Institute of Language and Thought of the U.S.S.R. Academy of Sciences. The situation is particularly unsatisfactory with respect to throwing light on the major question of the relationship between theoretical research and practical work on developing the language and writing systems of the peoples of the U.S.S.R., the practical teaching of languages in educational institutions, both higher and secondary.

It is utterly inadmissible that linguists doing research on the great Russian language took no part in the session's work. It was especially important that they participate, because it is precisely in this field that a struggle against anti-Marr traditions is extremely urgent.

Many participants in the session brought up the need for close coordination of the work of linguists, historians of material culture, philosophers, ethnographers, historians and others.

By way of self-criticism, it must be admitted that Soviet philosophers, especially [in] the Institute of Philosophy of the U.S.S.R. Academy of Sciences and [on] the magazine *Voprosy filosofii* have not yet given real help to linguists in solving pressing problems of Soviet linguistics.

Voprosy filosofii's attempt to shed light on urgent problems of modern linguistics (the article by Comrades Nikolsky and Yakovlev in No. 1, 1949) proved unsuccessful since this article, as the newspaper *Kultura i zhizn* justly pointed out, contained serious errors in fact and in principle.

The question of coordinating work in the field of linguistics in the various national republics is an extremely acute one. The need has arisen for the establishment of a special agency to throw much light on the theoretical and practical work of all linguistic institutions of the Soviet Union.

The results of the session show that we must have more principled, Bolshevist criticism and self-criticism which will make it possible to end the covert and overt attacks on Marr and to raise Soviet, materialist, Marrist linguistics to a higher level.

The Controversy in Pravda

[On May 9, 1950, *Pravda,* official newspaper of the Communist Party in the Soviet Union, opened its columns to a free controversy over Marxist linguistics with the following editorial note:]

In connection with the unsatisfactory state of Soviet linguistics, the editors consider it essential to organize an open discussion in *Pravda* in order through criticism and self-criticism to overcome the stagnation in the development of Soviet linguistics and to give correct direction to further scientific work in this field. . . . Beginning with this issue, *Pravda* will devote two pages weekly to articles discussing questions of linguistics.

[Between May 9 and June 20, 1950, the linguistics scholars of the Soviet Union engaged in a verbal battle over the theories of the Marrist school of linguistics. The controversy aroused great interest. The attacks upon Marr and his proponents grew increasingly polemical and self-assured; those who defended became increasingly confused and uncertain. Finally, on June 20, 1950, the argument was brought to a climax and a halt with a pronouncement, in the form of a letter to the editors of *Pravda,* by J. Stalin.]

J. STALIN: ON MARXISM IN LINGUISTICS [2]

A group of youthful comrades has suggested to me that I express my opinion in the press on linguistic problems, particularly where Marxism in linguistics is concerned. I am not a linguist and, of course, I cannot fully satisfy the comrades. As for Marxism in linguistic as well as other social sciences, I am directly concerned with this. I have therefore consented to reply to a number of questions asked by the comrades.

Question: Is it true that language is a superstructure over a base?

Answer: No, it is not true.

The base is the economic structure of society at a given stage of its development. The superstructure comprises the political, legal, religious, artistic and philosophical views of society and their corresponding political, legal and other institutions.

Every base has its corresponding superstructure. The base of the feudal order has its own superstructure, its political, legal and other views and the institutions corresponding to them; the capitalist base has its superstructure; the socialist has its superstructure. If the base changes and is eliminated, then its superstructure changes and is eliminated after it; if a new base is born, then a superstructure corresponding to it is born after it.

In this respect language differs radically from the superstructure. Take, for example, Russian society and the Russian language. During the past 30 years the old capitalist base has been liquidated in Russia and a new, socialist base constructed. Correspondingly, the superstructure over the capitalist base has been eliminated and a new superstructure created corresponding to the socialist base. Consequently, the old political, legal, etc., institutions have been replaced by new, socialist ones. Despite this, however, the Russian language has remained basically the same as it was before the October revolution.

What changes occurred during this period in the Russian language? To a certain extent the vocabulary of the Russian language changed, in the sense that a large number of new words and expressions were added which had appeared as a result of the development of a new, socialist mode of production, the appearance of a new state, a new socialist culture, a new public opinion and morality and, finally, as a result of the development of science and technology. A number of words and expressions underwent a change in meaning and acquired new significance. A certain number of obsolete words disappeared from the vocabulary. As for the basic lexical fund and

[2] From *Pravda,* June 20, 1950, pp. 3–4.

the grammatical structure of the Russian language, which comprise the basis of the language, after the elimination of the capitalist base they were not only not eliminated and replaced by a new basic lexical fund and a new grammatical structure, but, on the contrary, were retained in their entirety and remained without any serious alterations. They were retained precisely on the basis of the contemporary Russian language.

To continue. The superstructure is generated by the base, but this by no means signifies that it merely reflects the base, that it is passive, neutral and indifferent to the fate of its base, to the fate of classes, to the character of the system. On the contrary, having put in an appearance, it then becomes a most active force which contributes vigorously to the formation and consolidation of its base, takes all steps to assist the new order to drive the old base and the former classes into the dust and liquidate them.

It could not be otherwise. The superstructure is created by the base to serve it, to help it actively in taking shape and growing strong, to struggle vigorously to get rid of the old base and its old superstructure which have outlived their time. The superstructure has merely to renounce its role as servitor, to switch from the active defense of its base to an attitude of indifference to it, to an attitude of an equal approach to the classes for it to lose its quality and cease to be a superstructure.

In this respect language differs radically from superstructure. Language is generated not by one base or another, by the old base or the new within a given society, but by the entire historic development of society and the history of the bases over the centuries. It is created not by any one class but by the whole society, by all classes of society, by the efforts of hundreds of generations. It is created not to meet the needs of any one class but of the whole society, of all classes in society. This is precisely why it is created as the language of the whole people, as a society's single language, common to all members of the society. In view of this, the role of language as a servant, as a means of communication for people consists not in serving one class to the detriment of other classes but in equal service to the entire society, to all classes in society. Strictly speaking, this is the reason why language can serve equally both the old, dying order and the new, emerging one, both the old base and the new, both exploiters and the exploited.

It is no secret that the Russian language served Russian capitalism and Russian bourgeois culture before the October revolution just as well as it now serves the socialist system and the socialist culture of Russian society.

The same holds true of Ukrainian, Belorussian, Uzbek, Kazakh, Georgian, Armenian, Estonian, Latvian, Lithuanian, Moldavian, Tatar, Azerbaidzhanian, Bashkir, Turkmenian and the other languages of the Soviet nations which served the old bourgeois systems in those nations as well as they are now serving the new, socialist system.

It cannot be otherwise. Language exists, it is created, to serve society as a whole in the capacity of a means of communication for people, to be common to the members of a society and one and the same for the society, serving the members of the society equally, regardless of their class position. Language has only to depart from this position with respect to the entire people, language has only to show preference for and render support to a particular social group, to the detriment of other social groups of the society for it to lose its quality, for it to cease to be a means of communication of people in a society, for it to become the jargon of a particular social group, for it to degenerate and doom itself to extinction.

In this respect language, while differing fundamentally from the superstructure, is not, however, different from the tools of production, machinery, say, which can serve both capitalism and socialism equally. . . .

Thus: (a) a Marxist cannot regard language as a superstructure over a base; (b) to confuse language with superstructure is to commit a grave error.

Question: Is it true that language has always been and remains of a class nature; that a single, non-class language common to a whole society and a whole people does not exist?

Answer: No, it is not true.

It is easy to see that there can be no question of a class language in a society without classes. The primitive clan society did not have classes and hence there could not have been a class language in it. There language was general. There was a single language for the whole collective. The objection that a class should be understood as any human collective, including the primitive commune, is not an objection but a play on words not meriting refutation.

As for subsequent development, from clan languages to tribal, from tribal languages to the languages of peoples and from the languages of peoples to national languages—everywhere, at every stage of development, language, as a means of communication for people in society, was common and single for the society, serving the members of society equally, regardless of social position.

Here I have in mind not the empires of the slave-owning and medieval periods, say the empire of Cyrus and Alexander the Great, or the empires of Caesar and Charlemagne, which did not have their own economic base and were temporary and unstable military and administrative combinations. These empires not only did not possess but could not have possessed a single language understandable to all members of society. They were a conglomeration of tribes and peoples who lived their own lives and had their own languages. Consequently, I am not referring to these empires and their like but to the tribes and peoples which comprised the empires and possessed their own economic bases and their own languages, which had developed in very ancient times. History shows that the languages of these tribes and peoples were not class languages but languages of the whole people, common for the tribes and peoples and understandable to them.

Of course, along with them were dialects and local tongues, but the single common language of the tribe or people predominated over them and made them subordinate.

Later on when capitalism appeared and feudal disunity was overcome, when the national market was formed, peoples developed into nations and the languages of peoples into the languages of nations. History shows that national languages are not class languages but are common to the whole people, common to the members of nations and one and the same for the nation.

I stated above that as a means of communication among people in society a language serves equally all classes in society and in this respect is, in a manner of speaking, indifferent to classes. But people, particular social groups and classes, are anything but indifferent to language. They try to use language for their own interest, to impose their own special vocabulary, terminology, their own special expressions, upon it. The uppermost layer of the propertied classes, divorced from the people and hating them, stand out particularly in this respect. Such are the aristocracy of the nobility and the upper strata of the bourgeoisie. "Class" dialects, jargons and salon "languages" developed. The literature [on the subject] not infrequently wrongly qualifies these dialects and jargons as languages and refers to "the language of the nobility," "the language of the bourgeoisie," in contrast to "the language of the proletariat," or "the language of the peasantry." Strange as it may seem, it was for this reason that some of our comrades reached the conclusion that a national language was a fiction and that only class languages actually existed.

I maintain that nothing could be more erroneous. Can these dialects and jargons be considered languages? Absolutely not. This is, first of all, because these dialects and jargons do not have their own grammar and basic lexical fund. They borrow them from the national language. Secondly, because the dialects and jargons circulate within a narrow sphere among the upper strata of a particular class and are totally worthless as a means of communication for people, for society as a whole. What do they actually have? They have a selection of certain specific words which reflect the specific tastes of the aristocracy or the upper strata of the bourgeoisie; a certain number of expressions and turns of speech distinguished for their refinement, gallantry, and free of the "coarse" expressions and figures of speech of the national language, and, finally, a certain number of foreign words. Everything basic, however, that is, the great majority of words and the grammar, are taken from the national language, common to the whole people. Consequently dialects and jargons are ramifications of the common national language of the people, are lacking in any independence as languages and are doomed to stagnation. To believe that dialects and jargons can develop into independent languages which are able to drive out and replace the national language is to lose sight of historical perspective and depart from the Marxist position.

Marx has been referred to and one place has been cited from his article "Holy Max" where he wrote that the bourgeois had his "own language," that this language "is the product of the bourgeoisie," that it is permeated with the spirit of mercantilism and of buying and selling. With this quotation some comrades would like to prove that Marx allegedly believed in the class nature of language and denied that a single national language existed. If these comrades had approached the question objectively they should also have quoted another place in the same article "Holy Max" where Marx, referring to the ways in which a single national language is formed, speaks of the "concentration of dialects into a single national language resulting from economic and political concentration."

Marx, consequently, admitted the need for a *single* national language as the superior form to which dialects, as lower forms, were subordinate.

In this event, what can the language of the bourgeois be, which in Marx's words "is the product of the bourgeoisie." Did Marx consider it a language just the same as a national language with its own special language structure? Could he have considered it to be such a language? Of course not! Marx simply wanted to say that the bourgeois had profaned the single national language with its vocabulary of cheap commercialism, that the bourgeois, consequently, had his own cheap commercial jargon.

The result is that these comrades have distorted Marx's point. They distorted it by quoting Marx not as Marxists but as pedants without looking into the essence of the matter.

References are made to Engels and to the quotation from his pamphlet *The Condition of the Working Class in England* where Engels says that ". . . in the course of time the British working class has become an entirely different people from the British bourgeoisie," that "the workers speak a different dialect and have different ideas and notions, different mores and moral principles, a different religion and different politics from the bourgeoisie." On the basis of this quotation certain comrades have concluded that Engels denied the need for a national language common to the whole people, that he consequently advocated the "class nature" of language. It is true that Engels is here speaking not of a language but of a dialect, fully comprehending that a dialect, as a ramification of the national language, cannot replace the national language. But evidently these comrades are not very sympathetic to the existence of a difference between language and dialects.

It is obvious that this quotation has been inappropriately cited since Engels is here speaking not of "class languages" but principally about class ideas, notions, mores, moral principles, religion and politics. It is perfectly true that the ideas, notions, mores, moral principles, religion and politics of the bourgeois and proletariat are directly opposite. But what has the national language or the "class" nature of language to do with this? Can the presence of class contradictions in society serve as an argument in favor of the "class nature" of language, or against the need for a single national language? Marxism holds that a common language is one of the most important characteristics of a nation, knowing well that there are class contradictions within a nation. Do the aforementioned comrades recognize this Marxist thesis? . . .

Reference is made to the fact that at one time the feudal lords in England "for centuries" spoke French while the English people spoke English, and that this circumstance is allegedly an argument in favor of the "class nature" of language and against the need for a language common to the whole people. This is not an argument, however, but a kind of anecdote. Firstly, all the feudal lords did not speak French at that time, but only a small upper stratum of English feudal lords attached to the court and in the counties. Secondly, it was not some special "class language" they spoke but ordinary French common to the whole people. Thirdly, it is known that the affection of French later disappeared without a trace, yielding to the English language of the whole people. Do these comrades maintain that "for centuries" the English feudal lords communed with the English people through the medium of interpreters, that they did not use English, that an English language did not then exist for the whole people, that at that time the French language was anything more important in England than the language of the salon, current only in a narrow circle of the upper layer of the English aristocracy? How can one deny the existence of and need for a language common to the whole people on the basis of such anecdotal "arguments"?

At one time Russian aristocrats also flirted with French at the Tsar's court and in the salons. It was their boast that while speaking Russian they hiccuped in French, that they could speak Russian only with a French accent. Does this mean that there was no common Russian language in Russia at the time, that a language common to the whole people was a fiction at that time whereas "class languages" were the reality?

Here our comrades make at least two mistakes.

The first mistake is that they confuse language and superstructure. They hold that if superstructure is of a class nature, then language too should be of a class nature and not common to the people as a whole. But I have already remarked above that language and superstructure are two different concepts and that a Marxist cannot admit of their confusion.

The second mistake is that these comrades regard the contradictory nature of the interests of the bourgeoisie and the proletariat, their violent class warfare, as the disintegration of society and the break of all ties between the hostile classes. They maintain that since society has fallen apart and there is no longer a single society but only classes, a single language for society, a national language, is also superfluous. What then remains if society has fallen apart and there is no longer a national language common to the whole people? Classes and "class languages" remain. Every "class language" will, understandably, have its own "class" grammar,—a "proletarian" grammar, a "bourgeois" grammar. True, such grammars do not exist in reality but these comrades are not embarrassed by this. They believe that such grammars will appear.

There were once "Marxists" among us who maintained that the railroads which remained in our country after the October revolution were bourgeois, that we Marxists ought not to use them, that they should be torn up and new "proletarian" railroads built. For this they earned the sobriquet of "troglodytes."

Of course such a primitive anarchistic view of society, classes and language has nothing in common with Marxism. But there can be no doubt whatever that it exists and still lives in the minds of certain of our confused comrades.

It is, of course, wrong to say that because of the existence of a violent class struggle society has allegedly split into classes which are economically no longer associated with each other in one society. On the contrary. As long as capitalism exists the bourgeoisie and the proletariat will be connected with each other by every economic tie as parts of a single capitalist society. The bourgeoisie cannot live and grow rich without having hired workers at its disposal; the proletariat cannot continue its existence without hiring out to the capitalists. The termination of all economic ties between them signifies the end of any production. The end of all production, moreover, leads to the ruin of society, to the ruin of the classes themselves. It is understandable that no class will want to undergo annihilation. Class struggle, therefore, no matter how acute, cannot result in the disintegration of society. Only ignorance in Marxist problems and utter failure to comprehend the nature of language could have suggested to certain of our comrades the fairy tale about the disintegration of society, about "class" languages and "class" grammars.

Furthermore they refer to Lenin and recall that Lenin recognized the existence of two cultures under capitalism, the bourgeois and the proletarian, that the slogan of a national culture under capitalism was a nationalistic slogan. All this is correct and Lenin here was absolutely right. But what has the "class nature" of language to do with this? They cite Lenin's remarks on two cultures under capitalism, evidently desiring to make the reader believe that the presence of two cultures in society, bourgeois and proletarian, means that there must also be two languages, since language is associated with culture; consequently, Lenin was denying the need for a single national language; Lenin was consequently holding a brief for "class" languages. Here these comrades make the error of identifying and confusing language with culture. But culture and language are two different things. Culture may be both bourgeois and socialist whereas language as a means of communication is always common to a whole people and can serve both bourgeois and socialist culture. Is it not true that Russian, Ukrainian and Uzbek are now serving the socialist culture of these nations just as satisfactorily as they served their bourgeois cultures before the October revolution? Thus these comrades are profoundly in error when they declare that the presence of two different cultures leads to the formation of two different languages and to the denial that a single language must exist.

When he spoke of two cultures, Lenin was proceeding from precisely that thesis that the presence of two cultures cannot lead to the denial of a single language and the formation of two languages, that language must be single. When the members of the Bund charged Lenin with denying the need for a national language and treating culture as "nationless," Lenin, as is known, abruptly protested and declared that he was fighting against bourgeois culture and not against a national language, the need for which he considered indisputable. Certain of our comrades have strangely wandered into the footsteps of the Bundists.

As for a single language, the need for which it is alleged that Lenin denied, we ought to heed the following words of Lenin:

Language is an extremely important means of human communication; the unity of language and its unimpeded development constitute one of the most important conditions for an organization of trade which will be really free and broad corresponding to contemporary capitalism and for a free and broad grouping of population according to all individual classes.

It turns out that the esteemed comrades have distorted Lenin's views.

Finally they refer to Stalin. They cite a quotation from Stalin to the effect that "the bourgeoisie and its nationalistic parties have been and remain the cardinal directing force of these nations in this period." All this is correct. The bourgeoisie and its nationalistic party really do control bourgeois culture just as the proletariat and its internationalist party control proletarian culture. But what does the "class nature" of language have to do with this? Surely these comrades must know that a national language is a form of national culture, that a national language can serve both bourgeois and socialist culture. Can it be that our comrades are not aware of the well-known Marxist formula that contemporary Russian, Ukrainian, Belorussian and other cultures are socialist in content and national in form, that is, in language? Do they agree with this Marxist formula?

The mistake our comrades make here is that they fail to see the difference between culture and language and do not understand that the content of culture changes with each new period in society's development while language remains basically the same language throughout several periods, serving equally both the new culture and the old.

SUMMARY

Hence: (a) language as a means of communication has always been and remains one and the same for society and common to its members; (b) the existence of dialects and jargons does not refute but confirms the existence of a language common to the whole people of which they are ramifications and to which they are subordinate; (c) the formula of the "class nature" of language is an erroneous, un-Marxist formula. . . .

Question: Was Pravda right in opening a free discussion of linguistic problems?

Answer: It did the right thing. . . . It can already be said that the discussion has been a great benefit. The discussion has made it clear, first of all, that both in the center and in the republics a regime has dominated in linguistic bodies not typical of science and men of science. The slightest criticism of the state of affairs in Soviet linguistics, even the most timid attempts to criticize the so-called "new teaching" in linguistics, was persecuted and stifled by the directors of linguistic circles. Valuable scholars and research workers in linguistics were removed from their positions and reduced in status for criticism of the heritage of N. Ya. Marr and for the slightest disapproval of his teaching. Linguists were moved up into responsible positions not according to their qualifications in the field but as they gave unconditional recognition to N. Ya. Marr's teaching.

It is universally recognized that no science can develop and flourish without a struggle of opinions, without free criticism. But this universally recognized rule has been ignored and trampled upon most unceremoniously. A self-contained group of infallible leaders has developed which has begun to ride rough-shod and behave in the most arbitrary manner after guaranteeing itself against any possible criticism.

An example: the so-called "Baku course" (lectures which N. Ya. Marr delivered in Baku) which the author himself rejected and forbade to be republished was, however, at the orders of the caste of leaders (Comrade Meshchaninov calls them "pupils" of N. Ya. Marr) republished and included without any reservations among the textual aids recommended for students. This means that the students were cheated by being given the rejected "course" as a worthy text. Were I not convinced of the honesty of Comrade Meshchaninov and other linguists I should say that such behavior was equivalent to wrecking.

How could this have happened? This happened because the Arakcheyev-like regime established in linguistics cultivates irresponsibility and encourages such disorders.

The discussion has proved extremely useful mainly because it has brought to light this Arakcheyev-like regime and smashed it to bits.

But the usefulness of the discussion does not end here. The discussion has not only smashed the old regime in linguistics. It has also brought to light the incredible confusion in views on the most important problems of linguistics which reigns among leading circles in this branch of science. Before the discussion began, they were silent and ignored the unwholesome situation in linguistics. But after the discussion began, it became impossible for them to keep silent and they were compelled to stand forth in the pages of the press. Well? It turned out that N. Ya. Marr's teaching contained a whole series of gaps, mistakes, inaccurately formulated problems, incompletely elaborated theses. One may ask why is it that the "pupils" of N. Ya. Marr have spoken up on this score only now, after the discussion has begun? Why did they show no concern for this earlier? Why is it that they did not speak openly and honestly on the subject earlier, as befits scientists? Recognizing "certain" errors of N. Ya. Marr, the "pupils" of N. Ya. Marr, it appears, think that Soviet linguistics can be further developed only on the basis of the "refined" theory of N. Ya. Marr which they consider Marxist. Please preserve us from the "Marxism" of N. Ya. Marr. N. Ya. Marr really did want to and tried to be a Marxist, but he did not succeed in becoming a Marxist. He was merely a simplifier and vulgarizer of Marxism, like the followers of the "Proletkult" or "RAPP."

N. Ya. Marr introduced into linguistics an erroneous, un-Marxist formula of language as a superstructure. He confused himself; he confused linguistics. It is impossible to develop Soviet linguistics on the basis of an incorrect formula.

N. Ya. Marr introduced into linguistics another formula, also wrong and un-Marxist, regarding the "class nature" of language. He confused himself; he confused linguistics. It is impossible to develop linguistics on the basis of a wrong formula which contradicts the entire history of peoples and languages.

N. Ya. Marr introduced into linguistics an immodest, boastful, arrogant tone, not characteristic of Marxism and leading to the wholesale and irresponsible rejection of everything in linguistics before N. Ya. Marr.

N. Ya. Marr noisily fulminated against the method of comparative historical analysis as "idealist." Nonetheless it must be said that, notwithstanding its substantial shortcomings, the method of comparative historical analysis is still better than the really idealist four-element analysis of N. Ya. Marr. Since the former is an impetus to work, to study languages, and the second is an impetus to lying on top of the oven and reading teacups about the notorious four elements.

N. Ya. Marr arrogantly dismissed any attempt to study groups (families) of languages as a manifestation of the theory of the "protolanguage." It cannot be denied, however, that language kinship, for example, of such nations as the Slavs is beyond dispute, that the study of the linguistic kinship of these nations could be of great benefit to linguistics in studying the laws of the development of language. Understandably, the "protolanguage" theory has nothing to do with this matter.

To listen to N. Ya. Marr, and particularly his "pupils," one might think that there was no linguistics before N. Ya. Marr, that linguistics began with the appearance of N. Ya. Marr's "new teaching." Marx and Engels were considerably more modest. They believed that their dialectical materialism was the product of the development of sciences, philosophy included, over preceding periods.

Thus, the discussion was also of benefit to the extent that it brought to light ideological lacunae in Soviet linguistics.

It is my belief that the sooner our linguistics frees itself of N. Ya. Marr's errors, the sooner it can emerge from the crisis in which it now finds itself.

The liquidation of the Arakcheyev-like regime in linguistics, the repudiation of N. Ya. Marr's mistakes and the inculcation of Marxism in linguistics —such is, in my opinon, the way which would make it possible to instill new health in Soviet linguistics.

PROFESSOR N. YAKOVLEV: LET US CORRECT MISTAKES IN OUR WORK [3]

The appearance in the pages of *Pravda* of J. V. Stalin's article "On Marxism in Linguistics" is a real triumph for Soviet science and a cause of celebration not only for us Soviet linguists but also for our historians, ethnographers, and philosophers. For the first time in history a work is published which is wholly dedicated to Marxist-Leninist teaching on language and illuminates the basic theoretical problems of linguistics.

At the base of all true science, including linguistics, must stand a correct Marxist-Leninist methodology. Nevertheless many linguists have not devoted enough attention to the mastery of this methodology. Therefore, despite the tremendous assistance which the development of science in the U.S.S.R. has been constantly given and is still given by the Party and the government, we Soviet linguists have to this day not always been able to figure out the basic problem of our science, the problem of what language is. This was particularly true of the works of the author of this article.

In revealing the radical difference between language and superstructure, J. V. Stalin discovered the basic defect in the work of many linguists who incorrectly considered language as an ideological superstructure on an economic base.

J. V. Stalin's exhaustively complete, profound and clear solution of the basic problem of the radical difference between language and superstructure has become the only methodological weapon with whose aid we can now confidently build a Marxist-Leninist linguistics.

One can express confidence that, having mastered Marxism-Leninism, in a very short time Soviet linguists will overcome in their research work the inadequacies of the comparative-historical method and will be able to apply in their field the method of historical materialism.

[3] From *Pravda,* July 4, 1950, p. 4.

It was only in the course of the free discussion in the pages of *Pravda* that the errors of N. Ya. Marr were revealed in all their nakedness and unsightliness. Comrade Stalin has shown that these errors were not accidental but made up a whole system of erroneous, pseudoscientific theses: language as superstructure, the "class nature" of language, the utterly idealist four-element analysis, the wholesale libeling of the comparative-historical method and of all attempts to study related groups (families) of languages and so on.

N. Ya. Marr's grossest errors made up a whole system of incorrect views and fully justify the characterization of N. Ya. Marr drawn by Comrade Stalin: "Marr really did want to and tried to be a Marxist, but he did not succeed in becoming a Marxist. He was merely a simplifier and vulgarizer of Marxism, like the followers of the 'Proletkult' or 'RAPP.' "

As a consequence of the "Arakcheyev-like regime," which began in linguistics while N. Ya. Marr was still alive, many scholars (not only linguists, but ethnographers, archeologists and historians as well) turned out to have lost their common sense and a correct criterion in evaluating N. Ya. Marr's works.

One must admit that the work written by me jointly with Prof. V. K. Nikolsky, "The Basic Theses of N. Ya. Marr's Doctrine of Language" (*Voprosy filosofii,* No. 1, 1949), contains in the opinion of both authors excessive praise of obviously erroneous theses of N. Ya. Marr.

Equally erroneous is another one of my articles "Marr as Citizen and Scholar—on the Fifteenth Anniversary of His Death" (*Scholarly Notes of the Kabardin Scientific Institute,* Vol. V, 1950). In addition, in a number of my specialized works—*Grammar of the Adighe Language* (1941), *Grammar of the Kabardinian-Cherkess Language* (1949), and others—one can find occasional uncritical references to N. Ya. Marr's mistaken theses. All this places upon me the greatest responsibility, having perceived these erroneous parts, to correct them through an accurate methodology and a scientific criticism of Academician N. Ya. Marr's pseudoscientific theses in my future works.

Comrade Stalin says: "Recognizing 'certain' errors of N. Ya. Marr, the 'pupils' of N. Ya. Marr it appears, think that Soviet linguistics can be further developed only on the basis of the 'refined' theory of N. Ya. Marr which they consider Marxist."

I think that all who, like us, erred terribly about Marr's "Marxism," might well remember the old Latin proverb: "All men can make mistakes but only fools persist in their errors." One learns from mistakes. I intend to correct my errors honestly in future work.

Armed with the Stalinist teaching on language, Soviet linguists are now placed in the front ranks of fighters for progressive materialist science. All who prize the success of Soviet linguistics will warmly greet Comrade Stalin's concluding words:

"The liquidation of the Arakcheyev-like regime in linguistics, the repudiation of N. Ya. Marr's mistakes and the inculcation of Marxism in linguistics —such is, in my opinion, the way which would make it possible to instill new health in Soviet linguistics."

ACADEMICIAN I. MESHCHANINOV: LETTER TO THE EDITORS [4]

In J. V. Stalin's remarkable work "On Marxism in Linguistics" we Soviet linguists have received for the first time an extremely lucid definition of the nature of language and of the further paths of development of the Soviet science of language.

The majority of us Soviet linguists, and especially myself, were so firmly convinced that language was a phenomenon of a superstructural nature that we did not even make any effort to think over those definitions of superstructures and their relation to the base which are contained in the Marxist-Leninist classics. Hence the erroneousness of many of our other theoretical theses.

Our recognition of the superstructural nature of language inevitably led to the incorrect assertion of its class nature, of its development through "upheavals" and consequently of the incorrect evaluation of the role of language hybridization as the basis of language formation and development. Following the same path, we were unable to understand truly the historical process of the formation of peoples and the development of languages. The extremely exaggerated evaluation of Marr's role in the development of Soviet linguistics, his elevation to the position of being almost the only positive figure not only in this field but in a whole series of related disciplines, follows from the above. Hence, also, the contemptuous attitude to the heritage of all Russian linguistics antecedent to Marr.

These and many other errors of Marr himself and of his pupils, particularly myself, actually led to stagnation in Soviet linguistics. We feared like the plague any application of the comparative-historical method, thinking naively that such attempts inevitably would lead to a return to the formalist-idealist ideas of the last century's science. We were unable to understand correctly the basis of language, its specific essence. The attempts made to study the grammatical structure of languages were indiscriminately proclaimed formalistic and met with direct opposition from the representatives of that linguis-

[4] From *Pravda,* July 4, 1950, p. 4.

tic regime which Comrade Stalin quite correctly labeled as Arakcheyev-like. Insistently and, unfortunately, not without some "success" the subject matter of linguistics was artificially torn from the urgent requirements of linguistic development and directed into bygone ages.

In his article Comrade Stalin laid a foundation for Soviet linguistics and opened a new era in its history; only after we had carefully thought through the nature of language as disclosed in that article could we who had followed Marr too uncritically see the error of the theoretical path taken by our investigations, a path along which we had led the young generation. The positive aspects of our work directed toward a thorough study of the vocabularies and grammatical structures of the languages of our multinational motherland were drowned in these vulgar errors.

The invaluable aid of Comrade Stalin calls forth deep and sincere gratitude in the hearts of Soviet linguists. He has liberated Soviet linguistics from stagnation and led it onto the broad path of truly scientific creativity.

We are confronted with a difficult but honorable and responsible task—to follow unswervingly Comrade Stalin's indications and to reorganize radically our investigative work on the foundation of a thorough mastery of the methodological and theoretical principles of Marxism-Leninism.

Let us remember firmly and follow unhesitatingly the wise words of our great leader and coryphaeus of science: "The liquidation of the Arakcheyev-like regime in linguistics, the repudiation of N. Ya. Marr's mistakes and the inculcation of Marxism in linguistics—such is, in my opinion, the way that would make it possible to instill new health in Soviet linguistics."

PROFESSOR N. CHEMODANOV: LETTER TO THE EDITORS [5]

In the light of Comrade Stalin's work "On Marxism in Linguistics" I must admit the utter erroneousness of my article "The Paths of Development of Soviet Linguistics" printed in *Pravda* of May 23, 1950, which reflected my mistakes in the basic problems of linguistics.

My fundamental error consists in my incorrect, un-Marxist view of language as a social superstructure on the base, in erroneously identifying language with social ideology and considering it to be a class phenomenon. Incorrectly, I considered N. Ya. Marr's theory on language basically Marxist and held that, freed of certain errors, it represented the general line of development of linguistics.

Now, after Comrade Stalin's article, it has become clear to me that this is not at all true. Comrade Stalin's brilliant new work is a tremendous event,

[5] From *Pravda,* July 4, 1950, p. 4.

a turning point in the development of social sciences. Among Marxist-Leninist classics on linguistics it is the most outstanding, the fullest and most systematic exposition of Marxism in this field of knowledge.

Comrade Stalin's work has created a firm theoretical foundation for Soviet linguistics and has destroyed the confusion in points of view which has existed until now. Soviet linguists can only be grateful to Comrade Stalin for fatherly assistance.

Now, after the publication of Comrade Stalin's work, the task is to realize the errors which were made [and then] to assume decisively and unconditionally the Marxist positions formulated by Comrade Stalin and in our practical scientific and educational work to transform Comrade Stalin's indications into life.

ALFREDO ROCCO

FASCISM—to use that term in its general sense to denote those modern totalitarian movements of a specifically non-Marxist character of which Fascism in Italy and Nazism in Germany were the archetypes—was always permeated with a thoroughgoing hostility to reason, both in human discourse and as a regulating principle of social relations. Although fascism often reinforced itself by appeal to traditional sentiments of patriotism or religion, its real attraction lay in its rejection of all accepted values. And although it used the rationalized framework of the modern state to consolidate power, it achieved that power without offering a reasoned set of policies designed to solve the great economic, social, and political problems of the age. Fascism had no theory. It was only after the fascist dictatorship was established that it was felt necessary, or expedient, to offer a rationalization or apologia. This was especially true in Italy where, years after the "March on Rome," an attempt was made to provide the dictatorship with some measure of intellectual substance and respectability. In this attempt Alfredo Rocco (1875–1935) was of considerable importance, for he was the chief ideologue of Mussolini's regime.

Before the advent of Mussolini's dictatorship in Italy, Rocco was a jurist and professor of law as well as a prominent member of the right-wing Nationalist Party. After the "March on Rome" that party, under the leadership of Rocco and others, came over to the Fascist camp. In 1924, Rocco was rewarded for his services by being made president of the Chamber of Deputies, and in 1925 he was appointed Minister of Justice, a position of decisive importance in a state that rejected the traditional rule of law. In that post Rocco guided the revision of the Penal Code from 1925 to 1930, a code that invoked heavy penalties even for the mildest criticism of the Fascist regime, and supervised a purge of the civil service. He justified that purge in the following words:

"It is an unavoidable necessity of the State, that all those who belong to public administration must not only observe with scrupulous regularity the specific duties of their office, but further carry out every activity in whatever form, with intimate, convinced, and sincere devotion to the State, in the particular positive order which it assumes at a determinate historic phase of its development. This follows from the very nature of the relationship of public employment, according to the fundamental conception of it, as laid down by the national Government, as a militia into which one enters and in which one has the title to remain only when conscience, which inspires and upholds work, responds to the impulses not of an enforced exterior discipline, but to a spontaneous spiritual persuasion, concentrated in the oath. . . . This supreme exigency implies that the public official must be considered as unsatisfactory for his duties, not only for the material inobservance of single legislative or regulation dispositions, which discipline bureaucratic action, but also for attitudes which contrast with the national spirit, from which those dispositions, like any other law of the State, have drawn their life." (*La Transformazione dello stato.*)

The following selection is from a speech first delivered by Rocco at Perugia, Italy, in 1925. The address had the express approval of Mussolini and may be regarded as an official expression of Fascist ideology, manufactured to order. It appears here in the translation of Dino Bigongiari which was published by the Carnegie Endowment for International Peace (1926).

1926

THE POLITICAL DOCTRINE OF FASCISM

FASCISM AS ACTION, AS FEELING, AND AS THOUGHT

Much has been said, and is now being said for or against this complex political and social phenomenon which in the brief period of six years has taken complete hold of Italian life and, spreading beyond the borders of the Kingdom, has made itself felt in varying degrees of intensity throughout the world. But people have been much more eager to extol or to deplore than to understand—which is natural enough in a period of tumultuous fervor and of political passion. The time has not yet arrived for a dispassionate judgment. For even I, who noticed the very first manifestations of this great development, saw its significance from the start and participated directly in its first doings, carefully watching all its early uncertain and changing developments, even I do not feel competent to pass definite judgment. Fascism is so large a part of myself that it would be both arbitrary and absurd for me to try to dissociate my personality from it, to submit it to impartial scrutiny in order to evaluate it coldly and accurately. What can be done, however, and it seldom is attempted, is to make inquiry into the phenomenon which shall not merely consider its fragmentary and adventitious aspects, but strive to get at its inner essence. The undertaking may not be easy, but it is necessary, and no occasion for attempting it is more suitable than the present one afforded me by my friends of Perugia. Suitable it is in time because, at the inauguration of a course of lectures and lessons principally intended to illustrate that old and glorious trend of the life and history of Italy which takes its name from the humble saint of Assisi, it seemed natural to connect it with the greatest achievement of modern Italy, different in so many ways from the Franciscan

---

This selection has been reprinted from Alfredo Rocco, "The Political Doctrine of Fascism," *International Conciliation,* No. 223 (Oct., 1926), pp. 393–415, by permission of the Carnegie Endowment for International Peace.

movement, but united with it by the mighty common current of Italian History. It is suitable as well in place because at Perugia, which witnessed the growth of our religious ideas, of our political doctrines and of our legal science in the course of the most glorious centuries of our cultural history, the mind is properly disposed and almost oriented towards an investigation of this nature.

First of all let us ask ourselves if there is a political doctrine of Fascism; if there is any ideal content in the Fascist state. For in order to link Fascism, both as concept and system, with the history of Italian thought and find therein a place for it, we must first show that it is thought; that it is a doctrine. Many persons are not quite convinced that it is either the one or the other; and I am not referring solely to those men, cultured or uncultured, as the case may be and very numerous everywhere, who can discern in this political innovation nothing except its local and personal aspects, and who know Fascism only as the particular manner of behavior of this or that well-known Fascist, of this or that group of a certain town; who therefore like or dislike the movement on the basis of their likes and dislikes for the individuals who represent it. Nor do I refer to those intelligent and cultivated persons, very intelligent indeed and very cultivated, who because of their direct or indirect allegiance to the parties that have been dispossessed by the advent of Fascism, have a natural cause of resentment against it and are therefore unable to see, in the blindness of hatred, anything good in it. I am referring rather to those—and there are many in our ranks too—who know Fascism as action and feeling but not yet as thought, who therefore have an intuition but no comprehension of it.

It is true that Fascism is, above all, action and sentiment and that such it must continue to be. Were it otherwise, it could not keep up that immense driving force, that renovating power which it now possesses and would merely be the solitary meditation of a chosen few. Only because it is feeling and sentiment, only because it is the unconscious reawakening of our profound racial instinct, has it the force to stir the soul of the people, and to set free an irresistible current of national will. Only because it is action, and as such actualizes itself in a vast organization and in a huge movement, has it the conditions for determining the historical course of contemporary Italy.

But Fascism is thought as well and it has a theory, which is an essential part of this historical phenomenon, and which is responsible in a great measure for the successes that have been achieved. To the existence of this ideal content of Fascism, to the truth of this Fascist logic we ascribe the fact that though we commit many errors of detail, we very seldom go astray on fundamentals, whereas all the parties of the opposition, deprived as they are of an informing, animating principle, of a unique directing concept, do very often wage their war faultlessly in minor tactics, better trained as they are in parliamentary and journalistic manoeuvres, but they constantly break down on the important issues. Fascism, moreover, considered as action, is a typically Italian phenomenon and acquires a universal validity because of the existence of this coherent and organic doctrine. The originality of Fascism is due in great part to the autonomy of its theoretical principles. For even when, in its external behavior and in its conclusions, it seems identical with other political creeds, in reality it possesses an inner originality due to the new spirit which animates it and to an entirely different theoretical approach.

COMMON ORIGINS AND COMMON BACKGROUND OF MODERN POLITICAL DOCTRINES: FROM LIBERALISM TO SOCIALISM

Modern political thought remained, until recently, both in Italy and outside of Italy under the absolute control of those doctrines which, proceeding from the Protestant Reformation and developed by the adepts of natural law in the XVII and XVIII centuries, were firmly grounded in the institutions and customs of the English, of the American, and of the French Revolutions. Under different and sometimes clashing forms these doctrines have left a determining imprint upon all theories and actions both social and political, of the XIX and XX centuries down to the rise of Fascism. The common basis of all these doctrines, which stretch from Longuet, from Buchanan, and from Althusen down to Karl Marx, to Wilson and to Lenin is a social and state concept which I call mechanical or atomistic.

Society according to this concept is merely a sum total of individuals, a plurality which breaks up into its single components. Therefore the ends of a society, so considered, are nothing more than the ends of the individuals which compose it and for whose sake it exists. An atomistic view of this kind is also necessarily anti-historical, inasmuch as it considers society in its spatial attributes and not in its temporal ones; and because it reduces social life to the existence of a single generation. Society becomes thus a sum of determined individuals, viz., the generation living at a given moment. This doctrine which I call atomistic and which appears to be anti-historical, reveals from under a concealing cloak a strongly materialistic nature. For in its endeavors to isolate the present from the past and the future, it rejects the spiritual inheritance of ideas and sentiments which each generation receives from those preceding and hands down to the following generation, thus destroying the unity and the spiritual life itself of human society.

This common basis shows the close logical connection existing between all political doctrines; the substantial solidarity, which unites all the political movements, from Liberalism to Socialism, that until recently have dominated Europe. For these political schools differ from one another in their methods, but all agree as to the ends to be achieved. All of them consider the welfare and happiness of individuals to be the goal of society, itself considered as composed of individuals of the present generation. All of them see in society and in its juridical organization, the state, the mere instrument and means whereby individuals can attain their ends. They differ only in that the methods pursued for the attainment of these ends vary considerably one from the other.

Thus the Liberals insist that the best manner to secure the welfare of the citizens as individuals is to interfere as little as possible with the free development of their activities and that therefore the essential task of the state is merely to coordinate these several liberties in such a way as to guarantee their coexistence. Kant, who was without doubt the most powerful and thorough philosopher of liberalism, said "man, who is the end, cannot be assumed to have the value of an instrument." And again "justice, of which the state is the specific organ, is the condition whereby the freedom of each is conditioned upon the freedom of others, according to the general law of liberty."

Having thus defined the task of the state, Liberalism confines itself to the demand of certain guarantees which are to keep the state from overstepping its functions as general coordinator of liberties and from sacrificing the freedom of individuals more than is absolutely necessary for the accomplishment of its purpose. All the efforts are therefore directed to see to it that the ruler, mandatory of all and entrusted with the realization, through and by liberty, of the harmonious happiness of everybody, should never be clothed with undue power. Hence the creation of a system of checks and limitations designed to keep the rulers within bounds; and among these, first and foremost, the principle of the division of powers, contrived as a means for weakening the state in its relation to the individual, by making it impossible for the state ever to appear, in its dealings with citizens, in the full plenitude of sovereign powers; also the principle of the participation of citizens in the lawmaking power, as a means for securing, in behalf of the individual, a direct check on this, the strongest branch, and an indirect check on the entire government of the state. This system of checks and limitations, which goes by the name of constitutional government, resulted in a moderate and measured liberalism. The checking power was exercised only by those citizens who were deemed worthy and capable, with the result that a small élite was made to represent legally the entire body politic for whose benefit this régime was instituted.

It was evident, however, that this moderate system, being fundamentally illogical and in contradiction with the very principles from which it proceeded, would soon become the object of serious criticism. For if the object of society and of the state is the welfare of individuals, severally considered, how is it possible to admit that this welfare can be secured by the individuals themselves only through the possibilities of such a liberal régime? The inequalities brought about both by nature and by social organizations are so numerous and so serious, that, for the greater part, individuals abandoned to themselves not only would fail to attain happiness, but would also contribute to the perpetuation of their condition of misery and dejection. The state therefore cannot limit itself to the merely negative function of the defense of liberty. It must become active, in behalf of everybody, for the welfare of the people. It must intervene, when necessary, in order to improve the material, intellectual, and moral conditions of the masses; it must find work for the unemployed, instruct and educate the people, and care for health and hygiene. For if the purpose of society and of the state is the welfare of individuals, and if it is just that these individuals themselves control the attainment of their ends, it becomes difficult to understand why Liberalism should not go the whole distance, why it should see fit to distinguish certain individuals from the rest of the mass, and why the functions of the people should be restricted to the exercise of a mere check. Therefore the state, if it exists for all, must be governed by all, and not by a small minority: if the state is for the people, sovereignty must reside in the people: if all individuals have the right to govern the state, liberty is no longer sufficient; equality must be added: and if sovereignty is vested in the people, the people must wield all sovereignty and not merely a part of it. The power to check and curb the government is not sufficient. The people must be the government. Thus, logically developed, Liberalism leads to Democracy, for Democracy contains the promises of Liberalism but oversteps its limitations in that it makes the action of the state positive, proclaims the equality of all citizens through the dogma of popular sovereignty. Democracy therefore necessarily implies a republican form of government even though at times, for reasons of expediency, it temporarily adjusts itself to a monarchical régime.

Once started on this downward grade of logical deductions it was inevitable that this atomistic theory of state and society should pass on to a more advanced position. Great industrial developments and the existence of a huge mass of working men, as yet badly treated and in a condition of semi-servitude, pushed the labor problem violently to the fore. Social inequalities, possibly endurable in a régime of domestic industry, became intolerable after the industrial revolution. Hence a state of affairs which towards the middle of the last century appeared to be both cruel and threatening. It was therefore natural that the following question should be raised: "If the state is created for the welfare of its citizens, severally considered, how can it tolerate an economic system which divides the population into a small minority of exploiters, the capitalists, on one side, and an immense multitude of exploited, the working people, on the other?" No! The state must again intervene and give rise to a different and less iniquitous economic organization, by abolishing private property, by assuming direct control of all production, and by organizing it in such a way that the products of labor be distributed solely among those who create them, viz., the working classes. Hence we find Socialism, with its new economic organization of society, abolishing private ownership of capital and of the instruments and means of production, socializing the product, suppressing the extra profit of capital, and turning over to the working class the entire output of the productive processes. It is evident that Socialism contains and surpasses Democracy in the same way that Democracy comprises and surpasses Liberalism, being a more advanced development of the same fundamental concept. Socialism in its turn generates the still more extreme doctrine of Bolshevism which demands the violent suppression of the holders of capital, the dictatorship of the proletariat, as means for a fairer economic organization of society and for the rescue of the laboring classes from capitalistic exploitation.

Thus Liberalism, Democracy, and Socialism, appear to be, as they are in reality, not only the offspring of one and the same theory of government, but also logical derivations one of the other. Logically developed Liberalism leads to Democracy; the logical development of Democracy issues into Socialism. It is true that for many years, and with some justification, Socialism was looked upon as antithetical to Liberalism. But the antithesis is purely relative and breaks down as we approach the common origin and foundation of the two doctrines, for we find that the opposition is one of method, not of purpose. The end is the same for both, viz., the welfare of the individual members of society. The difference lies in the fact that Liberalism would be guided to its goal by liberty, whereas Socialism strives to attain it by the collective organization of production. There is therefore no antithesis nor even a divergence as to the nature and scope of the state and the relation of individuals to society. There is only a difference of evaluation of the means for bringing about these ends and establishing these relations, which difference depends entirely on the different economic conditions which prevailed at the time when the various doctrines were formulated. Liberalism arose and began to thrive in the period of small industry; Socialism grew with the rise of industrialism and of world-wide capitalism. The dissension therefore between these two points of view, or the antithesis, if we wish so to call it, is limited to the economic field. Socialism is at odds with Liberalism only on the question of the organization of production and of the division of wealth. In religious, intellectual, and moral matters it is liberal, as it is liberal and democratic in its politics. Even the anti-liberalism and anti-democracy of Bolshevism are in themselves purely contingent. For Bolshevism is opposed to Liberalism only in so far as the former is revolutionary, not in its socialistic aspect. For if the opposition of the Bolsheviki to liberal and democratic doctrines were to continue, as now seems more and more probable, the result might be a complete break between Bolshevism and Socialism notwithstanding the fact that the ultimate aims of both are identical.

FASCISM AS AN INTEGRAL DOCTRINE OF SOCIALITY ANTITHETICAL TO THE ATOMISM OF LIBERAL, DEMOCRATIC, AND SOCIALISTIC THEORIES

The true antithesis, not to this or that manifestation of the liberal-democratic-socialistic conception of the state but to the concept itself, is to be found in the doctrine of Fascism. For while the disagreement between Liberalism and Democracy, and between Liberalism and Socialism lies in a difference of method, as we have said, the rift between Socialism, Democracy, and Liberalism on one side and Fascism on the other is caused by a difference in concept. As a matter of fact, Fascism never raises the question of methods, using in its political praxis now liberal ways, now democratic means and at times even socialistic devices. This indifference to method often exposes Fascism to the charge of incoherence on the part of superficial observers, who do not see that what counts with us is the end and that therefore even when we employ the same means we act with a radically different spiritual attitude and strive for entirely different results. The Fascist concept then of the nation, of the scope of the state, and of the relations obtaining between society and its individual components, rejects entirely the doctrine which I said proceeded from the theories of natural law developed in the course of the XVI, XVII, and XVIII centuries and which form the basis of the liberal, democratic, and socialistic ideology.

I shall not try here to expound this doctrine but shall limit myself to a brief résumé of its fundamental concepts.

Man—the political animal—according to the definition of Aristotle, lives and must live in society. A human being outside the pale of society is an inconceivable thing—a non-man. Humankind in its entirety lives in social groups that are still, today, very numerous and diverse, varying in importance and organization from the tribes of Central Africa to the great Western Empires. These various societies are fractions of the human species each one of them endowed with a unified organization. And as there is no unique organization of the human species, there is not "one" but there are "several" human societies. Humanity therefore exists solely as a biological concept not as a social one.

Each society on the other hand exists in the unity of both its biological and its social contents. Socially considered it is a fraction of the human species endowed with unity of organization for the attainment of the peculiar ends of the species.

This definition brings out all the elements of the social phenomenon and not merely those relating to the preservation and perpetuation of the species. For man is not solely matter; and the ends of the human species, far from being the materialistic ones we have in common with other animals, are, rather, and predominantly, the spiritual finalities which are peculiar to man and which every form of society strives to attain as well as its stage of social development allows. Thus the organization of every social group is more or less pervaded by the spiritual influxes of: unity of language, of culture, of religion, of tradition, of customs, and in general of feeling and of volition, which are as essential as the material elements: unity of economic interests, of living conditions, and of territory. The definition given above demonstrates another truth, which has been ignored by the political doctrines that for the last four centuries have been the foundations of political systems, viz., that the social concept has a biological aspect, because social groups are fractions of the human species, each one possessing a peculiar organization, a particular rank in the development of civilization with certain needs and appropriate ends, in short, a life which is really its own. If social groups are then fractions of the human species, they must possess the same fundamental traits of the human species, which means that they must be considered as a succession of generations and not as a collection of individuals.

It is evident therefore that as the human species is not the total of the living human beings of the world, so the various social groups which compose it are not the sum of the several individuals which at a given moment belong to it, but rather the infinite series of the past, present, and future generations constituting it. And as the ends of the human species are not those of the several individuals living at a certain moment, being occasionally in direct opposition to them, so the ends of the various social groups are not necessarily those of the individuals that belong to the groups but may even possibly be in conflict with such ends, as one sees clearly whenever the preservation and the development of the species demand the sacrifice of the individual, to wit, in times of war.

Fascism replaces therefore the old atomistic and mechanical state theory which was at the basis of the liberal and democratic doctrines with an organic and historic concept. When I say organic I do not wish to convey the impression that I consider society as an organism after the manner of the so-called "organic theories of the state"; but rather to indicate that the social groups as fractions of the species receive thereby a life and scope which transcend the scope and life of the individuals identifying themselves with the history and finalities of the uninterrupted series of generations. It is irrelevant in this connection to determine whether social groups, considered as fractions of the species, constitute organisms. The important thing is to ascertain that this organic concept of the state gives to society a continuous life over and beyond the existence of the several individuals.

The relations therefore between state and citizens are completely reversed by the Fascist doctrine. Instead of the liberal-democratic formula, "society for the individual," we have "individuals for society," with this difference however: that while the liberal doctrines eliminated society, Fascism does not submerge the individual in the social group. It subordinates him, but does not eliminate him; the individual as a part of his generation ever remaining an element of society however transient and insignificant he may be. Moreover the development of individuals in each generation, when coordinated and harmonized, conditions the development and prosperity of the entire social unit.

At this juncture the antithesis between the two theories must appear complete and absolute. Liberalism, Democracy, and Socialism look upon social groups as aggregates of living individuals; for Fascism they are the recapitulating unity of the indefinite series of generations. For Liberalism, society has no purposes other than those of the members living at a given moment. For Fascism, society has historical and immanent ends of preservation, expansion, improvement, quite distinct from those of the individuals which at a given moment compose it; so distinct in fact that they may even be in opposition. Hence the necessity, for which the older doctrines make little allowance, of sacrifice, even up to the total immolation of individuals, in behalf of society; hence the true explanation of war, eternal law of mankind, interpreted by the liberal-democratic doctrines as a degenerate absurdity or as a maddened monstrosity.

For Liberalism, society has no life distinct from the life of the individuals, or as the phrase goes: *solvitur in singularitates.*[1] For Fascism, the life of society overlaps the existence of individuals and projects itself into the succeeding generations through centuries and millennia. Individuals come into being, grow, and die, followed by others, unceasingly; social unity remains always identical to itself. For Liberalism, the individual is the end and society the means; nor is it conceivable that the individual, considered in the dignity of an ultimate finality, be lowered to mere instrumentality. For Fascism, society is the end, individuals the means, and its whole life consists in using individuals as instruments for its social ends. The state therefore guards and protects the welfare and development of individuals not for their exclusive interest, but because of the identity of the needs of individuals with those of society as a whole. We can thus accept and explain institutions and practices, which like the death penalty, are condemned by Liberalism in the name of the preeminence of individualism.

The fundamental problem of society in the old doctrines is the question of the rights of individuals. It may be the right to freedom as the Liberals would have it; or the right to the government of the commonwealth as the Democrats claim it, or the right to economic justice as the Socialists contend; but in every case it is the right of individuals, or groups of individuals (classes). Fascism on the other hand faces squarely the problem of the right of the state and of the duty of individuals. Individual rights are only recognized in so far as they are implied in the rights of the state. In this preeminence of duty we find the highest ethical value of Fascism.

THE PROBLEMS OF LIBERTY, OF GOVERNMENT, AND OF SOCIAL JUSTICE IN THE POLITICAL DOCTRINE OF FASCISM

This, however, does not mean that the problems raised by the other schools are ignored by Fascism. It means simply that it faces them and solves them differently, as, for example, the problem of liberty.

There is a Liberal theory of freedom, and there is a Fascist concept of liberty. For we, too, maintain the necessity of safeguarding the conditions that make for the free development of the individual; we, too, believe that the oppression of individual personality can find no place in the modern state. We do not, however, accept a bill of rights which tends to make the individual superior to the state and to empower him to act in opposition to

[1] [That is, everything is reduced to particulars.]

society. Our concept of liberty is that the individual must be allowed to develop his personality in behalf of the state, for these ephemeral and infinitesimal elements of the complex and permanent life of society determine by their normal growth the development of the state. But this individual growth must be normal. A huge and disproportionate development of the individual of classes, would prove as fatal to society as abnormal growths are to living organisms. Freedom therefore is due to the citizen and to classes on condition that they exercise it in the interest of society as a whole and within the limits set by social exigencies, liberty being, like any other individual right, a concession of the state. What I say concerning civil liberties applies to economic freedom as well. Fascism does not look upon the doctrine of economic liberty as an absolute dogma. It does not refer economic problems to individual needs, to individual interest, to individual solutions. On the contrary it considers the economic development, and especially the production of wealth, as an eminently social concern, wealth being for society an essential element of power and prosperity. But Fascism maintains that in the ordinary run of events economic liberty serves the social purposes best; that it is profitable to entrust to individual initiative the task of economic development both as to production and as to distribution; that in the economic world individual ambition is the most effective means for obtaining the best social results with the least effort. Therefore, on the question also of economic liberty the Fascists differ fundamentally from the Liberals; the latter see in liberty a principle, the Fascists accept it as a method. By the Liberals, freedom is recognized in the interest of the citizens; the Fascists grant it in the interest of society. In other terms, Fascists make of the individual an economic instrument for the advancement of society, an instrument which they use so long as it functions and which they subordinate when no longer serviceable. In this guise Fascism solves the eternal problem of economic freedom and of state interference, considering both as mere methods which may or may not be employed in accordance with the social needs of the moment.

What I have said concerning political and economic Liberalism applies also to Democracy. The latter envisages fundamentally the problem of sovereignty; Fascism does also, but in an entirely different manner. Democracy vests sovereignty in the people, that is to say, in the mass of human beings. Fascism discovers sovereignty to be inherent in society when it is juridically organized as a state. Democracy therefore turns over the government of the state to the multitude of living men that they may use it to further their own interests; Fascism insists that the government be entrusted to men capable of rising above their own private interests and of realizing the aspirations of the social collectivity, considered in its unity and in its relation to the past and future. Fascism therefore not only rejects the dogma of popular sovereignty and substitutes for it that of state sovereignty, but it also proclaims that the great mass of citizens is not a suitable advocate of social interests for the reason that the capacity to ignore individual private interests in favor of the higher demands of society and of history is a very rare gift and the privilege of the chosen few. Natural intelligence and cultural preparation are of great service in such tasks. Still more valuable perhaps is the intuitiveness of rare great minds, their traditionalism and their inherited qualities. This must not however be construed to mean that the masses are not to be allowed to exercise any influence on the life of the state. On the contrary, among peoples with a great history and with noble traditions, even the lowest elements of society possess an instinctive discernment of what is necessary for the welfare of the race, which in moments of great historical crises reveals itself to be almost infallible. It is therefore as wise to afford to this instinct the means of declaring itself as it is judicious to entrust the normal control of the commonwealth to a selected élite.

As for Socialism, the Fascist doctrine frankly recognizes that the problem raised by it as to the relations between capital and labor is a very serious one, perhaps the central one of modern life. What Fascism does not countenance is the collectivistic solution proposed by the Socialists. The chief defect of the socialistic method has been clearly demonstrated by the experience of the last few years. It does not take into account human nature, it is therefore outside of reality, in that it will not recognize that the most powerful spring of human activities lies in individual self-interest and that therefore the elimination from the economic field of this interest results in complete paralysis. The suppression of private ownership of capital carries with it the suppression of capital itself, for capital is formed by savings and no one will want to save, but will rather consume all he makes if he knows he cannot keep and hand down to his heirs the results of his labors. The dispersion of capital means the end of production since capital, no matter who owns it, is always an indispensable tool of production. Collective organization of production is followed therefore by the paralysis of production since, by eliminating from the productive mechanism the incentive of individual interest, the product becomes rarer and more costly. Socialism then, as experience has shown, leads to increase in consumption, to the dispersion of capital and therefore to poverty. Of what avail is it, then, to build a social machine which will more justly distribute wealth if this very wealth is destroyed by the construction of this machine? Socialism committed an irreparable error when it made of private property a matter of justice while in truth it is a problem of social utility. The recognition of individual property rights, then, is a part of the Fascist doctrine not because of its individual bearing but because of its social utility.

We must reject, therefore, the socialistic solution but we cannot allow the problem raised by the Socialists to remain unsolved, not only because justice demands a solution but also because the persistence of this problem in liberal and democratic régimes has been a menace to public order and to the authority of the state. Unlimited and unrestrained class self-defense, evinced by strikes and lockouts, by boycotts and sabotage, leads inevitably to anarchy. The Fascist doctrine, enacting justice among the classes in compliance with a fundamental necessity of modern life, does away with class self-defense, which, like individual self-defense in the days of barbarism, is a source of disorder and of civil war.

Having reduced the problem to these terms, only one solution is possible, the realization of justice among the classes by and through the state. Centuries ago the state, as the specific organ of justice, abolished personal self-defense in individual controversies and substituted for it state justice. The time has now come when class self-defense also must be replaced by state justice. To facilitate the change Fascism has created its own syndicalism. The suppression of class self-defense does not mean the suppression of class defense which is an inalienable necessity of modern economic life. Class organization is a fact which cannot be ignored but it must be controlled, disciplined, and subordinated by the state. The syndicate, instead of being, as formerly, an organ of extra-legal defense, must be turned into an organ of legal defense which will become judicial defense as soon as labor conflicts become a matter of judicial settlement. Fascism therefore has transformed the syndicate, that old revolutionary instrument of syndicalistic socialists, into an instrument of legal defense of the classes both within and without the law courts. This solution may encounter obstacles in its development; the obstacles of malevolence, of suspicion of the untried, of erroneous calculation, etc., but it is designed to triumph even though it must advance through progressive stages.

HISTORICAL VALUE OF THE DOCTRINE OF FASCISM

I might carry this analysis farther but what I have already said is sufficient to show that the rise of a Fascist ideology already gives evidence of an upheaval in the intellectual field as powerful as the change that was brought about in the XVII and XVIII centuries by the rise and diffusion of those doctrines of *ius naturale* [2] which go under the name of "Philosophy of the French Revolution." The philosophy of the French Revolution formulated certain principles, the authority of which, unquestioned for a century and a half, seemed so final that they were given the attribute of immortality. The influence of these principles was so great that they determined the formation of a new culture, of a new civilization. Likewise the fervor of the ideas that go to make up the Fascist doctrine, now in its inception but destined to spread rapidly, will determine the course of a new culture and of a new conception of civil life. The deliverance of the individual from the state carried out in the XVIII century will be followed in the XX century by the rescue of the state from the individual. The period of authority, of social obligations, of "hierarchical" subordination will succeed the period of individualism, of state feebleness, of insubordination.

This innovating trend is not and cannot be a return to the Middle Ages. It is a common but an erroneous belief that the movement, started by the Reformation and heightened by the French Revolution, was directed against mediaeval ideas and institutions. Rather than as a negation, this movement should be looked upon as the development and fulfillment of the doctrines and practices of the Middle Ages. Socially and politically considered the Middle Ages wrought disintegration and anarchy; they were characterized by the gradual weakening and ultimate extinction of the state, embodied in the Roman Empire, driven first to the East, then back to France, thence to Germany, a shadow of its former self; they were marked by the steady advance of the forces of usurpation, destructive of the state and reciprocally obnoxious; they bore the imprints of a triumphant particularism. Therefore the individualistic and anti-social movement of the XVII and XVIII centuries was not directed against the Middle Ages, but rather against the restoration of the state by great national monarchies. If this movement destroyed mediaeval institutions that had survived the Middle Ages and had been grafted upon the new states, it was in consequence of the struggle primarily waged against the state. The spirit of the movement was decidedly mediaeval. The novelty consisted in the social surroundings in which it operated and in its relation to new economic developments. The individualism of the feudal lords, the particularism of the cities and of the corporations had been replaced by the individualism and the particularism of the bourgeoisie and of the popular classes.

The Fascist ideology cannot therefore look back to the Middle Ages, of

[2] [*Natural law.*]

which it is a complete negation. The Middle Ages spell disintegration; Fascism is nothing if not sociality. It is if anything the beginning of the end of the Middle Ages prolonged four centuries beyond the end ordinarily set for them and revived by the social democratic anarchy of the past thirty years. If Fascism can be said to look back at all it is rather in the direction of ancient Rome whose social and political traditions at the distance of fifteen centuries are being revived by Fascist Italy.

I am fully aware that the value of Fascism, as an intellectual movement, baffles the minds of many of its followers and supporters and is denied outright by its enemies. There is no malice in this denial, as I see it, but rather an incapacity to comprehend. The liberal-democratic-socialistic ideology has so completely and for so long a time dominated Italian culture that in the minds of the majority of people trained by it, it has assumed the value of an absolute truth, almost the authority of a natural law. Every faculty of self-criticism is suppressed in the minds and this suppression entails an incapacity for understanding that time alone can change. It will be advisable therefore to rely mainly upon the new generations and in general upon persons whose culture is not already fixed. This difficulty to comprehend on the part of those who have been thoroughly grounded by a different preparation in the political and social sciences explains in part why Fascism has not been wholly successful with the intellectual classes and with mature minds, and why on the other hand it has been very successful with young people, with women, in rural districts, and among men of action unencumbered by a fixed and set social and political education. Fascism moreover, as a cultural movement, is just now taking its first steps. As is the case with all great movements, action regularly outstrips thought. It was thus at the time of the Protestant Reformation and of the individualistic reaction of the XVII and XVIII centuries. The English revolution occurred when the doctrines of natural law were coming into being and the theoretical development of the liberal and democratic theories followed the French revolution.

At this point it will not be very difficult to assign a fitting place in history to this great trend of thought which is called Fascism and which, in spite of initial difficulties, already gives clear indication of the magnitude of its developments.

The liberal-democratic speculation both in its origin and in the manner of its development appears to be essentially a non-Italian formation. Its connection with the Middle Ages already shows it to be foreign to the Latin mind, the mediaeval disintegration being the result of the triumph of Germanic individualism over the political mentality of the Romans. The barbarians, boring from within and hacking from without, pulled down the great political structure raised by Latin genius and put nothing in its place. Anarchy lasted eight centuries during which time only one institution survived and that a Roman one—the Catholic Church. But, as soon as the laborious process of reconstruction was started with the constitution of the great national states backed by the Roman Church the Protestant Reformation set in followed by the individualistic currents of the XVII and XVIII centuries, and the process of disintegration was started anew. This anti-state tendency was the expression of the Germanic spirit and it therefore became predominant among the Germanic peoples and wherever Germanism had left a deep imprint even if afterward superficially covered by a veneer of Latin culture. It is true that Marsilius from Padua is an Italian writing for Ludwig the Bavarian, but the other writers who in the XIV century appear as forerunners of the liberal doctrines are not Italians: Occam and Wycliff are English; Oresme is French. Among the advocates of individualism in the XVI century who prepared the way for the triumph of the doctrines of natural law in the subsequent centuries, Hotman and Languet are French, Buchanan is Scotch. Of the great authorities of natural law, Grotius and Spinoza are Dutch; Locke is English; l'Abbé de St. Pierre, Montesquieu, d'Argenson, Voltaire, Rousseau, Diderot and the encyclopaedists are French; Althusius, Pufendorf, Kant, Fichte are German.

Italy took no part in the rise and development of the doctrines of natural law. Only in the XIX century did she evince a tardy interest in these doctrines, just as she tardily contributed to them at the close of the XVIII century through the works of Beccaria and Filangieri.

While therefore in other countries such as France, England, Germany, and Holland, the general tradition in the social and political sciences worked in behalf of anti-state individualism, and therefore of liberal and democratic doctrines, Italy, on the other hand, clung to the powerful legacy of its past in virtue of which she proclaims the rights of the state, the preeminence of its authority, and the superiority of its ends. The very fact that the Italian political doctrine in the Middle Ages linked itself with the great political writers of antiquity, Plato and Aristotle, who in a different manner but with an equal firmness advocated a strong state and the subordination of individuals to it, is a sufficient index of the orientation of political philosophy in Italy. We all know how thorough and crushing the authority of Aristotle was in the Middle Ages. But for Aristotle the spiritual cement of the state is "virtue," not absolute virtue but political virtue, which is social devotion. His state is made up solely of its citizens, the citizens being either those who defend it with their arms or who govern it as magistrates. All others who provide it with the materials and services it needs are not citizens. They become such only in the corrupt forms of certain democracies. Society is therefore divided into two classes, the free men or citizens who give their time to noble and virtuous occupations and who profess their subjection to the state, and the laborers and slaves who work for the maintenance of the former. No man in this scheme is his own master. The slaves belong to the freemen, and the freemen belong to the state.

It was therefore natural that St. Thomas Aquinas the greatest political writer of the Middle Ages should emphasize the necessity of unity in the political field, the harm of plurality of rulers, the dangers and damaging effects of demagogy. The good of the state, says St. Thomas Aquinas, is unity. And who can procure unity more fittingly than he who is himself one? Moreover the government must follow, as far as possible, the course of nature and in nature power is always one. In the physical body only one organ is dominant—the heart; in the spirit only one faculty has sway—reason. Bees have one sole ruler; and the entire universe one sole sovereign—God. Experience shows that the countries which are ruled by many perish because of discord while those that are ruled over by one enjoy peace, justice, and plenty. The states which are not ruled by one are troubled by dissensions, and toil unceasingly. On the contrary the states which are ruled over by one king enjoy peace, thrive in justice and are gladdened by affluence. The rule of the multitudes can not be sanctioned, for where the crowd rules it oppresses the rich as would a tyrant.

Italy in the Middle Ages presented a curious phenomenon: while in practice the authority of the state was being dissolved into a multiplicity of competing sovereignties, the theory of state unity and authority was kept alive in the minds of thinkers by the memories of the Roman Imperial tradition. It was this memory that supported for centuries the fiction of the universal Roman Empire when in reality it existed no longer. Dante's *De Monarchia* deduced the theory of this empire conceived as the unity of a strong state . . . [and concluded] that the individual must sacrifice himself for his country. . . .

The Roman tradition, which was one of practice but not of theories—for Rome constructed the most solid state known to history with extraordinary statesmanship but with hardly any political writings—influenced considerably the founder of modern political science, Niccolò Machiavelli, who was himself in truth not a creator of doctrines but a keen observer of human nature who derived from the study of history practical maxims of political import. He freed the science of politics from the formalism of the scholastics and brought it close to concrete reality. His writings, an inexhaustible mine of practical remarks and precious observations, reveal dominant in him the state idea, no longer abstract but in the full historical concreteness of the national unity of Italy. Machiavelli therefore is not only the greatest of modern political writers, he is also the greatest of our countrymen in full possession of a national Italian consciousness. To liberate Italy, which was in his day "enslaved, torn and pillaged," and to make her more powerful, he would use any means, for to his mind the holiness of the end justified them completely. In this he was sharply rebuked by foreigners who were not as hostile to his means as they were fearful of the end which he propounded. He advocated therefore the constitution of a strong Italian state, supported by the sacrifices and by the blood of the citizens, not defended by mercenary troops; well-ordered internally, aggressive and bent on expansion. "Weak republics," he said, "have no determination and can never reach a decision." (Disc. I. c.38) "Weak states were ever dubious in choosing their course, and slow deliberations are always harmful." (Disc. I. c.10) And again: "Whoso undertakes to govern a multitude either in a régime of liberty or in a monarchy, without previously making sure of those who are hostile to the new order of things builds a short-lived state." (Disc. I. c.16) And further on "the dictatorial authority helped and did not harm the Roman republic" (Disc. I. c.34), and "Kings and republics lacking in national troops both for offense and defense should be ashamed of their existence." (Disc. I. c.21) And again: "Money not only does not protect you but rather it exposes you to plundering assaults. Nor can there be a more false opinion than that which says that money is the sinews of war. Not money but good soldiers win battles." (Disc. II. c.10) "The country must be defended with ignominy or with glory and in either way it is nobly defended." (Disc. III. c.41) "And with dash and boldness people often capture what they never would have obtained by ordinary means." (Disc. III. c.44) Machiavelli was not only a great political authority, he taught the mastery of energy and will. Fascism learns from him not only its doctrines but its action as well.

Different from Machiavelli in mental attitude, in cultural preparation, and in manner of presentation, G. B. Vico must yet be connected with the great Florentine from whom in a certain way he seems to proceed. In the heyday of "natural law" Vico is decidedly opposed to *ius naturale* and in his attacks against its advocates, Grotius, Seldenus and Pufendorf, he systematically assails the abstract, rationalistic, and utilitarian principles of the XVIII century. As Montemayor justly says:

While the "natural jurists," basing justice and state on utility and interest and grounding human certitude on reason, were striving to draft permanent codes and construct the perfect state, Vico strongly asserted the social nature of man, the ethical character of the juridical consciousness and its growth through the history of humanity rather than in sacred history. Vico therefore maintains that doctrines must begin with those subjects which take up and explain the entire course of civilization. Experience and not ratiocination, history and not reason must help human wisdom to understand the civil and political régimes which were the result not of reason or philosophy, but rather of common sense, or if you will of the social consciousness of man

and farther on

to Vico we owe the conception of history in its fullest sense as *magistra vitae*,[3] the search after the humanity of history, the principle which makes the truth progress with time, the discovery of the political "course" of nations. It is Vico who uttered the eulogy of the patrician "heroic hearts" of the "patres patriae," first founders of states, magnanimous defenders of the commonwealth and wise counsellors of politics. To Vico we owe the criticism of democracies, the affirmation of their brief existence, of their rapid disintegration at the hands of factions and demagogues, of their lapse first into anarchy, then into monarchy, when their degradation does not make them a prey of foreign oppressors. Vico conceived of civil liberty as subjection to law, as just subordination of the private to the public interests, to the sway of the state. It was Vico who sketched modern society as a world of nations each one guarding its own imperium, fighting just and not inhuman wars. In Vico therefore we find the condemnation of pacifism, the assertion that right is actualized by bodily force, that without force, right is of no avail. . . .

It is not difficult to discern the analogies between these affirmations and the fundamental views and the spirit of Fascism. Nor should we marvel at this similarity. Fascism, a strictly Italian phenomenon, has its roots in the Risorgimento and the Risorgimento was influenced undoubtedly by Vico.

It would be inexact to affirm that the philosophy of Vico dominated the Risorgimento. Too many elements of German, French, and English civilizations had been added to our culture during the first half of the XIX century to make this possible, so much so that perhaps Vico might have remained unknown to the makers of Italian unity if another powerful mind from Southern Italy, Vincent Cuoco, had not taken it upon himself to expound the philosophy of Vico in those very days in which the intellectual preparation of the Risorgimento was being carried on.

An adequate account of Cuoco's doctrines would carry me too far. Montemayor, in the article quoted above, gives them considerable attention. He quotes among other things Cuoco's arraignment of Democracy: "Italy has

[3] [That is, the governing principle of life.]

fared badly at the hand of Democracy which has withered to their roots the three sacred plants of liberty, unity, and independence. If we wish to see these trees flourish again let us protect them in the future from Democracy."

The influence of Cuoco, an exile at Milan, exerted through his writings, his newspaper articles, and Vichian propaganda, on the Italian patriots is universally recognized. Among the regular readers of his *Giornale Italiano* we find Monti and Foscolo. Clippings of his articles were treasured by Mazzini, and Manzoni, who often acted as his secretary, called him his "master in politics."

The influence of the Italian tradition summed up and handed down by Cuoco was felt by Mazzini whose interpretation of the function of the citizen as duty and mission is to be connected with Vico's doctrine rather than with the philosophic and political doctrines of the French Revolution.

"Training for social duty," said Mazzini,

> is essentially and logically unitarian. Life for it is but a duty, a mission. The norm and definition of such mission can only be found in a collective term superior to all the individuals of the country—in the people, in the nation. If there is a collective mission, a communion of duty . . . it can only be represented in the national unity.

And farther on:

> The declaration of rights, which all constitutions insist in copying slavishly from the French, express only those of the period . . . which considered the individual as the end and pointed out only one half of the problem

and again,

> assume the existence of one of those crises that threaten the life of the nation, and demand the active sacrifice of all its sons . . . will you ask the citizens to face martyrdom in virtue of their rights? You have taught men that society was solely constituted to guarantee their rights and now you ask them to sacrifice one and all, to suffer and die for the safety of the "nation?"

In Mazzini's conception of the citizen as instrument for the attainment of the nation's ends and therefore submissive to a higher mission, to the duty of supreme sacrifice, we see the anticipation of one of the fundamental points of the Fascist doctrine.

Unfortunately, the autonomy of the political thought of Italy, vigorously established in the works of Vico, nobly reclaimed by Vincenzo Cuoco, kept up during the struggles of the Risorgimento in spite of the many foreign influences of that period, seemed to exhaust itself immediately after the unification. Italian political thought, which had been original in times of servitude, became enslaved in the days of freedom.

A powerful innovating movement, issuing from the war and of which Fascism is the purest expression, was to restore Italian thought in the sphere of political doctrine to its own traditions which are the traditions of Rome. This task of intellectual liberation, now slowly being accomplished, is no less important than the political deliverance brought about by the Fascist Revolution. It is a great task which continues and integrates the Risorgimento; it is now bringing to an end, after the cessation of our political servitude, the intellectual dependence of Italy.

Thanks to it, Italy again speaks to the world and the world listens to Italy. It is a great task and a great deed and it demands great efforts. To carry it through, we must, each one of us, free ourselves of the dross of ideas and mental habits which two centuries of foreign intellectualistic tradition have heaped upon us; we must not only take on a new culture but create for ourselves a new soul. We must methodically and patiently contribute something towards the organic and complete elaboration of our doctrine, at the same time supporting it both at home and abroad with untiring devotion. We ask this effort of renovation and collaboration of all Fascists, as well as of all who feel themselves to be Italians. After the hour of sacrifice comes the hour of unyielding efforts. To our work, then, fellow countrymen, for the glory of Italy!

HANNAH ARENDT

FOR THE LAST six years or so, a group of American, British, and French historians have been classifying and selecting for publication some four hundred tons of captured Nazi documents, enough to stuff twelve Nissen huts to the very brim. This is only a fraction of the documents in our hands; some of these have already been published, for example, the Graebe Memorandum (appended to the following selection), which was introduced as evidence during the Nuremberg trials of German war criminals. But information, mere accumulation of data, does not necessarily yield understanding, and as the facts of the Nazi regime come to light, and as we learn more of developments within the Soviet orbit, we realize that our capacity for comprehending these political phenomena of the twentieth century is inadequate. There is little, after all, in the history of Western civilization, from the viewpoint that history has been studied in the past two hundred years, which would prepare us for the terror of the Graebe Memorandum, remembering that this was not an individual aberration but the deliberate and even "normal" act of a political authority.

Not until the 1940's was it generally understood that the Nazis in Germany and to a lesser degree the Fascists in Italy, the Soviets in Russia, and perhaps now the Communists in China represent an utterly novel form of government and that they seek to establish a new type of society as well. Historians and social scientists have acknowledged this uniqueness by abandoning traditional concepts—such as dictatorship or tyranny—and substituting for them the term totalitarianism. The term is variously defined, but most students would agree that it connotes the unique culture of a political system of repression which employs and indeed depends upon the most advanced technological means of a highly industrialized mass society and which seeks to destroy the idea and the existence of the free individual or autonomous personality, as these have evolved in the Western world.

The deepening of our understanding of totalitarianism owes much to Hannah Arendt (b. 1906), a philosopher born and trained in Germany, who, after the Nazis had established their new order in Germany, fled abroad, coming in 1941 to the United States, where she now resides. In a great many articles and in her cogent book, *The Origins of Totalitarianism* (1951), Arendt has tried to analyze the roots and character of the totalitarian system. In the two essays which comprise the following selection, she discusses the necessary relation in totalitarianism between ideology and terror, maintaining that neither is cynically manipulated for rational goals, but that both together constitute the determining aspects of this new society. Her inquiry makes use of the tools and insights of a great many disciplines—history, sociology, psychology, as well as literature—and while specialists have not always agreed with all her premises (for example, that the Nazi and Soviet regimes can adequately be treated as but two forms of a single political system, even though such experts grant certain similarities between them) or with all her conclusions, it is perhaps significant that it was a philosopher, a nonspecialist, who was one of the first to begin the task of formulating a series of new political categories capable of rendering the facts of totalitarianism intelligible. Whatever the shortcomings of her approach, few critics will deny that she is unsurpassed in evoking the mood of human existence under totalitarianism, that underneath her philosophical and historical inquiry is an immediate and sympathetic sense of the tragic limitations of man in such a system. Faced with the "inanimate men," the human products of the Nazi and similar regimes, she proposes a new criterion for political judgment: "Will it lead to totalitarian rule or will it not?" and thus at once recalls the deepest warning of George Orwell (1903–1950) that no modern society is entirely immune from totalitarianism.

IDEOLOGY AND TERROR: A NOVEL FORM OF GOVERNMENT

The following considerations have grown out of a study of the origins, the elements and the functioning of that novel form of government and domination which we have come to call totalitarian. Wherever it rose to power, it developed entirely new political institutions and destroyed all social, legal and political traditions of the country. No matter what the specifically national tradition or the particular spiritual source of its ideology, totalitarian government always transformed classes into masses, supplanted the party system, not by one-party dictatorships, but by a mass movement, shifted the center of power from the army to the police, and established a foreign policy openly directed toward world domination. Present totalitarian governments have developed from one-party systems; whenever these became truly totalitarian, they started to operate according to a system of values so radically different from all others, that none of our traditional legal, moral, or common sense utilitarian categories could any longer help us to come to terms with, or judge, or predict its course of action.

If it is true that the elements of totalitarianism can be found by retracing the history and analyzing the political implications of what we usually call the crisis of our century, then the conclusion is unavoidable that this crisis is no mere threat from the outside, no mere result of some aggressive foreign policy of either Germany or Russia, and that it will no more disappear with the fall of Soviet Russia than it disappeared with the fall of Nazi Germany. It may even be that the true predicaments of our time will assume their

This selection has been reprinted from Hannah Arendt, "Ideology and Terror: A Novel Form of Government," *The Review of Politics*, Vol. 15, no. 3 (July, 1953), pp. 303–327, by permission of the publisher.

authentic form—though not necessarily the cruelest—only when totalitarianism has become a thing of the past.

It is in the line of such reflections to raise the question whether totalitarian government, born of this crisis and at the same time its clearest and only unequivocal symptom, is merely a make-shift arrangement, which borrows its methods of intimidation, its means of organization and its instruments of violence from the well-known political arsenal of tyranny, despotism and dictatorships, and owes its existence only to the deplorable, but perhaps accidental failure of the traditional political forces—liberal or conservative, national or socialist, republican or monarchist, authoritarian or democratic. Or whether, on the contrary, there is such a thing as the *nature* of totalitarian government, whether it has its own essence and can be compared with and defined like other forms of government such as Western thought has known and recognized since the times of ancient philosophy. . . .

If we consider this in terms of the history of ideas, it seems extremely unlikely. For the forms of government under which men live have been very few; they were discovered early, classified by the Greeks and have proved extraordinarily long-lived. If we apply these findings, whose fundamental idea, despite many variations, did not change in the two and a half thousand years that separate Plato from Kant, we are tempted at once to interpret totalitarianism as some modern form of tyranny, that is a lawless government where power is wielded by one man. Arbitrary power, unrestricted by law, yielded in the interest of the ruler and hostile to the interests of the governed, on one hand, fear as the principle of action, namely fear of the people by the ruler and fear of the ruler by the people, on the other—these have been the hallmarks of tyranny throughout our tradition.

Instead of saying that totalitarian government is unprecedented, we could also say that it has exploded the very alternative on which all definitions of the essence of governments have been based in political philosophy, that is the alternative between lawful and lawless government, between arbitrary and legitimate power. That lawful government and legitimate power, on one side, lawlessness and arbitrary power on the other, belonged together and were inseparable has never been questioned. Yet, totalitarian rule confronts us with a totally different kind of government. It defies, it is true, all positive laws, even to the extreme of defying those which it has itself established (as in the case of the Soviet Constitution of 1936, to quote only the most outstanding example) or which it did not care to abolish (as in the case of the Weimar Constitution which the Nazi government never revoked). But it operates neither without guidance of law nor is it arbitrary, for it claims to obey strictly and unequivocally those laws of Nature or of History from which all positive laws always have been supposed to spring.

It is the monstrous, yet seemingly unanswerable claim of totalitarian rule that, far from being "lawless," it goes to the sources of authority from which positive laws received their ultimate legitimation, that far from being arbitrary it is more obedient to these suprahuman forces than any government ever was before, and that far from wielding its power in the interest of one man, it is quite prepared to sacrifice everybody's vital immediate interests to the execution of what it assumes to be the law of History or the law of Nature. Its defiance of positive laws claims to be a higher form of legitimacy which, since it is inspired by the sources themselves, can do away with petty legality. Totalitarian lawfulness pretends to have found a way to establish the rule of justice on earth—something which the legality of positive law admittedly could never attain. The discrepancy between legality and justice could never be bridged because the standards of right and wrong into which positive law translates its own source of authority—"natural law" governing the whole universe, or divine law revealed in human history or customs and traditions expressing the law common to the sentiments of all men—are necessarily general and must be valid for a countless and unpredictable number of cases, so that each concrete individual case with its unrepeatable set of circumstances somehow escapes it.

Totalitarian lawfulness, defying legality and pretending to establish the direct reign of justice on earth, executes the law of History or of Nature without translating it into standards of right and wrong for individual behavior. It applies the law directly to mankind without bothering with the behavior of men. The law of Nature or the law of History, if properly executed, is expected to produce mankind as its end product; and this expectation lies behind the claim to global rule of all totalitarian governments. Totalitarian policy claims to transform the human species into an active unfailing carrier of a law to which human beings otherwise would only passively and reluctantly be subjected. If it is true that the link between totalitarian countries and the civilized world was broken through the monstrous crimes of totalitarian regimes, it is also true that this criminality was not due to simple aggressiveness, ruthlessness, warfare and treachery, but to a conscious break of that *consensus iuris*[1] which, according to Cicero constitutes a "people," and which, as international law, in modern times has constituted the civilized world insofar as it remains the foundation-stone of international relations even under the conditions of war. Both moral judgment and legal punish-

[1] [*Consent to the law.*]

ment presuppose this basic consent; the criminal can be judged justly only because he takes part in the *consensus iuris,* and even the revealed law of God can function among men only when they listen and consent to it.

At this point the fundamental difference between the totalitarian and all other concepts of law comes to light. Totalitarian policy does not replace one set of laws with another, does not establish its own *consensus iuris,* does not create, by one revolution, a new form of legality. Its defiance of all, even its own positive laws implies that it believes it can do without any *consensus iuris* whatever, and still not resign itself to the tyrannical state of lawlessness, arbitrariness and fear. It can do without the *consensus iuris* because it promises to release the fulfillment of law from all action and will of man; and it promises justice on earth because it claims to make mankind itself the embodiment of the law.

This identification of man and law, which seems to cancel the discrepancy between legality and justice that has plagued legal thought since ancient times, has nothing in common with the *lumen naturale* [2] or the voice of conscience, by which Nature or Divinity, as the sources of authority for the *ius naturale* [3] or the historically revealed commands of God, are supposed to announce their authority in man himself. This never made man a walking embodiment of the law, but on the contrary remained distinct from him as the authority which demanded consent and obedience. Nature or Divinity as the source of authority for positive laws are thought of as permanent and eternal; potitive laws were changing and changeable according to circumstances, but they possessed a relative permanence as compared with the much more rapidly changing actions of men; and they derived this permanence from the eternal presence of their source of authority. Positive laws, therefore, are primarily designed to function as stabilizing factors for the ever changing movements of men.

In the interpretation of totalitarianism, all laws have become *laws of movement.* When the Nazis talked about the law of Nature or when the Bolsheviks talk about the law of History, neither Nature nor History is any longer the stabilizing source of authority for the actions of mortal men; they are movements in themselves. Underlying the Nazis' belief in race laws as the expression of the law of Nature in man, is Darwin's idea of man as the product of a natural development which does not necessarily stop with the present species of human beings, just as under the Bolsheviks' belief in class-struggle as the expression of the law of History lies Marx's notion of society as the

[2] [*Natural light.*]
[3] [*Natural law.*]

product of a gigantic historical movement which races according to its own law of motion to the end of historical times when it will abolish itself.

The difference between Marx's historical and Darwin's naturalistic approaches has frequently been pointed out, usually and rightly in favor of Marx. This has led us to forget the great and positive interest Marx took in Darwin's theories; Engels could not think of a greater compliment to Marx's scholarly achievements than to call him the "Darwin of history." If one considers, not the actual achievement but, the basic philosophies of both men, it turns out that ultimately the movement of History and the movement of Nature are one and the same. Darwin's introduction of the concept of development into nature, his insistence that, at least in the field of biology, natural movement is not circular but unilinear, moving in an infinitely progressing direction, means in fact that nature is, as it were, being swept into history, that natural life is considered to be historical. The "natural" law of the survival of the fittest is just as much a historical law and could be used as such by racism as Marx's law of the survival of the most progressive class. Marx's class struggle on the other hand, as the driving force of history, is only the outward expression of the development of productive forces which in turn have their origin in the labor *force* of men. Labor, according to Marx, is not a historical but a natural-biological "force," namely man's "metabolism with nature" by which he conserves his individual life and reproduces the species. Engels saw the affinity between the basic convictions of the two men very clearly because he understood the decisive role which the concept of development played in both theories. The tremendous intellectual change which took place in the middle of the last century consisted in the refusal to view or accept anything "as it is" and in the consistent interpretation of everything as being only a stage of some further development. Whether the driving force of this development was called Nature or History is relatively secondary.

In these theories, the term "law" itself changed its meaning: from expressing the framework of stability within which human actions and motions can take place, it became the expression of the motion itself.

By lawful government we understand a body politic in which positive laws are needed to translate and realize the immutable *ius naturale* or the eternal commandments of God into standards of right and wrong. Only in these standards, in the body of positive laws of each country, do the *ius naturale* or the Commandments of God achieve their political reality. In the body politic of totalitarian government, this place of positive laws is taken by total terror, which is designed to translate into reality the law of movement of History or Nature. Just as positive laws, though they define transgressions, are independent of them—the absence of crimes in any society does not render laws superfluous but, on the contrary, signifies their most perfect rule—so terror in totalitarian government has ceased to be a mere means for the suppression of opposition, though it is also used for such purposes. Terror becomes total when it becomes independent of all opposition; it rules supreme when nobody any longer stands in its way. If lawfulness is the essence of non-tyrannical government and lawlessness is the essence of tyranny, then terror is the essence of totalitarian domination.

Terror is the realization of the law of movement; its chief aim is to make it possible for the force of Nature or of History to race freely through mankind, unhindered by any spontaneous human action. As such, terror seeks to "stabilize" men in order to liberate the forces of Nature or History. It is this movement which singles out the foes of mankind against whom terror is let loose, and no free action of either opposition or sympathy can be permitted to interfere with the elimination of the "objective enemy" of History or Nature, of the class or the race. Guilt and innocence become senseless notions; "guilty" is he who stands in the way of the natural or historical process which has passed judgment over "inferior races," over individuals "unfit to live," over "dying classes and decadent peoples." Terror executes these judgments, and before its court, all concerned are subjectively innocent: the murdered because they did nothing against the system, and the murderers because they do not really murder but execute a death sentence pronounced by some higher tribunal. The rulers themselves do not claim to be just or wise, but only to execute historical or natural laws; they do not apply laws, but execute a movement in accordance with its inherent law. Terror is lawfulness, if law is the law of the movement of some suprahuman force, Nature or History.

Terror as the execution of a law of movement whose ultimate goal is not the welfare of men or the interest of one man but the fabrication of mankind, eliminates individuals for the sake of the species, sacrifices the "parts" for the sake of the "whole." The suprahuman force of Nature or History has its own beginning and its own end, so that it can be hindered only by the new beginning and the individual end which the life of each man actually is.

Positive laws in constitutional government are designed to erect boundaries and establish channels of communication between men whose community is continually endangered by the new men born into it. With each new birth, a new beginning is born into the world, a new world has potentially come into being. The stability of the laws corresponds to the constant motion of all human affairs, a motion which can never end as long as men are born and die. The laws hedge in each new beginning and at the same time assure its freedom of movement, the potentiality of something entirely new and unpredictable; the boundaries of positive laws are for the political existence of man what memory is for his historical existence: they guarantee the pre-existence of a common world, the reality of some continuity which transcends the individual life span of each generation, absorbs all new origins and is nourished by them.

Total terror is so easily mistaken for a symptom of tyrannical government because totalitarian government in its initial stages must behave like a tyranny and raze the boundaries of man-made law. But total terror leaves no arbitrary lawlessness behind it and does not rage for the sake of some arbitrary will or for the sake of despotic power of one man against all, least of all for the sake of a war of all against all. It substitutes for the boundaries and channels of communication between individual men a band of iron which holds them so tightly together that it is as though their plurality had disappeared into One Man of gigantic dimensions. To abolish the fences of laws between men—as tyranny does—means to take away man's liberties and destroy freedom as a living political reality; for the space between men as it is hedged in by laws, is the living space of freedom. Total terror uses this old instrument of tyranny but destroys at the same time also the lawless, fenceless wilderness of fear and suspicion which tryanny leaves behind. This desert, to be sure, is no longer a living space of freedom, but it still provides some room for the fear-guided movements and suspicion-ridden actions of its inhabitants.

By pressing men against each other, total terror destroys the space between them; compared to the condition within its iron hand, even the desert of tyranny, insofar as it is still some kind of space, appears like a guarantee of freedom. Totalitarian government does not just curtail liberties or abolish essential freedoms; nor does it, at least to our limited knowledge, succeed in eradicating the love for freedom from the hearts of man. It destroys the one essential prerequisite of all freedom which is simply the capacity of motion which cannot exist without space.

Total terror, the essence of totalitarian government, exists neither for nor against men. It is supposed to provide the forces of Nature or History with an incomparable instrument to accelerate their movement. This movement, proceeding according to its own law, cannot in the long run be hindered; eventually its force will always prove more powerful than the most powerful forces engendered by the actions and the will of men. But it can be slowed down and is slowed down almost inevitably by the freedom of man, which even totalitarian rulers cannot deny, for this freedom—irrelevant and arbitrary as they may deem it—is identical with the fact that men are being born and that therefore each of them *is* a new beginning, begins, in a sense, the world anew. From the totalitarian point of view, the fact that men are born and die can be only regarded as an annoying interference with higher forces. Terror, therefore, as the obedient servant of natural or historical movement has to eliminate from the process not only freedom in any specific sense, but the very source of freedom which is given with the fact of the birth of man and resides in his capacity to make a new beginning. In the iron band of terror, which destroys the plurality of men and makes out of many the One who unfailingly will act as though he himself were part of the course of History or Nature, a device has been found not only to liberate the historical and natural forces, but to accelerate them to a speed they never would reach if left to themselves. Practically speaking, this means that terror executes on the spot the death sentences which Nature is supposed to have pronounced on races or individuals who are "unfit to live," or History on "dying classes," without waiting for the slower and less efficient processes of Nature or History themselves.

In this concept, where the essence of government itself has become motion, a very old problem of political thought seems to have found a solution similar to the one already noted for the discrepancy between legality and justice. If the essence of government is defined as lawfulness, and if it is understood that laws are the stabilizing forces in the public affairs of men (as indeed it always has been since Plato invoked Zeus, the God of the boundaries, in his *Laws*) then the problem of movement of the body politic and the actions of its citizens arises. Lawfulness sets limitations to actions, but does not inspire them; the greatness, but also the perplexity of laws in free societies is that they only tell what one should not, but never what one should do. The necessary movement of a body politic can never be found in its essence if only because this essence—again since Plato—has always been defined with a view to its permanence. Duration seemed one of the surest yardsticks for the goodness of a government. It is still, for Montesquieu, the supreme proof for the badness of tyranny that only tyrannies are liable to be destroyed from within, to decline by themselves, whereas all other governments are destroyed through exterior circumstances. Therefore what the definition of governments always needed was what Montesquieu called a "principle of action" which, different in each form of government, would inspire government and citizens alike in their public activity and serve as a criterion beyond the merely negative yardstick of lawfulness, for judging all action in public affairs. Such guiding principles and criteria of action are, according to Montesquieu, honor in a monarchy, virtue in a republic and fear in a tyranny.

In a perfect totalitarian government, where all men have become One Man, where all action aims at the acceleration of the movement of Nature or History, where every single act is the execution of a death sentence which Nature or History has already pronounced, that is, under conditions where terror can be completely relied upon to keep the movement in constant motion, no principle of action separate from its essence would be needed at all. Yet as long as totalitarian rule has not conquered the earth and with the iron band of terror made each single man a part of one mankind, terror in its double function as essence of government and principle, not of action, but of motion cannot be fully realized. Just as lawfulness in constitutional government is insufficient to inspire and guide men's actions, so terror in totalitarian government is not sufficient to inspire and guide human behavior.

While under present conditions totalitarian domination still shares with other forms of government the need for a guide for the behavior of its citizens in public affairs, it does not need and could not even use a principle of action strictly speaking, since it will eliminate precisely the capacity of man to act. Under conditions of total terror not even fear can any longer serve as an advisor of how to behave, because terror chooses its victims without reference to individual actions or thoughts, exclusively in accordance with the objective necessity of the natural or historical process. Under totalitarian conditions, fear probably is more widespread than ever before; but fear has lost its practical usefulness when actions guided by it can no longer help to avoid the dangers man fears. The same is true for sympathy or support of the regime; for total terror not only selects its victims according to objective standards; it chooses its executioners with as complete a disregard as possible for the candidate's conviction and sympathies. The consistent elimination of conviction as a motive for action has become a matter of record since the great purges in Soviet Russia and the satellite countries. The aim of totalitarian education has never been to instill convictions but to destroy the capacity to form any. The introduction of purely objective criteria into the selective system of the SS troops was Himmler's great organizational invention; he selected the candidates from photographs according to purely racial criteria. Nature itself decided, not only who was to be eliminated, but also who was to be trained as an executioner.

No guiding principle of behavior, taken itself from the realm of human action, such as virtue, honor, fear, is necessary or can be useful to set into motion a body politic which no longer uses terror as a means of intimidation, but whose essence *is* terror. In its stead, it has introduced an entirely new principle into public affairs that dispenses with human will to action altogether and appeals to the craving need for some insight into the law of movement according to which the terror functions and upon which, therefore, all private destinies depend.

The inhabitants of a totalitarian country are thrown into and caught in the process of Nature or History for the sake of accelerating its movement; as such, they can only be executioners or victims of its inherent law. The process may decide that those who today eliminate races and individuals or the members of dying classes and decadent peoples are tomorrow those who must be sacrificed. What totalitarian rule needs to guide the behavior of its subjects is a *preparation* to fit each of them equally well for the role of executioner and the role of victim. . . .

. . . The question we raised at the start of these considerations and to which we now return is what kind of basic experience in the living-together of men permeates a form of government whose essence is terror and whose principle of action is the logicality of ideological thinking. That such a combination was never used before in the varied forms of political domination is obvious. Still, the basic experience on which it rests must be human and known to men, insofar as even this most "original" of all political bodies has been devised by, and is somehow answering the needs of, men.

It has frequently been observed that terror can rule absolutely only over men who are isolated against each other and that, therefore, one of the primary concerns of all tyrannical government is to bring this isolation about. Isolation may be the beginning of terror; it certainly is its most fertile ground; it always is its result. This isolation is, as it were, pretotalitarian; its hallmark is impotence insofar as power always comes from men acting together, "acting in concert" (Burke); isolated men are powerless by definition.

Isolation and impotence, that is the fundamental inability to act at all, have always been characteristic of tyrannies. Political contacts between men are severed in tyrannical government and the human capacities for action and power are frustrated. But not all contacts between men are broken and not all human capacities destroyed. The whole sphere of private life with the capacities for experience, fabrication and thought are left intact. We know that the iron band of total terror leaves no space for such private life and that the self-coercion of totalitarian logic destroys man's capacity for experience and thought just as certainly as his capacity for action.

What we call isolation in the political sphere, is called loneliness in the sphere of social intercourse. Isolation and loneliness are not the same. I can be isolated—that is in a situation in which I cannot act, because there is nobody who will act with me—without being lonely; and I can be lonely—that is in a situation in which I as a person feel myself deserted by all human companionship—without being isolated. Isolation is that impasse into which men are driven when the political sphere of their lives, where they act together in the pursuit of a common concern, is destroyed. Yet isolation, though destructive of power and the capacity for action, not only leaves intact but is required for all so-called productive activities of men. Man insofar as he is *homo faber*[4] tends to isolate himself with his work, that is to leave temporarily the realm of politics. Fabrication (*poiesis,* the making of things), as distinguished from action (*praxis*) on one hand and sheer labor on the other, is always performed in a certain isolation from common concerns, no matter whether the result is a piece of craftsmanship or of art. In isolation, man remains in contact with the world as the human artifice; only when the most elementary forms of human creativity, which is the capacity to add something of one's own to the common world, are destroyed, isolation becomes altogether unbearable. This can happen in a world whose chief values are dictated by labor, that is where all human activities have been transformed into laboring. Under such conditions, only the sheer effort of labor which is the effort to keep alive is left and the relationship with the world as a human artifice is broken. Isolated man who lost his place in the political realm of action is deserted by the world of things as well, if he is no longer recognized as *homo faber* but treated as an *animal laborans*[5] whose necessary "metabolism with nature" is of concern to no one. Isolation then becomes loneliness. Tyranny based on isolation generally leaves the productive capacities of man intact; a tyranny over "laborers," however, as for instance the rule over slaves in antiquity, would automatically be a rule over lonely, not only isolated, men and tend to be totalitarian.

While isolation concerns only the political realm of life, loneliness concerns human life as a whole. Totalitarian government, like all tyrannies, certainly could not exist without destroying the public realm of life, that is, without destroying, by isolating men, their political capacities. But totalitarian domination as a form of government is new in that it is not content with this isolation and destroys private life as well. It bases itself on loneliness, on the experience of not belonging to the world at all, which is among the most radical and desperate experiences of man.

Loneliness, the common ground for terror, the essence of totalitarian gov-

[4] [That is, man as craftsman or artist.]

[5] [*Working animal.*]

ernment, and for ideology or logicality, the preparation of its executioners and victims, is closely connected with uprootedness and superfluousness which have been the curse of modern masses since the beginning of the industrial revolution and have become acute with the rise of imperialism at the end of the last century and the break-down of political institutions and social traditions in our own time. To be uprooted means to have no place in the world, recognized and guaranteed by others; to be superfluous means not to belong to the world at all. Uprootedness can be the preliminary condition for superfluousness, just as isolation can (but must not) be the preliminary condition for loneliness. Taken in itself, without consideration of its recent historical causes and its new role in politics, loneliness is at the same time contrary to the basic requirements of the human condition *and* one of the fundamental experiences of every human life. Even the experience of the materially and sensually given world depends upon my being in contact with other men, upon our *common* sense which regulates and controls all other senses and without which each of us would be enclosed in his own particularity of sense data which in themselves are unreliable and treacherous. Only because we have common sense, that is only because not one man, but men in the plural inhabit the earth can we trust our immediate sensual experience. Yet, we have only to remind ourselves that one day we shall have to leave this common world which will go on as before and for whose continuity we are superfluous in order to realize loneliness, the experience of being abandoned by everything and everybody.

Loneliness is not solitude. Solitude requires being alone whereas loneliness shows itself most sharply in company with others. Apart from a few stray remarks—usually framed in a paradoxical mood like Cato's statement . . . *numquam minus solum esse quam cum solus esset,* "never was he less alone than when he was alone," or never was he less lonely than when he was in solitude—it seems that Epictetus, the emancipated slave philosopher of Greek origin, was the first to distinguish between loneliness and solitude. His discovery, in a way, was accidental, his chief interest being neither solitude nor loneliness, but being alone (*monos*) in the sense of absolute independence. As Epictetus sees it . . . the lonely man (*eremos*) finds himself surrounded by others with whom he cannot establish contact or to whose hostility he is exposed. The solitary man, on the contrary, is alone and therefore "can be together with himself" since men have the capacity of "talking with themselves." In solitude, in other words, I am "by myself," together with my self, and therefore two-in-one, whereas in loneliness I am actually one, deserted by all others. All thinking, strictly speaking, is done in solitude and is a dialogue between me and myself; but this dialogue of the two-in-one does not lose contact with the world of my fellow-men because they are represented in the self with whom I lead the dialogue of thought. The problem of solitude is that this two-in-one needs the others in order to become one again: one unchangeable individual whose identity can never be mistaken for that of any other. For the confirmation of my identity I depend entirely upon other people; and it is the great saving grace of companionship for solitary men that it makes them "whole" again, saves them from the dialogue of thought in which one remains always equivocal, restores the identity which makes them speak with the single voice of one unexchangeable person.

G. H. Mead

Solitude can become loneliness; this happens when all by myself I am deserted by my own self. Solitary men have always been in danger of loneliness, when they can no longer find the redeeming grace of companionship to save them from duality and equivocality and doubt. Historically, it seems as though this danger became sufficiently great to be noticed by others and recorded by history only in the nineteenth century. It showed itself clearly when philosophers, for whom alone solitude is a way of life and a condition of work, were no longer content with the fact that "philosophy is only for the few" and began to insist that nobody "understands" them. Characteristic in this respect is the anecdote reported from Hegel's deathbed which hardly could have been told of any great philosopher before him: "Nobody has understood me except one; and he also misunderstood." Conversely, there is always the chance that a lonely man finds himself and starts the thinking dialogue of solitude. This seems to have happened to Nietzsche in *Sils Maria* when he conceived of *Zarathustra.* In two poems ("Sils Maria" and "Aus hohen Bergen") he tells of the empty expectation and the yearning waiting of the lonely until suddenly *"um Mittag wars, da wurde Eins zu Zwei . . ./ Nun feiern wir, vereinten Siegs gewiss,/ das Fest der Feste;/ Freund Zarathustra kam, der Gast der Gäste!"* ("Noon was, when One became Two . . . Certain of united victory we celebrate the feast of feasts; friend Zarathustra came, the guest of guests.")

What makes loneliness so unbearable is the loss of one's own self which can be realized in solitude, but confirmed in its identity only by the trusting and trustworthy company of my equals. In this situation, man loses trust in himself as the partner of his thoughts and that elementary confidence in the world which is necessary to make experiences at all. Self and world, capacity for thought and experience are lost at the same time.

The only capacity of the human mind which needs neither the self nor the other nor the world in order to function safely and which is as independent of experience as it is of thinking is the ability of logical reasoning whose premise is the self-evident. The elementary rules of cogent evidence, the truism that two and two equals four cannot be perverted even under the conditions of absolute loneliness. It is the only reliable "truth" human beings can fall back upon once they have lost the mutual guarantee, the common sense, men need in order to experience and live and know their way in a common world. But this "truth" is empty or rather no truth at all, because it does not reveal anything. (To define consistency as truth as some modern logicians do means to deny the existence of truth.) Under the conditions of loneliness, therefore, the self-evident is no longer just a means of the intellect and begins to be productive, to develop its own lines of "thought." That thought processes characterized by strict self-evident logicality, from which apparently there is no escape, have some connection with loneliness was once noticed by Luther (whose experiences in the phenomena of solitude and loneliness probably were second to no one's and who once dared to say that "there must be a God because man needs one being whom he can trust") in a little-known remark on the Bible text "it is not good that man should be alone": A lonely man, says Luther, "always deduces one thing from the other and thinks everything to the worst." . . . The famous extremism of totalitarian movements, far from having anything to do with true radicalism, consists indeed in this "thinking everything to the worst," in this deducing process which always arrives at the worst possible conclusions.

What prepares men for totalitarian domination in the non-totalitarian world is the fact that loneliness, once a borderline experience usually suffered in certain marginal social conditions like old age, has become an everyday experience of the evergrowing masses of our century. The merciless process into which totalitarianism drives and organizes the masses looks like a suicidal escape from this reality. The "ice-cold reasoning" and the "mighty tentacle" of dialectics which "seizes you as in a vise" appear like a last support in a world where nobody is reliable and nothing can be relied upon. It is the inner coercion whose only content is the strict avoidance of contradictions that seems to confirm a man's identity outside all relationships with others. It fits him into the iron band of terror even when he is alone, and totalitarian domination tries never to leave him alone except in the extreme situation of solitary confinement. By destroying all space between men and pressing men against each other even the productive potentialities of isolation are annihilated; by teaching and glorifying the logical reasoning of loneliness where man knows that he will be utterly lost if ever he lets go of the first premise from which the whole process is being started, even the slim chances that loneliness may be transformed into solitude and logic into thought are obliterated.

If it is true that tyranny bears the germs of its own destruction because it is based upon powerlessness which is the negation of man's political condition, then, one is tempted to predict the downfall of totalitarian domination without outside interference, because it rests on the one human experience which is the negation of man's social condition. Yet, even if this analogy were valid—and there are reasons to doubt it—it would operate only after the full realization of totalitarian government which is possible only after the conquest of the earth.

Apart from such considerations—which as predictions are of little avail and less consolation—there remains the fact that the crisis of our time and its central experience have brought forth an entirely new form of government which as a potentiality and an ever-present danger is only too likely to stay with us from now on, just as other forms of government which came about at different historical moments and rested on different fundamental experiences have stayed with mankind regardless of temporary defeats—monarchies and republics, tyrannies, dictatorships and despotism.

But there remains also the truth that every end in history necessarily contains a new beginning; this beginning is the promise, the only "message" which the end can ever produce. Beginning, before it becomes a historical event, is the supreme capacity of man; politically, it is identical with man's freedom. *Initium ut esset homo creatus est*—"that a beginning be made man was created" said Augustine. . . . This beginning is guaranteed by each new birth; it is indeed every man.

THE CONCENTRATION CAMPS

The SS has made the camp the most totalitarian society in existence up to now.—DAVID ROUSSET

There are three possible approaches to the reality of the concentration camp: the inmate's experience of immediate suffering, the recollection of the survivor, and the fearful anticipation of those who dread the concentration camp as a possibility for the future.

This selection has been reprinted from Hannah Arendt, "The Concentration Camps," *Partisan Review,* July, 1948, pp. 743–762, by permission of the publisher.

Immediate experience is expressed in the reports which "record but do not communicate" things that evade human understanding and human experience; things therefore that, when suffered by men, transform them into "uncomplaining animals" (*The Dark Side of the Moon,* New York, 1947). There are numerous such reports by survivors; only a few have been published, partly because, quite understandably, the world wants to hear no more of these things, but also because they all leave the reader cold, that is, as apathetic and baffled as the writer himself, and fail to inspire those passions of outrage and sympathy through which men have always been mobilized for justice, for "Misery that goes too deep arouses not compassion but repugnance and hatred" (Rousset).

Der SS-Staat by Eugen Kogon and *Les Jours de notre mort* by David Rousset are products of assimilated recollection. Both authors have consciously written for the world of the living, both wish to make themselves understood at any cost, and both have cast off the insane contempt for those "who never went through it," that in the direct reports so often substitutes for communication. This conscious good will is the only guaranty that those who return will not, after a brief period of sullen resentment against humanity in general, adapt themselves to the real world and become once more the exact same unsuspecting fools that they were when they entered the camps. Both books are indispensable for an understanding not only of the concentration camps, but of the totalitarian regime as a whole. They become useless and even dangerous as soon as they attempt a positive interpretation—Kogon because he cites apparent historical precedents and believes that the camps can be understood psychologically, Rousset because he seeks the consolation of an "extreme experience" in a kind of suffering which, strictly speaking, no longer permits of experience, and thus arrives at a meaningless affirmation of life that is extremely dangerous because it romanticizes and transfigures what must never under any circumstances be repeated on this earth. What is really true, on the contrary, was recently remarked by Isaac Rosenfeld in *The New Leader* (February 14, 1948):

> We still don't understand what happened to the Jews of Europe, and perhaps we never will. . . . By now we know all there is to know. But it hasn't helped . . . as there is no response great enough to equal the facts that provoked it. There is nothing but numbness, and in the respect of numbness we . . . are no different from the murderers who went ahead and did their business and paid no attention to the screams.

Fearful anticipation is the most widespread and perhaps the only fitting approach to the reality of the concentration camp. It certainly has a great deal to do with the attitudes of men under the totalitarian terror, although it always seems to go hand in hand with a remarkable and very characteristic uncertainty which impedes both rebellion and any clear, articulated understanding of the thing feared. Kogan reports: "Only a very, very few of those who entered a concentration camp for the first time had the slightest idea . . . of what awaited them. [Some] were prepared for the worst. But these ideas were always nebulous; the reality far exceeded them." The reason for the uncertainty was precisely that this reality was utterly incredible and inconceivable. In totalitarian regimes, uncertainty as well as fear is manufactured and fostered by the propagandistic treatment of the institution of terror. "There was hardly anything connected with the SS that was not kept secret. The biggest secret of all was the routine of the concentration camps . . . whose only purpose was to spread an anonymous terror of a general political character" (Kogon). Concentration camps and everything connected with them are systematically publicized and at the same time kept absolutely secret. They are used as a threat, but all actual reports about them are suppressed or denounced as fantastic.

It is not surprising that those who made terror the actual foundation of their power should know how to exploit it through publicity and propaganda. The surprising thing is that the psychological and political effects of this propaganda could survive the collapse of the Nazi regime and the opening up of the concentration camps. One would think that the eye-witness reports and, to an even greater degree, the works of ordered recollection which substantiate one another and speak directly to the reader, in Rousset's case most persuasively, should have punctured the propagandist claim that such things were absurd horror stories. This, as we all know, is not the case. Despite overwhelming proofs, anyone speaking or writing about concentration camps is still regarded as suspect; and if the speaker has resolutely returned to the world of the living, he himself is often assailed by doubts with regard to his own truthfulness, as though he had mistaken a nightmare for reality.

This doubt of people concerning themselves and the reality of their own experience only reveals what the Nazis have always known: that men determined to commit crimes will find it expedient to organize them on the vastest, most improbable scale. Not only because this renders all punishments provided by the legal system inadequate and absurd; but because the very immensity of the crimes guarantees that the murderers who proclaim their innocence with all manner of lies will be more readily believed than the victims who tell the truth. The Nazis did not even consider it necessary to keep this discovery to themselves. Hitler circulated millions of copies of his book in which he stated that to be successful, a lie must be enormous—which did not prevent people from believing him as, similarly, the Nazis' proclamations, repeated ad nauseam, that the Jews would be exterminated like bedbugs (i.e., with poison gas), prevented anybody from *not* believing them.

There is a great temptation to explain away the intrinsically incredible by means of liberal rationalizations. In each one of us, there lurks such a liberal, wheedling us with the voice of common sense. We attempt to understand elements in present or recollected experience that simply surpass our powers of understanding. We attempt to classify as criminal a thing which, as we all feel, no such category was ever intended to cover. What meaning has the concept of murder when we are confronted with the mass production of corpses? We attempt to understand the behavior of concentration camp inmates and SS men psychologically, when the very thing that must be realized is that the psyche (or character) *can* be destroyed even without the destruction of the physical man; that, indeed, as Rousset convincingly shows, psyche, character, or individuality seem under certain circumstances to express themselves only through the rapidity or slowness with which they disintegrate. The end result in any case is inanimate men, i.e., men who can no longer be psychologically understood, whose return to the psychologically or otherwise intelligibly human world closely resembles the resurrection of Lazarus—as Rousset indicates in the title of his book. All statements of common sense, whether of a psychological or sociological nature, serve only to encourage those who think it "superficial" to "dwell on horrors" (Georges Bataille, in *Critique,* January 1948).

If it is true that the concentration camps are the most consequential institution of totalitarian rule, "dwelling on horrors" would seem to be indispensable for the understanding of totalitarianism. But recollection can no more do this than can the uncommunicative eye-witness report. In both these genres there is an inherent tendency to run away from the experience; instinctively or rationally, both types of writer are so much aware of the terrible abyss that separates the world of the living from that of the living dead, that they cannot supply anything more than a series of remembered occurrences that must seem just as incredible to those who relate them as to their audience. Only the fearful imagination of those who have been aroused by such reports but have not actually been smitten in their own flesh, of those who are consequently free from the bestial, desperate terror which, when confronted by real, present horror, inexorably paralyzes everything that is not mere reaction, can afford to keep thinking about horrors. Such thoughts are useful only for the perception of political contexts and the mobilization of political passions. A change of personality of any sort whatever can no more be induced by thinking about horrors than by the real experience of horror. The reduction of a man to a bundle of reactions separates him as radically as mental disease from everything within him that is personality or character. When, like Lazarus, he rises from the dead, he finds his personality or character unchanged, just as he had left it.

Nor can horror or thinking about horrors become a basis for a political community or a party in the narrower sense. Attempts have failed to create a European elite with a program of inter-European understanding on the basis of the common experience of the concentration camp, much in the same way that similar attempts after the First World War failed to draw political consequences from the experience of the front-line soldier. In both cases it developed that the experiences themselves could impart only nihilistic platitudes, such as: "Victim and executioner are alike ignoble; the lesson of the camps is the brotherhood of abjection; if you haven't acted with the same degree of ignominy, it's only because you didn't have time . . . but the underlying rot that rises, rises, rises, is absolutely, terrifyingly the same" (Rousset). Political consequences like postwar pacifism followed from the universal fear of war, not from experience of the war. An insight, led and mobilized by fear, into the structure of modern war would have led not to a pacifism without reality, but to the view that the only acceptable ground for modern war is to fight against conditions under which we no longer wish to live—and our knowledge of the camps and torture chambers of totalitarian regimes has convinced us only too well that such conditions are possible. An insight into the nature of totalitarian rule, directed by our fear of the concentration camp, might serve to devaluate all outmoded political shadings from right to left and, beside and above them, to introduce the most essential political criterion for judging the events of our time: Will it lead to totalitarian rule or will it not?

In any case fearful anticipation has the great advantage that it dispels the sophistical-dialectical interpretations of politics, which all rest on the superstition that some good can come out of evil. Such dialectical acrobatics retained at least an appearance of justification as long as the worst evil that man could inflict on man was murder. But murder, as we know today, is still a limited evil. The murderer who kills a man who must die in any event, moves within the familiar realm of life and death, between which there is a necessary relation that is the basis of dialectics, although dialecticians are not always aware of it. The murderer leaves a corpse and does not claim that his victim never existed; he may obscure the traces of his own identity, but he does not efface the memory and grief of those who loved his victim; he destroys a life, but he does not destroy the very fact of its ever having existed.

The horror of the concentration and extermination camps can never be fully embraced by the imagination for the very reason that it stands outside of life and death. The inmates are more effectively cut off from the world of the living than if they were dead, because terror compels oblivion among those who know them or love them. "What extraordinary women you are here," exclaimed the Soviet police when Polish women insisted on knowing the whereabouts of their husbands who had disappeared. "In our country, when the husband is arrested, the wife sues for divorce and looks for another man" (*The Dark Side of the Moon*). Murder in the camps is as impersonal as the squashing of a gnat, a mere technique of management, as when a camp is overcrowded and is liquidated—or an accidental by-product, as when a prisoner succumbs to torture. Systematic torture and systematic starvation create an atmosphere of permanent dying, in which death as well as life is effectively obstructed.

The fear of the absolute Evil which permits of no escape knows that this is the end of dialectical evolutions and developments. It knows that modern politics revolves around a question which, strictly speaking, should never enter into politics, the question of all or nothing: of all, that is, a human society rich with infinite possibilities; or exactly nothing, that is, the end of mankind.

II

There are no parallels to the life of the concentration camps. All seeming parallels create confusion and distract attention from what is essential. Forced labor in prisons and penal colonies, banishment, slavery, all seem for a moment to offer helpful comparisons, but on closer examination lead nowhere.

Forced labor as a punishment is limited as to time and intensity. The convict retains his rights over his body; he is not absolutely tortured and he is not absolutely dominated. Banishment banishes only from one part of the world to another part of the world, also inhabited by human beings; it does not exclude from the human world altogether. Throughout history slavery has been an institution within a social order; slaves were not, like concentration camp inmates, withdrawn from the sight and hence the protection of their fellow men; as instruments of labor they had a definite price and as property a definite value. The concentration camp inmate has no price, because he can always be replaced and he belongs to no one. From the point of view of normal society he is absolutely superfluous, although in times of acute labor shortage, as in Russia and in Germany during the war, he is used for work.

The concentration camp as an institution was not established for the sake of any possible labor yield; the only permanent economic function of the camps has been the financing of their own supervisory apparatus; thus from the economic point of view the concentration camps exist mostly for their own sake. Any work that has been performed could have been done much better and more cheaply under different conditions. The example of Russia, whose concentration camps are usually referred to as forced labor camps, because the Soviet bureaucracy has given them this flattering title, shows most clearly that the main point is not forced labor; forced labor is the normal condition of the whole Russian proletariat which has been deprived of freedom of movement and can be mobilized anywhere at any time.

The incredibility of the horrors is closely bound up with their economic uselessness. The Nazis carried this uselessness to the point of open anti-utility when in the midst of the war, despite the shortage of rolling stock, they transported millions of Jews to the east and set up enormous, costly extermination factories. In the midst of a strictly utilitarian world the obvious contradiction between these acts and military expediency gave the whole enterprise an air of mad unreality.

However, such unreality, created by an apparent lack of purpose, is the very basis of all forms of concentration camp. Seen from outside, they and the things that happen in them can be described only in images drawn from a life after death, that is, a life removed from earthly purposes. Concentration camps can very aptly be divided into three types corresponding to three basic Western conceptions of a life after death: Hades, purgatory, and hell. To Hades correspond those relatively mild forms, once popular even in nontotalitarian countries, for getting undesirable elements of all sorts—refugees, stateless persons, the asocial and the unemployed—out of the way; as DP camps, which are nothing other than camps for persons who have become superfluous and bothersome, they have survived the war. Purgatory is represented by the Soviet Union's labor camps, where neglect is combined with chaotic forced labor. Hell in the most literal sense was embodied by those types of camp perfected by the Nazis, in which the whole of life was thoroughly and systematically organized with a view to the greatest possible torment.

All three types have one thing in common: the human masses sealed off in them are treated as if they no longer existed, as if what happened to them were no longer of any interest to anybody, as if they were already dead and some evil spirit gone mad were amusing himself by stopping them for a while between life and death before admitting them to eternal peace.

It is not so much the barbed wire as the skillfully manufactured unreality of those whom it fences in that provokes such enormous cruelties and ultimately makes extermination look like a perfectly normal measure. Everything that was done in the camps is known to us from the world of perverse, malignant fantasies. The difficult thing to understand is that, like such fantasies, these gruesome crimes took place in a phantom world, in a world in which there were neither consequences nor responsibilities; and finally neither the tormentors nor the tormented, and least of all the outsider, could be aware that what was happening was anything more than a cruel game or an absurd dream.

The films which the Allies circulated in Germany and elsewhere after the war showed clearly that this atmosphere of insanity and unreality is not dispelled by pure reportage. To the unprejudiced observer they are just about as convincing as the pictures of mysterious substances taken at spiritualist séances. Common sense reacted to the horrors of Buchenwald and Auschwitz with the plausible argument: "What crime must these people have committed that such things were done to them!"; or, in Germany and Austria, in the midst of starvation, overpopulation, and general hatred: "Too bad that they've stopped gassing the Jews"; and everywhere with the skeptical shrug that greets ineffectual propaganda.

If the propaganda of truth fails to convince the average Philistine precisely because it is too monstrous, it is positively dangerous to those who know from their own imaginings that they themselves are capable of doing such things and are therefore perfectly willing to believe in the reality of what they have seen. Suddenly it becomes evident that things which for thousands of years the human imagination had banished to a realm beyond human competence, can be manufactured right here on earth. Hell and purgatory, and even a shadow of their perpetual duration, can be established by the most modern methods of destruction and therapy. When people of this sort, who are far more numerous in any large city than we like to think, see these films, or read reports of the same things, the thought that comes to their minds is that the power of man is far greater than they ever dared to think and that men can realize hellish fantasies without making the sky fall or the earth open.

The one thing that cannot be reproduced is what made the traditional conceptions of hell tolerable to man: the Last Judgment, the idea of an absolute standard of justice combined with the infinite possibility of grace. For in the human estimation there is no crime and no sin commensurable with the everlasting torments of hell. Hence the discomfiture of common sense, which asks: What crime must these people have committed in order to suffer so inhumanly? Hence also the absolute innocence of the victims: no man ever deserved this. Hence finally the grotesque haphazardness with which concentration camp victims were chosen in the perfected terror state: such "punishment" can, with equal justice and injustice be inflicted on anyone.

III

In comparison with the insane end-result—concentration camp society—the process by which men are prepared for this end, and the methods by which individuals are adapted to these conditions, are transparent and logical. The insane mass manufacture of corpses is preceded by the historically and politically intelligible preparation of living corpses.

Juridical death

In another connection it might be possible, indeed it would be necessary, to describe this preparatory process as a consequence of the political upheavals of our century. The impetus and, what is more important, the silent consent to such unprecedented conditions in the heart of Europe are the products of those events which in a period of political disintegration suddenly and unexpectedly made hundreds of thousands of human beings homeless, stateless, outlawed and unwanted, while millions of human beings were made economically superfluous and socially burdensome by unemployment. This in turn could only happen because the rights of man, which had never been philosophically established but merely formulated, which had never been politically secured but merely proclaimed, have, in their traditional form, lost all validity.

Meanwhile, however, totalitarian regimes exploited these developments for their own purposes. In order to understand these purposes, we must examine the process of preparing living corpses in its entirety. After all, loss of passport, residence, and the right to work, was only a very provisional, summary preparation, which could hardly have produced adequate results. The first essential step was to kill the juridical person in man; this was done by placing the concentration camp outside the normal penal system, and by selecting its inmates outside the normal judicial procedure in which a definite crime entails a predictable penalty. Thus criminals, who for other reasons are an essential element in concentration camp society, are ordinarily sent to a camp only on completion of their prison sentence. Deviations from this rule in Russia must be attributed to the catastrophic shortage of prisons and to a desire, so far unrealized, to transform the whole penal system into a system of concentration camps.

The inclusion of criminals is necessary in order to make plausible the propagandistic claim that the institution exists for asocial elements. It is equally essential, as long as there is a penal system in the country, that they should be sent to camps only on completion of their sentence, that is, when they are actually entitled to their freedom. It is, paradoxically, harder to kill the juridical person in a man who is guilty of some crime than in a totally innocent. The stateless persons who in all European countries have lost their civil rights along with their nationality, have learned this only too well; their legal position improved automatically as soon as they committed a theft: then they were no longer without rights but had the same rights as all other thieves. In order to kill the juridical person in man, the concentration camp must under no circumstances become a calculable punishment for definite offenses. Criminals do not properly belong in the concentration camps; if nevertheless they constitute the sole permanent category among the inmates, it is a concession of the totalitarian state to the prejudices of society which can in this way most readily be accustomed to the existence of the camps. The amalgamation of criminals with all other categories has moreover the advantage of making it shockingly evident to all other arrivals that they have landed in the lowest level of society. It soon turns out, to be sure, that they have every reason to envy the lowest thief and murderer; but meanwhile the lowest level is a good beginning. Moreover it is an effective means of camouflage: this happens only to criminals and nothing worse is happening than what deservedly happens to criminals.

The criminals everywhere constitute the aristocracy of the camps. (In Germany, during the war, they were replaced in the leadership by the Communists, because not even a minimum of rational work could be performed under the chaotic conditions created by a criminal administration. This was merely a temporary transformation of concentration camps into forced labor camps, a thoroughly atypical phenomenon of limited duration. With his limited, wartime experience of Nazi concentration camps, Rousset overestimates the influence and power of the Communists.) What places the criminals in the leadership is not so much the affinity between supervisory personnel and criminal elements—in the Soviet Union apparently the supervisors are not, like the SS, a special elite of criminals—as the fact that only criminals have been sent to the camp in connection with some definite activity and that in them consequently the destruction of the juridical person cannot be fully successful, since they at least know why they are in a concentration camp. For the politicals this is only subjectively true; their actions, in so far as they were actions and not mere opinions or someone else's vague suspicions, or accidental membership in a politically disapproved group, are as a rule not covered by the normal legal system of the country and not juridically defined.

To the amalgam of politicals and criminals, with which concentration camps in Russia and Germany started out, was added at an early date a third element which was soon to constitute the majority of all concentration camp inmates. This largest group has consisted ever since of people who had done nothing whatsoever that, either in their own consciousness or the consciousness of their tormentors, had any rational connection with their arrest. In Germany, after 1938, this element was represented by masses of Jews, in Russia by any groups which, for any reason having nothing to do with their actions, had incurred the disfavor of the authorities. These groups, innocent in every sense, are the most suitable for thorough experimentation in disfranchisement and destruction of the juridical person, and therefore they are both qualitatively and quantitatively the most essential category of the camp population. This principle was most fully realized in the gas chambers which, if only because of their enormous capacity, could not be intended for individual cases but only for people in general. In this connection, the following dialogue sums up the situation of the individual: "For what purpose, may I ask, do the gas chambers exist?"—"For what purpose were you born?" (Rousset). It is this third group of the totally innocent who in every case fare the worst in the camps. Criminals and politicals are assimilated to this category; thus deprived of the protective distinction that comes of having done something, they are utterly exposed to the arbitrary.

Contrasting with the complete haphazardness with which the inmates are selected are the categories, meaningless in themselves but useful from the standpoint of organization, into which they are usually divided on their arrival. In the German camps there were criminals, politicals, asocial elements, religious offenders, and Jews, all distinguished by insignia. When the French set up concentration camps after the Spanish civil war, they immediately introduced the typical totalitarian amalgam of politicals with criminals and the innocent (in this case the stateless), and despite their inexperience proved remarkably inventive in devising meaningless categories of inmates. Originally devised in order to prevent any growth of solidarity among the inmates, this technique proved particularly valuable because no one could know whether his own category was better or worse than someone else's. In Germany this eternally shifting though pedantically organized edifice was given an appearance of solidity by the fact that under any and all circumstances the Jews were the lowest category. The gruesome and grotesque part of it was that the inmates identified themselves with these categories, as though they represented a last authentic remnant of their juridical person. It is no wonder that a Communist of 1933 should have come out of the camps more Communistic than he went in, a Jew more Jewish.

While the classification of inmates by categories is only a tactical, organizational measure, the arbitrary selection of victims indicates the essential principle of the institution. If the concentration camps had been dependent on the existence of political adversaries, they would scarcely have survived the first years of the totalitarian regimes. "The camps would have died out if in making its arrests the Gestapo had considered only the principle of opposition" (Kogon). But the existence of a political opposition is for a concentration camp system only a pretext, and the purpose of the system is not achieved even when under the most monstrous terror, the population becomes more or less voluntarily coordinated, i.e., relinquishes its political rights. The aim of an arbitrary system is to destroy the civil rights of the whole population, who ultimately become just as outlawed in their own country as the stateless and homeless. The destruction of a man's rights, the killing of the juridical person in him, is a prerequisite for dominating him entirely. For even free consent is an obstacle; and this applies not only to special categories such as criminals, political opponents, Jews, but to every inhabitant of a totalitarian state.

Any, even the most tyrannical, restriction of this arbitrary persecution to certain opinions of a religious or political nature, to certain modes of intellectual or erotic social behavior, to certain freshly invented "crimes," would render the camps superfluous, because in the long run no attitude and no opinion can withstand the threat of so much horror; and above all it would make for a new system of justice, which, given any stability at all, could not fail to produce a new juridical person in man, that would elude the totalitarian domination. The so-called "*Volksnutzen*"[1] of the Nazis, constantly fluctuating (because what is useful today can be injurious tomorrow) and the eternally shifting party line of the Soviet Union which, being retroactive, almost daily makes new groups of people available for the concentration camps, are the only guaranty for the continued existence of the concentration camps and hence for the continued total disfranchisement of man.

IV

The next decisive step in the preparation of living corpses is the murder of the moral person in man. This is done in the main by making martyrdom, for the first time in history, impossible. Rousset writes:

> How many people here still believe that a protest has even historic importance? This skepticism is the real masterpiece of the SS. Their great accomplishment. They have corrupted all human solidarity. Here the night has fallen on the future. When no witnesses are left, there can be no testimony. To demonstrate when death can no longer be postponed is an attempt to give death a meaning, to act beyond one's own death. In order to be successful, a gesture must have social meaning. There are hundreds of thousands of us here, all living in absolute solitude. That is why we are subdued no matter what happens.

The camps and the murder of political adversaries are only part of organized oblivion that not only embraces carriers of public opinion such as the spoken and the written word, but extends even to the families and friends of the victim. Grief and remembrance are forbidden. In the Soviet Union a woman will sue for divorce immediately after her husband's arrest in order to save the lives of her children; if her husband chances to come back, she will indignantly turn him out of the house. The Western world has hitherto, even in its darkest periods, granted the slain enemy the right to be remembered as a self-evident acknowledgment of the fact that we are all men (and *only* men). It is only because even Achilles set out for Hector's funeral, only because the most despotic governments honored the slain enemy, only because the Romans allowed the Christians to write their martyrologies, only because the Church kept its heretics alive in the memory of men, that all was not lost and never could be lost. The concentration camps, by making death itself anonymous—in the Soviet Union it is almost impossible even to find out whether a prisoner is dead or alive—robbed death of the meaning which it had always been possible for it to have. In a sense they took away the individual's own death, proving that henceforth nothing belonged to

[1] [That is, the political or social "needs" of the German "people" as arbitrarily determined by the dictatorship.]

him and he belonged to no one. His death merely set a seal on the fact that he had never really existed.

This attack on the moral person might still have been opposed by man's conscience which tells him that it is better to die a victim than to live as a bureaucrat of murder. The totalitarian governments have cut the moral person off from this individualist escape by making the decisions of conscience absolutely questionable and equivocal.

When a man is faced with the alternative of betraying and thus murdering his friends or of sending his wife and children, for whom he is in every sense responsible, to their death; when even suicide would mean the immediate murder of his own family—how is he to decide? The alternative is no longer between good and evil, but between murder and murder. In perhaps the only article which really gets to the core of this matter, Camus (in *Twice a Year,* 1947) tells of a woman in Greece, who was allowed by the Nazis to choose which among her three children should be killed.

Through the creation of conditions under which conscience ceases to be adequate and to do good becomes utterly impossible, the consciously organized complicity of all men in the crimes of totalitarian regimes is extended to the victims and thus made really total. The SS implicated concentration camp inmates—criminals, politicals, Jews—in their crimes by making them responsible for a large part of the administration, thus confronting them with the hopeless dilemma whether to send their friends to their death, or to help murder other men who happened to be strangers.

Once the moral person has been killed, the one thing that still prevents men from being made into living corpses is the differentiation of the individual, his unique identity. In a sterile form such individuality can be preserved through a persistent stoicism, and it is certain that many men under totalitarian rule have taken and are each day still taking refuge in this absolute isolation of a personality without rights or conscience. There is no doubt that this part of the human person, precisely because it depends so essentially on nature and on forces that cannot be controlled by the will, is the hardest to destroy (and when destroyed is most easily repaired).

The methods of dealing with this uniqueness of the human person are numerous and we shall not attempt to list them all. They begin with the monstrous conditions in the transports to the camps, when hundreds of human beings are packed into a cattle car stark naked, glued to each other, and shunted back and forth over the countryside for days on end; then continue upon arrival at the camp, the well-organized shock of the first hours, the shaving of the head, the grotesque camp clothing; and they end in the utterly unimaginable tortures so gauged as not to kill the body, at any event not quickly. The aim of all these methods, in any case, is to manipulate the human body—with its infinite possibilities of suffering—in such a way as to make it destroy the human person as inexorably as certain mental diseases of organic origin.

It is here that the utter lunacy of the entire process becomes most apparent. Torture, to be sure, is an essential feature of the whole totalitarian police and judiciary apparatus; it is used every day to make people talk. This type of torture, since it pursues a definite, rational aim, has certain limitations: either the prisoner talks within a certain time, or he is killed. But to this rationally conducted torture another, irrational, sadistic type was added in the first Nazi concentration camps and in the cellars of the Gestapo. Carried on for the most part by the SA, it pursued no aims and was not systematic, but depended on the initiative of largely abnormal elements. The mortality was so high that only a few concentration camp inmates of 1933 survived these first years. This type of torture seemed to be not so much a calculated political institution as a concession of the regime to its criminal and abnormal elements, who were thus rewarded for services rendered. Behind the blind bestiality of the SA, there often lay a deep hatred and resentment against all those who were socially, intellectually, or physically better off than themselves, and who now, as if in fulfillment of their wildest dreams, were in their power. This resentment, which never died out entirely in the camps, strikes us as a last remnant of humanly understandable feeling.

The real horror began, however, when the SS took over the administration of the camps. The old spontaneous bestiality gave way to an absolutely cold and systematic destruction of human bodies, calculated to destroy human dignity; death was avoided or postponed indefinitely. The camps were no longer amusement parks for beasts in human form, that is, for men who really belonged in mental institutions and prisons; the reverse became true: they were turned into "drill grounds" (Kogon), on which perfectly normal men were trained to be full-fledged members of the SS.

The killing of man's individuality, of the uniqueness shaped in equal parts by nature, will, and destiny, which has become so self-evident a premise for all human relations that even identical twins inspire a certain uneasiness, creates a horror that vastly overshadows the outrage of the juridical-political person and the despair of the moral person. It is this horror that gives rise to the nihilistic generalizations which maintain plausibly enough that essentially all men alike are beasts. Actually the experience of the concentration camps does show that human beings can be transformed into specimens of the human beast, and that man's "nature" is only "human" in so far as it opens up to man the possibility of becoming something highly unnatural, that is, a man.

After murder of the moral person and annihilation of the juridical person, the destruction of the individuality is almost always successful. Conceivably some laws of mass psychology may be found to explain why millions of human beings allowed themselves to be marched unresistingly into the gas chambers, although these laws would explain nothing else but the destruction of individuality. It is more significant that those individually condemned to death very seldom attempted to take one of their executioners with them, that there were scarcely any serious revolts, and that even in the moment of liberation there were very few spontaneous massacres of the SS men. For to destroy individuality is to destroy spontaneity, man's power to begin something new out of his own resources, something new that cannot be explained on the basis of reactions to environment and events. Nothing then remains but ghastly marionettes with human faces, which all behave like the dog in Pavlov's experiments, which all react with perfect reliability even when going to their own death, and which do nothing but react. This is the real triumph of the system—:

> The triumph of the SS demands that the tortured victim allow himself to be led to the noose without protesting, that he renounce and abandon himself to the point of ceasing to affirm his identity. And it is not for nothing. It is not gratuitously, out of sheer sadism, that the SS men desire this defeat. They know that the system which succeeds in destroying its victim before he mounts the scaffold . . . is incomparably the best for keeping a whole people in slavery. In submission. Nothing is more terrible than these processions of human beings going like dummies to their death. The man who sees this says to himself: "For them to be thus reduced, what power must be concealed in the hands of the masters," and he turns away, full of bitterness but defeated. (Rousset)

V

It is characteristic of totalitarian terror that it increases as the regime becomes more secured, and accordingly concentration camps are expanded as political opposition decreases. Totalitarian demands do not seem to be satisfied by political success in establishing a one-party state, and it seems as though political opposition were by no means the cause of terror but rather a barrier to its full development. This seems absurd only if we apply to modern totalitarian movements those standards of utility which they themselves expressly reject as obsolete, sentimental, and bourgeois.

If on the contrary we take totalitarian aspirations seriously and refuse to be misled by the common-sense assertion that they are utopian and unrealizable, it develops that the society of the dying established in the camps is the only form of society in which it is possible to dominate man entirely. Those who aspire to total domination must liquidate all spontaneity, such as the mere existence of individuality will always engender, and track it down in its most private forms, regardless of how unpolitical and harmless these may seem. Pavlov's dog, the human specimen reduced to the most elementary reactions, the bundle of reactions that can always be liquidated and replaced by other bundles of reactions that behave in exactly the same way, is the model "citizen" of a totalitarian state; and such a citizen can be produced only imperfectly outside of the camps.

The uselessness of the camps, their cynically admitted antiutility, is only apparent. In reality they are more essential to the preservation of the regime's power than any of its other institutions. Without concentration camps, without the undefined fear they inspire and the very well-defined training they offer in totalitarian domination, which has nowhere else been fully tested with all of its most radical possibilities, a totalitarian state can neither inspire its nuclear troops with fanaticism nor maintain a whole people in complete apathy. The dominating and the dominated would only too quickly sink back into the "old bourgeois routine"; after early "excesses," they would succumb to everyday life with its human laws; in short, they would develop in the direction which all observers counseled by common sense were so prone to predict. The tragic fallacy of all these prophecies originating in a world that was still safe, was to suppose that there was such a thing as one human nature established for all time, to identify this human nature with history and thus declare that the idea of total domination was not only inhuman but also unrealistic. Meanwhile we have learned that the power of man is so great that he really can be what he wishes to be.

It is in the very nature of totalitarian regimes to demand unlimited power. Such power can only be secured if literally all men, without a single exception, are reliably dominated in every aspect of their life. In the realm of foreign affairs new neutral territories must constantly be subjugated, while at home ever-new human groups must be mastered in expanding concentration camps, or, when circumstances require, liquidated to make room for others. Here the question of opposition is unimportant both in foreign and domestic affairs. Any neutrality, indeed any spontaneously given friendship is from the standpoint of totalitarian domination just as dangerous as open hostility, precisely because spontaneity as such, with its incalculability, is the greatest of all obstacles to total domination over man. The Communists of non-Communist countries, who fled or were called to Moscow, learned by bitter experience that they constituted a menace to the Soviet Union. Convinced Communists are in this sense, which alone has any reality today, just as ridiculous and just as menacing to the regime in Russia as for example the convinced Nazis of the Roehm faction were to the Nazis.

What makes conviction and opinion of any sort so ridiculous and dangerous under totalitarian conditions is that totalitarian regimes take the greatest pride in having no need of them, or of any human help of any kind. Men insofar as they are more than animal reaction and fulfillment of functions are entirely superfluous to totalitarian regimes. Totalitarianism strives not toward despotic rule over men, but toward a system in which men are superfluous. Total power can be achieved and safeguarded only in a world of conditioned reflexes, of marionettes without the slightest trace of spontaneity. Precisely because man's resources are so great, he can be fully dominated only when he becomes a specimen of the animal-species man.

Therefore character is a threat and even the most unjust legal rules are an obstacle; but individuality, anything indeed that distinguishes one man from another, is intolerable. As long as all men have not been made equally superfluous—and this has been accomplished only in concentration camps—the ideal of totalitarian domination has not been achieved. Totalitarian states strive constantly, though never with complete success, to establish the superfluity of man—by the arbitrary selection of various groups for concentration camps, by constant purges of the ruling apparatus, by mass liquidations. Common sense protests desperately that the masses are submissive and that all this gigantic apparatus of terror is therefore superfluous; if they were capable of telling the truth, the totalitarian rulers would reply: The apparatus seems superfluous to you only because it serves to make men superfluous.

They will not speak so frankly. But the concentration camps, and even more so the corpse factories invented by the Nazis speak only too clearly. Today, with population almost everywhere on the increase, masses of people are continuously being rendered superfluous by political, social, and economic events. At such a time the instruments devised for making human beings superfluous are bound to offer a great temptation: why not use these same instruments to liquidate human beings who have already become superfluous?

This side of the matter is only too well understood by the common sense of the mob which in most countries is too desperate to retain much fear of death. The Nazis, who were well aware that their defeat would not solve the problems of Europe, knew exactly what they were doing when, toward the end of the war—which by then they knew they had lost—they set up those factories of annihilation which demonstrated the swiftest possible solution to the problem of superfluous human masses. There is no doubt that this solution will from now on occur to millions of people whenever it seems impossible to alleviate political, or social, or economic misery in a manner worthy of man.

THE GRAEBE MEMORANDUM

I, Hermann Friedrich Graebe, declare under oath:

At Wiesbaden, on 10 November 1945 I made two statements describing as an eye-witness the execution of Jews on the former airport near Dubno, Ukraine, and the herding together, ill-treatment and killing of men, women and children of the former Ghetto at Rowno, Ukraine.

By way of corollary to these statements I depose as follows:

1. The SS-man acting as the executioner on the edge of the pit during the shooting of Jewish men, women and children on the airport near Dubno, wore an SS-uniform with a grey armband about 3 cm wide on the lower part of his sleeve with the letters "SD" in black on it, woven in or embroidered.

2. SS-Sturmbannfuehrer Dr. Puetz was in charge of the carrying out of the operation (Aktion) at Rowno during the night of 13 July 1942. I knew Dr. Puetz personally as the "Kommandeur der SP u. SD" [commander of the Security Police and Security Service] of Rowno, for I had had several discussions with him with a view to preventing a pogrom against the Jews [Judenaktion] at Sdolbunow, Misotsch and Ostrog. Dr. Puetz was introduced to me by the Area Commissioner Georg Marschall. In addition I definitely remember that a nameplate was fixed on the outside of the door to his office bearing his name and rank.

On the morning of 14 July I recognized three or four SS-men in the Ghetto, whom I knew personally and who were all members of the Security Service in Rowno. These persons also wore the armband mentioned above. I cannot recall their names, but, in my opinion, the foreman Fritz Einsporn must know their names, as, to my knowledge, he corresponded with them.

This selection has been reprinted from *Nazi Conspiracy and Aggression* (Washington, D.C., Office of the United States Chief of Counsel for Prosecution of Axis Criminality, United States Government Printing Office, 1946), Vol. V, pp. 696–699.

I make the foregoing statement in Wiesbaden, Germany, on 13 November 1945. I swear before God, that this is the absolute truth.

(s) Fr. Graebe

(t) HERMANN FRIEDRICH GRAEBE

Before me, Homer B. Crawford, being authorized to administer oaths, personally appeared Hermann Friedrich Graebe, who, being by me duly sworn through the interpreter Elisabeth Radzie-Jewska, made and subscribed the following statement:

I, Hermann Friedrich Graebe, declare under oath:

From September 1941 until January 1944 I was manager and engineer-in-charge of a branch office in Sdolbunow, Ukraine, of the Solingen building firm of Josef Jung. In this capacity it was my job to visit the building sites of the firm. Under contract to an Army Construction Office, the firm had orders to erect grain storage buildings on the former airport of Dubno, Ukraine.

On 5 October 1942, when I visited the building office at Dubno, my foreman Hubert Moennikes of 21 Aussenmuehlenweg, Hamburg-Haarburg, told me that in the vicinity of the site, Jews from Dubno had been shot in three large pits, each about 30 meters long and 3 meters deep. About 1500 persons had been killed daily. All of the 5000 Jews who had still been living in Dubno before the pogrom were to be liquidated. As the shootings had taken place in his presence he was still much upset.

Thereupon I drove to the site, accompanied by Moennikes and saw near it great mounds of earth, about 30 meters long and 2 meters high. Several trucks stood in front of the mounds. Armed Ukrainian militia drove the people off the trucks under the supervision of an SS-man. The militia men acted as guards on the trucks and drove them to and from the pit. All these people had the regulation yellow patches on the front and back of their clothes, and thus could be recognized as Jews.

Moennikes and I went directly to the pits. Nobody bothered us. Now I heard rifle shots in quick succession, from behind one of the earth mounds. The people who had got off the trucks—men, women, and children of all ages—had to undress upon the order of an SS-man, who carried a riding or dog whip. They had to put down their clothes in fixed places, sorted according to shoes, top clothing and underclothing. I saw a heap of shoes of about 800 to 1000 pairs, great piles of under-linen and clothing. Without screaming or weeping these people undressed, stood around in family groups, kissed each other, said farewells and waited for a sign from another SS-man, who stood near the pit, also with a whip in his hand. During the 15 minutes that

I stood near the pit I heard no complaint or plea for mercy. I watched a family of about 8 persons, a man and woman, both about 50 with their children of about 1, 8 and 10, and two grown-up daughters of about 20 to 24. An old woman with snow-white hair was holding the one-year old child in her arms and singing to it, and tickling it. The child was cooing with delight. The couple were looking on with tears in their eyes. The father was holding the hand of a boy about 10 years old and speaking to him softly; the boy was fighting his tears. The father pointed toward the sky, stroked his head, and seemed to explain something to him. At that moment the SS-man at the pit shouted something to his comrade. The latter counted off about 20 persons and instructed them to go behind the earth mound. Among them was the family, which I have mentioned. I well remember a girl, slim and with black hair, who, as she passed close to me, pointed to herself and said, "23." I walked around the mound, and found myself confronted by a tremendous grave. People were closely wedged together and lying on top of each other so that only their heads were visible. Nearly all had blood running over their shoulders from their heads. Some of the people shot were still moving. Some were lifting their arms and turning their heads to show that they were still alive. The pit was already ⅔ full. I estimated that it already contained about 1000 people. I looked for the man who did the shooting. He was an SS-man, who sat at the edge of the narrow end of the pit, his feet dangling into the pit. He had a tommy gun on his knees and was smoking a cigarette. The people, completely naked, went down some steps which were cut in the clay wall of the pit and clambered over the heads of the people lying there, to the place to which the SS-man directed them. They lay down in front of the dead or injured people; some caressed those who were still alive and spoke to them in a low voice. Then I heard a series of shots. I looked into the pit and saw that the bodies were twitching or the heads lying already motionless on top of the bodies that lay before them. Blood was running from their necks. I was surprised that I was not ordered away, but I saw that there were two or three postmen in uniform nearby. The next batch was approaching already. They went down into the pit, lined themselves up against the previous victims and were shot. When I walked back, round the mound I noticed another truckload of people which had just arrived. This time it included sick and infirm people. An old, very thin woman with terribly thin legs was undressed by others who were already naked, while two people held her up. The woman appeared to be paralyzed. The naked people carried the woman around the mound. I left with Moennikes and drove in my car back to Dubno.

On the morning of the next day, when I again visited the site, I saw about

30 naked people lying near the pit—about 30 to 50 meters away from it. Some of them were still alive; they looked straight in front of them with a fixed stare and seemed to notice neither the chilliness of the morning nor the workers of my firm who stood around. A girl of about 20 spoke to me and asked me to give her clothes, and help her escape. At that moment we heard a fast car approach and I noticed that it was an SS-detail. I moved away to my site. Ten minutes later we heard shots from the vicinity of the pit. The Jews still alive had been ordered to throw the corpses into the pit—then they had themselves to lie down in this to be shot in the neck.

I make the above statement at Wiesbaden, Germany, on 10th November 1945. I swear before God that this is the absolute truth.

Hermann Friedrich Graebe

Subscribed and sworn to before me at Wiesbaden, Germany, this 10 day of November 1945.

Homer B. Crawford
Major, AC
Investigator Examiner, War Crimes Branch

I, Elisabeth Radziejewska, being first duly sworn, state: That I truly translated the oath administered by Major Homer B. Crawford to Hermann Friedrich Graebe and that thereupon he made and subscribed the foregoing statement in my presence.

Elisabeth Radziejewska
Interpreter

Subscribed and sworn to before me at Wiesbaden, Germany, this 10 day of November 1945.

Homer B. Crawford
Major, AC
Investigator Examiner, War Crimes Branch

CONTEMPORARY CIVILIZATION: ITS PREDICAMENTS

3. THE WIDENING CIRCLE OF UPHEAVAL

JOSÉ ORTEGA Y GASSET

THE core of Ortega's thought is most fully set forth in *El tema de nuestro tiempo* (1923), translated from the Spanish by James Cleugh as *The Modern Theme* (1931). It is from the "supplementary" section of this book that the following selection is taken. In it, Ortega ascribes three successive cycles to human civilizations, which he identifies as the regimes of traditionalism, rationalism, and mysticism. Present-day Europe, he believes, is passing into its third cycle. This is the "sunset" period for revolutions, for bold rational and individualist assertion, an era when "vital resources weaken" and yield before "universal cowardice."

It would be erroneous to assume that Ortega is resigned to his prophecy or, however sharp his critique of rationalist excesses, that he endorses the mystical outlook. The key to his philosophy is offered in *The Modern Theme* as "perspectivism" and is summed up in the sentence, "I am myself and my circumstance." A man, that is—or for that matter a people at any moment in its history—is locked into a "perspective," a unique set of circumstances. The reason which informs action must be a "living reason" (*razón vital*) interacting with immediate circumstances, defining them and defined *by* them. It is needless here to explore Ortega's metaphysics, which is largely inspired by such German thinkers as Georg Simmel (1858–1918) and Edmund Husserl (1859–1938), or to assess its philosophic validity and usefulness. But it should be stressed that Ortega persistently tries to avoid the system-building, universalist rationalism which floats free of experienced reality and, at the same time, the easy relativism which indiscriminately undermines all criteria for moral action.

"The modern theme," writes Ortega, "is to subject reason to living, to localize it within the biological field, to subordinate it to the spontaneous." "Living reason" replaces "pure reason" as the proper mode of cognition. Yet his is not, he claims, another "vitalistic" theory in which reason retreats before a mystical *élan,* or random spirit. "Do not believe anyone who tells you that the inexpressible is of the most value in man," he warns in *Mocedades* (1941). "That is a very ancient lie of the mystics and of the confused enemies of man."

An understanding of what Ortega means by "living reason" illuminates the grounds of his apprehensions about the "mystical" era into which he alleges Europe to be entering. For the "mystagogue" traffics in dark secrets and mysteries which it is the philosopher's task to expose to light. We are to distinguish, however, between mysticism and religion. The primary meaning of "religion," Ortega asserts, derives not from *religare* (that is, *to bind* man to God) but from *religiosus,* meaning scrupulous, conscientious, not trifling. "To live not wantonly but warily—wary of a transcendental reality—is . . . the essential meaning of all religion. . . . The opposite of religion thus would be negligence, carelessness, indifference, laxity." Ortega accounts for the great centuries of the Roman Republic by its leaders' circumspection regarding precipitous action. Alive to the vastness of the reality which they faced, they submitted their projects to the judgment of the gods to await their "auspices"; thus *auspicium* became synonymous with *imperium*, or rule. "A fusion took place between the concepts of state and of belief. In politics, there are epochs of religion and epochs of negligence, of care and of carelessness, of probity and of frivolity." (*Concord and Liberty*, 1940.)

If, for the sake of speculation, one accepts Ortega's view that Europe's revolutionary sun has set, and that the shadows of "negligence" are gathering, it remains to examine the confrontation between Western man and the rest of the world. For in many lands a spirit of revolution imparted by Europe has yet to reach its zenith, and the "auspices" of age-old religions still abound.

THE SUNSET OF REVOLUTION

The Sabbath was made for man, not man for the Sabbath.—S. MARK II, 27.

For the purpose of defining an epoch it is not enough to know what has been done in it; it is also necessary for us to know what it has not done, what was, in fact, impossible in it. This may seem a singular requisite; yet such is the condition upon which our thought proceeds. To define is to exclude and deny. The more reality that is possessed by what we define, the more exclusions and denials we shall have to practise. Accordingly, the most profound definition of God, the supreme reality, is that given by the Indian Yajnavalkya: "Na iti, na iti." "Nothing of that kind, nothing of that kind." Nietzsche acutely observes that we are more influenced by what does not happen to us than by what does and, according to the Egyptian ritual of the dead, when the "double" abandons the corpse and has to perform its feat of self-definition before the judges of the world beyond the grave, it makes its confession contrariwise, that is to say, it enumerates the sins it has not committed. Similarly, when we declare that one of our acquaintances is an excellent person, do we mean anything except that he will not rob or kill us, and that if he does covet his neighbour's wife no one will be very much concerned about it?

The positive character with which we thus invest negation is nevertheless not simply a necessity inflicted by the peculiar temper of our intelligence. There is, at any rate in the case of living beings, a real vigour of negation which corresponds to the negative concept. If the Romans did not invent the motor-

---

This selection has been reprinted from *The Modern Theme* by José Ortega y Gasset by permission of W. W. Norton & Company, Inc., Copyright 1933 by W. W. Norton & Company, Inc., New York (pp. 99–127, 131–134).

car, that was no mere accident. One of the ingredients that play a part in Roman history is the incapacity of the Latin race in matters of technical detail. This was one of the most active factors in the decadence of the antique world.

An epoch is a repertory of positive and negative tendencies; it is a system of subtleties and perspicacities united to a system replete with blindness and dullness. There is not only the taste for certain things, but also the determination to have distaste for others. At the beginning of a new age the first thing we notice is the magical presence of these negative propensities, which initiate the elimination of the fauna and flora of the anterior epoch: so, in the flight of the swallows and in the fall of the leaves we first become aware of the presence of autumn.

In this sense there is no better qualification of the age now dawning upon our ancient continent than the recognition that in Europe revolutions are things of the past. Such recognition implies not only that they no longer exist in fact, but also that they can never exist again.

Perhaps the full significance comprised in this prognostication does not appear obvious at once for the reason that the current notion of revolution is a very vague one. Not long ago an excellent friend of mine, of Uruguayan nationality, assured me, with ill-concealed pride, that in less than a century his country had undergone forty revolutions. Evidently my friend was exaggerating. Educated, like myself and a good number of my readers, in an uncritical worship of the idea of revolution, he patriotically desired to adorn his national history with the greatest possible number of concrete instances. To this end, following a common custom, he called revolutionary every collective movement in which violence is employed against established power. But history cannot be content with such rough and ready notions. It requires more exact instruments and more sharply outlined concepts for its purpose of sound orientation in the forest of human occurrences. Not every violent measure against public power is revolution. It is not, for example, revolution when one part of society rebels against the governing class and violently substitutes others for them. The convulsions of the South American peoples are almost always of this type. If there is a very earnest desire to retain the title of revolution for them, we should not dream of inspiring a further example in order to thwart the desire in question: but we shall have to look for another name to denominate another class of processes of an essentially distinct type, to which belong the English revolution of the seventeenth century, the four French ones of the eighteenth and nineteenth, and in general all the public life of Europe between 1750 and 1900, which Auguste Comte had already, by 1830, proved to be "essentially revolutionary" in character and derivation. The same motives which induce people to think that there will be no more revolutions in Europe oblige them to believe that there have not yet been any in South America.

The least essential feature of true revolution is violence. It is not inconceivable, though it is hardly likely, that a revolution might run its whole course without a drop of blood being shed. Revolutions are not constituted by barricades, but by states of mind. Such states of mind do not occur in all ages; like fruits, they have their seasons. It is a remarkable fact that in all the great historical cycles of which we have sufficient knowledge—the Greek, Roman and European worlds, for instance—a point is reached at which not one revolution but a whole revolutionary era begins, which lasts two or three centuries before it finally disappears for good.

It shows a complete lack of historical perception to consider the risings of peasants and serfs in the Middle Ages as events foreshadowing modern revolutions. There is no real connection between the two types of phenomena. When the medieval man rebels it is against the abuses indulged in by his lords. The modern revolutionary, on the other hand, does not rebel against abuses but against usage or custom. Up to a short time ago histories of the French revolution began by representing the years round about 1780 as a time of misery and social depression with affliction rife in the lower classes and tyranny in the upper. In their ignorance of the specific structure of revolutionary eras people believed that the catastrophe could only be explained as a movement of protest against an antecedent oppression. It has now long been recognised that in the stage previous to the general rising the French nation enjoyed greater wealth and more even-handed justice than in the time of Louis XIV. It has been declared a hundred times that the revolution was formed in men's minds before it began in the streets. If a sound analysis had been made of what is implied by this expression, the physiology of revolution would have been discovered.

All revolutions, in effect, if they are true revolutions, presuppose a peculiar and unmistakable disposition of mind. To understand it properly one must turn to study the development of the great historical organisms which have completed their full cycle. We then find that in every one of those great composite movements mankind has passed through three distinct spiritual situations, or, in other words, that the life of the human psyche has gravitated successively towards three diverse centres.

The psyche passes from a traditional state of mind to a rationalist and from the latter to a mystical *régime*. These are, so to speak, the three different forms of psychic mechanism, the three distinct ways in which the mental apparatus of mankind pursues its function.

During the centuries in which some great historical conglomeration, such as Greece, Rome or our own continent of Europe, is in process of formation and organisation, what *régime* directs the spirit of its members? The answer given by facts is a most surprising one. It is when a people is young and in course of development that it is chiefly influenced by the past. At the first glance the contrary would appear to be the more natural state of affairs: one would suppose that an ancient people, with a long past behind them, would be most thoroughly subject to the claims of bygone days. This, however, is not the case. The decrepit nation is not in the slightest degree influenced by the past; on the other hand, in an adolescent population everything is done with an eye to the past. And it is not a short past that is envisaged, but one so long, and with so vague and remote a horizon, that no one has ever seen, or remembers, its commencement. It is, in brief, immemorial.

The psychology of peoples dominated by ancestral ideas and arrested, through one kind or another of historical malnutrition, in a permanently infantile stage of development is a curious study. One of the most primitive peoples in existence is the aboriginal Australian. If we investigate the way in which the intellectual activity of this people functions, we find that on being confronted with any sort of problem—for example, a phenomenon of nature —the Australian does not look for an explanation which is enough of itself to satisfy intelligence. In his mentality, to account for a fact such, for instance, as the existence of three rocks standing together on a plain, is to recall a mythological story which he has heard ever since he was a child, and according to which in antiquity, or, as the Australians say, in *alcheringa,* three men, who were once kangaroos, were changed into the stones in question. This explanation satisfies his mind precisely because it is not a reason or a thought which can be verified. Its validity consists in the fact that the individual intelligence creates it for itself, either as an original statement, or by repeating the ratiocination and observations which integrate it. The strength of reason is born of the conviction that it produces in the individual. Now, the Australian does not experience what we call individuality or, if so, he experiences it in the form and to the extent that a child does when it is left alone, abandoned by the family group. The primitive man only perceives the singularity of his person as solitude or disruption. The concept of individuality and everything based upon it only produces terror in him: it is a synonym, for him, of debility and insufficiency. Solidity and security are to be found only in the communal condition, whose existence is anterior to that of any individual: for the latter finds it ready-made for him as soon as he awakes to life. As the old men of the tribe had been equally conscious of it, it is considered to be of immemorial origin. It does each man's thinking for him by means of its treasure of myth and legend, transmitted by tradition; it creates his legal and social codes, his rites, dances and gestures. The Australian believes in the mythological explanation precisely because he has not invented it, precisely because he does not possess a sound reasoning faculty. The reaction of his intellect to the events of life does not consist in the immediate expression of a spontaneous thought of his own, but in reiterating a pre-existent and accepted formula. For these people thought, desire and feeling connote mere circulation through ready-made psychological channels, repetition of a hackneyed repertory of mental attitudes. The spontaneous, in this mode of existence, is fervent submission and adaption to accepted type, to the tradition in which the individual lives submerged, and which is, for him, immutable reality.

This is the traditionalist state of mind which has been operative in our own Middle Ages, and which directed the course of Greek history up to the seventh and Roman to the third century B.C. The content of these epochs is naturally much richer, more complex and more delicate than that of the mind of a savage; but the type of psychic mechanism and its method of functioning is the same. The individual invariably adapts his reactions to a communal repertory which he has received by transmission from a venerated past. The medieval man, when he has to decide upon a course of action, puts himself into relation with what his "fathers" did. The situation is identical, in this respect, with that prevailing in the mind of the child. The child, too, believes more in what it hears from its parents than in its own judgments. When an event is described in the presence of children they generally direct an interrogative look at their parents, as if to ask them whether the narrative is to be believed, whether it is "true" or a "story." The mind of the child, too, never gravitates to the centre of its own individuality: it clings to its progenitors in the same way as the medieval mind clings to the "usage and custom of our fathers." In no system of jurisprudence does customary law, or immemorial usage, possess such weight as it does in the systems which arise during historical formations and consolidations. The simple fact of antiquity is converted into a legal sanction. The foundation of jurisprudence is neither justice nor equity, but the irrational, by which I mean the purely material, fact of prolonged existence.

In the political world the traditionalist mind will be found living in respectful concurrence with what is already established which, precisely because it is established, possesses an invulnerable prestige: it is what we find ready-made for us when we are born; it is what our fathers did. When a new requirement presents itself it does not occur to anyone to reform the structure of established fact; what is done is to make room in the latter for the new fact and give it a permanent place in the immemorial body of tradition.

It is in the epochs characterized by the traditionalist mind that nations organize themselves. For this reason such periods are followed by an age of maturity, which is, in a certain sense, the hour of historical culmination. The body of the nation has reached its perfect development: it enjoys the use of all its organs and has accumulated a vast treasure of energies together with potentialities of a high order. A time comes when all this wealth begins to be expended, and such stages of history then appear to us particularly healthy and brilliant. We are more forcibly aware of our neighbour's health when he begins to turn it to account externally in various outstanding exploits or, in other words, when he begins to lose it by expenditure. Such ages are the splendid centuries of vital dilapidation. The nation is no longer content with its internal life, and an epoch of expansion is initiated.

With such an epoch coincide the first clear symptoms of a new state of mind. The traditionalist mechanism of the mind is about to be replaced by another mechanism of an opposite type—the rationalist.

We, too, in the present age are affected by traditionalism; but we must avoid confusing this type with what I have previously called traditionalism in this essay. Contemporary traditionalism is no more than a philosophic and political theory. The traditionalism of which I have spoken, on the contrary, is a reality; it is the real mechanism responsible for the functioning of men's minds during certain epochs.

So long as the empire of tradition lasts, each unit of mankind remains embedded in the close corporation of communal existence. He does nothing on his own account, apart from the social group. He is not the protagonist of his own acts; his personality is not his own, distinct from others; an identical mind is reproduced in each unit with the same thoughts, memories, desires and emotions. Hence, in traditionalist centuries figures of outstanding personal physiognomy are not, as a rule, to be found. All the members of the social body are more or less the same. The only important differences are those of position, rank, employment or class.

However, within this communal mind, whose texture is that of tradition, and which has its seat in each unit of the group, a small central nucleus begins, after a time, to form: this is the sentiment of individuality. It originates in a tendency antagonistic to that which the traditional mind has been moulding. The supposition, that the consciousness of private individuality was a primary notion and, so to speak, aboriginal in man, was quite erroneous. It used to be asserted that human beings are originally aware of themselves as individuals, and that the next step is to seek out other human beings with

Mead.

the object of associating with them. The truth is just the opposite. The subjective personality begins by feeling himself to be an element of a group, and it is only later that he proceeds to separate from it and achieve little by little the consciousness of his singularity. The "we" comes first, and then the "I." The latter is therefore endowed from its birth with the secondary character of secession. I mean by this that man proceeds to discover his individuality in proportion to the development of his conscious hostility to communism and opposition to tradition. Individualism and anti-traditionalism are one and the same psychological force.

This nucleus of individuality, germinating within the traditionalist mind like the larva of an insect in the core of a fruit, gradually grows to the dimensions of a new demand, principle or imperative, confronting tradition. On this view the traditional method of reacting intellectually—I hardly care to call it thought—consists in recalling the repertory of beliefs received from the forefathers of the group. On the other hand, the individualist method turns its back on all such accepted beliefs, repudiating them just because they are accepted, and aims instead at producing some new thought which is to be valued on the grounds, only, of its own independent content. Such a thought, not proceeding out of immemorial communistic life, not to be referred to "our fathers," an ideation lacking lineage, genealogy and the prestige of hereditary emblems, is obliged to derive its parentage from its own works, to sustain itself by its own convincing efficacy, by its purely intellectual perfections. In a word, it must be a Reason.

The traditionalist mind functioned under the guidance of a single principle and possessed a unique centre of gravity which was, in fact, tradition. But henceforward two antagonistic forces operate in the mind of each unit, viz., tradition and reason. Little by little the latter will go on gaining ground from the former: this means that spiritual life has been converted into an internal struggle and has exchanged its unitarian status for dissociation into two mutually inimical tendencies.

While the primitive mind accepts, as soon as it is born, the world which it finds already provided for it, the birth of individuality involves at once a negation of that world. But the subjective personality, in repudiating the traditional, finds itself obliged to reconstruct the universe through its own resources, i.e., its reason.

It is easy to see that in consequence of this necessity the human spirit may succeed in developing its intellectual faculty to a point nothing short of marvelous. These rationalist periods are always the most glorious epochs of human thought. The irrational myth is put on the shelf, and in its place the scientific conception of the cosmos proceeds to the erection of its admirable edifices of theory. The specific enjoyment to be derived from ideas makes itself felt, and an amazing virtuosity in their invention and management is acquired.

Man ends by believing that he possesses a sort of divine faculty capable of revealing to him, once and for all, the ultimate essence of phenomena. This faculty must be independent of actual experience, whose constant variations might induce modifications in the revelation expected. Descartes called this faculty *raison* or *pure intellection,* and Kant, more accurately, pure reason.

"Pure reason" is not the ordinary exercise of the understanding, but its method of functioning absolutely. When Robinson Crusoe applies his intelligence to the resolution of the urgent problems that await him on his desert isle he does not employ pure reason. He imposes on his intellect the task of adjusting itself to circumambient reality, and its actual function is reduced to the effective combination of truncated portions of such reality. Pure reason is, on the contrary, the state of the understanding when left to its own devices: it then constructs, on its own foundations, a number of prodigious weapons, of a sublime accuracy and rigidity. Instead of seeking contact with phenomena it ignores such contact, and tries to ensure the most exclusive fidelity to its own internal laws. Mathematics is the typical product of pure reason. Its concepts are elucidated once and for all, and there is no risk of reality contradicting them at some future date, for reality is not their source. In mathematics nothing is uncertain and approximate. Everything is clear, for everything stands at its highest point of expression. Greatness is infinite greatness, and smallness is absolute smallness. The straight line is radically straight, and the curve curves unadulterated. Pure reason never passes beyond the circle of superlatives and absolutes. Indeed, that is the reason why it is called pure. It is incorruptible and uncompromising. When it defines a concept it endows it with perfect attributes. It can only think in terms of the utmost limit, i.e., radically. As its operations are entirely self-reliant, it can give its creations the maximum polish without going to very much expense. In the same way, in the realm of political and social questions, it is in the habit of believing that it has discovered a civil constitution or a code which is perfect and definitive, and which alone deserves the names. This pure use of the intellect, this thinking *more geometrico* [1] is generally called rationalism. Perhaps it would be more enlightening to call it radicalism.

Everyone is unanimous in recognising that revolutions are not in essence anything but political radicalism. But perhaps it is not everyone who per-

[1] [*In the geometrical manner.*]

ceives the true sense of this formula. Political radicalism is not an original attitude; it is rather a consequence. It is not *radical* in politics because it is radical in *politics,* but because it is already radical in thought. This distinction, though it may have a frivolously super-subtle air, is decisive for the comprehension of the historical phenomenon which is properly styled revolutionary. The scenes which such phenomena invariably exhibit are signalized by such moving evidences of passion that we feel inclined to seek the origin of revolution in emotion. Some people will see the motive power of the impressive event in the explosion of a certain type of civic heroism. But Napoleon used to say: "Vanity made the revolution: liberty was only the pretext." I do not deny that both of these passions may be ingredients of revolution. But in all the great historical epochs there have been plenty of instances of heroism and vanity which do not necessarily lead to catastrophic outbreaks. For revolution to result from the operation of these two affective forces they must function in a spirit saturated with faith in pure reason.

This consideration enables us to account for the fact that in every great historical cycle a moment arrives when the revolutionary mechanism suddenly begins to act with uncontrollable violence. In Greece as in Rome, in England as on the continent of Europe, intelligence, in the pursuit of its normal development, reaches a stage at which it discovers its power of constructing, with means exclusively its own, theoretical edifices on a large scale and perfect in form. It had previously existed entirely upon the observations of the senses, which are for ever in a state of fluctuation, *fluctuans fides sensuum,* as Descartes, the father of modern rationalism, used to say, or upon the sentimentally interpreted prestige of political and religious tradition. But there now suddenly appears one of those ideological specimens of an architecture constructed by pure reason, such as the philosophic systems of the Greeks of the seventh and sixth centuries, the mechanics of Kepler, Galileo and Descartes, or the *Natural Law* of the seventeenth and eighteenth centuries. The transparency, precision, rigidity and integrity in systematisation of these compact spheres of ideas, manufactured *more geometrico,* are incomparable. From the intellectual point of view nothing more estimable can be imagined. It should be noted that the qualities I have enunciated are specifically intellectual; they might be called the professional virtues of the intelligence. It is, of course, true that there are many other values and attractive qualities in the universe which have nothing to do with the understanding, e.g., fidelity, honour, mystic fervour, solidarity with the past, authoritative power. But when the great rational creations arise men are already a little tired of such values. The new qualities, of an intellectual category, make an ardent and exclusive appeal to the human spirit. The result is a strange disdain for realities: men turn their backs to the latter and become the impassioned slaves of ideas as such. The perfection of the geometrical form of the idea intoxicates its devotees to the point of forgetting that, by definition, the business of the idea is to coincide with the reality of which it is the expression in the medium of thought.

The next step is the total inversion of spontaneous perspective. Ideas have so far been employed simply as instruments in the service of vital necessities. But now life is to take up the service of ideas. This radical reshuffling of the relations between life and idea is the true essence of the revolutionary spirit.

The subversive movements of the burgesses and peasants of the Middle Ages did not aim at the transformation of the political and social *régime* of the period: quite the reverse: they either limited themselves to accomplishing the reform of some abuse, or their object was the attainment of certain particular benefits or privileges within the framework of the established *régime;* they thus signified their approval of its general configuration. No one moderately well informed would venture to-day to compare the guilds and corporations of the thirteenth and fourteenth centuries with modern democracies. The latter have, it is true, appropriated much of the juridical technique that the guilds and corporations elaborated; but the spirits of the ancient and modern institutions are utterly different. It was with good reason that the city constitutions were called "charters" or "privileges" in Spain. The endeavour they symbolised was, precisely, the attempt to adjust the established *régime* to new necessities and desires, the idea of jurisprudence to life. The charter is a privilege, that is to say, it is a legally constituted vent for the new energy in the system of traditional powers. The point is that such energy, instead of transforming the system, is assimilated to it and implanted in its structure. The system, on its side, yields to and admits the newly introduced reality.

The political principles of the medieval burgess involved no more than the establishment, in opposition to the privileges of the nobility, of further privileges of similar type. The city guilds and the various corporations prided themselves on the possession of an even narrower, more suspicious and more egotistical spirit than that of the feudal lords. The highest authority on the life of the citizen in the Middle Ages—the Belgian, Henri Pirenne—notes that the corporations, in their most democratic epoch, practised an exclusiveness in their political life of an almost incredible character, and showed less hospitality to strangers and newcomers than had ever existed before. So much was this the case that "while the neighbouring rural communities increase in density the statistics of the burgess population within the city walls show no increase whatever." The strange phenomenon of a sparse urban population during these centuries is accordingly due to the resistance offered by the towns to the influx of fresh competitors for their liberties.

Far from trying to extend their legal code and institutions so as to include any considerable portion of the peasantry, the towns were more jealous in guarding their monopolies the more the popular *régime* achieved consolidation and development within their bounds. They endeavoured, moreover, to impose an extremely burdensome hegemony on the people of the free rural districts, treated them like subjects and, when the opportunity arose, violently compelled them to sacrifice themselves for the benefit of their dictators. . . . In short, then, we may conclude that the urban democracies of the Middle Ages were not and could not be anything but democracies comprising a privileged membership.

Now, democracy in the modern sense and privilege are the most complete contradiction that can be imagined. "It is not," pursues Pirenne,

that the theory of democratic government was unknown to the Middle Ages. The philosophers of the time formulated it clearly, in imitation of the ancient political writers. In Liége, in the midst of civil dissensions, the good canon Jean Hocsem examines quite seriously the respective merits of aristocracy, oligarchy and democracy, and finally gives his verdict in favour of the latter. Moreover, it is sufficiently well-known that more than one scholastic philosopher has formally recognised the sovereignty of the people and their right to dispose of political power. But these theories did not exercise the least influence upon the contemporary bourgeoisie. Their influence can, no doubt, be traced, during the fourteenth century, in certain political pamphlets and in a few literary works; it is, however, perfectly certain that they had not, at any rate in the Low Countries, the smallest influence on the Commune.

The idea that some "radicals" in Spain have had of connecting their own democratic politics with the rise of civic communities in the Middle Ages merely reveals the ignorance of history which is a permanent attribute, like some innate vice, of radicalism.

Modern democracy is not to be ascribed directly to any ancient democracy, neither the medieval nor the Greek nor the Roman. The only legacies of the classical democracies to our own age have been a misrepresented terminology, the general cast of their features, and their rhetoric. The procedure of the Middle Ages was to amend the existing *régime*. That of our own era, on the other hand, has been to organize revolutions; that is to say, instead of adapting *régime* to social reality we have made attempts to adapt the latter to the scheme of an ideal.

When the feudal lords, in their hunting expeditions, gallop over the farmer's crops and destroy them, the farmer feels a natural irritation and is anxious to retaliate, or at any rate to avoid such a misfortune in the future. But it does not occur to him that in order to prevent the repetition of so concrete an injury to his property or person it may be necessary to bring about a radical transformation of the entire organisation of society. In our own time, on the contrary, the deep resentment of the oppressed citizen is directed not so much against the oppressor himself as against the whole architecture of a universe in which such oppression is possible. For this reason I maintain that while the medieval man is irritated by abuses—of a *régime*—the modern man is irritated by usage, that is to say, by the *régime* itself.

The desire of the rationalist temperament is to mould the social body, at all costs, to the pentagraph of concepts framed by pure reason. In the view of the revolutionary the value of the law is pre-existent to its suitability to life. The good law is good by its own nature, like a pure idea. Accordingly, for the last century and a half European politics have been almost exclusively politics of ideas. A political philosophy concerned with realities and involving no anxiety for the triumph of an idea as such has hitherto seemed immoral. I do not at all mean by this that a political philosophy of private interest and ambition may not, in fact, have been practised surreptitiously. But the symptomatic feature of the matter is the fact that the political philosophy in question could not keep on its course and make its way without assuming the sanction of idealist colours and masking its true intentions.

Now, an idea framed without any other object than that of perfecting it as an idea, however much it may conflict with reality, is precisely what is called utopia. The geometrical triangle is utopia; nothing visible and tangible exists in which the definition of the triangle can find exact expression. Accordingly, utopianism is not an affection peculiar to a certain political doctrine, but the character appropriate to what pure reason elaborates. Rationalism, radicalism and the exercise of thought *more geometrico* are examples of utopianism. In science, perhaps, which is a contemplative function, utopianism may have a necessary and lasting mission to perform. The practice of politics, however, is a matter of realisation. How is it that the utopian spirit has not been found incompatible with politics?

The fact is that every revolution cherishes the entirely chimerical object of realising a more or less complete utopia. The plan inevitably fails. Its failure creates the twin and antithetical phenomenon of all revolutions, viz., counter-revolution. It would be interesting to prove the latter no less utopian than its antagonist and sister, even when less inspiring, warm-hearted and intelligent. Enthusiasm for pure reason will not admit defeat and returns to the charge. Another revolution breaks out, with yet another utopia, a modification of the first, inscribed upon its banners. There is a fresh failure and a fresh reaction; and so it goes on until the social conscience begins to suspect that the ill-success of these attempts is not due to the intrigues of their enemies, but to the contradictory elements inherent in the objects aimed at. Political ideas lose their glamour and attractive force. All that is facile and puerile in their schematic organisation begins to come to light. The utopian programme reveals its underlying formalism, its poverty and aridity in comparison with the delicious, abundant and splendid stream of life. The revolutionary era ends very simply, without phrases or gestures, in reabsorption by a new sensibility. To the political philosophy of ideas succeeds a political philosophy of concrete phenomena and men. We discover at last that life does not exist for the benefit of the idea, but that the idea, the institution, the rule exist for the benefit of life, or, as the Gospel has it, that "the Sabbath was made for man, not man for the Sabbath."

In particular—and this is a very important symptom—the whole business of politics comes to lose its character of urgency, disappears from the foreground of human interests and is permanently converted into a necessity of the same type as so many others, unavoidable, but not inspiring and not likely to be served with any degree of solemn and quasi-religious veneration. For it should be observed that in the revolutionary era political philosophy is found installed in the very centre of human preoccupations. There is no better apparatus for the registration of the hierarchy of our vital enthusiasms than death. The most important thing in our lives will always be that for which we are capable of dying. And the modern man has, in point of fact, risked his life at the barricades of revolution, thereby showing unmistakably that he expected politics to provide him with happiness. When the sunset of revolution commences this fervour of the previous generations appears to most people to be an evident aberration of the perspective of sentiment. Politics is not susceptible of exaltation to such high rank among hopes and devotions. The rationalist mind wrecked political science by expecting too much from it. When this thought begins to become general it puts an end to the era of revolution, to the political philosophy of ideas and the struggle for constitutional right.

The process has always been the same in Greece, in Rome, and in Europe. Laws are at first the effect of necessities, forces or dynamic combinations, but are soon converted into the expression of illusion and desire. Have juridical forms ever furnished men with the happiness they expected from them? Have the problems that originated them ever once been solved? Such are the suspicions now germinating at the roots of European consciousness and initiating a new type of spiritual mechanics which will replace the rationalist type as the latter supplanted that of the traditionalists. An anti-revolutionary epoch is beginning; but short-sighted people believe that a universal reaction is setting in. I am unaware of a single epoch of reaction throughout the whole era of history; there has never been such a thing. Reactions, like counter-revolutions, are casual and altogether transitory intervals, which derive their sustenance from vivid memories of the latest rebellion. Reaction is no more than a parasite of revolution. Such movements have already commenced in the southern periphery of Europe, and it is extremely probable that they will soon extend to the great nations of the centre and the north. But all that will be fugitive in character, little more than the noticeable oscillation that always precedes arrival at a new state of equilibrium. The revolutionary mind has never been succeeded in history by a reactionary mind, but rather—a more simple matter—by a disillusioned one. It is an inevitable psychological legacy of the splendid centuries of idealism and rationalism; those periods of organic dilapidation intoxicated with faith and self-assurance, those great topers of the beverages of utopia and illusion.

The physiognomy of the human mind in its traditionalist and revolutionary aspects . . . is undoubtedly in harmony with the development of European history from 1500 to our own day. The principal events of the latter centuries are too widely known for their concrete evidence to have failed to authenticate in the reader's mind the general scheme I have outlined of the configuration of the revolutionary spirit. But it is more interesting, it may even be called somewhat exciting, to observe that the same scheme is exactly reproduced in the other historical cycles of which we have any fairly definite knowledge. After this discovery the spiritual phenomenon of revolution acquires the character of a cosmic law of universal application, a stage through which every national body passes, and the transition from traditionalism to radicalism comes to resemble a biological rhythm pulsating irresistibly, so to speak, throughout history, after the manner of the rhythm of the seasons in vegetable life.

Let us, then, recall certain events in Greek and Roman history which fit with rare precision into the scheme I have described, and constitute its most adequate proof. This course will allow me, at the same time, to transcribe one or two paragraphs from great historians who, preoccupied exclusively with their own requirements and not, like myself, on the watch for historical generalisations, describe this or that moment in the life of Greece and Rome. If these authors, without troubling to look very closely at what they were doing, and without premeditation, have found themselves compelled to postulate behind the concrete case they are narrating the same mechanism of revolutionary spirit which I have defined as a universal stage in history, the coincidence will not be denied a demonstrative value of high rank.

In Greek and Roman history, up to some considerable time ago, an error was allowed to persist which is only now beginning to be corrected. Fundamentally, it was a belief that the hour of prosperity in Greece and in Rome coincides with the epoch which is the source of our abundant historical material. The whole of the earlier period was considered to have been a time of racial consolidation, prehistorical in the case of both nations. By an optical illusion very frequent in this field of investigation history confounds the non-existence of dates with the non-existence of events. A rectification of the error in question showed that the reality was very different from what had been supposed. The epochs concerning which a great deal of information begins to be accumulated are epochs in which historians already exist who undertake its preservation. Now, when historians begin to be found among a people it means that the people in question has already ceased to be young, that it is actually fully mature and may be taking its first steps to decadence. History, like a grape, is an autumnal delicacy.

The age at which the life of Greece and Rome becomes perfectly clear to us is already their September. The true history of the earlier period of these peoples, their youth and infancy, remains practically untouched. Accordingly, the face of the Greco-Roman image so ecstatically worshipped by the last few centuries was long past its prime; wrinkles had already installed upon it the geometrical designs which are the first indications of a cadaverous rigidity announcing the decline of life.

Mommsen was the first to rectify the perspective of Roman history. The great Eduard Meyer did the same, but to a more limited extent, with that of Greece. To the latter is due one of the most important and fertile innovations of historical thought. The division of universal history into ancient, middle and modern periods was a pentagraph dictated by convention and caprice and has, from the seventeenth century onwards, been hammered hard, so to speak, into the continuous body of history. Reconstructing Hellenic life, Meyer found that the Hellenes had passed through an epoch not unlike our own Middle Ages, and he ventured to speak of it as the Greek Middle Age. This discovery involved the transposition of the three ages of history to the historical cycle of each nation. Every people has its ancient, medieval and modern age. The practice of this view of history completely alters the significance of the traditional division into periods, and its three stages cease to be external, conventional or dialectical labels and assume a more real and, so to speak, biological significance. They are the infancy, youth and maturity of each people.

The Greek Middle Age comes to an end in the seventh century. This is the first period concerning which we possess any copious and exact information. There is, however, no question here of the birth of a nation. On the contrary, we are invited to witness the protracted dissolution of a people's long past and its awakening to a new age. Meyer sums up the position as follows:

The foundations of the medieval political constitution are destroyed. The dominion of the nobles is no longer an adequate expression of the prevailing circumstances; the interests of the governing and governed classes no longer coincide. The antique pattern of life, of law and of communities founded upon consanguinity loses its significance and becomes an obstruction. Men no longer necessarily remain members of the circle in which they were born. Everyone is master of his own fate; the individual emancipates himself socially, spiritually and politically. If a man cannot make his fortune in his own country he goes to seek it among foreigners. Affairs involving currency and revenues—the economics of finance begin during this epoch—are considered immoral, and everyone becomes aware of their disastrous effects; but no one can be indifferent to them, and the most conservative nobleman takes good care not to despise his profits. *Chremata, chremata aner*—money, money makes the man—is the motto of the times; and it is very significant that we find it put into the mouth of a Spartan (Alcaeus, frag. 49) or of an Argive (Pindar, Isthmians 2). Between the nobles and the labourers come the new industrial and mercantile classes, with their attendant corps of artisans, petty traders and seamen, among whom are conspicuous such adventurers as Archilochus of Thasos, who seek their fortunes wherever they can, and bear the double burden of calamity and subjection to an alien power. The cities grow bigger, for the peasants migrate to them so as to secure an easier livelihood; foreigners, too, who had no luck in their own country or had to go into exile on account of party struggles, settle in the towns. All combine in attacks upon the *régime* of the aristocrats. The peasants aspire to freedom from the intolerable burden of economic oppression; the newly rich citizens to participation in administrative power; the descendants of the immigrants, who are sometimes more numerous than the longer established citizens, claim equality of treatment with the hereditary inhabitants. All these elements are united under the name of *demos*,[2] as they were during the French Revolution under the name of *tiers état*.[3] Like the latter, the Greek *demos* does not constitute a unity, either through its position or through its political and social aims; it is only the common opposition of such heterogeneous elements to the "better sort" that maintains their alliance.

There can be no more exact parallel with the composition of modern nations on the eve of the revolutionary era. The more general distribution of money introduces capitalism. The rise of the latter is accompanied by that of imperialism. Soon afterwards comes the creation of great fleets. The wars of the mounted medieval nobles—I am now speaking of Greece—are replaced by others, not conducted on horseback or man to man. The *promachia*, or

[2] [*Common people.*]
[3] [*Third estate.*]

single combat, is succeeded by the great invention of the phalanx of hoplites, the body of infantry capable of tactical movements. At the same time the medieval system of dissociated units is brought to an end and all the Greeks begin to call themselves Hellenes. Under the unity of this name they come to feel their profound historical affinity.

Finally, it is in this age that the abrupt legislative changes in constitutions are introduced. Can the fact that these "invented" constitutions are always coupled with the name of some philosopher be due to mere chance? For it is, let us not forget, the century of the Seven Wise Men, and of the first Ionian and Dorian thinkers. Where there is radical alteration of laws and the establishment of new codes of conduct there is also to be noted, invariably, the manifest or covert presence of some "wise man." The Seven Wise Men are the seven great intellectual leaders of the epoch, the discoverers of reason or *logos* as opposed to *mythos* or tradition.

By a rare piece of good fortune our data enable us to witness, through documentary evidence, the first incarnation of the individualist and rational mentality in revolt against the mentality of tradition. The first thinker whose figure has come down to us in the light of complete historical authenticity is Hecataeus of Miletus, who wrote a book on the popular myths which then controlled the attitude of Greek civilisation. This work, of which only very inconsiderable fragments remain, begins as follows: "Thus speaks Hecataeus of Miletus. I write all this in accordance with what seemed to me to be the truth; for the legends of the Greeks are, in my opinion, contradictory and ridiculous." These words are the cockcrow of individualism, the bugle that sounds the *reveille* of the rationalist faith. Here, for the first time, we have an individual rebelling, in signal isolation, against tradition, that vast millenary world in which the mind of Greece had dwelt from time immemorial.

Reform succeeds reform for a whole century, till we reach the most celebrated innovation of all, that of Cleisthenes. This is how Wilamowitz-Moellendorff outlines the thought and the psychology of his author:

> Cleisthenes the Alcmaeonid, belonging to the most powerful of the rival noble families banished by Pisistratus, succeeded, with the help of Delphi and Sparta, in overthrowing the tyrant; he did not, however, take the latter's place, nor did he make Athens an aristocratic state, as Sparta hoped, but, again with the help of Delphi, endowed the city with a fully democratic constitution, the only one we are at all well acquainted with. For it was he, not Solon, who was its true creator. . . . Previous sanctions had been confined to unwritten law, religion and custom, but from this date written laws become the true kings. Yet such laws are not dead letters carved in stone, mere obstacles to freedom, but rules of widely accepted

validity, such as may be found engraven in the hearts of all enlightened citizens. The people alone have established them; but the people will not cancel them arbitrarily; they must be modified in legal form when they have ceased to be "just." The people have appropriated them by the act of pledging their obedience; but it is a legislator who has really made them. In order that the people might be induced to accept them willingly they had to face the same way as the people's thoughts and desires; but it was the legislator who hit upon the creative idea in the course of his self-communings; and just as in the humanitarianism of the old Attic law the mild and pious character of the wise poet, Solon, is clearly to be observed, so in the constitution of Cleisthenes there are traces of a violent type of logico-arithmetical constructive thought which invite the deduction of conclusions as to the temperament of their author. He must have elaborated a complete schematic synthesis of his plans during his banishment, and only admitted with reluctance a few rare compromises with reality when he found he could not extirpate it. His general tendencies, at any rate, have much in common with the arithmetical philosophic speculation which was then beginning and which was soon to lead to the doctrine of faith in the reality of numbers. Cleisthenes had, in fact, connections with Samos, the native city of the Pythagoreans. His violent radicalism derives obviously from the character of the sophists and philosophers, always fanatically determined to impose what is capable of logical proof on the real world in the interests of its salvation. Such castles in the air remind one immediately of the ephemeral constitutions of France prevailing in the interval between the fall of the old monarchy and the rise of Napoleon I.

I do not think I need add to this exposition. The reform of Cleisthenes is a typically revolutionary phenomenon, the most notable of a long series which comes to an end only with the advent of Pericles. After this date the most casual glance reveals the workings of the geometric mind, philosophic radicalism, and "pure reason."

The purpose of this essay was to show that the genesis of the revolutionary phenomenon must be sought in a determinate affection of the intelligence. Taine brought this idea to light when he enumerated the causes of the great revolution; on the other hand, he cancelled the value of his astute discovery by persuading himself that he was dealing with a habit peculiar to the mentality of France. He did not see that he was dealing with a general historical law. Every people whose development has not been violently interrupted reaches a rationalist stage in the course of its intellectual evolution. When rationalism has been converted into the ordinary method of mental procedure the revolutionary process breaks down automatically and inevitably. It does not, therefore, originate in the oppression of the lower classes by the upper, nor in the advent of an imaginary sensibility to more delicately balanced justice—such a belief is spontaneously rationalist and anti-historical—nor even when new social classes attain sufficient power to wrest supremacy from the hands of its traditional possessors. Certain facts which can be described in this way accompany the manifestation of the revolutionary spirit, but are rather its consequences than its causes. . . .

In the course of the sunset of revolution ideas gradually cease to be a primary factor in history and return to the negative status they had occupied in the preceding traditionalist age.

EPILOGUE ON THE MENTAL ATTITUDE OF DISILLUSION

The theme of the foregoing essay was confined to an attempt at a definition of the revolutionary spirit and an affirmation of its dissolution in Europe. But I said at the beginning of my discourse that such a spirit is a mere stage in the orbit that traverses every great historical cycle. It is preceded by a rationalist attitude and followed by a mystical, or, more precisely, by a superstitious frame of mind. Perhaps the reader feels some curiosity as to the nature of the delta of superstition into which the river of revolution is finally dissipated. It happens, however, that it is not possible to speak upon the subject except at length. The post-revolutionary epochs, after a very fugitive hour of apparent splendour, settle into a time of decadence. And decadences, like births, are enveloped, so far as history is concerned, in darkness and silence. History is accustomed to exercise a strange modesty, which makes it draw a pious veil over the imperfection of commencements and the disagreeable aspect of national decay. It is a fact that the events of the "hellenistic" epoch in Greece and of the middle and later Empire of Rome are little known to historians, while their very existence is scarcely suspected by the generality of educated men. It is not therefore in any way possible to refer to them in the form of a brief allusion.

It would only be by risking the imputation of innumerable misinterpretations that I would venture to satisfy the curiosity of the reader—but are there any curious readers in this country?—in the following words:

The traditionalist mind is a mechanism operating through credulity, for its whole activity consists in its reliance upon the unquestioned wisdom of the past. The rationalist mind breaks these bonds of credulity and replaces them with a fresh imperative: faith in individual energy, of which reason is the supreme instigator. But rationalism tries to do too much—in fact, aspires to the impossible. The proposal to substitute ideas for reality is admirable in its illusive electrical quality, but is always foredoomed to failure. An enterprise so disproportionately ambitious leaves a historical field behind it which becomes an area of disillusion. After the defeat of all his daring idealist aims man is left completely demoralised. He loses all spontaneous faith and does not believe in anything that works along manifest and disciplined lines. He respects neither tradition nor reason, neither collectivity nor the individual. His vital resources weaken because definitively, it is the beliefs we cherish that keep such resources at concert pitch. He has not sufficient strength in reserve to maintain a suitable attitude before the mystery of life and the universe. Physically and mentally he degenerates. In these epochs the human harvest is left to wither and the national populations dwindle. Not so much through famine, disease or other similar calamities as because the generative potency of man diminishes. Simultaneously, there is a decline in typically virile courage. Universal cowardice begins to prevail: a strange phenomenon which appeared equally in Greece and Rome and has not yet received its due emphasis. In times of security man possesses but half the measure of personal valour required to encounter the vicissitudes of life without disgrace. In such ages of waste valour becomes an unusual quality which is only possessed by a few. Its practice is made a profession whose exponents form a soldiery hostile to all public order and stupidly oppressive of the rest of the social body.

This universal cowardice becomes apparent in the most delicate and intimate recesses of the mind, and projects itself in all directions. Men are terrified once more by lightning and thunder, as they were in the most primitive times. No one relies on his own personal vigour to enable him to triumph over difficulties. Life is felt to be a formidable accident, in which man is dependent upon mysterious and occult wills, acting in accordance with the most puerile caprices. The debased mind is incapable of offering resistance to destiny, and turns to superstitious practices in the hope of propitiating these hidden powers. The most absurd rites attract the adhesion of the multitude. Rome submits to the dominion of all the monstrous divinities of Asia, which had been so honourably disdained two centuries before.

In short: the spirit of the time being incapable of maintaining itself in equilibrium by its own unaided efforts, searches for some spar that will save it from the wreck, and examines its environment with the anxious and cringing look of a dog, hoping it may find someone to help it. The superstitious mind is, in effect, a dog in search of a master. Men cannot now even remember the noble gestures of pride they once assumed; and the imperative of liberty that resounded in their ears for centuries would now be totally incomprehensible. On the contrary, they feel an incredible anxiety to be slaves. Slavery is their highest ambition: slavery to other men, to an emperor, to a sorcerer or to an idol. Anything rather than feel the terror of facing single-handed, in their own persons, the ferocious assaults of existence.

Perhaps the name that best suits the spirit that comes into being beyond the sunset of revolution is the term, spirit of slavery.

TRADITION AND PROTEST IN LATIN AMERICA

THE selections that follow are, first, an anthropological account of the people of rural Peru and, second, an ideological statement of their condition by a city-bred, Peruvian socialist intellectual. The data given by the American anthropologist Bernard Mishkin (b. 1913) make clear that a large segment of this population is Indian and that "Indian" is a socio-cultural more than a biological criterion. It is, moreover, among the traditional communities of the austere and mountainous "sierra," rather than on the commercial sugar and cotton haciendas of the fertile coastal valleys, that Indian culture traits show their tenacity. During the four centuries or more since the Spaniards conquered the Incan empire, of which Peru's Quechuan Indians formed a part, European ways have of course penetrated even the sierra. Peruvian society, however, still exhibits a range, a diversity, and discontinuities far in excess of those of Western industrial nations. It is in this respect that Peru typifies other "backward" or, less harshly, "underdeveloped" societies of Latin America, Africa, and Asia that contain perhaps a majority of the world's population.

The thorny problem of extending industrial and democratic benefits to so heterogeneous, inarticulate, and impoverished a people as Peru's was addressed by José Carlos Mariátegui (1895–1930) in "The Land Problem," one of his *Seven Essays Interpreting the Peruvian Reality* (1928), which, in the translation of Leonardo C. De Morelos, forms the second of these selections. Though a Marxist and leading Latin American spokesman for the Third International, Mariátegui was alive to the full spectrum of the European intellectual heritage, and in many realms—political, socio-economic, and cultural—strove to mediate between it and local "Indianism." Like sixteenth-century Catholicism, however, modern programs such as Marxism must be strategically modified if they are to achieve relevance to the earthbound life and timeless, animistic world of the Indian. In twentieth-century Peru the Indian and Occidental, the feudal and capitalistic, the colonial and national, the communalistic and (in Mariátegui's term) "demo-liberal" all coexist. Since Peru, like most of the modern world, corresponds to no historical "phase" of Western Europe or the United States, in Marxist or other idiom, Peruvian reformers characteristically drift into heavy-handed eclecticism. Mariátegui in particular—aware that the long-abused and culturally segregated Indians will not easily develop the "class consciousness" of the Occidental world, or respond to its rhetoric and inducements—reformulates Marxism in agrarian terms, showing something of a nostalgia for such diverse elements as Incan collectivism, medieval feudalism, theocratic Jesuit communalism, and more recent "demo-liberal" ideals. His endorsement of certain aspects of the Spanish heritage leads one to speculate on Mariátegui's suggestion that commercially more aggressive colonizers, such as the English, might better have prepared Peruvians for the modern age—especially in the light of Gandhi's appraisal, in a later reading, of the "civilization" which the English brought to India. Indeed Mariátegui, like Mishkin, implicitly raises the question as to whether the impinging industrial order, of which the English were the proconsuls, will sufficiently recompense the Peruvian Indian when it eventually destroys the remnants of his rich culture.

As Mariátegui points out, the Spaniards were unable to maintain, during their three hundred years of rule, the Incas' highly developed functionalism, productive efficiency, and husbanding of resources for the common welfare. Spanish administration did, however, recognize the Indians' unique culture and institutions, and made provision for their absorption into the empire as spiritual equals of the European. A violent Indian revolt toward the end of the colonial period (1780), led by a scion of the Incan rulers, was directed not against the king and Spanish hegemony, but against malfeasance of the king's agents in the New World. Peruvian independence (1824), moreover, was not effected by a popular revolution, but was simply the termination of two secessionist campaigns led by Bolívar from the north and San Martín from the south which had converged upon Peru and its viceregal capital, Lima.

The era that began at independence was only ostensibly a republican one. "The majority of the governments in the 115 years Peru has been a republic," one writer computed in 1936, "have been either revolutionary and dictatorial, or provisional. Of the eighty-seven administrations only twenty-two have been constitutional." Spain's partially effective safeguards for the Indian's land and way of life vanished after 1824, and Peru, in the words of another observer, fell under the dominance of "a reactionary church hierarchy; a small, colonial-minded, intellectual aristocracy; and a narrow, Lima-centered government group that forgets the provinces." This oligarchy, playing fast and loose with constitutional mechanisms carefully copied from those of Western democracies, has remained entrenched and preserved its bloodline as has no similar group in Latin America. Neither the Indian nor the mixed-breed, the mestizo, has come to symbolize—as in Mexico, for instance—a fresh spirit of national culture and aspiration.

Manuel González Prada (1846–1918) was one of the few nineteenth-century critics of the status quo, and his scathing essays gave impetus to the reform movement in which Mariátegui figured. Mariátegui himself, an impoverished tubercular from the slums of Lima, entered journalism, although his formal education had ended at the age of twelve. In 1918 he received a government fellowship to travel in Europe. Here he visited socialist leaders, became a convinced Marxist, and returned to Peru to help organize APRA (Popular American Revolutionary Alliance), a reform party which has been copied in other Latin American countries and has persistently opposed the entrenched oligarchy. Two years before his death in 1930 Mariátegui split with the "Apristas," and APRA, which had broken with international communism and was evincing a more pragmatic and "liberal" character, became dominated by the shrewd, forceful, highly popular and personalistic figure of Víctor Raúl Haya de la Torre (b. 1895). The initial planks of the Aprista program were: action against "Yankee imperialism," political unity of Latin America, nationalization of land and industry, internationalization of the Panama Canal, and solidarity with all peoples and oppressed classes.

Peru, unlike Mexico, has had no "Revolution." Socio-economic changes have been fragmentary and usually under oligarchic or military auspices. APRA, for much of its life an underground organization, had a period of legality and participation in government in 1945–48, only to be outlawed again after a military coup. Haya de la Torre was forced to take asylum in the Colombian embassy in Lima (1949); not until 1954, after Haya had become an international *cause célèbre,* did the Peruvian government allow him to go into political exile in Mexico. In so doing, however, the regime redeemed but one of many outstanding pledges to which, as one of the disparate bedfellows of an "anti-authoritarian" world coalition, it scrupulously professed its allegiance.

BERNARD MISHKIN: THE CONTEMPORARY QUECHUA

Of Peru's total population of 7,023,111 (Census of 1940), 2,847,196 or 40 percent of the population, were classified as Indians, and 3,283,360 as Mestizos. In the 1876 Census, the Indian component of the population was put at 57.6 percent of the total. These figures reveal a noteworthy trend. Peru, like others of its neighbors in the "Indo-American" bloc, is on the road to becoming a Mestizo country. . . .

It should be pointed out that the results of the 1940 Census do not pretend to describe the racial composition of the population in exact terms. No elaborate biological criteria were used to set off one group from the other, but rather an effort was made to indicate the larger divisions in the population on the basis of rough common-sense judgments. It was ascertained that 13 percent of the population personally filled in the blank on race; 87 percent were entered in one or the other racial categories by the census taker. Generally speaking, subjective factors such as personal preference, or arbitrary choice, seem to have played a large part in determining race designation. Cultural criteria doubtless were utilized to some extent. . . .

An extensive list of the cultural criteria that might fit the needs of the census taker in the field would include language spoken, type of settlement, utilization of land, amount of land owned, clothing worn, nature of religious worship, etc. Of all these, language is certainly the least complicated to deal with statistically and is of primary importance. . . .

The *Quechua*-speaking population, including bilingual persons, are exactly equal in number to the Spanish-speaking inhabitants of the country. Those

---

This selection has been reprinted from Bernard Mishkin, "The Contemporary Quechua," *Handbook of South American Indians* (Washington, U.S. Government Printing Office, 1947), Vol. II, pp. 411–416, 418–421, 423–425, 436, 442–443, 460–462.

speaking Spanish only are a minority of the whole population, and are concentrated mainly along the coast. . . .

Proficiency in handling Spanish and one of the Indian languages is often taken to be the mark of a Mestizo. Standing between the Spanish-speaking Coastal citizen and the Andean Indian, the Mestizo is the interpreter, the middleman, the social, economic, and political link between the two poles of Peruvian life. But the linguistic criterion alone does not define the limits of the Mestizo group; other cultural factors tending to give the Mestizo greater numerical as well as political importance come into play.

Whatever distinctions are made between Mestizo and Indian must depend for their validity upon the object of such distinctions. In reality, the two groups merge. A few European traits have penetrated to even the most isolated Indian cultures; similarly, certain concepts peculiarly Indian have found their way to the most conservative Spanish descendants. Except for a small and distinct element, which is wholly Western in its mode of life and thinking, the various levels that comprise Peruvian national culture are fluid in character, each spilling over into the next. Any segment of the population curve will contain groups representing varying degrees of Indian and Mestizo status. The same individual may be considered Indian from one point of view or be classified as a Mestizo from another. . . .

None of this denies the existence of the *Quechua* Indian as fundamental reality of contemporary Peru. In the popular sense, the *Quechua* Indian signifies a social problem of national import. Ethnologically speaking, the label is applied loosely to a Highland folk whose culture is an intricate complex of native and foreign elements, the end-product of historic growth and change. The *Quechua* Indian, it may be said, constitutes the peasantry of a nation. Hence, the ethnologist confronts not only a distinct culture but a distinct class. The *Quechua* Indian is not a primitive tribalist keeping to his circumscribed corner of the country. He has spread out through practically every Department and Province. . . .

Agriculture. Typical *Quechua* agriculture is characterized by adherence to a simple traditional technology and to an intricate division of labor, quite as much a survival as the technology. Generally, draft animals are not used, and the most complicated instrument used by the *Quechua* agriculturist is nothing more than a primitive digging stick whose only concession to modernity is the fact that it possesses an iron blade. Irrigation is known practically everywhere among the Indians, though it is practiced in the simplest way possible. Occasionally, types of terracing are used, which, however, are not infrequently of ancient construction.

Despite the Indian's great expenditure of effort in attempting to cultivate land of uneven fertility, he is able to extract relatively little reward for his labor. The land is too often poor and exhausted; the Indian's own poverty does not allow him to obtain adequate fertilizer; and undeveloped technology prohibits intensive cultivation and maximum utilization. Most important of all, artificial land scarcity has reduced *Quechua* landholdings to a point at which large numbers of Indians own insufficient or no land to meet their own food requirements.

Hacienda agriculture. Some reference must be made to Peruvian hacienda agriculture, which exists in the midst of the *Quechua* community and on which it depends for labor supply. In the majority of haciendas of the Andes, agricultural methods differ little from those found in the *Quechua* villages. Here, more often than not, the *colonos* and *yanaconas* [1] are left to their own devices by the *hacendado* [2] so long as they abide by their contracts, give their labor, and deliver to the hacendado his proper share of the total produce harvested. Farm technology is slightly more advanced, and it may be said justifiably that cultivation in these haciendas is commonly less efficient than in the community farmlands. Absentee landlords, lack of capital, poor communications and transportation facilities, and enormous size of holdings contribute to produce as low a yield per hectare [3] in the hacienda as in the community.

The situation is far different in the great Coastal haciendas and in a few model haciendas of the Sierra. Although mechanization of agriculture has not proceeded very far, large-scale irrigation together with detribalized farm labor has been responsible for a highly successful plantation agriculture. The typical Coastal hacienda is carefully managed in distinction to that of the Sierra. Private capital and government assistance are made available to them. A patronizing policy toward farm labor has created an effective, relatively healthy force of Mestizo and *Quechua* wage-laborers whose standard of living is patently superior to that of the free cultivators and sharecroppers of the Sierra. Finally, the Coastal haciendas produce crops—cotton, flax, sugarcane—almost exclusively for a world market. Prices translated into local terms signify tangible profits over the cost of production. . . .

Division and organization of labor. . . . The lending of labor in group

[1] [*Tenants* and *laborers.*]
[2] [*Hacienda owner.*]
[3] [Hectare = about 2.5 acres.]

work to form *masas* [4] is called working in *aine*. It is the most significant factor in the division of labor, running through all currents of Andean economic life. The mechanism of working in *aine* affects every member of the community since everyone must belong to a voluntary work party. Each member of a party, just as he can summon the others to work in his plot, must be ready to lend his labor when it is needed. Working in *aine* is not restricted to agricultural labor. Women will assist one another in domestic activities on an *aine* basis. Children who have been given the task of herding sheep in the *punas* [5] might be relieved by other children who will work in *aine*. They then may go off to play for the day, offering the same opportunity to their companions at some future time.

Reduced to simplest terms, *aine* means mutual assistance. It provides for an exchange of labor, man for man and day for day. . . .

With the atomization of land holdings, groups working in *aine* are much smaller than they had been previously. The few men who have accumulated large land holdings prefer to pay outright for labor. There are visible signs of the disintegration of the *aine* system. . . .

Practically all arable land in Peru is individually owned today. Usually there is no true *ejido,* or commons; nor are there pasture commons in many communities. Through a series of historic steps, collective landholdings have been transformed into privately owned plots. . . .

Those Indians who find their way to the haciendas to rent land or to seek work as farm laborers are drawn into complex economic relationships, some of which are of pre-Columbian origin. Those who are able to rent a parcel of land in an hacienda on a cash basis retain a certain independence. However, rentals for fixed fees are rare in Peru except in the case of Mestizos and Whites who rent an entire *finca* [6] or hacienda. . . .

The reasons for the prejudice against the system of rentals for cash lie in the Colonial fabric of Peruvian agrarian economy. The landlord of Colonial type, who is usually absent from his holdings and has little or nothing to do with the exploitation of his land, prefers to have the Indian not as a free agent but as a farm laborer of one type or another. . . .

Agricultural ritual. Agricultural ritual is highly developed among all *Quechua.* Offerings of coca [7] and liquor (aguardiente) are made periodically to the earth. Dates for planting are guided by phases of the moon, the full

[4] [*Work parties.*]

[5] [High, dry-grass country.]

[6] [*Farm.*]

[7] [Dried leaves of the coca plant, chewed by the Indian to dull his senses and increase his endurance.]

moon being regarded as particularly inauspicious. In August, the earth is thought to be alive, and it is necessary to make coca offerings to protect the people of the community from illness and the crops from destruction. . . .

Christian ritual plays an important role in protecting the crops against pests and the rigors of climate. Hail is fought off by burning incense and throwing holy water. Against "frost," bonfires are started in the fields. However, it should be noted that many Indians consider the bonfire (*conuy*) as a means of engaging the "frost" in physical combat and not of protecting the plants by raising the temperature in their vicinity. For this reason, bonfires frequently aggravate the "frost" rather than give relief. Frequently, the "frost" enraged by the deliberate resistance of the Indians, will destroy everything in the fields.

Worms and beetles and other insects are excommunicated. Numerous legends are associated with the various pests that attack plant life. Frequently, they embody the spirits of men, legendary or real, who have caused injury to the community. For rain, children are sent out to recite the "Misericordia," and to weep at the absence of water and rain. . . .

Markets. The market is still a fundamental institution in *Quechua* territory. Throughout the Andean republics, an Indian market is held once a week or more frequently in the capital of each district and in the urban centers. In the case of the towns, permanent daily markets are held, but these are in the hands of Mestizo traders and established merchants. . . .

Characteristic of *Quechua* trade in the market place is the pettiness of the transactions and the vendor's lack of diversified goods. Only the Mestizos display a variety of merchandise and a respectable quantity of it in their stands. They, of course, are professional traders whose full-time occupation it is to purchase goods wholesale, and sell in retail. The Indian customarily has merely the surplus of his own agricultural production or a few handicraft articles he has been able to make in his spare time. Basically, the Indian is exchanging a part of his own production for a part of the production of another Indian. The two are merely increasing the variety of goods each will use, and this is most frequently achieved without reference to a middleman or to the money economy.

Thus, in the plaza, it is often difficult to perceive who is the buyer and who the seller, since both are on equal terms. One woman sits before a tiny mound of potatoes; another, facing her, has opened a napkin containing a few ears of corn. There is silence and concentration as one studies the goods of the other. In a minute or two an agreement has been reached. The amounts to be bartered are pushed forward, *yapa* (overweight) is requested, and the transaction is completed. . . .

The Community. The normal-functioning *Quechua* community exhibits strong group feeling. Defense of community lands against encroachments of the hacienda is a rallying point for all the inhabitants. Even with growing individualization in the ownership of land, the loss of land by one member of the community is still regarded as a community calamity. The whole group feels weakened thereby and considers its future security endangered. In addition, the various family units which make up the community are united by kinship ties resulting from intermarriage. These ties exercise considerable weight in fortifying the common economic interests of the group. Cooperation in the performance of many day-to-day tasks, discussed above under the heading of *aine,* further adds to group cohesion. Religious expression in the fiestas and in the practice of magic ritual not only requires group participation but reveals, as well, a sense of community responsibility.

It is only when the community has been completely disrupted by outside economic pressures that this characteristic solidarity disappears. In North Peru, and in the Departments of Cuzco and Puno, the process of land diminution is reaching the stage which threatens the existence of the community itself. The communities are no longer able to unite for defense. Then, kinship obligations begin to break down. The landholdings are so reduced in size that mutual assistance to work them is no longer necessary. Poverty compels the inhabitants to put an end to a great deal of ceremonialism; social life is neglected. In the end, the political structure of the community becomes functionless, and those who still retain their land reside on it as individual farmers unconnected with any social unit. . . .

The *Quechua* community usually tends to be endogamous. Where marrying out of the community occurs, residence is likely to be patri-local. Endogamy is, of course, a highly desirable institution for agriculturists living in constant fear of losing their land, or of being invaded by outsiders who will further diminish the extent of available land. Marrying within the community gives security. The family holdings are maintained intact and strangers qualified to inherit do not appear in the community. . . .

The stranger is feared and hated. The entire community seems as if it is ready to contract and recoil in the face of any outsider attempting to work his way into the community. Anyone selling his plot of land to the stranger is considered almost a criminal. But such an event seldom comes to pass. The stranger realizes that he can gain little and risks a great deal if he attempts to work land in a community not his own. He will not receive assistance for work in the fields; no one will work in *aine* with him. He will be socially ostracized. Worst of all, every sorcerer in the community will practice the black art against him. This is the community's culminating attack on the stranger in their midst. . . .

Education. The *Quechua* child is taught to be submissive and to bow before authority, to distrust the outsider, to fear the Christian-pagan hierarchy of spirits and deities, and to struggle as best he can to gain a livelihood. Throughout his life, he remains hemmed in from all sides. His daily experiences together with subtle family indoctrination teach him that he has no weapon with which to defend himself and tend to produce the familiar *Quechua* personality—the sullen and resigned Indian who breaks through his protective shell on some fiesta days with the help of aguardiente or, from time to time, in avoidance of a paralysis born of desperation (it would seem to the onlooker), is thrown into spasms of violence.

But the *Quechua* also learns to be a good farmer, to carry on animal husbandry, and to work at the arts and crafts connected with his village and family. It is with these economic activities that the overt educative process is concerned. As we have described, the *Quechua* people show a certain competence and resourcefulness in getting a living from their farming. Despite ignorance of modern agricultural practice and lack of facilities, they have accumulated an extensive body of lore, much of it truly applicable to Andean conditions. This mixture of proved knowledge and superstition is passed on from generation to generation. The father sets himself the task of teaching his son all that he himself knows of his work with unsurpassed seriousness, and he does so patiently and deliberately. Boys of preschool age accompany their fathers to the fields, are taught the use of the various instruments, are encouraged to try their hand at the work, are given light duties to perform in a regular *aine,* and are paid the half wage due women and working children. Girls, likewise, are taught the household arts by their mothers with considerable care. Parents and grandparents both give daily instruction in spinning, in weaving, and in whatever other local arts are practiced. The common phenomenon of older siblings teaching the younger is to be seen everywhere among the *Quechua,* although parents and grandparents take the major responsibility for instructing the young.

Knowledge and instruction of a formal sort are beyond the reach of the majority of Peruvian *Quechua.* Very few Indians learn Spanish and fewer learn to read and write even poorly. Peru's population of 15 years of age and over totals to 3,595,800, of which 57.6 percent (2,071,637) are illiterate.

The national coefficient of illiteracy is given at 35.15 percent. As regards the school-age population of 1,464,664, only 35.15 percent of the children are receiving some type of instruction, while 64.85 percent are receiving none at all. . . .

The Sierra, although it is the most densely populated region of the country with the largest number of populated centers, is the most lacking in educational facilities. Enormous areas are to be found in which not one school exists. . . .

In those places where the Indians have access to schools, language proves to be an insuperable difficulty for the *Quechua* students. Instruction, in practically all cases, is given in Spanish. The *Quechua* students are unable to follow it and, after a brief but unsuccessful effort, are satisfied to devote themselves to tidying the school grounds and to physical education. Meanwhile, the teacher can concentrate his best efforts in behalf of the handful of Mestizo children who come from Spanish speaking homes. The teachers themselves complain of the situation, but there is no remedy until a system of education using *Quechua* as a medium of instruction is put into effect. . . .

Religion. Quechua religion today is essentially a special form of Catholicism. The Catholic ritual and theology has penetrated to the most isolated *Quechua* communities. Most of the surviving non-Catholic elements are coated over with a Catholic surface.

Just as in peasant Europe Catholicism was combined with local pagan worship, so the pre-Columbian religious forms throughout the Americas were frequently absorbed in local church practice. . . . [The] modern *Quechua* have not developed a highly integrated religion. The elements often do not jibe; there is no attempt to relate one element to another. In distinction to typical Mexican, or let us say, Guatemalan examples, *Quechua* religion appears to be a loose jumble of beliefs, ideas, and practices, disconnected and unsystematized.

Be this as it may, *Quechua* religion is not a negligible factor in the life of the community. The supernatural beings are closely involved in the economic and social life of the inhabitants. Ritual and ceremonialism are allied to the most practical and serious objectives of men and women. The public ceremonials are pivots and high points of communal life. Magic and curing enter into the whole field of human relations. Moreover, outside of Government, the Church is the only other great constant whose pressure is felt in every community. . . .

JOSÉ CARLOS MARIÁTEGUI: THE LAND PROBLEM

We who study and define the Indian problem from a socialist standpoint begin by declaring that the humanitarian and philanthropic points of view are absolutely superseded insofar as the old pro-Indian campaign constituted a prolongation of the missionary battles of Friar Bartolomé de Las Casas.[1] Our central effort is directed toward establishing the nature of the Indian problem as fundamentally economic. First of all, we attack the instinctive—and defensive—tendency of the creole or "misti" [2] to reduce it to a purely administrative, pedagogic, ethnic, or moral problem in order to avoid at all costs the economic plane. For this reason, the most absurd reproach which can be directed against us is that of lyricism, or of producing sheer literary exercise. By placing the socio-economic problem foremost, we adopt the least lyrical and literary attitude possible. We are not satisfied with reaffirming the right of the Indian to education, culture, progress, love, and Heaven. We begin by reaffirming categorically his right to the land. This reaffirmation, completely materialistic, should have been enough to prevent our being confused with the heirs or emulators of the gospel preached by the great Spanish Friar, a person whom we otherwise admire and esteem warmly in spite of our complete materialism.

And this problem of the land—which is clearly connected with the Indian problem—we also refuse to minimize or veil in an opportunistic manner. Just the opposite. As for me, I try to present it in perfectly clear and unmistakable terms.

The agrarian problem appears, above all, as the problem of liquidating feudalism in Peru. This liquidation should have been already accomplished by the demo-bourgeois regime formally established by the revolution of independence. But we in Peru have not had, in a hundred years as a republic, a truly bourgeois class, a truly capitalistic class. The old feudal class, camouflaged or disguised as republican bourgeoisie, has retained its position. The policy of breaking up large church estates, which was begun by the revolution of independence as a logical consequence of its ideology, did not lead to the development of the small properties. The old landholding class had not lost its control. . . . It is well known that disentailing tended to attack instead the community. And the fact is that during a century of republican

---

This selection has been reprinted from José Carlos Mariátegui, *7 ensayos de interpretación de la realidad peruana* (2nd ed., Lima, 1943), pp. 33–75.

[1] [Spanish Dominican missionary (1474–1566), appointed "Protector of the Indians."]

[2] [That is, the Peruvian "bourgeois."]

regime the larger agrarian property has increased and has gained strength in spite of the theoretical liberalism of our constitution and of the practical need for developing our capitalistic economy.

There are two signs of the surviving feudalism: latifundio [3] and servitude. These two expressions are co-existing and co-substantial, and their analysis leads to the conclusion that the servitude which weighs over the Indian cannot be eliminated without destroying the latifundio.

Once the agrarian problem of Peru is stated in these terms, there is no possibility of misleading distortions. It appears then in all its magnitude as a socio-economic (and therefore political) problem under the control of men who act on this plane of deeds and ideas. And it is useless to attempt to convert it, for example, into a technical-agricultural problem under the control of agricultural experts.

Everyone knows that the liberal solution of this problem would be, according to the individualist ideology, the breaking up of the latifundio in order to create small property holdings. Among us, the ignorance revealed at each step concerning the elemental principles of socialism is so limitless that it will never be useless or idle to insist that this formula—the breaking up of the latifundio in favor of the small property holder—is neither utopian, heretic, revolutionary, Bolshevist nor avant-garde, but rather that it is orthodox, constitutional, democratic, capitalistic, and bourgeois. And that it has its origin in the liberal theology which has inspired the constitutional statutes of all the demo-bourgeois states. And that in the countries of Central and Eastern Europe—where a war crisis [World War I] brought down the last walls of feudalism with the consent of Western capitalism, which since that time opposes this block of anti-Bolshevist countries precisely against Russia—in Czechoslovakia, Rumania, Poland, Bulgaria, etc., agrarian laws have been enacted which in principle limit land property to a maximum of 500 hectares.

In accord with my ideological position, I believe that the time for trying in Peru the liberal method, the individualistic formula, has already passed. Leaving aside doctrinal reasons, I fundamentally consider the following factor, which gives a peculiar character to our agrarian problem, as unanswerable and concrete: the survival of the community and of the elements of practical socialism in Indian life and agriculture.

But those who remain within the demo-liberal doctrine, if they truly seek a solution to the Indian's problem which would, first of all, free him from his servitude, can look to the Czech or Rumanian experience—in case the Mexican experiment should seem a dangerous example because of its inspiration

[3] [Large, quasi-feudal estate—or, hacienda.]

and methods. For them there is still time to advocate the liberal formula. If they should do so, they would at least assure the presence, in the debate on the agrarian problem called forth by the new generation, of the liberal thought, which, according to written history, has been governing Peruvian life since the foundation of the Republic. . . .

As far as the Indian problem is concerned, special reasons make quite imperative its subordination to the land problem. The Indian race is an agricultural race. The Inca people were rural dwellers, usually devoted to agriculture or herding. Industry and the arts had a domestic and rural character. The principle that "Life comes from the earth" was truer in the Peru of the Incas than among any other people. . . .

Incaic communism—which cannot be denied or belittled merely because it developed under the autocratic regime of the Incas—is therefore called agrarian communism. The fundamental characteristics of the Incaic economy—according to César Ugarte, who generally defines the traits of our historical process with great thoughtfulness—were the following:

Collective ownership of arable land by the "ayllu," or group of related families, although the land was divided into individual and non-transferable plots: collective ownership of waters, pasturage lands and forests by the "marca" or tribe, that is, by the federation of "ayllus" established around the same village; common cooperation in labor; individual appropriation of the harvest and fruits.

The destruction of this economy—and therefore of the culture which it nourished—is one of the most evident responsibilities of the colonial regime, not because it meant the destruction of indigenous ways, but because it did not substitute superior ones. The colonial regime disorganized and destroyed the Incaic agrarian economy but failed to replace it with a more productive one. Under an Indian aristocracy, the population comprised ten million people, with an efficient and organic state whose action reached all realms of society; under a foreign aristocracy, the natives were reduced to an anarchic and dispersed mass of a million people fallen into servitude and "fellahism." . . .

The Spaniard did not possess the colonizing characteristics of the Anglo-Saxon. The creation of the United States appears as the work of the pioneer. After the epic of the conquest Spain sent us, however, almost solely nobles, clergymen, and villains. The conquistadors were of a heroic breed; but not the colonizers. They considered themselves noblemen, not pioneers. Those who thought that the wealth of Peru lay in its precious metals transformed mining, with their use of forced labor, into an instrument for destroying human capital and for degrading agriculture. . . .

The colonizer, who settled in the mines rather than in the fields, possessed the psychology of a gold prospector. He was, therefore, not a creator of wealth. An economy, a society, is the product of those who colonize and work the land, not of those who precariously extract the treasure of its subsoil. The history of the prosperity and decadence of many colonial towns in the sierra, determined by the discovery and abandonment of mines quickly exhausted or discarded, clearly indicates that historic law working among us.

Perhaps the only squadrons of true colonizers sent us by Spain were the Jesuit and Dominican missions. Both groups, especially the Jesuits, created several interesting centers of production in Peru. The Jesuits united religious, political, and economic factors in their enterprise—not to the extent which they did in Paraguay, where they carried out their most famous and extensive experiment, but certainly in accordance with the same principles. . . . This aspect of colonization, like many others in our economy, has not been studied yet. It has been left to me, a convinced and avowed Marxist, to prove its existence. . . .

The [colonial] Laws of the Indies protected Indian property and recognized its communist organization. Legislation relative to the Indian "communities" was adapted to the need of leaving intact institutions or customs unrelated to the religious spirit or to the political nature of the colonial regime. The agrarian communism of the "ayllu," once the Incaic state had been destroyed, was not incompatible with either. Just the opposite. The Jesuits took advantage precisely of Indian communism in Peru, in Mexico, and to a still greater degree in Paraguay for purposes of catechizing. The medieval regime, in theory and in practice, reconciled feudal with communalistic property.

The recognition of the communities and of their economic customs by the Laws of the Indies not only reveals the realistic shrewdness of the colonial policies, but also conforms absolutely with feudal theory and practice. On the other hand, the provisions of colonial laws, which maintained the community's economic mechanism without inconveniences, naturally reformed those customs opposed to Catholic doctrine (trial marriage, etc.), and tended to convert the community into a cog of the administrative and fiscal machinery. The community could and should survive, for the greater glory and profit of the King and of the Church. . . .

The co-existence of "community" and latifundio in Peru is therefore clearly explained not only by the characteristics of the colonial regime, but also by the experience of feudal Europe. The community under this regime could not be really protected, however, but merely tolerated. The owner of a latifundio imposed upon the community the law of his despotic power, without any possible supervision by the state. The community survived, but under a regime of servitude. Before, it had been the state's cellular unit, guaranteeing the dynamism necessary for the welfare of its members. The colonial system petrified the community with landed estates, which were the basis of a new order that was alien to the destiny of the community.

The liberalism of the laws of the Republic, powerless to destroy feudalism and to create capitalism, was bound later to withhold the formal protection which had been granted by the absolutism of the colonial laws.

Let us now examine the land problem under the Republic. In order to clarify my assumptions regarding the agrarian question in this period, I must insist on a view . . . about the character of the war for independence in Peru. This revolution found Peru lagging in the formation of its bourgeoisie. In our country the elements of a capitalist economy were embryonic to a greater degree than in other American countries, where the revolution found a less larval, less incipient bourgeoisie.

If the revolution had been a movement of the Indian masses or had represented their claims to justice, it would necessarily have had an agrarian character. It has been clearly demonstrated that the French Revolution benefited especially the rural classes, from which it had to draw support in order to prevent the return of the old regime. Furthermore, this phenomenon seems generally as characteristic of the bourgeois revolution as of the socialist revolution, if one is to judge by the more clearly defined and lasting consequences of the overthrow of feudalism in Central Europe and of tsarism in Russia. Directed and carried out mainly by the urban bourgeoisie and proletariat, both revolutions have had the rural population as their immediate beneficiaries. Particularly in Russia, this class was the one which enjoyed the first fruits of the Bolshevik revolution, because in that country no bourgeois revolution had taken place to effect the prior liquidation of feudalism and absolutism, and the substitution of a demo-liberal regime.

But in order for the demo-liberal revolution to have had these results, two assumptions have been necessary: the existence of a bourgeoisie conscious of the objectives and interests of its actions, and the existence of a feeling among the rural classes favorable to revolution and, above all, to the assertion of their rights to the land under terms incompatible with the power of the landholding aristocracy. In Peru, to a lesser extent than in other American countries, the revolution for independence was not based on such assumptions. The revolution triumphed because of the enforced solidarity of the peoples who were rebelling against Spanish domination, and because world political and economic factors worked in their favor. The continent-wide nationalism of the Latin American revolutionaries was joined to that inevitable community of their destinies, equalizing the countries most advanced in their progress toward capitalism with those most backward on the same road. . . .

Instead of the conflict between the landowning nobility and merchant bourgeoisie, the Latin-American revolution produced their collaboration in many cases, at times because of the liberal ideas which had penetrated the aristocracy, and at others because the aristocracy saw in the revolution only a movement of emancipation from the Spanish crown. The rural population, which was Indian in Peru, did not have direct and active participation in the revolution, for the revolutionary program did not champion its cause.

Still, this program was inspired by the liberal ideology. The revolution could not do without principles which considered existent agrarian demands that were based on practical necessity and on the theoretical justice of freeing land ownership from feudal shackles. The Republic inserted these provisions in its statutes. Peru lacked a bourgeois class which could apply them in harmony with its economic interests, and its political and juridical doctrine. But the Republic—since this was the compelling trend of history—was bound to be constituted on liberal and bourgeois principles. The sole drawback was that the practical consequences of the revolution, with respect to agrarian property, were bound to halt within the limits fixed by the interests of the great landowners.

For this reason, the policy of breaking up agrarian property, imposed by the political principles of the Republic, did not attack the latifundio. And—although in compensation the new laws ordered the distribution of land to the Indians—on the other hand, it attacked the Indian "community" in the name of the liberal postulates.

Thus a regime was inaugurated which, whatever may have been its principles, aggravated to a degree the condition of the Indians instead of improving it. Nor was this the fault of the ideology which inspired the new policy and which, rightfully applied, would have put an end to feudal control of the land by converting the Indians into small landowners.

The new policy formally abolished forced and servile labor. It embraced a number of measures which meant the liberation of the Indian from serfdom. But as, on the other hand, it left untouched the power and strength of feudal property, it nullified its own measures designed to protect the small owner and the rural worker.

The landowning aristocracy maintained its advantages *de facto,* if not its privileges *de jure*. It continued as the dominant class in Peru. The revolution had not actually raised a new class to power. The professional and merchant bourgeoisie were too weak to govern. The abolition of serfdom did not advance, therefore, beyond a mere theoretical declaration, since the revolution had not touched the latifundio. And serfdom is merely one of the aspects of feudalism, not feudalism itself.

During the period of military caudillos which followed the independence revolution, a liberal policy toward agrarian property could not develop logically, even in outline. Military caudillos were the natural product of a revolutionary period which had been unable to create a new ruling class. Under these conditions power had to be exercised by the military leaders of the revolution who on one hand enjoyed the martial prestige of their laurels, and on the other were in a position to retain control of the government by force of arms. The caudillo could not of course escape the influence of class interests or of the opposing historical forces. He found support in both the inconsistent and rhetorical liberalism of the urban "demos" and the conservative colonialism of the landowning caste. He was inspired both by the group of orators and lawyers of urban democracy and by the writers and rhetoricians of the landed aristocracy. For, in the conflict of interests between liberals and conservatives, there was no direct and active agrarian demand forcing the liberals to include in their programs the redistribution of agrarian property.

Even so, this basic problem would have been observed and appreciated by a superior statesman, but none of our military bosses of this period had such stature. . . .

During the period of military caudillos, the landed aristocracy was strengthened at the expense of the urban "demos." With commerce and finance in the hands of foreigners, it was economically impossible for a vigorous urban middle class to emerge. Spanish education, radically alien to the objectives and needs of industrialism and capitalism, did not prepare businessmen or technicians, but lawyers, writers, theologians, etc. These persons, unless they felt a particular vocation for jacobinism or demagoguery, were bound to serve the interests of the landed class. Commercial capital, almost exclusively foreign, could do nothing except come to terms and become associated with this aristocracy, which, in addition, retained tacitly or explicitly its political control. . . .

We have seen already how the formal liberalism of republican legislation has been inactive except with respect to the Indian "community." It can be said that the concept of individual property has had an almost antisocial function in the Republic because of its conflict with the survival of the "community." In fact, if the dissolution and expropriation of the "community" had been decreed and achieved by a capitalism developing vigorously and independently, it would have appeared as imposed by economic progress. The Indian would then have passed from a mixed regime of communism and serfdom into a free system of wages. This change would have disoriented him somewhat, but it would have placed him on the road toward self-organization and emancipation as a class—along the road traveled by the other proletarian groups of the world. Instead, the gradual expropriation and absorption of the "community" by the latifundio on one side sank him deeper in bondage, and on the other destroyed the economic and juridical institution which partially protected the spirit and physical organization of his ancient civilization.

(. . . Modern communism is a different matter from Incaic communism. . . . The civilization of the Incas was agrarian; that of Marx and Sorel is industrial. In the former man was subject to nature. In the latter nature is at times subject to man. It is therefore absurd to compare the forms and institutions of one communism with those of the other. The only thing which can be observed is their essential similarity in the abstract, given the essential and material differences of time and space. And in order to make this comparison, we need a measure of historical perspective. . . .

Individual liberty is one aspect of the complicated liberal phenomenon. A realist critique can define it as the juridical base of a capitalist civilization —without freedom of choice no free traffic is possible, nor free competition, nor free industry. An idealist critique can define it as an acquisition of the human spirit in the modern age. In neither respect could this freedom prevail in Inca life. . . . The life and spirit of the Indian were not tormented by the desire for speculation and for intellectual creation. Neither were they subordinated to the need to engage in commerce, in contracts, in exchange. What use could the Indian make, therefore, of this freedom invented by our civilization? If the spirit of freedom was revealed to the Quechua, it was undoubtedly in a formula, or rather in an emotion, different from the liberal, jacobin, and individualistic formula of freedom. The revelation of freedom, like the revelation of God, varies with epochs, peoples, and climes. To identify the abstract idea of liberty with the concrete images of a liberty that wears a Phrygian cap—daughter of Protestantism and the Renaissance and the French Revolution—is to be ensnared by an illusion which depends perhaps from a mere philosophic, although not unselfish, astigmatism on the part of the middle class and its democracy.

. . . Autocracy and communism are incompatible in our times; but they were not so in primitive societies. Today a new order cannot renounce any of the moral advances achieved by modern society. Contemporary socialism—other epochs have had other types of socialism labeled by history with other names—is the antithesis of liberalism; but it is born from it and is nourished by its experience. Socialism does not disdain any of the intellectual conquests of liberalism, and does not mock or deride anything except its limitations. It recognizes and understands everything which is positive in the liberal idea; it condemns and attacks only those aspects which are negative or temporary. . . .

It is not possible to speak of tyranny in the abstract. A tyranny is a concrete fact. And it becomes real only to the degree in which it oppresses the will of a people or in which it opposes and smothers their vital impulse. In ancient times, on the contrary, an absolutist and theocratic regime often embodied and represented that will and that impulse. This seems to have been the case during the Inca empire. I do not believe that the Incas performed any miracles. I deem their political capacity to be evident; but I deem it no less evident that their work consisted in constructing the empire with the human material and moral elements supplied by the centuries. The ayllu—the community—was the cell of the empire. The Incas forged a unity, invented the empire, but did not create the cell. The juridical state organized by the Incas undoubtedly reproduced the preexisting natural state. The Incas did not hasten anything unduly. It is well that their achievement be praised; it is wrong to scorn and belittle the millennial labor of multitudes, of which that achievement is but one expression and consequence.) [4]

During the republican period, national writers and legislators have shown a more or less uniform tendency to condemn the "community" as a residue of a primitive society, or as a survival of the colonial system. This attitude has answered in some cases to the interests of the landholding bosses and in others to the individualistic and liberal thought which has automatically dominated an excessively verbalistic and impassioned culture. . . .

The Indian, in spite of one hundred years of laws under a republican regime, has not become an individualist. And this is not because the Indian resists progress, as is claimed by the easy generalizations of self-interested detractors. Rather, it depends on the fact that individualism, under a feudal system, does not find the necessary conditions for its support and development. Communism, on the other hand, has continued to be the only defense

[4] [The four preceding paragraphs, given here in parentheses, appear in the original as a footnote—*Trans.*]

for the Indian. Individualism cannot prosper, and in fact scarcely exists, except under a regime of free competition. And the Indian has never felt less free than when he has felt himself alone. . . .

THE "COLONIALISM" OF OUR COASTAL CULTURE

The extent of development reached by the industrialization of agriculture under a capitalistic regime and technique in the coastal valleys is chiefly attributable to the interest of British and American capital in Peru's production of sugar and cotton. The industrial or capitalistic aptitudes of the landowners are not a large factor in the spread of these crops. The owners devote their lands to the production of cotton or cane, financed or supported by powerful export firms.

The best lands in the coastal valleys are planted to cotton or cane, not because they are exactly suited to these crops, but because at this moment they are the only crops of importance to English and American merchants. Farm credit—completely subordinated to the economic interests of these firms until the National Farm Bank be established—does not encourage any other crop. The cultivation of food crops destined for the domestic market is generally in the hands of small owners and tenants. Only in the valleys near Lima, because of their proximity to important urban markets, do owners devote large farms to staple foods. In many cases staples are not grown on the sugar or cotton plantations even to the extent necessary to supply the local farm population.

The small proprietor or tenant finds himself impelled to grow cotton by this trend which disregards almost completely the particular needs of the national economy. The substitution of cotton for the traditional food crops in those coastal fields where small farms still exist has been one of the most obvious reasons for the rise in food costs in the coastal towns. . . .

A clear and urgent need of the Peruvian economy has for a long time demanded that the country produce wheat for its people's bread. Had this objective been attained, Peru would not have to continue paying abroad twelve or more million *soles* annually for the wheat consumed in the coastal cities. Why has this problem of our economy remained unsolved? . . .

The obstacle, the resistance to a final solution, lies in the very structure of the Peruvian economy. Its movements and development are subordinated to the interests and needs of the markets of London and New York. These markets consider Peru to be a storehouse of raw materials and a market for their own manufactured products. Peruvian agriculture therefore obtains credits and transportation only for those products which can find profitable sale in the big foreign markets. Foreign financiers are interested one day in rubber, another day in cotton, and another in sugar. Whenever London can obtain a product cheaper and in sufficient quantity from India or Egypt, the Peruvian suppliers are abandoned to their own fate. Our *latifundistas,* our landowners, whatever their illusions may be about their independence, in reality merely act as intermediaries or agents for foreign capital.

FINAL PROPOSITIONS

To the basic propositions already presented in this study regarding the contemporary aspects of the agrarian question in Peru, I must add the following:

1. The nature of land ownership in Peru appears as one of the major obstacles to the development of national capitalism. The percentage of lands worked by large or medium tenants, belonging to owners who have never managed their own farms, is extremely high. These landowners, completely alien to and removed from agriculture and its problems, live off their land rents without contributing either labor or brains to the economic activity of the country. They belong to the category of the aristocrat or landlord, a nonproducing consumer. Through inherited property rights they receive a rent income which may be considered as a feudal right. The farm tenant, on the other hand, more or less corresponds to the manager-type of a capitalist concern. Within a true capitalist system the surplus obtained by his enterprise should benefit himself as an "industrialist" and the capital financing his labor. The managing of land by a class of tenants imposes upon production the heavy load of sustaining an income not subject to a long-term decline in the value of farm products. The tenant generally does not find in this system all the stimuli necessary for maximum utilization of the lands, crops, and installations. The fear of an increase in rent on expiration of his contract prompts him to be niggardly in making investments. The ambition of the tenant farmer is of course to become a landowner; but his own industry contributes to increasing the value of the land for the benefit of the owner. The primitive conditions of farm credit in Peru preclude a more intensive, capitalistic expropriation of the land in favor of this class of "industrialists." For this reason, capitalistic use and industrialization of the land, which require for their full and free development the elimination of all feudal privileges, progress in our country by extremely slow degrees. A problem exists here which is evident not only from a socialist, but also from a capitalist point of view. Formulating a principle embodied in the agrarian program of the liberal French bourgeoisie, Edouard Herriot affirms that

"land demands the actual presence [of the owner]." It is not useless to point out that the West is not more advanced than the Orient in this respect, for Mohammedan law establishes, as Charles Gide observes, that "the land belongs to him who makes it produce and live."

2. In addition, the latifundio system prevalent in Peru stands as the most serious barrier to white immigration. For obvious reasons, the immigration which we can expect is that of farmers from Italy, Central Europe, and the Balkans. Western urban population emigrates in a much lesser scale, and, moreover, industrial workers know that there are few opportunities in Latin America. Furthermore, the European farmer does not come to Latin America to work as a farm hand, except in cases when high salaries enable him to lay aside considerable savings. And this is not the case in Peru. Not even the most wretched peasant in Poland or Rumania would accept the standard of living of our workers on the sugar or cotton plantations. His ambition is to become a small landowner. In order for our fields to attract this immigration, it is necessary to offer land equipped with living quarters, animals, implements, and ready access to railroads and markets. A Fascist official or propagandist who visited Peru about three years ago declared in the local newspapers that our system of large holdings was incompatible with a program of colonization and immigration capable of attracting the Italian peasant.

3. The infeudation of coastal agriculture to British and American capital and markets is opposed not only to its organization and development in accordance with specific needs of the national economy—that is, once the people are assured their staple foods—but also to the experimentation and adoption of new crops. The largest endeavor of this sort undertaken in the last few years—the tobacco plantations in Tumbes—has been made possible only through the intervention of the state. This fact supports better than any other the claim that the liberal policy of "laisser faire," which has proved so barren in Peru, must be definitively replaced by a social program for nationalizing the large sources of wealth.

4. The coastal agrarian system, in spite of the prosperous times it has enjoyed, has proven incapable of coping with the problems of rural health to the degree demanded by the state, which is of course quite moderate. The regulations imposed by the Department of Public Health on the landowners have failed to make them comply even with the measures for malaria control. There has not even been a general improvement on the smaller farms. It has been demonstrated that the coastal population has the highest rates of mortality and disease in the country (with the obvious exception of the

excessively unhealthy jungle regions). Demographic statistics for the rural district of Pativilca revealed three years ago a mortality rate higher than its birth rate. . . .

5. In the sierra, surviving agrarian feudalism is totally impotent as a source of wealth and progress. With the exception of sheep-raising enterprises which export wool, and a few others, the latifundio in the valleys and plains of the sierra has a miserable production record. Returns from the soil are meager and the methods of labor primitive. A local newspaper said recently that in the Peruvian sierra the owner appears relatively as poor as the Indian. This argument—which has no value within a criterion of relativity—far from justifying the existence of the owner, condemns him irrevocably because in modern economics—considered as an objective and concrete science—the only justification for capitalism and its captains of industry and finance lies in its function of creating wealth. On the economic level, the feudal lord or boss is the main culprit responsible for the scant yield of his domain. We have already seen how this landowner does not concern himself with the production, but with the profitable tenancy of his land. We have also seen how, even though his lands are the best, his indices of production are no higher than those obtained by the Indian with his primitive farming equipment on his marginal communal lands. As an economic factor, the owner is therefore entirely discredited.

6. As an explanation for this phenomenon, it is said that the economic conditions of agriculture in the sierra depend absolutely on the means of communication and transport. Those who reason in this way undoubtedly do not understand the organic and fundamental difference between a feudal or semi-feudal economy and a capitalist economy. They do not understand that the primitive patriarchal type of feudal landowner is substantially different from the type of the modern entrepreneur. On the other hand, rural bossism and the latifundio also form an obstacle to achieving the transportation system now planned by the state. The abuses and the interests of the bosses are totally opposed to a fair application of the law for conscripting men for public services. The Indian instinctively considers the law a weapon of the bosses. Under the Incaic regime, this duly allotted work on the roads would have been an obligatory public service, thoroughly compatible with the principles of modern socialism; within the colonial regime of latifundio and serfdom, this same service acquires the hateful characteristics of forced labor.

MOHANDAS K. GANDHI

ONE of the major indices of upheaval in the twentieth century has been the rapid development of revolutionary national movements in the Orient, and the concomitant collapse or contraction of European political and economic control of that area of the globe. The influence of Western civilization upon Eastern did not become significant until the nineteenth century. Although Western peoples had long been in contact with India and China—Greeks and Romans traded in the Orient before the birth of Christ, and commercial connections between the Mediterranean and the East were maintained after the decline of Roman power in Europe and the upsurge of Islam in the Middle East—it was not until the sixteenth century that Europeans began to enjoy a superiority in power over Oriental peoples. It was not until the eighteenth century that this superiority became decisive and not until the nineteenth that the Orient came to be dominated by West European states. But by the beginning of the twentieth century, of the large Asiatic nations only Japan and, to a lesser degree Thailand, could still claim real independence of the conflicting European imperial systems.

The impact of modern European civilization upon the diverse, intricate, and ancient cultures of Asia was most profound. In its penetration of the Orient, Western economic and military power everywhere induced changes in the Asiatic societies. Along with colonial rule, the rule of a distinct and foreign caste of white overlords, along with modern technology and capitalism, went specifically Western political and social ideas and ideological aspirations. The years just prior to the First World War witnessed the climax of European colonialism in the East; those same years saw also the development, at least among the educated and to a degree Westernized classes, in all Oriental countries of nationalist, anti-imperialist movements for independence, movements which, moreover, were often colored by demands for democratic political rights, for social equality and economic betterment. The involvement of the great European powers in the two World Wars provided the opportunity for these movements to become effective in the actual political arena.

The twentieth-century revolutions in the East have taken many courses and have produced many kinds of leaders. In India the most important figure was that of Mohandas K. Gandhi, whose ascetic life reflected the ancient Hindu goal of "living without desire," yet who was also dedicated to the modern principles of Indian freedom, unity, and peace. More than any contemporary, Gandhi profoundly stirred India's religious imagination; he also galvanized into successful action the newly developed forces of Indian nationalism.

Gandhi was born in 1869, in Probandar, India, of the *vaisya* or merchant caste. Educated first in Indian schools, he studied law in England, and achieved his early reputation in South Africa, where, before the First World War, he developed his almost religious method of "nonviolent noncooperation" in an epic battle to obtain, from the Boer and British ruling class, a measure of political and social justice for his fellow countrymen living in South and East Africa. From his African days to the end of his life, he was a controversial personage. Looked upon as a dangerous subversive by conservative Britons, he was held to be a "saint" by many cultivated Europeans. Called Mahatma ("great-souled") and adored as a holy man by tens of millions of Hindus, he was a master politician who combined the skills of a ward boss with the appeal of a charismatic leader. By conviction as well as inheritance a Hindu, he was influenced by Christ and Tolstoy, and his deepest concern was with that true "religion which underlies all religions." Rejecting the values of Western industrialized civilization and preaching the virtues of agrarian simplicity and handicraftsmanship, he was idolized by India's destitute masses. Yet his movement to force Britain to grant Indian independence was financed by some of India's most wealthy industrialists. Socialists regarded him as a reactionary bent upon preserving the exploitative class structure of India; even many among his own followers looked upon his economic thinking as atavistic. India's Moslems saw in Gandhi an enemy of their faith; at the same time Hindus of the Mashaba movement accused him of conspiring with Islamic leaders against men of his own religion.

Gandhi's weapons in the struggle for Indian independence ultimately were moral and psychological rather than physical; passive resistance, fasting, submission to imprisonment, were used with telling effect upon the British. Yet he often employed these same weapons against his own people when extremists turned from civil disobedience to more crude forms of insurrection and terrorism. An apostle of peace and a curious amalgam of European and Indian modes of thought, Gandhi, more than any other man, "changed the face of India" and was responsible for that country's final freedom from British rule. But almost at the moment of triumph, in 1948, he was assassinated by a Hindu fanatic who held him responsible for the division of the country into two states, Moslem Pakistan in the northwest and northeast and (predominately) Hindu India in the rest of the subcontinent.

The following selection is taken from Mohandas Gandhi's book *Indian Home Rule* (1919).

INDIAN HOME RULE

CHAPTER VI: CIVILISATION

READER: Now you will have to explain what you mean by civilisation.

EDITOR: It is not a question of what I mean. Several English writers refuse to call that civilisation which passes under that name. Many books have been written upon that subject. Societies have been formed to cure the nation of the evils of civilisation. A great English writer has written a work

---

This selection has been reprinted from M. K. Gandhi, *Indian Home Rule,* Ganesh & Co., Madras, 1919 (pp. 25–46, 65–75, 78–89, 92–102, 106–108) by permission of the publisher.

called *Civilisation: Its Cause and Cure.* Therein he has called it a disease.

READER: Why do we not know this generally?

EDITOR: The answer is very simple. We rarely find people arguing against themselves. Those who are intoxicated by modern civilisation are not likely to write against it. Their care will be to find out facts and arguments in support of it, and this they do unconsciously, believing it to be true. A man, whilst he is dreaming, believes in his dream; he is undeceived only when he is awakened from his sleep. A man labouring under the bane of civilisation is like a dreaming man. What we usually read are the works of defenders of modern civilisation, which undoubtedly claims among its votaries very brilliant and even some very good men. Their writings hypnotise us. And so, one by one, we are drawn into the vortex.

READER: This seems to be very plausible. Now will you tell me something of what you have read and thought of this civilisation?

EDITOR: Let us first consider what state of things is described by the word "civilisation." Its best test lies in the fact that people living in it make bodily welfare the object of life. We will take some examples. The people of Europe to-day live in better-built houses than they did a hundred years ago. This is considered an emblem of civilisation, and this is also a matter to promote bodily happiness. Formerly, they wore skins, and used as their weapons spears. Now, they wear long trousers, and, for embellishing their bodies, they wear a variety of clothing, and, instead of spears, they carry with them revolvers containing five or more chambers. If people of a certain country, who have hitherto not been in the habit of wearing much clothing, boots, etc., adopt European clothing, they are supposed to have become civilised out of savagery. Formerly, in Europe, people ploughed their lands mainly by manual labour. Now, one man can plough a vast tract by means of steam-engines, and can thus amass great wealth. This is called a sign of civilisation. Formerly, the fewest men wrote books that were most valuable. Now, anybody writes and prints anything he likes and poisons people's minds. Formerly, men travelled in waggons; now they fly through the air in trains at the rate of four hundred and more miles per day. This is considered the height of civilisation. It has been stated that, as men progress, they shall be able to travel in airships and reach any part of the world in a few hours. Men will not need the use of their hands and feet. They will press a button, and they will have their clothing by their side. They will press another button, and they will have their newspaper. A third, and a motorcar will be waiting for them. They will have a variety of delicately dished-up food. Everything will be done by machinery. Formerly, when people wanted to fight with one another, they measured between them their bodily strength; now it is possible to take away thousands of lives by one man working behind a gun from a hill. This is civilisation. Formerly, men worked in the open air only so much as they liked. Now, thousands of workmen meet together and, for the sake of maintenance, work in factories or mines. Their condition is worse than that of beasts. They are obliged to work, at the risk of their lives, at most dangerous occupations, for the sake of millionaires. Formerly, men were made slaves under physical compulsion, now they are enslaved by temptation of money and of the luxuries that money can buy. There are now diseases of which people never dreamt before, and an army of doctors is engaged in finding out their cures, and so hospitals have increased. This is a test of civilisation. Formerly, special messengers were required and much expense was incurred in order to send letters; to-day, anyone can abuse his fellow by means of a letter for one penny. True, at the same cost, one can send one's thanks also. Formerly, people had two or three meals consisting of home-made bread and vegetables; now, they require something to eat every two hours, so that they have hardly leisure for anything else. What more need I say? All this you can ascertain from several authoritative books. These are all true tests of civilisation. And, if anyone speaks to the contrary, know that he is ignorant. This civilisation takes note neither of morality nor religion. Its votaries calmly state that their business is not to teach religion. Some even consider it to be a superstitious growth. Others put on the cloak of religion, and prate about morality. But, after twenty years' experience, I have come to the conclusion that immorality is often taught in the name of morality. Even a child can understand that in all I have described above there can be no inducement to morality. Civilisation seeks to increase bodily comforts, and it fails miserably even in doing so.

This civilisation is irreligion, and it has taken such a hold on the people in Europe that those who are in it appear to be half-mad. They lack real physical strength or courage. They keep up their energy by intoxication. They can hardly be happy in solitude. Women, who should be the queens of households, wander in the streets, or they slave away in factories. For the sake of a pittance, half a million women in England alone are labouring under trying circumstances in factories or similar institutions. This awful fact is one of the causes of the daily growing suffragette movement.

This civilisation is such that one has only to be patient and it will be self destroyed. According to the teaching of Mahomed this would be considered a Satanic civilisation. Hinduism calls it the Black Age. I cannot give you an adequate conception of it. It is eating into the vitals of the

English nation. It must be shunned. Parliaments are really emblems of slavery. If you will sufficiently think over this, you will entertain the same opinion, and cease to blame the English. They rather deserve our sympathy. They are a shrewd nation and I, therefore, believe that they will cast off the evil. They are enterprising and industrious, and their mode of thought is not inherently immoral. Neither are they bad at heart. I, therefore, respect them. Civilisation is not an incurable disease, but it should never be forgotten that the English people are at present afflicted by it.

CHAPTER VII: WHY WAS INDIA LOST?

READER: You have said much about civilisation—enough to make me ponder over it. I do not now know what I should adopt and what I should avoid from the nations of Europe, but one question comes to my lips immediately. If civilisation is a disease, and if it has attacked England why has she been able to take India, and why is she able to retain it?

EDITOR: Your question is not very difficult to answer, and we shall presently be able to examine the true nature of Swaraj; [1] for I am aware that I have still to answer that question. I will, however, take up your previous question. The English have not taken India; we have given it to them. They are not in India because of their strength, but because we keep them. Let us now see whether these propositions can be sustained. They came to our country originally for purposes of trade. Recall the Company Bahadur. Who made it Bahadur? they had not the slightest intention at the time of establishing a Kingdom. Who assisted the Company's officers? Who was tempted at the sight of their silver? Who bought their goods? History testifies that we did all this. In order to become rich all at once, we welcomed the Company's officers with open arms. We assisted them. If I am in the habit of drinking Bhang, and a seller thereof sells it to me, am I to blame him or myself? By blaming the seller shall I be able to avoid the habit? And, if a particular retailer is driven away, will not another take his place? A true servant of India will have to go to the root of the matter. If an excess of food has caused me indigestion, I will certainly not avoid it by blaming water. He is a true physician who probes the cause of disease and, if you pose as a physician for the disease of India, you will have to find out its true cause.

READER: You are right. Now, I think you will not have to argue much with me to drive your conclusions home. I am impatient to know your further views. We are now on a most interesting topic. I shall, therefore, endeavour to follow your thought, and stop you when I am in doubt.

[1] [*Home rule.*]

EDITOR: I am afraid that, in spite of your enthusiasm, as we proceed further we shall have differences of opinion. Nevertheless, I shall argue only when you will stop me. We have already seen that the English merchants were able to get a footing in India because we encouraged them. When our princes fought among themselves, they sought the assistance of Company Bahadur. That corporation was versed alike in commerce and war. It was unhampered by questions of morality. Its object was to increase its commerce and to make money. It accepted our assistance, and increased the number of its warehouses. To protect the latter it employed an army which was utilised by us also. Is it not then useless to blame the English for what we did at that time? The Hindus and the Mahomedans were at daggers drawn. This, too, gave the Company its opportunity, and thus we created the circumstances that gave the Company its control over India. Hence it is truer to say that we gave India to the English than that India was lost.

READER: Will you now tell me how they are able to retain India?

EDITOR: The causes that gave them India enable them to retain it. Some Englishmen state that they took, and they hold, India by the sword. Both these statements are wrong. The sword is entirely useless for holding India. We alone keep them. Napoleon is said to have described the English as a nation of shop keepers. It is a fitting description. They hold whatever dominions they have for the sake of their commerce. Their army and their navy are intended to protect it. When the Transvaal offered no such attractions, the late Mr. Gladstone discovered that it was not right for the English to hold it. When it became a paying proposition, resistance led to war. Mr. Chamberlain soon discovered that England enjoyed a suzerainty over the Transvaal. It is related that some one asked the late President Kruger whether there was gold in the moon? He replied that it was highly unlikely, because, if there were, the English would have annexed it. Many problems can be solved by remembering that money is their God. Then it follows that we keep the English in India for our base self-interest. We like their commerce, they please us by their subtle methods, and get what they want from us. To blame them for this is to perpetuate their power. We further strengthen their hold by quarrelling amongst ourselves. If you accept the above statements, it is proved that the English entered India for the purposes of trade. They remain in it for the same purpose, and we help them to do so. Their arms and ammunition are perfectly useless. In this connection, I remind you that it is the British flag which is waving in Japan, and not the Japanese. The English have a treaty with Japan for the sake of their commerce, and you will see that, if they can manage it, their commerce will greatly expand in that country. They wish to convert the whole world into a vast market for their goods. That they cannot do so is true, but the blame will not be theirs. They will leave no stone unturned to reach the goal.

CHAPTER VIII: THE CONDITION OF INDIA

READER: I now understand why the English hold India. I should like to know your views about the condition of our country.

EDITOR: It is a sad condition. In thinking of it, my eyes water and my throat gets parched. I have grave doubts whether I shall be able sufficiently to explain what is in my heart. It is my deliberate opinion that India is being ground down not under the English heel but under that of modern civilisation. It is groaning under the monster's terrible weight. There is yet time to escape it, but every day makes it more and more difficult. Religion is dear to me, and my first complaint is that India is becoming irreligious. Here I am not thinking of the Hindu, and Mahomedan, or the Zoroastrian religion, but of that religion which underlies all religions. We are turning away from God.

READER: How so?

EDITOR: There is a charge laid against us that we are a lazy people, and that the Europeans are industrious and enterprising. We have accepted the charge and we, therefore, wish to change our condition. Hinduism, Islamism, Zoroastrianism, Christianity and all other religions teach that we should remain passive about worldly pursuits and active about godly pursuits, that we should set a limit to our worldly ambition, and that our religious ambition should be illimitable. Our activity should be directed into the latter channel.

READER: You seem to be encouraging religious charlatanism. Many a cheat has by talking in a similar strain led the people astray.

EDITOR: You are bringing an unlawful charge against religion. Humbug there undoubtedly is about all religions. Where there is light, there is also shadow. I am prepared to maintain that humbugs in worldly matters are far worse than the humbugs in religion. The humbug of civilisation that I endeavour to show you is not to be found in religion.

READER: How can you say that? In the name of religion Hindus and Mahomedans fought against one another. For the same cause Christians fought Christians. Thousands of innocent men have been murdered, thousands have been burned and tortured in its name. Surely, this is much worse than any civilisation.

EDITOR: I certainly submit that the above hardships are far more bearable than those of civilisation. Everybody understands that the cruelties you have named are not part of religion, although they have been practised in its name; therefore, there is no aftermath to these cruelties. They will always happen so long as there are to be found ignorant and credulous people. But there is no end to the victims destroyed in the fire of civilisation. Its deadly effect is that people come under its scorching flames believing it to be all good. They become utterly irreligious and, in reality, derive little advantage from the world. Civilisation is like a mouse gnawing while it is soothing us. When its full effect is realised, we will see that religious superstition is harmless compared to that of modern civilisation. I am not pleading for a continuance of religious superstitions. We will certainly fight them tooth and nail, but we can never do so by disregarding religion. We can only do so by appreciating and conserving the latter.

READER: Then you will contend that the Pax Britannica is a useless encumbrance?

EDITOR: You may see peace if you like; I see none.

READER: You make light of the terror that the Thugs, the Pindaris, the Bhils were to the country.

EDITOR: If you will give the matter some thought, you will see that the terror was by no means such a mighty thing. If it had been a very substantial thing, the other people would have died away before the English advent. Moreover, the present peace is only nominal, for by it we have become emasculated and cowardly. We are not to assume that the English have changed the nature of the Pindaris and the Bhils. It is, therefore, better to suffer the Pindari peril than that someone else should protect us from it, and thus render us effeminate. I should prefer to be killed by the arrow of a Bhil than to seek unmanly protection. India without such protection was an India full of valour. Macaulay betrayed gross ignorance when he libelled Indians as being practically cowards. They never merited the charge. Cowards living in a country inhabited by hardy mountaineers, infested by wolves and tigers must surely find an early grave. Have you ever visited our fields? I assure you that our agriculturists sleep fearlessly on their farms even to-day, and the English, you and I would hesitate to sleep where they sleep. Strength lies in absence of fear, not in the quantity of flesh and muscle we may have on our bodies. Moreover, I must remind you who desire Home Rule that, after all, the Bhils, the Pindaris, the Assamese and the Thugs are, our own countrymen. To conquer them is your and my work. So long as we fear our own brethren, we are unfit to reach the goal.

CHAPTER IX: THE CONDITION OF INDIA (CONTINUED): RAILWAYS

READER: You have deprived me of the consolation I used to have regarding peace in India.

EDITOR: I have merely given you my opinion on the religious aspect, but, when I give you my views as to the poverty of India you will perhaps begin to dislike me, because what you and I have hitherto considered beneficial for India no longer appears to me to be so.

READER: What may that be?

EDITOR: Railways, lawyers and doctors have impoverished the country, so much so that, if we do not wake up in time, we shall be ruined.

READER: I do now, indeed, fear that we are not likely to agree at all. You are attacking the very institutions which we have hitherto considered to be good.

EDITOR: It is necessary to exercise patience. The true inwardness of the evils of civilisation you will understand with difficulty. Doctors assure us that a consumptive clings to life even when he is about to die. Consumption does not produce apparent hurt—it even produces a seductive colour about a patient's face, so as to induce the belief that all is well. Civilisation is such a disease, and we have to be very wary.

READER: Very well, then, I shall hear you on the railways.

EDITOR: It must be manifest to you that, but for the railways, the English could not have such a hold on India as they have. The railways, too, have spread the bubonic plague. Without them, masses could not move from place to place. They are the carriers of plague germs. Formerly we had natural segregation. Railways have also increased the frequency of famines, because, owing to facility of means of locomotion, people sell out their grain, and it is sent to the dearest markets. People become careless, and so the pressure of famine increases. They accentuate the evil nature of man. Bad men fulfil their evil designs with greater rapidity. The holy places of India have become unholy. Formerly, people went to these places only with great difficulty. Generally, therefore, only the real devotees visited such places. Nowadays, rogues visit them in order to practice their roguery.

READER: You have given a one-sided account. Good men can visit these places as well as bad men. Why do they not take the fullest advantage of the railways?

EDITOR: Good travels at a snail's pace—it can, therefore, have little to do with the railways. Those who want to do good are not selfish, they are not in a hurry, they know that to impregnate people with good requires a long time.

But evil has wings. To build a house takes time. Its destruction takes none. So the railways can become a distributing agency for the evil one only. It may be a debatable matter whether railways spread famines, but it is beyond dispute that they propagate evil.

READER: Be that as it may, all the disadvantages of railways are more than counterbalanced by the fact that it is due to them that we see in India the new spirit of nationalism.

EDITOR: I hold this to be a mistake. The English have taught us that we were not one nation before, and that it will require centuries before we become one nation. This is without foundation. We were one nation before they came to India. One thought inspired us. Our mode of life was the same. It was because we were one nation that they were able to establish one kingdom. Subsequently they divided us.

READER: This requires an explanation.

EDITOR: I do not wish to suggest that because we were one nation we had no differences, but it is submitted that our leading men travelled throughout India either on foot or in bullock-carts. They learned one another's languages, and there was no aloofness between them. What do you think could have been the intention of those far-seeing ancestors of ours who established Shevetbindu Rameshwar in the South, Juggernaut in the South-East, and Hardwar in the North as places of pilgrimage? You will admit they were no fools. They knew that worship of God could have been performed just as well at home. They taught us that those whose hearts were aglow with righteousness had the Ganges in their own homes. But they saw that India was one undivided land so made by nature. They, therefore, argued that it must be one nation. Arguing thus, they established holy places in various parts of India, and fired the people with an idea of nationality in a manner unknown in other parts of the world. Any two Indians are one as no two Englishmen are. Only you and I and others who consider ourselves civilised and superior persons imagine that we are many nations. It was after the advent of railways that we began to believe in distinctions, and you are at liberty now to say that it is through the railways that we are beginning to abolish those distinctions. An opium-eater may argue the advantage of opium-eating from the fact that he began to understand the evil of the opium habit after having eaten it. I would ask you to consider well what I have said on the railways. . . .

CHAPTER XIII: WHAT IS TRUE CIVILISATION?

READER: You have denounced railways. . . . I can see that you will discard all machinery. What, then, is civilisation?

EDITOR: The answer to that question is not difficult. I believe that the civilisation India has evolved is not to be beaten in the world. Nothing can equal the seeds sown by our ancestors. Rome went, Greece shared the same fate, the might of the Pharaohs was broken, Japan has become westernised, of China nothing can be said, but India is still, somehow or other, sound at the foundation. The people of Europe learn their lessons from the writings of the men of Greece or Rome, which exist no longer in their former glory. In trying to learn from them, the Europeans imagine that they will avoid the mistakes of Greece and Rome. Such is their pitiable condition. In the midst of all this, India remains immovable, and that is her glory. It is a charge against India that her people are so uncivilised, ignorant and stolid, that it is not possible to induce them to adopt any changes. It is a charge really against our merit. What we have tested and found true on the anvil of experience, we dare not change. Many thrust their advice upon India, and she remains steady. This is her beauty; it is the sheet-anchor of our hope.

Civilisation is that mode of conduct which points out to man the path of duty. Performance of duty and observance of morality are convertible terms. To observe morality is to attain mastery over our mind and our passions. So doing, we know ourselves. The Gujariti equivalent for civilisation means "good conduct."

If this definition be correct, then India, as so many writers have shown, has nothing to learn from anybody else, and this is as it should be. We notice that mind is a restless bird; the more it gets the more it wants, and still remains unsatisfied. The more we indulge our passions, the more unbridled they become. Our ancestors, therefore, set a limit to our indulgences. They saw that happiness was largely a mental condition. A man is not necessarily happy because he is rich, or unhappy because he is poor. The rich are often seen to be unhappy, the poor to be happy. Millions will always remain poor. Observing all this, our ancestors dissuaded us from luxuries and pleasures. We have managed with the same kind of plough as it existed thousands of years ago. We have retained the same kind of cottages that we had in former times, and our indigenous education remains the same as before. We have had no system of life-corroding competition. Each followed his own occupation or trade, and charged a regulation wage. It was not that we did not know how to invent machinery, but our forefathers knew that, if we set our hearts after such things, we would become slaves and lose our moral fiber. They therefore, after due deliberation, decided that we should only do what we could with our hands and feet. They saw that our real happiness and health consisted in a proper use of our hands and feet. They further reasoned that large cities were a snare and a useless encumbrance, and that people would not be happy in them, that there would be gangs of thieves and robbers, prostitution and vice flourishing in them, and that poor men would be robbed by rich men. They were, therefore, satisfied with small villages. They saw that kings and their swords were inferior to the sword of ethics, and they, therefore, held the sovereigns of the earth to be inferior to the Rishis and the Fakirs. A nation with a constitution like this is fitter to teach others than to learn from others. This nation had courts, lawyers and doctors, but they were all within bounds. Everybody knew that these professions were not particularly superior; moreover, these *vakils* and *vaids* did not rob people; they were considered people's dependents, not their masters. Justice was tolerably fair. The ordinary rule was to avoid courts. There were no touts to lure people into them. This evil, too, was noticeable only in and around capitals. The common people lived independently, and followed their agricultural occupation. They enjoyed true Home Rule.

Go eat your rice

And where this cursed modern civilisation has not reached, India remains as it was before. The inhabitants of that part of India will very properly laugh at your new-fangled notions. The English do not rule over them nor will you ever rule over them. Those whose name we speak we do not know, nor do they know us. I would certainly advise you and those like you who love the motherland to go into the interior that has yet not been polluted by the railways, and to live there for six months; you might then be patriotic and speak of Home Rule.

Now you see what I consider to be real civilisation. Those who want to change conditions such as I have described are enemies of the country and are sinners.

READER: It would be all right if India were exactly as you have described it, but it is also India where there are hundreds of child widows, where two-year-old babies are married, where twelve-year-old girls are mothers and housewives, where women practise polyandry, where the practice of Niyog obtains, where, in the name of religion, girls dedicate themselves to prostitution, and where, in the name of religion, sheep and goats are killed. Do you consider these also symbols of the civilisation that you have described?

EDITOR: You make a mistake. The defects that you have shown are defects. Nobody mistakes them for ancient civilisation. They remain in spite of it. Attempts have always been made, and will be made, to remove them. We may utilise the new spirit that is born in us for purging ourselves of these evils. But what I have described to you as emblems of modern civilisation are accepted as such by its votaries. The Indian civilisation, as described by me has been so described by its votaries. In no part of the world, and under no civilisation, have all men attained perfection. The tendency of Indian civilisation is to elevate the moral being, that of the western civilisation is to propagate immorality. The latter is godless, the former is based on a belief in God. So understanding and so believing, it behoves every lover of India to cling to the old Indian civilisation even as a child clings to its mother's breast.

CHAPTER XIV: HOW CAN INDIA BECOME FREE?

READER: I appreciate your views about civilisation. I will have to think over them. I cannot take in all at once. What, then, holding the views you do, would you suggest for freeing India?

EDITOR: I do not expect my views to be accepted all of a sudden. My duty is to place them before readers like yourself. Time can be trusted to do the rest. We have already examined the conditions for freeing India, but we have done so indirectly; we will now do so directly. It is a world-known maxim that the removal of the cause of a disease results in the removal of the disease itself. Similarly, if the cause of India's slavery be removed, India can become free.

READER: If Indian civilisation is, as you say, the best of all, how do you account for India's slavery?

EDITOR: This civilisation is unquestionably the best, but it is to be observed that all civilisations have been on their trial. That civilisation which is permanent outlives it. Because the sons of India were found wanting, its civilisation has been placed in jeopardy. But its strength is to be seen in its ability to survive the shock. Moreover, the whole of India is not touched. Those alone who have been affected by western civilisation have become enslaved. We measure the universe by our own miserable foot-rule. When we are slaves, we think that the whole universe is enslaved. Because we are in an abject condition, we think that the whole of India is in that condition. As a matter of fact, it is not so, but it is as well to impute our slavery to the whole of India. But if we bear in mind the above fact, we can see that, if we become free, India is free. And in this thought you have a definition of Swaraj. It is Swaraj when we learn to rule ourselves. It is, therefore, in the palm of our hands. Do not consider this Swaraj to be like a dream. Hence there is no idea of sitting still. The Swaraj that I wish to picture before you and me is such that, after we have once realised it, we will endeavour to the end of our life-time to persuade others to do likewise. But such Swaraj has to be experienced by each one for himself. One drowning man will never save another. Slaves ourselves, it would be a mere pretention to think of freeing others. Now you will have seen that it is not necessary for us to have as our goal the expulsion of the English. If the English become Indianised, we can accommodate them. If they wish to remain in India along with their civilisation, there is no room for them. It lies with us to bring about such a state of things.

READER: It is impossible that Englishmen should ever become Indianised.

EDITOR: To say that is equivalent to saying that the English have no humanity in them. And it is really beside the point whether they become so or not. If we keep our own house in order, only those who are fit to live in it will remain, others will leave of their own accord. Such things occur within the experience of all of us.

READER: But it has not occurred in history.

EDITOR: To believe that what has not occurred in history will not occur at all is to argue disbelief in the dignity of man. At any rate, it behoves us to try what appeals to our reason. All countries are not similarly conditioned. The condition of India is unique. Its strength is immeasurable. We need not, therefore, refer to the history of other countries. I have drawn attention to the fact that, when other civilisations have succumbed, the Indian has survived many a shock.

READER: I cannot follow this. There seems little doubt that we shall have to expel the English by force of arms. So long as they are in the country, we cannot rest. One of our poets says that slaves cannot even dream of happiness. We are day by day becoming weakened owing to the presence of the English. Our greatness is gone; our people look like terrified men. The English are in the country like a blight which we must remove by every means.

EDITOR: In your excitement, you have forgotten all we have been considering. We brought the English, and we keep them. Why do you forget that our adoption of their civilisation makes their presence in India at all possible? Your hatred against them ought to be transferred to their civilisation. But let us assume that we have to drive away the English by fighting, how is that to be done?

READER: In the same way as Italy did it. What it was possible for Mazzini and Garibaldi to do, is possible for us. You cannot deny that they were very great men. . . .

CHAPTER XV: ITALY AND INDIA

EDITOR: . . . India can fight like Italy only when she has arms. You have not considered this problem at all. The English are splendidly armed; that does not frighten me, but it is clear that, to fit ourselves against them in arms, thousands of Indians must be armed. If such a thing be possible, how many years will it take? Moreover, to arm India on a large scale is to Europeanise it. Then her condition will be just as pitiable as that of Europe. This means, in short, that India must accept European civilisation, and if that is what we want, the best thing is that we have among us those who are so well trained in that civilisation. We will then fight for a few rights, will get what we can and so pass our days. But the fact is that the Indian nation will not adopt arms, and it is well that it does not.

READER: You are over assuming facts. All need not be armed. At first, we will assassinate a few Englishmen and strike terror; then, a few men who will have been armed will fight openly. We may have to lose a quarter of a million men, more, or less, but we will regain our land. We will undertake guerrilla warfare, and defeat the English.

EDITOR: That is to say, you want to make the holy land of India unholy. Do you not tremble to think of freeing India by assassination? What we need to do is to kill ourselves. It is a cowardly thought that of killing others. Whom do you suppose to free by assassination? The millions of India do not desire it. Those who are intoxicated by the wretched modern civilisation think these things. Those who will rise to power by murder will certainly not make the nation happy. Those who believe that India has gained by Dhingra's act and such other acts in India make a serious mistake. Dhingra was a patriot, but his love was blind. He gave his body in a wrong way; its ultimate result can only be mischievous.

READER: But you will admit that the English have been frightened by these murders, and that Lord Morley's reforms are due to fear.

EDITOR: The English are both a timid and a brave nation. She is, I believe, easily influenced by the use of gunpowder. It is possible that Lord Morley has granted the reform through fear, but what is granted under fear can be retained only so long as the fear lasts.

CHAPTER XVI: BRUTE-FORCE

READER: This is a new doctrine; that what is gained through fear is retained only while the fear lasts. Surely, what is given will not be withdrawn.

EDITOR: Not so. The Proclamation of 1857 was given at the end of a revolt, and for the purpose of preserving peace. When peace was secured and people became simple-minded, its full effect was toned down. If I ceased stealing for fear of punishment, I would re-commence the operation as soon as the fear is withdrawn from me. This is almost a universal experience. We have assumed that we can get men to do things by force and, therefore, we use force.

READER: Will you not admit that you are arguing against yourself? You know that what the English obtained in their own country they have obtained by using brute-force. I know you have argued that what they have obtained is useless, but that does not affect my argument. They wanted useless things, and they got them. My point is that their desire was fulfilled. What does it matter what means they adopted? Why should we not obtain our goal, which is good, by any means whatsoever, even by using violence? Shall I think of the means when I have to deal with a thief in the house? My duty is to drive him out anyhow. You seem to admit that we have received nothing, and that we shall receive nothing by petitioning. Why, then, may we not do so by using brute-force? And, to retain what we may receive we shall keep up the fear by using the same force to the extent that it may be necessary. You will not find fault with a continuance of force to prevent a child from thrusting its foot into fire? Somehow or other, we have to gain our end.

EDITOR: Your reasoning is plausible. It has deluded many. I have used similar arguments before now. But I think I know better now, and I shall endeavour to undeceive you. Let us first take the argument that we are justified in gaining our end by using brute-force, because the English gained theirs by using similar means. It is perfectly true that they used brute-force, and that it is possible for us to do likewise, but, by using similar means, we can get only the same thing that they got. You will admit that we do not want that. Your belief that there is no connection between the means and the end is a great mistake. Through that mistake even men who have been considered religious have committed grievous crimes. Your reasoning is the same as saying that we can get a rose through planting a noxious weed. If I want to cross the ocean, I can do so only by means of a vessel; if I were to use a cart for that purpose, both the cart and I would soon find the bottom. "As is the God, so is the votary" is a maxim worth considering. Its meaning has been distorted, and men have gone astray. The means may be likened to a seed, the end to a tree; and there is just the same inviolable connection between the means and the end as there is between the seed and the tree. I am not likely to obtain the result flowing from the worship of God by laying myself prostrate before Satan. If, therefore, anyone were to say, "I want to worship God, it does not matter that I do so by means of Satan," it would be set down as ignorant folly. We reap exactly as we sow. The English in 1833 obtained greater voting power by violence. Did they by using brute force better appreciate their duty? They wanted the right of voting, which they obtained by using physical force. But real rights are a result of performance of duty; these rights they have not obtained. We, therefore, have before us in England the farce of everybody wanting and insisting on his rights, nobody thinking of his duty. And, where everybody wants rights, who shall give them to whom? I do not wish to imply that they never perform their duty, but I do wish to imply that they do not perform the duty to which those rights should correspond; and, as they do not perform that particular duty, namely, acquire fitness, their rights have proved a burden to them. In other words, what they have obtained is an exact result of the means they adopted. They used the means corresponding to the end. If I want to deprive you of your watch, I shall certainly have to fight for it; if I want to buy your watch, I shall have to pay you for it; and, if I want a gift, I shall have to plead for it; and, according to the means I employ, the watch is stolen property, my own property, or a donation. Thus we see three different results from three different means. Will you still say that means do not matter?

Now we shall take the example given by you of the thief to be driven out. I do not agree with you that the thief may be driven out by any means. If it is my father who has come to steal, I shall use one kind of means. If it is an acquaintance, I shall use another, and, in the case of a perfect stranger, I shall use a third. If it is a white man, you will perhaps say, you will use means different from those you will adopt with an Indian thief. If it is a weakling, the means will be different from those to be adopted for dealing with an equal in physical strength; and, if the thief is armed from tip to toe, I shall simply remain quiet. Thus we have a variety of means between the father and the armed man. Again, I fancy that I should pretend to be sleeping whether the thief was my father or that strong armed man. The reason for this is that my father would also be armed, and I should succumb to the strength possessed by either, and allow my things to be stolen. The strength of my father would make me weep with pity; the strength of the armed man would rouse in me anger, and we should become enemies. Such is the curious situation. From these examples, we may not be able to agree as to the means to be adopted in each case. I myself seem clearly to see what should be done in all these cases, but the remedy may frighten you. I, therefore, hesitate to place it before you. For the time being, I will leave you to guess it, and, if you cannot, it is clear that you will have to adopt different means in each case. You will also have seen that any means will not avail to drive away the thief. You will have to adopt means to fit each case. Hence it follows that your duty is not to drive away the thief by any means you like.

Let us proceed a little further. That well-armed man has stolen your property, you have harboured the thought, you are filled with anger; you argue that you want to punish that rogue, not for your own sake, but for the good of your neighbours; you have collected a number of armed men, you want to take his house by assault, he is duly informed of it, he runs away; he, too, is incensed. He collects his brother-robbers, and sends you a defiant message that he will commit robbery in broad daylight. You are strong, you do not fear him, you are prepared to receive him. Meanwhile, the robber pesters your neighbours. They complain before you, you reply that you are doing all for their sake, you do not mind that your own goods have been stolen. Your neighbours reply that the robber never pestered them before, and that he commenced his depredations only after you declared hostilities against him. You are between Scylla and Charybdis. You are full of pity for the poor men. What they say is true. What are you to do? You will be disgraced if you now leave the robber alone. You, therefore, tell the poor men: "Never mind. Come, my wealth is yours, I will give you arms, I will teach you how to use them; you should belabour the rogue; don't you leave him alone." And so the battle grows; the robbers increase in numbers; your neighbours have deliberately put themselves to inconvenience. Thus the result of wanting to take revenge upon the robber is that you have disturbed your own peace; you are in perpetual fear of being robbed and assaulted; your courage has given place to cowardice. If you will patiently examine the argument, you will see that I have not overdrawn the picture. This is one of the means. Now let us examine the other. You set this armed robber down as an ignorant brother; you intend to reason with him at a suitable opportunity; you argue that he is, after all, a fellow-man; you do not know what prompted him to steal. You, therefore, decide that, when you can, you will destroy the man's motive for stealing. Whilst you are thus reasoning with yourself, the man comes again to steal. Instead of being angry with him, you take pity on him. You think that this stealing habit must be a disease with him. Henceforth, you, therefore, keep your doors and windows open; you change your sleeping-place, and you keep your things in a manner most accessible to him. The robber comes again, and is confused, as all this is new to him; nevertheless, he takes away your things. But his mind is agitated. He inquires about you in the village, he comes to learn about your broad and loving heart, he repents, he begs your pardon, returns you your things, and leaves off the stealing habit. He becomes your servant, and you find for him honourable employment. This is the second method. Thus, you see different means have brought about totally different results. I do not wish to deduce from this that robbers will act in the above manner or that all will have the same pity and love like you, but I wish only to show that only fair means can produce fair results, and that, at least in the majority of cases, if not, indeed, in all, the force of love and pity is infinitely greater than the force of arms. There is harm in the exercise of brute-force, never in that of pity. . . .

CHAPTER XVII: PASSIVE RESISTANCE

READER: Is there any historical evidence as to the success of what you have called soul-force or truth-force? No instance seems to have happened of any nation having risen through soul-force. I still think that the evil-doers will not cease doing evil without physical punishment.

EDITOR: The poet Tulsidas has said "Of religion, pity or love is the root as egotism of the body. Therefore, we should not abandon pity so long as we are alive." This appears to me to be a scientific truth. I believe in it as much as I believe in two and two being four. The force of love is the same as the force of the soul or truth. We have evidence of its working at every step. The universe would disappear without the existence of that force. But you ask for historical evidence. It is, therefore, necessary to know what history means. The Gujarati equivalent means: "It so happened." If that is the meaning of history, it is possible to give copious evidence. But, if it means the doings of kings and emperors, there can be no evidence of soul-force or passive resistance in such history. You cannot expect silver-ore in a tin-mine. History, as we know it, is a record of the wars of the world, and so there is a proverb among Englishmen that a nation which has no history, that is, no wars, is a happy nation. How kings played, how they became enemies of one another and how they murdered one another is found accurately recorded in history and, if this were all that had happened in the world it would have been ended long ago. If the story of the universe had commenced with wars, not a man would have been found alive to-day. Those people who have been warred against have disappeared, as, for instance, the natives of Australia, of whom hardly a man was left alive by the intruders. Mark, please, that these natives did not use soul-force in self-defence, and it does not require much foresight to know that the Australians will share the same fate as their victims. "Those that wield the sword shall perish by the sword." With us, the proverb is that professional swimmers will find a watery grave.

The fact that there are so many men still alive in the world shows that it is based not on the force of arms but on the force of truth or love. Therefore, the greatest and most unimpeachable evidence of the success of this force is to be found in the fact that, in spite of the wars of the world, it still lives on.

Thousands, indeed tens of thousands, depend for their existence on a very active working of this force. Little quarrels of millions of families in their daily lives disappear before the exercise of this force. Hundreds of nations live in peace. History does not, and cannot, take note of this fact. History is really a record of every interruption of the even working of the force of love or of the soul. Two brothers quarrel; one of them repents and reawakens the love that was lying dormant in him; the two again begin to live in peace; nobody takes note of this. But, if the two brothers, through the intervention of solicitors or some other reason, take up arms or go to law—which is another form of the exhibition of brute-force—their doings would be immediately noticed in the press, they would be the talk of their neighbours, and would probably go down to history. And what is true of families and communities is true of nations. There is no reason to believe that there is one law for families, and another for nations. History, then, is a record of an interruption of the course of nature. Soul-force, being natural, is not noted in history.

READER: According to what you say, it is plain that instances of the kind of passive resistance are not to be found in history. It is necessary to understand this passive resistance more fully. It will be better, therefore, if you enlarge upon it.

EDITOR: Passive resistance is a method of securing rights by personal suffering; it is the reverse of resistance by arms. When I refuse to do a thing that is repugnant to my conscience, I use soul-force. For instance, the government of the day has passed a law which is applicable to me. I do not like it. If, by using violence, I force the government to repeal the law, I am employing what may be termed body-force. If I do not obey the law, and accept the penalty for its breach, I use soul-force. It involves sacrifice of self.

Everybody admits that sacrifice of self is infinitely superior to sacrifice of others. Moreover, if this kind of force is used in a cause that is unjust, only the person using it suffers. He does not make others suffer for his mistakes. Men have before now done many things which were subsequently found to have been wrong. No man can claim to be absolutely in the right, or that a particular thing is wrong, because he thinks so, but it is wrong for him so long as that is his deliberate judgment. It is, therefore, meet that he should not do that which he knows to be wrong, and suffer the consequence whatever it may be. This is the key to the use of soul-force.

READER: You would then disregard laws—this is rank disloyalty. We have always been considered a law-abiding nation. You seem to be going even beyond the extremists. They say that we must obey the laws that have been passed, but that, if the laws be bad, we must drive out the law-givers even by force.

EDITOR: Whether I go beyond them or whether I do not is a matter of no consequence to either of us. We simply want to find out what is right, and to act accordingly. The real meaning of the statement that we are a law-abiding nation is that we are passive resisters. When we do not like certain laws, we do not break the heads of law-givers, but we suffer and do not submit to the laws. That we should obey laws whether good or bad is a new-fangled notion. There was no such thing in former days. The people disregarded those laws they did not like, and suffered the penalties for their breach. It is contrary to our manhood, if we obey laws repugnant to our conscience. Such teaching is opposed to religion, and means slavery. If the government were to ask us to go about without any clothing, should we do so? If I were a passive resister, I would say to them that I would have nothing to do with their law. But we have so forgotten ourselves and become so compliant that we do not mind any degrading law.

A man who has realised his manhood, who fears only God, will fear no-one else. Man-made laws are not necessarily binding on him. Even the government do not expect any such thing from us. They do not say: "You must do such and such a thing," but they say: "If you do not do it, we will punish you." We are sunk so low, that we fancy that it is our duty and our religion to do what the law lays down. If man will only realise that it is unmanly to obey laws that are unjust, no man's tyranny will enslave him. This is the key to self-rule or home-rule.

It is a superstition and an ungodly thing to believe that an act of a majority binds a minority. Many examples can be given in which acts of majorities will be found to have been wrong, and those of minorities to have been right. All reforms owe their origin to the initiation of minorities in opposition to majorities. If among a band of robbers, a knowledge of robbing is obligatory, is a pious man to accept the obligation? So long as the superstition that men should obey unjust laws exists, so long will their slavery exist. And a passive resister alone can remove such a superstition.

To use brute-force, to use gun-powder is contrary to passive resistance for it means that we want our opponent to do by force that which we desire but he does not. And, if such a use of force is justifiable, surely he is entitled to do likewise by us. And so we should never come to an agreement. We may simply fancy, like the blind horse moving in a circle round a mill, that we are making progress. Those who believe that they are not bound to obey laws which are repugnant to their conscience have only the remedy of passive resistance open to them. Any other must lead to disaster.

READER: From what you say, I deduce that passive resistance is a splendid weapon of the weak, but that, when they are strong, they may take up arms.

EDITOR: This is gross ignorance. Passive resistance, that is, soul-force, is matchless. It is superior to the force of arms. How, then, can it be considered only a weapon of the weak? Physical-force men are strangers to the courage that is requisite in a passive resister. Do you believe that a coward can ever disobey a law that he dislikes? Extremists are considered to be advocates of brute force. Why do they, then, talk about obeying laws? I do not blame them. They can say nothing else. When they succeed in driving out the English, and they themselves become governors, they will want you and me to obey their laws. And that is a fitting thing for their constitution. But a passive resister will say he will not obey a law that is against his conscience, even though he may be blown to pieces at the mouth of a cannon.

What do you think? Wherein is courage required—in blowing others to pieces from behind a cannon or with a smiling face to approach a cannon and to be blown to pieces? Who is the true warrior—he who keeps death always as a bosom-friend or he who controls the death of others? Believe me that a man devoid of courage and manhood can never be a passive resister.

This, however, I will admit: that even a man weak in body is capable of offering this resistance. One man can offer it just as well as millions. Both men and women can indulge in it. It does not require the training of an army; it needs no Jiu-jitsu. Control over the mind is alone necessary, and, when that is attained, man is free like the king of the forest, and his very glance withers the enemy.

Passive resistance is an all-sided sword; it can be used anyhow; it blesses him who uses it and him against whom it is used. Without drawing a drop of blood, it produces far-reaching results. It never rusts, and cannot be stolen. Competition between passive resisters does not exhaust. The sword of passive resistance does not require a scabbard. It is strange indeed that you should consider such a weapon to be a weapon merely of the weak. . . .

Passive resistance has been described in the course of our discussion as truth-force. Truth, therefore, has necessarily to be followed, and that at any cost. In this connection, academic questions such as whether a man may not lie in order to save a life, etc. arise, but these questions occur only to those who wish to justify lying. Those who want to follow truth every time are not placed in such a quandary, and, if they are, they are still saved from a false position.

Passive resistance cannot proceed a step without fearlessness. Those alone can follow the path of passive resistance who are free from fear, whether as to their possessions, false honour, their relatives, the government, bodily injuries, death.

These observances are not to be abandoned in the belief that they are difficult. Nature has implanted in the human breast ability to cope with any difficulty or suffering that may come to man unprovoked. These qualities are worth having, even for those who do not wish to serve the country. Let there be no mistake as those who want to train themselves in the use of arms are also obliged to have these qualities more or less. Everybody does not become a warrior for the wish. A would-be warrior will have to observe chastity, and to be satisfied with poverty as his lot. A warrior without fearlessness cannot be conceived of. It may be thought that he would not need to be exactly truthful, but that quality follows real fearlessness. When a man abandons truth, he does so owing to fear in some shape or form. The above four attributes, then, need not frighten anyone. It may be as well here to note that a physical-force man has to have many other useless qualities which a passive resister never needs. And you will find that whatever extra effort a swordsman needs is due to lack of fearlessness. If he is an embodiment of the latter, the sword will drop from his hand that very moment. He does not need its support. One who is free from hatred requires no sword. A man with a stick suddenly came face to face with a lion, and instinctively raised his weapon in self-defence. The man saw that he had only prated about fearlessness when there was none in him. That moment he dropped the stick, and found himself free from all fear.

JAWAHARLAL NEHRU

AMONG the leaders of the Indian independence movement, Gandhi was regarded with veneration, but also with dismay. For while Gandhi was the spirit of the struggle, his daily conduct of affairs was often inconsistent and visionary. Few educated Indians were prepared to follow their leader into the life of a religious ascetic, nor were they prepared to reject entirely those Western social, economic, and political techniques which might be useful in the solution of the grave problems which India faced. Most of Gandhi's lieutenants were men who had received their education in British schools; these men looked to Western institutions as well as to Indian traditions for guidance. The achievement of India's freedom may indeed have depended upon Mahatma Gandhi, but her survival as a state now depends on men of the type of Jawaharlal Nehru.

Born in Allahabad in 1889 of a wealthy Kashmiri Brahmin family, Nehru passed a lonely childhood under the direction of an English governess and tutor; the English tongue was almost more native to him than any Indian language. At sixteen years of age, Nehru, accompanied by his entire family, went to England, where he was enrolled in Harrow. From that "public school" he went to Cambridge for the classical education of a British aristocrat, and from there to two additional years of law study at the Inner Temple in London. During holidays and vacations, he toured widely on the Continent, and did not return to India until his education was completed.

Yet (as was the case also with Gandhi himself), this experience of England and Europe seemed to define and confirm Nehru's sense of being Indian. Almost immediately upon his return to his homeland he plunged into politics, becoming an ardent follower of Gandhi. In this enterprise he was aided by his father and mother, who were already engaged in the Indian independence movement. Young Nehru quickly emerged as one of the few leaders of the Congress (nationalist) Party to achieve a stature comparable to that of Gandhi. Throughout the 1920's, 1930's, and early 1940's, Nehru's life was dedicated to the goal of independence. It was spent in a fever of political activity, in civil disobedience campaigns, strikes, and agitations; these activities were punctuated periodically by prison sentences. In all he passed a full ten years within the walls of British jails. His father died as a result of imprisonment; his mother's death was in part caused by a beating she received at the hands of the British police. A man of quick temper and deeply emotional nature, Nehru still bore these ordeals with fortitude. Moreover they but increased his political stature among the Indians. Always suspicious of the Japanese and opposed to any form of totalitarianism, he was, nonetheless, jailed in 1942 for protesting the imperial mandate that made India a belligerent alongside Britain in World War II without the consent of the Indians. He spent the remainder of the war behind bars; but at the termination of hostilities he was released, partly because he was needed to maintain order in the country, partly because, with the election of a Labor government in Britain, some form of Indian independence now seemed inevitable. The final, hectic, and by no means non-violent campaign for freedom—a campaign aggravated by the bitter animosity of Moslem toward Hindu—now took place. In 1947 India (less Pakistan) was made a free republic with tenuous connections with the British Commonwealth of Nations. Jawaharlal Nehru became the new state's first prime minister.

The following selection consists, first, of letters which Nehru wrote to his daughter Indira and which were published in 1942 in his book *Glimpses of World History;* and, second, of an article which Nehru wrote, late in 1937, and which first appeared in the American journal *Foreign Affairs* (Jan., 1938).

GLIMPSES OF WORLD HISTORY

August 7, 1933

Of the writing of letters there is no end so long as pen and paper and ink hold out. And of writing on world happenings also there is no end, for this world of ours rolls on, and the men and women and children in it laugh and weep, and love and hate, and fight each other unceasingly. It is a story that goes on and on and has no ending. And in the to-day in which we live, life seems to be flowing faster than ever, its tempo is swifter, and changes come rapidly one after the other. Even as I write it changes, and what I write to-day may be out of date, distant, and perhaps out of place, to-morrow. The river of life is never still; it flows on, and sometimes, as now, it rushes forward, pitilessly, with a demon energy, ignoring our little wills and desires, making cruel mock of our petty selves, and tossing us about like straws on its turbulent waters, rushing on and on no one knows whither—to a great precipice which will shatter it into a thousand bits, or to the vast and inscrutable, stately and calm, ever-changing and yet changeless sea.

I have written already far more than I ever intended or than I ought to have done. My pen has run on. We have finished our long wandering and have completed the last long stage. We have reached to-day and stand on the threshold of to-morrow, wondering what it will be like when it also, in its turn, becomes to-day. Let us pause a little and look around the world. How does it stand on this seventh day of August nineteen hundred and thirty-three?

In India Gandhiji has again been arrested and sentenced and is back in

This selection has been reprinted from *Glimpses of World History* by Jawaharlal Nehru, Copyright, 1942 by The John Day Company, Inc., New York (pp. 936–940, 945–948) and used by permission of the publisher.

Yervada Prison. Civil Disobedience has been resumed, though in a restricted form, and our comrades go to gaol again. A brave and dear comrade, a friend whom I first met a quarter of a century ago when I was new at Cambridge, Jatindra Mohan Sen-Gupta, has just left us, dying as a prisoner of the British Government. Life merges into death, but the great work to make life worth living for the people of India goes on. Many thousands of India's sons and daughters, the most spirited and often the most gifted, lie in prison or internment camps, spending their youth and energy in conflict against the existing system which enslaves India. All this life and energy might have gone in a building up, in construction; there is so much to be done in this world. But before the construction must come destruction, so that the ground may be cleared for the new structure. We cannot put up a fine building on top of the mud walls of a hovel. The state of India to-day can best be appreciated by the fact that in certain parts of India in Bengal even the manner of dress is regulated by government order, and to dress otherwise means prison. And in Chittagong even little boys (and presumably little girls also) of twelve and upwards have to carry about identity cards with them wherever they go. I do not know if such an extraordinary order has ever been enforced elsewhere, even in Nazi-ridden Germany, or in a war area occupied by enemy troops. We are indeed a ticket-of-leave nation to-day under British rule. And across our north-west frontier our neighbours are being bombed by British aeroplanes.

Our fellow-countrymen in other countries have little honour shown to them; they are seldom made welcome anywhere. And this is not surprising, for how can they have honour elsewhere when they have no honour at home? They are being turned out of South Africa where they were born and bred, and some parts of which, especially in Natal, they had built up with their labour. Colour prejudice, racial hatred, economic conflict, all combine to make these Indians in South Africa castaways with no home or refuge. They must be shipped away to some other place, to British Guiana, or back to India, where they can but starve, or anywhere else, says the Government of the Union of South Africa, so long as they leave South Africa for good.

In East Africa, Indians have played a great part in building up Kenya and the surrounding territories. But they are no longer welcome there; not because the Africans object, but because the handful of European planters object to them. The best areas, the highlands, are reserved for these planters, and neither African nor Indian may possess land there. The poor Africans are far worse off. Originally all the land was in their possession and was their only source of income. Huge areas of this were confiscated by the government, and free grants of land were made to the European settlers. These settlers or planters are thus big landholders there now. They pay no income-tax and hardly any other tax. Almost the whole burden of taxation falls on the poor down-trodden African. It was not easy to tax the African, for he possesses next to nothing. A tax was put on certain necessaries of life for him, like flour and clothing, and indirectly he had to pay it when he bought them. But the most extraordinary tax of all was a direct hut and poll tax on every male over sixteen years old and his dependants, which included women. The principle of taxation is that people should be taxed out of what they earn or possess. As the African possessed practically nothing else, his body was taxed! But how was he to pay this poll tax of twelve shillings per person per year if he had no money? Therein lay the craftiness of this tax, for it forced him to earn some money by working on the plantations of the European settlers, and thus paying the tax. It was a device not only to get money, but also cheap labour for the plantations. So these unhappy Africans sometimes have to travel enormous distances, coming from the interior 700 or 800 miles away to the plantations near the coast (there are no railways in the interior and just a few near the coast), in order to earn enough wages to pay their poll tax.

There is so much more that I could tell you of those poor exploited Africans who do not even know how to make their voices heard by the outside world. Their tale of misery is a long one, and they suffer in silence. Driven off from their best lands, they had to return to them as tenants of the Europeans, who got the land free at the expense of these Africans. These European landlords are semi-feudal masters, and every kind of activity which they dislike has been suppressed. The Africans cannot form any association even to advocate reforms as the collection of any money is forbidden. There is even an ordinance proscribing dancing, because the Africans sometimes mimicked and made fun of European ways in their songs and dances! The peasantry are very poor, and they are not allowed to grow tea or coffee because this would compete with the European planters.

Three years ago the British Government solemnly announced that they were trustees for the African, and that in future he would not be deprived of his lands. Unfortunately for the Africans, gold was discovered in Kenya last year. The solemn promise was forgotten; the European planters made a rush for this land, turned out the African farmers, and started digging for gold. So much for British promises. We are told that all this will eventually work out for the advantage of the Africans, and that they are quite happy at losing their lands!

This capitalist method of exploiting a gold-bearing area is most extraordinary. People are actually made to run for it from a prescribed place, and each one takes possession of part of the area and then works it. Whether he finds much gold or not in that particular bit depends on his luck. This method is typical of capitalism. The obvious way to deal with a gold-field seems to be for the government of the country to take possession of it and work it for the advantage of the whole State. This is what the Soviet Union is doing with its gold-fields in Tadjikistan and elsewhere.

I have said something about Kenya . . . because we . . . [tend to ignore] Africa. . . . Remember it is a vast continent full of the African races who have been cruelly exploited by foreigners for hundreds of years, and are still exploited. They are terribly backward, but they have been kept down, and not given the chance to go ahead. Where this chance has been given them, as recently at a university founded on the west coast, they have made remarkable progress.

. . . [In] the countries of western Asia . . . and in Egypt, the struggle for freedom goes on in various forms and in various stages. So also in south-east Asia, in Farther India and Indonesia—Siam, Indo-China, Java, Sumatra and the Dutch Indies, the Philippine Islands. And everywhere, except in Siam, which is independent, the struggle has two aspects: the nationalist urge against foreign domination and the urge of the down-trodden classes for social equality or at least economic betterment.

In the Far East of Asia, giant China lies helpless before her aggressors, and is torn by internal dissension into many bits. One of her faces is turned towards communism, and the other is turned violently away from it, and meanwhile Japan marches forward, almost inexorably, and establishes her hold on large areas of Chinese territory. But China has survived many a mighty invasion and danger in the long course of her history, and there is little doubt that she will survive the Japanese invasion.

Imperialist Japan, semi-feudal, military-ridden, and yet industrially highly advanced, a strange mixture of the past and the present, nurses ambitious dreams of world empire. But behind these dreams lies the reality of threatening economic collapse and terrible misery for her teeming population, which is shut out from America and the vast uninhabited spaces of Australia. And a tremendous check to these dreams also lies in the hostility of the United States, the most powerful of modern nations. Soviet Russia is another powerful check to Japanese expansion in Asia. In Manchuria and over the deep waters of the Pacific Ocean many keen-eyed observers can already see the approaching shadow of a great war.

The whole of northern Asia is part of the Soviet Union, and is absorbed in planning and building a new world and a new social order. It is strange that these backward countries that civilization had left behind in its march, and where a kind of feudalism still prevailed, should have jumped forward to a stage which is ahead of the advanced nations of the West. The Soviet Union in Europe and Asia stands to-day a continuing challenge to the tottering capitalism of the western world. While trade depression and slump and unemployment and repeated crises paralyse capitalism, and the old order gasps for breath, the Soviet Union is a land full of hope and energy and enthusiasm, feverishly building away and establishing the socialist order. And this abounding youth and life, and the success the Soviet has already achieved, are impressing and attracting thinking people all over the world.

The United States of America, another vast area, is typical of the failure of capitalism. In the midst of great difficulties, crises, labour strikes, and unexampled unemployment, she is making a brave effort to pull together and preserve the capitalist system. The result of this great experiment remains to be seen. But whatever that may be, nothing can take away from America the great advantages that she possesses in her wide territories, rich in almost everything that man requires, and in her technical resources, which are greater than those of any other country, and in her skilled and highly-trained people. The United States, as also the Soviet Union, is bound to play a vastly important part in the world affairs of the future. . . .

August 8, 1933

. . . So you see what a curious chequer-board Europe is at present, with its conflicts and hatreds, and rival groups of nations glaring at each other. There is interminable talk of disarmament, and yet everywhere there is arming going on and new and terrible weapons of war and destruction are being invented. There is also plenty of talk of international co-operation, and conferences without number have been held. All to little purpose. The League of Nations itself is a pitiful failure, and the last effort to pull together at the World Economic Conference has also come and gone with no success. There is a proposal that the various countries of Europe, or rather Europe without Russia, should join together to form a kind of United States of Europe. The "Pan-Europe" movement this is called, and it is really an effort to form an anti-Soviet *bloc,* as well as to get over the innumerable difficulties and tangles due to there being such a large number of little nations. But national hatreds are far too powerful for any one to pay attention to such a proposal.

In reality each country is drifting farther apart from the others. The slump and world crisis have quickened this process by pushing all countries along the lines of economic nationalism. Each sits behind high tariff barriers and tries to keep out as far as possible foreign goods. It cannot, of course, keep out all foreign goods, because no country is self-sufficient—that is, capable of producing everything it requires. But the tendency is for it to grow or manufacture everything it needs. Some essential articles it may not be able to grow because of its climate. For instance, England cannot grow cotton or jute or tea or coffee and many other articles which require a warmer climate. This means that in future trade will be largely confined between countries having different climates, and therefore growing and making different articles. Countries manufacturing the same type of articles will have little use for each other's goods. Thus trade will go north and south, and not east and west, for climates vary north and south. A tropical country may deal with a temperate or cold country, but not two tropical countries with each other, or two temperate countries. Of course there may be other considerations also, such as the mineral resources of a country. But in the main the north and south considerations will apply to international trade. All other trade will be stopped by tariff barriers.

This seems to be an inevitable tendency to-day. It is called the final phase in the industrial revolution when each country is sufficiently industrialized. It is true that Asia and Africa are far from industrialized yet. Africa is too backward and too poor to absorb manufactured goods in any quantity. The three large areas which might continue to absorb such foreign goods are India, China, and Siberia. Foreign industrial countries are looking eagerly towards these three huge potential markets. Having been cut off from many of their usual markets, they are thinking of this "push towards Asia," in order to dispose of their surplus goods, and thus prop up their tottering capitalism. But it is not so easy to exploit Asia now, partly because of the development of Asiatic industries, and partly because of international rivalry. England wants to keep India as a market for her own goods, but Japan and the United States and Germany want a look in also. So also in China; and to add to this is her present disturbed state and want of proper communications, which make trade difficult. Soviet Russia is prepared to take quite a lot of manufactured goods from abroad if she is given credit and not asked to pay for them immediately. But very soon the Soviet Union will make almost everything it requires.

The whole past tendency has been towards greater interdependence between nations, a greater internationalism. Even though separate independent national States remained, an enormous and intricate structure of international relations and trade grew up. This process went so far as to conflict with the National States and with nationalism itself. The next natural step was a socialized international structure. Capitalism, having had its day, had reached the stage when it was time for it to retire in favour of socialism. But unhappily such a voluntary retirement never takes place. Because crisis and collapse threatened it, it has withdrawn into its shell and tried to reverse the past tendency towards interdependence. Hence economic nationalism. The question is if this can succeed, and even if it does so, for how long?

The whole world is a strange mix-up, a terrible tangle of conflicts and jealousies, and the new tendencies but increase the field of these conflicts. In every continent, in every country, the weak and the oppressed want to share in the good things of life which they themselves help to produce. They claim payment of their debt, long overdue to them. In some places they are doing so loudly and harshly and aggressively; in other places more quietly. Can we blame them if, angry and bitter at the treatment and exploitation they have been subjected to for so long, they act in a manner we do not like? They were ignored and looked down upon; no one took the trouble to teach them drawing-room manners.

This upheaval of the weak and the oppressed frightens the possessing classes everywhere, and they band themselves together to suppress it. And thus fascism grows and imperialism crushes all opposition. The fine phrases about democracy and the people's good and trusteeship retire into the background, and the naked rule of the possessing classes and vested interests becomes more obvious, and in many places it seems to meet with triumph. A harsher age appears, an age of iron and aggressive violence, for everywhere the fight is one of life and death between the old order and the new. Everywhere, whether it is in Europe or America or India, the stakes are high and the fate of the old regime hangs in the balance, even though for the moment it may be strongly entrenched. Partial reform does not meet or solve the problems of the day when the whole imperialist-capitalist system is shaken to its foundation and cannot even meet its liabilities or the demands made upon it.

All these innumerable conflicts, political, economic, racial, darken the world to-day, and carry the shadow of war with them. It is said that the greatest of these conflicts, the most fundamental of them, is the one between imperialism and fascism on the one side and communism on the other. These face each other all over the world, and between them there is no room for compromise.

Feudalism, capitalism, socialism, syndicalism, anarchism, communism—so many isms! And behind them all stalks opportunism! But there is also idealism for those who care to have it; not the idealism of empty fancies and an imagination run riot, but the idealism of working for a great human purpose, a great ideal which we seek to make real. Somewhere George Bernard Shaw has said:—

> This is the true joy in life, the being used for a purpose recognized by yourself as a mighty one; the being thoroughly worn out before you are thrown on the scrap heap; the being a force of nature, instead of a feverish, selfish little clod of ailments and grievances, complaining that the world will not devote itself to making you happy.

. . . The world has indeed become one single inseparable whole, each part influencing, and being influenced by, the other. It is quite impossible now to have a separate history of nations. We have outgrown that stage, and only a single world history, connecting the different threads from all the nations, and seeking to find the real forces that move them, can now be written with any useful purpose.

Even in past times, when nations were cut off from each other by many physical and other barriers, we have seen how common international and intercontinental forces shaped them. Great individuals have always counted in history, for the human factor is important in every crisis of destiny; but greater than any individual are the mighty forces at work which, almost blindly and sometimes cruelly, forge ahead, pushing us hither and thither.

So it is to-day with us. Mighty forces are at work moving the hundreds of millions of human beings, and they go ahead like an earthquake or some other upheaval of Nature. We cannot stop them, however much we may try, and yet we may, in our own little corner of the world, make some slight difference to them in speed or direction. According to our different temperaments we meet them—some frightened by them, others welcoming them, some trying to combat them, others submitting helplessly to the heavy hand of fate, while still others try to ride the tempest and control it a little and direct it, willingly facing the perils that this involves for the joy of helping actively in a mighty process.

There is no peace for us in this turbulent twentieth century, a third of which has already passed with its full complement of war and revolution. "The whole world is in revolution," says the great fascist, Mussolini. "Events themselves are a tremendous force pushing us on like some implacable will." And the great Communist, Trotsky, also warns us of this century not to expect too much of peace and comfort. "It is clear," he says, "that the twentieth century is the most disturbed century within the memory of humanity. Any contemporary of ours who wants peace and comfort before anything else has chosen a bad time to be born."

The whole world is in labour, and the shadow of war and revolution lies heavy everywhere. If we cannot escape from this inevitable destiny of ours, how shall we face it? Ostrich-like, shall we hide our heads from it? Or shall we play a brave part in the shaping of events and, facing risks and perils if need be, have the joy of great and noble adventure, and the feeling that our "steps are merging with those of history"? . . .

We have finished, my dear; the long story has ended. I need write no more, but the desire to end off with a kind of flourish induces me to write another letter—the Last Letter!

It was time I finished, for the end of my two-year term draws near. In three and thirty days from to-day I should be discharged, if indeed I am not released sooner, as the gaoler sometimes threatens to do. The full two years are not over yet, but I have received three and a half months' remission of my sentence, as all well-behaved prisoners do. For I am supposed to be a well-behaved prisoner, a reputation which I have certainly done nothing to deserve. So ends my sixth sentence, and I shall go out again into the wide world, but to what purpose? *A quoi bon?* When most of my friends and comrades lie in gaol and the whole country seems a vast prison.

What a mountain of letters I have written! And what a lot of good *swadeshi* [1] ink I have spread out on *swadeshi* paper. Was it worth while, I wonder? Will all this paper and ink convey any message to you that will interest you? You will say, yes, of course, for you will feel that any other answer might hurt me, and you are too partial to me to take such a risk. But whether you care for them or not, you cannot grudge me the joy of having written them, day after day, during these two long years. It was winter when I came. Winter gave place to our brief spring, slain all too soon by the summer heat; and then, when the ground was parched and dry and men and beasts panted for breath, came the monsoon, with its bountiful supply of fresh and cool rain-water. Autumn followed, and the sky was wonderfully clear and blue and the afternoons were pleasant. The year's cycle was over, and again it began: winter and spring and summer and the rainy season. I have sat here, writing to you and thinking of you, and watched the seasons go by, and listened to the pitapat of the rain on my barrack roof—

> *"O doux bruit de la pluie,*
> *Parterre et sur les toits!*
> *Pour un coeur qui s'ennuie,*
> *Oh! le chant de la pluie!"* [2]

[1] *Swadeshi* means made in one's own country.

[2] [*"Oh, sweet sound of the rain, / On streets and on roof-tops! / For a wearied heart, / Oh! the song of the rain!"*]

Benjamin Disraeli, the great English statesman of the nineteenth century, has written: "Other men condemned to exile and captivity, if they survive, despair; the man of letters may reckon those days as the sweetest of his life." He was writing about Hugo Grotius, a famous Dutch jurist and philosopher of the seventeenth century, who was condemned to imprisonment for life, but managed to escape after two years. He spent these two years in prison in philosophic and literary work. There have been many famous gaolbirds, the two best known perhaps being the Spaniard, Cervantes, who wrote *Don Quixote,* and the Englishman, John Bunyan, the author of *The Pilgrim's Progress*. . . .

The past brings us many gifts; indeed, all that we have to-day of culture, civilization, science, or knowledge of some aspects of the truth, is a gift of the distant or recent past to us. It is right that we acknowledge our obligation to the past. But the past does not exhaust our duty or obligation. We owe a duty to the future also, and perhaps that obligation is even greater than the one we owe to the past. For the past is past and done with, we cannot change it; the future is yet to come, and perhaps we may be able to shape it a little. If the past has given us some part of the truth, the future also hides many aspects of the truth, and invites us to search for them. But often the past is jealous of the future and holds us in a terrible grip, and we have to struggle with it to get free to face and advance towards the future.

History, it is said, has many lessons to teach us; and there is another saying that history never repeats itself. Both are true, for we cannot learn anything from it by slavishly trying to copy it, or by expecting it to repeat itself or remain stagnant; but we can learn something from it by prying behind it and trying to discover the forces that move it. Even so, what we get is seldom a straight answer. "History," says Karl Marx, "has no other way of answering old questions than by putting new ones."

The old days were days of faith, blind, unquestioning faith. The wonderful temples and mosques and cathedrals of past centuries could never have been built but for the overpowering faith of the architects and builders and people generally. The very stones that they reverently put one on top of the other or carved into beautiful designs, tell us of this faith. The old temple spire, the mosque with its slender minarets, the Gothic cathedral—all of them pointing upward with an amazing intensity of devotion, as if offering a prayer in stone or marble to the sky above—thrill us even now, though we may be lacking in that faith of old of which they are the embodiments. But the days of that faith are gone, and gone with them is that magic touch in stone. Thousands of temples and mosques and cathedrals continue to be built, but they lack the spirit that made them live during the Middle Ages. There is little difference between them and the commercial offices which are so representative of our age.

Our age is a different one; it is an age of disillusion, of doubt and uncertainty and questioning. We can no longer accept many of the ancient beliefs and customs; we have no more faith in them, in Asia or in Europe or America. So we search for new ways, new aspects of the truth more in harmony with our environment. And we question each other and debate and quarrel and evolve any number of "isms" and philosophies. As in the days of Socrates, we live in an age of questioning, but that questioning is not confined to a city like Athens; it is world-wide.

Sometimes the injustice, the unhappiness, the brutality of the world oppress us and darken our minds, and we see no way out. With Matthew Arnold, we feel that there is no hope in the world and that all we can do is to be true to one another.

> "For the world which seems
> To lie before us, like a land of dreams,
> So various, so beautiful, so new,
> Hath really neither joy, nor love, nor light,
> Nor certitude, nor peace, nor help for pain;
> And we are here, as on a darkling plain
> Swept with confused alarms of struggle and flight,
> Where ignorant armies clash by night."

And yet if we take such a dismal view we have not learnt aright the lesson of life or of history. For history teaches us of growth and progress and of the possibility of an infinite advance for man. And life is rich and varied, and though it has many swamps and marshes and muddy places, it has also the great sea, and the mountains, and snow, and glaciers, and wonderful starlit nights (especially in gaol!), and the love of family and friends, and the comradeship of workers in a common cause, and music, and books and the empire of ideas. So that each one of us may well say:—

> "Lord, though I lived on earth, the child of earth,
> Yet was I fathered by the starry sky."

It is easy to admire the beauties of the universe and to live in a world of thought and imagination. But to try to escape in this way from the unhappiness of others, caring little what happens to them, is no sign of courage or fellow-feeling. Thought, in order to justify itself, must lead to action.

"Action is the end of thought," says our friend Romain Rolland. "All thought which does not look towards action is an abortion and a treachery. If then we are the servants of thought we must be the servants of action."

People avoid action often because they are afraid of the consequences, for action means risk and danger. Danger seems terrible from a distance; it is not so bad if you have a close look at it. And often it is a pleasant companion, adding to the zest and delight of life. The ordinary course of life becomes dull at times, and we take too many things for granted and have no joy in them. And yet how we appreciate these common things of life when we have lived without them for a while! Many people go up high mountains and risk life and limb for the joy of the climb and the exhilaration that comes from a difficulty surmounted, a danger overcome; and because of the danger that hovers all around them, their perceptions get keener, their joy of the life which hangs by a thread, the more intense.

All of us have our choice of living in the valleys below, with their unhealthy mists and fogs, but giving a measure of bodily security; or of climbing the high mountains, with risk and danger for companions, to breathe the pure air above, and take joy in the distant views, and welcome the rising sun. . . .

THE UNITY OF INDIA

January, 1938

Most Americans, bred in the democratic tradition, sympathize with India's struggle for freedom. They dislike empire and imperialism and the domination and exploitation of one nation by another. And yet they are perplexed when they consider the Indian problem, wondering whether it is possible to build a united and progressive nation out of the seemingly infinite diversity that makes up the fabric of Indian life. They have heard so much of the separatist elements, of the conflicts of religion and culture, of the variety of languages, of the mediaeval conditions in the semi-feudal regions of the Indian States, of social cleavages, of the general backwardness of Indian life, that doubts assail them whether it is possible to harmonize all these in a free and independent India. Can democracy be built upon such insecure foundations? Could India stand together and free, if British rule were withdrawn?

This selection has been reprinted from Jawaharlal Nehru, *The Unity of India: Collected Writings, 1937–1940* by permission of The John Day Company, New York, publishers, pp. 11–26.

These hesitations and perplexities are natural. The questions in which they originate must be considered by us dispassionately, and we must attempt to find the right answers. Freedom for a nation and a people may be, and is, I believe, always good in the long run; but in the final analysis freedom itself is a means to an end, that end being the raising of the people in question to higher levels and hence the general advancement of humanity. The vital and most important problem that faces us in India is the appalling poverty of the people. Will political independence help us to diminish this, as well as the numerous ills that flow from it?

It is well to remember that the British have been in effective control of India for more than a hundred and fifty years and that during this period they have had almost complete freedom to act in any manner they chose. No democratic or any other kind of control in fact existed, the British Parliament being too far away and too ignorant to intervene. India was, and is, a rich country, rich in agricultural resources, mineral wealth, human material; only her people are poor. It was indeed the wealth of India that attracted hordes of foreign adventurers to her shores. With these resources and that human material, and following a century and a half of unchecked despotism, one is entitled to ask for substantial results. During this period Europe has changed out of recognition, Japan has transformed herself with amazing speed, America has become the wealthiest country in the world. But in India we still have grinding poverty, widespread illiteracy, a general absence of sanitation and medical relief—a lack, indeed, of all the good things of life. There are undoubtedly some good works which have followed British rule, notably in the field of irrigation. But how little they are compared to what they might have been!

It is idle to blame the Indian people for this when those people have been allowed no say in the matter. The very backwardness of a people is a condemnation of its government. With this patent result of British rule in India, little argument is needed to demonstrate its failure. But even admitting the failure, it is true that our present problems are no nearer solution. It nevertheless is well to bear the fact in mind, for the very structure of British imperialist rule has been, and is, such as to aggravate our problems and not solve any of them. And because these problems insistently demand solution we have to look for it outside the orbit of the British Empire.

India is smaller than the United States of America, yet it is a vast country and its population is far larger than that of the United States. Our problems therefore are continental. They are unlike those of the small countries of Europe. Till the advent of modern communications and modern methods of transport, it was very difficult for such a vast area to hold together politically for long. The United States grew and developed into a powerful unit, despite the vast area involved, because of the increase in transport and communications. If the United States had had a long history, going back hundreds and thousands of years before modern science and industry revolutionized life, probably the country would have been split up into many small national units, as happened in Europe. The fact that India was split up politically in the course of her long history was inevitable under the conditions then existing. Yet always the idea of the political unity of India persisted, and kings and emperors sought to realize it. Asoka indeed achieved unity two thousand years ago and built up an empire far greater than that of Britain in India to-day. It stretched right into Central Asia and included Afghanistan. Only a small part in South India remained outside, and this because of the horror of war and bloodshed that came over Asoka in the full flood of victory and conquest. Other rulers in the past tried to achieve the political unification of India and succeeded in some measure. But this desire for a unified political control of the whole country could not be realized in view of the lack of means and machinery. The coming of the British to India synchronized with the development in transport, communications and modern industry, and so it was that British rule succeeded at last in establishing political unity.

The desire for political unity, in India as in other countries before the advent of nationalism, was usually the desire of the ruler or the conqueror and not of the people as a whole. In India, where for long ages there had been a large measure of local self-government, the people were far more interested in their local freedom and rights than in the machinery of government at the top. Kings changed at the top, but the newcomers respected local rights and did not interfere with them. Because of this, conflicts between kings and people did not take place as in Europe; and later, under cover of this, kings gradually built up their autocratic power.

An all-India political unity thus was not possible in the past. What is far more important for us is to see what other more basic unifying or separatist features there were in Indian life. This will help us to understand the present and shape the future. Superficial observers of India, accustomed to the standardization which modern industry has brought about in the West, are apt to be impressed too much by the variety and diversity of India. They miss the unity of India; and yet the tremendous and fundamental fact of India is her essential unity throughout the ages. Indian history runs into thousands of years, and, of all modern nations, only China has such a continuous and ancient background of culture. Five to six thousand years ago the Indus Valley civilization flourished all over northern India and probably extended to the south also. Even then it was something highly developed, with millennia of growth behind it. Since that early dawn of history innumerable peoples, conquerors and settlers, pilgrims and students, have trekked into the Indian plains from the highlands of Asia and have influenced Indian life and culture and art; but always they have been absorbed and assimilated. India was changed by these contacts and yet she remained essentially her own old self. Like the ocean she received the tribute of a thousand rivers, and though she was disturbed often enough, and storms raged over the surface of her waters, the sea continued to be the sea. It is astonishing to note how India continued successfully this process of assimilation and adaptation. It could only have done so if the idea of a fundamental unity were so deep-rooted as to be accepted even by the newcomer, and if her culture were flexible and adaptable to changing conditions.

Vincent Smith, in his *Oxford History of India,* refers to what I have in mind: "India beyond all doubt possesses a deep underlying fundamental unity, far more profound than that produced either by geographical isolation or by political suzerainty. That unity transcends the innumerable diversities of blood, colour, language, dress, manners, and sect." And Sir Frederick Whyte, in *The Future of East and West,* also stresses this unity. He refers to the tremendous diversity of India and yet

> the greatest of all the contradictions in India is that over this diversity is spread a greater unity, which is not immediately evident because it failed historically to find expression in any political cohesion to make the country one, but which is so greatly a reality, and so powerful, that even the Musulman world in India has to confess that it has been deeply affected by coming within its influence.

This Indian background and unity were essentially cultural; they were not religious in the narrow sense of the word. That culture was not exclusive or intolerant to begin with; it was receptive and adaptable, and long ages of pre-eminence gave it deep roots and a solidarity which storms could not shake. It developed a beneficent attitude which, secure in its own strength, could afford to be tolerant and broadminded. And this very toleration gave it greater strength and adaptability. There was in it till almost the beginning of the Christian era a certain rationalism, something approaching a scientific outlook, which refused to tie itself down to dogmas. True, this culture and rationalism were largely confined to the upper classes, but they percolated down to the masses to some extent. Superstitions and dogmas and many an evil practice gradually crept in. Buddhism was a revolt against these. But the old way of life was still powerful, and it is one of the wonders of history how India succeeded in absorbing Buddhism without any physical conflict. Buddhism, which had spread throughout India and had made progress from Western Asia right across Central Asia to the Far East, gradually faded out of the land of its birth. The man who is supposed to be largely responsible for this was Shankaracharya, who lived in the eighth century after Christ. This amazingly brilliant young man travelled all over India arguing, debating, convincing large audiences, and in a few years (he died at the age of 32) changed the mental atmosphere of the country. The appeal was to reason and logic, not to force.

This practice of debate and conference over religious and other matters was common throughout India and there are records of many great gatherings from Kashmir in the north to the far south. Whatever the political divisions of the country, ideas spread rapidly and were hotly debated. India hung together culturally and the mental background of the people everywhere was much the same. Even the masses in different parts of the country were not dissimilar in thought and outlook. The chief places of pilgrimage fixed by Shankaracharya were situated at the four corners of India: Badrinath in the Himalayas in the north, Rameshwaram near Cape Comorin in the south, Dwarka in the west overlooking the Arabian sea, and Puri in the east, washed by the waters of the Bay of Bengal. There was continuous intercourse between the peoples of the different regions. India as a whole was their holy land.

It is interesting to compare the intolerance of Europe in matters religious to the wide tolerance prevailing almost throughout history in India. Christianity came to India in the first century after Christ, long before Europe knew much about it, and found a welcome and a home. There was no opposition whatever. Even now there flourish in India many early Christian sects which were crushed out of existence in Europe. There are the Nestorians, and various Syrian Christian sects. The Jews came to India also about eighteen hundred years ago or more, and were welcomed. They still carry on their community life and parts of an ancient city where they live are supposed to resemble old Jerusalem. The Zoroastrians also came to India, driven out of Persia, and made their home here, and have flourished ever since. The Moslems first came soon after the advent of Islam and they found ready admittance and welcome and full opportunities for propagating their faith. For centuries there was no conflict except on the frontiers; it was only when Moslems came as conquerors and raiders that there was conflict.

The coming of Moslem rule shook India. For a while there was a conflict between the old background and the new, but soon the old spirit of India began to assert itself and attempts began to be made to find a synthesis of the old and the new. Even in religion, most difficult subject of all, this attempt was repeatedly made by Nanak, Kabir and others. The Moslem rulers generally accepted the background of Indian life and culture, varied by Persian cultural ideas. There was no difficulty whatever in the adaptation of old Indian arts to new ideas. New styles grew up in architecture and painting which were a true synthesis of the two and yet were essentially Indian. So also in music. Even in dress a certain uniformity crept in, and a common language developed.

Thus the whole history of India for thousands of years past shows her essential unity and the vitality and adaptability of her culture. This vitality took her message in art and thought and religion to the Far East; it took the shape of great colonizing expeditions to Malaysia, to Java and Sumatra and the Philippines and Borneo, as the remains of great monuments there, a thousand years old, bear testimony.

Behind this cultural unity, and giving strength to it, was the ceaseless attempt to find a harmony between the inner man and his outer environment. To some extent this was the outlook of the Middle Ages in Europe. And yet it probably was something more. The profit motive was not so obvious and riches were not valued in the same way as elsewhere. Unlike as in Europe, honour was reserved for the man of intellect and the man who served the state or society, and the great soldier or the rich man took second and third place. Perhaps it was this want of stress on the outer environment that made India politically weak and backward, while external progress went forward so rapidly in the West.

This past record of Indian cultural solidarity does not necessarily help us to-day. It is present conditions that we have to deal with, and memories of what has been may be of little avail. But though that is perfectly true, yet an ancient people has deep roots in the past and we cannot ignore them. Both the good and the bad that we possess have sprung from those roots; they give us strength and inspiration; they also burden us and tie us down to many a harmful tradition and evil practice. India undoubtedly deteriorated and the vital urge in her began to weaken. Her power to assimilate and absorb became feebler, and the flexibility of her thought and structure gave place to rigidity. What was dynamic became more and more static. The rationalism and the scientific basis of her thought continued for a favoured few, but for others irrationalism and superstition held sway. Caste, which was a division of society by occupation, and which at the start was far from rigid, developed a fearful rigidity and became the citadel of social reaction and a basis for the exploitation of the masses. For a long time India stagnated, the strength had gone out of her, and it was inevitable that she should fall an easy prey to the better-equipped and more vital and technically advanced nations of the West.

The immediate result of this was the growth of conservatism, a further shrinking of India inside her shell in self-defence. British rule forwarded this process by crystallizing many a changing custom and giving it the force of law. Even more important in keeping India back was the economic structure which British rule built up. The feudal Indian State system, the gilded Maharajas and Nabobs, and the big landlord system are essentially British creations in India. We have them, to our misfortune, still with us. But this desire of the British rulers to keep a semi-feudal structure in India could not hold back the impact of new ideas and new conditions. The British themselves thrived in the East on the strength of the great impulse given to the world by the advent of industrialism, and India herself was inevitably affected by this impulse. For their own purposes and in order to entrench themselves, they built railways and the other accompaniments of a modern administration. They tried hard to stop the industrial growth of India, desiring to keep her as a producer of raw materials only and a consumer of British manufactured goods. But the industrial revolution had to spread to India, even though it came slowly because of the obstruction offered by the Government.

The British gave political unity to India. This had now become possible owing to the development of communications and transport. It was a unity of a common subjection, but it gave rise to the unity of common nationalism. The idea of a united and a free India gripped the people. It was not a superficial idea imposed from above, but the natural outcome of that fundamental unity which had been the background of Indian life for thousands of years. The difference that had crept in was the new emphasis on the political aspect. To combat this, the British Government tried to lay stress on the religious differences and adopted a policy which encouraged them and brought them into conflict with each other. It has had a measure of success, but nationalism, in India as in other countries of the East, is the dominant urge of the time and must triumph. This nationalism is being tempered today by the economic urge, but this is still further removed from the mediaeval outlook which thinks in terms of religious groupings in political affairs.

The growth of the powerful nationalist movement in India, represented by the National Congress, has demonstrated the political unity of India.

The last two decades have seen vast upheavals, in the nature of a peaceful rebellion, taking place throughout the length and breadth of the country and shaking the foundations of British rule. This voluntary organization, commanding the willing allegiance of millions, has played a great rôle in fixing the idea of Indian unity in the minds of our masses. The capacity for united action and disciplined sacrifice for a national ideal which the people have shown has demonstrated not only the probability of Indian unity but its actual existence. In India to-day no one, whatever his political views or religious persuasions, thinks in terms other than those of national unity.

There are differences, of course, and certain separatist tendencies, but even these do not oppose national freedom or unity. They seek to gain a special favour for their particular group and because of this they hinder sometimes the growth of the nationalist movement. Religious differences affect politics less and less, though still sometimes they distract attention. There is no religious or cultural conflict in India. What is called the religious or communal problem is really a dispute among upper-class people for a division of the spoils of office or of representation in a legislature. This will surely be settled amicably wherever it arises.

Language is alleged to divide India into innumerable compartments; we are told by the census that there are 222 languages or dialects in India. I suppose the census of the United States mentions a very large number of languages; the German census, I think, mentions over sixty. But most of these languages are spoken by small groups of people, or are dialects. In India, the absence of mass education has fostered the growth of dialects. As a matter of fact, India is a singularly unified area so far as languages are concerned. Altogether in the vast area of India there are a dozen languages and these are closely allied to each other. They fall into two groups—the Indo-Aryan languages of the north and centre and west, and the Dravidian languages of the east and south. The Indo-Aryan languages derive from Sanskrit and anyone who knows one of them finds it easy to learn another. The Dravidian languages are different, but each one of them contains fifty per cent. or more words from the Sanskrit. The dominant language in India is Hindustani (Hindi or Urdu) which is already spoken by a huge block of a hundred and twenty million people and is partly understood by scores of millions of others. This language is bound to become the all-India medium of communication, not displacing the great provincial languages, but as a compulsory second language. With mass education on behalf of the state this will not be difficult. Already due to talkies and the radio the range of Hindustani is spreading fast. The writer of this article has had occasion to address great mass audiences all over India and almost always, except in the south, he has used Hindustani and been understood. However numerous the difficult problems which India has to solve, the language problem clearly is not one of them. It is already well on the way to solution.

It will thus be seen that the forces working for Indian unity are formidable and overwhelming, and it is difficult to conceive of any separatist tendency which can break up this unity. Some of the major Indian princes might represent such a tendency; but they flourish not from their own inherent strength, but because of the support of the British power. When that support goes, they will have to surrender to the wishes of their own people, among whom the sentiment of national unity is widespread.

This does not mean that our problems are easy of solution. They are very difficult, as every major problem in the world today is difficult, and probably their solution will depend on international as well as on national factors. But the real problems of India, as of the rest of the world, are economic, and they are so interrelated that it is hardly possible to tackle them separately. The land problem is the outstanding question of India, and it is difficult to see any final solution of it without revolutionary changes in our agriculture and land system. Feudal relics and the big landlord system are hindrances to development and will have to go. The tiny holdings, averaging a fraction of an acre per person, are uneconomic and wasteful and too small for the application of scientific methods of agriculture. Large-scale state and collective or cooperative farms must be established instead, and this cannot be done so long as the vested interests in land are not removed. Even when this has been done the vast urban and rural unemployment will not be reduced. For that as well as for other obvious reasons we must push forward the industrialization of the country. This again requires the development of social services—education, sanitation, etc. And so the problem becomes a vast and many-sided one affecting land, industry and all departments of life, and we see that it can be tackled only on a nationally planned basis without vested interests to obstruct the planning. Therefore many of us think that a socialist structure is necessary, that in no other way can such planning be organized and pushed through.

But then the vested interests come in—here lies the real difficulty and the real conflict. Far the greatest of these is the City of London, representing British finance and industry. The Government of India is but its shadow when vital interests are concerned. In addition there are the imperial services and Indian vested interests, the princes and others. The new Constitution of India,[1] though giving a certain leverage in the provinces owing to the extension of the electorate, is essentially designed to protect these special interests and keep British imperialism in India intact. Even in the provinces real power rests with the Governors and the revenues are largely mortgaged to these interests. Such strength as there is behind the provincial governments comes far more from the organized national movement than from the Constitution Act. Fear of conflict with this movement, resulting possibly in the suspension of the Constitution, prevents too much interference with provincial governments. But the position is essentially unstable; conflicts are inherent in it. Besides, under the financial provisions and reservations really big schemes of social reform simply cannot be undertaken.

But by far the worst part of the Constitution is the proposed Federal structure, for it makes the feudal Indian States permanent and, in addition, gives them some power to interfere in the affairs of the rest of India. The whole conception of a union of imperialism, feudalism and democracy is incapable of realization and can only mean the entrenchment of all the reactionary elements. It must be remembered that the Indian State system is over a hundred years old and that during this century it has continued more or less unchanged. In this period Europe and the world have altered past recognition, and it is a monstrous imposition on us that we should be saddled permanently with feudal relics which prevent all growth. Hence the fierce opposition to the Federal structure and the Constitution Act as a whole.

The National Congress stands for independence and a democratic state. It has proposed that the constitution of a free India must be framed, without outside interference, by a Constituent Assembly elected on the basis of an adult franchise. That is the democratic way and there is no other way short of revolution which can bring the needed result. An Assembly so elected will represent the people as a whole and will be far more interested in the economic and social problems of the masses than in the petty communal issues which affect small groups. Thus it will solve without much difficulty the communal and other like problems. It will not solve so easily the economic problems, but the clash of interest there is similar to that found all over the world. In the world-wide conflict of ideas and politics, India stands for democracy and against Fascism and the totalitarian state. She stands

[1] The Constitution is embodied in the Government of India Act, 1935, passed by the British Parliament. It does not carry the consent of the Indian people and was imposed on India in the face of national opposition. The Constitution has become operative only in the provinces. The introduction of the Federal Central structure with its highly objectionable features has been successfully resisted by the Indian national movement up till now.

for peace and coöperation between nations and ultimately the building up of a world order.

Will an independent India be strong enough to protect herself from outside aggression and invasion? If India is strong enough to gain her freedom from British imperialism, which has so long been entrenched on her soil, it seems to follow that she will also be strong enough to resist fresh aggression. The strength of a nation is a relative affair, depending on a host of internal and external factors. Most independent countries today are not strong enough to stop by themselves the aggression of a Great Power. Even a Great Power might succumb to a combination of other Great Powers. Probably the United States is the only country so fortunately situated and so strong in every way as to be able to hope to resist successfully almost any hostile combination. The others rely for their independence partly on their own strength, but more so on a combination of circumstances.

India will, of course, take all necessary steps to strengthen her defences. For this she has the industrial and other necessary resources. Her policy will be one of friendship to her neighbours and others, and she will rigorously avoid conflict. The National Congress has already declared that in the event of Britain being involved in an imperialist war, India will not be a party to it. There is no doubt that India can build up a strong defence apparatus. Her army to-day, though lacking in Indian officers, is considered an efficient force. . . .

. . . [We] live in an abnormal world, full of wars and aggression. International law has ceased to be, treaties and undertakings have no value, gangsterism prevails unabashed among the nations. We realize that anything may happen in this epoch of revolution and wars, and that the only thing to be done to protect ourselves is to rely on our own strength at the same time that we pursue consciously a policy of peace. Risks have to be taken whatever the path we follow. These we are prepared to take, for we must.

We do not underestimate the difficulties before us. We have a hard task, hard because of external opposition, harder still because of our own weaknesses. It is always more difficult to fight one's own failings than the power of an adversary. We have to do both. We have social evils, with the authority of long tradition and habit behind them. We have within us the elements which have gone to build up Fascism in other countries. We have inertia and a tame submission to fate and its decrees. But we have also a new awakening of the vital spirit of India. The static uncreative period is over, a hunger for change and for the ending of misery and poverty has seized the masses. The world is shaken by war and alarms of war. No one knows what horror and inhuman cruelty and destruction—or human progress—the future holds for us. Be that as it may, India will no longer be merely a passive instrument of destiny or of another's will.

In the subconscious mind of India there is questioning, a struggle, a crisis. As of old, India seeks a synthesis of the past and the present, of the old and the new. She sees the new industrial civilization marching irresistibly on; she distrusts it and dislikes it to some extent, for it is an attack against and an upheaval of so much that is old; yet she has accepted that industrial civilization as an inevitable development. So she seeks to synthesize it with her own fundamental conceptions, to find a harmony between the inner man and his ever-changing outer environment. That harmony is strangely lacking in the whole world to-day. All of us seek blindly. Till we find it we shall have to march wearily through the deserts of conflict and hatred and mutual destruction.

MAO TSE-TUNG

THE twentieth-century revolutions in Asia have been primarily directed against the imperialism and colonialism of European states; even in such a case as the Chinese revolution of 1911, which overthrew the Manchu dynasty and established the Republic of China, the rebellion, while overtly aimed at native rulers, was motivated by disgust over the inability of the dynasty successfully to assert the dignity and sovereignty of China in the face of foreign attempts at domination. But in a true sense, even the program of the revolution itself reflected the impact of the West upon China; the revolutionary leaders were almost invariably inspired by Western examples and animated by political and social ideals formulated in Europe and America. Sun Yat-sen (1866–1925), founder of the Chinese Republic, was strongly under the influence of West European ideology; successive leaders of the Kuomintang, or Nationalist Party, affirmed their allegiance to his program, and the Kuomintang itself, despite the fact that it actually always ruled in an authoritarian manner, has also always paid lip service to liberal, parliamentarian aspirations. However, with the founding of the Chinese Communist Party in the early 1920's, an alternative and radical form of Western political and social ideology—"dialectical materialism"—entered the contest for the control of some five to six hundred million largely illiterate, tradition-minded Chinese peasants.

Mao Tse-tung, born of peasant stock in 1893, was associated with the Chinese Communist Party from its confused and inauspicious beginnings. A superb organizer and a flexible tactician of mass movements, Mao early recognized in the exploited condition of the Chinese countryside the powder of genuine social revolution. Even in the period 1923–1927, when doctrinaire Soviet Russian advisers were directing Chinese Communist efforts and when the Party itself was recognized as a legitimate segment of the dominant Kuomintang (1924), Mao insisted on developing landless peasant support along lines considered unorthodox by the Russian experts and revolutionary by the right-wing majority in the government. In 1927 tension between the radicals and conservatives in the Nationalist (Kuomintang) government, coupled with the success of General Chiang Kai-shek (b. 1886) in ending the internal anarchy that had consumed China since 1920, reached a breaking point when Chiang threw in his fortunes with the right-wing majority. Chiang outlawed the Communist Party, while the Party rose in revolt. There followed a civil war during which the Nationalist forces gradually beat down Communist resistance. In 1934–1935, the Party decided to cut its losses and, under the command of Mao Tse-tung, the Red Army undertook its famous "long march," a six-thousand-mile retreat in good order through Kweichow and Szechwan to northern Shensi. Mao Tse-tung was now chairman of the Soviet Republic of China and most powerful man in the Party. But the Communist movement had reached the nadir of its fortunes, isolated in a remote and primitive province; even Stalin had decided that the Chinese Communist cause was for the moment lost.

The Japanese invasion of China in 1937 and the outbreak of World War II resuscitated Communist hopes. In the interest of a united front against the invader, Chiang Kai-shek and Mao Tse-tung arranged an uneasy truce and Communists and Kuomintang cooperated, at least nominally, until 1946. But the strain of the long years of war, added to the internal erosion of Nationalist energy, proved too great for Chiang's government to sustain. For the first time fully backed by the Soviet Union, Mao abandoned the wartime coalition, and renewed the civil war. By 1949, Kuomintang power had evaporated on the mainland and Chiang was driven to a last refuge on the island of Taiwan (Formosa). Mao Tse-tung was now head of the new Communist People's Democratic Republic of China.

Although noted for his resiliency as a political leader, Mao Tse-tung is thoroughly impregnated with Leninist doctrine. He views the chaos of Chinese history since 1911 through the intellectual spectacles of "dialectical materialism." As the following selection, taken from an address which Mao delivered in 1937 at the Anti-Japanese Military and Political College in Yenan, reveals, Mao has always been assiduous in the attempt to apply Marxist-Leninist doctrine to the Chinese situation. This has often necessitated realignment and reinterpretation; yet always has Chinese Mao managed to maintain the fundamentals of that potent system of thought which was the product of a nineteenth-century German philosopher writing in London and of a Russian revolutionary writing mostly in Switzerland. From Mao Tse-tung's point of view, this merely demonstrates the unity of world history.

ON CONTRADICTION

The law of Contradiction in things, that is, the law of the unity of opposites, is the most basic law in materialist dialectics. Lenin said: "In its proper meaning, dialectics is the study of the contradiction within the very essence of things." Lenin often called this law the essence of dialectics; he also called it the kernel of dialectics. Therefore, in studying this law, we cannot but touch upon a wide range of subjects, upon a great number of problems of philosophy. If we can clear up all these problems, we shall arrive at a basic understanding of materialist dialectics. These problems are: the two world outlooks; the universality of contradiction; the particularity of contradiction; the principal contradiction and the principal aspect of a contra-

---

diction; the identity and the struggle of the aspects of a contradiction; the role of antagonism in contradiction.

In recent years, philosophical circles in the Soviet Union have subjected the idealism of the Deborin school to criticism. This has aroused great interest among us. Deborin's idealism has exerted a very bad influence in the Chinese Communist Party, and it cannot be said that dogmatic ways of thought in our Party have nothing to do with the style of work of this school. Thus our present study of philosophy should have as its principal objective the eradication of dogmatic ways of thought.

I. THE TWO WORLD OUTLOOKS

In the history of human knowledge, there have always been two views on the laws of development of the world: The metaphysical view and the dialectical view, which form two mutually opposed world outlooks. Lenin said: "The two basic (or two possible? or two historically observable?) conceptions of development (evolution) are: development as decrease and increase, as repetition, and development as a unity of opposites (the division of the one into mutually exclusive opposites and their reciprocal relation)." Lenin was referring to these two different world outlooks.

For a very long period of history, in China as well as in Europe, metaphysics formed part of the idealist world outlook and occupied a dominant position in human thought. In the early days of the bourgeoisie in Europe, materialism was also metaphysical. The Marxist materialist-dialectical world outlook emerged because the social economy of many European countries had entered the stage of highly-developed capitalism; because the productive forces, the class struggle, and the sciences all developed to a level unprecedented in history; and because the industrial proletariat had become the greatest motive force in historical development. Then, besides an openly avowed, extremely barefaced, reactionary idealism, vulgar evolutionism also emerged from the bourgeoisie to oppose materialist dialectics.

The so-called metaphysical world outlook or the world outlook of vulgar evolutionism means looking at the world from an isolated, static, and one-sided point of view. It regards all things in the world, their forms and their species, as forever isolated from one another and forever changeless. If any change is admitted, it is merely an increase or decrease in quantity or a transfer in space. Moreover, the cause of such an increase or decrease or transfer does not lie inside things, but outside them, that is, through propulsion by external forces. Metaphysicians hold that all varieties of things in the world, as well as their characteristics, have remained the same since the moment they came into being. Any subsequent change is a mere quantitative expansion or contraction. They hold that a thing can only be repeatedly reproduced as the self-same thing forever and cannot change into something of a different kind. In their eyes, capitalist exploitation, capitalist competition, the ideology of individualism in capitalist society, and so on, can all be found in the slave society of antiquity, or even in primitive society, and will continue to exist forever without any change.

As to the causes of social development, they find the explanation in conditions external to society like geography and climate. They naively seek outside the things themselves for the cause of their development, and repudiate the theory advanced by materialist dialectics that it is the contradictions inside things that cause their development. Therefore, they cannot explain the multiplicity of the quantities of things; nor can they explain the phenomenon of one quality changing into another. In Europe, this mode of thought existed as mechanistic materialism in the seventeenth and eighteenth centuries and as vulgar evolutionism at the end of the nineteenth and the beginning of the twentieth centuries. In China, the metaphysical mode of thought that "Heaven changes not, and the Way too changes not," was for a long time supported by the decadent feudal ruling classes. Imported from Europe in the last hundred years, mechanistic materialism and vulgar evolutionism have been supported by the bourgeoisie.

Contrary to the metaphysical world outlook, the materialistic-dialectical world outlook advocates the study of the development of things from the inside, from the relationship of a thing to other things. The development of things should be regarded as their internal and necessary self-movement, a thing in its movement and the things around it should be regarded as interconnected and interacting upon each other. The basic cause of the development of things does not lie outside but inside them, in their internal contradictions. The movement and development of things arise because of the presence of such contradictions inside all things. This contradiction within a thing is the basic cause of its development, while the interconnection of a thing with, and its interaction upon, other things are the secondary causes of its development. Thus materialist dialectics forcefully combats the theory of external causes of propulsion advanced by metaphysical mechanistic materialism and vulgar evolutionism. It is evident that purely external causes can only lead to the mechanical motion of things, that is, to changes in size and quantity, but cannot explain why things are qualitatively different in a thousand and one ways and why things change into one another. As a matter of fact, even a mechanical motion of things propelled by some external force is also brought about through their internal contradictions. Mere growth in plants and animals and their quantitative development are also chiefly caused by their internal contradictions.

Similarly, social development is chiefly due not to external, but to internal causes. Many countries exist under almost the same geographical and climatic conditions, yet the difference and unevenness in their development are extremely great. Tremendous social changes take place even in one and the same country, while its geography and climate have not changed. Imperialist Russia changed into the Socialist Soviet Union, and feudal, insulated Japan changed into imperialist Japan, although the geography and climate of these two countries have not changed. China, for long dominated by feudalism, has undergone great changes in the last hundred years and is now changing in the direction of a new China, liberated and free; yet her geography and climate have not changed. The geography and climate of the earth as a whole and of every part of it are also changing, but these changes obviously appear very small when compared with changes in society. In the former the changes manifest themselves in terms of tens of thousands or millions of years, while in the latter they manifest themselves in mere thousands, hundreds, tens, or even a few years or even months (as in times of revolution). According to the viewpoint of materialist dialectics, changes in nature are chiefly due to the development of the internal contradictions in nature. Social changes are chiefly due to the internal contradictions in society, namely, the contradiction between the productive forces and the relations of production, the contradiction between the classes, and the contradiction between the old and the new. It is the development of these contradictions that impels society forward and starts the process of the superseding of the old society by a new one.

Does materialist dialectics leave external causes out of account? Not at all. Materialist dialectics considers external causes as the condition of change and internal causes as the basis of change, external causes becoming operative through internal causes. In a suitable temperature an egg changes into a chicken, but no temperature can change a stone into a chicken because the fundamentals of the two things are different. There is a constant, interacting influence between the peoples of different countries. In the era of capitalism, especially in the era of imperialism and the proletarian revolution, interacting influences and stimulation—political, economic and cultural—between various countries have been extremely great.

The Socialist October Revolution ushered in a new epoch not only in Russian history but also in world history, exerting an influence on the internal changes in all countries of the world and, in a similar and yet particularly profound way, on the internal changes in China. Such changes, however, arose according to an inner necessity in those countries as well as in China. Two armies engage in battle; one is victorious and the other is defeated: Both victory and defeat are determined by internal causes. One is victorious either because of its strength or because of its correct command; the other is defeated either because of its weakness or because of its incompetent command: It is through internal causes that external causes become operative. In 1927 the Chinese big bourgeoisie defeated the proletariat, operating through the opportunism existing within the Chinese proletariat itself (within the Chinese Communist Party). When we liquidated this opportunism, the Chinese revolution resumed its advance. Later, the Chinese revolution again suffered severe blows from the enemy, because adventurism appeared within our party. When we liquidated this adventurism, our cause once more resumed its advance. Thus, if a political party is to lead the revolution to victory, it must rely upon the correctness of its own political line and the consolidation of its own organization.

The dialectical world outlook had already emerged in ancient times in both China and Europe. But ancient dialectics has something spontaneous and naive about it. Being based upon the social and historical conditions of those times, it could not fully explain the world, and was later supplanted by metaphysics. The famous German philosopher Hegel, who lived from the latter part of the eighteenth century to the early part of the nineteenth, made very important contributions to dialectics, but his is idealist dialectics. It was not until the great men of action of the proletarian movement, Marx and Engels, made a synthesis of the positive achievements in the history of human knowledge and, in particular, critically absorbed the rational elements of Hegelian dialectics, and created the great theory of dialectical materialism and historical materialism, that a great, unprecedented revolution took place in the history of human knowledge. Subsequently, this great theory has been further developed by Lenin and Stalin. As soon as it was introduced into China, this theory brought about tremendous changes in the sphere of Chinese thought.

This dialectical world outlook chiefly teaches man how to be good at observing and analyzing the movement in opposites of various things and, on the basis of such analyses, to point out the methods of resolving the contradictions. Consequently, it is of paramount importance for us to understand concretely the law of contradictions in things. . . .

III. THE PARTICULARITY OF CONTRADICTION

. . . The basic contradiction in the process of development of things, and the quality of the process determined by this basic contradiction, will not disappear until the process is completed; but the conditions of each stage in the long process of development of things often differ from those of another stage. The reason for this is that, while the nature of the basic contradiction in the development of things and the quality of the process have not changed, yet at the various stages in the long process of development, the basic contradiction assumes an increasingly intensified form. Besides, among the numerous big and small contradictions determined or influenced by the basic contradiction, some become intensified, some are temporarily or partially resolved or mitigated, and some emerge anew; consequently the process reveals itself as consisting of different stages. If people do not pay attention to the stages in the process of development of a thing, they cannot deal properly with its contradictions.

For example: At the time when capitalism of the era of free competition developed into imperialism, there was no change in the character of the two classes in fundamental contradiction, the proletariat and the bourgeoisie, or in the capitalist nature of such a society. However, the contradiction between these two classes became intensified, the contradiction between monopoly capital and non-monopoly capital emerged, the contradiction between metropolitan countries and colonies became intensified, and the contradiction between the capitalist countries, that is, the contradiction caused by the unevenness of their development, manifested itself in a particularly acute way, thus bringing about the special stage of capitalism, the stage of imperialism. The reason why Leninism is Marxism of the era of imperialism and of the proletarian revolution is that Lenin and Stalin have correctly explained these contradictions and correctly formulated the theory and tactics of the proletarian revolution for resolving them.

An examination of the process of the bourgeois-democratic revolution in China, which began with the Revolution of 1911, also reveals several special stages. In particular, the revolution in the period of its bourgeois leadership and the revolution in the period of its proletarian leadership are marked off from each other as two vastly different historical stages. That is, the leadership of the proletariat has basically changed the physiognomy of the revolution, and led to a readjustment in class relations, a tremendous stirring of the peasant revolution, a thoroughness in the anti-imperialist and anti-feudal revolution, the possibility of the transition from democratic revolution to Socialist revolution, and so on. All this could not possibly happen in the period when the revolution was under bourgeois leadership. Although there was no change in the nature of the basic contradiction of the whole process—in the anti-imperialist, anti-feudal, democratic-revolutionary nature of the process (with the semi-colonial, semi-feudal nature as the other aspect)—yet in this long period of some twenty years it has gone through several stages of development. Such great events as the failure of the Revolution of 1911 and the establishment of the regime of the Northern warlords, the establishment of the first national united front and the Revolution of 1924–27, the breaking up of the united front and the passing of the bourgeoisie into the counter-revolutionary camp, the wars between the new warlords, the agrarian revolutionary war, the establishment of the second national united front and the Anti-Japanese War. These stages contain such specific conditions as the intensification of some contradictions (for example, the agrarian revolutionary war and the Japanese invasion of the four Northeastern provinces); the partial or temporary solution of other contradictions (for example, the liquidation of the Northern warlords and our confiscation of the land of the landlords); and the fresh emergence of still other contradictions (for example, the struggle between the new warlords, the landlords' recovery of their land after our loss of the revolutionary bases in the south).

To study the particularity of the contradictions at every stage in the process of development of things, we must not only observe them in their interconnection and their totality, but we must consider each aspect of the contradiction at each stage of its development.

Take the Kuomintang and the Communist Party, for instance. As to the Kuomintang: In the period of the first united front it was revolutionary and vigorous and represented an alliance of various classes in the democratic revolution, because it carried out Sun Yat-sen's three cardinal policies of alliance with Russia, co-operation with the Communists, and assistance to the workers and peasants. After 1927, the Kuomintang turned in the opposite direction and became the reactionary bloc of the landlords and the big bourgeoisie. After the Sian Incident in December, 1936, it made another turn and began to move in the direction of cessation of the civil war and alliance with the Communist Party in joint opposition to Japanese imperialism. Such are the characteristics of the Kuomintang in its three stages. The formation of these characteristics is, of course, due to various causes.

As to the Chinese Communist Party in the period of the first united front, it was a party in its childhood and courageously led the Revolution of 1924–27, but it revealed itself as immature in the understanding of the nature, tasks, and methods of the revolution. Consequently, *Ch'en Tuhsiuism,* which appeared in the last period of this revolution, was able to have its effect and caused the defeat of this revolution. After 1927, the Communist Party again courageously led the agrarian revolutionary war and created the revolutionary army and revolutionary bases; however it also made mistakes of adventurism which brought serious losses to both the army and the bases. Since 1935, it has rectified these mistakes and led the new anti-Japanese united front; this great struggle is now developing. At the present stage the Communist Party is a party that has gone through the test of two revolutions and has acquired a rich store of experience. Such are the characteristics of the Chinese Communist Party in its three stages.

The formation of these characteristics is also due to various causes. Without studying these characteristics, we cannot understand the specific interrelations of the two parties at the various stages of their development: The establishment of the united front, the breaking up of the united front, and the establishment of another united front. But in order to study the various characteristics of the two parties, we must—this is even more fundamental—study the class basis of the two parties, the resultant contradictions between the two parties and other forces during different periods. For example, in the period of its first alliance with the Communist Party, the Kuomintang on the one hand stood in contradiction to foreign imperialism and therefore opposed imperialism; while on the other hand it stood in contradiction to the great masses of the people at home, and, though it verbally promised to give many benefits to the toiling people, in reality it gave them very few or even none at all. In the period when it carried on the anti-Communist war, it collaborated with imperialism and feudalism to oppose the great masses of the people, writing off all the benefits which the great masses of the people had won in the revolution and thus intensifying its own contradiction with the great masses of the people. In the present period of the Anti-Japanese War, the Kuomintang, standing in contradiction to Japanese imperialism, wants on the one hand to ally itself with the Communist Party, while on the other it does not slacken its struggle against, and its oppression of, the Communist Party and the Chinese people.

As to the Communist Party, no matter in which period, it always sides with the great masses of the people to oppose imperialism and feudalism; in the present period of the Anti-Japanese War, because the Kuomintang shows itself in favor of resisting Japan, the Communist Party has adopted a mild policy toward it and toward the domestic feudal forces. Because of these conditions, an alliance of the two parties is brought about at one time, and a struggle at another; and even during the period of the alliance between the two parties, there also exists a complicated state of affairs in which alliance and struggle take place at the same time. If we do not study the characteristics of these aspects of the contradiction, we shall not only fail to understand the relation between each of the two parties and other forces, but also fail to understand the interrelation of the two parties.

From this it can be seen that in studying the specific nature of any kind of contradiction—contradiction in various forms of motion of matter, contradiction in various forms of motion in every process of development, each aspect of the contradiction in every process of development, contradiction at the various stages of every process of development, and each aspect of the contradiction at the various stages of development—in studying the specific nature of all these contradictions, we must be free from any taint of subjective arbitrariness and must make a concrete analysis of them. Apart from a concrete analysis there can be no knowledge of the specific nature of any contradiction. We must at all times bear in mind Lenin's words: the concrete analysis of concrete conditions.

Marx and Engels were the first to supply us with an excellent model of such concrete analysis.

When Marx and Engels applied the law of contradiction in things to the study of the process of social history, they saw the contradiction between the productive forces and the relations of production; they saw the contradiction between the exploiting class and the exploited class, as well as the contradiction produced thereby between the economic basis and its superstructures such as politics and ideology; and they saw how these contradictions inevitably lead to different social revolutions in different class societies.

When Marx applied this law to the study of the economic structure of capitalist society, he saw that the basic contradiction of this society is the contradiction between the social character of production and the private character of ownership. This contradiction manifests itself in the contradiction between the organized character of production in individual enterprises and the unorganized character of production in society as a whole. The class manifestation of this contradiction is the contradiction between the bourgeoisie and the proletariat.

Because of the vastness of the scope of things and the limitlessness of their development, what is universality in one case is in another changed into particularity. On the other hand, what in one case is particularity is in another changed into universality. The contradiction contained in the capitalist system between the socialization of production and the private ownership of the means of production is common to all countries where capitalism exists and develops; as far as capitalism is concerned, this constitutes the universality of contradiction. However, this contradiction in capitalism is something pertaining to a certain historical stage in the development of class society in general; as far as the contradiction between the productive forces and the relations of production in class society in general is concerned, this constitutes the particularity of contradiction. But when Marx revealed by analysis the particularity of every contradiction in capitalist society, he simultaneously expounded more profoundly, more adequately, and more completely the universality of the contradiction between the productive forces and the relations of production in class society in general.

As the particular is connected with the universal, and as not only the particularity of contradiction but also the universality of contradiction is inherent in everything, universality thus existing in particularity, so, when we study a certain object we ought to try to discover both of these aspects and their interconnection, to discover the two aspects of particularity and universality within the object as well as their interconnection, and to discover the interconnection of this object with the many objects outside it. When Stalin explained the historical roots of Leninism in his famous work, *Foundations of Leninism,* he analyzed the international situation in which Leninism was born, and the various contradictions in capitalism which had reached their extreme under the conditions of imperialism. He analyzed how these contradictions made the proletarian revolution a question of immediate practice, and created favorable conditions for a direct onslaught upon capitalism. In addition, he analyzed the reasons why Russia became the home of Leninism, how tsarist Russia represented the focus of all the contradictions of imperialism, and why the Russian proletariat could become the vanguard of the international revolutionary proletariat. In this way, Stalin analyzed the universality of the contradiction in imperialism, showing how Leninism is Marxism of the era of imperialism and the proletarian revolution, and analyzed the particularity of the imperialism of tsarist Russia in the contradiction in general, showing how Russia became the birthplace of the theory and tactics of the proletarian revolution and how in such a particularity is contained the universality of contradiction. This kind of analysis by Stalin serves as a model in understanding the particularity and the universality of contradiction and their interconnection.

On the question of applying dialectics to the study of objective phenomena, Marx and Engels, and likewise Lenin and Stalin, have always taught people that they should not be tainted with any subjective arbitrariness and must discover, from the concrete conditions inherent in the objective actual movements, the concrete contradictions in those phenomena, the concrete role of each of the aspects of the contradictions, and the concrete interrelation of the contradictions. Because they have not taken such an attitude in study, our dogmatists can never be in the right. We must take warning from the failure of dogmatism, and learn to acquire such an attitude in study—there is no other method.

The relation between the universality of contradiction and the particularity of contradiction is the relation between the common character and the individual character of contradictions. By common character we mean that contradiction exists in all processes and runs through all processes from beginning to end. Contradictions are movements, are things, are processes, are thought. To deny the contradiction in things is to deny all. This is a universal principle which admits of no exceptions, in either ancient or modern times, in China or foreign countries. Hence the common character or absoluteness. But this common character is contained in all individual characters; without individual character there can be no common character. If all individual characters were removed, what common character would remain? Because each of the contradictions is particular, their individual characters are formed. All individual characters exist conditionally and temporarily, hence they are relative.

This principle of common character and individual character, of absoluteness and relativity, is the quintessence of the problem of the contradiction in things; not to understand it is equivalent to abandoning dialectics.

IV. THE PRINCIPAL CONTRADICTION AND THE PRINCIPAL ASPECT OF A CONTRADICTION

As regards the problem of the particularity of contradiction, there are still two sides which must be specially singled out for analysis, that is, the principal contradiction and the principal aspect of a contradiction.

In the process of development of a complex thing, many contradictions exist; among these, one is necessarily the principal contradiction the existence and development of which determine or influence the existence and development of other contradictions.

For example, in capitalist society, the two opposing forces in contradiction, the proletariat and the bourgeoisie, form the principal contradiction. This principal contradiction determines and influences the other contradictions—for example, the contradiction between the remnant feudal class and the bourgeoisie, between the rural petty bourgeoisie and the bourgeoisie, between the proletariat and the rural petty bourgeoisie, between the liberal bourgeoisie and the monopolistic bourgeoisie, between bourgeois democracy and bourgeois fascism, between the capitalist countries themselves, between imperialism and the colonies, etc.

In semi-colonial countries like China, the relationship between the principal contradiction and non-principal contradictions presents a complicated situation.

When imperialism wages a war of aggression against such a country, the various classes in that country, apart from the traitors, can temporarily unite to wage a national war against imperialism. At such a time, the contradiction between imperialism and that country becomes the principal contradiction, while all the contradictions among the various classes within that country (including the principal contradiction between the feudal system and the great masses of the people) are relegated temporarily to a secondary or subordinate position. Such was the case in China in the Opium War of 1840, the Sino-Japanese War of 1894, the Boxer War of 1900, and it is the case in the present Sino-Japanese War.

But in another situation, the relative positions of contradictions undergo a change. When imperialism does not apply the pressure of war, but adopts comparatively mild forms—political, economic, cultural, etc.—to carry on its oppression, the ruling classes in the semi-colonial countries will capitulate to imperialism; the two will form an alliance for the joint oppression of the great masses of the people. At such a time, the great masses of the people often adopt the form of civil war to oppose the alliance of imperialism and the feudal class, while imperialism often adopts indirect methods in helping the reactionaries in the semi-colonial countries to oppress the people without taking direct action. This reveals the special sharpness of the internal contradiction. Such has been the case in China in the revolutionary war of 1911, the revolutionary war of 1924–27, and the ten years' agrarian revolutionary war since 1927. Furthermore, the civil wars between the various reactionary ruling blocs in the semi-colonial countries, *e.g.,* the wars between the warlords in China, also belong to this category.

When a revolutionary civil war reaches the point of fundamentally threatening the existence of imperialism and its jackals—the domestic reactionaries—imperialism will often adopt methods other than those mentioned above in an endeavor to maintain its rule. It either tries to split up the revolutionary front from within or sends armed forces directly to help the domestic reactionaries. At such times, foreign imperialism and the domestic reactionaries stand completely in the open at one pole while the great masses of the people stand at another, thus forming the principal contradiction which determines or influences the development of other contradictions. The aid given by various capitalist countries to the Russian reactionaries after the October Revolution is a case of armed intervention. Chiang Kai-shek's betrayal in 1927 is a case of disintegrating the revolutionary front.

But whatever happens, there is no doubt at all that at every stage in the process of development, only one principal contradiction plays the leading role.

From this it can be seen that if in any process a number of contradictions exist, only one of them is the principal contradiction, playing the leading and decisive role, while the rest occupy a secondary or subordinate position. Thus, in studying any process—if it is a complicated process in which more than two contradictions exist—we must devote our whole energy to discovering its principal contradiction. Once this principal contradiction is grasped, any problem can be solved readily. This is the method Marx taught us when he studied capitalist society. When Lenin and Stalin studied imperialism and the general crisis of capitalism, and when they studied Soviet economy, they also taught us this method. Thousands of scholars and practical workers do not understand this method, with the result that, bewildered as if lost in a sea of mist, they cannot find the crux of a problem and naturally cannot find the method of resolving contradictions.

As we said above, we cannot treat all the contradictions in a process as equal, but must distinguish between the principal and the secondary contradictions, and pay particular attention to grasping the principal one. But, in any contradiction, whether principal or secondary, can we treat the two contradictory aspects as equal?

No, we cannot. In any contradiction, at any time, the development of the contradictory aspects is uneven. Sometimes there seems to be a balance of forces, but that is only a temporary and relative state; the basic state is unevenness. Of the two contradictory aspects, one must be the principal and the other secondary. The principal aspect is the one which plays the leading role in the contradiction. The quality of a thing is mainly determined by the principal aspect of the contradiction that has taken the dominant position.

But this state is not fixed; the principal and the non-principal aspects of a contradiction transform themselves into each other and the quality of a thing changes accordingly. In a certain process or at a certain stage in the development of a contradiction, the principal aspect is A and the non-principal aspect is B; at another stage of development or in another process of development, the roles are reversed—a change determined by the extent of the increase and decrease, respectively, in the intensity of the struggle of the two aspects of the contradiction in the development of a thing.

We often speak of "the superseding of the old by the new." The superseding of the old by the new is the universal, forever inviolable law of the world. A thing transforms itself into something else according to its nature and the conditions under which it finds itself and through different forms of leaping; that is the process of the superseding of the old by the new. Everything contains a contradiction between its new aspect and its old aspect, which constitutes a series of intricate struggles. As a result of these struggles, the new aspect grows and rises to become the thing that dominates, while the old aspect dwindles and becomes the thing that gradually approaches extinction. And the moment the new aspect has won the dominant position over the old aspect, the quality of the old thing changes into the quality of the new thing. From this it can be seen that the quality of a thing is mainly determined by the principal aspect of the contradiction that has won the dominant position. When the principal aspect of the contradiction that has won the dominant position undergoes a change, the quality of a thing changes accordingly.

In capitalist society, capitalism transformed itself from a force which occupied a subordinate position in the old era of feudal society into one that has won the dominant position, and the nature of society has also changed from feudal to capitalist. In the new era of capitalist society, feudal forces have been transformed from forces originally in the dominant position into subordinate forces, and then they gradually approached extinction; such is the case, for example, in Britain and France. With the development of the productive forces, the bourgeoisie has been transformed from a new class, playing a progressive role, into an old class, playing a reactionary role, until it is finally overthrown by the proletariat and is transformed into a class which is deprived of its private means of production and of its power, and which will then also gradually approach extinction. The proletariat, which is much more numerous than the bourgeoisie, and which grows up simultaneously with the bourgeoisie but is under its rule, is a new force. From its initial position subordinate to the bourgeoisie, it gradually grows stronger and becomes an independent class playing a leading role in history until finally it seizes political power and becomes the ruling class. At such a time, the nature of society changes from that of the old capitalist society into that of the new socialist society. This is the path that the Soviet Union has already traversed and that all other countries inevitably will traverse.

As regards the situation in China, while imperialism occupies the principal position in the contradiction which makes her a semi-colony, and oppressed the Chinese people, China has changed from an independent country into a semi-colony. But this state of affairs inevitably will change. In the struggle between the two sides, the strength of the Chinese people, which grows under the leadership of the proletariat, inevitably will change China from a semi-colony into an independent country, whereas imperialism will be overthrown and the old China will inevitably change into a new China.

The change of the old China into a new China also involves a change in the relation between the old forces of China's feudalism and the new forces of her people. The old feudal landlord class will be overthrown, and from being the ruler it will become the ruled; this class will also gradually approach extinction. Under the leadership of the proletariat the people will, from being the ruled, become the rulers. At the same time, the nature of Chinese society will undergo a change—that is, the old, semi-colonial and semi-feudal society will change into a new, democratic society.

Instances of such mutual transformations are found in our past experience. The Manchu dynasty, which had ruled China for nearly three hundred years, was overthrown during the Revolution of 1911, while the Revolutionary League under Sun Yat-sen's leadership won victory for a time. In the revolutionary war of 1924–27, the revolutionary forces in the South, the alliance between the Communist Party and the Kuomintang, grew from weakness to strength and won victory in the Northern Expedition, while the Northern warlords, once all-powerful, were overthrown. In 1927, the people's forces under the leadership of the Communist Party, suffering from the attacks of the Kuomintang reactionary forces, became very weak, but having eliminated opportunism within their ranks they gradually became stronger once more. In the revolutionary bases under the leadership of the Communist Party, the peasants have transformed themselves from being the ruled into the rulers, while the landlords have undergone an opposite transformation. It is always in such a manner that the new displaces the old in the world, that the old is superseded by the new, that the old is eliminated and the new is brought forth, or that the old is thrown off and the new ushered in.

At certain times in the revolutionary struggle, difficulties outweigh advantages; at such times, difficulties constitute the principal aspect of the contradiction and advantages the secondary aspect. But through the efforts of revolutionaries, difficulties can be gradually overcome, an advantageous new situation is created, and the difficult situation yields place to the advantageous one. Such was the case after the failure of the revolution in China in 1927 and during the Long March of the Chinese Red Army. In the present Sino-Japanese War, China is again in a difficult position; but we can change this state of affairs and bring about a fundamental change in the situation of both China and Japan. Conversely, advantages can also be transformed into difficulties, if the revolutionaries make mistakes. The victory of the Revolution of 1924–27 turned into a defeat. The revolutionary bases that had grown in the southern provinces after 1927 all suffered defeat in 1934.

Such also is the contradiction in our studies when we pass from ignorance to knowledge. At the very beginning of our study of Marxism, our ignorance or scanty knowledge of Marxism stands in contradiction to knowledge of Marxism. But as a result of industrious study, ignorance can be transformed into knowledge, scanty knowledge into considerable knowledge, and blindness in the use of Marxism into its masterly application.

Some people think that there are contradictions different from this. For example: In the contradiction between the productive forces and the relations of production, the productive forces are the principal aspect; in the contradiction between theory and practice, practice is the principal aspect; in the contradiction between the economic base and its superstructure, the economic base is the principal aspect; and there is no change in their respective positions. This is the view of mechanistic materialism, and not of dialectical materialism. True, the productive forces, practice, and the economic base generally manifest themselves in the principal and decisive role; whoever does not admit this, is not a materialist. But under certain conditions, such aspects as the relations of production, theory, and the superstructure, in turn, manifest themselves in the principal and decisive role; this must also be admitted. When the productive forces cannot be developed unless the relations of production are changed, the change in the relations of production plays the principal and decisive role. When, as Lenin put it, "without a revolutionary theory, there can be no revolutionary movement," the creation and advocacy of the revolutionary theory play the principal and decisive role. When certain work (this applies to any work) is to be done but there is as yet no directive, method, plan, or policy, defining the directive, method, plan, or policy is the principal and decisive factor. When the superstructure of politics, culture, and so on hinders the development of the economic base, political and cultural reforms become the principal and decisive factors.

In saying this, are we running counter to materialism? We are not, because we recognize that in the development of history as a whole material things determine spiritual things, social existence determines social consciousness. But at the same time, we also recognize and must recognize the reaction of spiritual things, the reaction of social consciousness on social existence, and the reaction of the superstructure on the economic base. This is not running counter to materialism; on the contrary, this is avoiding mechanistic materialism and firmly upholding dialectical materialism.

If, in studying the problem of the particularity of contradiction, we do not study these two conditions—the principal contradiction and the non-principal contradiction in the process, as well as the principal aspect and the non-principal aspect of a contradiction—that is, if we do not study the distinctive character of these two conditions of contradiction, we shall get bogged down in abstract studies and shall not be able concretely to understand the condition of a contradiction, and consequently we shall not be able to find the correct method of solving the contradiction. The distinctive character or particularity of these two conditions of contradiction represents the unevenness of the contradictory forces. There is nothing in the world that is absolutely even in its development, and we must oppose the theory of even development or the theory of equilibrium. At the same time, the concrete conditions of a contradiction and the change in the principal and non-principal aspects of a contradiction in its process of development, show precisely the force of the new things in superseding the old. The study of various conditions of unevenness in the contradiction, the study of the principal contradiction and the non-principal contradiction, of the principal aspect of the contradiction and the non-principal aspect of the contradiction, constitutes one of the important methods by which a revolutionary political party determines correctly its political and military strategic and tactical directives. All Communists should note this. . . .

VI. THE ROLE OF ANTAGONISM IN CONTRADICTION

. . . In human history, antagonism between the classes exists as a particular manifestation of the struggle within the contradiction, the contradiction between the exploiting class and the exploited class. The two mutually contradictory classes coexist for a long time in one society, be it a slave, a feudal, or a capitalist society, and struggle with each other; but it is not until the contradiction between the two classes has developed to a certain stage that the two sides adopt the form of open antagonism which develops into a revolution. In a class society, the transformation of peace into war is also like that.

The time when a bomb has not yet exploded is the time when contradictory things, because of certain conditions, coexist in an entity. It is not until a new condition (ignition) is present that the explosion takes place. An analogous situation exists in all natural phenomena when they finally assume the form of open antagonism to resolve old contradictions and produce new things.

It is very important to know this situation. It enables us to understand that in a class society revolutions and revolutionary wars are inevitable, that apart from them the leap in social development cannot be made, and the reactionary ruling classes cannot be overthrown so that the people will win political power.

Communists must expose the deceitful propaganda of the reactionaries that social revolution is unnecessary and impossible, and so on, and firmly uphold the Marxist-Leninist theory of social revolution, so as to help the people understand that social revolution is not only entirely necessary but also entirely possible, and that the whole history of mankind and the triumph of the Soviet Union all confirm this scientific truth.

However, we must study concretely the conditions of various kinds of struggle within the contradiction and should not inappropriately impose the above-mentioned formula on everything. Contradiction and struggle are universal, absolute, but the methods for resolving contradictions, that is, the forms of struggle, differ according to the differences in the nature of the contradictions. Some contradictions are characterized by open antagonism, some are not. Based on the concrete development of things, some contradictions, originally non-antagonistic, develop and become antagonistic, while some contradictions, originally antagonistic, develop and become non-antagonistic.

The contradiction between correct ideology and erroneous ideologies within the Communist Party is, as we said earlier, the reflection in the party of class contradictions when classes exist. In the beginning, or with regard to particular matters, such a contradiction need not immediately manifest itself as antagonistic. But with the development of the class struggle, it can also develop and become antagonistic. The history of the Communist Party of the Soviet Union shows us that the contradiction between the correct ideology of Lenin and Stalin and the erroneous ideologies of Trotsky, Bukharin, and others, was in the beginning not yet manifested in an antagonistic form, but subsequently developed into antagonism. A similar case occurred in the history of the Chinese Communist Party. The contradiction between the correct ideology of many of our comrades in the party and the erroneous ideologies of Chen Tu-hsiu, Chang Kuo-tao, and others was also in the beginning not manifested in an antagonistic form, but subsequently developed into antagonism. At present, the contradiction between the correct ideology and the erroneous ideologies in our party is not manifested in an antagonistic form, and, if comrades who have made mistakes can correct them, it will not develop into antagonism. Therefore, on the one hand the party must carry on a serious struggle against erroneous ideologies, and on the other it must give the comrades who have made mistakes sufficient opportunity to become aware of them. Under such conditions, struggles pushed to excess are obviously not appropriate. But if those people who have made mistakes persist in them and increase the gravity of their mistakes, then there is the possibility of such contradictions developing into antagonism.

Economically, in capitalist society (where the town under bourgeois rule ruthlessly exploits the countryside) and in the Kuomintang-ruled areas in China (where the town under the rule of foreign imperialism and the native, comprador, big bourgeoisie most savagely exploits the countryside), the contradiction between the town and the countryside is one of extreme antagonism. But in a socialist country and in our revolutionary bases, such an antagonistic contradiction becomes a non-antagonistic contradiction; and it will disappear when a communist society is realized.

Lenin said: "Antagonism and contradiction are utterly different. Under socialism, antagonism disappears, but contradiction exists." That is to say, antagonism is only a form of struggle within the contradiction, but not its universal form; we cannot impose the formula everywhere. . . .

CONTEMPORARY CIVILIZATION: ITS MORAL COMMITMENT

I. THE CONTEXT OF MORAL LIFE

JACQUES MARITAIN

IN the latter half of the nineteenth century, the Roman Catholic Church, like many of the institutions of the period, sought to preserve its integrity and to guarantee the perdurance of its historical prerogatives and authority, by meeting the various challenges put to it by the intense nationalisms of the era and by the social problems which the Industrial Revolution had created. But in addition to the problem of maintaining the allegiance of many who were torn by competing loyalties, and who found in secular faiths, like socialism, the more immediate possibilities of social action and reform, the Church had the special task of retaining the intellectual assent of many who found it difficult to reconcile such things as Darwinism and the historical discoveries of the higher criticism of the Bible, with the traditional Christian views of man, nature, and revelation. And numbers of intellectuals who did not defect, nonetheless felt that the Church must either modernize its teachings or fail to continue as a genuine spiritual option, that dogma must be construed historically rather than as eternally given, that the function of religious teaching must be pragmatically, rather than doctrinally justified, and that doctrine itself, should it conflict with science in any way, must concede its inadequacy to pronounce on matters of fact. Such were the tenets of Modernism, a movement within the Church itself, and such were the views condemned as a "summation of heresies" by Pope Pius X in 1907. Pius not only took a number of practical steps against the Modernist leaders, many of whom he excommunicated and many of whose writings he had placed on the Index, but he also sought to reassert the intellectual authority of Catholicism in the encyclical *Pascendi,* which ordained that "scholastic philosophy be made the basis of the sacred sciences." In this he only echoed the policy of his predecessor, Leo XIII, who established Thomism as the foundation of accepted Christian thought in his encyclical of 1879, *Aeterni Patris,* which urged that "the golden wisdom of St. Thomas . . . (be spread) far and wide for the defense and beauty of the Catholic faith, for the good of society, and for the advantage of all the sciences." Thus it was that Scholasticism, a philosophical movement which in the writings of its greatest representative, St. Thomas Aquinas (1225–1274), had been perhaps the most characteristic intellectual expression of medieval Europe, rose again to polemical importance after nearly six hundred years of relative obscurity. St. Thomas had achieved the remarkable feat of accommodating Christian dogma to an entirely new intellectual foundation, and squaring it with Aristotelianism, the best science of his time. Though Thomism was widely promoted in ensuing centuries, it failed to stand up against the programs of humanism and of the New Science of the seventeenth century; and no subsequent attempt was made by any significant Catholic thinker to carry on the creative and synthetic endeavors of St. Thomas. However deeply Thomistic forms of thought may have been embedded into the Catholic consciousness, the scholastic movement had long since degenerated into eclectic glossing on the old texts. But Neo-Scholasticism breathed a certain life into the older forms, and sought to provide a scholastic framework within which science might be interpreted, rather than to permit science and faith to develop independently as Modernism recommended. It is to this movement of thought that the French philosopher, Jacques Maritain (b. 1882), belongs; and he is generally recognized as its most original and philosophically creative spokesman.

Raised as a Protestant, Maritain was encouraged by the poet Charles Péguy (1873–1914) to study with Henri Bergson, then lecturing at the Sorbonne. Maritain was initially convinced by Bergson's insistence that rationalism was unsound, though he subsequently undertook to show the inadequacy of his mentor's theory of intuition. Later, in 1906, under the influence of the novelist Léon Bloy (1846–1917), both Maritain and his wife became converted to Catholicism, and the philosopher apparently found a spiritual peace and intellectual orientation which had evaded him heretofore. He undertook to reconstruct his own philosophy on Thomistic foundations, and to bring Thomism to bear upon contemporary issues of science, politics, and morals. His chief production, *The Degrees of Knowledge* (1932), contains a presentation of the unity of knowledge and especially of the basic compatibility of science and religion. Maritain's philosophy repudiates subjectivism of every sort, and proclaims the reality of universals, the absoluteness of moral and aesthetic values, and the objectivity of truth. All of this, according to him, can be discovered through the free use of reason.

In 1914 he was appointed professor at the Institut Catholique de Paris, and he has lectured widely in Europe and America. He has been visiting professor at the universities of Toronto and Chicago and at Columbia and Princeton. He served as French Ambassador to the Vatican from 1945 to 1948. A prolific writer, Maritain's best known works include *Art and Scholasticism* (1930), *Introduction to Philosophy* (1930), *The Degrees of Knowledge* (1932), *True Humanism* (1938), *Christianity and Democracy* (1944), from which the following selection has been taken, in a translation from the French by Doris C. Anson, and *Man and the State* (1951).

CHRISTIANITY AND DEMOCRACY

EVANGELICAL INSPIRATION AND THE SECULAR CONSCIENCE

. . . When at the end of the eighteenth century the Rights of Man were proclaimed in America and in France, and the peoples bidden to partake of the ideal of Liberty, Equality and Fraternity, a great challenge of the people, of the plain man, of the spirit of childhood and faith, and at the same time of an ideal

This selection has been reprinted from *Christianity and Democracy* by Jacques Maritain; Copyright 1944 by Charles Scribner's Sons; used by permission of the publishers, Charles Scribner's Sons, New York (pp. 42–74).

of universal generosity, was hurled in the political domain itself at the mighty of this world and their experienced skepticism. The evangelical impulse which thus erupted bore the imprint of a secularized Christianity; rationalist philosophy added to it illusions—which quickly became bloody—and assured mankind that the goodness of nature and reason alone would suffice for the coming of the great promise of justice and peace. But through these illusions the heart of man sensed a sacred truth: that the energies of the Gospel must pass into temporal life; that the good tidings heralded as throwing open heaven and eternal life ask also to transform the life of earthly societies in the very midst of its woes and its contradictions, that there are in the message of the Gospel political and social implications which must at all cost be unfurled in history.

And do you think that old Christian peoples would have gone to the trouble of starting revolutions and massacres, would have set out with all their household and the heritage of their labor if it had not been for the promised and so long awaited beatitudes? If it is a mirage to believe them within reach of the hand, it is not a mirage to set out after them. The Middle Ages sought with the Holy Empire to erect a fortress for God on earth. Today the poor and the oppressed are setting out for the land of justice and fraternity. To have awakened and then betrayed such a hope is a measure of the failure of the modern world. It would be a worse failure to renounce this hope, and to seek to uproot it from men's hearts. Hard experience has taught us that the kingdom of God is not meant for earthly history, but at the same time we have become aware of this crucial truth that it must be enigmatically prepared in the midst of the pains of earthly history.

Christianity announced to the peoples the kingdom of God and the life to come; it has taught them the unity of the human race, the natural equality of all men, children of the same God and redeemed by the same Christ, the inalienable dignity of every soul fashioned in the image of God, the dignity of labor and the dignity of the poor, the primacy of inner values and of good will over external values, the inviolability of consciences, the exact vigilance of God's justice and providence over the great and the small. It has taught them the obligation imposed on those who govern and on those who have possessions to govern in justice, as ministers of God, and to manage the goods entrusted to them to the common advantage, as God's stewards, the submission of all to the law of work and the call to all to share in the freedom of the sons of God. It has taught them the sanctity of truth and the power of the Spirit, the communion of the saints, the divine supremacy of redeeming love and mercy, and the law of brotherly love which reaches out to all, even to those who are our enemies, because all men, to whatever social group, race, nation or class they may belong, are members of God's family and adopted brothers of the Son of God. Christianity proclaimed that where love and charity are, there God is; and that it is up to us to make every man our neighbor, by loving him as ourselves and by having compassion for him, that is, in a sense, by dying unto ourselves for his sake. Christ cursed the rich and the Pharisees. He promised the poor, and those who suffer persecution for the sake of justice that they shall inherit the kingdom of heaven, the meek that they shall inherit the earth, those who mourn that they shall be comforted, those that hunger and thirst after justice that they shall be satisfied, the merciful that they shall obtain mercy, the pure in heart that they shall see God, the peace-makers that they shall be called sons of God. He declared that everything that is done to the meanest of His brothers is done to Him, He gave to His disciples the new commandment: to love one another as He Himself has loved them.

What then are the thoughts and aspirations which the Christian message has by degrees awakened in the depths of the conscience of peoples, and which moved along underground for centuries before becoming manifest? However misunderstood and distorted they may have become in the course of this hidden journey in the secular conscience, what are those truths of evangelical origin which this conscience henceforth linked and identified with the very idea of civilization?

If we seek to consider them in themselves, separating them from any erroneous contexts, we would say that by virtue of the hidden work of evangelical inspiration, the secular conscience has understood that human history does not go around in circles, but is set toward a goal and moves in a certain direction. Progress is not automatic and necessary, but threatened and thwarted; progress is not due to an advent of pure reason which would invalidate the entire heritage of the past, it is rather this very heritage which increases while it groans under the labor of all the human and divine energies in man. Progress does not lead to the recovery of Paradise by Revolution tomorrow, it tends to the carrying over of the structures of conscience and the structures of human life to better states, and this all through history up to the advent of the kingdom of God and the land of the resurrected, which is beyond history. Whether or not you believe in this advent, it is toward it that you are moving, if you believe in the forward march of humanity. And what at any rate has been gained for the secular conscience, if it does not veer to barbarism, is faith in the forward march of humanity.

Under the often misunderstood but active inspiration of the Gospel, the secular conscience has understood the dignity of the human person and has understood that the person, while being a part of the State, yet transcends the

State, because of the inviolable mystery of his spiritual freedom and because of his call to the attainment of supra-worldly possessions. The State's reason for existing is to help him in the acquisition of these possessions and of a truly human life. What has been gained for the secular conscience, if it does not veer to barbarism, is faith in the rights of the human person, as a human person, as a civic person, as a person engaged in social and economic life and as a working person; and it is faith in justice as a necessary foundation for common life, and as an essential property of the law, which is not a law if it is unjust. Proudhon believed that thirst for justice is the privilege of Revolution, and the object of attentive dread for the Church. The thirst for justice was imprinted in the soul of the Christian ages by the Gospel and the Church; it is from the Gospel and the Church that we learn to obey only if it is just to do so.

Under the inspiration of the Gospel at work in history, the secular conscience has understood the dignity of the people and of the common man. Faithful people, God's little people, kingly people, called to share in the work of Christ; people in the sense of the community of the citizens of a country, united under just laws; people in the sense of the community of manual labor and of the stock and resource of humanity in those who toil close to nature—the notion of the people which the secular conscience has gradually formed, stems from the meeting and mingling of all these elements, and it is from the heritage of Christendom that this notion proceeds. The people are not God, the people do not have infallible reason and virtues without flaw, the will of the people or the spirit of the people is not the rule which decides what is just or unjust. But the people make up the slowly prepared and fashioned body of common humanity, the living patrimony of the common gifts and the common promises made to God's creature—which are more profound and more essential than all the additional privileges and the social distinctions—and of the equal dignity and equal weakness of all as members of the human race. It is on the condition of existing in communion with the people that all efforts bear fruit in temporal history, and that the inspirational leadership which the people need keeps both its strength and its legitimacy. Awakened to a consciousness of himself by the movement of civilization, the man of common humanity knows today that his day has dawned, if only he triumphs over totalitarian corruption and is not devoured by it; and he knows that the idea of a caste, of a class or a race hereditarily constituted as ruling and dominant must give way to the notion of a community of free men, equal in rights and in labor, and to the notion of an élite of the mind of labor which stems from the people without cutting itself off from them, and which would truly be the flower and luxury of their vital energies. What has been gained for the secular conscience, if it does not veer to barbarism, is the sense of men's equality in nature and the relative equality which justice must establish among them, and the conviction that by means of the functional inequalities demanded by social life, equality must be reestablished on a higher level, and must fructify in everyone's possibility of acceding to a life worthy of man, in everyone's assured enjoyment of the elementary possessions, both material and spiritual, of such a life, and in the true participation of each one, according to his capabilities and his worth, in the common task and the common heritage of civilization.

By virtue of the hidden work of evangelical inspiration, the secular conscience has understood that the authority of the rulers, by the very fact that it emanates from the author of human nature, is addressed to free men who do not belong to a master, and is exercised by virtue of the consent of the governed. The dictates of authority are binding in conscience because authority has its source in God; but from the very fact that authority has its source in God and not in man, no man and no particular group of men has in itself the right to rule others. The leaders of the people receive this right from the creative and conservative principle of nature through the channels of nature itself, that is, through the consent or will of the people or of the body of the community, through which authority always passes before being invested in the leaders. And it is as vicars or representatives of the multitude that the holders of authority lead the multitude, and it is toward the common good of the multitude that they must lead it. It is contrary to nature for men, members of the same species, all equal before God and death, to be simple tools of political power—tools of a dictator, the only human person among a flock of organized slaves, or tools of a paternalist power, the only adult among a regiment of children. Once the man of common humanity has understood that he is born with the right to conduct his own life by himself, as a being responsible for his acts before God and the law of the community, how can the people be expected to obey those who govern unless it is because the latter have received from the people themselves the custody of the people's common good? What has been gained for the secular conscience, if it does not veer to barbarism, is the conviction that authority, or the right to exercise power, is held by the rulers of the earthly community only because the common consent has been manifested in them, and because they have received their trust from the people; and it is the conviction that the normal state to which human societies ought to aspire is a state in which the people will act as grown-ups or those come of age in political life.

By virtue of the hidden work of evangelical inspiration the secular conscience has understood that the political realm and the flesh and blood paraphernalia of the things that are Caesar's must nevertheless be subject to God and to justice, it has understood that the entire art of domination and all the crimes which the princes and the heads of nations carry out to conquer and consolidate their power can certainly give them power but inevitably turn out for the misfortune of the peoples. Christianity cast the net of the Gospel upon the Pagan Empire and the Pagan Empire died of it, for there is no quarter given between the evangelical law of the Son of God and the law of the Empire which sets itself up as God. Once man has understood that in the truth of things politics depends upon morality because its aim is the human good of the community, once he has understood that political life must conform to natural law and, according to the special conditions of its temporal object, even to the law of the Gospel, he sees at the same moment that to call for justice and law in politics is to call for a great revolution which will substitute for the power politics of the masters, men, States or nations, the politics of the common good over which the people themselves must watch as the chief interested parties. A community of free men cannot live if its spiritual base is not solely law. Machiavellianism and the politics of domination, in the sight of which justice and law are a sure means of ruining everything, are the born enemies of a community of free men. What has been gained for the secular conscience, if it does not veer to barbarism, is the condemnation of the politics of domination and of iniquitous and perverse means in the guidance of nations, the profound feeling that justice fosters order and injustice the worst disorder, and the conviction that the cause of the welfare and freedom of the people and the cause of political justice are substantially linked.

Under the often misunderstood or disfigured but active inspiration of the Gospel, the secular conscience has awakened not only to the dignity of the human person, but also to the aspirations and the élan which are at work in his depths. The person, in itself a root of independence, but immersed in the constraints emanating from material nature within and outside man, tends to transcend these constraints and gain freedom of autonomy and expansion. In the very realm of spiritual life the message of the Gospel has revealed to the human person that he is called to the perfect freedom of those who have become a single spirit and love with God, but in the realm of temporal life it is natural aspiration of the person to liberation from misery, servitude, and the exploitation of man by man, that the repercussions of the Gospel's message were to stimulate. When you know that we are all made for blessedness, death no longer holds any terror; but you cannot become resigned to the oppression and enslavement of your brothers, and you aspire, for the earthly life of humanity, to a state of emancipation consonant with the dignity of this life. What has been gained for the secular conscience, if it does not veer to barbarism, is the sense of freedom and the conviction that the forward march of human societies is a march toward the conquest of a freedom consonant with the vocation of our nature.

Finally under the inspiration of the Gospel at work in history, the secular conscience has understood that in the misfortunes and suffering of our existence, crushed by the iron laws of biological necessity and by the weight of the pride, injustice and wickedness of men, a single principle of liberation, a single principle of hope, a single principle of peace can stir up the mass of servitude and iniquity and triumph over it, because this principle comes down to us from the creative source of the world, stronger than the world: that brotherly love whose law was promulgated by the Gospel to the scandal of the mighty, and which is, as the Christian well knows, God's own charity diffused into the hearts of men. And the secular conscience has understood that in the temporal social and political order itself, not only is civic friendship, as the ancient philosophers knew it, the soul and the constitutive link of the social community (if justice is first of all an essential requirement, it is as a necessary condition which makes friendship possible), but this very friendship between citizens cannot prevail in actual fact within the social group if a stronger and more universal love, brotherly love, is not instilled in it, and if civic friendship, itself becoming brotherhood, does not overflow the bounds of the social group to extend to the entire human race. Once the heart of man has felt the freshness of that terrible hope, it is troubled for all time. If it fails to recognize its supra-human origins and exigencies, this hope runs the risk of becoming perverted and of changing into violence to impose upon all "brotherhood or death." But woe to us if we scorn this hope itself, and succeed in delivering the human race from the promise of brotherhood. The human race has been exalted by it, it will give it up only at the cost of becoming more fierce than before. This hope is holy in itself, it corresponds to the deepest and most ineradicable desires of human nature; it places souls in a communion of pain and longing with all the oppressed and the persecuted; it calls for heroism; it has a divine power for transforming human history. What has been gained for the secular conscience, if it does not veer to barbarism, is faith in the brotherhood of man, a sense of the social duty of compassion for mankind in the person of the weak and the suffering, the conviction that the political work par excellence is that of rendering common life better and more brotherly, and of working so as to make of the structure of laws, institutions and customs of this common life a house for brothers to live in.

THE TRUE ESSENCE OF DEMOCRACY

The ideas and the aspirations of which I have just spoken characterize the democratic state of mind and the democratic philosophy of man and society. And it is under the influence of the evangelical ferment at work in the world that they took shape in the secular conscience. During the nineteenth century and particularly in Europe, as a consequence of the most absurd of historical contradictions, these ideas and aspirations were involved in a so-called philosophy of the emancipation of thought which drained them of all substance, disavowed and disintegrated them, all the while pretending to "put out the stars" in the name of science, and to make a man a soulless ape for whom the accidents of zoölogical mutations turned out favorably. In themselves, however, these ideas and these aspirations remained and will always remain essentially linked to the Christian message and to the action of hidden stimulation which this message exercises in the depths of the secular conscience of the world.

That is why I said above that the democratic impulse burst forth in history as a temporal manifestation of the inspiration of the Gospel. Statesmen know this well, and it is not without reason that in their defense of democracy they are today invoking the Sermon on the Mount. In his message of January 4, 1939, which has been said to contain "the outline of that reconstruction in their moral philosophy which the democracies must undertake if they are to survive," President Roosevelt stressed the fact that democracy, respect for the human person, for liberty, and for international good faith find their soundest foundation in religion and furnish religion with its best guarantees. He recently affirmed that "we (the United Nations) shall seek . . . the establishment of an international order in which the spirit of Christ shall rule the hearts of men and of nations."

In an important speech delivered on May 8, 1942, Henry A. Wallace, the Vice-President of the United States, declared in turn: "The Idea of freedom . . . is derived from the Bible with its extraordinary emphasis on the dignity of the individual. Democracy is the only true political expression of Christianity." Toward the close of his life, Chateaubriand had expressed the same thought. And in his book, *The Two Sources of Morality and Religion,* Henri Bergson also stated that because in the republican slogan "the essential thing is fraternity," we must state that "democracy is evangelical in essence." To the misfortune and the confusion of ideas of the modern world, Rousseau and Kant dressed democratic thought up in their sentimental and philosophical formulas. We know, however, "how much Kant owed to his pietism, and

Rousseau to an interplay of Protestantism and Catholicism." The sources of the democratic ideal must be sought many centuries before Kant and Rousseau.

Not only does the democratic state of mind stem from the inspiration of the Gospel, but it cannot exist without it. To keep faith in the forward march of humanity despite all the temptations to despair of man that are furnished by history, and particularly contemporary history; to have faith in the dignity of the person and of common humanity, in human rights and in justice—that is, in essentially spiritual values; to have, not in formulas but in reality, the sense of and respect for the dignity of the people, which is a spiritual dignity and is revealed to whoever knows how to love it; to sustain and revive the sense of equality without sinking into a leveling equalitarianism; to respect authority, knowing that its wielders are only men, like those they rule, and derive their trust from the consent or the will of the people whose vicars or representatives they are; to believe in the sanctity of law and in the efficacious virtue—efficacious at long range—of political justice in face of the scandalous triumphs of falsehood and violence; to have faith in liberty and in fraternity, an heroical inspiration and an heroical belief are needed which fortify and vivify reason, and which none other than Jesus of Nazareth brought forth in the world.

Let us also consider the immense burden of animality, of egoism, and of latent barbarism that men bear within themselves and which keeps social life still terribly far from achieving its truest and most elevated aims. Let us realize this fact that the part of instinct and irrational forces is even greater in communal existence than in individual existence, and that at the moment when the people enter into history by claiming their political and social majority, large portions of humanity remain in a state of immaturity or suffer from morbid complexes accumulated in the course of time, and are still no more than the rough draft or the preparation of that fruit of civilization which we call a people. Let us understand that in order to enjoy its privileges as an adult in political life without running the risk of failure a people must be able to act grown-up: then we will understand that the era has still not passed when for democracy itself force—righteous force—aside from its normal role in the policing of societies, must also play a subsidiary role of protecting against the return of the instinct of domination, exploitation or anarchic egoism. And above all we will understand that, with a view to curtailing as much as possible and eliminating by degrees these subsidiary functions of force, more than ever democracy needs the evangelical ferment in order to be realized and in order to endure. The lasting advent of the democratic state of mind and of the democratic philosophy of life requires the energies of the Gospel to penetrate secular existence, taming the irrational to reason and becoming embodied in the vital dynamism of the tendencies and instincts of nature, in order to fashion and stabilize in the depths of the subconscious those reflexes, habits and virtues without which the intellect which leads action fluctuates with the wind and wasting egoism prevails in man. It was Joseph de Maistre who said:

> Wherever a religion holds sway, there slavery is sanctioned, and wherever the Christian religion weakens, the nation becomes, in exact proportion, less capable of general liberty. . . . Government alone cannot govern, it needs either slavery which reduces the number of active wills in the State, or divine force, which by a kind of spiritual grafting, destroys the natural harshness of these wills, and enables them to work together without harm to one another.

It is not enough for a population or a section of the population to have Christian faith and be docile to the ministers of religion in order to be in a position properly to judge political matters. If this population has no political experience, no taste for seeing clearly for itself nor a tradition of initiative and critical judgment, its position with respect to politics grows more complicated, for nothing is easier for political counterfeiters than to exploit good principles for purposes of deception, and nothing is more disastrous than good principles badly applied. And moreover nothing is easier for human weakness than to merge religion with prejudices of race, family or class, collective hatreds, passions of a clan and political phantoms which compensate for the rigors of individual discipline in a pious but insufficiently purified soul. Politics deal with matters and interests of the world and they depend upon passions natural to man and upon reason. But the point I wish to make here is that without goodness, love and charity, all that is best in us—even divine faith, but passions and reason much more so—turns in our hands to an unhappy use. The point is that right political experience cannot develop in people unless passions and reason are oriented by a solid basis of collective virtues, by faith and honor and thirst for justice. The point is that without the evangelical instinct and the spiritual potential of a living Christianity, political judgment and political experience are ill protected against the illusions of selfishness and fear; without courage, compassion for mankind, and the spirit of sacrifice the ever-thwarted advance toward an historical ideal of generosity and fraternity is not conceivable.

As Bergson has shown in his profound analyses, it is the urge of a love infinitely stronger than the philanthropy commended by philosophers which caused human devotion to surmount the closed borders of the natural social groups—family group and national group—and extended it to the entire human race, because this love is the life in us of the very love which has created being and because it truly makes of each human being our neighbor. Without breaking the links of flesh and blood, of self-interest, tradition and pride which are needed by the body politic, and without destroying the rigorous laws of existence and conservation of this body politic, such a love extended to all men transcends and at the same time transforms from within the very life of the group, and tends to integrate all of humanity into a community of nations and peoples in which men will be reconciled. For the kingdom of God is not miserly, the communion which is its supernatural privilege is not jealously guarded; it wants to spread and refract this communion outside its own limits, in the imperfect shapes and in the universe of conflicts, malice and bitter toil which make up the temporal realm. That is the deepest principle of the democratic ideal, which is the secular name for the ideal of Christendom. That is why, Bergson writes, "democracy is evangelical in essence and . . . its motive power is love."

Yet in the same way it also appears that the democratic ideal runs against the grain of nature, whose law is not evangelical love. ". . . They were false democracies, those cities of antiquity, based on slavery, relieved by this fundamental iniquity of the biggest and most excruciating problems." Democracy is a paradox and a challenge hurled at nature, at the thankless and wounded human nature whose original aspirations and reserves of grandeur it evokes. In the democratic ideal, and "in the democratic frame of mind" we must see, Bergson writes, "a great effort running against the grain of nature": which does not mean an effort contrary to nature, but an effort to straighten nature, an effort linked to the developments of reason and justice and which must take place in history under the influence of the Christian leaven; an effort which requires that nature and the temporal order be elevated by the action of this leaven within their own realm, in the realm of civilization's movement. If the development of machinery and the great conquests which we have seen in the realm of matter and technique demand "an increment of soul" in order to become true instruments of liberation, it is also by means of this increment of soul that democracy will be realized. Its progress is bound up with the spiritualization of secular existence.

The democratic philosophy of man and society has faith in the resources and the vocation of human nature. In the great adventure of our life and our history it is placing its stakes on justice and generosity. It is therefore betting on heroism and the spiritual energies. This idealism runs all the risks if it does not take its source sufficiently high and if at the same stroke it misjudges the harsh natural realities at the heart of which it must work, for then it dares not face the existence and power of evil because it does not feel within itself the strength to overcome them. But if it truly understands the dignity of man and his vocation; if it is cognizant of the power of truth and the power of love; if it has respect for the soul and an awareness of the soul's grandeur; if at the top of the scale of values it places the workings of the spirit and of freedom; and if it knows that the pursuit of happiness is mysteriously linked to self-sacrifice, because it is above all the pursuit of the fulfillment of the human being in love, and because material goods and abundance in communal life are to be sought first of all as the conditions and means of such a goal; if it knows that the work of temporal salvation and earthly emancipation of humanity is at one and the same time the work of a humanity ransomed for eternal life and of a Redeeming God whose blood passes into its veins, then the idealism inherent in democratic philosophy can face the fierceness of the laws of material nature, the weakness and the perversity of men and the reality of evil in the world, because it knows that there is in man and above man the wherewithal to overcome all that. Indeed, all that will be overcome only amidst many impurities and imperfections. That is precisely why we must want all the more strongly to overcome it.

The essential characteristics of the democratic philosophy of man and society, or of the humanist political philosophy, stand forth with the greatest clarity in their opposition to the slave philosophy. This humanist political philosophy may be identified by the features which I stressed above: inalienable rights of the person, equality, political rights of the people whose consent is implied by any political régime and whose rulers rule as vicars of the people, absolute primacy of the relations of justice and law at the base of society, and an ideal not of war, prestige or power, but of the amelioration and emancipation of human life—the ideal of fraternity. For this philosophy the political task is *par excellence* a task of civilization and culture; it tends above all to provide the common good of the multitude in such a way that the concrete person, not only within the category of the privileged, but in the whole mass, truly accedes to the measure of independence which is compatible with civilized life and which is assured alike by the economic guarantees of labor and property, political rights, civic virtues and the cultivation of the mind. The democratic philosophy thrives on the unceasing work of invention, criticism and demands of individual conscience—it thrives on it and it would die of it if it were not also living on the unceasing gift of self which must correspond to this unceasing work of criticism and demand; running counter to the natural bent of man's imagination, it denies to the rulers the right to consider themselves and be considered a superior race, and wills nevertheless that their authority be respected on a juridical basis. It does not admit that the State is a transcendent power incorporating within itself all authority and imposed from above upon human life; it demands that autonomous organs, in possession of authority commensurate with their function, emanate spontaneously from the civil community and from the tension existing between its diverse activities, and that the State—controlled by the nation—be nothing more than the highest organ of regulation, whose object is the common good as it concerns the totality as such.

Are we called upon now to define that form of government to which the principles of the humanist political philosophy naturally tend? This philosophy maintains that the human person as such is called upon to participate in political life and that the political rights of a community of free men must be firmly secured. That is why it claims the right of suffrage for all adult citizens, of whatever race and social condition, and demands also that a juridically formulated constitution determine the basic laws of the régime under which the people deliberately resolve to place their political life. The principles of the democratic philosophy of man and society can adjust themselves to a (constitutional) system of monarchic or oligarchic government. But by right, as in fact, it is to the republican system that these principles tend as their most normal expression—to a system of government which must link and attune to the democratic dominant of freedom and the progressive enfranchisement of the human being, the qualities of oneness and of the differentiation of values, which were the prevailing features of the monarchic régime and the aristocratic régime since transcended, and in which the legislative power must be exercised by the representatives of the people, and the executive power by delegates who are directly or indirectly appointed by the people and whose conduct of affairs is controlled by them.

According to the popular saying, the democratic régime is described as the régime of the sovereignty of the people. This expression is ambiguous, for in truth there is no sovereign nor absolute master in a democracy. It would be better to say that democracy is the régime wherein the people enjoy their social and political majority and exercise it to conduct their own affairs; or better still to say that democracy is "the government of the people, by the people, for the people." Which means that the people are then governed by men whom they themselves have chosen for functions of a determined nature and duration, and over whose management they maintain a regular control, first of all by means of their representatives and the assemblies thus constituted.

The error of individualistic liberalism lay in denying in principle to those elected by the people every real right of command, on the pretext that everyone must "obey himself alone": these elected officers then became holders of a power without authority, and at the very moment that they were governing the people, they were obliged to make the people believe them mere passive tools of the people. In reality they receive their charge from the people and must govern in communion with them, but they hold real authority within the limits of their functions. Another error lay in reducing the community to an atomized mass of individuals confronted with an all-powerful State in which the will of each one was supposed to engulf and annihilate itself and mystically come to life again in the form of the general will; the error lay furthermore in excluding the existence and the autonomy, the initiative and the rights proper to each group or community of a rank inferior to the State, and finally, in causing the very concept of common good and common task to vanish. These errors which correspond to the advent of the bourgeois class and ideology, far from becoming an integral part of democracy, are deadly to democracy. These errors paved the way to totalitarianism, as did complacency to mediocrity and the hegemony of political parties, which are not essential to democracy either, but which are the constant temptation of all democracies lacking spiritual vigor. By freeing itself from such errors, a new democracy will be restored to the genuine principles of democratic philosophy.

This new democracy will not come into being easily. Even the most just of wars is a crisis brought on by the process of *disintoxication,* and which may turn out badly. It breaks open all abscesses. We must burn out all the pre-war poisons and do away with those which the war itself will have produced. In depth this operation affects all the structures of civilization, in scope the entire world. Once the Pagan Empire has been laid waste, its putrefaction of moral nihilism, of sadistic brutality, and of frenzied ideas will not be swept away at one blow, nor yet the inexpiable hatreds that it will have awakened, nor the vast amount of cast-off and shameful illusions which its lackeys, put to flight, will have dropped along the road. We will also have to face ancient interests and ancient economic privileges everywhere defending themselves tenaciously; ancient ambitions and ancient errors still eager to prey on the democracies; and new risks emanating from hardened national instincts and blind claims of prestige, or from the desire to turn the misfortune of men to account for a gold mine of profits and for the hegemony of big business, or from the fancies of the ignorant who seek to refashion the map of the world according to the principles of geopolitics and organize the universe "rationally" without knowing that man has a soul. The intelligence of the best architects is baffled when confronted with a civilization to be rebuilt; a new international order to be established, restoring their destinies not only to liberated Europe, but to liberated China and emancipated India; a new disposition, equitable for all men, to be found for what we still call the Colonial Empires—and which will not be found unless there truly prevail the sense of moral responsibility toward the populations, of respect for their soul and their wishes, and of true human fellowship with them. It is to be hoped that a sufficiently extended period of trial and adjustment, controlled by international agencies, will give experience the time to enlighten reason. In truth the democracies have to contend at one and the same time with the Pagan Empire and with themselves. They must triumph over Hitler and over their own self-contradictions in the social and spiritual realms. And not only must they recover on the one hand their genuine social and political impulse, and on the other hand their genuine spiritual impulse, but they must reconcile the two—and to that end get rid of bitter prejudices and ill-will.

REINHOLD NIEBUHR

IN the recent past, interest among Protestants in the larger questions of theology has revived in order to explain the difficulties and paradoxes of twentieth-century life. While many modern Catholics, such as Maritain, have reexamined St. Thomas in their attempt to answer Modernist challenges, Protestant theologians such as Karl Barth (b. 1886) and Emil Brunner (b. 1889) in Europe and Reinhold Niebuhr (b. 1892) and the European-trained Paul Tillich (b. 1886) in the United States have drawn their strength from the older Augustinian tradition with its emphasis on the limitations of human nature and the gulf between the human and the divine.

Neo-Augustinianism or Neo-orthodoxy is to be understood as part of a general reaction against the mood of the rationalistic liberal humanism that has had so large an influence in Western thought since the eighteenth century. More narrowly, theologians like Reinhold Niebuhr, Vice President of Union Theological Seminary, New York, also reject much of liberal Protestantism which, in accommodating itself to the modern spirit, had in some degree become synonymous with a purely ethical impulse and secular moral commitments. Niebuhr has tried to bring Protestantism back to an eschatological view of reality, to make of it what it was for Augustine, Thomas, Luther, and Calvin, a doctrine of truth rather than solace.

From his Gifford lectures at Edinburgh on *The Nature and Destiny of Man* (2 vols., 1941–43) to his *The Irony of American History* (1952) Niebuhr has been concerned to bring Christian eschatology to bear on contemporary problems. Not so severely orthodox as Karl Barth, who sees no possibilities for man in history except in participation in the personal drama of salvation, Niebuhr has been sufficiently influenced by American pragmatic liberalism to construe the doctrine of original sin as implying only the impossibility of *perfect* justice within human history. As Niebuhr suggests, in the following selection drawn from his *Moral Man and Immoral Society* (1932), historically, man is ever involved in the dilemmas of power and subject to the excesses of egotism. Creativeness and possibility are not denied man; Utopia and transcendence of self are.

In Niebuhr's thought man is seen as both creature and creator, involved in the equally real worlds of time and eternity. He is historically conditioned, subject to the influences and temptations of his age and place; however, he is also free in the sense that his nature is not merely the sum of the environmental forces that play upon him but also made in the image of God and thus capable of choice, will, and possibility. All of human history and life is thus to be understood in the classic Christian sense of a struggle and tension between man's creatureness and creativeness, the flesh and the spirit, the claims of history and the claims of a transcendent and timeless order.

In his earlier writings Niebuhr proposed nonviolence as a basis for Christian politics. With the growth of totalitarianism he urged Christians to use power in the form of the State to prevent the triumph of Hitler and Stalin. He warned, however, that not even a democratic society or state could escape the limitations of its citizens. Like seventeenth-century English radicals and their nonconformist descendants, Niebuhr uses the doctrine of original sin to suggest a democratic polity. His political sentiments are best summarized in his belief that man's injustice makes democracy with its checks and balances and recallable decisions necessary, while man's justice, his ability to better himself by pragmatic choice, makes democracy possible.

MORAL MAN AND IMMORAL SOCIETY

THE RELIGIOUS RESOURCES OF THE INDIVIDUAL FOR SOCIAL LIVING

The hopes and expectations of an ideal society, through the development of the moral capacities of individual men, have proceeded from and been encouraged by the religious, as well as the rational, idealists. The belief that a revival of religion will furnish the resources by which men will extricate themselves from their social chaos is a perennial one, and it expresses itself even in an age in which the forces of religion are on the defensive against a host of enemies and detractors. It justifies a thorough examination of the relation of religion to the moral life, particularly since an increasing number of sensitive spirits, whose chief interest is in the social problem, regard religion as a hindrance rather than a help in redeeming society from its ills.

If the recognition of selfishness is prerequisite to the mitigation of its force and the diminution of its anti-social consequences in society, religion should be a dominant influence in the socialisation of man; for religion is fruitful of the spirit of contrition. Feeling himself under the scrutiny of an omniscient eye, and setting his puny will into juxtaposition with a holy and omnipotent will, the religious man is filled with a sense of shame for the impertinence of his self-centered life. The sentiment of contrition runs as a persistent motif of humility through all classical religious literature and expresses itself in all religious life. It may become so stereotyped and formalised that its inner vitality is lost, but even then it pays tribute to an inner necessity of the religious life.

Essentially religion is a sense of the absolute. When, as is usually the case, the

---

This selection has been reprinted from *Moral Man and Immoral Society* by Reinhold Niebuhr;

absolute is imagined in terms of man's own highest ethical aspirations, a perspective is created from which all moral achievements are judged to be inadequate. Viewed from the relative perspectives of the historic scene, there is no human action which cannot be justified in terms of some historic purpose or approved in comparison with some less virtuous action. The absolute reference of religion eliminates these partial perspectives and premature justifications. There is no guarantee against the interpretation of the absolute in terms of faulty moral insights; and human vice and error may thus be clothed by religion in garments of divine magnificence and given the prestige of the absolute. Yet there is a general development in the high religions toward an interpretation of the divine as benevolent will, and a consequent increase of condemnation upon all selfish actions and desires. In investing the heart of the cosmos with an ethical will, the religious imagination unites its awe before the infinitude and majesty of the physical world with its reverence for the ethical principle of the inner life. The inner world of conscience, which is in constant rebellion against the outer world of nature, is made supreme over the world of nature by the fiat of religion. Thus the Bechuana regarded thunder as the accusing voice of God and cried: "I have not stolen, I have not stolen, who among us has taken the goods of another?" And Jesus, in the sublime *naïveté* of the religious imagination at its best, interprets the impartiality of nature toward the evil and the good, which secular reason might regard as its injustice, as a revelation of the impartial love of God. The religious imagination, seeking an ultimate goal and point of reference for the moral urges of life, finds support for its yearning after the absolute in the infinitude and majesty of the physical world. The omnipotence of God, as seen in the world of nature, invests his moral character with the quality of the absolute and transfigures it into holiness. Since supreme omnipotence and perfect holiness are incompatible attributes, there is a note of rational absurdity in all religion, which more rational types of theologies attempt to eliminate. But they cannot succeed without sacrificing a measure of religious vitality.

The religious conscience is sensitive not only because its imperfections are judged in the light of the absolute but because its obligations are felt to be obligations toward a person. The holy will is a personal will. Philosophers may find difficulty in transferring the concept of personality, loaded as it is with connotations which are derived from the sense limitations of human personality, to the absolute. But these difficulties are of small moment to the poetic imagination of religion. It uses the symbols derived from human personality to describe the absolute and it finds them morally potent. Moral attitudes always develop most sensitively in person-to-person relationships. That is

Assumption

one reason why more inclusive loyalties, naturally more abstract than immediate ones, lose some of their power over the human heart; and why a shrewd society attempts to restore that power by making a person the symbol of the community. The exploitation of the symbolic significance of monarchy, after it has lost its essential power, as in British politics for instance, is a significant case in point. The king is a useful symbol for the nation because it is easier for the simple imagination to conceive a sense of loyalty toward him than toward the nation. The nation is an abstraction which cannot be grasped if fitting symbols are not supplied. A living person is the most useful and potent symbol for this purpose. In religion all the higher moral obligations, which are lost in abstractions on the historic level, are felt as obligations toward the supreme person. Thus both the personality and the holiness of God provide the religious man with a reinforcement of his moral will and a restraint upon his will-to-power.

The history of religion is proof of the efficacy of religious insights in making men conscious of the sinfulness of their preoccupation with self. There is nothing, that modern psychologists have discovered about the persistence of ego-centricity in man, which has not been anticipated in the insights of the great mystics of the classical periods of religion. Asceticism, which is at once the great vice and the great virtue of religion, is the proof of its sensitive realisation of the evil of self-will. Schopenhauer quite rightly interprets religious asceticism as the "denial of the will-to-live."

His will turns round, no longer asserts its own nature but denies it. . . . Voluntary and complete chastity is the first step in asceticism or the denial of the will-to-live. It thereby denies the assertion of the will which extends beyond the individual life. . . . Asceticism then shows itself further in voluntary and intentional poverty which is meant as a constant mortification of the will, so that the satisfaction of wishes, the sweet of life, shall not again arouse the will, against which self-knowledge has gained a horror.

It is interesting to note that rigorous mystics frequently arrive at estimates of the selfishness of human action, which bear striking similarity to the analysis of human motives made by naturalistic hedonists. "All generosity," declares Fenelon in a letter to Madame Maintenon, "all natural affection is only self-love of a specially subtle, delusive and diabolical quality. We must wholly die to all friendship." This judgment might be compared with the words of De Mandeville,

The humblest man alive must confess that the reward of a virtuous action, which is the satisfaction that ensues upon it, consists in a certain pleasure he procures to himself by the contemplation of his own worth; which pleasure, together with the occasion of it, are certain signs of pride, as looking pale and trembling at any imminent danger are symptoms of fear.

It cannot be denied that mysticism and asceticism involve themselves in every kind of absurdity in their attempt to root out the selfishness of which their mystical contemplation has made them conscious. The mystic involves himself not only in the practical absurdity of becoming obsessed with self, in the very fever of the effort to eliminate it, but in the rational absurdity of passing judgment upon even the most unselfish desires as being selfish because they are desires. "We must suppress our desires, even the desire for the joys of paradise," declares Madame Guyon. Bossuet, who traces down these morbid efforts of the mystics to achieve absolutely consistent disinterestedness, paraphrases their dominant sentiment in the words, "The desire for God is not God, therefore we close the door upon that as well." The mystics who attempted to satisfy their longing for absolute perfection in ascetic practice were involved in an even more difficult and irrational procedure. They destroyed life and society in the process of refining it. Both Christian and Buddhist ascetics, unable to disassociate selfish desire from the will-to-live, have stopped short only of complete physical annihilation in their effort to destroy desire. In the paradox of Christ, "Whoso seeketh to find his life shall lose it and he that loseth his life for my sake shall find it," the religious tension which drives toward asceticism is resolved by condemning self-seeking as a goal of life, but allowing self-realisation as a by-product of self-abnegation. This paradox has saved Christianity from the pessimistic denials of life which characterise Hinduism and Buddhism, more particularly the latter. Yet the difference between Western and Eastern religion is only one of degree. Asceticism remains a permanent characteristic of all religious life. It may degenerate into morbid moralities of various kinds, but its complete absence is a proof of a lack of vitality in religion. A sun warm enough to ripen the fruits of the garden must make some fruits overripe. Criticism of the ascetic note in religion, which regards it merely as an excrescence and not as an inevitable by-product of the religious yearning for the absolute, proceeds from a lack of understanding of the true nature of religion.

. . . It would be well to consider . . . [that] moral resource of religion, which tends to qualify and to destroy the subjectivism into which mysticism and asceticism easily fall. This is the religious emphasis upon love as the highest virtue. A rational ethic aims at justice, and a religious ethic makes love the ideal. A rational ethic seeks to bring the needs of others into equal consideration with those of the self. The religious ethic (the Christian ethic more particularly, though not solely) insists that the needs of the neighbor shall be met, without a careful computation of relative needs. This emphasis upon love is another fruit of the religious sense of the absolute. On the one hand religion absolutises the sentiment of benevolence and makes it the norm and ideal of the moral life. On the other hand it gives transcendent and absolute worth to the life of the neighbor and thus encourages sympathy toward him. Love meets the needs of the neighbor, without carefully weighing and comparing his needs with those of the self. It is therefore ethically purer than the justice which is prompted by reason. (Since it is more difficult to apply to a complex society it need not for that reason be socially more valuable than the rational principle of justice.) In part the religious ideal of love is fed and supported by viewing the soul of the fellowmen from the absolute and transcendent perspective. Your neighbor is a son of God, and God may be served by serving him. "What ye have done unto one of the least of these my brethren, ye have done unto me," said Jesus. "I have come to the stage of realisation in which I see that God is walking in every human form and manifesting himself alike in the sage and in the sinner," said the Indian saint Ramakrishna. It is religious insight, flowing from the capacity of the religious imagination to view the immediate and the imperfect from the perspective of the absolute and the transcendent, which prompted St. Francis to kiss the leper and to trust the robber; which persuaded Paul that "in Christ there is neither Jew nor Greek, neither bond nor free"; which inspired an old Indian saint to greet the soldier, who, in the time of the Indian mutiny, was about to put the cold steel of his bayonet into the body of the saint, with the words, "And thou too art divine." Nor does the religious appreciation of human personality reveal itself only in highly mystical natures. Unlike the spirit of asceticism, it manifests itself in more rationalised forms of religion. The Stoic doctrine of brotherhood was rooted in Stoic pantheism. Kant's maxim that human beings must always be treated as ends and never as means, is not the axiom of rational ethics that he supposes. It cannot be, in fact, consistently applied in any rational ethical scheme. It is rather, a religious ideal inherited from Kant's pietistic religious worldview. Religious reverence for human life is the mainspring of the idealism of as rationalistic a Christian as William Ellery Channing. He writes:

> I have felt and continually insisted that a new reverence for man was essential to the cause of social reform. There can be no spirit of brotherhood, nor true peace, any farther than men come to understand their affinity with and relation to God and the infinite purposes for which he gave them life. . . . None of us can conceive the change of manners, the new courtesy and sweetness, the mutual kindness, deference and sympathy, the life and efforts for social melioration, which are to spring up in proportion as man shall penetrate beneath the body to the spirit, and shall learn what the lowest human being is.

This logic impelled Channing to espouse the antislavery cause, just as a more mystical Christian, the Quaker, John Woolman, found slavery incompatible with his religious estimate of human personality as a facet of the divine. While, as Troeltsch properly maintains, religious idealism never arrives at equalitarian political ideals without the aid of rationalistic political thought, the doctrine of the transcendent worth of all human personality does tend to become transmuted into the idea of the equal worth of all personalities. This idea may achieve real ethico-political significance; though it must be confessed that its political possibilities are usually vitiated by the suggestion of religion, that equality before God need not imply equality in historic social relations. The religious sense of the absolute may, in this and in other instances, overreach itself and end by destroying the ethical possibilities which it has created.

The introspective character of religion, which results in the spirit of contrition also contributes to its spirit of love. Egoistic impulses are discovered and analysed in the profounder types of religious introversion. They are condemned with the greater severity because the critical eye of the self becomes the accusing eye of God in the mystical religious experience. This condemns selfishness more readily than it encourages love. It results in an ideal of disinterestedness rather than an ideal of benevolence. But it may offer strong support to the spirit of love by its critical attitude toward all egoism. A man's actions may be regarded as more benevolent than they really are from an external perspective, from which the hidden motives cannot be recognised. Even when they are known to be selfish they may gain approval from a social perspective. From the inner perspective neither this confusion nor this approval is possible. The alloy of egoism which corrupts all benevolence is isolated, and sometimes purged, from it by a rigorous internal analysis. Furthermore the social justification of egoism has no weight in this analysis. The actions and attitudes of the soul are judged in the light of an absolute moral ideal, and are found to fall short in comparison with it. Religious introspection may involve the soul in hopeless obsession with self, if escape from self is attempted without social reference. But the check which it places upon egoism is a potential support for the spirit of love.

If religion be particularly occupied with the absolute from the perspective of the individual, it is nevertheless capable of conceiving an absolute society in which the ideal of love and justice will be fully realised. There is a millennial hope in every vital religion. The religious imagination is as impatient with the compromises, relativities and imperfections of historic society as with the imperfections of individual life. The prophet Isaiah dreamed of the day when the lion and the lamb would lie down together, when, in other words, the law of nature which prompts the strong to devour the weak would be abrogated. The

religious idealists of both Egypt and Babylon had their visions of an ideal reign. Sometimes the contrast between the real and the ideal is drawn so sharply that the religious man despairs of the achievement of the ideal in mundane history. He transfers his hopes to another world. This is particularly true of religion influenced by Platonic idealism, in which the ideal world is always above and not at the end of human history. It was the peculiar genius of Jewish religious thought, that it conceived the millennium in this-worldly terms. The gospel conception of the kingdom of God represents a highly spiritualised version of this Jewish millennial hope, heavily indebted to the vision of the Second Isaiah. Wherever religion concerns itself with the problems of society, it always gives birth to some kind of millennial hope, from the perspective of which present social realities are convicted of inadequacy, and courage is maintained to continue in the effort to redeem society of injustice. The courage is needed; for the task of building a just society seems always to be a hopeless one when only present realities and immediate possibilities are envisaged. The modern communist's dream of a completely equalitarian society is a secularised, but still essentially religious, version of the classical religious dream. Its secularisation is partly a reaction to the unrealistic sentimentality into which the religious social hope degenerated in the middle-class religious community; partly it is the inevitable consequence of the mechanisation of modern life and the destruction of religious imagination. Though it is a secularised version of the religious hope, its religious quality is attested by its emphasis upon catastrophe. It does not see the new society emerging by gradual and inevitable evolutionary process. It is pessimistic about the present trends in society and sees them driving toward disaster; but its hope, as in all religion, grows out of its despair, and it sees the new society emerging from catastrophe. Evolutionary millennialism is always the hope of comfortable and privileged classes, who imagine themselves too rational to accept the ideal of the sudden emergence of the absolute in history. For them the ideal is in history, working its way to ultimate triumph. They identify God and nature, the real and the ideal, not because the more dualistic conceptions of classical religion are too irrational for them (though they are irrational); but because they do not suffer as much as the disinherited from the brutalities of contemporary society, and therefore do not take as catastrophic a view of contemporary history. The more privileged proletarians turn catastrophic Marxism into evolutionary socialism for the same reason. Religion is always a citadel of hope,

which is built on the edge of despair. Men are inclined to view both individual and social moral facts with complacency, until they view them from some absolute perspective. But the same absolutism which drives them to despair,

rejuvenates their hope. In the imagination of the truly religious man the God who condemns history will yet redeem history.

The undoubted moral resources of religion seem to justify the religious moralists in their hope for the redemption of society through the increase of religio-moral resources. In their most unqualified form, these hopes are vain. There are constitutional limitations in the genius of religion which will always make it more fruitful in purifying individual life, and adding wholesomeness to the more intimate social relations, such as the family, than in the problems of the more complex and political relations of modern society. The disrepute in which modern religion is held by large numbers of ethically sensitive individuals, springs much more from its difficulties in dealing with these complex problems than from its tardiness in adjusting itself to the spirit of modern culture. A society which is harassed with the urgent political and economic problems, which confront our contemporary world, is inclined to be scornful of any life-expression, which is not immediately relevant to its most urgent tasks. In that attitude it may be no more justified than are the religious sentimentalists, who insist that they have a panacea for every ill to which the human flesh is heir.

The religious sense of the absolute qualifies the will-to-live and the will-to-power by bringing them under subjection to an absolute will, and by imparting transcendent value to other human beings, whose life and needs thus achieve a higher claim upon the self. That is a moral gain. But religion results also in the absolutising of the self. It is a sublimation of the will-to-live. Though God is majestic and transcendent he is nevertheless related to man by both his qualities and his interest in man. His qualities are human virtues, raised to the *n*th degree. His interest in man remains even when, as in modern Barthian theology, he is described as the "wholly other." In religion man interprets the universe in terms relevant to his life and aspirations. Religion is at one and the same time, humility before the absolute and self-assertion in terms of the absolute. Naturalists, who accuse religion of either too much pride or of too abject self-depreciation, fail to understand this paradox of the religious life. Naturally the two elements are not always equally powerful. . . . The two emphases exist side by side in varying degrees in almost every expression of the religious life. Whether the religious sublimation of the will-to-live mitigates the sharpness of the conflict between the will-to-power of individuals on the historic level, by lifting the energy of life to a higher level and beguiling the soul to seek ultimate satisfactions in a transhistorical and supramundane world, is a difficult question to answer. In some respects this is the effect of the religious life. The modern radical, who regards religion as an opiate, justifies his indictment in terms of this characteristic of religion. On the other hand, the religious sanctification of the individual life and will, may make it a more resolute force in the historic situation. The power, by which the middle commercial classes defeated the landed aristocracy in the political and economic battles of the past three centuries, was partially derived from the puritan sense of the religious worth of personality and of the spiritual character of secular pursuits. . . . The fact seems to be that the religious sublimation of the will-to-live is also, or may be, an extension of that will in historic and social terms. The prizes of another world may prompt the weak man to resignation, but they will encourage the strong man to deeds of superhuman heroism.

The danger to social life of this impartation of absolute value to human life is most apparent when it expresses itself in the life of national and other groups rather than in individuals. There is a moral and social imagination in religion which invests the life of other nations with a significance as great as that which is claimed for one's own nation. But it is not as powerful and not as frequently expressed as the imagination which makes one's own nation the peculiar instrument of transcendent and divine purposes. The prophet Amos could cry in the name of the Lord, "Are ye not as the children of the Ethiopians unto me, saith the Lord?" But his was a voice in the wilderness among the many who regarded Israel as the special servant of God among the nations of the world. It is not religion which gives a special dignity and worth to the life of the nation to which one belongs. Patriotism is a form of piety which exists partly through the limitation of the imagination, and that limitation may be expressed by savants as well as by saints. The wise men of the nations were just as sedulous in proving, during . . . World War [I], that their particular nation had a peculiar mission to "culture" and to "civilisation" as were the religious leaders in asserting that the will of God was being fulfilled in the policy of their state. But since the claims of religion are more absolute than those of any secular culture the danger of sharpening the self-will of nations through religion is correspondingly greater.

Even when the religious sense of the absolute expresses itself, not in the sublimation of the will, but in the subjection of the individual will to the divine will, and in the judgment upon the will from the divine perspective, it may still offer perils to the highest social and moral life, even though it will produce some choice fruits of morality. One interesting aspect of the religious yearning after the absolute is that, in the contrast between the divine and the human, all lesser contrasts between good and evil on the human and historic level are obscured. Sin finally becomes disobedience to God and nothing else. Only rebellion against God, and only the impertinence of self-will in the sight of God, are regarded as sinful. One may see this logic of religion very clearly in the thought of Jonathan Edwards. "A crime is more or less heinous," he declares,

according as we are under greater or less obligation to the contrary. Our obligation to love, honor and obey any being is in proportion to its loveliness, honorableness and authority. But God is a being infinitely lovely because he has infinite excellence and beauty. So that sin against God, being a violation of infinite obligations, must be a crime infinitely heinous and so deserving of infinite punishment.

The sin which the religious man feels himself committing against God is indeed the sin of self-will; but his recognition of the fact may, but need not, have special social significance. So strong is the emphasis upon the God-and-man relationship in the religious conception of sin, that Rudolf Otto is able to interpret it entirely as a feeling of profanity before the sacred. This is probably an overstatement of the fact; for "the holy" achieves a connotation of the morally perfect in the development of religion and sin is correspondingly defined in moral terms. Nevertheless the tendency to lose moral distinctions in the emphasis upon the religious aspect of sin remains a permanent characteristic of vital religious life. In the modern Barthian revival of Lutheran orthodoxy the religious experience is practically exhausted in the sense of contrition. The emphasis upon the difference between the holiness of God and the sinfulness of man is so absolute that man is convicted, not of any particular breaches against the life of the human community, but of being human and not divine. Thus, to all intents and purposes, creation and the fall are practically identified and, everything in human history being identified with evil, the "nicely calculated less and more" of social morality lose all significance. It is interesting that Schleiermacher, the *bête noir* of the modern Barthians, interprets the relation of morality and religion in terms which explicitly confess what is implicit in the Barthian position but not as freely admitted. . . . The implicit pantheism of Schleiermacher's position is diametrically opposed to Barthian conceptions of divine transcendence and it results in making reverence rather than contrition the dominant religious feeling. But both result in an identical separation of religion and morality.

Augustine, writing about the two cities in his *De civitate Dei,* contrasts the religious and the secular in a similar vein; and moral differences are thereby obscured or effaced:

Two loves therefore have given origin to these two cities, self-love in contempt of God unto the earthly; love of God in contempt of one's self to the heavenly. The first seeketh the glory of man, and the latter desires God only, as the testimony of the conscience, the greatest glory. . . . In the earthly city the wise men follow either the goods of the body or mind or both, living according to the flesh . . . but in the other, this heavenly city, there is no wisdom of man but only the piety that serveth the true God and expecteth a reward in the society of the holy angels and men, that God may be all in all.

There is a form of religious piety in which religious sensitivity heightens the sense of sin, without destroying its moral connotation; in which the affront to God is the final, but not the only, crime of selfishness, and in which the worship of God is the crown, but not the only, manifestation of the self-conquered life. Such a relation between religion and ethics is found in the thought of Thomas Aquinas for instance. Nevertheless the tendency of religion to obscure the shades and shadows of moral life, by painting only the contrast between the white radiance of divine holiness and the darkness of the world, remains a permanent characteristic of the religious life.

This tendency has more than one dubious effect. It certainly tends very readily to a moral, social and political indifferentism. The individual, and more particularly society, are regarded as too involved in the sins of the earth to be capable of salvation in any moral sense. Usually the individual is saved by the grace of God, while society is consigned to the devil; that is, the social problem is declared to be insoluble on any ethical basis. Thus Augustine concludes that the city of this world is "compact of injustice," that its ruler is the devil, that it was built by Cain and that its peace is secured by strife. That is a very realistic interpretation of the realities of social life. It would stand in wholesome contrast to the sentimentalities and superficial analyses, current in modern religion, were it not marred by a note of defeatism. That note creeps easily into all rigorous religion, with its drift toward dualism. The injustices of society are placed into such sharp contrast with the absolute moral ideal, conceived by the individual conscience, that the religiously sensitised soul is tempted to despair of society. Religion thus degenerates into an asocial quest for the absolute. The soul seeks the perfection of God in either quietistic absorption or ascetic withdrawal from the world; and in each case perfection is defined and experienced in purely individualistic terms. Another possible alternative is to regard the absolute and the perfect as unattainable and to despair of achieving any virtue which would have significance in the sight of God. In that case the religious man is comforted by the experience of grace, an experience in which the religious life accepts the mercy and forgiveness of God as consolation for its failure, and turns defeat into victory by enjoying an anticipatory attainment of what is regarded as unattainable. In all these various forms religion heightens the tensions of life and then relaxes them. The moral tension of life is invariably imperilled in this process of religious relaxation. Religion draws the bow of life so taut that it either snaps the string (defeatism) or overshoots the mark (fanaticism and asceticism). The belief that the moral weaknesses of religion may be eliminated simply by increasing religious vitality is too simple to be true. The greater the vitality of religion, the more it may either support or endanger morality. It may create sensitivity and destroy moral vigor by the force of the same vitality.

Both the resources and the limitations of religion in dealing with the social problem, are revealed even more clearly in its spirit of love than in its sense of contrition. Religion encourages love and benevolence, as we have seen, by absolutising the moral principle of life until it achieves the purity of absolute disinterestedness and by imparting transcendent worth to the life of others. This represents a permanent contribution to the moral life which, despite limitations revealed in the more intricate and complex social relations, must be gratefully accepted as an extension and enlargement of the moral attitudes, usually expressed only in the more intimate relations. "If ye love them that love you, what reward have ye?" declared Jesus; and in the logic of those words the whole social genius of the Christian religion is revealed. The transcendent perspective of religion makes all men our brothers and nullifies the divisions, by which nature, climate, geography and the accidents of history divide the human family. By this insight many religiously inspired idealists have transcended national, racial and class distinctions.

The great seers and saints of religion have always placed their hope for the redemption of society in the possibility of making the love-universalism, implicit in religious morality, effective in the whole human society. When Celsus accused the early Christians of destroying the integrity of the empire by their moral absolutism, Origen answered: "There is no one who fights better for the king than we. It is true that we do not go with him to battle, but we fight for him by forming an army of our own, an army of piety, through our prayers to the Godhead. Once all men have become Christians then even the barbarians will be inclined to peace." It was a natural and inevitable hope in the early Christian community that the spirit of love, which pervaded the life of its own group, would eventually inform the moral life of the whole human race. That hope has been reborn again and again in the history of the Western world. Thousands of Christians, who keenly felt the World War [I] as an apostasy from the Christian spirit, consoled themselves with the thought that Christianity had not failed, because it had not been tried. The implication of this observation is that it will someday be tried. Not a few Christian historians have intimated that, but for the unhappy conversion of Constantine, which gave Christianity a premature popularity, the love spirit of the early Christian community might have been preserved for future history. All this leaves definite limitations of the human heart and imagination out of account. These limitations make it inevitable that the religious spirit of love should lose some of its force in proportion to the size of the communities which profess it, the impersonal and indirect character of social relations in which it operates, and the complexity of the situation which it faces. The Christian sects, such as the Quakers and other small religious communities, have preserved it more purely than the churches with their inclusive membership. It has characterised the lives of individual saints more than that of any religious communities, even small and intimate ones. All of which means that religion may increase the power and enlarge the breadth of the generous social attitudes, which nature prompts in the intimate circle; but that there are definite limits to its power and extension. All men cannot be expected to become rational. Those who achieve either excellence will always be a leavening influence in social life; but the political structure of society cannot be built upon their achievement. Religion may consolidate benevolent sentiments and lodge their force in the will, thus giving the whole character a consistent benevolence, more stable than the force of tender sentiments. Nevertheless even this goodwill depends for its encouragement and excitement upon personal contacts, and the relevation of need in vivid terms. We express our love most generously to those who have natural claims upon us, and to those who have no claims at all. The beggar, the completely disinherited, the needy at the ends of the earth, the lepers to whom Father Damien went and the children of the primeval forest, who are being served by Albert Schweitzer, these and our own kin are the inciters and prompters of the spirit of love; love is most active when the vividness or nearness of the need prompts those whose imagination is weak, and the remoteness of the claim challenges those whose imagination is sensitive. Love, which depends upon emotion, whether it expresses itself in transient sentiment or constant goodwill, is baffled by the more intricate social relations in which the highest ethical attitudes are achieved only by careful calculation. If it cannot find an immediate object it has difficulties in expressing itself. The same intellectual analysis which the complex situation requires may actually destroy the force of the benevolent impulse.

Furthermore there is always the possibility that the perfectionism, which prompts religious generosity, is more interested in the perfect motive than in ideal consequences. Preoccupation with motive is an unvarying characteristic of the religious life, which has its own virtues, but is also perilous to the interests of society. It is responsible for the many absurdities which have been committed in the name of religious philanthropy; absurdities which are inevitable when the benevolent spirit disregards the social consequences of generous action. The *Didache,* written in the second century, admonishes Christians to be uneasy until a beneficiary of their almsgiving appears. "Let thine alms sweat in thine hand until thou know to whom to give them," it declares.

The weaknesses of the spirit of love in solving larger and more complex problems become increasingly apparent as one proceeds from ordinary relations between individuals to the life of social groups. If nations and other social groups find it difficult to approximate the principles of justice . . . they are naturally even less capable of achieving the principle of love, which demands more than justice. The demand of religious moralists that nations subject themselves to "the law of Christ" is an unrealistic demand, and the hope that they will do so is a sentimental one. Even a nation composed of individuals who possessed the highest degree of religious goodwill would be less than loving in its relation to other nations. It would fail, if for no other reason, because the individuals could not possibly think themselves into the position of the individuals of another nation in a degree sufficient to insure pure benevolence. Furthermore such goodwill as they did possess would be sluiced into loyalty to their own nation and tend to increase that nation's selfishness. . . . No nation in history has ever been known to be purely unselfish in its actions. The same may be said of class groups with equal certainty. Religious idealism may qualify national policies, as much as rational idealism, but this qualification can never completely eliminate the selfish, brutal and antisocial elements, which express themselves in all intergroup life.

The religious idealist, confronted with these stubborn obstacles to the realisation of his ideals, is tempted either to leave the world of political and economic relations to take the course which natural impulse prompts, or to assume that his principles are influencing political life more profoundly than they really are. He is tempted, in other words, either to defeatism or to sentimentality. We have previously considered the social indifferentism which results from a too purely religious interpretation of sin. Very closely akin to this indifferentism is the defeatism which results not from a purely religious conception of good and evil but from a definition of the ideal in such pure moral terms (*i.e.,* absolute love) that the more complex political and economic relations are clearly outside of the pale of the religio-moral ideal. Religion, in short, may be indifferent toward or despair of the politico-moral problem not only when it makes an unequivocal contrast between the divine and the human but when, remaining on the human and moral level, it adopts a rigorous perfectionism in stating its moral ideal. The early church was defeatist in its attitude toward the "world," regarding the world as doomed and expressing its optimism in its millennial hopes. When these began to wane and the church was forced to assume responsibility for political and economic life, there was little disposition to challenge the basic social customs and relationships in the name of the Christian ideal. Slavery, injustice, inequality of wealth, war, these all were accepted as ordained by the "natural law" which God had devised for man's sinful state. Occasionally there was considerable confusion, whether such social arrangements, as slavery for instance, should be regarded as the fruit of man's condition or as the instrument which God uses to hold sin in check. At any rate the prevailing institutions were accepted, even though the church was quite conscious of the conflict between them and its own ideal. Its natural determinism, its faith that nothing in nature or history could exist without the explicit will of God, gave additional support to this tendency. The natural law might be of a lower order than the law of the gospel, but its institutions of state and property, of war and inequality were nevertheless ordained of God. It was left to the monastics, and in Protestant times to the sects, to incarnate the higher law. For the church, both Catholic and Protestant, the law of love was interpreted religiously rather than socially. It guaranteed equality before God, and therefore in the religious community; but this did not imply that the church would strive to realise an ideal of social justice in society. Luther in fact turned on the peasants of his day in holy horror when they attempted to transmute the "spiritual" kingdom into an "earthly" one by suggesting that the principles of the gospel had social significance.

The fact that slaves had rights of equality in the early church did not aid them in improving their civil status. The church left the institution of slavery undisturbed until economic forces transmuted it into the serfdom of the Middle Ages. The fact that individual Christians manumitted their slaves proves that the principles of the gospel could inspire individuals more readily than they could prompt social and political policies. To this day religious communities and churches pride themselves on ability to transcend economic and social inequalities within the pale of their organisation; but it does not follow that they will move vigorously against the social injustices in the larger society which they know to be in conflict with their religious and moral ideal.

This defeatism of religion is derived from a too consistent God-world, spirit-body dualism, in which the fact, that natural impulses in the economic and political life more under less restraint of reason and conscience than in the private conduct of individuals, persuades the religious man to despair of bringing any ethical values into them whatsoever. There is a certain realism in this defeatism, and it has its own virtues, when compared with the sentimentality derived from a too consistent monism, in which God and the world, the ideal and the real are identified. If defeatism is the besetting sin of both Catholic and Protestant orthodoxy, sentimentality is the peculiar vice of liberal Protestantism. By adjusting its faith to the spirit of modern culture it imbibed the evolutionary optimism and the romantic overestimates of human virtue, which characterized the thought of the Enlightenment and of the Romantic Movement. The vices are therefore not the peculiar vices of religion. But religion frequently adds a sentimental bathos to the illusions under which naturalistic monists live. "Ye are Gods, you are crystalline, your faces are radiant," cried Henry Ward Beecher to his congregation, illustrating how the Christian ethos may accommodate itself to naturalistic romanticism. His contemporary Walt Whitman, standing squarely in the romantic tradition, had the same estimate of the moral and spiritual worth of man: "I exist as I am: that is enough. Divine am I inside and out, and I make holy whatever I touch and am touched from."

The evolutionary optimism of the eighteenth and nineteenth centuries, and the sentimentalisation of the moral and social problem in romanticism, have affected religious idealism with particular force in America, because they suited the mood of a youthful and vigorous people, youth usually being oblivious of the brutality which is the inevitable concomitant of vitality. Furthermore the expanding economy of America obscured the cruelties of the class struggle in our economic life, and the comparative isolation of a continent made the brutalities of international conflict less obvious. Thus we developed a type of religious idealism, which is saturated with sentimentality. In spite of the disillusionment of the World War, the average liberal Protestant Christian is still convinced that the kingdom of God is gradually approaching . . . that the wealthy will be persuaded by the church to dedicate their power and privilege to the common good and that they are doing so in increasing numbers, that the conversion of individuals is the only safe method of solving the social problem, and that such ethical weaknesses as religion still betrays are due to its theological obscurantism which will be sloughed off by the progress of enlightenment.

It might be added that when the cruelties of economic and political life are thus obscured, and when the inertia, which every effort toward social justice must meet in any society, however religious or enlightened, remains unrecognised, there is always a note of hypocrisy, as well as sentimentality, in the total view. Those who benefit from social injustice are naturally less capable of understanding its real character than those who suffer from it. They will attribute ethical qualities to social life, if only the slightest gesture of philanthropy hides social injustice. If the disinherited treat these gestures with cynicism and interpret unconscious sentimentality as conscious hypocrisy, the privileged will be properly outraged and offended by the moral perversity of the recipients of their beneficences. Since liberal Protestantism is, on the whole, the religion of the privileged classes of Western civilisation, it is not surprising that its espousal of the ideal of love, in a civilisation reeking with social injustice, should be cynically judged and convicted of hypocrisy by those in whom bitter social experiences destroy the sentimentalities and illusions of the comfortable.

Religion, in short, faces many perils to the right and to the left in becoming an instrument and inspiration of social justice. Every genuine passion for social justice will always contain a religious element within it. Religion will always leaven the idea of justice with the ideal of love. It will prevent the idea of justice, which is a politico-ethical ideal, from becoming a purely political one, with the ethical element washed out. The ethical ideal which threatens to become too purely religious must save the ethical ideal which is in peril of becoming too political. Furthermore there must always be a religious element in the hope of a just society. Without the ultrarational hopes and passions of religion no society will ever have the courage to conquer despair and attempt the impossible; for the vision of a just society is an impossible one, which can be approximated only by those who do not regard it as impossible. The truest visions of religion are illusions, which may be partially realised by being resolutely believed. For what religion believes to be true is not wholly true but ought to be true; and may become true if its truth is not doubted.

Yet the full force of religious faith will never be available for the building of a just society, because its highest visions are those which proceed from the insights of a sensitive individual conscience. If they are realised at all, they will be realised in intimate religious communities, in which individual ideals achieve social realisation but do not conquer society. To the sensitive spirit, society must always remain something of the jungle, which indeed it is, something of the world of nature, which might be brought a little nearer the kingdom of God, if only the sensitive spirit could learn, how to use the forces of nature to defeat nature, how to use force in order to establish justice. Knowing the peril of corruption in this strategy, the religious spirit recoils. If that fear can be overcome religious ideals may yet achieve social and political significance.

Meanwhile it must be admitted that no society will ever be so just, that some method of escape from its cruelties and injustices will not be sought by the pure heart. The devotion of Christianity to the cross is an unconscious glorification of the individual moral ideal. The cross is the symbol of love triumphant in its own integrity, but not triumphant in the world and society. Society, in fact, conspired the cross. Both the state and the church were involved in it, and probably will be so to the end. The man on the cross turned defeat into victory and prophesied the day when love would be triumphant in the world. But the triumph would have to come through the intervention of God. The moral resources of men would not be sufficient to guarantee it. A sentimental generation has destroyed this apocalyptic note in the vision of the Christ. It thinks the kingdom of God is around the corner, while he regarded it as impossible as realisation, except by God's grace.

A day which confronts immediate problems of social reconstruction will have little understanding for this aspect of the religious life, this soaring of the soul beyond the possibilities of history. That appreciation can come only when the new and just society has been built, and it is discovered that it is not just. Men must strive to realise their individual ideals in their common life but they will learn in the end that society remains man's great fulfillment and his great frustration.

MIGUEL DE UNAMUNO

MIGUEL DE UNAMUNO Y JUGO was born in Balboa, in the Basque country of northern Spain, in 1864. It was a fitting birthplace for him who was to become the prince of paradox of Spanish letters. The Basque region was the most separatist one of western Europe's most regionalistic country; its Basque-speaking inhabitants spoke Spanish as a foreign tongue, and looked upon the Madrid government with suspicion and upon the Spanish "nation" as an unserviceable abstraction. At the same time, however, the workers and bourgeoisie of Bilbao, an expanding industrial and port city, had developed cosmopolitan attitudes and were alive to the need for centralized, national administration. It was no accident, then, that Unamuno's first book, *En torno al casticismo* (1895). was an effort to define the vital spirit of his country, to cut through the windy polemics between traditionalists, or *casticistas,* and Europeanizers. Like his younger contemporary Ortega y Gasset, Unamuno won early renown for his fresh and incisive insights into the national scene. Unlike Ortega, he came to lay increasing stress upon reinterpreting and reanimating the ancient vitalities of Spain. "What is the use of our wanting to make our thought modern and European when our language is neither European nor modern?" (*On Europeanization —Arbitrary Reflections,* 1906.) In deforming the spirit to meet some external standard, he continues, we neither make ourselves over into the other image nor succeed in being ourselves. Unamuno and Ortega, then, are the two loadstones of twentieth-century Spanish thought and letters—Ortega insisting on the need to cosmopolitanize, to Europeanize the mind of his country, Unamuno audaciously asserting that Spain can find itself only if it attempts to "Spaniardize" Europe.

Seen in larger perspective, Ortega's enterprise has been to redefine philosophic universals so as to restore their efficacy for construing experienced realities. Unamuno's was to redirect us to the urgency and immediacy of those realities, which bedevil our every effort at categorization. One can expect the outlook of an Unamuno, which provides the very stuff of artistic creation, to be bodied forth in "white-hot" paradoxes as soon as a more philosophic expression of it is essayed. And it is important to observe that among Unamuno's most significant works are his short novels, *Mist* (1914, English translation 1928) and *Three Exemplary Novels and a Prologue* (1920, English translation 1930), his poem *The Christ of Velásquez* (1920, English translation 1951), and his interpretive study *The Life of Don Quixote and Sancho* (1905, English translation 1927). Needless to say, Don Quixote and Sancho were key symbols for Unamuno. His was a mind which rejected Aristotle's featherless biped, Descartes's cogitating man, and the Manchesterian economic man—"a man neither of here nor there, neither of this age nor another, who has neither sex nor country, who is, in brief, merely an idea. That is to say, a no-man." (*Tragic Sense of Life,* 1913.) Unamuno's man was "of flesh and bone" or, in the title of one of his novels, "nothing less than a whole man." Such were Quixote and Sancho: Quixote who fights not for ideals but for the spirit, whose faith is essentially human because it issues from despair and incertitude, from the never resolved conflict of reason and immortal desire, and in whose heart seems to dwell the cry, "Lord, I believe; help thou my unbelief!" And Sancho, prototype of the rationalist who doubts his own reason—a whole and real man because his heroic faith in his master's knight-errantry is forged in the shadow of the doubt to which the Don's follies give rise.

The reader who takes up any of Unamuno's philosophic essays, such as his *The Tragic Sense of Life in Men and in Peoples* (1913, English translation 1921) or the following selection from his *The Agony of Christianity* (published in French 1925; Spanish edition 1931; English translation by Pierre Loving 1928), must be prepared for the wrench and shock of his prose. This mode of expression is determined largely by two circumstances. The first is that Unamuno is trying to rouse us to an awareness of the inexpressible, an awareness of the eternal antinomies between flesh and spirit, reason and lived experience, capacity and desire —an awareness alien to the realm of science, congenial only to that of *sabiduría*, "wisdom." The full life is the passionate life, and as such is "arbitrary" and self-justifying. Elsewhere Unamuno has written: "Passion and sensuality are incompatible; passion is arbitrary, logic is sensual. For logic is nothing but a form of sensuality." (*On Europeanization.*) A second determinant of Unamuno's style is his belief that the mere "rubbing together" of conventional attitudes hardens and thickens the protective shells of those who hold them; like corns, the shells grow larger with rubbing. "I do not like to rub against people but to clash against them; I do not like to approach people obliquely and glance off them at a tangent, but to meet them frontally, and if possible split them in two. It is the best service I can do them." (*Solitude,* 1905.)

Although heterodox, antidogmatic, and profoundly influenced by the personalistic, neo-Augustinian spiritual travail of the Dane Soren Kierkegaard (1813-1855), Unamuno remained unswervingly true to the image of Spain in the deep, communal faith of its preindustrial, pre-Renaissance age. Yet he knew that the simple, undoubting faith of the "charcoal burner" could never be his. Indeed, for Unamuno the vigor of medieval faith was that it sprang from despair as much as from certainty, and that it was interpolated with life and with reason. With this alchemy of faith, life, and reason Unamuno wished—quixotically, in both the literal and extended meanings, as he himself well knew—to rejuvenate, or to "Spaniardize" Europe. As for his personal creed: "My religion is to seek truth in life and life in truth, though in the knowledge that I shall not find them while I live; my religion is to struggle incessantly and tirelessly with the mystery; my religion is to wrestle with God from daybreak to nightfall." (*My Religion and Other Essays,* 1910.)

Unamuno was appointed professor of Greek at the University of Salamanca in 1891, and rector ten years later. In 1914 he was dismissed for political reasons, and in 1924 he was deported to the Canary Islands for his spirited attacks upon the monarchy and the dictatorship of General Primo de Rivera. The next six years he spent in France. In 1930 he returned to republican Spain, became a deputy to the Constituent Cortes, and in 1934 was declared rector of Salamanca for life. When the civil war broke out in July, 1936, Unamuno momentarily professed to see in Franco's rebels a breath of hope for stagnant, befuddled Spain, but he soon reversed this view in his speech inaugurating the academic year at Salamanca. He was immediately dismissed from his post and confined to his house under guard. He died of a cerebral stroke at the end of the year. Whether his life ended in the last hours of 1936 or the early ones of 1937 will never be known.

THE AGONY OF CHRISTIANITY

I. INTRODUCTION

. . . On Sunday, November 30, in this year of grace 1924, I attended the divine service of the Greek Orthodox Church of Saint Stephen, near where I live on the rue Georges Bizet. As I stood pondering, on the large painted bust of Christ which fills the tympanum, this sentence in Greek, "I am the Way, the Truth and the Life," I felt myself anew cast on an island; and I thought or, rather, dreamed, that the way and the life were not perhaps coterminous with the truth, and that there might indeed be some contradiction between truth and life, for truth has the power to slay us and life can preserve us in the path of error. And this led to the thought of the agony of Christianity, of the agony inherent in it and in each one of us. Can Christianity, indeed, be conceived as existing outside of us?

That is precisely where the tragedy lies. For truth is something collective, social, even civil; that which is true is that upon which we all agree. Christianity is something incommunicable. And that is why it agonizes within each one of us.

Agony, from the Greek *agonia,* signifying struggle. He agonizes who lives in a state of struggle, struggling against life itself. And against death. It is the prayer cried out by Saint Theresa of Jesus: "I die of not dying."

What I propose to lay bare here is my own agony, my Christian struggle, the agony of Christianity in me, its death and resurrection at every single moment of my inner life. . . .

Now, in the domain of things religious, and above all, in the domain of the Christian religion, it is impossible to treat of large general interests—religious, eternal, universal—without investing them with a personal or, I

This selection has been reprinted from *The Agony of Christianity* by Miguel de Unamuno (pp. 18–28, 31–32, 97–104, 106–110, 111–112, 113–119, 120–122, Payson and Clarke, Ltd., 1928) by permission of Harcourt, Brace & Company, Inc., New York.

should say, individual character. Every Christian, in order to disclose his Christianity, must needs address himself thus: *Ecce Christianus* as Pilate said: *Ecce Homo.* He must needs bare his Christian soul, which he forges for himself in the heat of the struggle, in his very agony of being a Christian. For man does not come into the world endowed with a soul; he dies with one, provided he has forged it for himself. And the goal of life is to forge a soul, an immortal soul. A soul that should in truth be our own handiwork. For when a man dies, he bequeaths a skeleton to the earth and a soul, a work of achievement, to history; provided he has lived, that is to say, provided he has wrestled with life that passes in order to attain life eternal.

And life—what is life? A far more tragic question than what is truth. For if truth cannot be defined since it is truth itself that does the defining, neither can we define life.

A French materialist, I am unable to recall now which one, asserted that life is an assemblage of functions that resist death. An agonistic, or if you prefer, a polemical definition. Life for him, therefore, meant struggle, agony. Against death, and also against truth, against the truth of death.

People speak of "the struggle for life": but that struggle for life is life itself, and, in sum, life is struggle.

Here is something to reflect upon: this is what the biblical legend in Genesis means when it relates how death came into the world through the sin of our first parents for that they wished to be like gods, that is, immortal through absorption of the knowledge of good and evil, of the knowledge which vouchsafes immortality. And afterward, according to the same legend, the first death was a violent one, a homicide, that of Abel by the hand of his brother Cain. And a fratricide too.

Many ask themselves how do the wild beasts—lions, tigers, panthers, hippopotami—die in the forests or the deserts which they inhabit; if they are slain or if they die what is called a natural death, seeking cover to perish in solitude, like the greatest saints. And so beyond doubt died the greatest saint of all, the unknown saint—unknown first of all to himself: he who was perhaps born already dead.

Life is a struggle; solidarity to preserve life is a struggle and manifests itself by means of a struggle. I can never tire of reiterating that what binds men most to each other is their discords. And what unites a man most with himself, what makes the intimate unity of our lives, is our inner discords, the innate contradictions of our discords. We finally make peace with ourselves, like Don Quixote, only to die.

And if this be true of physical or corporeal life, psychical or spiritual life in its turn consists of a struggle against eternal oblivion. And against history, which is God's thought on earth among men, lacks a supreme human finality and marches toward forgetfulness and the unknown. Every effort of man tends to bestow a human finality upon history, a superhuman finality, Nietzsche would have said, who conjured up that absurdity: social Christianity.

II. AGONY

Agony, accordingly, is a species of struggle. And Christ appeared bringing us agony, struggle and not peace, as he himself said.

> Think not that I am come to send peace on earth: I came not to send peace, but a sword. For I am come to set a man at variance against his father, and the daughter against her mother, and the daughter-in-law against her mother-in-law. And a man's foes shall be they of his own household. (Matt. x, 34–37.)

He remembered as he spoke that his own family, his mother and his brothers, had looked upon him as a madman quite beside himself, and that they had set out to lay hold on him. (Mark III, 21.) And he further said:

> I am come to send fire on the earth; and what will I, if it be already kindled? . . . Suppose ye that I am come to give peace on earth? I tell you, Nay; but rather division: for from henceforth there shall be five in one house divided, three against two, and two against three; the father shall be divided against the son, and the son against the father; the mother against the daughter, and the daughter against the mother; the mother-in-law against her daughter-in-law, and the daughter-in-law against her mother-in-law. (Luke XII, 49–54.)

What then of peace, it may be asked. For throughout other passages in the Gospels, and these yet more numerous and undoubtedly more explicit, peace is specifically referred to. But peace is, as we know, achieved through war and war is achieved through peace. And therein precisely consists the agony.

Some one might here point out that peace is life—or death—and that war is death—or life—for it is indeed a matter of little moment whether they are likened one to the other; and peace through war or war through peace, this is but life in death, death in life: agony.

Is this sheer conceptualism? Saint Paul is accordingly a conceptualist, and so are Saint Augustine and Pascal. The logic of the passion is a kind of logic that is at once rational, polemical, and agonistic. The Gospels, moreover, are swollen with paradoxes, with white-hot bones that sear the fingers.

As Christianity forever agonizes, so also does Christ. "Jesus will be in agony until the end of the world: do not be caught asleep then." Thus wrote

Pascal in the *Mystère de Jésus*. And he wrote those words in agony. For not to sleep is to dream wide-awake, to dream of agony; it is really to agonize.

They are terribly tragic, our crucifixes, our Spanish Christs. They represent the cult of Christ agonizing, not yet dead. Christ lying out-stretched in the sepulchre is the dead Christ, already become one with earth, become, as it were, peace, Christ dead, interred by other dead. But Christ on the cross, whom we worship, is the agonizing Christ, crying: "*Consummatum est!*"[1] It is to the Christ of the "My God, why hast Thou forsaken me?" (Matt. XXVII, 46), that agonizing believers turn. Among these you will find many who believe they are not doubting, who believe they are believing.

To doubt is to live, to struggle, to struggle for life and to live by struggle. I have already made reference to this in another of my works, recalling the passage of the Gospels where it is written: "Lord, I believe, help Thou my unbelief!" (Mark IX, 24.) A faith which does not continue to doubt is a dead faith.

What then is the meaning of doubt? *Dubitare* contains the same root—that of the adjectival numeral *duo,* two—as *duellum,* a struggle. Doubt, Pascalian doubt, agonistic or polemical, rather than the systematic doubt of Descartes, presupposes the duality of combat. I mean here the doubt of life (life-struggle) and not of way (way-method).

We have been trained by the catechism to believe in that which we have not seen. That is the basis of faith. To believe in that which we see—and that which we do not see—that is reason, science; and to believe in that which we will see—or will not see—is hope. And it is all summed up in belief. I affirm and I believe, in so far as I am a poet or creator, by gazing back into the past, digging into the recesses of memory; I deny, in so far as I am a rational being and a citizen, face to face with the present; and as a man and a Christian, I doubt, I struggle and agonize by casting my eyes toward an unrealizable future, toward eternity.

Among the Spanish people, an agonistic and polemical race, exists the cult of Christ agonizing; alongside it obtains the cult of Our Lady of Sorrows, with her heart pierced by seven swords. This is not the Italian *Pietà*. We do not so much support the cult of the Son who lies dead in the lap of his mother, as that of the Virgin Mother who agonizes in grief with her son gathered in her arms. It is the cult of the agony of the Mother.

There is also, to be sure, the cult of the Infant Jesus, the Child at the Breast, the cult of the Nativity, the life-giving Virgin, suckling her child. . . .

The suffering of monks and nuns, of celibates of both sexes, is not the

[1] [*It is consummated.*]

suffering of sex but of maternity and paternity, that is, of finality. They suffer because their flesh, which embraces the spirit, may not perpetuate itself, may not propagate itself. Feeling themselves close to death, to the end of the world, to their own doom, that is, they tremble in the desperate hope of the resurrection of the body.

The Trappists of Dueñas sang: *Mater creatoris, ora pro nobis!* Mother of the Creator! The human spirit yearns to create its creator, him who will endow it with eternal life. *Mater Creatoris!* Mother of the Creator! Behold the cry of anguish, the cry of agony.

The Virgin is called the "Mother of God," *deipara*. "And blessed is the fruit of her womb" (Luke I, 42), it is said of the Word without which was not anything made that was made. (John I, 3.) Not only the soul, but the body as well, the body which is to be resurrected, yearns to create the Word, in order that the Word may in its turn create the soul and render it eternal; and the body, the cradle and sepulchre of the soul, the body where the soul is born and dis-born, dies and dis-dies. To be dis-born is to die; and to dis-die is to be born. Such is the dialectic of agony.

Thus Christianity agonizes. . . .

VII. THE PRETENCE OF SOCIAL CHRISTIANITY

Social Christianity? The social kingdom of Jesus Christ which the Jesuits din into our ears? What traffic can Christianity, true Christianity, have with society here below, on the earth? What is this celebrated Christian democracy?

"My kingdom is not of this world," Christ said when he saw that the end of the world did not come to pass. And also "Render therefore unto Caesar the things which be Caesar's, and unto God the things which be God's." But it is necessary to recall the circumstances in which this cardinal sentence was pronounced.

Those who followed him to bring about his downfall conspired to ask him if it was lawful or not for them to pay tribute to Caesar, the invader, the enemy of the Jewish people, the temporal authority. If he said yes, he would be represented to his people as a bad Jew, a traitor to his people, and if he said no, he would be accused of sedition before the Roman authorities. When the question was put, Jesus asked for a piece of money and, pointing to the effigy, he asked: "Whose image and superscription hath it?" And they answered and said, "Caesar's." And he said: "Render unto Caesar the things which be Caesar's, and unto God the things which be God's." This can be interpreted as meaning: Give money to Caesar, to the world, to society; and give to God the soul which is to be resurrected with the body. Thus he evaded the socio-economic problem, he who said that it is more difficult for a camel to pass through the needle's eye than for a rich man to enter the kingdom of heaven; and he revealed that his good tidings had nothing in common with socio-economic or national questions, as little with democracy or international demagogy as with nationalism.

The fourth Gospel reveals why the scribes and Pharisees caused Christ to be condemned. Or rather, the pretext they put forth. It was for his anti-patriotism.

Then gathered the chief priests and Pharisees, a council, and said, What do we? for this man doeth many miracles. If we let him thus alone, all men will believe on him; and the Romans shall come and take away both our place and nation. And one of them named Caiphas, being the high priest that same year, said unto them, Ye know nothing at all, nor consider that it is expedient for us that one man should die for the people and that the whole nation perish not.

It is plain that they sought to destroy him because of his anti-patriotism, because his kingdom was not of this world, because he was not concerned with political economy, neither with democracy nor with patriotism.

But after the reign of Constantine, when the Romanization of Christianity began, when the letter not the word of the Gospel began to be changed into something resembling the twelve tables of the law, the Caesars set about to offer protection to the Father of the Son, to the God of Christ and of Christendom. And then that horrible thing known as Canon Law appeared. The judicial, mundane and social conception of so-called Christianity became in time a solid fact. Saint Augustine, man of the letter, was to start his career as a jurist, skilled in the law. Saint Paul was that also, and at the same time a mystic. The mystic and jurist contended with him. On the one side stood the law, on the other grace.

Law and duty are not Christian and religious but, as we know, legal concepts. The Christian is all grace and sacrifice. And for the contraption "Christian democracy" it is in the same category as blue chemistry. He who supports tyranny may be a Christian equally much as he who defends democracy or civil liberty. The Christian as Christian has nothing to do with such things.

Yet, since the Christian is a man in society, a civil being, a citizen, how can he fail to be interested in the social and civil life? Ah, Christianity exacts perfect solitude; the Christian ideal is the Carthusian who forsakes his father and mother and brothers for Christ, and gives up founding a family, gives up being a husband and father. If the human race is to persist, if Christianity is to persist in the sense of a social and civil community of Christians, if the Church is to persist, this ideal is impossible. And herein lies what is most terrible in the agony of Christianity.

You cannot situate in history what is anti-historic, what is the negation of history: neither the resurrection of the flesh nor the immortality of the soul, neither the Letter nor the Word, neither the Gospel nor the Bible. History signifies the burying of the dead so that we may live through them. It is the dead who lead us through our study of history, and the God of Christ is not a god of the dead but of the living.

Pure Christianity, evangelical Christianity, sets itself to find eternal life beyond the confines of history and encounters only the eternal silence which frightened Pascal, whose life proved a Christian agony. History is God's thought concerning the world of man.

The Jesuits, degenerate sons of Ignatius de Loyola, come chanting the ballad of the social kingdom of Jesus Christ, and, keeping always this political criterion in view, they seek to deal with political and socio-economic problems,—to defend private property, for example. Christ has nothing to do with socialism or with private property. Similarly, the thigh of the divine Anti-Patriot which was pierced by the lance and from which gushed blood and water, making a blind soldier believe, has nothing in common with the Sacred Heart of the Jesuits. The soldier was blind, to be sure; but he saw as soon as he was touched by the blood of him who had said that his kingdom was not of this world.

And those poor devils—devil: *diabolos,* prosecutor—who say that Jesus was a great democrat, a great revolutionary or a great republican! The passion of Christ still endures, for it is a terrible passion, is it not? to be compelled to suffer yourself to be travestied by some as a radical socialist, and by others as a nationalist, by some as a free-mason and still others as a Jesuit. Christ was in the eyes of the high priests, scribes and Pharisees of Judaism, a Jewish anti-patriot. . . .

Let it not be forgotten, albeit we utter it most reverently, that Christ was a celibate. This alone must have been enough to make him appear an anti-patriot to his biblical compatriots.

No. Democracy, civil liberty, dictatorship or tyranny have nothing to do with Christianity, any more than science has; the social work of Belgian Catholicism, for example, has no more to do with Christianity than has Pasteur. The Christian mission is not to resolve the socio-economic problem, that of poverty and wealth, of the redistribution of this world's goods; despite the fact that he who would redeem the poor from poverty must needs redeem the rich from wealth; he who would redeem the slave must needs redeem the tyrant, and will inevitably attack the death sentence, whereby he will redeem not the condemned man but the executioner. But all this does not partake of the Christian mission. Christ called unto him poor and rich, slaves and tyrants, the victim and the executioner. At the approach of doom, at the coming of death, what difference is there between riches and poverty, slavery and tyranny, the man who sentences, and the man who is executed? . . .

A Spanish priest, Jaime Balmes, wrote a book comparing Protestantism to Catholicism in their relation to civilization. Well, it may be possible to judge Protestantism and Catholicism in their bearing on civilization, but Christianity, evangelical Christianity, has nothing to do with civilization or with culture. Neither with Latin culture, written with a small *c,* curved and round, nor with the Germanic *Kultur,* with its capital *K,* whose four points jut out like barbed wire entanglements.

And as Christendom cannot live without civilization and culture, Christianity agonizes. And so does the Christian civilization, which is an innate contradiction. It is through this agony that both Christianity and the so-called Graeco-Roman or Western civilization, live. The death of one implies the death of the other. If the despairing and agonistic Christian faith were to die, our civilization would die. We must needs live in agony.

Pagan religions, State religions were political; Christianity is non-political. But as soon as it became Catholic, and moreover Roman, Christianity became paganized by its transformation into a State religion. There was at one stage even a Pontifical State! It became, in short, political. And its agony increased.

Is Christianity pacifist? The question seems devoid of sense. Christianity is above, or, if you prefer, below these worldly and purely moral—or perhaps purely political—distinctions between pacifism and bellicism, between militarism and civic order, between *si vis pacem, para bellum* and *si vis bellum, para pacem.*[2]

We have already seen that Christ said he had come to sow dissension among families, to bring fire and division and the sword. . . . But when he was ambushed on the Mount of Olives, and his disciples asked if they were to defend themselves with the sword, he answered that they should suffer it *this once,* and he healed the ear of him who had been wounded.

[2] [*If you desire peace, prepare for war* and *if you desire war, prepare for peace.*]

And he chided Peter who had drawn his sword and wounded Malchus, servant of the high priest, saying: "Put up again thy sword in its place, for all they that take the sword shall perish by the sword!"

The fourth Gospel, which is attributed to John, is the only one which tells us that he who drew his sword to defend the Master was Simon Peter, the rock on which the Roman Apostolic Catholic Church was built, the supposed founder of the dynasty which established the temporal power of the popes and preached the Crusades.

The fourth Gospel is considered the least historic in the materialistic or realistic sense of history; but in the profound sense, in the idealistic and personal sense, the fourth Gospel, the symbolic Gospel, is much more historic than the synoptic accounts. It was and continues to be the source of the agonistic history of Christianity.

Thus, in this Gospel, which is the most historic because it is the most symbolic of the four, and indeed the most living, Christ says to the symbolic founder of the pontifical Roman Catholic dynasty that he who draws the sword must perish by the sword. In September, 1870, the troops of Victor Emmanuel of Savoy entered, by the might of the sword, into pontifical Rome. And Catholic agony was increased on the day when the Vatican council proclaimed the Jesuitical doctrine of the infallibility of the Pope.

The militia of the Cross was founded on a militaristic dogma engendered in the thick of battle, in a company mustered by an old soldier, a military man who, wounded, was unfit for the militia of the sword. And within the Roman Church is discipline, *discipulina,* in which the disciple does not learn,—*non discit,*—but passively receives the ordination, the dogma, not the doctrine, from his master, or more than master, chief master, in conformity with the third decree of obedience which Loyola recommended to the Fathers and Brothers of Portugal. Ah, yes, that is indeed an agony!

Can the Roman Church be expected to preach peace? Lately the Spanish bishops, in a collective document, proclaimed war for the civil protectorate —protectorate! and civil!—which the royal Government of Spain, not the Spanish people, wanted to establish in Morocco. They called that war a *crusade!* And that is the name which it must bear, not so much for the cross which the soldiers have made into an emblem, as for that other cross which they brandish like a club and with which they break the heads of infidels. Terrible struggle and terrible agony! . . .

. . . War saddens and darkens the soul. Peace does, too. In the *Syllabus* there will perhaps be no positive article against war, but in the Gospels there are arguments against war and against peace, for war and for peace. It is simply that war and peace are the things of this world, which is not the kingdom of Christ. Abishag the Shunammite had nothing to do with the peaceful projects of Solomon or with the war between Solomon and Adonijah.

The struggle of Christianity, its agony, partakes neither of mundane war nor peace. It is futile to ask if mysticism is action or contemplation because it is active contemplation and contemplative action.

Nietzsche speaks of that which is beyond good and evil. Christianity is beyond war and peace. Or rather on this side of war and peace.

The Roman Church, or let us say Jesuitism, preaches peace, a peace which is the peace of conscience, implicit faith, passive submission. Leon Shestov says truly: "Let us remember that the earthly keys to the kingdom of heaven were bestowed upon Saint Peter and his successors, precisely because Peter knew enough to sleep, and slept while God, having descended among men, made ready to die on the cross." Saint Peter knew enough to sleep, or slept without knowing it. And Saint Peter was he who denied the Master until he was aroused by the crowing of the cock, who awakens sleepers.

VIII. ABSOLUTE INDIVIDUALISM

. . . We are told that Christianity and Western or Greco-Roman civilization will disappear simultaneously and another civilization—whether you like this expression or not—will supervene, by way of Russia and Bolshevism, an Asiatic civilization, with Buddhistic roots, in short a Communist civilization. For Christianity is radical individualism.

Yet the real father of Russian nihilist sentiment is Dostoievski, a despairing Christian, a Christian caught in the throes of agony.

But here we stumble into the fact that there are no concepts more contradictory in themselves and lending themselves to more contradictory applications than the concepts of individualism and communism, of anarchism and socialism. It is impossible to clarify anything by the use of these terms. Those who believe that they see clearly with the aid of these terms are benighted spirits. What would not the agonistic dialectic of Saint Paul have done with them!

Nothing is more universal than individuality. Yet the means by which people may understand one another on this plane no longer exist.

If the anarchists wish to live they must found a state, and communists must rally around individual liberty. The most radical individualists found a community. Hermits join together and form a monastery, that is, a convent of monks, *monachos,* of solitary souls. The solitaries must help each other. Bury their dead. What is more, they are committed to make history, since they do not produce children.

Yet only the hermit approaches the ideal of the individualistic life. A Spanish man of science, who, nearing sixty, set himself to learn to ride the bicycle, said to me that it was the most individualistic method of locomotion. "No, Don José," I replied, "the individualistic mode of locomotion is to walk alone, barefooted, in places where there are no roads." It is, in other words, to live alone, naked and in the desert.

Père Hyacinthe, after his rupture with the Roman Catholic Church, wrote that the Anglo-Saxon race is "the race of the strong and moral family, the race of free and energetic personality, the race of individual Christianity. . . ." It has often been said that Protestant Christianity, particularly Calvinist Christianity, is a creed of individualism. But individual Christianity exists only in celibacy; Christianity within the family is no longer pure Christianity, but a compromise with the age. To follow Christ, a man must abandon father and mother and brothers and wife and children, and if the continuation of the human race is thereby imperilled, so much the worse for it!

A universal monastery on the other hand is not viable; not viable, I mean, in the monastery which would house us all. Hence there are two classes of Christians: first, secular Christians, belonging to their age—*saecula* means generations—Christian citizens, those who bring up children in the sight of God; the other, pure Christians, those in orders, the *monachi,* inhabiting a cloister. The former propagate the flesh, and with it original sin; the latter, the solitary spirit. But one can bear the world into the cloister, the age into monastic order, and even retain the spirit of the cloister intact in the midst of the world.

Both these classes, when they are of a religious character, live in intimate contradiction, in agony. The monk, who preserves his virginity and withholds his fleshly seed in whose resurrection he believes, who is called *father* —or in the case of the nun, *mother*—dreams of the immortality of the soul and of survival in history. Saint Francis of Assisi thought that he would be remembered and talked about, but he was not a real solitary, a monk, *monachus;* he was rather a little brother, *fratello.* On the other hand, the civic Christian, good citizen, father of a family, so long as he feels himself living in history, wonders if his salvation is not thereby imperilled. And though the worldly man who immures himself—or who is immured—in a monastery, strikes us as tragic, the monk of the spirit, the solitary who perforce lives in his own age, is even more so.

The state of virginity is in the eyes of the Apostolic Roman Catholic Church a state more perfect in itself than that of marriage. It has made of marriage a sacrament, but only as a concession to the world, to history. In contrast, the men and women virgins who are vowed to the Lord live their lives anguished continually by the paternal and maternal instincts. In a convent of nuns it is natural to find a passionate cult centering around the infant Jesus, the child God.

Could Christianity—perhaps humanity—achieve its goal by constituting itself in the manner of a beehive or an ant-hill, with the fathers and mothers on one side and the sterile workers, the neuters, on the other? In the beehive and in the ant-hill the neuter bees and ants are those who toil and who bring up the new sex-endowed generation. With us it is ordinarily the father and mother who labour to maintain their progeny—the proletariat, those who create flesh and who produce the things which serve to perpetuate material life. But spiritual life? Among the Catholic peoples it is the monks and the nuns who keep alive the religious tradition, who rear the young. But as they must rear them to live in the world, in their own time, to become fathers and mothers of families, to adapt themselves to civic and political life, an innate contradiction arises in their education. One bee might instruct another bee in the art of constructing a cell, but it could not teach a hornet how to fecundate the queen-bee.

And this contradiction, innate in monastic education for the benefit of future citizens, reached its culmination in the Company called of Jesus. The Jesuits do not relish being called monks or brothers. A monk is a Benedictine or a Carthusian; a brother is a Franciscan or a Dominican. But since the Jesuits, in order to combat the Reformation, the force which secularized and generalized primary education, devoted themselves to the education of laymen, of citizens, of future fathers of families, the other religious orders followed their example and became jesuitized. They ended by regarding the service of education as an industry, the pedagogical industry. Instead of mendicants they became schoolmasters.

Thus Christianity, true Christianity, agonizes in the hands of these masters of the age. Jesuit pedagogy is a profoundly anti-Christian pedagogy. The Jesuit loathes the mystic. His doctrine of passive obedience, of the three degrees of obedience as expressed by Ignatius Loyola in his famous letter to the Fathers and Brothers of Portugal, is an anti-Christian and at bottom an anti-civic doctrine. With this sort of obedience, civilization becomes impossible, and progress as well. . . .

Napoleon said that within a century after his death Europe would turn either Cossack or republican. His meaning was doubtless akin to that of Père Hyacinthe (who was a Napoleon in his own fashion—the first was a son of Rousseau, the second of Chateaubriand) when he spoke in the same breath of ultramontanists and revolutionaries. But what neither of them, it seems, foresaw was that the Cossacks would turn republican and the republicans Cossack; ultramontanism would turn revolutionary and revolution ultramontanist. They anticipated neither Bolshevism nor Fascism. And all this immense confusion and chaos poor Spengler tries to explain away by the architectonic music of his downfall of the Occident (*der Untergang des Abendlandes*). Which is only another way of stating the agony of Christianity.

The yellow peril? The black peril? Peril has no colour. In so far as they participate in history, become civil and political—and warfare is, as Treitschke so aptly said, politics *par excellence*—desert-bred Mohammedans are being Christianized, becoming Christian. Which is to say, agonistic. Mohammedanism is agonizing in proselytism.

I said something about progress. Progress is not a religious value, but a civic value.

What is progress, after all? Has history a human,—or, better still, a divine —goal? Does it not live at every instant? For Christ, and for those who believed in the imminent end of the world, progress was empty of meaning. One does not progress in holiness. One cannot, to-day, in the twentieth century, be more saintly than in the second, fourth, or the eleventh century. A Christian does not believe that progress can bring nearer the salvation of the soul. Historic or civic progress is not the journey of the soul towards God. Hence another agony for Christianity.

The doctrine of progress is that of Nietzsche's superman, but the Christian is constrained to believe that the goal which he is endeavouring to reach is not the superman, but the immortal or Christian man.

Is there such a thing as progress after death? The Christian who believes in the resurrection of the flesh and who believes unqualifiedly in the immortality of the soul is obliged to ask himself that question over and over again. But the majority of simple evangelical believers like to imagine the other life as repose, as peace, as contemplative quietude, rather as "the eternalization of momentaneity," as the fusion of the past with the future, of memory and hope, in a sempiternal present. The other life or glory is for them a sort of monastery of families, a phalanstery. . . .

JEAN PAUL SARTRE

IN America the dislocations attendant upon World War II received little in the way of intellectual focus. But in France they brought a realignment of philosophical problems. "Existentialism Is a Humanism," originally delivered as a lecture by Jean Paul Sartre (b. 1905) in 1945, was the manifesto of the new philosophy. The following selection has been taken from the slightly revised version of the lecture which, in the translation of Bernard Frechtman, appeared in English under the title *Existentialism,* in 1947. Existentialism in its previous versions had seemed cramped by personal anxieties; classical French humanism, in contrast, had extolled the emancipation of man and his cultural flowering. Sartre's unprecedented equation of existentialism with humanism found encouragement in the widespread optimism which assigned the anxious struggles of the Resistance a pivotal role in the liberation and revivification of France. His denial that values precede actions generalized the contemporary feeling that the weight of tradition no longer encumbered France's political future. Yet neither the size nor the expectancy of Sartre's audience could be entirely attributed to a mood of political revival. The broader cultural significance of his existentialist philosophy seemed asserted by the vogue of his literary writings.

Sartre's literary efforts are summed up in a tetralogy of novels, *The Ways of Freedom,* in which he experimented with new techniques for rendering collisions between the process of individual reflection and the requirements of social action. These novels were not strictly autobiographical (in the manner of his own *Nausea,* 1938) but instead multiplied individual points of view until a social panorama (on the model of Dos Passos's *U.S.A.*) was obtained. Sartre went further than Dos Passos in reconstituting the novel as social history, for he tried to yield a sense of the disconcerting course of history by altering his literary techniques in handling its successive phases. Thus the first novel, *The Age of Reason* (1945), is deliberately traditional in its construction, for during the first phase his characters merely reflect so that their lives seem to retain private significance. But in the second novel, *The Reprieve* (1945), which covers the week of the Munich negotiations, their private reflections become public suspense over the impending course of history, and Sartre renders this transformation by overlapping the episodes of their different lives and shunting from one character to another in the middle of a paragraph or even of a sentence. The defeat of France in the third novel, *Death in the Soul* (1949), submerges his characters' reflections in history.

In the fourth novel, which will be set in the period of the Resistance, Sartre's characters will finally confront their individual responsibilities for social action. But Sartre has neither published this volume nor completed *Man,* which will be his philosophical delineation of these responsibilities.

The optimistic and expectant mood of the liberation of France was short-lived, and Sartre has himself expressed misgivings about "Existentialism Is a Humanism," in which he disposes of the problems of value and of action with such confident rapidity. Since the war he has attempted a more patient transition from his former reflective approach by concerning himself with the intervening problems of motives and choices. He has also attempted to keep up with historical events by editing the monthly magazine *Modern Times*. Characteristically he has been primarily concerned with writers' choosing to write, both in so far as their motives are features of the social history of the novel—*What Is Literature* (1947)—and in terms of their individual consciousness and endeavors, as in *Baudelaire* (1947) and *Jean Genêt* (1952). In his essays in social history he has been critical of the Marxist assumption that changes in the economic "substructure" determine the course of history independently of human reflection and choice. His "existential psychoanalyses" of literature are similarly undertaken in criticism of Freudian determinism.

EXISTENTIALISM

I should like on this occasion to defend existentialism against some charges which have been brought against it.

First, it has been charged with inviting people to remain in a kind of desperate quietism because, since no solutions are possible, we should have to consider action in this world as quite impossible. We should then end up in a philosophy of contemplation; and since contemplation is a luxury, we come in the end to a bourgeois philosophy. The communists in particular have made these charges.

On the other hand, we have been charged with dwelling on human degradation, with pointing up everywhere the sordid, shady, and slimy, and neglecting the gracious and beautiful, the bright side of human nature; for example, according to Mlle Mercier, a Catholic critic, with forgetting the smile of the child. Both sides charge us with having ignored human solidarity, with considering man as an isolated being. The communists say that the main reason for this is that we take pure subjectivity, the *Cartesian I think*, as our starting point; in other words, the moment in which man becomes fully aware of what it means to him to be an isolated being; as a result, we are unable to return to a state of solidarity with the men who are not ourselves, a state which we can never reach in the *cogito*.[1]

From the Christian standpoint, we are charged with denying the reality

---

This selection has been reprinted from *Existentialism* by Jean Paul Sartre (New York, The Philosophical Library, 1947), pp. 11–61 by permission of the publisher.

[1] [The reference is to Descartes's *Cogito ergo sum*, that is, *I think therefore I am*.]

and seriousness of human undertakings, since, if we reject God's commandments and the eternal verities, there no longer remains anything but pure caprice, with everyone permitted to do as he pleases and incapable, from his own point of view, of condemning the points of view and acts of others.

I shall try today to answer these different charges. Many people are going to be surprised at what is said here about humanism. We shall try to see in what sense it is to be understood. In any case, what can be said from the very beginning is that by existentialism we mean a doctrine which makes human life possible and, in addition, declares that every truth and every action implies a human setting and a human subjectivity.

As is generally known, the basic charge against us is that we put the emphasis on the dark side of human life. Someone recently told me of a lady who, when she let slip a vulgar word in a moment of irritation, excused herself by saying, "I guess I'm becoming an existentialist." Consequently, existentialism is regarded as something ugly; that is why we are said to be naturalists; and if we are, it is rather surprising that in this day and age we cause so much more alarm and scandal than does naturalism, properly so called. The kind of person who can take in his stride such a novel as Zola's *The Earth* is disgusted as soon as he starts reading an existentialist novel; the kind of person who is resigned to the wisdom of the ages—which is pretty sad—finds us even sadder. Yet, what can be more disillusioning than saying "true charity begins at home" or "a scoundrel will always return evil for good"?

We know the commonplace remarks made when this subject comes up, remarks which always add up to the same thing: we shouldn't struggle against the powers-that-be; we shouldn't resist authority; we shouldn't try to rise above our station; any action which doesn't conform to authority is romantic; any effort not based on past experience is doomed to failure; experience shows that man's bent is always toward trouble, that there must be a strong hand to hold him in check, if not, there will be anarchy. There are still people who go on mumbling these melancholy old saws, the people who say, "It's only human!" whenever a more or less repugnant act is pointed out to them, the people who glut themselves on *chansons réalistes;* these are the people who accuse existentialism of being too gloomy, and to such an extent that I wonder whether they are complaining about it, not for its pessimism, but much rather its optimism. Can it be that what really scares them in the doctrine I shall try to present here is that it leaves to man a possibility of choice? To answer this question, we must re-examine it on a strictly philosophical plane. What is meant by the term *existentialism?*

Most people who use the word would be rather embarrassed if they had to explain it, since, now that the word is all the rage, even the work of a musician or painter is being called existentialist. A gossip columnist in *Clartés* signs himself *The Existentialist,* so that by this time the word has been so stretched and has taken on so broad a meaning, that it no longer means anything at all. It seems that for want of an advance-guard doctrine analogous to surrealism, the kind of people who are eager for scandal and flurry turn to this philosophy which in other respects does not at all serve their purposes in this sphere.

Actually, it is the least scandalous, the most austere of doctrines. It is intended strictly for specialists and philosophers. Yet it can be defined easily. What complicates matters is that there are two kinds of existentialist; first, those who are Christian, among whom I would include Jaspers and Gabriel Marcel, both Catholic; and on the other hand the atheistic existentialists, among whom I class Heidegger, and then the French existentialists and myself. What they have in common is that they think existence precedes essence, or, if you prefer, that subjectivity must be the starting point.

Just what does that mean? Let us consider some object that is manufactured, for example, a book or a paper-cutter: here is an object which has been made by an artisan whose inspiration came from a concept. He referred to the concept of what a paper-cutter is and likewise to a known method of production, which is part of the concept, something which is, by and large, a routine. Thus, the paper-cutter is at once an object produced in a certain way and, on the other hand, one having a specific use; and one can not postulate a man who produces a paper-cutter but does not know what it is used for. Therefore, let us say that, for the paper-cutter, essence—that is, the ensemble of both the production routines and the properties which enable it to be both produced and defined—precedes existence. Thus, the presence of the paper-cutter or book in front of me is determined. Therefore, we have here a technical view of the world whereby it can be said that production precedes existence.

When we conceive God as the Creator, He is generally thought of as a superior sort of artisan. Whatever doctrine we may be considering, whether one like that of Descartes or that of Leibnitz, we always grant that will more or less follows understanding or, at the very least, accompanies it, and that when God creates He knows exactly what He is creating. Thus, the concept of man in the mind of God is comparable to the concept of paper-cutter in the mind of the manufacturer, and, following certain techniques and a conception, God produces man, just as the artisan, following a definition and a technique, makes a paper-cutter. Thus, the individual man is the realisation of a certain concept in the divine intelligence.

In the eighteenth century, the atheism of the *philosophes* discarded the idea of God, but not so much for the notion that essence precedes existence. To a certain extent, this idea is found everywhere; we find it in Diderot, in Voltaire, and even in Kant. Man has a human nature; this human nature, which is the concept of the human, is found in all men, which means that each man is a particular example of a universal concept, man. In Kant, the result of this universality is that the wild-man, the natural man, as well as the bourgeois, are circumscribed by the same definition and have the same basic qualities. Thus, here too the essence of man precedes the historical existence that we find in nature.

Atheistic existentialism, which I represent, is more coherent. It states that if God does not exist, there is at least one being in whom existence precedes essence, a being who exists before he can be defined by any concept, and that this being is man, or, as Heidegger says, human reality. What is meant here by saying that existence precedes essence? It means that, first of all, man exists, turns up, appears on the scene, and, only afterwards, defines himself. If man, as the existentialist conceives him, is indefinable, it is because at first he is nothing. Only afterward will he be something, and he himself will have made what he will be. Thus, there is no human nature, since there is no God to conceive it. Not only is man what he conceives himself to be, but he is also only what he wills himself to be after this thrust toward existence.

Man is nothing else but what he makes of himself. Such is the first principle of existentialism. It is also what is called subjectivity, the name we are labeled with when charges are brought against us. But what do we mean by this, if not that man has a greater dignity than a stone or table? For we mean that man first exists, that is, that man first of all is the being who hurls himself toward a future and who is conscious of imagining himself as being in the future. Man is at the start a plan which is aware of itself, rather than a patch of moss, a piece of garbage, or a cauliflower; nothing exists prior to this plan; there is nothing in heaven; man will be what he will have planned to be. Not what he will want to be. Because by the word "will" we generally mean a conscious decision, which is subsequent to what we have already made of ourselves. I may want to belong to a political party, write a book, get married; but all that is only a manifestation of an earlier, more spontaneous choice that is called "will." But if existence really does precede essence, man is responsible for what he is.

Thus, existentialism's first move is to make every man aware of what he is and to make the full responsibility of his existence rest on him. And when we say that a man is responsible for himself, we do not only mean that he is responsible for his own individuality, but that he is responsible for all men.

The word subjectivism has two meanings, and our opponents play on the two. Subjectivism means, on the one hand, that an individual chooses and makes himself; and, on the other, that it is impossible for man to transcend human subjectivity. The second of these is the essential meaning of existentialism. When we say that man chooses his own self, we mean that every one of us does likewise; but we also mean by that that in making this choice he also chooses all men. In fact, in creating the man that we want to be, there is not a single one of our acts which does not at the same time create an image of man as we think he ought to be. To choose to be this or that is to affirm at the same time the value of what we choose, because we can never choose evil. We always choose the good, and nothing can be good for us without being good for all.

If, on the other hand, existence precedes essence, and if we grant that we exist and fashion our image at one and the same time, the image is valid for everybody and for our whole age. Thus, our responsibility is much greater than we might have supposed, because it involves all mankind. If I am a workingman and choose to join a Christian trade-union rather than be a communist, and if by being a member I want to show that the best thing for man is resignation, that the kingdom of man is not of this world, I am not only involving my own case—I want to be resigned for everyone. As a result, my action has involved all humanity. To take a more individual matter, if I want to marry, to have children; even if this marriage depends solely on my own circumstances or passion or wish, I am involving all humanity in monogamy and not merely myself. Therefore, I am responsible for myself and for everyone else. I am creating a certain image of man of my own choosing. In choosing myself, I choose man.

This helps us understand what the actual content is of such rather grandiloquent words as anguish, forlornness, despair. As you will see, it's all quite simple.

First, what is meant by anguish? The existentialists say at once that man is anguish. What that means is this: the man who involves himself and who realizes that he is not only the person he chooses to be, but also a law-maker who is, at the same time, choosing all mankind as well as himself, can not help escape the feeling of his total and deep responsibility. Of course, there are many people who are not anxious; but we claim that they are hiding their anxiety, that they are fleeing from it. Certainly, many people believe that when they do something, they themselves are the only ones involved, and when someone says to them, "What if everyone acted that way?" they shrug their shoulders and answer, "Everyone doesn't act that way." But really, one should always ask himself, "What would happen if everybody looked at things that way?" There is no escaping this disturbing thought except by a kind of double-dealing. A man who lies and makes excuses for himself by saying "not everybody does that," is someone with an uneasy conscience, because the act of lying implies that a universal value is conferred upon the lie.

Anguish is evident even when it conceals itself. This is the anguish that Kierkegaard called the anguish of Abraham. You know the story: an angel has ordered Abraham to sacrifice his son; if it really were an angel who has come and said, "You are Abraham, you shall sacrifice your son," everything would be all right. But everyone might first wonder, "Is it really an angel, and am I really Abraham? What proof do I have?"

There was a madwoman who had hallucinations; someone used to speak to her on the telephone and give her orders. Her doctor asked her, "Who is it who talks to you?" She answered, "He says it's God." What proof did she really have that it was God? If an angel comes to me, what proof is there that it's an angel? And if I hear voices, what proof is there that they come from heaven and not from hell, or from the subconscious, or a pathological condition? What proves that they are addressed to me? What proof is there that I have been appointed to impose my choice and my conception of man on humanity? I'll never find any proof or sign to convince me of that. If a voice addresses me, it is always for me to decide that this is the angel's voice; if I consider that such an act is a good one, it is I who will choose to say that it is good rather than bad.

Now, I'm not being singled out as an Abraham, and yet at every moment I'm obliged to perform exemplary acts. For every man, everything happens as if all mankind had its eyes fixed on him and were guiding itself by what he does. And every man ought to say to himself, "Am I really the kind of man who has the right to act in such a way that humanity might guide itself by my actions?" And if he does not say that to himself, he is masking his anguish.

There is no question here of the kind of anguish which would lead to quietism, to inaction. It is a matter of a simple sort of anguish that anybody who has had responsibilities is familiar with. For example, when a military officer takes the responsibility for an attack and sends a certain number of men to death, he chooses to do so, and in the main he alone makes the choice. Doubtless, orders come from above, but they are too broad; he interprets them, and on this interpretation depend the lives of ten or fourteen or twenty men. In making a decision he can not help having a certain anguish. All leaders know this anguish. That doesn't keep them from acting; on the contrary, it is the very condition of their action. For it implies that they envisage a number of possibilities, and when they choose one, they realize that it has value only because it is chosen. We shall see that this kind of anguish, which is the kind that existentialism describes, is explained, in addition, by a direct responsibility to the other men whom it involves. It is not a curtain separating us from action, but is part of action itself.

When we speak of forlornness, a term Heidegger was fond of, we mean only that God does not exist and that we have to face all the consequences of this. The existentialist is strongly opposed to a certain kind of secular ethics which would like to abolish God with the least possible expense. About 1880, some French teachers tried to set up a secular ethics which went something like this: God is a useless and costly hypothesis; we are discarding it; but, meanwhile, in order for there to be an ethics, a society, a civilization, it is essential that certain values be taken seriously and that they be considered as having an *a priori* existence. It must be obligatory, *a priori,* to be honest, not to lie, not to beat your wife, to have children, etc., etc. So we're going to try a little device which will make it possible to show that values exist all the same, inscribed in a heaven of ideas, though otherwise God does not exist. In other words—and this I believe, is the tendency of everything called reformism in France—nothing will be changed if God does not exist. We shall find ourselves with the same norms of honesty, progress, and humanism, and we shall have made of God an outdated hypothesis which will peacefully die off by itself.

The existentialist, on the contrary, thinks it very distressing that God does not exist, because all possibility of finding values in a heaven of ideas disappears along with Him; there can no longer be an *a priori* Good, since there is no infinite and perfect consciousness to think it. Nowhere is it written that the Good exists, that we must be honest, that we must not lie; because the fact is we are on a plane where there are only men. Dostoievsky said, "If God didn't exist, everything would be possible." That is the very starting point of existentialism. Indeed, everything is permissible if God does not exist, and as a result man is forlorn, because neither within him nor without does he find anything to cling to. He can't start making excuses for himself.

If existence really does precede essence, there is no explaining things away by reference to a fixed and given human nature. In other words, there is no determinism, man is free, man is freedom. On the other hand, if God does not exist, we find no values or commands to turn to which legitimize our conduct. So, in the bright realm of values, we have no excuse behind us, nor justification before us. We are alone, with no excuses.

That is the idea I shall try to convey when I say that man is condemned to be free. Condemned, because he did not create himself, yet, in other respects is free; because, once thrown into the world, he is responsible for everything he does. The existentialist does not believe in the power of passion. He will never agree that a sweeping passion is a ravaging torrent which fatally leads a man to certain acts and is therefore an excuse. He thinks that man is responsible for his passion.

The existentialist does not think that man is going to help himself by finding in the world some omen by which to orient himself. Because he thinks that man will interpret the omen to suit himself. Therefore, he thinks that man, with no support and no aid, is condemned every moment to invent man. Ponge, in a very fine article, has said, "Man is the future of man." That's exactly it. But if it is taken to mean that this future is recorded in heaven, that God sees it, then it is false, because it would really no longer be a future. If it is taken to mean that, whatever a man may be, there is a future to be forged, a virgin future before him, then this remark is sound. But then we are forlorn.

To give you an example which will enable you to understand forlornness better, I shall cite the case of one of my students who came to see me under the following circumstances: his father was on bad terms with his mother, and, moreover, was inclined to be a collaborationist; his older brother had been killed in the German offensive of 1940, and the young man, with somewhat immature but generous feelings, wanted to avenge him. His mother lived alone with him, very much upset by the half-treason of her husband and the death of her older son; the boy was her only consolation.

The boy was faced with the choice of leaving for England and joining the Free French Forces—that is, leaving his mother behind—or remaining with his mother and helping her to carry on. He was fully aware that the woman lived only for him and that his going-off—and perhaps his death—would plunge her into despair. He was also aware that every act that he did for his mother's sake was a sure thing, in the sense that it was helping her to carry on, whereas every effort he made toward going off and fighting was an uncertain move which might run aground and prove completely useless; for example, on his way to England he might, while passing through Spain, be detained indefinitely in a Spanish camp; he might reach England or Algiers and be stuck in an office at a desk job. As a result, he was faced with two very different kinds of action: one, concrete, immediate, but concerning only one individual; the other concerned an incomparably vaster group, a national collectivity, but for that very reason was dubious, and might be interrupted en route. And, at the same time, he was wavering between two kinds of ethics. On the one hand, an ethics of sympathy, of personal devotion; on the other, a broader ethics, but one whose efficacy was more dubious. He had to choose between the two.

Who could help him choose? Christian doctrine? No. Christian doctrine says, "Be charitable, love your neighbor, take the more rugged path, etc., etc." But which is the more rugged path? Whom should he love as a brother? The fighting man or his mother? Which does the greater good, the vague act of fighting in a group, or the concrete one of helping a particular human being to go on living? Who can decide *a priori*? Nobody. No book of ethics can tell him. The Kantian ethics says, "Never treat any person as a means, but as an end." Very well, if I stay with my mother, I'll treat her as an end and not as a means; but by virtue of this very fact, I'm running the risk of treating the people around me who are fighting, as a means; and, conversely, if I go to join those who are fighting, I'll be treating them as an end, and, by doing that, I run the risk of treating my mother as a means.

If values are vague, and if they are always too broad for the concrete and specific case that we are considering, the only thing left for us is to trust our instincts. That's what this young man tried to do; and when I saw him, he said, "In the end, feeling is what counts. I ought to choose whichever pushes me in one direction. If I feel that I love my mother enough to sacrifice everything else for her—my desire for vengeance, for action, for adventure—then I'll stay with her. If, on the contrary, I feel that my love for my mother isn't enough, I'll leave."

But how is the value of a feeling determined? What gives his feeling for his mother value? Precisely the fact that he remained with her. I may say that I like so-and-so well enough to sacrifice a certain amount of money for him, but I may say so only if I've done it. I may say "I love my mother well enough to remain with her" if I have remained with her. The only way to determine the value of this affection is, precisely, to perform an act which confirms and defines it. But, since I require this affection to justify my act, I find myself caught in a vicious circle.

On the other hand, Gide has well said that a mock feeling and a true feeling are almost indistinguishable; to decide that I love my mother and will remain with her, or to remain with her by putting on an act, amount somewhat to the same thing. In other words, the feeling is formed by the acts one performs; so, I can not refer to it in order to act upon it. Which means that I can neither seek within myself the true condition which will impel me to act, nor apply to a system of ethics for concepts which will permit me to act. You will say, "At least, he did go to a teacher for advice." But if you seek advice from a priest, for example, you have chosen this priest; you already knew, more or less, just about what advice he was going to give you. In other words, choosing your adviser is involving yourself. The proof of this is that if you are a Christian, you will say, "Consult a priest." But some priests are collaborating, some are just marking time, some are resisting. Which to choose? If the young man chooses a priest who is resisting or collaborating, he has already decided on the kind of advice he's going to get. Therefore, in coming to see me he knew the answer I was going to give him, and I had only one answer to give: "You're free, choose, that is, invent." No general ethics can show you what is to be done; there are no omens in the world. The Catholics will reply, "But there are." Granted—but, in any case, I myself choose the meaning they have.

When I was a prisoner, I knew a rather remarkable young man who was a Jesuit. He had entered the Jesuit order in the following way: he had had a number of very bad breaks; in childhood, his father died, leaving him in poverty, and he was a scholarship student at a religious institution where he was constantly made to feel that he was being kept out of charity; then, he failed to get any of the honors and distinctions that children like; later on, at about eighteen, he bungled a love affair; finally, at twenty-two, he failed in military training, a childish enough matter, but it was the last straw.

This young fellow might well have felt that he had botched everything. It was a sign of something, but of what? He might have taken refuge in bitterness or despair. But he very wisely looked upon all this as a sign that he was not made for secular triumphs, and that only the triumphs of religion, holiness, and faith were open to him. He saw the hand of God in all this, and so he entered the order. Who can help seeing that he alone decided what the sign meant?

Some other interpretation might have been drawn from this series of setbacks; for example, that he might have done better to turn carpenter or revolutionist. Therefore, he is fully responsible for the interpretation. Forlornness implies that we ourselves choose our being. Forlornness and anguish go together.

As for despair, the term has a very simple meaning. It means that we shall confine ourselves to reckoning only with what depends upon our will, or on the ensemble of probabilities which make our action possible. When we want something, we always have to reckon with probabilities. I may be counting on the arrival of a friend. The friend is coming by rail or street-car; this supposes that the train will arrive on schedule, or that the street-car will not jump the track. I am left in the realm of possibility; but possibilities are to be reckoned with only to the point where my action comports with the ensemble of these possibilities, and no further. The moment the possibilities I am considering are not rigorously involved by my action, I ought to disengage myself from them, because no God, no scheme, can adapt the world and its possibilities to my will. When Descartes said, "Conquer yourself rather than the world," he meant essentially the same thing.

The Marxists to whom I have spoken reply, "You can rely on the support of others in your action, which obviously has certain limits because you're not going to live forever. That means: rely on both what others are doing elsewhere to help you, in China, in Russia, and what they will do later on, after your death, to carry on the action and lead it to its fulfillment, which will be the revolution. You even *have* to rely upon that, otherwise you're immoral." I reply at once that I will always rely on fellow-fighters in so far as these comrades are involved with me in a common struggle, in the unity of a party or a group in which I can more or less make my weight felt; that is, one whose ranks I am in as a fighter and whose movements I am aware of at every moment. In such a situation, relying on the unity and will of the party is exactly like counting on the fact that the train will arrive on time or that the car won't jump the track. But, given that man is free and that there is no human nature for me to depend on, I can not count on men whom I do not know by relying on human goodness or man's concern for the good of society. I don't know what will become of the Russian revolution; I may make an example of it to the extent that at the present time it is apparent that the proletariat plays a part in Russia that it plays in no other nation. But I can't swear that this will inevitably lead to a triumph of the proletariat. I've got to limit myself to what I see.

Given that men are free and that tomorrow they will freely decide what man will be, I can not be sure that, after my death, fellow-fighters will carry on my work to bring it to its maximum perfection. Tomorrow, after my death, some men may decide to set up Fascism, and the others may be cowardly and muddled enough to let them do it. Fascism will then be the human reality, so much the worse for us.

Actually, things will be as man will have decided they are to be. Does that mean that I should abandon myself to quietism? No. First, I should involve myself; then, act on the old saw, "Nothing ventured, nothing gained." Nor does it mean that I shouldn't belong to a party, but rather that I shall have no illusions and shall do what I can. For example, suppose I ask myself, "Will socialization, as such, ever come about?" I know nothing about it. All I know is that I'm going to do everything in my power to bring it about. Beyond that, I can't count on anything. Quietism is the attitude of people who say, "Let others do what I can't do." The doctrine I am presenting is the very opposite of quietism, since it declares, "There is no reality except in action." Moreover, it goes further, since it adds, "Man is nothing else than his plan; he exists only to the extent that he fulfills himself; he is therefore nothing else than the ensemble of his acts, nothing else than his life."

According to this, we can understand why our doctrine horrifies certain people. Because often the only way they can bear their wretchedness is to think, "Circumstances have been against me. What I've been and done doesn't show my true worth. To be sure, I've had no great love, no great friendship, but that's because I haven't met a man or woman who was worthy. The books I've written haven't been very good because I haven't had the proper leisure. I haven't had children to devote myself to because I didn't find a man with whom I could have spent my life. So there remains within me, unused and quite viable, a host of propensities, inclinations, possibilities, that one wouldn't guess from the mere series of things I've done."

Now, for the existentialist there is really no love other than one which manifests itself in a person's being in love. There is no genius other than one which is expressed in works of art; the genius of Proust is the sum of Proust's works; the genius of Racine is his series of tragedies. Outside of that, there is nothing. Why say that Racine could have written another tragedy, when he didn't write it? A man is involved in life, leaves his impress on it, and outside of that there is nothing. To be sure, this may seem a harsh thought to someone whose life hasn't been a success. But, on the other hand, it prompts people to understand that reality alone is what counts, that dreams, expectations, and hopes warrant no more than to define a man as a disappointed dream, as miscarried hopes, as vain expectations. In other words, to define him negatively and not positively. However, when we say, "You are nothing else than your life," that does not imply that the artist will be judged solely on the basis of his works of art; a thousand other things will contribute toward summing him up. What we mean is that a man is nothing else than a series of undertakings, that he is the sum, the organization, the ensemble of the relationships which make up these undertakings.

When all is said and done, what we are accused of, at bottom, is not our pessimism, but an optimistic toughness. If people throw up to us our works of fiction in which we write about people who are soft, weak, cowardly, and sometimes even downright bad, it's not because these people are soft, weak, cowardly, or bad; because if we were to say, as Zola did, that they are that way because of heredity, the workings of environment, society, because of biological or psychological determinism, people would be reassured. They would say, "Well, that's what we're like, no one can do anything about it." But when the existentialist writes about a coward, he says that this coward is responsible for his cowardice. He's not like that because he has a cowardly heart or lung or brain; he's not like that on account of his physiological make-up; but he's like that because he has made himself a coward by his acts. There's no such thing as a cowardly constitution; there are nervous constitutions; there is poor blood, as the common people say, or strong constitutions. But the man whose blood is poor is not a coward on that account, for what makes cowardice is the act of renouncing or yielding. A constitution is not an act; the coward is defined on the basis of the acts he performs. People feel, in a vague sort of way, that this coward we're talking about is guilty of being a coward, and the thought frightens them. What people would like is that a coward or a hero be born that way.

One of the complaints most frequently made about *The Ways of Freedom* can be summed up as follows: "After all, these people are so spineless, how are you going to make heroes out of them?" This objection almost makes me laugh, for it assumes that people are born heroes. That's what people really want to think. If you're born cowardly, you may set your mind perfectly at rest; there's nothing you can do about it; you'll be cowardly all your life, whatever you may do. If you're born a hero, you may set your mind just as much at rest; you'll be a hero all your life; you'll drink like a hero and eat like a hero. What the existentialist says is that the coward makes himself cowardly, that the hero makes himself heroic. There's always a possibility for the coward not to be cowardly any more and for the hero to stop being heroic. What counts is total involvement; some one particular action or set of circumstances is not total involvement.

Thus, I think we have answered a number of the charges concerning existentialism. You see that it can not be taken for a philosophy of quietism, since it defines man in terms of action; nor for a pessimistic description of man—there is no doctrine more optimistic, since man's destiny is within himself; nor for an attempt to discourage man from acting, since it tells him that the only hope is in his acting and that action is the only thing that enables a man to live. Consequently, we are dealing here with an ethics of action and involvement.

Nevertheless, on the basis of a few notions like these, we are still charged with immuring man in his private subjectivity. There again we're very much misunderstood. Subjectivity of the individual is indeed our point of departure, and this for strictly philosophic reasons. Not because we are bourgeois, but because we want a doctrine based on truth and not a lot of fine theories, full of hope but with no real basis. There can be no other truth to take off from than this: *I think; therefore, I exist.* There we have the absolute truth of consciousness becoming aware of itself. Every theory which takes man out of the moment in which he becomes aware of himself is, at its very beginning, a theory which confounds truth, for outside the Cartesian *cogito,* all views are only probable, and a doctrine of probability which is not bound to a truth dissolves into thin air. In order to describe the probable, you must have a firm hold on the true. Therefore, before there can be any truth whatsoever, there must be an absolute truth; and this one is simple and easily arrived at; it's on everyone's doorstep; it's a matter of grasping it directly.

Secondly, this theory is the only one which gives man dignity, the only one which does not reduce him to an object. The effect of all materialism is to treat all men, including the one philosophizing, as objects, that is, as an ensemble of determined reactions in no way distinguished from the ensemble of qualities and phenomena which constitute a table or a chair or a stone. We definitely wish to establish the human realm as an ensemble of values distinct from the material realm. But the subjectivity that we have thus arrived at, and which we have claimed to be truth, is not a strictly individual subjectivity, for we have demonstrated that one discovers in the *cogito* not only himself, but others as well.

The philosophies of Descartes and Kant to the contrary, through the *I think* we reach our own self in the presence of others, and the others are just as real to us as our own self. Thus, the man who becomes aware of himself through the *cogito* also perceives all others, and he perceives them as the condition of his own existence. He realizes that he can not be anything (in the sense that we say that someone is witty or nasty or jealous) unless others recognize it as such. In order to get any truth about myself, I must have contact with another person. The other is indispensable to my own existence, as well as to my knowledge about myself. This being so, in discovering my inner being I discover the other person at the same time, like a freedom placed in front of me which thinks and wills only for or against me. Hence, let us at once announce the discovery of a world which we shall call inter-subjectivity; this is the world in which man decides what he is and what others are.

Besides, if it is impossible to find in every man some universal essence which would be human nature, yet there does exist a universal human condition. It's not by chance that to-day's thinkers speak more readily of man's condition than of his nature. By condition they mean, more or less definitely, the *a priori* limits which outline man's fundamental situation in the universe. Historical situations vary; a man may be born a slave in a pagan society or a feudal lord or a proletarian. What does not vary is the necessity for him to exist in the world, to be at work there, to be there in the midst of other people, and to be mortal there. The limits are neither subjective or objective, or, rather, they have an objective and a subjective side. Objective because they are to be found everywhere and are recognizable everywhere; subjective because they are *lived* and are nothing if man does not live them, that is, freely determine his existence with reference to them. And though the configurations may differ, at least none of them are completely strange to me, because they all appear as attempts either to pass beyond these limits or recede from them or deny them or adapt to them. Consequently, every configuration, however individual it may be, has a universal value.

Every configuration, even the Chinese, the Indian, or the Negro, can be understood by a Westerner. "Can be understood" means that by virtue of a situation that he can imagine, a European of 1945 can, in like manner, push himself to his limits and reconstitute within himself the configuration of the Chinese, the Indian, or the African. Every configuration has universality in the sense that every configuration can be understood by every man. This does not at all mean that this configuration defines man forever, but that it can be met with again. There is always a way to understand the idiot, the child, the savage, the foreigner, provided one has the necessary information.

In this sense we may say that there is a universality of man; but it is not given, it is perpetually being made. I build the universal in choosing myself; I build it in understanding the configuration of every other man, whatever age he might have lived in. This absoluteness of choice does not do away with the relativeness of each epoch. At heart, what existentialism shows is the connection between the absolute character of free involvement, by virtue of which every man realizes himself in realizing a type of mankind, an involvement always comprehensible in any age whatsoever and by any person whosoever, and the relativeness of the cultural ensemble which may result from such a choice; it must be stressed that the relativity of Cartesianism and the absolute character of Cartesian involvement go together. In this sense, you may, if you like, say that each of us performs an absolute act in breathing, eating, sleeping, or behaving in any way whatever. There is no difference between being free, like a configuration, like an existence which chooses its essence, and being absolute. There is no difference between being an absolute temporarily localised, that is, localised in history, and being universally comprehensible.

This does not entirely settle the objection to subjectivism. In fact, the objection still takes several forms. First, there is the following: we are told, "So you're able to do anything, no matter what!" This is expressed in various ways. First we are accused of anarchy; then they say, "You're unable to pass judgment on others, because there's no reason to prefer one configuration to another"; finally they tell us, "Everything is arbitrary in this choosing of yours. You take something from one pocket and pretend you're putting it into the other."

These three objections aren't very serious. Take the first objection. "You're able to do anything, no matter what" is not to the point. In one sense choice is possible, but what is not possible is not to choose. I can always choose, but I ought to know that if I do not choose, I am still choosing. Though this may seem purely formal, it is highly important for keeping fantasy and caprice within bounds. If it is true that in facing a situation, for example, one in which, as a person capable of having sexual relations, of having children, I am obliged to choose an attitude, and if I in any way assume responsibility for a choice which, in involving myself, also involves all mankind, this has nothing to do with caprice, even if no *a priori* value determines my choice.

If anybody thinks that he recognizes here Gide's theory of the arbitrary act, he fails to see the enormous difference between this doctrine and Gide's. Gide does not know what a situation is. He acts out of pure caprice. For us, on the contrary, man is in an organized situation in which he himself is involved. Through his choice, he involves all mankind, and he can not avoid making a choice: either he will remain chaste, or he will marry without having children, or he will marry and have children; anyhow, whatever he may do, it is impossible for him not to take full responsibility for the way he handles this problem. Doubtless, he chooses without referring to pre-established values, but it is unfair to accuse him of caprice. Instead, let us say that moral choice is to be compared to the making of a work of art. And before going any further, let it be said at once that we are not dealing here with an aesthetic ethics, because our opponents are so dishonest that they even accuse us of that. The example I've chosen is a comparison only.

Having said that, may I ask whether anyone has ever accused an artist who has painted a picture of not having drawn his inspiration from rules set up *a priori*? Has anyone ever asked, "What painting ought he to make?" It is clearly understood that there is no definite painting to be made, that the artist is engaged in the making of his painting, and that the painting to be made is precisely the painting he will have made. It is clearly understood that there are no *a priori* aesthetic values, but that there are values which appear subsequently in the coherence of the painting, in the correspondence between what the artist intended and the result. Nobody can tell what the painting of tomorrow will be like. Painting can be judged only after it has once been made. What connection does that have with ethics? We are in the same creative situation. We never say that a work of art is arbitrary. When we speak of a canvas of Picasso, we never say that it is arbitrary; we understand quite well that he was making himself what he is at the very time he was painting, that the ensemble of his work is embodied in his life.

The same holds on the ethical plane. What art and ethics have in common is that we have creation and invention in both cases. We can not decide *a priori* what there is to be done. I think that I pointed that out quite sufficiently when I mentioned the case of the student who came to see me, and who might have applied to all the ethical systems, Kantian or otherwise, without getting any sort of guidance. He was obliged to devise his law himself. Never let it be said by us that this man—who, taking affection, individual action, and kind-heartedness toward a specific person as his ethical first principle, chooses to remain with his mother, or who, preferring to make a sacrifice, chooses to go to England—has made an arbitrary choice. Man makes himself. He isn't ready-made at the start. In choosing his ethics, he makes himself, and force of circumstances is such that he can not abstain from choosing one. We define man only in relationship to involvement. It is therefore absurd to charge us with arbitrariness of choice.

In the second place, it is said that we are unable to pass judgment on others. In a way this is true, and in another way, false. It is true in this sense, that, whenever a man sanely and sincerely involves himself and chooses his configuration, it is impossible for him to prefer another configuration, regardless of what his own may be in other respects. It is true in this sense, that we do not believe in progress. Progress is betterment. Man is always the same. The situation confronting him varies. Choice always remains a choice in a situation. The problem has not changed since the time one could choose between those for and those against slavery, for example, at the time of the Civil War, and the present time, when one can side with the Maquis Resistance Party, or with the Communists.

But, nevertheless, one can still pass judgment, for, as I have said, one makes a choice in relationship to others. First, one can judge (and this is perhaps not a judgment of value, but a logical judgment) that certain choices are based on error and others on truth. If we have defined man's situation as a free choice, with no excuses and no recourse, every man who takes refuge behind the excuse of his passions, every man who sets up a determinism, is a dishonest man.

The objection may be raised, "But why mayn't he choose himself dishonestly?" I reply that I am not obliged to pass moral judgment on him, but that I do define his dishonesty as an error. One can not help considering the truth of the matter. Dishonesty is obviously a falsehood because it belies the complete freedom of involvement. On the same grounds, I maintain that there is also dishonesty if I choose to state that certain values exist prior to me; it is self-contradictory for me to want them and at the same time state that they are imposed on me. Suppose someone says to me, "What if I want to be dishonest?" I'll answer, "There's no reason for you not to be, but I'm saying that that's what you are, and that the strictly coherent attitude is that of honesty."

Besides, I can bring moral judgment to bear. When I declare that freedom in every concrete circumstance can have no other aim than to want itself, if man has once become aware that in his forlornness he imposes values, he can no longer want but one thing, and that is freedom, as the basis of all values. That doesn't mean that he wants it in the abstract. It means simply that the ultimate meaning of the acts of honest men is the quest for freedom as such. A man who belongs to a communist or revolutionary union wants concrete goals; these goals imply an abstract desire for freedom; but this freedom is wanted in something concrete. We want freedom for freedom's sake and in every particular circumstance. And in wanting freedom we discover that it depends entirely on the freedom of others, and that the freedom of others depends on ours. Of course, freedom as the definition of man does not depend on others, but as soon as there is involvement, I am obliged to want others to have freedom at the same time that I want my own freedom. I can take freedom as my goal only if I take that of others as a goal as well. Consequently, when, in all honesty, I've recognized that man is a being in whom existence precedes essence, that he is a free being who, in various circumstances, can want only his freedom, I have at the same time recognized that I can want only the freedom of others.

Therefore, in the name of this will for freedom, which freedom itself implies, I may pass judgment on those who seek to hide from themselves the complete arbitrariness and the complete freedom of their existence. Those who hide their complete freedom from themselves out of a spirit of seriousness or by means of deterministic excuses, I shall call cowards; those who try to show that their existence was necessary, when it is the very contingency of man's appearance on earth, I shall call stinkers. But cowards or stinkers can be judged only from a strictly unbiased point of view.

Therefore though the content of ethics is variable, a certain form of it is universal. Kant says that freedom desires both itself and the freedom of others. Granted. But he believes that the formal and the universal are enough to constitute an ethics. We, on the other hand, think that principles which are too abstract run aground in trying to decide action. Once again, take the case of the student. In the name of what great moral maxim do you think he could have decided, in perfect peace of mind, to abandon his mother or to stay with her? There is no way of judging. The content is always concrete and thereby unforeseeable; there is always the element of invention. The one thing that counts is knowing whether the inventing that has been done, has been done in the name of freedom.

For example, let us look at the following two cases. You will see to what extent they correspond, yet differ. Take *The Mill on the Floss.* We find a certain young girl, Maggie Tulliver, who is an embodiment of the value of passion and who is aware of it. She is in love with a young man, Stephen, who is engaged to an insignificant young girl. This Maggie Tulliver, instead of heedlessly preferring her own happiness, chooses, in the name of human solidarity, to sacrifice herself and give up the man she loves. On the other hand, Sanseverina, in *The Charterhouse of Parma,* believing that passion is man's true value, would say that a great love deserves sacrifices; that it is to be preferred to the banality of the conjugal love that would tie Stephen to the young ninny he had to marry. She would choose to sacrifice the girl and fulfill her happiness; and, as Stendhal shows, she is even ready to sacrifice herself for the sake of passion, if this life demands it. Here we are in the presence of two strictly opposed moralities. I claim that they are much the same thing; in both cases what has been set up as the goal is freedom.

You can imagine two highly similar attitudes: one girl prefers to renounce her love out of resignation; another prefers to disregard the prior attachment of the man she loves out of sexual desire. On the surface these two actions resemble those we've just described. However, they are completely different. Sanseverina's attitude is much nearer that of Maggie Tulliver, one of heedless rapacity.

Thus, you see that the second charge is true and, at the same time, false. One may choose anything if it is on the grounds of free involvement.

The third objection is the following: "You take something from one pocket and put it into the other. That is, fundamentally, values aren't serious, since you choose them." My answer to this is that I'm quite vexed that that's the way it is; but if I've discarded God the Father, there has to be someone to invent values. You've got to take things as they are. Moreover, to say that we invent values means nothing else but this: life has no meaning *a priori*. Before you come alive, life is nothing; it's up to you to give it a meaning, and value is nothing else but the meaning that you choose. In that way, you see, there is a possibility of creating a human community.

Tabula rasa

I've been reproached for asking whether existentialism is humanistic. It's been said, "But you said in *Nausea* that the humanists were all wrong. You made fun of a certain kind of humanist. Why come back to it now?" Actually, the word humanism has two very different meanings. By humanism one can mean a theory which takes man as an end and as a higher value. Humanism in this sense can be found in Cocteau's tale *Around the World in Eighty Hours* when a character, because he is flying over some mountains in an airplane, declares, "Man is simply amazing." That means that I, who did not build the airplanes, shall personally benefit from these particular inventions, and that I, as man, shall personally consider myself responsible for, and honored by, acts of a few particular men. This would imply that we ascribe a value to man on the basis of the highest deeds of certain men. This humanism is absurd, because only the dog or the horse would be able to make such an over-all judgment about man, which they are careful not to do, at least to my knowledge.

But it can not be granted that a man may make a judgment about man. Existentialism spares him from any such judgment. The existentialist will never consider man as an end because he is always in the making. Nor should we believe that there is a mankind to which we might set up a cult in the manner of Auguste Comte. The cult of mankind ends in the self-enclosed humanism of Comte, and, let it be said, of fascism. This kind of humanism we can do without.

But there is another meaning of humanism. Fundamentally it is this: man is constantly outside of himself; in projecting himself, in losing himself outside of himself, he makes for man's existing; and, on the other hand, it is by pursuing transcendent goals that he is able to exist; man, being this state of passing-beyond, and seizing upon things only as they bear upon this passing-beyond, is at the heart, at the center of this passing-beyond. There is no universe other than a human universe, the universe of human subjectivity. This connection between transcendency, as a constituent element of man—not in the sense that God is transcendent, but in the sense of passing beyond—and subjectivity, in the sense that man is not closed in on himself but is always present in a human universe, is what we call existentialist humanism. Humanism, because we remind man that there is no law-maker other than himself, and that in his forlornness he will decide by himself; because we point out that man will fulfill himself as man, not in turning toward himself, but in seeking outside of himself a goal which is just this liberation, just this particular fulfillment.

From these few reflections it is evident that nothing is more unjust than the objections that have been raised against us. Existentialism is nothing else than an attempt to draw all the consequences of a coherent atheistic position. It isn't trying to plunge man into despair at all. But if one calls every attitude of unbelief despair, like the Christians, then the word is not being used in its original sense. Existentialism isn't so atheistic that it wears itself out showing that God doesn't exist. Rather, it declares that even if God did exist, that would change nothing. There you've got our point of view. Not that we believe that God exists, but we think that the problem of His existence is not the issue. In this sense existentialism is optimistic, a doctrine of action, and it is plain dishonesty for Christians to make no distinction between their own despair and ours and then to call us despairing.

SIGMUND FREUD

SIGMUND FREUD has contributed to modern thought one of its most extensive and provocative discourses on the nature of man and his social environment. During the first two decades of his work in psychology, Freud established the essential directions for the theory and practice of psychoanalysis. However, he continued to widen the scope of his theoretical evaluations, going beyond their immediate clinical application. This evolution of ideas is evident in his essay "Thoughts for the Times on War and Death" (1915), which comprises the following selection. For this work not only reveals Freud's abiding concern for the travails of contemporary civilization, but contains, as well, the germs of ideas which he was to elaborate in the succeeding twenty-five years in a number of important publications. At least two lines of thought are indicated in this study. One of them probes into the nature of the "external" determinants working upon the life of civilized man and was developed more fully in his later essays *Totem and Taboo* (1927), *Future of an Illusion* (1928), and *Civilization and Its Discontents* (1930). In diverse ways, these works pose the question of what role conventional practices, religions and social ideals, and culturally inherited illusions play in the organization and orientation of the developing human personality. The other motif to be found in "Thoughts for the Times on War and Death," which was further articulated in *Beyond the Pleasure Principle* (1922), *Ego and Id* (1923), and the *Problem of Anxiety* (1936), explores the "internal" revolution of man's psychic energies and the external struggle between the forces of life and death.

THOUGHTS FOR THE TIMES ON WAR AND DEATH

I. THE DISILLUSIONMENT OF THE WAR

Swept as we are into the vortex of this war-time, our information one-sided, ourselves too near to focus the mighty transformations which have already taken place or are beginning to take place, and without a glimmering of the inchoate future, we are incapable of apprehending the significance of the thronging impressions, and know not what value to attach to the judgments we form. We are constrained to believe that never has any event been destructive of so much that is valuable in the common wealth of humanity, nor so

---

This selection has been reprinted from Sigmund Freud, "Thoughts for the Times on War and Death," in *Collected Papers,* Vol. IV (pp. 288–317, Copyright 1925 by Hogarth Press, London) by permission of the publisher. The 1946 edition has been used.

misleading to many of the clearest intelligences, nor so debasing to the highest that we know. Science herself has lost her passionless impartiality; in their deep embitterment her servants seek for weapons from her with which to contribute towards the defeat of the enemy. The anthropologist is driven to declare the opponent inferior and degenerate; the psychiatrist to publish his diagnosis of the enemy's disease of mind or spirit. But probably our sense of these immediate evils is disproportionately strong, and we are not entitled to compare them with the evils of other times of which we have not undergone the experience.

The individual who is not himself a combatant—and so a wheel in the gigantic machinery of war—feels conscious of disorientation, and of an inhibition in his powers and activities. I believe that he will welcome any indication, however slight, which may enable him to find out what is wrong with himself at least. I propose to distinguish two among the most potent factors in the mental distress felt by non-combatants, against which it is such a heavy task to struggle, and to treat of them here: the disillusionment which this war has evoked; and the altered attitude towards death which this—like every other war—imposes on us.

When I speak of disillusionment, everyone at once knows what I mean. One need not be a sentimentalist: one may perceive the biological and psychological necessity of suffering in the economics of human life, and yet condemn war both in its means and in its aims, and devoutly look forward to the cessation of all wars. True, we have told ourselves that wars can never cease so long as nations live under such widely differing conditions, so long as the value of individual life is in each nation so variously computed, and so long as the animosities which divide them represent such powerful instinctual forces in the mind. And we were prepared to find that wars between the primitive and the civilized peoples, between those races whom a colour-line divides, nay, wars with and among the undeveloped nationalities of Europe or those whose culture has perished—that for a considerable period such wars would occupy mankind. But we permitted ourselves to have other hopes. We had expected the great ruling powers among the white nations upon whom the leadership of the human species has fallen, who were known to have cultivated world-wide interests, to whose creative powers were due our technical advances in the direction of dominating nature, as well as the artistic and scientific acquisitions of the mind—peoples such as these we had expected to succeed in discovering another way of settling misunderstandings and conflicts of interest. Within each of these nations there prevailed high standards of accepted custom for the individual, to which his manner of life was bound to conform if he desired a share in communal privileges. These ordinances, frequently too stringent, exacted a great deal from him, much self-restraint, much renunciation of instinctual gratification. He was especially forbidden to make use of the immense advantages to be gained by the practice of lying and deception in the competition with his fellow-men. The civilized state regarded these accepted standards as the basis of its existence; stern were its proceedings when an impious hand was laid upon them; frequent the pronouncement that to subject them even to examination by a critical intelligence was entirely impracticable. It could be assumed, therefore, that the state itself would respect them, nor would contemplate undertaking any infringement of what it acknowledged as the basis of its own existence. To be sure, it was evident that within these civilized states were mingled remnants of certain other races who were universally unpopular and had therefore been only reluctantly, and even so not to the fullest extent, admitted to participation in the common task of civilization, for which they had shown themselves suitable enough. But the great nations themselves, it might have been supposed, had acquired so much comprehension of their common interests, and enough tolerance for the differences that existed between them, that "foreigner" and "enemy" could no longer, as still in antiquity, be regarded as synonymous.

Relying on this union among the civilized races, countless people have exchanged their native home for a foreign dwelling-place, and made their existence dependent on the conditions of intercourse between friendly nations. But he who was not by stress of circumstances confined to one spot, could also confer upon himself, through all the advantages and attractions of these civilized countries, a new, a wider fatherland, wherein he moved unhindered and unsuspected. In this way he enjoyed the blue sea, and the grey; the beauty of the snow-clad mountains and of the green pasture-lands; the magic of the northern forests and the splendour of the southern vegetation; the emotion inspired by landscapes that recall great historical events, and the silence of nature in her inviolate places. This new fatherland was for him a museum also, filled with all the treasures which the artists among civilized communities had in the successive centuries created and left behind. As he wandered from one gallery to another in this museum, he could appreciate impartially the varied types of perfection that miscegenation, the course of historical events, and the special characteristics of their mother-earth had produced among his more remote compatriots. Here he would find a cool inflexible energy developed to this highest point; there, the gracious art of beautifying existence; elsewhere, the sense of order and fixed law—in short, any and all of the qualities which have made mankind the lords of the earth.

Nor must we forget that each of these citizens of culture had created for himself a personal "Parnassus" and "School of Athens." From among the great thinkers and artists of all nations he had chosen those to whom he conceived himself most deeply indebted for what he had achieved in enjoyment and comprehension of life, and in his veneration had associated them with the immortals of old as well as with the more familiar masters of his own tongue. None of these great figures had seemed to him alien because he had spoken another language—not the incomparable investigator of the passions of mankind, nor the intoxicated worshipper of beauty, nor the vehement and threatening prophet, nor the subtle mocking satirist; and never did he on this account rebuke himself as a renegade towards his own nation and his beloved mother tongue.

The enjoyment of this fellowship in civilization was from time to time disturbed by warning voices, which declared that as a result of long-prevailing differences wars were unavoidable, even among the members of a fellowship such as this. We refused to believe it; but if such a war indeed must be, what was our imaginary picture of it? We saw it as an opportunity for demonstrating the progress of mankind in communal feeling since the era when the Greek Amphictyones had proclaimed that no city of the league might be demolished, nor its olive-groves hewn down, nor its water cut off. As a chivalrous crusade, which would limit itself to establishing the superiority of one side in the contest, with the least possible infliction of dire sufferings that could contribute nothing to the decision, and with complete immunity for the wounded who must of necessity withdraw from the contest, as well as for the physicians and nurses who devoted themselves to the task of healing. And of course with the utmost precautions for the non-combatant classes of the population—for women who are debarred from war-work, and for the children who, grown older, should be enemies no longer but friends and cooperators. And again, with preservation of all the international undertakings and institutions in which the mutual civilization of peace-time had been embodied.

Even a war like this would have been productive of horrors and sufferings enough; but it would not have interrupted the development of ethical relations between the greater units of mankind, between the peoples and the states.

Then the war in which we had refused to believe broke out, and brought—disillusionment. Not only is it more sanguinary and more destructive than any war of other days, because of the enormously increased perfection of weapons of attack and defence; but it is at least as cruel, as embittered, as implacable as any that has preceded it. It sets at naught all those restrictions known as International Law, which in peace-time the states had bound themselves to observe; it ignores the prerogatives of the wounded and the medical service, the distinction between civil and military sections of the population, the claims of private property. It tramples in blind fury on all that comes in its way, as though there were to be no future and no goodwill among men after it has passed. It rends all bonds of fellowship between the contending peoples, and threatens to leave such a legacy of embitterment as will make any renewal of such bonds impossible for a long time to come.

Moreover, it has brought to light the almost unbelievable phenomenon of a mutual comprehension between the civilized nations so slight that the one can turn with hate and loathing upon the other. Nay, more—that one of the great civilized nations is so universally unpopular that the attempt can actually be made to exclude it from the civilized community as "barbaric," although it long has proved its fitness by the most magnificent co-operation in the work of civilization. We live in the hope that the impartial decision of history will furnish the proof that precisely this nation, this in whose tongue we now write, this for whose victory our dear ones are fighting, was the one which least transgressed the laws of civilization—but at such a time who shall dare present himself as the judge of his own cause?

Nations are in a measure represented by the states which they have formed; these states, by the governments which administer them. The individual in any given nation has in this war a terrible opportunity to convince himself of what would occasionally strike him in peace-time—that the state has forbidden to the individual the practice of wrong-doing, not because it desired to abolish it, but because it desires to monopolize it, like salt and tobacco. The warring state permits itself every such misdeed, every such act of violence, as would disgrace the individual man. It practises not only the accepted stratagems, but also deliberate lying and deception against the enemy; and this, too, in a measure which appears to surpass the usage of former wars. The state exacts the utmost degree of obedience and sacrifice from its citizens, but at the same time treats them as children by maintaining an excess of secrecy, and a censorship of news and expressions of opinion that renders the spirits of those thus intellectually oppressed defenceless against every unfavorable turn of events and every sinister rumour. It absolves itself from the guarantees and contracts it had formed with other states, and makes unabashed confession of its rapacity and lust for power, which the private individual is then called upon to sanction in the name of patriotism.

Nor may it be objected that the state cannot refrain from wrong-doing, since that would place it at a disadvantage. It is no less disadvantageous, as a general rule, for the individual man to conform to the customs of morality and refrain from brutal and arbitrary conduct; and the state but seldom proves able to indemnify him for the sacrifices it exacts. It cannot be a matter for astonishment, therefore, that this relaxation of all the moral ties between the greater units of mankind should have had a seducing influence on the morality of individuals; for our conscience is not the inflexible judge that ethical teachers are wont to declare it, but in its origin is "dread of the community" and nothing else. When the community has no rebuke to make, there is an end of all suppression of the baser passions, and men perpetrate deeds of cruelty, fraud, treachery and barbarity so incompatible with their civilization that one would have held them to be impossible.

Well may that civilized cosmopolitan, therefore, of whom I spoke, stand helpless in a world grown strange to him—his all-embracing patrimony disintegrated, the common estates in it laid waste, the fellow-citizens embroiled and debased!

In criticism of his disillusionment, nevertheless, certain things must be said. Strictly speaking, it is not justified, for it consists in the destruction of—an illusion! We welcome illusions because they spare us emotional distress, and enable us instead to indulge in gratification. We must not then complain if now and again they come into conflict with some portion of reality, and are shattered against it.

Two things in this war have evoked our sense of disillusionment: the destitution shown in moral relations externally by the states which in their interior relations pose as the guardians of accepted moral usage, and the brutality in behaviour shown by individuals, whom, as partakers in the highest form of human civilization, one would not have credited with such a thing.

Let us begin with the second point and endeavour to formulate, as succinctly as may be, the point of view which it is proposed to criticize. How do we imagine the process by which an individual attains to a higher plane of morality? The first answer is sure to be: He is good and noble from his very birth, his very earliest beginnings. We need not consider this any further. A second answer will suggest that we are concerned with a developmental process, and will probably assume that this development consists in eradicating from him the evil human tendencies and, under the influence of education and a civilized environment, replacing them by good ones. From that standpoint it is certainly astonishing that evil should show itself to have such power in those who have been thus nurtured.

But this answer implies the thesis from which we propose to dissent. In reality, there is no such thing as "eradicating" evil tendencies. Psychological—more strictly speaking, psycho-analytic—investigation shows instead that the inmost essence of human nature consists of elemental instincts, which are common to all men and aim at the satisfaction of certain primal needs. These instincts in themselves are neither good nor evil. We but classify them and their manifestations in that fashion, according as they meet the needs and demands of the human community. It is admitted that all those instincts which society condemns as evil—let us take as representatives the selfish and the cruel—are of this primitive type.

These primitive instincts undergo a lengthy process of development before they are allowed to become active in the adult being. They are inhibited, directed towards other aims and departments, become commingled, alter their objects, and are to some extent turned back upon their possessor. Reaction-formations against certain instincts take the deceptive form of a change in content, as though egoism had changed into altruism, or cruelty into pity. These reaction-formations are facilitated by the circumstance that many instincts are manifested almost from the first in pairs of opposites, a very remarkable phenomenon—and one strange to the lay public—which is termed the "ambivalence of feeling." The most easily observable and comprehensible instance of this is the fact that intense love and intense hatred are so often to be found together in the same person. Psycho-analysis adds that the conflicting feelings not infrequently have the same person for their object.

It is not until all these "vicissitudes to which instincts are subject" have been surmounted that what we call the character of a human being is formed, and this, we know, can only very inadequately be classified as "good" or "bad." A human being is seldom altogether good or bad; he is usually "good" in one relation and "bad" in another, or "good" in certain external circumstances and in others decidedly "bad." It is interesting to learn that the existence of "bad" impulses in infancy is often the actual condition for an unmistakable inclination towards "good" in the adult person. Those who as children have been the most pronounced egoists may well become the most helpful and self-sacrificing members of the community; most of our sentimentalists, friends of humanity, champions of animals, have been evolved from little sadists and animal-tormentors.

The transformation of "bad" instincts is brought about by two co-operating factors, an internal and an external. The internal factor consists in an influence on the bad—say, the egoistic—instincts exercised by erotism, that is, by the human need for love, taken in its widest sense. By the admixture of *erotic* components the egoistic instincts are transmuted into *social* ones. We learn to value being loved as an advantage for which we are willing to sacrifice other advantages. The external factor is the force exercised by up-bringing, which advocates the claims of our cultural environment, and this is furthered later by the direct pressure of that civilization by which we are surrounded. Civilization is the fruit of renunciation of instinctual satisfaction, and from each new-comer in turn it exacts the same renunciation. Throughout the life of the individual there is a constant replacement of the external compulsion by the internal. The influences of civilization cause an ever-increasing transmutation of egoistic trends into altruistic and social ones, and this by an admixture of erotic elements. In the last resort it may be said that every internal compulsion which has been of service in the development of human beings was originally, that is, in the evolution of the human race, nothing but an external one. Those who are born to-day bring with them as an inherited constitution some degree of a tendency (disposition) towards transmutation of egoistic into social instincts, and this disposition is easily stimulated to achieve that effect. A further measure of this transformation must be accomplished during the life of the individual himself. And so the human being is subject not only to the pressure of his immediate environment, but also to the influence of the cultural development attained by his forefathers.

La Marck

If we give the name of *cultural adaptability* to a man's personal capacity for transformation of the egoistic impulses under the influence of the erotic, we may further affirm that this adaptability is made up of two parts, one innate and the other acquired through experience, and that the relation of the two to each other and to that portion of the instinctual life which remains untransformed is a very variable one.

Generally speaking, we are apt to attach too much importance to the innate part, and in addition to this we run the risk of overestimating the general adaptability to civilization in comparison with those instincts which have remained in their primitive state—by which I mean that in this way we are led to regard human nature as "better" than it actually is. For there is, besides, another factor which obscures our judgement and falsifies the issue in too favourable a sense.

The impulses of another person are naturally hidden from our observation. We deduce them from his actions and behaviour, which we trace to motives born of his instinctual life. Such a conclusion is bound to be, in many cases, erroneous. This or that action which is "good" from the civilized point of view may in one instance be born of a "noble" motive, in another not so. Ethical theorists class as "good" actions only those which are the outcome of good impulses; to the others they refuse their recognition. But society, which is practical in its aims, is little troubled on the whole by this distinction; it is content if a man regulates his behaviour and actions by the precepts of civilization, and is little concerned with his motives.

We have seen that the external compulsion exercised on a human being by his up-bringing and environment produces a further transformation towards good in his instinctual life—a turning from egoism towards altruism. But this is not the regular or necessary effect of the external compulsion. Education and environment offer benefits not only in the way of love, but also employ another kind of premium system, namely, reward and punishment. In this way their effect may turn out to be that he who is subjected to their influence will choose to "behave well" in the civilized sense of the phrase, although no ennoblement of instinct, no transformation of egoistic into altruistic inclinations, has taken place within. The result will, roughly speaking, be the same; only a particular concatenation of circumstances will reveal that one man always acts rightly because his instinctual inclination compels him so to do, and the other is "good" only in so far and for so long as such civilized behaviour is advantageous for his own egoistic purposes. But superficial acquaintance with an individual will not enable us to distinguish between the two cases, and we are certainly misled by our optimism into grossly exaggerating the number of human beings who have been transformed in a civilized sense.

Civilized society, which exacts good conduct and does not trouble itself about the impulses underlying it, has thus won over to obedience a great many people who are not thereby following the dictates of their own natures. Encouraged by this success, society has suffered itself to be led into straining the moral standard to the highest possible point, and thus it has forced its members into a yet greater estrangement from their instinctual dispositions. They are consequently subjected to an unceasing suppression of instinct, the resulting strain of which betrays itself in the most remarkable phenomena of reaction and compensation formations. In the domain of sexuality, where such suppression is most difficult to enforce, the result is seen in the reaction-phenomena of neurotic disorders. Elsewhere the pressure of civilization brings in its train no pathological results, but is shown in malformations of character, and in the perpetual readiness of the inhibited instincts to break through to gratification at any suitable opportunity. Anyone thus compelled to act continually in the sense of precepts which are not the depression of instinctual inclinations, is living, psychologically speaking, beyond his means, and might objectively be designated a hypocrite, whether this difference be clearly known to him or not. It is undeniable that our contemporary civilization is extraordinarily favourable to the production of this form of hypocrisy. One might venture to say that it is based upon such hypocrisy, and that it would have to submit to far-reaching modifications if people were to undertake to live in accordance with the psychological truth. Thus there are very many more hypocrites than truly civilized persons—indeed, it is a debatable point whether a certain degree of civilized hypocrisy be not indispensable for the maintenance of civilization, because the cultural adaptability so far attained by those living to-day would perhaps not prove adequate to the task. On the other hand, the maintenance of civilization even on so questionable a basis offers the prospect of each new generation achieving a further-reaching transmutation of instinct, and becoming the pioneer of a higher form of civilization.

From the foregoing observations we may already derive this consolation—that our mortification and our grievous disillusionment regarding the uncivilized behavior of our world-compatriots in this war are shown to be unjustified. They are based on an illusion to which we had abandoned ourselves. In reality our fellow-citizens have not sunk so low as we feared, because they had never risen so high as we believed. That the greater units of humanity, the peoples and states, have mutually abrogated their moral restraints naturally prompted these individuals to permit themselves relief for a while from the heavy pressure of civilization and to grant a passing satisfaction to the instincts it holds in check. This probably caused no breach in the relative morality within their respective national frontiers.

We may, however, obtain insight deeper than this into the change brought about by the war in our former compatriots, and at the same time receive a warning against doing them an injustice. For the evolution of the mind shows a peculiarity which is present in no other process of development. When a village grows into a town, a child into a man, the village and the child become submerged in the town and the man. Memory alone can trace the earlier features in the new image; in reality the old materials or forms have been superseded and replaced by new ones. It is otherwise with the development of the mind. Here one can describe the state of affairs, which is a quite peculiar one, only by saying that in this case every earlier stage of development persists alongside the later stage which has developed from it; the successive stages condition a co-existence, although it is in reference to the same materials that the whole series of transformations has been fashioned. The earlier mental state may not have manifested itself for years, but none the less it is so far present that it may at any time again become the mode of expression of the forces in the mind, and that exclusively, as though all later developments had been annulled, undone. This extraordinary plasticity of the evolution that takes place in the mind is not unlimited in its scope; it might be described as a special capacity for retroversion—for regression—since it may well happen that a later and higher stage of evolution, once abandoned, cannot be reached again. But the primitive stages can always be re-established; the primitive mind is, in the fullest meaning of the word, imperishable.

What are called mental diseases inevitably impress the layman with the idea of destruction of the life of mind and soul. In reality, the destruction relates only to later accretions and developments. The essence of mental disease lies in a return to earlier conditions of affective life and functioning. An excellent example of the plasticity of mental life is afforded by the state of sleep, which every night we desire. Since we have learnt to interpret even absurd and chaotic dreams, we know that whenever we sleep we cast off our hard-won morality like a garment, only to put it on again next morning. This divestiture is naturally unattended by any danger because we are paralysed, condemned to inactivity, by the state of sleep. Only through a dream can we learn of the regression of our emotional life to one of the earliest stages of development. For instance, it is noteworthy that all our dreams are governed by purely egoistic motives. One of my English friends put forward this proposition at a scientific meeting in America, whereupon a lady who was present remarked that that might be the case in Austria, but she could maintain for herself and her friends that *they* were altruistic in their dreams. My friend, although himself of English race, was obliged to contradict the lady emphatically on the ground of his personal experience in dream-analysis, and to declare that in their dreams high-minded American ladies were quite as egoistical as the Austrians.

Thus the transformations of instinct on which our cultural adaptability is based, may also be permanently or temporarily undone by the experiences of life. Undoubtedly the influences of war are among the forces that can bring about such regression; therefore we need not deny adaptability for culture to all who are at the present time displaying uncivilized behaviour, and we may anticipate that the refinement of their instincts will be restored in times of peace.

There is, however, another symptom in our world-compatriots which has perhaps astonished and shocked us no less than the descent from their ethical nobility which has so greatly distressed us. I mean the narrow-mindedness shown by the best intellects, their obduracy, their inaccessibility to the most forcible arguments, their uncritical credulity for the most disputable assertions. This indeed presents a lamentable picture, and I wish to say emphatically that in this I am by no means a blind partisan who finds all the intellectual shortcomings on one side. But this phenomenon is much easier to account for and much less disquieting than that which we have just considered. Students of human nature and philosophers have long taught us that we are mistaken in regarding our intelligence as an independent force and in overlooking its dependence upon emotional life. Our intelligence, they teach us, can function reliably only when it is removed from the influences of strong emotional impulses; otherwise it behaves merely as an instrument of the will and delivers the inference which the will requires. Thus, in their view, logical arguments are impotent against affective interests, and that is why reasons, which in Falstaff's phrase are "as plenty as blackberries," produce so few victories in the conflict with interests. Psycho-analytic experience has, if possible, further confirmed this statement. It daily shows that the shrewdest persons will all of a sudden behave like imbeciles as soon as the needful insight is confronted by an emotional resistance, but will completely regain their wonted acuity once that resistance has been overcome. The logical infatuations into which this war has deluded our fellow-citizens, many of them the best of their kind, are therefore a secondary phenomenon, a consequence of emotional excitement, and are destined, we may hope, to disappear with it.

Having in this way come to understand once more our fellow-citizens who are now so greatly alienated from us, we shall the more easily endure the disillusionment which the nations, those greater units of the human race, have caused us, for we shall perceive that the demands we make upon them ought to be far more modest. Perhaps they are reproducing the course of individual evolution, and still to-day represent very primitive phases in the organization and formation of higher unities. It is in agreement with this that the educative factor of an external compulsion towards morality, which we found to be so effective for the individual, is barely discernible in them. True, we had hoped that the extensive community of interests established by commerce and production would constitute the germ of such a compulsion, but it would seem that nations still obey their immediate passions far more readily than their interests. Their interests serve them, at most, as rationalizations for their passions; they parade their interests as their justification for satisfying their passions. Actually why the national units should disdain, detest, abhor one another, and that even when they are at peace, is indeed a mystery. I cannot tell why it is. It is just as though when it becomes a question of a number of people, not to say millions, all individual moral acquirements were obliterated, and only the most primitive, the oldest, the crudest mental attitudes were left. Possibly only future stages in development will be able in any way to alter this regrettable state of affairs. But a little more truthfulness and upright dealing on all sides, both in the personal relations of men to one another and between them and those who govern them, should also do something towards smoothing the way for this transformation.

II. OUR ATTITUDE TOWARDS DEATH

The second factor to which I attribute our present sense of estrangement in this once lovely and congenial world is the disturbance that has taken place in our attitude towards death, an attitude to which hitherto we have clung so fast.

This attitude was far from straightforward. We were of course prepared to maintain that death was the necessary outcome of life, that everyone owes a debt to Nature and must expect to pay the reckoning—in short, that death was natural, undeniable and unavoidable. In reality, however, we were accustomed to behave as if it were otherwise. We displayed an unmistakable tendency to "shelve" death, to eliminate it from life. We tried to hush it up; indeed we even have the saying, "To think of something as we think of death." [1] That is our own death, of course. Our own death is indeed unimaginable, and whenever we make the attempt to imagine it we can perceive that we really survive as spectators. Hence the psycho-analytic school could venture on the assertion that at bottom no one believes in his own death, or to put the same thing in another way, in the unconscious every one of us is convinced of his own immortality.

As to the death of another, the civilized man will carefully avoid speaking of such a possibility in the hearing of the person concerned. Children alone disregard this restriction; unabashed they threaten one another with the eventuality of death, and even go so far as to talk of it before one whom they love, as for instance: "Dear Mama, it will be a pity when you are dead but then I shall do this or that." The civilized adult can hardly even entertain the thought of another's death without seeming to himself hard or evil-hearted; unless, of course, as a physician, lawyer or something of the sort, he has to deal with death professionally. Least of all will he permit himself to think of the death of another if with that event some gain to himself in freedom, means or position is connected. This sensitiveness of ours is of course impotent to arrest the hand of death; when it has fallen, we are always deeply affected, as if we were prostrated by the overthrow of our expectations. Our habit is to lay stress on the fortuitous causation of the death—accident, dis-

[1] The German saying is used as an equivalent for "incredible" or "unlikely."—Trans.

ease, infection, advanced age; in this way we betray our endeavour to modify the significance of death from a necessity to an accident. A multitude of simultaneous deaths appears to us exceedingly terrible. Towards the dead person himself we take up a special attitude, something like admiration for one who has accomplished a very difficult task. We suspend criticism of him, overlook his possible misdoings, issue the command: *De mortuis nil nisi bene;* [2] and regard it as justifiable to set forth in the funeral-oration and upon the tombstone only that which is most favourable to his memory. Consideration for the dead, who no longer need it, is dearer to us than the truth, and certainly, for most of us, is dearer also than consideration for the living.

The culmination of this conventional attitude towards death among civilized persons is seen in our complete collapse when death has fallen on some person whom we love—a parent or a partner in marriage, a brother or sister, a child, a dear friend. Our hopes, our pride, our happiness, lie in the grave with him, we will not be consoled, we will not fill the loved one's place. We behave then as if we belonged to the tribe of the Asra, who must die too when those die whom they love.

But this attitude of ours towards death has a powerful effect upon our lives. Life is impoverished, it loses in interest, when the highest stake in the game of living, life itself, may not be risked. It becomes as flat, as superficial, as one of those American flirtations in which it is from the first understood that nothing is to happen, contrasted with a Continental love-affair in which both partners must constantly bear in mind the serious consequences. Our ties of affection, the unbearable intensity of our grief, make us disinclined to court danger for ourselves and for those who belong to us. We dare not contemplate a great many undertakings which are dangerous but quite indispensable, such as attempts at mechanical flight, expeditions to far countries, experiments with explosive substances. We are paralysed by the thought of who is to replace the son with his mother, the husband with his wife, the father with his children, if there should come disaster. The tendency to exclude death from our calculations brings in its train a number of other renunciations and exclusions. And yet the motto of the Hanseatic League declared: "Navigare necesse est, vivere non necesse!" (It is necessary to sail the seas, it is not necessary to live.)

It is an inevitable result of all this that we should seek in the world of fiction, of general literature and of the theatre compensation for the impoverishment of life. There we still find people who know how to die, indeed, who are even capable of killing someone else. There alone too we can enjoy the

[2] [*Never speak ill of the dead.*]

condition which makes it possible for us to reconcile ourselves with death—namely, that behind all the vicissitudes of life we preserve our existence intact. For it is indeed too sad that in life it should be as it is in chess, when one false move may lose us the game, but with the difference that we can have no second game, no return-match. In the realm of fiction we discover that plurality of lives for which we crave. We die in the person of a given hero, yet we survive him, and are ready to die again with the next hero just as safely.

It is evident that the war is bound to sweep away this conventional treatment of death. Death will no longer be denied; we are forced to believe in him. People really are dying, and now not one by one, but many at a time, often ten thousand in a single day. Nor is it any longer an accident. To be sure, it still seems a matter of chance whether a particular bullet hits this man or that; but the survivor may easily be hit by another bullet; and the accumulation puts an end to the impression of accident. Life has, in truth, become interesting again; it has regained its full significance.

Here a distinction should be made between two groups—those who personally risk their lives in battle, and those who have remained at home and have only to wait for the loss of their dear ones by wounds, disease, or infection. It would indeed be very interesting to study the changes in the psychology of the combatants, but I know too little about it. We must stop short at the second group, to which we ourselves belong. I have said already that in my opinion the bewilderment and the paralysis of energies, now so generally felt by us, are essentially determined in part by the circumstance that we cannot maintain our former attitude towards death, and have not yet discovered a new one. Perhaps it will assist us to do this if we direct our psychological inquiry towards two other relations with death—the one which we may ascribe to primitive, pre-historic peoples, and that other which in every one of us still exists, but which conceals itself, invisible to consciousness, in the deepest-lying strata of our mental life.

The attitude of prehistoric man towards death is known to us, of course, only by inferences and reconstruction, but I believe that these processes have furnished us with tolerably trustworthy information.

Primitive man assumed a very remarkable attitude towards death. It was far from consistent, was indeed extremely contradictory. On the one hand, he took death seriously, recognized it as the termination of life and used it to that end; on the other hand, he also denied death, reduced it to nothingness. This contradiction arose from the circumstance that he took up radically different attitudes towards the death of another man, or a stranger, of an enemy, and towards his own. The death of the other man he had no objection to; it meant the annihilation of a creature hated, and primitive man had no scruples against bringing it about. He was, in truth, a very violent being, more cruel and more malign than other animals. He liked to kill, and killed as a matter of course. That instinct which is said to restrain the other animals from killing and devouring their own species we need not attribute to him.

Hence the primitive history of mankind is filled with murder. Even to-day, the history of the world which our children learn in school is essentially a series of race-murders. The obscure sense of guilt which has been common to man since prehistoric times, and which in many religions has been condensed into the doctrine of original sin, is probably the outcome of the blood-guiltiness incurred by primitive man. In my book *Totem und Tabu* (1913) I have, following clues given by W. Robertson Smith, Atkinson and Charles Darwin, attempted to surmise the nature of this primal guilt, and I think that even the contemporary Christian doctrine enables us to deduce it. If the Son of God was obliged to sacrifice his life to redeem mankind from original sin, then by the law of the talion, the requital of like for like, that sin must have been a killing, a murder. Nothing else could call for the sacrifice of a life in expiation. And if the original sin was an offence against God the Father, the primal crime of mankind must have been a parricide, the killing of the primal father of the primitive human horde, whose image in memory was later transfigured into a deity.

His own death was for primitive man certainly just as unimaginable and unreal as it is for any one of us to-day. But there was for him a case in which the two opposite attitudes towards death came into conflict and joined issue; and this case was momentous and productive of far-reaching results. It occurred when primitive man saw someone who belonged to him die—his wife, his child, his friend, whom assuredly he loved as we love ours, for love cannot be much younger than the lust to kill. Then, in his pain, he had to learn that one can indeed die oneself, an admission against which his whole being revolted; for each of these loved ones was, in very truth, a part of his own beloved ego. But even so, on the other hand, such deaths had a rightfulness for him, since in each of the loved persons something of the hostile stranger had resided. The law of ambivalence of feeling, which to this day governs our emotional relations with those whom we love most, had assuredly a very much wider validity in primitive periods. Thus these beloved dead had also been enemies and strangers who had aroused in him a measure of hostile feeling.

Philosophers have declared that the intellectual enigma presented to primitive man by the picture of death was what forced him to reflection, and thus that it became the starting-point of all speculation. I believe that here the philosophers think too philosophically, and give too little consideration to the primarily effective motives. I would therefore limit and correct this assertion: By the body of his slain enemy primitive man would have triumphed, without racking his brains about the enigma of life and death. Not the intellectual enigma, and not every death, but the conflict of feeling at the death of loved, yet withal alien and hated persons was what disengaged the spirit of inquiry in man. Of this conflict of feeling psychology was the direct offspring. Man could no longer keep death at a distance, for he had tasted of it in his grief for the dead; but still he did not consent entirely to acknowledge it, for he could not conceive of himself as dead. So he devised a compromise; he conceded the fact of death, even his own death, but denied it the significance of annihilation, which he had had no motive for contesting where the death of his enemy had been concerned. During his contemplation of his loved one's corpse he invented ghosts, and it was his sense of guilt at the satisfaction mingled with his sorrow that turned these new-born spirits into evil, dreaded demons. The changes wrought by death suggested to him the disjunction of the individuality into a body and a soul—first of all into several souls; in this way his train of thought ran parallel with the process of disintegration which sets in with death. The enduring remembrance of the dead became the basis for assuming other modes of existence, gave him the conception of life continued after apparent death.

These subsequent modes of existence were at first no more than appendages to that life which death had brought to a close—shadowy, empty of content, and until later times but slightly valued; they showed as yet a pathetic inadequacy. We may recall the answer made to Odysseus by the soul of Achilles:

> Erst in the life on the earth, no less than a god we revered thee,
> We the Achaeans; and now in the realm of the dead as a monarch
> Here dost thou rule; then why should death thus grieve thee, Achilles?
> Thus did I speak: forthwith then answering thus he addressed me,
> Speak not smoothly of death, I beseech, O famous Odysseus,
> Better by far to remain on the earth as the thrall of another;
> E'en of a portionless man that hath means right scanty of living,
> Rather than reign sole king in the realm of the bodiless phantoms.

Or in the powerful, bitterly burlesque rendering by Heine, where he makes Achilles say that the most insignificant little Philistine at Stuckert-on-the-Neckar, in being alive, is far happier than he, the son of Peleus, the dead hero, the prince of shadows in the nether world.

It was not until much later that the different religions devised the view of this after-life as the more desirable, the truly valid one, and degraded the life which is ended by death to a mere preparation. It was then but consistent to extend life backward into the past, to conceive of former existences, transmigrations of the soul and reincarnation, all with the purpose of depriving death of its meaning as the termination of life. So early did the denial of death, which above we designated a convention of civilization, actually originate.

Besides the corpse of the beloved were generated not only the idea of the soul, the belief in immortality, and a great part of man's deep-rooted sense of guilt, but also the earliest inkling of ethical law. The first and most portentous prohibition of the awakening conscience was: Thou shalt not kill. It was born of the reaction against that hate-gratification which lurked behind the grief for the loved dead, and was gradually extended to unloved strangers and finally even to enemies.

This final extension is no longer experienced by civilized man. When the frenzied conflict of this war shall have been decided, every one of the victorious warriors will joyfully return to his home, his wife and his children, undelayed and undisturbed by any thought of the enemy he has slain either at close quarters or by distant weapons of destruction. It is worthy of note that such primitive races as still inhabit the earth, who are undoubtedly closer than we to primitive man, act differently in this respect, or did so act until they came under the influence of our civilization. The savage—Australian, Bushman, Tierra del Fuegan—is by no means a remorseless murderer; when he returns victorious from the war-path he may not set foot in his village nor touch his wife until he has atoned for the murders committed in war by penances which are often prolonged and toilsome. This may be presumed, of course, to be the outcome of superstition; the savage still goes in fear of the avenging spirits of the slain. But the spirits of the fallen enemy are nothing but the expression of his own conscience, uneasy on account of his blood-guiltiness; behind this superstition lurks a vein of ethical sensitiveness which has been lost by us civilized men.

Pious souls, who cherish the thought of our remoteness from whatever is evil and base, will be quick to draw from the early appearance and the urgency of the prohibition of murder gratifying conclusions in regard to the force of these ethical stirrings, which must consequently have been implanted in us. Unfortunately this argument proves even more for the opposite contention. So powerful a prohibition can only be directed against an equally powerful impulse. What no human soul desires there is no need to prohibit; it is automatically excluded. The very emphasis of the commandment *Thou shalt not kill* makes it certain that we spring from an endless ancestry of murderers, with whom the lust for killing was in the blood, as possibly it is to this day with ourselves. The ethical strivings of mankind, of which we need not in the least depreciate the strength and the significance, are an acquisition accompanying evolution; they have then become the hereditary possession of those human beings alive to-day, though unfortunately only in a very variable measure.

Let us now leave primitive man, and turn to the unconscious in our own mental life. Here we depend entirely upon the psycho-analytic method of investigation, the only one which plumbs such depths. We ask what is the attitude of our unconscious towards the problem of death. The answer must be: Almost exactly the same as primitive man's. In this respect, as in many others, the man of prehistoric ages survives unchanged in our unconscious. Thus, our unconscious does not believe in its own death; it behaves as if immortal. What we call our "unconscious" (the deepest strata of our minds, made up of instinctual impulses) knows nothing whatever of negatives or of denials—contradictories coincide in it—and so it knows nothing whatever of our own death, for to that we can give only a negative purport. It follows that no instinct we possess is ready for a belief in death. This is even perhaps the secret of heroism. The rational explanation for heroism is that it consists in the decision that the personal life cannot be so precious as certain abstract general ideals. But more frequent, in my view, is that instinctive and impulsive heroism which knows no such motivation, and flouts danger in the spirit of Anzengruber's Hans the Road-Mender: "Nothing can happen to *me*." Or else that motivation serves but to clear away the hesitation which might delay an heroic reaction in accord with the unconscious. The dread of death, which dominates us oftener than we know, is on the other hand something secondary, being usually the outcome of the sense of guilt.

On the other hand, for strangers and for enemies, we do acknowledge death, and consign them to it quite as readily and unthinkingly as did primitive man. Here there does, indeed, appear a distinction which in practice shows for a decisive one. Our unconscious does not carry out the killing; it merely thinks it and wishes it. But it would be wrong entirely to depreciate this psychical reality as compared with actual reality. It is significant and pregnant enough. In our unconscious we daily and hourly deport all who stand in our way, all who have offended or injured us. The expression: "Devil take him!" which so frequently comes to our lips in joking anger, and which really means "Death take him!" is in our unconscious an earnest deliberate death-wish. Indeed, our unconscious will murder even for trifles; like the ancient Athenian law of Draco, it knows no other punishment for crime than death; and this has a certain consistency, for every injury to our almighty and autocratic ego is at bottom a crime of *lèse-majesté*.

And so, if we are to be judged by the wishes in our unconscious, we are, like primitive man, simply a gang of murderers. It is well that all these wishes do not possess the potency which was attributed to them by primitive man; in the cross-fire of mutual maledictions mankind would long since have perished, the best and wisest of men and the loveliest and fairest of women with the rest.

Psycho-analysis finds little credence among laymen for assertions such as these. They reject them as calumnies which are confuted by conscious experience, and adroitly overlook the faint indications through which the unconscious is apt to betray itself even to consciousness. It is therefore relevant to point out that many thinkers who could not have been influenced by psycho-analysis have quite definitely accused our unspoken thoughts of a readiness, heedless of the murder-prohibition, to get rid of anyone who stands in our way. From many examples of this I will choose one very famous one:

In *Le Père Goriot,* Balzac alludes to a passage in the works of J. J. Rousseau where that author asks the reader what he would do if—without leaving Paris and of course without being discovered—he could kill, with great profit to himself, an old Mandarin in Peking by a mere act of the will. Rousseau implies that he would not give much for the life of this dignitary. "*Tuer son mandarin*" has passed into a proverb for this secret readiness even on the part of ourselves to-day.

There is as well a whole array of cynical jests and anecdotes which testify in the same sense, such as, for instance, the remark attributed to a husband: "If one of us dies, I shall go and live in Paris." Such cynical jokes would not be possible unless they contained an unacknowledged verity which could not be countenanced if seriously and baldly expressed. In joke, as we know, even the truth may be told.

As for primitive man, so also for us in our unconscious, there arises a case in which the two contrasted attitudes towards death, that which acknowledges it as the annihilation of life and the other which denies it as ineffectual to that end, conflict and join issue—and this case is the same as in primitive ages—the death, or the endangered life, of one whom we love, a parent or partner in marriage, a brother or sister, a child or dear friend. These loved ones are on the one hand an inner possession, an ingredient of our personal ego, but on the other hand are partly strangers, even enemies. With the exception of only a very few situations, there adheres to the tenderest and closest of our affections a vestige of hostility which can excite an unconscious death-wish. But this conflict of ambivalence does not now, as it did then, find issue in theories of the soul and of ethics, but in neuroses, which afford us deep insight into normal mental life as well. How often have those physicians who practise psycho-analysis had to deal with the symptom of an exaggeratedly tender care for the well-being of relatives, or with entirely unfounded self-reproaches after the death of a loved person. The study of these cases has left them in no doubt about the extent and the significance of unconscious death-wishes.

The layman feels an extraordinary horror at the possibility of such feelings, and takes this repulsion as a legitimate ground for disbelief in the assertions of psycho-analysis. I think, mistakenly. No depreciation of our love is intended, and none is actually contained in it. It is indeed foreign to our intelligence as also to our feelings thus to couple love and hate, but Nature, by making use of these twin opposites, contrives to keep love ever vigilant and fresh, so as to guard it against the hate which lurks behind it. It might be said that we owe the fairest flowers of our love-life to the reaction against the hostile impulse which we divine in our breasts.

To sum up: Our unconscious is just as inaccessible to the idea of our own death, as murderously minded towards the stranger, as divided or ambivalent towards the loved, as was man in earliest antiquity. But how far we have moved from this primitive state in our conventionally civilized attitude towards death!

It is easy to see the effect of the impact of war on this duality. It strips us of the later accretions of civilization, and lays bare the primal man in each of us. It constrains us once more to be heroes who cannot believe in their own death; it stamps the alien as the enemy, whose death is to be brought about or desired; it counsels us to rise above the death of those we love. But war is not to be abolished; so long as the conditions of existence among the nations are so varied, and the repulsions between peoples so intense, there will be, must be, wars. The question then arises: Is it not we who must give in, who must adapt ourselves to them? Is it not for us to confess that in our civilized attitude towards death we are once more living psychologically beyond our means, and must reform and give truth its due? Would it not be better to give death the place in actuality and in our thoughts which properly belongs to it, and to yield a little more prominence to that unconscious attitude towards death which we have hitherto so carefully suppressed? This hardly seems indeed a greater achievement, but rather a backward step in more than one direction, a regression; but it has the merit of taking somewhat more into account the true state of affairs, and of making life again more endurable for us. To endure life remains, when all is said, the first duty of all living beings. Illusion can have no value if it makes this more difficult for us.

We remember the old saying: *Si vis pacem, para bellum.* If you desire peace, prepare for war.

It would be timely thus to paraphrase it: *Si vis vitam, para mortem.* If you would endure life, be prepared for death.

CONTEMPORARY CIVILIZATION: ITS MORAL COMMITMENT

2. POSSIBILITIES OF MORAL GROWTH

R. G. COLLINGWOOD

HISTORIAN, archaeologist, and philosopher, and Waynflete Professor of Metaphysical Philosophy at Oxford University (1935–1941), Robin George Collingwood (1889–1943) was a prolific author and one of Oxford's most notable teachers. Collingwood's passion for history dominated much of his intellectual career. He contributed a number of important historical and archaeological studies on the Roman period of Britain (*Roman Britain,* 1921; *Archaeology of Roman Britain,* 1930; *Roman Britain and the English Settlements,* 1936). And his interest in the historical orientation of the Italian philosopher Benedetto Croce (1866–1952) led him to translate the latter's *Autobiography* (1927) and his study on *Vico* (1913). In fact, Collingwood's enthusiasm for history established itself firmly in his philosophy (*Essay on Philosophical Method,* 1933; *Essay on Metaphysics,* 1940). For Collingwood the context of philosophic study must be circumscribed by historical considerations, and the basic assumptions shaping any philosophic outlook are, in the last analysis, historically conditioned. Collingwood regarded this approach to the analysis of philosophical ideas as a necessary and salutary answer to the skepticism and "irrationalism" which he felt grew out of the newer "analytical" and positivist philosophies beginning to gain an audience in England and, in particular, in Oxford, during his lifetime.

Though he wrote extensively on a great variety of philosophic issues, Collingwood produced no over-all, formal philosophical "system." However, a number of fresh and illuminating investigations into such diverse areas as art (*The Principles of Art,* 1938), politics (*The New Leviathan,* 1942), and history (*The Idea of History,* 1946) emerges from his published work to establish him as one of England's more prominent philosophers in the twentieth century.

The following selection is from his *The Idea of History,* which was published posthumously in 1946.

THE IDEA OF HISTORY

Part V: Epilegomena

6. HISTORY AND FREEDOM

We study history, I . . . [maintain], in order to attain self-knowledge. By way of illustrating this thesis, I shall try to show how our knowledge that

---

This selection has been reprinted from *The Idea of History* by R. G. Collingwood (pp. 315–334, Copyright 1946 by Oxford University Press), by permission of the publisher.

human activity is free has been attained only through our discovery of history.

. . . History has at last escaped from a state of pupilage to natural science. The disappearance of historical naturalism, however, entails the further conclusion that the activity by which man builds his own constantly changing historical world is a free activity. There are no forces other than this activity which control it or modify it or compel it to behave in this way or in that, to build one kind of world rather than another.

This does not mean that a man is always free to do what he pleases. All men, at some moments in their lives, are free to do what they want: to eat, being hungry, for example, or to sleep, being tired. But this has nothing to do with the problem to which I have referred. Eating and sleeping are animal activities, pursued under the compulsion of animal appetite. With animal appetites and their gratification or frustration history is not concerned. It makes no difference to the historian, as an historian, that there should be no food in a poor man's house; though it may and must make a difference to him as a man with feelings for his fellow creatures; and though as an historian he may be intensively concerned with the shifts by which other men have contrived to bring about this state of things in order that they should be rich and the men who take wages from them poor; and equally concerned with the action to which the poor man may be led not by the fact of his children's unsatisfied hunger, the fact, the physiological fact, of empty bellies and wizened limbs, but by his thought of that fact.

Nor does it mean that a man is free to do what he chooses; that in the realm of history proper, as distinct from that of animal appetite, people are free to plan their own actions as they think fit and execute their plans, each doing what he set out to do and each assuming full responsibility for the consequences, captain of his soul and all that. Nothing could be more false. Henley's rhyme does no more than utter the fantasy of a sick child who has discovered that he can stop himself crying for the moon by making believe that he has got it. A healthy man knows that the empty space in front of him, which he proposes to fill up with activities for which he accordingly now begins making plans, will be very far from empty by the time he steps into it. It will be crowded with other people all pursuing activities of their own. Even now it is not as empty as it looks. It is filled with a saturate solution of activity, on the point of beginning to crystallize out. There will be no room left for his own activity, unless we can so design this that it will fit into the interstices of the rest.

The rational activity which historians have to study is never free from compulsion: the compulsion to face the facts of its own situation. The more rational it is, the more completely it undergoes this compulsion. To be rational is to think; and for a man who proposes to act, the thing it is important to think about is the situation in which he stands. With regard to this situation, he is not free at all. It is what it is, and neither he nor anyone else can ever change that. For though the situation consists altogether of thought, his own and other people's, it cannot be changed by a change of mind on the part of himself or anyone else. If minds change, as they do, this merely means that with the lapse of time a new situation has arisen. For a man about to act, the situation is his master, his oracle, his god. Whether his action is to prove successful or not depends on whether he grasps the situation rightly or not. If he is a wise man, it is not until he has consulted his oracle, done everything in his power to find out what the situation is, that he will make even the most trivial plan. And if he neglects the situation, the situation will not neglect him. It is not one of those gods that leave an insult unpunished.

The freedom that there is in history consists in the fact that this compulsion is imposed upon the activity of human reason not by anything else, but by itself. The situation, its master, oracle, and god, is a situation it has itself created. And when I say this I do not mean that the situation in which one man finds himself exists only because other men have created it by a rational activity not different in kind from that by which their successor finds himself to be in it and acts according to his lights; and that, because human reason is always human reason, whatever may be the name of the human being in whom it works, the historian can ignore these personal distinctions and say that human reason has created the situation in which it finds itself. I mean something rather different from that. All history is the history of thought; and when an historian says that a man is in a certain situation this is the same as saying that he thinks he is in this situation. The hard facts of the situation, which it is so important for him to face, are the hard facts of the way in which he conceives the situation.

If the reason why it is hard for a man to cross the mountains is because he is frightened of the devils in them, it is folly for this historian, preaching at him across a gulf of centuries, to say "This is sheer superstition. There are no devils at all. Face facts, and realize that there are no dangers in the mountains except rocks and water and snow, wolves perhaps, and bad men perhaps, but no devils." The historian says that these are the facts because that is the way in which he has been taught to think. But the devil-fearer says that the presence of devils is a fact, because that is the way he has been taught to think. The historian thinks it a wrong way; but wrong ways of thinking are just as much historical facts as right ones, and, no less than they, determine the situation (always a thought-situation) in which the man who shares them is placed.

The hardness of the fact consists in the man's inability to think of his situation otherwise. The compulsion which the devil-haunted mountains exercise on the man who would cross them consists in the fact that he cannot help believing in devils. Sheer superstition, no doubt: but this superstition is a fact, and the crucial fact in the situation we are considering. The man who suffers from it when he tries to cross the mountains is not suffering merely for the sins of his fathers who taught him to believe in devils, if that is a sin; he is suffering because he has accepted the belief, because he has shared the sin. If the modern historian believes that there are no devils in the mountains, that too is only a belief he has accepted in precisely the same way.

The discovery that the men whose actions he studies are in this sense free is a discovery which every historian makes as soon as he arrives at a scientific mastery of his own subject. When that happens, the historian discovers his own freedom: that is, he discovers the autonomous character of historical thought, its power to solve its own problems for itself by its own methods. He discovers how unnecessary it is, and how impossible it is, for him, as a historian, to hand these problems over for solution to natural science; he discovers that in his capacity as historian he both can and must solve them for himself. It is simultaneously with this discovery of his own freedom as historian that he discovers the freedom of man as an historical agent. Historical thought, thought about rational activity, is free from the domination of natural science, and rational activity is free from the domination of nature.

The intimacy of the connexion between these two discoveries might be expressed by saying that they are the same thing in different words. It might be said that to describe the rational activity of an historical agent as free is only a roundabout and disguised way of saying that history is an autonomous science. Or it might be said that to describe history as an autonomous science is only a disguised way of saying that it is the science which studies free activity. For myself, I should welcome either of these two statements, as providing evidence that the person who made it had seen far enough into the nature of history to have discovered (a) that historical thought is free from the domination of natural science, and is an autonomous science, (b) that rational action is free from the domination of nature and builds its own world of human affairs, *Res Gestae,* at its own bidding and in its own way, (c) that there is an intimate connexion between these two propositions.

But at the same time I should find in either statement evidence that the person who made it was unable (or for some ulterior purpose had decided to profess himself unable) to distinguish between what a person says and what is implied in what he says: unable, that is, to distinguish the theory of language, or aesthetics, from the theory of thought, or logic; and was therefore committed, for the time being at least, to a verbalistic logic, in which the logical connexion between two thoughts which imply each other is confused with the linguistic connexion between two sets of words which "stand for the same thing."

I should see, too, that his attempt to burke the problems of logic by substituting for them problems in linguistics was not based on any very just appreciation of the nature of language, because I should see that, of two synonymous verbal expressions, he was assuming that one really and properly means the thing "for which it stands," while the other means this only for the insufficient reason that the person who uses it means that by it. All of which is very disputable. Rather than approve such errors, I should prefer to leave the matter where I have left it; to say that these two statements (the statement that history is an autonomous science and the statement that rational activity is free in the sense described) are not synonymous forms of words, but express discoveries neither of which can be made without making the other. And arising out of this, I will observe that the "free-will controversy" which was so prominent in the seventeenth century had a close connexion with the fact that the seventeenth century was the time when scissors-and-paste history in its simpler forms was beginning to dissatisfy people, and when historians were beginning to see that their own house needed setting in order or that historical studies ought to take example from the study of nature, and raise themselves to the level of a science. The desire to envisage human action as free was bound up with a desire to achieve autonomy for history as the study of human action.

But I do not leave the matter there; because I wish to point out that of the two statements I am considering, one is necessarily prior to the other. It is only by using historical methods that we can find out anything about the objects of historical study. No one will assert that he knows more than historians do about certain actions done in the past concerning which historians claim to have knowledge, and that he knows this in such a way that he can satisfy both himself and other people that that claim is groundless. It follows that we must first achieve a genuinely scientific and therefore autonomous method in historical study before we can grasp the fact that human activity is free.

This may seem contrary to facts; for surely, it will be said, many people were already aware that human activity is free, long before that revolution took place by which history raised itself to the level of a science. To this objection I will offer two answers, not mutually exclusive, but the one relatively superficial, the other, I hope, a little more profound.

(i) They were aware, perhaps, of human freedom; but did they grasp it?

Was their awareness a knowledge that deserved the name of scientific? Surely not; for in that case they would not only have been convinced of it, they would have known it in a systematic way, and there would have been no room for controversy about it, because those who were convinced of it would have understood the grounds of their conviction and been able to state them convincingly.

(ii) Even if the revolution by which history has become a science is only about a half-century old, we must not be deceived by the word "revolution." Long before Bacon and Descartes revolutionized natural science by expounding publicly the principles on which its method was based, people here and there had been using these same methods, some more often, some more rarely. As Bacon and Descartes so justly pointed out, the effect of their own work was to put these same methods within the grasp of quite ordinary intellects. When it is said that the methods of history have been revolutionized in the last half-century, this is what is meant. It is not meant that examples of scientific history will be sought in vain before that date. It is meant that whereas, earlier, scientific history was a thing of rare occurrence, hardly to be found except in the work of outstanding men, and even in them marking moments of inspiration rather than the even tenor of study, it is now a thing within the compass of everyone; a thing which we demand of everybody who writes history at all, and which is widely enough understood, even among the unlearned, to procure a livelihood for writers of detective stories whose lot is based upon its methods. The sporadic and intermittent way in which the truth of human freedom was grasped in the seventeenth century might, to say the least of it, have been a consequence of this sporadic and intermittent grasp on the method of scientific history.

7. PROGRESS AS CREATED BY HISTORICAL THINKING

The term "progress," as used in the nineteenth century when the word was much in people's mouths, covers two things which it is well to distinguish: progress in history, and progress in nature. For progress in nature the word "evolution" has been so widely used that this may be accepted as its established sense; and in order not to confuse the two things I shall restrict my use of the word "evolution" to that meaning, and distinguish the other by the name "historical progress."

"Evolution" is a term applied to natural processes in so far as these are conceived as bringing into existence new specific forms in nature. This conception of nature as evolution must not be confused with the conception of nature as process. Granted the latter conception, two views of natural process are still possible: that events in nature repeat one another specifically, the specific forms remaining constant through the diversity of their individual instances, so that "the course of nature is uniform" and "the future will resemble the past," or that the specific forms themselves undergo change, new forms coming into existence by modification of the old. The second conception is what is meant by evolution.

In one sense, to call a natural process evolutionary is the same thing as calling it progressive. For if any given specific form can come into existence only as a modification of one already established, the establishment of any given form presupposes that of which it is a modification, and so on. If a form b is a modification of a, and c of b, and d of c, the forms a, b, c, d, can only come to exist in that order. The order is progressive in the sense that it is a series of terms which can come into existence only in that order. To say this, of course, implies nothing as to why the modifications arise, or whether they are large or small. In this sense of the word "progress," progressive only means orderly, that is, exhibiting order.

But progress in nature, or evolution, has often been taken to mean more than this: namely the doctrine that each new form is not only a modification of the last but an improvement on it. To speak of improvement is to imply a standard of valuation. This, in the case of breeding new forms of domestic animals or plants, is intelligible enough: the value implied is the new form's utility for human purposes. But no one supposes that natural evolution is designed to produce such utilities; the standard implied, therefore, cannot be that. What is it?

Kant held that there was one form of value, and only one, that was independent of human purposes, namely the moral value of the good will. All other kinds of goodness, he argued, are merely goodness for some postulated purpose, but the goodness of morality does not depend on any postulated purpose, and thus moral goodness, as he put it, is an end in itself. On this view the evolutionary process has been truly progressive, because it has led through a determinate series of forms to the existence of man, a creature capable of moral goodness.

If this view is rejected, it is very doubtful whether any other standard of valuation can be found which would entitle us to call evolution progressive except merely in the sense of being orderly. Not because the idea of value finds no place in our view of nature, for it is difficult to think of any organism except as striving to maintain its own existence, and such effort implies that, at least for itself, its existence is not a mere matter of fact but something of value; but because all values seem merely relative. The archaeopteryx may in fact have been an ancestor of the bird, but what entitles us to call the bird an improvement on the archaeopteryx? A bird is not a better archaeopteryx, but something different that has grown out of it. Each is trying to be itself.

But the view of human nature as the noblest outcome of the evolutionary process did undoubtedly underlie the nineteenth-century conception of historical progress as guaranteed by a law of nature. That conception, in fact, depended on two assumptions or groups of assumptions. First, that man is or contains in himself something of absolute value, so that the process of nature in its evolution has been a progress in so far as it has been an orderly process leading to the existence of man. From this it followed that, since man obviously did not control the process leading to his own existence, there was in nature as such an inherent tendency towards the realization of this absolute value: in other words, "progress is a law of nature." Secondly, the assumption that man, as a child of nature, is subject to natural law, and that the laws of historical process are identical with the laws of evolution: that historical process is of the same kind as natural process. It followed that human history was subject to a necessary law of progress, in other words that of the new specific forms of social organization, art and science, and so forth, which it brings into existence each is necessarily an improvement on the last.

The idea of a "law of progress" may be attacked by denying either of these two assumptions. It may be denied that man has in him anything of absolute value. His rationality, it may be said, only serves to make him the most maleficent and destructive of the animals, and is rather a blunder or a cruel joke of nature than her noblest work; his morality is only (as the modern jargon goes) a rationalization or ideology which he has devised to conceal from himself the crude fact of his bestiality. From this point of view, the natural process that has led to his existence can no longer be regarded as a progress. But further: if the conception of historical process as a mere extension of natural process is denied, as it must be by any sound theory of history, it follows that there is no natural and in that sense necessary law of progress in history. The question whether any particular historical change has been an improvement must consequently be a question to be answered on its merits in each particular case.

The conception of a "law of progress," by which the course of history is so governed that successive forms of human activity exhibit each an improvement on the last, is thus a mere confusion of thought, bred of an unnatural union between man's belief in his own superiority to nature and his belief that he is nothing more than a part of nature. If either belief is true, the other is false: they cannot be combined to produce logical offspring.

Nor can the question, whether in a given case an historical change has or has not been progressive, be answered until we are sure that such questions have a meaning. Before they are raised, we must ask what is meant by historical progress, now that it has been distinguished from natural progress; and, if anything is meant, whether the meaning is one applicable to the given case we are considering. For it would be hasty to assume that, because the conception of historical progress as dictated by a law of nature is nonsensical, the conception of historical progress itself is therefore nonsensical.

Assuming, then, that the phrase "historical progress" may still have a meaning, we must ask what it means. The fact that it has suffered confusion through contamination with the idea of evolution does not prove it meaningless; on the contrary, it suggests that it has a certain basis in historical experience.

As a first attempt to define its meaning, we might suggest that historical progress is only another name for human activity itself, as a succession of acts each of which arises out of the last. Every act whose history we may study, of whatever kind it is, has its place in a series of acts where one has created a situation with which the next has to deal. The accomplished act gives rise to a new problem; it is always this new problem, not the old problem over again, which the new act is obliged to solve. If a man has discovered how to get a meal, next time he is hungry he must find out how to get another, and the getting of this other is a new act arising out of the old. His situation is always changing, and the act of thought by which he solves the problems it presents is always changing too.

This is no doubt true, but it is not to our purpose. It is just as true of a dog as of a man, that every meal must be a different meal: just as true, that every time a bee gathering honey visits a flower, it must be a different flower; just as true, that every time a body moving in a straight line or an open curve comes to a part of space, it must be a different part. But these processes are not historical processes, and to quote them as throwing light on the historical process would betray the old fallacy of naturalism. Moreover the novelty of the new situation and the new act is not a specific novelty, for the new act may be a new act of exactly the same kind (for example, setting the same snare again in the same place); so that we are not even discussing the evolutionary aspect of natural process, which is the point at which that process seems most akin to the historical. The search for a fresh meal takes place even in the most completely static or non-progressive society.

The idea of historical progress, then, if it refers to anything, refers to the coming into existence not merely of new actions or thoughts or situations belonging to the same specific type, but of new specific types. It therefore presupposes such specific novelties, and consists in the conception of these as improvements. Suppose, for example, a man or a community had lived on fish and, the fish-supply failing, had sought food in a new way, by digging for roots: this would be a change in the specific type of situation and activity, but it would not be regarded as a progress, because the change does not imply that the new type is an improvement on the old. But if a community of fish-eaters had changed their method of catching fish from a less to a more efficient one, by which an average fisherman could catch ten fish on an average day instead of five, this would be called an example of progress.

But from whose point of view is it an improvement? The question must be asked, because what is an improvement from one point of view may be the reverse from another; and if there is a third from which an impartial judgement can be passed on this conflict, the qualifications of this impartial judge must be determined.

Let us first consider the change from the point of view of the persons concerned in it: the older generation still practicing the old method while the younger has adopted the new. In such a case the older generation will see no need for the change, knowing as it does that life can be lived on the old method. And it will also think that the old method is better than the new; not out of irrational prejudice, but because the way of life which it knows and values is built round the old method, which is therefore certain to have social and religious associations that express the intimacy of its connexion with this way of life as a whole. A man of the older generation only wants his five fish a day, and he does not want half a day's leisure; what he wants is to live as he has lived. To him, therefore, the change is no progress, but a decadence.

It might seem obvious that by the opposite party, the younger generation, the change is conceived as a progress. It has given up the life of its fathers and chosen a new one for itself: it would not do this (one might suppose) without comparing the two and deciding that the new is better. But this is not necessarily the case. There is no choice except for a person who knows what both the things are between which he is choosing. To choose between two ways of life is impossible unless one knows what they are; and this means not merely looking on one as a spectacle, and practicing the other, or practicing one and conceiving the other as an unrealized possibility, but knowing both in the only way in which ways of life can be known: by actual experience, or by the sympathetic insight which may take its place for such a purpose. But experience shows that nothing is harder than for a given generation in a changing society, which is living in a new way of its own, to enter sympathetically into the life of the last. It sees that life as a mere incomprehensible spectacle, and seems driven to escape from sympathy with it by a kind of instinctive effort to free itself from parental influences and bring about the change on which it is blindly resolved. There is here no genuine comparison between the two ways of life, and therefore no judgement that one is better than the other, and therefore no conception of the change as a progress.

For this reason, the historical changes in a society's way of life are very rarely conceived as progressive even by the generation that makes them. It makes them in obedience to a blind impulse to destroy what it does not comprehend, as bad, and substitute something else as good. But progress is not the replacement of the bad by the good, but of the good by the better. In order to conceive a change as a progress, then, the person who has made it must think of what he has abolished as good, and good in certain definite ways. This he can only do on condition of his knowing what the old way of life was like, that is, having historical knowledge of his society's past while he is actually living in the present he is creating: for historical knowledge is simply the re-enactment of past experiences in the mind of the present thinker. Only thus can the two ways of life be held together in the same mind for a comparison of their merits, so that a person choosing one and rejecting the other can know what he has gained and what he has lost, and decide that he has chosen the better. In short: the revolutionary can only regard his revolution as a progress in so far as he is also an historian, genuinely re-enacting in his own historical thought the life he nevertheless rejects.

Let us now consider the change in question, no longer from the standpoint of those concerned in it, but from that of an historian placed outside it. We might hope that, from his detached and impartial point of view, he would be able to judge with some chance of fairness whether it was a progress or not. But this is a difficult matter. He is only deceived if he fastens on the fact that ten fish are caught where five were caught before, and uses this as a criterion of progress. He must take into account the conditions and consequences of that change. He must ask what was done with the additional fish or the additional leisure. He must ask what value attached to the social and religious institutions that were sacrificed for them. In short, he must judge the relative value of two different ways of life, taken as two wholes. Now, in order to do this, he must be able to enter with equal sympathy into the essential features and values of each way of life: he must re-experience them both in his own mind, as objects of historical knowledge. What makes him a qualified judge, therefore, is just the fact that he does not look at his object from a detached point of view, but re-lives it in himself.

We shall see, later, that the task of judging the value of a certain way of life taken in its entirety is an impossible task, because no such thing in its entirety is ever a possible object of historical knowledge. The attempt to know what we have no means of knowing is an infallible way to generate illusions; and this attempt to judge whether one period of history or phase of human life, taken as a whole, shows progress as compared with its predecessor, generates illusions of an easily recognizable type. Their characteristic feature is the labelling of certain historical periods as good periods, or ages of historical greatness, and of others as bad periods, ages of historical failure or poverty. The so-called good periods are the ones into whose spirit the historian has penetrated, owing either to the existence of abundant evidence or to his own capacity for reliving the experience they enjoyed; the so-called bad periods are either those for which evidence is relatively scanty, or those whose life he cannot, for reasons arising out of his own experience and that of his age, reconstruct within himself.

At the present day we are constantly presented with a view of history as consisting in this way of good and bad periods, the bad periods being divided into the primitive and the decadent, according as they come before or after the good ones. This distinction between periods of primitiveness, periods of greatness, and periods of decadence, is not and never can be historically true. It tells us much about the historians who study the facts, but nothing about the facts they study. It is characteristic of an age like our own, where history is studied widely and successfully, but eclectically. Every period of which we have competent knowledge (and by competent knowledge I mean insight into its thought, not mere acquaintance with its remains) appears in the perspective of time as an age of brilliance: the brilliance being the light of our own historical insight. The intervening periods are seen by contrast as, relatively speaking and in different degrees, "dark ages": ages which we know to have existed, because there is a gap of time for them in our chronology, and we have possibly numerous relics of their work and thought, but in which we can find no real life because we cannot re-enact that thought in our own minds. That this pattern of light and darkness is an optical illusion proceeding from the distribution of the historian's knowledge and ignorance is obvious from the different ways in which it is drawn by different historians and by the historical thought of different generations.

The same optical illusion in a simpler form affected the historical thought of the eighteenth century, and laid the foundations for the dogma of progress, as that was accepted in the nineteenth. When Voltaire laid it down that "all history is modern history," and that nothing could be genuinely known before about the end of the fifteenth century, he was saying two things at once: that nothing earlier than the modern period could be known, and that nothing earlier deserved to be known. These two things came to the same thing. His inability to reconstruct genuine history from the documents of the ancient world and the Middle Ages was the source of his belief that those ages were dark and barbarous. The idea of history as a progress from primitive times to the present day was, to those who believed in it, a simple consequence of the fact that their historical outlook was limited to the recent past.

The old dogma of a single historical progress leading to the present, and the modern dogma of historical cycles, that is, of a multiple progress leading to "great ages" and then to decadence, are thus mere projections of the historian's ignorance upon the screen of the past. But, setting dogmas aside, has the idea of progress no other basis than this? We have already seen that there is one condition on which that idea can represent a genuine thought, and not either a blind feeling or a mere state of ignorance. The condition is that the person who uses the word should use it in comparing two historical periods or ways of life, both of which he can understand historically, that is, with enough sympathy and insight to reconstruct their experience for himself. He must satisfy himself and his readers that no blind spot in his own mind, and no defect in his equipment of learning, prevents him from entering into the experience of either less fully than into the other's. Then, having fulfilled that condition, he is entitled to ask whether the change from the first to the second was a progress.

But when he asks this, what exactly is he asking? Obviously, he is not asking whether the second comes nearer to the way of life which he accepts as his own. By re-enacting the experience of either in his own mind he has already accepted it as a thing to be judged by its own standards: a form of life having its own problems, to be judged by its success in solving those problems and no others. Nor is he assuming that the two different ways of life were attempts to do one and the same thing, and asking whether the second did it better than the first. Bach was not trying to write like Beethoven and failing; Athens was not a relatively unsuccessful attempt to produce Rome; Plato was himself, not a half-developed Aristotle.

There is only one genuine meaning for this question. If thought in its first phase, after solving the initial problems of that phase, is then, through solving these, brought up against others which defeat it; and if the second solves these further problems without losing its hold on the solution of the first, so that there is gain without any corresponding loss, then there is progress. And there can be progress on no other terms. If there is any loss, the problem of setting loss against gain is insoluble.

According to this definition, it would be idle to ask whether any one period of history taken as a whole showed a progress over its successor. For the historian can never take any period as a whole. There must be large tracts of its life for which he has either no data, or no data that he is in a position to interpret. We cannot, for example, know what the Greeks enjoyed in the way of musical experience, though we know that they greatly valued it; we have not enough material; and on the other hand, though we have no lack of data about Roman religion, our own religious experience is not of such a kind as to qualify us for reconstructing in our own minds what it meant to them. We must select certain aspects of experience and confine our search for progress to these.

Can we speak of progress in happiness or comfort or satisfaction? Obviously not. Different ways of life are differentiated by nothing more clearly than by differences, between the things that people habitually enjoy, the conditions which they find comfortable, and the achievements they regard as satisfactory. The problem of being comfortable in a medieval cottage is so different from the problem of being comfortable in a modern slum that there is no comparing them; the happiness of a peasant is not contained in the happiness of a millionaire.

Nor does it mean anything to ask whether there is progress in art. The artist's problem, so far as he is an artist, is not the problem of doing what his predecessor has done and going on to do something further which his predecessor failed to do. There is development in art, but no progress: for though in the technical processes of art one man learns from another, Titian from Bellini, Beethoven from Mozart, and so on, the problem of art itself consists not in mastering these technical processes but in using them to express the artist's experience and give it reflective form, and consequently every fresh work of art is the solution of a fresh problem which arises not out of a previous work of art but out of the artist's unreflective experience. Artists do better or worse work in so far as they solve these problems well or ill; but the relation between good and bad art is not an historical relation, because the problems arise out of the flow of unreflective experience, and that flow is not an historical process.

In one sense, there is no progress in morality. The life of morality consists not in the development of moral codes, but in their application to individual problems of conduct, and to a great extent these problems, like those of art, arise out of unreflective experience. The course of our moral life is conditioned by the succession of our desires; and, though our desires change, they do not change historically. They arise out of our animal nature, and though this may change from youth to old age, or vary in different peoples and climates, its differences are part of the process of nature, not of history.

In another sense, however, there is or may be moral progress. Part of our moral life consists of coping with problems arising not out of our animal nature but out of our social institutions, and these are historical things, which create moral problems only in so far as they are already the expression of moral ideals. A man who asks himself whether he ought to take voluntary part in his country's war is not struggling with personal fear; he is involved in a conflict between the moral forces embodied in the institution of the State, and those embodied not merely in the ideal, but in the equally actual reality, of international peace and intercourse. Similarly the problem of divorce arises not out of the whims of sexual desire, but out of an unresolved conflict between the moral idea of monogamy and the moral evils which that ideal, rigidly applied, brings in its train. To solve the problem of war or of divorce is only possible by devising new institutions which shall recognize in full the moral claims recognized by the State or by monogamy, and shall satisfy those claims without leaving unsatisfied the further claims to which, in historical fact, the old institutions have given rise.

The same double aspect appears in the economic life. So far as that consists in finding from moment to moment the means of satisfying demands which spring not from our historical environment but from our nature as animals with certain desires, there can be no progress in it; that would be a progress in happiness or comfort or satisfaction, which we have seen to be impossible. But not all our demands are for the satisfaction of animal desires. The demand for investments in which I can put my savings to support me in old age is not an animal desire; it arises out of an individualistic economic system in which the old are supported neither statutorily by the State nor customarily by their families, but by the fruits of their own labour, and in which capital commands a certain rate of interest. That system has solved a good many problems, and therein lies its economic value; but it gives rise to a good many others which as yet it has failed to solve. A better economic system, one whose substitution for this would be a progress, would continue to solve the same problems which are solved by individualist capitalism, and solve these others as well.

The same considerations apply to politics and law, and I need not work out the application in detail. In science, philosophy, and religion the conditions are rather different. Here, unless I am mistaken, the question of coping with our animal nature and satisfying its needs does not arise. The problem is a single one instead of a double.

Progress in science would consist in the supersession of one theory by another which served both to explain all that the first theory explained, and also to explain types or classes of events or "phenomena" which the first ought to have explained but could not. I suppose that Darwin's theory of the origin of species was an example. The theory of fixed species explained the relative permanence of natural kinds within the recorded memory of man: but it ought to have held good for the longer stretch of geological time, and it broke down, too, for the case of selectively-bred animals and plants under domestication. Darwin propounded a theory whose claim to merit rested on its bringing these three classes under one conception. I need hardly quote the now more familiar relation between Newton's law of gravitation and that of Einstein, or that between the special and general theories of relativity. The interest of science, in relation to the conception of progress, seems to be that this is the simplest and most obvious case in which progress exists and is verifiable. For this reason, those who have believed most strongly in progress have been much in the habit of appealing to the progress of science as the plainest proof that there is such a thing, and often, too, have based their hope of progress in other fields on the hope of making science the absolute mistress of human life. But science is and can be mistress only in her own house, and forms of activity which cannot progress (such as art) cannot be made to do so by subjecting them, if that phrase meant anything, to the rule of science; whereas those which can must progress by finding out for themselves how to improve in doing their own work.

Philosophy progresses in so far as one stage of its development solves the problems which defeated it in the last, without losing its hold on the solutions already achieved. This, of course, is independent of whether the two are stages in the life of a single philosopher, or are represented by different men. Thus, suppose it true that Plato grasped the necessity for an eternal object, the world of Ideas or Idea of the God, and also for an eternal subject, the soul in its double function of knower and mover, as solutions for the problems with which his predecessors' work had left him confronted: but was baffled to say how these two were related; and suppose Aristotle saw that the problem of the relation between them, as Plato had stated it, or rather as he himself saw it in his long apprenticeship to Plato's teaching, could be solved by thinking of them as one and the same, pure intellectual being identical with its own object, and its knowledge of that object being its knowledge of itself; then, so far (though conceivably not in other respects) Aristotle's philosophy would mark a progress on Plato's, granted that by that new step Aristotle sacrificed nothing that Plato had achieved by his theory of Ideas and his theory of soul.

In religion, progress is possible on the same terms. If Christianity, bating no jot or title of what Judaism had won by its conception of God as one God, just and terrible, infinitely great over against man's infinite littleness and infinitely exacting in his demands on man, could bridge the gulf between God and man by the conception that God became a man in order that we might become God, that was a progress, and a momentous one, in the history of the religious consciousness.

In such senses and in such cases as these, progress is possible. Whether it has actually occurred, and where and when and in what ways, are questions for historical thought to answer. But there is one other thing for historical thought to do: namely to create this progress itself. For progress is not a mere fact to be discovered by historical thinking: it is only through historical thinking that it comes about at all.

The reason for this is that progress, in those cases (common or rare) when it happens, happens only in one way: by the retention in the mind, at one phase, of what was achieved in the preceding phase. The two phases are related not merely by way of succession, but by way of continuity, and continuity of a peculiar kind. If Einstein makes an advance on Newton, he does it by knowing Newton's thought and retaining it within his own, in the sense that he knows what Newton's problems were, and how he solved them, and, disentangling the truth in those solutions from whatever errors prevented Newton from going further, embodying these solutions as thus disentangled in his own theory. He might have done this, no doubt, without having read Newton in the original for himself; but not without having received Newton's doctrine from someone. Thus Newton stands, in such a context, not for a man but for a theory, reigning during a certain period of scientific thought. It is only in so far as Einstein knows that theory, as a fact in the history of science, that he can make an advance upon it. Newton thus lives in Einstein in the way in which any past experience lives in the mind of the historian, as a past experience known as past—as the point from which the development with which he is concerned started—but re-enacted here and now together with a development of itself that is partly constructive or positive and partly critical or negative.

Similarly with any other progress. If we want to abolish capitalism or war, and in doing so not only to destroy them but to bring into existence something better, we must begin by understanding them: seeing what the problems are which our economic or international system succeeds in solving, and how the solution of these is related to the other problems which it fails to solve. This understanding of the system we set out to supersede is a thing which we must retain throughout the work of superseding it, as a knowledge of the past conditioning our creation of the future. It may be impossible to do this; our hatred of the thing we are destroying may prevent us from understanding it, and we may love it so much that we cannot destroy it unless we are blinded by such hatred. But if that is so, there will once more, as so often in the past, be change but no progress; we shall have lost our hold on one group of problems in our anxiety to solve the next. And we ought by now to realize that no kindly law of nature will save us from the fruits of our ignorance.

HERBERT J. MULLER

HERBERT JOSEPH MULLER, from whose book *The Uses of the Past* (1952) the following selection has been taken, was born in Mamaroneck, New York, in 1905. He was educated at Cornell University where he obtained his Ph.D. in 1932. After teaching at Cornell from 1926 to 1935, he went to Purdue University where he became a professor of English in 1945. Although trained in literature and literary criticism, Muller has always been concerned to use a humane knowledge of history to counteract those who see in Western civilization a culture doomed and to assess that civilization's own achievements and chances of survival. Among Muller's works have been *Modern Fiction* (1937), *Science and Criticism* (1943), and *Thomas Wolfe* (1947).

THE USES OF THE PAST

III. THE ADVENTURE OF CIVILIZATION

1. The Costs of Civilization. . . . We cannot absolutely prove that it is better to be a civilized man than a caveman, or even that it is worth being a human being. We can say that if conscious life has no value, nothing has value and all thought is meaningless. No man in his senses really wishes to change places with a contented imbecile or a pig in his sty. But then we have to pay for our knowledge of good and evil. The price of conscious life is discontent, fear, and pain unknown to other animals. The conditions of civilized life are richer values and higher costs. By its more elaborate, complex organization of life a civilization provides more goods, both material and spiritual, than a primitive society can; and it thereby creates more tension, friction, instability, insecurity.

Adventure, as Whitehead maintained, is quite literally the key to civilization. This highest achievement of man is a "program for discontent." Likewise Toynbee suggests that the terms of the adventure may be summed up in Faust's wager with the Devil:

If ever time should flow so calmly on
Soothing my spirits in such oblivion
That in the pleasant trance I would arrest
And hail the happy moment in its course,
Bidding it linger with me . . .
Then willingly do I consent to perish.

By the grace of Goethe, Faust was saved, as civilizations have not been; but unlike them he stuck to the terms of the bargain. They have typically succumbed to complacency or conservatism, losing their creative energy or readiness for adventure; and only in stagnation and death can they approach the stable equilibrium they seek. The stablest element in human history is precisely the most primitive and formless—the peasant masses that have no real history. The great creative ages, on the other hand, have been conspicuously unstable. When bookmen celebrate the golden ages, now changeless, composed, and serene in splendor, they are apt to falsify the spirit of these ages; for no man who craves security and peace of mind would have been happy in Periclean Athens, Renaissance Italy, or Elizabethan England. . . .

Today, at any rate, there is no mistaking the necessity of adventure. The pace of revolution is strictly unprecedented; centuries in Egypt, China, and India, or even in Greece and Rome, brought less radical change than a lifetime today. We are all too aware of the risks, the costs we pay for the goods of our kind of civilization. For this reason, however, we are apt to magnify the costs, or to regard any costs as unprecedented. We forget that men have always had to live dangerously, above all when they were living near the height of their powers. So we might do well to review the distinctive means and ends of civilization, the main articles of its program for discontent. . . .

2. *The Material Basis of Civilization*. . . . To judge by all the available evidence, the rise of civilization was not a gift of the gods or a tribute to them. It was a technological affair, an economic enterprise inspired by practical motives. Through inventions and discoveries, men were able to take care of their physical wants more efficiently; in the leisure, comfort, and relative security thus achieved, they were able to develop social graces, fine arts, literate learning, and higher religions. In all civilizations before our own, agriculture remained the chief source of wealth; because most aristocracies were landed aristocracies, agriculture had more prestige than commerce—as it still does among literary devotees of the ancient cultural tradition. Nevertheless civilization flourished with the growth of industry and trade, which were far more extensive in antiquity than is commonly realized. The great adventure of Greek civilization in particular began as an adventure in trade, or specifically with the

Assumes leisure → good use of

exploitation of the humble grape and olive; the production of wine and olive oil enabled the enterprising Greeks to enter the world market and compete with the Phoenicians (one of the few known peoples whose brilliant culture was frankly identified with commerce, and organized to promote commerce). The first notable achievements in Greek poetry, philosophy, and science were contributed by Ionia, the colonial cities in Asia Minor that were the first to develop a thriving commerce. The glory of Greece reached its zenith in Athens, at the zenith of the Athenian adventure in economic imperialism. . . .

Commerce in turn is but one example of the division and diversification of labor resulting from the advance of technology and the accumulation of an economic surplus. Men are apt to underrate the very great gains this has made possible. Resenting their confinement to a particular task or regretting their dependence, they are fond of cultivating the illusion of being as self-sufficient as their pioneering ancestors by hunting their own game, building their own shacks. Yet specialization—by the individual and by the community—is the clearest index of human development. The self-sufficient man has little to contribute to the community, the self-sufficient community as little to contribute to other communities. Both may still be found—in the most primitive parts of the world. (One may even find "natural" economies so close to a bare subsistence that they cannot afford such specialists as the priest or witch-doctor.) Specialization alone has enabled the extraordinary man to discover and develop his genius, and the ordinary man to discover and develop his individuality.

As plainly, however, it may narrow, warp, and impoverish individuality. In our own world specialization has produced the machine-tender and the bookkeeper, the technician and the academician—the hordes of cultural illiterates and expert ignoramuses. It denies millions the opportunity of really creative work, the elemental satisfaction of saying, "I made this." . . . In short, division of labor naturally leads to excessive division, or sharp separation; and it brings us back to the familiar complex of good-and-evil. So too with commerce. All the energy, initiative, and daring that go into it help to promote the indolence and conservatism of privileged classes. Still plainer, commerce breeds fraud, greed, strife, war.

And so with the major problem, the everlasting problem, raised by the surplus wealth that made civilization possible. It posed the question who was to own the surplus, and for what purposes was it to be used. The historic answer has invariably been the creation of a hierarchy of classes, more or less rigid. In every civilization the wealth and the power that goes with it have been concentrated in the hands of a few. Among the early specialists were experts in consumption—a class whose chief functions included what Veblen called conspicuous consumption, or vicarious consumption for the edification of the producing classes. We may assume that the rise of privileged classes was largely unconscious, not a deliberate plot by greedy men. We may also assume that the problem of sharing the wealth, or approaching equity, will plague even the "classless society," since power has to be exercised by a few and is always liable to abuse. But the basic paradox remains that for great masses of men civilization has always meant less material well-being than primitive men usually enjoy. It has meant a man-made misery, which was aggravated by increasing inequality as in time the privileged came to exploit the masses more deliberately and systematically. And with the Industrial Revolution came still more glaring contradictions, of more wretched poverty and impotence amidst vastly increased wealth and power. An astounding triumph of technological efficiency created unemployment and want, bringing on periodic depressions and panics by producing more goods than could be sold, while millions needed those goods. For the first time in history, society has been plagued by abundance rather than scarcity.

. . . We may note another fundamental difference between modern civilization and its predecessors. The historic result of the material surplus has not been the constant class struggle pictured by Marxists, between the few who have and the many who have not. Although such class wars have broken out occasionally, as in ancient Greece and Rome, the significant struggles have usually been within the upper classes, involving kings, priests, warrior nobles, and in time wealthy merchants. Throughout most of history the peasant masses accepted their lowly status. Their infrequent rebellions, in times of extreme want or oppression, were blind uprisings, not planned revolutions in the name of democratic rights, and had no profound, lasting results. With the rise of democracy, however, the masses have become a real factor in the problem of sharing the wealth. Despite the marked inequalities, the advanced democracies have unquestionably raised the standard of living of the great majority of their citizens. The ordinary man now has opportunities for a richer life than he dreamed of in the past. What he does with these opportunities, how he conceives the rich life, is another problem. . . . But it would seem dishonest as well as futile for well-fed, well-clothed, well-housed intellectuals merely to deplore the common desire for material well-being.

3. *The City as Center and Symbol.* Among the literary tendencies of recent years has been the revolt against the City. . . . Always we read the same complaints, of the vulgarity, the artificiality, the immorality and irreligion, the

physical and spiritual squalor, the soullessness—the age-old follies and vices of Babylon, which in every age seem new. So the story is true, as far as it goes. The city is always vain and wicked enough to provoke the prophet of doom. "Wail, O inhabitants of the Mortar!"

Yet the old story is also superficial and vain—if we value civilization itself. *Civilization* means literally the making of cities and city life, and it is literally impossible without them. The village world has been relatively stable (at least until the Industrial Revolution) because of its inertia; what energy was left over from the labor of supporting life was spent in maintaining the ancient rites and customs, or resisting the new-fangled ones coming from without. The rise of the city has been the historic sign of a society on the march; it stimulated further adventure by bringing people together, pooling their efforts, promoting change by exchange, enlarging the world through contact with other peoples and cities. The great city became the center of unrest and disorder because it remained the center of creative activity. In time the poet or the philosopher might flee to the village (or more often the villa), but his very understanding and appreciation of nature were a product of the city; his work was inspired by it, addressed to it, circulated and preserved by it. Without London and Boston Thoreau could have had no Walden, or no spiritual interests to take there. Although civilization has always rested on the labor of the village world, its history is the history of Babylon, Jerusalem, Athens, Rome, Constantinople, Paris, London.

Even religion owes its highest achievements to the city. Simply because the village is conservative, orthodox, and pious, while the city is given to heresy and unrest, the higher religions have grown up in cities. Thus Jesus, the Galilean, went to Jerusalem to enact the climactic scenes of his failure and his triumph. His Apostles spread the gospel in the cities of the Roman Empire. The first great churches were established in the great cities of Ephesus, Antioch, Alexandria, and Rome, which among other things were famous for their mobs, their luxury, and their vice. The bulk of the early converts to Christianity came from the despised city rabble. The last to be converted were the peasants or "pagani"—who in the backward sections of Christendom still worship pagan deities, under the guise of patron saints. The village remains the stronghold of the old-time religion, which may not be good enough for the future.

Hence we might discount somewhat the notorious evils of city life—the life that has always attracted the more ardent, enterprising spirits from the countryside. Its popularity is not due simply to the inducements of the big money. It is doubtful whether the ordinary city-dweller is more grasping than the French peasant, say, or even the sturdy New Englander. Nor are his morals necessarily lower than the countryman's (apart from the latter's rude mode of education in the facts of life). As Morris Cohen observed, the stabler *mores* of the village do not permit the freedom that may be abused in the city; yet stability is not the *summum bonum,* and freedom is essential if morality is to be rational and responsible. Traditionalists are like to deplore city life because they have something of the attitude of the small-town moralist.

The basic truth, however, is that the city is a symbol of both the best and the worst in civilization, and all the risks of its bold presumptions. It is open to a much wider world than the village, and walled off from the natural world; by its variety, bustle, and commotion it stirs new interests and aspirations, and weakens old faiths and natural pieties. As the political capital, the seat of rule and misrule, it launches the national adventures in statesmanship and conquest, and loses the victories or squanders the spoils. As the social capital, it is the school of grace, urbanity, intrigue, and frivolity, the arts of living and of living on others. As the cultural capital, the marketplace of ideas, it is the birthplace of new movements in art and thought, which may mean regeneration or degeneration. . . .

4. *The Ambiguities of the Spiritual Achievement.* . . . We should do well to . . . [take] an ironic view of the spiritual achievements of man. For . . . [faith in them] is always vulnerable to the taunts of practical men, who may seem to get along well enough with their material wealth and coarse pleasures, and as vulnerable to the analysis of skeptics and cynics, who may ask what good has come of all this spiritual achievement, and how we know that it is good. The faith is always threatened as well by the falsities and absurdities of its disciples: the pursuit of virtue, truth, and beauty has inspired egregious evil, error, and ugliness. We should not be surprised to find that the highest manifestations of civilization have involved the deepest contradictions.

The historic source of these contradictions, Ralph Turner points out, was the invention of writing. Literate learning, the major means to intellectual growth and creative achievement, has also been a major aid to the conservative forces that resist growth and adventure. From the outset it encouraged a purely verbal kind of learning that was confused with natural knowledge, and a liturgical kind that discouraged free inquiry. It helped to standardize and sanctify the codes, classics, and scriptures that embalmed the ignorance and prejudice as well as the wisdom of the ancestors. As the possession of a privileged few—especially the priestly class—it consolidated the power of the upper classes, raising them still higher above the illiterate masses, who were condemned to blind obedience and blind worship.

One result of this aristocratic monopoly on learning has been an inevitable distortion of history. The records of the past, which reflect chiefly the interests of the upper classes, give only an incidental or indirect view of the life of the masses, the everyday business of hewing and hauling. Thus Gibbon wrote his celebrated description of the Roman Empire under Trajan, Hadrian, and the Antonines, as the period in the history of the world during which "the condition of the human race was most happy and prosperous"; but he was not actually talking about the "human race." He was describing the condition of the prosperous upper classes. There is some evidence that the great majority of the population—the peasants, the city proletarians, and the slaves—were not especially happy or prosperous at this time. The main point, however, is simply that we do not know and cannot know much about their lot. And so with all the other great empires. When the anonymous masses enter history it is chiefly to be slaughtered in battle, to die of famine or privation—to illustrate the failures of their betters; apart from these calamities we can only conjecture how contented they were under their priests and kings, and whether they enjoyed the golden ages. We have the mighty pyramids, but no first-hand account of the feelings of the wretches who built them. . . .

A related effect of the aristocratic monopoly was the cultivation of knowledge for decorative, honorific, esoteric, or sacred purposes, rather than practical or productive ones. Invented to facilitate business transactions, writing soon became the medium for transactions with the gods or the god-kings, and those who carried on this elevated business naturally looked down on the lowly business of the world, the vulgar doing and making of artisans, merchants, and slaves. Applied knowledge was not merely degraded but divorced from the higher learning; the "useful" was opposed to the philosophical and the spiritual. Hence the advance of science in the Western world was not a clear gain but a constant "problem": it jeopardized traditional beliefs that had been cut off from natural knowledge. Since the last century, to be sure, the tables have been turned. Now useful knowledge has become almost sacred, as the means to our wealth and power; our "institutions of higher learning" have been specializing in a practical training that is neither high nor learned. But the ancient aristocratic bias still persists. The immense visions of modern physics and astronomy are considered less imaginative than the most tortured imaginings of modern poets, less spiritual than the mildewed metaphors of conventional churchmen. In general, the limitations of modern culture are due not only to the narrowness of scientists and technicians, and the grossness of businessmen, but to the fastidious exclusiveness of literary and learned men, jealous of their traditional prerogatives as custodians of a higher or holier kind of truth.

Apart from the classiness of the classical, however, the glorious accomplishments of the mind and spirit have always had inglorious consequences. Today the conspicuous example is science. Its enormous extension of knowledge has meant not only a narrowing of consciousness for many specialists but an impoverishment of consciousness for the many others who have regarded its severely limited descriptions as complete explanations, the whole truth about the world. Its triumphant advance in the understanding and control of nature has weakened man's belief in his own importance in the cosmic scheme, or even in the reality of his spiritual values; many thinkers concluded that man is a mere mechanism whose behavior is blindly determined. More recently, the triumphs have culminated in discoveries about the subatomic world that appear to undermine the basic assumptions of uniformity and causality on which science has rested, and that give man a power which conceivably may destroy science and all its work. Altogether, the most successful instrument of human reason has shaken the faith in reason that has been the mainspring of Western civilization.

But the humanities have also been inhuman, or all too human, in their conceit. Religion everywhere has exhibited . . . paradoxes. . . . The higher religions have commonly grown out of the failures of civilization, bringing promises of eternal life to dying societies. Although they survive these societies they bear the marks of their defeatist origins; the most characteristic sign of their loftiness is the abasement of man and this earth, an other-worldly or life-denying spirit. They are therefore always liable to conflict with the creative forces of a flourishing society, and thence to profound inconsistencies or ignoble concessions. Above all, they are invariably corrupted by their worldly success. As they become popular their revolutionary spiritual ideals are translated into popular hopes, fears, and desires; the loftier they are, the wider is the gap between the idealism of their founders and the practice and belief of most of their followers. As they become institutionalized they suffer the fate of all other worldly institutions. A priesthood ceases to propagate new values and devotes itself primarily to conserving the old ones, piously reducing them to routine rituals and dead dogmas. An established church also tends to ally itself with other vested interests, and thus to become infected with the worldly pride it was born to combat. And the periodic reactions that follow—the efforts to reinterpret the original revelation or recapture the original purity—revitalize the faith at the cost of splintering it into more sects and further confusing the nature of the original revelation.

All such perversions of high tradition are intensified by traditionalism, the occupational disease of guardians of culture. The guardians tend to forget that tradition has always been the great enemy of the founders of great traditions: that Socrates was a radical who did corrupt the youth of Athens by impiously urging them to question the time-honored ways; or that the teachings of Christ were an outrage to precisely the most cultivated, respectable, God-fearing people of his time; or that the American Revolution was strictly a revolution, illegal, violent, and bloody. In particular, the traditionalists abuse our Western heritage by singling out some one school of thought as the "essential" or "true" tradition; whereas diversity and non-conformity are the very soul of this heritage. It is the richest tradition that man has ever known simply because it includes so many disparate elements from diverse sources, and has never been at rest.

Yet the last word must be spoken in piety. We have said enough about the abuses of the higher values to enable us, in realism and in honor, to declare their supreme value. While man is immensely indebted to the past for practical knowledge and skills, he cherishes the past for its contributions to the life of the mind or spirit. Ultimately he has never really honored the material wealth and power he has always sought. Reverently he recalls the great failures, ironically the mere conquests or triumphs of power. Assyria was a mighty empire, Sparta succeeded in dominating all Greece, the Mongols under the extraordinary Jenghiz Khan swept out of nowhere to conquer most of the known world. But who mourns the fall of Nineveh and Sparta, or the disappearance of the Mongols into the obscurity whence they came? Athens, Jerusalem, and Rome exemplified the limitations and excesses of great cultural achievement, all the paradoxes of glory and grandeur. But who rejoices at their fall? . . .

5. *The Conscious Individual*. . . . The emergence of the individual with a mind of his own may be considered . . . the chief justification of civilization. He also sums up its paradoxes. The individual has always been a threat to the social order that produced him. Now an inspired prophet introduces new ideas that disrupt settled ways of thinking and feeling; now an ambitious leader leads his society to conquest of other societies, or to disaster; now an impassioned rebel starts a revolution. The self-conscious individual is always prone, moreover, to be conscious chiefly of his selfish interests, and to exploit others for his own good. Hence many other individuals have suffered in civilization as prehistoric men did not. They have been conscious chiefly of injustice, oppression, tyranny, cruelty—of outrages on their new sense of rights.

Civilization has accordingly created the problem of adjusting rights and duties, harmonizing the interests of the individual and of the group. The most conspicuous and most difficult aspect of this problem is the political. Here we encounter the ancient, universal story of privilege and oppression, the long struggle for social justice and personal liberty, and the new complications introduced by the ideal of individualism. But the problem affects all spheres of culture. Religion usually demands conformity to a uniform faith, which may produce a serene piety, or may violate individual conscience and kill the religious spirit; the prophet crying in the wilderness may then unsettle the ancient faith, perhaps preparing the way for a nobler ideal, perhaps stirring up hysteria or fanaticism. Poetry and art usually impose conventional forms or modes, which may facilitate the expression of talent or may cramp the original genius; the individualist who rebels may be a great innovator or a mere eccentric. Even science now faces this problem. It has represented the closest approach to the presumable ideal in these matters: an international co-operative enterprise based on complete freedom of thought, in which the individual scientist freely subjects himself to a rigorous discipline that is never arbitrary or despotic; and makes his findings freely available to society. Hence scientists could zealously pursue the truth, innocently unconcerned about the consequences of their discoveries, almost unaware that they were shattering the traditional foundations of thought and revolutionizing their society. With their unlocking of atomic power, however, they have suddenly awakened to an urgent sense of social responsibility; while at the same time the state has limited their freedom of inquiry, and in Russia has prescribed the truths they must find.

At any given moment, this whole problem is a matter of stress. In a democratic society with a tradition of rugged individualism, and a perhaps excessive fear of all forms and constraints, one might stress that there is no such thing as an absolute individual with absolute rights. The individual is inseparable from his society, which has created his rights, furnished the materials for his prized individuality, furnished even the principles for his rebellion against it. Similarly one might remark that most of the great poets and artists of the past did not make a cult of self-expression, strain for originality, or proclaim the sovereign rights of genius; they managed to express themselves freely and fully enough while accepting conventional forms and modes, subordinating their art to the interests of religion or the state, or even remaining anonymous. Usually, however, this is not what most needs to be said. There has seldom been too much freedom for too many individuals, nor is such freedom the great menace today. Given the long historic record of oppression, the painfully slow, erratic growth of the ideal of personal liberty, the natural conservatism or inertia of mankind, the immense force of custom and convention, the vast reserves of ignorance and prejudice—given all the political and cultural pressures for conformity even in the advanced democracies, the final stress should be on the claims of the individual, the ideal freedom to think and act for oneself.

6. *The Meaning of History.* Time will tell, we say; but we may not be aware of the difference that is made by our very conception of time. To the Greeks and Romans time was characteristically a slow but inexorable enemy of man, telling the destruction of all his works. To the Hindu sage it was static or illusory, resembling a deep pool rather than a flow or a river; so the splash of history made ripples that vanished as they spread, distracting only the foolish. To the modern Westerner, on the contrary, time is all-important. He tells it, keeps it, lives by it punctually. In America he has a passion for making it and saving it (though what he saves it for may not be clear). It has been his great hope, in its promise of ever bigger and better things to come. And if he is now much less hopeful he has a more vivid sense of the horrors that time may bring. For him, in any event, things always keep moving. Time Marches On!

In short, our feeling about time—however vague or unconscious—ultimately involves a philosophy of history. It leads to a momentous question. Given all the drama of human history, what is the plot, the grand design, the final meaning of the whole show? Positivists will tell us that this is a meaningless question. Manifestly we cannot give it a precise, positive answer: we cannot state it in terms that permit either empirical verification or rigorous logical analysis. But neither can we escape it. Although we naturally come to it as we hope to make sense of history, we are forced to consider it if only because men persist in answering it. Thus Westerners have declared that history is progress, and in this faith have made extraordinary history. Today Communists are still so positive the drama will have a happy ending, in a classless society, that they threaten to precipitate a war which might make any society impossible, put a literal end to history. Others have . . . been led to reject the whole faith in progress—and their negations may also have positive consequences. Time will tell in any case; but what it will tell depends on what men say and do right now. . . .

. . . The theory of decline is the hoariest theory of history. Men used to locate Utopia in the remote past instead of the future—as in the Garden of Eden of Babylonian-Hebrew mythology, or the Golden Age of Hesiod. Even the sophisticated literature of the Greco-Roman world is shot through with the notion that civilization is a disease or degeneration. . . .

. . . [But these] theories of decline cannot be taken seriously as literal outlines of history. There is no evidence whatever of the historical existence of a Garden of Eden or Golden Age, or of an ideal primitive stage in evolution. Such fictions may be useful as metaphors, symbolizing the actual corruptions of civilization and the natural corruptibility of man, but it is essential to remember that they are fictions, pure and rather too simple. Usually they reflect a shallow view of history, or a sheer ignorance of it.

Hence the deepest thought of antiquity led rather to the conclusion that history is an endless cycle. Aristotle saw a continuous "coming to be and falling away"; he speculated that there had already been countless civilizations, which had passed through a uniform destiny. Stoics and Epicureans alike dwelt on the inevitable recurrences. The rational soul, wrote Marcus Aurelius, "considers the periodic destructions and rebirths of the universe, and reflects that our posterity will see nothing new, and that our ancestors saw nothing greater than we have seen." Or in the words of Ecclesiastes, "The thing that hath been, it is that which shall be; and that which is done is that which shall be done; and there is no new thing under the sun." This theory of cycles has been maintained by such Western thinkers as Bodin, Vico, and Nietzsche, and in our time has been given its most systematic, comprehensive formulation in Spengler's *Decline of the West*. Spengler argued that all civilizations necessarily pass through parallel stages and necessarily die a natural death—unless (like the Aztec) they are prematurely destroyed by accident.

Whether one is comforted or depressed by this fatalistic view of history is presumably a matter of temperament. Most thinkers have chosen to dwell on its pessimistic implications. . . . Men are disposed to take such a view of history, moreover, when they believe that their society is on the downswing, headed for catastrophe. Like the primitivists, the "cyclists" usually believed that the best days were behind them, and they had even less hope of the future. So we have the curious spectacle of civilized man forever marching with his face turned backward—as no doubt the cave-man looked back to the good old days when men were free to roam instead of being stuck in a damn hole in the ground. And so the theory of cycles has again become seductive, as men again fear the worst. Spengler, Sorokin, and Toynbee have presented different versions of it, but all agree that the West is on the decline.

The most obvious argument for this theory is its correspondence with the processes of birth, growth, decay, and death in the natural world. Given the fate of all other higher organisms, it seems reasonable to assume that a civilization cannot maintain itself indefinitely, but in time must age and die. Offhand, the theory also corresponds with the actual history of civilizations to date: all but our own have died, or have been dying. . . . Everywhere we find a momentous recurrence of the basic themes of selfishness and greed, fear and hate. But most pertinent is the evidence of cyclical movements within civilizations, the familiar patterns of rise and fall. In *Configurations of Cultural*

Growth, A. L. Kroeber surveys the major cultural achievements of all the great societies; and the most striking fact that emerges from his anthropological study is the fact of configuration and cycle.

About 1400, for example, the notable Dutch-Flemish school of painters arose suddenly, out of nowhere, with the Van Eycks; about 1700 the whole movement ended as suddenly, for Rembrandt, Hals, Teniers, Ruysdael, and the rest had died within a few years of one another; and ever since there has been practically no Dutch-Flemish painting of consequence. So it has been with all the major growths in art, literature, philosophy, and science. This phenomenon of the golden age is so familiar that we may forget how strange it is. All our knowledge of genetics indicates that the appearance of genius in any given society should be more or less constant—yet it never has been. Except for a very few isolated great men, such as John Scotus Erigena, genius has appeared only when there was a movement afoot; most potential greatness evidently goes to waste. And the movements appear to have specific limits as well as potentialities: they move to fulfilment, and then to exhaustion. All this implies a kind of predestination that Kroeber regrets. Nevertheless "the empirical data, over and over again, and with really remarkably few exceptions, compel the conclusion that there are whole arrays of events in the history of culture which are objectively describable only in terms of the metaphors of 'growth,' 'realization,' 'exhaustion,' and 'death,' as our vocabulary stands today."

This much seems clear. The picture as a whole, however, is not at all clear. Although we can make out configurations everywhere, they are irregular in their growth, diverse in their content, and inconstant in their associations. After medieval philosophy reached the end of its development, about 1350, there was no important philosophy in all Europe until the rise of the moderns with Descartes, after 1600: yet this long slump coincided with the Renaissance, a period of abounding intellectual activity. Kroeber's survey indicates that such apparent anomalies are the rule. Ancient Greece has fixed the common notion of a golden age as a rich growth in all fields of art and thought, a whole culture on the surge: but this glory has so profoundly impressed men because it was indeed unique. Thus the splendid Elizabethan Age produced no painting or sculpture to speak of, whereas the splendor of the Italian Renaissance was largely confined to the representative arts. Similarly there are conspicuous gaps in great civilizations. Egypt, Mesopotamia, and Japan produced no significant philosophy, Rome no science, Islam no painting, sculpture, or drama. Furthermore, the golden ages of culture appear to have no necessary connection with national expansion. Greek culture flowered before and after the little city-states had their brief hour of military glory; the Italians made their greatest contributions when their cities were torn by civil war and largely dominated by other countries; the Germans led all Europe under Beethoven, Goethe, and Kant while they were being overrun by Napoleon's armies, and their great creative period was over by 1870, when their great national expansion began.

Altogether, Kroeber can make out no "true law" in cultural history: "nothing cyclical, regularly repetitive, or necessary." And in the history of whole civilizations, regular cycles are still harder to find. Civilizations are much less discrete and homogeneous than the cyclical theory presupposes, and their geographical, political, and cultural components do not have a uniform destiny. . . . Historians cannot even agree on their location in time and space—Toynbee makes out at least twice as many civilizations as Spengler did. Neither can they agree on criteria for marking the peak of a society, or on the symptoms of growth and decay. And most dubious are the neat parallels, the efforts to make all societies swing through exactly the same cycle. On the face of it, civilizations start at different points, building on different pasts in different environments, exploiting different possibilities. Spengler, the most systematic exponent of this theory, kept his cycles orderly only by a Teutonic forcing and drilling of the facts, with a ruthless suppression of all unruly facts.

Above all, the *necessity* of the cycles is unproved, and unprovable on the basis of present knowledge. The only cause suggested by Spengler is a biological analogy that cannot bear scientific analysis. "The Biology of the future," he declared, "will undoubtedly find the point of departure for an entirely new formulation of its problems in the concept of the preordained life-span of the genus and species"—a span, he added, which is "a numerical value of almost mystical significance." Mystical is strictly the word for it. Biology gives no signs of accommodating him; and even if it attempted this new departure . . . it would not prove his point, since a society is neither a genus nor a species.

What biology still does teach is the theory of evolution; and this brings us back to the modern theory of progress. Although past societies were often complacent enough about their superiority over barbarians, there are only a few scattered hints of any hope for a continuous advance. The nearest thing to it was the Hebrew vision of the Messiah, which bred the Christian visions of the Millennium and the Second Coming, but these all depended upon a direct intervention by God; they stirred no hope that man, by his own efforts, could achieve a steady improvement of his earthly condition. Only with the rise of science did men begin to entertain seriously the possibility of progress. At length the possibility was transformed into a gospel, a certainty. History became a success story of a race that was bound to make good. "Progress is not an accident but a necessity," proclaimed Herbert Spencer. "What we call evil and immorality must disappear. It is certain that man must become perfect. . . . Always toward perfection is the mighty movement."

Now in the long evolutionary view, reaching back to the cave-man and ape-man, there unquestionably has been progress—always granted the assumption that it is worth being a human being. Man has achieved greater mastery of his natural environment, greater freedom of action, and thereupon has discovered the finer possibilities of life implicit in his distinctive power of consciousness. In historic times there have been clear gains in intellectual and spiritual as well as material wealth and power. Christian thinkers who now ridicule the faith in progress forget the assumption of progress in their own concept of "higher" religions, and of the progressive revelations of God through Abraham, Moses, and Christ; and hardly any thinker will deny that the religion of Jesus is loftier than that of Moloch. If all specific gains are disputable, there remains the general advance that man has made, from blind obedience to the totems and taboos of the tribe to conscious, reasoned loyalty to ideals of humanity. All the savagery that persists seems more frightful because it no longer seems inevitable or proper. In general, the tragic failures of civilization have left substantial residues of knowledge, skills, arts, ideas, ideals—of enduring goods that men do not willingly give up, once they are known, but that we are apt to forget because we take them for granted. . . .

7. *The Open Society.* What, then, is the meaning of history? . . . My answer . . . amounts to a basic assumption, a premise that should be laid face up on the table. Briefly, my answer is at once a negation and an affirmation. History has no meaning, in the sense of a clear pattern or determinate plot; but it is not simply meaningless or pointless. It has no certain meaning because man is free to give it various possible meanings.

His freedom is sharply limited, of course. Man has to choose within the conditions imposed by his biological structure, his natural environment, and his cultural heritage. He cannot do whatever he has a mind to, and at that his mind has been largely made up by his ancestors. For such reasons he is always prone to believe that history somehow makes itself, in spite of his efforts, by the automatic operation of natural laws or God's will. Still, at any moment he has a wide range of choices and is willy-nilly making more history, discovering the meanings of his past and determining the meanings of his future. The most significant "facts" he has to face are of man's own making. Marxism, for all its theoretical determinism, is the clearest illustration of how history is made by men's beliefs about what has happened, what is happening, and what should happen.

This insistence on human freedom is not simply cheering. It means that we have to keep making history, instead of leaning on it, and that we can never count on a final solution. It means the constant possibility of foolish or even fatal choices. Yet the dignity of man lies precisely in this power to choose his destiny. We may therefore welcome the conclusion that we cannot foretell the future, even apart from the possibility that it may not bear knowing. Uncertainty is not only the plainest condition of human life but the necessary condition of freedom, of aspiration, of conscience—of all human idealism.

It is the business of the future to be dangerous, Whitehead remarked; and we can always trust it to keep on the job. I again stress the uncertainties, however, because the dangers are always intensified by the pretensions to absolute certainty or finality. These are the ultimate source of corruption, the reason why the best becomes the worst and crusaders for heaven make a hell on earth. And none is more insidious than the principle of historical predestination. Knowing in advance how history is going to turn out, men climb on the bandwagon, ride the wave of the future. They can then indulge any policy, from supine resignation to ruthless violence. So the Communists can justify the most barbarous behavior: like hangmen, they are merely executing "the verdict of history." They corrupt morality at its very base by implying that it is man's duty to fight for the inevitable, or that historic might makes right. Even in self-sacrifice they are profoundly irresponsible. Our business as rational beings is not to argue for what is going to be but to strive for what ought to be, in the consciousness that it will never be all that we would like it to be.

Among the possible "meanings" of history . . . the most significant is the growth of this power of self-determination, or freedom to make history. I assume that for interpreting the past and choosing a future we must begin with a full acknowledgment of the claims of reason: a humble reason that makes no claim to finality or metaphysical certitude, because such claims cannot be rationally substantiated, and that recognizes its finiteness and fallibility; a proud reason that nevertheless maintains its authority as the final judge of all claims to truth, insisting that its tested knowledge is no less real and reliable because it is not a knowledge of ultimate reality, and that only by a further exercise of reason can its limitations and its fallacies be clearly discerned. We are not forced to choose between reason and faith in the conventional sense—we may choose between more or less reasonable faiths. The ideal of rationality in turn requires the ideal of freedom, the right to be an individual. A rational person is not merely one who has good habits or right principles, but one who knows what he believes and assumes the intellectual and moral responsibilities of his beliefs; and first he must be free to think for himself, make up his own mind. Although non-rational behavior may exhibit admirable qualities, such as the loyalty, fortitude, and daring found in barbarians, or even in the animal world, these qualities are not wholly admirable, or trustworthy, unless they are conscious, responsible choices. The only possible virtue in being a civilized man instead of a barbarian, an ignoramus, or a moron is in being a free, responsible individual with a mind of one's own.

The best society, accordingly, is that which is most conducive to the growth of such persons. It is what Karl Popper has called the "open society." It is an adventurous society that has broken with the universal, prehistoric custom of regarding ancient customs as magical or sacred, that views its institutions as man-made for human purposes and examines their suitability for these purposes, that welcomes variety and change instead of enforcing rigid conformity, and that accordingly provides its members with personal opportunities and responsibilities beyond mere obedience. It is Athens as opposed to Sparta. . . .

XI. CONCLUSION: THE USES OF THE FUTURE

2. *A Credo*. . . . And so with Western civilization as a whole. The familiar refrains about its "breakdown" may obscure the extraordinary unflagging creativeness that has made it the richest, most dramatic spectacle in history. It has maintained a high level of creative activity over a longer period of time than have previous societies, which rested on their oars after bursts of great achievement. In particular, as Whitehead observed, thought has been more creative. Whereas in other societies thought served chiefly to explain and conserve, Western man embarked on an endless "adventure of ideas" and put the ideas to work. He has thrived on the continuous disagreement and disharmony from which he has suffered; his life has always been charged with high tension. Since the dawn of the Middle Ages Europe has known the sense of crisis—the symptoms diagnosed by the specialists in "breakdowns." During its most complacent periods, such as the *ancien régime* and the Victorian age, revolutionary forces were agitating the more sensitive spirits and engendering further crises.

Now it may be that the long era of expansion is drawing to a close, and that even if we escape a universal catastrophe the future will be an era of contraction. All history might be charted in terms of such pendulum swings, which are the natural terms of action and reaction. An obvious sign in our time is the growth of totalitarianism—a "dynamic" reversion to the closed, tribal society. Another sign is the swelling appeal to religion, which might betoken a quest for spiritual freedom but looks more like a yearning for security and rest. At best, such tendencies to contraction represent a healthy desire to order, consolidate, and conserve, to restore community and natural piety, in a healthy recognition of the abuses of freedom and the limitations of reason. Yet we are not likely to enjoy the best, nor are we in a position to make consolidation the order of the day. Immediately we have to deal with another revolutionary development, in the unlocking of atomic energy; to conserve anything at all we shall have to make over our traditional institutions and policies. Given science, we must expect more revolutionary developments, in both our conceptions of the universe and our operations on it. We cannot count on history to repeat itself.

Hence I should stress first of all, in very general terms, our continued need of an adventurous spirit—of still more creative thought, bold, imaginative, experimental, self-reliant, critical of all "infallible" authority. This stress may seem unnecessary in an age notorious for its skepticism and irreverence, and at a moment when revolutionaries are the apparent menace. Nevertheless these revolutionaries are much less bold and independent than they appear, what with their childish faith in guaranteed totalitarian solutions. Our conservatives are even less enterprising than they appear; the frequent violence of their tactics masks a fearful timidity and unimaginativeness in their basic strategy, when not a downright panic. And we all have to be wary of another contradiction in our heritage. While the spirit of adventure has been the genius of Western thought, at its heart has remained the venerable assumption of a static, finished world, in which truth is timeless, standards are absolute and fixed, and human nature is always and everywhere the same. Our religion, our ethics, our poetry, our political and economic theory, our proverbs and maxims for daily life—our idealism and our common sense alike are steeped in this assumption, which is at variance both with our scientific knowledge of human history in an evolving world, and with the conditions of life in a revolutionary world.

All along I have been identifying the adventurous spirit with humanism, liberalism, rationalism, the scientific spirit, the ideals of freedom, individualism, and the "open society." Since these have constituted the distinctive faith of our secular civilization, I appear to be calling for business as usual, at the same old stand—the kind of business that has brought on the present crisis. I should therefore repeat that the adventure in freedom is inevitably precarious. Yet I deny that this faith is the main source of our folly and evil. In the world of affairs the obvious menace is the inveterate self-interest, individual and national, upon which all faiths have foundered. In the world of thought the chief menaces are the various forms of authoritarianism and irrationalism. The worst folly of liberals has been a facile optimism that blinked both the ancient evils and the new complexities.

Today they are apt to echo the common charge that "scientific philosophy" is the root of our evils. Science has indisputably inspired much narrow, harsh philosophy, and much pseudo-science; its disciples have often been inhuman. As inhuman, however, is the fashion of branding all the efforts of intelligence as sinful pride, and all the works of science as mere materialism. It appears that to study meteorology and scientific agriculture is to be materialistic, whereas to pray for rain and good crops is to be spiritual. Actually, both procedures have utilitarian motives; the immediate choice is between more or less intelligent, efficacious means of attaining human ends: and as for "higher values," pure science is a more disinterested, more genuinely spiritual activity than ordinary prayer or worship. At least science cannot be charged with the nationalism and imperialism that now threaten catastrophe. No war has ever been fought over scientific causes. No nation—least of all Soviet Russia—has proposed its aims or resolved its issues in a scientific spirit. Science has had very little to do, indeed, with the administration of our economic and political life. It remains the author of our major problem, in its gift of tremendous power that has been terribly abused; but for the wise use of this power we need more, not less, of the objective, dispassionate scientific spirit. For our philosophical purposes we need more of its integrity and its basic humility, its respect at once for fact and for mystery. . . . No product of social intercourse is more precious than reasonableness, or more essential to attaining and sharing the goods of life; for love itself is a partial sentiment that often goes wrong, leading to division, jealousy, and hatred.

In this spirit reason must then add that love and hatred remain more elemental. Its claims need to be qualified by modest ideas of its functions and its powers; its ideal product is not pure rationality but reasonableness. Traditional rationalism has taken too supercilious an attitude toward the instinctive, spontaneous life, the sentiment and passion that alone can give force to its ideals. In this century many social scientists have displayed an incredibly naïve confidence in the power of intelligence to control the "behavior patterns" with which they play, talking as if social conflict could be handled in the same way as infectious disease. Liberals generally have set their sights too high, overestimating the rationality and virtue of free men. Yet it is still reason that warns us against such unreasonable expectations. In its most mournful judgments of its frail powers it still proves its necessity, its responsibility, and its power.

To live intelligently, in short, we must recognize that man is not simply a "rational animal." To live decently we must also recognize that this definition of him is more adequate than such popular definitions as a beast of prey, an illusioned robot, or an imprisoned soul. He shares his basic drives and reflexes with other animals, and he may or may not have an immortal soul; what most plainly and positively distinguishes him from other animals is the power of conscious thought and responsible behavior. If we respect him at all we must treat him as if he were rational, and enlist his free consent in joint enterprises. The whole argument for liberty and democracy ultimately rests on Pascal's dictum that thought makes the whole dignity of man, and that the endeavor to think well is the basic morality. "The chief virtue of democracy," concluded Carl Becker, "and in the long run the sole reason for cherishing it, is that with all its defects it still provides the most favorable conditions for the maintenance of that dignity and the practice of that morality." . . .

All these ideals, once more, necessarily lead to disagreement, disquiet, disharmony, disorder, disunity. Still, such costs are not necessarily prohibitive. They seem more alarming because of the conservative disposition to be alarmed by all change, and to spare the past its troubles. Historically, there is no clear correlation between harmony and health, much less growth—no great society has realized the degree of spiritual unity common in primitive societies. Although freedom in thought and political life has always got societies into trouble, none have died of it; dying societies have been marked rather by rigidity, the traditionalism of which Rome in decline is the conspicuous example. The most encouraging sign in the Western world is that it not only recognizes the evils in its way of life but continues to struggle against them. It has not yet lost the pioneering spirit that has made its whole history a migration. There will always be some hope for it so long as it retains its distinctive hope that life on earth can and must be improved.

To this hope—to the whole humanistic endeavor—Christianity, finally, can lend strong support. Although it did not lead the way, it contributed the germinal ideals of spiritual freedom and equality. Today many of its leaders are outgrowing the traditional exclusiveness that has militated against its ideal of universal brotherhood. Some are willing to believe that religion too is properly an adventure—a progress toward more adequate conceptions of God and the spiritual life, instead of the final truth about them. Meanwhile Christianity remains the most accessible source of saving experience for the West. It can comfort, bind up wounds, and cure as no secular faith can. And simply because it is no longer a flaming, crusading faith it can preach more effectively its gospel of charity and humility, help to keep alive the possibilities of peace. Churchmen of all sects are combating the tendency of political and military leaders to buy slight tactical advantages at great moral cost (as Monte Cassino was blasted, to no gain whatever). The Christian conscience might avert the ultimate horror of a total war to preserve freedom—a war waged in a total disregard of the values that alone make freedom precious, and rehabilitation possible.

Nevertheless I have been arguing that Christianity does not constitute our best hope, at least for our earthly future. An established religion remains by nature a deeply conservative force, not a creative one. The churches have long brought up the intellectual rear of our civilization, and despite their awakened social conscience their claims to spiritual leadership are still weakened by their engrained tendency to resist new knowledge and aspiration. Most are still disposed to a dogmatic supernaturalism that saps the intellectual honesty and courage essential for a responsible idealism. Churchmen persistently narrow our choices by equating "religious" and "spiritual," obscuring all the shriveled, deformed spirituality to be found within the churches and all the healthy idealism to be found outside them. Much of what passes for religious faith today amounts to a side bet, covering a vague belief that "there must be something" or that man needs to believe (especially when in foxholes); often it verges on sentimentality—the indulgence of feeling without commitments in thought and action. Many churchmen are trying to reanimate such faith by exploiting the theology of crisis, the ethos of fear—preaching not merely humility but humiliation. Given the historic record, we cannot be simply heartened by the possibility that the future may belong to the churches again.

Humanism, or the religion of humanity, may not do either. Toynbee attacks it as peculiar, perverse, "even pathological." It is in fact peculiar enough—it has not had the chance of religion. No doubt it makes too heavy demands on human nature in its present state, especially when it asks men to put humanity above the tribe—something they have never succeeded in doing under the fatherhood of God. Yet I still hold that the Western humanistic faith is not perverse, and not so pathological as historic religion has often been. It has proved itself in many good men, by many good works. It has brought finer possibilities of life to masses of men who in the past could invest their hope only in a hypothetical life to come. The utter defeat of this cause would be the worst tragedy in history. Meanwhile the notorious pride of the modern world is dangerous because it is not a clear, proud faith in the dignity of man or in the uses of mind. The enemy today wears a mask of pride, but its true name is fear. . . .

BENJAMIN N. NELSON

THE FOLLOWING paper by Benjamin N. Nelson was originally delivered, in a more extended version, at a symposium on "Conflict in the Social Order" held in 1951 at the University of Minnesota. Since the author's conclusions are presented in the form of a kind of intellectual odyssey, there is no need here to specify the traditions which he finds congenial. It will be remarked, however, that many of the thinkers cited by Nelson are represented in the present volumes—indeed, his very title derives from Sigmund Freud's *The Future of an Illusion*. For the student, much of the suggestiveness of the following essay attaches to it as a working model of how data and concepts from such diverse realms as the social sciences, psychology and psychoanalysis, history, literature, philosophy, and religion—as well as from the morning newspaper—may be, if not "integrated" or "systematized," at least brought to interact within a quite personal perspective.

Some of the generalizations set forth in "The Future of Illusions" will be more aptly appraised when it is known that Nelson, a medieval scholar, has written a book called *The Idea of Usury* (1949), a documented "genealogy" of the Western concept of usury which shows the influence of Max Weber in developing its thesis that Western society has passed, in the words of the subtitle, "from tribal brotherhood to universal otherhood." In his epilogue to this work the author makes clear that, although he is apprehensive of the dilution which the notion of moral community undergoes when it is extended by "rationalist liberals" to embrace all mankind, he is equally mistrustful of the "organicist" leanings of such writers as Tönnies. The latter are correct, Nelson claims, in recognizing that the advent of a universalist, "capitalist" morality attenuates the moral bond of the tribal kindred. But they are misguided insofar as they urge, out of resentment rather than out of love and prudence, a reversion to introverted tribal moralities. Our present condition and ideals, however inappropriate to clannish brotherhood and mutuality, are not such as to warrant despair.

"A society which embodies recognizable norms for people in general is ethically superior to one in which there are privileges for the insiders, temporary concessions for good neighbors and strangers, and no obligations at all toward distant 'barbarians.' . . . Better the abhorred 'atomized individualism of bourgeois liberalism' than conflicting 'Brotherhoods of Blood and Soil.'

"Better still the Brotherhood of Man."

Benjamin N. Nelson was born in New York City in 1911, was graduated from the College of the City of New York in 1931, and received his Ph.D. in history from Columbia University in 1944. He has taught history and social sciences at these two institutions, as well as at Brooklyn, Queens, and Chicago. At present he is chairman of the European Heritage sequence in the Humanities program and co-chairman of the Social Science program in the Department of General Studies at the University of Minnesota. In addition to his book on usury, he has written articles for professional journals and is co-author of *Personality—Work—Community: An Introduction to Social Science* (1953).

THE FUTURE OF ILLUSIONS

I

If I were asked how one could become a psychoanalyst, I should answer, *through the study of his own dreams.*—SIGMUND FREUD

In Western society, as in any other, those who allow themselves or are permitted to express the representative thoughts of the culture have characteristically been constrained to function in one or another of the following roles:

1. The *pontiff* or *priest.*—At every time there are individuals who play the role of pontiff or priest whose central prerogative and responsibility it becomes to administer the *sacra*—the precious utensils and ideals of the culture—and to protect the holy mysteries, the so-called *arcana,* from the obtrusive gaze of illiterate and aggressive masses. It is not at all necessary that these guardians of the holies be men of the cloth. They may be persons of various professions—political, commercial, educational. Their job, as they conceive it, comes to be to mask the imponderables of the culture, to keep the pearls from being cast before swine. The behavior of the Roman pontiffs in concealing the sacred and mandatory legal forms of action in the early days of the Roman Republic is a case in point.

2. In reaction to this systematic protection or concealment of the mysteries of the culture, there have arisen in moments of great stress prophets whose role it becomes to *expose the mysteries* and to *conjure up a vision* of a world where men would see each other face to face, no longer as through a glass darkly. There is no prophet in the Western world who will not play the part of *conjurer,* who will not present to men's eyes the vision of a *utopia* in which happiness will abound, conflict cease, unity pervade, and self-interest disappear. Again, prophets are not necessarily whirling dervishes or overstimulated hermits. They may also appear in the guise of business men, secondary school teachers, lawyers, politicos, journalists, and, even, college professors.

This selection has been reprinted from Benjamin N. Nelson, "The Future of Illusions," *Psychoanalysis,* Vol. 2, No. 4 (Spring–Summer 1954), pp. 16–37, by permission of the publisher. Slight revisions have been made by the author for the present edition.

They will differ markedly among themselves with respect to the degree in which their exposure of the hitherto concealed mysteries and their descriptions of the perfections of the envisaged paradise is animated by what Nietzsche called *resentment.* But, there seems reason to suspect that all such conjurers have had some portion of resentment and all have had more than an insignificant measure of illusion.

What roles have there been—are there—in our culture for persons who desire neither to conceal nor in any aggressive and resentful fashion to expose the premises of the culture? What parts lie available to men who are concerned to tell man plain truths about some of the balky and intractable aspects of his fate here below and to persuade him wisely to use such resources as wisdom suggests to improve his lot, to the extent that it can be improved?

There have been no recognized roles for such activity in Western culture, except those of the clown or court fool and the privy councilor, both, it will be observed, confidential intimates of the King.

It is interesting that in the Orient a role has long existed in the form of the *sage* who considers it his responsibility to make man aware of the character of the persistent or recurrent truths about himself and his culture and to protect him from the excesses of nihilistic concealment and nihilistic exposure. The Western world has characteristically not had much room, if any, for sages. The reasons for this are too complex to explore at this juncture. Perhaps one of the most important of these reasons has been the incapacity of Western culture, as we have known it, to acknowledge the fact that men are mortal; social reality at least as difficult to penetrate as the starry heavens above; wisdom and justice painful, if not impossible, to achieve. Also, our culture has been devoted, inevitably, it would appear, to the indefinite prolongation of infancy, and we have not been able to protect ourselves against the infantilist conception that true wisdom shall come out of the mouths of babes. For these and other reasons, to be discussed presently, the civilization of the whole world appears beset by an activist dynamism to which it seems impossible to set plausible limits.

Only occasionally in the past and in the nineteenth and twentieth centuries have there occurred evidences of sufficient maturity within our culture to make it possible for persons to state without fear of ridicule or reprisal some of the fundamental facts concerning the recalcitrant features of human lot and the character of political society. In this connection one thinks of such men as Alexis de Tocqueville, John Stuart Mill, Jacob Burckhardt, Max Weber, Georg Simmel, Sigmund Freud, Nicolas Berdyaev, George Santayana, and others.

Coming now to the fruits of this dynamism and infantilism:

Through the history of so-called Western civilization, both in the Orient and Occident, one detects the paramount importance of planetary or cosmic myths of apocalypse, utopia, and final renovation, to which I shall henceforth refer as *apocalyptic cosmism* and *futurism*. The fascination over men's minds exerted by these overpowering dreams of a final and perfect rebirth is readily discovered in the successive philosophies of history and destiny-ideas of Western civilization. The whole of history, human and natural alike, has been conceived to exhibit either inevitable degeneration or inevitable and infinite progress—both, however, to be climaxed by a Millennial Age and final redemption.

There are any number of versions of the Heavenly City in Western culture, ranging from the ecstatic worshippers of Dionysus and the consecrated secret brotherhoods of Pythagoreans to the devotees of millennial communism in our own day. The variations in the faiths and liturgies of these sects are too numerous to mention. Here one must be content to recall only the major groupings: the early Christian communities described in the Acts of the Apostles; the Montanists, the Donatists, the new millennialists of Asia Minor described by Eusebius; the medley of Messianists, Adamites, Flagellants, Millennialists, Perfectionists, and spiritual Franciscans who appear in the Middle Ages; the Anabaptists of Münster, the Diggers and Fifth Monarchy Men in England, the Hutterites, Shakers, Quakers, Mormons (and in some respects even the early New England Puritans) of the early modern era; and latterly, the devotees of Communism, Fascism, Nazism, Pan-Slavism, Pan-Islamism, and other exponents of national or international dreams of collective redemption.

The precedents of this dream of final redemption are to be found in the patterns of sentiment and action of all cultures known to us. To speak only of so-called Western civilization, where its roots have apparently become ineradicable: Its accents are clear in the Old Testament and the New, the Hebrew Prophets, the Book of Daniel, the Acts of the Apostles, the Revelations of John, the teachings of the early Christian communities, the rules of medieval monastic orders, the notions underlying the theocratic conceptions of the medieval Church, the preachings of numerous heretics of the Middle Ages and modern era. One has only to recall the doctrines of the Calabrian prophet, Joachim of Floris (d. *ca.* 1202), he who proclaimed the imminence of a renovated Third Age—neither the Age of the Father, nor the Age of the Son, when a fortunate minority of monastic brethren enjoyed the freedom of the Gospel, but the Age of the Holy Spirit, in the animated words of

Ernst Troeltsch, "an age of the spirit and of freedom, of peace and absence of violence, of the humble and the poor, without social and class distinctions, without 'mine and thine.'" How many times has Joachim's notion of the redemptive Third Age reechoed in our own era! In subterranean ways, it has supplied the substance of and the dynamic for earthly visions of an all-powerful Third Rome. It is this to which appeal was made by the Holy Roman Empire, by Mussolini's Fascism, by Hitler's establishment of a Third—a thousand-year—Reich, and even by the dynasty of the Romanovs, who looked to Moscow to become the successor to the City of the Golden Horn and the City of the Tiber. Today, the dream of a last age of history deludes the followers of Stalin.

Other versions of these myths of final redemption have escaped notice because of the seeming absence of transcendental metaphors in their promise and program. We must not deceive ourselves into thinking that these necessitarian and inevitabilist views are peculiar to the present Soviet state, the self-styled Eastern democracies, or Oriental culture as a whole.

As a noted German Church historian, Ernst Benz, has recently remarked, Russian and Western European conceptions of man, though differing in detail from time to time, appear to belong together in a kind of dialectical tension. Both anthropologies, Eastern and Western, he remarks, are rooted in the same evangelical message and are complementary rather than exclusive. One who knows the elements of the developments of both cultures will not in the least be surprised by these observations.

Western culture is Judaeo-Christian to the core and reveals at every turn the insistent emphases of European Christianity. Russian culture, whatever its excesses, is no less Judaeo-Christian and reveals the insistent emphases of the Byzantine and Russian churches. Both, in their different ways, are permeated by chiliastic eschatologies, millennial expectations of god-manhood (*theosis*) symbolized in the mystery of the Incarnation. Both have developed versions of cosmic brotherhood of man and their sacramental oneness in an undivided state of community.

As one might anticipate, especially ingenious versions of eschatological thought are found in the writings of Hegel and Marx, who form a bridge between Western European and Russian thought. There can not be the slightest doubt about the significance of earlier theological and metaphysical traditions for the futuristic and cosmic projections of both Hegel and Marx.

Academic observers of the history of society have largely been deceived about the rhythms and characteristics of the cultural evolution of the so-called West. In their oversimplified and evidently distorted notions about intellectual and social progress, they have failed to recognize the dominance under different guises of the gospel of apocalyptic cosmism and futurism. The present ways of periodizing the history of Western civilization make the error of supposing that liberal intelligence steadily advanced at the expense of ancient myth in the eras of the Renaissance, the Reformation, the French, American, and Industrial Revolutions. A more sober view would at once suggest that these very designations prove the persistence of the myth of rebirth, of renovation, of apocalyptic futurism. It is customary to suppose that the intellectual individualism of the Renaissance, the Protestant concept of Christian liberty, the economic individualism associated with the development of commerce, the idea of political liberalism developing from the left-wing of the Reformation, represent a succession of attacks upon older traditions. It is also imagined that these new attitudes triumphed throughout the length and breadth of Western culture and that they now form the core of our institutions and ways of life. Two observations deserve to be made in this connection:

1. The various forms of individualism which are so often supposed to have been and still to be at war with one another can readily be seen to reveal an inner affinity. Their oppositions are the result of contingent rather than structural circumstances. Solipsistic individualism in its various versions has been one of the two dominant strains in Western culture. (As must already be apparent, familialistic collectivism has been the other.) There is a most peculiar affinity between the religious individualism of a St. Paul and the economic individualism of a Herbert Hoover. It would be easy to show that the so-called "rugged economic individualism" of some American "captains of industry" is more than an illustration of brutal self-assertion in the economic sphere. If it were merely that, it would be easy for culture to set limits to its actions. To the contrary, rugged economic individualism is principally an exhibit of a religious dream in secular guise. Any study of the life histories of the rugged individualists in our culture will readily show the crucial importance of the influence upon them of individualistic religious conceptions.

2. The notion that mythic futurist ideas and magical habits of mind disappeared with the advance of sober science and rational knowledge can now be described as a sheer misreading of the facts. We are indebted to the late Carl Becker for having proved so ingeniously that the eighteenth-century philosophers who supposed that they were exploding superstitions themselves designed a new Heavenly City with not substantially different materials.

We should go far astray, indeed, if we looked for cosmism and futurism only among sectarian enthusiasts. Some of the most dynamic myths of recent days have been those which have been masquerading in the guise of "level-headed" realism, efficient management, and experimental science. In truth, so-called scientific outlooks and "liberal" intelligence have contributed more than their fair share to the proliferation of apocalyptic myths of millennial assurances of a perennially glorified humanity, of Paradise Lost and Paradise Regained.

Not very many observers, however, have penetrated the forms which these illusions have taken in the recent history of the Western world. Perhaps the most widespread and least recognizable of these myths is the belief that technical power, so-called scientific management, organized intelligence combined with social engineering, will inevitably yield economic plenty, the more abundant life, and the eternal enjoyment of the (Four?) Freedoms of Man. In these hopes we recognize the myth of Prometheus Bound and Unbound, the dreams of Roger Bacon and Francis Bacon, the vision of the American, Frederick Winslow Taylor—the prophet of the stop-watch and the slide rule—and his fellow worker in the vineyards of the Lord, Frank Gilbreth, recently rescued from obscurity by being made the hero of the best-selling family romance *Cheaper by the Dozen,* written by two of his twelve children. (Possessed by a "compulsion to save time," Taylor hated to see workmen wilfully or unknowingly wasting time; by going about their tasks in their habitual and inefficient ways, hired hands appeared to Taylor to be resisting, indeed to be sabotaging the dictates of the machine. Gilbreth, a corpulent man, with a weak heart, hated to have to perform, or see others perform, needless motions —he wanted all work brought up to the waist. Between them, Taylor and Gilbreth established the logic of the mechanized industrial universe—time-motion analysis, and its attendant schemes, the belt-conveyor, the speed-up, the vast expansion of administrative personnel, and so forth.)

Moving versions of all these myths—of Prometheus Bound and Unbound, of Paradise Lost and Paradise Regained—will be found in Marx, whose strategic importance for the modern era lies in his incredible power to synthesize myths ancient and modern, as well as to depict the unsavory realities lying behind the mythical pretensions of others. The vision of Prometheus dominated Marx's mind as early as his student days at the University. His mature social thought, from the *Communist Manifesto* to the last pages he wrote in *Das Kapital,* is simply a cosmic projection of the Promethean legend.

II

> For there is a path to a world more beautiful, trodden in all ages and civilizations, the easiest and also the most fallacious of all, the dream. A promise of escape from the gloomy actual is held out to all; we have only to colour life with fancy, to enter upon the quest of oblivion, sought in the delusion of ideal harmony.—JOHAN HUIZINGA

These myths can be ultimately traced, I would guess, to men's nostalgic reminiscences of childhood. Since it seems evident that a great number of persons are utterly unwilling to admit the differences between rational goals and self-contradictory illusions, it might not be amiss to rehearse some observations made in a related connection by the master interpreter of dreams, Sigmund Freud.

"There is no one," Freud somewhere observes, "whose life is likely to be more difficult than he who presumes to awake people from their dreams." Such attempts, he explains, have been made three times in the history of modern European culture, once by himself, twice by men he regarded as his predecessors.

Copernicus, said Freud, with pardonable exaggeration, was the first man in modern European history to wake his neighbors from their dreams. Before the publication of the great Polish astronomer's major work, men did believe that the earth was stable in the center of the cosmos and that the sun and other planets revolved about the earth. Copernicus's heliocentric hypothesis rudely disturbed men's images of their place in the universe. All sorts of convictions appeared to collapse as a result of his suggestion that the earth revolves about the sun. Before the great fabric of institutions which rested on these convictions could be adjusted to the new outlook, Bruno had to die at the stake, and Galileo bow before the Inquisition.

The second episode to which Freud referred was the hypothesis advanced by Darwin concerning the evolution of species. If the Copernican thesis appears to deny the centrality of the earth in the universe and the central significance of the drama of redemption being played uniquely on the earth's surface, the Darwinian argument appeared to cast doubt upon the centrality of man's position in the "Great Chain of Being." Man appeared no longer to be the monarch of creation, the summit of the animal kingdom, but simply another mortal animal who had descended from lower species. Those who care to consult the debates at the time of Darwin's announcement will see that it was almost impossible for great numbers of men, scholars as well as laymen, to accept the suggestion of man's humanity, his animal origin, his mortality. The Darwinian teaching is still not universally accepted. Indeed, it is forbidden to be taught in some states of the Union.

The third episode in the awakening of man to reality, said Freud, involved himself. And his presumption, Freud suspected, might come to be considered as perhaps "the unkindest cut of all." For what did Freud do but suggest that man was not master *in his own house*—that is, that man's conscious mind was in the grip of unconscious drives and memory traces and that the conscious self (the Ego) was very far indeed from being the captain of the individual's destiny? How can any considerable number of people be persuaded to believe that? How can men win the courage and wisdom to forego the final illusion—the illusion that each of us enjoys central location with regard to himself and everything in this world? It is next to impossible to convince ordinary men and women, even university students, for that matter, that an individual may know less about himself than he might know about something or someone else, or that another person might come to know the roots of his personality better than he does himself.

To round out this long digression and draw the moral from Freud's revealing venture into history: Western culture has been acutely suffering from the domination of two seemingly distinct, but actually dynamically related, dreams:

1. The dream of the ecstatic, orgastic union of parents and children—this dream expresses the nostalgia of all who have been bred in the family. Where, one might ask, is the family in which fathers and sons, mothers and daughters, brothers and sisters have actually enjoyed an uninterrupted state of undivided community? Surely we must admit in our more sober moments that our childhood was not one of unmixed bliss. Why, then, do men permit themselves to dream against all evidence that the future holds the promise, if only we apply the right key, to a state of *utter harmony for all mankind?* The belief in this myth has already had the most tremendous consequences. Now that the range of "civilization" has become planetary, the risks to be run have grown to cosmic proportions, and the price of failure has come ultimately to be tantamount to the common ruin of all.

2. The second dream is the dream which we find reflected recurringly in the philosophy of absolute individualism, or what I prefer to describe as solipsism. In the solipsistic view, only the "I" is real. No one or nothing else here below is held to have reality, only the self. This myth, also, I would guess, originates in the experience of the child—except that this time, the ever-selective consciousness organizes the memories of misfortune and ends by

adopting an unqualified resentment against authority, whether rational or irrational. The child remembering in this case is the child who has rejected the authority of father and mother, who wishes to be utterly alone and independent of constraint.

These two myths, in their extreme forms, have dominated the whole of Western culture. Now I may be asked, how can society proceed without dreams? Must not youth be allowed to dream? Can old men live if these particular myths are shorn of their romance? I should hope that all men, young and old, might learn to orient themselves meaningfully to reality, without the illusory consolations of contradictory dreams for, if they cannot, then they must be prepared, like the alcoholic derelicts in Eugene O'Neill's *The Iceman Cometh,* to waste their lives in neurotic aggressions against themselves and others. If, at the present turn in history, the masses and classes alike cannot forego the luxury of such delusions, our civilization and culture have no future whatever. Is it so difficult to perceive the fact that the *price of illusion* has multiplied a thousand-fold during the last century? Even before the notion of an atomic bomb was ever dreamed of, Freud wrote in the last pages of his *Civilization and Its Discontents* (1930): "Men have brought their powers of subduing the forces of nature to such a pitch that by using them they could now very easily exterminate one another to the last man." Is it not clear that all of us —the "children of light" as well as the "children of darkness"—now have dreadful toys with which to play out our dreams of love and hate?

These myths—of Prometheus and Paradise—are common in the United States and the Soviet Union. They are now penetrating China and India, as they have already penetrated Japan.

Tomorrow, they may reign everywhere.

Wherever these myths take hold, they are accompanied, willy-nilly, by a new concept of human action and association which carried to its extreme can have no other end than the bureaucratic mentality and way of life: the notion of *impersonal* (bureaucratic) service to an *impersonal* (bureaucratic) end. The religious roots of this conception in Western religion will be familiar to those who have encountered the profound writings of Max Weber.

The mythical elements in the "secular" dreams of Paradise have managed to escape notice because they have been unconsciously secreted into the interstices of the dominant systems of economic and social thought and continue to be fashionably outfitted in the latest vocabulary of science.

In one or another form, the major social thinkers of the Western world have insisted either that there was a *pre-established harmony* of interests—we might call this *cosmic philharmonism*—or that with not too great effort there could be achieved some universally acceptable *artificial identification* of interests. If not religion, then science and the liberal temper, it is supposed, would surely discover ways of unifying and satisfying the totality of wants and interests of men, however much they might expand and however contradictory might be their expression. All of this, it is assumed, is capable of being managed without undue risk of grief, pain, and cost. In this task, science and communication are assumed to play a central role. The extension of scientific method to the understanding of society, it is premised, cannot but eventuate in resolving the problems which confront men. There is an utter failure to perceive the distinction between *solving the problems of science,* whether natural or social, and *solving the problems of society*. Through the extension of the channels of communications, it is anticipated, we may be assured of final truth, ultimate consensus, and the elimination of interest. "Peoples," as the populist mythographers like to say, have only to speak to "peoples" and all conflict will disappear.

Thus both cultures, Russian and American, are persuaded in the last analysis of the *ultimate* reconcilability of interests and the overcoming of conflict through communication. In the former case, the perfection of community is felt to demand the maximizing of *the intensity of the bond* which unites men one to another. Total communion, which I call *Unanimism,* is felt to be necessary for true community, and total community is felt to be necessary for true communication. In the case of our own land, community is supposed to develop as the outcome of a *willed* association of individuals who choose to communicate with one another. Community is presumed to follow inevitably upon the enlargement of the area of communication. In its most noted philosophical version, our outlook assumes that indefinite expansion of the channels of discussion and inquiry will inevitably yield consensus and solution of social problems. Without meaning to minimize the differences in cultural emphasis, it must be acknowledged that both peoples have universalizing aims and orientations. Both claim allegiance to "democracy" and "World Brotherhood."

It may be argued that I am attacking high aspirations. On the contrary, our culture has been beset from the very beginning, and is beset today, by an inability to distinguish between apocalyptic visions and plausible and fruitful ideals. In this connection one could cite the interesting illustration provided by the Swiss writer, Denis de Rougemont, in his challenging book, *Love in the Western World*. Since the twelfth century, de Rougemont argues, Western man has been under the domination of a myth of perfect and uninterrupted happiness through romantic love. (This state is, in principle, impossible of achievement.) This notion, de Rougemont supposes, was originally confined to the aristocratic groups of Southern French (Albigensian) culture and came only after considerable time to be shared generally by the less privileged classes. As time passed, he claims, the originally exclusive ideal of romantic love spread by suggestion and imitation, and it currently holds the world in thrall as a result of the universal influence of Hollywood films. Now there is no corner of life which is not influenced by the migration of romantic love from its original haunts. Romantic love has, indeed, not without reason, recently been alleged to be one of the most dynamic world religions of the present century.

Continues de Rougemont: From the very outset, it may seem odd to note, the pursuit of the perfection of romantic love has been assumed to know no other consummation than death. Perfect fulfillment occurs only in what Richard Wagner calls the *Liebestod,* the love-death. Is this not striking evidence of the grim ending which accompanies every human attempt to organize life on the basis of utter self-transcendence?

Another example of the permeating of our ideas by chiliastic aspirations would be the idea of "freedom from want." Without wishing in any way to disparage the motives of the architects of that phrase, I would insist that it is a jungle of confusions and illusions. So long as man preserves his humanity, so long indeed as he continues to be an animal, whether or not rational, he will continue to entertain wants which are incapable of satisfaction.

The notion of freedom from want would seem innocent enough did it not so readily lend itself to the proliferation of just those illusions I have been describing. There are many who suppose that human productivity has now expanded to the point of guaranteeing a minimum subsistence to all peoples of the world. It is assumed that if selfishness were to be replaced by selflessness, all men everywhere the world over could even now enjoy what is so vaguely called "freedom from want." This is simply not the case, as everyone knows who has at any time made a serious effort to think the problem through in concrete terms, with the aid of available statistics.

More significantly, the notion of "freedom from want" makes the absurd postulate that wants remain stable. The folly of this view was well known to Plato and Aristotle. In more recent days, the disturbing implications of this too generally neglected fact of the mobility of wants have been restated with profound insight by the French sociologist, Emile Durkheim, and by the contemporary economist, Professor Frank H. Knight. How can there be "freedom from want" when wants show so aggressively a tendency in our present culture to expand more rapidly than men's productive powers? If wants could be kept stable while the improvements of science and economic organization continued to promote ever larger outputs of goods and services, it might be possible for men to achieve something comparable to what may be implied in the essentially mythical phrase "freedom from want." But if wants were kept stable, could one be sure that the gross output would expand?

In any case, it is a sheer delusion to imagine that the only or even the most important source of human unhappiness at the present time is economic need. Our public discussions would gain greatly if more men were to perceive the myths involved in the notion of freedom from want.

To say that human life and culture, wherever they occur, are likely to reveal recalcitrant or recurrent features is not to say that men must resign themselves to live unloved or loveless lives, empty of joys and fulfilments. It is merely to say that human and social organisms may be expected to exhibit limits to their perfectibility. The frank facing-up to this fact is the best antidote I know for moderating the threat of the endless recurrence of what I have called *apocalyptic futurism*.

III

To rest upon a formula is a slumber that, prolonged, means death.
—OLIVER WENDELL HOLMES, JR.

It may be of some value to provide another illustration of the price men are now paying for the luxury of illusions. This illustration may be taken to involve another freedom, "freedom from fear." It hardly needs saying that it has been very difficult for the Western imagination, overstimulated as it has been by millennial expectations, to acknowledge the fact that men die. As Freud observed, the *Id* does not know of death and will not hear of it. Today, as millions face the prospect of death, our journals of opinion and newspapers carry comforting stories about discoveries made by science which seem to suggest that there is no reason whatever for men to die, as most now seem to do, before the age of seventy. It is hoped that the time will soon come when seventy will be the time of adolescence and humans will live to twice that time, one hundred and fifty. There is already evidence now being culled with ever greater intensity that some men have lived to be as old as Methuselah. Indeed, a recent newspaper article notifies us that scientists frankly do not understand why men die and are now entertaining the hope that they can be made to live forever, as apparently some of the micro-organisms do. It is difficult not to see in this simply another instance of the persistent dream of eternal life. One wonders how, if things are to be as they are, if the pace of life is to remain as most men now describe it—"simply killing"—how it can be anticipated *that they will want* to live as long as science trusts they can be made to live.

Another recent article reports that Professor Harold Urey, whose exploits in the creation of the atomic bomb are well known, has finally become persuaded that human life exists on other planets. It may well be that this conviction is the result of scrupulous scientific observations and inferences, but one may surely be allowed to suspect that the interpretation that will be put upon Professor Urey's announcement will have a peculiar color in the present hour. As men prepare themselves for the holocaust, they wish at least to be allowed to believe that if this world be destroyed, human life will persist elsewhere.

The revival, at the present time, of the old notion of a plurality of worlds has a transparent poignancy. As Professor A. O. Lovejoy has so brilliantly remarked, the men of the Middle Ages and the early modern era could not visualize and accept the possibility of plurality of worlds because it appeared to violate all their frames of reference and to allow for the possibility that the incarnation and redemption were not unique occurrences. Bruno died at the stake in the year 1600 principally because his visionary imaginings conflicted with prepotent assumptions concerning the divine plan for human and superterrestrial existence. We today have somehow escaped the limits of the older drama and in any case our need is so much greater. If we must perish, will it not be a consolation to know that on some other planet the great game in which we have been engaged will continue to be played under more fortunate auspices?

Not so easy, however, is the elimination of "want and fear." Those who live by science fiction have for many decades now assumed the likelihood of life on other planets and, indeed, have painted grim tales of interplanetary warfare. One of the most profound studies along these lines, which provides as brilliant a rendering of modern myths as can be found anywhere, can be read in the pages of the too-little-known Russian novel *We,* completed in 1922 by Eugene Zamiatin, forerunner of Aldous Huxley and George Orwell. It is no accident that the plot of the work centers in the massive preparations made by the people behind the "Green Wall," evidently the Communists, to bring happiness to the deluded people who live on the other side of the moon. What shall we say to this fable concerning the "freedom from want?"

The classes have known no better than the masses how to escape the production of illusions. Those who have held power, rank, and station in the Western world have either generally not cared, nor known how, to protect culture from the spread of illusions. Characteristically, in both the Orient and the Occident, ruling cadres have insisted upon establishing one or another version of the illusion of Paradise. In the modern world, they have insisted that Paradise was already available here below or could readily be achieved with no great effort. One is reminded of the behavior of the Romans in the so-called Golden Age of the Antonines, from 96 to 180 A.D., when aspirants to favor sought so desperately to conceal from themselves and from their mighty patrons that the Great Empire was at the very brink of destruction.

At every turn in history—today no less than yesterday—the wealthy and mighty deceive themselves by building Palaces of Pleasure which are inevitably called by the names of Versailles and Sans Souci, whether they be in the Ile de France, le Cap d'Antibes, or Miami Beach. Wherever established classes congregate—and this is as true for the established classes within Soviet society as it was for the Nazis and the Italian fascists, for Europe, the United States, and the Orient—they irresistibly exhibit their desire both to protect the mysteries of the society from the uninitiated and to conceal from themselves the evidence of its impending disintegration.

One who wishes to understand how profound are the illusions accepted and encouraged by the more favored classes at the present time has only to spend a week end with the travel section of the blessedly abundant Sunday edition of the New York *Times*. The reading of but one column and one advertisement should suffice to expose the gnawing pathos that pervades our culture. How desperate is the effort to find, if not for a week, then at least for a week end, some hideaway which is stocked with the world's goods and all of the dreamt of pleasures! It is not to be supposed that these advertisements are directed to the Four Hundred, or the Four Thousand, or the Four Hundred Thousand. They are now directed to all mankind without discrimination. Conrad Hilton is one of the great religious virtuosi of our time, and he has his parallels in Socialist Britain and in the Soviet Union. A world structured like ours must have its Paradise, if only for a week end. Since men are no longer sure that Paradise awaits at the end of the long journey, they must have it now. The more favored classes are no less urgent than are the visionary masses in this respect. All in deafening unison chant: "Heaven can wait. This is Paradise."

The highest strata build their castles on the cliffs; the middle classes painfully fashion their glass menageries in the flats; the least favored groups learn to dull their anxieties with the aid of strong draughts of heady pleasure—sadism, sex, and unblended whiskey. All alike lust for the Palaces of Pleasure. If children and mass-men cry for television sets, jet-propelled automobiles, and "dynaflow" frigidaires and washing machines—everything in our culture must get off the ground, be ready to zoom through the stratosphere at supersonic speeds—it is because all of us are incessantly taught to lust for these goods by those more fortunate in circumstance and by those who purvey the seemingly boundless supply of marvels over the mass media. Already the peoples of Asia and Africa are demanding to possess a full complement of the miraculous fruits of our productive system—our gleaming gadgets.

This cry on the part of everyone everywhere for an improved standard of living would surely merit our sympathy and support or would at least appear utterly innocent were it not so evidently tainted at its source by resentment and therefore destined to involve all mankind in the greatest of risks. The so-called "underdeveloped" nations of the world have served notice that they will no longer suffer foreign investment in the development of their resources. They will no longer endure "colonialism" and "imperialism," but insist upon possessing their own "arsenal of production," their own stock of absolute weapons. New contestants are flocking to enter the race for material supremacy whose goal becomes daily more difficult to fathom.

Unless now inconceivable miracles of social invention occur in the very near future, we are all destined to reap the harvest of a new crop of industrial wars. Instead of the universal expansion of productivity in accordance with the laws of "comparative advantage" so dear to economists, instead of the wise division of labor and reciprocally profitable patterns of resource utilization, we face the demand for autarchy on all fronts. In the name of national self-determination, all peoples are claiming control over their own resources and their own destinies—all of this being urged in the name of Justice. The maxim which prevails everywhere has become *Fiat Justitia, Pereat Mundus*—"Let there be justice, though the world perish."

Twice already within the present century, mankind has been embroiled in wars between those nations which were relatively early to industrialize and those which for one and another reason entered the race later in the day. It is not surprising that the laggard countries—especially those whose "economic progress" was long delayed by the hold of the feudal and familialistic institutions—have adopted the most stringent economic and political centralization in the hope of more rapidly outdistancing their more favored competitors. The totalitarian formations of Fascist Italy, Nazi Germany, and Bolshevik Russia have their precedent in the autarchic centralization of Imperial Germany. The succession of Four-, Five-, and Ten-Year plans are alleged to have their rationale in the need to mitigate the ravages associated with rapid modernization of communalistic agricultural societies. The new element in the situation, which now involves the world in the risk of common ruin, is the latter-day perfection of the technology of warfare. The most fateful achievement of the

Industrial and Scientific Revolution has been the vast expansion in the range and striking power of engines of destruction. There is no one anywhere who does not now wonder: Can the conflicts attendant upon the race for industrial and political supremacy be mediated through the establishment of more functional political and cultural forms? Or, must we anticipate that the availability and use of absolute weapons will presently become more general? For all we know, there may be no escape from this vicious circle in time to head off the oncoming catastrophe.

Throughout the Western world, but especially in these United States, the situation has a peculiar poignancy. Here, those more favored by circumstances do not actually know how to embody in their way of life a pattern which will cause them to be admired and respected both at home and abroad as truly representative of culture's highest ideals. It cannot be assumed that less favored persons and classes will of necessity rebel against their condition. The evident nihilism in the revolutionary and counterrevolutionary politics of our time results in no slight measure from the fact that those who are less favored have been taught to lust after the unobtainable, to consider themselves equal to every occasion, and have not been provided with any proper models of humane values. It may be a shame to have to confess this, but it is true for whatever reason—whether it be the fatal misconstructions of the creed of equality, the overevaluation of economic goods and income, the evident underestimation of the complex products of art, science, and social invention, or any other factor—there simply does not exist in the United States of America any body of persons who in any consistent way know how to act as paradigms or representative exemplars of our most precious values. There is no use blaming this upon the ravages of mass society. Long before the masses invaded the inner sanctum, the classes had abdicated. Mass men now traffic in the holy of holies.

These historical reveries have, for the moment, one primary purpose: to document my conviction that the present threat is only the first in a long new series of threats which are not likely to diminish in intensity and scope unless and until the peoples of the world manage to discover new ways of defining their expectations and scaling their values. I repeat, I have no desire to suggest that the present threat is not one of immense magnitude. What I protest is the assumption that its outcome will be decisive and the likelihood of its early recurrence negligible. These are hard words, but hard times call for hard words and there is surely nothing to be gained by the perpetration of still further illusions. Those concerned to conserve and promote free culture have great explorations to make, and it will take no one knows how much time to make them tolerably well. During that indefinable interval, our culture may expect regularly to be challenged by the thrusts of the devotees of apocalyptic and redemptive cosmism. *The least that one can do to assist in the works of reconstruction is to desist from giving sanction and encouragement to the spread of illusion.*

IV

> If you have no will for *human* association, I tell you that you are exposing civilization to the fate of dying in fearful agony.—PIERRE LEROUX

It seems to me evident, in short, that Western society is now in the midst of deep convulsions, the sources of which are obscure to most if not all of us. These convulsions did not originate in 1914, 1917, 1933, or in 1945, nor will they end in any foreseeable future. These are convulsions which stem from the evident incapacity of our society to achieve patterns of integration which artfully orchestrate the multitude of conflicting wants, needs, and interests which men and groups in the modern world have come to experience. The available schemes of association are either lapsing into anomic disorder or are being found to impose the killing yoke of uniformity.

The patterns of integration which once appeared to have afforded a tolerable measure of consensus or stability have evidently collapsed and men seek in the midst of violence to fabricate new ones. Since society cannot function without the presence of spirit, men will insist on collectively worshipping idols rather than suffer the agonies of rootlessness and despair. Where subtle and satisfying forms of organic solidarity are unavailable, men will seek to escape chaos by adopting or imposing the yoke of mechanism. To be truly viable, the forms of association must ingeniously pattern the claims of human nature, the expectations of men in society, the underlying functions of social life, and the changing requirements of culture. It is plain that a society founded on sheer egoism, a society which operates on too grand a scale, at too rapid a pace, will undergo atomization, anomic loss of a sense of belongingness. Such under-integration of the moral community and the spatial order may always be expected to generate pendular reactions.

If liberal society recurrently runs the risk of under-integration and absence of compelling loyalties and coherent motivations, totalitarian society offers us no other prospect than that of over-integration, the substitution of mechanism for spirit. The killing yoke of undivided oneness—*Unanimism*—is thrust at us because we cannot bear the ravages of total absence of community—*Inanimism.*

Intermediate ways which would allow for varying balances of individuality and community, between personality and social framework, have yet to be found. Numerous experiments have been conducted among small groups in various lands. All of these attempts have repeatedly run into difficulties either because they have adopted excessively simple views of man's ambiguous nature or because they have assumed the absolute necessity of single systems of belief and utter unity in the organization of motivations. I know of no modern or recent experiment in community, however elevated its articles of faith, which does not have totalitarian features or propensities.

Patterns of total integration, which frustrate men's stark pursuit of elemental joys, deny the evidence of men's variety, and abort or stereotype their mysterious groupings for creative novelties, are doomed to destruction. It makes no difference whether these schemes of total integration take the form of a vision of a cosmic brotherhood, a totalitarian race-nation-state, or a consecrated sectarian brotherhood within the pores or on the frontiers of a hateful civilization. These cautions are even relevant in a measure for those remarkable experiments in communitarianism which have recently grown either out of the Resistance movement in France and Italy or from pioneer undertakings in the new State of Israel. Anyone who wishes to discover for himself how difficult it is to reconcile individuality and social order, stability and progress, tradition and innovation, even under the most favorable auspices, has only to read recent writings by sympathetic participants and reporters concerning the Hutterites in the Dakotas, Montana, Canada, and Paraguay, and the experiment now being conducted by the high-minded American veterans in Macedonia, Georgia.

This much we know. No society can long survive if each of its members in the last analysis calls himself "I" and regards all others as a kind of inanimate "They." No society can long survive if each "I" is compelled to shout "We" in utter unanimity to the point of surrendering all sense of self and freedom. Eugene Zamiatin was prophetic in entitling his novel *We*. Throughout the world today, wherever disintegration is held in check by bureaucracy, men are compelled to cry "We." *Unanimism,* as we have said, the forcing of oneness in all ways of the spirit, is put in play to conceal *Inanimism,* the absence of spirit in society. It must be apparent that men wish neither to have to say "I" all of the time nor "We" all of the time, but that they are seeking blindly, without guidance or direction, for ways of achieving relationships which are mutualistic —ways which affirm the reality and validity of, yet seek to orchestrate the differences between, the *mine* and the *thine*.

The notion of subordination of personality to the collective will is a vicious and destructive illusion. A community which knows only a single person, a Super-Person, the "Big Brother," is a living death. A community, on the other hand, in which personality is compelled to act in utter isolation is certain to lose all sense of coherence.

May one not hope that schemes of reciprocity will arise in which, to paraphrase the writings of Martin Buber, the *I* and *thou* will echo to one another's integrity, where *ego* will not remain indifferent to or tyrannize over the *alter,* and the *alter* will not subordinate and constrain the *ego,* where men would be related as persons, rather than as objects. Such a society would inevitably be a personalist society, a community in which persons would strive to achieve *patterns of reciprocity* with one another. Such patterns of reciprocity simply cannot function where soulless bureaucracy prevails. It remains to be seen whether men will learn how to fashion multi-dimensional and mutualistic communities.

It hardly needs saying that such mutualistic communities will also be plagued by conflict. Conflict, as this essay has continued to insist, is at the very heart of life, resulting not simply from the malevolence of others, but also from the fact that men of the best will in the world seem to suffer incurably, so far as one can tell, from what William James called "a certain blindness" in perceiving the vitalities of others. Inevitably, the great American philosopher explained "each of us dichotomizes the Cosmos in a different place!" Men simply cannot live in one another's skin.

If all of this has been so well known for so long a time, how, we are again brought to ask, does one explain the persistence of the delusions which mark both the Communist and solipsistic schemes of social order? How account for the endless recurrence of the two contradictory ideas: the first, that utter coherence of men's wills and interests in all respects is the sole guarantee of community; the second, that the very notion of community is a fantasy and a snare, a restraint upon each person's inherent right to unfettered self-expression? To identify the sources of delusion so deep-rooted, we are not likely to go far astray if, in the spirit of Freud, we seek them in the nuclear experiences of men when they were children in the bosoms of their families. As earlier suggested, both of the myths under discussion bear evident traces of their derivation from nostalgic and regressive infantile reminiscences, if indeed, they do not go even farther back. It is not by accident that the collectivist dream has generally described itself as the *Brotherhood of Man,* whether or not under the Fatherhood of God. I am also saying that the image of a society founded upon the flight of the child from the home is also derived from infantile reminiscences. There is no child who has not longed for liberty, who has not suffered from arbitrary restraint, who has not longed for complete independence to do and live as he chooses. When this illusion becomes the cornerstone of social order, it produces utopian dreams of Anarchism and the not-so-utopian realities of "capitalist" society.

The family has, thus, been the breeding ground of the best and worst in human culture. It has been described as the source of Communism, at one and the same time the pattern and the justification for the Soviet Union's world-wide expansion. It would be just as true to describe the family as the spur to individualism for, as we have been taught by Freud, there is not a child who is not an anarchist and who will not rebel against the prepotent authority of the father. If the family has persisted for so many millennia and will persist so many more, it must be because it has managed to provide satisfactions and to perform functions which are not adequately perceived by either the Communists or the absolute individualists. The family is perhaps as significant an example of *mutualism* as Western society has known. It is evident that the secondary environment cannot, must not, be modeled too closely upon the image of a family, whether patriarchal or matriarchal, but it is also evident that a society which does not in some way embody the mutualistic strains of a family will simply not endure. I do not dare to speculate how we must proceed to develop the new patterns of integration so evidently needed for our time.

To summarize:

If our cosmos is to have a future, it must learn to do without its two most persistent illusions, apocalyptic cosmism and redemptive futurism. Mankind must cease to dream of building a utopian society which will transcend the bonds of time, the taint of place, and the limits of political society. It must learn to accept the fact that there never has been and never will be an undivided, wholly consecrated community here below or anywhere else in this cosmos where men are constituted as they are now and will, so far as one can now tell, forever be. It is the illusion of cosmism which persistently generates the illusion of futurism; it is the illusion of futurism which persistently generates the illusion of cosmism. Our culture stands now in peril of destruction because of the intensity and aggressiveness of those who entertain these intertwined illusions. Redemption will not come, as Reinhold Niebuhr has taught us to say, *in history* or *through history*. (I leave it to others to say whether redemption will occur *beyond history* or *outside history*.) There will be a *human* future only if an end is put to apocalyptic futurism.

May one anticipate that men in the Orient and the Occident alike can soon learn to live meaningful lives, without continually embracing over-mastering myths which drive them on relentlessly to the achievement of unobtainable goals? Is it to be expected that the millions can quickly learn to understand the difference between according tentative credence to rational possibilities of ideals and believing against all evidence in self-contradictory delusions? A historian of culture must at this time confess that there seems little likelihood that these desired eventualities will occur in the foreseeable future. Self-absorption in cosmic and futuristic myths is apparently too pleasurable an indulgence to forego. Dreams will long continue to provide headier thrills than the actual satisfactions of seemingly more primitive desires or the achievement of unspectacular rational goals.

In this impasse, one can only hope that strenuous efforts, ingenious contrivances, and fortunate auspices will all conspire to permit men to discover new ways of living without a surfeit of delusion. It is not suggested that illusions of all sorts can permanently be eliminated from all minds in all corners of the cosmos. Illusion is inexpugnable and the comforts which illusion provides are doubtless imperative for the very persistence of organized life. It would probably be the height of illusion to anticipate that all illusion could be eradicated. It is simply being suggested that the scope, the intensity, the range, the magnitude, the dynamism of illusion be checked in the interest of the preservation of human society. To repeat our refrain: *if the cosmos is to have a future, it must learn to do without apocalyptic futurism.*

With each passing day, the irony of our situation appears compounded geometrically by the fact that thinking men, in ever greater numbers, are now coming to perceive that the movement which now forces its futurism upon us is no better than a mass of hoary and discredited illusions.

We have been placed, as the poet reminds us, "on this isthmus of a middle state." And we must labor to discover ways of life appropriate to creatures so strangely situated. Long will be the way before we shall know how to be at one and the same time "sensual" and "spiritual"; "self-loving" and "selfless"; "cooperative" and "competitive"; earthy and unworldly;—dedicated to the ennoblement of life, but not blind to its evanescence; not waiting as fallen angels momentarily to be restored to a Paradise never intended for us nor supine and helpless in the face of fate as are the mindless microorganisms. Humanity has no chance to endure if society will not learn in this eleventh hour to become *humane*—to build fit habitations for humans—that is, natural persons, neither demons nor angels, but men with all their perfections and imperfections, wedded to time but not lost to eternity.

CONTEMPORARY CIVILIZATION: ITS MORAL COMMITMENT

3. IN PURSUIT OF A MORAL IDEAL

ERNST TROELTSCH

ERNST TROELTSCH (1865–1923) was one of the earliest sociologists to achieve academic respectability in Germany. He was a scholar of very broad achievements who might be classified as a historian, a theologian, or a philosopher as readily as he might be called a sociologist. In fact he served as professor of theology in two great German universities, Bonn and Heidelberg, and professor of philosophy at a third, Berlin. It was during the tenure of his professorship at Heidelberg (1894–1915) that he met Max Weber and was turned toward sociological studies. He carried these studies on, however, without abandoning his earlier interests and concerns, devoting himself now to the attempt to understand and interpret sociologically how theological and religious developments came to pass. More especially, in his major work in this field, *The Social Teachings of the Christian Churches* (first published in German in 1912 and in English in 1931), Troeltsch sought to discover, by sociological analysis of the history of Christianity, how far sociological factors could be held to determine the origin, development, and changes that had marked the course of that religion.

Philosophically, Troeltsch was a neo-Kantian who sought to assert that there is a specific religious content that is independent of and prior to experience. He found, however, that the more he attempted to justify the assertion of a religious *a priori,* the more he became aware of the religiously creative energies of social forces in history. The search for that which was uniquely religious and "given" in the nature of the universe led him dialectically back to a starting point in history, in time, rather than in the eternal, nontemporal, nonempirical. This philosophic insight he expressed in one of his most important books, *Christian Thought; Its History and Application* (first published in English in 1923 and in German in 1924).

In addition to his writings and his academic duties, in the last years of his life, after World War I, Troeltsch turned to politics. He was elected to the Prussian diet in 1919 and was named parliamentary undersecretary to the minister of education. From his position he influenced considerably, and in a consistently democratic direction, Prussian educational and religious policies.

The following selection is from the first of a series of two lectures on the theme *Christian Thought* which Troeltsch delivered, in German, at the University of London, in 1923 just before his death.

CHRISTIAN THOUGHT

THE MORALITY OF THE PERSONALITY AND OF THE CONSCIENCE

. . . [My] central theme concerns the relation between the endless movement of the stream of historical life and the need of the human mind to limit and to shape it by means of fixed standards. This is a question which arose for me in my early adult life in the domain of religious philosophy and theology, where not only historical and philosophical criticism, but, above all, the historical entanglements and the historical variability of Christianity so greatly increase the difficulty of finding firm principles for the living present. But the question very soon proved itself to be much more general than this. The same problem exists for the sum of all standards in general, and not only for the standards of the religious life in particular. In the State, in Society and in Economics, and also in Science and in Art, the same problem reappears. The so-called natural standards are in no way more firmly fixed than the standards which we call supernatural; and all attempts to fix the one from the side of the other are illusory from whichever side we may care to start our labor. And, over and above all this, the entire question is by no means the raising of a merely personal problem; it is a problem brought home to us by the entire situation of our times. It is the general mind of our times which finds itself shaken to its depths and in a state of change in almost every direction; and all this commotion is accompanied throughout by an almost alarming perspicacity in historical reflection and comparison. It is due to this position of affairs that considerations of an historical-philosophical kind again play the part to-day which they did before and after the French Revolution—in the age of Rousseau, Voltaire, and Herder, and again in the age of Hegel and of Comte.

Meanwhile, however, the historical horizon has become very much wider both in space and in time, and our knowledge of the past has become much more differentiated, more exact, and more objective. Our contemporary literature is full of comparative and evolutionary considerations varying from primitive man in the Ice Age down to the most modern European and Asiatic civilization, and from Australia and Central Africa to Europe, America, and Eastern Asia. The immense variety and movement apparent in this gigantic body of material for our historical comparisons at first profoundly interested us and broadened our minds, so long as it all could be easily comprised within the series of an evolutionary progress, and so long as our own

This selection has been reprinted from Ernst Troeltsch, *Christian Thought,* University of London Press, Ltd., London, 1923 (pp. 39–68), by permission of the publisher.

position, as the summit of this progress, remained beyond doubt. But the more difficult the construction of such an evolutionary series finally became, in the increasing exactitude of research, and the more our own proud present revealed alarming cleavages and gaps, the more did the problem I have attempted to indicate obtrude itself, both theoretically and practically, in a manner which compelled attention and evoked anxiety. The idea of a humane European order, expressing itself in the organization of the states and the societies appertaining to it, was dissolved by criticism, and gave way to all sorts of plans for the distant future, or to pessimism, or to purely materialist appreciation of interests which can only be realized by violence. Nietzsche spoke of the irruption of European nihilism, and the great Russian novelists turned away with horror from the West in its decomposition, the essence of which they conceived to be Criticism, Psychology, Evolution, and finally, despair of what is called Progress.

Behind all this lie the problems of the Philosophy of History—the problems of controlling and dominating the immense stream of historical life, a stream which grows continually more rapid and more extended, and not merely of constructing theoretically its successive stages, and its laws of movement. But this means, in other words, that History requires us to come to grips with the idea of an abiding system of values which shall give us our standards, even though every such system seems always to be undermined and washed away by this stream. But such a system of values is nothing else than what we call, in other words, the system of Ethics. Hence the great question is: what is the rôle and the significance of the system of Ethics for the great task of controlling and damming the historical movement, which, in itself, is simply boundless? And this is the question on which I should like to speak . . . [now].

I . . . [assume] in my [readers] a knowledge of the nature of modern historico-critical inquiry, and a sense of the consequences and dangers pertaining to such inquiry. This is perhaps, here in England, less intensively at work than it is amongst us on the Continent; and yet here also, as the religious, political, and social unrests and argumentations show, it is sufficiently strong not to find itself overcome any longer by simple appeals to tradition, custom, and political propriety. At bottom we are all, in our every fibre, aware of Historical Relativism; and there is no need, therefore, of any closer elucidation of its origin, nature, and effect. The most living problem of actual life consists in the question whether, and how far, a conceptually assured and clarified Ethic can master and limit this Historical Relativism.

Yet we must admit that, in the domain of Ethics, in its present form, the same problems which exist elsewhere recur in somewhat different shapes; and, indeed, further problems appear which arise from the inner nature and difficulty of the ethical idea itself.

The entire domain of the ethical standards has itself been drawn, by Modern Psychology, by Historical Relativism, and by Evolutionism, into the flow of things, and been made part and parcel of this Historicism. The impulse of modern-minded men, apparently all-powerful, towards simplification and deductions of a highly monistic type, has led to the derivation of the ethical standards themselves from instincts which are either pre-ethical or not yet ethical in character, just as Darwinism, enlarged into a philosophy, has attempted to derive apparently firm and purposive forms from crossings between the purposeless and accidental. After David Hume and Adam Smith had begun to explain the origin of the illusion of objective moral commands in a suggestive and acute manner, the proofs furnished by Sociology of the dependence of the ethical standards on the varying needs of society and the relations between Capital and Labor seemed definitely to complete this monistic explanation and derivation. This was the origin of Utilitarianism and Ethical Empiricism, in its numerous forms, though in the end it ceased to be able to furnish a foundation for any abiding system of Morality, and led to a general moral scepticism or to a mere Practicism or Pragmatism.

But it is not these questions which I would here consider. These questions stand or fall with the general theory of a Monistic Empiricism, which has taken it into its head to reduce all standards to accidents of the psychological mechanism, and to trace back all the imperative laws of first principles to natural, psycho-logical, or psycho-physical laws of the stream of consciousness, and this though in all other possible respects the world remains full of dualisms and pluralisms. Against this Monistic Empiricism we can but advance the old line of thought which Plato already advanced against the Sophists and Naturalists—a line of thought formulated afresh in modern times, more particularly by Kant, but already advanced before his time, in England by the school of Reid against the school of Hume and in France by Descartes against the Sceptics. Logically all moral, juristic, and aesthetic principles are and remain principles which oppose themselves to the flow of the psycho-logical determinist mechanism, and derive their right and their necessity from their significance and content, quite independently of their origin in the psychological concatenation. Not the "how?" of their genesis but the "that" of their objectively significant contents and of their logical connections is here decisive. This applies to all the domains concerned with standards, and therefore to the moral domain also. How the stream of consciousness can make such a continuous severance of itself into genetically explicable mechanisms and principles which themselves furnish their authority by their objectively significant contents—that is a further question, but it can alter nothing in the actual facts, which are entirely clear and decisive for the very possibility of all thinking.

It is not at this point that the problem lies. It lies in the fact that the principles which arise in this way are still also subject on their part to deep historical changes, and that they themselves are anything but simple, but, on the contrary, full of an interior tension and distinctly complex. The question of the origin of this fact would lead us too far into the further question of the interior developments of the spirit and all its incursions into the mere psychic life; but that is a metaphysical question and one which is perhaps incapable of explanation. I desire here to confine myself simply to the position of the facts as they lie before us; to accept the historical conditionality and complexity of the standards simply as a fact; and to analyse it only with the object of discovering how, in these circumstances, the principle which is at the same time a standard can nevertheless be attained for any and every present. And further I would desire, in following this procedure, to return from the broad and great conception of the standard principles in general to the particular ethical principles which were described in the beginning. The comparison of these ethical principles with the logical principles in which the autonomous independence of the postulate attains its greatest clearness is, after all, only a comparison. And although Kant has been particularly successful in making clear the ethical principles by means of this comparison, he has nevertheless pushed this comparison too far and approximated the ethical too closely to the logical. In reality we must see to it that, after this comparison has rendered all the services of which it is capable for the cognition of the autonomy which also belongs to the ethical, our attention is turned to the ethical phenomenon in its peculiarity.

Now the peculiarity of the ethical phenomenon consists in a quite extraordinary complexity of the ethical consciousness, the standards of which flow together from very different sources and directions, and the tensions within which, produced by these very differences, have always to be included together anew in a single final result. True, the logical also is not as simple and as free from tension as it appears to the man in the street. General Formal Logic, the Empirical Logic of the Sciences of Nature, and finally the Logic of Philosophy which brings the Many and their contradictions to unity, all arise from different sources and different directions of thought; and the drawing of them all together into a unity of outlook forms the eternal and special difficulty of all Philosophy. But these divisions of logical thought have nothing to do with the divisions within ethical thought, and they do not of themselves explain the complexities of the latter. In any case this is true for the facts which lie immediately to hand—facts which we have to analyse by a direct confrontation. If we follow this procedure, the decisive conclusion is the complexity of the Ethical Consciousness. This complexity is confirmed by every glance at experience and at historical reality; it is the real reason why a Science of Ethics is so immensely difficult, and why it has led less than all the other philosophical sciences, with the possible exception of Aesthetics, to abiding results and to general recognition. It is what we find mirrored, too, in the oppositions and contradictions between the ethical systems themselves; for they by no means spring only from a distinction between the empirical and the categorical derivation of the ethical standards, but arise quite as much from the internal objective tensions and complexities of Ethical Thought itself. True, this second side of the ethical problem has always attracted less notice than the first, which resounds in almost the entire literature of Ethics, from the time of the Greeks down to ourselves. This springs spontaneously from the natural impulse of Ethics to reach a single form of standard. But in itself the second series of differences is the more important, and in reality it lies far more at the root of the differences between the historical systems of Ethics, though it must be confessed that this has seldom been apprehended by their exponents.

Let us first attempt to draw out of this complex fabric the thread which lies most clearly before our eyes and promises to lead us more securely than any other to our end, to a universal and objective determination of the ethical standard.

This thread consists in the determinations of what we call Conscience; in the general moral demands of the traditional doctrine of the virtues and the duties; in the demands of personal moral dignity, of strength of character and self-conquest on the one hand, and of justice, benevolence, and public spirit on the other. We have thus to do with the old virtues, elaborated by the Socratic school and more precisely fixed by the Stoics, which later, under the influence of Christianity, appear more as divine demands and hence as duties. These are, in reality, the general formal standards which proceed from the nature of the Moral Consciousness. But if we are determined to deduce them more precisely from this consciousness, we shall not be able, like the most severe of the modern ethical thinkers, to deduce them simply from the universality and objectivity of the Moral Reason, or only and immediately from the conception of a categorical imperative. We shall have to consider that Ethics is an action; that all action is a realization of ends; and, therefore, that the unity of Ethics too can only be deduced from the end, as indeed even Kant finally realized in some of his incidental and auxiliary thinking. Now, the end of moral action which first appears in an obvious manner is the attainment and the defense of a free personality, which has its foundations in itself and possesses a certain unity of its own. The idea of personality is the decisive idea. Out of the flux and confusion of the life of the instincts, the unity and compactness of personality has first to be created and acquired.

No man is born a personality; everyone has first to make himself into a personality by obedience towards another instinct, which leads to unity and homogeneity. Freedom and creation constitute the secret of personality, but this self-creation of personality is, of course, no absolute creation in us finite creatures who emerge from the stream of life and consciousness. It is a creation which takes place in obedience and in devotion to an attraction towards emancipation from merely natural and accidental determination—an attraction to the imperative "ought" which is analogous to the attraction towards logical truth and correctness, and arises, like the latter, from the deeper spiritual levels of our being. So far it is a purely formal aim of independence from mere fate, and of self-determination from within, through the ideal of an internal unity and clarity of our being, which ought to be, and obliges us. It is a distinct and independent question what are to be the concrete single ends by which certain qualities are to be acquired that will strengthen and bring out the general independence. Our further inquiry will have to occupy itself with this further question, and it is from this point of view that the complexity of Ethics will appear in its fullest light. Hitherto this second question has not appeared upon our horizon; but, as the price for this simplicity of outlook, we have only to do with the purely formal end, with the unity, centrality, homogeneity, consistency and purity of intention of the personality, all considered as characteristics which ought to exist.

From this end or aim which ought to exist the particular demands of Ethics can be derived without difficulty as soon as we consider that, in the first place, this personality has to develop itself in a double direction, in a particular demeanor towards itself, and in a particular demeanor towards its neighbor; and that, in the second place, the characteristic of personality applies as a demand made not only of single men but also of communities, so that not only individual but also corporate personalities are required. But the demands, purely formal as they are in this nature, which arise in these several directions, can attain so great an independence as single demands that it is possible to forget, in consequence, the connection of them all with the fundamental end contained in the sense of obligation generally, and again the fact that this general end is intrinsically related to a concrete cultural subject-matter in which it has had to find the stuff for its activity. Such forgetfulness has often enough occurred, both practically and theoretically; and whenever it occurs the particular commandments each appear as something absolute, as something which is its own guarantee, whilst, in reality, they are only that through their connection with the general imperative on the one hand and with the particular subject-matter of action on the other.

As regards the dependence of the particular commandments upon the general commandment, ethical demeanor divides itself, in consequence of this connection, into duties towards oneself and duties towards one's neighbor, as traditional morality, formally perhaps somewhat offensively, but quite rightly as concerns the content, formulates its character. Action in regard to our own self demands first of all strict veracity or unison with oneself, the energy and the strength of character which expresses itself in an interconnected moral life, and the disposition which is directed to inner moral values in contradiction to all and every eudaemonism: in a word, the elaboration and the persistent defense of moral dignity. In regard to one's neighbor, moral action aims at the conception and the treatment of this neighbor as not only a means but, at the same time, an end in himself, who, precisely like ourselves, possesses or is called to the dignity of a human being. In this celebrated Kantian phrase, all that is essential is already expressed. In it is contained more especially the demand of justice—the justice which contemplates life and things, not only from its own standpoint, but also from the standpoint of other men, and, at the same time, is directed towards the recognition and the advancement of the moral dignity of the neighbor. This recognition is the justice which everywhere establishes a certain proportion, corresponding to the whole ethical value of the several persons, and allots their place in it according to the circumstances—to honor or loyal obedience, to gratitude or to blame, to resistance or to the influence of the educator. In so far as this justice is joy in the moral dignity of one's neighbor, or is education and aid brought to some incipient moral worth, it becomes kindness; and from this connection with justice even kindness and benevolence become a duty, which persists so long as we are not obliged to convince ourselves of the opposite and of the impossibility of improving our neighbor. All further moral theories and lists of the virtues and the duties, such as are dear to ancient and modern moralists, are only further elaborations of these simple fundamental ideas, and may be left untouched here.

As concerns the second kind of personality, the group, all the determinations of the morality of solidarity belong to it—a morality in which the natural consciousness of the group is transfigured into an ethically founded devotion to a moral, super-individual Whole. And in such a transfiguration it is, in the first instance, presupposed that this Whole itself—this family, tribe, class, corporation, nation, humanity—is no mere result of blood, or of nature, or of instincts and habits, but needs to be considered and felt as a community in certain ethical values, a community which ought to be; it is presupposed, in a word, that these several Wholes should not only be considered to exist, but should also really exist, as Wholes. The group, starting from its natural basis, is thus to develop into a special moral community through the union and inter-connection of its members; and the members are to feel their devotion to this community, not merely as an instinct of nature or of habit, but as a duty in which the individual grows to a height above himself, even to the sacrifice of himself for the Whole when that becomes necessary. We have here the overcoming of the selfishness of the group, a selfishness which is in no way more venerable, though it is certainly more natural, than the selfishness of the individual: it is the overcoming of the herd-instinct or the mere co-operation of interests. Such a transfiguration is not possible without a continuous criticism of the unity of the group and a continuous moral ennobling of it. Nor is it possible, again, to find the justification for the sacrifice and renunciation which are thus required in the advantage which the individual is to gain thereby; it can only be found in the obligation of the Whole to purity and dignity.

But wherein the ethical value of the group itself consists, and how it can be ennobled and spiritualized from within itself—that is still another question, which cannot yet be answered on the basis of these purely formal presuppositions, and leads to further ethical questions which must be answered in . . . [due course]. At this point we need only add that the same rules apply to the relations of the groups, or collective personalities, towards each other, as apply to the relations of single persons with one another. Moral regulation is certainly much more difficult of accomplishment for a group than it is for individuals, because the complexity of the relations and the distribution of responsibility are greater, and indeed the moralizing of the group in general is very much more difficult than the moralizing of individual men; but in principle we have to do with the same demands of justice and of kindness, of recognition and of education, of respect and of support. At this point the moral demand rises to the ideal of Humanity—of a community of all mankind in which the national groups are morally bound to each other and depend upon each other in the same way as the single social groups within the several nations. This is what constitutes the moral conception or ideal of Humanity, which is something different from the anthropological or geographical conception of the populations of the globe and the presumable relationship in blood of all creatures that bear the face of man. All these demands which are thus applied to group personalities are necessary consequences of the fundamental principle of Formal Ethics, as soon as this principle comes to be pressed to its last consequences. Hence these doctrines continually recur in all ethical systems as the doctrines of Humanity, of the Love of Mankind, of International Justice, of the Rights of Man, and of Progress. Ever since the age of the Stoics extended the horizon of Ethics in principle beyond the national range, these doctrines have really constituted moral demands of a universal validity, which have passed into Christian ideas of the morality of peoples and, again, into modern ideas of humanity and of progress towards moral purification and unity. But we have always to bear in mind that it is not simply men and groups, as so many natural beings, with which we have to do, but men and groups as rational beings and as personalities which have first to produce themselves by free acts of determination.

Is it, then, possible, and may we expect, that the historical stream of life can be defined and shaped for us in the light of these ideas which follow from the formal nature of moral obligation? Many moralists demand and maintain it: they postulate only, as its condition, that necessary self-conquest and that indispensable radicalism by which mere Nature and her instinctive confused egoism must be brought under the yoke. Others regard it as impossible; and they accordingly reject in their entirety the very assumptions of such a mental structure, which is contradicted, as they believe, by the totally different character of the actual process of reality.

It cannot be denied that the relation of these mental structures to actual history presents a difficult problem.

In the first place, we have to put to ourselves the question, "Do these demands, which spring from the timeless nature of obligation or reason, and are therefore perfectly objective, universal, and identical with reason itself—do they really and actually appear in history itself so universally and originally as on this theory they are bound to do?" In facing this question we can leave entirely out of account the extent of their realization, and even the possibility or impossibility of their realization; but in any case they must be universally diffused as demands (which, whether realized or no, are actually made).

An answer to the question would carry us far into evolutionary and sociological investigations, and especially into extremely difficult investigations of primitive man and his possible survivals and analogies. Such investigations are impossible in this connection; and they are also unnecessary. Reason, and the idea of personality—which is closely connected with reason —is still in process of growth, disengaging itself everywhere, even yet, from its natural basis; climbing upward from the preparatory stage of the natural life of instinct; and seeking to deliver itself from that stage, as it recognizes its opposition to it, in order to achieve its own independence. So far as its content is concerned, it is a matter of indifference when, where, and how this is done. This content, whenever it has grasped its own independence, proceeds to grow by its own independence, proceeds to grow by its own purely rational laws, and ceases to be determined by psychological factors. Such a "conversion" or "break through" must have happened in innumerable cases and places; and even to-day, in spite of all tradition and education, it must constantly happen afresh whenever an independent moral person, single or collective, is to burst its sheath. Even in regard to the primitive, investigation is steadily showing, with an ever-growing force, that moral demands of this order have actually developed themselves everywhere, in a greater or less degree of purity and perfection, to constitute the internal morality of exclusive groups. Regard for character, honesty, self-control, justice, and benevolence is a quality which naturally grows first within narrow groups, depending on personal intercourse and ready community of sentiment; and it is mixed with every possible religious and sociological motive. It is only in such groups that we find dominant that atmosphere of mutual confidence in which these moral demands can grow and be obeyed. Externally, and in the struggle of groups, there reigns an atmosphere of mistrust, in which, in the main, it is only the morality of courage, of group-solidarity, and, at best, of fidelity to engagements which can arise. Only when groups are very highly developed are they able to knit bonds of union which transcend the antagonism of groups, nations, and races—bonds which are woven of the stuff of pure humanity, and made by the extension of internal to international morality. Here again, when this point has been reached, the virtues and the duties already mentioned are constantly reappearing as decisive. Even yet, however, it is not so much groups themselves as it is particular individuals, of an advanced thought and an inward enlightenment, who are united and controlled by this morality of personality. Even to-day groups still remain, for the most part, in an atmosphere of mistrust and struggle for existence, according to the sociological law that masses find their bond of cohesion more readily in material interests and elementary passions than in the higher spiritual purposes and values. This defect has been to some extent remedied, but it has by no means been removed, by the great universal religions, by scientific enlightenment, by the interchange of philosophic thought, and by humanized international law. In the last few years we have ourselves had tragic experience of its existence.

I conclude that it is not the actual diffusion, or non-diffusion, of this universal morality which is the essential problem; it is the question of its real practicability. Now this morality is always, to begin with, a controlling and conquering of mere nature, from which it springs, but with which it struggles. In its essence it is a perpetual struggle and a perpetual creation. The very conception of this morality means that it can never be simply victorious. Victory would be the end of struggle and freedom: it would be the absolute and effortless necessity of the good and of reason; and that is something which we cannot picture to ourselves. And this is the reason why the religious always transcends the moral: why the highest ideal is elevated to an incomprehensible other-world of Love or to a passionless supra-moral peace of the spirit. But it is not only this essential element of struggle in all moral life which makes it impossible to disengage the moral from its admixture of natural instincts and natural needs, and which must always prevent its full realization. There is another reason. These instincts and needs have, and they continue to maintain, their own independent justification in the nature of man, as it struggles for room, for food, for life, for more life; and in man's earthly life they can never be completely excluded or rationally organized. The conflict between Nature and Morality, between the demands of subsistence and the shaping of moral personality, can never be completely solved. The most advanced theories which assume such a solution—the theories of communism and socialism—are consequently bound to assume two miracles: the miracle of a technique which puts Nature completely and adequately at the service of man, and which must include, as part of itself, the technique of proper regulation of the numbers of the population; and the miracle of a new education, which enthrones Reason and Morality, alike in the relations of individuals and of groups, completely above the natural turmoil of instincts and the tendency towards the struggle for existence. And both of these miracles are impossible even for the boldest of hopes. The practical attempts at the realization of such ideals have hitherto always shown that provision for natural necessities cannot be organized in this fashion; that technique fails utterly, and mass-starvation begins; that the tendency towards the struggle for existence must necessarily be diverted to some external outlet; and that fresh wars thus arise out of the gospel of peace. That is the lesson both of the French and Russian Revolutions.

In these circumstances there is no hope at all left for the realization of the moral idea of humanity by finally and completely damming and canalizing the stream of historical life through a morality which is timelessly valid and transcends history. Struggle remains to all eternity—struggle and yet again struggle—as the lot of the moral here on earth. Man is, and always will be, at once a natural and a rational being. Reconciliation can only be attained by a compromise which has always to be made afresh—a compromise which every agent must seek on his own account and at his own peril; a compromise which must always be especially difficult and involved in politics and the dealings of States with one another. The only possible line of action must be that of always realizing ethical purposes *as far as possible;* of enlisting in their services, in given circumstances, powerful natural instincts; and, in other circumstances, of leaving free play to natural forces which we cannot alter, and which perhaps we can only hope to capture again afterwards. What gives responsibility and ethical quality to our actions is just that, in a given situation, we undertake to find the right way *to the best of our knowledge and conscience,* and that we voluntarily make ourselves answerable for solving the conflict between Nature and Reason. The conformity of the moral with conviction, emphasized by Kant in his excessively idealistic Rationalism, does not consist in the pure intention of reasonableness—that may be present, and yet we may leave the actual process of action to take care of itself, and warm ourselves at our own virtue—but in the will to responsibility and decision, where the compromise between Nature and Reason is struck according to the circumstances of the moment. This is the goodwill which is in question, and not the abstract obedience to reason of the Stoics. . . . There are certainly cases in which any compromise would be immoral. But they are rare; and they always belong to the sphere of private and personal life. From the particularly complicated relations of public life it has never been possible to eliminate compromise utterly.

If this be the case, our main question in regard to the regulation of historic life by this morality can no longer be simply answered by a Yes or No. Historical Relativism can and must be limited from this point of view. It does not lead, and the knowledge of it does not lead, to a fundamental Amoralism. But the act of limitation itself is always and in every case an act which differs according to situation and circumstances, maturity of development and difficulties of life. It is a relative act, which only realizes absolute standards as far as possible, and bears in its bosom its own absolute quality only in the form of decision by the personal conscience and resolution. In this act or resolution account ought to be taken of the moral laws to the fullest possible extent. We must not make it easy or comfortable for ourselves; and in this respect, an advance may very well be both possible and desirable for humanity. In the act of decision we may thus certainly trace a factor of fundamental definition and precision of direction, but not a timeless, eternally valid, abstract programme, in the light of which, at any point, on the assumption of goodwill, the problem of historical perplexities can be solved, or which, again, as the final triumph of progress, can, in any conceivable future, perfectly organize the whole of humanity.

This serious recognition must be opposed to all moralizing abstraction about the philosophy of history. Even in this sphere, where we are dealing with the most universal, the most abstract, and the clearest factors of the ethical consciousness, we must confess that there is no possibility of any limitation of the historical stream of life which is finally valid. Limitation in this direction is much more readily possible for individuals than for groups, and even then the limitation remains an act of compromise, which is one with conscience. It is not for nothing that religion, which everywhere transcends all morality, teaches us that the pure will and devotion to an ideal world is sufficient for righteousness, and that life itself remains sinful—a mixture, that is to say, of nature and the divine life. Justification by faith is only a specifically religious expression for this universal relation of things. It is not for nothing that the religious idea places the individual, his decision and his salvation, in the foreground. He alone transcends history; and the inward union of the devout with one another is a heavenly object of longing or a monastic order, while it is only the ever-recurring mixture of light and darkness which suits earthly history. The kingdom of God, just because it transcends history, cannot limit or shape history. Earthly history remains the foundation and the presupposition of the final personal decision and sanctification; but in itself it goes on its way as a mixture of reason and natural instinct, and it can never be bound in any bonds except in a relative degree and for a temporary space.

JOSIAH ROYCE

A CALIFORNIAN who studied philosophy at Johns Hopkins and in imperial Germany, Josiah Royce (1855–1916) was an able, systematic exponent of the stern doctrine of "duty for duty's sake" in terms of absolute idealism. In one of his earliest essays, entitled "The Decay of Earnestness," written in California just before coming to Harvard, Royce challenged the reader thus: "Hast thou received into thy heart any ideal?" He continued with the plea: "Send us a thinker that can show us just what life is most worthy of our toil, just what makes man's destiny more than poor and comic, just what is the ideal we ought to serve." Himself an heir of Calvinism, but cut off from formal religion (he once explained that he did not attend church because "I might get a bias"), Royce wrote for the earnest, troubled folk of his generation who had strayed from orthodoxy but who still craved the sort of meaning and significance in life which religion had formerly supplied.

For his answer, Royce turned to an ancient tradition, that of the Christian golden rule and the Kantian categorical imperative, which he restated (in *The Religious Aspect of Philosophy,* 1885) as "insofar as in thee lies, act as if thou wert at once thy neighbor and thyself. Treat these two lives as one life." It is the task of ethics to point the way to a complete harmonizing of conflicting wills in the service of all sorts of "causes" which bring men together in such fields as science, art, religion, business, and politics. That total unification is made possible, in Royce's view, only because there is an underlying unity in nature: all the clashing struggles of men are ultimately "one life," one being, and one mind, the Absolute Moral Will.

As the reflective person looks at the conflicts of wills all around him, however, he naturally inclines toward ethical skepticism, and even toward pessimism. But it is Royce's burning conviction that a sufficiently intense study of this diversity will bring any resolute thinker into the safe harbor of the Absolute. This explains one of his most famous later sayings: "Pessimism is often regarded with horror, yet an earnest pessimist would be better than a sluggard of any creed."

Central to Royce's thinking was his concept of loyalty. In his *The Philosophy of Loyalty* (1908) Royce examined the nature of unifying "causes," and concluded that their key characteristic is "the good old Anglo-Saxon concept of loyalty." To be loyal to any cause is good, but any particular cause is "subjective." The only cause that is free from arbitrariness is that of loyalty itself. Hence the cause most worthy of loyalty is "loyalty to loyalty." The supreme ethical imperative is "Be loyal to loyalty." Act, in other words, so that by your action there is an increase in the amount of loyalty in the world.

Royce specified this idea of loyalty in many contexts. Thus in the series of lectures which he delivered at Lake Forest College, Illinois, in 1911, under the auspices of the William Bross Foundation, from the published version of which, *The Sources of Religious Insight* (1914), the following selection has been made, this concept was considered as a prime source of insight into fundamental religious attitudes.

THE SOURCES OF RELIGIOUS INSIGHT

V. THE RELIGION OF LOYALTY

... Our moral interests have a development which, in all its higher phases, runs at least parallel to the development of our religious interests, even in cases where the two sorts of interests seem to clash. The moral problems arise through certain interactions that take place between our individual and our social experience. The reason reviews these interactions and takes interest in unifying our plan of life. The will is always, from the very nature of the case, concerned in the questions that here arise. For whatever else morality is, it is certain that your morality has to do with your conduct, and that moral goodness cannot be yours unless your will itself is good. Wealth might come to you as a mere gift of fortune. Pleasure might be brought to you from without, so far as you have the mere capacity for pleasure. The same might appear to be true even in case of salvation, if, indeed, salvation is wholly due to saving grace. But moral goodness, if you can get it at all, requires your active cooperation. You can earn it only in case you do something to possess it. Its motto reads: "*Erwirb es um es zu besitzen.*" [1]

Therefore the moral question always takes the form of asking: What am I to do? The first contribution to the answer is furnished, upon all levels of our self-consciousness, by our individual experience. And one apparently simple teaching that we get from this source may be stated in a maxim which wayward people often insist upon, but which only the very highest type of morality can rationally interpret: "I am to do what I choose, in case only I know what I choose and am able to do it." From this point of view, my only limitations, at first sight, seem to be those set for me by my physical weakness. There are many things that, if I had the power, I should or might choose to do. But since I frequently cannot accomplish my will, I must learn to limit myself to what I can carry out. So far, I say, our individual experience, if taken as our sole moral guide, seems at first to point out the way.

---

[1] [*Earn it so as to possess it.*]

But this first teaching of our individual experience is by no means so simple as it seems. For the question arises: What is it, on the whole, that I choose to do? . . . [Each] of us is by nature so full of caprices and of various aims, that, left to ourselves, we live not only narrowly but inconsistently. Hence we spend much of our lives in finding out, after the fact, that what we chose to do at one moment of our lives has hopelessly thwarted what we intended to do at some other moment. Self-will then, left to itself means self-defeat. That is the lesson of life. And the question: What is it that, on the whole, I would choose to do if I had the power? is a question that individual experience, taken by itself, never answers in any steadily consistent way. Therefore, as we all sooner or later come to see, one of our most persistent limitations is *not* our physical weakness to accomplish what we choose, but our incapacity, when left to ourselves, to find out what it is that we propose and really choose to do. Therefore, just because individual experience, taken by itself, never gives steady guidance, we have to look elsewhere for a rule.

The question: What am I to do? is never in practice answered without consulting, more or less persistently, our social experience. Being what we are, naturally gregarious, imitative, and, when trained, conventional creatures, who, indeed, often fight with our kind, but who also love our kind, who not only cannot bear to be too much alone, but are simply helpless when wholly isolated from our fellows (unless we have already learned in their company the very arts that we may be able to use while we are alone), we can give no answer to the question: What is to be my choice? without pretty constantly consulting our social interests. And these interests are indeed plentiful and absorbing. But they too are naturally conflicting. And so, taken as they come, they give us no rule of life.

To be sure, the social will in general says to us: "Live with your fellows, for you cannot do without them. Learn from them how to live; for you have to live more or less in their way. Imitate them, co-operate with them, at least enough to win such ideas as will help you to know what you want and such skill as will make you best able to accomplish whatever, in view of your social training, you are led to choose. Do not oppose them too much, for they are many, and, if stirred up against you, can easily destroy you. Conform, then, to their will enough to get power to have your own way."

And so far our ordinary social will gives us more or less consistent counsel. But beyond such really rather barren advice (the counsel of an inane worldly prudence), our social experience, as it daily comes to us, has no single ideal to furnish, no actually universal rules to lay down. For, as I go about in social relations, sometimes I love my fellows and sometimes I feel antipathy for them. Sometimes I am full of pity for their woes and long to help them. Sometimes they are my rivals; and I then naturally try to crush them. There is thus no one social tendency that, as it comes to us in the course of our ordinary social experience, gives us sufficient guidance to tell us how to escape self-defeat. For my love and pity war with my social greed and with my rivalries. I am so far left to my chaos.

Thus, then, if I sum up my position, I indeed propose to do what I choose, in so far as I am able, and in so far as I can find out what it is that I choose and can avoid thwarting myself by my own choices. And the art of learning how to choose, and what to choose, and how to carry out my will, is for me, since I am gregarious, imitative, and conventionalised, a social art. But, on the other hand, no social art that I ordinarily learn is sufficient either to teach me my whole purpose in life, or to make a consistent self of me, or to lead me out of that chaos of self-thwarting efforts wherein so many men pass their lives.

. . . How real and how confused this chaos is, the daily record of certain aspects of the ordinary social life of men which you see in each morning's newspaper may serve to illustrate. These princes and peoples, these rebels and executioners, these strikers and employers, these lovers and murderers, these traders and bankrupts, these who seem for the moment to triumph and these who just now appear to be ground under the opponent's or the oppressor's heel, what arts of living were they and are they all following? Well, each in his way appears to have been choosing to have his own will; yet each, being a social creature, had learned from his fellows all his vain little arts of life. Each loved some of his fellows and was the rival of others. Each had his standards of living, standards due to some more or less accidental and unstable union of all the motives thus barely suggested. The news of the day tells you how some of these won their aims, for the moment, while others were thwarted. When I asked you to note, and what the reason of every man in his more enlightened moments shows him, is that each of these who at any moment was thwarted, precisely in so far as he had any will of his own at all, was defeated not only by his fellows, but by himself. For this special will of his was some caprice not large enough to meet his own ends. The career, for instance, of that man who failed in love or in business or in politics is wrecked. His reputation is lost. Well, it was his will, as a social being, to aim at just such a career and to value just that sort of reputation. Had he chosen to be a hermit, or a saint, or a Stoic, what would just such a career and such a reputation have been to him? How could he have lost unless he had sought? And his failure, to what was it due? No doubt to some choice of his own quite as much as to his rival's skill. He wanted freedom to carry on his own speculations. He got that freedom and lost his fortune. He wanted to be free to choose whom and how to love. He had his way and defeated his own aim. He chose to follow his ambitions. They have led him where he is.

Such are perfectly reasonable reflections upon the course of ordinary social conflicts. . . . [And] now this type of reflection appears as aiming to lead us to some practical rule for guiding our active life. For our attention is now fixed . . . on a rule for doing something in accordance with our own true will. This rule is, negatively stated, the following: Do *not* seek, either in your individual self as you are or in your social experience as it comes, for the whole truth either about what your own will is or about how you can get your aims. For if you confine yourself to such sources of moral insight, you will go on thwarting yourself quite as genuinely, even if by good luck, not quite as scandalously, as the bankrupt speculators and the strikers and the outcast oppressors, and the politicians and the murderers, and the deposed monarchs and the defeated revolutionists, of whom you read in the newspapers, have thwarted both their individual and their social will. In brief: Put not your trust in caprices, either individual or social. On the positive side, the rule here in question is: In order to find out what is your true choice, and how you can live without thwarting yourself, make your *principle* of life such that whatever fortune besets you, you can inwardly say: "I have not really failed, for I have acted as I intended, and also as I still intend to act, and have had my will whatever the consequences that fortune has brought to me, or however my momentary mood happens to change, or however this or that social caprice leads men to love or to despise me." Such is the moral insight that the first use of your reason, in thus reviewing life, suggests. Or, as the moral common-sense of the wise has often stated the rule here in question: So act that, upon any calm review of the sense of your individual and of your social life, you shall never have ground to regret the principle of your action, never have ground to say: "By choosing thus I thwarted my own will."

As you hear these statements, I hope that, reduced to their very lowest terms: *"So act as never to have reason to regret the principle of your action,"* they express a sort of counsel for life which is not strange to common-sense, even if it has received an abstract expression in the famous ethical philosophy of Kant. Only, as you will rightly insist, this counsel is indeed a seemingly hopeless counsel of perfection when it is addressed to the natural man, who merely has taken his instincts as he found them developing, and his social world as he has felt it fascinating or disturbing him, and who has then stumbled on, more or less prudently and obstinately trying to find out what it really is that he wants to do in life. Such a man will cry out: "But how shall I discover a principle of life such that, if I hold thereto, I shall never, upon any reasonable survey of life, regret following that principle?"

Here at length let life itself answer the question. As I was preparing these very words, and thinking what new instance to choose, in order to illustrate afresh the very principle that I have in mind, the newspaper of the day, side by side with its usual chronicle of unreason and disaster, reported the approaching end of a public servant. This public servant was Ida Lewis, who for fifty years was the official keeper of the Lime Rock lighthouse in Narragansett Bay. She had been known for more than fifty years for her early and later often-repeated heroism as a life-saver. And now she was at last on her death-bed. She has since died. I know nothing of her career but what public reports have told. So far as her duty required her at her post, she kept her light burning through all the nights and the storms of those many years. She saved, in all, upon various occasions, eighteen lives of those who were in danger from wreck. Her occupation thus had its perils. It had, what must have been much harder to endure, its steady call upon daily fidelity. It was, on the whole, an obscure and humble occupation; although by chance, as well as by reason of her skill and devotion, this particular lighthouse keeper was privileged to become in a sense famous. But certainly it could have been no part of her original plan to pursue a famous career. When we seek public prominence we do not select the calling of the lighthouse keeper. I do not know how she came to find this calling. She may not even have chosen it. But she certainly chose how to live her life when she had found it. What it means for the world to have such lives lived, a very little thought will show us. What spirit is needed to live such lives as they should be lived, we seldom consider, until such a public servant, dying with the fruits of her years to some extent known to the public, reminds us of our debt and of her devotion.

The newspaper in which I read of this case, in commenting upon its significance, also reported (I do not know how accurately) this incident, of which some of you may know more than I do. I quote the words:

> Forty-one years ago, Daniel Williams, keeper of the light at Little Traverse Bay, in Lake Michigan, went out in a boat for the rescue of a ship's crew in distress, and did not come back alive. For three days the storm continued. But his widow

did not forget other lives, and each night climbed the winding stairs and trimmed the lamp. This duty she discharged until the government learned the situation, when it authorised her to continue. And she is still at her post.

Lighthouse keepers are not the only people who live thus. There are countless lights kept alive in homes where want or weariness or stormy sorrow have long since and often entered, and have again and again seemed about to overwhelm, but where, after many years, faithful souls, well known to many of you, are, despite fortune, still at their post, with the light burning.

And now, I ask you, What is the spirit which rules such lives? It is a spirit which is familiar in song and story; for men always love to tell about it when they meet with impressive examples of its workings. What I regret is that, when men repeat such songs and stories, familiarity breeds, not indeed contempt (for our whole nature rejoices to think of such deeds), but a certain tendency to false emphasis. We notice the dramatic and heroic incidents of such lives, and are charmed with the picturesque or with the thrilling features of the tale. And so we seem to ourselves to be dealing mainly with anecdotes and with accidents. We fail sufficiently to consider that back of the exceptional show of heroism there has to be the personal character, itself the result of years of devotion and of training—the character that has made itself ready for these dramatic but, after all, not supremely significant opportunities. Only when we in mind run over series of such cases do we see that we are dealing with a spirit suited not only to great occasions, but to every moment of reasonable life, and not only to any one or two callings, but to all sorts and conditions of men.

The spirit in question is the one which is often well illustrated in the lives of warriors who willingly face death for their flag—if only they face death not merely as brutes may also face it (because their fighting blood is aroused), but as reasonable men face death who clearly see what conditions make it "man's perdition to be safe." There are two tests by which we may know whether the warriors really have the spirit of which I am speaking, namely, the spirit that was also, and quite equally, present in the widow who, in all the agony of a new grief, and through the storm that had taken away her husband, still climbed the lonely stairway and trimmed the lamp which he could never again tend. The first test that the warrior and the lighthouse tender are moved by the same spirit is furnished by the fact that those warriors who are rightly filled with this spirit are as well able to live by it in peace as in war; are, for instance, able even to surrender to the foe, when fortune and duty require them to do so—to surrender, I say, with the same calm dignity and unbroken courage that Lee showed in his interview with Grant at Appomattox, and that inspired him in the years of defeat and of new toils through which he had still to live after the war. That is, the warrior, if rightly inspired, is as ready for life as for death, is as ready for peace as for war; and despises defeat as much as danger—fearing only sloth and dishonour and abandonment of the service. The other test is whether the warrior is ready to recognise and to honour, with clear cordiality, this same spirit when it is manifested in another calling, or in another service, and, in particular, is manifested by his enemy. For then the warrior knows that warfare itself is only the accident of fortune, and that the true spirit of his own act is one which could be manifested without regard to the special occasion that has required him to face death just here or to fight on this side. If the spirit of the warrior bears these tests, his faithfulness is of the type that could be shown as well by the lonely light-tender in her grief as by the hero for whom glory waits.

And again, this spirit is the very one that martyrs have shown when they died for their faith; that patient mothers and fathers, however obscure and humble, show when they toil, in true devotion, for their homes. . . . And lest all these instances should impress you with the idea that the spirit in question has to do only with brilliant emotional colourings, such as those which fill our imaginations when we think of war, and of brave deaths, and of heroic triumph over grief, and of lovers' vows, let me turn at once to what some of you may think to be the other extreme of life. Let me say that, to my mind, the calm and laborious devotion to a science which has made possible the life-work of a Newton, or of a Maxwell, or of a Darwin is still another example, and a very great example, of this same spirit—an example full of the same strenuousness, the same fascinated love of an idealised object, and, best of all, full of the willingness to face unknown fortunes, however hard, and to abandon, when that is necessary, momentary joys, however dear, in a pursuit of one of the principal goods which humanity needs—namely, an understanding of the wonderful world in which we mortals are required to work out our destiny. It is not a superficial resemblance that the lighthouse tender and the scientific man both seek to keep and to spread light for the guidance of men.

The lighthouse tender, the mother, the warrior, the patriot, the martyr, the true lover, the scientific investigator—they all show, I insist, this same essential spirit.

Patient through the watches long,
Serving most with none to see;

superior to fortune because something that is worthier than any fortune seems to call them to their task. Such are undismayed in defeat. So Newton was undismayed when he looked for the needed confirmation of his theory in the motion of the moon and for the time failed. He worked on steadily, without any effort to win renown by hasty publication of possible explanations, until new advances of science showed why confirmation had so far been lacking and brought him what he needed. So Lee turned to the new life after the war. So the widow climbed the lonely stairway, despite her lost one, and because of her lost one. So the martyrs faced the lions. These all were sustained through long toil, or bewildering grief, by a spirit that tended to make them masters of their own lives and to bring them into unity with the master of all life.

We have illustrated the spirit. We now ask: What is the principle which dominates such lives? Is it or is it not a principle such, that one at any time wholly devoted to it could thereafter, upon a reasonable review of life, wisely regret having chosen to live thus? If it is not such a principle, if on the contrary it is a principle such that any reasonable view of life approves it, let us know what it is, let us detach it from the accidental conditions which at once adorn and disguise it for our imagination, let us read it so as to see how it applies to every sort of reasonable life—and then we shall be in possession of the solution of our moral problem. Then we shall know what it is that, if we are indeed rational, we really choose to do so soon as we learn how to live.

If we consider carefully any such faithful lives as I have just exemplified, we see that, however simple-minded and unreflective some of the people may be who learn to live in this way, the motives that guide them are such as will bear a great deal of thoughtful reflection.

The people whom I have in mind, and of whom such instances teach us something, are, in the first place, individuals of considerable wealth and strength of personal character. They certainly are resolute. They have a will of their own. They make choices. And so the contribution of their individual experience to their moral purpose is large. It would be wrong to say, as some do, that they are characterised by mere "altruism," but utter "self-forgetfulness," by "living solely for others." If you were on a wreck in a storm, and the lighthouse keeper were coming out to save you, you would take little comfort in the belief, if you had such a belief, that, since he was a man who had always "lived for others," he had never allowed himself the selfish delight of being fond of handling a boat with skill or of swimming for the mere love of the water. No, on the contrary, you would rejoice to believe, if you could, that he had always delighted in boating and in swimming, and was justly vain of his prowess on the water. The more of a self he had delightedly or with a just pride trained on the water, the more of a self he might have to save you with. When we are in desperate need, we never wish beings who, as some say, "have no thought of self" to help us in our plight. We want robust helpers who have been trained through their personal fondness for the skill and the prowess that they can now show in helping us. So individual self-development belongs of necessity to the people whose faithfulness we are to prize in an emergency. And if people resolve to become effectively faithful in some practical service, their principle of action includes individual self-development.

In the second place, people of the type whom I here have in mind have strong social motives. Their faithfulness is a recognition of the significance, in their eyes, of some socially important call. And this, of course, is too obvious a fact to need further mention.

But in the third place, these people are guided by a motive which distinguishes their type of social consciousness from . . . [mere] chance and fickle interests in this or that form of personal and social success. . . . A peculiar grace has been indeed granted to them—a free gift, but one which they can only accept by being ready to earn it—a precious treasure that they cannot possess without loving and serving the life that has thus endowed them—a talent which they cannot hide, but must employ to earn new usury—a talent which seems to them not to belong to themselves, but to their master, who will require it of them, increased. This grace, this gift, is what may be called their Cause. Sometimes it appears to them in winning guise, seen in the depths of the eyes of a beloved one, or symbolised by a flag, or expressed through a song. Sometimes they think of it more austerely, and name it "science," or "the service," or "the truth." Sometimes they conceive it expressly as a religious object, and call it, not unwisely, "God's will." But however they conceive it, or whatever name they give to it, it has certain features by which you may easily know it.

The Cause, for people of this spirit, is never one individual person alone, even if, as in the lover's case, the devoted person centres it about the self of one beloved. For even the lovers know that they transfigure the beloved being, and speak of their love in terms that could not be true, unless that which they really serve were much more than any one individual. The Cause for any such devoted servant of a cause as we have been describing *is some conceived, and yet also real, spiritual unity which links many individual lives in one, and which is therefore essentially superhuman, in exactly the sense in which we . . . [find] the realities of the world of the reason to be superhuman*. Yet the cause is not, on that account, any mere abstraction. It is a live something: "My home," "my family," "my country," "my service," "mankind," "the church," "my art," "my Science," "the cause of humanity," or, once more, "God's will,"—such are names for the cause. One thinks of all these objects as living expressions of what perfectly concrete and needy people want and require. But one also thinks of the cause as unifying many individuals in its service, and as graciously furnishing to them what they need, namely, the opportunity to be one in spirit. The cause, then, is something based upon human needs, and inclusive of human efforts, and alive with all the warmth of human consciousness and of human love and desire and effort. One also thinks of the cause as *superhuman in the scope, the wealth, the unity, and the reasonableness of its purposes and of its accomplishments.*

Such is the cause. That the individual loves it is, in any one case, due to the chances of his temperament and of his development. That it can be conceived and served is a matter of social experience. That it is more worthy to be served than are any passing whims, individual or social, is the insight which the individual gets whenever he surveys his life in its wider unities. That to serve it requires creative effort, that it cannot be served except by positive deeds is the result of all one's knowledge of it. That in such service one finds self-expression even in and through self-surrender, and is more of a self even because one gives one's self, is the daily experience of all who have found such a cause. That such service enables one to face fortune with a new courage, because, whatever happens to the servant of the cause, he is seeking not his own fortune, but that of the cause, and has therefore discounted his own personal defeats, is the result of the whole spirit here in question.

For such a practical attitude toward such a cause I know no better name than the good old word Loyalty. And hereupon we are ready for a statement of the principle which dominates loyal lives. All the foregoing cases were cases of loyalty. In each some one had found a cause, a live spiritual unity, above his own individual level. This cause is no mere heap or collection of other human beings; it is a life of many brethren in unity. The simplest statement of the principle of the loyal person was the maxim: *"Be loyal to your cause."* Somewhat more fully stated this principle would read: *"Devote your whole self to your cause."* Such a principle does not mean

"Lose yourself," or "Abolish yourself," or even simply "Sacrifice yourself." It means: "Be as rich and full and strong a self as you can, and then, with all your heart and your soul and your mind and your strength, devote yourself to this your cause, to this spiritual unity in which individuals may be, and (when they are loyal) actually are, united in a life whose meaning is above the separate meanings of any or of all natural human beings."

Yet even thus the principle which actually inspires every thoroughly loyal action has not been fully stated. For, as we have seen, the warriors, despite the fact that their duty requires them to compass if they can the defeat of their foes, best show their loyal spirit if they prize the loyalty of their foes and honour loyalty wherever they find it. We call such a spirit that honours loyalty in the foe a spirit of chivalry. You and I may remember that Lee was the foe of that Union in whose triumph we now rejoice. Yet we may and should look upon him as, in his own personal intent, a model of the spirit of true loyalty; for he gave all that he had and was to what he found to be his cause. Such an insight into the meaning of the loyalty of the foe, chivalry requires. Therefore, the true spirit of loyalty, including, as is reasonable, this spirit of chivalry, also requires us to state the principle of loyalty in a still deeper and more universal form. The true principle of loyalty is, in fact, a union of two principles. The first is: *Be loyal.* The second is: *So be loyal, that is, so seek, so accept, so serve your cause that thereby the loyalty of all your brethren throughout all the world, through your example, through your influence, through your own love of loyalty wherever you find it, as well as through the sort of loyalty which you exemplify in your deeds, shall be aided, furthered, increased so far as in you lies.*

Can this principle be acted out? Can it direct life? Is it a barren abstraction? Let the life and the deed of the lonely lighthouse keeper give the reply. Who, amongst us, whatever his own cause, is not instructed and aided in his loyalty by the faithful deed of such a devoted soul? Such people are then, in truth, not loyal *merely* to their own private cause. *They are loyal to the cause of all loyal people.* For, to an enlightened survey of life, all the loyal, even when chance and human blindness force them at any moment to war with one another, are, in fact, spiritual brethren. They have a common cause—the cause of furthering universal loyalty through their own choice and their own service. The spirit of chivalry simply brings this fact to mind. The loyal are inspired by the loyal, are sustained by them. Every one of them finds in the loyal his kindred, his fellow-servants. Whoever is concretely loyal, that is, whoever wholly gives himself to some cause that binds many human souls in one superhuman unity, is just in so far serving the cause not only of all mankind, but of all the rational spiritual world. I repeat then: The true principle of all the loyal is: *So be loyal to your own cause as thereby to serve the advancement of the cause of universal loyalty.*

Now of the principle thus formulated I assert that it is a principle fit to be made the basis of an universal moral code. There is no duty, there is no virtue whose warrant and whose value you cannot deduce from this one principle. Charity, justice, fidelity, decisiveness, strenuousness, truthfulness, efficiency, wise self-assertion, watchful self-restraint, patience, defiance of fortune, resignation in defeat, your daily social duties, your individual self-development, your personal rights and dignity, your obedience to the calls of duty, your justified self-sacrifices, your rational pride in the unique moral office to which you have individually been called—all these, I assert, can be rightly defined, defended, estimated, and put into practice through an accurate understanding and development of the principle of loyalty just laid down. . . .

Consider the lives of the loyal, in such examples as I have suggested to you, and . . . try for yourselves to see what they teach. To help you in such a consideration, I may here simply remind you that when one is not only loyal but enlightened, one cannot finally approve or accept any cause or any mode of living that, while seeming in itself to be a cause or a mode of living such as embodies the spirit of loyalty, still depends upon or involves contempt for the loyalty of other men, or a disposition to prey upon their loyalty and to deprive them of any cause to which they can be loyal. No loyalty that lives by destroying the loyalty of your neighbour is just to its own true intent. And that is why charity and justice are fruits of the loyal spirit. And that is why, if your cause and your loyal action are rightly accepted and carried out, the common interests of all rational beings are served by your loyalty precisely in so far as your powers permit. Whatever your special cause (and your special personal cause—your love, your home, or your calling—you must have), *your true cause is the spiritual unity of all the world of reasonable beings.* This cause you further, so far as in you lies, by your every deed.

And that also is why the principle of loyalty, once rightly defined and served by you—served with the whole energy and power of your personal self—is a principle that, upon any enlightened survey of your life you can never regret having served. This, then, is what we are seeking—an absolute moral principle, a guide for all action.

But even this is not the whole meaning of what the spirit of loyalty has to teach you. Your cause, thus concretely and yet universally defined, is something of which you can always, and now truthfully and without any pathetic fallacy, say, what Browning's lover said in the lyric . . .

World, how it walled about
Life with disgrace,
Till God's own smile came out
That was thy face.

For your cause can only be revealed to you through some presence that first teaches you to love this unity of the spiritual life. This presence will come to you in a beloved form, as something human, dear, vitally fascinating. It may be a person—a face—or a living community of human beings that first reveals it to you. You can, indeed, choose it as your cause. Your will is needed. Loyalty is no mere sentiment. It is the willing and practical and thorough-going devotion of a self to a cause. But you can never choose your cause until you have first found it. And you must find it in human shape. And you must love it before you can choose its service.

Therefore, however far you go in loyalty, you will never regard your loyalty as a mere morality. It will also be in essence a religion. It will always be to you a finding of an object that comes to you from without and above, as divine grace has always been said to come. Hence loyalty is a source not only of moral but of religious insight. The spirit of true loyalty is of its very essence a complete synthesis of the moral and of the religious interests. The cause is a religious object. It finds you in your need. It points out to you the way of salvation. Its presence in your world is to you a free gift from the realm of the spirit—a gift that you have not of yourself, but through the willingness of the world to manifest to you the way of salvation. This free gift first compels your love. Then you freely give yourself in return.

Therefore, the spirit of loyalty completely reconciles those bitter and tragic wrangles between the mere moralists and the partisans of divine grace. It supplies in its unity also the way to define, in harmonious fashion, the ideal of what your individual experience seeks in its need, of what your social world, groaning and travailing in pain together, longs for as our common salvation, of what the reason conceives as the divine unity of the world's meaning, of what the rational will requires you to serve as God's will. Through loyalty, then, not only the absolute moral insight, but the absolute religious insight, as you grow in grace and persist in service, may be and will be gradually and truthfully revealed to you.

For loyalty, though justifying no "moral holidays," shows you the will of the spiritual world, the divine will, and so gives you rest in toil, peace in the midst of care. And loyalty also, though leaving you in no mystic trance, displays to you the law that holds the whole rational world together; though showing you the divine grace, calls upon you for the strenuous giving of your whole self to action; though requiring of you no philosophical training, tells you what the highest reason can but justify; and, though concerned with no mere signs and wonders, shows you the gracious and eternal miracle of a spiritual realm where, whatever fortunes and miracles and divine beings there may be, you, in so far as you are loyal, are and are to be always at home.

And all this is true because the spirit of loyalty at once expresses your own personal need and reason, and defines for you the only purpose that could be justified from the point of view of one who surveyed all voluntary and rational life. This is the purpose to further the unity of whatever spiritual life you can influence, and to do this by your every rational deed, precisely in so far as your powers permit. This is a law for all rational beings. No angels could do more than this.

There is a famous word that Chaucer put into the mouth of his Griselda at the moment when her husband tried her patience with his last and utmost cruelty. That word, uttered by a woman to a mere individual human creature who happened to be her husband, seems helplessly pathetic and slavish enough. Yet Chaucer himself warns us that the old tale, truly interpreted, should be viewed as an allegory of the deeper relations between the soul and God. Even so, to many of our leading modern minds the allegory, when interpreted in this way, may seem harsh enough. Mere moralists may make light of it, because it seems opposed to the dignity of the moral spirit of individual self-respect. Only the partisans of a divine grace, administered through inscrutable divine decrees, would, you might suppose, still see any worth in so cruel an allegory. Nevertheless, this judgment of the allegory is false. Let a truly loyal being—our lighthouse keeper, for instance—our patriot or martyr, let Lee or Newton, let whoever is filled with the right spirit of loyalty—whoever, through the light that he trims, intends to lighten and to unify so much of the spiritual world as he can ever reach by his deed—let *such* a loyal being utter Griselda's word. Let him utter it as in the presence of the master of life, who offers to all the loyal the divine grace of finding themselves through their devotion to their cause. Let him address this word

As unto one that hears
A cry above the conquered years.

Let him utter this word as the summary and confession of his whole life of loyalty. And then Griselda's word is no longer slavish. It is full of the resolute courage, of the splendid contempt for mere fortune, of the unconquerable spiritual self-assertion, yes, it is full of the deathless will, which are of the very essence of loyalty, and which, indeed, must overcome and, in the eternal realm, do overcome the world.

Griselda's word was this:

> But certes, Lord, for none adversitie,
> To dien in this case it shall not be
> That I in herte and minde should aye repente,
> That I you gave my soul with whole intente.

Whoever thus addresses his word, not to a human individual, but as unto the master of life, and then, sincerely and persistently and lovingly, lives that word out in his life, has solved the religious paradox. From out the lonely and darkened depths of his personal finitude, from out the chaos of his social promptings and of his worldly ambitions, amid all the storms of fortune, "midst of hell's laughter and noises appalling," he has heard the voice of the Spirit. He has heard, and—however unlearned—he has understood. His own lamp is burning, and through his deed the eternal light shines in the darkness of this world.

JOHN DEWEY

DEWEY'S vision of an ideal community of scientists, governed by the moral code of the laboratory and funding their experiences through the generations for the benefit of all mankind, is applied in his discussions of religion to the formulation of the ideal possibilities of a community of all mankind. Through cooperative association humankind pools its experience, developing a fund of information to be worked and reworked by the method of intelligence toward the solution of many age-old problems in human relations. At the heart of this conception of religion lies a faith unlike that of traditional religions: a faith in human effort rather than supernatural guidance, in an unfolding revelation of human potentialities rather than in completed revelation. For Dewey, "God" is not a name for the begetter of all things and the cause of all experience, but the name for an *"active* relation between ideal and actual," and thus a relation which is natural rather than supernatural. Instead of setting apart a realm of the sacred from a realm of the profane, Dewey considers experience to be all of a piece, so that the same experience may be religious or not depending upon which aspect of its effect on us is stressed. What is "religious" in experience is not its beginning but its end, not what initiates it but how it is consummated.

The following selection has been taken from John Dewey's book *A Common Faith* which appeared in 1934, based on his Terry Lectures delivered at Yale University in the same year.

A COMMON FAITH

CHAPTER I: RELIGION VERSUS THE RELIGIOUS

. . . There is a difference between religion, *a* religion, and the religious; between anything that may be denoted by a noun substantive and the quality of experience that is designated by an adjective. It is not easy to find a definition of religion in the substantive sense that wins general acceptance. However, in the *Oxford Dictionary* I find the following: "Recognition on the part of man of some unseen higher power as having control of his destiny and as being entitled to obedience, reverence and worship."

This particular definition is less explicit in assertion of the supernatural

---

This selection has been reprinted from *A Common Faith* by John Dewey (Yale University Press, New Haven, 1934), pp. 3–5, 6, 9–11, 14–15, 23–28, 59–62, 64–74, 77–84, 87, by permission of the publishers.

character of the higher unseen power than are others that might be cited. It is, however, surcharged with implications having their source in ideas connected with the belief in the supernatural, characteristic of historic religions. Let us suppose that one familiar with the history of religions, including those called primitive, compares the definition with the variety of known facts and by means of the comparison sets out to determine just what the definition means. I think he will be struck by three facts that reduce the terms of the definition to such a low common denominator that little meaning is left.

He will note that the "unseen powers" referred to have been conceived in a multitude of incompatible ways. Eliminating the differences, nothing is left beyond the bare reference to something unseen and powerful. This has been conceived as the vague and undefined Mana of the Melanesians; the Kami of primitive Shintoism; the fetish of the Africans; spirits, having some human properties, that pervade natural places and animate natural forces; the ultimate and impersonal principle of Buddhism; the unmoved mover of Greek thought; the gods and semi-divine heroes of the Greek and Roman Pantheons; the personal and loving Providence of Christianity, omnipotent, and limited by a corresponding evil power; the arbitrary Will of Moslemism; the supreme legislator and judge of deism. And these are but a few of the outstanding varieties of ways in which the invisible power has been conceived.

There is no greater similarity in the ways in which obedience and reverence have been expressed. There has been worship of animals, of ghosts, of ancestors, phallic worship, as well as of a Being of dread power and of love and wisdom. Reverence has been expressed in the human sacrifices of the Peruvians and Aztecs; the sexual orgies of some Oriental religions; exorcisms and ablutions; the offering of the humble and contrite mind of the Hebrew prophet, the elaborate rituals of the Greek and Roman Churches. Not even sacrifice has been uniform; it is highly sublimated in Protestant denominations and in Moslemism. Where it has existed it has taken all kinds of forms and been directed to a great variety of powers and spirits. It has been used for expiation, for propitiation and for buying special favors. There is no conceivable purpose for which rites have not been employed.

Finally, there is no discernible unity in the moral motivations appealed to and utilized. They have been as far apart as fear of lasting torture, hope of enduring bliss in which sexual enjoyment has sometimes been a conspicuous element; mortification of the flesh and extreme asceticism; prostitution and chastity; wars to extirpate the unbeliever, and philanthropic zeal; servile acceptance of imposed dogma, along with brotherly love and aspiration for a reign of justice among men. . . .

The logic involved in getting rid of inconvenient aspects of past religions compels us to inquire how much in religions now accepted are survivals from outgrown cultures. It compels us to ask what conception of unseen powers and our relations to them would be consonant with the best achievements and aspirations of the present. It demands that in imagination we wipe the stage clean and start afresh by asking what would be the idea of the unseen, of the manner of its control over us and the ways in which reverence and obedience would be manifested, if whatever is basically religious in experience had the opportunity to express itself free from all historic encumbrances. . . .

. . . A religion . . . always signifies a special body of beliefs and practices having some kind of institutional organization, loose or tight. In contrast, the adjective "religious" denotes nothing in the way of a specifiable entity, either institutional or as a system of beliefs. It does not denote anything to which one can specifically point as one can point to this and that historic religion or existing church. For it does not denote anything that can exist by itself or that can be organized into a particular and distinctive form of existence. It denotes attitudes that may be taken toward every object and every proposed end or ideal.

Before, however, I develop my suggestion that realization of the distinction just made would operate to emancipate the religious quality from encumbrances that now smother or limit it, I must refer to a position that in some respects is similar in words to the position I have taken, but that in fact is a whole world removed from it. I have several times used the phrase "religious elements of experience." Now at present there is much talk, especially in liberal circles, of religious experiences as vouching for the authenticity of certain beliefs and the desirability of certain practices, such as particular forms of prayer and worship. It is even asserted that religious experience is the ultimate basis of religion itself. The gulf between this position and that which I have taken is what I am now concerned to point out.

Those who hold to the notion that there is a definite kind of experience which is itself religious, by that very fact make out of it something specific, as a kind of experience that is marked off from experience as aesthetic, scientific, moral, political; from experience as companionship and friendship. But "religious" as a quality of experience signifies something that may belong to all these experiences. It is the polar opposite of some type of experience that can exist by itself. . . .

The difference between an experience having a religious force because of what it does in and to the processes of living and religious experience as a separate kind of thing gives me occasion to refer to a previous remark. If this function were rescued through emancipation from dependence upon specific types of beliefs and practices, from those elements that constitute a religion, many individuals would find that experiences having the force of bringing about a better, deeper and enduring adjustment in life are not so rare and infrequent as they are commonly supposed to be. They occur frequently in connection with many significant moments of living. The idea of invisible powers would take on the meaning of all the conditions of nature and human association that support and deepen the sense of values which carry one through periods of darkness and despair to such an extent that they lose their usual depressive character. . . .

. . . According to the best authorities, "religion" comes from a root that means being bound or tied. Originally, it meant being bound by vows to a particular way of life—as *les religieux* were monks and nuns who had assumed certain vows. The religious attitude signifies something that is bound through imagination to a *general* attitude. This comprehensive attitude, moreover, is much broader than anything indicated by "moral" in its usual sense. The quality of attitude is displayed in art, science and good citizenship.

If we apply the conception set forth to the terms of the definition earlier quoted, these terms take on a new significance. An unseen power controlling our destiny becomes the power of an ideal. All possibilities, as possibilities, are ideal in character. The artist, scientist, citizen, parent, as far as they are actuated by the spirit of their callings, are controlled by the unseen. For all endeavor for the better is moved by faith in what is possible, not by adherence to the actual. Nor does this faith depend for its moving power upon intellectual assurance or belief that the things worked for must surely prevail and come into embodied existence. For the authority of the object to determine our attitude and conduct, the right that is given it to claim our allegiance and devotion is based on the intrinsic nature of the ideal. The outcome, given our best endeavor, is not with us. The inherent vice of all intellectual schemes of idealism is that they convert the idealism of action into a system of beliefs about antecedent reality. The character assigned this reality is so different from that which observation and reflection lead to and support that these schemes inevitably glide into alliance with the supernatural.

All religions, marked by elevated ideal quality, have dwelt upon the power of religion to introduce perspective into the piecemeal and shifting episodes of existence. Here too we need to reverse the ordinary statement and say that whatever introduces genuine perspective is religious, not that religion is something that introduces it. There can be no doubt (referring to the second element of the definition) of our dependence upon forces beyond our control. Primitive man was so impotent in the face of these forces that, especially in an unfavorable natural environment, fear became a dominant attitude, and, as the old saying goes, fear created the gods.

With increase of mechanisms of control, the element of fear has, relatively speaking, subsided. Some optimistic souls have even concluded that the forces about us are on the whole essentially benign. But every crisis, whether of the individual or of the community, reminds man of the precarious and partial nature of the control he exercises. When man, individually and collectively, has done his uttermost, conditions that at different times and places have given rise to the ideas of Fate and Fortune, of Chance and Providence, remain. It is the part of manliness to insist upon the capacity of mankind to strive to direct natural and social forces to humane ends. But unqualified absolutistic statements about the omnipotence of such endeavors reflect egoism rather than intelligent courage.

The fact that human destiny is so interwoven with forces beyond human control renders it unnecessary to suppose that dependence and the humility that accompanies it have to find the particular channel that is prescribed by traditional doctrines. What is especially significant is rather the form which the sense of dependence takes. Fear never gave stable perspective in the life of anyone. It is dispersive and withdrawing. Most religions have in fact added rites of communion to those of expiation and propitiation. For our dependence is manifested in those relations to the environment that support our undertakings and aspirations as much as it is in the defeats inflicted upon us. The essentially unreligious attitude is that which attributes human achievement and purpose to man in isolation from the world of physical nature and his fellows. Our successes are dependent upon the coöperation of nature. The sense of the dignity of human nature is as religious as is the sense of awe and reverence when it rests upon a sense of human nature as a coöperating part of a larger whole. Natural piety is not of necessity either a fatalistic acquiescence in natural happenings or a romantic idealization of the world. It may rest upon a just sense of nature as the whole of which we are parts, while it also recognizes that we are parts that are marked by intelligence and purpose, having the capacity to strive by their aid to bring conditions into greater consonance with what is humanly desirable. Such piety is an inherent constituent of a just perspective in life.

Understanding and knowledge also enter into a perspective that is religious in quality. Faith in the continued disclosing of truth through directed cooperative human endeavor is more religious in quality than is any faith in a completed revelation. It is of course now usual to hold that revelation is not completed in the sense of being ended. But religions hold that the essential framework is settled in its significant moral features at least, and that new elements that are offered must be judged by conformity to this framework. Some fixed doctrinal apparatus is necessary for *a* religion. But faith in the possibilities of continued and rigorous inquiry does not limit access to truth to any channel or scheme of things. It does not first say that truth is universal and then add there is but one road to it. It does not depend for assurance upon subjection to any dogma or item of doctrine. It trusts that the natural interactions between man and his environment will breed more intelligence and generate more knowledge provided the scientific methods that define intelligence in operation are pushed further into the mysteries of the world, being themselves promoted and improved in the operation. There is such a thing as faith in intelligence becoming religious in quality—a fact that perhaps explains the efforts of some religionists to disparage the possibilities of intelligence as a force. They properly feel such faith to be a dangerous rival.

Lives that are consciously inspired by loyalty to such ideals as have been mentioned are still comparatively infrequent to the extent of that comprehensiveness and intensity which arouse an ardor religious in function. But before we infer the incompetency of such ideals and of the actions they inspire, we should at least ask ourselves how much of the existing situation is due to the fact that the religious factors of experience have been drafted into supernatural channels and thereby loaded with irrelevant encumbrances. A body of beliefs and practices that are apart from the common and natural relations of mankind must, in the degree in which it is influential, weaken and sap the force of the possibilities inherent in such relations. Here lies one aspect of the emancipation of the religious from religion.

Any activity pursued in behalf of an ideal end against obstacles and in spite of threats of personal loss because of conviction of its general and enduring value is religious in quality. Many a person, inquirer, artist, philanthropist, citizen, men and women in the humblest walks of life, have achieved, without presumption and without display, such unification of themselves and of their relations to the conditions of existence. It remains to extend their spirit and inspiration to ever wider numbers. If I have said anything about religions and religion that seems harsh, I have said those things because of a firm belief that the claim on the part of religions to possess a monopoly of ideals and of the supernatural means by which alone, it is alleged, they can be furthered, stands in the way of the realization of distinctively religious values inherent in natural experience. For that reason, if for no other, I should be sorry if any were misled by the frequency with which I have employed the adjective "religious" to conceive of what I have said as a disguised apology for what have passed as religions. The opposition between religious values as I conceive them and religions is not to be bridged. Just because the release of these values is so important, their identification with the creeds and cults of religions must be dissolved.

CHAPTER III: THE HUMAN ABODE OF THE RELIGIOUS FUNCTION

. . . The core of religions has generally been found in rites and ceremonies. Legends and myths grow up in part as decorative dressings, in response to the irrepressible human tendency toward story-telling, and in part as attempts to explain ritual practices. Then as culture advances, stories are consolidated, and theogonies and cosmogonies are formed—as with the Babylonians, Egyptians, Hebrews and Greeks. In the case of the Greeks, the stories of creation and accounts of the constitution of the world were mainly poetic and literary, and philosophies ultimately developed from them. In most cases, legends along with rites and ceremonies came under the guardianship of a special body, the priesthood, and were subject to the special arts which it possessed. A special group was set aside as the responsible owners, protectors and promulgators of the corpus of beliefs.

But the formation of a special group having a peculiar relation to both the practices and the beliefs of religion is but part of the story. In the widest perspective, it is the less important part. The more significant point as regards the social import of religion is that the priesthoods were official representatives of some community, tribe, city-state or empire. Whether there was a priesthood or not, individuals who were members of a community were born into a religious community as they were into social and political organization. Each social group had its own divine beings who were its founders and protectors. Its rites of sacrifice, purification, and communion were manifestations of organized civic life. The temple was a public institution, the focus of the worship of the community; the influence of its practices extended to all the customs of the community, domestic, economic, and political. Even wars between groups were usually conflicts of their respective deities.

An individual did not join a church. He was born and reared in a community whose social unity, organization and traditions were symbolized and celebrated in the rites, cults and beliefs of a collective religion. Education was the induction of the young into community activities that were interwoven at every point with customs, legends and ceremonies intimately connected with and sanctioned by a religion. There are a few persons, especially those brought up in Jewish communities in Russia, who can understand without the use of imagination what a religion means socially when it permeates all the customs and activities of group life. To most of us in the United States such a situation is only a remote historic episode.

The change that has taken place in conditions once universal and now infrequent is in my opinion the greatest change that has occurred in religion in all history. The intellectual conflict of scientific and theological beliefs has attracted much more attention. It is still near the focus of attention. But the change in the social center of gravity of religion has gone on so steadily and is now so generally accomplished that it has faded from the thought of most persons, save perhaps the historians, and even they are especially aware of it only in its political aspect. For the conflict between state and church still continues in some countries.

There are even now persons who are born into a particular church, that of their parents, and who take membership in it almost as a matter of course; indeed, the fact of such membership may be an important, even a determining, factor in an individual's career. But the thing new in history, the thing once unheard of, is that the organization in question is a *special* institution within a secular community. Even where there are established churches, they are constituted by the state and may be unmade by the state. Not only the national state but other forms of organization among groups have grown in power and influence at the expense of organizations built upon and about a religion. The correlate of this fact is that membership in associations of the latter type is more and more a matter of the voluntary choice of individuals, who may tend to accept responsibilities imposed by the church but who accept them of their own volition. If they do accept them, the organization they join is, in many nations, chartered under a general corporation law of the political and secular entity.

The shift in what I have called the social center of gravity accompanies the enormous expansion of associations formed for educational, political, economic, philanthropic and scientific purposes, which has occurred independently of any religion. These social modes have grown so much that they exercise the greater hold upon the thought and interest of most persons, even of those holding membership in churches. This positive extension of interests which, from the standpoint of a religion, are non-religious, is so great that in comparison with it the direct effect of science upon the creeds of religion seems to me of secondary importance. . . .

Changes in practice that affect collective life go deep and extend far. They have been operating ever since the time we call the Middle Ages. The Renaissance was essentially a new birth of secularism. The development of the idea of "natural religion," characteristic of the eighteenth century, was a protest against control by ecclesiastic bodies—a movement foreshadowed in this respect by the growth of "independent" religious societies in the preceding century. But natural religion no more denied the intellectual validity of supernatural ideas than did the growth of independent congregations. It attempted rather to justify theism and immortality on the basis of the natural reason of the individual. The transcendentalism of the nineteenth century was a further move in the same general direction, a movement in which "reason" took on a more romantic, more colorful, and more collective form. It asserted the diffusion of the supernatural through secular life.

These movements and others not mentioned are the intellectual reflex of the greatest revolution that has taken place in religions during the thousands of years that man has been upon earth. For, as I have said, this change has to do with the *social* place and function of religion. Even the hold of the supernatural upon the general mind has become more and more disassociated from the power of ecclesiastic organization—that is, of any particular form of communal organization. Thus the very idea that was central in religions has more and more oozed away, so to speak, from the guardianship and care of any particular social institution. Even more important is the fact that a steady encroachment upon ecclesiastic institutions of forms of association once regarded as secular has altered the way in which men spend their time in work, recreation, citizenship, and political action. The essential point is not just that secular organizations and actions are legally or externally severed from the control of the church, but that interests and values unrelated to the offices of any church now so largely sway the desires and aims of even believers.

The individual believer may indeed carry the disposition and motivation he has acquired through affiliation with a religious organization into his political action, into his connection with schools, even into his business and amusements. But there remain two facts that constitute a revolution. In the first place, conditions are such that this action is a matter of personal choice and resolution on the part of individuals, not of the very nature of social organization. In the second place, the very fact that an individual imports or carries his personal attitude into affairs that are inherently secular, that are outside the scope of religion, constitutes an enormous change, in spite of the belief that secular matters *should* be permeated by the spirit of religion. Even if it be asserted, as it is by some religionists, that all the new movements and interests of any value grew up under the auspices of a church and received their impetus from the same source, it must be admitted that once the vessels have been launched, they are sailing on strange seas to far lands.

Here, it seems to me, is the issue to be faced. Here is the place where the distinction that I have drawn between a religion and the religious function is peculiarly applicable. It is of the nature of a religion based on the supernatural to draw a line between the religious and the secular and profane, even when it asserts the rightful authority of the Church and its religion to dominate these other interests. The conception that "religious" signifies a certain attitude and outlook, independent of the supernatural, necessitates no such division. It does not shut religious values up within a particular compartment, nor assume that a particular form of association bears a unique relation to it. Upon the social side the future of the religious function seems preëminently bound up with its emancipation from religions and a particular religion. Many persons feel perplexed because of the multiplicity of churches and the conflict of their claims. But the fundamental difficulty goes deeper.

In what has been said I have not ignored the interpretation put, by representatives of religious organizations, upon the historic change that has occurred. The oldest organization, the Roman Catholic church, judges the secularization of life, the growing independence of social interests and values from control by the church, as but one evidence the more of the apostasy of the natural man from God: the corruption inherent in the will of mankind has resulted in defiance of the authority that God has delegated to his designated representatives on earth. This church points to the fact that secularization has proceeded *pari passu* with the extension of Protestantism as evidence of the wilful heresy of the latter in its appeal to private conscience and choice. The remedy is simple. Submission to the will of God, as continuously expressed through the organization that is his established vicegerent on earth, is the sole means by which social relations and values can again become coextensive with religion.

Protestant churches, on the contrary, have emphasized the fact that the relation of man to God is primarily an individual matter, a matter of personal choice and responsibility. From this point of view, one aspect of the change outlined marks an advance that is religious as well as moral. For according to it, the beliefs and rites that tend to make the relation of man to God a collective and institutional affair erect barriers between the human soul and the divine spirit. Communion with God must be initiated by the individual's heart and will through direct divine assistance. Hence the change that has occurred in the social status of organized religion is nothing to deplore. What has been lost was at best specious and external. What has been gained is that religion has been placed upon its only real and solid foundation: direct relationship of conscience and will to God. Although there is much that is non-Christian and anti-Christian in existing economic and political institutions, it is better that change be accomplished by the sum total of efforts of men and women who are imbued with personal faith, than that they be effected by any wholesale institutional effort that subordinates the individual to an external and ultimately a worldly authority.

Were the question involved in these two opposed views taken up in detail, there are some specific considerations that might be urged. It might be urged that the progressive secularization of the interests of life has not been attended by the increasing degeneration that the argument of the first group implies. There are many who, as historical students, independent of affiliation with any religion, would regard reversal of the process of secularization and return to conditions in which the Church was the final authority as a menace to things held most precious. With reference to the position of Protestantism, it may be urged that in fact such social advances as have taken place are not the product of voluntary religious associations; that, on the contrary, the forces that have worked to humanize human relations, that have resulted in intellectual and aesthetic development, have come from influences that are independent of the churches. A case could be made out for the position that the churches have lagged behind in most important social movements and that they have turned their chief attention in social affairs to moral *symptoms,* to vices and abuses, like drunkenness, sale of intoxicants, divorce, rather than to the causes of war and of the long list of economic and political injustices and oppressions. Protest against the latter has been mainly left to secular movements.

In earlier times, what we now call the supernatural hardly meant anything more definite than the extraordinary, that which was striking and emotionally impressive because of its out-of-the-way character. Probably even today the commonest conception of the natural is that which is usual, customary and familiar. When there is no insight into the cause of unusual events, belief in the supernatural is itself "natural"—in this sense of natural. Supernaturalism was, therefore, a genuinely social religion as long as men's minds were attuned to the supernatural. It gave an "explanation" of extraordinary occurrences while it provided techniques for utilizing supernatural forces to secure advantages and to protect the members of the community against them when they were adverse.

The growth of natural science brought extraordinary things into line with events for which there is a "natural" explanation. At the same time, the development of positive social interests crowded heaven—and its opposite, hell—into the background. The function and offices of churches became more and more specialized; concerns and values that had been regarded, in an earlier contrast, as profane and secular grew in bulk and in importance. At the same time, the notion that basic and ultimate spiritual and ideal values are associated with the supernatural has persisted as a kind of vague background and aura. A kind of polite deference to the notion remains along with a concrete transfer of interest. The general mind is thus left in a confused and divided state. The movement that has been going on for the last few centuries will continue to breed doubleness of mind until religious meanings and values are definitely integrated into normal social relations.

The issue may be more definitely stated. The extreme position on one side is that apart from relation to the supernatural, man is morally on a level with the brutes. The other position is that all significant ends and all securities for stability and peace have grown up in the matrix of human relations, and that the values given a supernatural locus are in fact products of an idealizing imagination that has laid hold of natural goods. There ensues a second contrast. On the one hand, it is held that relation to the supernatural is the only finally dependable source of motive power; that directly and indirectly it has animated every serious effort for the guidance and rectification of man's life on earth. The other position is that goods actually experienced in the concrete relations of family, neighborhood, citizenship, pursuit of art and science, are what men actually depend upon for guidance and support, and that their reference to a supernatural and otherworldly locus has obscured their real nature and has weakened their force.

The contrasts outlined define the religious problem of the present and the future. What would be the consequences upon the values of human association if intrinsic and immanent satisfactions and opportunities were clearly held to and cultivated with the ardor and the devotion that have at times marked historic religions? The contention of an increasing number of persons is that depreciation of natural social values has resulted, both in principle and in actual fact, from reference of their origin and significance to supernatural sources. Natural relations, of husband and wife, of parent and child, friend and friend, neighbor and neighbor, of fellow workers in industry, science, and art, are neglected, passed over, not developed for all that is in them. They are, moreover, not merely depreciated. They have been regarded as dangerous rivals of higher values; as offering temptations to be resisted; as usurpations by flesh of the authority of the spirit; as revolts of the human against the divine.

The doctrine of original sin and total depravity, of the corruption of nature, external and internal, is not especially current in liberal religious circles at present. Rather, there prevails the idea that there are two separate systems of values. . . . The values found in natural and supernatural relationships are now, in liberal circles, said to be complementary, just as the truths of revelation and of science are the two sides, mutually sustaining, of the same ultimate truth.

I cannot but think that this position represents a great advance upon the traditional one. While it is open logically to the objections that hold against the idea of the dual revelation of truth, practically it indicates a development of a humane point of view. But if it be once admitted that human relations are charged with values that are religious in function, why not rest the case upon what is verifiable and concentrate thought and energy upon its full realization?

History seems to exhibit three stages of growth. In the first stage, human relationships were thought to be so infected with the evils of corrupt human nature as to require redemption from external and supernatural sources. In the next stage, what is significant in these relations is found to be akin to values esteemed distinctively religious. This is the point now reached by liberal theologians. The third stage would realize that in fact the values prized in those religions that have ideal elements are idealizations of things characteristic of natural association, which have then been projected into a supernatural realm for safe-keeping and sanction. Note the rôle of such terms as Father, Son, Bride, Fellowship and Communion in the vocabulary of Christianity, and note also the tendency, even if a somewhat inchoate one, of terms that express the more intimate phases of association to displace those of legal, political origin: King, Judge, and Lord of Hosts.

Unless there is a movement into what I have called the third stage, fundamental dualism and a division in life continue. The idea of a double and parallel manifestation of the divine, in which the latter has superior status and authority, brings about a condition of unstable equilibrium. It operates to distract energy, through dividing the objects to which it is directed. It also imperatively raises the question as to why having gone far in recognition of religious values in normal community life, we should not go further. The values of natural human intercourse and mutual dependence are open and public, capable of verification by the methods through which all natural facts are established. By means of the same experimental method, they are capable of expansion. Why not concentrate upon nurturing and extending them? Unless we take this step, the idea of two realms of spiritual values is only a softened version of the old dualism between the secular and the spiritual, the profane and the religious. . . .

Vested interests, interests vested with power, are powerfully on the side of the *status quo,* and therefore they are especially powerful in hindering the growth and application of the method of natural intelligence. Just because these interests are so powerful, it is the more necessary to fight for recognition of the method of intelligence in action. But one of the greatest obstacles in conducting this combat is the tendency to dispose of social evils in terms of general moral causes. The sinfulness of man, the corruption of his heart, his self-love and love of power, when referred to as causes are precisely of the same nature as was the appeal to abstract powers (which in fact only reduplicated under a general name a multitude of particular effects) that once prevailed in physical "science," and that operated as a chief obstacle to the generation and growth of the latter. Demons were once appealed to in order to explain bodily disease and no such thing as a strictly natural death was supposed to happen. The importation of general moral causes to explain *present* social phenomena is on the same intellectual level. Reinforced by the prestige of traditional religions, and backed by the emotional force of beliefs in the supernatural, it stifles the growth of that social intelligence by means of which direction of social change could be taken out of the region of accident. . . . Accident in this broad sense and the idea of the supernatural are twins. Interest in the supernatural therefore reinforces other vested interests to prolong the social reign of accident.

There is a strong reaction in some religious circles today against the idea of mere individual salvation of individual souls. There is also a reaction in politics and economics against the idea of *laissez faire.* Both of these movements reflect a common tendency. Both of them are signs of the growing awareness of the emptiness of individuality in isolation. But the fundamental root of the *laissez faire* idea is denial (more often implicit than express) of the possibility of radical intervention of intelligence in the conduct of human life. Now appeal for supernatural intervention in improvement of social matters is also the expression of a deep-seated *laissez-faireism;* it is the acknowledgment of the desperate situation into which we are driven by the idea of the irrelevance and futility of human intervention in social events and interests. Those contemporary theologians who are interested in social change and who at the same time depreciate human intelligence and effort in behalf of the supernatural, are riding two horses that are going in opposite directions. The old-fashioned ideas of doing something to make the will of God prevail in the world, and of assuming the responsibility of doing the job ourselves, have more to be said for them, logically and practically.

The emphasis that has been put upon intelligence as a method should not mislead anyone. Intelligence, as distinct from the older conception of reason, is inherently involved in action. Moreover, there is no opposition between it and emotion. There is such a thing as passionate intelligence, as ardor in behalf of light shining into the murky places of social existence, and as zeal for its refreshing and purifying effect. The whole story of man shows that there are no objects that may not deeply stir engrossing emotion. One of the few experiments in the attachment of emotion to ends that mankind has not tried is that of devotion, so intense as to be religious, to intelligence as a force in social action.

But this is only part of the scene. No matter how much evidence may be piled up against social institutions as they exist, affection and passionate desire for justice and security are realities in human nature. So are the emotions that arise from living in conditions of inequity, oppression, and insecurity. Combination of the two kinds of emotion has more than once produced those changes that go by the name of revolution. To say that emotions which are not fused with intelligence are blind is tautology. Intense emotion may utter itself in action that destroys institutions. But the only assurance of birth of better ones is the marriage of emotion with intelligence.

Criticism of the commitment of religion to the supernatural is thus positive in import. All modes of human association are "affected with a public interest," and full realization of this interest is equivalent to a sense of a significance that is religious in its function. The objection to supernaturalism is that it stands in the way of an effective realization of the sweep and depth of the implications of natural human relations. It stands in the way of using the means that are in our power to make radical changes in these relations. It is certainly true that great material changes might be made with no corresponding improvement of a spiritual or ideal nature. But development in the latter direction cannot be introduced from without; it cannot be brought about by dressing up material and economic changes with decorations derived from the supernatural. It can come only from more intense realization of values that inhere in the actual connections of human beings with one another. The attempt to segregate the implicit public interest and social value of all institutions and social arrangements in a particular organization is a fatal diversion.

Were men and women actuated throughout the length and breadth of human relations with the faith and ardor that have at times marked historic religions the consequences would be incalculable. To achieve this faith and *élan* is no easy task. But religions have attempted something similar, directed moreover toward a less promising object—the supernatural. It does not become those who hold that faith may move mountains to deny in advance the possibility of its manifestation on the basis of verifiable realities. There already exists, though in a rudimentary form, the capacity to relate social conditions and events to their causes, and the ability will grow with exercise. There is the technical skill with which to initiate a campaign for social health and sanity analogous to that made in behalf of physical public health. Human beings have impulses toward affection, compassion and justice, equality and freedom. It remains to weld all these things together. It is of no use merely to assert that the intrenched foes of class interest and power in high places are hostile to the realization of such a union. As I have already said, if this enemy did not exist, there would be little sense in urging *any* policy of change. The point to be grasped is that, unless one gives up the whole struggle as hopeless, one has to choose between alternatives. One alternative is dependence upon the supernatural; the other, the use of natural agencies.

There is then no sense, logical or practical, in pointing out the difficulties that stand in the way of the latter course, until the question of the alternative is faced. If it is faced, it will also be realized that one factor in the choice is dependence upon enlisting only those committed to the supernatural and alliance with all men and women who feel the stir of social emotion, including the large number of those who, consciously or unconsciously, have turned their backs upon the supernatural. Those who face the alternatives will also have to choose between a continued and even more systematic *laissez faire* depreciation of intelligence and the resources of natural knowledge and understanding, and conscious and organized effort to turn the use of these means from narrow ends, personal and class, to larger human purposes. They will have to ask, as far as they nominally believe in the need for radical social change, whether what they accomplish when they point with one hand to the seriousness of present evils is not undone when the other hand points away from man and nature for their remedy.

The transfer of idealizing imagination, thought and emotion to natural human relations would not signify the destruction of churches that now exist. It would rather offer the means for a recovery of vitality. The fund of human values that are prized and that need to be cherished, values that are satisfied and rectified by *all* human concerns and arrangements, could be celebrated and reinforced, in different ways and with differing symbols, by the churches. In that way the churches would indeed become catholic. The demand that churches show a more active interest in social affairs, that they take a definite stand upon such questions as war, economic injustice, political corruption, that they stimulate action for a divine kingdom on earth, is one of the signs of the times. But as long as social values are related to a supernatural for which the churches stand in some peculiar way, there is an inherent inconsistency between the demand and efforts to execute it. On the one hand, it is urged that the churches are going outside their special province when they involve themselves in economic and political issues. On the other hand, the very fact that they claim if not a monopoly of supreme values and motivating forces, yet a unique relation to them, makes it impossible for the churches to participate in promotion of social ends on a natural and equal human basis. The surrender of claims to an exclusive and authoritative position is a *sine qua non* for doing away with the dilemma in which churches now find themselves in respect to their sphere of social action.

. . . [Referring] to an outstanding historic fact[:] The coincidence of the realm of social interests and activities with a tribal or civic community has vanished. Secular interests and activities have grown up outside of organized religions and are independent of their authority. The hold of these interests upon the thoughts and desires of men has crowded the social importance of organized religions into a corner and the area of this corner is decreasing. This change either marks a terrible decline in everything that can justly be termed religious in value, in traditional religions, or it provides the opportunity for expansion of these qualities on a new basis and with a new outlook. It is impossible to ignore the fact that historic Christianity has been committed to a separation of sheep and goats; the saved and the lost; the elect and the mass. Spiritual aristocracy as well as *laissez faire* with respect to natural and human intervention, is deeply embedded in its traditions. Lip service—often more than lip service—has been given to the idea of the common brotherhood of all men. But those outside the fold of the church and those who do not rely upon belief in the supernatural have been regarded as only potential brothers, still requiring adoption into the family. I cannot understand how any realization of the democratic ideal as a vital moral and spiritual ideal in human affairs is possible without surrender of the conception of the basic division to which supernatural Christianity is committed. Whether or no we are, save in some metaphorical sense, all brothers, we are at least all in the same boat traversing the same turbulent ocean. The potential religious significance of this fact is infinite. . . .

The considerations put forward . . . [here] may be summed up in what they imply. The ideal ends to which we attach our faith are not shadowy and wavering. They assume concrete form in our understanding of our relations to one another and the values contained in these relations. We who now live are parts of a humanity that extends into the remote past, a humanity that has interacted with nature. The things in civilization we most prize are not of ourselves. They exist by grace of the doings and sufferings of the continuous human community in which we are a link. Ours is the responsibility of conserving, transmitting, rectifying and expanding the heritage of values we have received that those who come after us may receive it more solid and secure, more widely accessible and more generously shared than we have received it. Here are all the elements for a religious faith that shall not be confined to sect, class, or race. Such a faith has always been implicitly the common faith of mankind. It remains to make it explicit and militant.

GEORGE SANTAYANA

FROM 1881, when he first contributed to the magazine of the Boston Latin School, until his death in 1952, George Santayana wrote voluminously on many matters great and small. His life was a rich one, not in terms of spectacular events occurring to his person, but in terms of what he absorbed and what he produced. He was a sharp observer of his time and a deep student of the past, and he had the power to utilize the philosophic heritage in constructing an independent system. "Systematic" he was, from first to last, though hardly by the method of declaiming ponderously in each written work just where he stood on this or that problem. He pursued relentlessly the ramifications of ideas, constantly recasting his analyses; and in this respect he was, as he once half-facetiously stated, "a disciple of Socrates." In his polemical writings, infrequent as they were, Santayana could hit hard. But he was not destined to have wide appeal during his lifetime. His last twenty years of work were obscured by the shadow of an Anglo-American movement that rationalized its own piecemeal type of philosophizing into an exclusive norm; and earlier he addressed philosophers who, though systematic themselves, could not easily make contact with his subtle formulations of philosophic issues. Nor did his original, powerful style of writing gain him wide attention in the literary world, since it served primarily as the medium of a technical subject matter.

The most extensive in scope of Santayana's works are *The Life of Reason* in five volumes (1905–1906) and *Realms of Being* in four volumes (1927–1940), the latter work foreshadowed in 1923 by *Scepticism and Animal Faith*. Notable among his other books are *The Sense of Beauty* (1896), *Interpretations of Poetry and Religion* (1900), *Three Philosophical Poets* (1910), *Winds of Doctrine* (1913), *Dialogues in Limbo* (1926), and *Dominations and Powers* (1951). Santayana wrote several volumes of verse, including *Lucifer* (1924), a "theological tragedy"; many essays in literary criticism; and "a memoir in the form of a novel," *The Last Puritan* (1935). His autobiography, *Persons and Places,* in three volumes, appeared between 1944 and 1953. As an undergraduate between 1883 and 1886 Santayana contributed a large number of cartoons to the *Harvard Lampoon*. His early poems, translations, and essays in the *Harvard Monthly* revealed an aspect of his mind no more fundamental, however, than this comic spirit, which in one form or another permeated his work to the end. In 1889 he was appointed to teach at Harvard, becoming a junior colleague of William James and Josiah Royce. He retired from teaching in 1912—one old legend telling us that on a beautiful April afternoon he rose from his chair, said to his students, "Gentlemen, it is spring," and walked slowly from the classroom, never to be seen there again.

At the end of the last century, when Santayana was writing *The Life of Reason,* the "warfare of science with theology" was at its height in America. In the wake of the impressive nineteenth-century advance of physical and biological science, mechanistic explanation seemed preeminent and irresistible. But the conflicting viewpoints were nowhere expressed with philosophic rigor, imagination, and adequacy. The naturalistic outlook stimulated by scientific progress expressed itself chiefly in the form of a materialistic metaphysics that proved too impoverished to be accepted by major thinkers. The attitude of religious spokesmen was defensive, and for the most part took the form either of reiterating traditional arguments or of affirming the independence and inviolability of religious faith. It was in the atmosphere of this conflict that Santayana emerged with a startlingly comprehensive, poetic naturalism, the full impact of which, it would appear, is only now being realized.

Among the various challenging objectives at which Santayana aimed as early as *Interpretations of Poetry and Religion* was a reinterpretation of the relations between religion and science. He approached religion and science as forms of social experience, as historically established disciplines, and as inevitable phases of human consciousness. In this account, science and religion are regarded as no more opposed to each other than science and art. Religion, indeed, is understood as a species of art—it is the complex art of expressing, in mythological form and through social media, the ideal possibilities of man. Science describes and predicts the patterns of existence. Religion renders dramatically the pervasive moral values of human life. Science discovers and discriminates these values, while religion makes them poetically intense, vivid, and urgent. Religious myth and religious ritual are the vehicles by which the human sense of perfection is preserved and sustained. The traditional conflict of science and religion rests on the assumption —shown to be false, Santayana believed, by close examination of religious thought and practice in the past—that religion necessarily concerns itself with truths of fact, specifically with truths about a supranatural domain of existence. Santayana found the inspiration for his naturalism in Benedict Spinoza (1632–1677) and the Greeks, and regarded his philosophy as largely a transformation of their vision into contemporary terms. The essay reprinted below was originally read by him at The Hague to an audience commemorating the tercentenary of Spinoza's birth. It was first printed in *Septimana Spinozana* (1933).

Santayana liked the old Spanish saying, "I was born in Aragon, because such was the will of God; but if I had had my way, I would have been born in Aragon." Spain was the land of his birth (1863), and he would have chosen it to be, just as he chose to spend his last years in Italy. But every national tradition that he experienced left its mark on him. The volume *Character and Opinion in the United States* (1920) was only one of his written responses to the culture of America. *Soliloquies in England* (1922) fused reflection on complex philosophic problems with delicate perception of regional and historical realities. Santayana's was a truly universal mind, in the sense that it sought to recognize and express, within a broad perspective, the multifariousness of existence. Both his adversaries and his admirers called him Olympian, the former suspecting him of cynical escapism, the latter finding in his detachment the virtues of dispassionateness and candor. In the last analysis, however, he belonged not on some condescending height but where he says (in the following essay) that Luther and Spinoza belonged, "under the sky."

ULTIMATE RELIGION

Before this chosen audience, in this consecrated place, I may venture to pass over all subsidiary matters and come at once to the last question of all: What inmost allegiance, what ultimate religion, would be proper to a wholly free and disillusioned spirit? The occasion invites us to consider this question, and to consider it with entire frankness. Great as you and I may feel our debt to be to Spinoza for his philosophy of nature, there is, I think, something for which we owe him an even greater debt; I mean, the magnificent example he offers us of philosophic liberty, the courage, firmness, and sincerity with which he reconciled his heart to the truth. Any clever man may sometimes see the truth in flashes; any scientific man may put some aspect of the truth into technical words; yet all this hardly deserves the name of philosophy so long as the heart remains unabashed, and we continue to live like animals lost in the stream of our impressions, not only in the public routine and necessary cares of life, but even in our silent thoughts and affections. Many a man before Spinoza and since has found the secret of peace: but the singularity of Spinoza, at least in the modern world, was that he facilitated this moral victory by no dubious postulates. He did not ask God to meet him half way: he did not whitewash the facts, as the facts appear to clear reason, or as they appeared to the science of his day. He solved the problem of the spiritual life after stating it in the hardest, sharpest, most cruel terms. Let us nerve ourselves today to imitate his example, not by simply accepting his solution, which for some of us would be easy, but by exercising his courage in the face of a somewhat different world, in which it may be even more difficult for us than it was for him to find a sure foothold and a sublime companionship.

There is a brave and humorous saying of Luther's, which applies to Spinoza better, perhaps, than to Luther himself. When asked where, if driven out of the Church, he would stand, he replied: "Under the sky." The sky of Luther was terribly clouded: there was a vast deal of myth tumbling and thundering about in it: and even in the clear sky of Spinoza there was perhaps something specious, as there is in the blue vault itself. The sun, he tells us, seemed to be about two-hundred feet away: and if his science at once corrected this optical illusion, it never undermined his conviction that all reality was within easy reach of his thought. Nature was dominated, he assumed, by unquestionable

---

This selection has been reprinted from *Obiter Scripta* by George Santayana, eds. Justus Buchler and Benjamin Schwartz, Copyright 1936 by Charles Scribner's Sons; used by permission of the publishers (pp. 368–377).

scientific and dialectical principles; so that while the forces of nature might often put our bodily existence in jeopardy, they always formed a decidedly friendly and faithful object for the mind. There was no essential mystery. The human soul from her humble station might salute the eternal and the infinite with complete composure and with a certain vicarious pride. Every man had a true and adequate idea of God: and this saying, technically justified as it may be by Spinoza's definitions of terms, cannot help surprising us: it reveals such a virgin sense of familiarity with the absolute. There could not but be joy in the sweep of an intelligence that seemed so completely victorious, and no misgivings could trouble a view of the world that explained everything.

Today, however, we can hardly feel such assurance: we should be taking shelter in a human edifice which the next earthquake might shake down. Nor is it a question really of times or temperaments: anyone anywhere, if he does not wish to construct a plausible system, but to challenge his own assumptions and come to spiritual self-knowledge, must begin by abstention from all easy faith, lest he should be madly filling the universe with images of his own reason and his own hopes. I will therefore ask you today, provisionally, for an hour, and without prejudice to your ulterior reasonable convictions, to imagine the truth to be as unfavourable as possible to your desires and as contrary as possible to your natural presumptions; so that the spirit in each of us may be drawn away from its accidental home and subjected to an utter denudation and supreme trial. Yes, although the dead cannot change their minds, I would respectfully beg the shade of Spinoza himself to suspend for a moment that strict rationalism, that jealous, hard-reasoning, confident piety which he shared with the Calvinists and Jansenists of his day, and to imagine—I do not say to admit—that nature may be but imperfectly formed in the bosom of chaos, and that reason in us may be imperfectly adapted to the understanding of nature. Then, having hazarded no favourite postulates and invoked no cosmic forces pledged to support our aspirations, we may all quietly observe what we find; and whatever harmonies may then appear to subsist between our spirits and the nature of things will be free gifts to us and, so far as they go, unchallengeable possessions. We shall at last be standing unpledged and naked, under the open sky.

In what I am about to say, therefore, I do not mean to prejudge any cosmological questions, such as that of free will or necessity, theism or pantheism. I am concerned only with the sincere confessions of a mind that has surrendered every doubtful claim and every questionable assurance. Of such assurances or claims there is one which is radical and comprehensive: I mean, the claim to existence and to directing the course of events. We say conventionally that the future is uncertain: but if we withdrew honestly into ourselves and examined our actual moral resources, we should feel that what is insecure is not merely the course of particular events but the vital presumption that there is a future coming at all, and a future pleasantly continuing our habitual experience. We rely in this, as we must, on the analogies of experience, or rather on the clock-work of instinct and presumption in our bodies; but existence is a miracle, and, morally considered, a free gift from moment to moment. That it will always be analogous to itself is the very question we are begging. Evidently all interconnections and sequences of events, and in particular any consequences which we may expect to flow from our actions, are really entirely beyond our spiritual control. When our will commands and seems, we know not how, to be obeyed by our bodies and by the world, we are like Joshua seeing the sun stand still at his bidding; when we command and nothing happens, we are like King Canute surprised that the rising tide should not obey him: and when we say we have executed a great work and re-directed the course of history, we are like Chanticleer attributing the sunrise to his crowing.

What is the result? That at once, by a mere act of self-examination and frankness, the spirit has come upon one of the most important and radical of religious perceptions. It has perceived that though it is living, it is powerless to live; that though it may die, it is powerless to die; and that altogether, at every instant and in every particular, it is in the hands of some alien and inscrutable power.

Of this felt power I profess to know nothing further. To me, as yet, it is merely the counterpart of my impotence. I should not venture, for instance, to call this power almighty, since I have no means of knowing how much it can do: but I should not hesitate, if I may coin a word, to call it *omnificent:* it is to me, by definition, the doer of everything that is done. I am not asserting the physical validity of this sense of agency or cause: I am merely feeling the force, the friendliness, the hostility, the unfathomableness of the world. I am expressing an impression; and it may be long before my sense of omnipresent power can be erected, with many qualifications, into a theological theory of the omnipresence of God. But the moral presence of power comes upon a man in the night, in the desert, when he finds himself, as the Arabs say, alone with Allah. It re-appears in every acute predicament, in extremities, in the birth of a child, or in the face of death. And as for the unity of this power, that is not involved in its sundry manifestations, but rather in my own solitude; in the unity of this suffering spirit overtaken by all those accidents. My destiny is single, tragically single, no matter how multifarious may be the causes of my destiny. As I stand amazed, I am not called upon to say whether, if I could penetrate into the inner workings of things, I should discover omnificent power to be simple or compound, continuous or spasmodic, intentional or blind. I stand before it simply receptive, somewhat as, in Rome, I might stand before the great fountain of Trevi. There I see jets and cascades flowing in separate streams and in divers directions. I am not sure that a single Pontifex Maximus designed it all, and led all those musical waters into just those channels. Some streams may have dried up or been diverted since the creation; some rills may have been added today by fresh rains from heaven; behind one of those artificial rocks some little demon, of his own free will, may even now be playing havoc with the conduits; and who knows how many details, in my image, may not have been misplaced or multiplied by optical tricks of my own? Yet here, for the spirit, is one total marvellous impression, one thunderous force, confronting me with this theatrical but admirable spectacle.

Yet this is not all. Power comes down upon me clothed in a thousand phenomena; and these manifestations of power open to me a new spiritual resource. In submitting to power, I learn its ways; from being passive my spirit becomes active; it begins to enjoy one of its essential prerogatives. For like a child the spirit is attracted to all facts by the mere assault of their irrational presence and variety. It watches all that happens or is done with a certain happy excitement, even at the most fearful calamities. Although the essence of spirit may be merely to think, yet some intensity and progression are essential to this thinking; thinking is a way of living, and the most vital way. Therefore all the operations of universal power, when they afford themes for perception, afford also occasions for intellectual delight. Here will and intellect, as Spinoza tells us, coincide: for omnificent power flows in part through our persons; the spirit itself is a spark of that fire, or rather the light of that flame: it cannot have an opposite principle of motion. With health a certain euphoria, a certain alacrity and sense of mastery are induced in the spirit; and a natural effect of perspective, the pathos of nearness, turns our little spark for us into a central sun. The world moves round us, and we move gladly with the world. What if the march of things be destined to overwhelm us? It can not destroy the joy we had in its greatness and in its victory. There may even be some relief in passing from the troubled thought of ourselves to the thought of something more rich in life, yet in its own sphere and progression, untroubled: and it may be easier for me to understand the motion of the heavens and to rejoice in it than to understand or rejoice in my own motions. My own eclipse, my own vices, my own sorrows, may become a subject to me for exact calculation and a pleasing wonder. The philosophical eye may compose a cosmic harmony out of these necessary conflicts, and an infinite life out of these desirable deaths.

Does it not begin to appear that the solitude of a naked spirit may be rather well peopled? In proportion as we renounce our animal claims and commitments, do we not breathe a fresher and more salubrious air? May not the renunciation of everything disinfect everything and return everything to us in its impartial reality, at the same time disinfecting our wills also, and rendering us capable of charity? This charity will extend, of course, to the lives and desires of others, which we recognize to be no less inevitable than our own; and it will extend also to their ideas, and by a curious and blessed consequence, to the relativity and misery of our own minds. Yet this intellectual charity, since it is inspired by respect for the infinite, will by no means accept all views passively and romantically, as if they were equal and not subject to correction; but doing better justice to the holy aspiration which animates them in common, it will rise from them all, and with them all, to the conception of eternal truth.

Here we touch the crown of Spinoza's philosophy, that intellectual love of God in which the spirit was to be ultimately reconciled with universal power and universal truth. This love brings to consciousness a harmony intrinsic to existence: not an alleged harmony such as may be posited in religions or philosophies resting on faith, but a harmony which, as far as it goes, is actual and patent. In the realm of matter, this harmony is measured by the degree of adjustment, conformity, and cooperation which the part may have attained in the whole; in a word, it is measured by *health*. In the realm of truth, the same natural harmony extends as far as do capacity and pleasure in understanding the truth: so that besides health we may possess *knowledge*. And this is no passive union, no dead peace; the spirit rejoices in it; for the spirit, being, according to Spinoza, an essential concomitant of all existence, shares the movement, the *actuosa essentia* of the universe; so that we necessarily *love* health and knowledge, and *love* the things in which health and knowledge are found. In so far as omnificent power endows us with health, we necessarily love that power whose total movement makes for our own perfection; and in so far as we are able to understand the truth, we necessarily love the themes of an intense and unclouded vision, in which our imaginative faculty reaches its perfect function.

Of this religion of health and understanding Spinoza is a sublime prophet. By overcoming all human weaknesses, even when they seemed kindly or noble, and by honouring power and truth, even if they should slay him, he entered the sanctuary of an unruffled superhuman wisdom, and declared himself supremely happy, not because the world as he conceived it was flattering to his heart, but because the gravity of his heart disdained all flatteries, and with a sacrificial prophetic boldness uncovered and relished his destiny, however tragic his destiny might be. And presently peace descended; this keen scientific air seemed alone fit to breathe, and only this high tragedy worthy of a heroic and manly breast. Indeed the truth is a great cathartic and wonderfully relieves the vital distress of existence. We stand as on a mountaintop, and the spectacle, so out of scale with all our petty troubles, silences and overpowers the heart, expanding it for a moment into boundless sympathy with the universe.

Nevertheless, the moral problem is not solved. It is not solved for mankind at large, which remains no less distracted than it was before. Nor is it solved even for the single spirit. There is a radical and necessary recalcitrancy in the finite soul in the face of all this cosmic pomp and all this cosmic pressure: a recalcitrancy to which Spinoza was less sensitive than some other masters of the spiritual life, perhaps because he was more positivistic by temperament and less specifically religious. At any rate many a holy man has known more suffering than Spinoza found in the long work of salvation, more uncertainty, and also, in the end, a more lyrical and warmer happiness. For in the first place, as I said in the beginning, a really naked spirit cannot assume that the world is thoroughly intelligible. There may be surds, there may be hard facts, there may be dark abysses before which intelligence must be silent, for fear of going mad. And in the second place, even if to the intellect all things should prove perspicuous, the intellect is not the whole of human nature, nor even the whole of pure spirit in man. Reason may be the differentia of man; it is surely not his essence. His essence, at best, is animality qualified by reason. And from this animality the highest flights of reason are by no means separable. The very life of spirit springs from animal predicaments: it moves by imposing on events a perspective and a moral urgency proper to some particular creature or some particular interest.

Good, as Spinoza would tell us, is an epithet which we assign to whatsoever increases our perfection. Such a doctrine might seem egotistical, but is simply biological; and on its moral side, the maxim is a greater charter of liberty and justice than ever politician framed. For it follows that every good pursued is genuinely good, and the perfection of every creature equally perfection. Every good therefore is a good forever to a really clarified, just, and disinterested spirit; such a spirit cannot rest in the satisfaction of any special faculty, such as intelligence, nor of any special art, such as philosophy. That the intellect might be perfectly happy in contemplating the truth of the universe, does not render the universe good to every other faculty; good to the heart, good to the flesh, good to the eye, good to the conscience or the sense of justice. Of all systems an optimistic system is the most oppressive. Would it not be a bitter mockery if, in the words of Bradley, this were the best of possible worlds, and everything in it a necessary evil? The universal good by which the spirit, in its rapt moments, feels overwhelmed, if it is not to be a mystical illusion, cannot fall short of being the sum of all those perfections, infinitely various, to which all living things severally aspire. A glint or symbol of this universal good may be found in any moment of perfect happiness visiting any breast: but it is impossible unreservedly to love or worship anything, be it the universe or any part of it, unless we find in the end that this thing is completely good: I mean, unless it is perfect after its kind and a friend to itself, and unless at the same time it is beneficent universally, and a friend to everything else. Pure spirit would be lame and evidently biassed by some biological accident, if it did not love every good loved anywhere by anybody. These varied perfections are rivals and enemies in the press of the world, where there seems not to be matter or time enough for everything: but to impartial spirit no good can render another good odious. Physically, one good may exclude another: nature and natural morality must choose between them, or be dissolved into chaos: but in eternity the most opposite goods are not enemies; rather little brothers and sisters, as all odd creatures were to St. Francis. And that all these various perfections are not actually attainable is a material accident, painful but not confusing to a free spirit. Their contrariety increases sorrow but does not diminish love; the very pain is a fresh homage to the beauty missed, and a proof of loyalty; so that the more the spirit suffers the more clearly, when it unravels its suffering, it understands what it loves. Every perfection then shines, washed and clear, separate and uncontaminated: yet all compatible, each in its place, and harmonious. To love things spiritually, that is to say, intelligently and disinterestedly, means to love the love in them, to worship the good which they pursue, and to see them all prophetically in their possible beauty. To love things as they are would be a mockery of things: a true lover must love them as they would wish to be. For nothing is quite happy as it is, and the first act of true sympathy must be to move with the object of love towards its happiness.

Universal good, then, the whole of that to which all things aspire, is something merely potential; and if we wish to make a religion of love, after the manner of Socrates, we must take universal good, not universal power, for the object of our religion. This religion would need to be more imaginative, more poetical, than that of Spinoza, and the word God, if we still used it, would have to mean for us not the universe, but the good of the universe. There would not be a universe worshipped, but a universe praying; and the flame of the whole fire, the whole seminal and generative movement of nature, would be the love of God. This love would be erotic; it would be really love and not something wingless called by that name. It would bring celestial glimpses not to be retained, but culminating in moments of unspeakable rapture, in a union with all good, in which the soul would vanish as an object because, as an organ, it had found its perfect employment.

For there is a mystery here, the mystery of seeming to attain emotionally the logically unattainable. Universal good is something dispersed, various, contrary to itself in its opposite embodiments; nevertheless, to the mystic, it seems a single living object, the One Beloved, a good to be embraced all at once, finally and for ever, leaving not the least shred of anything good outside. Yet I think this mystery may be easily solved. Spirit is essentially synthetic; and just as all the known and unknown forces of nature make, in relation to experience and destiny, one single omnificent power; and just as all facts and all the relations between facts compose for the historical and prophetic mind one unalterable realm of truth; so exactly, for the lover, all objects of love form a single ineffable good. He may say that he sees all beauties in a single face, that all beauties else are nothing to him; yet perhaps in this hyperbole he may be doing his secret heart an injustice. Beauty here may be silently teaching him to discern beauty everywhere, because in all instances of love only the sheer love counts in his eyes: and in the very absoluteness of his love he may feel an infinite promise. His ecstasy, which passes for a fulfilment, remains a sort of agony: and though itself visionary, it may, by its influence, free his heart from trivial or accidental attachments and lead it instead to a universal charity. Beggars in Catholic and Moslem countries used to beg an alms, sometimes, for the love of God. It was a potent appeal; because God, according to the Socratic tradition, was the good to which all creation moved; so that anyone who loved deeply, and loved God, could not fail, by a necessary inclusion, to love the good which all creatures lived by pursuing, no matter how repulsive these creatures might be to natural human feeling.

Thus the absolute love of anything involves the love of universal good; and the love of universal good involves the love of every creature.

Such, in brief, seems to me the prospect open to a mind that examines its moral condition without any preconceptions. Perhaps an empirical critic, strictly reducing all objects to the functions which they have in experience, might see in my meagre inventory all the elements of religion. Mankind, he might say, in thinking of God or the gods have always meant the power in events: as when people say: *God willing*. Sometimes they have also meant the truth, as when people say: *God knows*. And perhaps a few mystics may have meant the good, or the supreme object of love, union with whom they felt would be perfect happiness. I should then have merely changed the language of traditional religion a little, translated its myths into their pragmatic equivalents, and reduced religion to its true essence. But no: I make no such professions: they would be plainly sophistical. The functions which objects have in experience no doubt open to us different avenues to those objects: but the objects themselves, if they exist, are not mere names for those functions. They are objects of faith and the religion of mankind, like their science, has always been founded on faith. Now there is no faith invoked in the examination of conscience which I have made before you this evening: and therefore, properly speaking, what I come to is not religion. Nor is it exactly philosophy, since I offer no hypotheses about the nature of the universe or about the nature of knowledge. Yet to be quite sincere, I think that in this examination of conscience there is a sort of secret or private philosophy perhaps more philosophical than the other: and while I set up no gods, not even Spinoza's infinite *Deus sive Natura* [God or Nature], I do not consider on what subjects and to what end we might consult those gods, if we found that they existed: and surely the aspiration that would prompt us, in that case, to worship the gods, would be our truest heart-bond and our ultimate religion.

If then any of us who are so minded should ever hear the summons of a liturgical religion calling to us: *Sursum corda, Lift up your hearts,* we might sincerely answer, *Habemus ad Dominum, Our hearts by nature are addressed to the Lord*. For we recognize universal power, and respect it, since on it we depend for our existence and fortunes. We look also with unfeigned and watchful allegiance towards universal truth, in which all the works of power are eternally defined and recorded; since in so far as we are able to discover it, the truth raises all things for us into the light, into the language of spirit. And finally, when power takes on the form of life, and begins to circle about and pursue some type of perfection, spirit in us necessarily loves these perfections, since spirit is aspiration become conscious, and they are the goals of life: and in so far as any of these goals of life can be defined or attained anywhere, even if only in prophetic fancy, they become glory, or become beauty, and spirit in us necessarily worships them: not the troubled glories and brief perfections of this world only, but rather that desired perfection, that eternal beauty, which lies sealed in the heart of each living thing.